Jeff Herman's

GUIDE TO
BOOK
PUBLISHERS,
EDITORS,
& LITERARY
AGENTS
2005

**Who they are!
What they want!
How to
win them
over!**

JEFF HERMAN

THE WRITER BOOKS

The Writer Books is an imprint of Kalmbach Trade Press, a division of Kalmbach Publishing Co. These books are distributed to the book trade by Watson-Guptill.

For all other inquiries, including individual orders or details on special quantity discounts for groups or conferences, contact:

Kalmbach Publishing Co.
21027 Crossroads Circle
Waukesha, WI 53187
(800) 533-6644

Printed in the United States of America

04 05 06 07 08 09 10 11 12 13   10 9 8 7 6 5 4 3 2 1

Publisher's Cataloging-in-Publication Data
(Prepared by The Donohue Group, Inc.)

Herman, Jeff, 1958-
  Jeff Herman's guide to book publishers, editors, & literary agents : who they are! what they want! and how to win them over! / Jeff Herman.—2005 ed. (2004)-

    v. ; cm.
    Annual
    ISSN: 1548-1344

1. Publishers and publishing—United States—Directories.   2. Publishers and publishing—Canada—Directories. 3. Editors—United States—Directories. 4. Editors—Canada—Directories. 5. Literary agents—United States—Directories. 6. Literary agents—Canada—Directories. 7. Authorship—Periodicals. I. Title: Guide to book publishers, editors, & literary agents II. Title: Book publishers, editors and literary agents.

Z475 .H47
070.5/025/73

Art Director: Lil Weber

ACKNOWLEDGEMENTS

There are many people who I am extremely grateful to for helping me to generate this huge body of work:

Deborah Herman, for understanding why I sometimes seem grouchy.

Colin Odell, for being a first-class gentleman, a hard worker, and a bit smarter than I asked him to be.

Miriam Tager, for being available, and for being excellent.

Amanda Allison, for always being around and eager to contribute.

Kristin Schneidler, for being a quick study and a top-notch editor.

Phil Martin, for valuable support and encouragement along the way.

Dick Christianson, for his vision.

Jamie Forbes, for helping to get it going a long time ago.

Ben Dominitz, for knowing and offering opportunities, and for taking risks.

DEDICATION

This, the 15th edition, is dedicated to writers, published or not, because it is upon their wings that all of us fly.

The power to publish is the power to create or destroy. It is not for the publishers to issue the call; that is determined by a source beyond them. By merits granted or earned, some will be chosen. The gates should therefore never be sealed, and those with the power to publish always revealed.

—An Anonymous Literary Agent

PUBLISHERS, EDITORS, AND LITERARY AGENTS

ADVICE FOR AUTHORS

RESOURCES FOR WRITERS

INTRODUCTION

Dear Writer,

This is the 15th edition of a book that has sold several hundred thousand copies since its first incarnation about 15 years ago. The idea for this book came to me in a moment of inspiration. I came to this business as a young man still in my 20s with little experience, and probably no right to call myself an agent. But I was just innocent enough not to know what I didn't know and shouldn't try. Youth gives us that special air pocket in which what we want to do fuels us into action, without the suffocations of logic or reason. To succeed, an agent needs to know editors, and I didn't know any. I looked for a book that listed who these people were and what types of work they acquired, but no such centralized source existed. So I compiled my contacts the old-fashioned way, cold-calling.

What I discovered is that some editors, certainly not all, had a disdain for hungry unproven writers. It surprised me that they actually did not want to have any contact with these people, unless they could somehow be "pre-certified" as someone that the editor might likely want to publish. It seemed as if some editors wanted to be cloistered within the chambers of a secret society, to which membership would only be offered to a select few. This web of legacies, pedigrees, and "secret handshakes," however, disqualified admission to too many people who had too many important ideas to share. And so I had the idea for this book. I envisioned it as a way for writers to have a little more information; a little more power; a little more of an opportunity to maybe get their words published.

What began as the *INSIDER'S GUIDE* became the *WRITER'S GUIDE* and is now *JEFF HERMAN'S GUIDE*. My original publisher was taken off the map by one of the multinational "gigantors," and this is my second year with a new publisher.

I encourage you to stay in touch with me about your ideas for this book, and your experiences with this book (whether negative or positive).

Thank you and may you realize all the success that you seek.

Best wishes,

Jeffrey H. Herman
THE JEFF HERMAN AGENCY, LLC
P.O. Box 1522
Stockbridge, MA   01262
Jeff@jeffherman.com
413-298-0077

ABOUT THE AUTHOR

Jeff Herman is the founder of The Jeff Herman Literary Agency, LLC. One of the most innovative agents in the book business, he represents more than 100 writers and has sold more than 500 titles in the United States and internationally. Herman has been extensively written and talked about in numerous print publications and broadcast programs, and he speaks at writer's conferences around the country. He is the coauthor with Deborah Levine Herman of *Write the Perfect Book Proposal*. Be sure to visit his high-content Web site at www.jeffherman.com.

CONTRIBUTORS

Deborah Levine Herman is vice president of The Jeff Herman Literary Agency and coauthor of *Write the Perfect Book Proposal: 10 Proposals That Sold and Why* (John Wiley & Sons) and *Spiritual Writing* (Beyond Words).

William Hamilton is the publisher at University of Hawaii Press.

Greg Ioannou is director of the Editorial Centre in Toronto, Ontario, Canada.

Jamie M. Forbes is a publishing and media consultant based in New York.

Morris Rosenthal is an author and translator. His computer books have been published in Chinese and Spanish editions, and you can visit his internationally recognized Web site at www.daileyint.com.

Toni Robino is a wonderful writer who is always there to help others write. Visit her Web site at www.withflyingcolors.com.

THE PUBLISHING
CONGLOMERATES

THE MULTINATIONAL CONGLOMERATED PUBLISHING ENTITIES

JEFF HERMAN

A long time ago, the U.S. book publishing business consisted of hundreds of mom-and-pop companies. Each was generally named for the individual(s) who founded the firm, and their respective catalogues reflected their own special tastes and sensibilities. Separately, none of these entities or individuals had the power to dictate the contemporary status or future direction of publishing. They were a thriving community of several hundred distinct pieces. Collectively, they comprised our nation's entire book publishing structure.

The revolution came and happened quickly. Some of us complained, but it didn't make any difference. It was a funny revolution in that it reversed the usual dynamic. Unlike the breaking away of exploited tribes from masters of conquest, which is revolution in its most romantic form, we watched as faceless and formless conquerors wrapped themselves around most of our precious tribes and soundlessly absorbed them into a small number of obese oceans. Perhaps those who might have cared the most saw gold before they saw the cost. Can we blame them? Should we even judge the result? Perhaps it is wiser to simply adjust.

Beginning with last year's edition of this book, we have consolidated the largest multinational publishing properties into their own section. It seemed right to do so, since consolidation has been their most striking feature. These companies possess the brand names of the firms they have acquired over the past three decades. It is safe to say that at least 70% of every dollar that an American consumer spends for a book goes to one of these firms. While some of the firms may be led by high-profile individuals or greatly influenced by multigenerational families that control large blocks of non-traded stock, it is also safe to say that these firms are greater than any one person or any unified collection of people. At the end of the day, it is the various pension funds and institutional investment firms that must be satisfied.

There are two other key features of multinational publishers. 1) Most of them are controlled by foreign interests. 2) The book publishing programs are an extremely small part of a much larger agenda, which includes movies, magazines, broadcast and cable channels, newspapers, music, and the Internet.

Do not let my irreverent or ominous tone chase you away. At all of these firms you will find hard-working, dedicated editors who want nothing more than the ability to publish good books. And they manage to achieve that. So join with them and adjust to the system as it is. The best thing you can do is get your book published.

This section is followed by a large number of independent and small houses, each of which is capable of doing as much, or more, than the big houses. The independent houses are not vestiges from a dead past. To the contrary, they keep the current publishing climate vibrant, and help create the future with their entrepreneurial and innovative ways. Don't ever think twice about joining them.

HARPERCOLLINS PUBLISHING GROUPS

HARPERCOLLINS GENERAL BOOKS GROUP

HARPERCOLLINS CHILDREN'S BOOKS GROUP

ZONDERVAN (SEE SEPARATE ENTRY IN RELIGIOUS PUBLISHERS)

10 E. 53rd Street, New York, NY 10022-5299

212-207-7000

www.harpercollins.com

HarperCollins Publishing Groups produces a broad variety of commercial, trade, professional, academic, and mass-market books in hardcover, paperback, and multimedia editions. As one of the largest English-language publishers in the world, HarperCollins is a subsidiary of News Corporation, which is owned by the Australia media giant Rupert Murdock. The main office is in New York, but publishing groups are also located in Canada, the U.K., and Australia, and imprints of various groups can be found across the United States.

HarperCollins' holdings include: Fox Broadcasting, Twentieth Century Fox, *TV Guide*, more than 128 newspapers, and other media interests worldwide.

Submissions: HarperCollins Publishers considers material submitted by literary agents and previously published authors. The house is currently not looking for poetry or academic books. Please note that 12 weeks or more may elapse before the editors are able to respond to proposals.

These guidelines apply to all submissions across the range of imprints.

HARPERCOLLINS GENERAL BOOKS GROUP

AMISTAD PRESS

AVON

CLIFF STREET BOOKS

ECCO PRESS

EOS

HARPERBUSINESS

HARPERCOLLINS

HARPERENTERTAINMENT

HARPERRESOURCE

HARPERSANFRANCISCO

PERENNIAL

PERFECTBOUND

QUILL

RAYO

REGANBOOKS

WILLIAM MORROW

From romance to religion, pop culture to perennial classics—in traditional print, audio, and e-books—HarperCollins imprints have it all.

AMISTAD PRESS

Amistad Press publishes works by and about people of African descent and on subjects and themes that have significant influence on the intellectual, cultural, and historical perspectives of a world audience. Formats include hardcover and paperback.

New releases include: *Shifting Through Neutral* by Bridgette Davis; *A Love Noir* by Erica Simone Turnipseed; *The Known World* by Edward P. Jones; *When Washington was in Vogue* by Edward Christopher Williams.

Dawn Davis, Editorial Director

Kelli Martin, Editor—Fiction

Stacey Barney, Assistant Editor

AVON BOOKS

Founded in 1941, Avon Books is the second-oldest paperback publishing house in the United States. Recently acquired by the HarperCollins Publishing Groups, Avon publishes titles for both adults and young readers. It is recognized for pioneering the historical romance category and continues to produce commercial literature for the broadest possible audience in mass-market paperback format.

Recent titles include: *I'm No Angel* by Patti Berg; *When He Was Wicked* by Julia Quinn; *Temporary Insanity* by Carroll Leslie; *Sweetest Taboo* by Carole Matthews; *Call Waiting* by Michelle Cunnah; *On The Couch* by Alissa Kwitney.

Titles representative of Avon Romance: *The Reluctant Suitor* by Kathleen E. Woodwiss; *A Necessary Bride* by Debra Mullens; *Beneath Silent Moon* by Tracy Grant; *Dancing at Midnight* by Julia Quinn; *Heaven, Texas* by Susan Elizabeth Phillips; *On a Wicked Dawn* by Stephanie Laurens; *An Affair to Remember* by Karen Hawkins.

Representative titles of Avon Mystery: *Ties that Bind* by Phillip Margolin; *The Samurai's Daughter* by Sujata Massey; *Bannerman's Ghosts* by John R. Maxim; *Engaged to Die* by Carolyn Hart.

Carrie Feron, Vice President and Executive Editor

Sarah Durand, Editor

Avon Romance Submission Guidelines

Avon does not read unsolicited manuscripts or proposals, but it does have a submissions process for budding romance writers and encourages them to send their query letters and synopses. Avon is currently looking for romances in the areas of historical romance, African American romance, and contemporary romance, including romantic suspense.

HISTORICAL ROMANCE
(100,000 words/approximately 400 ms. pages)

A man and a woman meet—she's like no other woman he's ever known. She tantalizes him in ways he never thought possible. . .and he'll stop at nothing to make her his forever.

"At Avon, we're seeking deliciously romantic historical novels for all parts of the list—Avon Romance, Avon Treasure, and Avon Superleader. These are love stories set primarily in Great Britain and the United States before 1900, and they are filled with all the promise and passion that Avon readers expect."

CONTEMPORARY ROMANCE
(100,000 words/approximately 400 ms. pages)

When Avon contemporary romance came on the scene, the face of romance changed forever.

"We seek stories of emotional complexity, written by authors with unique voices. Books with humor, drama, romantic suspense—all types and tones can be right for Avon."

AFRICAN AMERICAN ROMANCE—AVON ROMANTIC TREASURE
(90,000 words/approximately 380 pages)

"We have listened to many of our readers and are actively seeking romance with African American heroes and heroines. These should be contemporary love stories—approximately 90,000–100,000 words long—set in the United States. Each author will be packaged, and developed, individually."

How to Submit a Manuscript

"To submit your historical or contemporary romance, please query first. We strongly urge you to query by e-mail, no attachments, please. Your query should be brief, no more than a two-page description of your book. Do not send chapters or a full synopsis at this time. You will receive a response, either a decline or a request for more material, in approximately 1–2 weeks."

Please e-mail your query to avonromance@harpercollins.com.

CLIFF STREET BOOKS

Cliff Street Books publishes distinct, high-concept books that speak to a wide audience. This imprint, named for the house where the four Harper Brothers published Melville, Poe, Twain, Dickens, James, and Trollope. It publishes select titles in literary fiction and a broad range of nonfiction books on self-help, inspiration, social commentary, style, and fashion. Formats include hardcover, paperback, and multimedia.

Titles representative of the nonfiction list include: *Stroke-Free for Life: The Complete Guide to Stroke Prevention and Treatment* by David O. Wiebers; *Murder in Spokane: Catching a Serial Killer* by Mark Fuhrman; *Tournament Week: Inside the Ropes and Behind the Scenes on the PGA Tour* by John Strege; *Goddess* By Barbara Victor; *Kinky Friedman's Texas Etiquette* by Kinky Friedman.

Fiction titles include: *The Width of the Sea* by Michelle Chalfoun; *The Blind Side of the Heart* by Michael C. White; *Past Forgetting: My Memory Lost and Found* by Jill Robinson; *One of the Guys* by Robert Clark Young.

ECCO PRESS

Ecco Press currently publishes approximately 60 titles per year by such critically acclaimed authors as John Ashbery, Paul Bowles, Italo Calvino, Gerald Early, Louise Glück, Robert Hass, Zbigniew Herbert, Erica Jong, Cormac McCarthy, Czeslaw Milosz, Joyce Carol Oates, Josef Skvorecky, Mark Strand, and Tobias Wolff. The Press has also created a number of literary series that today enjoy a special celebrity in the world of book publishing.

Titles representative of the cooking, food, and wine category are: *The Antipasto Table* by Michele Scicolonean; *Invitation to Indian Cooking* by Madhur Jaffrey; *Bistros of Paris* by Robert and Barbara Hamburger; *The Book of Latin and American Cooking* by Ortiz Lambert and *The Book of Yogurt* by Sonia Uvezian.

Titles in the memoir/biography category include: *The Way of the Ship* by Derek Lundy; *Alaskan Wilderness* by Lynn Schooler; *The Story of America's Most Beloved Song* by

Steve Turner; *Death on the Black Sea: The Untold Story of the 'Struma' and World War II's Holocaust at Sea* by Douglas Frantz and Catherine Collins.

New titles include: *Celestial Harmonies* by Peter Esterhazy; *Take Me, Take Me With You* by Lauren Kelly; *Bobby Fischer Goes To War* by David Edmonds and John Eidinow; *His Brother's Keeper* by Jonathan Weiner.

Query letters and SASEs should be directed to:

Daniel Halpern, Vice President and Publisher

Julia Serebrinsky, Senior Editor

EOS

Eos, founded in 1998, has already gained a positive reputation for its progressive editorial style, not to mention its bold, "break the rules" packaging and innovative promotional campaigns. Named for the Greek goddess of the dawn, Eos is committed to "bringing new life to science fiction and fantasy." Bestselling Eos authors include: Raymond E. Feist, Anne McCaffrey, and Gregory Benford.

Harper Eos is a new branch of the Eos imprint offering exciting and innovative titles for the young adult sci fi and fantasy reader. The books are intended to be engaging enough to appeal to adults and include: *Fire-us Trilogy*, by Jennifer Armstrong and Nancy Butche; *The Books of Magic*, by Hillari Bell and *Sacred Sacrement* by Sherryl Jordan, author of several critically acclaimed and award-winning books including *The Raging Quiet*, a School Library Journal Best Book, and the ALA Best Books for Young Adults.

Recent Eos titles include: *Acorna's Truimph* by Anne McCaffrey and Elizabeth Ann Scarborough; *King of Foxes* by Raymond Feist; *The Ships of Air* by Martha Wells; *Forge of Heaven* by C.J. Cherryh; *The Locus Awards*, edited by Charles Brown.

HARPERBUSINESS

HarperBusiness produces innovative ideas and distinctive voices in the categories of general business, leadership, finances, entrepreneurship, and corporate strategies.

Recent titles include: *The Origin of Brands: Discover the Natural Laws of Product Innovation and Business Survival* by Al Ries and Laura Ries; *The Rising Tide: Why Tax Cuts are the Key to Prosperity and Freedom* by Lawrence Kudlow; *Culture and Prosperity: The Truth About Markets—Why Some Nations Are Rich But Most Remain Poor* by John Kay and *The Fall of Advertising and The Rise of PR* by Al Ries (reprint).

Send query letters with SASEs to:

Marion Maneker, Editorial Director

Edwin Tan, Associate Editor—business, narrative nonfiction, humor, self-help, the arts, and Access travel guides

HARPERCOLLINS

HarperCollins produces adult hardcover books, trade paperbacks, and mass-market paperback editions that cover the breadth of trade publishing categories, including feature biographies (celebrities, sports, and historical), business, mysteries and thrillers, popular culture, humor, inspiration, and how-to (including cookbooks and health), in addition to works in most reference categories.

HarperStyle specializes in illustrated works keyed to contemporary lifestyle, design, and culture.

Best-selling authors include: Dr. Robert C. Atkins, Michael Crichton, Bill Phillips, Emeril Lagasse, Tony Hillerman, Barbara Taylor Bradford, Leon Uris, Anne Rivers Siddons and Ursula K Le Guin.

Recent nonfiction titles include: *Truth and Beauty: A Friendship* by Ann Patchett; *Life in the Middle Ages* by James Atlas; *Blinded by Sunlight* by Matthew McAllester; *America the Vulnerable* by Stephen Glynn; *The Provence Cookbook* by Patricia Wells; *Italy in Small Bites* by Carol Field; *Freedom Just Around the Corner* by Walter A. McDougall; *The Birth of the Chess Queen* by Marilyn Yalom.

Recent fiction titles include: *Sleeping Beauty* by Phillip Margolin; *Four Souls* by Louise Erdrich; *Islands* by Anne River Siddons; *Sharpe's Escape* by Bernard Cornwell; *Eleven Minutes* by Paulo Coelho; *The Goodbye Summer* by Patricia Gaffney; *Killer Smile* by Lisa Scottoline; *Hear No Evil* by James Grippando.

Direct queries and SASEs to:

David Hirshey, Executive Editor—Pop culture, celebrity books, politics, current affairs

Hugh Van Dusen, Editor-in-Chief, HarperPerennial—History, biography, reference, humor, politics, spirituality, self-help, and fiction and nonfiction reprints and originals in quality paperback

Susan Friedland, Executive Editor—Food, cookbooks, literary history

Tim Duggan, Executive Editor—Serious nonfiction, literary fiction

HARPERENTERTAINMENT

HarperEntertainment lays claim to being "your #1 media source" for television, movies, celebrities, sports, and music, from Seinfeld to new franchises like Mystic Knights. This imprint boasts an all-star cast of brand-name products which include NASCAR, NBA, *The X-Files*, and *Titanic*. This line has a new look. It has more high profile memoirs, and continues to be the place for television and movie tie-ins. Harper Entertainment publishes 12-15 hardcovers per year with an edgier and sharper personality than its former middle America image.

Direct queries and SASEs to:

Mauro DiPreta, Executive Editor— Pop culture, humor and commercial nonfiction

Maureen O'Brien, Executive Editor—Fiction and nonfiction

HARPERRESOURCE

HarperResource publishes leading names and brands in the practical nonfiction and reference categories. With an emphasis on books of enduring quality that educate, inform, and motivate, HarperResource produces a wide range of resource books and reference guides, including college guides, field guides, Spanish dictionaries, film encyclopedias, and etiquette guides.

Recent titles include: *The Real Age Makeover: Take Years Off Your Looks and Add Them to Your Life* by Michael Roizen; *Essentially Lilly: A Guide to Colorful Entertaining* by Lilly Pulitzer; *Fire Your Boss* by Stephen Pollan and Mark Levine; *My Greatest Shot* by Ron Cherney and Michael Arkush; *8 Minutes in the Morning for Extra Easy Weight Loss* by Jorge Cruise (reprint).

Direct queries and SASEs to:

Toni Sciarra, Editor

Edwin Tan, Associate Editor

HARPERSANFRANCISCO

353 Sacramento Street, Suite 500, San Francisco, CA 94111

415-477-4400   fax: 415-477-4444

www.harpercollins.com/sanfran   e-mail: hcsanfrancisco@harpercollins.com

HarperSanFrancisco strives to be the preeminent publisher of titles on religion, spirituality, mind, body, and spirit in hardcover and mass-market paperback. This imprint is dedicated to "publishing books that both illuminate diverse religious traditions and spiritual journeys and offer paths toward personal growth and well-being." The scope ranges from inspiring fiction to non-fiction that explores your mind, body and spirit.

Recent Titles representative of this list: *Life Goes On* by Phillip Gulley; *The Secrets of Jin-Shei* by Alma Alexander; *100 Simple Secrets of Happy Families: What Scientists Have Learned and How You Can Use It* by David Niven; *A Faith Worth Believing: Finding New Life Beyond the Rules of Religion* by Tom Stella.

Query letters and SASEs should be directed to:

Stephen Hanselman, Publisher

Michael Maudlin, Editorial Director—Religious, inspiration and literature

John V. Loudon, Executive Editor—Religious studies, Biblical studies, psychology/personal growth, inspiration, Eastern religions, Buddhist and Christian spirituality.

Gideon Weil, Editor
Born: August 16, 1971.
Education: Vassar College–English Major.
Employment history/editor career path: I started out working in the weekly newspaper business at the New York Press. I then worked at Witherspoon Associates,

a literary agency, for four years, and I have now been at HarperSanFrancisco for four years.

Do you represent fiction? We do acquire fiction.

Do you represent nonfiction? Yes, inspiration, self-help, narrative nonfiction.

Do you require book proposals? If so, what do you look for in evaluating a book proposal? Yes, I like to see the structure of the book, sample chapters, and where it fits in the marketplace.

Are certain aspects of a book proposal given more weight than others? Sample chapters.

What process do you use for making a decision? What is the process for acquisition, is there a committee? Yes, it consists of the publisher, editorial staff, marketing and sales people.

What kinds of nonfiction books do you want to see less of? Memoirs with no direction.

Are you interested in work geared for the masses (readers of People, The Star, etc.)? Yes.

Are agents important? Why? Yes. Good agents make the process run smoothly.

Do you like new writers? What should new writers do to break into the business? Yes. Be confident in writing for an audience and know who your audience is. Read books. Know how to effectively get your point across to the reader. Take your time. Know why you are writing. Sell yourself in two paragraphs.

How should writers approach you? Through agents.

What are some common mistakes writers make? What really gets on your nerves? Laziness, putting little thought into something.

What can writers do to get your attention and to avoid the slush pile? Write good, clear, concise cover letters. Put your best foot forward.

What have been some of your craziest experiences with submissions? After I have rejected a project, having family members call and convince me of why I am making a mistake.

What have been some of your best experiences with writers or in your job? Developing a productive author/editor relationship is the most fulfilling part of the job.

What, if anything, makes you different from other editors? I make myself available to the author, I'm conscientious, I come from the agent side so I know what is important to authors. I can negotiate and know what the common problems are that writers have and know how to effectively solve them.

Any advice for writers? Be aggressive, sell yourself, get an agent. Nothing will happen if you are passive in this business. Be aggressive, but don't nag.

Renee Sedliar, Associate Editor
Born: October 28, 1970.
Education: B.A., English and Liberal Arts; M.A., Fine Arts and Creative Writing from the University of Michigan.

Employment history/editor career path: I have been at HarperSanFrancisco for seven years.

What would you be doing if you were not an editor? I would teach creative writing on a high school or undergraduate level.

What has been your most successful book that you have acquired to date? I've worked with Lynne Hinton, author of *Friendship Cake*, *The Things I Know Best*, and *Garden of Faith*.

What books have you acquired that make you the most proud? What books that you have acquired reflect the types of books you like to represent? The novels *The Monk Downstairs*, *Slow Way Home*, *The Still Point Dhommapoda*, and *The Hope Springs Series*.

Do you represent fiction? If so, what are you looking for? We're starting to do more fiction here but it must have a spiritual angle. Some of our titles include Lynne Hinton's books *The Treasure of Montsegur* and *The Monk Downstairs*.

Do you represent nonfiction? Yes. It must have a spiritual or inspirational tone.

Do you require book proposals? If so, what do you look for in evaluating a book proposal? Yes. I look for clarity, directness of purpose, creativity, how well authors know what they want to do (where they are going), author credentials, and sample material.

Are certain aspects of a book proposal given more weight than others? It's on a per-project basis—author credentials, sample chapters, timeliness of topic.

What process do you use for making a decision? What is the process for acquisition, is there a committee? Yes, we have weekly meetings with a committee composed of the editorial staff, publicity, marketing, and the publisher.

Are agents important? Why? Yes, they make the whole publishing process go much smoother. They know which editors to send what projects to, and they help authors to understand the publishing business.

Do you like new writers? What should new writers do to break into the business? Yes, I champion the underdog. I would say to break into the business, you need to get a good agent and pay attention to the market.

How should writers approach you? A query letter, sample chapters, outline with SASE.

What are some common mistakes writers make? What really gets on your nerves? Lack of knowledge about their material or the market. Lack of knowledge about what we publish. General sloppiness (typos in cover letters don't make a good impression).

What can writers do to get your attention and to avoid the slush pile? Have a topic that catches my attention or write about something that appeals to me. If it doesn't appeal to me but I know of a colleague that it does, I will pass it on to that person. I do try to read everything that comes across my desk.

What have been some of your craziest experiences with submissions? I've received some proposals with strangely creative content, making outrageous claims along the lines of things you would find in the tabloids.

What have been some of your best experiences with writers or in your job? Simply meeting and working with so many amazing, creative, and intelligent people.

Any advice for writers? Be conscientious, be neat and careful, pay attention to the market and whom you are sending material to, don't waste valuable time, and realize that there is a lot of work involved in writing a book.

PERENNIAL

Perennial publishes fiction and nonfiction originals and reprints in trade paperback format. Perennial's broad range includes everything from Matt Groening's *The Simpsons* to Thomas Moore's *Care of the Soul.*

Titles indicative of the nonfiction list include: *African Blood* by Alex Shoumatoff; *Mars and Venus in Touch* by John Gray; *The American Dream: Stories from the Heart of Our Nation* by Dan Rather; *Frida: A Biography of Frida Kahlo* by Hayden Herrera; *Happy Hours: Alcohol in a Woman's Life* by Devon Jersild; *Heart: A Natural History of the Heart-Filled Life* by Gail Godwin; *Who Owns Death?: Capital Punishment, the American Conscience, and the End of Executions* by Robert Jay Lifton and Greg Mitchell.

Titles representative of Perennial's literature and fiction list are: *Suicide's Girlfriend: A Novella and Short Stories* by Elizabeth Evans; *Too Many Men* by Lily Brett; *Watch by Moonlight* by Kate Hawks; *The Catsitters* by James Wolcott; *I Wish I Had a Red Dress* by Pearl Cleage; *The Justus Girls* by Evelyn "Slim" Lambright; *The Shape of Things to Come* by Maud Casey.

Recent releases include: *Blue Suburbia* by Lucy Albanese; *Ask Me Again Tomorrow* by Olympia Dukakis (reprint); *Roone* by Roone Arledge (reprint); *Almost Like Being in Love* by Steve Kluger; *Big Bratty Book of Bart* by Matt Groening.

PERFECTBOUND

PerfectBound is the e-book imprint at HarperCollins and publishes a diverse list of titles. Many of the e-book titles have special features that are unavailable in other editions.

QUILL

Quill reprints previously published books in mass-market paperback format.

RAYO

RAYO publishes hardcover and paperback books that exemplify the diversity within the Latino community, in both English and Spanish-language editions. RAYO's mission is "to connect culture with thought, invigorating tradition with spirit."

Titles representative of RAYO's select list include: *The Hispanic Condition: The Power of a People* by Ilan Stavans; *The Twelve Gifts of Birth* by Charlene Costanzo; *The*

Republic of East LA: Stories by Luis J. Rodriguez; *Does a Kangaroo Have a Mother Too? El Canguro Tiene Mama* by Eric Carle (Illustrator) and Teresa Mlawer (Translator); *The Wise Women of Havana* by Jose Raul Bernardo.

New releases include: *Celia: My Life* by Celia Cruz; *Burro Genius* by Victor Villasenor; *Unsettling* by Lynda Sandoval; *The Latino Wave* by Jorge Ramos.

REGANBOOKS

This imprint is known for its informal slogan "Not Just the Same Old Story." From politics to pop culture, health and fitness, to hot new fiction, wherever there's a zeitgeist, there's a Regan publishing campaign. ReganBooks boasts a stable of phenomenal and diverse bestselling authors, including Wally Lamb, Jackie Collins, Howard Stern, Robert Bork, Christopher Darden, Marilu Henner, and Dr. Barry Sears. The imprint was founded by one of publishing's most dynamic personalities, Judith Regan.

Titles indicative of the fiction list include: *The Power of a Teacup: A Story of Art, Love, and Sacred Gardens* by Lissi Kaplan; *Dark City Dames: The Wicked Women of Film Noir* by Eddie Muller; *The Return of the Sacred* by F. David Peat.

Nonfiction titles representative of ReganBooks include: *500 Questions to Ask Before You Ask Them to Bed: Finding the Right Mate by Asking the Right Questions* by Laurie L. Seale; *Child No More: A Memoir* by Xaviera Hollander; *8 Total Life Changes to Improve Your Body, Your Health, and Your Life Today!* by Jay Williams.

Recent releases include: *The Assistants* by Robin Lynn Williams; *The Other Man* by Michael Bergin; *God and Ronald Reagan* by Paul Kengor; *The New Basics: A to Z Baby and Child Care for the Modern Parent* by Dr. Michael Cohen; *Zone Meals in Seconds: 150 Fast and Delicious Recipes for Breakfast, Lunch and Dinner* by Dr. Barry Sears and Lynn Sears.

Direct queries and SASEs to:

Judith Regan, Publisher

Calvert Morgan, Editorial Director

WILLIAM MORROW

William Morrow, acquired in 1999 by HarperCollins Publishing, is one of the nation's leading publishers of general trade books, including bestselling fiction, nonfiction, and cookbooks. With such acclaimed authors as Sidney Sheldon, Mary Stewart, Robert Pirsig, Emeril Lagasse, and Cokie Roberts, Morrow continues its history of publishing quality books and remains committed to bringing the best of commercial hardcover literature to the broadest possible audience.

Representative titles in the biographies/memoirs category include: *Authorized Biography of Christopher Isherwood* by Peter Parker; *Michael Jordan* by Richard Brenner; *Back Then: Two Lives in 1950s New York* by Anne Bernays and Justin Kaplan; *One Perfect Op: An Insider's Account of the Navy Seal Special Warfare Teams* by Dennis C. Chalker, et al.

Titles indicative of William Morrow's literature and fiction list include: *Enough Rope: Collected Stories* by Lawrence Block; *The Middle Ages* by Jennie Fields; *Sleepyhead* byMark Billingham; *Breathing Room* by Susan Elizabeth Phillips; *Sons of Heaven* by Terrence Cheng; *The Body in the Bonfire: A Faith Fairchild Mystery* by Katherine Hall Page; *Unholy Order: A Paul Devlin Mystery* by William Heffernan.

Recent titles include: *Emily's Reasons Why Not* by Carrie Gerlach; *Divine Sarah* by Adam Brauer; *The Annuciation of Francesca Dunn* by Janis Hallowell; *The Perfect Play* by Audrey Unger; *The Ideal Bride* by Stephanie Laurens; *The Burglar on the Prowl* by Lawrence Block; *The Sons of Camelot* by Laurence Leamer.

Direct queries and SASEs to:

Carolyn Marino, Vice President, Editorial Director—commercial fiction, mysteries, suspense, and women's fiction

---

HARPERCOLLINS CHILDREN'S BOOKS GROUP

AVON

GREENWILLOW BOOKS

HARPERCOLLINS CHILDREN'S BOOKS

HARPERFESTIVAL

HARPERTROPHY

JOANNA COTLER BOOKS

LAURA GERINGER BOOKS

TEMPEST

10 E. 53rd St., New York, NY 10022

212-261-6500

AVON BOOKS

Avon Books is home to some of the most popular fiction being published in library binding and paperback formats for young readers. Romance, mystery, high adventure, and fantasy titles dominate this imprint's list. Avon also boasts successful series like Making Out, Animal Emergency, Get Real, and Enchanted Hearts. Authors representative of Avon are Bruce Coville, Beatrice Sparks, and Dave Duncan. Avon describes its list as "a kid-friendly best-selling commercial powerhouse."

Representative titles in the 4-8 age group include: *Get Well, Gators* by Joanna Cole and *Bravo, Amelia Bedelia!* by Herman Parish and Lynn Sweat (Illustrator). In young adult fiction they include: *Gwyneth and the Thief* (Avon True Romance) by Margaret Moore and *Anna and the Duke* (Avon True Romance) by Kathryn Smith.

GREENWILLOW BOOKS

Greenwillow, founded in 1974, publishes books in hardcover and library bindings for children of all ages. "We hope that at the heart of each book there is honesty, emotion, and depth conveyed by an author or artist who has something that is worth saying to children and who says it in a way that is worth reading."

Recent titles that are representative of their list include: *The Train of States* by Peter Sis; *Ida B.* by Katherine Hannigan; *A Crack in The Line* by Michael Lawrence; *The Oracle Betrayed* by Catherine Fisher; *Olive Ocean* by Kevin Henkes, Newbery Honor Award Recipient.

Direct query and SASE to:

Virgina Duncan, Vice-President/Publisher

HARPERCOLLINS CHILDREN'S BOOKS

HarperCollins Children's Books is known worldwide for its tradition of publishing quality books for children in hardcover, library binding, and paperback for children, from toddlers through teens. This imprint also boasts several successful series, such as: I Can Read, Math Start, and Let's Read and Find Out.

Titles representative of this list are: *Ten Go Tango* by Arthur Dorros and *I'm Not Going to Chase the Cat Today!* by Jessica Harper; *Big Bear Ball* by Joanne Ryder and Steven Kellogg (Illustrator); *The Firebird* by Jane Yolen and Vladimir Vasilevich Vagin (Illustrator) and *Danny and the Dinosaur Go to Camp* (I Can Read Book) by Syd Hoff (Illustrator).

Recent releases for ages 4-8 include: *I Already Know I Love You* by Billy Crystal and *My Grandson Lew* by Charlotte Zolotow.

Recent releases for ages 9-12 include: *Measle and The Wrathmonk* by Ian Ogilvy and *Carnivorous Carnival (Series of Unfortunate Events #9)* by Lemony Snicket and Brett Helquist (Illustrator).

Recent releases for teens: *Alice, I Think* by Susan Juby; *The Hunting of the Last Dragon* by Sherryl Jordan.

Send query letters and SASEs to:

Alix Reid, Vice-President

Margaret Anastas, Editorial Director at Large

Kate Morgan Jackson, Senior Vice President, Assoc. Publisher, Editor-in-Chief

Phoebe Yeh, Editorial Director

Elise Howard, Vice President and Director of Paperback Publishing

Barbara Lalicki, Senior Vice President and Editorial Director

Maria Modugno, Vice President and Editorial Director

Katherine Fegen, Editorial Director, Katherine Fegen Books

HARPERFESTIVAL

HarperFestival is home to books, novelties, and merchandise for very young children, from infants to 6-year-olds. Classic board books such as *Goodnight Moon* and *Runaway Bunny* established this list a decade ago. Today, Festival boasts programs such as HarperGrowing Tree and Heidi Murkoff's What to Expect Kids, as well as character-based programs such as Biscuit and Paddington Bear.

A few titles indicative of this list are: *My Little Pony*; *Spiderman 2* (movie tie-in) and *Let's Go, Baby-O!* by Marcia Leonard.

Emily Brenner, Editorial Director

HARPERTROPHY

HarperTrophy is a leading paperback imprint for children, producing original fiction and nonfiction, as well as paperback reprints of previously published titles. Currently with more Newbery and Caldecott winners than any other publisher, Harpertrophy has good reason to be proud. From picture books by Maurice Sendak to novels by Laura Ingalls Wilder, E. B. White, Katherine Paterson, and Beverly Cleary, Trophy continues its tradition of offering a broad list of the old and the new.

Titles representative of this list include: *Tumble Bumble* by Felicia Bond; *Betsy-Tacy* by Maud Hart Lovelace and *Cowboy Ghost* by Robert Newton Peck.

Emily Brenner, Editorial Director

JOANNA COTLER BOOKS

Joanna Cotler Books publishes literary and commercial picture books and fiction for all ages. Authors and illustrators include award winners, bestsellers, and luminaries such as Clive Barker, Francesca Lia Block, Sharon Creech, Jamie Lee Curtis, Laura Cornell, Patricia MacLachlan, Barbara Robinson, Art Spiegelman, Jerry Spinelli, and William Steig.

A few recent titles indicative of Joanna Cotler's list are: *Heartbeat* by Sharon Creech; *It's Hard To Be Five* by Jamie Lee Curtis; *Diary of a Worm* by Doreen Cronin.

Joanna Cotler, Senior Vice President and Publisher

LAURA GERINGER BOOKS

Laura Geringer Books was founded in the early 1990s to provide children with award-winning, best-selling, and innovative authors and artists who "push the envelope" and set new standards of excellence. Authors on this list include: William Joyce, Laura Joffe Numeroff, Felicia Bond, Bruce Brooks, Richard Egielski, and Sarah Weeks.

Recent titles include: *So Be It* by Sarah Weeks; *Toes* by Tor Seidler; *The Ugly Truckling* by David Gordon.

Laura Geringer, Senior Vice President and Publisher

TEMPEST

Tempest produces previously published books in both hardcover and paperback formats, as well as some original titles for young adults. It publishes "Great books for real teens, with characters, settings, and stories relevant to their own lives, minds, and spirits."

Recent titles include: *The Alison Rules* by Catherine Clark; *Cruise Control* by Terry Truman; *Please Don't Kill the Freshman* by Zoey Trope and *True Confessions of a Heartless Girl* by Martha Brooks.

Elise Howard, Vice President and Executive Publishing Director for Paperback Books

HOLTZBRINCK PUBLISHERS, LLC

FARRAR, STRAUS & GIROUX

HENRY HOLT AND COMPANY

ST. MARTIN'S PRESS

Holtzbrinck Publishers, LLC, the US subsidiary of German-based media and publishing company Verlagsgruppe Georg von Holtzbrinck, includes book divisions Farrar, Straus & Giroux, Henry Holt and Company, and St. Martin's Press.

FARRAR, STRAUS & GIROUX

FARRAR, STRAUS & GIROUX BOOKS FOR YOUNG READERS

HILL AND WANG

NORTH POINT PRESS

FABER AND FABER, INC..

19 Union Square West, New York, NY 10003

212-741-6900   fax: 212-206-5340

www.fsgbooks.com

Farrar, Straus & Giroux was founded in 1946 by Roger W. Straus. The firm is renowned for its international list of literary fiction, nonfiction, poetry, and children's books. Farrar, Straus & Giroux authors have won extraordinary acclaim over the years, including numerous National Book Awards, Pulitzer Prizes, and 21 Nobel Prizes in literature. Nobel Prize winners include: Knut Hamsun, Hermann Hesse, T. S. Eliot,

Par Lagerkvist, Francois Mauriac, Juan Ramon Jimenez, Salvatore Quasimodo, Nelly Sachs, Czeslaw Milosz, Elias Canetti, William Golding, Wole Soyinka, Joseph Brodsky, Camilo Jose Cela, Nadine Gordimer, Derek Walcott, and Seamus Heaney.

Poetry has always played a pivotal role on the Farrar, Straus & Giroux list, which boasts some of the greatest names in modern verse, ranging from Elizabeth Bishop, Ted Hughes, and Phillip Larkin to John Ashbery, Thom Gunn, and Les Murray.

Fiction has an even greater international reach, distinguished by Rosellen Brown, Jim Crace, Michael Cunningham, Jonathan Franzen, Carlos Fuentes, Peter Hoeg, Jamaica Kincaid, Bernard Malamud, Alice McDermott, Peter Nadas, Walker Percy, Richard Powers, Susan Sontag, Scott Turow, Mario Vargas Llosa, Tom Wolfe, and Lois-Ann Yamanaka.

History, art history, natural history, current affairs, and science round out a strong list in nonfiction, represented by Thomas Friedman, Philip Gourevitch, Roy Jenkins, Gina Kolata, Ben Macintyre, Louis Menaud, Giles Milton, and John McPhee.

Recent titles include: *Remains: Non-Viewable* by John Sacret Young; *After* by Claire Tristram; *Antipodes: Stories* by Ignacio Padilla; *A Sentimental Murder: Love and Madness in the Eighteenth Century* by John Brewer and *Redbone: Malice and Murder Inside Atlanta's Black Elite* by Ron Stodghill.

FSG's sales catalog and promotional endeavors include services for a number of smaller houses with literary orientations, such as Soho Press, Aperture, Harvill Press, and Graywolf Press.

Query letters and SASEs should be directed to:

Jonathan Galassi, President—fiction, nonfiction, art history, belles lettres, business, and poetry

John Glusman, Editor in Chief—literary fiction, thrillers, history, biography, science, politics and current events

Elisabeth Sifton, Vice President and Senior Editor—History, politics, current events and issues, biography, and literary fiction

Ayesha Ponde, Senior Editor—cultural and social issues, academics, fiction, narrative nonfiction, memoirs and multicultural projects

FARRAR, STRAUS & GIROUX BOOKS FOR YOUNG READERS

The FSG juvenile program Books for Young Readers publishes quality picture books and novels for children and young adults. Award-winning authors include Jack Gantos, Madeleine L'Engle, Louis Sachar, Uri Shulevitz, Peter Sis, David Small, William Steig and Sarah Stewart.

Recent titles include: *The Canning Season* by Polly Horvath; *The Tree of Life* by Peter Sis; *The Friend* by Sarah Stewart and David Small (illustrator).

Query letters and SASEs should be directed to:

Frances Foster, Publisher, Frances Foster Books

Margaret Ferguson, Vice President, Associate Publisher, and Editorial Director

Wes Adams, Executive Editor

Melanie Kroupa, Publisher, Melanie Kroupa Books

Beverly Reingold, Executive Editor

HILL AND WANG

Hill and Wang focuses on hard and softcover books of academic interest for both the trade market and the college market. The list is strong in American history, world history, and politics. Among its authors are Roland Barthes, Michael Burleigh, William Cronon, Langston Hughes, Robert Wiebe, and Eli Wiesel.

Representative titles include: *Murdering McKinley* by Eric Rauchway; *William Clark and the Shaping of the West* by Landon Y. Jones; *Pathfinder* by Tom Chaffin; *Pox Americana* by Elizabeth A. Fenn and *The Rehnquist Court* by Herman Schwartz.

Query letters and SASEs should be directed to:

Thomas LeBien, Publisher

NORTH POINT PRESS

The North Point Press specializes in hard and softcover literary nonfiction, with an emphasis on natural history, travel, ecology, music, food, and cultural criticism. Past and present authors include Peter Matthiessen, Evan Connell, Beryl Markahm, A. J. Liebling, Margaret Visser, Wendell Berry, and M. F. K. Fisher.

Representative titles include: *Dark Heart of Italy* by Tobias Jones; *Sonnets to Orpheus* by Rilke Maria Rainer; *A Sweet Quartet* by Fran Gage; *Yoga Mala* by Sri K. Pattabhi Jois; *To Reach the Clouds* by Philippe Petit.

FABER AND FABER, INC.

Faber and Faber Inc. offers a unique list of drama, film, poetry, and books of cultural interest. Among its authors are Pulitzer Prize winning playwrights David Auburn and Margaret Edson, as well as the British dramatists Tom Stoppard and David Hare.

Representative titles include: *Kubrick* by Michele Cement; *Our Lady of 121st Street and Other Plays* by Stephen Adly Guirgis; *The Hitchcock Murders* by Peter Conrad; *Moviemakers' Master Class* by Laurent Tirard and *Speak the Speech!* by Rhona Silverbush and Sami Plotkin.

Query letters and SASEs should be directed to:

Linda Rosenberg, Editor

HENRY HOLT AND COMPANY

HENRY HOLT FOR YOUNG READERS

EDGE BOOKS

REDFEATHER BOOKS

OWLETS PAPERBACKS

HENRY HOLT REFERENCE

JOHN MACRAE BOOKS

METROPOLITAN BOOKS

OWL BOOKS

TIMES BOOKS

21ST CENTURY BOOKS

115 West 18th Street, New York, NY 10011

212-886-9200

www.henryholt.com

One of the oldest publishers in the United States, Henry Holt is known for publishing high quality books, including those by such authors as Erich Fromm, Robert Frost, Hermann Hesse, Norman Mailer, Robert Louis Stevenson, Ivan Turgenev, and H. G. Wells. The publication program currently focuses on American and international fiction, biography, history, politics, science, psychology, health, and books for children. The firm was purchased by the German-based Holtzbrinck Group several years ago and merged with other recently purchased U.S. publishers.

Titles representative of Henry Holt's nonfiction list include: *American Road: The Story of an Epic Transcontinental Journey at the Dawn of the Motor Age* by Pete Davies; *American Son: A Portrait of John F. Kennedy, Jr.* by Richard Blow; *A Death in Texas: A Story of Race, Murder and a Small Town's Struggle for Redemption* by Dina Temple-Raston; *Balsamic Dreams: A Short but Self-Important History of the Baby Boomer Generation* by Joe Queenan; *Below Another Sky: A Mountain Adventure in Search of a Lost Father* by Rick Ridgeway; *Borrowed Finery: A Memoir* by Paula Fox; *The Bridge at No Gun Ri: A Hidden Nightmare from the Korean War* by Charles J. Hanley, Martha Mendoza, and Sang-hun Choe; *Bury My Heart at Wounded Knee: An Indian History of the American West* by Dee Brown; *Day of Infamy 60th Anniversary: The Classic Account of the Bombing of Pearl Harbor* by Walter Lord; *Dr. Eckener's Dream Machine: The Great Zeppelin and the Dawn of Air Travel* by Douglas Botting; *For Women Only: A Revolutionary Guide to Overcoming Sexual Dysfunction and Reclaiming Your Sex Life* by Dr. Jennifer Berman, Dr. Laura Berman, and Elisabeth Bumiller; *Home Lands: Portrait of the New Jewish Diaspora* by Larry Tye.

Titles representative of Henry Holt fiction: *Accidents in the Home* by Tessa Hadley; *Desert Burial* by Brian Littlefair; *The Bear in the Attic* by Patrick F. McManus; *Eva Moves the Furniture* by Margot Livesey; *Field Guide* by Gwendolen Gross; *The Good German* by Joseph Kanon; *Great American Plain* by Gary Sernovitz; *Greetings from the Golden State* by Leslie Brenner; *He Sleeps* by Reginald McKnight; *Iced* by Jenny Siler.

Recent nonfiction titles include: *In the Company of Soldiers: A Chronicle of Combat in Iraq* by Rick Atkinson; *The Importance of Being Famous: Behind the Scenes of the Celebrity-Industrial Complex* by Maureen Orth; *How Tough Could it Be? The Trials and Errors of a Sportswriter Turned Stay-at-Home Dad* by Austin Murphy.

Recent fiction titles include: *Saints at the River* by Ron Rash; *Prince Edward* by Dennis Mcfarland; *Missing Justice, A Samantha Kincaid Mystery* by Alafair Burke; *She Smiled Sweetly* by Mary Ann Tirone-Smith.

Direct query letters and SASEs to:

Jennifer Barth, Editor in Chief—Commercial and literary fiction, biography, memoir, narrative nonfiction and pop culture

HENRY HOLT AND COMPANY BOOKS FOR YOUNG READERS

Henry Holt and Company Books for Young Readers publishes a wide range of children's books, from picture books for preschoolers to fiction for young adults. Imprints include Edge Books, Redfeather Books, and Owlets Paperbacks.

Representative titles include: *Beach Patrol* by John O'Brien and Max Bilkins; *Mary Was a Little Lamb* by Gloria Rand and Ted Rand (Illustrator); *Humphrey's Bedtime* by Sally Hunter (Illustrator); *A Christmas Tree in the White House* by Gary Hines, Alexandra Wallner; *Air Show* by Anastasia Suen and Cecco Mariniello (Illustrator); *Army Ant Parade* by April Pulley Sayre and Rick Chrustowski (Illustrator); *Badger's New House* by Robin Muller (Illustrator); *Bug Cemetery* by Frances Hill and Vera Rosenberry (Illustrator); *Cat in the Manger* by Michael Foreman (Illustrator); *Ark in the Park* by Wendy Orr and Kerry Millard (Illustrator); *The Circus Lunicus* by Marilyn Singer; *The Copper Treasure* by Melvin Burgess and Richard Williams (Illustrator); *The Dollhouse Magic* by Yona Zeldis McDonough and Diane Palmisciano (Illustrator); *The Number Devil: A Mathematical Adventure* by Hans Magnus Enzensberger, et al.; *Ola's Wake* by B. J. Stone.

Direct queries and SASEs to:

Laura Godwin, Vice President and Publisher

JOHN MACRAE BOOKS

Nonfiction titles representative of John Macrae Books include: *Vermeer: A View of Delft* by Anthony Bailey; *Among the Bears: Raising Orphaned Cubs in the Wild* edited by Benjamin Gray Kilham; *Eisenhower: The Making of a Commander* by Carlo D'Este; *Eye of the Albatross: Views of the Endangered Sea* by Carl Safina; *The Artist's Wife* by Max Phillips; *The Mold in Dr. Florey's Coat* by Eric Lax ; *A Death in Brazil* by Peter Robb.

Direct queries and SASEs to:

John Macrae, Publisher

METROPOLITAN BOOKS

Metropolitan Books, established in 1995, publishes fiction and nonfiction of the highest quality, both American and international. This Henry Holt imprint is open to various genres, unconventional points of view, controversial opinions, and new voices. From short stories to social science, award winning novels to American politics, foreign fiction to cutting edge history and current affairs, Metropolitan is committed to diversity, distinction, and surprise.

Authors published by Metropolitan Books include: Ann Crittenden, Mike Davis, Barbara Ehrenreich, Susan Faludi, Orlando Figes, Michael Frayn, Eduardo Galeano, Atul Gawande, Todd Gitlin, Arlie Russell Hochschild, Michael Ignatieff, Orville Schell, and Tom Segev.

Titles representative of Metropolitan's nonfiction list include: *Black Earth City: When Russia Ran Wild (and So Did We)* by Charlotte Hobson; *Dr. Tatiana's Sex Advice to All Creation* by Olivia Judson; *Elvis in Jerusalem: Post-Zionism and the Americanization of Israel* by Tom Segev and Haim Watzman; *Media Unlimited: How the Torrent of Images and Sounds Overwhelms Our Lives* by Todd Gitlin; *The Mind of Egypt: History and Meaning in the Time of the Pharaohs* by Jan Assmann and Andrew Jenkins.

Titles indicative of Metropolitan fiction include: *The Beholder* by Thomas Farber; *Spies* by Michael Frayn; *The Appointment* by Herta Muller, et al.; *Housebroken: 3 Novellas* by Yael Hedaya, et al.; *Afterimage* by Helen Humphreys; *Dugan Under Ground* by Tom De Haven; *I Dreamed I Was a Ballerina* by Anna Pavlova and Edgar Degas.

Recent titles include: *The Italian Boy: A Tale of Murder and Body Snatching in 1830s London* by Sarah Wise; *Heavy Metal Freeway: California's Season in Hell* by Mike Davis; *The Empire Builders: America's New Foreign Policy Mandarins* by Tom Barry; *Sixteen Acres: The Outrageous Struggle for the Future of Ground Zero* by Philip Nobel and *The Lost Island: Alone Among the Fruitful and Multiplying* by Alfred Van Cleef.

Direct queries and SASEs to:

Sara Bershtel, Associate Publisher—Individualistic nonfiction and literary fiction

Riva Hocherman, Editor

OWL BOOKS

Owl Books reprints many of Henry Holt's nonfiction titles in trade paperback format, as well as producing original titles.

Titles representative of the Owl list include: *Fight Club* by Chuck Palahniuk (fiction, reprint); *Winning Scholarships For College* by Marianne Ragins; *The Pain Free Book: 6 Simple Steps to End Pain and Reclaim Your Active Life* by Harris H. McIlwain, M.D. and Debra Fulghum Bruce, M.D.; *Fire and Ashes: On the Front Lines Battling Wildfires* by John N. Maclean; *Why Zebras Don't Get Ulcers (3rd Edition)* by Robert M. Sapolsky.

PUBLISHING CONGLOMERATES

TIMES BOOKS

Times Books, launched in 2001, is the result of a copublishing agreement between Holt and the *New York Times*; its nonfiction list focuses on science, business, and current events.

Titles representative of this list include: *The Big Questions: Probing the Promise and Limits of Science* by Richard Morris, Ph.D.; *Courting Disaster: The Supreme Court and the Dangerous Unmaking of American Law* by Martin Garbus; *Future Evolution: An Illuminated History of Life to Come* by Peter Ward and Alexis Rockman; *How Race Is Lived in America: Pulling Together, Pulling Apart* by correspondents of the *New York Times*: Joseph Lelyveld, James Madison, Garry Wills, and Arthur M. Schlesinger, Jr.; *John Quincy Adams* by Robert V. Remini and Arthur M. Schlesinger, Jr.; *The New Rules of Personal Investing: How to Prosper in a Changing Economy* by Allen R. Myerson, Floyd Norris, and Gretchen Morgenson; *The Power of Babel: A Natural History of Language* by John McWhorter; *Sex: A Natural History* by Joann Ellison Rodgers; *The Tangled Wing: Biological Constraints on the Human Spirit* by Melvin Konner; *The Tending Instinct: How Nurturing Is Essential to Who We Are and How We Live* by Shelley E. Taylor; *The Turtle and the Stars: Observations of an Earthbound Astronomer* by Arthur Upgren, Ph.D.; *Writers on Writing: Collected Essays from the New York Times* by John Darnton.

Recent releases include: *Gay Marriage: Why it is Good For Gays, Good For Straights and Good For America* by Jonathan Rauch; *Human Nature: A Blueprint For Managing the Earth—By People, For People* by James Trefil; *Laboratory of Justice: The Supreme Court's 200 Year Struggle to Integrate Science and the Law* by David L. Faigman; *The Status Syndrome: How Social Standing Affects Our Health and Longevity* by Michael Marmot.

Direct queries and SASEs to:

Paul Golob, Editor

ST. MARTIN'S PRESS

ST. MARTIN'S PRESS TRADE

ST. MARTIN'S REFERENCE GROUP

175 Fifth Avenue, New York, NY 10010

212-674-5151

www.stmartins.com

Founded in 1952, St. Martin's Press—one of the ten largest general publishers in the United States and an important publisher of trade, mass-market, college, and global academic titles—is an international publisher with a broad and comprehensive program. St. Martin's is now part of the German-based international communications conglomerate Verlagsgruppe Georg von Holtzbrinck. Within its framework,

St.Martin's enjoys its long-standing tradition of editorial independence, as it operates from its historic environs in Manhattan's famed Flatiron Building.

St. Martin's publishes across the spectrum of trade nonfiction and hosts a wide range of popular and literary fiction. The house is particularly strong in a number of speciality areas, some with associated lines and imprints (including popular culture, international arts and letters, relationships, multicultural topics, science, business, and professional topics). St. Martin's is also known for a strong list of scholarly and reference titles and offers a solid lineup of college textbooks. It produces hardcover, trade paperback, and mass-market paper editions and also offers a line of calendars.

Representative titles include: *The Rise and Fall of the British Empire* by Lawrence James; *Topping From Below* by Laura Reese; *The Other Mrs. Kennedy* by Jerry Oppenheimer; *Farewell, I'm Bound to Leave You* by Fred Chappell; *In the Deep Midwinter* by Robert Clark; *The River Beyond the World* by Janet Peery; *Beyond Jennifer and Jason* by Linda Rose; *Mary Queen of Scotland and the Isles* by Margaret George; *The Sculptress* by Minette Walters; *Aaron Spelling: A Prime-Time Life* by Aaron Spelling; *To Build the Life You Want, Create the Work You Love* by Marsha Sinetar.

Recent titles include: *The Men We Became* by Robert Littell and *Saucer the Conquest* by Steven Conts.

Queries and SASEs should be directed to:

Charles Spicer, Executive Editor—Commercial fiction: crime, suspense, mysteries; nonfiction: true crime, biography and history. "When people ask me what I love about my job, the response is always the same: the variety of books and authors on my list makes every day a fascinating challenge. For me, being a generalist makes publishing both interesting and fun. My hardcover list encompasses bestselling commercial suspense fiction by authors like Stephen Coonts, Stephen J. Cannell, and James W. Hall as well as British authors Val McDermid and Julia Wallis Martin. I also publish works of history and biography, among them *The Rise and Fall of the British Empire* by historian Lawrence James and a biography of the last Czarina of Russia by acclaimed biographer Carolly Erickson. Popular nonfiction is another favorite of mine and two beautiful illustrated boks exemplify what I've done in this area: *Kennedy Weddings* by Jay Mulvaney and *At the Plaza: An Illustrated History of the World's Most Famous Hotel* by Curt Gathje. I am also a part of SMP Paperbacks where I oversee the True Crime Library imprint, which has long been the most successful publisher of nonfiction crime with many New York Times bestsellers and Edgar winners to its credit, including the paperback edition of *Jon Benet* by Steve Thomas and *To the Last Breath* by Carlton Stowers.

Michael Connor, Editor—Pop culture and general nonfiction. "I love not being pigeonholed into only publishing one kind of genre. My personal interests are as diverse as our list and I would hate to pass on a project I felt passion for because I was stuck working on one type of book. Mainly my acquisitions center around popular culture, with a mix of about 90% nonfiction to 10% fiction. I love projects that are focused around media, film, music, celebrity, fashion and probably anything on your shelves that you'd describe as young, now, sexy, and hip. As for fiction, it's true, I'm a guy that digs 'chick-lit' If it's fast-paced, screamingly funny, yet smartly written with a sharp eye that's tuned to today's culture, I'm excited. I'm also on the hunt for commercial gay fiction that can get men's minds as well as their hearts racing. Additionally, I look for journalists who would like to shape a column or article into a great read, licensing opportunities that can expand a brand into the world of books, and for my serious side, I enjoy relationship books, and practical service nonfiction."

Elizabeth Beier, Editor—General nonfiction. "What makes me wake up in the morning and stay up late with a pencil in my hand is the chance to bring in personalities from other worlds and help them transform what they're all about into terrific reading—a recent example is Doris Roberts of 'Everbody Loves Raymond' and her wonderful bestseller *Are You Hungry, Dear?* And I'm crazy about those charming and literate books that can gift wrap an issue for women everywhere—like our recent *Entre Nous: A Woman's Guide to Finding Her Inner French Girl* by Debra Ollivier and *The Between Boyfriends Book* by Cindy Chupack. I also marinate in pop culture, and love to acquire and edit books relating to movies, music, trends, and cultural icons. Most of the books I edit are nonfiction, but I eagerly make an exception for novelists that knock my socks off—a group that includes Tom Perotta, author of *Joe College* and the upcoming *Little Children*, and Alisa Valdes-Rodriguez, whose fresh and fast *The Dirty Girls Social Club* made a lot of readers happy last summer."

George Witte, Editor in Chief—Quality literary fiction and nonfiction of literary or intellectual interest. "As Editor-in-Chief, I'm responsible for managing our editors and helping them shape St. Martin's publishing list. . .St. Martin's editors acquire and publish across the spectrum of books; our list offers depth and breadth to all kinds of readers. During my twenty years here, I've taken particular pleasure in the number of first books we've published—many of those authors are now writing their fifth, tenth, fifteenth, even twentieth book for us. Discovery, energy, and commitment to authors are the driving forces of our house.

I continue to publish literary and commercial fiction for St. Martin's, as well as current affairs and issues, business, and serious narrative nonfiction. Recent acquisitions include the autobiography of a young man who escaped from slavery in the Sudan, a provocative discussion of contemporary Islam by a woman raised in the faith, a history of America's culture of therapy and its consequences, and novels by an Academy Award-winning actor, a Booker Prize finalist, and a BookSense best-selling author."

Hope Dellon, Executive Editor—Fiction: mysteries, serious historical novels; nonfiction: parenting, women's issues, psychology and biography. "I grew up reading mysteries and nineteenth-century fiction and to this day I tend to look for novels that are as strong in storytelling as they are in characters and prose. After studying English at Yale, I worked for legendary mystery editor Joan Kahn at Harper & Row, then joined St. Martin's in 1975. Since then I have published suspense fiction ranging from period mysteries, to modern twists on traditional British 'cozies,' to commercial thrillers. I love both contemporary and historical fiction that creates a detailed and compelling world. Some of my books include Margaret George's biographical novels, Bernard Cornwell's Arthurian trilogy, a retelling of *Pride & Prejudice* set up in contemporary Florida, and a continuation of Margaret Mitchell's *Gone with the Wind* that has been in the works for over five years. In nonfiction, my interests include biography, social history, and psychological memoirs. As the wife of a psychiatrist and mother of two daughters, I also find myself drawn to books on parenting, education, women's issues, and medicine."

Jennifer Weis, Executive Editor—Commercial fiction: women's, thrillers, romance; commercial nonfiction: people books, narrative nonfiction, cookbooks, self-help, health and parenting, humor and popular culture. "As an editor of commercial fiction and nonfiction, I am drawn to books that tell a story. Whether they are voice or plot driven, in fiction I am a fan of the page-turner, in serach of a novel that will strike a chord with its readership, whether it's a thriller, domestic drama, or purely commerical women's read. In nonfiction, I look for authors who have a platform, a niche, something provocative and timely to say, and who say it well. Of particular interest to me are all areas relating to women, such as health, relationships, psychology, and narrative memoir. In general, I look for books that will have a life in hardcover and paperback, and authors I can build into the bestsellers of tomorrow. I also look to generate many of my own ideas, which grow out of being a big magazine reader."

Kelley Ragland, Associate Editor—Commercial and serious nonfiction; literary nonfiction, especially related to women's or racial issues; parenting, psychology, biography, essays, popular and literary fiction and a wide range of mysteries, thrillers and suspense. "I began my career in publishing at St. Martin's Press in 1993, and now publish approximately 30 books a year. Mystery and suspense fiction make up 70% of my list, so it's been great to take part in starting and shaping St. Martin's Minotaur, our crime imprint. My taste in crime runs the gamut from cozy to hardboiled, but is becoming increasingly dark and more serious; in addition to series authors like Kris Nelscott, Dana Stabenow, and Linda Barnes, recent books include *The Barbed-Wire Kiss* by Wallace Stroby and *The Bridge of Sighs* by Olen Steinhauer. I also publish literary and popular fiction, all of which has in common the presence of a strong narrative voice. I've recently begun editing the bestselling novelist Jeffrey Archer. In nonfiction, my interest lies mainly in travel and outdoor/adventure titles; in this area, one recent title is *Looking for Alaska*, the latest book by Peter Jenkins. All in all, if a book sends chills up my spine, tells an enchanting story, launches the career of a promising writer, or takes me to a new place, it just might be my cup of tea."

Jennifer Enderlin, Senior Editor—Women's fiction, psychological suspense, general commercial fiction; commercial nonfiction (sex, relationships, psychology). Enderlin writes, "A friend of mine once said, "How can you read and edit all weekend long and then, when you're done, pick up a novel and read for fun?" And I thought to myself, how could I not? I grew up reading commercial women's fiction—haunting, romantic novels; sexy, hilarious novels; and three-hankie reads. I feel uneasy and incomplete if I don't have a book on me at all times—being stuck on a train with nothing to read is my idea of a nightmare! And commercial nonfiction (what I call 'talk show nonfiction') is another pleasure of mine: popular psychology, self-help, relationships, motivation/inspiration. In nonfiction, watching a promotable author deliver his or her message through the media, and then watching the direct correlation of media to sales, is utterly fascinating. Working with authors and developing projects from the idea stage to the final book is my dream job come true."

Born: June 10, 1967.

Education: B.A., in English from University of New Hampshire.

Employment history/editor career path: Started at Putnam/Berkley in 1989; moved to NAL/Dutton in 1991; moved to SMP in 1993.

Personal interests: Travel.

What would you be doing if you were not an editor? I'd still be reading if I weren't an editor. But maybe only 10 books a week. I'd like to work in a spa—it's the nurturing side of me.

What has been your most successful book that you have acquired to date? *High Five* by Janet Evanovich; *Never Be Lied to Again* by Dr. David Lieberman.

Do you represent fiction? If so, what do you look for? Yes. Commercial women's fiction.

Do you represent nonfiction? Yes.

Are agents important? Why? Yes. I love agents! They bring me great projects and they work hard. After all, they have to do the two hardest things on earth, seek (projects) and sell (projects).

Do you like new writers? What should new writers do to break into the business? Writers are some of the most hilarious, wonderful, inventive, intelligent people around. I feel privileged that I can work with them. On the downside, they can often be insecure, needy, unappreciative, and arrogant! But I'm sure they would say the same thing about editors.

Is there anything you would like to see changed in the industry? I would change dismal entry-level publishing salaries so that we don't lose the best and the brightest to the Internet.

Any additional thoughts? I love the fact that I get to read for a living! I love discovering new writers. I love seeing a book I've fought for, work in the marketplace. I hate the fact that every single weekend is occupied by work. People don't seem to understand that I do not read or edit in the office. Every submission is read at home, every bit of editing is done on the weekends. "Part 2" of my job begins weeknights at 7:30 P.M. and for 8 to 10 hours per day on the weekends.

ST. MARTIN'S PRESS TRADE

BEDFORD BOOKS

MINOTAUR

PALGRAVE

PICADOR USA

RENAISSANCE

STONEWALL INN EDITIONS

THOMAS DUNNE BOOKS

TOR, FORGE, & ORB

175 Fifth Avenue New York, NY 10010

212-674-5151   fax: 212-674-3179

BEDFORD

Bedford is a college publisher specializing in the humanities. Book categories include communication, English, history, music, religion, culture, linguistics, business, and technical writing.

Recent titles indicative of this list include: *Making Sense: A Real-World Rhetorical Reader (2nd Edition)* by Cheryl Glenn; *St. Martin's Guide to Writing (7th Edition)* by Risa Axelrod and Charles Cooper; *Research and Documentation in the Electronic Age* by Diana Hacker and Barbara Fister; *Thinking and Writing About Philosophy* by Hugo Bedau; *The Bedford Guide for College Writers* by X. J. Kennedy, et al. and *A Writer's Reference* by Diana Hacker.

Direct all queries and SASEs to:

Joan Feinberg, President

MINOTAUR

Minotaur is a mystery imprint created by St. Martin's Press in 1999. The name was suggested by editor Ruth Cavin, who says she loves the symbolism of the Greek mythological figure the Minotaur, a creature who guarded the fabled labyrinth and devoured anyone who entered (except for Theseus, of course).

Minotaur publishes mystery books with an emphasis on thrillers that range from very soft to very hard. Many of these books are police procedural, historical nonfiction, and true crime.

Titles representative of Minotaur's list include: *The Pillow Book of Lady Wisteria* by Laura Joh Rowland; *In the Bleak Midwinter* by Julia Spencer-Fleming; *A Mist of Prophe-*

cies by Steven Saylor; *The Bawdy Basket* by Edward Marston; *Buttons and Foes* by Dolores Johnson; *The Corporal Works of Murder* by Carol Anne O'Marie; *Hard Freeze: A Joe Kurtz Novel* by Dan Simmons; *Here Comes the Corpse* by Mark Richard Zubro; *The Irish Sports Pages* by Les Roberts; *Last Scene Alive* by Charlaine Harris ; *Medusa* by Skye Kathleen Moody.

Recent releases include: *Flat Crazy: A Blanco County Mystery* by Ben Rehder; *A Taint in the Blood: A Kate Shugak Novel* by Dana Stabenow; *Skin River* by Steven Sidor; *Tonight I Said Goodbye* by Michael Koryta; *Dry Heat: A David Mapstone Mystery* by Jon Talton; *Choke Point* by James C. Mitchell; *Bahamarama* by Bob Morris; *Please Do Feed the Cat* by Marion Babson; *Sherlock Holmes: The Hidden Years* by Michael Kurland.

PALGRAVE

Palgrave, created in October 2000 and formerly known as St. Martin's Press Scholarly and Reference Division, publishes monographs, and upper-level and graduate-level texts and sophisticated trade books for the general educated reader or scholar. It was created when St. Martin's Press Scholarly and Reference Division and Macmillan Press (UK) united their global publishing operations.

Palgrave publishes a wide range of nonfiction books in the humanities and social sciences. The list contains original works by many of the foremost academic writers and editors in the world, including several Nobel laureates. Books include specialized monographs that make original contributions to scholarship in their disciplines, upper-division supplemental texts and readers designed for classroom use, and trade titles written for a broad, educated, but nonacademic audience. Categories include: history, politics, literature and cultural studies, medieval studies, theater studies, education, religion, gender studies, anthropology, and Latino and Latin American studies.

Titles indicative of this list include: *A History of Censorship in Islamic Societies* by Trevor Mostyn; *A New Democracy* by Harry Shutt; *Arabia of the Bedouins* by Marcel Kurpershoek; *Dialogue of Civilizations* by Majid Tehranian and David W. Chappell; *Diplomacy and Murder in Tehran* by Lawrence Kelly; *Dracula* by Bram Stoker (edited by John Paul Riquelme); *The Cognition of Geographic Space* by Rob Kitchin and Mark Blades; *The Cult of Ivan the Terrible in Stalin's Russia* by Maureen Perrie; *The Effectiveness of EU Business Associations* by Justin Greenwood.

Recent titles include: *Perpetuating the Family Business: 50 Lessons Learned From the Long Lasting, Successful Families in Business* by John L. Ward; *The Korean Conundrum: America's Troubled Relations with North and South Korea* by Ted Galen Carpenter and Doug Bandow; *The British Museum Timeline of the Ancient World* by Katharine Wiltshire; *Ireland in the 20th Century* by Tim Pat Coogan.

Palgrave is also the U.S. distributor of the following U.K. publishers: Manchester University Press, I. B. Tauris, and Zed Books.

Direct query letters and SASEs to:

Michael Flamini, Vice President, Editorial Director

PICADOR USA

Picador USA was founded by St. Martin's Press in 1994. With an international cast of world-class authors, Picador (and its sibling Picador UK imprint) publishes hardcover and paperback editions, highlighting original titles as well as reprints.

Representative Picador USA titles include: *Ultimate Fitness: The Quest for Truth About Health and Exercise* (reprint) by Gina Kolata; *Positively Fifth Street: Murders, Cheetahs and Binion's World Series of Poker* (reprint) by James McManus; *See Under Love* by David Grossman; *Elegy for Iris* by John Bayley; *Father of the Four Passages* by Lois-Ann Yamanaka; *The Adversary* by Emmanuel Carrere; *Lost Geography* by Charlotte Bacon; *The Love of Stones* by Tobias Hill; *An Unexpected Light* by Jason Elliot and *The God Who Begat a Jackal* by Nega Mezlekia.

Query letters and SASEs should be directed to:

Frances Coady, Publisher

Diane Higgins, Editor. "As a passionate reader of both, I acquire quality fiction and nonfiction equally. I'm intrigued by the underlying, intricate network of themes that often influence both genres: the search for love, the struggle to incorporate faith and belief into modern life, and the courage to explore the dark side of family.

I am especially drawn to topics involving Catholicism, Judaism, feminism, liberal political issues, race relations, international culture and politics, and in general both fiction and nonfiction that deal with spirituality. Recently published or forthcoming are a plethora of notable titles, including the extraordinary holocaust memoir *The Pianist* by Wladyslaw Szpilman, a *New York Times* bestseller and the book on which the movie was based; *Wintering* by Kate Moses, a brilliant first novel based on the last weeks of Sylvia Plath's life; Tama Janowitz's edgy new novel, *Peyton Amberg*; as well as *Queenmaker* by India Edghill, a rich Biblical novel with the scope of *The Red Tent*; and *The Unhealed Wound: The Church, The Priesthood, and the Question of Sexuality* by Eugene Kennedy.

Before turning to editing full-time four years ago I was a publicity director, and that background affords me a heightened understanding of and expertise regarding the marketing potential of the books I acquire."

RENAISSANCE BOOKS

This St. Martin's Press imprint produces hardcover and paperbacks in nonfiction, as well as select literary titles.

Representative titles include: *Science, Sense, and Soul* by Casey Blood; *Blood and Bone Brigade* by Jana Abrams Karam; *One Bird, One Stone: American Zen Stories* by Sean Murphy; *17 Lies That Are Holding You Back & the Truth That Will Set You Free* by Steve Chandler; *Discovering Colorado* by Elizabeth P. Linebaugh; *Healing Hands and a Soldier's Heart: A Year in the Trenches with EMS* by Jana Abrams Karam; *The 90/10 Weight Loss Plan* by Joy Bauer; *Hollywood 101: The Film Industry* by Frederick Levy; *Reading Monarchs' Writing: The Poetry of Henry VIII, Mary Stuart, Elizabeth I, and James VI/I* edited by Peter C. Herman.

STONEWALL INN EDITIONS

Stonewall Inn Editions publishes works with a lesbian and gay cultural slant in hardcover and paperback editions. The house addresses such trade areas as current events and public interest, reference works, cultural affairs and literary anthologies. It also produces Stonewall Inn Studio Books (featuring graphically lavish and luxuriously produced gift volumes), and the Stonewall Inn Mysteries line. The scope of St. Martin's lesbian and gay interest list is not limited to works issued under the Stonewall Inn imprint.

Featured Stonewall Inn authors have included: Quentin Crisp, Larry Kramer, Paul Monette, Ethan Morden, Denise Ohio, Randy Shilts, Edmund White, and Mark Richard Zubro.

Popular titles from Stonewall Inn include: *The Violet Quill Reader: The Emergence of Gay Writing After Stonewall* edited by David Bergman; *Sportsdykes: Stories from On and Off the Field* by Susan Fox Rogers; *Dark Wind: A True Account of Hurricane Gloria's Assault on Fire Island* by John Jiler; *Another Dead Teenager (a Paul Turner mystery)* by Mark Richard Zubro; *Sacred Lips of the Bronx* by Douglas Sadonick; *End of the Empire* by Denise Ohio; *Drama Queen: A Gay Man's Guide to An Uncomplicated Life* by Patrick Price; *Dirty Pictures: Tom of Finland, Masculinity, and Homosexuality* by Micha Ramakers; *Half-Moon Scar* by Allison Green.

Keith Kahla, Editor. "Like many of my colleagues, I've been at St. Martin's for a while (fifteen years) and in that time I've worked on a very broad range of material. Currently my list is about 80% fiction, primarily thrillers (Joseph Finder, Robert Ludlum, Gayle Lynds), crime fiction (S. J. Rozan, Steven Saylor, William. G. Tapply), and literary fiction with an emphasis on gay/lesbian themes (Paul Russell, Brian Malloy). The nonfiction on my list is, if anything, more diverse. The main themes are some traditional 'New Age' works (astrology, tarot), divination systems (Medicine Cards, Tarot de Paris), occasional works of biography and history, and very occasionally, humor and anthologies.

But there is, to my mind, a clear unifying element to these disparate works. What draws me to a particular book is the quality of the writing and a distinct, compelling authorial voice. Editorially, I believe it isn't the topic, story, or 'hook' that is the determining factor for interesting and successful books—it's the execution of the work by a talented author."

THOMAS DUNNE BOOKS

In Thomas Dunne's more than 25 years at St. Martin's Press, he has published virtually every kind of book, from runaway bestsellers such as *The Shell Seekers* by Rosamunde Pilcher and *River God* by Wilbur Smith, to the critically acclaimed nonfiction of Robert Kaplan and Juliet Barker. The Thomas Dunne imprint produces roughly 150 titles per year and covers a wide array of interests that include commercial fiction, mysteries, military histories, biographies, divination, politics, philosophy, humor, literary fiction, and current events.

Nonfiction titles representative of this list include: *Arousal: The Secret Logic of Sexual*

Fantasies by Dr. Michael J. Bader; *Barbara Bush: Matriarch of a Dynasty* by Pamela Kilian; *Tigers of the Snow: How One Fateful Climb Made the Sherpas Mountaineering Legends* by Jonathan Neale; *You Don't Need Meat* by Peter Cox; *101 Damnations: The Humorists' Tour of Personal Hells* edited by Michael J. Rosen; *Alcohol: A History* by Griffith Edwards; *Soul Picnic: The Music and Passion of Laura Nyro* by Michele Kort; *The Way of Zen* by David Scott, et al.

Select fiction titles from Dunne's list include: *Area 7* by Matthew Reilly; *From the Heart of Covington* by Joan A. Medlicott; *Bronx Boy* by Jerome Charyn; *Flip-Flopped* by Jill Smolinski; *Drop Dead Gorgeous* by Anna Cheska; *Looking for Mary Gabriel* by Carole Lawrence; *A Week in Winter* by Marcia Wilett.

Recent releases include: *Slip Cue: A Talk Radio Mystery* by Joyce Krieg; *The Blighted Cliffs* by Edwin Thomas; *A Risk Worth Taking* by Robin Pilcher; *The Two Americas* by Stanley B. Greenberg; *Mullahs, Merchants and Militants* by Stephen Clain.

Queries and SASEs should be directed to:

Thomas L. Dunne, Vice President, Executive Editor, Publisher—Eclectic interests, commercial women's fiction, mysteries, military histories, biographies, divination systems, politics, philosophy, humor, literary fiction and current events

Peter Wolverton, Senior Editor and Associate Publisher—Fiction: commercial and popular literature, genre mysteries; and a wide range of nonfiction consistent with the Thomas Dunne list. "After trying out another house, I came back to Thomas Dunne Books to enjoy once more the freedom to publish a wide range of books. As Associate Publisher, I work to give every title we publish an additional dose of attention. During my 14 years in the business, I've published a variety of titles, but inevitably find myself drawn to sports books, thrillers, outdoor literature (a particular passion— I'm always looking for the next Stegner or Mosher), and nonfiction of all kinds. Over the last few seasons I've had great success and hit the *New York Times* bestseller list with *Gettysburg* by Newt Gingrich and William R. Forstchen, *Knight* by coach Bob Knight, and *The Junction Boys* by Jim Dent."

Ruth Cavin, Senior Editor; Associate Publisher—crime fiction, contemporary fiction, anecdotal science and medicine, novelties (quotation books). Cavin writes, "An editor gets 'What are you looking for' just about as often as an author gets 'Where do you get your ideas?' The first part of my answer has to be 'Not only mysteries,' since I have been typecast just that way. The second part is 'Something that excites me.' I'm lucky; like a kid in a candy store, I can point to anything and cry 'I'll take that!' so long as I think it will sell a reasonable number of copies. My list can go from a book about volcanologists ('One of the year's best science books,' says *Library Journal*) to *Mayflower Bastard*—the author is still working on his story of the pirate, spy, all-round scoundrel who was his ancestor; to Jerome Charyn's memoir about growing up in the Bronx ('It is no small accomplishment to be the Babel of the Bronx.'—*The New York Times Book Review*); to Christine Andreae's account of what she learned about life and death as a hospice volunteer. But though as 'Ms. Mystery' I may flirt with intriguing outsiders, having a roster of terrific crime novelists like Edgar Award-winner Steve Hamilton, Donna Andrews, Dale Wimberly, and so many more, every one a gem of the genre, my marriage to the mystery is still in the best of health."

Sign: Libra.

Employment history/editor career path: St. Martin's Press, 1988 to present; Walker Books 1979–1988; Two Continents Publishing, 1975–1979, freelance writer, Editor, author.

Personal interests: Theater, travel, children/grandchildren, people.

What would you be doing if you were not an editor? I would travel. I would probably also write. But I intend to keep my day job, because I love it. They will have to throw me or carry me out.

What has been the most successful book that you have acquired to date? I would have to look at the numbers, but what comes to mind is: Nonfiction: *Whoever Fights Monsters*, Robert K. Ressler and Tom Shachtman; Fiction: *A Grave Talent*, Laurie King.

What books have you acquired that make you the most proud? What books that you have acquired reflect the types of books you like to represent? I'm proud of a great many of them. I publish almost 50 books a year and have done so for the last dozen years; it would be too difficult to list them all. The only ones I'm considerably less proud of are those that were mistakes in judgment, in the sense that I saw potential I thought could be realized but wasn't, because the author and I could not agree, or the author was not able to do what I expected. But there are only a few of those. There are also books that I am certainly not ashamed of, but that I publish because I know people want them rather than that I would give them "A for Excellence." The types of books I like to represent are anything as varied, very well written, and imaginative as *Charles Todd: A Test of Wills* or *Afterzen* by Janwillem van de Wetering or *Volcano Cowboys* by Dick Thompson. I look for good books, fiction or nonfiction, that I feel are well worth reading, that others will enjoy, and that have a reasonable chance of commercial success.

Do you represent fiction? Yes, I publish fiction. Some mainstream novels, but it is difficult to launch a new mainstream novel unless something about it will help to sell it; if the author is known for something else, or if the house is very high on it and will spend money promoting it. David Corn's first novel, *Deep Background*, sold well because it's a terrific book; David had published a successful nonfiction book previously; his name is known as the longtime Washington editor of *The Nation*; he knows people whose "blurb" will impress bookstores and readers; it got terrific reviews; and David himself is a familiar on political talk shows. And even then, the book did only moderately well—but well above the usual for a first novel. Yet hope springs eternal, and if there is a wonderful book of fiction like *This Is Graceanne's Book* by P. L. Whitney or *Jenny Rose* by Mary Anne Kelly or *My Darling Elia* by Eugenie Melnyk, I publish it. Of course, all three authors had been published as mystery writers before. I have published novels from some "names"—for example, Herbert Gold, Jerome Charyn. You do keep trying if you believe in the book and the author understands not to give up that day job. Category books like mysteries are easier than mainstream novels to get out there when the author is unknown, because people who follow the category are actively looking for new writers and protagonists. I look for individuality, imagination, a fresh voice.

What do you want to see less of? Mysteries just like a hundred others.

Do you represent nonfiction? Yes, I publish nonfiction.

Do you require book proposals? If so, what do you look for in evaluating a book proposal? I require something, either a proposal, an outline, a writing sample, or a full manuscript. I will buy nonfiction on a proposal if the subject is one I think will find an audience, the author has some kind of credentials for writing about that subject, and I have an outline and enough writing sample to be confident about the author's style. I will not buy fiction on a proposal except from authors whose work I have published previously and know well, but if an author or agent wants to submit an outline and three chapters I will be able to tell whether I want to see the complete manuscript.

Are certain aspects of a book proposal given more weight than others? I suppose in nonfiction the subject/the content. But the outline and the writing style are very important.

What process do you use for making a decision? What is the process for acquisition, is there a committee? I read the proposal or manuscript. I sometimes ask colleagues for an opinion, although I don't always. I ask for the author's track record; other books published and sales and subrights figures if any, reviews, other writing background, publicity possibilities. (A good agent gives you these without being asked.) I then discuss the book and its attributes with my boss, Tom Dunne, and we arrive at a figure for an offer, with some knowledge of what to include in any necessary negotiation. If the money is more than usual, we get an estimated P & L from sales, production, and accounting and also consult our publisher and others in the house.

What kinds of nonfiction books do you want to see less of? I want to see nothing of inspirational, religious, psychological self-help, beauty, slimming diet, celebrity bios, all that commercial stuff that I know brings in a lot of money, but isn't for me.

Are you interested in work geared for the masses (readers of *People, The Star,* etc.)? No way.

Are agents important? *Why?* Yes, because the good ones winnow out the chaff and also know which editor is interested in what kinds of books. They understand the business and can be easier than an inexperienced author to deal with. But I also look at nonagented work.

Do you like new writers? What should new writers do to break into the business? It's not a question of like or not like. It's harder, of course; they have no following. But if their books are good and I feel they have a chance of selling, I'll delighted. If new writers want to write fiction, they have a better shot for publication by writing category books than mainstream, but they have to listen to their own desires.

How should writers approach you? Send a proposal or manuscript addressed to me. Be prepared to wait for an answer; I get hundreds of submissions. Do not call and ask if I've read it; when I've read it, you'll know. The call just puts it off further, when it is one of many. Do not send a query letter and nothing else for a work of fiction, there's no way I can judge fiction from a query letter unless the plot description is so incredibly awful, it rules out any desire to see the rest. It's easy to describe a plot, but a book made from that story can be dreadful or marvelous and there's no way a letter can indicate that.

What are some common mistakes writers make? What really gets on your nerves? If you mean in the actual writing, I can't say, except if they don't use some imagination instead of the same old same old. Some of the physical details really get on my nerves. Such as, giving me a pitch on how this book is going to be the grandest blockbuster of a bestseller I've ever published. Sending cover designs along. Not numbering the pages consecutively (numbering each chapter separately instead.) Single-spacing. Sending the book in a heavy and unwieldy binder, using expensive paper that makes the manuscript twice as heavy as good old copier paper. (Editors have to schlep the books around—home, to the baseball game, anywhere they can find a little time to read it.) Not keeping a copy for themselves in case we lose the one they sent.

What can writers do to get your attention and to avoid the slush pile? If a submission is addressed to me by my name, it will not land in the slush pile. I don't guarantee to read it all the way through, but it will get a read of a large-enough section to let me know whether or not it is something I want to pursue further.

What have been some of your craziest experiences with submissions? Annoying and funny: A woman who had the whole U.S. postal system looking for a manuscript we returned, not because she didn't have a copy (that would just have been a tragedy) but because she was sure that we had stolen it and were going to make a fortune by publishing it under our name. (This, I shall say gently, was highly unlikely even if we were inclined to cheat an author.) Sad: The factory worker who drove all the way overnight from somewhere in the Midwest to deliver by hand a (quite promising) six-page or so proposal for a memoir and was then going back that night so he could go to work the next day.

What have been some of your best experiences with writers or in your job? Above all, working for and with Tom Dunne. Meeting wonderful, very generous, interesting, and varied authors, so many that I can't start naming them here.

What, if anything, makes you different from other editors? Old age.

Is there anything you would like to see changed in the industry? Yes. I would like to see the publishers take the $27,000 they spend on a full-page ad in the *New York Times* to tell us about a book that already has six million copies out and use the money to bring some fine authors to the attention they are not getting and that they deserve. I'd like to find a way of convincing the reading public how their lives will be enriched if they raise their standards of and demands for good writing.

Any advice for writers? Writing a book is more than putting words down on paper; it requires a lot of thinking, a lot of discernment, constant observation of the way people behave, reading but not aping, and the primary motive: you must want to write that book. Wanting to have a published book is not enough, and wanting to make a fortune with a bestseller is adolescent and a futile way to go about it. Don't give up your day job.

TOR

This imprint, created in 1981, is known for its science fiction/fantasy list, including the bestselling Sword of Truth series by Terry Goodkind. Tor is an English word indicating an outcropping, butte, promontory, summit, peak, or high hill, which is representative of this list's goals and successes.

Titles indicative of this list include: *The Dragon's Son* by Margaret Weis; *Ender's Shadow* by Orson Scott Card; *Appleseed* by John Clute; *Argonaut* by Stanley Schmidt; *The Baron War* by Jory Sherman; *Beast Master's Ark* by Andre Norton and Lyn McConchie; *Blood Diamonds* by Jon Land; *Burning the Ice* by Laura J. Mixon.

Recent titles include: *The Dragon Quintet* edited by Marvin Kaye; *Wellspring of Chaos* by L.E. Modesitt Jr.; *Elegy for a Lost Star* by Elizabeth Hayden; *Gardens of the Moon* by Steve Erikson; *Dune: The Battle of Corrin* and *The Skinner* by Neal Asher.

The Official Tor Submissions Guidelines can be found at www.tor.com.

1. Submissions should be sent to Tor Books, 175 Fifth Avenue, New York NY 10010. Do not submit work on disk, tape, or other electronic media; do not submit work by e-mail.

2. Address unsolicited science fiction and fantasy submissions to Patrick Nielsen Hayden and unsolicited mainstream submissions to Melissa Singer.

3. Submit only the first three chapters of your book and a synopsis of the entire book. (We're not big on query letters, since we can't tell whether we'll like the book until we see a chunk of the manuscript.) And please make sure you send the first three chapters. No matter how good your synopsis is, it's difficult for us to get a good sense of the book from chapters 4, 17, and 32.

4. Your cover letter should state the genre of the submission and previous sales or publications, if relevant.

5. Never send us the only copy of your book. The U.S. Post Office is no more perfect than the rest of us, and things do get lost in the mail. Always put your name and address on the manuscript. In addition, your name, the manuscript title, and the page number should appear on every page of the manuscript. If you wish your manuscript to be returned, enclose a stamped, self-addressed envelope large enough to hold your submission; publishers are not responsible for returning submissions unaccompanied by return postage. If you do not wish your manuscript to be returned, please say so in the cover letter, and enclose a stamped, self-addressed, business-sized envelope for our reply. If you enclose a stamped, self-addressed postcard, we will return it to verify receipt of the manuscript.

6. Type your manuscript on plain white paper, double-spaced, using only one side of the page. Do not staple or otherwise bind your manuscript; a paper clip will suffice. If you use a computer and printer, do not submit low-resolution dot matrix printouts; they will not be read. Please do not use a fancy font (this is almost as difficult to read as the palest dot matrix), and please make sure you use a font large enough to read easily. Please turn off margin justification and proportional spacing; pages with ragged right margins are easier for us to read and easier for our production department to set.

7. Please indicate italics by underlining and indicate boldface by drawing a wavy line beneath the affected characters. Copy to be typeset needs to be marked in very specific ways, and if you use italics or boldface in the manuscript, they will still need to be marked up by production.

8. Please allow at least 4–6 months for your manuscript to be considered. If you haven't heard from us after four months and wish to make sure your manuscript got here, please write a letter stating the genre, the date of submission, and the title of the manuscript, rather than calling. We will respond promptly.

9. We do not accept simultaneous submissions.

FORGE BOOKS

Forge Books publishes nonfiction, thrillers, suspense, mystery historicals, and Westerns, targeted to the mainstream audience. Forge was created in 1993 as a new imprint to market contemporary books.

Among the books currently appearing under the Forge imprint are bestsellers like Harold Robbins's *The Predators*; technothrillers like Michael Cassutt's *Missing Man*; legal thrillers like Junius Podrug's *Presumed Guilty*; as well as mysteries like Kate Flora's *Death at the Wheel* and Bill Eidson's *The Guardian*. Its strong list of historical titles includes the bestselling *1916*, Morgan Llewelyn's novel of the Irish Troubles; *Railroad Schemes* by distinguished historical novelist Cecelia Holland

Tom Doherty, Publisher

ORB BOOKS

In 1992, Tom Doherty Associates created Orb Books in response to complaints from readers and booksellers that some of their favorite science fiction and fantasy backlist titles were no longer available. Consequently, Orb publishes trade paperbacks that have been previously published in Tor mass-market editions.

ST. MARTIN'S PAPERBACKS (MASS MARKET)

GRIFFIN TRADE PAPERBACKS

Griffin, a St. Martin's imprint, publishes trade paperbacks, with a strong emphasis in "how to" nonfiction, contemporary fiction, travel, biography, and current culture.

Titles indicative of Griffin's nonfiction list include: *Just How Smart Are You?* by Terry Stickels and Abbie F. Salny; *The Guide to Getting In* by Harvard Student Agencies; *How to Play Bass Guitar* by Laurence Canty; *Label Launch: A Guide to Independent Record Recording, Promotion, and Distribution* by Veronika Kalmar; *The New York Times Guide to Coin Collecting* by Ed Reiter.

Titles representative of the fiction list include: *The Griffin & Sabine Trilogy (Griffin & Sabine, Sabine's Notebook, and The Golden Mean)* by Nick Bantock; *Under Fire* by W. E.

B.Griffin; *Boogie Woogie* by Danny Moynihan; *Dispensing with the Truth* by Alicia Mundy; *The Key* by James N. Frey; *The Secrets of My Life* by Kathy McCoy.

Recent releases include: *I Love My Smith and Wesson* by David Bowker; *An Egg on Three Sticks* by Jackie Moyer Fischer; *Sock* by Penn Jillette.

ST. MARTIN'S REFERENCE GROUP

LET'S GO TRAVEL GUIDES

GOLDEN GUIDES AND GOLDEN FIELD GUIDES

ENCARTA

LET'S GO PUBLICATIONS

67 Mount Auburn Street, Cambridge, MA 02138

www.letsgo.com

Let's Go is a budget travel series that prides itself in being the "only guidebook publisher that updates its entire series each year." As a wholly owned subsidiary of Harvard Student Agencies, all Let's Go guides are written by full-time, degree-seeking Harvard students.

GOLDEN GUIDES AND GOLDEN FIELD GUIDES

Golden Guides are a series of small guidebooks on various aspects of nature. Printed in 5x 6 format, these guides are basic enough for beginners and informative enough for seasoned amateurs.

Titles include: *Endangered Animals* by George S. Fichte; *Tropical Fish: A Guide for Setting Up and Maintaining an Aquarium for Tropical Fish and Other Animals* (Golden Field Guide Series.) by Bruce W. Halstead, et al.; *Exploring Space* by Mark R. Chartrand and Ron Miller (photographer); *Poisonous Animals* (Golden Field Guide Series) by Edmund D. Brodie, et al.; *Bird Life: A Guide to the Behavior and Biology of Birds* by Stephen W. Kress,Ph.D., and John D. Dawson (illustrator); *Dinosaurs* by Eugene S. Gaffney and John Dawson; *North American Indian Arts* by Andrew Hunter Whiteford, et al.; *Mammals: A Guide to Familiar American Species* by Herbert S. Zim, Ph.D., et al.

ENCARTA

Encarta publishes the Encarta World Dictionary in a variety of languages.

PENGUIN GROUP (USA) INC.

AVERY

BERKLEY BOOKS GROUP

BLUEHEN BOOKS

DORLING KINDERSLEY

DUTTON

GOTHAM BOOKS

HPBOOKS

HUDSON STREET PRESS

JEREMY P. TARCHER

NEW AMERICAN LIBRARY/NAL

PENGUIN

PERIGEE BOOKS

PLUME

PORTFOLIO

PRICE STERN SLOAN

PRIME CRIME

PUTNAM

RIVERHEAD BOOKS

VIKING

PENGUIN PUTNAM BOOKS FOR YOUNG READERS

375 Hudson Street, New York, NY 10014

212-366-2000

Penguin Putnam is a leading U.S. adult and children's trade book publishing group, formed in 1996 as a result of the merger between Penguin Books USA and the Putnam Berkley Group. The Penguin Group, headquartered in the UK, is owned by Pearson plc, an international media group.

Penguin Putnam publishes under a broad range of imprints and trademarks, among them Berkley Books, Dutton, Grosset & Dunlap, New American Library, Penguin, Philomel, G. P. Putnam's Sons, Riverhead Books, and Viking.

The company possesses a distinctive list of best-selling authors, including: Dorothy

Allison, Melissa Bank, Saul Bellow, A. Scott Berg, Harold Bloom, Sylvia Browne, Tom Clancy, Robin Cook, Patricia Cornwell, Catherine Coulter, Clive Cussler, the Dalai Lama, Dick Francis, Sue Grafton, W. E. B. Griffin, Jan Karon, Robert Ludlum, James McBride, Terry McMillan, Arthur Miller, Jacqueline Mitchard, Toni Morrison, Kathleen Norris, Joyce Carol Oates, Suze Orman, Robert Parker, Nora Roberts, Maeve Binchy, John Sandford, Carol Shields, John Steinbeck, Amy Tan, Eric Jerome Dickey, Kurt Vonnegut, and Neale Donald Walsch.

Penguin Putnam is also a global leader in children's publishing, through its Books for Young Readers, with imprints such as Dial Books, Dutton, Grosset & Dunlap, Philomel, Puffin, G. P. Putnam's Sons, Viking, and Frederick Warne.

These imprints are home to Ludwig Bemelmans, Jan Brett, Eric Carle, Roald Dahl, Tomie dePaola, Hardie Gramatky, Eric Hill, Brian Jacques, A. A. Milne, and Tasha Tudor. Grosset & Dunlap issues such perennial favorites as *The Little Engine That Could* and the Nancy Drew and Hardy Boys series. (See separate entry for Penguin Putnam Books for Young Readers.)

Penguin Putnam houses Penguinclassics.com, an online community devoted to classic titles. The company also launched Penguin Lives, a series of short biographies about well-known historical and cultural figures, written by some of today's most respected authors. In addition, Penguin Putnam resumed its Pelican Shakespeare series, which has remained one of the best-selling series of Shakespeare's plays since the line was introduced in the mid-1960s.

AVERY

Avery's publishing program is dedicated primarily to complementary medicine, nutrition, and healthful cooking. It was established in 1976 as a college textbook publisher specializing in niche areas. Through a series of alliances, most notably with Hippocrates Health Institute, Avery began a program of health books by such authors as Ann Wigmore and Michio Kushi, whose work on macrobiotics helped propel the Avery list in the health food and alternative markets. The firm was acquired by the Penguin Group in 2000.

In addition to producing original titles in hardcover and paperback formats, Avery has a backlist of several hundred titles in trade and mass-market formats that includes works by pioneers in alternative healing, scientists, and health-care professionals involved in cutting-edge research.

Titles representative of the Avery list: *Dare to Lose: 4 Simple Steps to a Better Body* by Shari Lieberman, Ph.D., Nancy Bruning (Contributor); *The Edge: Ben and Joe Weider's Guide to Ultimate Strength, Speed, and Stamina* by Ben Weider, et al.; *Natural Highs: Supplements, Nutrition, and Mind/Body Techniques to Help You Feel Good All the Time* by Hyla Cass and Patrick Holford; *Aromatherapy: Essential Oils for Vibrant Health and Beauty* by Roberta Wilson; *Secrets from a Healthy Asian Kitchen* by Ying Chang and Ying Chang Compestine.

Direct your query letter and SASE to:

Megan Newman

BERKLEY BOOKS GROUP

ACE

BERKLEY BOOKS

JOVE

ACE BOOKS

Ace Books, founded in 1953 by A. A. Wyn, is the oldest continuously operating science fiction publisher in the United States. In 1982, Ace, which had been part of Grosset & Dunlap, was acquired by G. P. Putnam's Sons (later known as the Putnam Berkley Group), and soon became Berkley's science fiction imprint.

The combined backlists of Ace and Berkley made a powerful presence in the science fiction field, with Frank Herbert's best-selling Dune series, T. H. White's classic Arthurian novel *The Once and Future King* (which was the basis for the musical *Camelot*), and much of Robert A. Heinlein's adult fiction, including *Stranger in a Strange Land*. More recent important authors include Joe Haldeman, winner of the 1998 Hugo and Nebula awards for *Forever Peace*, and William Gibson, whose *Neuromancer* is credited with having introduced the concept of cyberspace.

Ace produces original titles in hardcover and mass-market paperback, as well as reprints previously published in hardcover and trade paperback fiction.

Recent titles include: *Coyote Rising* by Allen Steele; *Cleopatra 7.2* by Elizabeth Ann Scarborough; *The Winter Oak* by James A. Hetley; *Neuromancer* by William Gibson; *Polaris* by Jack McDevitt; *For Those Who Fell* by William C. Dietz; *Dragon's Treasure* by Elizabeth A. Lynn.

Direct query letters and SASEs to:

Susan Allison, Vice President, Editor in Chief of Ace Books—Science fiction, fantasy, horror, women's fiction

BERKLEY BOOKS

Berkley Books, under the leadership of President and Publisher Leslie Gelbman, publishes more than 500 titles per year under the Berkley, Jove, and Ace imprints, in mass-market paperback, trade paperback, hardcover, audiocassettes, and audio CD-ROM formats. Berkley publishes some of the country's bestselling authors, including Tom Clancy, Robin Cook, Patricia Cornwell, Catherine Coulter, and Nora Roberts.

Bestsellers include: *Last Man Down* by Richard Picciotto with Daniel Paisner; *Narcissus in Chains* by Laurell K. Hamilton; *Chosen Prey* by John Sandford; *Edge of Danger* by Jack Higgins; *It's Not About the Bike* by Lance Armstrong; *A Little Magic* by Nora Roberts; *The Sum of All Fears* by Tom Clancy; *Tom Clancy's Net Force: Cybernation*, created by Tom Clancy and Steve Pieczenik, written by Steve Perry.

Recent nonfiction titles on the Berkley list include: *The Science of Cold Case Files* by Katherine Ramsland; *So Many Books, So Little Time: A Year of Passionate Reading* by Sara Welson; *On Hallowed Ground: The Last Battle for Pork Chop Hill* by Bill McWilliams and *City Room* by Arthur Gelb.

Recent fiction titles include: *The Effect of Living Backwards* by Heidi Julavits; *Sacred Stone* by Clive Cussler and Craig Dirgo; *The Real Thing* by Kay Hooper; *Garrett in Wedlock* by Paul Mandelbaum; *The Cowboy with the Tiffany Gun* by Aaron Latham.

Direct query letters and SASEs to:

Leslie Gelbman, President of Mass Market Paperbacks—Wide range of projects in fiction and nonfiction. Works with such authors as Nora Roberts, Laura Kinsale, and Erich Segal.

Denise Silvestro, Executive Editor—Women's fiction and nonfiction, self-help, inspirational, spiritual, and New Age, popular culture, health

Gail Fortune, Executive Editor—Women's fiction, romance, and mystery

Tom Colgan, Executive Editor—Wide range of commercial fiction and nonfiction, including history, business, inspiration, biography, military, thrillers, adventure, and suspense.

Natalie Rosenstein, Vice President, Senior Executive Editor—General fiction and mystery.

Christine Zika, Senior Editor—Women's fiction, health, popular culture, historical and contemporary romance.

Allison McCabe, Senior Editor—Women's fiction, general fiction and nonfiction, commercial/literary works.

Cindy Hwang, Senior Editor—Women's fiction, popular culture, young adult, paranormal romance, historical romance, contemporary romance.

BLUEHEN BOOKS

BlueHen Books, established by Frederick Ramey and Greg Michalson, was launched in March 2000 and presented its debut list in the summer of 2001. BlueHen is "dedicated to introducing writers of quality fiction to a broad audience," and looks for books with compelling stories that are artfully told. BlueHen is the breeder's term for a thoroughbred mare that produces a long line of competitors.

Titles indicative of this growing list include: *Swim Naked, Defy Gravity and 99 Other Essential Things to Accomplish Before Turning 30* by Colleen Rush and *The Student Conductor* by Robert Ford.

Direct query letters and SASEs to:

Fred Ramey, Editor

Greg Michalson, Editor

DORLING KINDERSLEY

Dorling Kindersley is an international publishing company specializing in the creation of high-quality, illustrated information books; interactive software; TV programs; and online resources for children and adults. Founded in London in 1974, DK now has offices in the UK, United States, Australia, South Africa, India, France, Germany, and Russia.

In May 2000, DK was acquired by Pearson plc, an international media company. This acquisition saw DK join the Penguin Group, as Peter Kindersley stepped down from his executive role at DK and Anthony Forbes Watson became Chief Executive of both DK and Penguin UK.

DK is one of the world's premier publishers of illustrated reference books. Aiming to be a "complete 'cradle to grave' publisher that families can grow up with," DK produces books for children of all ages and books for adults covering a wide variety of subjects, including: child care, health, gardening, food and wine, travel, business, and sports. DK produces books in hardcover, trade paperback, and CD-ROM.

Recent titles that are representative of the DK list include: *DK Collector's Guides: Art Nouveau* by Judith Miller; *Fit Kids* by Neil Izenberg; *Defying Age* by Miriam Stoppard; *Organized Crime: An Inside Guide to the World's Most Successful Industry*; *The Pilates Promise* by Alycea Ungaro Anatomy.

DK also produces the Essential Science Series and Eyewitness Top 10 Travel guides. All DK books are produced in-house.

DUTTON

Dutton dates back to 1852, when Edward Payson Dutton founded a bookselling firm, E. P. Dutton, in Boston. Dutton currently publishes about 50 hardcover titles a year.

Dutton authors include: Maeve Binchy (*Scarlet Feather*), John Jakes (*On Secret Service*), Sylvia Browne (*Life on the Other Side* and *Past Lives, Future Healing*), Eric Jerome Dickey (*Between Lovers*), John Lescroart (*The Hearing*), Wendy Northcutt (*The Darwin Awards*), Darin Strauss (*Chang and Eng*), Barbara Parker (*Suspicion of Vengeance*), Dave Pelzer (*Help Yourself*), Randall Robinson (*The Debt*); Tracy Chevalier (*Girl with a Pearl Earring* and *Falling Angels*).

Recent titles include: *Good News, Bad News* by David Wolstencroft; *Off The Cuff* by Carson Kressley; *The Wendy Williams Experience* by Wendy Williams; *The Family Tree* by Carole Cadwalladr.

Direct query letters and SASEs to:

Brian Tart, Publisher, Editorial Director and Vice President

Laurie Chittenden, Senior Editor—Popular and commercial works in nonfiction and occasional fiction

Mitch Hoffman, Senior Editor—Mysteries, thrillers, narrative nonfiction, and humor

GOTHAM BOOKS

This imprint was started in 2001. The mission of Gotham Books, according to founder Bill Shinker, is to create a, "literary boutique with a commercial profile." It is completely devoted to nonfiction. Some of its first titles in early 2003 included: *Lite Cuisine* by Patti LaBelle; *Authentically Black: Essays for the Black Silent Majority* by John McWhorter; *Real Love* by Greg Baer. By 2004 the list expanded to 35 titles, including 20 originals. Its emphasis continues to be on narrative nonfiction, self-help, spirituality, business, sports, and travel writing.

Recent releases include: *Beautiful Bones without Hormones* by Dr. Leon Root and Betty Kelly Sargent; *Jim Morrison: Life, Death, Legend* by Stephen Davis; *Dark Nights of the Soul: A Guide to Finding Meaning During Life's Ordeals* by Thomas Moore; *The Obesity Myth: Why America's Obsession with Weight is Hazardous to Your Health* by Paul Campos; *I Call the Shots: Straight Talk About the Game of Golf Today* by Johnny Miller and Guy Yocum.

Direct query and SASE to:

William Shinker, Senior Vice President and Publisher

Lauren Marino, Executive Editor

Brendan Cahill, Editor

HPBOOKS

HPBooks, acquired by the Penguin Putnam Group as part of the purchase of Price Stern Sloan, originated in Tucson, Arizona as publishers of nonfiction books in the categories of cooking, automotive, photography, gardening, health, and child care. HPBooks now specializes in cooking and automotive titles, publishing about a dozen books per year in trade paperback and a few in hardcover. Among the stars of the list, Mable Hoffman's *Crockery Cookery* recently celebrated its 20th year in print with more than 5 million copies sold.

Recent titles representative of this list include: *1001 More High Performance Tech Tips* by Wayne Scraba; *How to Keep Your Minivan Alive!* By Mark Warner; *The PDQ (Pretty Darn Quick) Vegetarian Cookbook* by Donna Klein; *The Everyday Turkey Cookbook* by Franki Papai Secunda; *The Church Ladies' Celestial Suppers and Sensible Advice* by Brenda Rhodes Miller; *Half-Baked Gourmet: Desserts* by Tamara Holt.

Direct query letters and SASEs to:

John Duff, Publisher, Vice President, and Senior Editor

Michael Lufty, Editorial Director

HUDSON STREET PRESS

Hudson Street Press was founded in 2003. This new imprint focuses on finding a new perspective and a unique writing voice. It deals only in hardcover originals, while Plume handles their trade paperbacks. The subjects they consider include: narrative nonfiction (prescriptive only), sex, relationships, money, women's issues, health/diet, biography/memoir, science, and popular history.

Laureen Rowland, Editorial Director

JEREMY P. TARCHER

Jeremy P. Tarcher publishes some 50 titles annually in both hardcover and paperback, covering a broad spectrum of topics that range from current affairs, social commentary, literary nonfiction, and creativity to spirituality/religion, health, psychology, parenting, business, and other topics. It has had numerous national bestsellers including *Drawing on the Right Side of the Brain* and *Seven Years in Tibet*. Tarcher also produces paperback reprints of previously published titles.

Recent titles include: *World's End 2009* by Peter Lorie; *The Sound of Paper* by Julia Cameron; *What Are You Afraid Of?* by Lavinia Plonka; *Where Girls Come First* by Ilana DeBare; *Love and Law* by Ernest Holmes.

Direct query letters and SASEs to:

Joel Fotinos, Publisher

Sara Carder, Editor—Practical nonfiction and narrative nonfiction

Mitch Horowitz, Senior Editor—Focuses on new trends in spirituality, science, social thought, and personal growth

NEW AMERICAN LIBRARY/NAL

ONYX

ROC

SIGNET

New American Library—popularly known as NAL—publishes a diverse and exciting range of paperback books, including *New York Times* bestsellers by Maeve Binchy, Stuart Woods, John Lescroart, and Ken Follett. Under the Signet, Onyx, and Roc imprints, NAL publishes both fiction and nonfiction and has recently expanded its trade paperback and hardcover programs in addition to the core mass-market format.

As part of NAL's ongoing efforts to initiate new developments in areas of commercial fiction and nonfiction, its editors are looking for strong, innovative authors who offer distinctive voices and original ideas. They encourage writers to submit their work through an agent.

Claire Zion, Editorial Director

Ellen Edwards, Executive Editor

Doug Grad, Senior Editor

Dan Slater, Senior Editor

Martha Bushko, Editor

Anne Bohner, Editor

ONYX

Onyx produces mass-market and trade paperbacks, both reprints and originals. Titles representative of the list include: *Breach of Confidence* by Eben Paul Perison; *Death Rites* by Bruce Elliot; *Chasing Darkness* by Danielle Girard; *The Edge of Heaven* by Teresa Hill; *Final Justice* by Nancy Kopp; *Hometown Girl* by Mary Jane Meier; *Hush* by Anne Frasier; *Insomnia* by Robert Westbrook; *Manhattan South* by John MacKie; *Saving Souls* by Lucy Taylor; *Some Survive* by James Preston Girard.

ROC

Roc publishes reprints and originals, in both trade paperback and mass market formats.

Titles indicative of this list include: *Angry Lead Skies* by Glen Cook; *Belarus* by Lee Hogan; *The Darker Side* edited by John Pelan; *The Disappeared* by Kristine Kathryn Rusch; *Drinking Midnight Wine* by Simon R. Green; *Fallen Host* by Lyda Morehouse; *Orbis* by Scott Mackay; *Season of Sacrifice* by Mindy L. Klasky.

Recent releases include: *Dies the Fire* by S.M. Stirling; *The Last Light of the Sun* by Guy Gavriel Kay; *Nebula Awards Showcase* edited by Vonda McIntyre.

SIGNET

This imprint produces mass-market paperback reprints, as well as some original titles in mass-market paperback format.

Titles representative of the list include: *Always in My Heart* by Catherine Anderson; *Bait and Switch* by Larry Brooks; *The Alamosa* by Ralph Compton; *The Banished Bride* by Andrea Pickens; *Caywood Valley Feud* by Judson Gray; *Dead Man's Ghost* by Peter King; *Hazard* by Jo Beverly.

Direct query letters and SASEs to:

Kara Welsh, Vice President and Publisher of New American Library

PENGUIN PRESS

Penguin produces numerous fiction and nonfiction trade paperback reprints, as well as original titles in trade paperback format. Covering subjects such as literature, biography/memoir, history, science, business, psychology, popular reference, and self-help, the Penguin list now has more than 3,000 books in print in the U.S. Two series, Penguin Classics and Penguin Twentieth-Century Classics, comprise more than 1,300 titles, making Penguin the largest publisher of ancient and modern classic literature in the English-speaking world. The Penguin list continues to grow under the new leadership of Ann Godoff. It continues to embrace new writers.

Recent titles that are indicative of this list include: *The Anxiety of Everyday Objects* by Aurelie Sheehan; *Alexander Hamilton* by Ron Chernow; *How to Behave So Your Preschooler Will Too* by Evelyn Porreca Vuko (reprint); *The Practical Writer: From Inspiration to Publication* by Therese Eiben and Mary Gannon; *Monster Careers: How to Land the Best Job of Your Life* by Jeff Taylor and *Democracy Matters: Winning the Fight Against Imperialism* by Cornell West.

Direct query letters and SASEs to:

Ann Godoff, President and Publisher

Jane von Mehren, Editor-in-Chief—health and social issues, self-help, child care and parenting, nature, memoir, history, popular culture, and personal stories, as well as contemporary and historical literary fiction

Scott Moyers, Senior Editor

Tracy Locke, Associate Publisher

Michael Millman, Senior Editor—oversees the Penguin Classics and Twentieth-Century Classics, the Viking Portable Library, and the Penguin Nature Classics series

PERIGEE BOOKS

Perigee Books, originally created as the trade paperback imprint for G.P. Putnam's Sons, has featured an eclectic range of titles from practically every category of nonfiction in hardcover and trade paperback format.

Among the bestsellers are: *The Complete Guide to Prescription and Nonprescription Drugs*; *The Perigee Visual Dictionary of Signing*; *The Out-of-Sync Child*; *The Lyle Official Antiques Review*. Featured Perigee authors include Heloise, Vicki Iovine, and JoAnna Lund.

Recent titles include: *Women for Hire's Get-Ahead Guide to Career Success* by Troy Johnson and Robyn Freedman Spizman; *Single Jewish Female: A Modern Guide to Sex and Dating* by Leah Furman; *How to Say it to Seniors: Closing the Communication Gap with our Elders* by David Solie; *Budget Living Party Central: A Year's Worth of Fabulous Entertaining* by the editors of *Budget Living* magazine; *The Secret Life of Toddlers* by Jana Murphy; *Screenwriting is Storytelling* by Kate Wright; *Been There, Done That!* by Rob Cohen and David Wollock.

Direct query letters and SASEs to:

John Duff, Publisher and Senior Editor of Perigee

Michelle Howry, Editor—Spirituality, women's issues, health, relationships, and pop culture

Marian Lizzi, Editor—Prescriptive nonfiction, health/fitness, parenting, relationships and communication

Christel Winkler, Assistant Editor—New Age, alternative health, lifestyle, inspiration, general self-help, and books for teens and young professionals

PLUME

Plume, founded in 1970 as the trade paperback imprint of New American Library, is now recognized as one of the preeminent trade paperback imprints. Throughout its history, Plume has been dedicated to giving an opportunity to voices previously neglected by mainstream publishing. The pioneering program in multicultural literature, which began with Toni Morrison and Jamaica Kincaid, has expanded to include ground-breaking works by Latino, African American, and Asian American authors.

Plume publishes such writers as Julia Alvarez (*In The Name of Salomé*), Bernice McFadden (*Sugar*), Gish Jen (*Typical American*), Charles Johnson (*Middle Passage*), Gus Lee (*China Boy*), and August Wilson (*Fences*). Plume was also a pioneer in gay publishing with Edmund White's *A Boy's Own Story* and Andrew Holleran's *Dancer from the Dance*.

Plume's literary fiction boasts many bestselling and prize-winning authors, including: Dorothy Allison (*Bastard Out of Carolina*), Pat Barker (*Regeneration*), E. L. Doctorow (*Ragtime*), Joyce Carol Oates (*We Were the Mulvaneys*), and Tracy Chevalier (*Girl with a Pearl Earring*).

Quality nonfiction is another area in which Plume takes special pride, publishing Dave Pelzer (*A Man Named Dave*), Mary Catherine Bateson (*Composing a Life*), Russell Baker (*Growing Up*), Robert Coles (*The Moral Intelligence of Children*), Mark Mathabane (*Kaffir Boy*), and Bill McKibben (*The Age of Missing Information*).

Plume's backlist is diverse, including: *The Fountainhead*; *The Joy of Cooking*; *Todd Wilbur's Top Secret Recipes*; *Leading the Revolution*; *Neatest Little Guide to Investing* and *Dr. Richard Heller's Carbohydrate Addict's LifeSpan Program* (with more than 1.5 million copies sold).

New releases include: *The Savage Nation* by Michael Savage (reprint); *Lies and the Lying Liars Who Tell Them* by Al Franken; *The Piano Teacher* by Lynn York; *Cuba* by Emily Barr; *Weekend in Paris* by Robyn Sisman.

Direct query letters and SASEs to:

Trena Keating, Editor-in-Chief—Health, popular psychology, spirituality and narrative nonfiction

PORTFOLIO

Portfolio is a new imprint that deals exclusively in business books.

Adrain Zacheim, Editor

PRICE STERN SLOAN

Price Stern Sloan (PSS) produces humor, novelty formats, and children's books. (See entry for Penguin Putnam Books for Young Readers.) The company had tremendous success with a number of proprietary brands, among them Mad Libs. Price Stern Sloan was purchased by the Putnam Berkley Group in 1993, and in 1997 the offices were moved to New York. PSS also produces a list of desk calendars.

Direct query letters and SASEs to:

Jon Anderson, Publisher

Lisa Rojany, Editorial Director

PRIME CRIME

Prime Crime produces original fiction crime titles in hardcover, trade, and mass-market paperback format. It also publishes paperback reprints.

Recent titles from the Prime Crime list include: *The Jasmine Moon Murder* by Laura Childs; *Crewel Yule* by Monica Ferris; *Win, Place and Show* by Dick Francis; *Access Denied* by Donna Andrews; *Mrs. Hudson and the Spirits' Curse* by Martin Davies; *Wrapped up in Crosswords* by Nero Blanc.

PUTNAM

Putnam produces a broad range of nonfiction and fiction titles. Formats for original titles include hardcover, trade paperback, and audio cassette. Putnam also publishes paperback reprints.

Titles representative of Putnam's list include: *Acid Row* by Minette Walters; *Aromatherapy: Essential Oils for Vibrant Health and Beauty* by Roberta Wison; *The Arraignment* by Steve Martini; *You Cannot Be Serious* by John McEnroe; *The Burying Field* by Kenneth Abel; *By Way of Water* by Charlotte Gullick; *A Clean Kill* by Mike Stewart; *The Commander* by Patrick A. Davis; *Criminal Intent* by Sheldon Siegel; *Flashover* by Suzanne Chazin; *From Wall to Wall* by Susan Kuklin; *A Game of Spies* by John Altman.

Recent titles include: *R is for Ricochet* by Sue Grafton; *Bad Business: A Spenser Novel* by Robert B. Parker; *The Paid Companion* by Amanda Quick/Jayne Ann Krentz; *Hidden Prey* by John Sanford; *Blowout* by Catherine Coulter; *Visions in Death* by J.D. Robb/Nora Roberts; *Lost City* by Clive Cussler.

Direct query letters with SASEs to:

Christine Pepe, Vice President, Executive Editor—Women's fiction, mysteries, thrillers, suspense, general nonfiction and parenting

David Highfill, Senior Editor—Suspense, mysteries and mainstream novels and commercial nonfiction

Neil Nyren, Publisher, G. P. Putnam's Sons—Serious and commercial fiction and nonfiction

Jennifer Hershey, Editorial Director—Women's fiction, suspense, social history and travel/adventure

RIVERHEAD BOOKS

Riverhead Books produces quality fiction and groundbreaking nonfiction in hardcover and trade paperback format.

In the past, this house helped usher Nick Hornby's third novel, *How to be Good*, onto the *New York Times* bestseller list. It also launched the fiction debut of the memoirist Nuala O'Faolain, *My Dream of You* (also a *New York Times* bestseller), as well as a critically acclaimed first memoir by Rebecca Walker, *Black White and Jewish*. It has kept alive its tradition of publishing the works of today's most prominent spiritual leaders, with Thich Nhat Hanh's *Anger* and Ghelek Rimpoche's *Good Life, Good Death*. As Riverhead moves forward to the future, it continues to extend its vision to help readers enlarge their understanding of the world and their place in it.

Riverhead is quickly gaining a reputation as the house to watch for up-and-coming fiction writers. So far, Riverhead has launched Jennifer Belle (*Going Down; High Maintenance*), Junot Díaz (*Drown*), Alex Garland (*The Beach*), Nick Hornby (*High Fidelity; About a Boy; How to Be Good*), Danzy Senna (*Caucasia*), and Sarah Waters (*Tipping the Velvet; Affinity; Fingersmith*).

Nonfiction *New York Times* bestsellers from Riverhead include: Rachel Remen's *Inspiring Kitchen Table Wisdom*; Harold Bloom's *Shakespeare: The Invention of the Human*, which was a finalist for the National Book Award and the National Book Critics Circle Award; and two major *New York Times* bestsellers from financial guru Suze Orman, *The Road to Wealth* and *The Courage to Be Rich*.

Riverhead published the Dalai Lama's *The Art of Happiness* and *Ethics for the New Millennium*. Other spiritual books on Riverhead's list include Kathleen Norris's *The Cloister Walk* and *Amazing Grace* (also *New York Times* bestsellers); Stephen Batchelor's *Buddhism Without Beliefs* and Thich Nhat Hanh's three Buddhist classics *Living Buddha, Living Christ; Going Home;* and *Anger*.

Recent Riverhead titles include: *How to Get Into Law School* by Susan Estrich; *The Art of Happiness at Work* by Dalai Lama and Dr. Howard C. Cutler; *Everyday Grace: Having Hope, Finding Forgiveness and Making Miracles* by Marianne Williamson; *War Torn* by John Marks; *Anja the Liar* by Thomas Moran.

Direct query letters and SASEs to:

Julie Grau, Co-Editorial Director

Cindy Spiegel, Co-Editorial Director

Sean McDonald, Senior Editor

Susan Lehman, Editor

VIKING

Viking, founded in 1925, currently publishes approximately 100 books per year, both fiction and nonfiction, in hardcover format. The firm's name and its logo, a Viking ship drawn by Rockwell Kent, were chosen as symbols of enterprise, adventure, and exploration.

The house issues a broad range of literary titles, as well as commercial titles. Viking is recognized for "increasing the visibility of its established and more prominent authors, while orchestrating the successful launch of new and relatively unknown writers."

Titles representative of Viking's nonfiction list include: *America and Americans and Selected Nonfiction* by John Steinbeck, et al.; *Bamboozled at the Revolution: How Big Media Lost Billions in the Battle for the Internet* by John Motavalli; *Brown: The Last Discovery of America* by Richard Rodriguez; *The Career As a Path to the Soul* by David Rottman; *The Fall of Berlin 1945* by Antony Beevor; *From a Victorian Garden: Creating the Romance of a*

Bygone Age Right in Your Own Backyard by Michael Weishan and Cristina Roig.

Titles indicative of Viking's fiction list include: *Annie Dunne* by Sebastian Barry; *Ariel's Crossing* by Bradford Morrow; *City of Names* by Kevin Brockmeier; *The Clubhouse* by Anastasia Suen, et al.; *The Escher Twist: A Homer Kelly Mystery* by Jane Langton; *Evil River* by William S. Burroughs; *Forty-Seven Roses* by Peter Sheridan; *Fox Girl* by Nora Okja Keller; *Girl from the South* by Joanna Trollope; *Journey to the Well* by Vashti Murphy McKenzie; *Last Things* by David Searcy; *Red Rain* by Michael Crow and *Women About Town* by Laura Jacobs.

Viking also produces illustrated titles through its imprint, Viking Studio. Titles on Viking Studio's list include: *Blue Dog*; *The Secret Language of Birthdays*; *King: The Photobiography of Martin Luther King* by Charles Johnson; *Vanity Fair's Hollywood*; *The Pennyroyal Caxton Bible*, illustrated by Barry Moser.

Recent releases include: *The Food of Love* by Anthony Capella; *They Would Never Hurt a Fly: War Criminals on Trial in the Hague* by Slavenka Drakulic; *The Myth of Solid Ground: Earthquakes, Prediction and the Fault Line Between Reason and Faith* by David L. Ulin; *Ten Minutes From Normal* by Karen Hughes; *Farewell Jackie* by Ed Klein; *Namath* by Mark Kriegal; *The Dr's Wife* by Elizabeth Brundage; *Multiple Choice* by Claire Cook.

Direct query letters and SASEs to:

Rick Kot, Executive Editor—Commercial works in nonfiction and current affairs

Paul Slovak, Vice President Viking Publishing, Senior Editor, Associate Publisher—poetry, literary fiction, beat work (Kerouac and the like), intellectual nonfiction

Carolyn Carlson, Executive Editor—Narrative nonfiction, cultural history, biography, women's issues, commercial nonfiction, commercial and literary fiction, mysteries

Janet Goldstein, Executive Director—Nonfiction including family, work, spirituality, health, psychology, narrative nonfiction

Pamela Dorman, Executive Editor and Vice President—Commercial fiction, especially women's fiction and suspense; nonfiction interests include self-help and psychology, investigative stories and narrative nonfiction, popular inspiration, popular reference, and women's issues

Wendy Wolf, Executive Editor—Nonfiction, especially music, culture, humor, bio and current affairs

Ray Roberts, Senior Editor—Current affairs and history

Molly Stern, Senior Editor—Religion, faith, and biography

Megan Newman, Editor for Viking Studio Books

PENGUIN PUTNAM BOOKS FOR YOUNG READERS

ALLOYBOOKS

DIAL BOOKS FOR YOUNG READERS

DUTTON CHILDREN'S BOOKS (DUTTON, GROSSET & DUNLAP)

FREDERICK WARNE

G. P. PUTNAM'S SONS BOOKS FOR YOUNG READERS

GROSSET & DUNLAP

PHILOMEL BOOKS

PHYLLIS FOGELMAN BOOKS

PRICE STERN SLOAN

PUFFIN BOOKS

VIKING CHILDREN'S BOOKS

375 Hudson Street, New York, NY 10014

212-366-2000

Penguin Putnam Books for Young Readers produces titles for children of all ages. This house offers a wide array of distinctive divisions, imprints, and affiliates of Penguin Putnam's component houses, including Alloy Books, Dial Books for Young Readers, Frederick Warne, Grosset & Dunlap, Philomel, Phyllis Fogelman Books, Price Stern Sloan, Puffin Books, and Viking Children's Books.

Each imprint publishes a broad assortment of titles in a variety of formats, and each children's house is a recognized name in the industry. Together, these imprints form a powerhouse in children's book publishing.

ALLOYBOOKS

AlloyBooks, a new Penguin Putnam imprint aimed at teens, released its first four nonfiction titles in August 2000, including: *Slam*, a unique poetry anthology; *DIY Beauty*, a do-it-yourself beauty guide; *Dreams*, a funky dream interpretation manual; and *Any Advice?* a book packed with advice for teens from Alloy.com's advice experts.

Subsequent lists have included: *Spiritualized*, a personalized look at teen spirituality across the country; *This Book Is About Sex*, a frank and honest exploration of teen sexuality and advice on sex; *Who Do You Think You Are? 12 Methods for Analyzing the True You*, a fun collection of self-analysis methods ranging from astrology to chakras to body types; *Have a Nice Life*, a funny, offbeat fiction series by Scarlett MacDougal.

New titles include: *Daisy Comes Home* by Sarah Dessen; *Ruby's Beauty Shop* by Rosemary Wells; *Locomotion* by Jacqueline Woodson; *The Cat Ate My Gymsuit* by Paula Danziger.

Direct query letters and SASEs to:

Ileen Kreit, Publisher

DIAL BOOKS FOR YOUNG READERS

Dial Books for Young Readers is a hardcover trade children's book division publishing 50 titles per year for children from preschool age through young adult.

This Penguin Group (USA) Inc. imprint traces its roots to 1880 and the founding of *The Dial*, a monthly literary magazine that published such literary giants as e.e. cummings, T. S. Eliot, D. H. Lawrence, and Gertrude Stein. Since the children's list was launched in 1961, Dial has been known for books of high literary merit and fine design for readers of all ages. It has pioneered books for the young, including the first quality boardbooks published in the U. S. Dial introduced its Easy-to-Read series in 1979 to publish full-color early readers with popular children's book authors and artists, including James Marshall, creator of the Fox series.

Representative titles include: *River Between Us* by Richard Peck (a Book Award fianalist and winner of the Scott O'Dell Award); *Bronx Masquerade* by Nikki Grimes; *A Year Down Yonder* by Richard Peck.

Direct query letters and SASEs to:

Nancy Paulsen, Publisher

Lauri Hornik, Editorial Director, Associate Publisher

DUTTON CHILDREN'S BOOKS

Dutton Children's Books is one of the oldest continually operating children's publishers in the U. S. Edward Payson Dutton opened the doors of his Boston bookshop in 1852 and shortly thereafter began to release "fresh and entertaining" books for young readers.

Nearly 150 years later, Dutton's tagline, "Every book a promise," reflects the imprint's mission to create high-quality books that will transport young readers. Today, the Dutton list looks very different, but its commitment to excellence,freshness, and entertainment has not changed.

Best-selling single titles include: *Wheels on the Bus* by Paul O. Zelinsky and *Dinosaur Roar!* by Paul Stickland, and licensed books published with such partners as Dream-Works/SKG, Hallmark-owned Interart's Holly Pond Hill, Radio Flyer, and Little Souls.

The recent list includes: *Creation* by Gerald McDermott; *Walter the Farting Dog: Trouble at the Yard Sale* by William Kotzwinkle; *Guitar Girl* by Sara Manning.

Direct query letters and SASEs to:

Stephanie Owens Lurie, President and Publisher

Lucia Monfried, Senior Editor

Meredith Mundy Wasinger, Editor

Michele Coppola, Editor

Julie Strauss-Gabel, Editor

FREDERICK WARNE

Frederick Warne was founded in 1865 by a bookseller turned publisher who gave his own name to the firm. The hallmarks of the publishing program are beautifully produced editions of historic original works, such as Beatrix Potter, plus lively spin-off books ranging from baby record books and treasuries to boardbooks and novelty titles.

G. P. PUTNAM'S SONS BOOKS FOR YOUNG READERS

G. P. Putnam's Sons Books for Young Readers publishes about 50 trade hardcover books for children per year, including lively, accessible picture books and some of today's strongest voices in fiction. It publishes popular novels and picture books from some of the top names in children's books today.

G. P. Putnam's Sons is the home of celebrated picture-book creators Tomie dePaola, Jan Brett, Eric Hill, Rachael Isadora, Maira Kalman, Keiko Kasza, and Peggy Rathmann. Award-winning authors for older readers include Joan Bauer, Paula Danziger, Jean Fritz, Vicki Grove, Suzy Kline, Robin McKinley, Jacqueline Woodson, and Laurence Yep.

G. P. Putnam's Sons Books for Young Readers is accepting manuscripts.

Guidelines for Manuscript Submissions

PICTURE BOOKS
Accepts full picture book manuscripts for review. Art should not be sent until specifically requested.

FICTION (MIDDLE-GRADE, CHAPTER BOOKS, YOUNG ADULT)
Send a query letter before submitting fiction. Include a synopsis and one to three sample chapters. Query letters and sample chapters will be circulated among the editors and the entire work will be requested upon interest.

NONFICTION
Send a query letter before submitting nonfiction. Include a synopsis and 1–2 sample chapters, as well as a table of contents. Query letters and sample chapters will be circulated among the editors and the entire work will be requested upon interest.

Direct all submissions to:
Putnam Children's Editorial, Manuscript Editor
345 Hudson Street, 14th Floor, New York, NY 10014

GROSSET & DUNLAP

Grossett & Dunlap produces about 125 mass-market children's books each year in hardcover, paperback, library binding, and other formats. Since the 1940s, in addition to the original Nancy Drew and Hardy Boys series, Grosset has published the Illustrated Junior Library. This collection of hardcover editions of *Little Women*, *Tom Sawyer*, and more than 20 other classics is a mainstay of practically every bookstore selling children's books.

Known for originality, quality, and value, Grosset & Dunlap currently publishes many well-known book lines, including the All Aboard Reading series of leveled paperpack readers and Reading Railroad, paperback 8 x 8s. Another Grosset series that continues to sell well is Dish, a middle grade series.

Grosset & Dunlap Series include: Smart About Art (all about art for kids 5-9); Katie Kazoo; Strawberry Shortcake and Who Was...(a biography series for kids 8-11)

Direct query letters and SASEs to:

Debra Dorfman, President and Publisher

Bonnie Bader, Editor Director

PHILOMEL BOOKS

Philomel Books was created in the early 1980s from World Publishing Books for Young People by editor and publisher Ann Beneduce. Beneduce was a pioneer in choosing books that would sell to both trade and institutional markets, so for the new list she chose the name Philomel, a term for an English nightingale that literally means "love of learning." The name implied that these books would be distinguished, beautiful in concept and form, fine enough to be sought as gifts, and original and handsome enough to be bought by libraries and schools. Titles are published in hardcover, as well as with school and library binding.

Philomel published Caldecott-winners *Owl Moon* by Jane Yolen and John Schoenherr and *Lon Po Po* by Ed Young. It became the primary publisher of popular artist-author Patricia Polacco, who created *Pink and Say*, *Chicken Sunday*, and many other biographical folk-like tales. Philomel was honored with *New York Times* Best Illustrated Awards for *Cats Are Cats* by Ed Young and *Fox's Dream* by Tejima.

The Philomel list has also included popular and respected novels. In the late 1980s it became a leader in the field of fantasy with Brian Jacques's Redwall books, a series now 11 books deep and growing. The trend toward quality fiction continues, with such titles as *The Lost Years of Merlin* by T. A. Barron; *The Lost Flower Children* by Janet Taylor Lisle; *I Am Mordred* by Nancy Springer.

Other worlds, of one form or another, have always been of interest to Philomel. It has published a lot of historical fiction, such as Sally Keehn's *I Am Regina* and Stephen Menick's *The Muffin Child*. The imprint also supports books with a social conscience, such as *Be Good to Eddie Lee* by Virginia Fleming and Floyd Cooper, and *Choosing Up Sides* by John H. Ritter, a recipient of the 1999 International Reading Award for Older Readers. Publishing books and ideas that celebrate a child's potential—indeed, human potential—in worlds past and present is Philomel's goal.

Titles indicative of this list include: *One Rainy Day* by Valeri Gorbachev; *I Invited a Dragon to Dinner: And Other Poems to Make You Laugh Out Loud* by Chris L. Demarest (Illustrator); *Tanya and the Red Shoes* by Patricia Lee Gauch and Satomi Ichikawa (Illustrator); *Elefantina's Dream* by X. J. Kennedy and Graham Percy (Illustrator); *Anna Sunday* by Sally M. Keehn; *The Tribes of Redwall: Badgers* (The Tribes of Redwall Series) by Brian Jacques and Peter Standley (Illustrator); *Things Not Seen* by Andrew Clements; *The Kingfisher's Gift* by Susan Williams Beckhorn; *Birdbrain Amos* by Michael Delaney; *Point Blank: An Alex Rider Adventure* by Anthony Horowitz; *The Girl in the Cage* by Jane Yolen and Robert J. Harris.

Direct query letters and SASEs to:

Michael Green, Associate Publisher and Editorial Director

PRICE STERN SLOAN

Price Stern Sloan (PSS) was founded in Los Angeles in the early 1960s to publish the Mad Libs series that Roger Price and Leonard Stern had concocted during their stint as writers for Steve Allen's *Tonight Show*. Along with their partner Larry Sloan, they expanded the company into a wide variety of publishing categories, especially children's books, novelty formats, and humor. The company had tremendous success with a number of proprietary brands, many of which flourish to this day; among them, Mad Libs, Wee Sing, Mr. Men & Little Miss, Serendipity, Crazy Games, and Doodle Art.

The company was purchased by the Putnam Berkley Group in 1993, and in 1997 the offices were moved to New York. With about 75 titles per year, Price Stern Sloan continues to publish successfully its proprietary brands, as well as titles that fall into the preschool children's mass merchandise categories. PSS also produces a successful annual list of desk calendars and occasional humor titles for the adult market.

Among PSS authors are: Pamela Beall, Arthur Bloch, Stephen Cosgrove, Dan Greenburg, Roger Hargreaves, Susan Nipp, Jan Pienkowski, and Charles Reasoner.

Titles indicative of this list include: *Aladdin* by Melissa Tyrrell, et al.; *Amazing Alphabet Maze Book* by Patrick Baldus (Illustrator); *The Ants Go Marching* (Wee Sing Board Books) by Susan Hagan, et al.; *The Big Burger Book* by Jocelyn Jamison; *Cinderella* (Hank the Cowdog # 40) by Melissa Tyrrell, et al.; *The Dinosaur Store* (Welcome to Eurekaville) by Sylvia Branzei, et al.; *Easter Treats* by Leigh Harris; *Five Little Ghosts* by William Boniface and Jerry Smath (Illustrator); *The Ghost Hunter's Handbook* by Rachel Dickinson; *Haunted Mad Libs* by Roger Price, et al.; *How to Be a Pig* by Ima Swine and Shelly Meredith (Illustrator); *The Mighty Big Book of Travel Games* by Dina Anastassio, et al. and *Muffin Dragon* by Stephen Cosgrove and Robin James (Illustrator).

In addition to producing original titles, Price Stern Sloan also reissues previously published books.

Direct query letters and SASEs to:

Jon Anderson, Publisher

PUFFIN BOOKS

Puffin Books was founded on a strong literary tradition and a commitment to publishing a successful mix of classic children's fiction, as well as some of the best new literature for children. Over the years, Puffin has transformed from a small, yet distinguished, paperback house into one of the largest, most diverse, and successful children's publishers in the business, publishing everything from picture books to ground-breaking middle-grade and teen fiction. In addition to publishing new editions of quality literary fiction, Puffin has started several original series with broad commercial appeal.

During the 1980s, Puffin Books produced quality paperback editions of Viking titles, aggressively acquired titles for paperback publication from outside publishing houses, reprinted Puffin UK titles, and maintained a backlist packed with award-winning children's literature, including Robert McCloskey's Caldecott Medal winner *Make Way For Ducklings*, Ludwig Bemelmans's beloved Caldecott Honor book *Madeline*, and Don Freeman's classic *Corduroy*.

In 1988, Penguin merged with New American Library and Dutton, creating a new powerhouse Puffin list. Incorporating titles from three hardcover imprints, Viking Children's Books, Dial Books for Young Readers, and Dutton Children's Books, Puffin drew on the strength of its expanded list to launch the Puffin Easy-to-Read series, as well as—in a major joint venture with Puffin UK—a newly redesigned Puffin Classics series. The 1996 merger of Penguin Books with the Putnam Berkley Group, and the subsequent incorporation of Putnam's PaperStar imprint with Puffin, cemented Puffin's long-standing position as one of the leading children's paperback publishers in the business.

Puffin produces titles for young readers in every age group: lift-the-flaps and picture books for young children, Puffin Easy-to-Reads for first-time readers, Puffin Chapters and the best in historical and contemporary fiction for middle-graders, and critically acclaimed novels for older readers under the Speak imprint.

In recent years, Puffin Books has published several *New York Times* and *Publishers Weekly* bestsellers, including the fantasy romp *Which Witch?* by Eva Ibbotson; *Rules of the Road* (a Newbery Honor Book) by Joan Bauer; *A Long Way From Chicago* (a Newbery Honor Book) by Richard Peck; Tomie dePaola's first chapter book *26 Fairmount Avenue* (a Newberry Honor Book); *Speak* (National Book Award Finalist and Printz Honor Book) by Laurie Halse Anderson. Lost classics like Elizabeth Goudge's *The Little White Horse* are finding a new generation of fans in Puffin. And Jon Scieszka's hilarious Time Warp Trio series keeps middle-grade readers in stitches, as Puffin's highly addictive original fiction series Sweep breaks new ground for teen readers.

Puffin is also expanding its list of original books for younger children with holiday lift-the-flap books designed to explore cultural traditions. Younger children love Claire Masurel and Susan Calitri's adorable bunny Emily, star of such charming lift-the-flaps as *Emily's Dance Class*, *Emily and Her Baby-Sitter*, and the doll set *Emily's Ballet Box*.

Noted Puffin picture book authors and illustrators include: *The Gingerbread Boy* by Ludwig Bemelmans and illustrator Jan Brett; *The Very Hungry Caterpillar* by Eric Carle;

Strega Nona by Tomie dePaola; *The Snowy Day* by Ezra Jack Keats and *Max and Ruby* by Rosemary Wells and Paul O. Zelinsky.

Middle-graders and teen readers devour books by Puffin. Titles include: *Time Cat* and *The Chronicles of Pyrdain* by Lloyd Alexander; *Charlie and the Chocolate Factory* by Roald Dahl; *Amber Brown* by Paula Danziger; *The Outsiders* by S. E. Hinton; *Pippi Longstocking* by Astrid Lindgren; *Roll of Thunder, Hear My Cry* by Mildred D. Taylor; *Miracle's Boys* by award-winning author Jacqueline Woodson.

Direct query letters and manuscripts with SASEs to:

Sharyn November, Senior Editor

VIKING CHILDREN'S BOOKS

Viking Children's Books, founded in 1933, publishes approximately 60 titles per year, ranging from books for very young children, such as board and lift-the-flap books, to sophisticated fiction and nonfiction for teens. The current Viking list is known for such classic characters as Madeline, Corduroy, Pippi Longstocking, Roald Dahl's Matilda, Rosemary Wells's Max & Ruby, The Stinky Cheese Man, Cam Jansen, and Froggy. Viking publishes the entire works of Ezra Jack Keats, including *The Snowy Day*, winner of the Caldecott Medal and Robert McCloskey, author of *Make Way for Ducklings*, also a Caldecott winner.

Throughout Viking's history, it has been known for innovation as well as for a dedication to quality books that has created the rich backlist the house enjoys. Viking has published 10 Newbery Medal winners and 10 Caldecott Medal winners, more than any other publishing house, as well as 27 Newbery Honor books, 33 Caldecott Honor books, and an American Book Award winner. Sixteen Viking books have been recognized as *New York Times* Best Illustrated Books. Two Viking books have received the Coretta Scott King Award, two have been Batchelder Honor books, four have received the Christopher Medal, and two authors, S. E. Hinton and Richard Peck, have received the Margaret A. Edwards Award for bodies of work that included Viking titles.

In 1985, Viking won the Carey Thomas Award for creative publishing, the first children's list to receive this award. Viking has been nominated twice for the *LMP* Award for Best Children's list.

Among the ground-breaking titles published by Viking are: *The Outsiders* (1969), still the best-selling young adult book ever published; *The Snowy Day* (1963), which brought multicultural books mainstream recognition; and *The Stinky Cheese Man* (1992), widely hailed for its innovative design.

Recent releases include: *Felicity Wishes: Little Book of Everyday Wishes* by Emma Thomson and *One Little Lamb* by Elaine Greenstein.

Direct query letters and SASEs to:

Regina Hayes, Publisher

RANDOM HOUSE, INC.

MAJOR RANDOM HOUSE DIVISIONS INCLUDE:

RANDOM HOUSE INFORMATION GROUP

RANDOM HOUSE TRADE PUBLISHING GROUP

MAJOR PUBLISHING GROUPS:

BALLANTINE PUBLISHING GROUP

BANTAM DELL PUBLISHING GROUP

CROWN PUBLISHING GROUP

DOUBLEDAY BROADWAY PUBLISHING GROUP

KNOPF PUBLISHING GROUP

RANDOM HOUSE CHILDREN'S BOOKS

1745 Broadway, New York, NY 10019

212-751-2600

Random House Inc., a division of the Bertelsmann Book Group of Bertelsmann AG, is the world's largest English-language general trade book publisher. Founded in 1925, Random House has grown into an intricate web of divisions, publishing groups, and imprints. The span of this house's titles runs both wide and deep, including a broad array of categories in both commercial fiction and nonfiction. Random House publishes titles in hardcover, trade paperback, mass-market paperback, audio, electronic, and digital, for adults, young adults, and children.

When Random House, Inc., was acquired by Bertelsmann in 1998, the imprints of the former Random House, Inc., and those of the former Bantam Doubleday Dell were joined to form the Bantam Dell Publishing Group. Random House, Inc.'s other publishing groups include Ballantine Books, the Crown Publishing Group, the Doubleday Broadway Publishing Group, the Knopf Publishing Group, the Random House Audio Publishing Group, Random House Children's Books, the Random House Diversified Publishing Group, the Random House Information Group, the Random House Trade Publishing Group, and Random House Ventures.

Random House only accepts manuscripts submitted by an agent. It does not accept unsolicited submissions, proposals, manuscripts, or submission queries via e-mail at this time.

RANDOM HOUSE INFORMATION GROUP

FODOR'S TRAVEL PUBLICATIONS

LIVING LANGUAGE

PRINCETON REVIEW

RANDOM HOUSE ESPAÑOL

RANDOM HOUSE PUZZLES & GAMES

RANDOM HOUSE REFERENCE PUBLISHING

A division of Random House, Inc., the Information Group publishes a well-developed list of consumer reference and dictionary titles, language study courses and academic test preparation titles. For a full list of Random House Information Group titles please visit the Random House website at www.randomhouse.com.

FODOR'S TRAVEL PUBLICATIONS

Fodor's Travel Publications, the world's largest English-language travel information publisher, has more than 440 travel titles to destinations worldwide. Fodor's Travel Publications is a unit of Fodor's LLC, a subsidiary of Random House, Inc., and its parent company, Bertelsmann AG, one of the world's largest media companies. For more information about Fodor's, visit its website at www.fodors.com.

Fodor's publishes niche market travel guidebooks, as well as more traditional guides that offer practical information on popular destinations worldwide. Fodor's publishes over 14 different series to address every type of travel experience imaginable. These include the flagship Gold Guides series, Fodor's FYI, Escape, Around the City with Kids, To Go, and Fodor's Road Guides USA.

Recent titles include: *Great Canadian Vacations*, *Athens: The Collected Traveler*; *Where to Weekend: Boston*; *Fodor's African Safari*, and *Alaska Ports of Call*.

LIVING LANGUAGE

Living Language is one of the most well-known names in both foreign-language and English-language instruction, and publishes courses that meet a variety of needs. Living Language offers a wide range of programs, including Complete Basic Courses; the All-Audio, Ultimate, In-Flight, and English for New Americans series; and the popular Daily Phrase & Culture Calendars. The Living Language line includes books, cassettes, CDs, and videos in 23 languages.

PRIMA GAMES

The world's leader in electronic entertainment publishing, Prima Games publishes strategy guides for PC and console games and has more than 38 million strategy games in print. For a full list of titles, visit the Prima Games website at www.primagames.com. If you're an experienced strategy guide author or an expert gamer who loves to write, please send a resume and writing sample to Prima Games, 3000 Lava Ridge Court, Roseville, CA 95661.

RANDOM HOUSE ESPAÑOL

Random House Español publishes Spanish-language books covering many subjects, including biography, history, health care, reference, self-help, spiritual and astrological, and practical how-to books. Further augmenting these offerings, Random House Español distributes titles from the diverse publishing programs of Random House's affiliate Spanish-language publishing companies: Plaza & Jans in Spain and Mexico, as well as Sudamericana in Argentina. With this combined strength, Random House Español offers one of the largest and most diverse lists of Spanish-language books available in the U. S.

RANDOM HOUSE PUZZLES & GAMES

Random House Puzzles & Games publishes crossword puzzle books, including those drawn from the pages of the *Los Angeles Times*, the *Boston Globe*, and the *New York Times*. The imprint also has a line of Dell Crossword puzzle books, as well as trivia books on baseball by Jeffrey and Doug Lyons. The Princeton Review imprint publishes books that help students sharpen their academic skills, prepare for standardized tests, and gain entrance into college and graduate school. Representative titles include: *Cracking the SAT*, *The Best 331 Colleges*, and *Word Smart*, the flagship title of The Princeton Review's "Smart" series.

RANDOM HOUSE REFERENCE PUBLISHING

Random House Reference Publishing is a leading publisher of reference works in both print and electronic formats. Its lexicography program is highly regarded for its inclusion of new words in the English language earlier than most other reference publishers.

Classic titles include: *Random House Webster's College Dictionary*; *Random House Webster's Unabridged Dictionary*; *Random House Roget's College Thesaurus*; *Random House Historical Dictionary of American Slang*.

Random House Reference also publishes a line of trade reference titles including: *Verbal Advantage* by Charles Elster, *Finding a Place Called Home: A Guide to African-American Genealogy and Historical Identity* by Dr. Dee Parmer Woodtor, and *The Random House Treasury of Best-Loved Poems*.

THE RANDOM HOUSE TRADE PUBLISHING GROUP

RANDOM HOUSE TRADE BOOKS

VILLARD BOOKS

STRIVER'S ROW

THE MODERN LIBRARY

RANDOM HOUSE TRADE BOOKS

Random House Trade Books publishes trade fiction and nonfiction covering a broad scope of literary and commercial appeal. Since 1995, it has published three of the best-selling books of all time: *My American Journey* by Colin Powell, *Midnight in the Garden of Good and Evil* by John Berendt, and *The Greatest Generation* by Tom Brokaw.

This group has also become a showcase for fiction and nonfiction authors publishing for the first time. Titles include: *April Witch* by Majgull Axelsson; *A Collection of Beauties at the Height of Their Popularity* by Whitney Otto; *Consent* by Ben Schrank; *A Future Perfect* by John Micklethwait and Adrian Wooldridge; *The God of Small Things* by Arundhati Roy.

Recent titles include: *In an Uncertain World: Tough Choices From Wall Street to Washington* by Robert Rubin and Jacob Weisberg; *Present Value* by Sabin Willett; *Reds: McCarthyism in Twentieth Century America* by Ted Morgan; *Bruce Springsteen's America* by Robert Coles.

Dan Manaker, Executive Editor-in-Chief

Kate Medina, Executive Editor

Jonathan Karp, Editor-in-Chief of Random imprints, Senior Vice President—memoirs, history, current events, business and self-help

Lee Boudreaux, Senior Editor—Literary and commercial fiction, women's issues, and narrative nonfiction

Bob Loomis, Executive Vice President, Executive Editor

VILLARD BOOKS

Villard Books publishes a general fiction and nonfiction list that is known for its titles in sports, personal narrative, cooking, and fiction with a new voice.

Launched in 1983, Villard publishes into many categories and attracts attention for its exciting and diverse list of authors and titles, including: The Travel Detective books by *Today Show* and NBC travel expert Peter Greenberg; *Shakey*, the only authorized biography of rock-and-roll legend Neil Young by Jimmy McDonough; Melissa Etheridge's autobiography, *Take-no-prisoners*; *Into Thin Air* by Jon Krakauer; *Never Die*

Easy by Walter Payton with Don Yaeger; *The Tribeca Grill Cookbook* by Don Pintabona.

Recent nonfiction titles include: *Buff Moms: The Complete Guide to Fitness for Mothers of All Ages* by Sue Fleming; *Lads: A Memoir of Manhood* by Dave Itzkoff; *The Mysterious Stranger* by David Blaine; *Motherhood and Hollywood* by Patricia Heaton; *Hold the Enlightenment* by Tim Cahill; *Dear Rhonda* by Demitri Kornegay.

Recent fiction title include: *Slick* by Daniel Price; *Donorboy* by Brendan Halpin; *The Holy Road* by Michael Blake; *No More Mr. Nice Guy* by C. Kelly Robinson; *Dream in Color* by Darlene Johnson; *Slave to Fashion* by Rebecca Campbell; *Meant to Be* by Rita Coburn Whack.

Bruce Tracy, Editorial Director

STRIVERS ROW

This imprint is dedicated to publishing African American fiction and nonfiction in trade paperback format. It is named for the street dubbed "Strivers Row"—West 138th and 139th Streets between Adam Clayton Powell and Frederick Douglass Boulevards—which was largely inhabited by first generation African American professionals during the time of the Harlem Renaissance. Its mission is to publish quality African American literature that captures the same spirit of hope, creativity, and promise as its namesake.

Striver's Row titles include: *Sorority Sisters* by Tajuana "TJ" Butler; *The Hearts of Men* by Travis Hunter; *Black Coffee* by Tracy Price-Thompson; *Rich Minds, Rich Rewards* by Valorie Burton; *Between Brothers* by C. Kelly Robinson.

Melody Guy, Senior Editor

THE MODERN LIBRARY

The Modern Library, known for publishing American classics, has expanded its program to include trade paperbacks and series of classics in various subject areas with distinguished guest editors. These include: Jon Krakauer's Exploration Series, Caleb Carr's War Series, Martin Scorsese's Movie Series, Steve Martin's Humor and Wit Series, and Ruth Reichl's Food Series.

Recent titles include: *The Reformation* by Patrick Collinson and *Truman Capote—Other Voices, Other Rooms* by Truman Capote.

THE BALLANTINE PUBLISHING GROUP

BALLANTINE BOOKS

DEL REY

DEL REY/LUCAS BOOKS

FAWCETT

IVY

ONE WORLD

PRESIDIO PRESS

WELLSPRING

The Ballantine Publishing Group is a Random House division that publishes hardcover, trade paperback, and mass-market paperback books. Founded in 1952, Ballantine was acquired by Random House in 1973.

Its imprints include: Ballantine Books, Del Rey, Del Rey/Lucas Books, Fawcett, Ivy, One World, Wellspring, and Presido Press.

BALLANTINE BOOKS

Ballantine Books publishes commercial fiction and general nonfiction, including health, diet, psychology, history, and biography.

The mass-market list includes such best-selling authors as John Case, Robert Crais, Fannie Flagg, Sue Grafton, Kristin Hannah, John Irving, Jonathan Kellerman, Richard North Patterson, Anne Perry, Anne Rice, Edward Rutherfurd, and Anne Tyler.

Recent titles include: *The Romanov Prophecy* by Steve Berry; *Shoulder the Sky* by Anne Perry; *We Got Fired and It's the Best Thing that Ever Happened to Us* by Harvey Mackay; *To the Last Man: A Novel of the First World War* by Jeff Shaara.

Gina Centrello, President and Publisher

Nancy Miller, Executive Editor for Group—Self-help, world affairs, parenting and narrative nonfiction

Maureen O'Neal, Vice President, Editorial Director of Trade Paperback—Diet/health, childcare/parenting, cooking and commercial fiction

Linda Marrow, Vice President and Editorial Director—Women's fiction, thrillers and suspense

Elisabeth Kallick Dyssegaard, Executive Editor—Women's issues, literary fiction and nonfiction

Joe Blades, Vice President and Executive Editor—Fiction, mysteries, suspense, and pop culture with emphasis on film

DEL REY & DEL REY/LUCAS BOOKS

Del Rey publishes science fiction, fantasy, and alternate history in hardcover, trade paperback, and mass-market paperback formats.

Del Rey/Lucas Books published the novelizations of the first three *Star Wars* films, plus an array of other *Star Wars* fiction and nonfiction titles. Since October 1997, Del Rey has been publishing novels of the films in the New Jedi Order fiction program and nonfiction books, in both the new and the classic *Star Wars* programs. Titles include: *Star Wars Episode 1: The Phantom Menace* by Terry Brooks; *The New Jedi Order: Vector Prime* by R. A. Salvatore; *Star Wars: Cloak of Deception* by James Luceno.

Recent titles include: *The Language of Power* by Rosemary Kirstein; *Gateway* by Frederik Pohl; *Exultant* by Stephen Baxter; *High Druid of Shannara: Tanequil* by Terry Brooks.

Betsy Mitchell, Vice President and Editor-in-Chief

FAWCETT BOOKS

Fawcett Books publishes a wide spectrum of fiction, with an emphasis on mysteries, thrillers, and suspense. Its mass-market paperback list includes such titles as: *Midnight Voices* by John Saul; *Final Round* by William Bernhardt; *A Caress of Twilight* by Laurell K. Hamilton; *Death in the Family* by Jill McGown.

IVY

Ivy is a mass-market paperback imprint that publishes both fiction and nonfiction books, including Ballantine's mass-market romance books.

The fiction list includes: *McCloud's Woman* by Patricia Rice; *A Piece of Heaven* by Barbara Samuel; *Texas Rich* by Fern Michaels; *Heart and Soul* by Sally Mandel; *Kiss and Tell* by Cherry Adair; *Highland Bride* by Janet Bieber; *The Trials of Angela* by Millie Criswell.

Nonfiction titles from Ivy include: *Utmost Savagery* by Col. Joseph H. Alexander; *Unnatural Death: Confessions of a Medical Examiner* by Michael M. Baden, M.D.

ONE WORLD

One World publishes multicultural titles, including subjects of African American, Asian, Latin, and Native American interest across all categories and formats.

Recent titles include: *Dying in the Dark* by Valerie Wilson Wesley; *The Red Moon* by Kuwana Haulsey; *My Heart Will Cross This Ocean: My Story, My Son, Amadou* by Kadiatou Diallo and Craig Wolff; *Every Shut Eye* by Colleen Dixon; *Angel of Harlem* by Kuwana Haulsey.

Melody Guy, Senior Editor

PRESIDIO PRESS

Presidio Press deals primarily in themes of war and the military. Recent titles include:

Ace of Aces: The Life of Captain Eddie Rickenbacker by H. Paul Jeffers; *Letters From Vietnam* edited by Bill Adler; *High Noon in the Cold War: Kennedy, Khrushchev and the Cuban Missle Crisis* by Max Frankel; *A Look Over My Shoulder: A Life in the Central Intelligence Agency* by Richard Helms and William Hood.

Zachary Schisgal, Senior Editor

WELLSPRING

Formed in 1999, Wellspring is one of the newer Ballantine imprints. It publishes new titles and repackaged classics from Ballantine's backlist in the categories of spirituality, health sciences, psychology, Eastern philosophy, holistic health, nutrition, yoga, and mythology.

Representative titles include: *The Herbal Epicure* by Carole Ottesen; *The Jesus Sutras* by Martin Palmer; *Barefoot on Holy Ground* by Gloria D. Karpinski; *Jivamukti Yoga* by Sharon Gannon and David Life.

BANTAM DELL PUBLISHING GROUP

BANTAM

DELACORTE PRESS

DELL

DELTA

THE DIAL PRESS

FANFARE

ISLAND

SPECTRA

1745 Broadway, New York NY 10019

212-751-2600

Bantam Dell Publishing Group publishes a broad spectrum of adult fiction and nonfiction, including frontlist commercial category, literary works, specialty titles, and genre fiction.

BANTAM

Bantam is one of the largest mass-market paperback publishers and also publishes titles in hardcover and trade paperback.

Nonfiction titles include: *It Doesn't Take a Hero* by General H. Norman Schwarzkopf; *Emotional Intelligence* by Daniel Goleman; *Seinlanguage* by Jerry Seinfeld; *The Wisdom of Menopause* by Christine Northrup; *Advanced Cinematherapy* by Nancy Peske and Beverly West; *The Dream Dictionary* by Tony Crisp; *Astrology for the Soul* by Jan Spiller ; *American Sign Language Dictionary* by Elaine Costello, Ph.D.

Bantam's fiction list includes: commercial novels, mysteries, thrillers, suspense, science fiction and fantasy, romance, women's fiction, and select literary works. The hardcover fiction list includes such novelists as Dean Koontz, Tom Robbins, Elizabeth George, Iris Johansen, Tami Hoag, Diane Mott Davidson, George R. R. Martin, Michael Palmer, and Luanne Rice. Bantam mass-market and trade paperback authors include Louis L'Amour, Maya Angelou, Jean Auel, Sandra Brown, Pat Conroy, Nora Roberts, Tom Wolfe, Kay Hooper, Lisa Gardner, and Rita Mae Brown.

Recent titles include: *Firestorm* by Iris Johansen; *Whisker of Evil* by Rita Mae Brown; *The Taking* by Dean Koontz; *Kill the Messenger* by Tami Hoag; *A Road Through the Mountain* by Elizabeth McGregor; *Forty Signs of Rain* by Kim Stanley Robinson; *Hondo* by Louis L'Amour; *Walking Raphael* by Leslie Forbes.

Direct queries and SASEs to:

Toni Burbank, Executive Editor—Self-help, spirituality and health

Ann Harris, Senior Editor—Inspirational

Kate Miciak, Executive Editor—Mysteries, thrillers and narrative nonfiction

Wendy McCurdy, Senior Editor—Women's fiction and romance

DELACORTE PRESS

Delacorte Press focuses on hardcover frontlist releases. Delacorte's categories include self-help, self-actualization, popular psychology, child care, politics, true crime, and current issues and events.

Delacorte's trade paperback fiction includes commercial novels, romance, historical, mystery, and futuristic works.

Nonfiction titles include: *Far Appalachia* by Noah Adams; *Aches & Pains* by Maeve Binchy; *For the Bride* by Colin Cowie; *The Promise of Sleep* by William C. Dement, M.D., Ph.D., and Christopher Vaughn; *How to Think Like Leonardo Da Vinci* by Michael Gelb; *More Grandmothers Are Like Snowflakes, No Two Are Alike* by Janet Lanese.

Fiction titles include: *No Man's Mistress* by Mary Balogh; *A Summer to Remember* by Mary Balogh; *The Thief-Taker* by T. F. Banks; *Thief of Souls* by Ann Benson; *Sometimes I Dream in Italian* by Rita Ciresi; *Gone for Good* by Harlan Coben; *The Palace of Tears* by Alev Lytle Croutier; *The Smoke Jumper* by Nicholas Evans.

Recent titles include: *Unlucky in Law* by Perri O'Shaugnessy; *Mina* by Jonathan Creely; *A Season for the Dead* by David Hewson; *The Book of Joe* by Jonathan Tropper; *Slightly Dangerous* by Mary Balogh; *The Immortal Highlander* by Karen Marie Moning; *Second Chance* by Danielle Steel.

DELL

Dell is a long-standing leader in publishing adult fiction and nonfiction in trade paperback format. Dell is home to the bestselling novelist Danielle Steel, who is published in Delacorte hardcover. Other writers who are published in mass market by Dell include: John Grisham, Thomas Harris, Nicholas Evans, Diana Gabaldon, Sara Paretsky, Belva Plain, Perri O'Shaughnessy, Harlan Coben, and Homer Hickam.

Recent titles include: *Summer of the Big Bachi* by Naomi Hirahara; *The Sun Road* by Hannah Macdonald; *Breakfast at Stephanie's* by Sue Margolis; *Call the Devil By His Oldest Name* by Sallie Bissell.

Danielle Perez, Senior Editor

DELTA

Delta publishes fiction and nonfiction in trade paperback format. Nonfiction titles are often biographies or memoirs, whereas the fiction list leans toward literary and short story collections.

Titles include: *Confessions of a Shopaholic* by Sophie Kinsella; *Giovanni's Room* by James Baldwin; *Paradise Park* by Allegra Goodman.

THE DIAL PRESS

The Dial Press, an imprint of Bantam Dell Publishing Group, publishes literary fiction and nonfiction. This includes works by Allegra Goodman, Caroline Knapp, Elizabeth McCracken, Michael Paterniti, David Schickler, and Katie Roiphe.

Dial Press author Justin Cronin won the Hemingway Foundation/PEN Award for First Fiction for *Mary and O'Neil*, a collection of connected short stories. Elizabeth McCracken won the L. L. Winship/PEN New England Prize for her second novel, *Niagara Falls All Over Again*.

Other titles indicative of this list are: *American Chica* by Marie Arana; *Franklin Flyer* by Nicholas Christopher; *Crow Lake* by Mary Lawson.

Recent titles include: *The Rule of Four* by Ian Caldwell and Dustin Thomason; *Can You Keep A Secret?* by Sophie Kinsella; *Reproduction is the Flow of Love* by Lauren Grodstein.

FANFARE

Fanfare publishes women's fiction and romance, featuring adventure, suspense, historical settings, and Westerns. Titles are produced in hardcover, paperback, and trade paperback.

Representative titles include: *To Kiss a Spy* by Jane Feather and *Dream Island* by Josie Litton.

ISLAND

Formerly Dell Island, this imprint publishes paperback fiction with an emphasis on mystery, romance, and suspense.

Titles include: *City of Light* by Lauren Belfer and *A Woman of Passion* by Virginia Henley.

SPECTRA

Spectra's slogan is "Speculative Fiction, Speculative Fact." This imprint of the Bantam Dell Publishing Group publishes science fiction and fantasy books in trade paperback and mass-market paperback.

Recent titles include: *Forty Signs of Rain* by Kim Stanley Robinson; *I, Robot* by Isaac Asimov; *Lord of the Shadows* by Jennifer Fallon; *A Choir of Ill Children* by Tom Piccirilli; *Thomas the Rhymer* by Ellen Kushner.

Anne Lesley Groell, Editor

CROWN PUBLISHING GROUP

CLARKSON POTTER/PUBLISHERS

CROWN BOOKS

CROWN BUSINESS

HARMONY BOOKS

SHAYE AREHEART BOOKS

THREE RIVERS PRESS

1745 Broadway, New York, NY 10019

Crown publishes a variety of trade-oriented fiction and nonfiction titles in hardcover and paperback. Acquired by Random House in 1988, Crown incorporates a number of Random House imprints and acquisitions that together make up the Crown Publishing Group. Crown imprints include: Harmony Books, the Crown imprint, Crown Business, Clarkson Potter, Shaye Areheart Books, and Three Rivers Press.

CLARKSON POTTER/PUBLISHERS

Although its interests vary, Clarkson Potter is a leader in beautifully illustrated nonfiction books about cooking, gardening, and interior design. Its authors include Martha Stewart, Mario Batali, Chris Casson Madden, and Ina Garten.

Titles representative of this list include: *You Can Do It Small Spaces: Decorating to Make Every Inch Count* by Christopher Lowell; *Sailing Style: Design Ideas from Ship to Shore* by Tricia Foley; *The Summer House Cookbook: Everything You Need to Cook at Your Summer House and Entertain in Your own Backyard* by Debra Ponzek and Geralyn

Delaney Graham; *The Lobster Roll and Other Pleasures of Summer by the Beach* by Jodi Della Famena and Andrea Terrys.

New offerings include: *Indian Home Cooking* by Suvir Saran and Stephanie Lyness; *Clean Like A Man: Housekeeping for Men. . .and the Women Who Love Them* by Tom McNulty; *The Keys to Unlocking Your Personal Decorating Style* by Chris Casson Madden.

Direct query and SASE to:

Annetta Hanna, Senior Editor—Design, gardening, biography, popular culture, how-to style and decorating books

Pam Krauss, Editorial Director—Cooking and food, how-to style and decorating books, gardening, narrative nonfiction

Chris Pavone, Senior Editor—Mostly cookbooks, with a focus on single-subject books and trendsetting authors; also, some projects in decorating, pets, cultural history and male-oriented subjects

Rosy Ngo, Editor—Branded books (Pillsbury, etc.), popular culture, urban history, cooking and transportation

CROWN

Crown's fiction list and works of cultural and literary interest are exemplified by *Another City, Not My Own: A Novel in the Form of a Memoir* by Dominick Dunne; *When Elephants Dance* by Tess Uriza Holthe; *Sloppy Firsts* by Megan McCafferty; *Guenevere* by Rosalind Miles; *Nappily Ever After* by Trisha R. Thomas.

The Crown Group's nonfiction encompasses popular titles in biography, history, art, pop culture, contemporary culture, crime, sports, travel, popular and literary science, languages, spirituality, cookbooks, self-help, how-to, antiques and collectibles, as well as popular reference works.

The Crown nonfiction list includes: *IBM and the Holocaust* by Edwin Black; *Tupac Shakur* by the editors of *VIBE* magazine; *Blinded by the Right* by David Brock; *Justice* by Dominick Dunne; *Lest We Forget: The Passage From Africa to Slavery and Emancipation* by Graham Hancock, and Suzanne Somers' diet and fitness series.

Recent titles include: *Blood Done Sign My Name* by Timothy B. Tyson; *Journey From the Land of No: A Girlhood Caught in Revolutionary Iran* by Roya Hakakian; *Sarah* by Marek Haller; *Rammer Jammer Yellow Hammer: A Journey Into the Heart of Fan Mania* by Warren St. John.

Direct queries and SASEs to:

Kristin Kiser, Editorial Director—Prescriptive and narrative nonfiction, pop culture, women's issues and diet/health

Caroline Sincerbeaux, Editor—Social/cultural history, biography, memoir, fiction with emphasis on people in their 20s and 30s, and science narratives, (particulary medicine)

CROWN BUSINESS

Crown Business is one of the leading publishers of business titles, producing titles by authors such as Charles Schwab, Suze Orman, Ram Charan and Michael Hammer. It publishes both traditional and cutting-edge business books, such as *The Deviant Advantage: How Fringe Ideas Become Mass Market* by Ryan Mathews and Watts Walker; *Customers.com* by Patricia Seybold; *Execution: The Discipline of Getting Things Done* by Larry Bossidy and Ram Charan.

Representative titles include: *Your Marketing Sucks* by Mark Stevens; *The Five Patterns of Extraordinary Careers: The Guide for Achieving Success and Satisfaction* by James M. Citrin and Richard A. Smith; *It Pays to Talk: How to Have the Essential Conversations with Your Family About Money and Investing* by Carrie Schwab-Pomerantz and Charles R. Schwab.

New releases include: *Life 2.0: How People Across the Country are Transforming Their Lives to Make Their Own American Dream* by Rich Karlgaard and *MBA in a Box: The Practical Guide to the Big Ideas of Business* by Joel Kurtzman, Glenn Rifkin and Victoria Griffith.

John Mahaney, Executive Editor

HARMONY BOOKS

Harmony Books is a market leader in the area of mind, body, and spirit, as well as biography/memoir, science, and general narrative nonfiction. Its critically acclaimed and best-selling authors include: Stephen Jay Gould, Caroline Myss, Deepak Chopra, and Suzanne Finstad.

Harmony's solid literary nonfiction list includes: *How to Know God* by Deepak Chopra; *Emotional Alchemy* by Tara Bennett-Goleman; *Bhagavad Gita* translated by Stephen Mitchell; *I Have Landed* by Stephen Jay Gould; *The Salmon of Doubt* by Douglas Adams.

Recent releases include: *Song of the Gorilla Nation* by Dawn Prince-Hughes; *House on the River: A Summer Journey* by Nessa Rapoport; *Cursed by a Happy Childhood: Tales of Growing Up, Then and Now* by Carl Lennertz; *Heft on Wheels: A Field Guide to Doing 180* by Mike Magnuson; *Everything Happens for a Reason: Finding the True Meaning of the Events in Our Lives* by Mira Kirshenbaum.

Bell Tower (a division of Harmony Books) publishes titles from many sacred traditions—"books that nourish the soul, illuminate the mind, and speak to the heart." Authors include Stephen Levine, Bernie Glassman, Ram Dass, and Rabbi Joseph Telushkin.

Harmony Books does not accept manuscripts without agent representation.

Shaye Areheart, Vice President and Publisher

Toinette Lippe, Editorial Director, Bell Tower

Kim Kanner Meisner, Senior Editor

SHAYE AREHEART BOOKS

Shaye Areheart Books is devoted to contemporary literary and commercial fiction. Authors include: Chris Bohjalian, Craig Nova, Jeanne Ray, John Smolens, Sheri Reynolds, and Maggie Estep.

Shaye Areheart books embraces a typically more vanguard literary tone. Titles deal with quality fiction and nonfiction.

Recent titles include: *Within Arm's Reach* by Ann Napolitano and *Cruisers* by Craig Nova.

Shaye Areheart Books does not accept manuscripts without agent representation.

Shaye Areheart, Publisher

THREE RIVERS PRESS

Three Rivers Press publishes trade and hardcovers as well as reprints of books issued initially in hardcover by the other Crown imprints.

Titles representative of the list include: *I Hope You Have a Good Life* by Campbell Armstrong; *Kick Me* by Paula Feig; *Black Rubber Dress* by Lauren Henderson; *We Got the Neutron Bomb* by Mark Spitz; *Black Planet* by David Shields; *Aha!* by Jordan Ayan.

Recent releases include: *Little Sugar Addicts: End the Mood Swings, Meltdowns, Tantrums and Low Self-Esteem in Your Child Today* by Kathleen Des Maisons; *Waking Beauty* by Elyse Friedman; *Gargantuan: A Ruby Murphy Mystery* by Maggie Estep; *Liquor* by Poppy Z. Brite; *The Self-Destruction Handbook: 8 Simple Steps to an Unhealthier You* by Adam Wasson and Jessica Staman.

Three Rivers Press is also a strong force in the area of antiques and collectibles books. It is the home of Ralph and Terry Kovel, as well as the popular guides from the House of Collectibles.

Query letters and SASEs should be directed to:

Becky Cabaza, Editorial Director—Health, fitness, parenting, humor, business, pop science, narrative nonfiction

Carrie Thornton, Editor—Pop culture, music, humor, gay and lesbian, dating/relationships, fiction and film

THE DOUBLEDAY BROADWAY PUBLISHING GROUP

BROADWAY BOOKS

CURRENCY

DOUBLEDAY

DOUBLEDAY RELIGIOUS PUBLISHING

HARLEM MOON

MAIN STREET BOOKS

NAN A. TALESE

1745 Broadway, New York, NY 10019

212-751-2600

A division of Random House, The Doubleday Broadway Publishing Group is known for its strong commercial lists in both fiction and nonfiction. This group continues to maintain a strong presence in the marketplace.

One of the notable changes is that Anchor Books left Doubleday to join Vintage Books, creating Vintage Anchor, currently part of the Knopf Publishing Group. Meanwhile, Broadway Books, a newer imprint, is quickly becoming a well-known division with both writers and book buyers. The Doubleday Broadway Publishing Group publishes titles in hardcover, paperback, and audio formats.

BROADWAY BOOKS

Broadway generates a variety of nonfiction including: celebrity autobiography and biography; historical, political, and cultural biography and memoirs; politics and current affairs; multicultural topics; popular culture; cookbooks, diet, and nutrition; consumer reference, business, personal finance, and popular psychology, spirituality, and women's issues. The house also provides selective commercial/literary frontlist fiction, primarily by established or highly promotable authors.

Broadway's emporium strategy involves publishing unique, marketable books of the highest editorial quality by authors who are authorities in their field and who use their credibility and expertise to promote their work.

Broadway Books began operation in mid-1995, with a mission to publish high-quality nonfiction hardcovers and trade paperbacks. In 1999 it was merged with Doubleday to form the Doubleday Broadway Publishing Group.

The publishing house's namesake street and logo (a diagonally bisected letter B) are emblematic of the publisher. Broadway is New York's oldest thoroughfare and runs obliquely through the diversity of Manhattan's multicultural neighborhoods—from the original harbor and the financial district, along the city's centers of government to the theater, retail shops, musical establishments, and educational and medical institutions.

Representative titles of Broadway's list include: *Catch Me If You Can* by Frank Abangnale; *Tuesdays With Morrie: An Old Man, a Young Man, and Life's Greatest Lesson* by Mitch Albom; *A Girl Named Zippy: Growing Up Small in Mooreland, Indiana* by Haven Kimmel; *The O'Reilly Factor* by Bill O'Reilly; *Bella Tuscany* by Frances Mayes; *Fair Ball* by Bob Costas; *Life Makeovers* by Cheryl Richardson; *Smart Women Finish Rich* by David Bach; *Under the Tuscan Sun* by Frances Mayers; *A Walk in the Woods* by Bill Bryson; *Vegetarian Cooking for Everyone* by Deborah Madison; *The Minimalist Cooks at Home.*

Recent titles include: *Coastal Cooking with John Shields* by John Shields; *Howling at the Moon: The Odyssey of an Out-of-Control Music Mogul in an Age of Excess* by Walter Yetnikoff; *Blood From Stones: The Secret Financial Network of Terror* by Douglas Farah; *The Right Address* by Caroline Doyle-Karasyov and Jill Kargman; *To Have and to Hold* by Jane Green.

Broadway does not accept unsolicited manuscripts; only agented works will be considered.

Jennifer Josephy, Executive Editor—Cookbooks and general nonfiction

Ann Campbell, Editor—Narrative nonfiction, women's history, women's fiction, health, fitness, spirituality, armchair travel, and politics

Charles Conrad, Vice President and Executive Editor—New nonfiction projects: popular culture, social history, and literary nonfiction; contemporary literary and quality fiction; in charge of trade-paperback reprints

Rebecca Cole, Associate Editor—New nonfiction, pop culture, social history, parenting, young, edgy nonfiction, and cultural criticism

Gerald Howard, Vice President and Editorial Director—Narrative nonfiction and unusual literary fiction

Patricia Medved, Senior Editor—Parenting, self-help, consumer reference, and health

Kristine Puopolo, Senior Editor—Literary nonfiction, self-help, spirituality, health, and fitness

CURRENCY

Currency publishes hardcover business books in a variety of categories, including business narrative, biography, general business, marketing/sales, careers, personal finance and investing, leadership, and entrepreneurship.

Titles indicative of this list are: *Power Failure: The Inside Story of the Collapse of Enron* by Mimi Swartz (reprint); *The Finish Rich Workbook* by David Rich; *The New Law of Demand and Supply* by Rick Kash; *Managing for the Short Term* by Chuck Martin; *A Stake in the Outcome* by Jack Stack and Bo Burlingham; *Creative Destruction* by Richard Foster and Sarah Kaplan; *The Art of Innovation* by Thomas Kelley; *The Fifth Discipline* by Peter M. Senge; *Speed is Life* by Bob Davis; *The 80/20 Principle* by Richard Koch; *The Great Game of Business* by Jack Stack and Bo Burlingham; *The Secret Handshake* by Kathleen Kelley Reardon, Ph.D.; *The Anatomy of Buzz: How to Create Word of Mouth Marketing* by Emanuel Rosen; *Zoom: How 12 Exceptional Companies Are Navigating the Road to the Next Economy* by Jim Citrin.

Send query letters with SASEs to:

Roger Scholl, Editor

DOUBLEDAY

Doubleday, now with more than a century in the publishing business, remains one of the world's most renowned houses. Perhaps best known for its strong commercial list in fiction and nonfiction, Doubleday continues to be a dominating force in mainstream popular nonfiction, in addition to books of literary note.

Representative titles in Doubleday fiction include: *The Summons* by John Grisham; *Three Weeks in Paris* by Barbara Taylor Bradford; *Palladio* by Jonathan Dee; *Choke* by Chuck Palahniuk; *The Treatment* by Mo Hayder; *The Hostage* by Robert Crais; *Beacon Street Mourning* by Diane Day; *Cold and Pure and Very Dead* by Joanne Dobson.

Recent fiction includes: *Death March* by Lincoln Child; *Princes of Ireland* by Edward Rutherfurd; *Circle of Grace* by Penelope J. Stokes.

Doubleday nonfiction categories run as broad as they run deep, including biography and autobiography, artists and photography, current affairs, political science, public affairs, philosophy, ethics, family, marriage, sports and recreation, health, history, home and garden, and self-help.

Recent nonfiction titles include: *Sore Winners (and the rest of us) in George Bush's America* by John Powers and *Women Make the Best Salesmen* by Marion Luna Brem.

Direct query letters and SASEs to:

Deb Futter, Vice President—Women's issues, narrative nonfiction, biography and fiction

Jason Kaufman, Senior Editor—Thrillers, action adventure, true crime and narrative nonfiction

DOUBLEDAY RELIGIOUS PUBLISHING

Doubleday Religious Publishing produces select titles in hardcover, as well as makes some books available as e-books. Categories cover spirituality and religion, including Christianity, Buddhism, and Judaism.

Sample titles include: *Miracles at the Jesus Oak* by Craig Harline; *Lord, Have Mercy* by Scott Hahn; *A Place at the Table* by William Elliot; *It's Not the Same Without You* by Mitch Finley; *The Mountain of Silence* by Kyriacos C. Markides; *The New Stations of the Cross* by Megan McKenna; *The Living Christ* by Harold Fickett; *Religions for Peace* by Francis Cardinal Arinze; *Angels & Dragons* by Molly Wolf; *The Divine Hours* by Phyllis Tickle; *It's a God Thing* by Luis Palau; *Soul Survivor* by Philip Yancey; *God Underneath* by Edward L. Beck; *Spiritual Survival Guide* by Charles Shields and Cynthia

Ferrell; *Hail, Holy Queen* by Scott Hahn; *Exploring Jewish Tradition* by Rabbi Abraham B. Witty and Rachel J. Witty.

Recent releases include: *Fumbling* by Kerry Egan; *The Book of Mormon* translated by Joseph Smith; *The Questions of Jesus* by John Dear.

Michelle Rapkin, Vice President and Director

HARLEM MOON

Harlem Moon within the Doubleday Group is an imprint focused primarily on quality African American writing. Authors include: Lynne Duke, Veronica Chambers, Connie Briscoe, E. Lynn Harris, Kenji Jasper, Alonzo Westbrook, Steven Barboza, Bertice Berry, and Nicole Bailey-Williams.

Representative fiction titles include: *Gumbo* edited by Marita Golden and E. Lynn Harris; *Sapphire's Grave* by Hilda Gurley-Highgate; *The Queen of Harlem* by Brian Keith Jackson; *Dakota Grand* by Kenji Jasper; *Cosmopolitan Girls* by Charlotte Burley and Lyah Beth LeFlore; *Dad Interrupted* by Van Whitfeild.

Nonfiction titles include: *Beautylicious* by Jeyne M. Raines; *Saving the Race* by Rebecca Carroll; *The End is Just the Beginning* by Reverend Arlene Churn, Ph.D.; *Strength for Their Journey* by Robert L. Jackson, MD and Paulette Stanford, MD; *Seven Soulful Secrets* by Stephanie Stokes Oliver; *Having It All?* by Veronica Chambers; *Why We Make Movies* by George Alexander.

Direct query letters and SASEs to:

Janet Hill, Executive Editor and Vice President

Clarence Haynes, Assistant Editor

MAIN STREET BOOKS

Main Street Books publishes a wide array of nonfiction and select fiction titles in hardcover and trade paperback format.

Titles representative of the fiction list include: *Dead Solid Perfect* by Dan Jenkins; *The Green* by Troon McAllister; *Compass of the Heart: A Novel of Discovery* by Priscilla Cogan; *Outside Providence* by Peter Farrelly; *A Crack Up at the Race Riots* by Harmony Korine.

Nonfiction titles representative of Main Street Books include: *How to Make Your Child a Reader for Life* by Paul Kropp; *10 Natural Remedies That Can Save Your Life* by James F. Balch, M.D.; *Healing Signs: The Astrological Guide to Wholeness and Well-Being* by Ronnie Gale Dreyer; *Kosher Sex: A Recipe for Passion and Intimacy* by Shmuley Boteach; *The Wedding Dress Diet: Lose Weight and Look Great on Your Wedding Day and Beyond* by Robyn Flipse and Jacqueline Shannon; *Writing to Win: The Legal Writer* by Steven D. Stark; *Teaching Tolerance: Raising Open-Minded Empathetic Children* by S. Bullard and *Four Magic Moves to Winning Golf* by Joe Dante.

NAN A. TALESE

Formed in 1990, Nan A. Talese/Doubleday is committed to publishing quality fiction and nonfiction, both in terms of its authors and the production of its books.

This literary trade paperback imprint is known for its new authors of fiction and nonfiction, as well as for the authors Nan Talese has published for many years. Nan Talese is a Senior Vice President of Doubleday and the Publisher and Editorial Director of Nan A. Talese/Doubleday.

Among its writers are Peter Ackroyd, Margaret Atwood, Pinckney Benedict, Thomas Cahill, Kevin Canty, Lorene Cary, Pat Conroy, Jennifer Egan, Mia Farrow, Antonia Fraser, David Grand, Nicola Griffith, Aleksandar Hemon, Thomas Keneally, Alex Kotlowitz, Robert MacNeil, Ian McEwan, Gita Mehta, George Plimpton, Edvard Radzinsky, Mark Richard, Nicholas Shakespeare, Barry Unsworth, and Gus Van Sant.

Representative titles include: *Faithful* by Davitt Sigerson; *Searching for El Dorado* by Marc Herman; *Property* by Valerie Martin; *Country of Cold* by Kevin Patterson; *Nowhere Man* by Aleksandar Hermon; *Atonment* by Ian McEwan; *A Million Little Pieces* by James Frey.

This imprint does not accept unagented/unsolicited submissions.

Sean McDonald, Editor

THE KNOPF PUBLISHING GROUP

ALFRED A. KNOPF

ANCHOR BOOKS

EVERYMAN'S LIBRARY

PANTHEON BOOKS

SCHOCKEN BOOKS

VINTAGE ANCHOR PUBLISHING

1745 Broadway, New York, NY 10019

ALFRED A. KNOPF

Alfred A. Knopf was founded in 1915 by Alfred and his wife, Blanche. Knopf, well-known as a publisher of distinguished hardcover fiction and nonfiction, is also well known by its logo, the running dog, officially referred to as a "coursing Borzoi"

Knopf was quoted as saying, "The coursing Borzoi has always been our trademark. . .From the very beginning we have frequently been asked the meaning of the word Borzoi and what it has to do with books. When I started in business, the publisher I admired most was London's William Heinemann, and the sign of a Heinemann book was a windmill. Since a windmill obviously had nothing to do with books, I saw no reason why we could not adopt the Borzoi as our mark."

Knopf nonfiction categories include: biography, history, nature, travel, cooking, and select poetry. It also publishes the National Audubon Field Guides, the illustrated culture and travel companions, the Knopf Guides and the Knopf City Guides.

Recent nonfiction titles include: *My Life* by Bill Clinton; *Powerful Medicines: The Benefits, Risks and Costs of Prescription Drugs* by Jerry Avorn; *A Meal Observed* by Andrew Tod Hunter; *Lost Recipes* by Marion Cunningham.

Recent fiction titles include: *Villages* by John Updike; *Amateur Marriage* by Anne Tyler; *Port Mungo* by Patrick McGrath; *Good Faith* by Jane Smiley.

Send query letters and SASEs to:

Ann Close, Senior Editor—Literary fiction, geography, social and cultural history

Gary Fisketjon, Editor—Literary fiction; varied serious nonfiction interests

Jane Garrett, Editor—U. S. history, some European and Middle Eastern history, craft and hobby books

Jonathan Segal, Senior Editor—Twentieth-century history, contemporary events, biography and health

Judith Jones, Senior Editor and Vice President—Literary fiction, cookbooks, cultural history and the arts

Deb Garrision, Poetry Editor at Knopf, Senior Editor of Pantheon

ANCHOR BOOKS

Anchor Books is the oldest trade paperback publisher in America. It was founded in 1953 by Jason Epstein with the goal of making inexpensive editions of modern classics widely available to college students and the adult reading public. Today, Anchor's list boasts award-winning history, science, women's studies, sociology, and quality fiction. Authors published by Anchor Books include: Susan Sontag, Natalie Angier, Thomas Cahill, Ian McEwan, Anne Lamott, and Margaret Atwood.

Representative fiction titles include: *The No. 1 Ladies' Detective Agency* by Alexander McCall Smith; *Ella Minnow Pea* by Mark Dunn; *Highwire Moon* by Susan Straight and *Juno & Juliet* by Julian Gough.

Representative nonfiction titles include: *Marie Antoinette* by Antonia Fraser; *The Radical Center* by Ted Halstead and Michael Lind; *Red Dust* by Ma Jian; *Carnage and Culture* by Victor Davis Hanson; *A Field Guide to Germs* by Wayne Biddle.

New fiction titles include: *What Becomes of the Brokenhearted* by E. Lynn Harris and *The Whole Story: And Other Stories* by Ali Smithof.

New nonfiction titles include: *Bush Versus the Environment* by Robert S. Devine and *Americana* by Hampton Sides.

EVERYMAN'S LIBRARY

Everyman's Library publishes a series of world literature classics. The series has grown to hundreds of volumes and also includes lines of Children's Classics and Pocket Poets.

Pnin by Vladmir Nabokov is from this list.

PANTHEON BOOKS

Pantheon handles nonfiction books in catagories such as: current events, international affairs, contemporary culture, literary criticism and the arts, popular business, psychology, travel, nature, science, and history. The house has a strong list in contemporary fiction, poetry, and drama. Pantheon also offers the Fairytale and Folktale Library.

Pantheon was founded in 1942 by Helen and Kurt Wolff, refugees from Nazi Germany. "Building on its tradition of publishing important works of international fiction in translation and groundbreaking works of social policy, Pantheon now publishes quality fiction and nonfiction in a wide range of areas."

Representative titles include: *Captives* by Linda Colley; *Scavenger Hunt* by Robert Ferrigno; *Interracial Intimacies* by Randall Kennedy; *Yoga For People Who Can't Be Bothered to Do It* by Geoff Dyer; *A Dangerous Place: California's Unsettling Fate* by Marc Reisner; *The Hills at Home* by Nancy Cark; *The Hermit in Paris* by Italo Calvin; *There Are No Shortcuts* by Rafe Esquith; *Persepolis* by Marjane Satrapi.

New releases include: *Persepolis 2* by Marjane Satrapi; *Disarming Iraq* by Hans Blix; *Victorine* by Catherine Texier; *The Full Cupboard of Life: More From the #1 Ladies Detective Agency* by Alexander McCall Smith; *The Pecking Order: Which Siblings Succeed and Why* by Dalton Conley.

Direct query letters and SASEs to:

Dan Frank, Editorial Director—Timely nonfiction

Deb Garrison, Senior Editor

SCHOCKEN BOOKS

Schocken publishes books of Jewish interest in the following areas: history, biography, memoir, current affairs, spirituality, religion, philosophy, politics, sociology, and fiction. Founded in Berlin in 1931 by Salman Schocken, a department store magnate, bibliophile, and ardent Zionist, Schocken Verlag was closed down by the Nazis in 1938. Salman Schocken founded Schocken Books in the U. S. in 1942. The company became a division of Random House in 1987.

Recently published books include: *The Choice: Poland 1939-1945* by Irene Eber and *Women's Diaries of The Westward Journey* by Lillian Schlissel.

Altie Karper, Editor

VINTAGE ANCHOR PUBLISHING

Vintage Anchor Publishing is the trade paperback arm of the Knopf Publishing Group and consists of Vintage Books and Anchor Books.

Vintage Books' publishing list includes a wide range, from world literature to contemporary fiction and distinguished nonfiction, featuring such writers as William Faulkner, Vladimir Nabokov, Albert Camus, Ralph Ellison, Dashiell Hammett, William Styron, A. S. Byatt, Philip Roth, Richard Ford, Cormac McCarthy, Alice Munro, David Guterson, and Arthur Golden.

Representative titles include: *All I Could Get* by Scott Lasser; *India* by V.S. Naipaul; *Lake Effect* by Rich Cohen; *Pobby and Dingan* by Ben Rice; *The Praise Singer* by Mark Renault; *Rapture* by Susan Minot; *Wetware* by Craig Nova.

Send query letters and SASEs to:

Martin Asher, Editor in Chief

RANDOM HOUSE CHILDREN'S BOOKS

Random House Children's Books consists of two editorial divisions and their respective imprints, series, and licenses: the Knopf Delacorte Dell Young Readers Group and the Random House Young Readers Group.

KNOPF DELACORTE DELL YOUNG READERS GROUP

ALFRED A. KNOPF

BANTAM

CROWN

DAVID FICKLING BOOKS

DELACORTE PRESS

DELL DRAGONFLY

DELL LAUREL-LEAF

DELL YEARLING BOOKS

DOUBLEDAY

WENDY LAMB BOOKS

Representative titles from these imprints are: *It Was You Blue Kangaroo* by Emma Chichester Clark; *The Silver Charm: A Folktale from Japan* by Robert D. San Souci, Illustrated by Yoriko Ito; *Spider on the Floor* by Raffi; *Goodnight Monster* by Ian

Whybrow,Illustrated by Ken Wilson-Max; *They Called her Molly Pitcher*, a true tale of an American Revolution heroine by Cynthia Von Buhler; *Trout and Me* by Susan Shreve.

RANDOM HOUSE YOUNG READERS GROUP

BEGINNER BOOKS

DISNEY

FIRST TIME BOOKS

LANDMARK BOOKS

LUCASBOOKS

PICTUREBACKS

SESAME WORKSHOP

STEP INTO READING

STEPPING STONES

Random House Children's Books produces books for preschool children through young adult, in all formats from boardbooks to activity books to picture books and novels.

Random House Children's Books publishes the mega-selling Dr. Seuss Books (more than 400 million copies sold) and other well-known licenses, such as Arthur, the Berenstain Bears, Disney, Sesame Workshop, and Thomas the Tank Engine.

Random House also publishes many of children's favorite authors, including Judy Blume, Robert Cormier, Madeleine L'Engle, Leo Lionni, Mary Pope Osborne, Gary Paulsen, Tamora Pierce, Philip Pullman, Faith Ringgold, and Jerry Spinelli. Random House is the publisher of Christopher Paul Curtis's novel *Bud, Not Buddy*, winner of the 2000 John Newbery Medal and the Coretta Scott King Author Award, and David Almond's novel *Kit's Wilderness*, winner of the 2001 Michael L. Printz Award.

In August 2001, Random House, Inc., acquired all the book-publishing properties of Golden Books Family Entertainment, which produces storybooks, coloring and activity books, puzzle books, educational workbooks, reference books, novelty books, and chapter books. The Golden Books publishing program features Blue's Clues, Rugrats, Bob the Builder, and Barbie, and the Little Golden Books series publishes classic favorites such as *Pat the Bunny* and *The Poky Little Puppy*.

Random House has made a promising venture with Disney Publishing Worldwide to create a new line of books based on Disney properties and featuring characters like Mickey Mouse, Winnie the Pooh, and Cinderella. This imprint, Disney Books for

Young Readers, was launched in January of 2001, and features a wide array of books that includes coloring and activity books, storybooks, novelty books, and early readers. All of these books draw upon classic Disney films, such as *The Little Mermaid*, *The Lion King*, *Atlantis*, and *Monsters, Inc.*

Random House has a number of book series specifically designed for young readers, including the Stepping Stones first chapter book series: Marvin Redpost; A to Z Mysteries, the Magic Tree House; Junie B. Jones; Replica; Dinoverse; and Francine Pascal's Sweet Valley High Senior Year, a popular series aimed at middle-grade and young adult readers.

In addition to series, Random House Children's Books publishes popular fiction including: *Anne of Green Gables*, *Where the Red Fern Grows*, and *The Phantom Tollbooth*, as well as Newbery Honor and Medal winning books such as: *The Watsons Go to Birmingham 1963*, *Lily's Crossing*, *Holes*, *A Wrinkle in Time*, *The Giver*, *The Dark-Thirty* and *Shabanu*. The Random House list also features Caldecott Honor and Medal winning books, including: *Tar Beach*, *Time Flies*, *Song and Dance Man*, and the late Leo Lionni's *Frederick*, *Swimmy*, and *Alexander and the Wind-Up Mouse*.

Recent releases include: *The Golden Sleepy Book* by Margaret Wise; *The Animals of Farmer Jones* by Richard Scarry and *Disney's Build Your Own Haunted Mansion*.

Query letters and SASEs should be directed to:

Janet Schulman, Editor-at-Large

Nancy Siscoe, Executive Editor, Knopf/Crown

Mallory Loehr, Editor in Chief, Random House

Dennis Shealy, Senior Editor, Disney Books

SIMON & SCHUSTER

SIMON & SCHUSTER ADULT PUBLISHING GROUP

SIMON & SCHUSTER CHILDREN'S PUBLISHING

1230 Avenue of the Americas, New York, NY 10020

212-698-7000

Simon & Schuster, the publishing operation of Viacom Inc., is a global leader in the field of general-interest publishing and is dedicated to providing the best in fiction and nonfiction for consumers of all ages, across all printed, electronic, and multimedia formats. Its divisions include the Simon & Schuster Adult Publishing Group, Simon & Schuster Children's Publishing, Simon & Schuster New Media, Simon & Schuster Online, Simon & Schuster U.K., and Simon & Schuster Australia.

SIMON & SCHUSTER ADULT PUBLISHING GROUP

ARCHWAY

ATRIA

PB PRESS

   FREE PRESS

   POCKET BOOKS

   WASHINGTON SQUARE PRESS

SCRIBNER

SIMON & SCHUSTER

The Simon & Schuster Adult Publishing Group was formed when the Simon & Schuster Trade Division was combined with Pocket Books. PB Press took its place alongside the other hardcover-only imprints in the Adult Publishing Group. Simon & Schuster, Scribner, the Free Press, and Simon & Schuster and Pocket Books will now publish primarily in the mass-market and original trade paperback formats. As this program now moves forward as PB Press, the house is expected to extend the range of books that it publishes and increase its output, while maintaining its track record as a commercial publishing house.

Today, Simon & Schuster publishes a wide variety of bestsellers across all formats and has more than 50,000 backlist titles and 52 Pulitzer Prize winners. In 1999, Simon & Schuster published 59 *New York Times* bestsellers, including: Bob Woodward's *Shadow*; Barbara Delinsky's *Coast Road* and *Lake News*; Stephen King's *The Girl Who Loved Tom Gordon*; Frank McCourt's *'Tis* and Iyanla Vanzant's *Yesterday I Cried*. By June 2000, Simon & Schuster already had 31 titles on the *New York Times* bestseller lists, including: Dave Eggers's *A Heartbreaking Work of Staggering Genius*; Mary Higgins Clark's *We'll Meet Again*; and Jeffery Deaver's *The Devil's Teardrop*.

Simon & Schuster has formed lasting relationships with top-selling authors such as Stephen King and Clive Cussler, creating innovative deals that promise maximum profit potential and that are revolutionary departures from the traditional economics of the publishing industry. Simon & Schuster has also tapped MTV Network's youth-oriented audience with several publishing programs. Pocket Books and MTV: Music Television joined forces to create the MTV Books imprint in 1995, which has produced several *New York Times* bestsellers.

ARCHWAY

Archway produces titles in digital format. Titles indicative of this growing list include: *Heath Ledger: The Heath Is On!* by Nancy Krulik; *Marion Jones: The Fastest Woman in the World* by Bill Gutman; *Night of the Pompon* by Sarah Jett; *Viking Claw* by Michael Dahl.

PB PRESS

THE FREE PRESS

POCKET BOOKS

ATRIA

THE WASHINGTON SQUARE PRESS

PB Press, under the direction of Executive Vice President and Publisher Judith M. Curr, is a hardcover imprint at Simon & Schuster. PB Press imprints include: the Free Press, Pocket Books, and the Washington Square Press.

THE FREE PRESS

The Free Press publishes nonfiction cutting-edge works in social thought, politics, current affairs, history, science, psychology, religion and spirituality, music, and a broad business list. It also produces college textbooks. Titles are produced in hardcover format.

Titles representative of this list include: *Origin of the American Revolution* by Bernard Knollenberg; *Pension Fund* by Peter Dietz; *Changing the Rules: Adventures of a Wall Street Maverick* by Muriel Siebert and Aimee Lee Ball; *American: Beyond Our Grandest Notions* by Chris Matthews; *A Century of Triumph: The History of Aviation* by Christopher Chant, illustrated by John Batchelor; *Confessions of a Political Anarchist: Why the Two Party System Doesn't Work—And How We're Going to Fix It* by Bill Hillsman; *Piano Notes: The Hidden World of the Pianist* by Charles Rosen and *Origins of Existence: How Life Emerged in the Universe* by Fred Adams, illustrated by Ian Schoenherr.

New releases include: *No Ordinary Matter* by Jenny McPhee; *General Ike: A Personal Reminiscence* by John S.D. Eisenhower; *Presidential Leadership*, a *Wall Street Journal* Book; *Vamped* by David Sosnowski; *The Way of Go: 8 Ancient Secrets for Success in Business and Life* by Troy Anderson; *Broken: The Troubled Past and Uncertain Future of the FBI* by Richard Gid Powers; *The Laws of Money: Five Timeless Secrets to Get Out and Stay out of Financial Trouble* by Suze Orman; *The Ultimate Weight Solution for Teens: 7 Keys to Weight Freedom* by Jay McGraw.

Direct query letters and SASEs to:

Martha K. Levin, Vice President, Publisher

Liz Stein, Senior Editor—Memoir

Amy Scheibe, Editor—Fiction

Fred Hills, Senior Editor—General business, motivation, health, medical, spirituality, current issues, history and true crime

Dominick Anfuso, Editoral Director—General nonfiction, history, politics, business and careers

Bruce Nichols, Vice President, Senior Editor—Serious nonfiction

Leslie Meredith, Editor—Animals, spirituality, health, and pop science

POCKET BOOKS

Pocket Books, founded in 1939, was America's first publisher of paperback books. Today, Pocket is producing general-interest fiction and nonfiction books in mass-market paperback, trade paperback, and hardcover format.

Representative titles include: *The Summerhouse* by Jude Deveraux; *The Camino* by Shirley MacLaine; *The Astrology of Time* by Gary Goldschneider; *Good in Bed* by Jennifer Weiner; *Maggody and the Moonbeams* by Joan Hess; *Larousse French English Dictionary, Canadian Edition* by Larousse; *Mercy* by Julie Garwood; *Bad Boy: The Influence of Sean "Puffy" Combs on the Music Industry* by Ronin Ro; *The Core* by Dean Wesley Smith.

Recent releases include: *Blown Away* by Caitlin Kelly; *All the Women I've Loved* by Byron Harmon; *Going to Pless* by Megan McAndrew; *Fourplay* by Brenda L. Thomas; *Almost Like Being in Love* by Christina Dodd.

Direct query letters and SASEs to:

Micki Nuding, Editor

Christina Boys, Editor

ATRIA

The Atria imprint, established in 2002, embraces a mix of nonfiction, especially biography and celebrity memoirs and fiction. It is the hardcover imprint for Pocket Books.

Recent titles include: *Homesick: A Memoir of Family Food and Finding Hope* by Jenny Lauren; *Asphalt* by Carl Hancock; *One for My Baby* by Tony Parsons; *My Sister's Keeper* by Jodi Picoult; *Bad Men* by John Connolly; *Hoax* by Robert K. Tanenbaum; *Growing Up Healthy* by Joan Lunden and Myron Winick.

Direct query letters and SASEs to:

Emily Bestler, Vice President and Executive Editorial Director—Commercial fiction and nonfiction

Greer Hendricks, Senior Editor—Literary and commercial fiction, narrative nonfiction, memoir and lifestyle

Tracy Behar, Vice President and Editorial Director—Health/fitness, spirituality/inspirational, self-help and narrative nonfiction

Malaika Adero, Senior Editor—Literary fiction, narrative nonfiction, health and fitness, spirituality, memoir, biography, African American interests, art and culture

Luke Dempsey, Senior Editor—Narrative nonfiction, sports (especially baseball and golf), popular culture, literary and commercial fiction and popular history

Brenda Copeland, Associate Editor—Literary and commercial fiction (especially Canadian voices), narrative nonfiction, practical self-help and personal development, astrology, parenting, and health

SCRIBNER

Scribner produces fiction and nonfiction titles in hardcover format. Categories include: general fiction, history, military, social science, popular culture, and self-help.

Titles representative of this list include: *Mistress to An Age: A Life of Madame De Stael* by J. Christopher Herold; *Four Sisters of Hofei: A History* by Annping Chin; *Odysseus in America: Combat Trauma and the Trials of Homecoming* by Jonathan Shay; *Romancing the Ordinary: A Year of Simple Splendor* by Sarah Ban Breathnach; *Blood on the Tongue: A Crime Novel* by Stephen Booth.

Recent releases include: *Brick Lane* by Monica Ali; *Murder at a Vineyard Mansion* by Philip R. Craig; *Living History* by Hillary Rodham Clinton; *Monday Mourning* by Kathy Reichs; *The Tarnished Eye* by Judith Guest; *An Alchemy of Mind: The Marvel and Mystery of the Brain* by Diane Ackerman; *Sex, Drugs and Cocoa Puffs: A Low Culture Manifesto* by Chuck Klosterman.

Send query letters with SASEs to:

Beth Wareham, Editor—Cookbooks

Nan Graham, Vice President and Editor-in-Chief—American literary fiction; fiction about clashing cultures, Third World and European; nonfiction interests include contemporary social and political issues, women's studies, historical and literary biography, and biographies of artists

Susan Moldow, Executive Vice President and Publisher—Areas consistent with house interest

SIMON & SCHUSTER

Simon & Schuster publishes fiction and nonfiction in hardcover format.

Titles representative of this list include: *The Conquerors: Roosevelt, Truman and the Destruction of Hitler's Germany* by Michael R. Beschloss; *Down by the River: Drugs, Money, Murder, and Family* by Charles Bowden; *Going with the Grain: A Wandering Bread Lover Takes a Bite Out of Life* by Susan Seligson; *The Gold Swan* by James Thayer; *The Greatest Minds and Ideas of All Time* by Will Durant; *An Illustrated Dictionary of Tatting* by Judith Connors.

Recent releases include: *Buddy Cooper Finds a Way* by Neil Connelly; *White Hot* by Sandra Brown; *Making Work Work: New Strategies for Surviving and Thriving at the Office* by Julie Morgenstern; *Letters to My Daughters* by Mary Matalin; *Tastes Like Chicken* by Lolita Files; *Hark: A Novel of the 87th Precinct* by Ed McBain; *Cold Case Squad* by Edna Buchanan; *Nighttime is My Time* by Mary Higgins Clark.

Send query letters and SASEs to:

Amanda Murray, Senior Editor—Hardcover nonfiction, both narrative and practical; subjects include memoir, women's issues, popular reference, beauty, inspiration, entertainment and mind/body/health.

Alice Mayhew, Editorial Director, Simon & Schuster Trade Division—Politics, current events, contemporary biographies and memoirs

Geof Kloske, Senior Editor—Serious nonfiction

Rob Weisbach, Editor-at-Large

Mary Sue Rucci, Senior Editor—Commercial fiction and nonfiction

Michael Korda, Editor in Chief—Commercial fiction and nonfiction

SIMON & SCHUSTER TRADE PAPERBACKS

FIRESIDE

SONNET

TOUCHSTONE

TV BOOKS

Simon & Schuster Trade Paperbacks division is comprised of several imprints, including Fireside and Touchstone Books.

FIRESIDE

Fireside publishes nonfiction titles in trade paperback format, as well as reissuing paperback books previously published in hardcover format. Categories include: crafts and hobbies, self-help, motivational, health/fitness, healing, games and word puzzles, humor, political, and other general nonfiction.

Titles representative of this list include: *2003 American Guide to U.S. Coins: The Most Up-to-Date Coin Prices Available* by Charles F. French and Scott Mitchell (editor); *Always My Child: A Parent's Guide to Understanding Your Gay, Lesbian, Bisexual, Transgendered, or Questioning Son or Daughter* by Kevin Jennings and Pat Shapiro (Contributor); *American Yoga Association Beginner's Manual* by Alice Christensen; *Best Alternative Medicine* by Dr. Kenneth Pelletier, et al.; *Dream Big! A Roadmap for Facing Life's Challenges and Creating the*

Life You Deserve by Deborah Rosado Shaw; *Finding Hope When a Child Dies: What Other Cultures Can Teach Us* by Sukie Miller; *More George W. Bushisms: More of Slate's Accidental Wit and Wisdom of Our 43rd President* by Jacob Weisberg; *The Journey: A Road Map to the Soul* by Brandon Bays.

Recent releases include: *Lead or Get Off the Pot! The 7 Secrets of a Self-Made Leader* by Pat Croce with Bill Lyon; *Weight Watchers Greatest Hits: 250 Classic Recipes From the Sixties to Today* by Weight Watchers International, Inc.; *Going Gray, Looking Great! The Modern Guide to Unfading Glory* by Diana Lewis Jewell; *Found: The Best Lost, Tossed and Forgotten Items From Around the World* by Davy Rothbart; *Take a Walk on the Dark Side: Rock and Roll Myths, Legends and Curses* by R. Gary Patterson.

Send query letters with SASEs to:

Cherise Davis, Editor—Craft of writing, branded nonfiction, career development, education, health, self-help, American history, illustrated books, humor, pop/youth/hip hop culture, personal memoir, and home decorating

Doris Cooper, Senior Editor—Narrative nonfiction, women's issues, psychology and self-help, sports and fitness (especially the outdoors), health, quirky business, relationships (from romantic to familial), and literary fiction

Matt Walker, Associate Editor—Movies, rock, pop culture, literary fiction, and literate nonfiction for Gen-X readers, chess, crosswords/games, offbeat science and history

Trish Todd, Vice President and Editor-in-Chief—Humor, self-help, child care, health, and psychology

TOUCHSTONE

Touchstone publishes nonfiction trade paperbacks in all categories of history, politics, military, political science, biography, and autobiography.

Titles representative of Touchstone's list include: *Hemingway on Fishing* by Ernest Hemingway (edited by Nick Lyons); *The Kennedy White House: Family Life and Pictures, 1961-1963* by Carl Sferrazza Anthony; *No More Words: A Journal of My Mother, Anne Morrow Lindbergh* by Reeve Lindbergh; *The Rehnquist Choice: The Untold Story of the Nixon Appointment That Redefined the Supreme Court* by John W. Dean; *Dixie: A Personal Odyssey Through Events That Shaped the Modern South* by Curtis Wilkie; *President Nixon: Alone in the White House* by Richard Reeves.

Recent releases include: *The Marriage Bed* by Regina McBride; *1215: The Year of Magna Carta* by Danny Danziger and John Gillingham; *A Secret Word* by Jennifer Paddock; *All The President's Spin: George W. Bush, the Media and the Truth* edited by Ben Fritz and Bryan Keefer.

SIMON & SCHUSTER CHILDREN'S PUBLISHING

AAA BOOKS

ALADDIN PAPERBACKS

ATHENEUM BOOKS FOR YOUNG READERS

LITTLE SIMON

MARGARET K. MCELDERRY

MINSTREL

NICK JR.

SIMON & SCHUSTER BOOKS FOR YOUNG READERS

SIMON PULSE

SIMON SPOTLIGHT

1239 Avenue of the Americas, New York, NY 10020

AAA BOOKS

AAA Books publishes titles for children of all ages, from babies through teens, in hardcover and paperback formats.

A few titles representative of this list include: *The Easter Chicken* by Lisa Funari Willever, et al.; *Chumpkin* by Lisa Funari Willever, et al.; *Early Poems* by A. F. Moritz.

ALADDIN PAPERBACKS

Aladdin Paperbacks publishes juvenile fiction and nonfiction early readers, chapter books, and middle grade books.

Titles representative of Aladdin's list include: *Ten Dragon* by D.J. Machale; *Wind and Snow* by Marion Dane Bauer; *Mars Year One: Marooned!* by Brad Strickland and Thomas E. Fuller; *Albert's Birthday* by Leslie Tryon; *Brave Norman* by Andrew Clements, illustrated by Donald Cook.

This imprint does not accept unsolicited manuscripts.

Ellen Krieger, Vice President and Associate Publisher

ATHENEUM BOOKS FOR YOUNG READERS

Atheneum produces new titles in fiction, nonfiction, and poetry for preschool to high school age children. Formats include hardcover and paperback. Categories include: history, action/adventure, social situations, family, military and wars, humor, friendship, and general nonfiction. Atheneum also reissues top-sellers and classics.

Titles representative of this list include: *Fight for Freedom: The American Revolution* by Benson Bobrick; *Clever Beatrice* by Margaret Willey, illustrated by Heather Solomon; *Dovey Coe* by Frances O'Roark Dowell; *America* by E.R. Frank; *Blubber* by Judy Blume; *Red Badge of Courage* by Stephen Crane, illustrated by Wendell Minor.

Send query letters with SASEs to:

Caitlyn Dlouhy, Executive Editor

Ginee Seo, Vice President and Associate Publisher

LITTLE SIMON

Little Simon produces nonfiction and novelty books for juveniles in hardcover and trade paperback formats.

Titles representative of this list include: *Chicka Chicka ABC* by Bill Martin Jr. and John Archambault, illustrated by Lois Ehert; *Goodnight Sweet Butterflies* by Dawn Bentley, illustrated by Heather Cahoon; *What's on the Beach* by Jo Lodge; *Little Chick* illustrated by Salina Yoon.

This imprint no longer accepts unsolicited manuscripts.

Cindy Eng, Editorial Director

Erin Molta, Senior Editor

MARGARET K. MCELDERRY BOOKS

Margaret K. McElderry Books publishes fiction and nonfiction for young children and juveniles in hardcover format.

Representative titles include: *Dilly Duckling* by Claire Freedman, illustrated by Jane Chapman; *The Legend of Buddy Bush* by Sheila P. Moses; *Musical Beds* by Mara Bergman, illustrated by Marjolein Pottie.

Send query letters with SASEs to:

Emma K. Dryden, Vice President and Editorial Director

MINSTREL

Minstrel publishes fiction and nonfiction for readers ages 8-12 in mass-market paperback, school and library binding, and digital formats.

Titles representative of this list include: *The Broadway Ballplayers #4: Sideline Blues* by Maureen Holohan; *Bub Moose* by Carol Wallace, et al.; *The Case of the Twin Teddy Bears* by Carolyn Keene; *The Castle Conundrum* by Franklin W. Dixon.

NICK JR.

Nick Jr. is a recent line of preschool and young adult books, associated with the Nickelodeon TV network. The creation of Nick Jr. was the largest licensing launch in children's publishing history.

SIMON & SCHUSTER BOOKS FOR YOUNG READERS

Simon & Schuster Books for Young Readers publishes fiction and nonfiction titles for children of all ages, from preschool through teens, in hardcover format.

Titles representative of the nonfiction list include: *Apolo Anton Ohno: My Story* by Apolo Anton Ohno, with Nancy Richardson; *Nibbles and Me* by Elizabeth Taylor and *Let's Try It Out with Freezing and Melting* (Let's Try It Out #7) by Seymour Simon and Nicole Fauteux, illustrated by Doug Cushman.

Fiction titles in this house span the spectrum from social situations and self-esteem, to animals and pets, action and adventure, holidays and festivals, science fiction, fantasy, African American, and other ethnic stories. Titles indicative of the fiction list include: *Because of Anya* by Margaret Peterson Haddix; *Eloise Takes a Bawth* by Kay Thompson, illustrated by Hilary Knight; *Henry and Mudge and the Tall Tree House* by Cynthia Rylant; *Please, Baby, Please* by Spike Lee and Tonya Lewis Lee, illustrated by Kadir Nelson.

Send query letters with SASEs to:

David Gale, Editorial Director—Middle-grade and young adult novels—looks for sharp writing and fresh voices. Does not want to consider standard young-adult problem novels or romances, but is interested in more unusual, hard-hitting, and literary young adult novels.

Kevin Lewis, Editor—Picture books (both short texts for younger readers and longer texts for older readers), interesting and fresh nonfiction for all age groups, and middle-grade novels with a distinctive voice

SIMON PULSE

Simon Pulse produces juvenile fiction titles in mass-market paperback and hardcover formats. Many of this imprint's books have movie or television tie-ins, such as: *Buffy the Vampire Slayer Script Book* (Season 2, Vol. 3).

Categories include: historical and medieval fiction, espionage, family, siblings, social situations, and self-esteem.

Titles representative of Simon Pulse include: *Princess of Pop* by Cathy Hopkins (series); *Betrayed* (Fearless #24) by Francine Pascal; *Dark Vengeance* by Diana G. Gallagher; *The Queen of Everything* by Deb Caletti; *Endangered Species* by Nancy Holder and Jeff Mariotte; *Hounded by Baskervilles* (Sabrina the Teenage Witch #45) by Mercer Warriner.

SIMON SPOTLIGHT

Simon Spotlight publishes hardcover and mass-market paperback fiction books tied to Viacom properties such as *Rugrats* and *The Busy World of Richard Scarry*.

Other titles indicative of Simon Spotlight's list include: *Dora Loves Boots* by Alison Inches; *SpongeBob Square Pants, Fish Happens* by Tricia Boczkowski; *Look and Find!* by Susan Kantor, illustrated by Joe Ewers; *The Wild Thornberrys Movie* by Cathy East Dubowski; *Bob* by Lauryn Silverhardt, illustrated by Barry Goldberg.

Not accepting unsolicited manuscripts at this time.

Tricia Boczkowski, Executive Editor

Jennifer Bergstrom, VP, Associate Publisher

Sheri Tan, Executive Editor

Beth Bracken, Assistant Editor

TIME WARNER TRADE BOOK PUBLISHING GROUP

LITTLE, BROWN AND COMPANY

WARNER BOOKS

Time & Life Building, 1271 Avenue of the Americas, New York, NY 10020

212-522-7200

www.twbookmark.com

LITTLE, BROWN AND COMPANY

BACK BAY BOOKS

BULFINCH PRESS

LITTLE, BROWN AND COMPANY BOOKS FOR CHILDREN AND YOUNG ADULTS

Time & Life Building, 1271 Avenue of the Americas, New York, NY 10020

212-522-8700

Boston office: (Bulfinch Press)

3 Center Plaza, Boston, MA 02108

617-227-0730   fax: 617-263-2857

Little, Brown and Company (founded in 1837) originated as an independent house with a Boston home base, and earned renown as a publisher with a dynamic, commercially successful line as well as an outstanding literary list. Now a subsidiary of Time Warner, it functions autonomously, primarily from within the Time & Life building (where its main trade offices reside), and releases titles under its stately colophon image of an eagle-topped column. Bulfinch Press (a division still based in Boston) is one of the leading houses to specialize in fine-arts publishing and illustrated volumes.

Representative titles include: *The Pregnancy Book* by William Sears, MD, and Martha Sears, RN; *Stokes Beginner's Guide to Dragonflies* by Donald and Lillian Stokes; *The Sailor's Handbook* by Halsey C. Herreshoff; *The Dream Workbook* by Jill Morris; *As Always, Jack: A Wartime Love Story* by Emma Sweeney; *Bad Boy Brawly Brown* by Walter Mosley; *City of Bones* by Michael Connelly; *In the Walled Gardens* by Alice Sebold.

Recent releases include: *Maternal Desire: On Children, Love and the Inner Life* by Daphne De Marnette; *The Interrogators: Inside the Secret War Against Al Qaeda* by Chris Hogan and Greg Miller; *Here Kitty Kitty* by Jardine Libaire; *The Big Love* by Sarah Dunn; *3rd Degree* by James Patterson.

Little, Brown maintains an extensive backlist, which is especially strong in literary fiction and nonfiction. Little, Brown distributes its own titles, as well as those of a changing list of other publishing houses both large and small, including Arcade Publishing, Bilingual Books, Food and Wine, Hyperion Books, and Miramax.

Query letters and SASEs should be directed to these New York editors:

Terry Adams, Vice President and Director, Trade Paperbacks, began his career in book publishing as a floater at Farrar, Straus & Giroux. He then worked for many years as Editor and Advertising Manager at Alfred A. Knopf before joining Little, Brown in 1996. Among the writers he has worked with are Breena Clarke, Julian Barnes, Harold Brodkey, Craig Childs, Katherine Dunn, Denis Johnson, the Monks of New Skete, J. F. Powers, and Wendy Wasserstein. Contact him at **Terry.Adams@twbg.com**.

Reagan Arthur, Senior Editor, joined Little, Brown in May 2001. She was formerly a Senior Editor at Picador and St. Martin's Press. Her Little, Brown acquisitions include books by international bestsellers Ian Rankin and Kate Atkinson, story collections by Oscar Casares and Elizabeth Crane, and non-fiction from *McSweeneys* and *Forward* contributor Jennifer Traig and *Atlantic Monthly's* Caitlin Flanagan. Contact her at **Reagan.Arthur@twbg.com**.

Asya Muchnick, Editor, joined Little, Brown in January 2001, and has edited novelists Alice Sebold (*The Lovely Bones*), Carolyn Parkhurst (*The Dogs of Babel*), and Elise Blackwell (*Hunger*), and nonfiction by Lisa Hilton (*Athénaïs: The Life of Louis XIV's Mistress*), William Poundstone (*How Would You Move Mount Fuji?*), and Asne Seierstad (*The Bookseller of Kabul*). Recent acquisitions include a look at how rulers through the ages have collected rare and exotic animals by art historian Marina Belozerskaya, a meditation on the meaning of suffering by *New Yorker* and *Harper's* contributor Peter Trachtenberg, and first novels by Jardine Libaire and Thomas O'Malley. Previously, she was at Knopf. Contact her at **Asya.Muchnick@twbg.com**.

Bill Phillips, Consulting Editor, has spent more than 35 years with Little, Brown and is one of the most acclaimed editors of our time. The writers he has edited include Nelson Mandela, George Stephanopoulos, James Carroll, Gavin DeBecker, Norm Abram, Berkeley Breathed, Donald Spoto, Phillip Lopate, Anne Bernays, Justin Kaplan, Dan Wakefield, Deirdre Bair, Pete Hamill, Jimmy Breslin, Robert Lacey, Robert Inman, Steven Gaines, Herman Wouk, and Malcolm Gladwell. Although he retired, Bill continues to work for Little, Brown as a Consulting Editor, editing several books per year and considering selected projects for publication. Bill works out of his home, and queries can be addressed to him at **wphillipsl @earthlink.net.**

Michael Pietsch, Senior Vice President and Publisher, has worked with the novelists Martin Amis, Peter Blauner, Michael Connelly, Martha Cooley, Tony Earley, Janet Fitch, Mark Leyrier, Rick Moody, Walter Mosley, James Patterson, George Pelecanos, Alice Sebold, Anita Shreve, Nick Tosches, David Foster Wallace, and Stephen Wright, the nonfiction writers John Feinstein, Peter Guralnick, and David Sedaris, and the cartoonist R. Crumb. Prior to joining Little, Brown in 1991, Michael worked at Harmony Books and before that at Scribner, where he edited a posthumous memoir by Ernest Hemingway, *The Dangerous Summer*. Contact him at **Michael.Pietsch@twbg.com.**

Geoff Shandler, Executive Editor. Currently among the many authors he has worked with are James Bradley, John le Carré, Robert Dallek, Tom Shales, Ann Blackman, Robert Wright, William Least Heat-Moon, Gary Giddins, James Miller, Doug Stanton, Elaine Shannon, Elizabeth Royte, Eileen Welsome, and Luis Urrea. His numerous bestsellers and award winners include *An Unfinished Life*, *Flyboys*, *Blind Man's Bluff*, *Black Mass*, *Paris in the Fifties*, and *In Retrospect*. Geoff primarily acquires histories, biographies and journalism. Contact him at **Geoff.Shandler@twbg.com.**

Claire H. Smith, Assistant Editor, is looking for sharp, unusual fiction and nonfiction having to do with social history, culture, expression, and risk-takers of all kinds. She is interested in a wide variety of subjects, ranging from language acquisition to twins, the natural world, hip-hop, feminism, and yard sale fashion. Claire has edited a number of books including the forthcoming *This is Burning Man* and *2DO Before I Die* and has also assisted Judy Clain in working with such authors as Elisabeth Robinson, Nic Kelman, Lynn Freed, and Simon Mawer. She has been with Little, Brown since the summer of 2000, prior to which she worked at Morgan Stanley. Contact her at **Claire.Smith@twbg.com.**

Mary Tondorf-Dick, Senior Managing Editor, joined the company in 1973 and edits biographer Peter Kurth, Susan Branch, Donald and Lillian Stokes, Henry Horenstein, the Bartlett's series of reference work and a broad range of nonfiction. She lives outside of Boston. Contact her at **Mary.Tondorf-Dick@twbg.com.**

Judy Clain, Senior Editor, joined Little Brown in 1998. She began her career as a film agent and was the Sony executive on *Deep End of the Ocean* and *Donnie Brasco*. She has edited novelists including Jody Shields (*The Fig Eater*), Simon Mawer (*The Fall*), Elisabeth Robinson (*The True and Outstanding Adventures of the Hunt Sisters*), and Robb Forman Dew (*The Evidence Against Her*). She has also edited narrative nonfiction by Kien Nguyen (*The Unwanted*) and Daphne de Marneffe (*Maternal Desire*) among others. Contact her at **Judy.Clain@twbg.com.**

Liz Nagle, Assistant Editor, is interested in a wide range of narrative nonfiction, especially history, biography, culture, and popular science. The editor of several books including Robert Lacey's *Great Tales From English History* and David Stafford's *Ten Days to D-Day*, Liz has also assisted Geoff Shandler in working with Robert Dallek, James Bradley, Dean King, and others. Prior to joining Little, Brown in 2000, she worked at Basic Books. Contact her at **Elizabeth.Nagle@twbg.com.**

Michael Mezzo, Assistant Editor, is interested in inventive literary fiction and narrative nonfiction, especially about music and pop culture. He edited *Super Flat Times*, a story collection by Matthew Derby, and has worked with Reagan Arthur on books by Joanna Scott, Elizabeth Crane, Ian Rankin, and Kate Atkinson among others. Prior to joining Little, Brown in June 2000, he worked at a literary agency and several magazines. Contact him at **Michael.Mezzo@twbg.com**.

Pat Strachan, Senior Editor, joined Little, Brown in September, 2002. Most recently at Houghton Mifflin, she began her career at Farrar, Straus & Giroux, where she worked as an editor for 17 years. She was then a fiction editor at *The New Yorker*, returning to book publishing in 1991. She has received the PEN/Roger Klein Award for Editing. Among the prose writers she has edited are Elizabeth Benedict, Harold Bloom, Ian Frazier, James Kelman, Jamaica Kincaid, Wendy Lesser, Rosemary Mahoney, John McPhee, David Nasaw, Edna O'Brien, Peter Orner, Padgett Powell, Marilynne Robinson, Jim Shepard, Tatyana Tolstaya, and Tom Wolfe. Her Little, Brown books include fiction on the fall 2003 and spring 2004 lists by Christina Adam, Kathryn Davis, Michelle de Kretser, Lucia Nevai, and Michael Redhill. She is acquiring literary fiction and general nonfiction. Contact her at **Pat.Strachan@twbg.com**.

Maja Thomas, Vice President and Publisher of Time Warner AudioBooks, joined the TWBG ten years ago, and has worked with authors Jack Welch, Madeleine Albright, and David Sedaris to adapt their stories for the audio medium. She is also the editor of the A+Audio series of guides to literary and musical classics. Contact her at **Maja.Thomas@twbg.com**.

BACK BAY BOOKS

Back Bay Books is a Little, Brown trade paperback imprint that accents contemporary fiction. Back Bay titles are generally cataloged with the core Little, Brown list.

Representative titles for Back Bay include: *All The Finest Girls* by Alexandra Styron; *Believing It All: Lessons I Learned from My Children* by Marc Parent; *The Cabal and Other Stories* by Rick Moody; *Fire in the Lake: The Vietnamese and the Americans in Vietnam* by Frances FitzGerald; *Shooting the Moon* by David Harris.

BULFINCH PRESS

Bulfinch Press is a Little, Brown and Company division based in Boston that specializes in fine arts, architecture, photography, and design, as well as in finely produced collections of literary classics and illustrated volumes with a historical, cultural, or geographical accent. The house produces lush hardcover and paperback volumes, as well as merchandise lines, including posters and calendars.

Representative titles of the Bulfinch list include: *Allure* by Diana Vreeland; *Antarctica: A Year at the Bottom of the World* by Jim Mastro; *The Breathing Field: Yoga as Art* by Wyatt Townley; *Cape Light* by Joel Meyerowitz; *Colefax & Fowler's Interior Inspirations* by Roger Banks-Pye and Dorothea Lange.

Recent releases include: *The Arts and Crafts Companion* by Pamela Todd; *Leslie Linsley's Decoupage: Design, Create, Display* by Leslie Linsley; *Voices of Valor: D-Day June 6, 1944* by Douglas Brinkley and Ronald J. Drez.

LITTLE, BROWN AND COMPANY BOOKS FOR CHILDREN AND YOUNG ADULTS

Three Center Plaza, Boston, MA 02108

617-227-0730

Little, Brown's children's books division produces picture books, boardbooks, pop-up and lift-the-flap editions, chapter books, and general fiction and nonfiction titles for middle and young-adult readers. This division also issues resource guides and reference titles in careers, social issues, and intellectual topics for higher grade levels and the college-bound. Marc Brown's *Arthur* books and Matt Christopher's sports series are especially successful. The house offers volumes in Spanish language and in dual Spanish/English editions and is on the lookout for multicultural titles.

Representative titles include: Caldecott winner *Saint George and the Dragon* illustrated by Trina Schart Hyman; Newbery winner *Maniac Magee* by Jerry Spinelli; *Toot & Puddle* by Holly Hobbie; *Daisy and the Egg* by Jane Simmons; *Kevin and His Dad* by Irene Smalls ; *The Jolly Pocket Postman* by Janet and Allen Ahlberg.

Recent releases include: *Blow Out the Moon* by Libby Koponen; *You're Not My Real Mother!* by Molly Friedrich; *New Baby Train* by Woody Guthrie; *Blonde Ambition: An A-list Novel* by Zoey Dean; *Best Friends for Never* by Lisi Harrison; *Doctor Illuminatus* by Martin Booth; *Spy High: The Serpent Scenario* by A.J. Butcher.

Prospective authors please note that Little, Brown's children's division does not accept unsolicited manuscripts directly from authors. Manuscripts must go through an agent.

Jennifer Hunt, Editor

WARNER BOOKS

MYSTERIOUS PRESS

TIME WARNER AUDIO BOOKS

WARNER ASPECT

WARNER FAITH

WARNER BUSINESS

Founded in 1961, Warner Books is a division of Time Warner Communications. It publishes trade nonfiction and commercial fiction. Warner produces mass-market, trade paperback and hardcover originals, as well as reprints. Warner's nonfiction categories include: biography, business, cooking, current affairs, history, house and home, humor, popular culture, psychology, self-help, sports, games books, and general reference. Warner fiction accents the popular approach and includes frontlist commercial novels and works in the categories of mystery and suspense, fantasy and science fiction, action thrillers, horror, and contemporary and historical romance. Warner Books handles its own distribution and distributes book products from other publishers.

Titles representative of the Warner list include: *The Sopranos Family Cookbook* by Allen Rucker and Michele Scicolone; *The Polio Paradox* by Richard L. Bruno, H.D., Ph.D.; *The Cross Legged Knight* by Candace Robb; *Chasing Rainbows* by Barry Friedman, James H. Collins and Gary Diamond; *The Miracles of Santo Fico* by D.L. Smith; *No Jesus, No Peace—Know Jesus, Know Peace* by Two Seekers; *What Clients Love* by Harry Beckwith; *Night Blooming* by Chelsea Quinn Yarbro; *The Kingmaker* by Brian Haig.

Recent releases include: *Brag! The Art of Tooting Your Own Horn Without Blowing It* by Peggy Klaus; *The Feiner Points of Leadership* by Michael Feiner; *How to Grow When Markets Don't* by Adrian Slywotsky; *The Oil Factor: Protect Yourself and Profit From the Coming Energy Crisis* by Stephen Leeb.

Diana Baroni, Executive Editor, has been with Warner Books for 10 years. She acquires fiction and nonfiction titles for the hardcover and paperback lists, with a focus on health, self-help, diet, and women's issues. Her books include: the *New York Times* bestsellers *Nice Girls Don't Get the Corner Office* by Lois Frankel, Ph.D.; *Satisfaction: The Art of the Female Orgasm* by Kim Cattrall and Mark Levinson; *The Wrinkle Cure* by Dr. Nicholas Perricone; *Live Now, Age Later* by Isadore Rosenfeld, MD; *Dr. Shapiro's Picture Perfect Weight Loss* by Dr. Howard Shapiro; *Kathy Smith's Moving Through Menopause* by Kathy Smith. Contact her at **Diana.Baroni@twbg.com.**

Dan Ambrosio, Associate Editor, was a newspaper reporter before coming to Warner Books in 1997. His areas of interest include business, sports, military history, true crime, adventure, pop culture, humor, and commercial fiction. The books he has edited include *Kiss: Behind the Mask, Triathlete Magazine's Complete Triathlon Book,* and *The Harvard Lampoon's Guide to College Admissions,* as well as a number of titles in the ongoing *Rich Dad* series, including the *Wall Street Journal* and *Business Week* bestsellers *Real Estate Riches* and *Real Estate Loopholes.* Contact him at **Dan.Ambrosio@twbg.com.**

Beth de Guzman, Editorial Director of Mass Market, has spent 17 years in publishing and has held positions at Berkley Books, Silhouette Books, and Bantam Books. She has edited over 30 *New York Times* bestsellers. At Warner Books, she oversees the mass-market program and acquires commercial fiction and nonfiction. She is the editor of Faye Kellerman; *USA Today* best-selling romance author Sandra Hill; romantic suspense author Annie Solomon; the parenting book *When We're in Public, Pretend You Don't Know Me;* the upcoming memoir *FBI Girl;* and chick-lit novel *Time Out for Good Behavior.* Contact her at **Beth.DeGuzman@twbg.com.**

Amy Einhorn, Editorial Director of Trade Paperbacks, also acquires hardcovers such as the *New York Times* best-selling novel *Good Grief* by Lolly Winston. She has worked at Warner for eight years, and previously held positions at Farrar, Straus & Giroux, Villard, Poseidon, and Pocket Books/Washington Square Press. Her areas of interest include high-end quality fiction, smart chick-lit (the upcoming *Conversations with the Fat Girl*), commercial nonfiction such as the *New York Times* bestseller *The Red Hat Society*, women's quirky narrative nonfiction such as *Belle du Jour*, Susan Jane Gilman's *Kiss my Tiara*, Gilman's memoir *Hypocrite in a Pouffy White Dress* (which Frank McCourt raves about), and parenting. Contact her at **Amy.Einhorn@twbg.com**.

Rick Horgan, Vice President and Executive Editor, has edited numerous bestsellers as well as books that have been nominated for the Edgar, Nebula, and Bram Stoker awards. His authors have included Bill Gates, Maria Shriver, Oliver North, Isaac Asimov, John Madden, Grace Slick, Jay Leno, Fran Drescher, Peter Maas, Jeffrey Archer, David Baldacci, John Lescroart, Dale Brown, David Morrell, and Brian Haig. His acquisition categories include commercial fiction, narrative nonfiction, politics, social critiques, inspiration/philosophy, fitness/nutrition, and business books. Contact him at **Rick.Horgan@twbg.com**.

Caren Karmatz Rudy, Senior Editor, has been at Warner Books for 11 years. Her areas of interest are women's commercial fiction and women's interest nonfiction. Her nonfiction focus is on lifestyle, relationships, parenting, women's issues, and memoir, while in fiction she looks for a strong narrative voice and topical subjects. Some of the bestsellers she has worked on include *AmandaBright@Home* by Danielle Crittenden, *Swell: A Girl's Guide to the Good Life* by Ilene Rosenzweig and Cynthia Rowley, *Behind the Smile: My Journey Out of Postpartum Depression* by Marie Osmond and Marcia Wilkie, and multiple books by Sarah Ban Breathnach, Ellen Fein, and Sherrie Schneider. Contact her at **Caryn.Karmatz-Rudy@twbg.com**.

Karen Kosztolnyik, Senior Editor, worked at Harlequin/Silhouette for five years before coming to Warner Books. In addition to working on the women's fiction/romance imprint, Warner Forever, she acquires fiction and nonfiction for all divisions including mass market, trade paperback, and hardcover. Her acquisition interests are romance, women's fiction, chick lit, suspense, and nonfiction concerning women's issues and pop culture. She is the editor of the *New York Times* bestseller Carly Phillips, *USA Today* bestseller Wendy Corsi Straub writing as Wendy Markham, *How to Meet Cute Boys* novelist Deanne Kizis, romantic suspense author Karen Rose, historical romance author Claire Delacroix, and Megan Crane, author of the chick-lit novel *English as a Second Language*. Contact her at **Karen.Kosztolnyik@twbg.com**.

Jamie Raab, Senior Vice President and Publisher, has worked at Warner Books for the past 18 years and currently oversees the publication of all Warner titles. She has a particular fondness for fiction, narrative nonfiction, and current affairs, and the authors she has edited include Nicholas Delblanco, Nelson DeMille, Henry Louis Gates ,Jr., Jane Goodall, Olivia Goldsmith, Billie Letts, Brad Meltzer, Michael Moore, Rosie O'Donnell, Nicholas Sparks, Jon Stewart, and Lalita Tademy. Contact her at **Jamie.Raab@twbg.com**.

Denise Stinson, Editor-at-Large, acquires all genres of African American Christian fiction for Walk Worthy Press. She is frantically searching for the Latina Terry McMillan, and is also interested in commercial self-help business books, high-profile autobiographies, and books on women's issues. Contact her at **Denise.Stinson@twbg.com**.

Les Pockell, Associate Publisher, has held editorial positions at St. Martin's Press, Doubleday, Kodansha International, and the Book-of-the-Month Club in addition to Warner Books. He is generally involved in acquiring and editing backlist nonfiction titles, though he has been known to dabble in fiction, especially mysteries. In his spare time, he is an anthologist, having edited, among other titles, *The 100 Best Poems of All Time* (Warner, 2001). Contact him at **Les.Pockell@twbg.com**.

Colin Fox, Associate Editor, has worked at Warner for more than 4 years. He has edited titles by such authors as Lou Dobbs, Tucker Carlson, Henry Louis Gates, Jr., Donald E. Westlake, and the founders of *Vice* magazine. He has a broad range of interests, but is particularly focusing on acquiring political books and those dealing with current events. He's also a huge fan of commercial fiction, narrative nonfiction, sports, popular science, business, and humor. Contact him at **Colin.Fox@twbg.com**.

Rick Wolff, Vice President, Executive Editor, edits both fiction and nonfiction and oversees the Warner Business Books imprint. His nonfiction tastes are eclectic, ranging from autobiography, politics, adventure, and education to sports, personal finance, and business management. On the fiction side, he looks primarily for thrillers and high-concept fiction. Some of his best-selling authors include Jack Welch, Tiger Woods, Robert Kiyosaki, Roger Angell, Robert Whiting, Bill Geist, Peter Maas, Herb Cohen, Tim Green, and Adrian Slywotzky. Contact him at **Rick.Wolff@twbg.com**.

Born: July 14, 1951.

Education: Harvard, 1973; Long Island University, M.A., 1985.

Employment history/editor career path: Warner books for the last seven years; Macmillan Books seven years before that; and the Alex Hamilton Institute eight years before that.

Personal interests: I'm fairly eclectic—everything from sports to psychology to reading books. But most of my spare time is devoted to my wife and our three children. Our lives revolve around them.

What would you be doing if you were not an editor? Probably writing books instead of editing them.

What has been your most successful book that you have acquired to date? I would say *Politically Correct Fairy Tales*—a humorous hardcover that was on the *New York Times* list for close to two years and was number one for a few weeks. That book sold more than four million copies worldwide. The author was James Finn Garner. Also, *How I Play Golf* by Tiger Woods and the *Rich Dad, Poor Dad* books by Roger Kiyosaki.

What books have you acquired that make you the most proud? What books that you have acquired reflect the types of books you like to represent? I'd say *Pros and Cons: The Criminals Who Play in the NFL* (Warner, 1999). Also, *You Gotta Have Wa* by Robert Whiting, about the Japanese obsession with baseball (Macmillan, 1987). *Rich Dad, Poor Dad*, which is on the list right now—financial advice from Robert Kiyosaki.

Do you represent fiction? If so, what do you look for? Yes. Strictly big-time commercial fiction. Warner has a very short fiction list, so whatever we acquire, it has to smell like a bestseller.

What do you want to see less of? Can't say. After all, *Politically Correct Fairy Tales* came in the slush pile.

Do you represent nonfiction? Yes—I handle business, sports, humor, psychology, biography, finances, and so on.

Do you require book proposals? If so, what do you look for in evaluating a book proposal? A book proposal is a must. I don't have the time to chat about "ideas" for a book over the phone or in e-mail.

Are certain aspects of a book proposal given more weight than others? It has to be well written by an author with top credentials, who is committed to promoting the book, and the idea behind the book has to be fresh and different.

What process do you use for making a decision? What is the process for acquisition, is there a committee? If a proposal gets past my review, I take it to the general editorial meeting to get more readings. If it makes the cut there, I take it to the publisher's review meeting for a determination of whether we should pursue it and for how much.

What kinds of nonfiction books do you want to see less of? At Warner, which is a major frontlist house, unless the book can break out in a major way for us, it probably isn't right for us. That usually means most general midlist nonfiction won't work for us.

Are you interested in work geared for the masses (readers of *People*, *The Star*, etc.)? Depends on the stars and how popular they are.

Are agents important? Why? Of course. To help develop proposals, to help the author understand the publishing process, and to work with the editor to make sure the book is a success.

Do you like new writers? What should new writers do to break into the business? Write for newspapers and magazines. Build from that.

How should writers approach you? Through an agent. I wish I had more time to chat with writers who aspire to be published, but unfortunately, I just don't.

What are some common mistakes writers make? What really gets on your nerves? Not promoting their books. Assuming that they can place demands on their editor and other people in the publishing house.

What can writers do to get your attention and to avoid the slush pile? Get an agent.

What have been some of your craziest experiences with submissions? I once put a clause in a contract with the author, a woman in her early 20s, that she couldn't lose her virginity until her book was published. And she signed the contract.

What have been some of your best experiences with writers or in your job? Most of them become lifelong friends and trusted colleagues. That's a major part of the job.

What, if anything, makes you different from other editors? I'm smarter and better looking than my editorial colleagues.

Is there anything you would like to see changed in the industry? I wish the production process could be speeded up with books. It seems silly to have to wait eight or nine months to get a book published after the manuscript is completed.

Any additional thoughts? One of the great aspects of book publishing is that you never know when a new talent is going to be discovered. That's what drives me—I'm always on the lookout for that next great writer.

MYSTERIOUS PRESS

The formerly independent Mysterious Press publishes a distinguished list of mystery, suspense, and crime novels, as well as selected crime nonfiction and reference.

Recent releases include: *Thieves' Dozen* by Donald Westlake; *The Dangerous Hour* by Marcia Muller; *The Surrogate Thief* by Archer Mayor; *See Isabelle Run* by Elizabeth Bloom; *The Accusers* by Lindsey Davis.

Kristen Weber, Associate Editor, moved to Mysterious Press from the subsidiary rights department of Warner Books and currently oversees the publication of all Mysterious Press titles. Authors she has edited include M.C. Beaton, Lindsey Davis, Margaret Maron, Marcia Muller, David Rosenfelt, and Kate White. Upcoming titles include *False Profits* by Patricia Smiley and *Forcing Amaryllis* by Louise Ure. She is looking for the complete range of crime novels—traditional, noir, thrillers, or private eye—and is especially interested in dark chick-lit mysteries. Contact her at **Kristen.Weber@twbg.com**.

WARNER ASPECT

Warner Aspect specializes in future fiction, science fiction, and fantasy.

Recent titles include: *Gloriana, or the Unfulfill'd Queen* by Michael Moorcock; *Horizon Storms* by Kevin J. Anderson; *The Sunborn* by Gregory Benford.

Jaime Levine, Editorial Director, works with such authors as David and Leigh Eddings, Walter Mosley, Nalo Hopkinson, and Gregory Benford. Outside of Aspect, her interests lie with thrillers and dark fiction. Past acquisitions include Thomas Monteleone's Borderlands trilogy and novels by Douglas Preston and Lincoln Child. Contact her at **Jaime.Levine@twbg.com**.

WARNER VISION

Warner Vision books are generally high profile mass-market releases.

WARNER FAITH

Warner Faith is an imprint that deals with faith, spirituality, and religion.

Recent titles include: *Seven Things That Steal Your Joy* by Joyce Meyer; *To A Child Love is Spelled T-i-m-e* by Mac Anderson and Lance Wubbels; *Today Matters* by John C. Maxwell; *The American Prophecies: Ancient Scriptures Reveal Our Nation's Future* by Michael D. Evans.

SECTION TWO

INDEPENDENT U.S. PRESSES

INDEPENDENT U.S. PRESSES

JEFF HERMAN

As an agent, I get to see things a bit differently then I would as a writer. As discussed elsewhere, publishing houses have more or less fallen into two huge categories: the "globalized" conglomerates, and everyone else. The former can be counted on the fingers of one hand, yet they constitute at least half of all trade book revenues. The latter are countless in number and always expanding like an unseen universe.

Some of these players—the "micro-presses" not included here—have revenues that could be rivaled by a nine-year-old's lemonade stand. Some here, on the other hand, are eight-figure operations.

Together the "independents" are the other half of the game. As a unified force, they are smaller than they were a decade ago, and are likely to keep getting smaller. But as their market-share shrinks, their indispensability only grows.

The choice of the word "independent" reflects the best word I could come up with, but it's not a perfect description. There are shades of gray, as in all things. Here you will find a few imprints of major houses that I felt operate in a particularly independent fashion. There are also cases where an independent house is distributed by one of the large mega-publishers, and it is listed here rather than with its large umbrella house.

If you have any questions, just look in the index. That should at least lead you to the location where that publisher is listed.

In the end, it's quality that counts, not quantity. And the long-term consequences of the growing consolidation in the industry are not clear yet. Dominance leads to comfort, which leads to inertia. When the asteroids return, it's the ponderous dominators who will be the first to fall.

But it wasn't me who predicted that the meek will inherit the Earth.

So welcome to the world of the independent publisher. Rest assured, we have been very careful not to include any vanity publishers or "fly-by-nights" who will take your money and promise the world without any intention of delivering. The publishing houses we have included are established and reputable.

In general, though not exclusively, as a group they tend to be slightly more open to direct queries and proposals from authors, rather than requiring that work be submitted through agents, as will be more the case with the larger publishers. However, if they say they do not accept unsolicited work, heed that advice and proceed accordingly to your search for the right agent who can help you get through the door.

For some, an independent press might be a stepping-stone to a glorious career as the chosen few published by the mega-presses. For others, the right independent house is exactly the right place to be. Often, a smaller press is able to offer more editorial attention, more authorial involvement throughout the process, and a more focused, long-term involvement with specialized audiences of readers and their communities.

It all depends—on you, your work, and on the methods of the publisher involved. So study each listing that seems of possible interest and look closely at their books.

In all cases, be sure to scrutinize their guidelines and prepare your material carefully. You want to put your best foot forward, and a clear query, followed by a well-written, well-organized proposal, is just as important for a small house as for a large one.

2.13.61 PUBLICATIONS, INC.

PO Box 1910, Los Angeles, CA 90078

1-800-992-1361   fax: 323-969-8791

www.two1361.com   email: two1361@aol.com

Founded in 1988, 2.13.61 Publications, Inc. offers new fiction and creative narratives, creative prose nonfiction, poetry, cultural events and critical works, photographic books, and audiovisual products.

Titles from 2.13.61 include *Devil's Knot: The True Story of the West Memphis Three* by Mara Leveritt; *Unwelcomed Songs* by Henry Rollins; *Reach* by Don Bajema; *King Ink* by Nick Cave; *Virtual Unreality* by Exene Cervenka; *Smile, You're Traveling*; *Solipsist*; *Do I Come Here Often?*; *Black Coffee Blues*; *The First Five*; *See a Grown Man Cry*; *Get in the Van*; *Eye Scream*, all by Henry Rollins; *Letters to Rollins* by Rob Overton; *The Cowardice of Amnesia* by Ellyn Maybe; *Go Tell the Mountain* by Jeffrey Lee Pierce; *Reach* and *Boy in the Air* by Don Bajema; *Attack God Inside* by Tricia Warden; *The Consumer* by Michael Gira; *Fish in a Barrel* by Peter Milne; *Dream Baby Dream* by Stephanie Chernikowski; *Planet Joe* by Joe Cole; *Metallica* (photographs by Ross Halfin); *Rosey the Baby Killer* by Bill Shields.

Oh, incidentally: It's no big secret, but this operation is under the watchful eye of none other than poet-rocker Henry Rollins himself. Want to start a contest? Guess what 2.13.61 means; a fancy facsimile of Henry Rollins's birth certificate goes to the winner.

The company distributes to the trade through Publishers Group West. Query letters and SASEs should be directed to:

Carol Bua, Director

ABBEVILLE PUBLISHING GROUP

ABBEVILLE KIDS

ARTABRAS

CANOPY BOOKS

CROSS RIVER

116 W. 23rd Street Suite 500, New York, NY 10011

646-375-2039   fax: 646-375-2040

www.abbeville.com

Abbeville is renowned for finely produced, award-winning volumes in the areas of fine arts, art history, architecture, graphic arts, design, lifestyle, cuisine, handicrafts, nature, collectibles, popular culture, sports, and illustrated historical works. Abbeville also produces postcard books, stationery items, pop-up children's books, artists' portfolios, and titles in biography, letters, literature, and humor. Abbeville issues hardcover and trade paperback editions—all published with attention to quality in design, illustration, and production standards. Abbeville Publishing Group includes Abbeville Press, Abbeville Kids, Artabras, Edition Stemmle, Touring Club of Italy, Skira, Van der Meer, and Flammarion. Abbeville Kids is the house's children's imprint (see subentry). Tiny Folios is a line of small, handsome, reasonably priced gift volumes. Editions Abbeville is the house's enterprising French imprint. Artabras is a house imprimatur for specially priced promotional/premium volumes. Abbeville is the exclusive distributor for English-language publications, based in Zurich, and for the Touring Club of Italy, Skira, and Van der Meer. They are publishers of fine art and photographic books.

Abbeville Publishing Group is an international firm with offices in New York and Paris. Abbeville upholds a tradition of bookmaking established by the publisher Harry N. Abrams, who with his son Robert E. Abrams started Abbeville Press (in 1977) subsequent to the purchase of the eponymous publishing house Harry N. Abrams, Inc. by the Times Mirror Company (see entry for Abrams in this directory).

Representing the Abbeville list: *Thomas Eakins, His Life and Art* by William Innes Homer; *Raphael* by Pierluigi De Vecchi; *Pacific Legacy, Image and Memory from World War II in the Pacific* by Rex Alan Smith and Gerald A. Meehl; *Wristwatch Annual 2003* edited by Peter Braun; *Women Writers* by Rebecca Hazell; *The Russians Emerge* by Heidi Hollinger; *L'Amour Fou, Photography and Surrealism* by Rosalind Krauss, Jane Livingston, and Dawn Ades.

Tiny Folios accents miniature books—for those who love gifts that come in small packages. Series titles: *Treasures of the Addison Gallery of American Art* by Adam D. Weinberg; *100 Classic Cocktails* by Barry Shelby; *Paul Cezanne* by Karen Wilkin; *Revelations, Art of the Apocalypse* by Nancy Grubb; *The Great Book of French Impressionism* by Diane Kelder.

Artabras (quality books at bargain prices) titles: *Ansel Adams: The National Park Service Photographs*; *The Beggarstaff Posters* by Colin Campbell; *California Gardens, Creating a New Eden* by David C. Streatfield; *Colt: An American Legend* by R. L. Wilson; *Goddesses in Art* by Lanier Graham.

Abbeville Press distributes its own books throughout the United States. Unsolicited manuscripts are rarely accepted, but query letters and SASEs can be directed to:

Susan Costello, Editorial Director—Gardening, nature, folk art, general nonfiction

Christopher Lyon, Executive Editor—Fine arts, general nonfiction

Kerrie Baldwin, Assistant Editor—Children's, general nonfiction

ABBEVILLE KIDS

Abbeville Kids produces a lineup designed to introduce younger folk to the world of art and design—as well as to hone the tastes of younger artists and connoisseurs. Abbeville Kids offers breakthrough series of interactive, inquiry-based books designed to teach children about art by looking at the world and about the world by looking at art. Abbeville Kids also offers books with a broader scope that cover the finer pleasures of living and life.

Titles from Abbeville Kids: Abbeville Animals series; *About How Artists See: America, East West South Midwest* by Colleen Carroll; *Letters From Felix* by Annette Langen; *Felix Explores the Planet* by Annette Langen; *Heroines: Great Women Through The Ages* by Rebecca Hazell; *Sebastian* by Vanessa Julian-Ottie; *In The Paint* by Patrick Ewing and Linda L. Louis.

ABRAMS

100 Fifth Avenue, New York, NY 10011

212-206-7715   fax: 212-645-8437

www.abramsbooks.com

Abrams publishes in the fields of fine art, architecture, design; anthropology, archaeology, ethnology, and culture; gardening and the home; literary and art criticism; world history; travel and the natural sciences; creative use of technology and new media.

The Abrams list accents fine illustrated volumes, mainly in hardcover, with some trade paperback editions and series, as well as a selection of works in electronic format. Many Abrams books are published in cooperation with institutions such as museums, foundations, or art galleries; these works bring together top-quality illustrative materials and text written by experts. Abrams publishes a strong seasonal list of new titles and maintains an extensive backlist.

Abrams was founded in 1949 as an independent house (then known as Harry N. Abrams, Inc.) and has been a subsidiary of the Times Mirror Company from 1977 to 1997. In that year, Abrams was acquired by Groupe Latingy (now La Martiniere Groupe). From its inception, the firm has been among the leaders in the field of fine bookmaking in the areas of art, design, and illustrated works.

From Abrams: *American Art 1908-1947: From Winslow Homer to Jackson Pollack* edited by Eric de Chassey; *American Arts and Crafts Textiles* by Dianne Ayres, Timothy Hansen, Beth Ann McPherson, and Tommy Arthur McPherson II; *American Anthem Masterworks from the American Folk Art Museum* by Stacy C. Hollander, Brooke Davis Anderson, and Gerard C. Wertkin; *Ann Hamilton* by Joan Simon; *Balthus Catalogue Raisonne of the Complete Works* by Virginie Monnier, edited and with an essay by Jean Clair, with the authorization of Balthus; *Blue Sky: The Art of Computer Animation* by Peter Weishar; *California Fashion: From the Old West to New Hollywood* by Marian Hall, with Marjorie Cane and Sylvia Sheppard; *Camille Claudel: A Life* by Odile Ayral-Clause; *Chocolate Riches from the Rainforest* by Robert Burleigh; *Blur: The Making of Nothing* by Elizabeth Diller and Ricardo Scofidio; *Elegant Eating: Four Hundred Years of Dining in Style*, a Victoria and Albert Museum Publication edited by Philippa Glanville and Hilary Young; *Envisioning Architecture: Drawings from The Museum of Modern Art*, a Museum of Modern Art Book edited by Matilda McQuaid, with an introduction by Terence Riley; *Flowers A to Z: A Practical Guide to Buying-Growing-Cutting-Arranging* by Cecelia Heffernan, photographs by T.K. Hill; *The Hall of Time: Frescoes of Light*, installations by Bill Viola, a Guggenheim Museum Publication, text by John Hanhardt; *Hollywood Moms: Photographs* by Joyce Ostin, Introduction by Carrie Fisher; *Hunt Slonem, An Art Rich and Strange* by Donald Kuspit; *Mathew Barney, The Cremaster Cycle*, a Guggenheim Museum Publication, texts by Nancy Spector and Neville Wakefield; *Paris Pictured*, a Royal Academy of Arts Publication by Julian Stallabrass; *Photography Transformed: The Metropolitan Bank & Trust Collection*, essay by Klaus Kertess; *Second-Hand Style: Finding and Renewing Antique Treasures* by Cris Dupouy, translated by Molly Stevens; *Studios by the Sea: Artists of Long Island's East End* by Bob Colacello, photographs by Jonathan Becker; *Tiaras Past & Present*, a Victorian and Albert Museum Publication by Geoffrey Munn; *Wallace Putnam* by Francis M. Naumann, foreward by Kristina U. Amadeus; *Whitney: American Visionaries, Selections from the Whitney Museum of American Art*, a Whitney Museum of American Art Publication, introduction by Maxwell L. Anderson.

Abrams children's books include *Babar and the Succotash Bird* by Laurent de Brunhoff; *Hello Kitty, Hello World*; *Sally Goes to the Beach* by Stephen Huneck; *The Worst Band in the Universe* by Graeme Base.

Abrams trade paperback lines include Discoveries (books covering history, archaeology, natural history, culture, and the arts, over the full range of house subject areas of interest).

Titles here: *Alexander the Great* by Pierre Briant; *The Aztecs* by Serge Gnuzinski; *The Birth of Greece* by Pierre Leveque; *Einstein* by Francoise Balibar.

It should be noted that Abrams is a specialist house and acquires projects on a highly selective basis that gives particular weight to such factors as the national or international renown and credentials of participant artists, photographers, and writers.

Abrams distributes its own books in the U. S. and Canada.

Query letters and SASEs should be directed to:

Eric Himmel, Editor-in-Chief

Mark Magowan, Publisher

ACADEMY CHICAGO PUBLISHERS

363 West Erie Street, Chicago, IL 60610

312-751-7300/1-800-248-7323   fax: 312-751-7306

www.academychicago.com   e-mail: info@academychicago.com

Established in 1975, Academy Chicago publishes general nonfiction, art, history, and cultural studies, as well as fiction (including mysteries). The house also offers a line of classic reprints. A small press with an inspired list, Academy Chicago is a major player in American letters.

Nonfiction from Academy Chicago includes popular works with an emphasis on contemporary culture, current events, and historical interpretation. Titles here: *Sharon: Israel's Warrior-Politician* by Sigalit Zetouni and Jordan Miller; *Over Sand & Sea* by Patrick Pfister; *Looking Backward: Stories from Chicago's Jewish Past* by Walter Roth; *Women With Wings: Female Flyers in Fact and Fiction* by Mary Cadogan; *The Celtic and Scandinavian Religions* by J. A. MacCulloch; *Ireland: A Concise History from the Twelfth Century to the Present Day* by Paul Johnson; *Night Witches: The Amazing Story of Russia's Women Pilots in World War II* by Bruce Myles.

The Academy Chicago program in fiction and letters encompasses English-language originals, often with a historical or cultural hook; a solid number of these titles feature the mystery and suspense modes. Academy Chicago also publishes a variety of contemporary and vintage novels in translation.

Frontlist fiction includes *A Fly Has a Hundred Eyes* by Aileen G. Baron; *Letters in the Attic* by Bonnie Shimko; *Poets, Martyrs & Satyrs: New and Selected Poems: 1959-2001* by Jordan Miller; *Cutter's Island* by Vincent Panella; *The Marquise & Pauline: Two Novellas* by George Sand (translated by Sylvie Charron and Sue Huseman); *Murder at Heartbreak Hospital* by Henry Slesar; *A Writer of Books* by George Paston (pen name of Emily Morse Symonds); *The Man Who Once Played Catch with Nellie Fox* by John Manderino; *Freedom in the Dismal* by Monifa A. Love; *Death and Blintzes* by Dorothy and Sidney Rosen; *Leone Leoni* by George Sand; *Homer's Daughter* by Robert Graves; *The Monkey's Paw: And Other Tales of Mystery and the Macabre* by W. W. Jacobs (compiled and with an introduction by Gary Hoppenstand); *In a Dark Wood Wandering: A Novel of the Middle Ages* by Hella S. Haasse (translated by Anita Miller); *Thirteen Uncollected Stories* by John

Cheever (edited by Franklin H. Dennis); *Indiana* by George Sand (translated by George Burnham Ives); *The White Guard* by Mikhail Bulgakov (translated by Michael Glenny); *The Fat Woman's Joke* by Fay Weldon; *The Life and Times of Deacon A. L. Wiley* by Gregory Alan-Williams; *The Perfect Murder* by H. R. F. Keating.

Academy Chicago is the American publisher of the successful British series of humorous and profound Miss Read novels, including *Fresh from the Country*.

Academy Chicago handles its own distribution. Query letters and SASEs should be directed to:

Anita Miller, Senior Editor

Jordan Miller, Vice President and Editor

ADAMS MEDIA CORPORATION

57 Littlefield Street, 2nd Floor, Avon, MA 02322

508-427-7100   fax: 508-427-6790

www.adamsmedia.com

Adams Media Corporation was sold last year by its founder, Robert Adams, to F & W Publications, and seems to be following the same innovative trajectories it has always pursued. Adams has experienced dramatic growth over the past few years and, looking to the future, is poised for even greater title acquisition, higher store presence, and increased marketing sales and media clout. One of the fastest-growing publishers in the country, the now mid-sized trade house publishes approximately 150 books per year. Adams has created a truly unique and distinct publishing universe with magnificent cover designs, eye-catching trademark brands, high-quality content, and competitive retail packaging.

The Adams Editorial Group is now structured to accommodate both best-selling single titles and powerhouse series publishing programs for the trade, mass-market, special sales, gift markets, library sales, and other burgeoning outlets and channels.

In the single-title area, the publisher has had tremendous success in the areas of self-help, women's issues, relationships, spirituality, popular psychology, personal finance, business management, and pets. Adams also considers proposals with broad popular appeal and unique marketing hooks in the areas of parenting, cooking, careers, fitness/leisure how-to, and sales/marketing how-to.

Sample titles include: *Please Stop Laughing At Me . . .* by Jodee Blanco; *Bring Back The Man You Fell In Love With* by Carolyn Bushong, L.P.C.; *The Church Potluck Supper Cookbook* by Elaine Robinson; *The Tao of Poker* by Larry W. Phillips; *College Grad Job Hunter 5th Edition* by Brian D. Krueger, C.P.C.; *Teen Torment* by Patricia Evans; *A Cup Of Comfort* edited by Colleen Sell; *Cat Miracles* by Brad Steiger and Sherry Hansen; *Real Life, Here I Come* by Autumn McAlpin; *Health Spa Cuisine* by Lynn Nicholson and Tracy A.

INDEPENDENT U.S. PRESSES

Smith; *Sales Talk* by Len Serafino; *Small Miracles for Families* by Yitta Halberstam and Judith Leventhal; *The Birth Order: How to Better Understand Yourself and Others* by Cliff Isaacson and Kris Radish; *The Complete Guide to Pregnancy After 30* by Carol Winkelman; *25 Sales Skills They Don't Teach You in Business School* by Stephan Schiffman; *The Road to CEO* by Sharon Voros; *IT Sales Boot Camp: Sure-Fire Techniques for Selling Technology Products to Mainstream Companies* by Brian Giese; *Guerrilla Publicity* by Jay Conrad Levinson, Rick Frishman, and Jill Lublin.

Among the company's single title backlist hot sellers are *Selling to VITO, 2nd Edition* by Anthony Parinello; *The Verbally Abusive Relationship* by Patricia Evans; *God Is My CEO* by Larry Julian.

The Adams Series Publishing Program continues to yield unparalleled results and now has an in-house acquisitions and development team to keep up with the insatiable market demand. The staff is actively seeking professional writers to build upon the phenomenal success of the flagship Everything series, which now boasts over 160 titles in more than a dozen publishing categories, including parenting, cooking, hobbies, spirituality, New Age, personal finance, pets, weddings, relationships, careers, gardening, and more. Among the series' top sellers are *The Everything Pregnancy Book*, *The Everything Baby Names Book*, *The Everything Bartenders Book*, *The Everything Dreams Book*, *The Everything Money Book*, *The Everything Wedding Book*, *The Everything Etiquette Book*, *The Everything Cat Book*, *The Everything Astrology Book*, and *The Everything Barbecue Book*.

New Everything titles include: *The Everything Gardening Book*; *The Everything Landscaping Book*; *The Everything Golf Instruction Book*; *The Everything Creative Wedding Book*; *The Everything Homebuying Book*; *The Everything Catholicism Book*; *The Everything Mafia Book*; *The Everything Fishing Book*.

While shorter in terms of title count than the Everything series, with only five books, the Small Miracles franchise has sold millions of copies and continues to enlighten readers around the world. Authors Yitta Halberstam and Judith Leventhal have assembled an astonishing collection of remarkable coincidences in *Small Miracles*, *Small Miracles II*, *Small Miracles for Women*, *Small Miracles of Love and Friendship*, and *Small Miracles for the Jewish Heart*.

Among Adams's many other series are: Streetwise, which now features two dozen business books, ranging from *Streetwise Managing People* to *Streetwise Internet Business Plan*; Heartwarmers by Azriela Jaffe, now firmly established with a third title, *Heartwarmers of Spirit*; Fastread, a series for people with limited reading time; Knock Em' Dead, a series of career books by Martin Yate; as well as Job Banks, Adams Almanacs, The 100 Best (Stocks, Mutual Funds, etc.), Mr. Cheap's, and 365 Ways to . . . .

Adams orchestrates its own worldwide distribution network. In the U.S. Adams distributes directly to bookstore chains and independents and also operates through wholesales and jobbers; in the UK and elsewhere in the world, the publisher distributes via overseas distributors.

Query letters with SASEs should be directed to:

Gary M. Krebs, Publishing Director—Handles a variety of trade properties, both in series and single title; will often pass to appropriate editors

Jill Alexander, Senior Editor—Business and careers.

Danielle Chiotti, Editor—Self-help, New Age, relationships, teens.

Kate Epstein, Associate Editor—Inspiration, pets, cooking, hobbies, parenting.

Kate Burgo, Project Editor—Acquires for series programs

Gina Mazilli, Project Editor—Series programs.

Paula Munier, Director of New Product Development (new brands, new series, unique packages in all categories).

ADDISON WESLEY LONGMAN PUBLISHING COMPANY

Addison Wesley is now strictly a textbook publisher.

ALGONQUIN BOOKS OF CHAPEL HILL (A DIVISION OF WORKMAN PUBLISHING COMPANY)

PO Box 2225, Chapel Hill, NC 27515

919-767-0108

www.algonquin.com

This division of Workman Publishing Company has a primarily literary orientation in commercial fiction and nonfiction. The house list represents the American tradition, ranging from the homespun to the avant-garde. Algonquin Books of Chapel Hill presents its titles in hardcover and trade paper editions with a look and feel befitting the publisher's emphasis on both the classical and contemporary—books designed to be comfortably handled when read. The Algonquin editorial organization operates from both the Chapel Hill and New York Workman offices.

Algonquin nonfiction includes: *100 Birds and How They Got Their Names* by Diana Wells, illustrated by Lauren Jarrett; *100 Flowers and How They Got Their Names* by Diana Wells; *100 Vegetables and Where They Came From* by Woys Weaver; *The Accidental Buddhist: Mindfulness, Enlightenment, and Sitting Still* by Dinty W. Moore; *Ambushed* by Ian Stewart; *American Mom: Motherhood, Politics, and Humble Pie* by Mary Kay Blakely; *At Sea In The City* by William Kornblum and Pete Hamill; *The Bad Daughter* by Julie Hilden; *Bark if You Love Me* by Louise Bermikow; *Billy Ray's Farm* by Larry Brown.

Algonquin fiction and literary works: *An Actual Life* by Abigail Thomas; *An Amer-*

ican Outrage by G.K. Wuori; *Balls* by Nanci Kincaid; *Best of the South, from Ten Years of New Stories from the South* by Shannon Ravenel; *Big Fish* by Daniel Wallace; *A Blessing On The Moon* by Joseph Skibell; *The Blue Hour* by Elizabeth Evans; *Body of Knowledge* by Carol Dawson; *Boulevard* by Jim Grimsley; *The Cage* by Audrey Schulman; *Carolina Moon* by Jill Mccorkle; *The Cheer Leader* by Jill Mccorkle.

Algonquin Books of Chapel Hill is distributed by the parent Workman Publishing Company.

Query letters and SASEs should be directed to:

Elisabeth Scharlatt, Publisher

Shannon Ravenel, Editorial Director, Shannon Ravenel Books

ALPHA BOOKS

201 West 103rd Street, Indianapolis, IN 46290

317-581-3500

375 Hudson Street, New York, NY 10014

212-366-2000

www.idiotguides.com

Alpha Books, an imprint of Pearson Education (one of the largest international publishing and media companies in the world) publishes the popular series, The Complete Idiot's Guides.

With over 400 titles already in print, The Complete Idiot's Guides is one of the most easily recognizable "how-to" title series in the world. Despite the dizzying success of the series, ideas and manuscripts are continually welcomed.

Best-selling topics include: personal finance, business, health/fitness, foreign language, New Age, relationships, and computers.

For a complete list of titles, visit the publisher's website—or check out any major bookstore in your area, where the series is sure to be displayed prominently on the shelves.

Marie Butler-Knight, Publisher (IN office)

Renee Wilmeth, Senior Editor (IN office)

Ms. Randy Ladenheim-Gil, Editor (NY office)

AMACOM (AMERICAN MANAGEMENT ASSOCIATION)

1601 Broadway, New York, NY 10019-7420

212-586-8100   fax: 212-903-8168   customer service: 1-800-262-9699

www.amanet.org

AMACOM publishes business and management books, primarily for a professional readership. AMACOM trade nonfiction lines include works that cover the fields of accounting and finance, career, customer service, management issues, general business and management, human resources, management skills, international business, manufacturing, organization development, strategy, information and communication technology, personal finance, marketing, advertising and public relations, personal development, small business, supervision, sales and sales management, and training.

Managers in large and small companies are encouraged to use AMACOM books as an inexpensive and effective way to improve their effectiveness, make their organizations more competitive, keep up with current trends and thinking, energize their staff, and inspire employees at all levels.

Titles from AMACOM: *The Lead Generation Handbook* by Robert W. Bly; *Building, Leading, and Managing Strategic Alliances* by Frank A. Kuglin; *Delivering Knock-Your-Socks-Off Service* by Ron Zemke; *Leading At The Edge* by Dennis N. T. Perkins; *Preparing for the Project Management Professional Certification Exam* by Michael W. Newell, PMP, ESP; *How To Develop an Employee Handbook* by Joseph W. R. Lawson; *101 Sample Write-Ups For Documenting Employee Performance Problems* by Paul Falcone; *Auditing Your Human Resources Department* by John H. McConnell; *Business-Driven Compensation Policies* by Robert L. Heneman; *The Sales Compensation Handbook* edited by Stockton B. Colt; *The Complete Guide to Conflict Resolution in the Workplace* by Marick F. Masters and Robert R. Albright; *The Interpersonal Skills Toolkit* by Terry Gillen; *Wireless Inc.* by Craig Settles; *The Workplace Learner* by William J. Rothwell; *Seven Steps to a Sucessful Business Plan* by Al Coke.

Prospective writers might keep in mind the AMACOM readership profile (not to typecast, but rather to offer guidelines): AMACOM readers are definitely not mass-market consumers; they want specialized materials and information on business issues that concern them most. AMACOM book buyers want more than a quick fix. They crave in-depth ideas and practical approaches they can try out on the job. They like to be on the leading edge and get a jump on the competition. They do not want second-hand information. They want to go straight to the source.

AMACOM distributes its own products through multiple marketing channels, including retail trade, direct marketing, special sales, and international sales (through McGraw-Hill). Query letters and SASEs should be directed to:

Adrienne Hickey, Executive Editor—General and human resource management, organization development, leadership, strategy

Jacquelyn Flynn, Executive Editor, Business biography and history, self-help, training and development, technology, finance.

Ellen Kadin, Senior Acquisitions Editor—Career skills, sales and marketing, customer service, self-development

---

AMERICAN PSYCHIATRIC PUBLISHING, INC.

1000 Wilson Boulevard, Suite 1825, Arlington, VA 22209-3901

1-800-368-5777   fax: 202-789-2648

www.appi.org

In March 2001, American Psychiatric Publishing, Inc. (APPI), fomerly American Psychiatric Press, Inc., celebrated its 20th anniversary. At that time, APPI had published more than 800 titles, launched five journals, and merged all publishing operations of the American Psychiatric Association into a single corporation entity known as American Psychiatric Publishing, Inc.

American Psychiatric Publishing, Inc., publishes professional, reference, and trade books, as well as college textbooks. The press's spheres of interest include the behavioral and social sciences, psychiatry, and medicine. The house publishes a mid-sized booklist in hardcover and trade paper and also produces a number of professional journals; selected reference works are issued in electronic formats (including diskettes and CD-ROMs).

Although by far the major portion of the American Psychiatric list is geared toward the professional and academic markets, the house catalogs a small number of books in the areas of patient information and books for the general public, among which are selected titles marketed through trade channels.

Representative of the American Psychiatric popular-interest list: *Integrated Treatment of Psychiatric Disorders* edited by Jerald Kay, MD; *Pain: What Psychiatrists Keen to Know* edited by Mary Jane Massie, MD; *Infant and Toddler Mental Health: Models of Clinical Intervention With Infants and Their Families* by J. Martin Maldonado-Duran, MD; *Evaluation and Management of Sleep Disorders, 3rd edition* by Martin Reite, MD, John Ruddy, MD, and Kim Nagel, MD; *Neurobiology of Violence, 2nd edition* by Jan Volavka, MD, P.h.D.; *Treating Trauma Survivors With PTSD* edited by Rachel Yehuda, PhD

Professional titles from American Psychiatric: *The American Psychiatric Publishing Textbook of Clinical Psychiatry, Fourth Edition* (edited by Robert E. Hales, MD, M.B.A., and Stuart C. Yudofsky, MD); *A Research Agenda for DSM-V* (edited by David J. Kupfer, MD, Michael B. First, MD and Darrel A. Regier, MD. ,M.P.H.)

Practice Guidelines (a series developed to improve patient careand assist with clinical decision-making) titles: *American Psychiatric Association Practice Guidelines for the*

Treatment of Psychiatric Disorders; Quick Reference to the American Psychiatric Association Practice Guidelines for the Treatment of Psychiatric Disorders; American Psychiatric Association Practice Guideline for the Treatment of Patients With Borderline Personality Disorder; American Psychiatric Association Practice Guideline for the Treatment of Patients With Bipolar Disorder, 2nd Edition.

American Psychiatric Publishing is also the publisher of the profession's acknowledged clinical guidebook, *Diagnostic and Statistical Manual of Mental Disorders (4th edition, text revision)*, also known as *DSM-IVTR*.

American Psychiatric Publishing distributes through several regional distribution services. Query letters and SASEs should be directed to:

Robert E. Hales, MD, M.B.A., Editor-in-Chief

Claire Reinburg, Editorial Director

AMERICAN PSYCHOLOGICAL ASSOCIATION, INC.

750 First Street, NE, Washington, DC 20002-4242

1-800-374-2721/202-336-5500

www.apa.org   e-mail: order@apa.org

The American Psychological Association (founded in 1892) is the major psychological organization in the United States. Areas of American Psychological Association publishing interest include virtually all aspects of the field of psychology: methodology, history, student aids, teaching, health, business strategies, violence, personality, and clinical issues. APA publications include books, journals, publishing resources, continuing-education/home-study programs, audiocassettes, videotapes, and databases.

The information resources produced by APA are grounded in a long publishing tradition of scholarly and professional works that encompass diverse topics and applications in the arena of human behavior, from basic research to practical therapies, including the teaching curriculum of psychology, as well as the contributions of psychology to progressive education, from personality disorders to implications for psychology of public policies.

On the APA list: *Determining Damages: The Psychology of Jury Awards* by Edie Greene, PhD and Brian H. Bornstein, PhD; *Flourishing: Positive Psychology and the Well-Lived* edited by Corey L. M. Keyes, PhD and Jonathan Haidt, PhD; *Getting Monitored in Graduate School* by W. Brad Johnson and Jennifer M. Huwe; *Inventing Personality: Gordon Allport and the Science of Selfhood* by Ian A. M. Nicholson, PhD; *Law & Mental Professionals: Arizona, 2nd Edition* by Michael Owen Miller, PhD, JD, Bruce D. Sales, PhD, JD and Javier Delgado, JD; *Models of Intelligence Perspectives* edited by Robert J.

Sternberg, PhD, Jaques Lautrey, PhD, and Todd I. Lubart, PhD; *The Scientific Study of Dreams: Neural Networks, Cognitive Development, and Content Analysis* by G. William Dornhoff, PhD; *Visual Perception: The Influence of H. W. Leibowitz* edited by Jeffrey Andre, PhD, D. Alfred Owens, PhD, and Lewis O. Harvey, Jr., PhD; *Emotions and Life: Perspectives From Psychology, Biology, and Evolution* by Robert Plutchik, PhD; *Methodological Issues and Strategies on Clinical Research, 3rd Edition* by Alan E. Kazdin PhD; *The Professor's Guide to Teaching: Psychological Principles and Practices* by Donelson R. Forsyth, Phd; *A Psychology of Human Strengths: Fundamental Questions and Future Directions* and *Future Directions for a Positive Psychology* edited by Lisa G. Aspinwall, PhD and Ursula M. Staudinger, PhD; *Stress Management Intervention for Women With Breast Cancer, Stress Management Intervention for Women With Breast Cancer: Therapist's Manual* and *Stress Management Intervention for Women With Breast Cancer: Participant's Workbook* by Michael H. Antoni, PhD; *Trauma and Substance Abuse: Causes, Consequences, and Treatment of Comorbid Disorders* edited by Paige Ouimette, PhD and Pamela J. Brown, PhD; *The Breast Cancer Notebook: The Healing Power of Reflection* by Ava Louise Stanton, LCSW and Geoffrey M. Reed. PhD; *Group Psychotherapy for Women With Breast Cancer* by James L. Spira, PhD, MPH, ABPP and Geoffrey M. Reed, PhD; *Integrating Aging Topics Into Psychology: A Practical Guide for Teaching Undergraduates* edited by Susan Krauss Whitbourne, PhD and John C. Cavanaugh, PhD; *Up Close and Personal: The Teaching and Learning of Narrative Research* edited by Ruthellen Josselson, PhD, Amia Lieblich, PhD, and Dan P. McAdams, PhD

A publication of the American Psychological Association that has wide influence in all areas of scholarly publishing, especially the social and behavioral sciences, is the *Publication Manual of the American Psychological Association* (now in its 4th edition), a resource that guides writers and editors through manuscript preparation and production. Query letters and SASEs should be directed to:

Julia Frank-McNeil, Director, APA Books

AMERICAN SOCIETY FOR TRAINING AND DEVELOPMENT (ASTD) BOOKS

1640 King Street, PO Box 1443, Alexandria, VA 22313-2043

703-683-8100   fax: 703-683-8103

www.astd.org   e-mail: customercare@astd.org

American Society for Training and Development (ASTD) Books is a business-information specialist. Among ASTD's major categories are workplace learning and performance, human resource development, training, management development, career development, workforce issues, consulting, teamwork, technology, games, and problem solving and creativity. In addition to books, ASTD offers training kits, diagnostic tools, presentation materials, games and simulations, videos, audiocassettes, and computer software.

Founded in 1944, ASTD Books is the book-publishing wing of The American Society for Training and Development, a nonprofit membership organization. The house's professional books cover such areas as employee education, training, and development; human resource development; organization management; career development; and performance improvement. Within this business arena, ASTD strives to put forth a list that represents the most current topics, the most innovative techniques, and the most gifted authors in the field.

Books listed in the ASTD catalog are reviewed and selected by a distinguished and professional peer group.

Titles from ASTD: *Training Design and Delivery* by Geri E. Mcardle; *Training on the Job* by Diane Walter; *Performance Intervention Maps: 36 Strategies for Solving Your Organization's Problems* by Ethan Sanders and Sivasailam "Thiagi" Thiagarajan; *Evaluating the Impact of Training* by Scott B. Parry; *The Targeted Evaluation Process: A Performance Consultant's Guide* by Wendy L. Combs and Salvatore V. Falletta; *ISD from the Ground Up: A No-Nonsense Approach to Instructional Design* by Chuck Hodell; *Project Management for Trainers: Stop "Winging It" and Get Control of Your Training Projects* by Lou Russell; *Managing Web Based Training: How to Keep Your Program on Track and Make It Successful* by Alan L. Ellis, Ellen D. Wagner, and Warren R. Longmire; *In Action: Leading Knowledge Management and Learning* by Dede Bonner; *Interactive Distance Learning Exercises That Really Work!* by Karen Mantyla; *Distance Learning: A Step-by-Step Guide for Trainers* by Karen Mantyla and Rick Gividen.

ASTD's new E-Learning series includes: *Project Managing E-Learning* by William E. Shackelford; *Implementing E-Learning* by Jay Gross and Lance Dublin; *Leading E-Learning* by William Horton; *Selling E-Learning* by Darin E. Harley; *Designing E-Learning* by Saul Carliner; *Evaluating E-Learning* by William Horton; *Using E-Learning* by William Horton.

ASTD Books distributes its own list via a catalog, easy ordering and an online store. Some ASTD books are available through other publishing houses. ASTD also distributes and copublishes books from a variety of other business-oriented publishers, including McGraw-Hill, Jossey-Bass, Berrett-Koheler, and others. ASTD also distributes through Amazon.com.

Writers: If you are working on a book targeted to trainers that you think ASTD might like to publish, please contact (703-683-9205). Guidelines for submitting a book proposal are available upon request. Query letters and SASEs should be directed to:

Mark Morrow, Senior Acquisitions Editor

Ruth Stadius, Director of Publications

ANDREWS MCMEEL PUBLISHING

4520 Main Street, Kansas City, MO 64111-7701

1-800-851-8923 fax: 816-932-6749

www.amuniversal.com/amp/

Founded in 1970, Andrews McMeel Publishing is an Andrews McMeel Universal company that publishes a wide assortment of general trade nonfiction books and gift books, humor (including cartoon books), and calendars. Areas of interest include popular culture and lifestyles, psychology and self-help, health and medicine, New Age and inspiration, and women's issues. Andrews McMeel publishes over 100 calendars each year in day-to-day, wall, and desk-diary format.

Titles from Andrews McMeel: *I Am the Greatest* by Karl Evanzz; *Teachers Photographs* by Gary Firstenberg; *Everyone Has a Right to Live* by Jerry Gay; *Another Day in Cubicle Paradise (a Dilbert Book)* by Scott Adams; *Yoga for Men* by Bruce Eric and Van Horn; *Now* by Patrick Regan; *Dogma* by Kim Levin and Erica Salmon; *New-Found Friends* by Rachael Hale; *Burn This Book. . .and Move On with Your Life* by Jessica Hurley; *Pure* by Anne Geddes; *Where Joy Begins* by Chris Shea; *Star Signs: Good Fortune Good Sex* by Michele Knight; *The Mommy Journal* by Tracy Broy; *Zelda Rules on Love* by Carol Gardner and Shane Young; *A Dog's Book of Truths* by Nancy LeVine; *Goodness Gracious* by Roxie Kelley and Shelly Reeves Smith.

The line of gift books includes: *The Blue Day Book* by Bradley Trevor Greive; *Mom, You Rule!* by Cate Holly; *Famous Black Quotes on Sisters* by Janet Cheatham Bell; *The Joy of Fatherhood* by Thomas Kinkade; *What? Another Birthday!!* by John McPherson; *Life Strategies from the Art of War* by Philip Dunn.

Tiny Tomes are tiny, of course—as well as topical, traditional, tactile, tempting, and targeted. These teeny books from Andrews and McMeel are less than half the size of the house's little gift books—the tactile allure of these palm-size volumes is said to be irresistible. Titles include: *Mom: You're the Greatest; A Tiny Treasury of African Proverbs; Sex: A Book of Quotations; The Little Book of Coffee.*

Each volume in the Cader Unstamped Books line presents 16 sheets of exquisitely designed and printed stamps. Use them to personalize and decorate correspondence, collect them, or frame them. Titles here include *Nature Unstamped; Holidays Unstamped; Angels Unstamped.*

Agents, please query. No unsolicited manuscripts are accepted. Query letters should be directed to:

Christine Schillig, Vice President and Editorial Director—General nonfiction, all categories

Dorothy O'Brien, Assistant Vice President and Managing Director—Humor and general nonfiction

Patty Rice, Senior Editor and Editorial Director—Gift books and general nonfiction

Jean Lucas, Editor—General nonfiction, illustrated books, humor, New Age

Jennifer Fox, Editor—General nonfiction, gift books, humor

Education: B.A. in Journalism from University of Missouri-Columbia.

Employment history/editor career path: Began as an Editorial Assistant at Andrews McMeel in 1996.

Do you represent fiction? No.

Do you represent nonfiction? Yes.

Do you require book proposals? If so, what do you look for in evaluating a book proposal? Yes. Solid summary, outline of book, competition, author bio, and sample text.

What process do you use for making a decision? What is the process for acquisition, is there a committee? I usually get a couple of reads from other editors before taking it to an acquisitions meeting with the committee.

What kinds of nonfiction books do you want to see less of? Parenting, business, serious self-help.

Are you interested in work geared for the masses (readers of *People*, *The Star*, etc.)? Yes, very much so.

Are agents important? Why? Yes, they're great for screening the material and sending it to the right publishing houses. They are also helpful in dealing with difficult authors.

How should writers approach you? They should approach me with a hook—what makes their idea different and saleable.

What are some common mistakes writers make? What really gets on your nerves? Writers who expect a great deal of attention and publicity for a small book. Writers who don't trust the publisher to make the right decisions. Writers who are too hands-on.

What have been some of your best experiences with writers or in your job? Working with talented, hard-working, and professional writers whose books actually succeed. Then, signing up more books with those authors.

Any advice for writers? Any way to improve the system for you? Any additional thoughts? I'm always looking for gift books, light self-help, pop culture, and humor books. Remember to get an agent.

THE ANONYMOUS PRESS, INC.

332 Bleecker Street, New York, NY 10014

Best known for the underground classic *Sleeping with the President: My Intimate Years with Bill Clinton* by Gennifer Flowers, this house maintains a purely underground mystique and reality. "Conspiracy theories" seems to be its reason for existence, and much of its product seems to be published under other (untraceable) imprints. Whatever they are, in all the years they have been in business, no author complaints of fraud or misrepresentation have ever been recorded.

Query letters and SASEs should be directed to:

(**Mr.**) **Gilchrist** (**Chris**) **Bonner**, Acquisitions (surely an alias)

THE APEX PRESS

THE BOOTSTRAP PRESS

Council on International and Public Affairs

777 United Nations Plaza, Suite 3C, New York, NY 10017

1-800-316-2739

www.cipa-apex.org   email: cipany@igc.apc.org

Branch office:

Box 337, Croton-on-Hudson, NY 10520

Apex accents nonfiction titles in such fields as corporate accountability, grassroots and worker participation, and intercultural understanding. One special publishing focus is on economic and social justice, human rights, and the impact of technology on contemporary society.

Introduced in 1990, The Apex Press is an imprint of the nonprofit research, education, and publishing group Council on International and Public Affairs (CIPA). Apex publishes hardcover and paperback books that provide critical analyses of and new approaches to significant economic, social, and political issues in the United States, other industrialized nations, and the Third World.

The Council on International and Public Affairs was founded in 1954 and is a nonprofit research, education, and publishing group. The Council seeks to further the study and public understanding of problems and affairs of the peoples of the United States and other nations of the world through conferences, research, seminars and workshops, publications, and other means.

From Apex Press: *Building Union,* by Peter Kellman, illustrated by Matt Wuerker; *Defying Corporations, Defining Democracy* edited by Dean Ritz; *The Elite Consensus* by George Draffan; *The Good Neighbor Handbook* by Sanford J. Lewis; *Grassroots Journalism: A Practical Manual* by Eesha Williams; *Greenwash: The Reality Behind Corporate Environmentalism* by Jed Greer & Kenny Bruno; *Washington's New Poor Law* by Gertrude Schaffner & Shelia D. Collins; *A New Democracy* by Harry Shutt; *Rethinking Globalization* by Martin Khor; *The Taliban* by Peter Marsden; *Voices Of Sanity* by Kamla Bhasin, Smitu Kothari & Bindia Thapar, editors; *Another American Century* by Nicholas

Guyatt; *Hungry For Trade* by John Madeley; *Protect or Plunder?* by Vandana Shiva; *Planet Champions* by Jack Yost; *In The Net* by Jim Watch; *Naming the Enemy* by Amory Starr; *The Rise and Fall of Economic Liberalism* by Frederic F. Clairmont; *Inhuman Rights: The Western System and Global Human Rights Abuses* by Winin Pereira; *Washington's New Poor Law: Welfare "Reform" and the Roads Not Taken, 1935—1996* by Sheila D. Collins and Gertrude Schaffner Goldberg;

The Apex Press handles its own distribution; the house catalog includes books and additional resources (including videos) from a number of publishers worldwide.

THE BOOTSTRAP PRESS

The Bootstrap Press (inaugurated in 1988) is an imprint of Intermediate Technology Development Group of North America (ITDG/North America) in cooperation with the Council on International and Public Affairs.

Bootstrap's publishing interest focuses on social economics and community economic change; the house covers small-scale and intermediate-scale or appropriate technology in both industrialized and emerging countries, with an aim to promote more just and sustainable societies. Its books explore business and industry theory and how-to, gardening and agriculture, building and construction, and communications.

Titles from Bootstrap: *Work Empowerment* edited by Jon Wisman; *Greening Cities: Building Just and Sustainable Communities* by Joan Reolofs; *Building Sustainable Communities: Tools and Concepts for Self-Reliant Economic Change* by C. George Benello, Robert Swann, and Shann Turnbull; *Chicken Little, Tomato Sauce and Agriculture: Who Will Produce Tomorrow's Food?* by Joan Dye Gussow.

Titles of Intermediate Technology Publications (London), previously distributed by the Bootstrap Press, are now available through Stylus Publishing.

Bootstrap publications are distributed with those of sibling operation the Apex Press. Query letters and SASEs should be directed to:

Judi Rizzi, Publications Manager

Ward Morehouse, President

APPLAUSE THEATRE & CINEMA BOOKS

151 West 46th Street, 8th Floor, New York, NY 10036

212-575-9265   fax: 646-562-5852

Established in 1983, Applause Theatre Book Publishers produces a list geared to fields of stage, cinema, and the entertainment arts. Applause produces collections, compendiums, biographies, histories, resource books, reference works, and guides keyed to the needs of the house's wide readership of seasoned pros, rookies, and aficionados.

The Applause program covers hardback and paperback editions, among them a number of generously illustrated and well-produced works. Applause issues stage plays and screenplays (many in translation and many in professional working-script format) that run the gamut from the classical repertory to contemporary works in drama, comedy, and musicals. Applause also offers audio works and a video library. The publisher's backlist is comprehensive (it has never declared a single title out of print and goes back to press for as few as 500 copies of a backlist standby).

Special-production volumes encompass works that detail the background and history behind the creation of works for stage and screen, in addition to containing complete scripts.

Titles from Applause: *The Real Life of Laurence Olivier* by Roger Lewis; *An Actor and His Time* by John Gielgud; *Ralph Richardson: An Actor's Life* by Garry O'Connor; *Seats: The Insider's Guide to the Performing Arts and Sports in New York* by Sandy Millman; *The Other Way: An Alternative Approach to Acting and Directing* by Charles Morowitz; *Fundamental Acting: A Practical Guide* by Paul Kuritz; *Theatre on the Edge: New Visions, New Voices* by Mel Gussow; *The Smart Set: George Jean Nathan and H. L. Mencken* by Thomas Quinn Curtiss; *London Theatre Walks* by Jim DeYoung; *Paul Scofield* by Garry O'Connor; *An Actor's Dickens* by Beatrice Manley; *Stones in His Pockets* by Marie Jones; *Political Stages* (edited by Emily Mann and David Roessel); *This Man & Music* by Anthony Borgess; *More Power to You* by Robert Cohen.

For theatrical professionals and students as well, Applause offers: *Acting in Film* (from the Applause Acting Series) by Michael Caine; *Telling Moments: 15 Gay Monologues* by Robert C. Reinhart; *The Actor and the Text* by Cicely Berry; *The Secret of Theatrical Space* by Josef Svoboda.

Applause Theatre Books are distributed by Hal Leonard Corporation. Query letters and SASEs should be directed to:

Glenn Young, Publisher

Mark Glubke, President

ARCADE PUBLISHING

141 Fifth Avenue, New York, NY 10010

212-475-2633   fax: 212-353-8148

www.arcadepub.com   e-mail: info@arcadepub.com

Arcade Publishing (founded in 1988 by Jeannette and Richard Seaver) produces commercial and literary nonfiction, as well as selected poetry. Nonfiction standouts include issue-oriented titles, contemporary human-interest stories, and cultural historical works. Arcade's fiction list includes entrants in such categories as mystery, suspense, and thrillers. Arcade's program leans toward learned and enlightened reading.

From Arcade: *A Season with Verona* by Tim Parks; *The Soldier's Return* by Melvyn Bragg; *Altered Land* by Jules Hardy; *The Ascent of Eli Israel* by Jon Papernick; *Hidden Minds* by Frank Tallis; *Silvermeadow* by Barry Maitland; *Music of a Life* by Andrei Makine; *The Obvious Diet* by Ed Victor; *Scrolling Forward* by David Levy; *Mercy Among the Children* by David Adams Richards; *A Dog Called Perth* by Peter Martin; *Duke of Egypt* by Margriet de Moor; *Bin Laden* by Adam Robinson; *Riot: A Love Story* by Shashi Tharoor; *Imperial Legend* by Alexis Troubetzkoy; *The Freemasons* by Jasper Ridley. Arcade Publishing is distributed by Little, Brown.

Prospective authors please note that Arcade does not accept unsolicited submissions. Query letters and SASEs should be directed to:

Calvert Barksdale, Senior Editor, Senior Vice President and General Manager—All areas of house interest

Jeannette Seaver, Executive Editor, Publisher, Marketing Director—Literary fiction; nonfiction including: history, politics, literary criticism, cookbooks; illustrated books

Richard Seaver, President and Editor-in-Chief—Literary fiction; nonfiction including: history, politics, literary criticism, illustrated books

Greg Comer, Editor

Susan Hayes, Director of Production

Darcy Falkenhagen, Associate Editor

Casey Ebro, Publicity Associate, Assistant Editor

JASON ARONSON INC., PUBLISHERS

230 Livingston Street, Northvale, NJ 07647

1-800-782-0015   fax: 201-767-1576

www.aronson.com

This revered publisher, of important and serious books relevant to psychology, sociology and Judaica, has ceased to acquire and publish new works.

AVALON BOOKS

160 Madison Avenue, New York, NY 10016

212-598-0222 fax: 212-979-1862

www.avalonbooks.com e-mail: avalon@avalonbooks.com

Avalon Books (not to be confused, though it often is, with the Avalon Publishing Group) produces fiction lines primarily for distribution to library and institutional markets on a subscriber basis. Avalon editions are wholesome family stories in the following categories: traditional mysteries; mainstream romance; career romance; historical romance, traditional genre Westerns. Avalon produces a line of literary classics in reprint (on the Airmont Classics imprint).

Avalon Books (a subsidiary of Thomas Bouregy & Company, founded in 1950) publishes a primarily hardcover fiction list. The house emphasis on new original novels caters to the tastes and preferences of the all-important library readership; stories should consist of those likely to be of high interest to the patrons of this core market.

From the Avalon list: *Training Tommy* by Barbara Meyers; *Heart on a String* by Lois Carnell Alexander; *A Wanted Man* by Nancy J. Parra; *Dreams Don't Last* by Joyce and Jim Lavene; *Shannon's Ride* by Charles E. Friend; *Way Out West* by Blanche Marriott; *A Catered Affair* by Carolyn Matkowsky; *The Gambling Man* by Kent Conwell; *Maggie's Mistake* by Carolyn Brown; *A Taste of Death* by Mary Ellen Hughed; *The Mad Herringtons* by Jane Myers Perrine; *Emma's Folly* by Carolyn Brown; *The Marshal's Destiny* by C. H. Admirand; *Save Your Heart for Me* by Joye Ames; *Painted Lady* by Lucinda Baker; *That Saturday Feeling* by Ingrid Betz; *Hannah and the Horseman* by Johnny D. Boggs; *The Night Next Door* by Charlene Bowen; *Chasing Charlie* by Kathy Carmichael; *Lights of Love* by Roni Denholtz; *Growing Season* by Mike Gaherty; *In a Wink* by Lacey Green; *Imperfect Together* by Amanda Harte; *Making the Call* by Pat Hines; *Forever and a Day* by Patricia Johnston; *Romantic Doctor* by Terry McDermid; *Emerald Sky* by Gerry O'Hara; *Lasting Love* by Tara Randel; *Coming Home* by Nadia Shworan; *The Secret of Spring Hollow* by Jan Weeks.

Distribution is primarily through library sales. Query letters and SASEs should be directed to:

Mira Son, Editor

Erin Cartwright, Editorial Director
Born: January 20.
Education: B.A., in English and History from the University of Delaware.
Employment history/editor career path: I grew up in the Bahamas, and I always knew I wanted to be a novelist and live in New York City. I discovered that I liked to edit much more than I liked the actual writing, so I became an Editor. I started out at *Details* magazine. I moved from there to Simon & Schuster for five years and then to HarperCollins for three years. I have been Senior Editor at Avalon Books for four

years.

Personal interests: Biking, running, snowboarding, traveling, and writing.

What would you be doing if you were not an editor? Teaching.

What books have you acquired that make you the most proud? What books that you have acquired reflect the types of books you like to represent? *Love Is Friendship Caught on Fire* by Guy Zona. *Everything* by Carolyn Porown.

Do you represent fiction? If so, what do you look for? Yes. Romance, mysteries, Westerns. I look for good writing, good stories, believable characters, and something that has a different edge to it.

Do you represent nonfiction? No.

Do you require book proposals? If so, what do you look for in evaluating a book proposal? No book proposal, but I do ask for a brief synopsis and the first three chapters with an SASE. If I like what I see, I will then request the entire manuscript.

What process do you use for making a decision? What is the process for acquisition, is there a committee? There is not a committee, but I will give the manuscript to about two or three people to also read. If they agree that it is a good buy, we will then discuss it in more detail.

Are agents important? Why? Yes, they are important for people who have published multiple books. I think first-time authors don't necessarily need an agent, it's when you decide to move on with more books, to the bigger houses, with a complicated contract, that you need an agent.

Do you like new writers? What should new writers do to break into the business? Yes. Most of my authors are first- or second-time authors. I think it's always good to have a fresh voice. To break into the business, you should take writing classes, always write, never give up even when the rejections are pouring in, and have others read and critique your work.

How should writers approach you? Go to the *LMP* or similar resources and find out what my submission guidelines are. Always give away the ending to your story in your cover letter to me; you don't have to "hook" an editor.

What are some common mistakes writers make? What really gets on your nerves? I tend to see the same kind of romances over and over again. There are too many cowboy romance stories. I don't like when the characters get killed in the stories in car accidents. It bothers me when people don't do their homework and submit something outside of my guidelines.

What can writers do to get your attention and to avoid the slush pile? Follow my submission guidelines.

What have been some of your craziest experiences with submissions? I've gotten some pretty weird stuff from people in prison. Manuscripts sent in from teenagers.

What have been some of your best experiences with writers or in your job? I have recently bought an author's first book—she's 80 years old! She just started writing about 10 years ago and was thrilled! This is the most wonderful feeling—to get to be the one to make someone's day.

What, if anything, makes you different from other editors? I am willing and happy to give anyone a chance. I will work with you even if everything is not perfect the first time around. If you have talent, and I don't feel I can buy your manuscript, I will take the time to suggest other editors who may like to take a look.

Is there anything you would like to see changed in the industry? I would like to see authors make more money.

Any advice for writers? Keep writing, do your homework, find out everyone's submission guidelines, and never quit! Keep writing and submitting until someone says "yes," because eventually someone will.

AVALON PUBLISHING GROUP

BLUE MOON BOOKS (SEE SEPARATE LISTING)

CARROLL & GRAF PUBLISHERS, INC. (SEE SEPARATE LISTING)

MARLOWE & COMPANY

SEAL PRESS (SEE SEPARATE LISTING)

THUNDER'S MOUTH PRESS

245 West 17th Street, New York, NY   10011

646-375-2570   fax: 646-375-2571

www.avalonpub.com

AVALON TRAVEL PUBLISHING

1400 65th Street, Suite 250 Emeryville, CA 94608

www.travelmatters.com   e-mail: info@travelmatters.com

The Avalon Publishing Group (not to be confused, though it often is, with Avalon Books, the firm described above) combines six unique firms—Avalon Travel Publishing, Blue Moon Books, Carroll & Graf Publishers, Thunder's Mouth Press, Marlowe & Company, and Seal Press. Each component maintains its own distinct publishing process and staff, and all are distributed by Publishers Group West.

AVALON TRAVEL PUBLISHING

Avalon Travel Publishing guides feature a combination of practicality and spirit, offering a unique traveler-to-traveler perspective perfect for an afternoon hike, around-the-world journey, or anything in-between. Avalon Publishing Group publishes many guides by Rick Steves.

Representative of Avalon Travel Publishing: (Series): Moon; Foghorn Outdoors,

Rick Steves; Road Trip USA; The Common Dog Lover's Companion; The Practical Nomad; Adapter Kit. (Titles): *100 Best Small Art Towns in America: Discover Creative Communities, Fresh Air, and Affordable Living, 3rd edition* by John Villani; *Are We Moving to Mars?* by Anne Schraff; *Asia in New York City: A Cultural Travel Guide*; *Big Book of Adventure, 4th Ed* by James Simmons; *Rick Steves' Europe Through the Back Door* by Rick Steves; *Road Trip USA: Cross-Country Adventures on America's Two-Lane Highways* by Jamie Jensen; *Travelers' Tales Greece* edited by Larry Habegger and Sean O'Reilly.

MARLOWE & COMPANY

Marlowe & Company focuses on personal growth, spirituality, psychology, self-help, health, and healthful cooking. Marlowe & Company is involved in a copublishing venture with Balliett & Fitzgerald called Illumina Books, which draws therapy and self-help from the world's finest literature.

Representative of Marlowe & Company: *Apache, The Sacred Path to Womanhood* by John Annerino; *Are You Ready for Lasting Love?: A Personal Guide to Creating Fulfilling Relationships* by Paddy Welles; *Fata Morgana* by William Kotzwinkle; *Fellini: A Life* by Hollis Alpert; *Feminist Political Theory: An Introduction* by Bryson; *Fire in the Sky* by Walton; *Gay Star Signs* by Max Bowman; *Good Fats, Bad Fats: An Indispensable Guide to All the Fats You're Likely to Encounter* by Rosemary Stanton; *Good Stress, Bad Stress: An Indispensable Guide to Identifying and Managing Your Stress* by Barry Lenson.

THUNDER'S MOUTH PRESS

Thunder's Mouth Press publishes adult trade books in a variety of subject areas, concentrating most heavily on popular culture, film, music, current events, contemporary culture, biography/personality, fantasy, role-playing games, the arts, and popular reference. Thunder's Mouth Press copublishes, with Balliett and Fitzgerald, Adrenaline Books, which features a series of anthologies written about extreme adventure sports and stories, and Adrenaline Classics, reprints of adventure classics. Thunder's Mouth also collaborates with the National Institute on an imprint called Nation Books, which features selections from this premier independent magazine of politics and culture.

Representative of Thunder's Mouth Press: *Adonis: Masterpieces of Erotic Male Photography* by Michelle Olley; *Al-Qaeda: The Terror Network that Threatens the World* by Jane Corbin; *All for Love* by Ved Mehta; *Art of Screenwriting: An A to Z Guide to Writing a Successful Screenplay* by William Packard; *Art of the Fillmore: The Poster Series 1966-1971* by Bill Graham; *Ayahuasca: Hallucinogens, Consciousness, and the Spirit of Nature* by Metzner; *Baby Driver* by Jan Kerouac.

Avalon Publishing Group is unable to accept unsolicited manuscripts or queries at this time. Query letters and SASEs should be directed to:

Neil Ortenberg, Thunder's Mouth Press

Matthew Lore, Marlowe & Company

Claiborne Hancock, Carroll & Graf

Heather Tidrick, Avalon Travel Publishing

BAEN PUBLISHING ENTERPRISES (BAEN BOOKS)

PO Box 1403, Riverdale, NY 10471

718-548-3100

www.baen.com   jimbaen@baen.com

Baen publishes science fiction and fantasy writing. The house's new releases are generally published in mass-market paperback format with targeted lead titles produced in trade paper and hardcover editions. Baen is a prominent publisher of series in science fiction and fantasy and also publishes a notable lineup of collections and anthologies geared to various subgenre traditions and the works of individual writers.

Founded in 1984, Baen Publishing Enterprises concentrates its concise list on its proven categories of publishing strength. Baen's roster of writers includes James P. Hogan, John Ringo, David Weber, Marion Zimmer Bradley, Lois McMaster Bujold, John Dalmas, Robert A. Heinlein, Mercedes Lackey, Anne McCaffrey, Eric Flint, Spider and Jeanne Robinson.

From Baen: *March to the Stars* by David Weber and John Ringo; *Give Me Liberty* by Martin Harry Greenberg and Mark Tier; *The Excalibur Alternative* by David Weber; *Melchior's Fire* by Jack L. Chalker; *The Independent Command* by James Doohan; *Empress of Light* by James C. Glass; *The Cold Equations* by Tom Godwin; *Advance & Retreat* by Harry Turtledove; *Orphans of the Sky* by Robert A Heinlein's; *In The Rift* by Marion Zimmer Bradley.

Baen Books is distributed by Simon & Schuster. Query letters and SASEs should be directed to:

James Baen, Editor-in-Chief

Toni Weisscoft, Executive Editor

BASKERVILLE PUBLISHERS

2711 Park Hill Dr. Fort Worth, TX 76109

817-923-1064   fax: 817-921-9114

www.baskervillepublishers.com   e:mail: info@baskervillepublishers.com

Baskerville Publishers has been around since 1992, but stopped publishing in 1997. The company was purchased by Ron Moore and moved to Ft. Worth, Texas to pursue titles of fine literary fiction and nonfiction. Their mission will be to publish the best fiction available and also unusual titles for lovers of serious music.

The first "new" list was released in spring of 2003. Titles included: *Great Voices,*

Volume Six: Placido Domingo: My Operatic Roles by Helena Matheopoulos; *Great Voices, Volume Seven: Lauritz Melchior: The Golden Years of Bayreuth* by Ib Melchior; *Fairy Tale* by Walt Foreman; *The Land Between* by Cathryn Hankla; *How I Became a Fisherman Named Pete* by David Spencer.

Send queries and SASEs to:

Ronald E. Moore, Owner/Publisher

Jeff Putnam, Editor

BARRICADE BOOKS INC.

185 Bridge Plaza North, Suite 308-A, Fort Lee, NJ 07024

201-944-7600   fax: 201-944-6363

www.barricadebooks.com   e-mail: customerservice@barricadebooks.com

Barricade's publishing interests include arts and entertainment; how-to/self-help; biography, history, politics, and current events; humor; natural sciences; New Age, occult, and religion; psychology, health, and sexuality; recreation; and true crime.

Barricade Books was founded in 1991 by the veteran publisher Lyle Stuart, who had previously founded Lyle Stuart Inc. (Lyle Stuart Inc. was sold and eventually became the Carol Publishing Group before Carol closed its doors in late 1999.) Barricade Books was launched in order to continue the tradition begun in 1956 when Lyle Stuart became a publisher. That tradition is to specialize in books other publishers might hesitate to publish because they are too controversial.

Barricade sought bankruptcy protection in 1999 due to an expensive libel suit against it by Las Vegas gambling tycoon Steve Wynn, but the firm continues full operations.

Barricade publisher Carole Stuart is the author of a number of successful books, including *I'll Never Be Fat Again* and *Why Was I Adopted?* She has worked in book publishing her entire adult life. Lyle Stuart is a former newspaper reporter who launched his career as a book publisher with $8,000 that he won in a libel action against Walter Winchell. Stuart sold that company three decades later for $12 million. The Barricade catalog expands this tradition with a roster of freethinking writers that is perhaps unrivaled in the international commercial-publishing arena. Barricade's list is exemplary of publishing courage in action.

From Barricade: *Power Beyond Reason: The Mental Collapse of Lyndon Johnson* by D. Jablow Hersham, and Gerald Tolchin, PhD; *Every Midget Has An Uncle Sam Costume: Writing For A Living* by Donald Bain; *Rancho Mirage* by Aram Saroyan; *Dr. Fischer's Little Book of Big Medical Emergencies* by Stuart Fischer, MD; *The CIA's Control of Candy Jones* by Donald Bain; *People and Other Animals* by Norma A. Donner; *Job Finder's Guide (3rd Edition)* by Les Krantz; *Murder of a Mafia Daughter* by Cathy Scott; *A Pictor-*

ial History of Vaudeville by Bernard Sobel; *Moving to Las Vegas* by John L. Smith; *The Hidden Documents of Zionism* by Lenni Brenner; *Murder at the Conspiracy Convention* by Paul Krassner; *My Bride Guide* by Judith Ann Graham; *I Escaped From Auschwitz* by Rudolf Vrba; *Surviving Terrorism* by Rainer Stahlberg; *My Face for the World to See* by Liz Renay; *The Complete Book Of Dreams* by Leonard R. N. Ashley; *Paul Pellicoro on Tango*; *The Gay Wicca Book* by Bruce K. Wilborn; *The Complete Book of Sex Magic* by Leonard R. N. Ashley; *Your Skin From A to Z* by Jerome Z. Litt; *The Dictionary of Sexual Slang* by Leonard R. N. Ashley; *Celebrities In Hell* by Warren Allen Smith; *Jobs Rated Almanac* by Les Krantz.

Query letters and SASEs should be directed to:

Carole Stuart, Publisher

BARRON'S/BARRON'S EDUCATIONAL SERIES, INC.

250 Wireless Boulevard, Hauppauge, NY 11788

1-800-645-3476   fax: 631-434-3723

www.barronseduc.com   e-mail: info@barronseduc.com

Barron's hosts a broad publishing operation that encompasses books in business and finance; gift books; cooking, family, health, gardening, nature, pets, and retirement lifestyle; selected titles in arts, crafts, and hobbying; and computer books and software. The house also highlights a children's line.

Founded in 1941, Barron's was originally known for its comprehensive line of study notes and test-preparation guides in business, literature, and languages, as well as standardized tests in individual subject and professional fields. The house offers a number of practical business series, retirement and parenting keys, programs on skills development in foreign languages (as well as in English), and specialty reference titles in allied areas of interest.

Barron's cookbooks address international cuisines as well as healthful cookery. Dictionaries of health-related terms and many other specialized topics are also offered. Under the rubric of special-interest titles, Barron's produces series on arts and crafts techniques, biographies of well-known artists, and home and garden titles. Books on pets and pet care include numerous titles keyed to particular breeds and species of birds, fish, dogs, and cats.

Children's and young adult books and books of family interest include series on pets, nature and the environment, dinosaurs, sports, fantasy, adventure, and humor. Many of these are picture storybooks, illustrated works, and popular reference titles of general interest.

Barron's children's and young adult titles include: *Amazing Christmas Mosaics* by Sarah Kelly; *Animal Shapes Kitten Illustrated* Rachael O'Neal; *Adios Chi Chi* by C.

Amato; *A La Granja (Farm)* by J. M. Parramon; *Again!* by John Prater; *101 Games for Spring* by Joseph M. Allue; *Bach* by Ann Rachlin and Tony Hart; *Bertie Bones* by Tim Wood; *By the Light of the Moon* by Gina Erickson, MA, and Kelli C. Foster, PhD; *Chunky Farm Horse* by Emily Bolam; *Dinosaurs* by Dougal Dixon; *Guess Who's Hiding!* by Ana Martin-Larranaga; *Into Space* by Kate Petty; *Penguins* by Judith Hodge and Susan Brocker; *Teatime Piglet* by Steve Bland.

Barron's offers an extensive general-interest series lineup of interest to students and educators: Masters of Music series, Megascope series, Bravo series, the History series, the Natural World series, and Literature Made Easy series.

From Barron's: *A Century of Car Design* by Penny Sparke; *Business Banking* by Theodore A. Platz Jr. and Thomas Fitch; *Cooking With the Stars* by Rick Ameil; *All Stitched Up* by Jane Crowfoot; *100 Tactics for Office Politics* by Casey Hawley; *The Art of Styling Sentences* by Ann Longknife PhD,. and K. D. Sullivan; *Oven-Baked Vegetarian Dishes* by Gabriele Redden; *501 French Verbs* by Christopher Kendris; *American History to 1877* by Robert D. Geise, M. Ed.; *Halloween* by Marie-Laure Mantoux and Frederique Crestin-Billet; *American Sign Language The Easy Way* by David Stewart, Ed. D.

Barron's handles its own distribution. Send query letters with SASEs to:

Mark Miele, Managing Editor

Max Reed, Senior Editor

Linda Turner, Senior Editor

BEACON PRESS

25 Beacon Street, Boston, MA 02108

617-742-2110   fax: 617-742- 3097

www.beacon.org

Beacon is primarily a publisher of nonfiction works (along with some fiction). Beacon's areas of publishing interest include contemporary affairs; gender, ethnic, and cultural studies; the life of the mind and spirit; history; science; and the spectrum of global and environmental concerns. The publisher also hosts a short, strong list of titles in literary essays and poetry. The house no longer publishes children's titles. Beacon Press tenders an extensive backlist.

Beacon Press has been a light of independent American publishing since 1854, when the house was established by the Unitarian Universalist Church. The Beacon Press list is presented as a complement to corporate publishing's rapt attention to commercially correct topics and as a publishing platform for those whose search for meaning draws them to fresh points of view. Indeed, the house's estimable reputation thrives on the diversity and divergence of the ideas and stances advanced by Beacon authors.

Beacon titles: *Bread of Three Rivers* by Sara Mansfield Taber; *Breakfast Epiphanies* by

David Anderson; *Choosing Naia* by Mitchell Zuckoff; *Children Who See Too Much* by Betsy McAlister Groves; *The Condemnation of Little B* by Elaine Brown; *Everybody Was Kung Fu Fighting* by Vijay Prashad; *Flying Colors* by Tim Lefens; *Free for All* by Wendy Kaminer; *Gathering Power* by Paul Osterman; *Going Public* by Michael Gecan; *Homefront* by Catherine A. Lutz; *I'll Be Short* by Robert B. Reich; *I Wanna Take Me a Picture* by Wendy Ewald; *Lester Leaps In* by Douglas Henry Daniels; *A Mind of Winter* edited by Robert Atwan; *A Modern Buddhist Bible* by Donald S. Lopez, Jr.; *The Passionate Learner* by Robert L. Fried; *The Place of Tolerance in Islam* by Khaled Abou El Fadl; *The Power of Nonviolence, A Beacon Anthology*; *Proverbs of Ashes* by Rita Nakashima and Rebecca Ann Parker; *Repair* by Elizabeth V. Spelman; *Revers Beach Elergy* by Roland Merullo; *Schools That Do Too Much* by Etta Kralovec; *Sustainable Planet* edited by Juliet Schor and Betsy Taylor; *The Thief of Happiness* by Bonnie Friedman.

Scholarly highlights: Beacon's new editions of *Gnostic Religion* by Hans Jonas; *The Woman in the Body: A Cultural Analysis of Reproduction* by Emily Martin; *The Ethnic Myth* and *Turning Back* by Stephen Steinberg; *Broken Spears: The Aztec Account of the Conquest of Mexico* by Miguel Leon-Portillo.

Writers, please note these Beacon titles that address themes in the writing life: *Ruined by Reading: A Life in Books* by Lynne Sharon Schwartz; *Writing as a Way of Healing: How Telling Our Stories Transforms Our Lives* by Louise DeSalvo; *The Thief of Happiness* by Bonnie Friedman.

Beacon Press is distributed to the trade by Houghton Mifflin. Query letters and SASEs should be directed to:

Helene Atwan, Editorial Director

PETER BEDRICK BOOKS

156 Fifth Avenue, New York, NY 10010

212-206-3738   fax: 212-206-4741

e-mail: bedrick@panix.com

Bedrick's list focuses on popular reference works in history, folklore and mythology, and women's studies; the Bedrick children's list accents highly illustrated nonfiction, including several ongoing series in world history and cultures, and numerous educational titles.

Peter Bedrick Books was established in 1983, following the founder's long and successful association with Schocken Books. Today a midsized publishing house with a fetching swan logo, Bedrick still has a personal touch—evident from the first Bedrick list, which featured adult and children's books and introduced the initial three titles in the Library of the World's Myths and Legends.

Special from Bedrick: *The World of the Pirate* by Valerie Garwood (illustrated by

Richard Berridge); *The World of Native Americans* by Marion Wood (illustrated by Antonella Pastorelli and Federico Michelli); *The Atlas of the Classical World* by Piero Bardi (illustrated by Paola Ravaglia and Matteo Chesi); *The Atlas of World Cultures* by Brunetto Chiarelli and Anna Lisa Bebi (illustrated by Paola Ravaglia); *Slavery: From Africa to the Americas* by Christine Hatt.

The Inside Story series offers titles filled with full-color cutaway illustrations and informative text. Notable entrants here: *The Roman Colosseum* by Fiona Macdonald (illustrated by Mark Bergin); *A Renaissance Town* by Jacqueline Morley (illustrated by Mark Peppe).

First Facts Series titles: *First Facts About the American Frontier* and *First Facts About the Ancient Romans* by Fiona MacDonald; *First Facts About the Ancient Egyptians* and *First Facts About the Vikings* by Jacqueline Morley.

Peter Bedrick Books has been acquired by NTC/Contemporary Publishing. The house does not accept any unsolicited manuscripts. Query letters and SASEs should be directed to:

Peter Bedrick, President and Publisher

MATTHEW BENDER & COMPANY, INC.

744 Broad Street, Newark, NJ 07102

973-820-2000/1-800-833-9844   fax: 518-487-3584

www.bender.com

Matthew Bender & Co, Inc. produces works in the fields of law, accounting, banking, insurance, and related professions. Areas of Bender concentration include general accounting, administrative law, admiralty, bankruptcy, civil rights law, computer law, elder law, employment/labor, environmental, estate and financial planning, federal practice and procedure, government, health care, immigration, insurance, intellectual property, law-office management, personal injury/medico-legal, products liability, real estate, securities, taxation, and worker's compensation.

Bender (founded in 1887), a member of the Reed Elsevier plc group, is a specialist publisher of professional information in print and electronic format. Bender publishes general references as well as state-specific works. Bender produces treatises, textbooks, manuals, and form books, as well as newsletters and periodicals. Many Matthew Bender publications are available in the CD-ROM format (Authority CD-ROM libraries make available the most comprehensive and accurate information for the practice of law) on the Internet and on LexisNexis.

Bender has served professionals for more than 100 years and has achieved its unique status as a specialty publisher in diverse areas of the law. Bender combines in-house editorial talent and publishing ties with the foremost experts in the legal profession to produce a product that will fit its customers' needs. Practicing attorneys often serve as contributing legal writers in their areas of expertise. Matthew Bender is one of the world's leading publishers of legal analysis and case law and pours this experience and expertise into more than 500 publications in print and electronic formats and serves professionals in more than 160 countries.

Bender considers itself an essential partner with law professionals, providing integrated information, resources, and tools, and delivering that information in formats that help its customers reach solutions with confidence.

Representative titles from Bender: *Attorney's Dictionary of Patent Claims* by Irwin M. Aisenberg; *Chisum on Patents* by Donald S. Chisum; *Copyright Law, Fifth Edition, 2000* by Craig Joyce, William Patry and Peter Jaszi; *ADA Compliance Manual for Employers, Second Edition* by Maurenn F. Moore; *Americans with Disabilities Act: Employee Rights and Employer Obligations* by Jonathan R. Mook, Esq. ; *California Employer's Compliance Review, Second Edition* by Lee T. Paterson; *Drafting Employment & Termination Agreements* by Laurie E. Leader; *Employment Screening* by Lex K. Larson; *International Employment Law* by Dennis Campbell, Center for International Legal Studies, General Editor; *Labor Law* by The Publisher's Editorial Staff; *Asset Based Financing: A Transitional Guide* by Howard Ruda; *Bank Holding Company Compliance Manual* by Joseph G. Beckford.

Bender handles its own distribution. Query letters and SASEs should be directed to:

The Editorial Department

BERRETT-KOEHLER PUBLISHERS

235 Montgomery Street, Suite 650, San Francisco, CA 94104-2916

415-288-0260   fax: 425-362-2512

www.bkconnection.com   e-mail: bkpub@bkpub.com

Berrett-Koehler's nonfiction program accents the areas of work and the workplace, business, management, leadership, career development, entrepreneurship, human resources, and global sustainability. Instituted in 1992, Berrett-Koehler is an independent press that produces books, periodicals, journals, newsletters, and audiocassettes.

The Berrett-Koehler booklist is produced in well-crafted, ecologically aware hardcover and paperback editions.

Berrett-Koehler stands for a commitment to produce publications that support the movement toward a more enlightened world of work and more free, open, humane, effective, and globally sustainable organizations. The house is committed to do publications that challenge conventional views of work and management, that create new lenses for understanding organizations, that pioneer new purposes and values in business, and that open up new sources of guidance for today's complex work world.

Berrett-Koehler's focus is to make each book it publishes successful. This seems natural, yet goes against the prevailing "numbers game" model in conglomerate publishing—put out large numbers of titles and see which ones succeed with little support from the publisher. Unfortunately, most conglomerates' titles do not succeed and have only a short shelf life before they go out of print. Berrett-Koehler is committed to keeping books in print far longer than the big publishers' norm, and, in fact, none of the titles from its first five years have gone out of print. The key to making each book successful and keeping books in print is Berrett-Koehler's marketing through multiple channels in addition to bookstores (such as direct mail, corporate sales, and association sales). This not only supports bookstore sales, but also provides an ongoing life for books when their bookstore shelf life is past.

Titles: *Accountability* by Rob Lebow and Randy Spitzer; *Be a Sales Superstar* by Brian Tracy; *Big Vision, Small Business* by Jamie S. Walters; *Change Is Everyone's Business* by Pat McLagan; *Creating Leaderful Organizations* by Joseph A. Raelin; *Dreamcrafting* by Paul Levesque and Art McNeil; *How to Make Collaboration Work* by David Straus; *Responsible Restructuring* by Wayne F. Cascio; *The 4-Dimensional Manager* by Julie Straw; *The Book of Agreement* by Stewart Levine; *The Inclusion Breakthrough* by Frederick A. Miller; *The Quest for Authentic Power* by G. Ross Lawford; *The Success Case Method* by Robert O. Brinkerhoff; *Why Decisions Fail* by Paul C. Nutt.

Bestselling titles from Berrett-Koehler include: *Get Paid More and Promoted Faster* by Brian Tracy; *The 3 Keys to Empowerment* by Ken Blanchard, John P. Carlos, Alan Randolph; *Fun Works* by Leslie Yerkes; *Downshifting* by John D. Drake; *Hands-On-Training* by Gary R. Sisson; *Abolishing Performances Appraisals* by Tom Coens and Mary Jenkins.

Berrett-Koehler tends its own multichanneled distribution, through bookstores, direct-mail brochures, catalogs, a toll-free telephone-order number, book clubs, association book services, e-books, and special sales to business, government, and nonprofit organizations; the house is distributed to the trade via Publishers Group West. Query letters and SASEs should be directed to:

Jeevan Sivasubramaniam, Managing Editor

Steven Piersanti, Publisher

BLOOMBERG PRESS

100 Business Park Drive, PO Box 888, Princeton, NJ 08542-0888

609-279-7049/1-800-388-2749   fax: 917-369-8288

www.bloomberg.com/books   e-mail: press@bloomberg.com

Bloomberg publishes books in finance, personal finance, business, economics, management, investments, financial planning, and related categories. House imprints and specialty lines include Bloomberg Professional Library (primarily for financial professionals), Bloomberg Personal Bookshelf (consumer-oriented personal finance and investing titles), and books on small businesses and entrepreneurship.

Bloomberg Press (founded in 1996) is part of Bloomberg L.P., a global, multimedia-based information service that combines news, data, and analysis for financial markets and businesses. The parent company runs a real-time financial-information network, as well as a number of news-service operations (supplying news and stories to, among other clients, reporters, editors, and news bureaus), and radio, Web, and television enterprises (Bloomberg Radio, Bloomberg.com, Bloomberg Television).

The goal at Bloomberg Press has been to cut through the technical static of the markets and provide a clear picture. Bloomberg Press books pack a lot of practical information. They are designed to be functional as well as factual, organized to take the reader's busy schedule into account. Authors are prominent authorities and financial journalists. Bloomberg publishes books for brokers, traders, portfolio managers, analysts, money managers, CEOs, CFOs, bankers, and other professionals, as well as for small-business people, consultants, and sophisticated investors worldwide. Subject areas include investment intelligence, portfolio management, markets, financial analytics, and economic analysis of use to traders and other financial professionals.

Representative titles: *New Thinking in Technical Analysis* by Rick Bensignor; *Tales from the Boom-Boom Room* by Susan Antilla; *Getting Started as a Financial Planner* by Jeffery H. Rattier; *Deena Katz on Practice Management* by Deena B. Katz; *The New Yorker Book of Golf Cartoons* edited by Robert Mankoff; *201 Great Ideas for Your Small Business* by Jane Applegate; *Zero Gravity 2.0* by Steve Harmon; *Profit in the Futures Markets!* by Arthur H. Rosenbloom.

Categories for consumers include investing; managing personal wealth; choosing products and services, including insurance, health care, banking services, and real estate; personal-finance reference, education, use of personal computers for investment decisions, and online information; and other topics, from a personal-finance angle such as credit, taxes, and estate planning.

Titles include: *Investing in Small-Cap Stocks* by Christopher Graja and Elizabeth Ungar, PhD; *Investing 101* by Kathy Kristof; *In Defense of Free Capital Markets* by David F. DeRosa; *The Pied Pipers of Wall Street* by Benjamin Cole.

Bloomberg markets its products and services internationally through a variety of creative outlets, including traditional print venues as well as electronic distribution. Bloomberg Press is distributed by W. W. Norton & Company.

Query letters and SASEs should be directed to:

Jared Kieling, Editorial Director

Tracy Tait, Associate Editor

Kathleen Peterson, Senior Acquisitions Editor

BLUE MOON BOOKS

(A Subsidiary of the Avalon Publishing Group)

161 William Street, 16th floor, New York, NY 10038

646-325-2570

www.avalonpub.com

Blue Moon's website contains a complete listing of available books and cover art. Blue Moon's erotica includes some of the finest novels and stories in the field. Blue Moon Books also publishes selected trade fiction and nonfiction. Blue Moon Books was established in 1987 by Barney Rosset, the trailblazing publisher who earlier founded Grove Press and developed that enterprise into a house of international literary, cultural, and commercial renown.

Blue Moon titles: *66 Chapters about 33 Women* by Michael Hemmingson; *Amanda* by Timothy Taylor; *Aphrodizza* by Richard Manton; *Arabella* by James Holmes; *Birch Fever* by Martin Pyx; *Blind Lust* by Maurice Gautier; *Blue Angel Confessions* by Margarete von Falkensee; *Blue Butterfly* by Don Winslow; *Burn* by Michael Perkins; *Captive's Journey* by Richard Manton; *Captured* by Anonymous; *Dancing Fawns* by Patrick Henden; *Dark Games* by Michael Perkins; *Degenerates* by Ray Gordon; *Departure of the Golden Cross* by Olga Tegora; *Dorothea* by Patrick Henden; *Drama* by Michael Hemmingson; *Dream Boat* by Richard Manton; *Five Men* by Tiffany Boots; *Flesh on Fire* by Lloyd Darden; *Gabriela and the General* by Daniel Vian; *Girl School* by Ray Gordon; *Green Girls* by Olga Tegora; *Hard Drive* by Stanley Carten.

In addition to fervid classical romances, Blue Moon offers erotic works with such contemporary themes as psychosexual suspense; the house offers a significant listing of erotic fiction by women.

Blue Moon Books oversees its own distribution. The house no longer accepts unsolicited submissions. All work must be submitted by literary agents.

MARION BOYARS PUBLISHING

U.K. Office:

Marion Boyars Publishing,

24 Lacy Road, London SW15 INL, England, U.K.

www.marionboyars.co.uk   e-mail: marion.boyars@talk21.com

Note: Marion Boyars's New York office at 237 East 39th Street, New York, NY 10016, is for publicity only. All editorial is handled in the U.K.

Founded in 1978, The Marion Boyars publishing program gives preeminence to fine writing and is open to considering the highest level of expression in virtually any category. Areas of particular accomplishment are in the fields of fiction, belles lettres, memoirs, literary criticism, biography, music, theater, sociology, and travel. Marion Boyars Publishing has achieved international renown and commercial presence in letters with an individualist precision and personalized disposition. Marion Boyars releases a moderate-sized seasonal list; the house tends a strong backlist. Though not technically a United States publishing house (projects emanate editorially from the London base), Boyars presents writers whose works may have more of an international appeal than a strictly commercial-American flavor. The publisher acquires on the basis of enthusiasm for a given work—and this is not necessarily based on projections of huge initial sales. Indeed, Marion Boyars herself has remarked that overlooked books and translations are often the house's jewels.

Representative of fiction titles: *The Eskimo in the Net* by Gerard Beirne; *The Ghost in the Eiffel Tower* by Oliver Bleys; *Fox Girl* by Nora Okja Keller; *The Demon* by Hubert Selby Jr; *L.I.E.* by David Hollander. Nonfiction: *The Art of the Siesta* by Thierry Paquot; *Belly Dancer* by Tina Hobin; *Memoirs of a Beatnik* by Diane Di Prima; *Women Travel Writers Diary 2003* edited by Ken Hollings and Julia Silk.

Marion Boyars Publishing is distributed by Consortium Saint Paul, MN. Query letters and SASEs should be directed to:

Cathy Kilgarriff, President, Editor-in-Chief—Fiction submissions are accepted through literary agents only

Julia Silk, Fiction Editor

Ken Hollings, Nonfiction and Chief Editor

BOYDS MILLS PRESS

(A Subsidiary of Highlights for Children)

815 Church Street, Honesdale, PA 18431

570-253-1164/1-800-490-5111

www.boydsmillspress.com   e-mail: Admin@boydsmillspress.com

Boyds Mills produces books for children, picture books, novels, nonfiction, and poetry—nonsensical verse, as well as more serious fare. The press promotes a solid seasonal list of new titles and hosts a hefty backlist. Boyds Mills Press (founded in 1990) is a subsidiary of Highlights for Children, Inc.

Boyds Mills wants books that challenge, inspire, and entertain young people the world over. Boyds Mills has published such international bestsellers as *Dougal Dixon's Dinosaurs* (over a dozen editions in 10 languages, plus multivolume spinoffs).

Boyds Mills releases: *On the Trail of Lewis and Clark: A Journey Up the Missouri River* by Peter Lourie; *Some Folks Like Cats: and Other Poems* by Ivy O. Eastwick, illustrated by Mary Kurnick Maass; *Black-eyed Suzie* by Susan Shaw; *Ali and the Magic Stew* by Shulamith Levey Oppenheim; *Jemma's Journey* by Trevor Romain; *Travel Puzzles & Games* by Jeffrey A. O'Hare; *Rivers: Nature's Wondrous Waterways* by David L. Harrison; *Wild Wings: Poems for Young People* by Jane Yolen; *Craft, Puzzle, & Activity Books* by the editors of *Highlights for Children*; *At the Mouth of the Luckiest River* by Arnold Griese; *Bats! Strange and Wonderful*; *Am I Naturally This Crazy?* by Sara Holbrook; *Bicycle Riding: and Other Poems* by Sandra Olson Liatsos.

Among featured Boyds Mills authors is Jane Yolen, award-winning author of more than 170 books. A sampling of her titles includes: *All in the Woodland Early: An ABC Book*; *Before the Storm*; *How Beastly! A Menagerie of Nonsense Poems*; *An Invitation to the Butterfly Ball: A Counting Rhyme*; *Jane Yolen's Mother Goose Songbook*; *Weather Report: A Book of Poems*; *Street Rhymes Around the World*; *Once Upon Ice*; *Water Music*; *Color Me a Rhyme*.

Boyds Mills Press handles its own distribution. Query letters and SASEs should be directed to:

Kent L. Brown, Jr., Publisher

Clay Winters, President

Larry Rosler, Editorial Director

Jan Cheripko, Assistant to the Publisher

Shirley Brinkerhoff, Publishing Assistant

BRASSEY'S INC.

22841 Quicksilver Drive, Dulles, VA 20166

703-661-1548   fax: 703-661-1547

www.brasseysinc.com

Brassey's Inc. is a leading publisher in history (especially military history), biography, defense, national and international affairs, foreign policy, military reference, and intelligence. The Brassey's Sports imprint publishes trade titles related to various sports topics.

Brassey's titles include: *Madness, Malingering, and Malfeasance* by R. Gregory Lande; *Hockey's Most Wanted* by Floyd Conner; *Pro Basketball Prospectus* by John Hollinger; *Espionage's Most Wanted* by Tom E. Mahl; *Gettysburg* by Richard A. Sauers; *Dominance* by Eddie Epstein; *Nerve Center* by Michael K. Bohn; *String Music* by Chris Dortch; *Flying Through Time* by Jim Doyle; *The First Reich* by David Stone; *Afghan Wars* by Edgar O'balance; *Images of Kursk* by Nikolas Cornish; *The Masters* by David Sowell; *Snake*

Pilot by Randy R. Zahn; *Pro Football Prospectus 2002* by Sean Lahman and Todd Greanier; *War of the Flea* by Robert Taber; *TV's Most Wanted* by Robert M. Browning, Jr.; *Baseball Prospectus: 2002 Edition* by Joseph Sheehan et al.; *Tennis Confidential: Today's Greatest Players, Matches, and Controversies* by Paul Fein; *Playing Hurt: Evaluating and Treating the Warriors of the NFL* by Pierce E. Scranton, Jr., MD; *Blue Ribbon College Football Yearbook: 2002 Edition* edited by Chris Dortch; *Basketball's Most Wanted: The Top 10 Books of Hoops' Outrageous Dunders, Incredible Buzzer-Beaters, and Other Oddities* by Floyd Connor.

Query letter with SASE should be directed to:

Donald Jacobs, Senior Assistant Editor

Don McKeon, Vice President and Publisher
Born: April 15, 1952.
Education: B.A., English, College of Holy Cross.

Employment history/editor career path: My editorial career path had several detours, but the route was basically as follows: bookstore Clerk, Proofreader and Copy Editor, Managing Editor of a monthly defense and foreign affairs magazine, and then Publishing Manager of what was then Pergamon-Brassey's International Defense Publishers, Inc. I have been with Brassey's for 14 years.

Personal interests: Reading (of course), volleyball, and motorcycling.

What would you be doing if you were not an editor? I'd possibly be working in international development. I served in the Peace Corps in West Africa after college.

What has been your most successful book that you have acquired to date? *Baseball Prospectus* by Chris Kahrl et al., a highly praised and entertaining annual analysis of baseball statistics, from the major league level down to the lowest minor leagues. Sales have improved each year, and now we're developing a *Football Prospectus* and a *Hockey Prospectus*.

What books have you acquired that make you the most proud? What books that you have acquired reflect the types of books you like to represent? I'm most proud of our books that make a real contribution to the literature, such as *Dien Bien Phu: The Epic Battle America Forgot* by Howard R. Simpson and *One War at a Time: The International Dimensions of the American Civil War* by Dean B. Mahin. Other books that reflect the types of books I like to represent include *Baseball Prospectus* by Chris Kahrl et al.; *Military Geography* by John M. Collins; *A Mind in Prison: The Memoir of a Son and Soldier of the Third Reich* by Bruno Manz; *A Chain of Events: The Government Cover-Up of the Black Hawk Incident and the Friendly-Fire Death of Lt. Laura Piper* by Joan L. Piper; *The Outpost War: The U.S. Marine Corps in Korea, 1952* by Lee Ballenger. I should add that I am now seeking more titles that can be used in courses at the military academies, in ROTC units, and at the military postgraduate schools.

Do you represent fiction? Brassey's no longer publishes fiction.

What do you want to see less of? Since we no longer publish fiction, I'd naturally like to see no more proposals for novels. Also, with all due respect to veterans, I'd like to see fewer proposals for unremarkable wartime memoirs. They must be unique and well written.

Do you represent nonfiction? Brassey's publishes nonfiction in the following areas: history (especially military history), world and national affairs, foreign policy, defense, intelligence, and biography. In addition, Brassey's is now developing books about transportation (especially automobiles) and about the personalities and events of national and international athletic competition.

Do you require book proposals? If so, what do you look for in evaluating a book proposal? We do require book proposals. We ask for a one-page synopsis, a table of contents or outline, 1–2 sample chapters, authors' thoughts on the book's market and competition, their qualifications, and photocopies of any sample photos. In evaluating proposals, besides deciding whether the topic itself interests us, we look for clarity and organization and for relevance in the author's credentials.

Are certain aspects of a book proposal given more weight than others? A proposal by an author with a strong publishing record will certainly get our attention.

What process do you use for making a decision? What is the process for acquisition, is there a committee? The first hurdle, I reject perhaps 95 percent of submissions out of hand. The rest are discussed at an editorial meeting, where the decision is made whether to have the proposal or manuscript read by outside experts. We regularly consult an informal network of authorities in our publishing areas.

Are you interested in work geared for the masses (readers of *People, The Star,* etc.)? We are interested to some degree in work geared to the masses, but only if it's somehow related to our core list. For example, this year we're publishing an account by a mother whose daughter, an Air Force officer, was killed in a friendly-fire incident and who fought government bureaucracies for years for accountability. Stories such as this have broad general appeal.

Are agents important? Why? Agents are important to publishers because they presumably don't waste their time on projects of little value, and the better agents know what kind of projects will be of interest to specific publishers.

Do you like new writers? What should new writers do to break into the business? We've had a lot of success with first-time authors, although it's usually easier to work with an author who already knows the game. I'm not sure what to suggest to new authors who want to break into the business except that perhaps they should find a new angle on a topic of broad interest and be able to summarize their project in 25 words or less.

How should writers approach you? By mail or e-mail, although we do not open unsolicited attached files. Please note that our new address is 22841 Quicksilver Drive, Dulles, VA 20166. I can be reached by e-mail at Don@BooksIntl.com.

What are some common mistakes writers make? What really gets on your nerves? Perhaps the biggest mistake I see is some authors' compulsion to use all the information dredged up during the book's research. They just cannot bring themselves to throw anything away. Authors should continually ask themselves how important each fact is to their thesis. What does it add? As to what really gets on my nerves, I'd have to say authors who don't make deadlines, who are disorganized, and who don't fact-check their own work.

What can writers do to get your attention and to avoid the slush pile? Potential authors could provide me with their proposal in a brief, clear, concise cover letter that tells me what the book is about, why it would be important, why it would sell, and why they are the proper person to write it.

What have been some of your craziest experiences with submissions? I can't think offhand of any particular example of a crazy submission experience, but we do occasionally receive those kinds of proposals on which every marginless page is completely filled with tiny handwriting and contains references to an extremely personal relationship with God.

What have been some of your best experiences with writers or in your job? My best publishing experiences have been with authors of memoirs—people who have led exemplary, sometimes courageous lives—some of whom I now consider friends.

What, if anything, makes you different from other editors? Although I've never been an author, I believe I have the ability to look at the publishing process from the author's perspective and can empathize with that individual. I wouldn't be doing my job if I always agreed with the authors, of course, but I'm patient, and many authors have said they enjoy working with me. Brassey's prides itself on its repeat authors.

Is there anything you would like to see changed in the industry? I wouldn't mind if the industry were more lucrative at the lower editorial and production levels so that it attracted and retained more bright young people.

Any advice for writers? Any way to change the system for you? Any additional thoughts? I would advise authors to remember who their main audience is and to write for that group, but also to try to get feedback from people who would not normally read their kind of book. Different perspectives can be valuable.

GEORGE BRAZILLER, INC.

171 Madison Avenue, New York, NY 10016

212-889-0909

George Braziller accents fine editions in art and design, architecture, and art movements and history. The house also publishes selected literary titles, as well as philosophy, science, history, criticism, and biographical works. The house hosts a solid backlist.

George Braziller, Inc. (founded in 1955), is perhaps most widely known for original fine books in the fields of art and architecture. Much of Braziller's fiction and poetry is foreign literature in translation, although the publisher does publish original literary novels (such as works by Janet Frame) and works in the English language that have received initial publication elsewhere.

Braziller also has a strong interest in literary criticism and writing relating to the arts, in addition to a small selection of contemporary and modern poetry. Essential Readings in Black Literature is a Braziller series that features world-class writers from around the globe. Other Braziller series include Library of Far Eastern Art and New Directions in Architecture.

From Braziller: *Impressionism: Reflections and Perceptions* by Meyer Schapiro; *Painted Prayers: The Book of Hours in Medieval and Renaissance Art* by Roger S. Wieck; *Picturing Hong Kong: Photography 1855—1910* by Roberta Wue, Edwin K. Lai, and Joanna Waley-Cohen; *The Gallery of Maps in the Vatican* by Lucio Gambi (translated by Francoise Pouncey Chiarini); *Georgia O'Keeffe: A Celebration of Music and Dance* by Katherine Hoffman; *Dreamings: The Art of Aboriginal Australia* (edited by Peter Sutton).

Great Frescoes of the Italian Renaissance series (10 volumes of the world's major fresco cycles from the early 14th–17th centuries): *Giotto: The Schrovegnia Chapel, Padua* by Bruce Cole; *The Brancacci Chapel, Florence* by Andrew Ladis; *Raphael: The Stanza Della Segnatura, Rome* by James Beck; *Ambrogio Lorenzetti: The Palazzo Pubblico, Siena* by Randolph Starn; *Andrea Mantegna: Padua and Mantua* by Keith Christiansen; *Piero Della Francesca: San Francesco, Arezzo* by Marilyn Aronberg Lavin; *Annibale Carracci: The Farnese Gallery, Rome* by Charles Dempsey; *Fra Angelico: San Marco, Florence* by William Hood; *Luca Signorelli: The San Brizio Chapel, Orvieto* by Jonathan B. Riess; *Michelangelo: The Sistine Chapel Ceiling, Rome* by Loren Partridge.

Braziller titles are distributed by W. W. Norton & Co. Query letters and SASEs should be directed to:

George Braziller, Publisher

BURNHAM PUBLISHERS

111 North Canal Street, Suite 955, Chicago, IL 60606

312-930-9446

Burnham (formerly Nelson-Hall) publishes college textbooks in political science, sociology, and mass communications.

Samples of recent Burnham titles include: *Living Off Crime* by Ken Tunnell; *Three Black Generations at the Crossroads* by Lois Benjamin; *Cities in the Third Wave* by Leonard Ruchelman; *History of Nazi Germany* by Joseph Bendersky. Virtually all of our authors are college professors at various institutions around the nation.

Burnham handles its own distribution and welcomes manuscript submissions (please write directly to Burnham for proposal guidelines). Query letters and SASEs should be directed to:

Richard Meade, General Manager

CAREER PRESS

NEW PAGE BOOKS

3 Tice Road, PO Box 687, Franklin Lakes, NJ 07417

201-848-0310/1-800-227-3371   fax: 201-848-1727

www.careerpress.com and www.newpagebooks.com

Career Press is established as a hard-driving, entrepreneurial publisher of essential career, business, reference, and personal finance titles. The still-independent company celebrated its 15th anniversary in March 2000. The year 2000 also saw a new Career Press imprint called New Page Books, which features general nonfiction books centered in these categories: weddings, Judaica, New Age, self-help, and health.

Between the two imprints, Career Press published 65 titles in 2000. There is an active backlist of more than 200 strong-selling and well-promoted titles. The publisher promotes aggressively and resourcefully and stocks booksellers with titles geared to receive major nationwide publicity.

Career Press highlights: *The Know-it-all's Guide to Life* by John T. Walbaum; *Superstar Sales Secrets* by Barry J. Farber; *6 Steps to Free Publicity* by Marcia Yudkin; *Brain Storm* by Jason R. Rich; *Executive Job Search Handbook* by Robert F. Wilson; *101 Smart Questions to Ask on Your Interview* by Ron Fry; *How to Protect and Manage Your 401 (k)* by Elizabeth Opalka, CPA, Esq.; *PowerSpeak* by Dorothy Leeds; *Positive Cash Flow* by Robert A. Cooke; *Top Telemarketing Techniques* by Ellen Bendremer; *Stress-free Performance Appraisals* by Sharon Armstrong and Madelyn Applebaum; *Reinvent Your Career* by Susan Wilson Solovic; *Superstar Sales Manager's Secret* by Barry Farber; *Master Math: Solving Word Problems* by Brita Immergut; *Your MBA Game Plan* by Omari Bouknight and Scott Shrum; *Better Grammar in 30 Minutes a Day* by Constance Immel and Florence Sacks; *Better Sentence Writing in 30 Minutes a Day* by Dianna Campbell; *Better Vocabulary in 30 Minutes a Day* by Edie Schwager; *Hiring* by Richard S. Deems, PhD; *Phone Power* by Doc Morey; *The Power of Innovative Thinking* by Jim Wheeler; *Motivation and Goal Setting* by Jim Cairo; *Motivational Minutes* by Don Essig.

New Page highlights: *Crop Circles: Signs of Contact* by Colin Andrews; *Soul Sex* by Pala Copeland and Al Link; *Mastering Candle Magick* by Patricia Telesco; *Exploring Numerology* by Shirley Lawrence, Msc.D.; *Earth Magic* by Marion Weinstein; *Maiden Magick* by C.C. Brondwin; *Secrets of the Amazon Shamans* by Michael Peter Langevin; *Exploring Chakras* by Susan G. Shumsky; *Hans Holzer's The Supernatural* by Hans Holzer; *Pain Relief for Life* by Al Skrobisch, C.N.M.T.; *Star Power* by Rob MacGregor and Megan MacGregor; *Pagans and the Law* by Dana D. Eilers; *OsteoPilates* by Karena Lineback; *We Are All in Shock* by Stephanie Mine, PhD; *The Natural Woman's Guide to Hormone Replacement Therapy* by M. Sara Rosenthal, PhD; *Dunwich's Guide to Gemstone Sorcery* by Gerina Dunwich.

Go to careerpress.com for complete information. Career Press distributes its own list. Query letters and SASEs should be directed to:

Ronald Fry, President

Michael Lewis, Acquisitions Editor

Stacey Franks, Editorial Director

CAROL PUBLISHING GROUP

This large and respected independent house went bankrupt and permanently shut its doors in late 1999. It is missed.

CARROLL & GRAF PUBLISHERS, INC.

245 West 17th Street, New York, NY 10011

646-375-2570   fax: 646-375-2571

www.carrollandgraf.com

Carroll & Graf publishes commercial trade nonfiction and literary and commercial fiction (including a strong list in mystery and suspense). Carroll & Graf (founded in 1983) is a compact house with a catalog as select and well targeted as it is diverse. In addition to its original titles, Carroll & Graf reprints American classics and genre works, along with foreign literature in translation. The house issues a full raft of genre-specific anthologies. Carroll & Graf produces hardcover, trade paper, and mass-market paperback editions.

Carroll & Graf nonfiction emphasizes contemporary culture, current events, and issue-oriented perspectives (including investigative accounts, political and historical works, and top-end true crime); business, finance, and economics; self-improvement; humor and games; and high-interest topical reference.

In fiction and the literary arts, Carroll & Graf produces mainstream novels; tales of the supernatural, fantasy, and science fiction and is particularly adventuresome in suspense categories, publishing an array of titles that runs from traditional mysteries to future-horror crime thrillers with a literary bent.

Titles from Carroll & Graf: *According to Queeney* by Beryl Bainbridge; *Across the Bridge* by Gallant; *After the First Death* by Lawrence Block; *Air Burial: A Novel* by Jean Shields; *Babylon Revisited: The Screenplay* by Fitzgerald; *Bad Dreams* by Kim Newman; *Beats: A Literary Reference* by Matt Theado; *Beyond the Grave* by Muller & Pronzini;

Birthday Boys by Beryl Bainbridge; *Bride of Newgate* by John Carr; *Brief History of British Kings and Queens* by Mike Ashley; *Brief History of Fighting Ships* by David Davis; *Brief History of the Druids* by Peter Ellis; *Bunuel* by Stephen Baxter; *Burnt Orange Heresy* by Charles Willeford; *Buyer Beware* by John Lutz; *Byrne* by Anthony Burgess; *Café on the Nile* by Bartle Bill; *Cannibal Who Overate* by Penecost; *Cardinal Richelieu: And the Making of France* by Anthony Levi; *Cheerfulness Breaks In* by Angela Thirkell; *Choosing Joy* by Gary Noll; *Christmas Pudding* by Nancy Mitford; *Close to the Wind* by Pete Goss; *Coffin for Dimitrios* by Eric Ambler; *Cogan's Trade* by George V. Higgins; *Compendium of Skirts: Fiction* by Phyllis Moore; *Complete History of Jack the Ripper* by Philip Sugden; *Compulsion* by Levin; *Coward's Kiss* by Lawrence Block.

Mammoth Books is a line from Carroll & Graf that accents quantity as well as quality: The Mammoth list includes literary anthologies, works of topical appeal, and specialist interests. Titles here: *The Mammoth Book of New Sherlock Holmes Adventures* edited by Mike Ashley; *The Mammoth Book of the Third Reich at War* edited by Michael Veranov; *The Mammoth Book of Chess* by Graham Burgess; *The Mammoth Book of Carnival Puzzles* by David J. Bodycombe; *The Mammoth Book of Fortune Telling* by Celestine.

Carroll & Graf books is now completely owned by its distributor, Publishers Group West.

Carroll & Graf no longer accepts unsolicited submissions. The house only accepts agented submissions. Query letters and SASEs should be directed to:

Philip Turner, Editor

CATBIRD PRESS

16 Windsor Road, North Haven, CT 06473

203-230-2391

Catbird Press is no longer accepting submissions of any kind.

CCC PUBLICATIONS

9725 Lurline Avenue, Chatsworth, CA 91311

818-718-0507   fax: 818-718-0655

www.whyleavethehouse.com

Founded in 1983, CCC Publications accents nonfiction trade books in crisply targeted categories: relationships, self-help/how-to, humor, inspiration, humorous inspirational titles, age-related and over-the-hill titles, games and puzzles, party books, cartoon books, gift books and merchandise, gag and blank books—and a group of titles mischievously cataloged as On the Edge. CCC publishes a number of books by best-selling author Jan King.

CCC produces primarily trade paperbacks, smaller gift-size editions, accessories (such as bags and bookmarks), and a line of audio works (including collections of answering-machine messages and sound effects).

In addition to books, CCC Publications also has a sidelines division: CCC Novel Tease Apparel Co. is one of the largest producers of embroidered occasion merchandise. Our themes include Bridal, New Parent, Baby, Age-Related, Anniversary, Over-the-Hill, Maternity, Graduation & Prom, and novelty items. Our fiber-optic design division is producing light-up caps and jackets for numerous major accounts.

On the CCC list: *Golfaholics* by Bob Zahn; *So, You're Getting Married* by Fred Sahner (illustrated by Lennie Peterson); *The Last Diet Book: You'll Ever Need!* by Dr. David Fisch; *Why God Makes Bald Guys* by Lennie Peterson; *Are We Dysfunctional Yet?* by Randy Glasbergen; *You Know He's a Two-Timing, Egomaniacal, Womanizing, Slimeball When . . .* by Jon Michaels; *Technology Bytes!* by Randy Glasbergen; *Love Dat Cat: 150 Wonderful Things You Can Do for Your Cat* by Jill Kramer; *How to Survive a Jewish Mother: A Guilt-Ridden Guide* by Steven Arnold; *Red-Hot Monogamy in Just 60 Seconds a Day* by Patrick T. Hunt, MD; *50 Ways to Hustle Your Friends* by Jim Karol.

From On the Edge: *Men Are Pigs, Women Are Bitches* by Jerry King; *The Definitive Fart Book* by Desmond Mullan; *The Very Very Sexy Adult Dot-to-Dot Book* by Tony Goffe; *The Complete Wimp's Guide to Sex* by Jed Pascoe.

Jan King books: *Over the Hill . . . Deal with It!*; *Ladies, Start Your Engines: The Secrets for Restoring Romance, Passion and Great Sex in Your Relationship*; *Why Men Don't Have a Clue*; *Hormones from Hell*; *Killer Bras (and Other Hazards of the 50s)*.

CCC orchestrates its own distribution. Query letters and SASEs should be directed to:

Cliff Carle, Editorial Director

Mark Chutick, Publisher

CHAPMAN AND HALL

Wolters-Kluwer Academic Publishers has purchased Chapman and Hall. The Chapman and Hall office has been closed.

CHAPTERS PUBLISHING

222 Berkeley Street, Boston, MA 02116

617-351-3855

Chapters specializes in books on cooking and nutrition, health and fitness, gardening, nature, country living, and home and family (including a series of weekend-projects books). The house offers a line of calendars with themes linked to its overall publishing interests. Chapters productions are recognized for their excellent book design and feature top-quality paper and binding.

Chapters Publishing (founded in 1991) publishes a select number of new titles each season and tends toward larger print runs; many Chapters titles enjoy sales through established book clubs. Chapters' evolution as a small commercial press has been markedly winning; and writers might note that the publisher's advances are generally comparable with those expected of large houses.

On the Chapters list: *The Joy of Coffee: The Essential Guide to Buying, Brewing and Enjoying* by Corby Kummer; *The New Games Treasury: More Than 500 Indoor and Outdoor Favorites with Strategies, Rules and Traditions* by Merilyn Dimonds Mohr; *The Complete Italian Vegetarian Cookbook: 350 Essential Recipes for Inspired, Everyday Eating* by Jack Bishop; *Mission Furniture You Can Build: Authentic Techniques and Designs for the Home Woodworker* by John Wagner; *Passing Strange: True Tales of New England Hauntings and Horrors* by Joseph A. Citro; *Eating Thin for Life: Food Secrets and Recipes from People Who Have Lost Weight and Kept It Off* by Anne M. Fletcher, M.S., R.D.; *Just the Weigh You Are: How to Be Fit and Healthy, Whatever Your Size* by Steven Jonas, MD, and Linda Konner; *Tender Roses for Tough Climates* by Douglas Green; *Hummingbird Gardens: Attracting Nature's Jewels to Your Backyard* by Nancy L. Newfield and Barbara Nielsen; *Orchid Simplified: An Indoor Gardening Guide* by Henry Jaworski.

Among Chapters series: Simply Healthful Cookbooks (recipes for tasty, healthful dishes without a lot of fuss and bother); How to Spot...(books written by professional naturalists that give a thorough description of a specific animal's habitat, range, diet, and breeding habits to increase amateur naturalists' enjoyment of animal watching).

The Curious Naturalist Series promotes works (in handsome trade paperback editions) from some of North America's finest naturalist writers, such as Peter Mathiessen, R. D. Lawrence, Adrian Forsyth, and Sy Montgomery. Titles here include: *A Natural History of Sex: The Ecology and Evolution of Mating Behavior* by Adrian Forsyth; *Birds of Tropical America* by Steven J. Hilty; *Nature's Everyday Mysteries: A Field Guide to the World in Your Backyard* by Sy Montgomery; *Shark! Nature's Masterpiece* by R. D. Lawrence; *The Wind Birds: Shorebirds of North America* by Peter Mathiessen.

Chapters Publishing is now part of Houghton Mifflin Company. Query letters and SASEs should be directed to:

Lori Galvin-Frost, Assistant Managing Editor—Cookbooks

CHELSEA GREEN PUBLISHING COMPANY

PO Box 428, Gates-Briggs Building # 205, White River Junction, VT 05001

802-639-4099   fax: 802-295-6444

www.chelseagreen.com   e-mail: info@chelseagreen.com

Chelsea Green publishes trade nonfiction in natural gardening and food, energy and shelter, nature and the environment, and regional books (including travel, social issues, history, and culture). Chelsea Green projects include a publishing co-venture with Real Goods Trading Company, designated by the imprimatur Real Goods Independent Living Book.

Chelsea Green Publishing Company (founded in 1984) is a compact, independent firm of individualistic spirit; the house continues to hone its publishing program through a small number of new seasonal releases (in hardcover and trade paper formats) and a hardy backlist. Chelsea Green's goal is to improve the visibility of sustainability by showing that even a small, home-based business can be instrumental in bringing about social change on a global scale.

On the Chelsea Green list: *The Grape Grower: A Guide to Organic Viticulture* by Lon Rombough; *The Solar House: Passive Heating and Cooling* by Dan Chiras; *Elder House: Planning Your Best Home Ever* by Adelaide Altman; *Extreme Simplicity: Homesteading in the City* by Christopher and Dolores Nyerges; *The Organic Life: Confessions of a Suburban Homesteader* by Joan Dye Gussow; *Low-Impact Forestry: Forestry as if the Future Mattered* by Mitch Lansky; *Justice on Earth: Earthjustice and the People it Has Served* by Tom Turner; *Freewheeling Homes: The House that Jack Built* by David Pearson; *Secrets of Salsa: A Bilingual Cookbook* by The Mexican Women of Anderson Valley; *The Hand-Sculpted: A Practical and Philosophy Guide to Building a Cob Cottage* by Ianto Evans, Michael G. Smith, and Linda Smiley; *Pesto Manifesto: Recipes for Basil and Beyond* by Lorel Nazzaro; *A Cafecito Story: El Cuento del Cafecito* by Julia Alvarez; *A House of Straw: A Natural Building Odyssey* by Carolyn Roberts; *The Lost Language: The Ecological Importance of Plant Medicines to Life on Earth* by Stephen Harrod Buhner.

Chelsea Green handles its own distribution and distributes for a number of other small, innovative independent presses such as Green Books, Ltd.; Orwell Cove; Otto-Graphics; Ecological Design Press; Harmonious Press; and Seed Savers Exchange. Query letters and SASEs should be directed to:

Hannah Silverstein, Production Editor

Stephen Morris, President and Publisher

Alan Berolzheimer, Acquisitions Editor

Jim Schley, Editor-in-Chief (Editor off the Grid)
Born: November 13, 1956.

Education: I went to Dartmouth College and have a B.A. in Literature and Creative Writing, a minor in Native American studies, and a M.A. in Poetry from Warren

Wilson College.

Employment history/editor career path: I have always loved books so I knew early on that I wanted to teach or be involved in publishing. I started as an intern at *New England Review* magazine and climbed very quickly up the ladder to become an Editor.

Personal interests: Reading, books, being outside, hiking, camping, activist politics; I built my house from scratch.

What would you be doing if you were not an editor? It's impossible for me to imagine, but I would probably be teaching or doing some kind of freelance work.

What has been your most successful book that you have acquired to date? *The Straw Bale House* by Athena Stein et al.

What books have you acquired that make you the most proud? What books that you have acquired reflect the types of books you like to represent? *Gaviotias* by Alan Weisman.

Do you represent fiction? If so, what do you look for? Yes. *Hammer. Nail. Wood* by Thomas Glynn; *Toyle*, which is a diary of someone working construction.

Do you represent nonfiction? Yes, unusual how-to books, gardening, building.

Do you require book proposals? If so, what do you look for in evaluating a book proposal? Yes, I need something written. In some cases I can help the author to do this, but in most I would expect to see an outline, writing samples, and so on.

What process do you use for making a decision? What is the process for acquisition, is there a committee? Yes, there is a committee made up of the publisher, editor-in-chief, acquiring editor, and the production and marketing team.

What kinds of nonfiction books do you want to see less of? I would like to see fewer submissions of material that we do not handle. We publish books that are related to ecology in some way. It needs to have something to do with environmentalism for us to take a look at it.

Are you interested in work geared for the masses (readers of *People*, *The Star*, etc.)? No.

Are agents important? Why? Yes, I think they are important. I've learned a lot about agents over the last couple of years; due to higher advances, they seem to be around more and more. Agents are very editor-savvy, they can think editorially and have good marketing skills. In most cases they are more sophisticated about the publishing business than the author, which helps to make the process go as smoothly as possible.

Do you like new writers? What should new writers do to break into the business? Yes, we publish many first-time authors. To break into the business an author should learn how to write. Start out by getting something published in magazines, newspapers, and so on.

How should writers approach you? Look at our website, www.chelseagreen.com, for our guidelines. To approach me, send me a letter or an e-mail. I would rather have something in writing than a phone call.

What are some common mistakes writers make? What really gets on your nerves? Writers concentrate so much sometimes on their subject, they forget about all the other aspects of writing. To be a writer, you need to have more than a good idea and it takes more than saying, "Everyone I know loves this idea!"

What can writers do to get your attention and to avoid the slush pile? Our slush pile is quite thin. But to avoid it, be clear and articulate and have a unique idea. We're a writer-friendly house and try to keep the slush to a minimum.

What have been some of your craziest experiences with submissions? Someone once brought me an idea for a book that was all about using human feces as fertilizer.

What have been some of your best experiences with writers or in your job? I love being an editor and working with my colleagues. I love the working relationship between the author and the editor. The editor gets to learn all aspects of a writer, that individual's strengths, weaknesses, and so on. Some authors turn into your best friends.

What, if anything, makes you different from other editors? I'm a very literary person, I read on my own time, I bring the skills of being a literary editor to a practical level.

Is there anything you would like to see changed in the industry? I can't answer what I would change, but I can tell you what not to change. What I would not like to see is the intimacy that reading represents for some people being lost.

Any advice for writers? Be clear, be inventive, and take pleasure in the task.

CHELSEA HOUSE PUBLISHERS

(A Subsidiary of Haights Cross Communications)

1974 Sproul Road, Suite 400, Broomall, PA 19008-0914

610-353-5166/1-800-848-2665   fax: 610-359-1439

www.chelseahouse.com   e-mail: info@chelseahouse.com

The entire Chelsea House catalog is available on the Internet.

Chelsea House produces books for older children and young adults, as well as books for elementary school students. The Chelsea House program accents the educational and institutional market in history, young adult nonfiction, reference works, and literary criticism, as well as some works of broader appeal. Books on the Chelsea House list are most often produced in library-bound hardcover volumes, with some titles offered in trade paperback editions.

The editorial focus is on biography, culture, and history (American and worldwide). Broad interest areas include multicultural studies, social studies, literary criticism/English, general biography, mythology, sports, science, health/drug education, art, Spanish-language books, economics/business and personal finance, and law.

This approach is underscored by developmental marketing of such series as the Asian American Experience, Folk Tales and Fables, the Immigrant Experience, Lives of the Physically Challenged, Milestones in Black American History, Mysterious Places,

Pop Culture Legends, Science Discoveries, and Sports Legends.

Chelsea House Publishers was originally instituted (founded in 1967) as a small press (then located in New York City) devoted to trade and reference titles on American history and popular culture. The company was bought in 1983 by Main Line Book Company, a library distributor based in suburban Philadelphia—whereupon the house's emphasis turned toward nonfiction for a young-adult readership.

Chelsea House series and highlights:

Famous Figures of the Civil War Era: *Jefferson Davis; Frederick Douglas; Ulysses S. Grant; Robert E. Lee; Abraham Lincoln*; Children of the World; Civil War Leaders; Egyptian Kings and Queens; Classical Deities; Good Luck Symbols and Talismans; Greetings of the World.

Cats and Dogs: A Basic Training, Caring, and Understanding Library: *Kittens & Cats; Skin Care for Cats; The Myth & Magic of Cats; The Well Trained Dog; Adopting a Dog; The Perfect Retriever; Traveling with Dogs; Puppy Training.*

Funtastic Science Activities for Kids: *Sound Fundamentals; Electricity & Magnetism Fundamentals; Heat Fundamentals.*

Major World Nations: *Albania, Argentina, Australia, Vietnam, West Bank, West Indies, Zimbabwe.*

Overcoming Adversity: *Tim Allen; Jim Carrey; James Earl Jones; Abraham Lincoln; William Penn.*

Superstars of Film: *Robert DeNiro; Johnny Depp; Brad Pitt; Keanu Reeves; John Travolta.*

They Died Too Young: *Kurt Cobain; Jimi Hendrix; Bruce Lee; John Lennon; Elvis Presley.*

Great Disasters: *Reforms and Ramifications; The Bombing of Hiroshima; The Exxon Valdez; Pearl Harbor; Three Mile Island; The Titanic.*

Male/Female Sports Stars: Baseball Legends: *Roger Clemens, Randy Johnson, Chipper Jones, Mark McGwire, Larry Walker*; Superstars of Men's Figure Skating; Superstars of Men's Track and Field; Superstars of Women's Golf; Superstars of Women's Tennis; Superstars of Women's Gymnastics.

The Illustrated Living History Series: *Tall Ships of the World; Woodland Indians; Revolutionary Medicine; Homebuilding and Woodworking in Colonial America.*

Women of Achievement: *Madeleine Albright; Hillary Rodham Clinton; Diana, Princess of Wales; Rosie O'Donnell; Elizabeth Taylor; Barbara Walters.*

Women Writers of English and Their Words: *Native American Women Writers; Jewish Women Fiction Writers; Asian-American Women Writers; British Women Fiction Writers of the 19th Century.*

Explorers of New Worlds: *Daniel Boone, Vasco de Gama; Lewis and Clark; Juan Ponce de Leon; The Viking Explorers.*

Crime, Justice, and Punishment: *Detectives, Private Investigators, and Bounty Hunters; Hate Crimes; The Jury System.*

Who Wrote That? Series: *Louisa May Alcott* by Elizabeth Silverthorne; *Betsy*

Byars by Rita Cammarano; *Roald Dahl* by Charles J. Shields; *Theodor Geisel (Dr. Seuss)* by Tanya Dean; *Gary Paulsen* by Elizabeth Paterra; *Mythmaker: The Story of J.K. Rowling* by Charles J. Shields.

Behind The Camera: *James Cameron* by Bonnie McMeans; *Ron Howard* by Hal Marcovitz; *Spike Lee* by Charles J. Shields; *George Lucas* by Charles J. Shields; *Rob Reiner* by Therese DeAngelis; *Stephen Spielberg* by Elizabeth Sirimarco.

Administrative, editorial, and warehousing facilities are currently located in the Philadelphia area. Query letters and SASEs should be directed to:

Sally Cheney, Editor-in-Chief

Kim Shinners, Director of Production

Pamela Loos, Manufacturing Manager

Sara Davis, Art Director

CHRONICLE BOOKS

CHRONICLE CHILDREN'S BOOKS

85 Second Street, Sixth Floor, San Francisco, CA 94105

415-537-3730/415-537-4441/1-800-722-6657   fax: 415-537-4470

www.chroniclebooks.com   e-mail: frontdesk@chroniclebooks.com

It was announced in late 1999 that this respected, independent firm was acquired from its corporate parent by the Associate Publisher, Nion McEvoy. McEvoy is the great-grandson of Michel de Young, who cofounded the San Francisco Chronicle with his brother Charles in 1865.

Founded in 1968, Chronicle Books publishes 300 new titles each year across its three divisions—Adult Trade, Children's, and Gift—in the subject areas of food, photography, art, architecture, interior design, gardening, pop culture, and fiction. It also distributes the publishing programs of the Princeton Architectural Press, North South Books, and innovative KIDS.

Chronicle's areas of interest include architecture and fine arts, design, photography, history and popular culture, the outdoors lifestyle (cuisine, pets, travel, home, and family), business and finance, and sports; the house issues a separate catalog for its children's books and for the gift list.

Chronicle Books was initially best known for its glossy paperback series of illustrated theme cookbooks. Since that era, Chronicle has gradually ventured further afield and currently publishes general nonfiction in both hardback and paperback. Chronicle Books also publishes selected fiction and literary works.

The Chronicle program features many selections of California regional interest (food, architecture, outdoors), with a focus on San Francisco and the Bay Area in particular (on both frontlist and backlist). The publisher has expanded its regional scope: Chronicle is open to an increasing variety of titles keyed to areas and travel destinations worldwide. Chronicle scored major bestseller hits with Nick Bantock's Griffin & Sabine fiction trilogy: *Griffin & Sabine*, *Sabine's Notebook*, and *The Golden Mean*.

Representative Chronicle titles: *The Bad Girl's Guide to the Party Life* by Cameron Tuttle; *The Beatles Anthology* by The Beatles; *The Bridesmaid Guide: Etiquette, Parties, and Being Fabulous* by Kate Chynoweth; *Christmas Trees: Fun and Festive Ideas* by Peter Cole; *Girl Culture: Photographs* by Lauren Greenfield; *I, Me, Mine* by George Harrison; *Our House Journal: The Story of Our Home* by Sacheverell Darling and Benjamin Darling; *Poetry Dog Tags* by Clare Ultimo; *Stars in the Darkness* by Barbara Joosse; *The Worst-Case Scenario Survival Handbook: Holidays*.

CHRONICLE'S CHILDREN'S BOOKS

Chronicle's children's lineup has a reputation for high quality and innovation in traditional and not-so-traditional formats.

From the Chronicle children's list: *ABC Block Books Illustrated* by Susan Estelle Kwas; *52 Activities in Nature* by Lynn Gordon and Bob Filipowich; *The Amazing Game Board Book* by Shereen Gertel Rutman (illustrated by John Clementson); *Art Activity Pack: Renoir* by Mila Boutan; *Hush Little Baby* by Sylvia Long; *If I Had a Horse* by Jonathan London (illustrated by Brooke Scudder); *Desert Dwellers: Native People of the American Southwest* by Scott Warren; *The Clubhouse Crew's Joker's Bag of Tricks* by Anne Civardi and Ruth Thomson (illustrated by Mark Oliver); *The Merchant of Marvels and the Peddler of Dreams* by Frederick Clement; *Beneath the Sea in 3-D* by Mark Blum; *Star Wars, The Empire Strikes Back*, and *Return of the Jedi* by John Whitman (illustrated by Brandon McKinney); *A Rainbow at Night: The World in Words and Pictures by Navajo Children* by Bruce Hucko.

Query letters and SASEs should be directed to:

Victoria Rock, Director and Associate Publisher—Children's books

Alan Rapp, Associate Editor—Adult Trade

Bill LeBlond, Editorial Director—Cookbooks

Christine Carswell, Associate Publisher—Adult Trade

Jay Schaefer, Editorial Director—Literature

Leslie Jonath, Senior Editor—Gardening, crafts, lifestyle

Sarah Malarkey, Executive Editor—Popular culture: all areas

Mikyla Brunder, Editor—Craft/lifestyle

Kerry Tessaro, Editor—Gift

Leigh Anna Mendenhall, Editor—Children's, calendars

Lisa Campbell, Editorial Assistant—Adult Trade

Lisa McGuinness, Associate Editor—Children's

Samantha McFerrin, Editorial Assistant—Children's
Amy Treadwell, Editorial Assistant—Adult Trade
Ann Wilson, Managing Editor—Gift
Anne Bunn, Assistant Editor—Adult Trade
Beth Weber, Managing Editor—Children's
Brenda Modliszewski, Editorial Assistant—Gift
Doug Ogan, Editorial Assistant—Adult Trade
Jodi Davis, Assistant Editor—Adult Trade
Bill LeBlond, Editor—Cookbooks
Carey Jones, Assistant Editor—Gift
Christine Amini, Editorial Assistant—Gift
Dean Burrell, Managing Editorial Director—Adult Trade
Jan Hughes, Associate Managing Editor— Adult Trade
Kerry Colburn, Executive Editor—Gift
Leslie Davisson, Editorial Assistant—Adult Trade
Steve Mockus, Associate Editor—Adult Trade

CITY LIGHTS PUBLISHERS

261 Columbus Avenue, San Francisco, CA 94133

415-362- 8193   fax: 415-362-4921

www.citylights.com   e-mail: staff@citylights.com

City Lights publishes literary essays and criticism, biography, philosophy, literary fiction (including first novels) and poetry, and books on political and social issues, as well as artistically ecumenical volumes featuring both words and visual images.

City Lights Booksellers and Publishers (founded in 1953 by the poet-publisher Lawrence Ferlinghetti) is a San Francisco treasure, its bookstore a North Beach landmark and, above all else, a resolute cultural institution and self-embodied tradition. City Lights initially featured the Pocket Poets series, which introduced such writers as Gregory Corso, Allen Ginsberg, Jack Kerouac, and other Beats to a wider audience. Since then, as successive literary generations have commenced and terminated, City Lights remains most assuredly commercially viable.

Highlights from City Lights: *Aureole: An Erotic Sequence* by Carole Maso; *Perversions Of Justice: Indigenous Peoples and Angloamerican Law* by Ward Churchill; *The World's Embrace: Selected Poems* by Abdellatif Laabi (Translated from French by Victor Reinking, Anne George, and Edris Makward; *Picnic Grounds* by Oz Shelach; *The End of Youth* by Rebecca Brown; *Indigenous: Growing up Californian* by Chris Mazza; *The Beat Generation in San Francisco: A Literary Journey* by Bill Morgan; *Globalize Liberation: How to Uproot the System and Build a Better World* edited by David Solnit; *Life Studies, Life Stories: Drawings* by Lawrence Ferlinghetti; *San Francisco Poems* by Lawrence Ferlinghetti; *Love Works* by Janice Mirikitani; *Instant Karma* by Mark Swartz; *Sealed In Stone* by Toni Maraini; *September 11 and the U.S. War: Beyond the Curtain of Smoke* edited by Roger Burbach and Ben Clarke; *The Terrorism Trap: September 11 and Beyond* by Michael Parenti; *Atet A.D.* by Nathaniel Mackey; *Another City: Writing from Los Angeles* edited by David L. Ulin; *Almost Blue* by Carlo Lucarelli (translated by Oonagh Stransky).

Each fall, the publisher issues *City Lights Review: Annual Journal of Literature and Politics*, which brims with original poetry, essays, and fiction.

City Lights is distributed by Consortium Book Sales and Distribution and has its own in-house mail-order fulfillment department. Query letters and SASEs should be directed to:

Elaine Katzenberger, Acquisitions Editor—Latin American literature, women's studies, fiction

James Brook, Acquisitions Editor—Nonfiction

Nancy J. Peters, Publisher and Executive Editor

Robert Sharrard, Acquisitions Editor—Poetry and literature

CLEIS PRESS

PO Box 14684, San Francisco, CA 94114

415-575-4700/1-800-780-2279   fax: 415-575-4705

www.cleispress.com   e-mail: cleis@cleispress.com

Founded in 1980, Cleis Press publishes books on sexual politics and self-help, lesbian and gay studies and culture, feminism, fiction, erotica, humor, and translations of world-class women's literature. Cleis titles cross-market from niches of gender and sexuality to reach the widest possible audiences.

Projects from Cleis Press garner numerous awards and reviews—and include many best-selling books. The house is committed to publishing the most original, creative, and provocative works by women (and a few men) in the United States and Canada.

From the Cleis list: *Annie Sprinkle: Post Porn Modernist, My Twenty-Five Years as a Multimedia Whore* by Annie Sprinkle; *The Diary of a Political Idiot: Normal Life in Belgrade* by Jasmina Tesanovic; *Curbside Boys* by Robert Kirby; *An American in Paris* by Margaret Vandenburg; *Speaking Sex to Power: The Politics of Pleasure & Perversity* by Patrick Califia-Rice; *Beebo Brinker* by Ann Bannon; *The Hardly Boys in A Ghost in the Closet, 2nd ed.*

by Mabel Maney; *Carrie's Story* by Molly Weatherfield; *Betty & Pansy's Severe Queer Review of New York* by Betty and Pansy.

Cleis Press is represented to the book trade by Publishers Group West. Query letters and SASEs should be directed to:

Felice Newman, Publisher and Acquisitions Editor

Frédérique Delacoste, Publisher and Acquisitions Editor

CLEVELAND STATE UNIVERSITY POETRY CENTER

1983 East 24th Street, Cleveland, OH 44115-2440

216-687-3986/1-888-278-6473   fax: 216-687-6943

www.csuohio.edu/poetrycenter   e-mail: poetrycenter@csuohio.edu

Cleveland State University Poetry Center was begun in 1962 at Fenn College (which became Cleveland State in 1964); the center initiated its book-publishing program in 1971. The press publishes poets of local, regional, and international reach, generally under the aegis of one or another of the center's ongoing series. Under its flying-unicorn logo, CSU Poetry Center most often publishes trade paper editions, but has also offered some titles in hardbound. The press generally produces a limited number of new titles each year. In addition, the house maintains a full backlist.

CSU Poetry Center presents a variety of styles and viewpoints—some with evident sociopolitical bent, others with broadly inspirational themes, and others notable for their strong individualistic inflections. The Poetry Center sponsors the Poetry Forum workshop and presents programs of public readings.

The center sponsors an annual poetry contest; please contact the CSU Poetry Center for submission guidelines.

Before the Blue Hour by Deirdre O'Connor was selected by Marie Howe as the contest winner from 856 manuscripts in the 2001 competition. The competition is extremely tough and the Poetry Center recommends that poets publish some individual poems in magazines and literary journals before submitting to this series. It is also recommended that prospective entrants review some of the work that the Poetry Center publishes.

Recent books from the Poetry Center: *The Largest Possible Life* by Alison Luterman; *The Book of Orgasms* (Imagination series) by Nin Andrews; *Attendant Ghosts* by George Looney; *A Short History of Pets* by Carol Potter. Shorter volumes and chapbooks: *Almost Home* by Susan Grimm; *The Book of Snow* by Mary Moore; *Troubled by an Angel* by Elizabeth Murawski; *Enough Light to Steer By* by Steven Reese. The full range of publications from CSU Poetry Center Press includes award-winning volumes from established poets and releases from accomplished new writers. On the CSU list: *Willow from the Willow* by Margaret Young; *Before the Blue Hour* by Deirdre O'Connor; *The Dry*

Season by Gaspar Pedro Gonzalez; *The Largest Possible Life* by Alison Luterman; *Games & Puzzles* by Barbara Tanner Angell; *Blood Stories* by Martha Ramsey; *Hurdy-Gurdy and Hammerlock* by Tim Seibles; *Order, or Disorder* by Amy Newman; *Refinery* by Claudia Keelan; *Fugitive Colors* by Chrystos; *Lives of the Saints and Everything* by Susan Firer; *The Long Turn Toward Light* by Cleveland poet and artist Barbara Tanner Angell; *At Redbones* by Thylias Moss; *The Sioux Dog Dance: Shunk ah weh* by Red Hawk.

Poetry Center books are distributed through Partners Book Distributing, Ingram, and Spring Church Book Company.

The Poetry Center accepts manuscripts only from November 1–February 1 in connection with the Center's annual competition ($20 entry fee; full manuscripts only). For complete guidelines, send request plus SASE, or visit www.csuohio.edu/poetrycenter.

SASEs should be directed to:

Ted Lardner, Director

Rita Grabowski, Director

COBBLEHILL BOOKS

See Penguin Putnam, Inc.

COFFEE HOUSE PRESS

27 North Fourth Street, Suite 400, Minneapolis, MN 55401

612-338-0125   fax: 612-338-4004

www.coffeehousepress.org

Coffee House produces contemporary poetry, short fiction, and novels. The press is a source of contemporary writing that is challenging and thought-provoking, funny and furious, wildly diverse, even downright wacky, vibrant, and lyrical.

Coffee House Press is a nonprofit publisher dedicated to presenting visionary books of contemporary literature by diverse authors. The mission of Coffee House Press is to promote exciting, vital, and enduring authors of our time; to delight and inspire readers; to increase awareness of and appreciation for the traditional book arts; to enrich our literary heritage; and to contribute to the cultural life of our community.

Coffee House Press publishes books that advance the craft of writing; books that present the dreams and ambitions of people who have been underrepresented in published literature; books that help build a sense of community; and books that help to shape our national consciousness.

Coffee House descends from what was originally (in the 1970s) a letterpress specialty firm, with a small list and an intimate circle of readers. The publisher then introduced titles geared toward an expanded readership; happily, conviviality and craft remain in strong evidence. Coffee House Press (established in 1984) is a publisher of trade titles and fine editions in a program that features a creative approach to the publishing arts. The house colophon is a steaming book, which is chosen to let the reader know (as the Coffee House motto runs) "where good books are brewing."

Titles from Coffee House: *Miniatures* by Norah Labiner; *Bingo Under the Crucifix* by Laurie Foos; *The White Palazzo* by Ellen Cooney; *My Love, My Love or The Peasant Girl* by Rosa Guy; *Gorgeous Chaos, New and Selected Poems: 1965-2001* poems by Jack Marshall; *Little Casino* by Gilbert Sorrentino; *Some of Her Friends That Year, New and Selected Stories* by Maxine Chernoff; *You Never Know* by Ron Padgitt; *Red Suburb* poems by Greg Hewett; *The Mermaid that Came Between Them* by Carol Ann Sima; *Transcircularities, New and Selected Poems* by Quincy Troupe.

Coffee House books are printed on acid-free paper stock and have sewn bindings for long life and comfortable reading—as well they might, for the house features a comprehensive and enduring backlist.

Coffee House Press oversees its own marketing and sales network with the assistance of regional representatives; trade distribution is handled by Consortium. Query letters and SASEs should be directed to:

Allan Kornblum, Editor and Publisher

Christopher Fischbach, Managing Editor

Anitra Budd, Editorial Assistant

Chris Martin, Interim Publicist and Editorial Assistant

COLLECTOR BOOKS

(A Division of the Schroeder Publishing Company)

5801 Kentucky Dam Road, Paducah, KY 42001

270-898-6211   fax: 270-898-8890

www.collectorbooks.com   e-mail: editor@collectorbooks.com

Mailing address:

PO Box 3009, Paducah, KY 42002-3009

Collector Books produces books for collectors in such fields as Depression glass, glassware, pottery and porcelain, china and dinnerware, cookie jars and salt shakers, stoneware, paper collectibles, Barbie dolls, dolls, toys, quilts, tools and weapons, jewelry and accessories, furniture, advertising memorabilia, bottles, Christmas collectibles, cigarette lighters, decoys, doorstops, and gas station memorabilia.

Collector Books (founded in 1969) is a division of Schroeder Publishing Company. Collector Books is dedicated to bringing the most up-to-date information and values to collectors in an attractive, high-quality format. Books are designed to be practical, easy-to-use tools that assist dealers and collectors in their pursuit of antiques and collectibles. Collector's publications are liberally illustrated editions, generally filled with histories, production facts and lore, research sources, and identification information. Collector Books also produces inventory ledgers for professional dealers and avid collectors.

The house produces a midsized list of new offerings each year and maintains a sizable backlist. Springing from its original principles of offering quality products, customer satisfaction, giving customers the most for their dollar and one-day sudden service, Collector Books has grown from one title on fruit jars to over 500 titles, and from a firm of two employees to over 70. Fueled by strong customer support, the publisher's list of new releases continues its recent growth.

Every August, Collector publishes *Schroeder's Antiques Price Guide*, which features more than 50,000 listings and hundreds of photographs for identification and current values, as well as background and historical information.

Sample titles: *Complete Price Guide to Watches* by Cooksey Shugart, Tom Engle, and Richard E. Gilbert; *Collector's Guide to Made in Japan Ceramics, Book IV* by Carole Bess White; *Florence's Glassware Pattern Identification Guide Vol III* by Gene and Cathy Florence; *The Glass Candlestick Book, Vol 1* by Tom Felt and Elaine and Rich Stoer; *Hot Wheels: The Ultimate Redline Guide* by Jack Clark and Robert P. Wicker; *The Standard Antique Clock Value Guide* by Alex Wescott; *Encyclopedia of Bisque Nancy Ann Storybook Dolls*, Elaine M. Pardee and Jackie Robertson; *Garage Sale and Flea Market Annual, 9th Edition* by Bob and Sharon Huxford; *Schroeder's Collectible Toys* by Bob and Sharon Huxford; *Collector's Guide to Lunch Boxes* by Carole Bess White and L. M. White; *Flea Market Trader* by Bob and Sharon Huxford; *Collectible Glassware from the 40s, 50s, & 60s* by Gene Florence; *Collecting Blue Willow* by M. A. Hoffman; *Toy Car Collector's Guide* by Dana Johnson; *Vintage Golf Collectibles* by Ronald John.

Collector Books looks for its authors to be knowledgeable people who are considered experts within their fields. Writers who feel there is a real need for a book on their collectible subject and have available a large comprehensive collection are invited to contact the publisher at the house's mailing address.

Collector Books distributes its own list, targeting particularly bookstore buyers and antiques-trade professionals. Collector Books operates an especially strong mail-order program and purveys selected works from other publishers, including out-of-print titles in the collectibles and antiques field. Query letters and SASEs should be directed to:

Billy Schroeder, Publisher

Lisa Stroup, Editor

CONARI PRESS

368 Congress St.

Boston, MA 02210

617-542-1324   fax: 617-482-9676

www.conari.com   e-mail: orders@redwheelweiser.com

In July 2002 Conari Press became an imprint of the Red Wheel/Weiser publishing company. About the addition of Conari to their company, Red Wheel/Weiser president Michael Kerber says, "This is an exciting development for us. We have considered a number of companies over the past year and none offered as many positive opportunities as Conari."

Attracted by Conari's strong backlist and distinct editorial emphasis on relationships, self-awareness, spirituality, and the family, Red Wheel/Weiser expects its presence in the spiritual living and self-help market to dramatically increase. Conari's Berkeley offices have been closed and all operations have moved to Red Wheel/Weiser's locations in Boston and New York. Conari still plans to be a distinct imprint.

Recent titles include: *Be Generous* by David Marell; *The Woman's Book of Courage* by Sue Patton Thoele; *The Naptime Book* by Cynthia MacGregor; *Safe Passage* by Molly Fumia; *It Takes a Certain Type to be a Writer* by Erin Barrett and Jack Mingo.

Conari Backlist highlights: *200 Ways to Raise a Girl's Self-Esteem* by Will Glennon; *365 Days of Love* by Daphne Rose Kingma; *Animal Angels* by Stephanie Laland; *Aromatherapy Through the Seasons* by Judith Fitzsimmons and Paula M. Bouquet; *The Art of Dreaming* by Jill Mellick; *Attitudes of Gratitude in Love* by M.J. Ryan; *Buddhist Acts of Compassion* compiled by Pamela Bloom; *Getting Over Getting Mad* by Judy Ford; *Expecting Baby* by Judy Ford; *Gifts with Heart* by Mary Beth Sammons; *A Grateful Heart* by M. J. Ryan; *House Magic* by Ariana; *How to Live in the World and Still Be Happy* by Hugh Prather; *The Pleasure Zone* by Stell Resnick, PhD; *Random Acts of Kindness* by the Editors of Conari Press.

Conari is distributed to the trade by Publishers Group West; gift store distribution is handled through Sourcebooks, Inc.

Query letters and SASEs should be directed to:

Julie Kessler, Editorial Assistant

CONTEMPORARY BOOKS

(A Division of McGraw-Hill)

2 Penn Plaza, 20th Floor, New York, NY 10121

212-512-2000

www.mhcontemporary.com

Contemporary Books offers a general nonfiction lineup that accents the areas of self-improvement, personal finance, health, and lifestyle. The list is particularly strong in sports, parenting, and self-help. Contemporary Books also has a major concentration in the foreign language area.

Originally an independent press, Contemporary Books (established in 1947) was part of the Tribune New Media organization and an imprint of NTC/Contemporary Publishing Company. The Tribune's book group was bought by McGraw-Hill in 2000.

Contemporary has branched out from a former emphasis on sports titles to a program broad in scope that includes hardcover and trade paperback editions.

From Contemporary: *Raising Resilient Children* by Robert Brooks and Sam Goldstein; *The No-Cry Sleep Solution* by Elizabeth Pantley; *The Hollywood Book of Death* by James Robert Parish; *The Making of the Super Bowl* by Don Weiss; *Lost on Everest: The Search for Mallory and Irving* by Peter Firstbrook; *Stages of the Soul* by Father Paul Keenana; *Coaching Yourself to Success* by Talane Miedaner; *Lapsing into a Comma* by Bill Walsh; *Unbelievably Good Deals and Great Adventures You Absolutely Can't Get Unless You're Over 50* by Joan Heilman (which is coming out in its 12th edition); *MHC Interactive: GED; Assessment Program for the GED; GED Satellite Series; Complete GED; GED Exercise Books; MHC Interactive: Pre-GED; TABE forms 7 & 8; TABE Español; Skills Assessment Module; Basic Skills Interactive; Foundations Reading; Grammar Write Away; Number Power; Number Sense; Math Solutions; Real Numbers; BetterReader System; New Reader Bookstore; On the Edge; Essentials of Reading; Thumbprint Mysteries; Expressions & Viewpoints; Reading & Writing Handbooks: 1000 Instant Words; Phonics Patterns; Introductory Word Book; Writer's Manual; How To Teach Reading; Word Power 1, 2, & 3; Exercising Your English; Writing and Reading the Essay; Short Cuts; Take Charge; Everyday English; Writing Matters; Writing to Learn; Citizenship Now; Uncle Sam Activity Book; Put English to Work.*

Contemporary's series of discount guides—Buying Retail Is Stupid!—is geared toward buying everything at up to 80 percent off retail; works include information on all aspects of discount shopping (mail order, outlets, resale stores, auctions, government surplus sales).

Contemporary Books also distributes books for the American Diabetes Association and *The Sporting News.*

Query letters and SASEs should be directed to:

Judith McCarthy, Senior Editor—General trade and reference

Michelle Pezzuti, Editor—Health, relationships, self help/how to.

CONTINUUM INTERNATIONAL PUBLISHING GROUP

15 East 26th Street, New York, NY   10010

212-953-5858   fax: 212-953-5944

www.continuumbooks.com   e-mail: info@continuum-books.com

Continuum's Web site contains details on forthcoming, current, and previously published titles, as well as links to Chiron Publications, Daimon Publications, Spring Publications, and Paragon House.

Continuum International publishes general trade books, texts, scholarly monographs, and reference works in the areas of literature and the arts, psychology, history and social thought, women's studies, and religion. Continuum offers more than 250 new publications a year, as well as 3,500 established backlist titles.

Continuum's broad focus integrates the fields of literature and criticism, psychology and counseling, religion, women's studies, and social issues of contemporary public interest. The house is known for its select line of books in popular and scholarly approaches to religion and philosophy. The Frederick Ungar imprint specializes in literature, film, and the performing arts.

Continuum and Crossroad Publishing Company were editorially independent components of the Crossroad/Continuum Publishing Group from 1980 into the early 1990s, since which time Continuum has pursued its own independent publishing trajectory now with a London office of former Cassell Academic and religion titles. (For Crossroad Publishing, see entry in the Religious, Spiritual & Inspirational Publishers section.)

From the Continuum trade list: *Underneath A Harlem Moon* by Iain Cameron Williams; *Suffer the Little Children* by Mary Raftery and Eoin O'Sullivan; *London Crossing* by Mike Phillips; *Cuban Fire* by Isabelle Leymarie; *French Cinema* by Remi Fournier Lanzoni; *Leni Riefenstahl* by Rainer Rother; *A Low Dishonest Decade* by Paul N. Hehn; *Journey Through the Night* by Jakob Littner and Kurt Nathan Grubler; *Invisible Woman* by Ika Hugel-Marshall; *The Dignity of Difference* by Jonathan Sacks; *Arranging the Score* by Gene Lees; *Undercurrents by The Wire*; *A New History of Jazz* by Alyn Shipton; *Fantabulosa* by Paul Baker; *Weather in the Century* by Philip Eden; *The Guerilla Film Makers Movie Blueprint* by Chris Jones; *All About Oscar* by Emanuel Levy; *Saying Goodbye to Daniel* by Juliet Cassuto Rothman; *Change for the Better* by Elizabeth Wilde McCormick; *Regeneration* by Jane Polden; *You're Not What I Expected* by Polly Young-Eisendrath; *Undressing Feminism* by Ellen Klein; *The Radiance of Being* by Allan Combs; *The Bearskin Quiver* by Gregory McNamee; *Hitler's Bureaucrats* by Yaacov Lozowick; *Unholy Alliance* by Peter Levenda.

Continuum is distributed through Books International. Continuum also distributes the distinguished publishing programs of Chiron Publications, Daimon Publications, Spring Publications, and Paragon House. Query letters and SASEs should be directed to:

Evander Lomke, Vice President and Managing Editor—Psychological counseling, history and the arts, literary criticism, current affairs, women's studies

Frank Oveis, Vice President and Senior Editor—Academic religious and Biblical studies, world religions, spirituality

David Barker, Commissioning Editor

COPPER CANYON PRESS

PO Box 271, Port Townsend, WA 98368

360-385-4925/877-501-1393   fax: 360-385-4985

www.coppercanyonpress.org   e-mail: contact@coppercanyonpress.org

The Copper Canyon mission is to publish poetry distinguished in both content and design, within the context of belief that the publisher's art—like the poet's—is sacramental. Copper Canyon Press (founded in 1972) publishes in hardcover and paperback.

Within this ambitious vision, there are limitations; Copper Canyon generally does not sign many new writers. The house assigns its resources to furthering its established roster. The publisher's success in its aim is proven through abundant and continuing recognition of its authors via honors, awards, grants, and fellowships.

Copper Canyon Press publishes a list with such titles as these: *Cool, Calm, and Collected* by Carolyn Kizer; *Waiting for Sweet Betty* by Clarence Major; *The Caged Owl* by Gregory Orr; *The Complete Poems of Kenneth Rexroth* by Kenneth Rexroth; *The Smallest Muscle in the Human Body* by Alberto Rios; *Steal Away* by C.D. Wright; *Reversible Monuments* by Monica de la Torre; *The Poet's Child* by Michael Wiegers; *Disaffections* by Cesare Pavese; *The Truth Squad* by Dennis Schmitz; *Contradictions* by Alfred Corn; *World Hotel* by Reetika Vazirani; *Always Beginning* by Maxine Kumin; *Armored Hearts* by David Bottoms; *August Zero* by Jane Miller; *Below Cold Mountain* by Joseph Stroud; *Black Iris* by Denise Levertov; *The Book of Questions* by Pablo Neruda; *Carrying Over* by Carolyn Kizer; *Communion* by Primaus St. John; *Daughter's Latitude* by Karen Swenson; *Death Son* by Thomas McGrath; *East Window* by W. S. Merwin; *Exiled in the Word* by Jerome Rothenberg and Harris Lenowitz; *Heart of Bamboo* by Sam Hamill; *Iris of Creation* by Marvin Bell; *Like Underground Water* by Edward Lueders; *The Leaf Path* by Emily Warn.

Copper Canyon distributes to the trade via Consortium.

Manuscripts for first, second, or third books are considered only in conjunction with the Hayden Carruth Award. Contact the press with an SASE for the entry form in September; submissions are accepted during the month of November, and the winner will be announced in February. The winner of the first Hayden Carruth Award is Sascha Feinstein for his poems *Blues Departures*. Visit our website at www.ccpress.org for details.

All queries must include an SASE. We do not accept manuscript queries by e-mail. Copper Canyon generally does not sign many new writers. Query letters and SASEs should be directed to:

Sam Hamill, Editor

Michael Wiegers, Managing Editor

Thatcher Bailey, Publisher

Mary Jane Knecht, Associate Publisher

CRISP PUBLICATIONS

1200 Hamilton Court, Menlo Park, CA 94025

650-323-6100/1-800-442-7477

www.crisplearning.com

Crisp Publications produces nonfiction business books and media packages; topics include management, personal improvement, human resources, communications, creativity, customer service, sales, small businesses, financial planning, adult literacy and learning, careers, and retirement and life planning. The house is known for a number of successful lines: 50-Minute Book a series in small-business ventures, and other business titles keyed to use of new media.

Crisp Publications (founded in 1985) is a specialist in target business publishing and is equally expert at marketing the resultant product. Crisp offers an extensive selection of training programs (including self-study formats) that incorporate books, manuals, and audiovisual materials. The house's aim is to provide high-quality, cost-effective books and videos that can help business organizations succeed in competitive times.

The 50-Minute Book is Crisp's signature designation for books produced with the concept of being concise, easily read, and readily understood through personal involvement with exercises, activities, and assessments. Other Crisp lines are the Quick Read Series, the Small Business and Entrepreneurship Series, and the Crisp Management Library.

Highlights from Crisp: Crisp's Fifty-Minute series books are concise guides intended to be "read with a pencil" and are designed for quick, easy to access information. Sample titles from the Fifty-Minute Series include: *Accountability*; *The Accounting Cycle*; *Achieving Job Satisfaction*; *The Art of Communicating*; *Basic Business Math*; *Concentration!*; *Conducting a Needs Analysis*; *Coping With Workplace Change*; *Creating a Learning Organization*; *Customer Satisfaction*; *Managing For Commitment*; *Men and Women*; *New*

Employee Orientation; Rightful Termination; Risk Taking; Self-Managing Teams; Sexual Harassment in the Workplace; Writing a Human Resource Manual.

Sample titles from the Professional Series include: *Adapting to Change; Closing Sales & Winning the Customer's Heart; Competency and the Learning Organization; Copyediting; Information Design Desk Reference; Invent!; Managing Differences; Take The Work and Love It; Virtual HR.*

Crisp Publications distributes through a commission sales force. Query letters and SASEs should be directed to:

George Young, Editor

DALKEY ARCHIVE PRESS

Illinois State University, Campus 8905, Normal, IL 61790-8905

309-438-7555   fax: 309-438-7422

www.dalkeyarchive.com   e-mail: contact@dalkeyarchive.com

Dalkey Archive (founded in 1984) is dedicated to breakthrough artistic expression in fiction. Dalkey's writers are among the most influential stylists on the printed page. Dalkey Archive Press is a division of the Center for Book Culture.

From the Dalkey Archive list: *The Age of Wire and String* by Ben Marcus; *Take Five* by D. Keith Mano; *Cigarettes* and *Tlooth* by Harry Mathews; *Excitability* by Diane Williams; *A Short Rhetoric for Leaving the Family* by Peter Dimock; *The Polish Complex* by Tadeusz Konwicki (introduction by the translator Richard Lourie); *The Dick Gibson Show* by Stanley Elkin; *Pushkin House* by Andrei Bitov; *Chromos* by Felipe Alfau; *Odile* by Raymond Queneau.

Dalkey Archive distributes through Chicago Distribution Center. Query letters and SASEs should be directed to:

Chad Post, Editor

DAW BOOKS, INC.

375 Hudson Street, New York, NY 10014

212-366-2096

www.dawbooks.com   e-mail: daw@penguinputnam.com

DAW Books publishes science fiction, fantasy, science fantasy, future fiction and future fantasy, dark suspense, and horror. DAW publishes mass-market paperbound originals and reprints, as well as hardcovers and trade paperbacks.

The DAW line includes masterful genre-keyed anthologies that showcase some of the most respected writers in their respective literary provinces. DAW typically produces a medium-sized seasonal list of new titles. The DAW backlist is replete with successful individual titles, along with a host of perennially selling series.

DAW Books (founded in 1971) is at the forefront of the literary categories and genres in which it specializes. The house is affiliated with Penguin Putnam, Inc.

Now, more than 25 years and more than a thousand titles later, DAW has a well-deserved reputation for discovering and publishing the hottest talents in the industry. Many stars of the science fiction and fantasy field made their debuts in the pages of a DAW book, including Tad Williams, C. J. Cherryh, Mercedes Lackey, Melanie Rawn, C. S. Friedman, Jennifer Roberson, and Tanith Lee.

From DAW Books: *Explorer* and *Defender* by CJ Cherryh; *The Forbidden Circle* by Marion Zimmer Bradley; *Apprentice Fantastic* edited by Martin H. Greenberg and Russell Davis; *Take a Thief: A Novel of Valdemar* by Mercedes Lackey; *The Dragons of the Cuyahoga* by S. Andrew Swann; *The Lion Throne* by Jennifer Roberson; *Past Imperfect* edited by Martin H. Greenberg and Larry Segriff; *Otherland: Sea of Silver Light* by Tad Williams.

DAW distribution is through an affiliation with Penguin USA. Query letters and SASEs should be directed to:

Peter Stampfel, Submissions Editor

DEACONESS PRESS

See Fairview Press.

DEARBORN TRADE PUBLISHING

(A Kaplan Professional Company)

30 South Wacker Drive, Chicago, IL 60606-1719

312-836-4400/1-800-245-2665   fax: 312-836-1021

www.dearborn.com   e-mail: trade@dearborn.com

Dearborn Trade Publishing is the nation's premier provider of personal finance, investment, real estate, general business, management resources and resources for consumers, professionals and sales and marketing.

Dearborn has constantly been redefining and refining its direction ever since the trade division started actively publishing practical how-to books for consumers and investors in 1986. Prior to that, the company (founded in 1967) focused on training for financial professionals in real estate, insurance, and securities. Dearborn remains the premier provider of prelicensing, continuing professional education, and training in the financial services and real estate industries. Dearborn Trade publishes titles intended for individual book buyers, whether they are general consumers or CEOs of corporations. Specific topics including personal finance, securities, trading, tax issues, estate planning, consumer real estate, general management, corporate biographies, business leader biographies, entrepreneurship, sales, and marketing.

From Dearborn: *The Communication Catalyst* by Mickey Connolly and Richard Rianoshek, PhD; *Everyone is a Customer* by Jeffery Shuman, Janice Twombly, David Rottenberg; *The Ernst & Young Entrepreneur Of The Year Award Keys to Winning in Business* by Gregory K. Ericksen; *Cause Marketing* by Joe Marconi; *Blue's Clues for Success: The 8 Secrets Behind a Phenomenal Business* by Diane Tracy; *The Power of DFSS* by Subir Chowdhury; *Always Think Big* by Thomas N. Duening and John M. Ivancevick; *Low Risk Real Estate Investments* by Peter Conti and David Finku.

Query letters and SASEs should be directed to

Cynthia Zigmund, Vice President and Publisher

Mary B. Good, Acquisitions Editor—Consumer real estate and finance

Jon Malysiak, Management and general business

Michael Cunningham, Sales and marketing

Jacquelyn Posek, Editorial Assistant

IVAN R. DEE, PUBLISHER

NEW AMSTERDAM BOOKS

J. S. SANDERS

1332 North Halsted Street, Chicago, IL, 60622-2694

312-787-662   fax: 312-787-6269

www.ivanrdee.com   e-mail: elephant@ivanrdee.com

Ivan R. Dee is a serious nonfiction publisher specializing in history, politics, biography, literature, philosophy, and theatre. For the most part Ivan R. Dee tries to publish provocative and authoritative titles aimed at the intelligent layperson. Its books are reviewed regularly in the *New York Times*, the *Washington Post*, the *Los Angeles Times*, the *New York Review of Books*, the *Wall Street Journal*, the *New Republic*, and other influential publications.

Founded in 1988, Ivan R. Dee became a part of the Rowman & Littlefield Publishing Group in 1998 and continues to work out of the company's location in Chicago. Ivan R. Dee also has a solid backlist and two distinct imprints: New Amsterdam Books and J. S. Sanders Books.

Among notable published authors are Roger Angell, Isaiah Berlin, Robert Brustein, Anthony Burgess, John Gross, Raul Hilberg, Gertrude Himmelfarb, Aldous Huxley, Hilton Kramer, Richard Schickel, Budd Schulberg, and John Simon.

Ivan R. Dee titles include: *Are Cops Racist?* by Heather Mac Donald; *Can't Anybody Here Play This Game?* by Jimmy Breslin; *Wilfred Owen* by Dominic Hibberd; *The Philosopher's Secret Fire* by Patrick Harpur; *Finding Out* by Leo Bogart; *The Struggle For Greece, 1941-1949* by C. M. Woodhouse; *Forged In War* by Warren F. Kimball.

New Amsterdam titles include: *Alvar Aalto* by Malcolm Quantrill; *Art in the Cold War* by Christine Lindsey; *Janet Backhouse* by The Bedford Hours; *Camille Pissarro* by Richard Thomson.

J. S. Sanders titles: *Bedford Forrest and His Critter Company* by Andrew Nelson Lytle; *Jefferson Davis* by Allen Tate; *John Brown* by Robert Penn Warren; *Adventures of Captain Simon Suggs* by Johnson Jones Hooper; *The Collected Stories* by Caroline Gordon.

DELACORTE PRESS

See Bantam Dell Publishing Group.

DELL PUBLISHING

See Bantam Dell Publishing Group.

THE DERRYDALE PRESS

4720 Boston Way, Lanham, MD 20706

301-459-3366   fax: 301-429-5748

www.derrydalepress.com

The Derrydale Press was founded in 1927 by Eugene V. Connett III and then quickly became America's preeminent publisher of books on outdoor sports. An avid sportsman himself, Connett sought out manuscripts by the leading sportsmen and sportswomen of his generation, for whom he published books of the highest quality materials.

Sample titles: *True North* by Jack Kulpa; *My Privileged Life* by Thady Ryan; *With Rifle and Petticoat* by Kenneth Czech; *Tigers of the Sea* by Colonel Hugh D. Wise; *A Vision of Paradise* by Elizabeth Ballantine and Stephen Lash; *Foxhunting with Melvin Poe* by Peter Winants.

The Derrydale Press currently has over 150 titles in print and continues to publish in the areas of fishing, hunting, equestrian sports, sporting art, the outdoors, and other aspects of nature. The Derrydale Press is an imprint of the Rowman & Littlefield Publishing Group, whose sister company, National Book Network (NBN), is responsible for the distribution of Derrydale books.

Please direct query letters with SASEs to:

Bethany Perry

ENTREPRENEUR PRESS

2445 McCabe Way, 4th Floor, Irvine, CA 92614

949-261-2325   fax: 949-261-7729

www.smallbizbooks.com   e-mail: jcalmes@entrepreneur.com

Entrepreneur Press, a division of Entrepreneur Media, Inc., publishes trade books offering practical advice and inspirational success stories for business owners and aspiring entrepreneurs. Our areas of expertise include instructional business books, motivational, management, marketing, new economy, e-commerce, and personal finance titles that appeal to a broad spectrum of the business book-buying audience. Steady sellers include: *Start Your Own Business*, the *Entrepreneur* magazine's Start-Up Series; *Power Tools for Women in Business: 10 Ways to Succeed in Life and Work*; *At Work with Thomas Edison: 10 Business Lessons from America's Greatest Innovator*.

Sample trade titles: *Success for Less; How To Be a Teenage Millionaire; Extreme Entrepreneur* by Mark Baven; *Ben Franklin's 12 Rules of Management* by Blaine McCormick; *Creative Selling* by Dave Donelson; *At Work With Thomas Edison* by Blaine McCormick; *Power Tools for Women in Business* by Aliza Sherman.

Sample Business Guide titles include: *Clothing; Automobile Detailing; Bar/Tavern; Bed & Breakfast; Bridal Consultant; Car Wash; Child Care Service; Cleaning Service; Consulting Service; Crafts Business; e-Business; Event Planning Service; Freight Brokerage Business; Growing Your Business; Herb Farming; Home Inspection Service; Information Consultant; Mail Order Business; Medical Claims Processing; Network Marketing; Self Publishing*.

Entrepreneur Press books are distributed to the trade by NBN. Query letters and SASEs should be directed to:

Jere Calmes, Editorial Director

M. EVANS & COMPANY, INC.

216 East 49th Street, New York, NY 10017

212-688-2810   fax: 212-486-4544

www.mevans.com   e-mail: editorial@mevans.com

The M. Evans frontlist features high-profile offerings in topical issues, investigative stories in politics, business, and entertainment, and popular biography. The core Evans program accents popular nonfiction books in the areas of health and fitness, human relationships, business and finance, and lifestyle and cuisine. Evans also issues a small list in popular fiction. The house tends a strong and varied backlist.

M. Evans and Company (founded in 1963) thrives as a selective trade publisher (in hardcover and trade paperback) with a clear, constantly honed commercial focus in its favored market niches.

Evans list is exemplified by: *Dr. Atkins' New Diet Revolution* by Robert C. Atkins, MD; *Class Acts* by Mary Mitchell; *Hidden Agenda* by Martin Allen; *Medicine of the Five Rings* by Robert Rister; *How to Start a Magazine* by James B. Kobak; *Riding in Prime Time* by Sarah Montague. Paperbacks: *The Any Diet Diary*; *The Botox Book* by Everett Lautin, MD and Suzanne Levine, D.M.P. with Kathryn Lance; *Facing Your Fifties* by Gordon Ehlers, MD and Jeff Miller; *Medicinal Mushrooms* by Georges M. Halpern, MD, PhD, and Andrew H. Miller; *Private Heart (An Art Harding mystery)* by Robert Bailey; *Down the Common* by Ann Baer. Nonfiction titles include: *Parent School* by Jared L. Biederman; *Dr. Atkins' New Diet Revolution*; *Baby Love* and *The Mighty Toddler* by Robin Barke.

M. Evans books are distributed to the trade via National Book Network. Query letters and SASEs should be directed to:

(Ms.) **P.J. Dempsey**, Senior Editor—Health, parenting, biography, cookbooks

FACTS ON FILE

132 West 31st Street, 17th Floor, New York, NY 10001

212-967-8800/1-800-322-8755   fax: 212-967-9196/1-800-678-3633

www.factsonfile.com   e-mail: Custserv@factsonfile.com

Facts On File specializes in reference and information titles in a broad popular range, including science, nature, technology, world history, American history, business, popular culture, fashion, design, sports, health, current affairs and politics, and the environment—in addition to general reference works. Facts On File offers a broad selection of historical and cultural atlases, dictionaries, and encyclopedias geared toward professional as well as popular interests and is one of the pioneers of the electronic multimedia-publishing frontier.

Facts On File (founded in 1940) is a dynamic popular-reference publisher. The house has many award-winning titles to its credit, and many Facts On File publications feature an innovative production approach. The publisher is extremely well tuned to specific category markets, which it targets with marked commercial consistency.

Facts On File has made a renewed commitment to its goal of becoming the premier print and electronic reference publisher in the industry. It is striving to be a beacon and a guide for librarians, teachers, students, parents, and researchers to look to for award-winning materials, cutting-edge trends, and innovative products. This is the publisher to be sought when the requirements are nebulous and the transitions are turbulent.

The year 1998 brought the launch of the trade imprint Checkmark Books. It was created to provide booksellers and consumers with quality resources focused on topics such as business, careers, fitness, health and nutrition, history, nature, parenting, pop culture, and self-help.

Facts On File titles include: *Career Opportunities in Banking, Finance and Insurance* by Thomas Finch; *Career Opportunities in Health Care* by Shelly Field; *Career Opportunities in Law and the Legal Industry* by Susan Echaore-McDavid; *Career Opportunities in Politics, Government, and Activism* by Joan Axelrod-Contrada, foreword by Senator John Kerry; *Career Opportunities in the Fashion Industry* by Peter Vogt; *Encyclopedia of American Law* by David Schultz; *Encyclopedia of American Prisons* by Carl Sifakis; *Encyclopedia of JFK* by Benson; *Encyclopedia of Kidnappings* by Michael Newton; *The Facts on File Dictionary of Astronomy*; *The Encyclopedia of Child Abuse*; *New Complete Book of Herbs, Spices & Condiments*; *The Encyclopedia of Schizophrenia and Other Psychotic Disorders*; *British English from A to Zed*; *Edgar Allan Poe A to Z*; *The Literary 100*; *Words to Rhyme With*; *Career Opportunities for Writers*; *The Executors' Handbook*; *Best Baby Names in the World*; *Black Belt Tae Kwon Do*; *Forbidden Films*; *Athletic Scholarships*; *Career Ideas for Kids Who Like Money*.

The On File program is an award-winning collection of reference materials. Spanning virtually every subject in the middle- and high-school curricula, each On File contains hundreds of images that visually depict complex subjects in a way that will both engage and inform young people. Even students at the elementary and college levels will find the material useful. Filled with hundreds of exciting hands-on activities, projects, exercises, and experiments, On File binders encourage critical thinking and allow students to actively participate in their educational process.

Facts On File utilizes individualized marketing and distribution programs that are particularly strong in the areas of corporate, institutional, and library sales. Query letters and SASEs should be directed to:

Jeff Soloway, Senior Editor—Reference books: language and literature

Laurie Likoff, Editorial Director—Family, parenting, trade books, science, music, history

Nicole Bowen, Executive Editor—Reference books: American history and culture, multicultural; and nonfiction young-adult reference books about history,

American culture and history, music, women's studies

Jim Chambers, Editor-in-Chief—Trade books, entertainment subjects, and reference books on entertainment subjects, TV, movies, Broadway, sports, and health; Ferguson Imprint, career titles

Frank Darmstadt, Senior Editor—Reference books, science, technology, nature

Claudia Schab, Editor—World history, religion

Owen Lancer, Editor-in-Chief—Reference books, geography, military, politics and government, history, law

FAIRVIEW PRESS

2450 Riverside Avenue, Minneapolis, MN 55454

612-672- 4180/ 1-800-544-8207   fax: 612-672-4980

www.fairviewpress.org   e-mail: press@fairview.org

Fairview Press publishes books and related materials that educate individuals and families about their physical, emotional, and spiritual health and motivate them to seek positive changes in themselves and their communities.

Fairview Press (formerly Deaconess Press; founded in 1988) is a division of Fairview Health Services, a community-focused health system affiliated with the University of Minnesota.

Imprints of Fairview Press include Fairview Publications (medical/technical) and the Center for Spirituality and Healing (integrative medicine and spirituality).

On the Fairview list: *Karma and Happiness* by Miriam E. Cameron, PhD, RN (foreword by His Holiness the Dalai Lama); *Navigating Through a Strange Land* edited by Tricia Ann Roloff; *The Cancer Poetry Project* edited by Karin B. Miller; *Staying Strong* by Lorie A Schleck; *Choices at the End of Life* by Linda Norlander, RN, MS and Kerstin McSteen, RN, MS; *The New Nursing Homes* by Marilyn Rantz, PhD, Lori Popejoy, RN and Mary Zwygart-Stauffer, PhD; *The Complete Mall Walker's Handbook* by John Bland, MD, with Jenna Colby, RD, LD; *A Senior's Guide to Personal Safety* by Janee Harteau and Holly Keegel; *Help Me Say Goodbye* by Janis Silverman; *A Garden of Love and Healing* by Marsha Olson, MA; *In Sickness and in Health* by Gail Lynch; *Saying Goodbye* by Marge Heegaard.

Fairview Press operates through a variety of sales venues; the press is distributed to the trade through National Book Network. Query letters and SASEs should be addressed to:

Lane Stiles, Director

Stephanie Billecke, Editor

FANTAGRAPHICS BOOKS

7563 Lake City Way NE, Seattle, WA 98115

206-524-1967/1-800-657-1100   fax: 206-524-2104

www.fantagraphics.com   e-mail: fbicomix@fantagraphics.com

Fantagraphics produces comics and comic art. The house accents a list of mainstream, classic, and borderline offerings in this specialty arena and also purveys a strong line of erotic comics and books. Fantagraphics Books (inaugurated in 1976) produces trade paperbacks, hardbound editions, and quality fine-art album editions of graphic productions, in addition to comic books, comics-related magazines, and a line of gift items dedicated to this most accessible literary form.

The Fantagraphics roster features some of the finest cartoonists of America and around the world. Included are reprints of classic newspaper comic-strip series—as well as works by underground masters, political satirists, artists in the realms of science fiction and fantasy, and emerging young Turks in the field.

Comics creators cataloged by Fantagraphics include Peter Bagge, Vaughn Bode, Daniel Clowes, Guido Crepax, Robert Crumb, Dame Darcy, Kim Deitch, Julie Doucet, Jules Feiffer, Frank Frazetta, Drew Friedman, Rick Geary, Los Bros. Hernandez, Peter Kuper, Terry LeBan, Douglas Michael, Joe Sacco, Gilbert Shelton, Art Spiegelman, Ralph Steadman, Basil Wolverton, and Wallace Wood.

Fantagraphics projects: *Dead End* by Thomas Ott; *Black Hole #10* by Charles Burns; *Hate Annual #3* by Peter Bagge; *Death & Candy* by Max Anderson; *T.O.T.T.* by Thomas Ott; *Angry Youth Comix #4* by Johnny Ryan; *The R. Crumb Sketchbook* by Robert Crumb; *Raisin Pie #1* by Rick Altergott and Ariel Bordeaux; *Weasel #5* by Dave Cooper; *Love & Rockets Vol. 2#5* by Los Bros. Hernandez; *20th Century Eightball* by Dan Clowes; *Meatcake #12* by Dame Darcy; *Burn Bitchy Burn* by Roberta Gregory; *Latest Issue: Naughty Bits #36* by Roberta Gregory; *Pecilia* by Richard Sala; *Schhh!* by Jason; *The Stuff of Dreams* by Kim Deitch.

Fantagraphics distributes its own list and catalogs selections from a number of other comics- and graphics-oriented publishers, in addition to audio CDs, computer CD-ROMs, videotapes, and books, posters, and calendars. Query letters should be accompanied by short, carefully selected samples.

Michael Dowers, Submissions Editor

FOUR WALLS EIGHT WINDOWS

39 West 14th Street, Suite 503, New York, NY 10011

212-206-8965   fax: 212-206-8799

www.4w8w.com   e-mail: edit@4w8w.com

Four Walls Eight Windows offers a select seasonal list in creative nonfiction and literary fiction oriented toward topical issues and current culture. The house is known for journalistic forays into progressive politics, experimental fiction that features a stylistic and intellectual edge (including illustrated narrative), American and world culture expressed and portrayed through the essay, penetrating literary and critical studies, and individualistic poetry.

This is a publisher with a list far from the norm: Four Walls Eight Windows catalogs cultural artifacts in book form. The house hosts a healthy backlist laden with critically acclaimed, accomplished sellers, as well as an array of literary reprints.

Four Walls Eight Windows (established in 1987) was founded by John Oakes and Daniel Simon. Repeat: Contrary to speculation, when Dan Simon split to found the independent press Seven Stories (in early 1995; see separate entry for Seven Stories in this directory), John Oakes did not even contemplate a name change to Two Walls Four Windows.

Representative titles from Four Walls include: *Veiled Threat* by Sally Armstrong; *The Hacker and the Ants* by Rudy Rucker; *Little Doors* by Paul Di Filippo; *Puerto Rican Cuisine in America* by Oswald Rivera; *The Neanderthal's Necklace* by Juan Luis Arsuaga; *The Struggle with the Angel* by Jean-Paul Kauffmann; *Everyone in Silico* by Jim Munroe; *Homecoming* by Natasha Radojcic-Kane; *The Man in the Gray Flannel Suit* by Sloan Wilson; *Vegetarianism* by Colin Spencer; *Entanglement* by Amir D. Aczel; *Craze* by Jessica Warner; *One Nation Under Gods* by Richard Abanes; *Steal This Book* by Abbie Hoffman; *Headbanger* by Hugo Hamilton; *The Angel Quickest for Flight* by Steven Kotler; *Here Comes the Bride* by Jaclyn Geller; *The Autobiography of Abbie Hoffman* by Abbie Hoffman; *Before the Big Bang: The Origins of the Universe and the Nature of Matter* by Ernest J. Sternglass; *Sizzling Chops and Devilish Spins* by Jerome Charyn; *The Prisoners of Cabrera* by Denis Smith; *Death in Paradise* by Tony Blache and Brad Schreiber; *Synners* by Pat Cadigan; *The Bone Museum* by Wayne Grady; *The Jaguar Hunter* by Lucius Shepard; *The Thank You Book* by Carole Stuart.

Four Walls Eight Windows books are distributed to the trade by Publishers Group West; foreign rights are administered by Writers House. Query letters and SASEs should be directed to:

Jofie Ferrari-Adler, Associate Editor

FOXROCK, INC.

61 Fourth Avenue, New York, NY 10003

fax: 212-673-1039

www.foxrock.com   e-mail: evergreen@nyc.rr.com

Foxrock was formed in 1994 by Barney Rosset, John G. H. Oakes, and Dan Simon. Since operations began in 1994, Foxrock has published books and distributed video-tapes. Foxrock, Inc., features fine writing in both hardcover and paperback. Foxrock hosts literary anthologies, poetic works, shorter and longer fiction, as well as general trade titles.

On the Foxrock list: *The Pearl* by Anonymous; *In Broken Wigwag* by Sushi Asano; *Exploits of a Young Rakehell* by Guillaume Apollinaire Amorous; *The Story of Venus and Tannhauser* by Aubrey Beardsley & John Glassco; *Eleutheria* by Samuel Beckett; *Stirrings Still* by Samuel Beckett; *Brazen* by Ghislaine Dunant; *The Man Sitting in the Corridor* by Marguerite Duras; *Jew Boy* by Alan Kaufman; *Lo's Diary* by Pia Pera; *Triangulation from a Known Point* (poetry) by Ruth Danon; *New and Selected Poems 1930–1990* by Richard Eberhart; *The Colors of Infinity* (poetry) by Donald E. Axinn.

The Foxrock Line has republished a number of classic literary compilations: *The Olympia Reader* and *The New Olympia Reader* (edited by Maurice Girodias) are filled with ribald and erotic writings first published in Paris by the germinal publisher of Olympia Press, Maurice Girodias; these volumes feature the work of such authors as Jean Genet, Henry Miller, Chester Himes, Lawrence Durrell, William S. Burroughs, Gregory Corso, George Bataille, John Cleland, Pauline Réage, Samuel Beckett, and the Marquis de Sade. Blue Moon Publisher Barney Rosset, along with associates, has edited *Evergreen Review Reader 1957–1966*, featuring selections from *Evergreen*, America's fabled journal of literary provocateurism.

Query letters and SASEs should be directed to:

Barney Rosset, President

Astrid Myers, Publisher's Assistant

FREE SPIRIT PUBLISHING

217 Fifth Avenue North, Suite 200, Minneapolis, MN 55401-1299

612-338-2068/1-800-735-7323   fax: 612-337-5050

www.freespirit.com   e-mail: help4kids@freespirit.com

Free Spirit Publishing produces trade nonfiction arenas keyed to parenting, child and adolescent development, the family, education, and relationships. Areas of special concentration: self-help for kids; self-help for teens; gifted and talented education, learning differences (LD), creative learning, parenting and teaching, social action, service learning, school success. Free Spirit Publishing offers creative learning materials that enrich the lives of children and teens.

Free Spirit publications include issue-focused guides for students, educators, parents, mental health professionals, children, and teens. The publisher (founded in 1983) has been particularly successful with its Self-Help for Kids and Self-Help for Teens lines of books and educational materials. Free Spirit also catalogs posters and other creative learning wares.

Free Spirit highlights: *101 Giraffe Heroes: Ready-to-Read Scripts About People Sticking Their Necks Out for the Common Good* by The Giraffe Project; *Boy v. Girl? How Gender Shapes Who We Are, What We Want, and How We Get Along* by George Abrahams, PhD and Shelia Ahlbrand; *Children's Dream Dictionary: How to Interpret Your Children's Dreams* by Amanda Cross; *Cunning, Devious, and Mesmerizing Mind-Bending Puzzles* by Terry Stickles; *Don't Sweat It! Every Body's Answers to Questions You Don't Want to Ask: A Guide for Young People* by Marguerite Crump, M.A., M.Ed; *Grades 10-12 Giraffe Heroes Program Resource Guide* by The Giraffe Project.

Free Spirit's distribution is through the trade market, as well as direct to schools and other youth-serving venues. Query letters and SASEs should be directed to:

Sid Farrar, Executive Editor

Liz Stein, Editor

Douglas J. Fehlen, Acquisitions Assistant

W. H. FREEMAN AND COMPANY PUBLISHERS

COMPUTER SCIENCE PRESS

SCIENTIFIC AMERICAN BOOKS

41 Madison Avenue, New York, NY 10010

212-576-9400/1-800-903-3019   fax: 212-689-2383

www.whfreeman.com

W. H. Freeman represents a tradition of outstanding and innovative publishing in the sciences. Freeman books often display superb graphics and fine design. W. H. Freeman and Company (established in 1946) is a sister company of Scientific American, Inc. The house logs a trusty backlist.

From Freeman: *Discovering the Universe* by Neil F. Comins and William J. Kaufmann; *Exploring Human Geography* by Margaret Pearce; *EarthInquiry: Earthquakes and Plate Boundaries* by the American Geological Institute; *EarthInquiry: Long-Term Climate

Change by William F. Ruddiman; *Geometry: Seeing, Doing, Understanding 3rd ed.* by Harold R. Jacobs; *The Practice of Statistics, 2nd ed* by Dan Yates, David Moore, and Daren S. Starnes; *BioStats Basics* by James L. Gould; *Modern Genetic Analysis* by Anthony Griffiths, William Gelbart, Richard Lewontin, and Jeffrey Miller; *General Chemistry* by American Chemical Society; *Physical Chemistry* by Peter Atkins and Julio DePaula; *Chemical Principles* by Peter Atkins and Loretta Jones; *Bridging to the Lab* by Loretta Jones and Roy Tasker.

W. H. Freeman oversees its own distribution. Query letters and SASEs should be directed to:

Clancy Marshall, Acquisitions Editor—Chemistry

Jason Noe, Sponsoring Editor—Life Science

Terri Ward, Acquisitions Editor—Mathematics

Sara Tenney, Publisher—Life Science and geography

FULCRUM PUBLISHING

16100 Table Mountain Parkway, Suite 300, Golden, CO 80403-5093

303-277-1623/1-800-992-2908

www.fulcrum-books.com   e-mail: fulcrum@fulcrum-books.com

Fulcrum publishes general trade nonfiction books, with emphasis on gardening, nature, and the outdoors; food; travel guides; business and the environment; Colorado and the Rockies; parenting; health; humor; and American history, world history, and cultural history.

Fulcrum imprints and lines include the Library of Congress series of Americana, educational books (for children and adults), and the Starwood line of books and calendars; the house also issues selected audiocassettes on the Fulcrum Audio Book imprint. Native American writers and subjects are a vital part of the Fulcrum program.

Fulcrum Publishing (founded in 1984) is a growing firm with an ambitious list. It is the Fulcrum vision to produce works that provide a link to the experiences and wisdom of the past. This image fits in neatly with the publisher's characterization of the editorial relationship:

"In his autobiography, Anthony Trollope wrote, 'Of all the needs that a book has, the chief need is that it be readable.' When that happens, it is due to excellent writers and professional and understanding editors. It is difficult and sometimes lonely being a writer, but a good editor is a supporter, a confidant, a representative of the reader, and often can assist the writer in producing a book far better than the writer is capable of creating alone. Sometimes the changes are obvious, sometimes subtle, but they are always aimed at making the book readable. Bob Baron, Publisher, would like to praise and thank Fulcrum's dedicated editors who have made all of its 250 books possible and who have tried to achieve the standards of Trollope."

This is good news for Fulcrum readers, and good news for writers, too. Fulcrum supports a hefty backlist.

Special Fulcrum projects: *The Book in America* by Richard Clement, which used the vast resources in the Library of Congress to trace the history of the American book. *All the World's a Stage*, a volume that combines writing from William Shakespeare with the calligraphy and full-color illustrations of Dorothy Boux. Fulcrum is working with colleagues in England to celebrate the building of the new Globe Theatre in London. *Faces of a Nation: The Rise and Fall of the Soviet Union, 1917–1991*, is a photo essay featuring Dmitri Daltermants, Russia's most famous photographer, with text by noted historian Theodore H. Von Laue.

On the Fulcrum list: *The Intuitive Gardener: Finding Creative Freedom in the Garden* by Marilyn Raff; *Evolution, Creationism, and Other Modern Myths: A Critical Inquiry* by Vine Deloria, Jr.; *Red Delta: Fighting for Life at the End of the Colorado River* by Charles Bergman; *The Edge of Enchantment: Sovereignty and Ceremony in Huatulco, Mexico* by Alicia Maria Gonzalez (photographs by Robert Ysais); *Surviving with Heart: Six Steps to Helping Patients and Caregivers Take Charge of Their Heart Care* by Darrell Trout and Ellen Welch; *A Road of Her Own: Women's Journeys in the West* by Marlene Blessing.

Fulcrum Publishing handles its own distribution. Query letters and SASEs should be directed to:

Bob Baron, President and Publisher

Charlotte Baron, Vice President

Dianne Howie, Vice President

Marlene Blessing, Editor in Chief

Daniel Forrest-Bank, Managing Editor

Susan Zernial, Editor—Education

T. J. Baker, Acquisitions Editor—Projects consistent with the house list

F&W BOOKS

4700 E. Galbraith Road, Cincinnati, OH 45236

513-531-2690   fax: 513-531-0798

www.fwpublications.com

F&W Books (a division of F&W Publications, founded in the early 1900s) is a large publisher of special-interest magazines and books. Through recent acquisitions of Krause Publications and other purchases, it has become one of the largest publishers of books for hobbyist and enthusiast interests in crafts, scrapbooking, art, antiques and collectibles, and other pastimes. The company is directed by William F. Reilly, past chairman of Macmillan, Inc. and Primedia.

Imprints include Krause Publications (see separate listing), David & Charles (crafts, equestrian, and railroading), North Light Books (decorative painting and fine art), HOW Design Books (graphic design), Warman's (antiques and collectibles), Betterway Books (consumer reference and genealogy), Memory Makers (scrapbooking), Popular Woodworking Books, and Writer's Digest Books (see separate listing).

F&W Books markets its products through trade channels, direct mail, and through the company's affiliated magazines. It also operates its own consumer book clubs in its areas of interest.

David Lewis, Executive Vice President, Book Division, Product Development

GARRETT PUBLISHING

384 South Military Trail, Deerfield Beach, FL 33442

954-480-8543   fax: 954-698-0057

www.garrettpub.com   e-mail: info@garrettpub.com

Garrett's focus is on books in business, finance, law, and personal finance. Garrett books are practical, often featuring a self-help/how-to approach that highlights sample forms, ready-to-use templates, checklists, instructions, resources, and informative examples. A major Garrett imprint is E-Z Legal Books.

Garrett Publishing (founded in 1990) is on the lookout for authors with marketable projects: authors who are expert in their fields and know how to get their point across clearly and enthusiastically. Garrett's marketing department is staffed with professionals skilled in publicity, promotions, advertising, and editorial services. Garrett promotes its authors' books through print advertising, television appearances, and radio spots. The house offers competitive advances and royalties.

With sales representatives located strategically across the United States, Garrett's books are available in the giant trade bookseller chains and are obtainable from major wholesalers and distributors. Over the past several seasons, the publisher has expanded its retail distribution.

Representative of the Garrett program: *Asset Protection Secrets; How to Settle with the IRS For Pennies on the Dollar, 2nd Edition; Building Your Financial Fortress: How to Protect Your Assets from the 10 Deadly Threats to Your Wealth!; The Limited Partnership Book.*

Garrett Publishing distributes through its own house operation, as well as via such outlets as Quality Book Distributors, Ingram, and Baker and Taylor. Query letters and SASEs should be directed to:

Dr. Arnold Goldstein, Editor/Owner

GENERAL PUBLISHING GROUP

This young West Coast start-up fell victim to the harsh realities of independent publishing and closed shop.

THE GLOBE PEQUOT PRESS

246 Goose Lane #200, PO Box 480, Guilford, CT 06437-0833

203-458-4500/1-800-820-2329   fax: 1-800-508-8938

www.globepequot.com   e-mail: info@globepequot.com

Globe Pequot Press (founded in 1947) is a specialist in travel and outdoor recreation, with additional interest in cooking, personal finance, and home-based business. The publisher accents titles marketed to both trade and specialty market slots.

Within this program, Globe Pequot looks for works in a number of important categories: travel books—regional and special-interest travel guides; family adventure guides; travel annuals, accommodations guides, itinerary-format guides, and travel how-to's; outdoor recreation—any outdoor sport, how-to, and where-to guides; and home-based business. Authors should have firsthand experience running the featured home-based business.

In the travel arena, Globe Pequot is well regarded for several bestselling series and also distributes for a number of travel-specialist houses. Among Globe Pequot lines: Quick Escapes (weekend and day trips keyed to metropolitan areas or regions); Romantic Days and Nights; Recommended Bed & Breakfasts; Fun with the Family Guides; Cadogan Guides to destinations worldwide for the discriminating traveler; and the popular Off-the-Beaten-Path series. Globe Pequot also updates a variety of annuals, among them *Europe by Eurorail*. Globe Pequot's regionally keyed books also cover such interest areas as biking, hiking, mountaineering, skiing, and family activities in the wilderness and on the beach.

Globe Pequot representative titles: Travel Books: *London-Paris*, 2nd ed.; *The Complete Guide to the National Park Lodges*, 3rd ed.; *Insiders' Guide to Williamsburg-Jamestown*, 11th ed.; *Chicago Off the Beaten Path*, 1st ed.; *100 Best All-Inclusive Resorts of the World*, 2nd ed.; *Hostels USA*, 4th ed.

Outdoor recreation books: *World Atlas of Saltwater Fishing* (hardcover); *Hiking Sequoia and Kings Canyon National Parks*; *Watching Wildlife: Trips, Gear and Great Places*; *Central Appalachian Wildflowers*; *Mountain Biking Moab*; *Foraging New England*. Other subjects: *Honor Our Flag* by David Singleton; *Legendary Lighthouses, Vol. III* by John Grant and Ray Jones; *Quotable New York* by Gregg Stebben; *The SAS Fighting Techniques*

Handbook by Terry White; *Remembering Charles Kuralt* by Ralph Grizzle. Berlitz Categories and titles: General Language Study: *Basic English for Spanish*. Language For Travel: *African Phrase Book*. Language For Business: *Greek Cassette Pack*. Language Reference: *1,000 German Words*. Berlitz Pocket Guides: *Athens Pocket Guide*. Executive Travel Guide: *Business Travel Guide to Europe*. Berlitz Kids: *Berlitz Kids Adventures With Nicholas: A Visit To Grandma*.

Globe Pequot was purchased in early 1997 by Morris Communications Corporation, a privately held company (founded in 1795) with nationwide, diversified holdings in newspaper and magazine publishing, radio, outdoor advertising, and computer services. Query letters and SASEs should be directed to:

Mary Norris, Executive Editor, Acquisitions consistent with house list

Shelley Wolf, Submissions Editor—General submissions

Laura Strom, Executive Editor—Travel submissions
Born: April 24.
Education: B.A., English Literature.
Employment history/editor career path: I started out in an unrelated industry out of college, but shortly after that I worked in an entry-level position at a vanity press and then shortly after that I moved to Connecticut and got an editorial/proofreading position. Four years later Globe Pequot was hiring, and I have been with the company for 11 years.
Personal interests: Traveling, swing dancing, gardening, being outdoors.
What would you be doing if you were not an editor? I would be a farmer.
What has been your most successful book that you have acquired to date? A companion book to a PBS genre on legendary lighthouses (Fall 1998); it's been back to press four times.
What books have you acquired that make you the most proud? What books that you have acquired reflect the types of books you like to represent? The companion book is one of them, also a book titled *New York Neighborhoods*, which is a food lovers' guide to the ethnic community by Elenor Berman (1999). I also developed a romantic travel book called *Romantic Days and Nights*.
Do you represent fiction? If so, what do you look for? No.
Do you represent nonfiction? Yes. In our specific areas (travel).
Do you require book proposals? If so, what do you look for in evaluating a book proposal? Yes. First I look to see if it's something we actually publish; well-credentialed authors; new ideas that can be sold into nontrade; any previous writing experience.
Are certain aspects of a book proposal given more weight than others? We look for excellent writing, the marketability and promotability of the author.
What process do you use for making a decision? What is the process for acquisition, is there a committee? We do have a committee that meets every couple of weeks and the Acquisitions Editors usually present the new ideas to the committee. The committee is made up of sales representatives, as well as our administration and editorial staff. We discuss new ideas that we have, and if everyone agrees, we do a thor-

ough competition search, and so on.

What kinds of nonfiction books do you want to see less of? Motor home travel books.

Do you think that agents are important? Why? Yes, agents are really important. They tend to represent some of the better authors. We also work with unagented authors or previous authors of ours.

Do you like new writers? What should new writers do to break into the business? Yes, especially for our regional guidebooks. New writers are often very enthusiastic.

How should writers approach you? With a query letter via snail mail.

What are some common mistakes writers make? What really gets on your nerves? Query letters that sound like they are a sales pitch or gimmick.

What can writers do to get your attention and to avoid the slush pile? Be polite, undemanding, do periodic follow-ups by e-mail or through the mail. No phone calls.

What have been some of your best experiences with writers or in your job? Working with authors who really know how to write.

What, if anything, makes you different from other editors? I really care about my authors.

DAVID R. GODINE, PUBLISHER, INC.

9 Hamilton Place, Boston, MA 02108

617-451-9600   fax: 617-350-0250

www.godine.com   e-mail:info@godine.com

Godine publishes trade nonfiction in such areas as history and criticism, typography and graphic arts, art and architecture, horticulture, cooking, Americana, and regional-interest books. The house also publishes fiction (including mysteries), literature and essays, and poetry, as well as children's books. Godine offers a line of classic works in reprint, as well as works in translation.

The Godine program is committed to quality. Godine specializes in attentively produced hardcover and trade paperback editions. The house issues a small catalog of new titles each year, while maintaining an active backlist. Godine's imprints include Country Classics, Double Detectives, and Nonpareil Books.

David R. Godine, Publisher, Inc. (founded in 1969), was started in an abandoned cow barn, where founder David R. Godine both worked and lived; the expanding operation later moved to Boston.

Godine has intentionally kept itself small, its list eclectic, and its quality consistently high, with a stronger concentration on titles with backlist potential (particularly nonfiction). The house maintains its fortunate position of being able to ask:"What do we really believe is superior?" rather than "What are we confident will sell?" The editors at Godine have learned to trust their instincts. By staying small, this house is lucky enough to have kept most of its goals attainable. It does not need to sell 10,000 copies of a book to make money. It does not need to put authors on tour or to indulge in massive hype. Good books, like water, find their own levels. It sometimes takes years, but it is inevitable.

In short, David R. Godine, Publisher, remains what it was 30 years ago: a true cottage industry, surviving on a very small budget, and doing what it does and what it knows best: publishing books that matter for people who care.

Titles from Godine: *At the Edge of Light* by David Travis; *Bear* by Marian Engel; *A Century for the Century* by Martin Hunter & Jerry Kelly; *A Cottage Garden Alphabet*, woodcuts by Andrea Wisnewski; *English Pleasure Gardens* by Rose Standish Nichols, introduction by Judith B. Tankard; *Gloucestermen Stories* by Jams B. Connolly; *Lines* by Olin Stephens, foreward by J. Carter Brown, introduction by Knight Coolidge; *The Last Buffalo Hunter* by Jake Mosher; *Lotte Jacobi* by Peter Moriarty; *New England Days*, photographs by Paul Caponigro, foreword by Aprile Gallant; *Peace in the House* by Faye Moskowitz; *The Penelopeia* by Jane Rawlings, illustrated by Heather Hurst; *The Picts & the Martyrs* by Arthur Ransome; *Sledding on Hospital Hill*, poems by Leland Kinsey; *Something's Not Quite Right* by Guy Billout; *The Man Who Liked Slow Tomatoes* by K.C. Constantine; *Missee Lee* by Arthur Ransome; *Age of Wonders* by Aharon Appelfeld & translated by Dalya Bilu; *Anatomy of a Typeface* by K.C. Constantine; *Calligraphic Flourishing* by William Hildebrandt; *The Sacrificial Years* by Walt Whitman.

Query letters and SASEs should be directed to:

The Editorial Department

GRAYWOLF PRESS

2402 University Avenue, Suite 203, Saint Paul, MN 55114

651-641-0077   fax: 651-641-0036

www.graywolfpress.org   e-mail: wolves@graywolfpress.com

Graywolf publishes poetry, fiction, and nonfiction and essays. Graywolf produces works by writers past and present, with particular emphasis on the scene of contemporary international letters, as well as a line of literary anthologies and reissues. Graywolf hosts a solid backlist of featured titles.

The Graywolf Press trade motto is "Creative writing for creative reading." This distinctive approach to publishing signifies Graywolf Press as an independent, not-for-profit publisher dedicated to the creation and promotion of thoughtful and imaginative contemporary literature essential to a vital and diverse culture.

Graywolf backs up its authors and its literary claims with publishing prowess: the

Graywolves have been successful in finding an audience for their works, and the Graywolf Press list has been augmented, confirming the achievement of a program that runs contrary to the stream of contemporary commercial publishing.

Begun in 1974, Graywolf Press exemplifies the small-scale independent American literary house. The publisher's wolf pack logo marks a list rippling with award-winners and critical endorsement.

The Graywolf Forum series was launched with the publication of *Graywolf Forum One: Tolstoy's Dictaphone: Technology and the Muse*, a collection of new essays edited by Sven Birkerts (author of the hotly debated Gutenberg Elegies).

Graywolf sample titles include: *Without an Alphabet, Without a Face* by Saadi Youssef (translated by Khaled Mattawa); *Avoidance* by Michael Lowenthal; *Deposition* by Katie Ford; *Blind Huber* by Nick Flynn; *Early Morning, Remembering My Father, William Stafford* by Kim Stafford; *Famous Builder* by Paul Lisicky; *The House in Eccles Road* by Judith Kitchen; *Can Poetry Matter? Essays on Poetry and American Culture* by Diana Gioia; *Owning It All* by William Kittredge; *Trespass* by Grace Dane Mazur; *Eat Quite Everything You See* by Leslie Adrienne Miller; *Heart-Side Up* by Barbara Dimmick; *Still Life with Waterfall* by Eamon Grennan; *The Complete French Poems of Rainer Maria Rilke* translated by A Poulin, Jr.; *No Shelter, The Selected Poems of Pure Lopez-Colome* translated by Forrest Gander; *Bellocq's Ophelia* by Natasha Trethewey; *Crying at the Movies, A Film Memoir* by Madelon Sprengnether; *Too Bright to See & Alma* by Linda Gregg.

Graywolf Press utilizes a network of regional sales representatives; books are proffered to the trade through Consortium Book Sales and Distribution. Query letters and SASEs should be directed to:

Katie Dublinski, Editor—Fiction

Anne Czarniecki, Executive Editor—Fiction and Nonfiction

Daniel Kos, Publishing Assistant

Fiona McCrae, Publisher

GROVE/ATLANTIC, INC.

ATLANTIC MONTHLY PRESS

GROVE PRESS

841 Broadway, New York, NY 10003

212-614-7860   fax: 212-614-7886

www.groveatlantic.com

Grove/Atlantic publishes trade nonfiction and fiction; these works often display a contemporary cultural bent or an issue-oriented edge. Grove Press and Atlantic Monthly

Press, two previously independent houses, are united under the Grove/Atlantic, Inc., corporate crest. Grove/Atlantic operates from the former Grove headquarters on Broadway (with Atlantic having relocated from its previous digs at nearby Union Square West). Grove/Atlantic operates essentially as one house, while maintaining the distinction of two major imprints. (See separate subentries further on for both Atlantic Monthly Press and Grove Press.)

Grove/Atlantic holds a tradition of publishing arresting literature—from the writing of Samuel Beckett and William S. Burroughs to Jean Genet and Marguerite Duras, from John Kennedy Toole and J. P. Donleavy to Henry Miller and Jeanette Winterson. The house initiated an aggressive program to repackage these modern classics, as well as to return to print the work of such celebrated writers as Terry Southern, Robert Coover, Jerzy Kosinski, Frederick Barthelme, Patricia Highsmith, Aharon Appelfeld, Barry Hannah, and Kenzaburo Oe. In a marketplace it sees as increasingly dominated by ephemera, Grove/Atlantic is committed to publishing serious books that last and to introducing classic books to a new generation of readers.

Subsequent to the previously noted Grove/Atlantic merger—with Atlantic most decidedly the major partner—speculation was that Atlantic had bought Grove essentially for Grove's extensive, internationally renowned backlist; Atlantic would presumably vampirize Grove's backlist, then cast aside the dry husk of Grove Press to any interested bidders. Happily, such tiresome prognostications have not come to pass; the publishing image of Grove/Atlantic is, if anything, more finely honed under the auspices of the umbrella house.

Titles from Grove/Atlantic include: *Gould's Book of Fish* by Richard Flanagan; *Old Flames* by John Lawton; *Eden* by Olympia Vernon; *The Devil That Danced on the Water* by Aminatta Forna; *Dumped* by Delores Max; *Dorian* by Will Self; *Wagons West, The Epic Story of America's Overland Trails*; *Fair Warning* by Robert Olen Butler; *The Siege* by Helen Dunmore; *Saddam Hussein* by Efraim Karsh; *Ice Cream* by Helen Dunmore; *In the Shape of a Boar* by Lawrence Norfolk; *The Inquisitor's Manual* by Antonio Lobo; *Only One Thing Missing* by Luis Manuel Ruiz; *Somersault* by Kenzaburo Oe; *Transforming Leadership* by James MacGregor; *The Pleasure of Eliza Lynch* by Anne Enrights; *August Frost* by Monique Roffey; *Goodnight, Nobody* by Michael Knight; *I, Lucifer* by Glen Duncan; *Parliament of Whores* by P. J. O'Rourke; *Scotland* by Magnus Magnusson; *Into Tibet* by Thomas Laird; *Labyrinth* by Randall Sullivan; *Birders* by Mark Cocker; *The Dark Clue* by James Wilson; *Living with Saints* by Mary O'Connell; *Howard Katz* by Patrick Marber; *The Hothouse* by Harold Pinter.

Amy Hundley, Editor

Brando Skyhorse, Editor

Daniel Maurer, Assistant Editor

ATLANTIC MONTHLY PRESS

Atlantic Monthly Press paces the spectrum of commercial categories, publishing hardcover and trade paperback editions in memoirs, belles lettres, history, social sciences, current affairs, natural history, ethnology, lifestyle, fashion, and cuisine, in addition to literary and popular fiction. AMP authors have over the years garnered an enormous wealth of recognition for their work, including Pulitzers, Nobels, and National Book Awards. The AMP Traveler series encompasses nonfiction works that offer unstinting looks at nations, cultures, and peoples of the world.

Atlantic Monthly Press has long been representative of the highest aims of American publishing—with a list that features quality writing, fine production, and strong commercial presence. Atlantic Monthly Press was inaugurated originally (in 1917) to be primarily a book-publishing vehicle for writers associated with *Atlantic Monthly* magazine. From 1925 through 1984 the press was an imprint of Boston's Little, Brown. Atlantic Monthly Press was bought by Carl Navarre in 1985, and under current owner-publisher Morgan Entrekin (who bought out Navarre in 1991), AMP (now in consort with Grove) continues as a leading force in American letters.

Prospective authors please note that Grove/Atlantic no longer accepts unsolicited material.

GROVE PRESS

Grove Press accents trade nonfiction and fiction with a sharp cultural consciousness and literary flair. The house continues to expand on its powerful backlist base by engaging at the forefront of publishing trends: Grove publishes a line of feature-film screenplays and has instituted a new poetry series.

Grove Press was founded in 1951 by literary trailblazer Barney Rosset, who established a tradition of enterprising lists that featured some of the finest and most fearless writing from around the globe. This literary institution was purchased by Ann Getty in 1985; in league with the British-based house of Weidenfeld & Nicholson, the publisher (briefly) operated under the sobriquet Grove Weidenfeld. With the early retreat of the Weidenfeld interests, the fate of Grove was a popular topic of publishing tattle—rumored by some to be perpetually on the block, both prior and subsequent to the house's merger with Atlantic Monthly Press.

Throughout these corporate shifts, Grove nevertheless extended its distinguished reputation, with a masterly mix of backlist offerings, as well as with commercially successful and stimulating new titles—as befits the Grove tradition.

The Grove nonfiction list covers biography and memoirs, popular culture worldwide, literary criticism, history, and politics.

Grove/Atlantic Monthly editors acquire in all areas consistent with house description. Prospective authors please note that Grove/Atlantic no longer accepts unsolicited material. However, you may still send a query or (occasionally) talk directly with an editor before sending a manuscript. Query letters and SASEs should be directed to:

Joan Bingham, Executive Editor

Morgan Entrekin, Publisher

HARCOURT INC.

HARCOURT TRADE CHILDREN'S BOOKS

HARVEST BOOKS

San Diego office:

525 B Street, Suite 1900, San Diego, CA 92101-4495

619-231-6616

New York office:

15 East 26th Street, New York, NY 10010

212-592-1000

www.harcourtbooks.com

The Harcourt trade division publishes the gamut of nonfiction categories, as well as some serious and commercial fiction, in hardcover and paperback editions. Special lines include Harcourt's Judaica backlist, literary works in translation, the Harvest imprint (which accents American and international literature and culture in trade paper originals and reprints), Gulliver Books (popular works in hardcover and trade paper for readers of all ages.

Harcourt (founded in 1919) has through the decades evolved into a publishing house of prodigious reach. Harcourt's multidimensional sprawl encompasses offices in such diverse locations as Chicago, Orlando, San Diego, Toronto, and New York. Although the trade-publishing program was trimmed markedly through the late 1980s into the early 1990s, Harcourt (formerly Harcourt Brace Jovanovich) remains particularly potent in the arena of educational materials and texts, as well as professional reference.

Among Harcourt subsidiaries are Academic Press, Johnson Reprint (scholarly and special-interest titles), W. B. Saunders (professional and academic medical publications), and Holt, Rinehart, & Winston (focusing on the educational market from elementary through university levels).

On the Harcourt list: *Last Man Out* by Melissa Fay Greene; *Alva & Irva* by Edward Carey; *Game Time* by Roger Angell (edited by Steve Kettman); *Slow Air*, poems by Robin Robinson; *Anything Can Happen* by Roger Rosenblatt; *Crabwalk* by Gunter Grass; *Bay Of Tigers* by Pedro Rosa Mendez; *October Men* by Roger Kahn; *Midsummer* by Marcelle Clements; *Scout's Honor* by Peter Applebome; *Star of the Sea* by Joseph O'Connor; *Mind Over Matter* by K.C. Cole; *The Secrets of the Vaulted Sky* by David Berlinsky; *The Other Side of Silence* by Andre Brink; *Changing Planes* by Ursula K. Le Guin; *Elsewhere in the Land of Parrots* by Jim Paul; *Lucca* by Jens Christian Grondahl; *Kartography* by Kamila Shamsie; *Personality* by Andrew O'Hagan; *Breaking Her Fall* by Stephen Goodwin; *Big If* by Mark Costello; *Sunday Jews* by Hortense Calisher;

The Demon and the Angel by Edward Hirsch; *Odd Girl Out* by Rachel Simmons; *The Missing Piece* by Antoine Bello; *Hester Among the Ruins* by Binnie Kirshenbaum; *Life of Pi* by Yann Martel; *Tales of Protection* by Erik Fosnes Hansen; *Boxing* by George Plimpton; *When I Was a Young Man* by Bob Kerry; *Mermaids Explained* by Christopher Reid; *Lost Legends of New Jersey* by Rederick Reiken; *Rails Under My Back* by Jeffery Renard Allen; *Scandalmonger* by William Safire; *Journey to Portugal* by Jose Saramago; *Nebula Awards Showcase 2001* by Robert Silverberg; *Jumping Fire* by Murray A. Taylor; *Confessions of Mycroft Holmes* by Marcel Theroux; *Half Empty, Half Full* by Susan C. Vaughan.

Harcourt handles its own distribution. Send query letters with SASEs to:

Walter Bode, Senior Editor—Literary fiction and nonfiction

Ann Patty, Executive Editor—Literary fiction, women's fiction

Daniel H. Farley, Vice President and Publisher (New York and San Diego)—Adult trade books

Jane Isay, Editor in Chief (New York)—Nonfiction books; hardcover originals; also works intended for the Harvest trade paper line

Drenka Willen, Editor (New York)—Literary fiction, translations; some poetry

HARCOURT TRADE CHILDREN'S BOOKS

GULLIVER BOOKS

GULLIVER GREEN

RED WAGON BOOKS

Harcourt children's categories include picture books, easy readers, nonfiction, fiction, poetry, big books, older readers, and reference books.

Harcourt produces a full offering of children's books in hardcover and paperback. Many Harcourt titles are presented as books for all ages—intended to embrace a wide readership range.

The house features several distinct imprints for young readers. Among them: Gulliver Books, Gulliver Green, Gulliver Books in Paperback, Red Wagon Books, Magic Carpet Books, Harcourt Big Books, Harcourt Creative Curriculum Connections, and the paperback lines Odyssey and Voyager Books—along with a lineup of author videos. Libros Viajeros is the Voyager line of Spanish-language books.

On the Harcourt children's list: *Babies on the Go* by Linda Ashman (illustrated by Jane Dyer); *Bubba and Beau* by Kathi Appelt (illustrated by Arthur Howard); *One Wide Sky* by Deborah Wiles (illustrated by Tim Bowers); *Ella Sarah Gets Dressed* by Margaret Chodos-Irvine; *B Is for Bulldozer* by June Sobel (illustrated by Melissa Iwai); *Hoptoad* by Jane Yolen (illustrated by Karen Lee Schmidt); *Rub-a-Dub Sub* by Linda Ashman (illustrated by Jeff Mack); *One Dark Night* by Lisa Wheeler (illustrated Ivan Bates); *The Complete Adventures of Big Dog and Little Dog* by Dav Pilkey.

Unsolicited manuscripts are no longer accepted. Editors now work exclusively through literary agents.

HARVEST BOOKS

Harvest Books, the trade paperback imprint of Harcourt Inc., offers the best from the house's illustrious 77-year publishing history, as well as from its distinguished present.

Harvest Books publishes fiction, nonfiction, and poetry by some of the most exciting writers and celebrities of our time. Many Harcourt hardcovers are published simultaneously in paperback by Harvest Books. Representative titles include: *The Years with Laura Diaz* by Carlos Fuentes; *Reading Magic* by Mem Fox; *Jell-O: A Biography* by Carolyn Wyman; *The Only Investment Guide You'll Ever Need* by Andrew Tobias; *The Tao of Elvis* by David Rosen; *Field Guide* by Gwendolen Gross; *The Columnist* by Jeffrey Frank; *Snow Mountain Passage* by James D. Houston.

Although Harcourt has greatly reduced its acquisitions of commercially oriented titles, the house is still active in the trade arena. Query letters and SASEs should be directed to:

André Bernard, Editor in Chief, Harvest Books

Katie Hesford, Editor

Jen Charat, Editor

HARLEQUIN BOOKS/SILHOUETTE BOOKS

HARLEQUIN BOOKS

SILHOUETTE BOOKS

RED DRESS INK

233 Broadway, Suite 1001, New York, NY 10279

212-553-4200

Harlequin and Silhouette publish romance novels, love stories, and women's fiction. With commanding emphasis on these interrelated categories, the publisher is always experimenting with inventive, distinctive lines that explore new approaches to the age-old tradition of tales of amour.

The Harlequin Books New York office issues several Harlequin series; the rest of the list is published from the Harlequin Enterprises base in Ontario, Canada (please see directory of Canadian publishers and editors), and the house's United Kingdom branch (contact information for which is listed under the Harlequin listing in the Canadian section). Silhouette Books (a division of Harlequin with editorial offices in New York) is profiled in a separate subentry further on.

Both Harlequin and Silhouette provide editorial guidelines for writers who wish to submit manuscripts for publishing consideration. Included in these materials are series requirements—including tips for authors regarding plot and character (some of which are applicable to other fiction-genre areas), as well as nuts-and-bolts advice pertaining to the preferred physical properties of manuscripts they review.

HARLEQUIN BOOKS

Harlequin Books is an innovator—not only in the romance category field, but in defining and refining the market for women's fiction in general. The Harlequin enterprise continues to access that important market sector through venues that range from direct marketing to discount-department-store wire racks to the woodgrained shelves of major book-chain superstores.

A précis of the Harlequin Books American lines follows.

Harlequin American Romance is an exciting series of passionate and emotional love stories—contemporary, engrossing, and uniquely American. These are longer, satisfying novels of conflict and challenge, stories of modern men and women dealing with life and love in today's changing world. Harlequin American Romance offers a lineup of contemporary, upbeat, action-packed novels, set in a world where everything is possible—not problem-based or introspective. These stories feature a characteristically self-assured, perceptive American woman as heroine. The hero is a dynamic American man who is irresistible, whether he's rough around the edges, earthy, slick, or sophisticated. Sizzling repartee and one-upmanship are hallmarks of the characters' attraction.

Because romance is all about mystery, Harlequin Intrigue offers something unique in the world of romance fiction: a compelling blend of romance, action, and suspense. These complex contemporary stories are chock-full of dynamic drama in the finest Harlequin tradition. Harlequin Intrigue is an exciting presentation of romance within such genre formats as a hidden identity, woman-in-jeopardy, whodunits, and thrillers. The love story is central to the mystery at the level of the novel's premise. The heroine and her hero must be indispensable to solving the mystery or completing whatever adventure they undertake. Their lives are on the line, as are their hearts.

Harlequin Historicals are tales of yesterday written for today's women. This distinctly different line delivers a compelling and quickly paced love story with all the scope of a traditional historical novel. Passionate romance and historical richness combine to give Harlequin Historicals a unique flavor. Harlequin Historicals are conceived as sweeping period romances and range from Medieval sagas to lighthearted Westerns and everything in between. These romance titles should be authentically detailed and realistic (to provide atmosphere, rather than a history lesson). Heroes and heroines are equally strong-willed, with their relationship the focus of the story. The writing should be rich and evocative, with the characters bringing the material alive so that the reader may connect with and appreciate the attributes of the historical setting. The story focus is on the heroine and how one man changes her life forever; the stories must have depth and complexity: Subplots and important secondary characters are necessary items here.

Sample bestsellers: (publisher included) *Spanish Disco* by Erica Orloff (Red Dress Ink Relationship); *Jackpot Baby* by Muriel Jensen (Harlequin American Romance); *Sister Found* by Joan Johnston (MIRA Romance); *Along Came Trouble* by Sherryl Woods (MIRA Romance); *Lionhearted* by Diana Palmer (Silhouette Romance); *An*

Arranged Marriage by Peggy Moreland (Silhouette Special Releases); *Dangerous* by Nora Roberts (Silhouette Special Releases).

Length of manuscript and level of sensuality vary from series to series; contact Harlequin for detailed editorial guidelines. When corresponding with Harlequin, please specify the series for which your manuscript is intended. Query letters and SASEs should be directed to:

Denise O'Sullivan, Associate Senior Editor, Harlequin Intrigue

Melissa Endlich, Associate Editor

Melissa Jeglinski, Associate Senior Editor, Harlequin American Romance

Tara Gavin, Editorial Director

Tracy Farrell, Senior Editor/Editorial Coordinator, Harlequin Historicals and Steeple Hill Love Inspired

Ann Leslie Tuttle, Associate Editor

Kim Nadelson, Associate Editor

Tina Colombo, Associate Editor

Priscilla Berthiaume, Associate Editor

SILHOUETTE BOOKS

Silhouette Books publishes adult category romances set in a contemporary milieu. Authors must indicate with their submissions for which series their work is intended. Silhouette Books was previously a major competitor of Harlequin Enterprises, its current parent company. A summary of the Silhouette romance lines follows.

Silhouette Romance is the house's original line of romance fiction. Silhouette Romance novels are contemporary, tender, emotional stories for today's reader, featuring the challenges and changes that occur as a couple falls in love. The wonder of a reassuring romance is that it can touch every woman's heart, no matter her age or experience. Although the hero and the heroine do not make love unless married, continuing sexual tension and strong romantic and emotional awareness keep the reader engaged. Silhouette encourages writers to come up with fresh twists to classic themes, as well as innovative, original stories. New writers are always welcome.

Silhouette Desire is a passionate, powerful, and provocative series with a strong emotional impact. Built on believable situations about how two people grow and develop, the plots capture the intensity of falling in love and explore the emotional and physical aspects of a meaningful relationship. Silhouette Desire accents the sensuous side of romance. These books are written for today's woman, whether innocent or experienced. The conflict should be emotional, springing naturally from within the characters. The characters do not have to be married to make love, but lovemaking is not taken lightly. New slants on classic formulas are welcome. Secondary characters and subplots must blend with the core story.

Silhouette Special Edition novels are substantial, contemporary romances that explore issues that heighten the drama of living and loving through true-to-life characters and compelling, romantic plots. Sophisticated and packed with emotion, these novels are for every woman who dreams of building a home with a very special man. With grace, courage, and determination, each of these vivacious heroines is empowered to be all that she can—lover, wife, mother—as she makes her dreams come true. Sensuality may be sizzling or subtle. The plot can run the gamut from the wildly innovative to the comfortably traditional. The novel's depth and emotional richness should contribute to the overall effect of a very special romance between unforgettable, fully developed characters.

Silhouette Intimate Moments features characters swept into a passionate world that is larger than life. These novels explore new directions by setting the core romance within the framework of today's mainstream novels: glamour, melodrama, suspense, and adventure, even occasionally paranormal. Let your imagination be your guide. Excitement is the key to a successful intimate moment novel. Your reader should be swept along with your characters as emotions run high against the backdrop of a compelling, complex, and always dramatic plot. Manuscript length and other series requirements vary; detailed editorial guidelines are available from the publisher. When querying, please specify the series for which your work is intended. Query letters and SASEs should be directed to:

Gail Chasan, Editor

Joan Marlow Golan, Senior Editor, Silhouette Desire

Karen Taylor Richman, Senior Editor, Silhouette Special Edition

Leslie Wainger, Executive Senior Editor, Silhouette Intimate Moments

Lynda Curnyn, Editor

Mary Theresa Hussey, Senior Editor, Silhouette Romance

Tara Gavin, Editorial Director

Julie Barnett, Editor

Susan Litman, Associate Editor

Diane Grecco, Assistant Editor

Kim Nadelson, Editor

Allison Lyons, Associate Editor

Mavis Allen, Associate Senior Editor

Stephanie Maurer, Assistant Editor

Patience Smith, Editor

Stacy Boyd, Associate Editor

Farren Jacobs, Associate Editor—Red Dress Ink

Margaret O'Neill Marbury, Senior Editor, Red Dress Ink

The Editorial Staff, Harlequin/Silhouette/Mills and Boon/Steeple Hill:

Born/Sign: Editorial age range is from early 20s to over 50, and we include every sign of the zodiac.

Employment history/editor career path: It varies with the editor. Some of the senior editorial staff have been with the company over 20 years; some of the junior and senior staff have worked at other publishing houses, both in romance publishing and other genres.

Personal interests: Responses include: Reading (of course!); walking; aerobics; fishing; salsa dancing; squash; art and sculpture; theater; architecture; interior design; dining out; psychology; travel; photography; watching television and movies; kids; playing the stock market.

What would you be doing if you were not an editor? Responses include: Unhappy accountant who reads romances at every opportunity; personal trainer and fitness instructor; veterinarian; archaeologist; film camera person; architect; classical actress or drama coach; librarian; teacher; bookstore employee; researcher; or producer for a website.

What has been your most successful book that you have acquired to date? We are proud of the success of a wide variety of authors who write or have written category romances for one or more of our various series and imprints and of the dedication to their readership that has led to many of our original authors, including some who've gone on to major mainstream success, to continue to contribute to our category lines. The honors garnered by our authors include positions on the *New York Times*, *USA Today*, and *Publishers Weekly* bestseller lists, as well as numerous awards such as the coveted RITA awards bestowed by the Romance Writers of America.

What books have you acquired that make you the most proud? What books that you have acquired reflect the types of books you like to represent? We're proud of all our books, and we're especially proud that in order to satisfy the demands of our readership—to be something beloved and familiar they can rely on, as well as something fresh and unique that will capture their imagination—we've more than doubled our output of incremental offerings during the past 10 years and increased the number of series as well. These devoted readers can count on our books to both celebrate their values and provide a respite from the daily stress and demands of their lives, reinvigorating their spirit. Harlequin celebrated its 50th anniversary in 1999; Silhouette is celebrating its 20th anniversary in 2000; and Mills & Boon has been publishing romance novels for more than 7 decades. Our category publishing activity has steadily increased and continues to be vibrant in 24 languages in more than 100 international markets.

Do you represent fiction? If so, what do you look for? Yes. We are always looking for writers with a distinctive, appealing, and upbeat voice who can create vivid, sympathetic characters and offer fresh approaches to the classic romance themes, along with compelling storytelling.

What do you want to see less of? It's not what you do, but how you do it—but keep in mind that we are a romance publisher. A happy ending is a must. Also, while there may be other elements in our romance novels, like a mystery or secondary plot, the focus must be on the love story between the hero and heroine. Please note that we do not accept e-mailed submissions or multiple submissions.

Do you represent nonfiction? No. We publish category romance, including inspirational romance, all of which is fiction.

Do you require book proposals? If so, what do you look for in evaluating a book proposal? Yes. We ask for a query letter that includes a word count and pertinent facts about the author as a writer, including familiarity with the romance genre and publishing history, and what series the project is appropriate for, as well as a brief synopsis (no more than two single-spaced pages). When we request a submission, we want to see a complete manuscript from unpublished authors and a proposal consisting of the first three chapters and an outline from published authors. We look for a clear idea of both plot and characters and an exciting new author voice.

Are certain aspects of a book proposal given more weight than others? A distinctive, appealing voice and compelling characterization are distinguishing factors that often get an editor's attention.

What process do you use for making a decision? What is the process for acquisition, is there a committee? If the proposal works for us, we ask to see the complete manuscript from unpublished authors and an outline and three sample chapters from previously published authors. The submission may be sent to an outside reader for evaluation before being considered in house. Both an acquiring editor and the senior editor of the series for which the work is targeted have to read and approve the submission in order for it to be bought.

Are you interested in work geared for the masses (readers of *People*, *The Star*, etc.)? With romance novels comprising close to half of all mass-market books sold, the romance genre continues its decades-long domination of the marketplace. As the world's largest publisher of category romance novels, Harlequin, with its imprints Harlequin, Silhouette, Steeple Hill, Mills & Boon, and its foreign language imprints, constantly strives to meet the needs of its growing marketplace.

Are agents important? Why? Harlequin/Silhouette/Mills & Boon are looking for romance authors with fresh, compelling voices. An agent is not necessary—we consider each and every submission, whether it comes in over the transom or from an agent—but we urge interested authors to research the genre fully and write in for our current guidelines before sending us any material. For over 15 years, most of our lines have requested unagented authors to send query letters with SASEs, while agented authors skip the query letter stage in favor of complete manuscripts (new authors) and proposals (published authors). Both methods have resulted in publication and long-term careers with us for large numbers of authors.

Do you like new writers? What should new writers do to break into the business? Yes! We publish new authors all the time within all of our series. A talented writer will bring her own special magic to whatever type of romance she writes, and a talented editor will discern it.

How should writers approach you? After reviewing our submission requirements on our website, eHarlequin.com, or sending in an SASE and request for our guidelines, please send a query letter and 2-page synopsis to the romance series you're targeting. Information can also be obtained from libraries, which often carry writers' guides, and some authors join writers' organizations—one specifically focused on romance writers and writing is Romance Writers of America (RWA).

What are some common mistakes writers make? What really gets on your nerves? Some new writers take too long to get into their story, whereas ideally the reader should be hooked from page one. If the most compelling material is "saved" for chapter 3 or 4, it's too late. Within the shorter category romances, new writers sometimes neglect to focus on the hero and heroine and allot too many pages to minor characters. Too often writers are not aware of our guidelines or lack an understanding of category romance and submit manuscripts that are inappropriate for our series. Swooning, passing-out heroines are a thing of the past and are not welcome. We do publish "bodice rippers." New writers will sometimes stagnate because they can't put aside a rejected manuscript and start writing a new one. Be aware that many category writers experience a few rejections before they make their first sale. Our biggest headaches are the result of contracted manuscripts not being delivered in a timely fashion, especially when we aren't given adequate notice of delays.

What can writers do to get your attention and to avoid the slush pile? Read widely in the series you've targeted. Research our books before submitting your manuscript. All of our guidelines are available at our website, eHarlequin.com. Keep in mind, too, that ultimately it is the emotional appeal of a given story, not its trendiness or lack thereof, that makes it a reader's favorite.

What have been some of your best experiences with writers or in your job? We are proud that authors who were among the original authors for each of our imprints are still writing for us, and that close to 100 of our current authors have published 20 or more books with Harlequin/Silhouette, Mills & Boon, or both. We value as well the many letters we get from readers telling us how much our books mean to them and the ways in which our authors' stories have touched and even changed their lives.

What, if anything, makes you different from other editors? The strength of our brand allows us to acquire never-before-published authors and publish them effectively. And while our titles must, of course, always meet our readers' expectations, because we are a unique publisher, we can let authors experiment with stories that never would have been published at a midlist house. We also publish many authors and many books from each author and, therefore, work with her editorially to develop her voice and a successful career. Within category romance, we offer our authors a variety of options to accommodate their particular talents and styles—their books may be contemporary or historical; tender or sexy; short enough to be read in one sitting or longer and more complex; pure romance or romance with elements of mystery, suspense, or paranormal; stand-alone books or miniseries; and in addition to category romance, we also offer authors the opportunity to contribute to short story anthologies and to write single titles that often evolve from a popular miniseries.

Is there anything you would like to see changed in the industry? We'd like to see a heightened perception of the romance genre and an elimination of negative bias against romance. In terms of author relations, we would like to see a timely delivery of manuscripts, as well as a willingness to work with the publisher to find effective solutions to problems.

Any advice for writers? Any way to improve the system for you? Any additional thoughts? Please keep in mind that inadequately thought-through or unsaleable submissions take up significant editorial time and lengthen response time. Authors who are responsive to reader tastes and present polished, professionally presented material avoid this.

THE HARVARD COMMON PRESS

535 Albany Street, Boston, MA 02118

617-423-5803   fax: 617-695-9794

www.harvardcommonpress.com

e-mail: orders@harvardcommonpress.com

Harvard Common Press accents trade nonfiction in the areas of food, home and the family, small-business guides, travel, and lifestyle, and in addition offers a select list of children's books.

The Harvard Common Press (founded in 1976) is a smaller house devoted to the publication of general nonfiction books in hardcover and trade paperback; the press maintains a solid backlist. The company colophon features a representation of a classical javelin thrower on the run—emblematic of the house's athletic publishing vigor.

Harvard Common issues the Best Places to Stay series as part of its travel line; the Gambit Books imprint covers how-to business titles geared to starting up and operating enterprises such as small restaurants, small newspapers, and small theaters, as well as alternative careers for teachers. Parenting and the family are sectors where Harvard Common shows particular traditional success.

Titles: *Apple Pie Perfect: 100 Delicious and Decidedly Different Recipes for America's Favorite Pie* by Ken Haedrich; *Real Stew: 300 Recipes for Authentic Home-Cooked Cassoulet, Gumbo, Chili, Curry, Minestrone, Bouillabaisse, Stroganoff, Goulash, Chowder, and Much More* by Clifford A. Wright; *The Ultimate Rotisserie Cookbook: 300 Mouthwatering Recipes for Making the Most of Your Rotisserie Oven* by Diane Phillips; *Party Nuts! 50 Recipes for Spicy, Sweet, Savory, and Simply Sensational Nuts that Will Be the Hit of Any Gathering* by Sally Sampson; *Eula Mae's Cajun Kitchen: Cooking Through the Seasons on Avery Island* by Eula Mae Dore and Marcelle R. Bienvenu; *Icebox Pies: 100 Scrumptious Recipes for No-Bake No-Fail Pies* by Lauren Chattman; *Lemonade: 50 Cool Recipes for Classic, Flavored, and Hard Lemonade and Sparklers* by Fred Thompson; *Iced Tea: 50 Recipes for Refreshing Tisanes, Infusions, Coolers, and Spiked Teas* by Fred Thompson; *The Wild Vegetarian Cookbook: A Forager's Guide (in the Field or in the Supermarket) to Preparing and Savoring Wild (and Not So Wild) Natural Foods, with More than 500 Recipes* by "Wildman" Steve Brill; *Fish & Shellfish, Grilled & Smoked: 300 Foolproof Recipes for Everything from Amberjack to Whitefish, Plus Really Good Rubs, Marvelous Marinades, Sassy Sauces, and Sumptuous Sides* by Karen Adler and Judith Fertig.

Query letters and SASEs should be directed to:

Bruce Shaw, President

Pam Hoenig, Executive Editor

Valerie Cimino, Managing Editor

Jodi Marchowsky, Production Editor

HEALTH COMMUNICATIONS, INC.

3201 Southwest 15th Street, Deerfield Beach, FL 33442

954-360-0909/1-800-441-5569   fax: 954-360-0034

www.hci-online.com

Health Communications features nonfiction trade titles in relationships, spirituality, health, empowerment, self-help, inspiration, esteem, and psychology. The publisher has achieved notable success with topical approaches to personal growth, women's issues, addiction and other compulsive behaviors, abuse and trauma, family relationships and healing.

Health Communications (founded in 1976) publishes with the intent to provide direction for the journey of living. The publisher's issue-orientation is apparent in a list that addresses a family spectrum of interest, encompassing books geared to be read by early readers through adults, as well as targeted market interest segments. Health Communications publishes books in affordable hardcover and trade paperback editions and also produces a line of audiobooks.

Health Communications operates in tandem with sister companies US Journal and US Journal Training. The program brings together professional caregivers and the broader community in a publishing forum that embraces books, journals, pamphlets, and conferences.

Exemplifying the Health Communications list: *The Schwarzbein Principle II: The Transition* by Dr. Diana Schwarzbein; *A Teen's Guide To Living Drug-Free* by Bettie B Youngs, PhD, Jennifer Leigh Youngs and Tina Moreno; *Health is a Choice. Learn How to Choose It!* by Raymond Francis, M.Sc with Kester Cotton; *Change Almost Anything in 21 Days* by Ruth Fishel; *The Power of Focus: How to Hit Your Business, Personal and Financial Targets with Absolute Certainty* by Jack Canfield, Mark Victor Hansen, and Les Hewitt; *Chicken Soup for the Teenage Soul on Love and Friendship* by Jack Canfield, Mark Victor Hansen, and Kimberly Kirberger; *You're Every Sign!* By Phyllis Firak-Mitz, M.A; *Addic-*

tive Relationships: Reclaiming Your Boundaries by Joy Miller; *An Adult Child's Guide to What's Normal* by John Friel, PhD, and Linda Friel, M.A.; *Before It's Too Late: Helping Women in Controlling an Abusive Relationship* by Robert J. Ackerman, PhD, and Susan E. Pickering; *Healing the Human Condition* by Charles L. Whitfield; *Healing the Child Within: Discovering and Recovery for Adult Children of Dysfunctional Families* by Charles L. Whitfield; *Gentle Reminders for Co-Dependents* by Mitzi Chandler; *From the First Bite: A Complete Guide to Recovery from Food Addiction* by Kay Sheppard; *Learning to Love Yourself* by Sharon Wegscheider-Cruise; *Lifeskills for Adult Children* by Janet Woitlitz, Ed.D., and Alan Gurner, M.A.; *Perfect Daughters: Adult Daughters of Alcoholics* by Robert J. Ackerman; *Time for Joy* by Ruth Fishel; *Eternal Blessings* by Brahma Kurmaris; *Pearls of Wisdom* by Dadi Janki; *The Soulful Money Manual: 9 Keys to Being Effective, Happy and at Peace with Money* by Richard Mitz; *Becoming a Father* by John L. Hart, PhD; *Fun Facts About Cats* and *Fun Facts About Dogs* by Richard Torregrossa; *How to Change Your Life* by Ernest Holmes and Michael Beckwith; *Lives Charmed: Intimate Conversations with Extraordinary People* by Linda Sivertsen; *Taste Berries for Teens* by Bettie B. Youngs, PhD, and Jennifer Leigh Youngs; *Struggle for Intimacy* by Janet C. Woitiz; *The Lost Boy* by Dave Pelzer; *Healing Shame That Binds You* by John Bradshaw.

Health Communications published *Chicken Soup for the Soul: 101 Stories to Open the Heart and Rekindle the Spirit* (written and compiled by Jack Canfield and Mark Victor Hansen), an entertaining, uplifting work that features selections from a wide variety of writers. As this book goes to press, the original Chicken Soup has been an international bestseller for several years. This book has spawned a number of successful Chicken Soup collections. Indeed, if imitation is the sincerest form of flattery, the number of works with allied themes that currently appear under other publishers' imprints is a genuine tribute from the industry to this popular genre originated by the authors and Health Communications. More titles in this series: *Chicken Soup for the Christian Soul: 101 Stories to Open the Heart and Rekindle the Spirit* by Jack Canfield, Mark Victor Hansen, Patty Aubery, and Nancy Mitchell; *Chicken Soup for the Woman's Soul: 101 Stories to Open the Hearts and Rekindle the Spirits of Women* by Jack Canfield, Mark Victor Hansen, Jennifer Read Hawthorne, and Marci Shimoff; *Condensed Chicken Soup for the Soul* by Jack Canfield, Mark Victor Hansen, and Patty Hansen.

Health Communications distributes its own list. Query letters and SASEs should be directed to:

Allison Janse, Senior Editor

Lisa Drucker, Senior Editor

Susan Tobias, Editor

Christine Belleris, Editorial Director
Sign: Leo.
Education: B.A., Journalism, from the University of Colorado.
Employment history/editor career path: I have always been interested in reading and writing. After I graduated from college, I was a Legislative Assistant for a U.S. congressman in Washington, D.C., for about four years. I decided I didn't want to stay in politics, so I started doing freelance work for the *Colorado Statesman*. I then moved to

Boca Raton, Florida, and started working at SIRS, publishing research material. I then came to Health Communications, where I have been employed for eight years.

Personal interests: Reading, writing, running, bicycling; I have a two-year-old and a new baby on the way.

What would you be doing if you were not an editor? I would be a travel writer.

What has been your most successful book that you have acquired to date? *The Schwarzbein Principle.*

What book have you acquired that makes you the most proud? What books that you have acquired reflect the types of books you like to represent? *The Immune Spirit* and *Not Just One in Eight.*

Do you represent fiction? If so, what do you look for? Yes, we do occasionally, but not much. Visionary fiction, New Age.

Do you represent nonfiction? Yes, self-help, books for teenagers, books on healthy aging, and anything that is new and different.

Do you require book proposals? If so, what do you look for in evaluating a book proposal? Yes, I look for two sample chapters, a table of contents, a detailed profile of the author, and marketing ideas. It has to be well written, neat, and follow our guidelines.

Are certain aspects of a book proposal given more weight than others? It helps if the authors are experts in their field, but we use a strategy known as HERT. H stands for healing. E, the author is an expert. R stands for whether the material is readable. T is timely. We need the proposal to meet all of these categories.

What process do you use for making a decision? What is the process for acquisition, is there a committee? We use the HERT system and, yes, we have a committee. The committee meets once a month and consists of staff from sales, marketing, e-public relations, and the editorial department.

What kinds of nonfiction books do you want to see less of? Personal memoirs that can't help a general audience.

Are you interested in work geared for the masses (readers of *People*, *The Star*, etc.)? Yes.

Are agents important? Why? Yes, they are very important. They bring a higher caliber of authors and manuscripts to us. They can "weed-out" all the material that is not what we're looking for.

Do you like new writers? What should new writers do to break into the business? Yes, we're always looking for new writers. I would say to join a writers group and try to publish some work in periodicals.

How should writers approach you? First, send me a query letter in the mail. If I like the material, I will call you to request the manuscript.

What are some common mistakes that writers make? What really gets on your nerves? When people call after you've asked them not to call. Most authors don't realize just how busy editors are. When authors don't do their homework and send me material that we don't even publish (i.e., poetry). When authors send unsolicited material without an SASE and expect that we will return it. We read unsolicited material as a courtesy, not an obligation.

What can writers do to get your attention and to avoid the slush pile? The way to get my attention is to send a professional-looking package with a well-written proposal inside.

What have been some of your craziest experiences with submissions? Getting gifts with the submissions. I've gotten everything from cookies, to stuffed animals, gum, rocks, you name it. A colleague of mine once received a dozen red roses.

What have been some of your best experiences with writers or in your job? Getting to know people. I always have good professional advice in this profession (diet, therapy). I'm always learning new things and I love to develop a wonderful relationship with the authors.

What, if anything, makes you different from other editors? I'm a good listener and am good at compromise. It's important in this job and business that you are willing to "bend" a little.

Is there anything that you would like to see changed in the industry? I would like to see less consolidation of bookstores; I like the independent bookstores.

Any advice for writers? Be persistent. Don't get discouraged because one person turned you down, and get many different viewpoints.

HIDDENSPRING

997 Macarthur Blvd, Mahwah, New Jersey 07430

201-825-7300

www.hiddenspringbooks.com

HiddenSpring is the general trade imprint of Paulist Press. Launched in the fall of 2000, HiddenSpring publishes a broad range of non-fiction "with a spiritual twist," ranging from biography, history, business, science, to self-help, inspirational, gardening and travel. HiddenSpring publishes 8 to 10 titles per year.

Recent titles include: *Francis of Assisi: A Revolutionary Life* by Adrian House; *Conversation: How Talk Can Change Our Lives* by Theodore Zeldin; *The Voice of the Irish: The Story of Christian Ireland* by Michael Staunton; *The Art of Spiritual Rock Gardening* by Donna Schaper; *Sacred Water: The Spiritual Source of Life* by Nathaniel Altman; *The Age of the Cloister: The Story of Monastic Life in the Middle Ages* by Christopher Brooke; *The Spiritual Traveler: England, Scotland, Wales* by Martin Palmer; *The Spiritual Traveler: New York City* by Edward Bergman; *The Spiritual Traveler: Boston and New England* by Jana Riess.

Send manuscripts, queries, and SASE's to:

Jan-Erik Guerth, Editorial Director

HILL STREET PRESS, LLC

191 East Broad Street, Suite 209, Athens, GA 30601-2848

706-613-7200/1-800-295-0365   fax: 706-613-7204

www.hillstreetpress.com   e-mail: info@hillstreetpress.com

Hill Street Press was founded in May 1998 and currently has 50 titles in print. Hill Street Press is a publisher of regional focus and international interest. We plan to increase our number of literary and popular fiction titles, ranging from the hard-edged to the homespun, as our backlist grows. HSP is particularly interested in nonfiction titles of various kinds, particularly contemporary issues. We do not publish poetry, children's or juvenile literature, science fiction, or romance. We are nationally and internationally distributed through LCP/InBook and Source Books and sell to all major chains and independents, as well as through the major e-commerce outlets.

Representative titles include: *The University of Georgia Trivia Book* by F.N. Boney; *Atlanta: An Illustrated History* by Andy Ambrose; *Mother of the Disappeared: An Appalachian Birth Mother's Journey* by Karen Salyer McElmurray; *The Barbarian Parade, or Pursuit of an Un-American Dream* by Kirby Gann; *Chicken Dreaming Corn* by Roy Hoffman; *Southern Belly: The Ultimate Food Lover's Companion to the South* by John T. Edge; *Bevelyn Blair's Everyday Cookies* by Bevelyn Blair; *The Quotable South* by Al Dixon; *Sleeping with Soldiers: In Search of the Macho Man* by Rosemary Daniell; *Essentials* by Jean Toomer; *Damn Good Dogs! The Real Story of Uga, University of Georgia's Bulldog Mascots* by Sonny Seiler & Kent Hannon; *Music Makers: Portraits and Song from the Roots of America* by Tim Duffy; *The Best of The Oxford American: Ten Years from the Southern Magazine of Good Writing* by Marc Smirnoff, editor; *Hints and Pinches* by Eugene Walter; *The Grit Cookbook* by World-Wise, *Down-home Recipes* by Jessica Greene & Ted Hafer.

Please direct query letters with SASEs to:

Patrick Allen, Senior Editor

HIPPOCRENE BOOKS

171 Madison Avenue, New York, NY 10016

212-685-4371   fax: 212-779-9338

www.hippocrenebooks.com   e-mail: hippocrene.books@verizon.net

Hippocrene accents history, military science, international literature, music, travel, cuisine, and scholarly Judaica and Polonica. The house offers selected works in the areas of current affairs and popular culture, in addition to a comprehensive line of foreign-language dictionaries. The house publishes dictionaries and instruction books in over 100 languages. Hippocrene Books (founded in 1971) publishes hardcovers and trade paperbacks.

Hippocrene has undertaken publication of the works of Polish writer Henryk Sienkiewicz (1905 Nobel Laureate in literature) in English translation.

Hippocrene titles for the general trade: *You Can't Do Business (or Most Anything Else) Without Yiddish* by Leon H. Gildin; *Wedded Strangers: The Challenges of Russian-American Marriages, Expanded Edition* by Lynn Vision; *Jews in Old China, Expanded Edition* by Sidney Shapiro; *Greece: An Illustrated History* by Tom Stone; *China: An Illustrated History* by Yong Ho.

Hippocrene Books prides itself on being the foremost United States publisher of international cookbooks and foreign-language dictionaries.

Titles include: *The Cuisine of the Caucasus Mountains* by Kay Shaw Nelson; *Cooking With Cajun Women: Recipes and Remembrances from South Louisiana Kitchens* by Nicole Fontenot & Alicia Fontenot Vidrine; *A Taste of Turkish Cuisine* by Nur Ilkin and Sheilah Kaufman; *A Taste of Syria* by Virginia Jerro Gerbino and Philip Kayal; *The Best of Taiwanese Cuisine* by Karen Hulene Bartell; *Flavors of Burma: Cuisine and Culture from the Land of Golden Pagodas* by Susan Chan; *Taste of Pyrenees, Classic and Modern* by Marina Chang; *International Dictionary of Gastronomy* by Guido Gomez de Silva; *Mongolian-English/English-Mongolian Dictionary and Phrasebook* by Aariimaa Baasanjav Marder; *Uzbek-English/English-Uzbek Dictionary and Phrasebook* by Nicholas Awde, William Dirks, Umida Hikmatullaeva; *Dictionary of Maya Hieroglyphs* by John Montgomery; *How to Read Maya Hieroglyphs* by John Montgomery; *Beginner's Swedish* by Scott Mellor; *Romania: An Illustrated History* by Nicolae Klepper; *Moscow: An Illustrated History* by Kathleen Murrell.

Hippocrene offers practical and concise dictionaries, as well as unabridged and comprehensive dictionaries, specialty dictionaries, proverbs dictionaries, and standard dictionaries in over 100 languages.

Mastering Advanced... guides make up a line that offers the student reasonably priced, contemporary foreign-language instruction. The Hippocrene Beginner's series is designed for students with little or no background in a foreign language. The goal of each volume is to provide readers with a basic knowledge to travel independently, speak and understand, and read and write essential words.

Hippocrene distributes its own list. Direct query letters and SASEs to:

Carol Chitnis-Gress, Managing Editor—Oversees international cooking, travel, library of world folklore, and general history titles

George Blagowidow, President and Editorial Director

Paul Simpson, Associate Editor—Oversees illustrated histories, series, international proverbs

Caroline Gates, Associate Editor—Oversees all foreign-language dictionaries and learning guides

HOUGHTON MIFFLIN COMPANY

CLARION BOOKS

COLLEGE DIVISION

GREAT SOURCE

CHAPTERS PUBLISHING (SEE SEPARATE LISTING)

HOUGHTON MIFFLIN BOOKS FOR CHILDREN

INTERNATIONAL DIVISION

MCDOUGAL LITTELL

RIVERSIDE PUBLISHING COMPANY

SCHOOL DIVISION

SUNBURST TECHNOLOGY

TRADE AND REFERENCE DIVISION

Boston office:

222 Berkeley Street, Boston, MA 02116-3764

617-351-5000

www.hmco.com

New York office:

215 Park Avenue South, New York, NY 10003

212-420-5800

Houghton Mifflin produces general trade nonfiction and fiction in hardcover and paperback, as well as a strong general-reference list. Mariner is a trade-paperback imprint covering house interests in fiction and nonfiction. Children's divisions include Houghton Mifflin Books for Children and the editorially independent juveniles' imprint Clarion Books (see subentries further on). The backlist of formerly independent Ticknor & Fields has been incorporated into the core Houghton Mifflin catalog.

Houghton Mifflin (founded in 1832) is one of the grand names of the American publishing tradition. The house's renowned leaping-dolphin emblem embellishes a distinguished list.

Houghton Mifflin nonfiction encompasses mainstream titles in such areas as current events, international affairs, business, journalism, lifestyle and travel, and natural history.

Reference works from Houghton Mifflin include *American Heritage Dictionary of the English Language* (an excellent resource for American writers); *The Columbia Encyclope-*

dia (copublished with Columbia University); *Cannon's Concise Guide to Rules of Order.* Houghton Mifflin is known for publishing the ever-popular *American Heritage Dictionary.*

Also on the Houghton Mifflin list nature series that include the Peterson Field Guides and Best Places to Stay Guides.

Popular Houghton Mifflin nonfiction: *Why I Am A Catholic* by Garry Wills; *The New Dictionary of Cultural Literacy* edited by Hirsch, Kett, and Trefil; *Baking in America* by Greg Patent; *Naked in the Promised Land* by Lillian Faderman; *Yankees Century* by Glenn Stout and Richard A Johnson; *A Human Being Died That Night* by Pumla Gobodo-Madikizela; *Fat Land* by Greg Crister; *The Apprentice* by Jacques Pepin; *Dark Star Safari* by Paul Theroux.

Fiction and works with literary and cultural scope: *Bay of Souls* by Robert Stone; *The Book of Salt* by Monique Truong; *The Winter Queen* by Jane Stevenson; *The Guru of Love* by Samrat Upadhyay; *July, July* by Tim O'Brien; *Long For This World* by Michael Byers.

The publisher also issues selected works of poetry, including *Time & Money: New Poems* by William Matthews; *Nature: Poems Old and New* by May Swenson.

Houghton Mifflin distributes its own list. Agented material to:

Eamon Dolan, Executive Editor (New York)—Business, technology, nonfiction; travel guides

Elaine Pfefferbilt, Editor at Large (New York)—Philosophy, history, biography, general nonfiction; literary fiction; nonfiction consistent with the house list

Harry L. Foster, Jr., Senior Editor (Boston)—Nature and history

Janet Silver, Vice President, and Publisher (Boston)—Literary nonfiction and fiction; nonfiction: biographies, arts and culture, women's issues; focus on developing writers

Laura van Dam, Science Editor (Boston)—Hard science, medicine, technology; practical nonfiction

Rux Martin, Senior Editor (Boston)—Cooking

Anton Mueller, Senior Editor (Boston)—Literary fiction, political/cultural nonfiction

Brandy Vickers, Assistant Manager, Mariner Paperbacks (Boston)

Heidi Pitlor, Editor (Boston)—Literary fiction

Lisa White, Associate Director (Boston)—Field guides

Deanne Urmy, Senior Editor—Science, nature, serious nonfiction

Frances Tenenbaum, Imprint Editor/Senior Editor Houghton Mifflin (Boston)—Gardening books; Oversees Taylor gardening guides and Tasha Tudor books

Education: University of Michigan and Columbia School of Journalism.

Employment history/editor career path: I have worked here for over 25 years. I started as a journalist and then moved on to work for a small publisher. I then worked for a small book club and was writing a book on gardening and wildflowers. Soon after, I moved out of Long Island and came to work for Houghton Mifflin.

Personal interests: Gardening, nonfiction editing, I love editing—don't like writing.

What would you be doing if you were not an editor? I don't know—I don't even want to think about it.

What has been your most successful book that you have acquired to date? *Tasha Tudor's Garden* by Tovah Martin and Richard Brown. It's a large, beautiful book that is full of color. I am also the editor of a whole series of gardening books called The Taylor's Guide to Gardening.

What books have you acquired that make you the most proud? What books that you have acquired reflect the types of books you like to represent? I am the Editor for three books by Henry Mitchell, a late columnist of the *Washington Post*. He is one of the most opinionated writers in gardening.

Do you represent nonfiction? Yes.

Do you require book proposals? If so, what do you look for in evaluating a book proposal? Yes, from people I don't know. Subject is the first thing, writing is the second. What is the salability of the project? It must have a unique voice.

What process do you use for making a decision? What is the process for acquisition, is there a committee? Because I'm the "expert" on gardening at Houghton Mifflin, I'm the one who usually reads the gardening books. I might go to other people who may be interested, such as the sales/marketing division. We do have an acquisitions committee.

Are agents important? Why? Yes and no. I work with some agents and I also work with people who do not have agents.

How should writers approach you? Not by phone.

What are some common mistakes writers make? What really gets on your nerves? When writers tell me that their project is unique, when I know that it's not. I don't like books that are rehashes, the same thing over and over again. I also don't like books that are manufactured in the author's head. As far as gardening books, it gets on my nerves when people have just taken it up, and they want to tell everyone else about it.

What can writers do to get your attention and to avoid the slush pile? If you write it directly to me, it doesn't go to the slush pile.

What have been some of your craziest experiences with submissions? My assistant usually goes through everything first, so she sees most of the "crazy" submissions.

What have been some of your best experiences with writers or in your job? I have some wonderful writers who turn out to be my best friends. I have recently found out that an organization that is giving a book party for one of my authors is actually giving the party for both of us. That's never happened to me before.

Is there anything that you would like to see changed in the industry? Yes, the whole industry.

CLARION BOOKS

215 Park Avenue South, 10th floor, New York, NY 10003

212-420-5800

Clarion publishes books geared for the youngest readers up through the early teen years. Clarion Books is an award-winning children's book division that is editorially independent of Houghton Mifflin's other lines.

On Clarion's list in fiction and picture books: *The Three Pigs* by David Wiesner; *Riding the Tiger* by Eve Bunting (illustrated by David Frampton); *A Pocketful of Poems* by Nikki Grimes (illustrated by Javaka Steptoe); *The Secrets of Ms. Snickle's Class* by Laurie Miller Hornik (illustrated by Debbie Tilley); *A Single Shard* by Linda Sue Park; *Sigmund Freud: Pioneer of the Mind* by Catherine Reef; *Heroine of the Titanic: The Real Unsinkable Molly Brown* by Elaine Landau.

Query letters and SASEs should be directed to:

Dinah Stevenson, Vice President and Editorial Director

Jennifer Greene, Editor

Lynne Polvino, Associate Editor

Jennifer Wingertzahn, Editor

HOUGHTON MIFFLIN BOOKS FOR CHILDREN

The Houghton Mifflin children's-book division stands out with a broad list that addresses topics of wide import; at all reading levels, the Houghton program accents works of thematic complexity and emotional depth. Imprints and lines include Walter Lorraine Books (illustrated and novelty titles) and Sandpiper Paperbacks.

Houghton Mifflin Books for Children publishes hardcover and paperback titles from picture books for the youngest readers to fiction for young adults, audio products, foldout books, boardbooks, lift-the-flap books—and the house showcases a brace of successful authors as well. Caldecott and Newbery medallions abound in the tradition of Houghton Mifflin Books for Children.

Representing Houghton Mifflin titles: Picture books: *Score One for the Sloths* by Helen Lester, illustrated by Lynn Munsinger; *The Strange Egg* by Mary Newell DePalma, illustrated by the author; *The Race of the Birkebeiners* by Lisa Lunge-Larsen, illustrated by Mary Azarian; *I Live in Tokyo: A Japanese Calendar* by Mari Takabayashi; *Animals in Flight* by Robin Page, illustrated by Steve Jenkins. Novels: *Breaking Through* by Francisco Jimenez; *Goose Chase* by Patrice Kindl; *When I Was Older* by Garret Freymann-Weyr.

Query letters and SASEs should be directed to:

Andrea Davis, VP and Publisher

Margaret Raymo, Acquisitions Editor (Boston)

HUMANICS PUBLISHING GROUP

HUMANICS LEARNING

PO Box 7400, Atlanta, GA 30309

404-874-1930   fax: 404-874-1976

www.humanicspub.com and www.humanicslearning.com

e-mail: info@humanicslearning.com

The Humanics publishing program covers the categories of self-help, how-to, psychology, human relations, health and nutrition, creative expression (in art, crafts, literature), education, humor, and spirituality. Special emphasis is on subjects such as personal growth, love and relationships, environment, peace, and Taoism. Market areas of concentration include elementary child and child development, teachers' resource books, child care, and the family.

Humanics produces children's books under the Humanics Children's House imprint. The Humanics line of teachers' resource books and materials in child development is directed in part to colleges and institutional markets; popular works in this arena are published under the Humanics Learning imprint.

Humanics Publishing Group (founded in 1976) publishes a small- to medium-sized list of paperback trade books, a line of special fine editions, and audiocassettes.

Humanics titles: *Lion Taming: On Being a Visionary Leader* by Don Johnson; *Becoming an Invitational Leader: A New Approach to Professionalism and Personal Success* by William W. Purkey, Ed.D and Betty L. Siegel, PhD; *Love, Sex, and Passion For the Rest of Your Life: How to Create the Ultimate Relationship* by David Ryback; *How to Get Kids to Do What You Want: The Power and Promise of Solution-Focused Parenting* by Bill Crawford, PhD; *From Chaos to Calm: Dealing With Difficult People vs. Them Dealing With You* by Bill Crawford, PhD; *Playful Mind: Bringing Creativity to Life* by James Downtown, Jr; *Character in Chief* by John M. Berecz; *All Stressed Up and Nowhere to Go: A Guide to Dealing with Stress & Creating a Purposeful Life* by Bill Crawford, PhD; *Spiral of Shame* by Jeanne Peterson & Marcie Goldman.

The Humanics Tao series offers a variety of titles: *The Tao of Calm: 81 Meditations for Everyday Living* by Pamela Metz, Ed.D.; *The Tao of Gender: Lao Tzu's* Tao Te Ching *Adapted for a New Age* by Tarynn Witten; *The Tao of Loss and Grief: Lao Tzu's* Tao Te Ching *Adapted for New Emotions* by Pamela Metz; *The Tao of Gardening: A Collection of Reflections Adapted from Lao Tzu's* Tao Te Ching by Pamela Metz.

Humanics oversees its own distribution. Query letters and SASEs should be directed to:

Arthur Bligh, Acquisitions Editor—Adult trade books.

HUMANICS LEARNING

The accent at Humanics Learning is on original stories and tales targeted for younger readers, in a program geared primarily toward illustrated works. The Fun E. Friends series is one of the house's successful lines. Humanics produces guides for caregivers and educators under the Humanics Learning logo.

On the Humanics Learning list: *Super Simple Science for Preschoolers* by Marvin Tolman and Lou Boothe; *Peace in Any Language: Celebrating Our Diversity* by Jeannine Perez; *Playful Traditions: A Jewish Preschool Book of Holiday Games and Ideas* by Marcia Shemaria Green; *Before and After School Activities: A Teachers Guide to Community Organization* by Gary B. Wilson; *Clean Air Activities* by The Clean Air Conservancy.

Titles for teachers and caregivers under the Humanics Learning imprint: *Science, Math and Nutrition for Toddlers: Setting the Stage for Lifelong Skills* by Rita Schrank; *The Planet of the Parental Classroom: A Parent's Guide for Teaching Your Baby in the Womb* by Rene Van De Carr and Marc Lehrer; *Teaching Terrific Twos* by Terry Graham and Linda Camp; *The Infant and Toddler Handbook* by Kathryn Castle; *Toddlers Learn by Doing* by Rita Schrank.

Query letters and SASEs should be directed to:

Arthur Bligh, Humanics Learning

HUMAN KINETICS

1607 North Market Street, PO Box 5076, Champaign, IL 61825-5076

217-351-5076/1-800-747-4457   fax: 217-351-1549

www.humankinetics.com

Human Kinetics produces works in recreational and competitive sports, physical education, sports medicine, and fitness. Human Kinetics (founded in 1974) offers a list of trade and academic works (including college textbooks) that covers a wide range of athletic pursuits, with books geared for professional-level coaches, trainers, and participants, in addition to serious leisure-time athletes. Human Kinetics has established the Human Kinetics Foundation to issue grants promoting youth sports and school physical education.

A notable HK imprint is YMCA of America Books. Human Kinetics books are issued primarily in trade paperback editions, with special editions in hardcover. The press also publishes a number of periodicals in its areas of interest. Human Kinetics bills itself as the premier publisher for sports and fitness.

Sample bestsellers: *Strength Ball Training* by Lorne Goldenberg and Peter Twist; *Directing Youth Sports Programs* by Rainer Martens; *Power Eating* by Susan M. Kleiner, PhD and Maggie Greenwood-Robinson; *Diets Designed for Athletes* by Maryann Karinch; *The Softball Coaching Bible*; *Managing Sports Organizations* by Dr. Ruben Acosta;

Exercise Prescription: A Case Study Approach to the ACSM Guidelines by David Swain and Brian Leutholtz; *Coaching Youth Baseball, 3rd Edition*.

Human Kinetics oversees its own distribution. Query letters and SASEs should be directed to:

Rainer Martens, Publisher and President

Holly Gilly, Vice President of Publication

Leigh LaHood, Managing Editor

Coree Schutter, Editorial Coordinator

Jennifer Walker, Editorial Coordinator

HYPERION

DISNEY PRESS

HYPERION BOOKS FOR CHILDREN

MIRAMAX BOOKS

ABC DAYTIME BOOKS

ESPN BOOKS

THEIA

77 W. 66th Street, New York, NY 10023-6298

212-456-0100

Hyperion Books for Children offices:

114 Fifth Avenue, New York, NY 10011-5690

212-633-4400

Hyperion (founded in 1991) publishes commercial fiction, literary works, and frontlist nonfiction in the areas of popular culture, health and wellness, business, current topical interest, popular psychology, self-help, and humor. The house publishes books in hardcover, trade paperback, and mass-market paperback formats. Hyperion operates a strong children's program that encompasses Hyperion Paperbacks for Children and Disney Press (see subentry for Hyperion Books for Children further on). Miramax Books (see separate subentry further on) concentrates on projects that tie in with the world of film.

Hyperion is part of Disney—the transnational corporate entity noted for its bountiful theme parks, hotels, and resorts, as well as its considerable ledger of film and television enterprises (including ABC, ESPN, Touchstone, Miramax, and Disney studies). Disney launched Hyperion as a full-fledged, well-funded book-publishing division, and the house's top-of-the-line reputation commenced with its initial well-chosen list.

Representing Hyperion: *Lucky Man* by Michael J. Fox; *Still Woman Enough* by Loretta Lynn; *It's Not Business, It's Personal* by Ronna Lichtenberg; *My Country Versus Me* by Wen Ho Lee, with Helen Zia; *Outsmarting Female Fatigue* and *Outsmarting the Female Fat Cell—After Pregnancy* by Debra Waterhouse, M.P.H, R.D.; *Simplify Your Work Life* by Elaine St. James; *Around the World in a Bad Mood* by Rene Foss; *In Every Kid There Lurks a Tiger* by Rudy Duran and Rick Lipsey; *In the Company of Angels* by N. M. Kelby; *The Knitting Goddess* by Deborah Bergman; *Tracy Porter's Home Style* by Tracy Porter; *Dr. Timothy Johnson's On Call Guide to Men's Health* by Dr. Timothy Johnson; *How to Become a Great Boss* by Jeffry J. Fox; *ESPN "The Magazine" Presents Answer Guy* by Answer Guy; *The Lifetime Love and Sex Quiz Book* by Dr. Pepper Swartz; *The Memory Bible* by Gary Small, MD; *Sam Choy's Polynesian Kitchen* by Sam Choy; *The Art of Deception* by Ridley Pearson; *Girls Will Be Girls* by JoAnn Deak, PhD, with Teresa Barker.

Hyperion hardcover and trade paperback books are distributed to the trade by Little, Brown; Warner Books handles special sales, as well as the mass-market paperback list.

Hyperion is not currently accepting unsolicited manuscripts. Any materials received will be returned without review.

Gretchen Young, Executive Editor

Mark Chat, Associate Editor

(Ms.) Leslie Wells, Executive Editor

Michael DiCapua, Publisher—Michael DiCapua Books, a new imprint within Hyperion's Children's Program, formerly an imprint at HarperCollins

Peternelle Van Arsdale, Executive Editor

Will Schwalbe, Editor in Chief

HYPERION BOOKS FOR CHILDREN

HYPERION PAPERBACKS FOR CHILDREN

DISNEY PRESS

The children's book division of Hyperion publishes titles for younger readers through young adult via a number of series, imprints, and lines. On the Hyperion children's division list are volumes that are finely designed and luxuriously produced in hardcover and paperback.

Hyperion Books for Children produces illustrated fairy tales, picture storybooks, poetry, illustrated fiction, calendars, and activity books—many of which are lavish, inventively presented works. Disney Press concentrates on illustrated works that tie in with Disney children's cinema classics, old and new—including series novelizations and books with cinematically conceived formats.

From Hyperion Books for Children: *McDuff and the Baby* by Rosemary Wells (illustrated by Susan Jeffers); *Dinorella: A Prehistoric Fairytale* by Pamela Duncan Edwards (illustrated by Henry Cole); *Pat the Beastie Hand Puppet* by Henrik Drescher; *Breakfast at the Liberty Diner* by Daniel Kirk; *The Secret of the Lost Kingdom* by Michael Bolton (illustrated by David Jermann); *William Wegman Puppies* by William Wegman; *The Peacock's Pride* by Melissa Kajpust (illustrated by Jo Anne Kelly); *The Bone Man: A Native American Modoc Tale* by Laura Simms (illustrated by Michael McCurdy); *Phoebe and the Spelling Bee* by Barney Saltzberg; *The Little Mermaid* by Hans Christian Anderson (illustrated with Disney Archival Art); *Teddy's Christmas: A Pop-up Book with Mini Christmas Cards* by Margie Palatini (illustrated by Mike Reed); *El árbol de Navidad/The Christmas Tree* by Alma Flor Ada (illustrated by Terry Ybañez); *The Farolitos of Christmas* by Rudolfo Anaya (illustrated by Edward Gonzalez); *Armadillos Sleep in Dugouts: And Other Places Animals Live* by Pam Muñoz Ryan (illustrated by Diane deGroat); *The Buried City of Pompeii: What It Was Like When Vesuvius Exploded* by Shelley Tanaka (illustrated by Greg Ruhl); *The Wonder Worm Wars* by Margie Palatini; *Sons of Liberty* by Adele Griffin; *Wolf Shadows* by Mary Casanova.

Other noteworthy titles: *Tim Burton's Vincent* by Tim Burton; illustrated by the author (his first picture book, which he wrote and illustrated, was *The Nightmare Before Christmas*); *Anastasia's Album* by Shelley Tanaka (edited by Hugh Brewster; the true story of the youngest daughter of Czar Nicholas II of Russia and her incredible life, told through her own snapshots, diaries, and letters); *On Board the Titanic: An I Was There Book* by Shelly Tanaka (illustrated by Ken Marschall; true-story account of the famous ocean liner's fate told through the eyes of two young survivors).

Fiendly Corners by E. W. Leroe is a new Hyperion series that features paperback originals with eye-popping die-cut covers: *Fiendly Corners No. 1: Monster Vision; Fiendly Corners No. 2: Pizza Zombies; Fiendly Corners No. 3: Revenge of the Hairy Horror; Fiendly Corners No. 4: Nasty the Snowman.*

Hyperion is proud to announce an ongoing series of FamilyPC books designed to grow as families grow. The FamilyPC book series is intended as the absolute best option for parents who want to get the most productivity and fun out of their home computers—in tandem with the Editors of award-winning *FamilyPC* magazine. Titles: *The FamilyPC Guide to Homework* by Gregg Keizer and the Editors of *FamilyPC*; *The FamilyPC Software Buyer's Guide* by Kurt Carlson, Valle Dwight, and the Editors of *FamilyPC*; *The FamilyPC Guide to Cool PC Projects* by Sam Mea and the Editors of *FamilyPC*.

Disney Press produces a lineup that includes picture books, boardbooks, pop-up books, novels, and activity books. Many of these works are derived from such successful Disney cinematic productions as *101 Dalmatians, The Hunchback of Notre Dame, The Lion King, Beauty and the Beast, James and the Giant Peach, Aladdin, Pocahontas, Lady and the Tramp, Bambi, The Mighty Ducks,* and *The Little Mermaid.*

Special Hyperion project: *Since the World Began: Walt Disney World's First 25 Years* by Jeff Kurtti. This work celebrates the 25th anniversary of the Disney World theme park. The book is a lavish, entertaining, and absolutely unique history of Walt's city of dreams—and the world's most popular tourist destination.

Hyperion Books for Children and products from Disney Press are distributed to the trade by Little, Brown.

Hyperion Books for Children is not currently accepting unsolicited manuscripts. Any materials received will be returned without review.

Andrea Cascardi, Associate Publisher

Gretchen Young, Editor—Also works with core Hyperion adult-trade list

Ken Geist, Associate Publisher

Lisa Holton, Vice President and Publisher

Wendy Lefkon, Executive Editor—Disney-related projects.—Has own Disney imprint

MIRAMAX BOOKS

Miramax Books accents titles keyed to cinema—as a profession, industry, lifestyle, or avocation. The Miramax imprint develops a wide range of markets within this interest area. The Miramax list includes select original fiction (usually with a high-concept media link, or at least a halfway-celebrity author), reprints of novels that serve as the basis for films, and other movie tie-in projects.

From Miramax Books: *From Dusk Till Dawn* (a script by Quentin Tarantino); *The Last of the High Kings* (novel keyed to a film project) by Ferdia MacAnna; a currently untitled dark-comic novel by David Lipsky (author of *The Pallbearer*); *The Piano* (a script by Jane Campion); *The Postman* (a script by Antonio Skarmeta); *Jane Eyre* by Charlotte Brontë (classic fiction produced in a film tie-in reprint edition); *Pulp Fiction* (a script by Quentin Tarantino and Roger Avary).

Miramax Books is not currently accepting unsolicited manuscripts. Any materials received will be returned without review.

INDUSTRIAL PRESS

200 Madison Avenue, New York, NY 10016

212-889-6330/1-888-528-7852   fax: 212-545-8327

www.industrialpress.com   e-mail: induspress@aol.com

Industrial Press produces scientific works, technical handbooks, professional guides, and reference books in the areas of engineering, manufacturing processes and materials, design engineering, and quality control. In addition to professional books, Industrial Press produces basic textbooks in its fields of interest.

Industrial Press (founded in 1883) is a leading specialist house in the professional, scientific, and scholarly publishing arenas. The publisher typically offers about a dozen handpicked new titles a year, in addition to its ongoing backlist of established sellers.

Industrial Press continues to offer its classic *Machinery's Handbook* by Erik Oberg, Franklin D. Jones, Holbrook L. Horton, and Henry H. Ryffel (elaborated from the Green-McCauley original in both print and CD-ROM), along with a companion guidebook (in fully revised formats).

Representative of the Industrial Press list: *Art of Gear Fabrication* by Prem H. Daryani; *Asset Maintenance Management: A Guide to Developing Strategy and Improving Performance* by Alan Wilson; *CNC Machining and Programming Handbook, 2nd Edition* by Peter Smid; *Complete Guide to Predictive and Preventive Maintenance* by Joel Levitt; *Dimensional Management: A Comprehensive Introduction* by Mark Curtis; *Glossary of Metalworking Terms* by Dick Pohanish; *Metal Stamping Process* by Jim Szumera.

Industrial Press handles its own distribution.

Industrial Press is expanding its list of professional and educational titles and also starting a new program in electronic publishing. For guidelines and suggestions regarding submitting proposals, check out the website or contact:

John F. Carleo, Marketing Director and Editor

ISLAND PRESS

Editorial office:

1718 Connecticut Avenue, NW, Suite 300, Washington, DC 20009

202-232-7933/1-800-828-1302   fax: 202-234-1328

www.islandpress.org   e-mail: info@islandpress.org

West Coast operations:

58440 Main Street, PO Box 7, Covelo, CA 95428

fax: 707-983-6414

service@islandpress.org

Island Press issues books for resource conservation professionals and activists. The Island Press list is keyed to topics and issues in ecology, conservation, nature, regional studies, science (including biology and natural sciences), landscape architecture, land use, education, policy and planning, economics, and reference. Island publishes hardcover and trade paperback editions. The Shearwater Books imprint accents books of mainstream trade appeal and topical interest in hardbound and trade paper.

Island Press (founded in 1979; a subsidiary of Center for Resource Economics) pronounces itself "the environmental publisher." Many Island Press books are authored in association with research groups, funds, and institutes with environmental focus.

From Island Press: *Achieving Sustainable Freshwater Systems* by Marjorie M. Holland; *Alone* by Richard E. Byrd; *Animal Behavior and Wildlife Conservation* by Marco Festa-

Bianchet; *The Atlantic Forest of South America* by Conservation International/ Center for Applied Biodiversity Science/Carlos Galindo-Leal; *Beyond the Last Village* by Alan Rabinowitz; *Climate Affairs* by Michael H. Glantz; *The Coming Democracy* by Ann Florini; *Community Forestry in the United States* by Mark Barker; *Drafting a Conservation Blueprint* by Craig R. Groves; *The Empty Ocean* by Richard Ellis; *Epicurean Simplicity* by Stephanie Mills; *Health and Community Design* by Lawrence D. Frank; *The Land We Share* by Eric T. Freyfogle; *Natural Assets* by James K. Boyce.

Titles from Shearwater: *Fishcamp: Life on an Alaskan Shore* by Nancy Lord (illustrated by Laura Simonds Southworth); *Kinship to Mastery: Biophilia in Human Evolution and Development* by Stephen R. Kellert; *The Value of Life: Biological Diversity and Human Society* by Stephen R. Kellert; *The Others: How Animals Made Us Human* by Paul Shepard.

Island Press handles its own distribution.

Acquisitions are made primarily through the Washington office. Initial contact names and locations should be confirmed prior to any query. Query letters and SASEs should be directed to:

Barbara Dean, Executive Editor—Biology, environmental restoration, ecosystem management, forestry, and sustainable agriculture books that are written for practitioners, scholars, undergraduate and graduate students, and general readers

Dan Sayre, Vice President and Publisher

Jonathon Cobb, Executive Editor, Shearwater Books

Todd Baldwin, Senior Editor—Marine affairs, energy policy, climate change, local governance

Heather Boyer, Editor—Human Habitat List—Landscape, architecture

Barbara Youngblood, Developmental Editor

James Nuzum, Assistant Editor

Laura Carrithers, Editorial Assistant

Kathryn Jergovish, Editorial Assistant

JOSSEY-BASS, INC., PUBLISHERS (A WILEY COMPANY)

PFEIFFER & COMPANY

989 Market Street, San Francisco, CA 94103

415-433-1740   fax: 415-433-1711

www.pfeiffer.com

Jossey-Bass, Inc., Publishers (established in 1967), produces nonfiction in professional and advanced trade categories covering business, management, and administration in public and nonprofit sectors, as well as issues in psychology, social and health sciences, religion, and education. One major Jossey-Bass division is Pfeiffer & Company. The house sustains an extensive backlist and publishes specialist journals in fields allied to editors.

The firm was acquired by John Wiley & Sons in 1999.

Pfeiffer & Company is a formerly independent business-and-workplace specialist press acquired by Jossey-Bass in 1996 (see subentry for Pfeiffer & Company).

Jossey-Bass has an editorial commitment to provide useful, leading-edge resources grounded in research and proven in practice. These works present substantive ideas that will help individuals and organizations to learn, develop, and improve their effectiveness.

The Jossey-Bass publishing niche accents theory-to-practice books for thinking professionals, often in larger corporations, who are progressive, curious, and in a position to influence their organizations. Most J-B books are grounded in primary research by the authors and are aimed at the twin concerns of development of the organization as a whole and the individuals within the organization.

Jossey-Bass sells via a half-dozen channels; about 20 to 25 percent of J-B business and management titles get general-market trade-bookstore distribution while the balance is sold through direct mail, direct to corporations, via catalog companies, through agency bookstore accounts (mostly large, independent professional booksellers), and for use in college-level courses.

Titles: *A New Beginning for Pastors and Congregations: Building an Excellent Match Upon Your Shared Strengths* by Kennor L. Callahan; *On Becoming a Servant Leader: The Private Writings of Robert K. Greenleaf* by Don M. Frick and Larry C. Spears; *Our Lives as Torah: Finding God in Our Own Stories* by Carol Ochs; *Living with Paradox: Religious Leadership and the Genius of Double Vision* by Newton Malony; *Jewish Spiritual Guidance: Finding Our Way to God* by Carol Ochs and Kerry Olitzky; *Reaching for Higher Ground in Conflict Resolution* by E. Ranklin Dukes, Marina A. Piscolish, and John B. Stephens; *Resolving Personal and Organizational Conflict* by Kenneth Cloke and John Goldsmith; *Narrative Mediation: A New Approach to Conflict Resolution* by John Winslade and Gerald Monk; *Peace Skills* by Alice Frazer Evans, Robert A. Evans, and Ronald S. Kraybill; *Collaborating: Finding Common Ground for Multiparty Problems* by Barbara Gray; *Work and Motivation* by Victor H. Vroom; *Working Scared: Achieving Success in Trying Times* by Kenneth N. Wexley and Stanley B. Silverman; *Working with Family Businesses: A Guide for Professionals* by David Bork, Dennis T. Jaffe, Sam H. Lane, and Leslie Dashew; *Visionary Leadership: Creating a Compelling Sense of Direction for Your Organization* by Burt Nanus; *Telecommuting: A Manager's Guide to Flexible Work Arrangements* by Joel Kugelmass; *Thought Leaders: Insights on the Future of Business* by Joel Kurtzman; *Strategic Pay: Aligning Organizational Strategies and Pay Systems* by Edward E. Lawler.

A representative Drucker Foundation Future series book: *The Leader of the Future: New Visions, Strategies, and Practices for the Next Era* (edited by Frances Hesselbein, Marshall Goldsmith, and Richard Beckhard; foreword by Peter F. Drucker). This Drucker Foundation Future series book asks the leaders of today to imagine the leadership of tomorrow.

Books from Warren Bennis Executive Briefing series: *The 21st Century Organization: Reinventing Through Reengineering* by Warren Bennis and Michael Mische; *Why Leaders Can't Lead: The Unconscious Conspiracy Continues* by Warren Bennis; *Fabled Service: Ordinary Acts, Extraordinary Outcomes* by Betsy Sanders; *The Absolutes of Leadership* by Philip B. Crosby.

Query letters and SASEs should be directed to:

Susan Williams, Editor—Business management/leadership

Lesley Iura, Senior Editor—Education

Alan Rinzler, Executive Editor—Psychology/self-improvement

Julianna Gustafson, Editor—Self-improvement with a spirituality component

Mark Kerr, Editor—Education books, religion, anything related to the evangelical Christian marketplace

Cedric Crocker, Executive Editor—Global business, strategy, and e-business models

Kathe Sweeney, Editor—Creativity/innovation, entrepreneurship (especially women), growing companies, post start-up, high-tech management, women in business, communications, transitions, third age, leadership development (CCL) and work/life balance

PFEIFFER & COMPANY

Pfeiffer's trade business list targets such areas as career/personal development and general business/management. Pfeiffer also produces a dynamic array of training games, simulation/experiential-learning leader's manuals, computer software/CD-ROMs, and audio- and videocassettes.

Pfeiffer & Company (formerly an independent business-and-workplace specialist press acquired by Jossey-Bass in 1996) is an international house that specializes in business topics directed particularly toward trainers, consultants, and managers. With offices in Amsterdam, Johannesburg, London, Sydney, and Toronto, in addition to its former U.S. home in San Diego, Pfeiffer & Company is adamantly global. As an imprint of Jossey-Bass Inc., Publishers, Pfeiffer & Company offers innovative products for Human Resource Development.

From Pfeiffer & Company: *Getting Together: Icebreakers and Group Energizers* by Lorraine L. Ukens; *Feeding the Zircon Gorilla and Other Team Building Activities* by Sam Sikes; *Team Players and Teamwork: The New Competitive Business Strategy* by Glenn M. Parker; *The Skilled Facilitator: Practical Wisdom for Developing Effective Groups* by Roger M. Schwarz; *Leading with Soul: An Uncommon Journey of Spirit* by Lee G. Bolman and Terrence E. Deal; *Empowerment Takes More Than a Minute* by Ken Blanchard, John P. Carlos, and Alan Randolph.

Query letters and SASEs should be directed to:

Susan Rachmeier, Associate Editor—Management, careers, training

KALMBACH BOOKS

THE WRITER BOOKS

21027 Crossroads Circle, P.O. Box 1612, Waukesha, WI 53187-1612

262-796-8776   fax: 262-798-6468

www.kalmbach.com   e-mail: books@kalmbach.com

Founded in 1933, Kalmbach Publishing Co. publishes and distributes high-quality consumer and trade magazines and books covering hobby, special interest, and leisure-time subjects.

Kalmbach Books publishes nonfiction how-to and reference titles on railroading, model railroading, toy train collecting and operating, and scale modeling. Recently, Kalmbach Books has teamed with the editors of *Bead&Button* to produce a well-received series of beading and jewelry-making booklets and launch a new line of books.

Recent titles include: *Chic & Easy Beading: 100 Fast and Fun Fashion Jewelry Projects*; *Beaded Pictures*; *Faces of Railroading* by Carl Swanson; *The Art of Lionel Trains* by Roger Carp; *Rio Grande Through the Rockies* by Mike Danneman; *Realistic Model RR Operations* by Tony Koester; *DCC Made Easy* by Lionel Strang; *Basic Painting and Weathering for Model Railroaders* by Jeff Wilson; *Mid-Sized and Manageable Track Plans* by Iain Rice; *Toy Train Layout from Start to Finish* by Stan Trzoniec; *Command Control For Toy Trains* by Neil Besougloff; *Toy Train Memories* by John Grams.

The Writer Books imprint publishes nonfiction paperback titles on all phases of writing and selling the written work. Recent titles include: *The Writer's Handbook*, edited by Elfrieda Abbe; *Making the Perfect Pitch: How to Catch a Literary Agent's Eye* by Katharine Sands; *The Interviewer's Handbook* by John Brady; *The Romance Writer's Handbook* by Rebecca Vinyard; *Take Joy: A Book for Writers* by Jane Yolen; *Ready, Aim, Specialize! Create Your Own Writing Specialty and Make More Money* by Kelly James-Enger; *The Writer's Guide to Writing Your Screenplay* by Cynthia Whitcomb; *The Writer's Guide to Selling Your Screenplay* by Cynthia Whitcomb.

Since 1887, both aspiring and professional writers have looked to *The Writer* magazine as a practical guide to instruct, inform, and inspire them in their work. The Writer is renowned for the annually updated reference resource *The Writer's Handbook* (edited by Elfrieda Abbe).

The Writer Books is not accepting new submissions at this time. Query letters and SASEs for other topics should be directed to:

Candice St. Jacques, Editor-in-Chief

Kristin Schneidler, Crafts Editor

Julia Gerlach, Assistant Editor—Beading and jewelry-making

Amy Glander, Assistant Editor

KENSINGTON PUBLISHING CORPORATION

PINNACLE BOOKS

ZEBRA BOOKS

DAFINA BOOKS

CITADEL BOOKS

CITADEL PRESS

850 Third Avenue, 16th Floor, New York, NY 10022-6222

212-407-1500

www.kensingtonbooks.com

The Kensington, Zebra, and Pinnacle programs cover all major categories of commercial and popular trade nonfiction and fiction. Kensington nonfiction is strong in issue-oriented investigatory works of topical interest, humor, health, self-help and awareness, true crime, and popular biography. Areas of fiction concentration include romance fiction (historical and contemporary), horror, mystery and suspense, thrillers, and women's fiction.

Kensington is one of the largest independently owned book publishers. Kensington Publishing Corporation is home to such divisional imprints as Kensington Books (primarily hardcover and trade paperback originals), along with Zebra and Pinnacle (mainly mass-market paperback editions, as well as selected hardcovers). Long a leader in the paperback category arena, the house has expanded its publishing emphasis along the commercial spectrum; under the Kensington and Zebra/Pinnacle banners, the house is a vital hardcover presence. Kensington recently bought the Carol Publishing Group's backlist.

The Kensington mass-market imprint publishes quality and commercial fiction and nonfiction, both original titles and reprints.

Zebra Books (founded in 1975) and its sibling house Pinnacle Books (acquired in 1987) publish a colossal list of mass-market paperback originals that spans the spectrum of mainstream and genre categories. Zebra and Pinnacle also produce mass-market reprints of hardcover originals, as well as fiction and nonfiction in trade paper and designated high-profile titles in original hardcover editions.

The paperback-originals division of the house maintains a firm backlist of books—however, in keeping with mass-market rack tradition, titles that don't move are soon gone.

Kensington continues its romance program under such imprints, series, and lines as Bouquet Romance, Regency Romance, Historical Romance, and Arabesque (a line of multicultural romances).

Sample Kensington titles: *Baby Momma Drama* by Carl Weber; *The Ways of Black*

Folks by Lawrence Ross; *Death By Chocolate* by G. A. McKevett; *This Must Be Love* by Kasey Michaels; *After Sundown* by Amanda Ashley; *Notorious* by Laura Parker; *While You Slept* by Wendy Burge; *Strong Spirits* by Alice Duncan; *Dangerous Attractions* by Colleen Easton; *Wildwood* by Drusilla Campbell; *Callus On My Soul* by Dick Gregory and Shelia Moses; *Andrew and Joey* by Jamie James; *Hot Blood XI* by Jeff Gelb and Michael Garrett; *Too Much Temptation* by Lori Foster; *Blueberry Muffin Murder* by Joanne Fluke; *She Loves Me Not* by Wendi Corsi Staub.

Representative Zebra titles: *The Lion in Glory* by Shannon Drake; *Velvet is the Night* by Elizabeth Thomas; *Simply Irresistible* by Kristine Grayson; *Don't Tell a Soul* by Susan McClafferty; *The Butterfly Garden* by Mary Campisi; *Shades of Midnight* by Linda Fallon.

From Pinnacle: *Love Me to Death* by Steve Jackson; *Code Name: Coldfire* by William W. Johnstone; *Crimson Night* by Trisha Baker; *At the Edge* by David Dun.

Kensington oversees its own distributional operations. All listed Kensington editors have a wide range of interests in fiction and nonfiction; some of their personal specialties are noted as follows. Query letters and SASEs should be directed to:

John Scognamiglio, Editorial Director, Fiction—Historical romance, Regency romance, women's contemporary fiction, gay fiction and nonfiction, mysteries, suspense, mainstream fiction

Karen Thomas, Editorial Director, Dafina/Arabesque—African American fiction and nonfiction

Kate Duffy, Editorial Director, Romance and Women's fiction—Historical romance, Regency romance, Brava erotic romance, women's contemporary fiction

Lee Heiman, Consulting Editor—Alternative health

Bruce Bender, Managing Director, Citadel Press—Popular nonfiction, film, television, Wicca, gambling, current events

Margaret Wolf, Senior Editor, Citadel Press—Psychology, women's issues, women's health, entertainment, current events, cookbooks

Bob Shuman, Senior Editor, Citadel Press—politics, military, Wicca, business, Judaica, sports

Amy Garvey, Consulting Editor—Historical romance, Regency romance, women's fiction

Michaela Hamilton, Editor in Chief—Thrillers, mysteries, mainstream fiction, true crime, current events

Elaine Sparber, Senior Editor—Health, alternative health, pets, New Age, self-help

Richard Ember, Editor, Citadel Press—Biography, film, sports, New Age, spirituality

Miles Lott, Assistant Editor—Mainstream fiction, thrillers, horror, women's fiction, general nonfiction, popular culture, entertainment

Lisa Filippattos, Consulting Editor—Contemporary and historical romance,

Regency romances, Brava erotic romance, women's fiction, thrillers.

Gary Goldstein, Editor, General nonfiction.

KÍVAKÍ PRESS, INC.

PO Box 1053, Skyland, NC 28776

828-274-7941   fax: 828-274-7943

www.kivakipress.com   e-mail: info@kivakipress.com

Kívakí Press is a small house with a focus on three editorial areas: environmental restoration; community renewal and education; and personal and holistic healing. Kívakí exists to provide people with practical strategies for restoring their ecosystems, for reconnecting with their places and local cultures, and for renewing their bodies holistically. Kívakí addresses academic, holistic health, and environmental book markets. Located in the mountains of North Carolina, the press produces a small number of new titles on a seasonal basis to add to a strong backlist.

Indicative of Kívakí interest: *A Wilder Life: Essays from Home* by Ken Wright; *The Company of Others: Essays in Celebration of Paul Shepard* (edited by Max Oelschlaeger); *Look to the Mountain: An Ecology of Indigenous Education* by Gregory Cajete; *Seasons of Change: Growing Through Pregnancy and Birth* by Suzanne Arms; *Restoration Forestry: An International Guide to Sustainable Forestry Practices* (edited by Michael Pilarski); *Flora of the San Juans: A Field Guide to the Mountain Plants of Southwestern Colorado* by Sue Komarek; *Sacred Land Sacred Sex: Rapture of the Deep—Concerning Deep Ecology and Celebrating Life* by Dolores Lachapelle; *Deep Powder Snow* by Dolores Lachapelle.

Kívakí oversees its own distribution, including direct mail-order, and a trade distribution network that utilizes the facilities of several national fulfillment and distribution firms. Query letters and SASEs should be directed to:

Fred Gray, Publisher

KRAUSE PUBLICATIONS

700 East State Street, Iola, WI 54990-0001

1-888-457-2873/715-445-2214   fax: 715-445-4087

www.krause.com

Krause is a large publisher of trade nonfiction, with a concentration in antiques, collectibles, sewing, ceramics, crafts, and hobbies, as well as technical and professional topics (in such areas as engineering). Series include Contemporary Quilting, Creative Machine Arts, and a full lineup of consumer/trade titles that lists current market values for a wide range of antiques and collectibles (usually in periodically updated editions).

Representative of the list: *100 Years of Vintage Watches* by Dean Judy; *2003 Brookman Stamp Price Guide* edited by David S. Macdonald; *2003 Price Guide to Contemporary Collectibles and Limited Editions, 8th ed.* edited by Mary L. Sieber; *2003 Standard Catalog of Baseball Cards, 12th ed.* edited by Bob Lemke; *American Dream Cars* by Mitchel J. Frumkin and Phil Hall; *Antique Trader Antiques & Collectibles 2003 Price Guide* edited by Kyle Husfloen; *Cindy Walter's Snippet Sensations Christmas Celebration* by Cindy Walter; *The Essential Guide to Practically Perfect Patchwork* by Michele Morrow Harer; *Hunting Dogs* by Russell A. Graves; *Renuzit Decorating With Fragrance* by Cindy Groom-Harry and Craft Marketing Connections, Inc; *Camping Digest* by Janet Groene; *Colorful Quilts for Kids* by Beth Wheeler; *The Cutting Edge* by Vivian Peritts; *Fishing Digest* edited by Dennis Thornton; *Glass A to Z* by David Shotwell; *Granny Quilts* by Darlene Zimmerman; *Hunting North American Big Game* by Durwood Hollis; *Kids 1st Scrapbooking* by Krause Publications; *Model Railroading With M.T.H. Electric Trains* by Rob Adelman; *Motifs for Crazy Quilting* by J. Marsha Michler; *Ragged-Edge Flowers* by Laura Farson; *Schuco Classic Tin Toys* by Chris Knox.

Query letters and SASEs should be directed to:

Deb Faupel, Editor, Book Division

Don Johnson, Vice President of Publishing, Magazines and periodicals

LATIN AMERICAN LITERARY REVIEW PRESS

PO Box 17660, Pittsburgh, PA 15235

412-824-7903   fax: 412-824-7909

www.lalrp.org   e-mail: latin@angstrom.net

Latin American Literary Review Press produces reference books, trade books, and specialty publications in Latin American interest and studies. The press produces books in art, architecture, literature, and poetry; history, biography, and natural science; country studies (Spain, Europe, United States, Latin America); and children's books.

Latin American Literary Review Press (founded in 1980) is an independent house that is particularly vigorous in such fields as Latin American literature in English translation, Spanish-language art books, and literary criticism in Spanish. The press also publishes the journal *Latin American Literary Review*, the only journal in the United States devoted solely to the study of Latin American literature.

Representative titles in fiction and literature: *Beer Cans in the Rio de la Plata* by Jorge Stamadianos; *Clara* by Luisa Valenzuela (translated by Andrea Labinger); *The Cuban*

Mile by Alejandro Hernandez Diaz (translated by Dick Cluster); *Musicians and Watchmakers* by Alicia Steimberg (translated by Andrea Graubart); *Pichka Harawikuna: Five Quechua Poets* edited by J. Noriega Bernuy (English translations by Maureen Ahern); *Sultry Moon* by Mempo Giardinelli (translated by Patricia J. Duncan); *To Die In Berlin* by Carlos Cerda (translated by David Davis); *UL: Four Mapuche Poets* edited by Cecilia Vicuca (English Translation by John Bierhorst); *Yo-Yo Boing!* by Giannina Braschi; *Scent of Love* by Edla van Steen (translated by David S. George); *The Island of Cundeamor* by Rene Vazquez Diaz (translated by David Davis); *The Medicine Man* by Francisco Rojas Gonzalez (translated by Robert S. Rudder and Gloria Ajona); *The Song of the Distant Root* by Elizabeth Subercaseaux (translated by John J. Hassett); *Strange Forces* by Leopoldo Lugones (translated by Gilbert Alter-Gilbert); *The Tenth Circle* by Mempo Giardinelli (translated by Andrea Labinger); *The Eye That Looks At Me* by Loreina Santos Silva (translated by Carys Evans-Corrales).

Latin American Literary Review Press has its own in-house distribution operation; in addition, the house markets through direct-mail catalog dissemination and utilizes a variety of national and regional distribution houses. Major markets include public libraries, trade booksellers, and university and college libraries. Latin American Literary Review Press handles distribution for a number of domestic and international presses. Query letters and SASEs should be directed to:

Yvette E. Miller, President and Editor in Chief

Maria G. Trujillo, Assistant Editor

LEARNING EXPRESS

900 Broadway, Suite 604, New York, NY 10003

212-995-2566   fax: 212-995-5512

www.learnatest.com

Learning Express is a leading publisher of print and online test preparation, career guidance, and basic skills materials. LearnATest.com/Library, its online interactive resource, offers practice tests and exercises for academic and career exams. Books are distributed by Delmar/Thomson Learning.

Sample titles include: *Basic Skills; Business Writing Help Center; Career Resources; Civil Service; College Preparation; Cosmetology; Elementary School Grade 4; EMS; Firefighter; GED; Graduate School Entrance; Healthcare; High School Grades 9-12; Law Enforcement; Middle School Grades 5-8; Military; Nursing; Online Courses; Online Spanish Courses; Parent Resources; Postal Services; Real Estate; Teaching; Technical and Career College; U.S. Citizenship.*

Query letters and SASEs should be directed to:

Jennifer Farthing, Senior Editorial Producer

LEISURE BOOKS

276 Fifth Avenue, Suite 1008, New York, NY 10001

212-725-8811   fax: 212-532-1054

www.dorchesterpub.com

Leisure's publishing program centers on mass-market paperback originals in fiction, with a short list of hardcover reprints. Leisure's category fiction embraces historical romance, horror, technothrillers, thrillers, and Westerns.

Leisure hosts a fine list from established genre writers and also offers works from newer authors; the house publishes several brand-name category series and issues a notable number of deluxe double editions. The innovative Love Spell line has defined new market territory with experimental marketing slates in paranormal, futuristic, time travel, legendary lovers, perfect heroes, and faerie-tale romance. Love Spell, which is developing a new line of humorous contemporary romance, recently launched a new line of gothic romances. Leisure Books (founded in 1970) and Love Spell are divisions of Dorchester Publishing Company.

Indicative of Leisure Books interest: *Forever Autumn* by Bobbi Smith; *Lord of the Hunt* by Ann Lawrence; *Hannah's Half-Breed* by Heidi Betts; *Princess Charming* by Beth Pattillo; *The Restless Dead* by Hugh B. Cave; *Road to Hell* by Gerald Houarner; *Against All Enemies* by Maj. B. Woulfe, USMC; *Spirit Rider* by Cotton Smith; *The Key* by Lynsay Sands; *The Geraldi Trail* by Max Brand; *Track of a Killer* by Stephen Overholser; *Deadly Season* by Tim Champlin; *From Boardwalk With Love* by Nina Bangs; *A Stranger's Desire* by Kimberly Raye; *Keeper Of The Light* by Janeen O' Kerry; *To Tame A Renegade* by Connie Mason; *Savage Destiny* by Cassie Edwards; *Danelaw* by Susan Squires; *The Wild Irish West* by Joan Avery; *A Treasure To Hold* by Kathleen McCarthy; *Haunter* by Charlee Jacob; *Laughing Man* by M. Wright; *Black Hat Butte* by John D. Nesbitt; *The Thorn & the Thistle* by Julie Moffett; *Once They Wore the Gray* by Johnny D. Boggs; *Gambler's Row* by Les Savage, Jr; *Stage Trails West* by Frank Bonham; *Dr. Yes* by Lisa Cach; *The Selkie* by Melanie Jackson; *Highland Fling* by Tess Mallory.

Leisure is distributed by Hearst Distribution Group. Query letters and SASEs should be directed to:

Alicia Condon, Editorial Director

Christopher Keeslar, Senior Editor

Don D'Auria, Senior Editor

Leah Hultenschmidt, Editorial Assistant

Ashley Kuehl, Editorial Assistant

Kate Seaver, Associate Editor

LIFELINE PRESS

SEE ALSO: REGNERY PUBLISHING, INC.

One Massachusetts Avenue NW, Washington, DC 20001

202-216-0600   fax: 202-216-0612

LifeLine Press is a new imprint of Regnery Publishing, which is dedicated to health, wellness, and child care. The press is committed to publishing the latest ground-breaking medical research in the fields of alternative health, nutrition, wellness, and child development. LifeLine's mission is "to provide timely and accurate information for consumers concerned about their health." LifeLine Press is committed to building a successful partnership with authors that could lead to the publication of not only the authors's first books, but their second and third books as well.

Sample titles include: *Life is Hard, Food is Easy* by Linda Spangle, R.N., M.A.; *The Nashville Diet* by Marilyn Tucker, D. Ph; *The Complete Medical Guide for the Family Caregiver* edited by Jeffery A. West, MD; *Epidemic* by Meg Meeker, MD; *Breaking the Rules of Aging* by David A. Lipschitz, MD, P.h.D.; *Diet Simple* by Katherine Tallmadge; *Healing Outside the Margins* by Carole O'Toole and Carolyn B. Hendricks, MD; *The Cornell Illustrated Encyclopedia of Health,* general editor Antonio M. Grotto Jr. MD, D.Phil; *Stop Living Life Like an Emergency!* by Diane Sieg, R.N.; *The Smart Weigh* by Pamela M. Smith, RD; *Warning Signs* by John Kelly with Brian J. Karem; *Every Heart Attack is Preventable* by Michael Mogadam, MD; *Higher Purpose* by Tom Whittaker; *Unglued & Tattooed* by Sara Trollinger with Mike Yorkey; *Living with Diabetes* by Nicole Johnson; *Heart Sense for Women* by Stephen Sinatra, MD; *The Diet Trap* by Pamela Smith, R.D.; *Low-Fat Lies* by Kevin Vigilante, MD, M.P.H. and Mary Flynn, P.h.D.

Query letters and SASEs should be directed to:

Mike Ward, Associate Publisher

Molly L. Mullen, Editor

LONELY PLANET PUBLICATIONS

150 Linden Street, Oakland, CA 94607

510-893-8555   fax: 510-893-8563

www.lonelyplanet.com   e-mail: info@lonelyplanet.com

Lonely Planet specializes in travel guides, phrasebooks, maps, atlases, restaurant guides, activity guides, and other specialist travel series, covering every country in the world and with options for a full range of budgets and styles. There are over 600 Lonely Planet publications produced in offices in Melbourne, Australia, Oakland, California, London, and Paris.

Lonely Planet's Shoestring Guides are the world's best-selling budget guides. Designed for the long-haul independent traveler, these cover either entire continents or large sections of entire continents.

Travel Guides are in-depth country or regional guides and include options and budget information for all types of travelers.

Condensed Guides are ideal pocket guides when time is tight, with quick-view maps, full color throughout, top sights, and the best places to stay, eat, and shop, all in a pocket-sized format.

CitySync is Lonely Planet's series of digital city guides for Palm and other PDAs. The series is currently available as a download, on CD-ROM, or as a Handspring module and a Palm Travel Pak card.

Walking Guides are for those who believe the best way to see the world is on foot, from family strolls to difficult treks, with reliable maps and essential travel information.

Cycling Guides map out the best bike routes, long and short, in day-to-day detail. Includes advice on staying healthy, bike maintenance, places to stay and eat, bike shops, and innovative maps with detailed cues to each ride and elevation charts.

Watching Wildlife guides are packed with advice on where, when, and how to view a region's wildlife, with photos of more than 300 species and engaging insights into their lives and environments.

Pisces guides explore the world's great diving and snorkeling areas and include full-color photos throughout, practical information on activities above and below the water, and listings of diving services and resorts. Each guide also includes health and safety tips and site details such as depth, visibility, levels of difficulty, and marine life you're likely to see.

Phrasebooks cover essential words and phrases, two-way dictionaries, local script for easy reference, and much more in pocket-sized format.

Lonely Planet also produces a limited series of hardcover, beautifully designed and produced, illustrated gift books on travel. Titles in this series include *Chasing Rickshaws*; *Sacred India and the Shape of Perfection*; *Buddhist Stupas in Asia*.

Other series from Lonely Planet include Read This First, Healthy Travel, City Maps, World Foot, Out to Eat, as well as videos, calendars, and other merchandise.

Lonely Planet's website includes over 300 Destinations Profiles—well-researched and up-to-date reports on countries, cities, islands, and regions—complete with maps and photographs. In addition, www.lonelyplanet.com's Thorn Tree has become the center of the independent travel community, with over 5,000 postings a day on hundreds of travel topics.

The people at Lonely Planet (founded in 1975) strongly believe that travelers can make a positive contribution to the countries they visit, both through their appreciation of the countries' culture, wildlife, and natural features and through the money they spend. In addition, Lonely Planet makes a direct contribution to the countries and regions it covers. Since 1986 a percentage of the income from each book has been donated to ventures such as famine relief in Africa, aid projects in India, agricultural projects in Central America, Greenpeace's efforts to halt French nuclear testing in the Pacific, and Amnesty International.

As the publisher's message suggests: "I hope we send the people out with the right attitude about travel. You realize when you travel that there are many different perspectives about the world, so we hope these books will make people more interested in what they see. These are guidebooks, but you can't really guide people. All you can do is point them in the right direction.'

Lonely Planet produces an anecdotal and informative travel newsletter and distributes its own list in America through its U. S. office. The Lonely Planet Publications editorial division is located in Australia—though manuscripts and proposals are given preliminary consideration at the stateside contact address. Query letters and SASEs should be directed to:

Eric Kettunen, U.S. Manager (at United States office)

LONGSTREET PRESS

2974 Hardman Court, Atlanta, GA 30305

404-254-0110   fax: 404-254-0016

www.longstreetpress.com   e-mail: info@longstreetpress.net

Longstreet publishes general nonfiction and fiction (often with a Southern regional accent), self-help, gardening, sports, health, photography, art, calendars, and gift books.

Titles from Longstreet include: *Call to Glory* by Michael J. Gilhuly, MD& Marilyn Gilhuly; *Fuqua* by J.B. Fuqua; *Will's War* by Janice Woods Windle; *Month-by-Month Gardening in Atlanta* by Don Hastings and Chris Hastings; *The Bowden Way* by Bobby Bowden with Steve Bowden; *Atlanta Cooks* by Melissa Libby; *Penley* by Steve Penley; *By Fate or By Faith: A Personal Story* by Isaac Goodfriend; *A Girl's Guide to a Guy's World* by Jennifer Babbit and Samantha Bank; *Small Blessings: A Book of Prayers for Children* by Don Harp; *Trees for the South* by Don Hastings; *Sweet Words to God* by Rabbi Arnold Goodman; *Forever Green: A History and Hope of the American Forest* by Chuck Leavell; *Family Estrangements: How They Begin, How to Mend Them, How to Cope with Them* by Barbara LeBey; *The Thank You Book and The Thank You Book for Kids* by Ali Lauren Spizman; *Bobby Jones: Extra!* (compiled by Sidney L. Matthew); *Down the Fairway* by Robert T. Jones and O. B. Keeler.

Longstreet publishes the popular Jeff Foxworthy's *You Might Be a Redneck If . . . ,* which now has more than one million copies in print. Other Foxworthy books include *Red Ain't Dead; Games Rednecks Play; Check Your Neck; You're Not a Kid Anymore; Redneck Classic; The Final Helping of You Might Be a Redneck If . . .*

Longstreet oversees its own distribution. Please note that due to a recently down-sized acquisitions department, Longstreet currently is not accepting unsolicited or unagented manuscript submissions.

Query letters and SASEs should be directed to:

Ann Lovet, Editorial and Publicity Assistant

Scott Bard, Publisher and President

LOOMPANICS UNLIMITED

Box 1197, Port Townsend, WA 98368

360-385-2230   fax: 360-385-7785

www.loompanics.com   e-mail: editorial@loompanics.com

Loompanics Unlimited produces books of nonfiction trade interest, in addition to professional and special-interest nonfiction. The Loompanics list accents practical self-help and how-to, contemporary and historical culture, and sociopolitical and issue-oriented works. The house offers a selective fiction list (primarily, reprints of hitherto overlooked masterworks).

Loompanics offers books in such categories as underground economy, tax "avoision," money-making opportunities, individual privacy, fake identification, Big Brother is watching you, conducting investigations, crime and police science, locks and lock-smithing, self-defense, revenge, guns, weapons, bombs and explosives, guerrilla warfare, murder and torture, survival, self-sufficiency, head for the hills, gimme shelter, health and life extension, paralegal skills, sex, drugs, rock and roll, intelligence increase, science and technology, heresy/weird ideas, anarchism and egoism, work, mass media, censorship, reality creation, self-publishing—and an enigmatic category of works classified solely as miscellaneous.

Since its foundation in 1973, Loompanics titles have been among the most controversial and unusual publications available, and the publishing program has produced recognized classics in a number of fields.

Many Loompanics publications test the edge of the free-speech envelope—and often do so with humorous subversiveness and literary zest; some of the more treacherous materials are clearly intended exclusively for amusement, informational, or scholarly reference purposes.

Loompanics features: *Secrets of Methamphetamine Manufacture* by Uncle Fester; *The Outlaw's Bible* by E. X. Boozhie; *Take No Prisoners: Destroying Enemies with Dirty and Malicious Tricks* by Mack Nasty; *Gaslighting: How to Drive Your Enemies Crazy* by Victor Santoro; *Poison Pen Letters* by Keith Wade; *Identity Theft: The Cyber Crime of the Millennium* by John Q. Newman; *Sex, Drugs & the Twinkie Murders* by Paul Krassner; *Anarchic Harmony: The Spirituality of Social Disobedience* by William J. Murray; *Principia Discordia:*

Or How I Found the Goddess and What I Did to Her When I Found Her by Malaclypse the Younger; *How to Sneak into the Movies* by Dan Zamudio; *Practical LSD Manufacture* by Uncle Fester; *Secondhand Success: How to Turn Discards into Dollars* by Jordan L. Cooper; *Uberhaker! How to Break into Computers* by Carolyn Meinel; *The Politics of Consciousness: A Practical Guide to Personal Freedom* by Steve Kubby; *Stoned Free: How to Get High Without Drugs* by Patrick Wells, with Douglas Rushkoff; *You Are Going to Prison (a survival guide)* by Jim Hogshire.

From the arena of literary fiction: *The Gas* (another classic literary work in reissue) by Charles Platt.

Some backlist Loompanics hits: *Bad Girls Do It! An Encyclopedia of Female Murderers* by Michael Newton (author of *Serial Slaughter: What's Behind America's Murder Epidemic?*); *Still At Large: A Casebook of 20th Century Serial Killers* and *Psychedelic Shamanism* by Jim DeKorne; *Secrets of a Superhacker* by an incognito information superhighwayman known as the Knightmare; *Shadow Merchants: Successful Retailing Without a Storefront* by Jordan L. Cooper; *The Art & Science of Dumpster Diving* by John Hoffman (with original comix by Ace Backwords); *Community Technology* by Karl Hess; *How to Obtain a Second Passport and Citizenship and Why You Want To* by Adam Starchild; *The Rape of the American Constitution* by Chuck Shiver; *The Wild and Free Cookbook* by Tom Squire; *Travel-Trailer Homesteading Under $5,000* by Brian D. Kelly; *Screw the Bitch: Divorce Tactics for Men* by Dick Hart; *Natural Law: Or Don't Put a Rubber on Your Willy* by Robert Anton Wilson.

Special Loompanics compilations: *Loompanics' Greatest Hits: Articles and Features from the Best Book Catalog in the World* (edited by Michael Hoy); *Loompanics Unlimited Live! in Las Vegas* (edited by Michael Hoy).

Loompanics Unlimited is editorially a reclusive house. Writers who wish to work with Loompanics should note that its business is the printed word, and potential authors should approach Loompanics through the printed word (via mail—do not telephone or e-mail proposals or submissions). The publisher also notes that the press tends toward small advances and works through literary agents only on occasion.

The Loompanics Unlimited direct-order catalog (emblazoned with the publisher's freebooter-spaceship colophon) depicts a wealth of titles from its own list, as well as select offerings from other houses, in a luscious newsprint format that includes graphics, essays, and short fiction, along with blurbs from reviewers and satisfied customers testifying to the potency of the house's list and the efficacy of the Loompanics distribution and fulfillment services.

Query letters and SASEs should be directed to:

Michael Hoy, President

THE LYONS PRESS

246 Goose Lane, PO Box 480, Guilford, CT 06437

203-458-4500   fax: 203-458-4668

www.lyonspress.com   e-mail: info@lyonspress.com

The Lyons Press, now an imprint of the Globe-Pequot Press, produces trade nonfiction, especially books on country living, horses, fly fishing, adventure, travel, military history, natural history, and outdoor recreation and sports; the house also produces works aimed at regional interests worldwide, selected literary fiction and essays, and reference. Recently, the house has widened its mandate quite a bit past fly fishing books.

From Lyons Press: *Terrible Angel* by Dermot McEvoy; *101 Fly Fishing Tips* by Lefty Kreh; *A River Seen Right* by Michael Baughman; *A Wedding Gift* by Timothy Foote; *An Honest Angler* by Sparse Grey Hackle; *Basic Fly Tying* by Dick Taller; *Bass Bug Fishing* by William Tapply; *Bass Wisdom* by Homer Circle; *In the Mountains of Heaven* by Mike Tidwell; *No Picnic on Mount Kenya* by Felice Benuzzi; *Of Men and Mountains* by William Douglas; *A Man Escaped* by Andre Devigny; *Assault In Norway* by Thomas Gallagher; *Bodyguard of Lies* by Anthony Cave Brown; *Brady's Civil War* by Webb Garrison; *Delilah* by Marcus Goodrich; *How They Won the War in the Pacific* by Edwin Hoyt; *Jutland* by John Campbell; *Country Houses and How to Build Them* by Daniel Atwood; *Fences, Gates, and Bridges* by George Martin; *Outwitting Contractors* by Bill Adler; *Pearls of Country Wisdom* by Deborah Tukua; *A Passion for Vegetables* by Paul Gayler; *An Omelette and a Glass of Wine* by Elizabeth David; *Cast Iron Cooking* by A. D. Livingston; *Cold-Smoking & Salt-Curing Meat, Fish & Game* by A. D. Livingston; *Honey From A Weed* by Patience Gray; *Country Breads of the World* by Linda Collister and Anthony Blake.

Fiction and literature: *Ice Hunter* (mystery) by Joseph Heywood; *Dry Rain* (stories) by Pete Fromm; *Travers Corners* (stories about the Lake Wobegon of fly fishing) by Scott Waldie.

The company logo shows a leaping trout poised gracefully midair over the publisher's ingenious LP colophon. Lyons Press produces 340 new titles and keeps a substantial backlist.

Query letters and SASEs should be directed to:

Jay Cassell, Editorial Director—Fishing, hunting, sports, adventure, history, gardening, home improvement, cooking, popular culture, fiction

George Donahue, Senior Editor—Adventure travel, business, current affairs, fiction, history, martial arts, military, Native Americans, nature, sports/fitness

Tom McCarthy, Senior Editor—Sports, history/military history, popular culture

Jay McCullough, Editor—History, military history, espionage, travelogue, fiction, fly fishing, fly tying techniques, and current events

Ann Treistman, Editor—Nature, animals, narrative nonfiction, cooking, health and fitness, women's sports

MACADAM/CAGE

155 Sansome Street, suite 550, San Francisco, CA 94104-3615

866-986-7470   fax: 415-986-7414

www.macadamcage.com

Founded in 1998 by David Poindexter, MacAdam/Cage Publishing is a successful trade publisher with offices in both Denver and San Francisco. Its aim as a publisher is to produce quality fiction and nonfiction, and it are committed to finding and publishing new and talented writers.

After acquiring the successful independent publisher, MacMurray & Beck, in 1999, MacAdam/Cage Publishing is considered to be a prime example of successful independent publishing in America. Notable authors from MacAdam/Cage include Patricia Henley, William Gay, and Susan Vreeland. For the future MacAdam/Cage will continue its innovative approach to marketing but will also will stay committed to introducing new and exciting authors from around the world.

Sample titles include: *Between Two Deserts* by Germaine Shames; *Stories from the Blue Moon Café* edited by Sonny Brewer; *Clara Mondschein's Melancholia* by Anne Raeff; *The Secret of Hurricanes* by Theresa Williams; *The Cartoonist's Handbook* by Craig Clevenger; *Welcome to Higby* by Mark Dunn; *What It Means to Love You* by Stephen Elliott; *Sparrowhawk Book Two: Hugh Kenrick* by Edward Cline; *The Toaster Broke, So We're Getting Married* by Pamela Holm; *The Cancer Monologue Project* by Tanya Taylor and Pamela Thompson; *The Pains of April* by Frank Hollon; *Bite the Stars* by Eliza Clark; *A Life Without Consequences* by Stephen Elliot; *The Perpetual Ending* by Kristen den Hartog; *Dream of the Blue Room* by Michelle Richmond; *Beautiful Girls* by Beth Ann Bauman; *Sleep Toward Heaven* by Amanda Ward; *The Anomalies* by Joey Goebel; *Reunion* by Michael Oren; *Sunset Terrance* by Rebecca Donner.

For new writers seeking to submit work, writer's guidelines can be found on the website. Query and SASE's go to:

Anna Streitfeld, Nonfiction Editor

MCFARLAND & COMPANY, INC., PUBLISHERS

Box 611, Jefferson, NC 28640-0611

336-246-4460   fax: 336-246-5018

www.mcfarlandpub.com   e-mail: info@mcfarlandpub.com

McFarland & Company, Inc., Publishers, is an independent nontrade publisher specializing in general reference, performing arts (especially film, radio, television, and theater), baseball, popular culture, automotive history, chess, Appalachian studies, history (U.S., Civil War, world), international studies, criminal justice, women's studies, and African American studies. Publishes nonfiction only, around 200 titles per year.

Titles include: *The History of Television, 1942-2000* by Albert Abramson; *Baseball Drills for Young People* by Dirk Baker; *Scapegoats* by Christopher Bell; *The Dinosaur Filmography* by Mark F. Berry; *The Braff Silent Short Film Working Papers* by Richard E. Braff; *Architectural Acoustics* Christopher N. Brooks; *The Norman Conquest of Southern Italy and Sicily* by Gordon S. Brown; *Serial Killer Cinema* by Robert Cettl; *Baseball and Richmond* by W. Harrison; *Human Prehistory in Fiction* by Charles De Paolo; *The Coon-Sanders Nighthawks* by Fred W. Edmiston; *The Politics and Plays of Bernard Shaw* by Judith Evans; *The Old Breed of Marine* by Abraham Felber; *The Mummy Unwrapped* by Thomas M. Feramisco; *For the Good of the Country* by David L. Fleitz; *Special Use Vehicles* by George Green; *The Negro Leagues* by Leslie A. Heaphy; *Anti-Communism and Popular Culture in Mid-Century America* by Cyndy Hendershot; *Black Threads* by Kyra E. Hicks; *Walter Penn Shipley* by John S. Hilbert.

Query letters and SASEs should be directed to:

Robert Franklin, President and Editor-in-Chief

Virginia Tobiassen, Editor

Steve Wilson, Senior Editor
Born: November 27, 1968.
Education: B.A., summa cum laude, in English, UNC-Chapel Hill, 1991.
Employment history/editor career path: Started at McFarland as an Assistant Editor shortly after college; no prior publishing experience.
Personal interests: Automotive history, Southern literature, woodworking, scale automotive modeling.

What books have you acquired that make you the most proud? What books that you have acquired reflect the types of books you like to represent? Two works, both coincidentally on North Carolina history, come to mind: Fred Mallison's *The Civil War on the Outer Banks* and R. G. (Hank) Utley and Scott Verner's *The Independent Carolina Baseball League, 1936–1938: Baseball Outlaws.* They're both labors of love, the kind of lifelong research efforts that can only be accomplished by someone deeply involved with the subject material. Moreover, they're both charming and fascinating. Both books also represent unknown marketing quantities that performed well.

Do you represent fiction? No.

Do you represent nonfiction? Yes, exclusively.

Do you require book proposals? If so, what do you look for in evaluating a book proposal? If the manuscript is complete when the author first contacts us, we generally invite the entire manuscript if it sounds plausible. At the opposite extreme, we're willing to launch a discussion based on nothing more than an idea, particularly if we have worked with the author before. At some point prior to a contract offer, we do need a proposal, though—preferably an outline, length estimate, draft of introduction or preface, two sample chapters, and description of special elements such as illustrations or appendices. We look for authoritative and complete coverage of a subject that is not already exhausted; competent research and organization; and reliability (we don't want to be forced to verify absolutely every fact and spelling).

Are certain aspects of a book proposal given more weight than others? Yes, but they vary according to the type of book. In a work of film reference, for example, we look hard at the depth of filmographic data; in a biography, the freshness of the material tends to be a key factor; in a book of library cartoons, the question is whether they're funny.

What process do you use for making a decision? What is the process for acquisition, is there a committee? All members of our editorial staff are involved in acquisitions. Proposals are distributed as they arrive, and the editors meet once a week to discuss the new proposals they've received.

What kinds of nonfiction books do you want to see less of? We do not publish devotional works, stories of personal triumph over adversity, theories about the functioning of the cosmos (a very frequent offering), or children's books, all of which are proposed to us regularly.

Are you interested in work geared for the masses (readers of *People*, *The Star*, etc.)? Generally, no. Our market consists of (1) libraries and (2) individuals with a strongly focused interest in any of several specialty subjects (film, old-time radio, baseball, chess, automotive history, and others).

Are agents important? Why? From our perspective, no. We use a standard contract that does not vary from book to book, so an agent has no real negotiating role in signing a contract with us. Communication with an author is smoother, too, when it is direct.

Do you like new writers? What should writers do to break into the business? We do like new writers. Perhaps as many as half our authors had not published a book before coming to McFarland, and many have gone on to publish several successful books with us. (We enjoy a very high rate of repeat authors.) For breaking in with a publisher like us, the best advice to a new author is to find a fresh, interesting subject and produce a fairly substantial sample before contacting us. Our website lists some useful guidelines.

How should writers approach you? The traditional query letter, followed up by a formal proposal if we express interest, is hard to beat. We accept queries by telephone or even by e-mail (no attachments please), but a letter tends to make the best impression.

What are some common mistakes writers make? What really gets on your nerves? Writers are better off not phoning every few days to see if we've looked at a proposal yet. We're really quite prompt—we respond inside of two weeks in most cases, and it almost never takes us more than a month—but some authors can't stand even that wait. The innocent "Have you gotten to my proposal yet?" question is almost impossible to answer by phone. We receive too many proposals to remember them all instantly (especially before actually looking through them), and a given proposal may be with any of four or five of us. An author who phones two or three times in the short period before we can reply signals a possible "personality problem."

What have been some of your craziest experiences with submissions? Authors re-proposing previously rejected manuscripts three or four times or writing us under a different name after a rejection. One or two have refused to reveal the subject of the manuscript without a commitment of interest and a written confidentiality agreement.

What have been some of your best experiences with writers or in your job? Well, there's really nothing more satisfying than a happy author. Editors sometimes forget the sheer work that goes into a manuscript. When an author's long labor has produced something really good, we've done our job right and turned out a beautiful book, and the author senses that we've made the manuscript better, I feel good. That sense of productive partnership is enormously rewarding.

THE MCGRAW-HILL COMPANIES, INC.

MCGRAW-HILL/OSBORNE MEDIA

MCGRAW-HILL PROFESSIONAL

ACCESS MED BOOKS

BUSINESS MCGRAW-HILL

INTERNATIONAL MARINE

RAGGED MOUNTAIN PRESS

SCHAUM'S MCGRAW HILL

WRIGHT GROUP/MCGRAW-HILL (SEE SEPARATE ENTRY)

2 Penn Plaza, New York, NY 10121

212-512-2000 fax: 212-904-6096

For over 100 years, McGraw-Hill has been publishing nonfiction titles in a wide range of categories. In addition to a long list of fiction titles, McGraw-Hill operates specialty programs in a variety of professional, business, and educational fields such as health care, law, high-tech industries, and textbooks for primary school through college. This house publishes the following: books for professional, institutional, and trade markets; journals geared to core areas of interest; and seminar and group workshop materials. It also issues a broad selection of electronic products, including e-books and CD-ROMs.

While still geared toward business and professional titles, McGraw-Hill continues to venture into the broader range of commercial trade arenas, including aviation, careers, cooking, computing, engineering, architecture, foreign language, general, self-help, medical, science, mathematics, sports, recreation, and telecommunications.

McGraw-Hill distributes for all its divisions. Query letters and SASEs should be directed to:

MCGRAW-HILL/OSBORNE MEDIA

2600 Tenth Street, Sixth Floor, Berkeley, CA 94710

McGraw-Hill/Osborne Media produces self-paced computer training materials, including user and reference guides, titles on business and technology, and high-level but practical titles on networking, programming, and Web development tools. McGraw-Hill/Osborne Media is the official press of Oracle, Corel, Global Knowledge, J. D. Edwards, Intuit, and RSA Security, Inc., and has a strategic publishing relationship with ComputerWorld. McGraw-Hill/Osborne Media is focusing on consumer support, emerging technologies, and innovative applications for developing future computer books.

McGraw-Hill/Osborne Media is known for its series, including: The Complete Reference Series, A Beginners Guide Series, All in One Series, and Certification Press Series.

Titles indicative of this list: *C# Programming Tips & Techniques* by Charles Wright and Kris Jamsa; *Learn to Program with Visual Basic.NET* by John Smiley; *Oracle 9i New Features* by Robert Freeman; *Mike Meyers' Network+ Certification Passport* by Michael Meyers and Nigel Kendrick; *OCP Oracle9i Database New Features for Administrators Exam Guide* by Daniel Benjamin; *DSL Survival Guide* by Lisa Lee; *Home Networking Survival Guide* by David Strom; *FrontPage 2002 Virtual Classroom* by David Karlins.

Direct query letters and SASEs to:

Scott Rogers, Editor-in-Chief; Scott_Rogers@mcgraw-hill.com

MCGRAW-HILL PROFESSIONAL

McGraw-Hill Professional focuses on professional, reference, and trade publishing. This division produces general-interest books, study guides, software, multimedia, and online products.

This broad list includes titles in business, economics, computers, education, family and relationships, foreign language study, health and fitness, history, language arts and disciplines, mathematics, medical, nature, nonclassifiable, psychology and psychiatry, science, self-help, social science, sports and recreation, technology, engineering, transportation, and travel.

General titles span the categories of art; body, mind, and spirit; cooking; crafts and hobbies; family and relationships; gardening; health and fitness; history; house and home; humor; music; nature; performing arts; photography; and self-help.

Titles indicative of McGraw-Hill Professional: *Fit from Within: 101 Simple Secrets to Change Your Body and Your Life—Starting Today and Lasting Forever* by Victoria Moran; *The No-Cry Sleep Solution: Gentle Ways to Help Your Baby Sleep Through the Night* by Elizabeth Pantley; *Model Mommy: Vendela's Plan for Emotional Support, Exercise, and Eating Right After Having a Baby* by Vendela Kirsebom; *Dealing with People You Can't Stand: How to Bring Out the Best in People at Their Worst* by Rick Brinkman and Rick Kirschner; *Beating Depression: The Journey to Hope* by Maga Jackson-Triche, Kenneth Wells, and Katherine Minnium; *Ten Secrets of Successful Men That Women Want to Know* by Donna Brooks and Lynn Brooks; *The September 11 Syndrome: Seven Steps to Getting a Grip in Uncertain Times* by Harriet Braiker; *Teach Yourself World Faiths, New Edition* by Paul Oliver; *Teach Yourself Film Making* by Tom Holden; *Table for One Chicago* by Michael Kaminer and Amy LaBan.

Aviation titles: *Safe Air Travel Companion* by Dan McKinnon; *Once a Fighter Pilot* by Jerry Cook; *Rescue Pilot* by Dan McKinnon; *Profit Strategies for Air Transportation* by George Radnoti; *Handling In-Flight Emergencies* by Jerry Eichenberger; *Ace the Technical Pilot Interview* by Gary Bristow.

Career titles: *Ace the IT Resume!* by Paula Moreira and Robyn Thorpe; *201 Best Questions to Ask on Your Interview* by John Kador; *101 Best Resumes to Sell Yourself* by Jay Block; *The Career Survival Guide Making Your Next Career Move* by Brian O'Connell; *Occupational Outlook Handbook, 2002–2003 Edition* by U.S. Department of Labor.

Engineering and Architecture titles representative of this list: *McGraw-Hill's National Electrical Safety Code Handbook* by David Marne; *Master Handbook of Video Production* by Jerry Whitaker; *Lineman's and Cableman's Handbook* by Thomas Shoemaker and James Mack; *Architects on Architects* by Susan Gray; *Interior Design Handbook of Professional Practice* by Cindy Coleman, *Interior Design* Magazine; *TAB Electronics Build Your Own Robot Kit* by Myke Predko and Ben Wirz; *Build a Remote-Controlled Robot* by David Shircliff; *Structures of Our Time: 31 Buildings That Changed Modern Life* by Roger Shepherd.

Direct query letters and SASEs to:

Judy Bass—Telecommunications; judy_bass@mcgraw-hill.com

Shelley Carr—Aviation, technical trades; shelley_carr@mcgraw-hill.com

Steve Chapman—Electrical engineering, telecommunications, video/audio; steve_chapman@mcgraw-hill.com

Scott Grillo—TAB electronics, embedded systems, electrical wiring; scott_grillo@mcgraw-hill.com

Larry Hager—Civil engineering, industrial engineering, quality engineering, construction; larry_hager@mcgraw-hill.com

Ken McCombs—Chemical engineering, environmental engineering, mechanical engineering, fire science; kenneth_mccombs@mcgraw-hill.com

Marjorie Spencer—Telecommunications, networking; marjorie_spencer@mcgraw-hill.com

Cary Sullivan—Architecture, landscape architecture, interior design, urban design; cary_sullivan@mcgraw-hill.com

ACCESS MED BOOKS

2 Penn Plaza, 12th Floor, New York, NY 10121-2298

fax: 212-904-6045

Access Med Books produces select medical titles. A few representative titles include *Cosmetic Dermatology Principles and Practice* by Leslie Baumann; *Spine Surgery: A Practical Atlas* by F. Todd Wetzel and Edward Hanley, Jr.; *Harrison's Internet Edition* by Eugene Braunwald, Anthony Fauci, Dennis Kasper, Stephen Hauser, Dan Longo, and J. Jameson; *Cardiology at a Glance* by Johnny Lee and Paul Lee; *Operative Obstetrics* by Larry Gilstrap, F. Cunningham, and J. Peter VanDorsten; *Goodman & Gilman's: The Pharmacological Basis of Therapeutics* by Joel Hardman, Lee Limbird, and Alfred Gilman.

Direct query letters and SASEs to:

Martin Wonsiewicz, Publisher—Specialty: Clinical medicine; martin_wonsiewicz@mcgraw-hill.com

Jack Farrell, Publisher and Sales Manager—Specialty: Medical education products; jack_farrell@mcgraw-hill.com

Mikael Engebretson, Publisher—Specialty: Online publishing (including Harrison's Online); mikael_engebretson@mcgraw-hill.com

BUSINESS MCGRAW-HILL

2 Penn Plaza, New York, New York 10121

212-512-2000   fax: 212-904-6096

Business McGraw-Hill publishes trade and professional titles in business, finance, entrepreneurship, marketing, training, human resources, investing, management, advertising, sales, and communication.

Representative of the Business McGraw-Hill list: *Financial Planning for the Utterly Confused* by Joel Lerner; *Short Cycle Selling: Beating Your Competitors in the Sales Race* by Jim Kasper; *Valuing Wall Street* by Andrew Smithers and Stephen Wright; *Software Rules: How the Next Generation of Enterprise Applications Will Increase Strategic Effectiveness* by Mark Barrenechea; *Investing in Separate Accounts* by Erik Davidson and Kevin Freeman; *The Rumsfeld Way: The Leadership Wisdom of a Battle-Hardened Maverick* by Jeffrey Krames; *Character Counts* by John Bogle; *Six Sigma for Managers* by Greg Brue; *The Welch Way* by Jeffrey Krames; *Streetsmart Guide to Managing Your Portfolio* by Frank Yao, Bret Xu, Kenneth Doucet, and Patrick Adams.

Direct query letters and SASEs to:

Mary E. Glenn, Editorial Director—Management and management theory, self-help with a business focus, some marketing and sales; topical books with global appeal that can cross over into serious nonfiction

Philip Ruppel, Publisher—All areas indicated in house description, including marketing, management, quality, human resources, training, operations management

Donya Dickerson-Associate Editot—General business

INTERNATIONAL MARINE

PO Box 220, Camden, ME 04843-0220

207-236-4837   fax: 207-236-6314

www.internationalmarine.com

International Marine has been publishing books about boats since 1970. Located near the Rockport and Camden harbors of midcoast Maine, IM has published more than 200 titles covering everything from boat and engine maintenance, to boat handling and seamanship, to nautical adventures that are stranger than fiction. This division's slogan is "The best books about boats."

Titles representative of this list: *The Ship and the Storm: Hurricane Mitch and the Loss of the Fantome* by Jim Carrier; *The Boat Doctor: A Boating Magazine Book* by Allen Berrien, *One Minute Guide to the Nautical Rules of the Road* by Charlie Wing; *The Voyager's Handbook: The Essential Guide to Bluewater Cruising* by Beth A. Leonard.

Direct query letters and SASEs to:

Jon Eaton, Editorial Director; Jonathan_Eaton@mcgraw-hill.com

Alex Barnett, Acquisitions; alex_barnett@mcgraw-hill.com

RAGGED MOUNTAIN PRESS

PO Box 220, Camden, ME 04843-0220

207-236-4837   fax: 207-236-6314

www.raggedmountainpress.com

Ragged Mountain Press publishes informative titles on outdoor activities and pursuits from fly fishing to outdoor cooking, sea kayaking to survival techniques, survival methods to RV living.

This division produces between 20 and 23 books each year. Titles indicative of this list: *The Backpacker's Handbook* by Chris Townsend; *The Baffled Parents' Guide to Great Baseball Drills* by Jim Garland; *The Essential Outdoor Gear Manual: Equipment Care, Repair, and Selection* by Annie Getchell, et al.; *The Essential Wilderness Navigator: How to Find Your Way in the Great Outdoors* by David Seidman; *Great Basketball Drills: A Baffled Parent's Guide* by James Garland; *Scuba Diving: A Woman's Guide* by Claire Walter; *The-*

Last Log of the Titanic by David G. Brown (digital).

> Direct query letters and SASEs to:
>
> **Jon Eaton**, Editorial Director; Jonathan_Eaton@mcgraw-hill.com
>
> **Alex Barnett**, Acquisitions; alex_barnett@mcgraw-hill.com

MEADOWBROOK PRESS

5451 Smetana Drive, Minnetonka, MN 55343

952-930-1100/1-800-338-2232   fax: 952-930-1940

www.meadowbrookpress.com

Meadowbrook publishes books with a family outlook, encompassing the areas of pregnancy and child care, parenting, health, the environment, business, travel, cooking, reference, party-planning, and children's-activity books. Meadowbrook Press (established in 1975) is a small trade-oriented house that has particular success pinpointing such specialty markets as baby names, family humor, and the facts of life.

Sample titles: *Discipline without Shouting or Spanking* by Jerry Wyckoff, Ph.D and Barbara C. Unell; *Reflections for Expectant Mothers* by Ellen Sue Stern; *Reflections for Newlyweds* by Ellen Sue Stern; *When I Grow Up. . .*created by Bruce Lansky; *Playing for Pride* by Timothy Tocher; *The Best of Girls to the Rescue* selected by Bruce Lansky; *Reflections for New Mothers* by Ellen Sue Stern; *Funny Little Poems for Funny Little People* by Bruce Lansky; *Quality Time Anytime* by Penny Warner; *The Children's Busy Book* by Trish Kuffner; *Smart Start for Your Baby* by Penny Warner; *Long Shot* by Timothy Tocher; *The Mocktail Bar Guide* by Frank Thomas and Karen L. Brown; *The Aliens Have Landed!* by Kenn Nesbitt; *Free Stuff for Kids 2002* by the Free Stuff Editors; *Pregnancy, Childbirth, and the Newborn (Revision)* by Penny Simkin, Janet Whalley, and Ann Keppler; *Our Bundle of Joy* by Bruce Lansky. From the Meadowbrook backlist: *The Joy of Sisters* by Karen Brown; *Free Stuff for Kids* (in periodically updated editions) by the Free Stuff Editors; *Eating Expectantly* by Bridget Swinney; *The Toddler's Busy Book* by Trish Kuffner; *Storybook Parties* by Penny Warner; *The Best Bachelorette Party Book* by Becky Long; *Pregnancy, Childbirth and the Newborn* by Penny Simkin and Janet Whalley; *52 Romantic Evenings* by Liya Lee Oertel.

Meadowbrook Press is distributed by Simon & Schuster. Query letters and SASEs should be directed to:

Bruce Lansky, Publisher

MEGAN TINGLEY BOOKS

Three Center Plaza, Boston, MA 02108

Megan Tingley Books, an imprint of Little, Brown and Company (see separate listing in Publishing Conglomerates), publishes mainly picture books, with some fiction and nonfiction for middle-grade and young adult readers. This imprint does not consider "genre" novels for publication (including mystery, romance, and science fiction).

Titles from Megan Tingley include *Look Alikes* by Joan Steiner; *Just Like a Baby* by Rebecca Bond; *The Girls' Guide to Life* by Catherine Dee; *Define Normal* by Anne Peters; *This Land Is Your Land* by Woody Guthrie and Kathy Jakobsen; *You Read to Me, I'll Read to You* by Mary Ann Hoberman and Michael Emberley; *It's Okay to Be Different* by Todd Parr; *Twin Tales: The Magic and Mystery of Multiple* by Donna M. Jackson.

While the submission guidelines for Megan Tingley Books remain the same as Little Brown's, unpublished authors may submit one-page query letters for fiction and nonfiction. Please mark the envelope "Query" and address to:

Alvina Ling, Editorial Assistant, Megan Tingley Books, Little Brown & Company, Three Center Plaza, Boston, MA 02108; Include an SASE for response

Mary Gruetzke, Assistant Editor

MERCURY HOUSE, INC.

PO Box 192850, San Francisco, CA 94119-2850

415-626-7874   fax: 415-626-7875

www.mercuryhouse.org   e-mail: mercury@mercuryhouse.org

Mercury House produces a list strong in contemporary fiction, world literature in translation, literary classics, Asian literature and philosophy, cultural studies, film and performing arts, current affairs, nature and environment, and general nonfiction. The press issues hardcovers and trade paperbacks.

Mercury House (a nonprofit corporation founded in 1984) is a publisher guided by literary values; categories of house interest encompass quality fiction; biographies and autobiographies; history and narrative nonfiction; multiethnic and cross-cultural literary expression (including essays and true-life narratives, as well as fiction); arts and entertainment; literary travel. The Mercury House logo is a graphic representation of a winged manuscript scroll in flight.

Fiction titles include: *Manhattan Music* by Meena Alexander; *Profane Friendship* by Harold Brodkey; *The Diary of Emily Dickinson* by Jamie Fuller; *Dirty Bird Blues* by Clarence Major; *The Men's Club* by Leonard Michaels.

Literature & Essay: *House With the Blue Bed* by Alfred Arteaga; *Life Sentences: Writers, Artists, & AIDS* by Thomas Avena; *Who Owns the West?* by William Kittredge.

Translation: *The Harp and the Shadow* by Alejo Carpenter; *Multiple Child* by Andree Chedid (translated by Judith Radke); *Camille Claudel* by Anne Debee (translated by Carol Cosman); *The Slave Trail* by Alain Gerber.

Culture: *No Pictures in My Grave: A Spiritual Journey in Sicily* by Susan Caperna Lloyd; *Tantra: The Art of Conscious Loving* by Charles & Caroline Muir.

Nature: *Earth Keepers: What You Need To Know About the Environment* by Leslie Baer-Brown & Bob Rhein; *Temporary Homelands* by Alison Hawthorne Deming; *The Face of the Deep* by Thomas Farber.

Mercury House distributes through Consortium. Please check its website for information about submissions policies at www.mercuryhouse.org.

K. Janene-Nelson, Executive Director

Jeremy Bigalke, Project Editor

Justin Edgar, Project Editor

MICROSOFT PRESS

One Microsoft Way, Redmond, WA 98052-6399

206-882-8080/1-800-677-7377

http://mspress.microsoft.com

Microsoft Press specializes in solution-oriented computer books—especially those relating to the corpus of Microsoft products, the Microsoft operating system, and selected titles pertaining to the Apple Macintosh world. Microsoft Press lists titles in general personal-computer applications, programming, and general-interest computing areas. The house brochure features books, book-and-software packages (including diskettes and CD-ROMs), and training videos. Microsoft Press (founded in 1983) is a product unit within the Microsoft Corporation and a leading source of comprehensive self-paced learning, training, evaluation, and support resources designed to help everyone from developers and IT professionals to end users get the most from Microsoft technology. Users can choose from more than 250 current titles in print, multimedia, and network-ready formats—learning solutions made by Microsoft. More information is available at http://mspress.microsoft.com.

Microsoft Press titles are constantly updated and released in newly revised versions in order to anticipate advances in hardware and software systems, as well as the underlying technology to which they pertain. The house aims to produce information that is reliable, timely, and easy to use so that readers can get their work done faster and without frustration.

Series from Microsoft Press include: *Designing and Implementing .NET Web Services with Microsoft ASP.NET* by Andrea Saltarello, Mario Zucca, and Pierre Greborio; *Programming Microsoft Outlook and Microsoft Exchange 2003, Third Edition* by Thomas Rizzo.

The Mastering series is a line of CD-ROM-based interactive training titles created to help intermediate and advanced developers' master tasks and concepts for writing sophisticated solutions with Microsoft tools.

A representative general reference work is *Microsoft Press Computer Dictionary*.

Microsoft Press distributes its own books; the list is also available through electronic mail via CompuServe. Query letters and SASEs should be directed to:

Alex Blanton, Acquisitions Editor—Bookidea@microsoft.com

MILKWEED EDITIONS

1011 Washington Avenue South, Suite 300, Minneapolis, MN 55415

612-332-3192/1-800-520-6455   fax: 612-215-2550

www.milkweed.org and www.worldashome.org

Milkweed publishes fiction, essays, literature, poetry anthologies, and poetry, as well as literary nonfiction about the natural world in its The World as Home publishing program. Milkweeds for Young Readers is the house's children's line. Milkweed Editions (instituted in 1984) presents a personalized small-house approach that accents high standards of content and production.

Milkweed was founded (in 1979) as a nonprofit literary press, publishing with the intention of making a humane impact on society, in the belief that literature is a transformative art uniquely able to convey the essential experiences of the human heart and spirit. The house presents distinctive voices of literary merit in handsomely designed, visually dynamic books, exploring the ethical, cultural, and aesthetic issues that free societies must continually address.

Under Emilie Buchwald (Publisher/CEO), the house maintains its position to make a humane impact on society. Milkweed Editions offers an award-winning list of distinctive literary voices, with a line of handsomely designed, visually dynamic volumes that address ethical, cultural, and aesthetic issues.

Milkweed publishes diverse, nonhomogeneous literary books that take artistic and financial risks and that give readers access to the richness, aliveness, and possibilities afforded by the written word. Milkweed exists to publish, promote, and keep alive this important literature for readers today and in the future.

The company's continued marketing success augments the publisher's stance in support of exceptional books with appeal to discerning readers. Milkweed Editions hosts a substantial backlist of hardcovers, paperbacks, and chapbooks.

Poetry: *The Porcelain Apes of Moses Mendelssohn* by Jean Nordhaus; *Turning Over the Earth* by Ralph Black; *Song of the World Becoming: Poems New & Collected 1981—2001* by Pattiann Rogers.

Nonfiction about the natural world: *Stories from Where We Live: The Gulf Coast* edited by Sara St. Antoine; *Roofwalker* by Susan Power; *Ecology of a Cracker Childhood* by Janisse Ray; *Swimming with Giants* by Anne Collet; *Brown Dog of the Yaak* by Rick Bass; *Boundary Waters: The Grace of the Wild* by Paul Gruchow.

Milkweed fiction titles: *The Return of Gabriel* by John Armistead; *Thirst and Pu-239 and Other Russian Fantasies* by Ken Kalfus; *Falling Dark* by Tim Tharp; *My Lord Bag of Rice* by Carol Buy; *Hell's Bottom, Colorado* by Laura Pritchett.

Milkweed is the publisher of Susan Straight's acclaimed *Aquaboogie: A Novel in Stories* (among a number of novels-in-stories projects). Contact the editorial department for information pertaining to the Milkweed Prize for Children's Literature and the Milkweed National Fiction Prize.

Books from Milkweed Editions are available via direct order from the publisher; the house's titles are distributed to the trade through Publishers Group West.

MILKWEEDS FOR YOUNG READERS

Milkweeds for Young Readers produces children's books of literary merit that embody humane values. Books that ask the most of young readers, the publisher maintains, have the staying power to influence them for a lifetime. Milkweed also produces a series of teaching guides.

Titles from Milkweed's children's program: *The Boy with Paper Wings* by Susan Lowell; *Emma and the Ruby Ring* by Yvonne MacGrory; *No Place* by Kay Haugaard; *Parents Wanted* by George Harrar; *The $66 Summer* by John Armistead; *The Ocean Within* by V. M. Caldwell; *The Secret of the Ruby Ring* by Yvonne MacGrory.

Query letters and SASEs should be directed to:

Elisabeth Fitz, First Reader

Emilie Buchwald, Publisher

Greg Larson, Fiction Editor

THE MOUNTAINEERS BOOKS

1001 Southwest Klickitat Way, Suite 201, Seattle, WA 98134

206-223-6303/1-800-553-4453   fax: 206-223-6306

www.mountaineerbooks.org   e-mail: mbooks@mountaineers.org

The Mountaineers produces adventure narratives, mountaineering histories and guides, hiking, rock-climbing books, and instructional guides to the outdoors and winter trekking, focused on the Pacific Northwest.

The Mountaineers (founded in 1906) is a conservation and outdoor-activity group with a mission to explore, study, preserve, and enjoy the natural beauty of the outdoors.

The Mountaineers Books was founded in 1961 as a nonprofit publishing program of the club. The Mountaineers sponsors the Barbara Savage/Miles from Nowhere Memorial Award competition for outstanding unpublished nonfiction adventure-narrative manuscripts. The initial title offered by Mountaineers Books, *Mountaineering: The Freedom of the Hills,* is still in print in a fully revised edition.

Series from Mountaineers: *The Beckoning Silence* by Joe Simpson; *Climbing: Expedition* by Phil Powers and Clyde Soles; *Don't Get Bitten* by Buck Tilton, MS; *Don't Get Eaten* by Dave Smith; *The Settler Way* by John D. G. Gorby (foreword by Jim Detterline); *Morpha: A Rain Forest Story* by Michael Tennyson (Illustrated by Jennifer H. Yoswa); *Nature In the City: Seattle* by Kathryn True and Maria Dolan; *Bugaboo Rock: A Climbing Guide* by Randall Green and Joe Bensen; *Richard Bangs: Adventure Without End* by Richard Bangs; *Tom Crean* by Michael Smith; *The Boardman Tasker Omnibus* by Boardman and Tasker; *The Hard Years Joe Brown; The Game of Ghosts* by Joe Simpson; *Arctic National Wildlife Refuge: Seasons of Life and Land* by Subhankar Banerjee (foreword by Jimmy Carter); *Extreme Rock and Ice: 25 of the World's Great Climbs* by Garth Hattingh; *Everest: Eighty Years of Triumph and Tragedy (2nd edition)* by Peter and Leni Gillman; *River Running (2nd edition)* by Verne Huser; *Hiking the Triple Crown* by Karen Berger; *Fearless on Everest: The Quest for Sandy Irvine* by Julie Summers; *Conquistadors of the Useless: From the Alps to Annapurna* by Lionel Terray.

Guidebooks include: *Best Hikes in California's North Sierra; 100 Hikes in Yosemite National Park; Best Short Hikes Sierra; Glacier National Park and Waterton Lakes National Park; Best Short Hikes In Northwest Oregon; Best Short Hikes in Washington's South Cascades and Olympics; Best Loop Hikes Washington.*

Winners of the Barbara Savage "Miles from Nowhere" competition (biennial award for a previously unpublished adventure narrative manuscript): *Himalayan Passage: Seven Months in the High Country of Tibet, Nepal, China, India, and Pakistan* by Jeremy Schmidt (photographs by Patrick Morrow); *American Discoveries: Scouting the First Coast-to-Coast Recreational Trail* by Dudley and Seaborg. Winners of Barbara Savage award include *Where the Pavement Ends* by Erika Warmbrunn; *Spirited Waters: Soloing South Through the Inside Passage* by Jennifer Hahn.

The Mountaineers Books distributes its list via direct orders and also utilizes the services of regional and national wholesalers and trade representatives. The American Alpine Club Press is now distributed by the Mountaineers Books.

Query letters and SASEs should be directed to:

Laura Drury, Acquisitions Assistant

David Emblidge, Editor in Chief

Cassandra Conyers, Acquisitions Editor

Christine Hosler, Assistant Acquisitions Editor

MOYER BELL LIMITED

54 Phillips Street, Wickford, RI 02852

401-294-0106   fax: 401-294-1076

www.moyerbell.com   e-mail: info@moyerbell.com

Moyer Bell Limited specializes in literary works, reference works, and books in art and design. Many general-interest nonfiction works from this smaller house evidence a high-interest cultural or public-issues slant. Within this specialty arena, Moyer Bell produces original titles, reprints, and translations. The house also maintains a strong commitment to poetry. The Asphodel Press imprint was founded as a nonprofit organization in 1990 and concentrates on fine literary titles.

Moyer Bell Limited was established in 1984 by Jennifer Moyer and Britt Bell; this notably independent house (with a U.K. base in London, in addition to its U.S. operations) has received worldwide accolades for its roster of fine writers and stylish product.

Moyer Bell nonfiction: *Writing in Time: A Political Chronicle* by Jonathan Schell; *The Art Book of Lucien Pissarro* by Lora Urbanelli; *Don't Look Back: A Memoir* by Patrick O'Connor; *Walking to LaMilpa: Living in Guatemala with Armies, Demons, Abrazos, and Death* by Marcos McPeek Villatoro; *The New Genetics: Challenges for Science, Faith, and Politics* by Roger L. Shinn; *In the Wake of Death: Surviving the Loss of a Child* by Mark Cosman; *Rebirth of Thought: Light from the East* by Ruth Nanda Anshen; *A Trifle, a Coddle, a Fry: An Irish Literary Cookbook* by Veronica Jane O'Mara and Fionnuala O'Reilly.

Fiction and literary titles: *The Only Piece of Furniture in the House* by Diane Glancy; *The Orchard on Fire* by Shena Mackay; *The Raven: With the Philosophy of Composition* by Edgar Allan Poe (poetry and essay; illustrated by Alan James Robinson); *Peace Breaks Out, Private Enterprise, and The Demon in the House* by Angela Thirkell (granddaughter of Edward Burne-Jones and a cousin of Rudyard Kipling); *Peony* by Pearl S. Buck.

On Moyer Bell's reference book list are the periodically revised *Grant Seekers Guide* by James McGrath Morris and Laura Adler. From Asphodel Press: *Directory of Literary Magazines* (updated annually) by the Council of Literary Magazines and Presses.

Moyer Bell Limited books are distributed to the trade by Publishers Group West.

Britt Bell, Editor and Publisher

MUSEUM OF NEW MEXICO PRESS

Deliveries and physical address:

228 East Palace Avenue, Santa Fe, NM 87501

505-827-6454   fax: 505-827-5741

www.museumofnewmexico.org

Mailing address:

PO Box 2087, Santa Fe, NM 87504-2087

e-mail: mwachs@oca.state.nm.us, agallegos@oca.state.nm.us

Museum of New Mexico Press is a nationally distributed publisher affiliated with the Museum of New Mexico. Museum of New Mexico Press publishes high-quality illustrated books on the arts and culture of the Southwest, such as Native America, the Hispanic Southwest, 20th-century fine art, folk art from around the world, Latin American arts, nature and gardening, architecture and style, folklore.

Sample titles: *Masks of Mexico* by Barbara Mauldin; *Indian Basketmakers of the Southwest* by Larry Dalrymple; *Benigna's Chimayo* by Don Usner; *Navajo Spoons* by Cindra Kline; *Maiolica Ole* by Florence C. Lister and Robert H. Lister.

Query letters and SASEs should be directed to:

Mary Wachs, Editorial Director

Anna Gallegos, Director

MUSTANG PUBLISHING COMPANY

PO Box 770426, Memphis, TN 38177

901-684-1200   fax: 901-684-8713

e-mail: MustangPub@aol.com

Mustang produces trade nonfiction books in hardcover and paperback. Mustang is especially successful with its lines of specialty how-tos and titles in the fields of humor, games, outdoor recreation, sports, travel, and careers. Mustang Publishing Company (founded in 1983) is a modest-sized house with a concise publishing vision and compactly tailored list.

Representative titles: *101 Classic Jewish Jokes: Jewish Humor from Groucho Marx to Jerry Seinfeld* by Robert Menchin (illustrated by Joel Kohl); *Dear Elvis: Graffiti from Graceland* by Daniel Wright; *Lucky Pants and Other Golf Myths* by Joe Kohl; *The Complete Book of Golf Games* by Scott Johnston; *How to Be a Way Cool Grandfather* by Verne Steen.

Mustang's specialty books include those geared to expansive lifestyles. Titles here: *Wonders to Behold: The Visionary Art of Mytrice West* edited by Carol Crown; *101 Classic Jewish Jokes* by Robert Menchin (illustrated by Joe Kohl); *Lucky Pants* by Joe Kohl (introduction by Dave Barry); *The Complete Book of Beer Drinking Games* by Andy Griscom, Ben Rand, and Scott Johnston; *The Hangover Handbook* by Nic van Oudtshoorn; *Hawaii for Free* by France Carter; *DC for Free* by Brian Butler; *The Southwest for Free* by Greg and Mary Jane Edwards; *Working in T.V. News* by Carl Filoreto with Lynn Setzer; *Let's Blow Thru Europe* by Thomas Neenan and Greg Hancock; *Northern Italy: A Taste of Trattoria* by Christina Baglivi.

The "For Free" series is a godsend for people scared by the high cost of travel and for everyone who loves a bargain. Each book describes hundreds of terrific things to do and see, and nothing costs one single penny, lire, franc, or pfennig. Titles: *Europe for Free*, *London for Free*, and *DC for Free* by Brian Butler; *The Southwest for Free* by Mary Jane and Greg Edwards; *Hawaii for Free* by Frances Carter; *Paris for Free (or Extremely Cheap)* by Mark Beffart.

The touring and travel list also includes: *Festival Europe! Fairs and Celebrations Throughout Europe* by Margaret M. Johnson; *The Nepal Trekker's Handbook* by Amy R. Kaplan, with Michael Keller; *Europe on 10 Salads a Day* by Mary Jane and Greg Edwards; plus, the hilariously revised and expanded edition of *Let's Blow Thru Europe: How to Have a Blast on Your Whirlwind Trip Through Europe* by Thomas Neenan and Greg Hancock.

A solid group of Mustang books targets a higher education-bound audience, including series for students and graduate-school applicants, often geared toward particular professional curricula: *The One Hour College Applicant* by Lois Rochester and Judy Mandell; *Medical School Admissions: The Insider's Guide* by John A. Zebala and Daniel B. Jones.

The Essays That Worked series inspires thousands of students to write the best essays they can. There's also lots of practical advice on the application process. Titles: *Essays That Worked for College Applicants* and *Essays That Worked for Business Schools* (edited by Boykin Curry and Brian Kasbar); *Essays That Worked for Law Schools* (edited by Boykin Curry).

Representative career title: *Working in T.V. News: The Insider's Guide* by Carl Filoreto, with Lynn Setzer; *Medical School Admissions: The Insider's Guide (4th edition)* by John Zebala, Daniel Jones, and Stephanie Jones.

Mustang also offers Alan and Theresa von Altendorf's general reference *ISMs: A Compendium of Concepts and Beliefs from Abolitionism to Zygodactylism*.

Writers should note that Mustang welcomes book proposals on almost any nonfiction topic. The publisher prefers to see an outline and two to three sample chapters and urges authors to be sure to enclose a self-addressed stamped envelope (the ubiquitous SASE) with each submission. No phone calls, please.

Mustang's books are distributed through National Book Network. Query letters and SASEs should be directed to:

Rollin A. Riggs, President and Publisher

THE NAIAD PRESS

PO Box 10543, Tallahassee, FL 32302

850-539-5965   fax: 850-539-9731

www.naiadpress.com

Naiad publishes lesbian and feminist fiction, essays, poetry, short stories, humor, translations, and bibliographies. The Naiad emphasis in category fiction includes stylish and traditional mysteries, espionage thrillers, adventure yarns, science fiction, fantasy, romances, historical fiction, erotica, and Westerns. Naiad Press (established in 1973) remains joyously the oldest and largest lesbian publishing company in the world, going from one title to being the publisher of more than 400 books.

Naiad has been particularly innovative among book-publishing operations in the development of specialized target-marketing techniques. The house has expanded its media presence to become active in the wider arena of audio books, videos, and theatrical film. The romantic fiction *Claire of the Moon*, by Nicole Conn (writer and director of the feature film of the same name), represents a groundbreaking Naiad project that embraces documentary, music, and storytelling in cinema, video, audiocassette, CD, and print. Naiad Books maintains a comprehensive backlist.

Nonfiction from Naiad: *Dancing In the Dark* edited by Barbara Grier; *Erotic Naiad* edited by Barbara Grier; *Lady Be Good* edited by Barbara Grier; *Lesbiana* by Barbara Grier; *Out for Blood* edited by Brownsworth & Redding; *Out for More Blood* edited by Brownsworth & Redding; *Romantic Naiad* by Barbara Grier; *Sex Variant Women in Literature* by Jeanette Foster; *Sapphistory* by Pat Califia; *For Love and for Life and Intimate Portraits of Lesbian Couples* by Susan Johnson; *There's Something I've Been Meaning to Tell You* by Loralee MacPike.

Sample Naiad fiction and belles lettres: *Daughters of a Coral Dawn* by Katherine V. Forrest; *Kate Delafield Trilogy* and *Curious Wine* by Katherine V. Forrest; *Both Sides* by Saxon Bennett; *Claire of the Moon* by Nicole Conn; *Greener than Grass* by Jennifer Fulton; *City Lights Country Candles* by Penny Hayes; *Car Pool* by Karin Kallmaker; *Cherished Love* by Evelyn Kennedy; *Dawn of the Dance* by Marianne Martin; *Window Garden* by Janet McClellan; *Yes I Said Yes I Will* by Judith McDaniel; *The Finer Grain* by Denise Ohio; *The Other Woman* by Ann O'Leary; *Endless Love* by Lisa Shapiro; *The Drive* by Trisha Todd; *Piece of My Heart* by Julia Watts.

The women of Naiad Press continue in pursuit of their essential goal—to make sure that someday, any woman, anyplace, can recognize her lesbianism and be able to walk into a bookstore and pick up a book that says to her: "Yes, you are a lesbian and you are wonderful." With that aim in mind, Naiad has adopted the following slogan for use in its potent mailing-list campaigns: Lesbians always know; if it's a book by Naiad Press, it's a book you want to own.

Naiad Press books are available directly from the publisher via a toll-free telephone-order number and from the following distributors as well: Bookpeople, LPC Group, Borders, and Ingram.

Query letters and SASEs should be directed to:

Barbara Grier, Chief Executive Officer

NATIONAL GEOGRAPHIC SOCIETY BOOKS

1145 17th Street Northwest, Washington, DC 20036

202-857-7000   fax: 202-429-5727

National Geographic Society Books' motto is "to diffuse geographic knowledge." Books are distributed by Simon & Schuster. National Geographic Society Books is interested in any type of book written from a geographic perspective.

Sample titles include: *Last Climb: The Legendary Everest Expeditions of George Mallory* by David Breashears and Audrey Salkeld; *Return to Midway* by Robert D. Ballard; *Cuba* by David Alan Harvey; *Shackleton: The Antarctic Challenge; Eyewitness to the 20th Century.*

Query letters and SASEs should be directed to:

Kevin Mulroy, Vice President and Director of Book Division

NAVAL INSTITUTE PRESS

291 Wood Road, Annapolis, MD 21402-5035

410-268-6110   fax: 410-269-7940

www.usni.org

Naval Institute Press features trade books, in addition to the house's targeted professional and reference titles. Areas of NIP interest include how-to books on boating, navigation, battle histories, and biographies, as well as occasional selected titles in fiction (typically with a nautical adventure orientation). Specific categories encompass such fields as seamanship, naval history and literature, the Age of Sail, aviation, aircraft, World War II naval history, ships and aircraft, current naval affairs, naval science, and general naval resources and guidebooks. Bluejacket Books is a trade-paperback imprint that includes time-honored classics as well as original titles. Naval Institute Press also publishes a line of historical and contemporary photographs and poster art.

Naval Institute Press, situated on the grounds of the United States Naval Academy, is the book-publishing imprint of the United States Naval Institute, a private, independent, nonprofit professional society for members of the military services and civilians who share an interest in naval and maritime affairs. USNI was established in 1873 at the Naval Academy in Annapolis; the press inaugurated its publishing program in 1898 with a series of basic guides to United States naval practice.

Titles from Naval Institute Press: *Admirals in the Age of Nelson* by Lee Bienkowski; *Age of Sail Annual* by Nicholas Tracy; *American Naval History, 3rd Edition* by Jack Sweetman; *Battleship Bismarck* by Burkard Baron von Mullenheim-Rechberg; *The Battleship Warspite* by Ross Watton; *Cochrane* by Donald Thomas; *Commodore Ellsworth P. Bertholf* by C. Douglas Kroll; *Cruise of the Lanikai* by Kemp Tolley; *El Dorado Canyon* by Joseph T. Stanik; *From Annapolis to Scapa Flow* by Edward L. Beach Sr. and Edward L. Beach Jr.; *German Aircraft of the Second World War* by J.R. Smith and Anthony Kay; *In the Hands of Fate* by Dwight R. Messimer; *Latitude* by Bill Carter and Merri Sue Carter; *Luftwaffe Seaplanes, 1939–1945* by Chris Goss and Bernd Rauchbach; *Green Berets in the Vanguard: Inside Special Forces 1953–1963* by Chalmers Archer, Jr.; *Punk's War* (novel) by Ward Carroll; *Death on the Hellships: Prisoners at Sea in the Pacific War* by Gregory F. Michno.

Fighter Squadron at Guadalcanal by Max Brand is a lost classic, published 50 years after the author's death. Now after more than 50 years and a string of fortunate coincidences, Brand's stirring firsthand account of the 212th Marine Fighter Squadron's operations at Guadalcanal in 1942 has been published.

The Naval Institute Guide to the Ships and Aircraft of the U.S. Fleet (17th edition) by Norman Polmar is indispensable to anyone needing technical data and program information on the contemporary U.S. Navy.

Bluejacket Books is an exciting series of fiction and nonfiction titles available in affordable paperback editions. Titles: *A Country Such as This* by James Webb; *A Sense of Honor* by James Webb; *Around the World Submerged: The Voyage of the Triton* by Edward L. Beach; *Midway: The Battle that Doomed Japan, the Japanese Navy's Story* by Mitsuo Fuchida and Masatake Okumiya; *Reminiscences* by Douglas MacArthur; *Teddy Roosevelt's Great White Fleet* by James R. Reckner.

Naval Institute Press handles its own distribution. Query letters and SASEs should be directed to:

Eric Mills, Acquisitions Editor

Sara Sprinkle, Editorial Assistant for Acquisitions

Thomas J. Cutler, Senior Acquisitions Editor

Paul Wilderson, Executive Editor

NEW HORIZON PRESS

SMALL HORIZONS

34 Church Street, Liberty Corner, NJ 07938

908-604-6311   fax: 908-604-6330

www.newhorizonpressbooks.com   e-mail: nhp@newhorizonpressbooks.com

Mailing address:

PO Box 669, Far Hills, NJ 07931

New Horizon Press: Real people…incredible stories. That's right—the New Horizon list accents true-life events with narrative nonfiction accounts told by actual participants. In its broader program, the house addresses topics of social concern, including corporate and professional responsibility, behavioral diversity, and politics, as well as personal self-help, how-to, and mainstream business books.

New Horizon Press (established in 1983) was originally an imprint of Horizon Press; now a separate publishing entity, New Horizon Press is remarkable for its pinpoint commercial vision in the arena of nonfiction stories of courageous individuals. These incredible tales of real people display an intense human-interest appeal and often embody an investigative journalistic stance that probes related public issues. The house maintains a solid backlist that is particularly strong in self-help titles.

New Horizon is configured as a small press: Projects are often initiated with restrained author advances; more money accrues to the writer through subsequent sales. The publisher has had conspicuous success in expanding the scope of its projects via targeted promotion, advertising, touring, and subsidiary rights, both in print via book-club selections and in the electronic arena in the form of related television docudramas, talk show appearances by authors, and feature items on television journals.

From the New Horizon list: *Changing Course* by Jeanne Marie Lutz; *13 Days of Terror* by Greg Williams; *Cool It!* by Dr. Michael Hershon; *Grave Undertakings* by Alexandria K. Mosca; *The SeXX Factor* by Marilou Ryder, Ed. and Judith Briles, PhD; *Race Against Evil* by David Race Bannon; *There's a Skunk in My Bunk* by Joseph T. McCann (art by Thomas Gerlach); *Women of Divorce* by Susan Shapiro Barash; *Cheaters* by Raymond B. Green with psychological input by Marcella Bakur Weiner, Ed. D.; *Setting Yourself Free* by SaraKay Smullens; *Shattered Bonds* by Cindy Band and Julie Malear; *The Mouse Family's Most Terrible, Terrifying Day* by Dr. Joan S. Dunphy; *Grave Accusations*; *CastOff*; *Whispers of Romance, Threats of Death*; *ER—Enter At Your Own Risk: How to Avoid Dangers Inside the Emergency Room*; *Swallowing a Bitter Pill: How Prescription and Over-the-Counter Drug Abuse Is Ruining Lives—My Story*.

New Horizon Press is distributed by National Book Network, Inc. Query letters and SASEs should be directed to:

INDEPENDENT U.S. PRESSES

Joan S. Dunphy, Editor in Chief

Sign: Leo/Virgo.

Education: PhD, from Miami University; English, Psychology, and Philosophy.

Employment history/editor career path: Assistant Professor at Rutgers University.

Personal interests: Reading, rock specimens.

What would you be doing if you were not an editor? Teaching English at a college level and writing.

What has been your most successful book that you have acquired to date? Black Widow/False Arrest.

What books have you acquired that make you the most proud? What books that you have acquired reflect the types of books you like to represent? In Africa with Schweitzer; My Life on the Streets.

Do you represent fiction? No.

What do you want to see less of? Nonfiction generalized manuscripts on the educational system, life, and so forth, and so on.

Do you represent nonfiction? Yes.

Do you require book proposals? If so, what do you look for in evaluating a book proposal? A subject matter that matters.

Are certain aspects of a book proposal given more weight than others? The plot and whether the author is the prime mover of the action.

What process do you use for making a decision? What is the process for acquisition, is there a committee? No committee, but we meet to discuss the merits, or lack of, on manuscripts we feel deserve attention.

Are you interested in work geared for the masses (readers of *People*, *The Star*, etc.)? Yes. I believe as Virgil said: Oftentimes the common people see 'rightly.'

Are agents important? Why? At times, very. Often an agent can recognize and send us the real essence of a true story, whereas the author who has lived it may not recognize its significance.

Do you like new writers? What should new writers do to break into the business? Since we are geared toward finding modern heroes who've made a difference, changing the status quo and present problems, we like new writers and subjects.

How should writers approach you? In writing, send: query, chapter synopsis, and at least two chapters. Please don't call.

What are some common mistakes writers make? What really gets on your nerves? Trying to get the editor's attention by diffuse methods (i.e., My story is the most dramatic, heartrending tale ever written, and then not saying what it is).

What can writers do to get your attention and to avoid the slush pile? Tell the story. In a synopsis tell us why it's important and make sure it is.

What have been some of your craziest experiences with submissions? The niece of Mary Phagan, a young girl murdered in the South, whose death brought back the KKK, sent a one-pager with red ink stains in the shape of tears. However, her story became the basis for a strong book and Emmy Award-winning mini-series.

What have been some of your best experiences with writers or in your job? Meeting brave and significant people who have fought for what they believe in.

What, if anything, makes you different from other editors? I look for true stories with social issues, and we are willing, if we find them, to do heavy rewriting in house.

Is there anything you would like to see changed in the industry? First and foremost: more diversity. I would like to see more interdisciplinary accords between film, Internet, and print so that the publishing industry does not vanish.

Any advice for writers? Any way to improve the system for you? For writers: Do not embellish, simplify. For the critics: Remember, the books that have transcended their times were often ridiculed or overlooked in them. And for our industry: "Change is here; it's not going away, it's gonna keep on happening; so, let's find a way to adapt to it."

SMALL HORIZONS

Small Horizons is an imprint offering self-help books for children, written by teachers and mental-health professionals.

Small Horizons Self-Help Books for Children titles include: *The Words Hurt* by Chris Loftis (art by Catherine Gallagher); *Up and Down the Mountain* by Pamela Leib Higgins (art by Gail Zawacki); *The Special Raccoon* by Kim Carlisle; *The Stick Family: Helping Children Cope with Divorce* by Natalie Reilly; *I Am So Angry, I Could Scream: Helping Children Deal with Anger* by Laura Fox; *The Boy Who Sat by the Window: Helping Children Cope with Violence* by Chris Loftis; *There's a Skunk in My Bunk: Teaching Children Tolerance for Others* by Dr. Joseph McCann.

NEWMARKET PRESS

18 East 48th Street, New York, NY 10017

212-832-3575   fax: 212-832-3629

www.newmarketpress.com   e-mail: mailbox@newmarketpress.com

Newmarket concentrates on general nonfiction, accenting such categories as contemporary issues, history, biography, psychology, parenting, health, nutrition, cooking, personal finance, and business. A major Newmarket program salutes classic literary figures, other media, and performing arts, featuring titles in film (including shooting scripts) and music. Newmarket also issues occasional works of high-interest fiction (the house was the original publisher of the hardcover edition of Michael Blake's novel *Dances with Wolves*).

Newmarket Press (founded in 1981) is a division of Newmarket Publishing and Communications Company. The house produces books in hardcover, trade paper, and mass-market paperback editions.

General trade titles: *Condi* by Antonia Felix; *Gods and Generals: The Shooting Script* by Ronald F. Maxwell; *Success at Life* by Ron Rubin and Stuart Avery Gold; *Dragon Spirit* by Ron Rubin and Stuart Avery Gold; *Laughing Allegra* by Anne Ford; *The Healing Touch For Cats* by Dr. Michael W. Fox; *The Healing Touch For Dogs* by Dr. Michael W. Fox; *The Words of Peace* edited by Irwin Abrams; *The Smart Chicken & Fish Cookbook* by Jane Kinderlehrer; *The West Wing Script Book* by Aaron Sorkin; *Fly Away Home* by Patricia Hermes, Robert Rodat, and Vincent McKewin; *Kids and Sports* by Eric Small, MD, FAAP; *Submerged* by Daniel Lenihan; *Tea Chings* by Ron Rubin, Stuart Avery Gold, and the Republic of Tea; *The Antioxidant Save-Your-Life Cookbook* by Jane Kinderleher and Daniel A. Kinderleher, MD; *The Totally Awesome Business Book for Kids* by Adriane G. Berg and Arthur Berg Bochner; *Whose Body Is It Anyway?* by Joan Kenley, PhD (edited by John C. Arpels); *The Matrix* by Larry Wachowski and Andy Wachowski; *How Do We Tell the Children?* by Dan Schaefer and Christine Lyons.

Film-related books: *Adaptation: The Shooting Script* by Charlie Kaufman and Donald Kaufman; *Chicago-From Stage to Screen, The Illustrated Story and Lyrics* introduction by Bill Condon, Rob Marshall, and Martin Richards; *Gods and Monsters: The Shooting Script* by Bill Condon; *Dreamcatcher: The Shooting Script* by Lawrence Kasdan and William Goldman; *X-Men 2* (introduction by Bryan Singer).

Newmarket distributes its list through W. W. Norton & Company. No children's titles. Query letters and SASEs should be directed to:

Keith Hollaman, Executive Editor

Esther Margolis, President and Publisher

Shannon Berning, Assistant Editor

NOLO.COM

950 Parker Street, Berkeley, CA 94710

510-549-1976/1-800-728-3555

www.nolo.com

Nolo.com, formerly Nolo Press, presents a glittering array of self-help titles in law and business. The house promotes a related list in lifestyle, recreation, travel, and retirement. Nolo also produces law-form kits, legal software, electronic books, and videotapes.

Nolo's consumerist perspective encompasses homeowners, landlords, and tenants; going to court; money matters; estate planning and probate; business; legal reform; patents, copyrights, and trademarks; employee rights and the workplace; family matters; immigration; research and reference; older Americans; and humor titles.

Nolo.com is the pioneer publisher of self-help legal books and software. The house (started in 1971) was founded by two Legal Aid lawyers who were fed up with the public's lack of access to affordable legal information and advice. Convinced that with good, reliable information, Americans could handle routine legal problems without hiring an attorney, they began writing plain-English law books for the general readership.

Nolo led off its first list with *How to Do Your Own Divorce in California* and has been going strong since, with a steady stream of titles addressing consumer needs in a wide range of general and specialist areas. Whereas lawyers have historically sold information only to the few who can afford their services, Nolo aims to provide comprehensive low-cost information to the public at large.

The Nolo website (www.nolo.com) is an award-winning destination for consumers, businesspersons, and not a few lawyers. *The Nolo Encyclopedia*, available free on the site, gives plain English answers to commonly asked questions. All of Nolo's books and software can be downloaded from the site or ordered in hard copy. Nolo also offers "e-Guides," "e-Form Kits," and "Web Forms," which are electronic products that allow users to buy legal information and tools "by the drink."

All Nolo publications are regularly revised and are issued in updated editions, and the publisher maintains a hardy backlist. Most Nolo titles are written by practicing attorneys who are specialists in their fields of authorship. A major portion of the Nolo list exhibits a national orientation, while some titles are specifically geared to regional markets.

Representative titles: *Make Your Own Living Trust* by Attorney Denis Clifford; *Patent It Yourself* by Attorney David Pressman; *The Lawsuit Survival Guide: A Client's Companion to Litigation* by Attorney Joseph L. Matthews; *Form Your Own Limited Liability Company* by attorney Anthony Mancuso; *Plan Your Estate* by Dennis Clifford and Cora Jordan; *License Your Invention: Take Your Great Idea to Market with a Solid Legal Agreement* by Attorney Richard Stim; *Every Landlord's Legal Guide* by Marcia Stewart and attorneys Ralph Warner and Janet Portman; *WillMaker: 50-state Estate-Planning Software*; *Patent It Yourself (revised edition)* by Attorney David Pressman.

Social, community, career, lifestyle, and issue-oriented titles: *Get a Life: You Don't Need a Million to Retire Well* by Ralph Warner; *The Copyright Handbook: How to Protect and Use Written Works* by Stephen Fishman; *How to Buy a House in California* by Attorney Ralph Warner, Ira Serkes, and George Devine; *Stand Up to the IRS* by Frederick W. Daily; *Dog Law* by Mary Randolph; *Neighbor Law: Fences, Trees, Boundaries & Noise* by Cora Jordan; *A Legal Guide for Lesbian and Gay Couples* by Hayden Curry, Denis Clifford, and Robin Leonard; *The Independent Paralegal's Handbook* (revised edition) by Attorney Ralph Warner; *How to Mediate Your Dispute: Find a Solution You Can Live with Quickly and Cheaply Outside the Courtroom* by Peter Lovenheim.

Some humor: *29 Reasons Not to Go to Law School* by Ralph Warner, Toni Ihara, and Barbara Kate Repa; *Poetic Justice: The Funniest, Meanest Things Ever Said About Lawyers* (edited by Jonathan and Andrew Roth); *The Devil's Advocates: The Unnatural History of Lawyers* by Andrew and Jonathan Roth.

Nolo.com distributes its own books to the trade (along with selected titles from other publishers) and also utilizes several distribution services; in addition, Nolo sells to consumers via direct mail and from its Web site and operates its own bookstore in Berkeley. Query letters and SASEs should be directed to:

Marsha Stewart, Editor

W. W. NORTON AND COMPANY, INC.

COUNTRYMAN PRESS/BACKCOUNTRY PUBLICATIONS

500 Fifth Avenue, New York, NY 10110

212-354-5500   fax: 212-869-0856

www.wwnorton.com and www.countrymanpress.com

Norton publishes trade nonfiction and belles lettres, as well as works for professional and academic markets. W. W. Norton (founded in 1923) offers prime-caliber publications in all areas of its trade program; the house is equally esteemed for its line of college texts and professional reference titles.

W. W. Norton produces hardcover and trade paperback editions under its celebrated gliding-seagull colophon, as well as through a variety of imprints, including Liveright and Countryman. Norton nourishes a comprehensive backlist of books in all areas of its publishing interest.

Norton nonfiction accents trade titles in topics of current interest, with a range of works featuring the popular as well as scholarly approach to fields, including cultural criticism, biography, psychology, history, economics, politics, natural history, the sciences, fine arts and design, photography, and lifestyle. Norton also offers a line of books for enthusiasts of sailing and publishes Blue Guide travel books.

Nonfiction from Norton: *A Murder in Virginia: Southern Justice on Trial* by Suzanne Lebsock; *The Fur Person: Gift Edition* by May Sarton; *The Pushcart Prize XXVII: Best of the Small Presses, 2003 Edition* edited by Bill Henderson; *American Architecture: An Illustrated Encyclopedia* by Cyril M. Harris; *Art Held Hostage: The Story of the Barnes Collection* by John Anderson; *I Will Be Cleopatra: An Actress's Journey* by Zoe Caldwell; *Wall Street* by Robert Gambee; *Nelson Mandela's Favorite African Folktales* by Nelson Mandela; *Encyclopedia of Urban Legends* by Jan Harold Brunvand; *Harvard and the Unabomber: The Education of an American Terrorist* by Alston Chase; *The Natural History of the Rich: A Field Guide* by Richard Conniff; *A Secret History of the IRA* by Ed Maloney; *Four Seasons in Five Senses: Things Worth Savoring* by David Mas Masumoto; *America's Black Architects and Builders* by Stephen A. Kliment; *The Country Houses of David Adler* by Steven M. Salny; *New York for New Yorkers, 2nd edition* by Liza M. Greene; *Between Lives: An Artist and Her World* by Dorothea Tanning; *Basil Street Blues: A Memoir* by Michael Holroyd; *The Life of Jung* by Ronald Hayman; *Next: The Invisible Revolution* by Michael Lewis; *Latinos: A Biography of the People* by Earl Shorris; *The Bush Dyslexicon* by Mark Crispin Miller.

In fiction and literary writing, Norton publishes novels, poetry (including the Norton Anthologies series), and short story collections—from established, distinguished scribes and from a select few marketable new voices. In addition, the house publishes critical essays, biographies, and literary histories. The Norton fiction list covers classical, modern, contemporary, and experimental styles, as well as novels showing a mainstream commercial profile; the Norton program also encompasses mystery and suspense fiction.

Examples from the Norton fiction list: *I, the Divine* by Rabih Alameddine; *The Collected Stories of Isaac Babel* by Isaac Babel; *Servants of the Map: Stories* by Andrea Barrett; *The Curious Case of Benjamin Button, Apt. 3W: Fiction* by Gabriel Brownstein; *Strange Fire: A Novel* by Melvin Jules Bukiet; *A Memory of War: A Novel* by Frederick Busch; *Lucy: A Novel* by Ellen Feldman; *The Patience of Rivers: A Novel* by Joseph Freda; *Waiting for an Angel: A Novel* by Dara Horn; *The Collected Stories of Joseph Roth* by Joseph Roth; *The Fur Person: Gift Edition* by May Sarton; *Babe in Paradise: Fiction* by Marisa Silver; *Porno* by Irvine Welsh.

Norton poetry includes: *Call Me Ishmael Tonight: A Book of Ghazals* by Agha Shahid Ali; *A Coast of Trees* by A. R. Ammons; *Local Visitations: Poems* by Stephen Dunn; *Landscape with Chainsaw: Poems* by James Lasdun; *Blackbird Singing: Lyrics and Poems, 1963–1999* by Paul McCartney; *Collected Poems 1951–1971* by A. A. Ammons; *Landscape with Chainsaw: Poems* by James Lasdum; *Last Blue: Poems* by Gerald Stern; *The Making of a Poem: A Norton Anthology of Poetic Forms* (edited by Mark Strand and Eavan Boland); *A Mayan Astronomer in Hell's Kitchen: Poems* by Martin Espada; *Worldly Hopes: Poems* by A. R. Ammons.

Works of speculative literary configuration: *The Coral Sea* (poetry, fiction, and essay) by Patti Smith; *In Short: A Collection of Brief Creative Nonfiction* (edited by Judith Kitchen and Mary Paumier Jones); *Sudden Fiction (Continued): 60 New Short-Short Stories* (edited by Robert Shepard and James Thomas); *When the Air Hits Your Brain: Tales of Neurosurgery* by Frank Vertosick; *Wise Women: Over 2,000 Years of Spiritual Writing* by Women (edited by Susan Cahill); *Holy Land: A Suburban Memoir* by D. J. Waldie.

W. W. Norton distributes its own list and handles distribution for its subsidiaries and imprints, as well as for a number of other publishers. Norton's distribution network includes Chapters Publishing, Countryman Press, Ecco Press, Liveright Publishing Corporation, New Directions Books, the New Press, Pushcart Press, the Taunton Press, Thames and Hudson, and Verso.

Query letters and SASEs should be directed to:

Alane Mason, Editor—Serious nonfiction for a general audience, particularly cultural and intellectual history; some illustrated books; literary fiction and memoir

Amy Cherry, Senior Editor—History, biography, women's issues, African American, health, fiction

Angela von der Lippe, Senior Editor—Trade nonfiction; serious works in behavioral sciences, earth sciences, astronomy, neuroscience, education

Carol Houck Smith, Editor at Large—Literary fiction, travel memoirs, behavioral sciences, nature

Edwin Barber, Senior Editor—Acquires for the full range of house interests

Jill Bialosky, Senior Editor—Literary fiction, biographies, memoirs, poetry

Jim Mairs, Senior Editor—History, illustrated books, photography

Robert Weil, Executive Editor—Literature in translation, intellectual history, social science, German and Jewish interests

Starling Lawrence, Editor in Chief—Acquires for the full range of house interests

W. Drake McFeely, President—Nonfiction of all kinds, particularly science and social science

Maria Guarnaschelli, Senior Editor—Cookbooks, serious nonfiction

COUNTRYMAN PRESS/BACKCOUNTRY PUBLICATIONS

New England office:

PO Box 748, Woodstock, VT 05091

fax: 802-457-1678

Countryman specializes in travel, regional history, recreation, gardening, nature, environment, how-to, regional hiking, walking, bicycling, fishing, cross-country skiing, and canoeing guides. Imprints include Countryman Press and Backcountry Guides.

Countryman (founded in 1973) has been on the cusp of the small, regional press initiative that has enriched the North American publishing scene through editorial acumen and niche-marketing panache. Now affiliated with W. W. Norton & Company, Countryman remains editorially independent.

Representative Countryman titles: *Eating New England* by Juliette Rogers and Barbara Radcliffe Rogers; *New Jersey's Great Gardens* by Arline Zatz; *Maine: An Explorer's Guide* by Chris Tree; *The Soul of Vermont* by Richard Brown; *The Granite Kiss* by Kevin Gardner; *American Rock* by Don Moller; *The King Arthur Flour Cookbook* by Brita Sands; *The Battered Stars* by Howard Coffin.

Backcountry Guides: *The Other Islands of New York City* by Sharon Seitz and Stuart Miller; *The Soul of Vermont* by Richard W. Brown; *The California Coast* by Donald Neuwirth and John J. Osborn, Jr; *50 Hikes in the Lower Hudson Valley* by Stella Green and Neil Zimmerman; *Sea Kayaking the Maine Coast* by Dorcas Miller; *Back Road Bicycling in Connecticut* by Ann-Marie Fusco.

Sales and distribution for Countryman are handled by the parent corporation, W. W. Norton. Query letters and SASEs should be directed to:

Kermit Hummel, Editorial Director

OAK TREE PRESS

2743 S. Veterans Parkway #135, Springfield, IL, 62704-6402

217-824-8001   fax: 217-824-3424

www.oaktreebooks.com   e-mail: info@oaktreepress.com

Oak Tree Press is an independent publisher of a wide variety of fiction and nonfiction, with a concentration on the mystery genre. Founded in 1998 to offer a counterpoint to shrinking publishing opportunities, Oak Tree maintains its welcoming attitude toward new authors. Since 1999, the publisher has sponsored the Dark Oak Mystery Contest and published the winning entry. Timeless Love, an imprint for romance novels, was introduced in July 2001.

Oak Tree policies include dynamic cover design, aggressive outreach, strong backlist promotion, and an open editorial policy. We will consider almost any subject—so long as there is no gratuitous violence against women.

Trade fiction titles include: *An Affinity For Murder* by Anne White; *Hearts Across Forever* by Mary Montague; *Red Room Rendezvous* by Paulette Crain; *Eagle Rising* by Mary Montague Sikes; *Mid-Life Mojo: A Guide for the Newly Single Male* by Robert M. Davis; *The Hunt* by Christine Rose; *From Russia, My Love* by Brian Reubendall; *The Damned Never Die* by J. McKay; *Callie and the Dealer and A Dog Named Jake* by Wendy Howell Mills; *An Affinity for Murder* by Anne White.

Under the Timeless Love imprint: *Hearts Across Forever* by Mary Montague Sikes.

In addition, Oak Tree is re-releasing a number of classic out-of-print titles from Odie Hawkins, beginning with Ghetto Sketches in spring 2001.

Nonfiction titles include *Of Weeds and Views* by Frances U. Crain; *Mid-Life Mojo: A Guide for the Newly Single Male* by Robert M. Davis, PhD; *Business Buyer's Handbook* by Jim Calkins.

In spring of 2001, Oak Tree made an entry into the audio and music realm through its sister company, WEGOTSKILLZ music, which will distribute and produce the work of independent artists.

Oak Tree Press handles its own marketing, sales, and distribution. Query letters with SASEs should be directed to:

Billie Johnson, Publisher

Sarah Wasson, Editorial Assistant

THE OVERLOOK PRESS

141 Wooster Street, New York, NY 10012

845-679-6838   fax: 845-679-8571

www.overlookpress.com   e-mail: overlook@netstep.net

Overlook focuses on general nonfiction and offers a respected line in fiction, belles lettres, and poetry. The nonfiction purview encompasses biography, crafts, how-to, fine arts, architecture, design, Hudson Valley regionals, cookbooks, and natural history. The house releases a limited number of titles directed toward the young reader.

The Overlook Press was founded in 1971 by Peter Mayer (until recently also Chief Executive of the Worldwide Penguin Group) and his father. Overlook is a smaller publisher with a diverse and select list. Under its enigmatic logo (a mythical beast in cartouche that calls to mind a winged elephantine species), Overlook produces books in special fine editions, hardcover, and trade paperback. The house nurtures a thriving backlist that features such titles as the business-martial arts classic *Book of Five Rings* by Miyamoto Musashi (translated by Victor Harris); *The Gormenghast Trilogy* by Mervyn Peake; *Tiny Houses* by Lester Walker.

Overlook was founded with the intent to publish against the grain. Here was a new publishing company that did not exactly imitate the policies of large companies. The editors did not pursue bestsellers; they wanted good-sellers. And they believed in the backlist. They did not want to be a niche publisher, just a small general publisher. They wanted to publish books that very likely had been "overlooked" by larger houses—although the Overlook name actually came from a mountain in Woodstock, New York.

Overlook made a name by publishing useful books in areas where none existed. It published the first book on wood stoves in the early 1970s, anticipating a major trend; when the house produced the first book on Kendo published in the United States (*A Book of Five Rings*)—who knew it would become famous as a metaphor for business strategy?

In 1977, Overlook launched the Ivory Press to publish unusual books in the visual arts, joining Tusk paperbacks in the Overlook family of imprints.

Overlook's authors roster is one of the finest in the land. Fiction: Paul West, Geoff Nicholson, Steve Weiner, Richard Foreman, Robert Schneider, David Shapiro, and Paul Auster. Film books: Howard Koch, Peter Bogdanovich, Ian McKellen, Derek Jarman, Ang Lee, Guin Turner, Rose Troche, Michael Ritchie, Cyril Collard, and Bruce Robinson. Nonfiction: Buckminster Fuller, Erving Goffman, Martin Esslin, Armond White, and Howard Jacobson. Design: Milton Glaser, Raymond Loewy, Terence Conran, Osborne and Little, Judith Miller, and Caroline Wrey.

Overlook titles include: *Billy* by Pamela Stephenson; *The Defection of A.J. Lewinter* by Robert Littell; *Samuel Beckett* by Gerry Dukes; *Top of My Lungs* by Natalie Goldberg; *The Short Life & Happy Times of the Shmoo* by Al Capp; *The Destruction of the Bismarck* by David J. Bercuson and Holgar H. Herwig; *It's Not Over 'Til It's Over* by Al Silverman;

Freddy the Pig Series by Walter R. Brooks; *The Complete Book of the Winter Olympics* by David Wallechinsky; *Jitney* by August Wilson; *Their First Time in the Movies* by Les Krantz; *The Royal Physician's Visit* by Per Olav Enquist; *The Destruction of the Bismark* by David Bercuson and Holger Herwig; *The Reconstructionist* by Josephine Hart; *The Girl from the Golden Horn* by Kurban Said; *Secret Agent* by David Stafford; *Green* by Benjamin Zucker; *The King of Limbo* by Adrianne Harun; *Deception in War* by Jon Latimer; *Shardik* by Richard Adams; *Wilson* by David Mamet; *Film Posters of the 80s* edited by Tony Nourmand and Graham Marsh; *The Yellow Sailor* by Steve Weiner; *The Poetry and Life of Allen Ginsberg* by Ed Sanders.

In 2002 Ardis Publishers was acquired by The Overlook Press. For now, Ardis will continue publishing academic and scholarly subjects like English Language translations, reference works, and critical assessments of Russian Literature. There website is www.ardisbooks.com.

Ardis titles include: *Day Equals Night* by Valeria Narbikova; *Escape Hatch: Two Novellas* by Vladimir Makanin; *Portfel* by Alexander Sumerkin.

Overlook Press is distributed by Penguin Puntam, Inc. Query letters and SASEs should be directed to:

Peter Mayer, Publisher

Tracy Karns, Editor

PALADIN PRESS

Paladin Enterprises, 7077 Winchester Circle, Boulder, CO 80301

303-443-7250   fax: 303-442-8741

www.paladin-press.com   e-mail: service@paladin-press.com

Paladin issues new titles and reprints in such categories as new identity, personal freedom, espionage and investigation, weapons, military science, revenge, humor, special forces, survival, martial arts, action careers, sniping, knives and knife fighting, locksmithing, self-defense, police science, silencers, and history and culture relating to the previous fields, as well as selected general-interest books. Paladin also purveys a video library. Paladin Press (established in 1970) is a division of Paladin Enterprises.

Certain Paladin titles exhibit a markedly subversive approach and are intended as high-edge, satiric amusement. It should be further noted that particular works on the Paladin list contain material that may be restricted in some jurisdictions and are sold for academic, research, or informational reference purposes only.

Frontlist catalog entrants: *Adventure Travels in the Third World* by Jeff Randall and Mike Perrin; *Aluminum Foil Deflector Beanie* by Lyle Zapato; *Iaido Sword* by Richard W. Babin, BS, MD; *Home Workshop Knifemaking* with Wally Hayes; *Martial Marksmanship* with Andy Stanford and Michael D. Janich; *Rural Surveillance* by Van Ritch; Secrets

From the Ninja Grandmaster by Stephen K. Hayes and Masaaki Hatsumi; *The Snubby Revolver* by Ed Lovette; *Art of the Rifle* by Jeff Cooper; *Glock Exotic Weapons System*; *Expedient Homemade Firearms* by P. A. Luty; *Weapon Tests and Evaluations* by Peter G. Kokalis; *Boston's Gun Bible* by Boston T. Party; *Stopping Power: A Practical Analysis of the Latest Handgun Ammunition* by Evan P. Marshall and Edwin J. Sanow; *Surviving Street Patrol: The Officer's Guide to Safe and Effective Policing* by Steve Albrecht; *The Passport Report: Over 100 Ways and Many Good Reasons to Obtain a Second Foreign Passport* by Dr. W. G. Hill.

Highlights from the backlist (including all-time Paladin hits): *Protect Your Assets: How to Avoid Falling Victim to the Government's Forfeiture Laws* by Adam Starchild; *Running a Ring of Spies: Spycraft and Black Operations in the Real World of Espionage* by Jefferson Mack; *SWAT Battle Tactics: How to Organize, Train, and Equip a SWAT Team for Law Enforcement or Self-Defense* by Pat Cascio and John McSweeney; *Body for Sale: An Inside Look at Medical Research, Drug Testing, and Organ Transplants and How You Can Profit from Them* by Ed Brassard.

Paladin Press looks for original manuscripts on combat shooting, firearms and exotic weapons, personal and financial freedom, military science, and other action topics. For more information, call or write the publisher for a copy of the Author Style Guide and Insider Newsletter.

Paladin Press distributes its own list and in addition services individual orders via toll-free ordering numbers, mail order, and its Web site. Query letters and SASEs should be directed to:

Jon Ford, Editorial Director

PATHFINDER PRESS

410 West Street, New York, NY 10014

212-741-0690   fax: 212-727-0150

www.pathfinderpress.com   e-mail: pathfinderpress@compuserve.com

The Pathfinder program catalogs such fields as black and African studies; women's rights; the Cuban revolution in world politics; revolutionaries and working-class fighters; fascism, big business, and the labor movement; Russia, Eastern Europe, and the Balkans; scientific views of politics and economics; trade unions: past, present, and future; United States history and political issues; Latin America and the Caribbean; the Middle East and China; and art, culture, and politics. Pathfinder titles often suggest such streams of thought as populism, internationalism, utopianism, socialism, and communism.

Pathfinder Press (established in 1940) issues books, booklets, pamphlets, posters, and postcards keyed to issues affecting working people worldwide. Pathfinder produces titles in English, Spanish, French, Swedish, Farsi, Greek, Icelandic, and Russian. Pathfinder distributes the journal *New International*.

The Pathfinder Mural that once adorned the company's editorial and manufacturing digs in Manhattan's Far West Village featured a depiction of a gargantuan printing press in action, as well as portraits of revolutionary leaders whose writings and speeches are published by Pathfinder; this community cultural icon represented the work of more than 80 artists from 20 countries.

Representative Pathfinder books: *Episodes of the Cuban Revolutionary War, 1956–1958* by Ernesto (Che) Guevara (firsthand account of the military campaigns and political events that culminated in the January 1959 popular insurrection that overthrew the U.S.-backed dictatorship in Cuba); *Lenin's Final Fight: Speeches and Writings, 1922–1923* by V. I. Lenin; *In Defense of Marxism: The Social and Political Contradictions of the Soviet Union* by Leon Trotsky; *The Second Declaration of Havana* by Fidel Castro.

On Pathfinder's staunch backlist: *Bolivian Diary* by Ernesto (Che) Guevara; *Peru's Shining Path: Anatomy of a Reactionary Sect* by Martín Koppel; *Lenny Bruce: The Comedian as Social Critic and Secular Moralist* by Frank Kofsky; *The Revolution Betrayed: What Is the Soviet Union and Where Is It Going?* by Leon Trotsky; *The Politics of Chicano Liberation* (edited by Olga Rodriguez); *Polemics in Marxist Philosophy* by George Novack; *The Communist Manifesto* by Karl Marx and Frederick Engels; *Cuba's Internationalist Foreign Policy, 1975–1980* by Fidel Castro; *To Speak the Truth: Why Washington's "Cold War" Against Cuba Doesn't End* by Fidel Castro and Che Guevara; *How Far We Slaves Have Come! South Africa and Cuba in Today's World* by Nelson Mandela and Fidel Castro; *Che Guevara: Economics and Politics in the Transition to Socialism* by Carlos Tablada.

Newer titles: *Malcolm X Talks to Young People*; *Marianas in Combat* by Tete Puebla; *De la Sierra del Escambray al Congo* by Victor Dreke; *Capitalism's World Disorder* by Jack Barnes; *What the 1987 Stock Market Crash Foretold* by Jack Barnes, Leon Trotsky, and Mary Alice Waters.

Pathfinder's *New International* is a magazine of Marxist politics and theory. Many of the articles that appear in *New International* are available in Spanish, French, and Swedish. The magazine is a numbered series in trade paperback format.

Special Pathfinder series include *Malcolm X: Speeches and Writings*, as well as written works and spoken words from James P. Cannon, Eugene V. Debs, Farrell Dobbs, Carlos Fonseca, Mother Jones, Rosa Luxemburg, Nelson Mandela, Fidel Castro, and Ernesto (Che) Guevara; the house also publishes the works of Karl Marx, Frederick Engels, V. I. Lenin, and Leon Trotsky.

A number of bookstores around the world distribute Pathfinder's titles and offer membership in a readers' club for an annual fee (entitling members to enjoy special Pathfinder discounts); individual orders are payable via Visa and MasterCard. Pathfinder Press distributes its own publications in the United States and worldwide primarily through its own fulfillment centers.

Query letters and SASEs should be directed to:

Michael Taber, Editorial Director—Projects consistent with the Pathfinder list

PEACHPIT PRESS (A DIVISION OF PEARSON EDUCATION)

1249 Eighth Street, Berkeley, CA 94710

510-524-2178/1-800-283-9444   fax: 510-524-2221

www.peachpit.com   e-mail: tell@peachpit.com

Peachpit is a specialist computer-publishing house with a list in personal computing and desktop publishing for business and recreational users. Peachpit publishes books and book/software packages (including CD-ROM products) that tackle basic practical tasks and troubleshooting, as well as advanced applications.

Peachpit covers a number of categories: general introductory works on computing, general works about the Macintosh computer system, Macintosh Bible series, Visual Quick Start series, On the Web series, the Real World series, the Non-Designer's series, desktop publishing, graphics, Windows and its applications, word processing, and related topics. Many Peachpit releases are keyed to particular proprietary products.

Visual Quick Start Guides provide exactly what the title implies: a fast, simple way to get up and running with a new program—which is perhaps the secret to the popularity of this successful line.

Peachpit's editorial approach is to make the computing world relevant, make it dramatic, and make it fun. Peachpit authors are at the forefront of ongoing technological developments and trends in computer hardware and software development and are masterful at teasing out the nuances of end-user potential in print.

Publisher's statement: Peachpit is not only in the book business and not only a player on the computer-business stage; Peachpit is also in the teaching business. In addition to trade bookstores and computer venues, Peachpit hits a variety of market sectors, such as schools and educational enterprises (including evening classes and adult education); library, institutional, and corporate consumers; and end-user and professional groups.

Peachpit Press (founded in 1986) was acquired by Addison-Wesley in late 1994, and the house is now a division of Pearson Education. Within this corporate structure, Peachpit maintains its independent editorial stance and gains financial and distributional leverage from the new ownership to the benefit of Peachpit's worthy list.

Titles from *Peachpit: Adobe Photoshop Master Class: John Paul Caponigro* by John Caponigro; *Certified Macromedia ColdFusion MX Developer Study Guide* by Ben Forta; *The Macintosh iLife* by Jim Heid; *Color Correction for Avid Xpress*; *Designing Web Site Interface Elements* by Eric Eaton; *Introduction to Avid Xpress DV 3.5 Effects*; *The Little iTunes*; *Adobe Acrobat 5 Master Class*; *After Effects 5.5 Hands-On Training*; *Excel X for Mac OS X: Visual Quickstart Guide*; *Illustrator 10 for Windows and Macintosh: Visual QuickStart Guide*; *Mac 911*; *Macromedia Flash ActionScripting: Advanced Training from the Source*; *The Painter 7 Wow! Book*; *Real World Adobe Illustrator 1.0*; *Stop Stealing Sheep and Find Out How Type*

Works, 2nd Edition; *REALbasic for Macintosh: Visual Quickstart Guide.*

Peachpit Press is distributed through the parent company Pearson Education. Query letters and SASEs should be directed to:

Nancy Aldrich-Ruenzel, Publisher

Marjorie Baer, Executive Editor

Cliff Colby, Executive Editor

Nancy Davis, Editor-in-Chief

Becky Morgan, Editor

Nikki Echler McDonald, Editor

Suki Gear, Editor

Serena Herr, Editor

Jill Lodwig, Editor

Karen Reichstein, Associate Editor

PEACHTREE PUBLISHERS, LTD.

PEACHTREE CHILDREN'S BOOKS

1700 Chattahoochee Avenue, Atlanta, GA 30318-2112

404-876-8761   fax: 404-875-2578

www.peachtree-online.com   e-mail: hello@peachtree-online.com

Peachtree publishes children's books and general trade and offers a substantial and growing children's list. Peachtree has a concentration in markedly innovative books in self-help, self-awareness, health, and parenting. A special area of Peachtree publishing interest encompasses regional topics, including the American South in general and the state of Georgia in particular.

Peachtree Publishers (established in 1978) is a midsize house that produces books in hardcover and trade paperback editions. Peachtree hosts a hardy backlist.

From Peachtree: *Cooking in the New South* by Anne Byrn; *Curtis Aikens' Guide to the Harvest* by Curtis G. Aikens; *After Eli* by Terry Kay; *Charlie's Story* by Maeve Friel; *Christmas in Georgia* by Celestine Sibley; *Head Above Water* by S. L. Rottman; *The Heart of a Distant Forest* by Philip Lee Williams; *Hero* by S. L. Rottman; *Jessie and Jesus and Cousin Claire* by Raymond Andrews; *The Last Radio Baby: A Memoir* by Raymond Andrews; *Beyond Birdwatching: More Than There Is To Know About Birding* by Ben, Cathryn and John Sill; *Cats Vanish Slowly* by Ruth Tiller; *Grandma U* by Jeanie Franz Ransom; *Kiss a Mule, Cure a Cold* by Evelyn Childers; *Mothers Are Always Special* by Celestine Sibley; *Retire & Rejoice* by Blackie Scott; *Southern Is. . .*by Mary Norton Kratt;

Wishing by Ruth Tiller (illustrated by Deborah Santini); *Cheap Psychological Tricks: What to Do When Hard Work, Honesty, and Perseverance Fail!* by Perry Buffington. Standout Peachtree projects: *Out to Pasture* by Ellie Leland Wilder (a five-volume series of tales from FairAcres Retirement Home); *To Dance with the White Dog* by Terry Kay; *Hiking Trails of the North Georgia Mountains* by Tim Homan; *Cooking in the New South: A Modern Approach to Traditional Southern Fare* by Anne Bryn.

Peachtree distributes its own list to the trade with the assistance of regional sales representatives. Query letters and SASEs should be directed to:

Helen Harris, Editorial Department

PEACHTREE CHILDREN'S BOOKS

Children's editions from Peachtree encompass award-winning illustrated storybooks for younger readers, as well as a select group of works directed toward parents. Peachtree Jr. is a line of chapter books targeted for ages 8 years and up. The AllStar SportStory series combines contemporary tales with sports history and statistics. Freestone is a line of novels for today's teenagers, ages 12 to 16.

Standout Peachtree Children's Books: *About Amphibians; About Arachnids; About Birds; About Fish; About Insects; About Mammals; About Reptiles* by Cathryn Sill, illustrated by John Sill; *Agatha's Feather Bed: Not Just Another Wild Goose Story* by Carmen Agra; *Aliens from Earth: When Animals and Plants Invade Other Ecosystems* by Mary Batten (illustrated by Beverlyn Doyle); *Anna Casey's Place in the World* by Adrian Fogelin; *The Boy Who Thought He Was a Teddy Bear* by Jeanne Willis; *The Bushwacker: A Civil War Adventure* by Jennifer Jason Garrity (illustrated by Paul Bachem); *Eleanor's Story: An American Girl in Hitler's Germany* by Eleanor Ramrath Garner; *The Misfits* series by Mark Delaney; *Seaman: The Dog Who Explored the West with Lewis and Clark* by Gail Langer Karwoski; *The Horned Toad Prince and Three Armadillies Tuff* by Jackie Hopkins; *While You Were Sleeping* and other books by John Butler.

Query letters and SASEs should be directed to:

Helen Harris, Editorial Department

PELICAN PUBLISHING COMPANY

PO Box 3110, Gretna, LA 70054-3110

504-368-1175/1-800-843-1724 (orders)   fax: 504-368-1195

www.pelicanpub.com   e-mail: editorial@pelicanpub.com

Pelican Publishing Company (founded in 1926) produces a general trade list with special interests in travel and lifestyle guides, Americana, cookbooks, art, architecture, photography, humor, sports, and motivational and inspirational titles. Many Pelican titles offer a regional or cultural perspective in such areas as the American South, Civil War history, Louisiana and the New Orleans environs, and Irish and Scottish American heritage. Pelican produces a short menu of children's books and offers a select group of fiction works, many of which have a regional or historical twist.

Pelican's travel series include the Maverick Guides (for the independent traveler—these guides include history, customs, language, and attractions, as well as current prices and recommendations for accommodations, dining spots, etc.), the Marmac Guides (up-to-date information on population, services, recreation, accommodations, and restaurants in various American cities), At Cost Travel Guide series (for the value-conscious traveler), and the Pelican Guide series (designed to give the discriminating traveler insight into some of the most interesting locations within the United States).

Other Pelican series include the Majesty Architecture series, the New Orleans Architecture series, the Best Editorial Cartoons of the Year series, the Editorial Cartoonists series, the Cruising Guides series, and the Clovis Crawfish Series for kids.

From Pelican: *Darina Allen's Ballymaloe Cooking School Cookbook* by Darina Allen; *The Ballymaloe Bread Book* by Tim Allen; *Douglas Southall Freeman* by David E. Johnson; *Firefighter's Night Before Christmas* by Kimbra Cutlip (illustrated by James Rice); *Pennsylvania Dutch Night Before Christmas Coloring Book* by Chet Williamson (illustrated by James Rice); *The Boy with a Wish* by Harry B. Knights (illustrated by Calico World Entertainment); *Ghost Army of World War II* by Jack M. Kneece; *The Warlord's Beads* by Virginia Walton Pilegard (illustrated by Nicholas Debon); *Mardi Gras Treasures: Float Designs of the Golden Age* by Henri Schindler.

Pelican's Top-30 list includes *See You at the Top* by Zig Ziglar; *The Justin Wilson Cook Book, The Justin Wilson Gourmet and Gourmand Cookbook*, and *Justin Wilson's Outdoor Cooking with Inside Help*, all by Justin Wilson.

Representing the Pelican's children's list favorites: *The Warlord's Fish* by Virginia Walton Pilegard (illustrated by Nicolas Debon); *Upsie Downsie, Are You Asleep?* written and illustrated by Jane Dillon; *Phoebe Clappsaddle and the Tumbleweed Gang* by Melanie Chrismer (illustrated by Virginia Marsh Roeder); *Clarence Thomas, Fighter with Words* by David R. Collins (illustrated by Celia Lauve); *Pennsylvania Dutch Night Before Christmas* by Chet Williamson (illustrated by James Rice); *Why Cowgirls Are Such Sweet Talkers* by Laurie Lazzaro Knowlton (illustrated by James Rice); *Lucky O'Leprechaun Comes to America*, written and illustrated by Jana Dillon.

Pelican Publishing Company handles its own distribution. Query letters and SASEs should be directed to:

Nina Kooij, Editor-in-Chief

THE PERMANENT PRESS/SECOND CHANCE PRESS

4170 Noyac Road, Sag Harbor, NY 11963

631-725-1101

www.thepermanentpress.com   e-mail: info@thepermanentpress.com

Founded in 1978 by copublishers Judith and Martin Shepard, the Permanent Press produces expressive, vital, and exciting nongenre fiction. The sine qua non here for titles is that they be artfully written. The Permanent Press publishes 12 books per year in cloth editions only. Selected out-of-print books are released in reprint under the Second Chance Press imprint.

Judith and Martin Shepard have endeavored to bring out quality writing, primarily fiction, without regard to authors' reputations or track records. The publisher presents a handpicked list in which it firmly believes. Such dedication is not without payoff: Permanent Press titles generate considerable and favorable word of mouth among readers and booksellers and reap the kinds of reviews that pique wide interest (particularly in the realm of subsidiary rights).

While publishing only 12 books per year, Permanent Press has, since 1986, gained 49 literary awards for its titles (including an American Book Award and a National Book Award finalist). The press has launched the careers of such novelists as Bill Albert, Larry Duberstein, David Galef, Andrew Klavan, Howard Owen, Sandra Scofield, and William Browning Spencer. Permanent has published a Nobel Prize winner (Halldor Laxness) and a Nobel Prize nominee (Berry Fleming). This is the house that gave a fresh start to Clifford Irving after his misadventures involving the Howard Hughes "autobiography," by publishing Irving's account of that episode (*The Hoax*).

To celebrate Permanent's 20th year, the list presents 20 titles (8 more than it has ever done before) selected from the more than 8,000 submissions received: 16 novels, 3 works of nonfiction, and a short-story collection.

Fiction on the Permanent Press list: *Africa Speaks* by Mark Goldblatt; *The Spoiler* by Domenic Stansberry; *The Rail* by Howard Owen; *The Food Taster* by Ugo DiFonte; *An Unclean Act* by Dean Burgess; *Fresh Eggs* by Rob Levandoski; *Townie* by John Butman; *UnderSurface* by Mitch Cullin; *Attempted Chemistry* by Jeff Gomez; *Toucan Whisper, Toucan Sing* by Robert Wintner; *Naked Singularity* by Victoria N. Alexander; *Hail To The Chiefs: Presidential Mischief, Morals, and Malarkey from George W to George W* by Barbara Holland; *Marginalia* by Doran Larsen; *Natural Bridges* by Debbie Lynn McCampbell; *The Trap* by Rink van der Velde (originally published in the Netherlands in 1966); *Geometry of Love* by Joan Fay Cuccio; *Up, Down, & Sideways and Life Between Wars* by Robert H. Patton; *The Deer Mouse* by Ken Grant; *The Speed of Light* by Susan Pashman; *Bending Time* by Stephen Minot (short stories); *Queen of the Silver Dollar* by Edward Hower; *Apology for Big Rod* by Charles Holdefer; *They Don't Play Stickball in Milwaukee* by Reed Farrel Coleman.

News from the subrights front: *Résumé with Monsters* (science fiction) by William Browning Spencer has garnered foreign rights in at least two countries—Germany and Italy. The film option for *An Occasional Hell* (mystery) by Randall Silvis became an official purchase when the cameras started to roll.

The house has also brought back all the original works (and some new ones) by Marco Vassi—works that gained Vassi a reputation as the best erotic writer of his generation. The Vassi Collection is a 10-volume offering of erotic fiction that has hitherto been long out of print and generally unavailable. Titles in the Vassi Collection: *The Stoned Apocalypse*; *Mind Blower*; *The Gentle Degenerate*; *The Saline Solution*; *Contours of Darkness*; *The Devil's Sperm Is Cold*; *The Sensual Mirror*; *Slave Lover*. More from Vassi: *A Driving Passion*; *The Erotic Comedies*; *The Other Hand Clapping*.

Permanent Press handles its own distribution. Query letters and SASEs should be directed to:

Judith Shepard, Editor and Copublisher

PERSEA BOOKS, INC.

853 Broadway, Suite 604, New York, NY 10003

212-779-7668

www.perseabooks.com   e-mail: info@perseabooks.com

Persea produces a discriminating list in trade and reference nonfiction, fiction, belles lettres, and poetry. Persea's categories include essays, memoirs, literary criticism, novels and stories, fine arts, art history, scholarly works, social sciences, and gender and cultural studies.

Persea Books (founded by Michael Braziller in 1975) is an independently owned press. The house's titles in the arts are brought out in handsomely designed and produced editions. Persea's contemporary literature has an international cast of eminent writers.

Entrants from the Persea program: *The Best of Animals* by Lauren Grodstein; *Leviathan with a Hook: Poems* by Kimberly Johnson; *Poems of Nazim Hikmet* and *Human Landscapes from My Country* translated by Randy Blasing and Mutlu Konuk; *Poems of Paul Celan* translated by Michael Hamburger; *Imagining America* edited by Wesley Brown and Amy Ling; *Exiled Memories* by Pablo Medina; *A Brief Conversion and Other Stories* by Earl Lovelace; *Living on the Margins* (edited by Hilda Raz); *On Leaf and Flower* (edited by Charles Dean and Clyde Wachsberger); *Promise Hill* by Helen Falconer; *The Holocaust Kid* by Sonia Pileer; *A Man and a Woman and a Man* by Savyon Liebrecht; *Fishing for Chickens* (edited by Jim Heynen); *The Return of Felix Nogara* by Pablo Medina.

Persea shares office space with and is distributed by W. W. Norton & Company. Query letters and SASEs should be directed to:

Karen Braziller, Editorial Director

Gabriel Fried, Associate Editor

PERSEUS BOOKS GROUP

BASIC BOOKS

BASIC CIVITAS BOOKS

COUNTERPOINT PRESS

DA CAPO PRESS

FISHER BOOKS

PERSEUS PUBLISHING

PUBLICAFFAIRS

WESTVIEW PRESS

Perseus Books Group (Headquarters)

10 E. 53rd Street, New York, NY 10022

Massachusetts office:

11 Cambridge Center, Cambridge, MA 02142

The Perseus Books Group was founded in 1997 on the ideal of creating a new publishing model that allows more "quality" titles to be published, without forgoing financial success. This group has eight member publishers, each with a distinct focus and individual strengths. Each Perseus Books Group member company is editorially independent and individually focused, although they each share the common mission of "publishing books that matter."

Perseus Books Group publishes major nonfiction works, as well as literary fiction. It has also developed a backlist in a wide variety of categories.

BASIC BOOKS

387 Park Avenue South, New York, NY 10016-8810

Basic Books has survived the half-century mark and continues to thrive throughout the turbulence of changes, most recently becoming a member of the Perseus Books Group in 1997. Known for its titles in psychology, history, philosophy, politics, sociology, and anthropology, Basic Books prides itself on "taking the most exciting thinkers of our time and introducing them to a wider reading audience." This house produces serious nonfiction in hardcover and trade paperback formats, often authored by pioneers, scholars, or leaders in respective fields.

Representative titles include: *A Problem from Hell: America and the Age of Genocide* by Samantha Power; *Heartbreak: The Political Memoir of a Feminist Militant* by Andrea Dworkin; *The Tsar's Last Armada* by Constantine Pleshakov; *So Others Might Live* by Terry Golway; *The Mystery of Capital: Why Capitalism Succeeds in The West and Fails Everywhere Else* by Hernando de Soto; *The Dawn of Universal History* by Raymond Aron; *The Health of the Country: How American Settlers Understood Themselves and Their Land* by Conevery Bolton Valencius; *The Psychology of* The Sopranos: *Love, Death, Desire and Betrayal in America's Favorite Gangster Family* by Glen O. Gabbard; *The Company of Critics* (reissue) by Michael Walzer; *Little Red Riding Hood Uncloaked: Ten Moral Tales from the Forest* by Catherine Orenstein; *Three Roads to Quantum Gravity* by Lee Smolin; *Acquiring Genomes: A Theory of the Origins of Species* by Lynn Margulis; *Significant Others* by Craig Stanford; *High Noon: 20 Global Issues, 20 Years to Solve Them* by Jean-François Rischard; *The Other Path* by Hernando de Soto; *Sunlight at Midnight St. Petersburg and The Rise of Modern Russia* by W. Bruce Lincoln.

Direct queries and SASEs to:

Liz Maguire, Editor—Cultural history and current affairs

Joann Miller, Editor—Psychology, law, women's studies and current affairs

William Frucht, Editor—Science, economics, technology, and social change

Vanessa Mobley, Editor—Politics and current affairs, with a special interest in investigative reporting

John Donatich, Publisher

Stephen Bottum, Managing Editor

BASIC CIVITAS BOOKS

10 E. 53rd Street, New York, NY 10022-5299

212-207-7600   fax: 212-207-7703

Directed by Henry Louis Gates, Jr., Basic Civitas Books is devoted to publishing original voices in a broad range of African and African American studies. Titles are produced in hardcover and trade paperback formats.

Recent titles indicative of this list: *The Cornel West Reader* by Cornel West; *Africana: The Encyclopedia of the African and African American Experience* by Kwame Anthony Appiah, Henry Louis Gates, Jr. (Editor); *The Hip Hop Generation: The Crisis in African American Culture* by Bakari Kitwana; *Out There: Mavericks of Black Literature* by Darryl Pinckney; *Freedom: Freedom in the Making of Western Culture* by Orlando Patterson.

Marnie Cochran, Senior Editor—Health, parenting, general self-help/how-to

Amanda Cook, Senior Editor—Popular science

COUNTERPOINT PRESS

1627 I Street NW, Suite 500, Washington, DC 20006

202-887-0363/202-393-8088

Counterpoint Press is the "original" member of the Perseus Books Group and is well-known for its literary fiction and essays from new and established voices, including Wendell Berry, Frederick Barthelme, Evan Connell, Gary Snyder, and James Salter. Counterpoint Press publishes serious literary work, with an emphasis on natural history, science, philosophy and contemporary thought, history, art, poetry, and fiction. Counterpoint produces books in hardcover as well as paperback format.

Although short in years, Counterpoint is already long in awards. Authors published under this imprint have received the PEN/Faulkner Award, the National Book Critics Circle Award, the Bollingen Poetry Prize, the T. S. Eliot Award, the PEN Translation Prize, the Bay Area Book Reviewers Award, the Robert Kirsch Lifetime Achievement Award from the Los Angeles Times, the Lannan Lifetime Achievement Award, and the Harold Morton Landon Prize from the Academy of American Poets.

Fiction titles representative of this list include *Bending Heaven: Stories* by Jessica Francis Kane; *The Moth Diaries: A Novel* by Rachel Klein; *Sparrow Nights* by David Gilmour; *Stanley Park* by Timothy Taylor; *Three Short Novels* by Wendell Berry; *The Memory Room* by Mary Rakow; *Running After Antelope* by Scott Carrier; *Odds* by Patty Friedmann; *Cassada* by James Salter.

Nonfiction titles indicative of this list: *Critical Injuries* by Joan Barfoot; *On the Wing: A Young American Abroad* (memoir) by Nora Sayre; *The Room Lit by Roses: A Journal of Pregnancy and Birth* by Carole Maso; *Watershed: The Undamming of America* by Elizabeth Grossman; *With Bold Knife and Fork* by M. F. K. Fisher; *Castaways of the Image Planet: Movies, Show Business, Public Spectacle* by Geoffrey O'Brien; *Reporting Back: Notes on Journalism* by Lillian Ross; *Works on Paper: The Craft of Biography and Autobiography Writing* by Michael Holroyd; *Body Toxic: An Environmental Memoir* by Suzanne Antonetta; *Following the Sun: From Andalusia to the Hebrides* by John Hanson Mitchell.

Counterpoint Press does not accept unsolicited manuscripts. Query letters and SASEs should be directed to:

Editorial and Publicity, 717 D Street NW, Suite 203, Washington, DC 20004 (202-393-8088; fax 202-393-8488)

Jack Shoemaker, Publisher

Trish Hoard, Executive and Editorial Associate

DA CAPO PRESS

11 Cambridge Center, Cambridge MA 02142

617-252-5200

Da Capo, founded in 1975, has begun moving into original publishing, in addition to continuing its tradition of publishing key reprints in the areas of music and history. Da Capo became a member of the Perseus Books Group in 1999 and maintains offices in

Cambridge, Massachusetts, and Manhattan. The house has earned acclaim for its titles in music, particularly jazz, but also classical, pop, rock, blues, and Celtic. Other nonfiction categories, published in hardcover and paperback, are American and world history, film, dance, theater, literature, art and architecture, sports, and African American studies.

Representative titles in general history, American history, European history, and military history include *Crazy Rhythm* by Leonard Garment; *Zin: The History and Mystery of Zinfandel* by David Darlington; *A History of Celibacy* by Elizabeth Abbott; *The Salem Witch Trials Reader* and *A Delusion of Satan: The Full Story of the Salem Witch Trials* by Frances Hill; *My Day: The Best of Eleanor Roosevelt's Newspaper Columns*; *Allies for Freedom & Blacks on John Brown* by Benjamin Quarles; *The Last Madam: A Life in the New Orleans Underworld* by Christine Wiltz; *The Templars: The Dramatic History of the Knights Templar* by Piers Paul Read; *A Rum Affair: A True Story of Botanical Fraud* by Karl Sabbagh; *A History in Fragments: Europe in the 20th Century* by Richard Vinen; *The Sisters of Henry VIII* by Maria Perry; *Allies: Pearl Harbor to D-Day* by John S. D. Eisenhower; *Foot Soldier: A Combat Infantryman's War in Europe* by Roscoe C. Blunt.

Titles indicative of Da Capo's rich music list include: *Like Young: Jazz, Pop, Youth, and Middle Age* by Frances Davis; *The Da Capo Jazz and Blues Lover's Guide* by Christiane Bird; *Satchmo: The Genius of Louis Armstrong* by Gary Giddins; *Kind of Blue* by Ashley Kahn; *Backbeat: Earl Palmer's Story* by Tony Scherrman; *Jazz in the Bittersweet Blues of Life* by Wynton Marsalis and Carl Vigeland; *The Dylan Companion* by Elizabeth Thomson and David Gutman; *A Cure for Gravity: A Musical Pilgrimage* by Joe Jackson; *Beat Punks* by Victor Bockris; *Can't You Hear Me Calling? The Life of Bill Monroe, Father of Bluegrass* by Richard D. Smith; *My First 79 Years* by Isaac Stern; *Celtic Music: A Complete Guide* by June Skinner Sawyers; *Hank Williams, Snapshots from the Lost Highway* by Colin Escott and Kira Florita.

Other nonfiction titles on this list: *Sports Guy* by Charles P. Pierce; *Friday Night Lights* by H. G. Bissinger; *What a Time It Was: The Best Sportswriting of W. C. Heinz*; *The Leaf and the Cloud* by Mary Oliver; *The Nick Tosches Reader*; *The Autobiography of Joseph Stalin* by Richard Lourie; *About Town: The New Yorker and the World It Made* by Ben Yagoda; *Endangered Species: Writers Talk About Their Craft, Their Visions, Their Lives* by Lawrence Grobel.

Authors on Da Capo's eclectic backlist include Duke Ellington, Harrison Salisbury, Walker Evans, Gary Giddins, Loretta Lynn, Groucho Marx, Nick Tosches, Diana Vreeland, Louis Armstrong, Eleanor Roosevelt, Peter Guralnick, Mary Oliver, H. G. Bissinger, Nat Hentoff, Ned Rorem, Joe Jackson, John S. D. Eisenhower, Albert Murray, Dore Ashton, Jonathan Schell, and Donald Spoto.

Da Capo Press accepts unsolicited manuscripts. Please send your query letter, SASEs, and/or manuscript to:

Marnie Cochran, Editor

FISHER BOOKS

Fisher Books, the most recent addition of the Perseus Books Group, publishes nonfiction guides to pregnancy and parenting, as well as popular guides to health and nutrition, in hardcover and paperback format.

Titles representative of this list include *Baby and Toddler Learning Fun: 50 Interactive and Developmental Activities to Enjoy with Your Child* by Sally R. Goldberg, PhD; *Getting the Lead Out: The Complete Resource for Preventing and Coping with Lead Poisoning* by Irene Kessel, et al.; *Custom Auto Interiors* by Don Taylor and Ron Mangus; *Your Pregnancy Questions & Answers* by Glade B. Curtis, MD, et al.; *Dr. Paula's Good Nutrition Guide for Babies, Toddlers, and Preschoolers: Answers to Parents' Most Common Questions Plus Help for Coping with Fussy Eaters* by Paula M. Elbirt, MD; *Living with Anxiety: A Clinically Tested Step-by-Step Plan for Drug-Free Management* by Bob Montgomery and Laurel Morris; *Your Pregnancy After 35* by Glade B. Curtis MD, et al.; *The Mediterranean Heart Diet: How It Works and How to Reap the Health Benefits, with Recipes to Get You Started* by Helen V. Fisher, et al.; *Being Happy Being Married: A Guide to Building a Better Relationship* by Lee Schnebly, M.Ed.; *Raising Confident Boys: 100 Tips for Parents and Teachers* by Elizabeth Hartley; *Fiber and Your Health* by Jeanette Parsons Egan; *Nurturing Yourself and Others: Learn How to Fill Your Life with Happiness* by Lee Schnebly; *Landscape Plants for Dry Regions: More Than 600 Species from Around the World* by Warren D. Jones and Charles Sacamano.

Direct queries and SASEs to:

Helen Fisher, Publisher

PERSEUS PUBLISHING

Recently the Perseus imprint has ceased to exist. The science, business, and general non-fiction parts of the Perseus imprint became part of the Basic imprint, and the new collaborative is called Perseus Basic Books. Health parenting, and reference/how-to titles are now part of the newly formed Perseus De Capo Press.

Marnie Cochran, Senior Editor—Health, parenting, general self-help/how-to

Amanda Cook, Senior Editor—Popular science

PUBLICAFFAIRS

250 West 57th Street, Suite 1321, New York, NY 10107

212-397-6666

PublicAffairs publishes original nonfiction works by field experts from journalists and politicians, to political dissidents and leaders in the arts. Perhaps it is most well known for the success of *Blind Man's Bluff: The Untold Story of American Submarine Espianage* which became a major bestseller.

PublicAffairs produces titles from authors such as Jane Alexander, Jim Lehrer, Boris Yeltsin, Vladimir Putin, and Andy Rooney.

Titles indicative of this list: *Gracefully Insane: The Rise and Fall of America's Premier Mental Hospital* by Alex Beam; *The Cat from Hue* by John Laurence; *Booknotes* by Brian Lamb; *Henry Ford and the Jews* by Neil Baldwin; *The Oligarchs* by David E. Hoffman; *Washington* by Meg Greenfield, et al.; *What Dying People Want: Practical Wisdom for the End of Life* by David Kuhl; *The Courage of Strangers: Coming of Age with the Human Rights Movement* by Jeri Laber; *A Soldier of the Revolution* by Ward S. Just; *Horse of a Different Color: A Tale of Breeding Geniuses, Dominant Females, and the Fastest Derby Winner Since Secretariat* by Jim Squires; *A Great, Silly Grin: The British Satire Boom of the 1960s* by Humphrey Carpenter; *The Underboss: The Rise and Fall of a Mafia Family* by Gerard O'Neill, et al.; *Vietnam, Now: A Reporter Returns* by David Lamb; *First Off the Tee: Presidential Hackers, Duffers and Cheaters from Taft to Bush* by Don Van Natta Jr.

Direct query letters and SASEs to:

Kate Darnton, Senior Editor—Current events, biographies, memoirs, women authors

WESTVIEW PRESS

5500 Central Avenue, Boulder, CO 80301-2877

303-444-3541

Westview Press, formerly part of HarperCollins, is in its third decade of publishing and is known for its textbooks and general audience non-fiction trade titles.

This press was founded in 1975 by Frederick A. Praeger and Maurice B. Mitchell in the basement of their Boulder, Colorado, home on Westview Drive. Though its first list published only 9 books, four years later the list had grown to 169 and kept growing. In 1981 all departments were relocated to the present location on Central Avenue. Under the direction and leadership of Fred Praeger, and guided by the motto "Books That Matter," Westview Press continues to grow and prosper. According to Praeger at the time, "We see our future as a sort of knowledge supermarket, where service is enthusiastic, efficient, fast, and highly professional, handling knowledge and information produced by the scholarly and scientific community."

Westview Press produced a wide array of academic and professional books, in addition to undergraduate- and graduate-level texts in the social sciences and humanities. The meat of its broad political science program is the Dilemmas in American Politics, Dilemmas in World Politics, and Transforming American Politics series, which include valuable contributions to these fields, such as Paula McClain and Joseph Stewart Jr.'s *Can We All Get Along?*; Gareth Porter and Janet Welsh Brown's *Global Environmental Politics*; Ted Gurr and Barbara Harff's *Ethnic Conflict in World Politics*; and Sandy Maisel's *The Parties Respond*. The sociology publishing program at Westview is also among the best in academia. Westview has published classics like Jay MacLeod's *Ain't No Makin' It*; David Wagner's *Checkerboard Square*, winner of the 1993 C. Wright Mills Award; and Charles Lemert's *Social Theory*.

Westview is particularly well known for its titles in area studies literature, with bestselling texts like *Latin American Politics* and *Development*, edited by Howard J. Wiarda and Harvey F. Kline; *A History of the Modern Middle East* by William Cleveland; *A Concise History of the Middle East* by Arthur Goldschmidt, Jr.; *Modern Japan: A Historical Survey* by Mikiso Hane; *Latin America: Its Problems and Its Promise*, edited by Jan Knippers Black.

In 1997, Westview acquired IconEditions, a respected HarperCollins art criticism and art history list formerly under the direction of Cass Canfield, Jr. These impeccably produced volumes are now known as WestviewPress/IconEditions, and Westview will continue to offer the classic Icon backlist titles, as well as take the list forward to publish new works of quality and scholarship.

In the last three years, Westview has become a recognizable and respected force in trade and general nonfiction publishing, with the release of titles like: *Sun Tzu's Art of War* by Ralph Sawyer; *Blood Diamonds* by Greg Campbell; *This is Cuba* by Shibley Telhami; *The Stakes* by Peter Wallison. Westview is committed to publishing these books and others like them as the press dances on the cutting edge of nonfiction trade publishing.

Westview's success, according to founder Fred Praeger, "will be measured by the contribution we can make to the harmony, the balance, and the survivability of this world."

Westview Press is not accepting any unsolicited packages or letters. Query letters and book proposals may be sent electronically to wvproposal@perseusbooks.com.

Holly Hodder, Vice President and Publisher

Jill Rothenberg, Senior Editor—Sociology, current affairs, gender studies

Karl Yambert, Senior Editor—Anthropology, archaeology, area studies

Sarah Warner, Senior Editor—religion, philosophy

Steve Catalano, Senior Editor—History and politics

PETERSON'S

2000 Lenox Drive PO Box 67005, Lawrenceville, NJ 08648

877-433-8277/609-896-1800   fax: 609-896-1811

www.petersons.com

Peterson's is the country's largest educational information/communications company, providing the academic, consumer, and professional communities with books, software, and online services in support of lifelong education access and career choice. Founded in 1966, Peterson's publishes such well-known references as its annual guides to graduate and professional job hunting programs, colleges and universities, financial aid, private schools, standardized test-prep, summer programs, international study, executive education, job hunting, and career opportunities, as well as a full line of software offering career guidance and information for adult learners. Many of Peterson's reference works are updated annually. Peterson's is a Thomson company.

Peterson's markets strongly to libraries and institutions, as well as to the corporate sector.

Newly authored frontlist titles include: *Basic Guidelines Set 2003-4 Vol, 15th Edition; Game Plan for Distance Learning, 1st Edition; Complete Financial Aid Kit-3 Vol, 200th edition; Get A Jump! What's Next After High School?; Summer Jobs for Students, 51st edition; The Ultimate College Survival Guide* by Janet Farrar Worthington and Ronald Farrar; *The Ultimate Job Search Guide* by Paul L. Dyer; *The Ultimate New Employee Survival Guide* by Ed Holton; *The Ultimate Home Office Survival Guide* by Sunny Baker and Kim Baker. Authored backlist titles include *The Colorblind Career* by Ollie Stevenson; *Portfolio Power* by Martin Kimeldorf; *How to Write a Winning Personal Statement for Graduate and Professional School* by Richard J. Seltzer; *Paralegal* by Barbara Bernardo; *Virtual College* by Pam Dixon; *Financing Graduate School* by Patricia McWade; *Smart Parents' Guide to College* by Dr. Ernest Boyer and Paul Boyer.

Query letters and SASEs should be directed to:

Eileen Fiore, Executive Assistant, Research and Editorial Development—Interests consistent with house list

Ian Gallagher, Senior Editor—Test preparation

POMEGRANATE COMMUNICATIONS, INC.

Box 6099, Rohnert Park, CA 94927

707-586-5500/1-800-227-1428   fax: 707-586-5518

www.pomegranatecommunications.com   e-mail: info@pomegranate.com

Pomegranate publishes an attractive array of graphically lavish books and specialty items geared to interests such as fine art, contemporary art, architecture, travel, ethnic culture, and crafts. Pomegranate is among the premier publishers of calendars of all types and stripes, posters and poster art, note cards, games and puzzles, specialty sets, and popular topical card decks.

Sample titles include *Sunday Afternoon, Looking for the Car: The Aberrant Art of Barry Kite* by Alan Bisbort; *Cultivating Sacred Space: Gardening for the Soul* by Elizabeth Murray; *CatDreams* by B. Kliban; *Maxfield Parrish: A Retrospective* by Laurence S. Cutler and Judy Goffman Cutler; *Edward Hopper's New England* by Carl Little; *The Collectible Art of Susan Seddon Boulet*. The Little Wright Books Series showcases the work of Frank Lloyd Wright, with each volume focusing on a particular topic. Titles by Carla Lind: *Frank Lloyd Wright's California Houses; Frank Lloyd Wright's First Houses; Frank Lloyd Wright's Public Buildings; Frank Lloyd Wright's Prairie Houses; Frank Lloyd Wright's Lost*

Buildings; Frank Lloyd Wright's Fireplaces; Frank Lloyd Wright's Dining Rooms.

Pomegranate is an independent house and operates its own distributional network, including foreign representation worldwide. Query letters and SASEs should be directed to:

Submissions Department

PRESIDIO PRESS

PO Box 1764, Novato, CA 94948-1764

415-898-1081   fax: 415-898-0383

Presidio is known for works in such areas as general military history, American history, aviation, biography and memoirs, world wars, Korean War, Vietnam, African American studies, military theory, and professional studies. Presidio also issues a small number of superior fiction titles that favor a military-historical milieu.

Presidio Press (founded in 1974) is America's foremost publisher of military history. The house emphasizes both popular and scholarly works, especially those with potential for backlist endurance. Presidio publishes in hardcover and quality paperback editions.

Nonfiction from Presidio: *Shadow Flights: America's Secret Air War Against the Soviet Union: A Cold War History* by Curtis Peebles; *Black Sheep One: The Lie of Gregory "Pappy" Boyington* by Bruce Gamble; *With the Old Corps in Nicaragua* by George B. Clark; *Formidable Enemies: The North Korean and Chinese Soldier in the Korean War* by Kevin Mahoney; *Carlson's Raid: The Daring Assault on Makin* by George W. Smith; *Spirit, Blood, and Treasure: The American Cost of Battle in the 21st Century* (edited by Donald Vandergriff); *Somalia on Five Dollars a Day: A Soldier's Story* by Martin Stanton; *Beyond the Rhine: A Screaming Eagle in Germany* by Donald R. Burgett; *A Few Good Men: The Fighting Fifth Marines: A History of the USMC's Most Decorated Regiment* by Ronald J. Brown; *His Time in Hell: A Texas Marine in France: The World War I Memoir of Warren R. Jackson* (edited by George B. Clark); *What They Didn't Teach You About the 60s* by Mike Wright; *Afternoon of the Rising Sun: The Battle of Leyte Gulf* by Kenneth I. Friedman.

Presidio's Gulf War memoir *She Went to War: The Rhonda Cornum Story* by flight surgeon Rhonda Cornum, as told to Peter Copeland, garnered considerable subsidiary-rights interest—including a high-profile television-movie.

Presidio Press titles, as well as those associated imprints (such as British military publisher Greenhill Books), are distributed to the book trade in the United States and Canada through National Book Network. Query letters and SASEs should be directed to:

Acquisitions Editors

PROFESSIONAL PUBLICATIONS, INC.

1250 Fifth Avenue, Belmont, CA 94002-3863

650-593-9119/ 1-800-426-1178   fax: 650-592-4519

www.ppi2pass.com   e-mail: info@ppi2pass.com

Professional Publications publishes titles in engineering, architecture, and interior design, as well as works aimed toward the broader business and professional trade arena. The house produces books and educational aids (such as audiocassettes, videos, software, and study guides) for the professional market.

Professional Publications (established in 1981) earned initial success with examination-preparation packages (reference manuals, ancillary workbooks, sample exams, and solved problem books) for the professional engineering license examination given to applicants in the major engineering disciplines. Once this niche market was secured, the house branched into wider publishing territory.

On the Professional Publications list: *Six-Minute Solutions for Electrical & Computer PE Exam Problems*; *Structural Engineering Reference Manual*; *FE Review Manual*, *Civil Engineering Reference Manual*, and *Mechanical Engineering Reference Manual*, all by Michael R. Lindeburg; *Interior Construction and Detailing for Designers and Architects and Interior Design Reference Manual*, both by David K. Ballast.

Professional Publications oversees its own distribution. Query letters and SASEs should be directed to:

Aline S. Magee, Acquisitions Editor

PROMETHEUS BOOKS

59 John Glenn Drive, Amherst, NY 14228-2197

716-691-0133/1-800-421-0351   fax: 716-564-2711

www.prometheusbooks.com   e-mail: editorial@prometheusbooks.com

Prometheus catalogs works with challenging stances on contemporary issues. The house is particularly strong in popular science, science and the paranormal, biblical criticism, religion and politics, politics and current events, consumer health and fitness, philosophy, humanism, free thought, sports, human sexuality, sexual autobiography, literature, literary history, popular culture, creation versus evolution, religion, and education, as well as reference works in allied fields and occasional works of fiction. Prometheus also publishes books for young readers, produces a line of titles on human aging, and serves the educational market with several series of modestly priced classics in reprint (including Great Books in Philosophy, Literary Classics, and Great Minds). The house offers select works in electronic format.

Prometheus Books (established in 1969) produces an ambitious frontlist that embraces a wide range of perennially popular nonfiction topics; more enduring titles are backlisted indefinitely.

Prometheus also publishes the following periodicals: *Scientific Review of Alternative Medicine* (a peer-reviewed medical journal providing objective, scientific assessments of the treatments, methods, and hypotheses of unconventional medicine—the realm of acupuncture, homeopathy, herbal therapies, therapeutic touch, "miraculous" cancer treatments, and more); *Nutrition Forum* (bimonthly newsletter on the frontline of the anti—health fraud movement); *The Journal for the Critical Study of Religion, Ethics, and Society* (articles in the area of religious studies and scholarly assessments of society, ethics, and culture that have a bearing on the understanding of religion; the journal seeks to promote a broadly humanistic understanding of culture).

On the Prometheus list: *100 Greatest African Americans* by Molefi Kete Asante; *Aging in Good Health* edited by Sue E. Levkoff, Yeon Kyung Chee, and Shohei Noguchi; *Atheism, Morality, and Meaning* by Michael Martin; *Babbitt* by Sinclair Lewis; *Bare Bones* by Augusto Sarmiento, MD; *Can We Be Good Without God?* by Robert Buckman, MD; *Caring for the Dying* edited by Robert M. Baird and Stuart E. Rosenbaum; *Controlling Technology* edited by Eric Katz, Andrew Light, and William B. Thompson; *Darkwater: Voices from Within the Veil* by W. E. B. Du Bois; *Dear Professor Einstein* edited by Alice Calaprice; *Eldercare 911* by Susan Beerman, M.S.W. and Judith Rappaport-Musson, C.S.A.; *Extract from Captain Stormfield's Visit to Heaven* by Mark Twain; *Flat Earth? Round Earth?* By Theresa Martin; *For a "Christian America"* by Ruth Murray Brown; *Gandhi* by G. B. Singh; *Highway Terror* by Paul Eberle; *Mothers and Their Adult Daughters* by Karen L. Fingerman, PhD; *Perfect Planet, Clever Species* by William C. Burger; *Philosophical Dictionary* by Mario Bunge; *Quantum Legacy* by Barry Parker; *Soldier of Fortune 500* by Steve Romaine; *The Culture of Extinction* by Frederic L. Bender.

Prometheus Books introduces the Literary Classics line. This is a series of attractive, moderately priced paperback editions of classic authors (in both poetry and prose) whose works embody free inquiry and free thought. Titles here: *The Turn of the Screw: The Lesson of the Master* by Henry James; *The Awakening* by Kate Chopin; *Main Street* by Sinclair Lewis; *The Confidence Man* by Herman Melville.

Please note: Though known primarily as a house that operates on an advance/royalty arrangement, Prometheus has on occasion offered agreements to authors through which the author invests cooperatively in the costs and thus subsidizes publication.

Prometheus distributes its own list. Queries and SASEs should be directed to:

Steven L. Mitchell, Editorial Director

Mark Hall, PhD, Managing Editor/Creative Marketing Coordinator
Born/sign: May 29, 1952; Gemini.
Education: PhD from the University of Pennsylvania in Ancient Near Eastern Studies; B.A. in Classics from the University of New York in Buffalo.
Employment history/editor career path: I originally went to grad school for

ancient history with the intent of teaching on a university level. I found out while in school that few positions were available in the area that I specialized in; nonetheless, I finished the degree. In 1990 I applied to Prometheus Books and got the job. I started as the Production Manager and then went on to edit trade books. The production demand to edit trade books was much too high for me, so I eventually left and went to marketing. I also do freelance medical editing for John Wiley & Sons in the department of psychology.

Personal interests: Ancient Near Eastern History, archaeology, history of the Bible, following modern fiction. I used to write poetry, so I try to keep up with that.

What would you be doing if you were not an editor? If there had been good opportunities in academics, I would love to be in that field.

What has been your most successful book that you have acquired to date? Prometheus is known for its midlist books.

What books have you acquired that make you the most proud? What books that you have acquired reflect the types of books you like to represent? *End of Days* by Erna Paris, which is a story of expulsion of the Jews in Spain at the time of Ferdinand and Isabella. She is a wonderful presenter and can do so in a way that is in great detail and has very interesting twists.

Do you represent fiction? If so, what do you look for? Prometheus doesn't publish much fiction.

What do you want to see less of? Works that tend to be narcissistic, self-indulgent, or that talk about boredom of the wealthy.

Do you represent nonfiction? Yes.

Do you require book proposals? If so, what do you look for in evaluating a book proposal? Yes. I look for a good, brief synopsis of what the book is about, a table of contents, a sample chapter, who is the competition. I don't usually like to see the entire manuscript.

What process do you use for making a decision? What is the process for acquisition, is there a committee? The Editor in Chief looks at almost every serious submission. We have recently hired two Acquisitions Editors to present material to the committee.

What kinds of nonfiction books do you want to see less of? Self-help, psychology, diet books, New Age, committed scientific evaluations.

Are agents important? Why? Agents are a fact of life in this business. They bring important authors to my attention.

Do you like new writers? Sometimes.

How should writers approach you? With a simple query letter. I would advise authors that sending a proposal on the first attempt is totally inappropriate.

What can writers do to get your attention and to avoid the slush pile? Do your homework.

What have been some of your craziest experiences with submissions? I once received a submission from a man who was recounting his experience 25 years ago in the Himalayas. He was searching for the meaning of life and went up the mountain and almost died. He was then rescued by a hermit and the hermit revealed to him the secrets of the universe.

What have been some of your best experiences with writers or in your job? Steve Allen, who wrote *Dumbth*, has been wonderful to work with. Peter Ustinov has also been a great joy to work with.

What, if anything, makes you different from other editors? My background in ancient eastern history.

Is there anything you would like to see changed in the industry? I would like to see less of a tendency to go with the conglomerates. The rise of Barnes & Noble and Borders, limiting the bookselling markets.

PUSHCART PRESS

Box 380, Wainscott, NY 11975

631-324-9300

Pushcart Press (established in 1972) is a small, personalized house that is emblematic of the mission to provide useful as well as entertaining trade books and reference volumes directed primarily toward writers, editors, small publishers, and literary aficionados; Pushcart Press is also a dedicated forum for fiction and nonfiction works of literary merit, and the house list includes many award-winning volumes.

Pushcart is known as the house that issues the established annual literary anthology *The Pushcart Prize: Best of the Small Presses*, in addition to the classic *The Publish-It-Yourself Handbook: Literary Tradition and How-to Without Commercial or Vanity Publishers* (both works edited by Pushcart Publisher Bill Henderson). *The Pushcart Book of Essays* (edited by Anthony Brandt) expands the house's line of exemplary writing collections.

Ongoing Pushcart Press publishing projects include the Literary Companion series and the Editors' Book Award series.

Titles from Pushcart: *To a Violent Grave: An Oral Biography of Jackson Pollock* by Jeffrey Potter; *Yeshua: The Gospel of St. Thomas* by Alan Decker McNary; *Garden State: A Novel* by Rick Moody; *Imagine a Great White Light* by Sheila Schwartz; *Writing for Your Life* by Sybil Steinberg; the anonymous *Autobiography of an Elderly Woman* (with an afterword by Doris Grumbach); *The Tale of the Ring: A Kaddish* by Frank Stiffel.

Pushcart Press is distributed by W. W. Norton. Query letters and SASEs should be directed to:

Bill Henderson, President

RED WHEEL/WEISER

368 Congress Street, 4th Floor, Boston, MA 02210

617-542-1324   fax: 617-482-9676

www.redwheelweiser.com

Red Wheel/Weiser's traditional interests are self-transformation, alternative healing methods, meditation, metaphysics, consciousness, magic, astrology, tarot, astral projection, Kabbalah, earth religions, Eastern philosophy and religions, Buddhism, t'ai chi, healing, and Tibetan studies.

The publisher has observed the many paths that lead to personal transformation and strives to publish books to help many different people find the paths that are right for them. Red Wheel/Weiser specializes in books relating to all facets of the secret and hidden teachings worldwide.

This distinguished publisher of occult and spiritual books was purchased last year. Its newest incarnation promises much of the familiar, with a more commercial flair.

Frontlist titles include: *Stillness, Daily Gifts of Solitude* by Richard Mahler; *Be Generous* by David Marell; *The Celestial Guide to Every Year of Your Life* by Z Budapest and Diana L. Paxson; *Gay Witchcraft* by Christopher Penczak; *The Office Sutras* by Maria Menter; *Will Work for Food or $* by Bruce Moody; *One God, Shared Hope* by Maggie Oman Shannon; *The Woman's Book of Courage* by Sue Patton Thoele; *Wonderful Ways to Love a Child* by Judy Ford (foreword by Amanda Ford); *The Naptime Book* by Cynthia MacGregor; *How to Get a Good Reading from a Psychic Medium* by Carole Lynne; *A Witch's Book of Answers* by Eileen Holland and Cerelia; *Heart Sense* by Paula M. Reeves, PhD; *The Celtic Book of Seasonal Meditations* by Claire Hamilton; *Sacred Beat* by Patricia Telesco and Don Two Eagles Waterhawk; *Tarot D' Amour* by Kooch Daniels and Victor Daniels; *The Power to Write* by Caroline Joy Adams; *Once and Future Myths* by Phil Cousineau; *Soul Mission Life Vision* by Alan Seale; *Single Female Pilgrim Seeks Spiritual Sustenance* by Suzanne Clores; *Safe Passage* by Molly Fumia; *A Way Forward* by Anna Viogt and Nevill Drury; *Spiritual Cleansing* by Draja Mickaharic; *Reality Works* by Chandra Alexander; *Intuition @ Work & at Home and Play* by James Wanless; *The Wise Earth Speaks to Your Spirit* by Janell Moon; *Beginner's Guide to Mediumship* by Larry Dreller; *Spirit Allies* by Christopher Penczak; *Gypsy Magic* by Patrinella Cooper; *Wiccan Wisdomkeepers* by Sally Griffyn; *Kitchen Witchery* by Marilyn Daniel; *The Virtual Pagan* by Lisa McSherry; *Everyday Tarot* by Gail Fairfield; *Tea Cup Reading* by Sasha Fenton.

Red Wheel/Weiser handles its own distribution and distributes selected titles from other houses; the Red/Wheel Weiser distribution catalog lists titles from more than 200 publishers.

Query letters with SASEs should be directed to:

Jan Johnson, Publisher

Robyn Heisey, Associate Publisher

REGNERY PUBLISHING, INC.

One Massachusetts Avenue, NW, Washington, DC 20001

202-216-0600/1-888-219-4747   fax: 202-216-0612

www.regnery.com   e-mail: editorial@regnery.com

Areas of Regnery publishing interest include contemporary politics, current events, public issues, biography, history, and alternative health; the house is open to projects with broad trade appeal by promotable authors with strong media CVs.

Regnery Publishing Inc. (formerly Regnery Gateway, founded in 1947) is a growing midsize house that produces primarily nonfiction projects in hardcover and quality paper editions. Regnery Gateway was acquired by Phillips Publishing International and is part of Phillips's Eagle Publishing subsidiary, which produces public-policy periodicals and operates the Conservative Book Club. A major accent of Regnery's program is to feature books that offer a Washington-insider purview. The house is also traditionally strong in paperbound reprints for the college market. Regnery Publishing supports a strong backlist. In 1997, Regnery launched LifeLine Press, which will concentrate on alternative health books.

For the past six years Regnery has released more bestsellers-per-title-published than any publisher in America, including, in 2002 four books on the *New York Times* bestseller list, including the nation's #1 bestseller. In a market that sees 50,000 or more new titles annually, Regnery is quite proud of its continued success considering they employ only 15 people and release, on average, 40 new books per year.

The Phillips corporate connection enables Regnery to promote titles through such venues as Phillips's Human Events newspaper and to take advantage of the parent company's expertise in direct-mail and special-market sales.

From the Regnery Publishing trade list: *When I Was a Kid, This Was a Free Country* by G. Gordon Liddy; *Good Enough to Be Great* by Josh Barr; *Breakdown* by Bill Gertz; *Fighting Back* by Bill Sammon; *Invasion* by Michelle Malkin; *Shooting Straight* by Wayne LaPierre and James Jay Bake; *Goodbye, Good Men* by Michael S. Rose; *Kill It and Grill It* by Ted and Shemane Nugent; *Shakedown: Exposing the Real Jesse Jackson* by Kenneth R. Timmerman; *What's So Great About America* by Dinesh D'Souza; *Bias* by Bernard Goldberg; *Life if Hard, Food is Easy* by Linda Spangle, R.N., M.A.; *Breaking the Rules of Aging* by David A. Lipschitz; *Gods, Guns, and Rock & Roll* by Ted Nugen.

Indicative of this house's heritage is founder Henry Regnery's choice of his publisher's mark—the gateway that serves as colophon for books published by Regnery. This gateway is a graphic representation of the Porta Nigra in Trier, Germany, a Roman gate constructed about A.D. 300, when Trier was a colonial capital city of the Roman Empire. As such, the gateway symbolizes the passage from barbarous realms into the world of civilization.

Regnery Publishing is distributed to the trade by National Book Network. Query letters and SASEs should be directed to:

Alfred S. Regnery, President

Harry Crocker, Executive Editor

RIZZOLI INTERNATIONAL PUBLICATIONS

300 Park Avenue South, New York, NY 10010-5399

212-982-2300

Rizzoli catalogs titles in fine arts, architecture, crafts, culinary arts, decorative arts, design, fashion, the home, gardens, landscaping, travel, and photography. Rizzoli also offers selected titles in sports and the performing arts.

The Rizzoli catalog offers titles from additional publishers in the arts and literary arena, including Angel City Press, Collectors' Press, Vendome, PBC International, Villegas Editores, Ipso Facto, and Merrell.

Rizzoli International (founded in 1976) is one of the exclusive set of cosmopolitan publishers renowned for finesse in the bookmaking craft. The house interest embraces artistic realms worldwide, throughout history as well as in the contemporary arena.

Rizzoli's consummately produced volumes feature graphics of the highest quality and are offered in hardback and trade paperback editions. (Please see entry for Universe Publishing.)

Titles from Rizzoli: *Fifth Avenue: The Best Address* by Jerry Patterson; *The Sensual Home* by Ilse Crawford (photographs by Martyn Thompson); *John Galliano: Romantic, Realist and Revolutionary* by Colin McDowell; *Architectural Glass Art: Form and Technique in Contemporary Glass* by Andrew Moor; *German Expressionism: Art and Society* by Stephanie Barron and Wolf-Dieter Dube; *East Meets West: Global Design for Contemporary Interiors* by Kelly Hoppen (photographs by Bill Batten); *Secret Gardens of Santa Fe* by Sydney LeBlanc (photographs by Charles Mann); *Living by Design: A Country House & Garden* by John Stefanidis (photographs by Fritz von der Schulenburg); *Diving: The World's Best Sites* by Jack Jackson.

PBC International titles: *New American Style* by Mike Strohl; *Kitchens: Lifestyle and Design* by James W. Krengel and Bernadette Baczynski; *Designing with Light: The Creative Touch* by Dr. Carol Soucek King, PhD; *Color: Details and Design* by Terry Trucco; *Magazines Inside and Out* by Steven Heller and Teresa Fernandes.

Rizzoli International Publications is distributed to the trade in the U. S. by St. Martin's Press; Canadian distribution is handled through McClelland & Stewart.

The house acquires new projects on an extremely selective basis. Query letters and SASEs should be directed to:

Isabel Venero, Editor—Art and general trade books

Liz Sullivan, Senior Editor—Art, culinary arts

David Morton, Senior Editor—Architecture

RODALE, INC.

400 South Tenth Street, Emmaus, PA 18098-0099

610-967-5171/1-800-813-6627

www.rodalepress.com

Rodale, Inc. (founded in 1932), specializes in books on the following topics: health and wellness; sports and fitness; gardening and organic lifestyles; home arts such as cooking, quilting, and sewing; practical spirituality and inspiration; self-improvement; and selected general interest titles. Rodale, Inc., publishes hardcover and trade paperback books and some video products.

Rodale publishes several award-winning magazines, including *Men's Health, Prevention, Organic Gardening, Runner's World, Bicycling,* and *Backpacker.*

Rodale published two *New York Times* bestsellers in *2000: Dr. Shapiro's Picture Perfect Weight Loss* by Dr. Howard Shapiro and *The Wrinkle Cure* by Dr. Nicholas Perricone.

Other recent books from Rodale include: *Find Love, Hope, and Joy in Everyday Life!* by Ardath Rodale; *Lose Weight the Smart Low-Carb Way* by Bettina Newman R.D., and Joachim David; *Joey Green's Magic Brands: 1,185 Brand-New Uses for Brand Name Products* by Joey Green; *The Testosterone Advantage Plan* by Lou Schuler; *Joey Green's Amazing Kitchen Cures* by Joey Green; *Rodale's Illustrated Encyclopedia of Organic Gardening* by Pauline Pears; *Ann Lovejoy's Organic Garden Design School* by Ann Lovejoy; *Try and Make Me* by Ray Levy, PhD, and Bill O'Hanlon, with Tyler Norris Goode; *The Immunity Pleasure Connection* by Carl Chametski, PhD, and Francis Brennan, PhD; *Run with the Champions* by Marc Bloom; *Another Shot* by Joe Kita; *The Green Pharmacy Anti-Aging Prescription* by Dr. James A. Duke; *The Joint Health Prescription* by James Rippe, MD

Rodale distributes books through multiple channels: direct mail, retail sales, book clubs, and so on. St. Martin's Press distributes Rodale titles to the book trade. Query letters and SASEs should be directed to:

Tami Booth, Vice President and Editor in Chief—Self-help, psychology, narrative nonfiction, women's health, health-related fiction

Ellen Phillips, Executive Editor—Home arts, tips, pets

Mary South, Deputy Editor—Narrative nonfiction, psychology, emotional and mental health, healing, sociology

Jeremy Katz, Editor—Men's Health

Margot Shupf, Editor—Organic Living

Anne Gaudinier, Senior Editor—Direct rights acquisitions for direct mail sales

Susan Berg, Editor—Senior health, herbal remedies, natural health, nutrition

Lou Cinquino, Senior Editor—Parenting, history

Mariska van Aalst, Associate Editor—Self-help, psychology, women's health issues, narrative nonfiction, health-related fiction

Karen Bolesta, Editor—Quilting, knitting

Kathy Everleth, Associate Editor—Cooking

Stepahie Tade, Executive Editor—Areas consistent with Rodale catalogue.

ROUTLEDGE (AN IMPRINT OF TAYLOR & FRANCIS BOOKS)

29 West 35th Street, New York, NY 10001-2299

212-216-7800   fax: 212-564-7854

www.routledge.com   e-mail: info@routledge.com

Routledge accents current events, communications, media, cultural studies, education, self-improvement, world political and cultural studies, philosophical thought, economics, feminist theory, gender studies, history, and literary criticism. The house produces trade nonfiction and academic works.

Routledge produces adult nonfiction in the humanities and social sciences. Routledge specialties include projects that give a vanguard twist to topical issues. Routledge imprints include Theatre Arts Books.

Founded in 1977 as Methuen Inc., and then as part of Routledge and Chapman and Hall (as a subsidiary of International Thompson Organization), the house held to the overall profile of a commercial publisher, abreast of trends in scholarship and general public interest, as it issued strong lines of trade and academic books. Routledge (with a concentration in the contemporary trade arena) is now separate from Chapman and Hall, which was purchased by Wolters-Kluwer Academic Publishers and has since been closed. Routledge is now an imprint of Taylor & Francis Books.

Routledge titles: *Journalism After September 11th* edited by Barbie Zelizer and Stuart Allan; *The Heart of War* by Gwyn Prins; *War of Words* by Sandra Silberstein; *Genes: A Philosophical Inquiry* by Gordon Graham; *War Without End* by Dilip Hiro; *The Complete Grimm's Fairy Tales* by Jacob and Wilhelm Grimm; *Stores and Tales* by Hans Christian Anderson; *Book of Nonsense* by Edward Lear; *British Folk Tales and Legends: A Sampler* by Katherine M. Briggs; *Hitler's Black Victims* by Jacob and Wilhelm Grimm; *India-Pakistan in War and Peace* by J.N. Dixit; *Israel's Wars: A History Since 1947* by Ahron Bergman; *The Open Society and its Enemies* by Karl Popper; *Emmeline Pankhurst* by June Purvis; *Striptease Culture: Sex, Media, and the Democratisation of Desire* by Brian McNair; *Alternative Approaches to Education: A Guide for Parents and Teachers* by Fiona Carnie; *The Almanac of British Politics* by Robert Waller and Byron Criddle; *Twin and Triplet Psychology: A Professional Guide to Working with Multiples* by Audrey Sandbank; *Punk Rock: So*

INDEPENDENT U.S. PRESSES

What? The Cultural Legacy of Punk Rock by Roger Sabin; *TV Living: Television Culture and Everyday Life* by David Gauntiett and Anneaen Hill; *The Atlantic* by Paul Butel; *101 Philosophy Problems* by Martin Cohen.

Query letters and SASEs should be directed to:

Linda Hollick, Vice President and Publisher

Bill Germano, Vice President and Publisher, Director—Humanities

Sylvia Miller, Publishing Director—Reference

Eric Nelson, Editor—Politics

Ilene Kalish, Senior Editor—Sociology, criminology and women's studies

Richard Carlin, Executive Editor—Music and dance

David McBride, Editor—Geography/urban studies

Damian Treffs, Editor—Religion

Karen A. Wolny, Publishing Director—Social sciences and history

Matthew Byrnie, Editor—Media, literary studies

George Zimmar, Executive Editor—Behavioral science

Emily Loeb, Associate Editor—Behavioral science

RUNNING PRESS BOOK PUBLISHERS

RUNNING PRESS BOOKS FOR CHILDREN

125 South 22nd Street, Philadelphia, PA 19103-4399

215-567-5080   fax: 215-568-2919

www.runningpress.com

Running Press is part of the Perseus Book Group.

Running Press shows flair in the areas of popular culture and arts, lifestyle, popular science, hobby how-to, and popular-interest reference titles. Running Press produces a singular line of specialty items that include bookstore-counter impulse-sale wares, striking free-standing exhibition units for kids' books, and a gleaming array of display and promotional titles (especially on the Courage Books imprint.)

Running Press Book Publishers (founded in 1972) publishes hardcover and paperback trade books in general nonfiction. The house, in addition, issues audiocassettes, stylized journals, diaries, bookplates, Miniature Editions, generously appointed educational-entertainment kits, and postcard books. Running Press products are associated with sleek production, as well as a sometimes humorous or insouciant air. Running Press maintains a solid backlist.

Sample Running Press titles: *46 Pages* by Scott Liell; *When Boston Won the World Series* by Bob Ryan; *The Game of Life* by Lou Harry; *The Relationship Tool Kit* by Ellen Sue Stern; *No More Mr. Nice Guy* by Robert A. Glover, Ph. D.; *Let's Talk About Sex* by Felicia Zopol; *The Cocktail Jungle* by Nicole Beland; *The Martini Companion* by Gary Ryan and Mardee Haidin Regan; *The Easy-Bake Oven* by David Hoffman; *The Ultimate Mixer Cookbook* by Rosemary Moon and Katie Bishop; *The Golf Voodoo Kit* by Michael Corcoran; *The Fortune Telling Handbook* by Dennis Fairchild; *The Joy of Knitting Companion* by Lisa R. Myers; *Strange Fruit* by David Margolick; *I Feel Great and You Will Too!* and *110%: 110 Stategies for Feeling Great Every Day!* by Pat Croce; *My Soul Has Grown Deep* by John Edgar Wideman; *Ceviche!* by Guillermo Pernot with Aliza Green; *Danny Boy* by Malachy McCourt; *On the Shoulders of Giants* by Stephen Hawking.

Running Press Miniature Edition books are delightful little books that fit in the palm of your hand; more than 32 million copies have been sold worldwide. The list covers an astonishing range of subjects: *7 Habits of Highly Effective People*; *9 Steps to Financial Freedom*; *Golf for Dummies*; *As a Man Thinketh* by James Allen; *An Alphabet of Animals* by Chistopher Wormell; *Yoga for Dummies* by George Feuerstein, Ph. D. and Larry Payne, Ph. D.; *Friends 4-Ever*; *Job Hunting for Dummies* by Robert Half and Max Messmer; *Aprons* by Joyce Cheney.

Running Press Miniature Editions has recently expanded to include book-plus-product kits. These latest palm-sized kits are fun and interactive, and they make great gifts! Titles include *The Serenity Kit*; *Wishing Stones*; *Mini Sunflower Garden*; *The Ornamental Grass Kit*; *The Art of the Love Letter*; *The Mini Bonsai Kit*; *The Mini Fondue Kit*; *The Mini Origami Kit*; *The Mini Voodoo Kit*; *The Sushi Box*.

Courage Books is the promotional imprint of Running Press, producing eye-catching volumes that can be advertised by booksellers as attractive, reasonably priced items. Sample Courage titles: *Big Book of Dinosaurs* by Robert Walters; *Christmas Treasury* by Christian Birmingham; *Log Home* by Nancy Mohr; *Complete Encyclopedia of Golf Techniques* edited by Paul Foston; *Indian* by Todd Rafferty; *Library of Classic Horror Stories*; *Fishing Essentials for Dummies* by Peter Kaminsky; *Grill It!* by Annette Yates; *Harley Davidson: The Ultimate Machine* by Tod Rafferty; *Tiger Woods: A Pictorial Biography* by Hank Gola; *Diana: The People's Princess* by Peter Donnelly; *Mother Teresa: The Pictorial Biography*; *Streisand: The Pictorial Biography* by Diana Karanikas Harvey and Jackson Harvey; *The Flowering of American Folk Art 1776–1876* by Joan Lipman and Alice Winchester; *Mothers: A Loving Celebration* (edited by Tara Ann McFadden, featuring excerpts from works by Mark Twain and Toni Morrison); *The Good Sex Book* by Dr. Paul Brown and Christine Kell.

Running Press participates in a joint publishing program with M. Shanken Communications, Inc., publishers of *Wine Spectator* and *Cigar Aficionado* magazines. Titles available: *California Wine: A Comprehensive Guide to the Wineries, Wines, Vintages and Vineyards of America's Premier Winegrowing State* by James Laube; *Ultimate Guide to Buying Wine*; *Guide to Great Wine Values $10 and Under*; *Buying Guide to Premium Cigars*.

Running Press distributes its own list. Direct query letters and SASEs to:

Jennifer Kasius, Editor, all areas consistent with stated house interests.

RUNNING PRESS BOOKS FOR CHILDREN

Running Press Books for Children features finely engineered pop-up books, foldouts, small-format editions, kits, coloring books, and how-tos—in stand-alone editions and numerous series.

Running Press created the Fit-a-Shape series (books for preschoolers that teach basic concepts using three-dimensional objects that fit matching shapes); the Gem series (captivating, fact-filled titles, each with vast amounts of information in a handy format); Five-Minute Mysteries (that test your powers of observation and deductive reasoning); Treasure Chests (expeditions into ancient cultures); Action Books (informative texts and components for exploring science and creating projects); Discovery Kits (read about a specific subject, such as a radio; then build your own); Book Buddy, created by Penny Dann (each title in this series features a die-cut corner where a soft-fabric Book Buddy lives); and Start Collecting (each title includes a guide that explains the history of the category, famous specimens, a poster, and tips on how to begin collecting).

SASQUATCH BOOKS

119 S. Main suite 400, Seattle, WA, 98104

206-467-4300/1-800-775-0817   fax: 206-467-4301

www.sasquatchbooks.com   e-mail: books@sasquatchbooks.com

Sasquatch specializes in books on travel, regional interest, gardening, guidebooks, nature, the outdoors, and food and wine. Sasquatch is broadening its Pacific Northwest regional concentration to include California. Additional areas of Sasquatch interest include literary nonfiction, especially in subject areas related to the house's core interests.

Sasquatch Books (founded in 1979) is known for a string of small-press successes. Among these: the Best Places travel series (Northwest Best Places; Northern California Best Places), the Cascadia Gardening series, and the Art Wolfe photo books.

Books from Sasquatch: *Plant Life* by Valerie Easton; *Making Gardens Works of Art* by Keeyla Meadows; *Bears of Alaska* by Erwin and Peggy Bauer; *Great Lodges of the National Parks: The Companion Book to the PBS Television Series* by Christine Barnes; *Pacific Grilling* by Denis Kelly; *The Northwest Essential Cookbook* by Greg Atkinson; *The Kingston Hotel Café Cookbook* by Judith Weinstock; *The Food Lover's Guide to Seattle* by Katy Calcott; *Northwest Berry Cookbook* by Kathleen Desmond Stang; *Cooking with Artisan Bread* by Gwenyth Bassetti and Jean Galton; *The Border in Bloom* by Ann Lovejoy; *The Year in Bloom* by Ann Lovejoy; *Winter Gardening* by Binda Colebrook.

Titles in the Best Places series: *Best Places Destinations Central California Coast* by Judith Babcock Wylie; *Best Places Destinations Marin* by Joanne Miller; *Best Places Inside*

Out Oregon: A Best Places Guide to the Outdoors by Terry Richard; *Northwest Budget Traveler: Cheap Eats, Cheap Sleeps, Affordable Adventure* (edited by Nancy Leson); *The Northwest Best Places Cookbook: Recipes from the Outstanding Restaurants and Inns of Washington, Oregon, and British Columbia* by Cynthia Nims and Lori McKean.

Sasquatch Books is distributed through a network of regional sales representatives. Jennie McDonald can be reached at Sasquatch Books, 1563 Solano Avenue, Box 364, Berkeley, CA, 94707.

Query with a SASE. No electronic queries or phone calls. Hard copy only. Respond in 3 months. Query letters and SASEs should be directed to: The Editors.

Suzanne De Glan, Senior Editor

Gary Luke, Editorial Director

SCHOLASTIC, INC.

ORCHARD BOOKS

555 Broadway, New York, NY 10012

212-343-6100

www.scholastic.com

Scholastic publishes quality hardcover picture books, middle-grade and young adult fiction, and some nonfiction.

The house publishes trade hardcover and also educational lines in hardcover and paperback editions, and owns a solid niche in electronic publishing. In addition, Scholastic Prep (founded in 1920), issues magazines, operates classroom book clubs, and offers computer software.

Scholastic's high-end hardcover imprints include Blue Sky Press, Scholastic Press, and Acedina Books. Cartwheel publishes boardbooks and novelties for pre-K.

Scholastic created the Literacy Place and Solares lines: These two core-curriculum reading and language-arts programs are for English and Spanish languages. Scholastic spent six years developing these programs because the publishers believe that teachers and children need and deserve a coherent plan of skills development (including phonics), better assessment, and, of course, the best children's literature.

Wiggleworks and Wiggleworks Español for grades K–2 (a complete early literacy system) are geared to raise reading scores. These programs use books and other educational technology that help emerging readers develop fluency, confidence, and control by reading, writing, listening, and speaking.

Solares is an innovative K–6 reading and language program in Spanish. Children read a wide variety of quality fiction that includes works originally written in Spanish, as well as classics translated from English and other languages. Solares provides a solid foundation for literacy through a program of explicit, intentional skills instruction that includes phonics.

Scholastic handles its own distribution.

FYI, here's the standard response "UNs" (Unagented/unsolicited writers) might encounter from Scholastic and other over-burdened presses.

Dear Writer,

Due to the overwhelming volume of submissions Scholastic Press receives, we regret that we are unable to accept any unsolicited manuscripts at this time. Scholastic Press considers only requested material or submissions from agented and/or previously published authors. Individual editors may also consider manuscripts from writers they meet at SCBWI conferences.

All solicited/requested submissions should by typed, double-spaced copies of your original work and accompanied by an SASE for return. Please allow 4–6 months for review.

Sincerely,

The Editors

> Picture book manuscripts, query letters, and SASEs should be directed to:
>
> **Liz Szabla**, Editorial Director
>
> **Dianne Hess**, Executive Editor
>
> **Tracy Mack**, Executive Editor
>
> **Lauren Thompson**, Senior Editor

ORCHARD BOOKS

557 Broadway, New York, NY 10012-3999

212-951-2649

Orchard Books produces mainstream trade children's fiction books, many of them illustrated works—and here again, award-winning titles and authors abound. Storybooks, boardbooks, novelty books, picture books, and middle grade and young adult novels are among areas of particular house emphasis.

Orchard emphasizes individual trade titles. Representative titles: *Clem's Chances* by S. Levitin; *Mouse in Love* by Kraus, Arvego, and Dewey; *Stepping Out with Grandma Mac* by Grimes and Angelo; *Flora's Blanket* by Glori; *One Monday* by A. Huntington; *Born in the Breezes* by Lasky and Krudoz; *Case Closed: The Real Scoop on Detective Work* by Meltzer.

Query letters and SASEs should be directed to:

Ken Geist, Vice President and Editorial Director

Amy Griffin, Senior Editor

SEAL PRESS

300 Queen Anne Avenue N. #375, Seattle, WA 98109

206-722-1838   fax: 206-285-9410

www.sealpress.com

Seal Press is dedicated to promoting the work of women writers. It is currently focusing its acquisitions in women's nonfiction titles (see the list that follows); in the past, it has published a wide range of fiction; poetry; and titles in women's studies, lesbian studies, sports, the outdoors, popular culture, parenting, self-help, and health.

Seal Press books enjoy a reputation for high literary quality, and the list often features finely designed, well-produced editions in hardcover and trade paperback. Seal Press supports a hardy backlist.

Founded in 1976, Seal is a smaller house that has leaped into its third decade of publishing with the same enthusiasm and mission that inspired the first book bearing the Seal name. More than 150 books later, the publishing business, as well as the cultural climate surrounding feminism, has changed considerably. Seal remains editorially agile and responsible to the industry's current challenges. Recent Seal books evidence the shifting signposts of feminism and an ever-expanding range of women's interests.

Seal is currently focusing its acquisitions in two successful series in its publishing program: the Adventura and Live Girls series. The Adventura line contains lively outdoor adventure and travel books; the Live Girls series features both fiction and nonfiction, with a focus on third-wave feminism concerns.

The Live Girls series was launched in 1995 with the publication of *Listen Up: Voices from the Next Feminist Generation* (edited by Barbara Findlen, and recently released in a new expanded edition). The series includes such recent titles as *Yentl's Revenge: The Next Wave of Jewish Feminism* (edited by Jill Corral and Lisa Miya-Jervis); *Breeder: Real Life Stories from the New Generation of Mothers* (edited by Ariel Gore and Bee Lavender); *Valencia* by Michelle Tea; *Cunt: A Declaration of Independence* by Inga Muscio. This line features edgy writing by young women who wield their own brands of modern feminism and apply their realities to an established, yet necessarily fluid, movement for social change.

Adventura Books is a series that captures women's outdoor and travel experiences with some of the finest writing of its kind. Adventura blazes a literary trail and encourages the spirit of adventure in every woman. Some Adventura series titles: *Dream of a Thousand Lives: A Sojourn in Thailand* by Karen Connelly; *Journey Across Tibet* by Sorrel Wilby; *A Woman Alone: Travel Tales from Around the Globe* (edited by Faith Conlon, Christina Henry de Tessan, and Ingrid Emerick); *The Unsavvy Traveler: Women's Comic Tales of Catastrophe* (edited by Rosemary Caperton, Anne Mathews, and Lucie Ocenas); *Girl in the Curl: A Century of Women in Surfing* by Andrea Gabbard; *Pilgrimage to India: A Woman Revisits Her Homeland* by Pramila Jayapal; *No Hurry to Get Home: The Memoir of the* New Yorker *Writer Whose Unconventional Life and Adventures Spanned the Twentieth*

Century by Emily Hahn.

For an up-to-date listing of Seal Press's current acquisitions focus and editorial needs, please see Seal Press's submission guidelines and calls for submissions at www.sealpress.com.

Seal Press is distributed to the trade by Publishers Group West. Query letters and SASEs should be directed to:

Faith Conlon, Publisher and Editor

Leslie Miller, Senior Editor

Anne Mathews, Managing Editor

SELF-COUNSEL PRESS

1704 North State Street, Bellingham, WA 98225

360-676-4530   fax: 360-676-4549

www.self-counsel.com   e-mail: orderdesk@self-counsel.com

Vancouver editorial office:

1481 Charlotte Road, North Vancouver, BC Canada V7J 1H1

604-986-3366

Self-Counsel was recently purchased by Entrepreneur Press. Self-Counsel produces business how-to, legal reference, self-help, and practical popular psychology. Topical areas include entrepreneurship, the legal system and you, business training, the family, and human resources development and management. The house also produces titles geared to lifestyles and business and legal issues in Florida, Oregon, and Washington.

Self-Counsel Press (founded in 1977) is a smaller house dedicated to providing well-researched, up-to-date books (primarily trade paperbacks), as well as cassettes and work kits. The company's trade motto is "Our business is helping business people succeed." Self-Counsel's expertly written books do not just tell people what to do; they show them—step by step—how to do it. Kick Start Guides is a lineup of pocket-size titles designed for business travelers. The Start and Run list shows how to start and run a number of different kinds of small-business ventures.

Self-Counsel books cover everything from business to finance, legal matters to family matters, in language that everyone can understand. Self-Counsel prides itself on delivering concise, easy-to-understand books and audio, offering the practical information you need, whether it is for helpful legal tips, succeeding in business, or personal self-help issues.

Self-Counsel also offers legal books covering national issues, as well as books that cover legal matters in Florida, Oregon, and Washington. Other topics include retirement, personal self-help, and lifestyles.

From Self-Counsel: *Tax This!* by Scott M. Estill; *Business Writing Basics* by Jane Watson; *What Your Lawyer Doesn't Want You to Know* by Douglas Eikermann; *Immigrating to the U.S.A.* by Dan P. Danilov; *Rightfully Yours* by Gary A. Shulman; *So You Wanna Buy a Car. . .Insider Tips for Saving Money and Your Sanity* by Bruce Fuller and Tony Whitney; *Start and Run a Profitable Mail-Order Business* by Robert W. Bly; *Start and Run a Profitable Tour Guiding Business* by Barbara Braidwood, Susan Boyce, and Richard Cropp; *First-Time Sales Rep: Sound Like a Pro, Act Like a Pro, Sell Like a Pro!* by Wayne Vanwyck.

Kick Start Guides is a series of handy pocket-sized guides developed for the business traveler. Each guide is written for a specific country and is designed to help readers kick-start themselves into action as soon as they arrive at their destination. The Guides are also helpful tools for entrepreneurs on the lookout for overseas business opportunities.

The Start and Run series offers step-by-step business plans and shows how to set up shop, sell products or services, hire employees, get financing, design marketing strategies, and identify legal considerations for a variety of different enterprises. The Start and Run Series includes titles keyed to bed-and-breakfast, the crafts business, freelance writing, secondhand bookstores, student-run businesses, and the gift-basket business.

Self-Counsel Press operates its own distribution services. Query letters and SASEs should be directed to:

Diana R. Douglas, President (Vancouver Office)

Ruth Wilson, Managing Editor (Vancouver Office)

SEVEN STORIES PRESS

140 Watts Street, New York, NY 10013

212-226-8760

www.sevenstories.com

Seven Stories publishes trade nonfiction, commercial literature, and popular reference works. The house's signature is a provocative edge in literature, current events, contemporary culture, biography, personality, memoirs, and inventive writing of all stripes (including classic reprints). In 2000, a Spanish-language imprint, Siete Cueulos Editorial, was founded.

Seven Stories Press was founded by publisher Dan Simon in 1996. Simon was previously cofounder (with John Oakes) of Four Walls Eight Windows (see separate entry). Seven Stories' publishing assets include backlist properties formerly catalogued by Four Walls.

Some titles from Seven Stories: *Radical Walking Tours of New York City* by Bruce

Kayton; *Against War with Iraq* by Jennie Green, Barbara Olshansky, and Michael Ratner; *Power and Terror* by Noam Chomsky; *Masters of War* by Clara Nieto; *Germs, Biological Warfare, Vaccinations* by James Feast and Dr. Gary Null; *The Few Things I Know About Glafkos Thrassakis* by Vassilis Vassilikos; *11 de Septiembre* by Noam Chomsky; *The Eden Express* by Mark Vonnegut; *The Solitude of Compassion* by Jean Giono; *Censored 2003* by Peter Phillips; *Ohio Angels* by Harriet Scott Chessman; *I Refuse to Die* by Koigi wa Wamwere; *Dead Heat* by Tom Athanasiou and Pail Baer; *Israel/ Palestine* by Tanya Reinhart; *Catfight* by Leora Tanenbaum; *Media Control* by Noam Chomsky; *Silencing Political Dissent* by Nancy Chang; *Urban Injustice* by Dr. David Hilfiker; *Exorcising Terror* by Ariel Dorfman; *Grand Central Winter: Stories from the Street* by Lee Stringer; *Nonconformity: Writing on Writing* by Nelson Algren; *Dark Alliance: The CIA, the Contras and the Crack Cocaine Explosion* by Gary Webb; *Profit Over People* by Noam Chomsky.

Distribution to the trade for Seven Stories is handled by Publishers Group West. Query letters and SASEs should be directed to:

Jill Schoolman, Associate Editor

M. E. SHARPE

80 Business Park Drive, Armonk, NY 10504

914-273-1800   fax: 914-273-2106

www.mesharpe.com

M. E. Sharpe publishes across the range of social and political sciences, including law, literature, area studies, women's studies, multicultural studies, business, comparative politics, and international and developmental economics. Special Sharpe focus is on Asian, Slavic, Eastern European, and Latin American studies, business (international and domestic), economics, political science, history, sociology, comparative public-policy analysis, and studies of the former Soviet Union.

M. E. Sharpe (founded in 1959) is a privately held company that produces trade books, reference books, scholarly and academic works, business books, and professional books in hardcover and paperback.

M. E. Sharpe has long been known for its area studies program covering Russia, Eastern Europe, and Asia. Expanding on that excellent publishing tradition, Sharpe has inaugurated programs in Latin American, American, African, and European studies, as well as related disciplines of comparative studies, women's studies, and literature, to provide a comprehensive understanding of today's world.

M. E. Sharpe chooses titles and authors that will define future debates about the political, economic, and social issues faced by various global regions and their peoples. Titles are selected by the editors to represent the most innovative and critical thinking in their respective disciplines.

Along with the primarily scholarly works, M. E. Sharpe publishes major single and multivolume reference works under the Sharpe Reference imprint; books aimed at the professional market are generally under the Sharpe Professional stamp.

The Sharpe list thus encompasses original research, policy studies, translations, reference compendiums, popular literature, classic reprints, and books that lend themselves to slots in the trade market. Sharpe started as a publisher of academic and professional journals and, by the late 1970s, had begun expansion into book publishing.

Books from Sharpe: *People's Lawyers: Crusaders for Justice in American History* by Diana Klebanow and Franklin Jonas; *The Vietnamese War: Revolution and Social Change in the Mekong Delta 1930-1975* by David Elliott; *The Infrastructure of Play: Building the Tourist City* by Denis R. Judd; *Biographical Dictionary of Chinese Women: The Twentieth Century, 1912-2000* by Lily Xiao Hong Lee; *Handbook of Workplace Spirituality and Organizational Performance* edited Robert A Giacalone and Carole L. Jurkiewick; *North Korea Handbook* edited by Yonhap News Agency, Seoul (Translated by: Monterey Interpretation and Translation Services, Heung-kook Park, President); *Computers, Visualization, and History: How New Technology Will Transform Our Understanding of the Past* by David J. Staley; *Explorations in Environmental Political Theory: Thinking About What We Value* edited by Joel J. Kassiola; *Public Broadcasting and the Public Interest* edited by Michael P. McCauley Eric E. Peterson, B. Lee Artz, and DeeDee Halleck; *Franklin D. Roosevelt and the Formation of the Modern World* edited by Thomas C. Howard and William D. Pederson; *Dictionary of the Political Thought of the People's Republic of China* by Henry Yuhuai He; *Elite Politics in Contemporary China* by Joseph Fewsmiht; *Eyewitness to Massacre: American Missionaries Bear Witness to Japanese Atrocities in Najing* by Editors Kaiyan Zhang and Martha Lund Smally; *The Negotiation Handbook* by Patrick J. Cleary.

It also highlights titles of the practical how-to variety on its Sharpe Professional list. Sharpe sells and promotes its titles both nationally and internationally; the house is a recognized industry leader in worldwide distribution. A large portion of Sharpe's sales comes from direct marketing; in addition, the house pursues a variety of means to sell its list, such as libraries, universities, trade and institutional bookstores, and catalogs.

M. E. Sharpe orchestrates its own distribution network, including stateside regional sales representatives, library-market specialists, and international wholesalers and reps. Query letters and SASEs should be directed to:

Patricia Loo, Editor—Asian studies

Patricia A. Kolb, Editorial Director—European and Russian studies, political science

Lynn Taylor, Executive Editor

Todd Hallman, Executive Editor—Sharpe Reference, cultural studies

Harry Briggs, Executive Editor—Management and public administration

SIERRA CLUB BOOKS

SIERRA CLUB BOOKS FOR CHILDREN

85 Second Street, San Francisco, CA 94105

415-977-5500   fax: 415-977- 5799

www.sierraclub.org/books

Sierra Club publishes works in the categories of nature, appropriate technology, outdoor activities, mountaineering, health, gardening, natural history, travel, and environmental issues. Sierra Club series include the Adventure Travel Guides, Sierra Club Totebooks, Naturalist's Guides, Natural Traveler, the John Muir Library, and Guides to the Natural Areas of the United States. Sierra Club Books has a strong division that publishes works geared to children and young adults (see subentry for Sierra Club Books for Children).

Membership in the Sierra Club, founded in 1892 by John Muir, has for more than a century stood in the forefront of the study and protection of the earth's scenic, environmental, and ecological resources; Sierra Club Books is part of the nonprofit effort the club carries on as a public trust. The house publishes hardcover and paperback books, many of them finely illustrated.

Sierra Club Books has the proud tradition of publishing books that are worldwide messengers for the Sierra Club mission: "To explore, enjoy and protect the wild places of the Earth; to practice and promote the responsible use of the Earth's ecosystems and resources; to educate and enlist humanity to protect and restore the quality of the natural and human environment; and to use all lawful means to carry out these objectives."

The books represent the following areas: the finest in outdoor photographic artistry; fervent and thought-provoking discussions of ecological issues; literary masterworks by the highest-caliber naturalist authors; authoritative handbooks to the best recreational activities the natural world can offer. Today, the need to protect and expand John Muir's legacy is greater than ever—to help stop the relentless abuse of irreplaceable wilderness lands, save endangered species, and protect the global environment.

On the Sierra Club list: *Downhill Slide* by Hal Clifford; *Beluga Café* by Jim Nollman; *Mother Earth* edited by Judith Boice; *The River Why* and *My Story as Told by Water: Confessions, Druidic Rants, Reflections, Bird-Watchings, Fish Stalkings, Visions, Song and Prayers Refracting Light from Living Rivers in the Age of the Industrial Dark* by David James Duncan; *Ancient Futures* by Helena Norberg-Hodge; *At the Cutting Edge- The Crisis in Canada's Forests* by Elizabeth May; *Breaking Gridlock* by Jim Motavalli; *Forward Drive: The Race to Build "Clean" Cars for the Future* by Jim Motavalli (foreword by Ed Begley, Jr.); *The Stations of Still Creek* by Barbara J. Scott.

Sierra Club Books are distributed to the book trade by University of California Press. Query letters and SASEs should be directed to:

Danny Moses, Editor-in-Chief—Nature writing; environmental issues; nonfiction literary works dealing with nature, environment, cultural anthropology, history, travel, and geography; fiction and poetry that are clearly related to natural or environmental themes

Linda Gunnarson, Senior Editor—Areas consistent with house list

SIERRA CLUB BOOKS FOR CHILDREN

Sierra Club Books for Children publishes primarily nonfiction, along with selected fiction keyed to subject areas that generally reflect the overall Sierra Club house emphasis.

Titles here: *Desert Giant: The World of the Saquaro Cactus* by Barbara Bash; *Tree of Life: The World of the African Baobab; And Then There Was One* by Margery Facklam; *Animals You Never Even Heard Of* by Patricia Curtis.

Desert Dog by Tony Johnston (full color paintings by Robert Wentherford); *The Waterfall's Gift* by Joanne Ryder (illustrated in full color by Richard Jesse Watson).

Sierra Club Books for Children are distributed to the trade by Gibbs Smith, Publisher.

We are currently not accepting proposals or manuscripts.

GIBBS SMITH, PUBLISHER

PO Box 667, Layton, UT 84041

801-544-9800   fax: 801-546-8853

www.gibbs-smith.com

Gibbs Smith publishes general trade nonfiction, including interior decorating, Western lifestyle, architecture, and nature. Gibbs Smith also produces a line of children's outdoor activity books and picture books. The house has a strong emphasis on home and health literature of the Western United States, including cowboy humor and poetry. The publisher's architecture program features a work on the classic Blacker House written by Randell Makinson.

The house produces books in fine hardcover and trade paper editions and offers distinctive lines of gift books keyed to the publisher's interest areas.

Gibbs Smith, Publisher (founded in 1969) is a house with a resourceful spirit. The company's mission statement: To enrich and inspire humankind. Gibbs Smith looks for new projects that contribute to and refresh this spirit. Gibbs Smith believes that the single most important quality for both writer and publisher is passion: with that come a sense of great purpose; an unusually heightened interest in the subject matter and in the task—whether it be writing or publishing. As Gibbs M. Smith writes: "It is a great privilege to work from our old barn office in the Rocky Mountains and have our books enter the literary bloodstream of the world."

High on the Gibbs Smith list: *The Lesson* by Carol Lynn Pearson (illustrated by Kathleen Peterson); *French by Design* by Betty Lou Phillips; *Camps and Cottages* by Molly Hyde English; *Bungalow Bathrooms* by Jane Powell.

Gibbs Smith publishes a seasonal-holiday sampler modeled on Moore's classic poem "'Twas the Night Before Christmas." Subjects include teachers, grandmas, grandpas, dads, cats, dogs, fishermen, and golfers in Texas, Chicago, Seattle, Florida, and California.

Sample titles: *Bob Wade's Cowgirls* by Bob Wade; *101 Things to Do With a Cake Mix* by Stephanie Dircks Ashcraft; *My Vacation Album* by Candice and Richard Elton (illustrated by Fran Lee); *Cool Chick's Guide to Baseball* by Lisa Martin; *Villa Décor* by Betty Lou Phillips; *American Grub* by Lynn Kuntz and Jan Fleming (illustrated by Mark A. Hicks); *Mexican Details* by Karen Witynski and Joe P. Carr; *Prefab* by Allison Arieff and Bryan Burkhart; *Riding on a Range: Western Activities for Kids* by G. Lawson Drinkard (illustrated by Fran Lee); *Blueprint Small: Creative Ways to Live With Less* by Michelle Kodis; *Cabin and Camps* by Ralph Kylloe; *Ordinary Mary's Extraordinary Deed* by Emily Pearson (illustrated by Fumi Kosaka); *Arts and Crafts* by W.G. Sutherland; *Consider the Butterfly: Your Life Through Meaningful Coincidence* by Carol Lynn Pearson; *Herd of Cows! Flock of Sheep!* By Rick Walton (illustrated by Julie Olson).

Of interest to children and family: *Bullfrog Pops!* by Rick Walton (illustrated by Chris McAllister); *Fishing in a Brook* by Lawson Drinkard (illustrated by Fran Lee); *Trekking on a Trail* by Linda White (illustrated by Fran Lee).

Gibbs Smith, Publisher, distributes its own list and utilizes a network of regional sales representatives. Query letters and SASEs should be directed to:

Madge Baird, V. P. Editorial—Interior design, Western, architecture

Suzanne Taylor, Senior Editor—Interior design, children's, gift books

Linda Nimori, Editor

Kathy Gurchiek, Associate Editor

Jennifer Adams, Children's Book Editor

SOHO PRESS

853 Broadway, New York, NY 10003

212-260-1900

www.sohopress.com

Soho publishes trade nonfiction and fiction. Nonfiction covers areas such as literary criticism, international affairs, and memoirs. This compact house is also distinguished for its formidable list of contemporary fiction (often with a literary bent), which includes mysteries and historical reprints. The Soho train of interest also verges into travel, autobiography, and the social sciences.

Soho Press (founded in 1986) publishes a superior roster of hardcover and softcover trade books. Many of the house's titles have achieved marked critical and commercial success, including Oprah winner and National Book Award nominee Edwidge Danticat, author of *The Farming of Bones* and *Breath, Eyes and Memory*.

Fiction and literary arts from Soho: *A Loyal Character Dancer* by Qiu Xiaolong; *Saturn's Return to New York* by Sara Gran; *Senseless* by Stona Fitch; *Lipstick and Other Stories* by Alex Kuo; *Egg Woman's Daughter* by Mary Chan Ma-lai; *Shanghai* by Christopher New; *Border Dogs* by Karen Palmer; *Riding a Tiger* by Robert Abel; *Patrol to the Golden Horn* by Alexander Fullerton; *The Blooding of the Guns* by Alexander Fullerton; *The Officer's Ward* by Marc Dugain; *Tokyo, City on the Edge* by T. Crowell and S.F. Morimura; *Latitudes of Melt* by Joan Clark; *The Chinese Box* by Chistopher New; *Cheung Chau Dog Fanciers' Society* by Alan B. Pierce; *Grace* by Eleanor McCallie Cooper and William Liu; *Gloria* by Keith Maillard; *The Gravity of Sunlight* by Rosa Shand; *Death of a Red Heroine* by Qiu Xialong; *The Sixteen Pleasures* by Robert Hellenga; *The Twins* by Tessa De Loo; *Adrian Mole: The Cappuccino Years* by Sue Townsend.

Soho mysteries: *The Amsterdam Cops* by Janwillem van de Wetering; *The Vault and The Reaper* by Peter Lovesey; *The Tattoo Murder Case* by Akimitsu Takagi (translated by Deborah Boehm); *The Whispering Wall* and *The Souvenir* by Patricia Carlon.

Crime books: *Some Bitter Taste* by Magdalen Nabb; *Property of Blood* by Magdalen Nabb; *The Reaper* by Peter Lovesey; *Detective Inspector Huss* by Helen Tursten; *Death of a Nationalist* by Rebecca Pawel.

The Hera Series presents reprints of historical fiction that feature strong female characters. Hera series titles: *Lady of the Reeds* by Pauline Gedge; *Stealing Heaven: The Love Story of Heloise and Abelard* by Marion Meade.

Soho Press books are distributed to the trade by Farrar, Straus & Giroux. Query letters and SASEs should be directed to:

Juris Jurjevics, Publisher

Laura Hruska, Associate Publisher

SOURCEBOOKS, INC.

SOURCEBOOKS CASABLANCA

SOURCEBOOKS HYSTERIA

SOURCEBOOKS LANDMARK

SOURCEBOOKS MEDIA FUSION

SPHINX PUBLISHING

Illinois office:

1935 Brookdale Road, Suite 139, Naperville, IL 60563

1-800-43-BRIGHT   fax: 630-961-2168

Connecticut office:

955 Connecticut Avenue, #5310, Bridgeport, CT 06607

203-333-9399   fax: 203-367-7188

New York Office:

101 Fifth Avenue, 11th Floor, New York, NY 10003

212-414-1701

www.sourcebooks.com   e-mail: info@sourcebooks.com

Founded in 1987, Sourcebooks's mission is to reach as many people as possible with books that will enlighten their lives. In 2000, Sourcebooks was named one of the fastest-growing private companies by *Inc.* magazine in its Inc. 500 list. Sourcebooks is the only publisher on this year's list. Sourcebooks also won the 2000 Blue Chip Enterprise Award.

Sourcebooks has strong distribution into the retail market—bookstores, gift shops, and specialty stores whose primary product is something other than books—and provides tremendous editorial, sales, marketing, and publicity support for its authors. The house follows a somewhat out-of-date model for book publishing that makes its passion for books central. In short, Sourcebooks believes in authorship. The house works with authors to develop great books that find and inspire a wide audience. Sourcebooks believes in helping to develop authors' careers and recognizes that a well-published, successful book is often a cornerstone. The company seeks authors who are as committed to success as it is.

Its fiction imprint, Sourcebooks Landmark, publishes a variety of titles. It is interested first and foremost in books that have a story to tell. Sourcebooks is currently reviewing only agented fiction manuscripts.

For nonfiction, Sourcebooks is interested in books that will establish a unique standard in their area. The house looks for books with a well-defined, strong target market.

Its publishing list includes most nonfiction categories, such as entertainment, sports, general self-help, psychology, business (particularly small business, marketing, and management), parenting, health and beauty, reference, biographies, gift books, and women's issues.

Recent titles: *101 Things Every Kid Should Do Growing Up* by Alecia T. Devantier; *The Sunny Day Rainy Day Book of Family Fun* by Silvana Clark; *365 Games Babies Play* by Sheila Eillison; *An American Summer* by Frank Deford; *What Successful People Know about Conflict Resolution* by Timothy E. Ursiny, PhD; *The Entrepreneur's Legal Guide* by Paul H. Cooksey; *Gay & Lesbian Rights* by Brette McWhorter; *Homeowner's Rights* by Mark Warda; *How to Buy Your First Home* by Diana Brodman Summers; *The Kingfisher's Call* by John Reed; *The Last Boy* by Robert H. Lieberman; *Natural Weight Loss* by Lewis Harrison; *The Money Dragon* by Pam Chun; *Profit from Intellectual Property* by James L. Rogers; *Protect Your Patent* by James L. Rogers; *Soft Sell* by Tim Connor; *Traveler's Rights* by Alexander Anolik.

Sourcebooks is not currently publishing children's books, but it does keep an active list of artists and illustrators.

Please direct query letters with SASEs to Sourcebooks, Editorial Submissions, PO Box 4410, Naperville, IL 60567-4410:

Hillel Black, (NY) Executive Editor—Commercial and literary fiction, thrillers, suspense, love stories, historical fiction, and mysteries; in nonfiction, history, biography, autobiography, science, medicine, relationship books

Deborah Werksman, (CT) Editorial Manager —Gift books, innovative formats, humor, love, dating, relationships, wedding books, self-help, women's interest, parenting, gift books

Peter Lynch, Editor, Popular reference, business, general non-fiction consistent with house list

Todd Stocke, Editor, Mixed-media (books combined with audio, video or disk products)

Dianne Wheeler, (IL)—Division Manager of Sphinx Publishing; titles that cover legal topics to interest the lay customer

STACKPOLE BOOKS

5067 Ritter Road, Mechanicsburg, PA 17055-6921

1-800-732-3669   fax: 717-796-0412

Stackpole specializes in nature and the outdoors, crafts and hobbies, fly fishing, sporting literature, history (especially military history), military reference, and works geared to the Pennsylvania region.

Stackpole Books publishes editions that are created lovingly, with striking design. When selecting projects to produce, the publisher determines what readers need and how these needs will be met through a proposed project's fresh perspective. Stackpole signs expert authors, juggles production schedules, and commits the personalized verve to make the dream real. Stackpole believes in perfectionism and care—when focused upon the practical—as keys to successful publishing.

Stackpole Books was established in 1933 as Stackpole & Sons, a small family-owned publishing enterprise. The house acquired the Military Service Publishing Company in 1935 and has continued to grow into additional publishing areas, while remaining attuned to its original publishing vision.

On the Stackpole list: *Arnhem* by Robert Jackson; *Biography of a Battalion* by James A. Huston; *Bombers Over Berlin* by Alan W. Cooper; *Combat Legend: A6M Zero* by Robert Jackson; *Combat Legend: De Havilland Mosquito* by Robert Jackson; *Fighting the Bombers* edited by David C. Isby; *Guderian* by Kenneth Macksey; *Cold War Hot* edited by Peter G. Tsouras; *Combat Legend: F-117 Nighthawk* by Paul Crickmore; *The Conquest of the Missouri* by Joseph Mills Hanson (introduction by Paul Hedren); *Emergency* by Stanley Stewart; *The 24th Wisconsin Infantry in the Civil War* by William J. K. Beaudot; *Annals of the Army of the Cumberland* by John Fitch; *Debris of Battle* by Gerard A. Patterson; *The Teutonic Knights* by William Urban; *Vital Guide: Abbey Ruins of Medieval England and Wales* by Gunter Endres and Graham Hobster; *Vital Guide: Ancient Crete* by Diane Canwell; *Adventures with the Connaught Rangers 1809-1814* by William Grattan; *Charge!* by Digby Smith; *Imperial Glory* edited by David Markham; *The Nelson Encyclopedia* by Colin White; *Wellington Invades France* by Ian Robertson; *Guide to Military Installations, 6th Edition* by Dan Cragg; *Swamp Doctor: The Diary of a Union Surgeon in the Virginia and North Carolina Marshes* by Thomas Lowry; *A Good Horse Has No Color: Searching Iceland for the Perfect Horse* by Nancy Marie Brown; *The Guide and the CEO* by M. David Detweiler; *Real Alaska: Finding Our Way in the Wild Country* by Paul Schullery; *The Half Not Told: The Civil War in a Frontier Town* by Preston Filbert.

From the Who's Who in British History series: *Who's Who in Tudor England, 1485–1603, Volume 1* by C. R. N. Routh; *Who's Who in Victorian Britain, 1851–1901, Volume 1* by Roger Ellis; *Who's Who in Early Medieval England* by Christopher Tyermand; *Who's Who in Late Medieval England* by Michael Hicks.

From the Pennsylvania Trail of History Guides: *Erie Maritime Museum and U.S. Brig Niagara; Brandywine Battlefield; Pennsbury Manor; Conrad Weiser Homestead; Hope Lodge; Mather Mill.*

Exploring the Appalachian Trail series titles: *Hikes in Northern New England* by Michael Kodas, Andrew Weegar, Mark Condon, and Glenn Scherer; *Hikes in Southern New England* by David Emblidge; *Hikes in the Mid-Atlantic States* by Glenn Scherer and Don Hopes; *Hikes in the Virginias* by David Lillard and Gwyn Hicks; *Hikes in the Southern Appalachians* by Doris Gove.

Stackpole distributes its own books, as well as a list of titles from U.K. and U.S. publishers. Query letters and SASEs should be directed to:

Col. Ed Skender (Ret.), Editor—Military reference

Judith Schnell, Editorial Director—Outdoor sports; fly fishing

Kyle Weaver, Editor—Pennsylvania

Chris Evans, Editor—History

Mark Allison, Editor—Nature
Born: 1964.
Education: B.A., English, Penn State University.
Employment history/editor career path: Started as an Editorial Assistant at Stackpole after working as a writer and proofreader.
Personal interests: Photography; reading books out of my line.

What books have you acquired that make you the most proud? What books that you have acquired reflect the types of books you like to represent? Books with a long shelf life. We want to keep an author's work in print forever.

Do you represent fiction? No.

What do you want to see less of? Imitations of successful titles, Harvey's Penick's *Little Red Book*-style treatments for subjects other than golf.

Do you represent nonfiction? Yes, exclusively.

Do you require book proposals? If so, what do you look for in evaluating a book proposal? I require a proposal or a sample chapter with a cover letter, no magic formula. I look for demonstrated expertise in the subject matter, demonstrated skill as a writer, and evidence of commitment to the project.

Are certain aspects of a book proposal given more weight than others? The writing itself and the description of what the book is all about—which must be well thought out, exact, and clearly presented.

What process do you use for making a decision? What is the process for acquisition, is there a committee? (1) Investigation and research by the editor. (2) Input from sales and marketing. (3) Review and discussion by the editorial board.

What kinds of nonfiction books do you want to see less of? Books that are heavy on design and photography/art, but skimpy on content.

Are you interested in work geared for the masses (readers of *People, The Star*, etc.)? Our readers usually have a keen interest in the activities or subject matter our lines cover: birding, fly fishing, Civil War history, and so on.

Are agents important? Why? We usually deal directly with authors, but have good working relationships with a few agents who know our lines. We sometimes get proposals from agents that are so far out of our lines that I wonder what purpose they are serving.

Do you like new writers? What should new writers do to break into the business? We publish a number of new writers, who should establish their expertise and perhaps an audience by writing for magazines and newspapers before tackling a book.

How should writers approach you? Query and proposal or query and sample chapter are the best ways. I personally don't like e-mail queries.

What are some common mistakes writers make? What really gets on your nerves? Focus on design and presentation of the book, instead of on the content.

What can writers do to get your attention and to avoid the slush pile? Straight-

INDEPENDENT U.S. PRESSES

forward presentation of the project in our line, author expertise.

What have been some of your craziest experiences with submissions? A querying author once refused to reveal the subject matter of his "top secret" project until a contract was signed.

Any advice for writers? Try to stay enthusiastic and realistic and remember that the author and publisher should be working toward the same goal.

STERLING PUBLISHING COMPANY

387 Park Avenue South, New York, NY 10016-8810

212-532-7160

www.sterlingpub.com   e-mail: info@sterlingweb.com

Sterling Publishing was recently purchased by the book chain conglomerate Barnes & Noble. This is significant as is the first time a major bookstore chain has purchased an actual book publisher.

Sterling emphasizes general popular reference and information books, science, nature, arts and crafts, architecture, home improvement, history, humor, health, self-help, wine and food, gardening, business and careers, social sciences, sports, pets, hobbies, drama and music, psychology, occult, New Age, and military-science books. Sterling also publishes games, puzzles, and children's books.

The current scope of the Sterling Publishing Company program includes a wide range of nonfiction practical approaches, including informative how-to books in gardening, crafts, and woodworking; books on military history; art and reference titles; and activity and puzzle books for the kids. The house (founded in 1949) hosts a formidable backlist.

Representative Sterling titles: *10 Minute Decorating* by Susan Ure; *The 12-Month Gardener* by Jeff Ashton; *90 Days To Stress-Free Living* by C. Shealy; *Above All, Courage* by Max Arthur; *African Visions* by Mirella Ricciardi; *The American Civil War* and *The Wars of the Nineteenth Century* by Brian Reid and John Keegan; *Ancient Trees* by Anna Lewington and Edward Parker; *Arrival of the Gods* by Erich van Daniken; *The Art of Bonsai Design* by Colin Lewis; *The Art of Rowena* by Doris Vallejo; *The Art of War* by Martin van Crevald and John Keegan; *Ashtanga Yoga* by Vickie Willis; *The Astrological History of the World* by Marjorie Orr; *Ballroom Dancing* by Paul Bottomer; *Baseball* by Alan Smith and Alan Bloomfield; *The Beaded Home* by Katherine Aimone; *A Beginners Guide to Digital Photography* by Adrian Davies; *The Beginner's Guide Human Anatomy* by James Horton; *Bookbinding Basics* by Paola Rosati; *Building Great Sheds* by Danielle Truscott; *By Hand* by Janice Kilby; *Capture the Moment* by Stephen Swain; *Christmas Past and Presents* by Christine Austin; *Classic Joints with Powder* by Yeung Chan; *Gemstones of the World* by Walter Schumann; *Romantic Massage* by R. J. Nikola, L.M.T.; *Zen Wisdom:*

Daily Teaching from the Zen Masters by Timothy Freke; *The Truth About Alien Abductions* by Peter Hough and Moyshe Kalman; *The Mystic Grail: The Magical World of the Arthurian Quest* by John Matthew.

On the Sterling children's book list: *Animal Snuggles: Cozy Kitten* by Shaheen Bilgrami and Emma Lake; *Asterix and the Actress* by Albert Uderzo; *Baseball* by Alan Smith and Alan Bloomfield; *Beginning Wrestling* by Bruce Curtis; *Brain Games For Babies, Toddlers, and Twos* by Jackie Silberg; *Brainstrains: Clever Logic Puzzles* by Norman Willis; *Cars & Trucks Dot-To-Dot* by Evan Kimble and Lael Kimble; *Cartooning For Kids* by Mike Artell; *Science Crafts for Kids: 50 Fantastic Things to Invent & Create* and *Nature Crafts for Kids: 50 Fantastic Things to Make with Mother Nature's Help* by Gwen Diehn and Terry Krautwurst; *The Great Rubber Stamp Book: Designing, Making, Using* by Dee Gruenig; *Cat Crafts: More Than 50 Purrfect Projects* by Dawn Cusick; *Dog Crafts: More Than 50 Grrreat Projects* by Bobbe Needham.

Query letters and SASEs should be directed to:

Steve Magnuson, Acquisitions Editor

STEWART, TABORI & CHANG

115 West 18th Street, New York, NY 10111

212-519-1200   fax: 212-519-1230

Stewart, Tabori, & Chang publishes luxuriously produced titles about love, food, spirituality, divination, history, comic art, music, and Christmas. The house offers top-notch specialty merchandise such as calendars, cards, journals, and engagement books. Terrail is an imprint in collaboration with Editions Terrail that publishes a line of art books at reasonable prices. The Essential Gardens library is a line accenting a wide range of topical-interest editions. The publisher offers a solid list of new seasonal titles and supports an impeccably select backlist.

Stewart, Tabori & Chang books are produced in hardcover and trade paperback editions. Booksellers especially appreciate the quality product signified by the publisher's prancing-bison trade logo—these books on display in a bookstore can draw significant point-of-purchase interest from customers. The house trade motto: "The heart and soul of illustrated books."

Stewart, Tabori & Chang (founded in 1981 by Andy Stewart, Lena Tabori, and Nai Chang), recently part of the publishing stable of Peter Brant (owner of the magazines *Interview, Art in America,* and *Antiques*), is now a division of U.S. Media Holdings, Inc.

From Stewart, Tabori & Chang: *The All American Cheese and Wine Book* by Laura Werlin (photographs by Andy Ryan); *Grilling & Barbecuing* by Denis Kelly (photographs by Maren Caruso); *The Fine Art of Advertising* by Barry Hoffman; *The Cottage Book* by Carol Bass (photographs by Dennis Welsh); *Pickled* by Lucy Norris (photographs by Elizabeth Watt); *How to Photograph Your Life* by Nick Kelsh; *Perfect Feet* by Dr. Stuart Mogul with Jacqueline DeMontravel (photographs by Ericka McConnell); *Lightweights* by Sharon Montrose; *Simply Dog* and *Simply She* by Maria Peevey and Megan Weinerman; *The Secrets of Pistoulet* by Jana Kolpen (designed by Mary Tiegreen); *From My Grandmother's Kitchen* by Charlotte de Saint Alban; *Everything for Baby* by Adelaide D'andigne (photographs by Alain Gelberger); *Giuliano Bugialli's Food of Naples* by Giuliano Bugialli (photographs by Andy Ryan); *Collecting African American History* by Elvin Montgomery; *I Dream a World* by Brian Lanker; *Life Doesn't Frighten Me* by Maya Angelou (paintings by Jean-Michel Basquiat); *Mary Cassatt* by Debra N. Mancoff; *Paintings in the Louvre* by Sir Lawrence Gowing; *Healthy 1-2-3* by Rozanne Gold (photographs by Anita Calero); *The Glory of Roses* by Allen Lacy (photographs by Christopher Baker); *Colors of Provence* by Michel Bicha (photographs by Heinz Angermayr); *Quick Cooking with Pacific Flavors* by Hugh Carpenter and Teri Sandison; *Goddess: A Celebration in Art and Literature* (edited by Jalaja Bonheim); *Little Moments of Happiness* by Elisabeth Brami and Philippe Bertrand; *Greece: The Dawn of the Western World* by Furio Durando.

The Essential Garden Library series encompasses gardening titles covering a variety of subjects and formats. Each book in the series features Stewart, Tabori & Chang quality in writing, photography, and production. Numbered chronologically, these books are uniform in height and width to stand next to one another in the reader's garden library. Some titles: *Herbs* by George Carter (photographs by Marianne Marjerus); *Getting Ready for Winter and Other Fall Tasks* by Stephen Bradley.

Stewart, Tabori & Chang distributes to the trade via Publishers Resources; in addition, the house uses a network of independent regional sales representatives. Query letters and SASEs should be directed to:

Alexandra Childs, Assistant Editor

Linda Sunshine, Editorial Director

Mary Kalamaras, Editor

SYBEX, INC.

1151 Marina Village Parkway, Alameda, CA 94501

510-523-6840   fax: 510-523-1766

www.sybex.com   e-mail: info@sybex.com

Sybex was founded in 1976 and is the oldest publisher of computer books, as well as the largest independent computer book publisher. Sybex also publishes a wide range of computer-based training and Web-based training products. It publishes trade computer books for all levels and all types of users. Sybex offers high-quality tutorials and references in all main software areas, including certification, programming, graphics, business applications, operating systems, and games. The company has wide distribution in all major retail bookstores, mass-market outlets, and warehouse clubs and enjoys superior worldwide distribution.

The Sybex catalog features certification titles for technical professionals; the Mastering series for beginning, intermediate, and advanced users; *Strategies and Secrets* for gamers; *I Didn't Know You Could Do That!* for intermediate users; *Complete* for beginning to intermediate users; *Developer's Guides* for professional programmers and developers; and *Jumpstart* and *Visual Jumpstart* for beginners.

Recent titles: *Mastering Lotus Notes* and *Domino 6* by Scot Haberman, Andrew Falciani, Matt Riggsby, and Cate McCoy; *ColdFusion MX Developer's Handbook* by Raymond Camden and Arman Danesh; *CCSA NG: Check Point Certified Security Administrator Study Guide* by Justin Menga; *Maya 4.5 Savvy* by John Kundert-Gibbs, Peter Lee, Dariush Derakhshani, Mark Bamforth, Keith Reicher, Perry Harovas; *The Art of Maya* by Alias Wavefront; *Impossible Creatures: Sybex Official Strategies & Secrets* by Doug Radcliffe and Dan Irish; *The Hidden Power of Photoshop Elements 2* by Richard Lynch; *Visual Basics.NET Developers Handbook* by Evangelos Petroutsos, Mark Ridgeway; *Maya Character Animation* by Jae-jin Choi; *Mastering Microsoft Project 2002* by Gini Courter, Annette Marquis, and Michael Miller; *Photoshop 7 Learning Studio* by Steve Romaniello; *Flash MX Learning Studio* by Ethan Waltrall; *PC Disaster and Recovery* by Kate J. Chase; *Digital Video Essentials: Shoot, Transfer, Edit, Share* by Erica Sadun.

Bestsellers include *CCNA Study Guide* by Todd Lammle; *Mastering Windows 2000 Server, 3rd edition*, and *The Complete PC Upgrade and Maintenance Guide, 11th Edition* by Mark Mianasi; *MCSE Window 2000 Core Requirements Study Guides* by James Chellis and other authors; *Pokemon Gold and Silver Pathways to Adventure* by Jason Rich.

Sybex handles its own distribution. Query letters and SASEs should be directed to:

Jordan Gold, Vice President and Publisher—He will direct you to the appropriate associate publisher and acquisitions editor who is responsible for the particular product or topic area; any book or series idea may be directed to his attention. He will also help you in any publishing-related matter.

THE TAUNTON PRESS

63 South Main Street, PO Box 5506, Newtown, CT 06470-5506

203-426-8171   fax: 203-426-3434

www.taunton.com

The Taunton Press is known for its high-quality, authentic books and magazines. For more than 20 years, it has published leading magazines, such as *Fine Woodworking* and *Fine Gardening*. Taunton started out publishing woodworking books, but then grew to include fiber arts, home design, building and remodeling, gardening, and cooking. Taunton is a small publishing company, but has a strong market reach through its parent company, Publisher's Group West. Taunton currently publishes 35–40 frontlist titles each year, with an active backlist of more than 250 books.

Recent titles: *The Distinctive Home* by Jeremiah Eck; Slipcase Set: *The Not So Big House Collection* by Sarah Susanka; *Not So Big Solutions for Your Home* by Sarah Susanka; *Updating Classic America: Bungalows* by M. Caren Connolly and Louis Wasserman; *Taunton's Home Workspace Idea Book* by Neal Zimmerman; *Patterns of Home* by Murray Silverstein, Max Jacobson, and Barbara Winslow; *Children's Furniture Projects* by Jeff Miller; *Building Fireplace Mantels* by Mario Rodriguez; *Roofing with Asphalt Shingles* by Mike Guertin; *Taunton's Lawn Guide* by John Fech.

Query letters and SASEs should be directed to:

Jim Childs, Publisher

TEN SPEED PRESS/CELESTIAL ARTS

CELESTIAL ARTS

TRICYCLE PRESS

PO Box 7123, Berkeley, CA 94707

510-559-1600/1-800-841-2665   fax: 510-524-1052

www.tenspeed.com

Ten Speed/Celestial Arts publishes practical nonfiction in cooking, business, careers, women's issues, parenting, health, self-discovery, leisure and lifestyle, humor, outdoors, house crafts, and popular reference. Tricycle Press (see subentry) is Ten Speed/Celestial's children's division. Ten Speed Press/Celestial Arts publishes hardcover and paperback titles; the house also produces a line of posters and novelty items.

Ten Speed Press (founded in 1971) gained success with *Anybody's Bike Book* by Tom Cuthbertson—the first book the publisher produced. This classic work has been revised and updated several times and is emblematic of the type of reference book that Ten Speed Press publishes so well. With the acquisition of the Celestial Arts subsidiary (see subentry), the house obtained the midsize status that set the platform for subsequent expansion of the list. Throughout this growth, Ten Speed has been renowned for its small press publishing savvy.

Ten Speed/Celestial is selective in acquiring new works and procures in part on the basis of projected endurance: The hardy backlist and announcements of revised editions read as fresh and bright as many houses' new releases.

Ten Speed is noted for the individualist expression of the American culture as voiced by the house's authors. Many Ten Speed titles feature unconventional approaches to the subject matter at hand—making creativity an enduring Ten Speed/Celestial Arts hallmark. Among its perennial sellers, Ten Speed publishes *What Color Is Your Parachute?* and other career-related works by Richard Bolles; *The Moosewood Cookbook* by Mollie Katzen; and *How to Shit in the Woods* by Kathleen Meyer.

Ten Speed titles: *Afghanistan* by Vladislav Tamarov; *African Kings* by Daniel Lane; *Cabernet* by Charles O'Rear; *Creaking Creativity* by Michael Michalko; *Manipulative Memos* by Arthur D. Rosenburg and Ellen Thorn Fuchs; *Negotiating Your Salary* by Jack Chapman; *The Small Investor* by Jim Gard; *Common Sense Supervision* by Roger Fulton; *Song of the Meadowlark* by James Eggert; *The 50-Mile Rule* by Judith Brandt; *Elvgren: His Life and Art* by Max Allan Collins and Drake Elvgren; *How Wal-Mart Is Destroying America (and the World)* by Bill Quinn; *Allergy-Free Gardening* by Thomas L. Ogren; *Eating to Save the Earth* by Ken Jacobsen and Linda Riebel, Ph. D.; *Energy Exercises* by Emma Mitchell; *Hit Below the Belt* by F. Ralph Berberich; *Sleep Disorders* by Herbert Ross, D.Ac., and Keri Brenner, L.Ac., with Burton Goldberg; *Abby and Her Sisters* by Melanie Bellah; *A Marriage Made in Heaven* by Vatsala Sperling and Ehud Sperling; *The Moonlight Chronicles* by Dan Price; *Journal to the Soul for Teenagers* by Rose Offner; *Protect This Girl* by Zoe Stern; *Surviving High School* by Michael Riera, PhD; *The Teen Spell Book* by Jamie Wood; *Be Your Own Literary Agent* by Martin P. Levin; *The History of Mystery* by Max Allan Collins.

Ten Speed Press/Celestial Arts handles its own distribution. Query letters and SASEs should be directed to:

Kirsty Melville, Publisher

Lorena Jones, Editorial Director

CELESTIAL ARTS

The Celestial Arts program homes toward titles in self-discovery, nutrition, fitness, general health, spirituality, popular psychology, relationships, healing, pregnancy, parenting, gay and lesbian issues, practical how-to, kitchen arts, and general trade nonfiction.

Celestial Arts was founded as an independent house in 1966 and was acquired by Ten Speed Press in 1983. The house produces an individual line of hardcover and trade paperback books, along with calendars, maps, poster art, personal journals, and engagement books.

On the Celestial Arts roster: *Bestfeeding* by Mary Renfrew, Chloe Fisher, and Suzanne Arms; *Living Juicy* by Sark; *Uncommon Sense for Parents with Teenagers* by Mike Riera; *Natural Superwoman* by Rosamon Richardson; *Hit Below the Belt: Facing Up to Prostate Cancer* by F. Ralph Berberich, MD; *Natural Alternatives to HRT Cookbook* by Marilyn Glenville; *Positively Gay* (edited by Betty Berzon, PhD); *The Detox Diet* by Elson M. Haas, MD

Celestial Arts is distributed by Ten Speed Press/Celestial Arts. Query letters and SASEs should be directed to:

Jo Ann Deck, Publisher

TRICYCLE PRESS

Tricycle is devoted to books and posters for kids and their grown-ups. Tricycle Press was started in 1993 to unify and expand the house's children's list (previously divided between parent Ten Speed and sister Celestial Arts). Tricycle Press, in addition to its own roster of originals, catalogs appropriate backlist selections from Ten Speed and Celestial Arts.

Tricycle is committed to publishing projects that reflect the creative spirit of the parent company, Ten Speed Press, and its publishing partner, Celestial Arts.

Titles from Tricycle: *Q Is for Quark* and *G Is for Googol* by David Schwartz; *Pretend Soup* and *Honest Pretzels* by Mollie Katzen; *Hey Little Ant* by Phillip and Hannah Hoose; *The Pumpkin Blanket* by Deborah Turney Zagwyn; *We Can Work It Out: Conflict Resolution for Children* by Barbara K. Polland; *Crashed, Smashed, and Mashed: A Trip to Junkyard Heaven* by Joyce Slayton Mitchell and Steven Borns.

No query letters. Manuscript guidelines can be found online at www.tenspeed.com. Send complete picture book manuscripts, and sample chapters and outlines for middle-grade novels or other longer works with an SASE to:

Nicole Geiger, Publisher

THAMES AND HUDSON

500 Fifth Avenue, New York, NY 10110

212-354-3763   fax: 212-398-1252

www.thamesandhudsonusa.com   e-mail: info@thames.wwnorton.com

Thames and Hudson publishes popular and scholarly works, as well as college texts in the fine arts, archaeology, architecture, biography, crafts, history, mysticism, music, photography, and the sciences.

Thames and Hudson (founded in 1977) is an international producer of well-crafted nonfiction trade books in hardcover and trade paperback under its double-dolphin logo. Though a portion of the publisher's list is originated through the New York editorial office, the greater part of Thames and Hudson's titles are imports via the house's United Kingdom branch.

From Thames and Hudson: *Genesis of the Pharaohs* by Toby Wilkinson; *Treasures of the American Arts and Crafts Movement 1890-1920* by Tod M. Volpe, Beth Cathers, and Alastair Duncan; *The Complete Gods and Goddesses of Ancient Egypt* by Rishard H. Wilkinson; *Figuring It Out* by Colin Renfrew; *Glenn Murcutt: Works and Projects 1969-2001* by Francoise Fromonot; *Practically Minimal* by Maggie Toy; *American Art* by Wally Caruana; *Egon Schiele: Drawings and Watercolors* by Jane Kallir; *The Prospect from Paris* by Raymond Mason; *Art Deco Textiles: The French Designers* by Alain-Rene Hardy; *Hip Hotels USA* by Herbert Ypma; *Chronicle of the Roman Republic* by Philip Matyszak;

Power and Profit: The Merchant in Medieval Europe by Peter Spufford; *The Ganges* by Raghubir Singh; *The Christian World: A Social and Cultural History* edited by Geoffrey Barraclough; *The Titanic Way: Art, Science, Ritual* by Ajit Mookerjee and Madhu Khanna; *The Shinning Textiles: The French Designers* by Alain-Rene Hardy; *The Essential Samuel Beckett* by Enoch Brater; *Street Graphics New York* by Barry Dawson.

Thames and Hudson is distributed to the trade by W. W. Norton. The house also offers an 800 ordering number and has in-house fulfillment services for purchases by individual consumers.

Query letters and SASEs should be directed to:

Peter Warner, President

THEATRE COMMUNICATIONS GROUP, INC.

355 Lexington Avenue, New York, NY 10017-0217

212-697-5230

www.tcg.org   e-mail: tcg@tcg.org

Theatre Communications Group is interested in theater-related works.

Sample titles: *Accomplices* by Simon Bent; *Alien Creature* by Linda Griffiths; *Contemporary American Monologues: Men* by Todd London; *A Carol Dublin* by TCG; *Masterclass: Volume One: Men* edited by Dean Carey; *Solo Speeches for Under 12s* by Shaun McKenna; *Theater, Aristocracy, and Pornocracy* by Karl Toepfer.

TIMBERWOLF PRESS

202 N. Allen Drive Suite A, Allen, TX 75013

972-644-7098

www.TwolfPress.com   e-mail: info@twolfpress.com

Founded in 1994 by Patrick Seaman, Timberwolf Press started out as a software company, publishing a Windows Database version of the bestselling trade reference *The Insider's Guide to Book Editors, Publishers, and Literary Agents* by Jeff Herman. The software was called Writer's Desktop Database for Windows and is now in its fourth annual release.

In 1995, Patrick became affiliated with the premiere Internet broadcasting company AudioNet (http://www.AudioNet.com). While searching for content to broadcast on AudioNet, Seaman asked a writing acquaintance, Jim Cline, to produce an audio version of a novel that Jim was working on at the time. In late 1995, this project gave birth to the first serialized audio-novel on the Internet. Thanks to the Internet, it received fan mail from around the world.

Sample titles: *Blood & Iron* by Dan MacGregor; *Soldier of the Legion* by Marshall S. Thomas; *Bradamant* by Ron Miller; *All The Tea* by Ken Carodine; *Calculated Risk* by Denise Tiller; *A Small Percentage* by Jim Cline; *Writing Excellence #1: Writing 101* by Timberwolf Press; *Seed of Fear* by Patrick Seaman.

In 1997, Timberwolf Press expanded from a software and multimedia publishing company to the world of print publishing when it released Jim Cline's epic military science fiction novel in a hardback edition: *A Small Percentage.*

A sequel to *A Small Percentage* is in the works, as well as other science fiction and techno-thriller titles.

Query letters and SASEs should be directed to:

Eve McClellen, Senior Editor

Jennifer Mikhail, Editor at Large

Patrick Seaman, Publisher

J. N. TOWNSEND, PUBLISHING

4 Franklin Street, Exeter, NH 03833

603-778-9883/1-800-333-9883   fax: 603-772-1980

www.jntownsendpublishing.com   e-mail: jntown@mediaone.net

J. N. Townsend is a small publisher with a successful line of titles about pets, wildlife, nature, and country living. Townsend (founded in 1986) initially published in softcover format only and issued its first hardcover title in 1994. The house has thrived on the basis of short press runs and by keeping titles alive on a full backlist.

From Townsend: *Duffy: Adventures of a Collie* by Irving Townsend; *Goat Song: My Island Angora Goat Farm* by Susan Basquin; *A Cat's Life: Dulcy's Story*, as told to Dee Ready; *Who Ever Heard of a HORSE in the HOUSE?* by Jacqueline Tresl; *The Ugly Dachshund (6th printing)* by G. B. Stern; *Regards, Rodeo: The Mariner Dog of Cassi (2nd printing)* by Alan Armstrong (illustrations by Martha Armstrong).

J. N. Townsend Publishing presents the latest book by Era Zistel, *The Good Year*; she writes about her life with animals in the Catskill Mountains of New York. Other Zistel titles: *Gentle People*; *Wintertime Cat*; *Orphan*; *A Gathering of Cats*; *Good Companions.*

Celebrating a third printing is *Separate Lifetimes: A Collection* by Irving Townsend (illustrated by Judith Roberts-Rondeau). This collection of essays is particularly cherished by readers who have suffered the loss of an animal companion. *Separate Lifetimes* was the first book published by the press in 1986 as a memorial to the publisher's father.

Townsend books are distributed to the trade by Alan C. Hood and Company. Query letters and SASEs should be directed to:

Jeremy Townsend, Editor

TUTTLE PUBLISHING

153 Milk Street, Boston, MA 02109

617-951-4080   fax: 617-951-4045

www.tuttlepublishing.com

Tuttle Publishing is America's leading independent publisher of Asian-interest books and the premier publisher of English-language books in Japan. Tuttle's imprints strive to span the East and West with market-leading books on cooking, martial arts, Eastern philosophy, spiritual development, Asian culture, design, and language learning.

Its publications include such renowned books as: *75 Block Downs: Refining Karate Technique* by Rick Clark; *The ABCs of Origami: Paper Folding for Children* by Claude Sarasas; *An Introduction to Zen Training: Sanzen Nyumon* by Roy Yoshimoto (translator) Dogen Hosokawa (translator) and Omori Sogen; *Basic Japanese Conversation Dictionary* by Samuel E. Martin; *Basic Tagalog for Foreigners and Non-Tagalogs* by Paraluman S. Aspillera; *Batam Travel Map: Third Edition* by Periplus; *Beyond the Known: The Ultimate Goal of the Martial Arts* by Tri Thing Dang; *Blue and White Japan* by Yutaka Satoh (photographer) and Amy Sylvestor Katoh; *Complete Asian Cookbook* by Charmaine Solomon (foreword by Ken Hom); *Concise English-Korean Dictionary: Romanized* by Joan V. Underwood; *Exciting India* by Bikram Grewal (photographer Henry Wilson).

Query letters with SASEs should be directed to:

Ed Walters, Publishing Director

Jennifer Lantagne, Acquisitions Editor

UNITED PUBLISHERS GROUP/UPG

HASTINGS HOUSE

GATES & BRIDGES

JUDD PUBLISHING

ROSSET-MORGAN BOOKS

50 Washington Street, Norwalk, CT 06854

203-838-4083   fax: 203-838-4084

www.upub.com   e-mail: info@upub.com

United Publishers Group/UPG produces a number of trade nonfiction lines and selective fiction through several affiliated imprints. The group includes Hastings House (Daytrips travel guides), Gates & Bridges (works with multicultural/global themes), Judd Publishing (illustrated editions), and Rosset-Morgan Books (books with a literary or cultural perspective).

United Publishers Group (founded in 1996) and its imprints conduct their programs from offices in several locations, including Connecticut, Washington, D.C., and Manhattan. UPG is a subsidiary of the German-based Peter Leers Group, a privately held real-estate and insurance amalgamate.

Henno Lohmeyer (UPG publisher) opened the house by acquiring several previously independent publishing firms and by securing the U.S. rights to a number of international publishing properties. Plans are to build the publishing group through a number of robust boutique imprints, rather than by combining editorial operations.

From Hastings House: *The Truth About Fiction Writing* by William Appel and Denise Sterrs; *Test Your Bible Power* by Jerry Agel; *Passion for Wine: The Ultimate Guide* by Paul Lirette.

Gates & Bridges is a new imprint that features works that exemplify the essential image: "gates to new worlds...bridges between continents." From Gates &Bridges: *Land of the Ascending Dragon: Rediscovering Vietnam* (photo essay) by Paul Martin (photographs by Seven Raymer); *The Opera Quiz Book: Everything You Always Wanted to Know About the Greatest Art Form Ever Invented by Mankind* by Michael Walsh.

United Publishers Group distributes through Publishers Group West. Initial queries to UPG may be directed to the main-entry address. Query letters and SASEs should be directed to:

Henno Lohmeyer, Publisher and Editor, Gates and Bridges—Works from an international perspective; regional markets; commercial and trade nonfiction

Hy Steirman, Editor in Chief, Hastings House—Presides over Hastings House (now featuring Daytrips travel guides)

Ruina W. Judd, Editor in Chief, Judd Publishing—Illustrated books

UNIVERSE PUBLISHING

CHILDREN'S UNIVERSE

300 Park Avenue South, New York, NY 10010-5399

212-982-2300

Universe produces books in art history and appreciation, architecture and design, photography, fashion, sports, alternative culture, and performing arts. Universe Publishing also takes on selected high-interest projects in literary writing and criticism, and the occasional human- or social-interest title in illustrated format. The Universe Publishing emphasis (through individual titles and a number of successful series) is on works of popular, as well as scholarly, interest in the arts worldwide and the arts and artists of the Western and European tradition from prehistoric to contemporary times.

Universe Publishing (founded in 1956; formerly a wing of Phaidon Universe) is an affiliate division of Rizzoli International. Imprints and associated publishers include Universe, Children's Universe, Universe Calendars, Vendome, and Universe Publishing. Among Universe's products are illustrated gift books, children's books, children's paper products, calendars, address books, and diaries.

Universe titles: *The Internet Design Project: The Best of Graphic Art on the Web* by Patrick Burgoyne and Liz Faber; *All-American: A Tommy Hilfiger Style Book* by Tommy Hilfiger, with David A. Keeps; *Secrets of Skating* by Oksana Baiul; *Gymnastics: Balancing Acts* by Christina Lessa; *Camera Ready: How to Shoot Your Kids* by Arthur Elgort; *Intimate Landscapes: The Canyon Suite of Georgia O'Keeffe* by Dana Self, in association with the Kemper Museum of Contemporary Art & Design; *The Romance of California Vineyards* by Molly Chappellet (photographs by Daniel D'Agostini); *Weekends with the Impressionists: A Collection from the National Gallery of Art, Washington* by Carla Brenner.

Universe Publishing and Vendome Press combine on special series lines: Universe of Fashion; Universe of Design; Universe of Art. Beautifully printed and designed—and reasonably priced—these books are geared to appeal equally to novice and expert.

Universe of Fashion offerings are introduced by Grace Mirabella (of magazine fame); each volume deals with the works of great 20th-century couturiers. These books connect the worlds of art, couture, and society with stories of legendary designers. Titles: *Coco Chanel* by Francois Baudot; *Dior* by Marie-France Pocha; *Yves Saint Laurent* by Pierre Bergé; *Valentino* by Bernadine Morris; *Versace* by Richard Martin.

From Universe of Design: *Ferrari* and *Pininfarina* by Lionel Froissard; *Cartier* by Philippe Trétiack.

The Universe of Art series features shifting, distinctive approaches. Some titles focus on an important facet in the work of an individual legendary master, generally a period or place that encapsulates the essence of a lifetime's work. Titles: *Matisse in Nice* by Xavier Girard; *Renoir's Nudes* by Isabelle Cahn; *Degas Backstage* by Richard Kendall; *Cézanne in Provence* by Denis Coutagne. Other titles in this series feature celebrity authors writing on celebrated artists: *Jasper Johns* by Leo Castelli; *Andy Warhol* by Bob Colacello.

From Vendome: *House & Garden Book of Country Rooms* by Leonie Highton; *Secrets of the Harem* by Carla Coco; *Treasures from Italy's Great Libraries* by Lorenzo Crinelli; *Churches of Rome* by Pierre Grimal (photographs by Caroline Rose); *The Grand Canal* by Umberto Franzoi (photographs by Mark Smith).

Universe is distributed to the trade by St. Martin's. Query letters and SASEs should be directed to:

Charles Miers, Publisher—Calendars, graphic products; Children's Universe projects

Elizabeth Johnson, Senior Editor—Art, architecture, women's studies

CHILDREN'S UNIVERSE

Children's Universe produces a variety of inventive products, ranging from book-and-toy packages to storybooks, to hide-and-seek books (with moveable parts), cut-out puppets, posters, masks, and make-it-yourself gift boxes. These are finely designed books and are produced in sturdy editions to withstand carefree handling.

Books from Children's Universe: *Skateboard Monsters* by Daniel Kirk; *Ravita and the Land of Unknown Shadows* (story by Marietta and Peter Brill; illustrated by Laurie Smollett Kutscera); *Head Trips* by Sara Schwartz; *First Steps in Paint: A New and Simple Way to Learn How to Paint* by Tom Robb; *Dinosaur Cowboys Puppet Theatre* by Judy Lichtenstein; *The ABCs of Art* (with a wall frieze version) by the National Gallery of Art, London (with flash cards by the National Gallery of Art, Washington, D.C.).

VERSO, INC.

180 Varick Street, New York, NY 10014-4606

212-807-9680   fax: 212-807-9152

www.versobooks.com   e-mail: versony@versobooks.com

Verso accents trade nonfiction and literary fiction. Areas of Verso scope include: contemporary issues and culture; history and biography; investigative works; world literature and thought in translation; continental, postmodernist, and deconstructivist philosophy and criticism; and humor. Verso produces hardcover and trade paperback editions, as well as occasional special merchandise lines such as calendars and cards.

Verso, Inc. (founded in 1968), is an international house; the United Kingdom headquarters operates from London offices and the major editorial acquisitions program is centered in the United Kingdom. The downtown New York wing is responsible for

Stateside promotion, marketing, sales, and distribution. Over the past several seasons the U.S. list has gained increasing presence.

Titles from Verso: *Parecon: Life After Capitalism* by Michael Albert; *The Humanist Controversy and Other Texts* by Louis Althusser; *Extra Time: World Politics Since 1989* by Perry Anderson; *Figures in the Forest* by Perry Anderson; *Debating Cosmopolitics* edited by Daniele Archibugi; *Debating Empire* by Gopal Balakrishnan; *Modern Times, Ancient Hours: Working Lives in the Twenty-first Century* by Pietro Basso; *Unfinished Business: South Africa, Apartheid, and Truth* by Terry Bell with Dumisa Buhle Ntsebeza; *Shooting People: Adventures in Reality TV* by Sam Brenton and Reuban Cohen; *Thinking Past Terror: Islamism and Critical Theory on the Left* by Susan Buck-Morss; *Figures of Dissent: Critical Essays on Fish, Spivak, Zizek and Others* by Terry Eagleton; *Soccer in Sun and Shadow* by Eduardo Galleano; *The No-Nonsense Guide to Indigenous Peoples* by Lotte Hughes; *Time Will Tell: Memories* by Yvonne Kapp; *Critique of Everyday Life, Vol. III* by Henri Lefebvre; *Freud and the Non-European* by Edward Said.

Verso distributes to the trade through W. W. Norton (U.S.), Penguin Canada (Canada), and Marston Book Services (U.K. and the rest of the world).

Query letters and SASEs for the United States concerns and interests of Verso, Inc., should be directed to:

Niels Hooper, Managing Editor

WALKER & COMPANY

WALKER & COMPANY BOOKS FOR YOUNG READERS

435 Hudson Street, New York, NY 10014

212-727-8300 fax: 212-727-0984

Walker publishes trade nonfiction and mystery fiction. Nonfiction emphasis includes science, history, health, nature, self-help, business, and entrepreneurship. Frontlist fiction accents mysteries. Walker produces a list of large-print Judaica and Christian inspirational titles; books for children range from preschool picture books to books for young adults (please see subentry for Walker & Company Books for Young Readers).

Walker & Company (established in 1959) is a concentrated powerhouse with a hard-hitting, diverse list; especially strong are Walker's market niches in history and science, health, mysteries, large-print religious and inspirational titles, and children's books that complement a broad, carefully chosen selection of adult nonfiction titles.

Walker operates on the publishing credo that what often separates the success of one book from another is the ability to execute an effective marketing strategy; what then separates one house from another is the ability to execute many such strategies—often simultaneously—season upon season.

Walker & Company was founded by the intrepid Sam Walker, who expressed the view "there cannot be a surfeit of good taste." Such faith in editorial content remains at the heart of the firm today, under the current leadership of publisher George Gibson. Underlying the house's publishing strategy is a commitment to quality of product. This two-pronged assault on the marketplace thus relies on compositional and literary depth, as well as on the ability to capitalize on the potential appeal of such works.

Walker nonfiction titles: *Longitude* by Dava Sobel; *Cod* by Mark Kurlansky; *The Boxer Rebellion* by Diana Preston; *Macular Degeneration* by Robert D'Amato; *Sweeping Changes* by Gary Thorp; *The Procrastinator's Handbook* by Rita Emmett; *Overcoming Overspending: A Winning Plan for Spenders and Their Partners* by Olivia Mellan with Sherry Christie; *The Joy of Pi* by David Blatner; *Fermat's Enigma: The Epic Quest to Solve the World's Greatest Mathematical Problem* by Simon Singh; *E = MC$_2$: A Biography of the World's Most Famous Equation* by David Bodanis; *Burnelleschi's Dome* by Ross King.

In fiction, Walker is admired for its standout approach to category books (a significant number of which are first novels) in mysteries. (Walker discontinued its lines in such genres as Western thrillers, romances, and adventure novels.)

On the Walker list in fiction: *The Wrong Dog* by Rachel Alexander and Dash; *Dark Coulee* by Mary Logue; *Bluebottle* by James Sallis; *Little Miss Evil* by Lev Raphael; *Nordic Nights* by Lise McClendon; *Blood Country* by Mary Logue; *Killing Cassidy: A Dorothy Martin Mystery* by Jeanne M. Dams; *Eye of the Cricket: A Lew Griffin Mystery* by James Sallis; *The Ice Pick Artist: A Carl Wilcox Mystery* by Harold Adams; *Five Card Stud: A Jake Hines Mystery* by Elizabeth Gunn.

Walker's guidelines for manuscript submission to its genre lists include valuable hints for fiction authors in general and category writers in particular; the sheet for Walker mysteries notes such tips as the editorial view that the mystery novel is a game between author and reader, an entertaining puzzle to be savored and solved; the mystery must be primary (with such nuances as romantic interest secondary); the mystery-novel story line must be rooted in the real world (and not imbued with supernatural overtones); and manuscripts should in general respect the conventions of the genre.

Authors please note: Materials submitted without an SASE will not be returned.

Walker handles marketing, sales, and distribution for its own list. Query letters and SASEs should be directed to:

George Gibson, Publisher—Nonfiction in all Walker areas, including science, nature, parenting, education, business, health, sourcebooks

Jacqueline Johnson, Editor—Nonfiction

Michael Seidman, Editor—Mysteries; no romantic suspense or horror stories

WALKER AND COMPANY BOOKS FOR YOUNG READERS

Walker and Company Books for Young Readers maintains a backlist in addition to its seasonal offerings of new books. The house caters to a variety of young-reader markets from preschooler picture books to fiction and nonfiction for young adults.

Walker titles for young readers: *The Singers* by Dennis Brindell Fradin (illustrated by Michael McCurdy); *Zooflakes ABC* by Will Howell; *You're a Good Sport, Miss Malarkey* by Judy Finchler and Kevin O'Malley; *Tulsa Burning* by Anna Myers; *Walk Away Home* by Paul Many; *Naming the Cat* by Laurence Pringle (illustrated by Katherine Potter); *Until I Met Dudley: How Everyday Things Really Work* by Roger McGough (illustrated by Chris Riddell); *Trapped by the Ice: Shackleton's Amazing Antarctic Adventure* by Michael McCurdy; *The Keeping Room* by Anna Myers.

Query letters and SASEs should be directed to:

Emily Easton, Publisher

Jim Travaglini, Editor

The previous two editors acquire children's books. They are especially interested in young science, photoessays, historical fiction for middle grades, biographies, current affairs, and young-adult nonfiction.

WATSON-GUPTILL PUBLICATIONS

770 Broadway, New York, NY, 10001

646-654-5500   fax: 646-654-5487

www.watsonguptill.com   e-mail: info@watsonguptill.com

Watson-Guptill produces titles in art instruction and technique, graphic design, fine arts, photography, crafts, environmental and interior design, lifestyle, popular culture, architecture, music, theater, and film. Manuals and handbooks abound on the Watson-Guptill booklist, as do annual design reviews geared to these specialized fields.

Watson-Guptill's imprints include Amphoto, Billboard Books, and Back Stage Books. The publisher maintains an extensive backlist and is a leading publisher in its areas of interest. Watson-Guptill Publications (founded in 1937) is a division of VNU Business Media.

The Watson-Guptill imprint addresses art instruction and graphic design, architecture, interior design, and planning. Amphoto produces instructional volumes from leading photographers. Billboard Books vends authoritative, up-to-the-minute books on every aspect of music and entertainment. Back Stage Books purveys informative reference and instruction books in the performing arts.

Sample titles: *30 Bridges* by Matthew Wells; *Draw and Paint Your Pet* by Susie Wynne; *Citizen Brand* by Marc Gobe; *Action Man Files* by John Michlig; *Dried Flowers* by Hilary Mandleburg and Stephen Woodhams; *Flash Frames* by Laurie Dolphin and Stuart Shapiro; *Bohemian Style* by Elizabeth Wilhide; *How to Heal* by Jeff Kane, MD; *Old Money* by Nelson W. Aldrich; *Film Facts* by Patrick Robertson; *Creative Exposure Control* by Les Meehan; *The Complete Guide to Book Marketing* by David Cole.

Watson Guptill also produces titles in these subjects: Home, Architecture, Art Technique, Business, Children's Books, Crafts, Comics & Cartoons, Fine Arts, Graphic Design, Interior Design, Money Matters, Performing Arts, Photography, and Writing.

Watson-Guptill distributes its own list. Query letters and SASEs should be directed to:

Bob Nirkind, Executive Editor, Billboard Books—Music, film, television, and popular culture

Candace Raney, Executive Editor—Fine art, art technique, cartooning, and comic book art

Mark Glubke, Editor, Back Stage Books—Crafts and interior design, theater

Victoria Craven, Senior Editor, Amphoto and Lifestyle

Julie Mazor, Senior Editor—Children's books

Joy Aquilino, Senior Editor—Crafts

JOHN WILEY & SONS

WILEY CHILDREN'S BOOKS

111 River Street, Hoboken, NJ 07030

201-748-6000   201-748-6088

www.wiley.com   e-mail: info@wiley.com

Wiley is best known in the areas of (in alphabetical order): architecture and design, biography, black interests, business and management, careers, children's and young adult nonfiction, computers, finance, health, history, hospitality, investment, nature, parenting, psychology, science, and tax. The publisher maintains a reputation for publishing top-drawer professional and popular works, in addition to academically oriented works in business and the sciences. Wiley publishes in hardcover and trade paperback editions.

John Wiley & Sons (founded in 1807) is an independent, global publisher of print and electronic products, specializing in textbooks and educational materials for colleges and universities, scientific and technical books and journals, and professional and consumer books and subscription services. The company has publishing, marketing, and distribution centers in the United States, Canada, Europe, Asia, and Australia.

From the Wiley trade list: *Taxes for Dummies* by Eric Tyson and David J. Silverman; *Everyday Negotiation: Navigating the Hidden Agendas in Bargaining* by Deborah M. Kolb and Judith Williams; *The Knowledge Activist's Handbook: Adventures from the Knowledge Trenches* by Victor Newman; *Memory: A Self-Teaching Guide* by Carol Turkington;

Truffles: Ultimate Luxury, Everyday Pleasure by Rosario Safrina and Judith Sutton; *Culinary Artistry* by Andrew Dornenburg and Karen Page; *Chef's Book of Formulas, Yields, and Sizes, 2nd edition* by Arno Schmidt; *The International Menu Speller* by Kenneth N. Anderson and Lois E. Anderson; *Seasons of Grace: The Life-Giving Practice of Gratitude* by Alan Jones and John O'Neil; *Toddler Troubles: Coping with Your Under 5s* by Jo Douglas; *Behind the Burga: Our Life in Afghanistan and How We Escaped to Freedom* by Batya Swift Yasgur; *Elizabeth & Georgiana: The Duke of Devonshire and His Two Duchesses* by Caroline Chapman; *The Death of Spin* by George Pitcher; *The Native American World* by Donna Hightower-Langston; *The American West* by Larry Schweikart and Bradley J. Birzer; *The Education of a Speculator* by Victor Niederhoffer; *Jacqueline Bouvier: An Intimate Memoir* by John H. Davis; *Jerusalem in the Twentieth Century* by Martin Gilbert; *Superchefs: Signature Recipes from America's New Royalty* by Karen Gantz Zahler; *Would-Be Worlds: Breaking the Complexity Barrier with the New Science of Simulation* by John L. Casti; *Sister Power: How Phenomenal Black Women Are Rising to the Top in a Race-Conscious Society* by Patricia Reid-Merritt; *Goodbye, Descartes: The End of Logic and the Search for a New Cosmology of the Mind* by Keith Devlin.

Wiley's website has the latest information on new books, journals, and other publications, along with special promotions and publicity.

John Wiley & Sons handles its own distribution. Query letters and SASEs should be directed to:

Larry Alexander, Publisher—Business/management

Bob Ipsen, Publisher—Computer books; technology-related topical nonfiction

Gerard Helferich, Publisher—General interest books

Carole Hall, Editor in Chief—African American books

Debra Englander, Editor—Financial and investment subjects

Hana Umlauf Lane, Senior Editor—History, biography

Mike Hamilton, Senior Editor—Career development, small businesses, real estate

Tom Miller, Executive Editor—Health, self-improvement, spirituality

Steven Power, Executive Editor—Science

Matthew Holt, Executive Editor—business narratives, business biographies, management and leadership, human resources, self-help, motivation, change management, project management and finance.

Jeff Golick, Editor—Science and reference

Richard Narramore, Editor, General business

David Pugh, Editor, Personal finance

WILEY CHILDREN'S BOOKS

Wiley Children's Books show the house motto: "Discovering the world up close." Wiley children's titles offer an in-depth approach to subjects at hand, be it the natural world, science and technology, or witty fun-and-games experimental projects. Branches in the Wiley children's family include the Earth-Friendly series, Janice VanCleave's science lines (including the Science for Every Kid series), Flying Start, the House of Science, and Spend the Day series.

Some titles: *Black Stars of the Civil Rights Movement* by Jim Haskins; *Janice VanCleave's Guide to the Best Science Fair Projects* by Janice VanCleave; *Secrets of Ancient Cultures: The Maya—Activities and Crafts from a Mysterious Land; The Mash and Smash Cookbook: Fun and Yummy Recipes Every Kid Can Make* by Marian Buck-Murray; *What Makes the Grand Canyon Grand? The World's Most Awe-Inspiring Natural Wonders* by Spencer Christian and Antonia Felix; *Science in Seconds with Toys: Over 100 Experiments You Can Do in Ten Minutes or Less* by Jean Potter; *Janice VanCleave's Insects and Spiders: Mind-Boggling Experiments You Can Turn into Science Fair Projects* by Janice VanCleave; *The New York Public Library Amazing African American History* by Diane Patrick Wexler.

Query letters and SASEs should be directed to:

Kate Bradford, Senior Editor, Professional and Trade Division—Science, nature, children's nonfiction

---

WILLIAMSON PUBLISHING COMPANY

1355 Church Hill Road, PO Box 185, Charlotte, VT 05445-0185

802-425-2102/1-800-234-8791   fax: 802-425-2199/1-800-304-7224

e-mail: info@williamsonbooks.com

Williamson's books help children succeed by helping them to discover their creative capacity. Kids Can!, Little Hands, Kaleidoscope Kids, Quick Starts for Kids, and Good Times books encourage curiosity and exploration with irresistible graphics and open-ended instruction. The house publishes hands-on learning books in science and nature, arts and crafts, math and history, cooking, social studies and more, featuring new Kaleidoscope Kids and Kids Can! titles. Its publishing program is committed to maintaining excellent quality while providing good value for parents, teachers, and children.

Williamson Publishing Company (founded in 1983) is known for a wide variety of works and viewpoints, united through an enthusiastic, upbeat, purposeful how-to approach. Williamson typically produces 16 new titles each year and commands a comprehensive backlist.

Titles from Williamson: *Awesome Ocean Science!* by Cindy Littlefield; *Great Games!* by Sam Taggar; *The Lewis & Clark Expedition* by Carol Johmann; *Make Your Own Christmas Ornaments* by Ginger Johnson; *Drawing Horses* by Don Mayne; *Felt Crafts* by Peg Blanchette & Terri Thibault; *Paper-Folding Fun!* by Ginger Johnson; *First Aid* by Karen Buhler Gale, RN; *All Around Town* by Judy Press; *At the Zoo!* by Judy Press;

Garden Fun! by Vicky Congdon; *40 Knots to Know* by Emily Stetson; *Draw Your Own Cartoons!* by Don Mayne; *Best-Ever Cookies!* by Sarah A. Williamson; *Birdhouses & Feeders* by Robyn Haus; *Fun Frames!* by Matt Phillips; *Hairwear* by Diane Baker; *Yo-Yo!* by Ron Burgess; *Be a Clown* by Ron Burgess; *Teddy Bears & Teddy Clothes* by Sue Mahren; *Scrapbooks & Photo Albums!* by Laura Check; *Jazzy Jewelry* by Diane Baker; *Kids' Books of Weather Forecasting* with Mark Breen and Kathleen Friestad; *Real-World Math for Hands-on Fun!* by Cindy A. Littlefield; *Kids Cook!* by Sarah Williamson and Zachary Williamson; *Super Science Concoctions* and *Gizmos & Gadgets* by Jill Frankel Hauser.

Williamson Publishing prides itself on publishing books that are acclaimed by teachers, kids, parents, and those in the publishing industry. A few of the many awards the house has won include *Mexico!* (American Bookseller Pick of the Lists); *Kids Make Music!* (Parents' Choice Gold Award; Benjamin Franklin Best Juvenile Nonfiction Award); *Fun with My 5 Senses* (Parents' Choice Gold Award); *Gizmos & Gadgets* (Benjamin Franklin Best Education/Teaching Book Award; 2000 American Institute of Physics Science Writing Award; American Bookseller Pick of the Lists).

Williamson Publishing distributes its own list and works through a number of regional book sales representatives. Query letters and SASEs should be directed to:

Susan Williamson, Editorial Director

WILLOW CREEK PRESS

PO Box 147, 9931 Highway 70 West, Minocqua, WI 54548

1-800-850-9453   fax: 715-358-7010

www.willowcreekpress.com   e-mail: books@willowcreekpress.com

Willow Creek Press is a fast-growing, small press company that publishes high-quality books mainly related to pets, the outdoors, wildlife, hunting, fishing, and cooking. The house is also interested in videos and calendars.

Sample titles: *Encyclopedia of North American Sporting Dogs; Bird Dog* by Ben O. Williams; *Drink* by Susy Atkins and Dave Broom; *What Dogs Teach Us* by Glenn Droomgoole; *Golden Rules* by Denver Bryan.

Query letters and SASEs should be directed to:

Tom Petrie, Publisher

Andrea Donner, Managing Editor

WORKMAN PUBLISHING COMPANY

ARTISAN/GREENWICH WORKSHOP PRESS

SEE ALSO ALGONQUIN BOOKS OF CHAPEL HILL

708 Broadway, New York, NY 10003-9555

212-254-5900   fax: 212-254-8098

www.workmanweb.com   e-mail: info@workman.com

Workman publishes commercial nonfiction with an accent on lifestyle areas of cooking, food and wine, health and exercise, how-to, sports, pregnancy and child care, cats, and related popular reference. The house is known for a precisely targeted selection of games and puzzles, cartoon books, and specialty merchandise such as gift books, calendars, journals, and diaries. General trade nonfiction hits the high points of most how-to/self-help categories, business, careers, and personal finance, and provides some quirky works that strike a contemporary note in the popular culture. Workman hosts an outstanding line of children's books.

Workman also lists titles in popular science, satire and humor, self-discovery, fun and games, hobbies and handicrafts, gardening and the home, and travel. Workman imprints and divisions include Artisan and Greenwich Workshop Press (which stress lifestyle, crafts, and design; see subentry.) In 1988 Workman acquired Algonquin Books of Chapel Hill, which specializes in American fiction and belletristic nonfiction.

Workman Publishing Company (started in 1967) is adept at a marketing, sales, and promotional style that features such results as eye-catching counter displays for booksellers and racks devoted entirely to Workman lines.

Highlights from Workman: *The Last Girls* by Lee Smith; *Take A Load Off Your Heart* by Joe Piscatella and Barry Franklin, PhD; *The Power of the Purse* by Anna Johnson; *God, A Guide for Seekers* by David Schiller; *The Barbecue Bible* by Steven Raichlen; *Beer-Can Chicken* by Steven Raichlen; *The Cake Mix Doctor* by Anne Byrn; *Chocolate From the Cake Mix Doctor* by Anne Byrn; *Philadelphia Chickens* by Sandra Boynton and Michael Ford; *What To Expect When You're Expecting* by Heidi E. Murkoff, Arlene Eisenberg, and Sandee E. Hathaway; *The Silver Palate Cookbook* by Julee Rosso and Sheila Lukins; *Non Campus Mentis* by Anders Henriksson; *Desperation Dinners! Home-Cooked Meals for Frantic Families in 20 Minutes Flat* by Beverly Mills and Alicia Ross; *Children Learn What They Live* by Dorothy Law Nolte, PhD, with Rachel Harris, PhD

Calendars and diaries are often theme-keyed to other arenas of Workman publishing interest. Many calendar lines tie in with Workman's successful series in lifestyle, inspiration, nature, games and puzzles, humor, sports, cats, and dogs.

Of interest to young readers and the family: *Brain Quest* and *The Magic Locket* by Elizabeth Koda-Callan; *Peek-A-Boo, Lizzy Lou! A Daytime Book and Muppet Puppet* by Lauren Attinelo (illustrated by author; puppet by Rolie Krewson); *Barnyard Dance* by

Sandy Boynton.

Workman Publishing Company handles its own distribution. Query letters and SASEs should be directed to:

Peter Workman, President—Oversees entire program; acquires in all areas consistent with list

Susan Bolotin, Editor in Chief—Acquires in all areas consistent with list

Suzanne Rafer, Editor—Cookbooks, humor, family issues; children's activity books

David Allender, Editor, Children's books.

Katie Workman, Associate Publisher, Cookbooks

ARTISAN/GREENWICH WORKSHOP PRESS

Workman's Artisan division specializes in lifestyle titles; the Artisan list includes titles from the Greenwich Workshop Press imprint (crafts and the arts), as well as calendars and other specialty merchandise. Artisan and Greenwich Workshop Press together accent crafts, home, garden, and design, each with its own distinctive editorial approach and publishing lines.

On the Artisan list: *The Ford Century* by Russ Banham (foreword by Paul Newman); *Melons for the Passionate Grower* by Amy Goldman; *Shooting Under Fire* by Peter Howe; *A Return to Cooking* by Eric Ripert and Michael Ruhlman; *Anatomy of a Dish* by Diane Forley and Catherine Young; *Explorations* by Royal Geographical Society; *Learning To See* by Vicente Wolf; *Pierre Franey Cooks with His Friends* by Pierre Franey with Claudia Franey Jensen (photographs by Martin Brigdale and Jean Cazals); *French Tarts: 50 Savory and Sweet Recipes* by Linda Dannenberg (photographs by Guy Bouchet; illustrated by Vavro); *Portobello Cookbook* by Jack Czarnecki (photographs by Alexandra Maldonado); *Fresh Cuts: Arrangements with Flowers, Leaves, Buds & Branches* by Edwina von Gal (photographs by John Hall; foreword by Ken Druse); *Picasso's One-Liners* (single-line drawings by Pablo Picasso); *Cowgirl Rising* (paintings by Donna Howell-Sickles; text by Peg Streep; introduction by Teresa Jordan); *The Glory of Flight: The Art of William S. Phillips* (paintings by William S. Phillips; text by Edwards Park; introduction by Stephen Coonts).

Artisan is the publisher of the Audubon Society's calendar line and distributes books for Eating Well Books (from *Eating Well* magazine).

Ann Bramson, Editor

WRIGHT GROUP/MCGRAW-HILL

19201 120th Avenue, NE, Bothell, WA 98011

1-800-345-6073/1-800-523-2371

www.wrightgroup.com

Wright Group/McGraw-Hill (founded in 1980) is a leading publisher of educational books for elementary school and junior high curricula. Wright series lines include Sunshine, Foundations, Heritage Readers, Woodland Mysteries, the Writing Project, Visions: African American Experiences, the Evangeline Nicholas Collection, Story Vine, Fast Track Reading, and Doors to Discovery.

Wright Group/McGraw-Hill publishers believe that after the parents' role, teachers are the most important people in the life of a child. The teacher who empowers a child to read fulfills the greatest purpose.

Wright educational tools feature the "whole language" approach to reading; Wright hosts a wide range of books in science and social studies, as well as professional books for educators. The house has a full slate of books geared to the Spanish-language market.

The SUNSHINE program is a core instructional reading program with more than 1,000 books for children. SUNSHINE includes fiction, nonfiction, poetry, plays, collections, traditional tales, and more. SUNSHINE features a mix of talented authors and illustrators from cultures and countries around the world. SUNSHINE is also available in Spanish.

The Foundations program introduces a powerful intervention system for use by classroom teachers. Foundations offers immediate intervention for children who are having problems learning to read and write.

Heritage Readers is an integrated literature and language-arts program for K–8 students. Heritage Readers are illustrated by renowned artists from the past and present and feature stories from the classic literary legacies of many cultures.

Woodland Mysteries is a collection of 30 high-interest novels designed especially for discouraged readers and ESL students.

The Writing Project complements and extends any language-arts program. Using their own life experience, students structure their writing from authentic writing models that incorporate various styles, forms, and functions.

Visions: African American Experiences is a guide-reading program for young students that brings together a collaborative team of African American educators, authors, and illustrators.

The Evangeline Nicholas Collection introduces students to rich multi-ethnic characters and true-to-life urban settings. Story Vine is a line that weaves tales of the American continent. These multicultural books include contemporary stories, traditional stories, and a memoir.

Wright Group/McGraw-Hill also offers professional books for teachers: *Think Big!*

Creating Big Books with Children by Cynthia Johnson; *Whole Learning: Whole Child* by Joy Cowley; *Student Portfolios: A Practical Guide to Evaluation* by Lindy Vizyak; *Literacy Learning: A Revolution in Progress* by David B. Doake; *The Spelling Teacher's Book of Lists* by Joe Phenix.

Wright Group/McGraw-Hill handles its own distribution. Please check our website for current submission acceptance status.

WRITER'S DIGEST BOOKS

4700 E. Galbraith Road, Cincinnati, OH 45236

513-531-2222   fax: 513-531-4744

www.writersdigest.com   e-mail: writersdig@fwpubs.com

Writer's Digest Books is owned by the F&W Publishing Group. Writer's Digest produces books to help writers, poets, artists, songwriters, and photographers develop their talent, hone their professional skills, and—of course—sell their work. The publisher pursues this mission by issuing a list of guidebooks, how-to, reference, and professional titles in hardcover and paperback editions.

Sample titles: *Snoopy's Guide to the Writing Life* edited by Barnaby Conrad (foreword by Monte Schultz); *45 Master Characters* by Victoria Schmidt; *Beginnings, Middles, and Ends* by Nancy Kress; *Building Better Plots* by Robert Kernen; *Characters & Viewpoint* by Orson Scott Card; *Conflict, Action and Suspense* by William Noble; *2003 Poet's Market* edited by Nancy Breen; *Creating Poetry* by John Drury.

Query letters and SASEs should be sent to:

David Lewis, Sr. Vice President, New Products

SECTION THREE

UNIVERSITY PRESSES

THE UNIVERSITY AS PUBLISHER

FROM ACADEMIC PRESS
TO COMMERCIAL PRESENCE

WILLIAM HAMILTON

You nod as you glance at the ads in the book reviews, you are aware of the spots you heard or saw on radio and late-night television, and you recognize the authors from television interviews and radio call-in shows. So you know that today's university presses publish much more than scholarly monographs and academic tomes.

Although the monograph is—and will always be—the bread and butter of the university press, several factors over the past quarter century have compelled university presses to look beyond their primary publishing mission of disseminating scholarship. The reductions in financial support from parent institutions, library-budget cutbacks by federal and local governments, and the increasing scarcity of grants to underwrite the costs of publishing monographs have put these presses under severe financial pressure. The watchword for university presses, even in the 1970s, was survival.

While university presses were fighting for their lives, their commercial counterparts also experienced difficult changes. The commercial sector responded by selling off unprofitable and incompatible lists or merging with other publishers; many houses were bought out by larger concerns. Publishers began to concentrate their editorial and marketing resources on a few new titles that would generate larger revenues. Books that commercial publishers now categorized as financial risks, the university presses saw as means of entry into new markets and opportunities to revive sagging publishing programs.

Take a look through one of the really good bookstores in your area. You'll find university press imprints on regional cookbooks, popular fiction, serious nonfiction, calendars, literature in translation, reference works, finely produced art books, and a considerable number of upper-division textbooks. Books and other items normally associated with commercial publishers are now a regular and important part of university press publishing.

There are approximately 100 university presses in North America, including U.S. branches of the venerable Oxford University Press and Cambridge University Press. Of the largest American university presses—California, Chicago, Columbia, Harvard, MIT, Princeton, Texas, and Yale—each publishes well over 100 books per year. Many of these titles are trade books that are sold in retail outlets throughout the world.

The medium-sized university presses—approximately 20 fit this category—publish between 50 and 100 books a year. Presses such as Washington, Indiana, Cornell, North Carolina, Johns Hopkins, and Stanford are well established as publishers of important works worthy of broad circulation.

All but the smallest university presses have developed extensive channels of distribution, which ensure that their books will be widely available in bookstores and wherever serious books are sold. Small university presses usually retain larger university presses or commissioned sales firms to represent them.

University Press Trade Publishing

The two most common trade areas in which university presses publish are (1) regional titles and (2) nonfiction titles that reflect the research interests of their parent universities.

For example, University of Hawaii Press publishes approximately 30 new books a year with Asian or Pacific Rim themes. Typically, 8 to 10 of these books are trade titles. Recent titles have included Japanese literature in translation, a lavishly illustrated book on Thai textiles, books on forms of Chinese architecture, and a historical guide to ancient Burmese temples. This is a typical university press trade list—a diverse, intellectually stimulating selection of books that will be read by a variety of well-informed, responsive general readers.

For projects with special trade potential, some of the major university presses enter into copublishing arrangements with commercial publishers—notably in the fields of art books and serious nonfiction with a current-issues slant—and there seems to be more of these high-profile projects lately.

Certain of the larger and medium-sized university presses have in the past few years hired editors with experience in commercial publishing to add extra dimensions and impact to the portion of their program with a trade orientation.

It's too early to know whether these observations represent trends. Even if so, the repercussions remain to be seen. Obviously, with the publishing community as a whole going through a period of change, it pays to stay tuned to events.

University Press Authors

Where do university press authors come from? The majority of them are involved in one way or another with a university, research center, or public agency, or are experts in a particular academic field. Very few would list their primary occupation as author. Most of the books they write are the result of years of research or reflect years of experience in their fields.

The university press is not overly concerned about the number of academic degrees following its trade book authors' names. What matters is the author's thoroughness in addressing the topic, regardless of his or her residence, age, or amount of formal education. A rigorous evaluation of content and style determines whether the manuscript meets the university press's standards.

University Press Acquisition Process

Several of the other essays in this volume provide specific strategies for you to follow to ensure that your book idea receives consideration from your publisher of choice—but let me interject a cautionary note: The major commercial publishers are extremely difficult to approach unless you have an agent, and obtaining an agent can be more difficult than finding a publisher!

The commercial publishers are so overwhelmed by unsolicited manuscripts that you would be among the fortunate few if your proposal or manuscript even received a thorough reading. Your unagented proposal or manuscript will most likely be read by an editorial assistant, returned unread, or thrown on the slush pile unread and unreturned.

An alternative to the commercial publisher is the university press. Not only will the university press respond; but the response will also generally come from the decision maker—the acquisitions editor.

Before approaching any publisher, however, you must perform a personal assessment of your expectations for your book. If you are writing because you want your book to be on the bestseller list, go to a medium to large commercial press. If you are writing to make a financial killing, go to a large commercial publisher. If you are writing in the hope that your book will be a literary success, contribute to knowledge, be widely distributed, provide a modest royalty, and be in print for several years, you should consider a university press.

Should a University Press Be Your First Choice?

That depends on the subject matter. It is very difficult to sell a commercial publisher on what appears on the surface to be a book with a limited market. For example, Tom Clancy was unable to sell *The Hunt for Red October* to a commercial publisher because the content was considered too technical for the average reader of action-adventure books. Clancy sent the manuscript to a university press that specialized in military-related topics. Naval Institute Press had the foresight to see the literary and commercial value of Clancy's work. As they say, the rest is history. Tom Clancy created the present-day technothriller genre and has accumulated royalties well into the millions of dollars. Once Clancy became a known commodity, the commercial publishers began courting him. All of his subsequent books have been published by commercial houses.

How do you find the university press that is suitable for you? You must research the university press industry. Start by finding out something about university presses. In addition to the listings in the directory of publishers and editors appearing in this book, most university presses are listed in *Literary Market Place*.

A far better and more complete source is *The Association of American University*

Presses Directory. The AAUP directory offers a detailed description of each AAUP member press, with a summary of its publishing program. The directory lists the names and responsibilities of each press's key staff, including the acquisitions editors. Each press states its editorial program—what it will consider for publication. A section on submitting manuscripts provides a detailed description of what the university press expects a proposal to contain. Another useful feature is the comprehensive subject grid, which identifies more than 125 subject areas and lists the university presses that publish in each of them.

An updated edition of *The Association of American University Presses Directory* is published every fall and is available for a nominal charge from the AAUP central offices in New York City or through its distributor, University of Chicago Press.

Most university presses are also regional publishers. They publish titles that reflect local interests and tastes and are intended for sale primarily in the university press's local region. For example, University of Hawaii Press has more than 250 titles on Hawaii. The books—both trade and scholarly—cover practically every topic one can think of. Books on native birds, trees, marine life, local history, native culture, and an endless variety of other topics can be found in local stores, including chain bookstores.

This regional pattern is repeated by university presses throughout the country. University of Washington Press publishes several titles each year on the Pacific Northwest and Alaska. Rutgers University Press publishes regional fiction. University of New Mexico Press publishes books on art and photography, most dealing with the desert Southwest. Louisiana State University Press publishes Southern history and literature. Nebraska publishes on the American West.

Almost all university presses publish important regional nonfiction. If your book naturally fits a particular region, you should do everything possible to get a university press located in that region to evaluate your manuscript.

Do not mistake the regional nature of the university press for an inability to sell books nationally—or globally. As mentioned earlier, most university presses have established channels of distribution and use the same resources that commercial publishers use for book distribution. The major difference is that the primary retail outlets for university press books tend to be bookstores associated with universities, smaller academic bookstores, specialized literary bookstores, and independent bookstores that carry a large number of titles.

Matching books to buyers is not as difficult as you might think. Most patrons of university press bookstores know these stores are likely to carry the books they want.

Traditionally, very few university press titles are sold through major chain bookstores outside their local region. Even so, this truism is subject to change. Some of the biggest bookstore chains are experimenting with university press sections in their large superstores.

What to Expect at a University Press

You should expect a personal reply from the acquisitions editor. If the acquisitions editor expresses interest, you can expect the evaluation process to take as long as 6 to 8 months. For reasons known only to editorial staffs—commercial, as well as those of university presses—manuscripts sit and sit and sit. Then they go out for review, come back, and go out for review again!

Once a favorable evaluation is received, the editor must submit the book to the press's editorial board. It is not until the editorial board approves the manuscript for publication that a university press is authorized to publish the book under its imprint.

A word about editorial boards: The imprint of a university press is typically controlled by an editorial board appointed from the faculty. Each project presented to the editorial board is accompanied by a set of peer reviews, the acquisitions editor's summary of the reviews, and the author's replies to the reviews. The project is discussed with the press's management and voted upon.

Decisions from the editorial board range from approval, through conditional approval, to flat rejection. Most university presses present to the editorial board only those projects they feel stand a strong chance of acceptance—approximately 10 to 15 percent of the projects submitted annually. So if you have been told that your book is being submitted to the editorial board, there's a good chance that the book will be accepted.

Once a book has been accepted by the editorial board, the acquisitions editor is authorized to offer the author a publishing contract. The publishing contract of a university press is quite similar to a commercial publisher's contract. The majority of the paragraphs read the same. The difference is most apparent in two areas—submission of the manuscript and financial terms.

University presses view publishing schedules as very flexible. If the author needs an extra 6 to 12 months to polish the manuscript, the market is not going to be affected too much. If the author needs additional time to proofread the galleys or page proofs, the press is willing to go along. Why? Because a university press is publishing for the long term. The book is going to be in print for several years. It is not unusual for a first printing of a university press title to be available for 10 or more years. Under normal circumstances the topic will be timeless, enduring, and therefore of lasting interest.

University presses go to great lengths to ensure that a book is as close to error-free as possible. The academic and stylistic integrity of the work is foremost in the editor's mind. Not only the content, but the notes, references, bibliography, and index should be flawless—and all charts, graphs, maps, and other illustrations perfectly keyed.

It does not matter whether the book is a limited-market monograph or serious nonfiction for a popular trade. The university press devotes the same amount of care to the editorial and production processes to ensure that the book is as accurate and complete as possible. Which leads us to the second difference—the financial terms.

Commercial publishers follow the maxim that time is money. The goal of the organization is to maximize shareholder wealth. Often the decision to publish a book is based solely on financial considerations. If a book must be available for a specific season in order to meet its financial goals, pressure may be applied to editorial by marketing, and editorial in turn puts pressure on the author to meet the agreed-upon schedule. This pressure may result in mistakes, typos, and inaccuracies—but will also assure timely publication and provide the publisher with the opportunity to earn its expected profit. At the commercial publishing house, senior management is measured by its ability to meet annual financial goals.

University presses are not-for-profit organizations. Their basic mission is to publish books of high merit that contribute to universal knowledge. Financial considerations are secondary to what the author has to say. A thoroughly researched, meticulously documented, and clearly written book is more important than meeting a specific publication date. The university press market will accept the book when it appears.

Do not get the impression that university presses are entirely insensitive to schedules or market conditions. University presses are aware that certain books—primarily textbooks and topical trade titles—must be published at specific times of the year if sales are to be maximized. But less than 20 percent of any year's list would fall into such a category.

University Presses and Author Remuneration

What about advances? Royalties? Surely, university presses offer these amenities—which is not to suggest they must be commensurate with the rates paid by commercial houses.

No and yes. No royalties are paid on a predetermined number of copies of scholarly monographs—usually 1,000 to 2,000.

A royalty is usually paid on textbooks and trade books. The royalty will be based on the title's sales revenue (net sales) and will usually be a sliding-scale royalty, ranging from as low as 5 percent to as high as 15 percent.

As with commercial publishers, royalties are entirely negotiable. Do not be afraid or embarrassed to discuss them with your publisher. Just remember that university presses rarely have surplus funds to apply to generous advances or high royalty rates. However, the larger the university press, the more likely you are to get an advance for a trade book.

Never expect an advance for a monograph or supplemental textbook.

When Considering a University Press

When you're deciding where to submit your manuscript, keep the following in mind. University presses produce approximately 10 percent of the books published in the United States each year. University presses win approximately 20 percent of the annual major book awards. Yet university presses generate just 2 percent of the annual sales revenue.

So if you want to write a book that is taken seriously and will be carefully reviewed and edited; if you want to be treated as an important part of the publishing process and want your book to have a good chance to win an award; and if you are not too concerned about the financial rewards—then a university press may very well be the publisher for you.

CAMBRIDGE UNIVERSITY PRESS

40 West 20th Street, New York, NY 10011-4211

212-924-3900/1-800-872-7423   fax: 212-691-3239

www.cup.org

The Cambridge list includes hardcover and paperback titles of topical contemporary general interest, as well as academic import, in the fields of literature, art, music, religion, history, philosophy, economics, the classics, mathematics, and the behavioral, biological, physical, social, and computer sciences. One of publishing's old guard, Cambridge University Press (founded in 1534) is now a major international operation that holds fast to a long commitment to quality.

Cambridge University Press is the printing and publishing house of the University of Cambridge. It is a charitable enterprise required by university statute to devote itself to printing and publishing in the furtherance of the acquisition, advancement, conservation, and dissemination of knowledge in all subjects; to the advancement of education, religion, learning, and research; and to the advancement of literature and good letters.

Special imprints include Cambridge Film Classics and the popularly priced Canto line. Cambridge also produces some titles for young readers and publishes a full range of academic and popular reference works. Cambridge is strong in the reprint area, offering editions of anthologies and compilations, as well as individual classic works.

Cambridge publishes more than 2,000 new titles each year. Recent titles include: *Modern Compiler Implementation in Java* by Andrew Appel; *Shakespeare from Cambridge*; *The Skeptical Environmentalist* by Bjorn Lomborg Ph.D.; *Infotech English for Computer Users* by Santiago Remacha Esteras; *Noam Chomsky* by Noam Chomsky; *D. H. Lawrence*; *Concepts In Programming Languages* by John C. Mitchell; *Russian and East European Studies*; *The Cruelty of Morality* by Elliot Turiel; *Hands-on Astronomy* by Herve Burillier and Christophe Lehenaff (translated by Klaus Brasch and Michael Covington); *A History of Iraq* by Charles Tripp.

The house hosts a strong reference list, including *The Cambridge International Dictionary of English* (edited by Paul Procter).

Cambridge University Press handles its own distribution.

Query letters and SASEs should be directed to:

Adam Black, Editor—Physical sciences

Roger Astley, Editor—Mathematics

Beatrice Rehl, Editor—Arts and classics

Andrew Winnard, Editor—Linguistics

Deborah Goldblatt, Senior Editor—ESL (English as a second language) books

Ellen Carlin, Editor—Engineering

Frank Smith, Publishing Director—Social sciences

Alan Harvey, Editor—Mathematics and computer science

Lewis Bateman, Editor—Political science

Lothlorien Homet, Editor—Computing

Mary Child, Editor—Social sciences

Mary Vaughn, Publishing Director—ESL (English as a second language) books

Matt Lloyd, Editor—Earth sciences

Katrina Halliday, Editor—Life science

Philip Laughlin, Editor—Psychology

Scott Parris, Editor—Economics

Terry Moore, Publishing Director—Humanities

COLUMBIA UNIVERSITY PRESS

61 West 62nd Street, New York, NY 10023

212-459-0600   fax: 212-459-3678

www.columbia.edu/cu/cup/press/

Columbia hosts a roster of trade and specialty titles, including distinguished lines in Asian studies, literary studies, social work, history, earth sciences, and film and media studies. Columbia's publishing interests also include current events, public issues, popular culture and fine arts, gay and lesbian studies, history, the sciences, literature, religion, and Asian studies. Columbia University Press (established in 1893) publishes a slate of general-interest titles in addition to its established list of scholarly, academic, and scientific works. Also on the roster is a number of standard reference works geared for the institutional and academic market. The press produces books in hardcover and trade paperback editions and nurtures a healthy backlist.

Among Columbia highlights: *Autobiography of a Geisha* by Sayo Masuda; *Books, Banks, Buttons* by Chiara Frugoni; *The Breaking Jewel* by Makoto Oda; *Breathing Spaces* by Nancy N. Chen; *Buddhism and Science* by B. Alan Wallace; *The City Trilogy* by His-kuo Chang; *Eastern Europe Since 1945* by Harold B. Segel; *Designing Women* by Lucy Fischer; *Desolation and Enlightenment* by Ira Katznelson; *The End of the Soul* by Jennifer Hecht; *The Great Nation* by Colin Jones; *The Literature of Lesbianism* by Terry Castle; *A Dictionary of Maqiao* by Han Shaogong; *Freedom on My Mind* by Manning Marable; *Hollywood from Vietnam to Reagan.. and Beyond* by Robin Wood; *Judaism in America* by Marc Lee Raphael; *Language in Danger* by Andrew Dalby; *A Short History of Opera, 4th edition* by Donald J. Grout; *Slow Food* by Carlo Petrini; *Time Passing* by Sylviane Agacinski; *Voice of America* by Alan L. Heil Jr.; *The Wealth of Nature* by Robert L. Nadeau; *Fluid*

Boundaries by William F. Fisher; *The Fine Art of Copyediting, Second Edition* by Elsie Myers Stainton; *Gendering World Politics* by J. Ann Tickner; *Milton and the Rabbis* by Jeffrey Shoulson; *New Immigrants in New York* (edited by Nancy Foner); *Palatable Poison* (edited by Laura Doan and Jay Prosser); *Piracy, Slavery & Redemption* (edited by Daniel J. Vitkus); *The Poetry of Sylvia Plath* (edited by Claire Brennan); *Practicing Religion in the Age of the Media* (edited by Stewart M. Hoover and Lynn Schofield Clark); *Shaky Ground* by Alice Echols; *Travels in Manchuria and Mongolia* by Yosano Akiko; *Up from Invisibility* by Larry Gross; *Voices of Revolution* by Rodger Streitmatter; *Wondrous Difference* by Alison Griffiths. Sample paperback titles: *The Aging Brain* by Lawrence Whalley; *Antitrust and the Formation of the Postwar World* by Wyatt Wells; *Between East and West* by Luce Irigaray; *Class Act* by Cholly Atkins.

From Columbia reference: *The Columbia Encyclopedia* (edited by Jay Parini); *The Columbia Guide to Standard American English* by Kenneth G. Wilson.

Columbia University Press distributes its own list and handles distribution for a number of other academically oriented publishers, including East European Monographs, Edinburgh University Press, and Kegan Paul International.

Query letters and SASEs should be directed to:

Wendy Lochner, Senior Executive Editor—Religion, medieval studies, and anthropology

Robin C. Smith, Senior Executive Editor—Science

Jennifer Crewe, Editorial Director—Literature, film, and Asian studies

John Michel, Senior Executive Editor—Social work, journalism

Peter Dimock, Senior Executive Editor—History and political science

James Warren, Executive Editor—Reference

CORNELL UNIVERSITY PRESS

Sage House, 512 East State Street, Ithaca, NY 14850

607-277-2338   fax: 607-277-2397

www.cornellpress.cornell.edu

Cornell publishes trade nonfiction, in addition to a wide range of academic and scholarly titles. The press's Comstock Books series continues a tradition of excellence in natural history. The ILR Press imprint focuses on labor and workplace issues. Cornell University Press (begun in 1869) is the oldest university press in the United States.

Representing the Cornell program: *The 100 Most Notable Cornellians* by Glenn C. Altschuler, Isaac Kramnick and R. Laurence Moore; *Affirmative Exclusion* by Jean-Loup Amselle (translated by Jane Marie Todd); *A Grand Strategy for America* by Robert J. Art; *Heidegger's Roots: Nietzsche, National Socialism and The Greeks* by Charles Bambach; *Ger-*

many's War and the Holocaust by Omer Bartov; *The Transmission of Affect* by Teresa Brennan; *Fables of Modernity* by Laura Brown; *Better a Shrew Than a Sheep* by Pamela Allen Brown; *Driving the State* by Delores M. Byrnes; *Amakudari* by Richard A. Colignon and Chikako Usui; *Changing Prospects* edited by Marianne Doezema; *Worked Over* by Dimitra Doukas; *A Field Guide to Bacteria* by Betsey Dexter Dyer; *Ariadne's Thread: A Guide to International Tales Found in Classical Literature* by William Hansen; *Korean Workers: The Culture and Politics of Class Formation* by Koo Hagen; *The Real World of Employee Ownership* by John Logue, Jacquelyn Yates, and William Greider; *The Victorian Homefront: American Thought and Culture, 1860–1880* by Louise L. Stevenson; *The Countryside in the Age of the Modern State: Political Histories of Rural America* by Catherine McNicol Stock and Robert D. Johnston; *Claiming the City: Politics, Faith and the Power of Place in St. Paul* by Mary Lethert Wingerd.

Cornell University Press distributes its own list.

Query letters and SASEs should be directed to:

Frances Benson, Editorial Director—Business, labor, workplace issues, health care

Bernhard Kendler, Executive Editor—Classics, literature, art history, archaeology, Egyptology, drama and film studies

Roger Haydon, Senior Editor—Political science, international relations, Asian studies, philosophy

Sheryl Englund, Acquisitions Editor—American history, American studies, anthropology, regional books, sociology

DUKE UNIVERSITY PRESS

905 West Main Street, Suite 18 B , Durham, NC 27701

919-687-3600   fax: 919-688- 4574

www.dukeupress.edu

Areas of Duke's publishing scope include cultural studies; literary studies; Latin American and Caribbean studies; legal studies; history; East European, Soviet, and post-Soviet studies; German studies; environmental studies; and history of economics. Post-Contemporary Interventions is a series that features imaginative world-class thinkers on culture, media, and global society.

Duke University Press (founded in 1921) publishes scholarly, trade, and textbooks in hardcover and trade paperback editions and maintains a strong backlist. Duke also publishes a number of academic journals, including *MLQ: Modern Language Quarterly*.

On the Duke list: *Terror and History* by Van Gosse; *September 11—A Public Emergency?* by Ella Shohat, Stefano Harney, Randy Martin, Timothy Mitchell, and Fred

Moten; *Dissent from the Homeland* edited by Stanley Hauerwas and Frank Lentriccia; *The Treatment* by Martha Stephens; *Emperors in the Jungle* by John Lindsay-Poland; *Feminism Without Borders* by Chandra Talpade Mohanty; *Benjamin Now: Critical Encounters with the Arcades Project* by Kevin McLaughlin and Philip Rosen; *The Scandal of the State* by Rajeswari Sunder Rajan; *Telling to Live: Latina Feminist Testimonials* by the Latina Feminist Group; *Gender and Sexuality in Latin America* by Gilbert M. Joseph; *Women on the Verge: Japanese Women, Western Dreams* by Karen Kelsky; *An Absent Presence: Japanese Americans in Postwar American Culture, 1945–1960* by Caroline Chung Simpson; *Millennial Japan* by Tomiko Yoda and Harry Harootunian; *Orientations: Mapping Studies in the Asian Diaspora* by Kandace Chuh and Karen Shimakawa; *Harbin and Manchuria: Place, Space and Identity* by Thomas Lahusen; *Labors Appropriate to Their Sex: Gender, Labor and Politics in Urban Chile 1900–1930* by Elizabeth Quay Hutchinson; *The Grooves of Change: Eastern Europe at the Turn of the Millennium* by J. F. Brown; *Crime and Punishment in Latin America: Law and Society Since Late Colonial Times* by Ricardo D. Salvatore, Carlos Aguirre, and Gilbert M. Joseph; *Publishing the Family* by June Howard.

Duke University Press oversees its own distribution.

Query letters and SASEs should be directed to:

Kenneth A. Wissoker—Editor-in-Chief

Christine K. Dahlin—Senior Editorial Assistant

J. Reynolds Smith—Executive Editor

Sharon Parks Torian—Senior Editorial Assistant

Valerie Millholland—Editor

Miriam Angress—Assistant Editor

Rachel Allen—Editor

THE FEMINIST PRESS AT THE CITY UNIVERSITY OF NEW YORK

365 Fifth Avenue, New York, NY 10016

212-817-1593   fax: 212-817-1593

www.feministpress.org

The publishing horizon at the Feminist Press includes biographies, cross-cultural studies, fiction, reprints, history/sociology, interdisciplinary texts, literary anthologies, resources and reference works, educational materials, middle-grade and young adult books, and women's studies (including several notable series). The house hosts a reprint program, but does not publish original fiction or poetry. It also supports a feminist journal, *Women's Studies Quarterly*. The Feminist Press publishes in hardcover and paperback editions and moves a backlist both heady and deep through special sales, including holiday mailings.

The Feminist Press maintains its aim to express and celebrate differences within the cultural context of humanity; in so doing, the house has held the publishing forefront with a series of important works that brings fresh dimensions to the attention of readers. Founded in 1970 at the crest of the second wave of American feminism, the press led off with a list that concentrated on a program to reestablish hitherto overlooked women's literary classics, aligned with an additional focus on literature of United States working-class women. The house's agenda has expanded gradually to encompass such themes as growing up female, women artists, and the family, as well as the publication of academic and general-interest works with an international cast of authors in varied disciplines and literary forms.

Highlights from Feminist Press: *Among the White Moon Faces: An Asian-American Memoir of Homelands* by Shirley Geok-lin Lim; *The New Lesbian Studies: Into the 21st Century* (edited by Bonnie Zimmerman and Toni A. H. McNaron); *Families As We Are: Conversations from Around the World* by Perdita Huston; *Women of Color and the Multicultural Curriculum* (edited by Liza Fiol-Matta and Miriam K. Chamberlain).

In fiction and literature: *The Binding Vine* by Shashi Deshpande; *Earthsong* by Suzette Haden Elgin; *Joss and Gold* by Shirley Geok-lin Lim; *The Judas Rose* by Suzette Haden Elgin; *The Rape of Site* by Lindsey Collen; *Wall Tappings* (edited by Judith A. Scheffler); *Women on War* (edited by Daniela Gioseffi); *Red Sand, Blue Sky* by Cathy Applegate; *A Clear Spring* by Barbara Wilson; *Women Confronting the New Technologies* (edited by Lee Quinby); *Still Alive* by Ruth Kluger.

A special-production volume from Feminist Press is *Long Walks and Intimate Talks*, with stories and poems by Grace Paley and paintings by Vera B. Williams.

The Feminist Press list is distributed to the trade in the United States via Consortium Book Sales & Distribution.

Submission guidelines can be found at www.feministpress.org.

Query letters and SASEs should be directed to:

Jean Casella, Publisher/Director

GALLAUDET UNIVERSITY PRESS

800 Florida Avenue NE, Washington, DC 20002-3695

202-651-5488   fax: 202-651-5489

http://gupress.gallaudet.edu

Gallaudet offers titles in categories such as communication, language arts, deaf culture and history, employment and law, audiology and speech reading, instructional materials, literature, parenting, and professional books, as well as a special concentration in sign language (including American Sign Language). The publisher maintains an extensive backlist.

Imprints of Gallaudet University Press include Clerc Books and Kendall Green Publications. Among areas of current publishing emphasis are audiology, sociolegal issues in special education, English as a second language (ESL), and signed children's books in English; the house also markets a line of videotapes.

The publishing program of Gallaudet University Press (founded in 1968) exemplifies the educational mission of Gallaudet University through an accent on issues pertinent to deafness. Gallaudet University Press publishes scholarly, educational, and general-interest titles, as well as children's books.

Among Gallaudet's list: *Deaf People in Hitler's Europe* edited by Donna F. Ryan and John S. Schuchman; *Damned for Their Difference* by Jan Branson and Don Miller; *Ethics in Mental Health and Deafness* edited by Virginia Gutman; *The Parent's Guide to Cochlear Implants* by Patricia M. Chute and Mary Ellen Nevins; *The American Sign Language Handshape Starter* by Richard A. Tennant and Marianne Gluszak Brown; *The Deaf Way II Anthology* edited by Tonya M. Stremlau; *Turn-Taking, Fingerspelling, and Contact in Signed Languages*; *Baby's First Signs* and *More Baby's First Signs* by Kim Votry and Curt Waller; *A Mighty Change: An Anthology of Deaf American Writing, 1816–1864* by Christopher Krentz; *Language in Hand: Why Sign Came Before Speech* by William C. Stokoe; *Orchid of the Bayou: A Deaf Woman Faces Blindness* by Cathryn Carroll and Catherine Hoffpauir Fischer; *Inner Lives of Deaf Children* by Martha Sheridan.

Gallaudet University Press books are distributed via Chicago Distribution Center. Query letters and SASEs should be directed to:

Ivey Pittle Wallace, Assistant Director

HARVARD BUSINESS SCHOOL PRESS

60 Harvard Way, Boston, MA 02163

617-783-7636   fax: 617-783-7489

New York office:

509 Madison Avenue, 15th floor, New York, NY 10022

212-873-9280

www.hbsp.harvard.edu

Our mission at Harvard Business School Press is straightforward: to be the source of the most influential ideas and conversations that shape business worldwide. Yet it addresses an enormous ambition. We understand that our books—however thoughtful, provocative, and enlightening—will become influential only when their ideas are brought to bear on our daily business activities. No matter how savvy the marketing, attractive the packaging, or aggressive the sales force, at the end of the day only the ideas themselves can make a difference in the thoughts, practice, and conversations of business book readers.

Among our titles: *How Customers Think* by Gerald Zaltman; *Customer Driven IT* by David Moschella; *Expectations Investing* by Alfred Rappaport and Michael J. Mauboussin; *Connecting the Dots* by Cathleen Benko and F. Warren McFarlan; *A Company of Citizens* by Brook Manville and Josiah Ober; *Working Identity* by Herminia Ibarra; *Primal Leadership* by Daniel Goleman; *Out of the Box* by John Hagel III; *The Heart of Change* by John P. Kotter and Dan S. Cohen; *Greeks and Geezers* by Warren G. Bennis and Robert J. Thomas; *The Money of Invention* by Paul A. Gompers and Josh Lerner; *Information Markets: What Businesses Can Learn from Financial Innovation* by William J. Wilhelm Jr. and Joseph D. Downing; *The Harvard Business School Guide to Careers in Finance 2002*; *Harvard Business Review on Turnarounds*; *The Loyalty Effect: The Hidden Force Behind Growth, Profits, and Lasting Value* by Frederick F. Reichheld; *The Infinite Asset: Managing Brands to Build New Value* by Sam Hill and Chris Lederer; *Marketing Moves: A New Approach to Profits, Growth and Renewal* by Philip Kotler, Dipak C. Jain, and Suvit Maesincee; *The Elephant and the Flea: Reflections of a Reluctant Capitalist* by Charles Handy; *Total Access: Giving Customers What They Want in an Anytime, Anywhere World* by Regis McKenna.

Established in 1984, the Press currently has more than 300 titles in print. Our publishing program combines the high standards of a university press with the aggressive marketing of a trade publisher to deliver the best of contemporary thinking in business and management to the widest possible audience. Manuscripts considered for publication by the Press are reviewed by peers, a process unique in trade publishing that ensures the quality and relevance of books that carry the Harvard Business School Press imprint.

In September 2002 Harvard Business School began a partnership with the Center for Public Leadership, headed by David Gergen at Harvard's Kennedy School of Government. The goal is to develop a co-branded line of books focusing on leadership for the common good. The partnership will allow Harvard Business School Press to publish books on public leadership with wide appeal and relevance for general interest readers. With the Center for Public Leadership, HBS Press hopes to define effective leadership in the 21st century whether in groups, organizations, communities, or nations.

Harvard Business School Press titles are consistently recognized by publishing industry awards and annual "best book" round-ups, among them, the *Financial Times*/Booz, Allen & Hamilton Best Business Book of 1997 for *The Innovator's Dilemma* by Clayton Christensen; *Business Week's* Ten Best Books of the Year awards; *Library Journal's* Best Books of the Year awards; and Soundview Executive Book Summaries' Thirty Best Books of the Year. In 1994, *Business Week* hailed *Competing for the Future* by Gary Hamel and C. K. Prahalad the "year's best management book."

Harvard Business School Press titles regularly garner significant national media attention in publications such as *Business Week*; *The Economist*; *Fortune, Inc.*; *Wired*; the

New York Times; The Financial Times; USA Today; and *The Wall Street Journal.* Several books have appeared on the national *Business Week* Bestseller List, including *Competing for the Future, The Loyalty Effect, Leading Change, Net Gain, Real Time, Unleashing the Killer App, Net Worth,* and *The Innovator's Dilemma.* Press titles also regularly appear on many regional bestseller lists, including those of the *Denver Post, Philadelphia Inquirer,* and *San Francisco Chronicle.*

Harvard Business School Press is a business unit of Harvard Business School Publishing, a wholly owned, not-for-profit subsidiary of the Harvard Business School that is headquartered in Boston, Massachusetts. Harvard Business School Publishing offers material in a variety of platforms and delivery methods that reflect its extension of the educational mission of the Harvard Business School and its access to leading authors and companies. Other business units of Harvard Business School Publishing include Harvard Business Review, Academic Cases & Reprints, Conferences, e-Learning, and Newsletters, which publishes *Harvard Management Update, Harvard Management Communications Letter,* and *The Balanced Scorecard Report.*

Query letters and SASEs should be sent to:

Carol Franco, Vice President, HBS Publishing, Director, HBS Press

Hollis Heimbouch, Editorial Director

Kirsten D. Sandberg, Executive Editor (NY)

Melinda Adams Merino, Senior Editor

Jacqueline Murphy, Senior Editor

Suzanne Rotondo, Senior Editor (NY)

Jeff Kehoe, Editor

HARVARD UNIVERSITY PRESS

79 Garden Street, Cambridge, MA 02138

401-531-2800/1-800-406-9145   fax: 617-495-5898/1-800-962-4983

www.hup.harvard.edu   e-mail: contact_HUP@harvard.edu

Harvard's publishing categories include current events, cultural affairs, the arts, history, psychology, literary studies (including selected poetry), the sciences, legal studies, and economics. Harvard's special series have included such lines as the Twentieth Century Fund, the Global AIDS Policy Coalition, and the Developing Child series.

Harvard University Press (started in 1913) is currently the largest academic press in the United States. Harvard University Press produces a large number of trade-oriented general-interest books for an eclectic readership, while maintaining its core program to provide a balanced offering of scholarly works in a range of academic fields. Harvard's extensive list is published in hardcover and trade paperback editions.

Featured Harvard titles: *The Deadly Truth* by Gerald N. Grob; *Paris: Capital of the World* by Patrice Higonnet (translated by Arthur Goldhammer); *Consciousness and the Novel* by David Lodge; *Strangers Within* by Susan Miller; *How Sex Changed* by Joanne Meyerowitz; *The Road of Excess* by Marcus Boon; *American Empire* by Andrew J. Bacevich; *Look Homeward: A Life of Thomas Wolfe* by David Donald; *Gaylaw: Challenging the Apartheid of the Closet* by William N. Eskridge; *History's Memory: Writing America's Past 1880–1980* by Ellen Fitzpatrick; *Japan Encyclopedia* by Louis Frederic; *American Agriculture in the Twentieth Century* by Bruce L. Gardner; *Unequal Freedom: How Race and Gender Shaped American Citizenship and Labor* by Evelyn Nakanao Glenn; *Teaching in America: The Slow Revolution* by Gerald Grant; *Separation of Church and State* by Philip Hamburger; *The Union Divided: Party Conflict in the Civil War North* by Mark E. Neelym Jr.

Harvard University Press handles its own distribution.

The publisher will not consider unsolicited poetry or fiction.

Query letters and SASEs should be directed to:

Elizabeth Knoll, Senior Editor for the Behavioral Sciences—Behavioral sciences, earth sciences, astronomy, neuroscience, education

Joyce Seltzer, Senior Executive Editor—History, contemporary affairs. Contact Joyce Seltzer at: 150 Fifth Avenue, Suite 625, New York, NY 10011; 212-337-0280.

Lindsay Waters, Executive Editor for the Humanities—Literary criticism, philosophy, film studies, cultural studies

Margaretta Fulton, General Editor for the Humanities—Classics (including Loeb Classics), religion, music, art, Jewish studies, women's studies

Michael A. Aronson, Senior Editor, Social Sciences—Economics, political science, sociology, law, some business

Michael Fisher, Executive Editor for Science and Medicine—Medicine, science (except astronomy), neuroscience

Kathleen McDermott, Senior Editor—History and social sciences

HOWARD UNIVERSITY PRESS

2225 Georgia Avenue NW, #718, Washington, DC 20059

202-238-2570   fax: 202-588-9849

www.founders.howard.edu/hupress

The Howard University Press program addresses the conditions, concerns, and contributions of African Americans, other African diasporic populations, and other people of color worldwide—including cultural expressions, geopolitical topics, and historical studies. Howard University Press (founded in 1972) produces scholarly and general nonfiction works in the areas of history, biography, economics, sociology, political science, education, contemporary affairs, communications, the arts, and literature. Howard University Press generally publishes a select group of new titles per year in hardcover and trade paperback editions. The press maintains a diverse backlist.

Indicative of the Howard University Press publishing program: *First Freed: Washington, D.C. in the Emancipation Era* edited by Elizabeth Clark-Lewis; *An American Paradox: Politics and Justice in America* by Patrick J. Gallo; *Barbara C. Jordan: Selected Speeches* edited by Sandra Parham; *The Black Seminole Legacy and North American Politics, 1693–1845* by Bruce Edward Ywyman; *Black Writers and Latin America Cross-Cultural Affinities* by Richard Jackson; *Genocide in Rwanda: A Collective Memory* edited by John A. Berry and Carol Pott Berry; *The Jamaican Crime Scene: A Perspective* by Bernard Headley; *Basic Currents of Nigerian Foreign Policy* by Mae C. King; *We Paid Our Dues: Women Trade Union Leaders of the Caribbean* by A. Lynn Bolles; *African Americans and U.S. Policy Toward Africa* by Elliott P. Skinner; *Captain Paul Cuffe's Logs and Letters, 1808–1817: A Black Quaker's "Voice from Within the Veil"* edited by Rosalind Wiggins; *An African Victorian Feminist: The Life and Times of Adelaide Smith Casely Hayford, 1869–1960* by Adelaide Cromwell.

On the literary, cultural, and artistic front: *Social Rituals and the Verbal Art of Zora Neale Hurston* by Lynda Marion Hill; *The Dramatic Vision of August Wilson* by Sandra Shannon; *Ancient Songs Set Ablaze: The Theatre of Femi Osofisan* by Sandra L. Richards; *Black Drama in America* edited by Darwin T. Turner; *Modern Negro Art* by James A. Porter.

Howard University Press handles distribution through its own in-house marketing department; fulfillment is handled through Johns Hopkins University Press.

The publisher will not consider unsolicited fiction or poetry. Please contact Howard University Press Editorial Department prior to sending any correspondence, including queries. Direct queries and SASEs to:

D. Kamili Anderson, Director of the Press

INDIANA UNIVERSITY PRESS

601 North Morton Street, Bloomington, IN 47404-3797

812-855-8817/1-800-842-6796   fax: 812-855-8507

www.indiana.edu/~iupress/   e-mail: iupress@indiana.edu

Indiana University Press (founded in 1950) publishes books of serious trade interest, as well as titles directed toward scholarly and academic audiences. The press addresses such subjects as African and Afro-American studies, Russian studies, music, philosophy, regional and cultural studies, military history, political science and international affairs, popular culture and the arts, semiotics, science and technology, environmental issues and natural history, Jewish studies, paleontology, Middle East studies, classics, anthropology, and gender studies. Indiana University Press also publishes fiction in translation. IUP produces hardcover and paperback editions.

Indiana University Press issues a number of prestigious series, among them Middle East Studies, Studies in Continental Thought, Theories of Contemporary Culture, Blacks in the Diaspora, Arab and Islamic Studies, and Medical Ethics. The house is home to a variety of academic journals, including *Africa Today*, *Jewish Social Studies*, and a number of journals in feminist studies.

On the IUP list: *African Voices in the African Heritage* by Betty M. Kuyk; *Africans in Colonial Mexico* by Herman L. Bennett; *Going Places* by Carlos Arnaldo Schwantes; *Apartheid's Festival* by Leslie Witz; *The Herron Chronicle* by Harriet G. Warkel, Martin F. Krause and S.L. Berry; *Naipaul's Strangers* by Dagmar Barnouw; *Put the Moose on the Table* by Randall L. Tobias and Todd Tobias; *Dan Ge Performance* by Daniel B. Reed; *The Essential Earthman* by Henry Mitchell; *No Place Like Home?* by Jennifer A. Parks; *Forging Peace* by Monroe E. Price and Mark Thompson; *Blood, Land, and Sex* by Lyda Favali and Roy Pateman; *Tank Driver* by J. Ted Hartman; *Ice Age Cave Faunas of North America* edited by Blaine W. Schubert, Jim I. Mead and Russell Wm. Graham; *The Monuments of Ancient Egypt*; *Fortress Conservation*; *Female, Jewish and Educated*; *Painted in Words*; *Together and Apart in Brzezany*; *Mothers of the Nation*; *Guitar Towns*; *Singing, Acting, and Movement in Opera*; *Becoming John Dewey*; *Gaining Ground*; *King of the Crocodylians*; *Derrida and Husserl*; *A Short History of African Philosophy*; *The Puzzle Instinct*; *Monon*.

Indiana University Press distributes its own list, as well as books produced by the Indiana Historical Society and the British Film Institute; IUP also serves as regional sales representative for several other university presses.

Query letters and SASEs should be directed to:

Janet Rabinowich, Editorial Director—Russian and East European studies, African studies, Middle Eastern and Judaic studies, philosophy

Robert Sloan, Senior Sponsoring Editor—Science, military history, U.S. history, African American studies, and religion

Linda Oblack, Assistant Sponsoring Editor

Richard Higgins, Assistant Sponsoring Editor

Jane Quinet, Assistant Sponsoring Editor

Michael Lundell, Sponsoring Editor—Classical studies, ancient history, medieval and Renaissance studies, film, folklore, and literature

Dee Mortensen, Sponsoring Editor—African studies, Caribbean and Black diaspora studies, philosophy, and women's studies (literary and cultural)

Gayle Sherwood, Sponsoring Editor—Music

Rebecca Tolen, Assistant Sponsoring Editor—Anthropology

THE JOHNS HOPKINS UNIVERSITY PRESS

2715 North Charles Street, Baltimore, MD 21218-4363

410-516-6900   fax: 410-516-6968

www.press.jhu.edu

The Johns Hopkins University Press (founded in 1878) issues a strong list of contemporary-interest titles and academic trade books, as well as scholarly, technical, and professional works, and select course books, reference books, and books of regional interest. The Press publishes in such diverse academic areas as literary criticism, ancient studies, religious studies, political science, and history of and current trends in medicine, science, and technology.

Johns Hopkins titles: *Evolution of New York City Subways* by Gene Sansone; *The Great Marsh* by David W. Harp and Tom Horton; *Maryland Basketball* by Paul McMullen; *The Physics of Hockey* by Alain Hache; *Adolescent Depression* by Francis Mark Mondimore, M.D.; *Architecture and Town Planning In Colonial North America* by James D. Kornwolf; *It Happened on Washington Square* by Emily Kies Folpe; *Camelot at Dawn* photographs by Orlando Suero; *Silent Screens* by Michael Putnam; *My House Is Killing Me! The Home Guide for Families with Allergies and Asthma* by Jeffrey C. May; *Zeppelin! Germany and the Airship, 1900–1939* by Guillame de Syon; *Saving the Bay: People Working for the Future of the Chesapeake* by Ann E. Dorbin (photographs by Richard A. K. Dorbin); *The Universities of the Italian Renaissance* by Paul F. Grendler; *The Tradition of the Trojan War in Homer and the Epic Cycle* by Jonathan Burgess; *The Rule of Law in America* by Ronald A. Cass; *Higher Education Law: The Faculty* by Steven G. Poskanzer; *Trauma and Its Representations: The Social Life of Mimesis in Post-Revolutionary France* by Deborah Jenson.

Johns Hopkins produces a number of specialty lines, such as the American Moment series of undergraduate course books in American history, the American Land Classics series of facsimile reprint editions, and Complete Roman Drama in Translation. The Johns Hopkins University Press handles its own distribution with the support of regional sales representatives.

The press will not consider unsolicited poetry or fiction.

Query letters and SASEs should be directed to:

Trevor Lipscombe, Editor-in-Chief—Physics and Astronomy

Henry Y. K. Tom, Executive Editor—Sociology, religious studies, economics, development, European history, sociology, political science

Vincent Burke, Acquisitions Editor—Biology and Life Sciences

Jacqueline C. Wehmueller, Executive Editor—Trade medical books for an educated general audience; books in higher education; history of medicine; reference books

UNIVERSITY PRESSES

Wendy Harris, Medical Editor—Medicine (hard science for medical professionals), public health, bioethics
Juliana McCarthy, Managing Editor
Robert Brugger, History Editor—American history, history of science and technology, regional titles, documentary editions
Michael Lonegro, Assistant Editor

LOUISIANA STATE UNIVERSITY PRESS

PO Box 25053, Baton Rouge, LA 70894-5053
225-578-6294/1-800-861-3477   fax: 1-800-305-4416
www.lsu.edu/lsupress   e-mail: lsupress@lsu.edu

Areas of Louisiana State University Press interest include Southern history, the American Civil War, African American history, United States history, Latin American history, European history, philosophy and politics, art, architecture and design, photography, literary voices of the South, American literature, general criticism and European literature, music, natural history, and medicine. LSU offers a wide variety of regional books (not limited to Louisiana environs), as well as concentrations in contemporary fiction, poetry, and literary criticism. The house produces hardcover and trade paperback editions and maintains a solid backlist. Louisiana State University Press (founded in 1935) publishes a primarily academic and scholarly list, along with a good number of general-interest titles.

From LSU Press: *Being-in-Christ and Putting Death in its Place* by Miles Richardson; *Doctor Quintard, Chaplain C.S.A. and Second Bishop of Tennessee* edited by Sam Davis Elliot; *Legacy of Disunion* edited by Susan-Mary Grant and Peter J. Parish; *Mother Love* by Candace Flynt; *The Magic Striptease* by George Garrett; *Sweetbitter* by Reginald Gibbons; *Such Was the Season* by Clarence Major; *Let the Bastards Go* by Joe Morris Doss; *Old Hickory's War* by David S. Heidler and Jeanne T. Heidler; *Memoirs of My Life* by Pierre Clement de Laussat (translated by Agnes-Josephine Pastwa, O.S.F.); *Do I Owe You Something* by Michael Mewshaw; *Tenderness Shore* by Meredith Stricker; *Girocho* by John Henry Poncio and Marlin Young; *My Diary North and South* by Eugene H. Berwanger; *Grant, Lee, Lincoln and the Radicals: Essays on Civil War Leadership* by Grady McWhiney; *Autumn of the Heartland: The Army of Tennessee, 1861–1862* by Thomas Lawrence Connelly; *Gardening in the Humid South* by Edmund N. O'Rourke Jr. and Leon C. Standifer; *Peter Taylor: A Writer's Life* by Hubert H. McAlexander; *Birds of the Gulf Coast* by Brian K. Miller and William R. Fontenot; *An Honorable Estate: My Time in the Working Press* by Louis D. Rubin Jr.; *John Marshall and the Heroic Age of the Supreme Court* by R. Kent Newmyer; *New Orleans Yesterday and Today: Third Edition* by Walter

G. Cowan, et al.; *Our People and Our History: Fifty Creole Portraits* by Rodolphe Lucien Desdunes; *Along the River Road: Revised and Expanded Edition* by Mary Ann Sternberg; *Dixiana Moon* by William Price Fox; *The Annunciation* by Ellen Gilchrist; *A Recent Martyr* by Valerie Martin; *Set in Motion* by Valerie Martin; *A Sacrificial Zinc* by Matthew Cooperman; *Strangers to Their Courage* by Alice Derry; *Icon and Evidence* by Margaret Gibson; *Anvil, Clock & Last* by Paulette Roeske; *A Word in Your Ear* by Monroe Spears.

Louisiana State University Press oversees a distributional network that uses the services of regional university presses and book-distribution companies, as well as independent sales representatives. The Press will not consider unsolicited poetry or any original fiction.

Query letters and SASEs should be directed to:

MaryKatherine Callaway, Director

THE MIT PRESS

5 Cambridge Center, Cambridge, MA 02142

617-253-5646   fax: 617-258-6779

The MIT Press publishes nonfiction titles in the forefront of such fields as contemporary art, architectural studies, science, environmental studies, computer science and artificial intelligence, cognitive science and neuroscience, linguistics, and economics and finance. The house produces scholarly and professional works, in addition to educational textbooks and books for a general audience. The MIT Press was founded in 1961 as the publishing wing of the Massachusetts Institute of Technology.

Representative titles from MIT Press include: *A Scientist Speaks* by Karl Taylor Compton; *Abel's Proof* by Peter Pesic; *The Accident of Art* by Paul Virilio; *Action and Recreation* by Jean Starobinski; *Actors* by Gul Agha; *Advanced Research in VLSI* by Jonathan Allen and F. Thompson Leighton; *Affinity, That Elusive Dream* by Mi Gyung Kim; *The Algebraic Mind* by Gary F. Marcus; *America as Second Creation* by Davis E. Nye; *Analytical Development Economics* by Kaushik Basu; *Art and Technology in the Nineteenth and Twentieth Centuries* by Pierre Francastel (translated by Randall Cherry); *Artificial Love* by Paul Shepheard; *Asset Price Bubbles* by William C. Hunter, George G. Kaufman and Michael Pomerleano; *Bandwagon Effects in High Technology Industries* by Jeffrey H. Rohlfs; *Beyond Late Development* by Alice H. Amsden and Wan-wen Chu; *A Ghost's Memoir* by John McDonald; *Advances in Neural Information Processing Systems 14* by Thomas G. Dietterich, Suzanna Becker, and Zoubin Ghahramani; *American Economic Policy in the 1990s* by Jeffrey A. Frankel and Peter R. Orszag; *Architectural Encounters with Essence and Form in Modern China* by Peter G. Rowe and Seng Kuan; *The Arts at Black Mountain College* by Mary Emma Harris; *Barriers to Riches* by Stephen L. Parente and Edward C. Prescott; *Belief's Own Ethics* by Jonathan E. Adler; *Borders and*

Brethren by Brenda Shaffer.

The MIT Press also publishes 40-odd specialist journals such as *The Drama Review*, *The Washington Quarterly*, and *October*. The Bradford Books imprint accents titles representing the frontiers of cognitive science and neuroscience.

The MIT Press distributes its own list and handles distribution for several other publishers (including Zone Books and AAAI Press).

Query letters and SASEs should be directed to:

Ellen W. Faran, Acting Editor-in-Chief

Tom Stone, Linguistics and Cognitive Science Editor

Clay Morgan, Environmental Science Editor

Douglas Sery, Computer Science Editor

Barbara Murphy, Neurosciences Editor

Robert Prior, Computer Science Editor

Roger Conover, Architecture and Design Editor

Elizabeth Murry, Economics, Finance, and Business Editor

Sara Meirowitz, Associate Editor, Science, Technology & Society

John Covell, Economics, Finance, and Business Editor

NEW YORK UNIVERSITY PRESS

858 Broadway, 3rd floor, New York, NY 10003-4812

212-998-2575   fax: 212-995-3833

www.nyupress.org   e-mail: nyupress.feedback@nyu.edu

New York University Press covers the fields of law and politics, history, American history, religion and Jewish studies, psychology, gender studies, sociology, cultural studies, media studies, literary criticism, urban studies, anthropology, race and ethnic studies, business, and New York regional affairs.

New York University Press (founded in 1916) offers a list laden with works of wide contemporary appeal for the general reader; NYU also maintains a strong presence in the scholarly and professional arena. Major series include titles catalogued under Fast Track (general-interest contemporary issues and affairs): Critical America; Sexual Cultures: New Directions from the Center for Gay and Lesbian Studies; Cultural Front; The World of War; The Religion, Race and Ethnicity series; New Perspectives on Jewish Studies; Essential Papers in Jewish Studies; Essential Papers in Psychoanalysis; and Qualitative Studies in Psychology. NYU publishes hardcover and paperback editions and supports a vigorous backlist.

From the NYU program: *The Atheist* by Bryan F. Le Beau; *The New Encyclopedia of Judaism* edited by Geoffrey Wigoder, Fred Skolnick and Shmuel Himelstein; *The New H.N.I.C.* by Todd Boyd; *An Interpretation of the Qur'an* (translated by Majid Fakhry); *Love the Sin* by Janet R. Jakobsen and Ann Pellegrini; *Irving Howe* by Gerald Sorin; *Dancing at Halftime* by Carol Spindel; *Going South* by Debra L. Schultz (foreword by Blanche Wiesen Cook); *Hollywood v. Hard Core* by Jon Lewis; *Fat History* by Peter N. Strearns; *Dreaming of Fred and Ginger* by Annette Kuhn; *Queer Latinidad* by Juana Maria Rodriguez; *Praxis for the Poor* by Sanford F. Schram; *Talking Trash* by Julie Engel Manga; *Black Gay Man* by Robert Reid-Pharr; *Lure of the Sinister: The Unnatural History of Satanism* by Gareth J. Medway; *The Practical Guide to Aging* by Christine K. Cassel; *TechniColor: Race, Technology, and Everyday Life* edited by Alondra Nelson, Thuy Linh N. Tu and Alicia Headlman Hines; *Reflections: The Life and Writings of a Young Blind Woman in Post-Revolutionary France* by Therese-Adele Husson (translated by Catherine Kudlick and Zina Weygand).

NYU Press is the exclusive North American distributor for Berg Publishers, Monthly Review Press, Lawrence & Wishart, and Rivers Oram (Pandora).

NYU Press Prize winners include *The Marvelous Adventures of Pierre Baptiste: Father and Mother, First and Last* (fiction) by Patricia Eakins, and *The Alphabet of Desire* (poetry) by Barbara Hamby.

New York University Press handles distribution through its own sales office, as well as a network of regional sales and marketing representatives.

Query letters and SASEs should be directed to:

Eric Zinner, Editor-in-Chief—Literary criticism and cultural studies, media studies, history, anthropology

Ilene Kalish, Sociology, Politics, and Anthropology

Jennifer Hammer, Editor—Religion and psychology

Deborah Gershenowitz, Editor—American History to 1900, American Military History, American Business History, Law

OHIO UNIVERSITY PRESS

180 Pressey Hall, 1070 Carmack Road, Columbus, OH 43210-1002

740-593-1155   fax: 740-593-4536

www.ohiostatepress.org

Ohio University Press areas of interest encompass literary criticism, philosophy, African studies, history, international, regional and cultural studies, and Frontier Americana. The press also publishes fiction reprints and anthologies. Poetry issued through the Swallow Press imprint certifies the house's outstanding presence in this literary niche.

Ohio University Press (established in 1964) produces scholarly and academic works, as well as a line of general-interest titles. OU Press publishes in hardcover and paperback. The house backlist is comprehensive.

On the OU Press list: *Guest Appearances and Other Travels in Time and Space* by Peter I. Rose; *From Blackjacks to Briefcases* by Robert Michael Smith; *The Virgin and The Dynamo* by Bailey Van Hook; *The Ceramic Career of M. Louise McLaughlin*; *Shakespeare at the Cineplex* by Samuel Crowl; *Two Hundred Women from Ohio* by Jacqueline Jones Royster; *Follow the Blue Blazes* by Robert J. Pond; *Solving for X* by Robert B. Shaw; *One Unblinking Eye* by Norman Williams; *The Inclusive Corporation* by Griff Hogan; *In the Work of Their Hands is Their Prayer* by Joel Daehnke; *One-Smoke Stories* by Mary Austin; *Vernon Lee* by Christa Zorn; *Tensions of Empire* by Ken'ichi Goto; *Broken Lives and Other Stories* by Anthonia C. Kalu; *Dared and Done: The Marriage of Elizabeth Barrett and Robert Browning* by Julia Markus; *Death and Taxes: The Complete Guide to Family Inheritance Planning* by Randell C. Doane and Rebecca G. Doane; *Deprived of Unhappiness* by Sam Pickering; *Brave Are My People: Indian Heroes Not Forgotten* by Frank Waters (foreword by Vine Deloria Jr.); *RFD* by Charles Allen Smart (foreword by Gene Logsdon); *The Watchers* by Memye Curtis Tucker; *Ruskin's Mythic Queen: Gender Subversion in Victorian Culture* by Sharon Aronofsky Weltman; *The Absent Man: The Narrative Craft of Charles W. Chesnutt*; *The Complete Works of Robert Browning, Volume XVI: With Variant Readings and Annotations* edited by Susan Crowl and Roma A. King Jr.; *Word Play Place: Essays on the Poetry of John Matthias* edited by Robert Archambeau.

Ohio University Press oversees its own sales and distribution.

Query letters and SASEs should be directed to:

Heather Lee Miller, PhD, Acquisitions Editor

Malcolm Litchfield, Acquisitions Editor

Eugene O'Connor, PhD, Acquisitions Editor

OXFORD UNIVERSITY PRESS

198 Madison Avenue, New York, NY 10016

212-726-6000

www.oup-usa.org

Oxford's list is especially prominent in the subject areas of life science, world history (both ancient and modern), United States history, law, philosophy, religion, psychology, classics, literature, engineering, politics, sociology, economics, finance, business and management, and music.

Oxford University Press is the world's largest university press. It publishes 3,000 new books a year and has a presence in more than 50 countries. Founded in 1478, Oxford is an international publisher of trade, scholarly, professional, and reference titles in the humanities, the arts, science, medicine, and social studies in hardcover and paperback editions. OUP also publishes college textbooks, English as a second language educational materials, and children's books, as well as a number of journals.

Oxford titles include: *All Shook Up* by Glenn Altschuler; *Personal States* by Catherine Alexander; *Art History: A Very Short Introduction* by Arnold Dana; *Bilingualism in Ancient Society* by J.N. Adams; *The Legend of Nandan* by Indira Parthasarathy; *Conversation Medicine* by Alonso Aguirre; *Applied Scholastic Hydrogeology* by Yoram Rubin; *1089 and All That* by David Acheson; *Victorian Detective Stories* by Michael Cox; *The Argument from Injustice* by Robert Alexy; *Broadway Yearbook, 1999–2000* by Steven Suskin; *The Oxford Book of Travel Stories* by Patricia Craig; *Superconductivity* by J. F. Annett; *Musorgsky* by David Brown; *Oresteia* by Aeschylus; *All That Makes A Man* by Stephen Berry; *Korean Cinema* by Frances Gateward; *Terrestrial Field Dissipation Studies* by Arthur Ellen; *The Ingredients* by Philip Ball; *Sundials at Greenwich* by Hester Higton; *The Lost World of Pompeii* by Colin Amery; *Methods in Agriculture Chemical Analysis* by N. T. Faithfull; *Inroads into Burma* by Gerry Abbott; *Sport in Australian History* by Daryl Adair; *Tourism and Spatial Transformation* by G. J. Ashworth; *Tourism in Spain* by M. Barke; *The Oxford Companion to the Wines of North America* by Bruce Cass; *Rome* by Amanda Claridge; *Spain* by Roger Collins; *The Temple Tiger and More Man-Eaters of Kumaon* by Jim Corbett; *World Leisure Participation* by G. Cushman; *The Classical Cookbook* by Andrew Dalby; *The A–Z of Sailing Terms, Second Edition* by Ian Dear; *Traditional Chinese Clothing* by Valery M. Garrett; *Trends in Outdoor Recreation, Leisure and Tourism* by W. C. Gartner; *Sou' West in Wanderer IV* by Eric C. Hiscock; *Budapest* by Michael Jacobs; *Travelers' India* by H. K. Kaul.

Oxford's New York office is editorially independent of the British home office and handles distribution of its own list, as well as titles originating from Oxford's branches worldwide.

Query letters and SASEs should be directed to:

Niko Pfund, Academic Publisher

Joan Bossert, Associate Publisher—Science and professional books

Catharine Carlin, Associate Publisher—Psychology

Martha Cooley, Editor—Business

Paul Donnelly, Executive Editor—Business, finance, economics

Dedi Felman, Editor—Politics, criminology, law, sociology

Susan Ferber, Editor—American and world history, art history

Kirk Jensen, Executive Editor—Life sciences

Peter C. Gordon, Editor—Chemistry, Chemical Engineering, Geography, Physics, Computer Sciences

Clifford W. Mills, Editor—Agriculture/Soil Science, Astronomy, Atmospheric Science, Environmental Sciences

UNIVERSITY PRESSES

Sharon Liu, Associate Editor—Chemistry

Stephen McGroarty, Associate Editor—Economics

Elissa Morris, Editor—Literary studies, classics, media studies, cultural studies, gay/lesbian studies, literature, African American studies

Peter Ohlin, Editor—Linguistics, philosophy

Cynthia Read, Senior Editor—Religion

Peter Ginna, Trade Editorial Director—American history

Tim Bartlett, Senior Editor—Political science, sociology, current events

Elda Rotor, Editor—Literature, cultural studies, art, photography, architecture

Nancy Toff, Editorial Director—Children's and young adult books

Jeff House, Executive Editor—Medicine

Fiona Stevens, Senior Editor—Psychiatry, medicine, neuroscience

Donald Kraus, Executive Editor—Bibles

PRINCETON UNIVERSITY PRESS

41 William Street, Princeton, NJ 08540

609-258-4900   fax: 609-258-6305

www.pup.princeton.edu

U.K. office:

3 Market Place, Woodstock, Oxfordshire OX20 1SY, U.K.

(011) 44-1993-814500

Princeton University Press, founded in 1905, has a particularly strong focus in such areas as popular culture and fine arts, current affairs, literary biography, European history, political science, economics, and natural history. Princeton University Press publishes trade and general-interest books, in addition to a list of scholarly and scientific works that span the academic spectrum. Popular Princeton lines include the Bollingen series and Princeton Science Library. Princeton publishes hardcover and paperback editions and hosts a comprehensive backlist.

Princeton titles: *Freedom and Its Betrayal* edited by Henry Hardy; *Human Rights as Politics and Idolatry* by Michael Ignatieff; *Identity in Democracy* by Amy Gutmann; *The Power of Denial* by Bernard Faure; *The Shi'is of Iraq* by Yitzhak Nakash; *The Silver Lining* by Seth R. Reice; *The Encyclopedia of Ancient Egyptian Architecture* by Dieter Arnold; *Marine Mammals of the North Atlantic* by Carl Christian Kinze; *A Photographic Guide to the Birds of Indonesia* by Morten Strange; *Democracy and the Foreigner* by Bonnie Honig;

Birds of Western and Central Africa by Ber van Perlo; *Charles Taylor* by Ruth Abbey; *Sexual Identities, Queer Politics* edited by Mark Blasius; *Financing the American Dream: A Cultural History of Consumer Credit* by Lendol Calder; *Diplomacy of Conscience: Amnesty International and Changing Human Rights Norms* by Ann Marie Clark; *Asset Pricing* by John H. Cochrane; *The Secular Mind* by Robert Coles; *Winslow Homer and the Critics: Forging a National Art in the 1870s* by Margaret C. Conrads; *Home Team: Professional Sports and the American Metropolis* by Michael N. Danielson; *Learning and Expectations in Macroeconomics* by George W. Evans and Seppo Honkapohja; *How the Leopard Changed Its Spots: The Evolution of Complexity* by Brian Goodwin; *The Necessary Nation* by Gregory Jusdanis.

The Bollingen Series, established in 1941, is sponsored by the Bollingen Foundation and has been published by Princeton since 1967. Bollingen titles are works of original scholarship, translations, or new editions of classics. An ongoing Bollingen project is Mythos: The Princeton/Bollingen series in world mythology. Titles include *Psychology of Kundalini Yoga* by C. G. Young; *On the Laws of the Poetic Art* by Anthony Hecht; *The Survival of the Pagan Gods: The Mythological Tradition and Its Place in Renaissance Humanism and Art* by Jean Seznec.

Books from the Princeton Science Library include *Infinity and the Mind* by Rudy Rucker; *A Natural History of Shells* by Geerat J. Vermeij; *Total Eclipses of the Sun* by J. B. Zirker.

Princeton University Press handles distribution through the offices of California/Princeton Fulfillment Services, as well as regional sales representation worldwide.

Query letters and SASEs should be directed to:

Peter Dougherty, Economics Editor and Publisher

Walter Lippincott, Director

Sam Elworthy, Editor-in-Chief

Robert Kirk, Senior Editor—Natural history

Ian Malcolm, Philosophy, Political Theory, and Sociology Editor

Chuck Myers, Political Science, Law, and Classics Editor

Brigitta van Rheinberg, Senior Editor—History and Religion Editor—Twentieth-century American history, non-American history, and religion (Jewish and Asian studies)

Richard Baggaley (U.K. office), European Publishing Director—Finance and economics

Fred Appel, Associate Editor—Music, anthropology, and literature

Vickie Kearn, Senior Editor—Mathematics

Ingrid Gnerlich, Editor—Physical sciences

Tim Sullivan, Editor—Sociology, economics, organizational behavior

Hanne Winarsky, Editor—Literature, art

UNIVERSITY PRESSES

RUTGERS UNIVERSITY PRESS

100 Joyce Kilmer Avenue, Piscataway, NJ 08854

732-445-7762 ext. 605

http://rutgerspress.rutgers.edu

Rutgers subject areas include African American studies, American history, anthropology, art and architecture, Asian American studies, environment and ecology, European history, gay and gender studies, geography, health and medicine, history of medicine and science, literature and literary criticism, media studies, multicultural studies, New Jerseyana, peace studies, poetry, religion, and sociology.

Rutgers University Press (founded in 1936) publishes a list of general-interest trade books in addition to scholarly titles in the humanities and social sciences, as well as books with a regional American bent.

Representing the nonfiction Rutgers list: *Midnight Dreary: The Mysterious Death of Edgar Allan Poe* by John Evangelist Walsh; *Talking Leadership: Conversations with Powerful Women* edited by Mary S. Hartman; *The Truth That Never Hurts: Writings on Race, Gender, and Freedom* by Barbara Smith; *Surviving Modern Medicine: How to Get the Best from Doctors, Family and Friends* by Peter Clarke and Susan H. Evans; *Mortal Men: Living with Asymptomatic HIV* by Richard MacIntyre (foreword by Stephen Lacey); *Heresy in the University: The Black Athena Controversy and the Responsibilities of American Intellectuals* by Jacques Berlinerblau; *How Jews Became White Folks and What That Says About Race in America* by Karen Brodkin; *Consuming Environments: Television and Commercial Culture* by Mike Budd, Steve Craig, and Clay Steinman.

Rutgers features the Touring North America guidebook series, which focuses on regional landscapes. Titles: *Beyond the Great Divide: Denver to the Grand Canyon*; *Megalopolis: Washington, DC, to Boston*.

New Jerseyana from Rutgers includes *Roadside New Jersey* by Peter Genovese; *Murdered in Jersey* by Gerald Tomlinson; *Teenage New Jersey, 1941–1975* (edited by Kathryn Grover); *The New Jersey State Constitution: A Reference Guide* by Robert F. Williams.

Rutgers University Press handles its own distribution.

Query letters and SASEs should be directed to:

Audra Wolfe, Science editor

Kristi Long, Social Sciences and religion editor

Melanie Halkias, History and Asian American Editor

Molly Baab, Editorial Assistant

Adi Hovav, Editorial Assistant

Leslie Mitchner, Associate Director and Editor-in-Chief—Humanities, literature, film, communications

STANFORD UNIVERSITY PRESS

1450 Page Mill Road, Palo Alto, CA 94304-1124

650-723-9434   fax: 650-725-3457

www.sup.org

Stanford produces a notable line of titles in the fields of new technology, the global political and natural environment, postmodern philosophy and psychology, gender studies, and international issues, as well as a number of books (many in translation) dealing with current cultural and literary theory. A major Stanford publishing concentration is in the Asian American and Pacific Rim fields of studies.

Stanford University Press (started in 1925) produces trade and scholarly books in literature, the social sciences, religion, history, political science, anthropology, and natural science in hardcover and paperback editions.

Highlights from Stanford: *The Wild God of the World* edited by Albert Gelpi; *Islam in a Globalizing World* by Thomas W. Simons, Jr.; *Diary of a Contraband* by William B. Gould IV; *Private Life Under Socialism* by Yunxiang Yan; *Decisive Encounters* by Odd Arne Westad; *The Difference "Difference" Makes* edited by Deborah L. Rhode; *Can One Live After Auschwitz?* by Theodor W. Adorno; *Theories of Social Order* edited by Michael Hechter and Christine Horne; *Silicon Valley, Women, and the California Dream* by Glenna Matthews; *Managing Ethics in Business Organizations* by Linda Klebe Trevino and Gary R. Weaver; *Controlling Immigration* edited by Wayne A. Cornelius, Takeyuki Tsuda, Philip L. Martin, and James F. Hollifield; *Creating a Strategic Human Resources Organization* edited by Edward E. Lawler III and Susan Albers Mohrman; *Organization Strategy, Structure, and Process* by Raymond E. Miles and Charles C. Snow; *The External Control of Organizations* by Jeffrey Pfeffer and Gerald R. Salancik; *Asian Security Order* edited by Muthiah Alagappa; *Taking Our Pulse: The Health of America's Women* by Iris F. Litt, M.D.; *The Cable Car in America* by George W. Hilton; *The Fall of the Packard Motor Car Company* by James A. Ward; *From Immigrant to Ethnic Culture: American Yiddish in South Philadelphia* by Rakhmiel Peltz; *Caught by History: Holocaust Effects in Contemporary Art, Literature, and Theory* by Ernst Van Alphen; *Desiring Women Writing: English Renaissance Examples* by Jonathan Goldberg.

Stanford University Press books are distributed by Cambridge University Press Distribution Center.

Query letters and SASEs should be directed to:

John Feneron, Managing Editor—Asian literature

Amanda Moran, Acquisitions Editor— Law, political science, and public policy. In particular, technology and law; human rights; intellectual property; jurists; comparative law; environmental law; American politics and political history.

Martha Cooley, Acquisitions Editor— Economics, finance, and business

Kate Wahl, Acquisitions Editor—Sociology, Anthropology, Education, and Middle Eastern Studies

Kimberly Brown, Associate Editor

Carmen A Borbon-Wu, Associate Editor

Muriel Bell, Senior Editor—Asian studies, political science, anthropology

Norris Pope, Director—Latin American studies, history, Victorian studies, natural sciences

---

SYRACUSE UNIVERSITY PRESS

621 Skytop Road, Suite 110, Syracuse, NY 13244-5290

315-443-5534   fax: 315-443-5545

http://syracuseuniversitypress.syr.edu/   e-mail: talitz@syr.edu

Syracuse University Press (founded in 1943) hosts a publishing program that accents scholarly, general, and regional (New York and New England) nonfiction interests, as well as literature and criticism. Syracuse has a particular presence in Irish studies, Iroquois studies, Middle Eastern studies, studies in peace and conflict resolution, history of the medieval period, and historical American utopianism and communitarianism.

On the Syracuse list: *Black Baseball* by Michael E. Lomax; *Athena's Daughters* edited by Frances Early and Kathleen Kennedy; *The West Wing* edited by Peter C. Rollins and John E. O'Connor; *What a Life!* edited by Gershon Freidlin; *A Due Voci* edited by Julie Grossman, Ann M. Ryan, and Kim Waale; *The Church Universal and Triumphant* by Bradley C. Whistle; *The Albert Schweitzer–Helene Bresslau Letters, 1902–1912* edited by Rhena Schweitzer Miller; *Verandahs of Power* by Garth Andrew Myers; *Yeats and the Visual Arts* by Elizabeth Bergmann Loizeaux; *Irish Women Writers Speak Out* by Caitriona Moloney and Helen Thompson; *The Madness of Art* by Robert Phillips; *A Reader's Guide to William Faulkner* by Edmond L. Volpe; *Adirondack Vernacular* by Robert Bogdan; *America in the Seventies* by Stephanie A. Slocum-Schaffer; *The Erie Canal Reader, 1790-1950* edited by Roger W. Hecht; *Act and Idea in the Nazi Genocide* by Berel Lang; *A Drive to Israel* by Ali Salem; *Situation Negative* by Hasan Basri Danisman; *Insects and Mites Injurious to Crops in Middle Eastern Countries* by Abdul Mun'im S. Talhouk; *Middle East Contemporary Survey* edited by Bruce Maddy-Weitzman; *Crossing Highbridge: A Memoir of Irish America* by Maureen Waters; *Under the Spell of Arabia* (photographs by Mathias Oppersdorff); *Gertrude Bell: The Arabian Diaries, 1913–1914* (edited by Rosemary O'Brien); *Women in Muslim Family Law* by John L. Esposito with Natana DeLong-Bas.

Titles in the Reader's Guide series: *A Reader's Guide to Walt Whitman* by Gay Wilson Allen; *A Reader's Guide to Joseph Conrad* by Frederick R. Karl; *A Reader's Guide to William Butler Yeats* by John Unterecker; *A Reader's Guide to Dylan Thomas, A Reader's Guide to James Joyce* and *A Reader's Guide to Finnegan's Wake* by William York Tindall; *A Reader's Guide to Samuel Beckett* by Hugh Kenner.

Syracuse University Press distributes its list via its own in-house offices and utilizes a variety of distribution services worldwide.

Syracuse University Press does not wish to receive unsolicited manuscripts.

Mary Shelden Evans, Executive Editor—e-mail: msevans@syr.edu

John J. Fruegwirth, Managing Editor

D.J. Whyte, Assistant Managing Editor

Tim Hayes, Assistant Editor

Marian Buda, Copy Editor

Kay Steinmetz, Copy Editor

TEXAS A&M UNIVERSITY PRESS

John H. Lindsey Building, Lewis Street, College Station, TX, 77843-4354

1-800-826-9811   fax: 1-800-617-2421

www.tamu.edu/upress/   e-mail: d-vance@tamu.edu

Texas A&M University Press (founded in 1974) publishes scholarly nonfiction, regional studies, art, economics, government, history, environmental history, natural history, social science, United States–Mexican borderlands studies, veterinary medicine, women's studies, and military studies. A special portion of the Texas A&M list accents Texas photography, history, and literature.

Texas A & M nonfiction: *Along Forgotten River* by Geoff Winningham; *America's Frontier Culture* by Ray A. Billington; *The Bootlegger's Other Daughter* by Mary Cimarolli; *The Buffalo Soldier Tragedy of 1877* by Paul H. Carlson; *Builders* by Joseph A. Pratt and Christopher J. Castaneda; *The Empty Schoolhouse* by Luther Bryan Clegg; *Lone Star Confederate* edited by George Skoch and Mark W. Perkins; *San Antonio on Parade* by Judith Berg Sobre; *Agent for the Resistance* by Herman Bodson; *A Dark and Bloody Ground* by Edward G. Miller; *Leadership in the Crucible* by Kenneth E. Hamburger; *The Art of Tom Lea* compiled by Kathleen G. Hjerter; *Like Sex with Gods* by Bayla Singer; *Behind Every Choice is a Story* by Gloria Feldt with Carol Trickett Jennings; *Every Good Boy Does Fine* by Timothy Lackawski; *More Space Than Anyone Can Stand* by William Notter; *The Second Dune* by Shelby Hearon; *Secret Lives* by Catherine Browder; *Slim* by Ruth Linnea Whitney; *Time Between Trains* by Anthony Bukoski; *Insects of the Texas Lost Pines* by Stephen Welton; *Legends and Love of Texas Wildflowers* by Elizabeth Silverthorne; *Reflections on the Neches* by Geraldine Ellis Watson; *Between Law and Politics* by Richard Pacelle, Jr.; *Land of the Desert Sun: Texas' Big Bend Country* by D. Gentry Steele.

Texas A&M University Press manages its own distribution network and handles distribution for several other regional, academically oriented presses.

Query letters and SASEs should be directed to:

Mary Lenn Dixon, Editor-in-Chief—e-mail: mary-dixon@tamu.edu

Shannon Davies, Senior Editor—e-mail: smdavies@aol.com

Jim Sadkovich, Acquisitions Editor—e-mail: j-sadkovich@tamu.edu

Stephanie George, Assistant Managing Editor

Jennifer Ann Hutt, Assistant Editor

Diana L. Vance, Editorial Assistant, Acquisitions

Janet Mathewson, Editorial Assistant, Copyeditor

UNIVERSITY OF ARIZONA PRESS

355 S. Euclid, Suite 103, Tucson, AZ 85719

520-621-1441   fax: 520-621-8899

www.uapress.arizona.edu

University of Arizona Press (founded in 1959) publishes works of general as well as academic interest, related primarily to the scholarly emphasis of the university's programs in Southwest regional culture and natural history. Fields of publishing concentration include general nonfiction about Arizona, the American West, and Mexico; wider categories encompass the American Indian and Latin America, anthropology, and archaeology.

From the Arizona program: *Centuries of Decline During the Hohokam Classic Period at Pueblo Grande* by David R. Abbott; *Adventuring in Arizona* by John Annerino; *When We Arrive: A New Literary History of Mexican America* by Jose F. Aranda; *Edward Abbey* by James M Cahalan; *Mexican Murals in Times of Crisis* by Bruce Campbell; *Work Done Right* by David Dominguez; *Southern Arizona Nature Almanac* by Roseann Beggy Hanson and Jonathan Hanson; *Salvadorans in Costa Rica: Displaced Lives* by Bridget Hayden; *Telling Stories the Kiowa Way* by Gus Palmer, Jr.; *Linking Human Rights and Environment* by Romina Picolotti and Jorge Daniel Taillant; *Talking Birds, Plumed Serpents and Painted Women: Ceramics of Casas Grandes* edited by Joanne Stuhr; *Dining at the Lineman's Shack* by John Weston; *Barren, Wild, and Worthless* by Susan J. Tweit; *The Political Ecology of the Colorado River Delta, 1940-1975* by Evan R. Ward; *Homol'ovi: An Ancient Hopi Settlement Cluster* by E. Charles Adams; *Backcountry Pilot: Flying Adventures with Ike Russell* by Thomas Bowen; *Moving from the Margins: A Chicana Voice on Public Policy* by Adela de la Torre; *Western Pueblo Identities* by Andrew Duff; *Mexican Americans and the U.S. Economy* by Arturo Gonzalez.

University of Arizona Press handles its own distribution and also distributes titles originating from the publishing programs of such enterprises and institutions as Oregon State University Press, the Arizona State Museum, and other archaeological and environmental consulting firms.

Query letters and SASEs should be directed to:

Patti Hartmann, Acquiring Editor, Humanities—Native American literature and studies, Latina/o literature and studies, environmental writing, Western and environmental history, Latin American studies

Allyson Carter, Acquiring Editor, Social Sciences and Sciences— Anthropology, archaeology, ethnohistory, Southwest studies, environmental studies, conservation biology, natural history, popular astronomy, space sciences, geography

UNIVERSITY OF ARKANSAS PRESS

McIlroy House, 201 Ozark Avenue, Fayetteville, AR 72701

479-575-3246   fax: 479-575-6044

www.uapress.com   e-mail: uapress@uark.edu

University of Arkansas Press (begun in 1980) features titles in Middle Eastern studies, civil rights studies, poetry, literary criticism, history, regional studies, natural science, political science, and popular culture. The house issues a moderate list of new books each season (in both hardcover and paperback editions), while tending a hardy backlist.

Indicative of the Arkansas list: *Bearing Witness* edited by George E. Lankford; *With Fire and Sword* by Thomas A. DeBlack; *Angry Voices* translated by Mohamed Enani; *After Communism* edited by Donald R. Kelley; *The Light of the Home* by Harvey Green with the assistance of Mary-Ellen Perry; *A Year at the Fights* by Thomas Hauser; *The Forayers or The Raid of the Dog Days: selected fiction of William Gilmore Simms; Lyon College, 1872–2002* by Brooks Blevins; *A Photographer of Note* by Robert Cochran; *Sports Wars: Athletes in the Age of Aquarius* by David W. Zang; *The Artificial Southerner: Equivocations and Love Songs* by Philip Martin; *Blood in Their Eyes: The Elaine Race Massacres of 1919* by Grif Stockley; *A Beautiful Sickness: Reflections on the Sweet Science* by Thomas Hauser; *The Ozarks: Land and Life, 2nd Edition* by Milton D. Rafferty; *Roads to Dystopia: Sociological Essays on the Postmodern Condition* by Stanford M. Lyman.

Poetry titles: *Changeable Thunder* by David Baker; *The Selected Letters of John Gould Fletcher* edited by Leighton Rudolph and Ethel C. Simpson; *All Things, Seen and Unseen* by Dan Masterson; *Stars at Noon: Poems from the Life of Jacqueline Cochran* by Enid Shomer; *Collected Poems, 1952-1999* by Robert Mezey; *The Apple that Astonished Paris* by Billy Collins.

University of Arkansas Press distributes its own list.

Query letters and SASEs should be directed to:

John Coghlan, Acting Director and Production Manager

Lawrence S. Malbey, Director and Editor

UNIVERSITY OF CALIFORNIA PRESS

2120 Berkeley Way, Berkeley, CA 94720-1012

510-642-4247   fax: 510-643-7127

www.ucpress.edu

University of California Press (founded in 1893) publishes a solid general-interest list, in addition to its substantial contributions to academic publishing. The house maintains a broad program that encompasses scholarly and classical studies, humanities and the arts, medicine and science, the environment, popular historical and contemporary culture and issues, and language and linguistics. The press has major concentrations in such specialty areas as California and the West; the Pacific Ocean region, including the Pacific Rim; Asian studies; Oceania; and Latin America. University of California Press also publishes literary fiction, letters, and poetry.

University of California titles include: *Eating Apples* by Dale Peterson; *Surviving Freedom: After the Gulag* by Janusz Bardach and Kathleen Gleeson; *Adventuring Along the Lewis and Clark Trail* by Elizabeth Grossman; *Raven's End: A Novel* by Ben Gadd; *Pather Panchali* by Vidya Borooah; *L. A. Confidential* by Manohla Dargis; *Sharks, Rays, and Chimaeras of California* by David Ebert; *This Land Is Our Land: Immigrants and Power in Miami* by Alex Stepick, Max Castro, Guillermo Grenier, and Marvin Dunn; *Himalayas: An Aesthetic Adventure* by Pratapadita Pal; *Singular Women: Writing the Artist* edited by Kristen Frederickson and Sarah E. Webb; *Homosexuality in Greece and Rome: A Sourcebook of Basic Documents* edited by Thomas K. Hubbard; *The Real Environmental Crisis: Why Poverty, Not Affluence, Is the Environment's Number One Enemy* by Jack M. Hollander; *LifePlace: Bioregional Thought and Practice* by Robert Thayer; *Safe Food: Bacteria, Biotechnology, and Bioterrorism* by Marion Nestle; *Early India: From the Origins to AD 1300* by Romila Thapar; *Chinese Visions of Family and State, 1915-1953* by Susan Glosser; *Taming the Elephant: Politics, Government, and Law in Pioneer California* edited by John F. Burns and Richard J. Orsi; *Food Politics: How the Food Industry Influences Nutrition and Health* by Marion Nestle; *Empire and Revolution: The Americans in Mexico Since the Civil War* by John Mason Hart.

University of California Press distributes its own list.

Query letters and SASEs should be directed to:

Deborah Kirshman, Editor—Fine arts

Doris Kretschmer, Executive Editor—Natural history, biology

Lynne Withey, Editor—Middle Eastern studies, world history

Monica McCormick, Editor—African studies and American studies

Laura Cerruti, Poetry, literature, classical studies

Chuck Crumly, Organismal biology, ecology, evolution, environment

Naomi Schneider, Executive Editor—Sociology, politics, gender studies, ethnic studies, Latin American studies

Sheila Levine, Editorial Director—Asian studies and European history, food

Stan Holwitz, Assistant Director—Anthropology

Stephanie Fay, Editor—Fine arts

Mary Francis, Editor—Music

Blake Edgar, Editor—Environmental science, biology, archaeology, viticulture

Reed Malcom—Religion, political science

UNIVERSITY OF CHICAGO PRESS

1427 East 60th Street, Chicago, IL 60637-2954

773-702-7700   fax: 773-702-9756

www.press.uchicago.edu   e-mail: marketing@press.uchicago.edu

University of Chicago Press (founded in 1891) specializes in the arts, humanities, and social sciences. Above all a scholarly and academic house, Chicago nonetheless has a noteworthy list of books intended for a wider readership. Major areas of Chicago publishing interest are history, regional Chicago and Illinois books, literary studies, philosophy and linguistics, anthropology, archaeology, art, architecture, music, religion, business and economics, media studies, political science, sociology, psychology, education, legal studies, gender studies, popular culture, and publishing, along with selected titles in the biological and physical sciences.

Titles from University of Chicago Press: *Sloan Rules: Alfred P. Sloan and the Triumph of General Motors* by David Farber; *Spying with Maps: Surveillance Technologies and the Future of Privacy* by Mark Monmonier; *Kafka Goes to the Movies* by Hanns Zischler; *Glass: A World History* by Alan Macfarlane; *Henry Miller, Happy Rock* by Brassaï; *Just Electronics: Creating a Fair Electoral Process in the United States* by Dennis F. Thompson; *Home Front: American Flags from Across the United States* by Peter Elliott; *The Chicago Guide to Communicating Science* by Scott L. Montgomery; *The Culture of Islam: Changing Aspects of Contemporary Muslim Life* by Lawrence Rosen; *What Is What Was* by Richard Stern; *The Greatest Killer: Smallpox in History* by Donald R. Hopkins; *Making Patriots* by Walter Berns; *Free to Die for Their Country: The Story of the Japanese American Draft Resisters in World War II* by Eric L. Muller; *Dancing at Armageddon: Survivalism and Chaos in Modern Times* by Richard G. Mitchell Jr.; *The Rules of the Global Game: A New Look at US International Economic Policymaking* by Kenneth W. Dam; *For the Love of Mike: More of the Best of Mike Royko* by Mike Royko; *The Moment of Complexity: Emerging Network Culture* by Mark C. Taylor.

Paperback titles: *Two Jews on a Train: Stories from the Old Country and the New* by Adam Biro; *Making Patriots* by Walter Berns; *Marlborough: His Life and Times, Book One* by Winston S. Churchill; *A Stroll with William James* by Jacques Barzun; *The Fourth Great Awakening and the Future of Egalitarianism* by Robert William Fogel; *Where the Buffalo Roam: Restoring America's Great Plains* by Anne Matthews; *Global Sex* by Dennis Altman; *Conversations with Picasso* by Brassaï.

University of Chicago Press distributes its own list.

Query letters and SASEs should be directed to:

Alan Thomas, Editor—Literary criticism and theory, religious studies

Christie Henry, Editor—Biological science

Douglas Mitchell, Editor—Sociology, history, gay and lesbian studies

Geoffrey Huck, Editor—Economics, linguistics, classics

John Tryneski, Editor—Political science, law, education

Kathleen Hansell, Editor—Music

Linda Halvorson, Editorial Director

Susan Bielstein, Editor—Art, architecture, classics, women's studies

Catherine Rice, Editor—History, philosophy, and social studies of science

T. David Brent, Editor—Anthropology, philosophy, psychology

Robert P. Devens, Associate Editor

Margaret Hivnor, Paperback Editor

Randolph Petilos, Assistant Editor

J. Alex Schwartz, Senior Editor

UNIVERSITY OF GEORGIA PRESS

330 Research Drive, Athens, GA 30602-4901

706-369-6130   fax: 706-369-6131

www.ugapress.uga.edu   e-mail: books@ugapress.uga.edu

University of Georgia Press (established in 1938) publishes a solid list of mainstream-interest books, in addition to its specialized roster of academic, scholarly, and scientific publications. Georgia trade-book titles accent fiction and literature, biography and memoirs, history, current affairs, and regional titles; the house's academic emphasis overlaps these areas of concentration, in a program that features scholarly nonfiction, poetry, short fiction, regional studies, and novels. The press publishes hardcover and trade paperback editions.

Representative of the Georgia list: *The Afro-American Tradition in Decorative Arts* by John Michael Vlach; *The American College and University* by Frederick Rudolph; *Aquatic and Wetland Plants of the Southeastern United States* by Robert K. Godfrey and Jean W. Wooten; *Berry Benson's Civil War Book* by Berry Benson, edited by Susan Williams Benson; *The Bible According to Mark Twain* by Mark Twain, edited by Howard G. Baetzhold and Joseph B. McCullough; *The Bourbaki Gambit* by Carl Djerassi; *Common Places* edited by Dell Upton and John Michael Vlach; *Cultural Theory and Popular Culture* edited by John Storey; *Ozark Wildflowers*; *The Violence of the Morning*; *Another Beauty*; *Apalachee*; *Two Cities*; *"Wild Apples" and Other Natural History Essays*; *Remembering Heaven's Face*; *Canada and the United States*; *Essays on Nature and Landscape*; *God and the Imagination*; *Seas of Gold, Seas of Cotton*; *Nations Divided*.

Backlist favorites: *American Plants for American Gardens: Plant Ecology—The Study of Plants in Relation to Their Environment* by Edith A. Roberts and Elsa Rehmann; *Why the South Lost the Civil War* by Richard E. Beringer, Herman Hattaway, Archer Jones, and William N. Still Jr.

The New Georgia Guide is filled with essays, tours, maps, and other resources keyed to Georgia's heritage and culture.

University of Georgia Press sponsors the Flannery O'Connor Award for Short Fiction. (Please write for entry requirements and submission guidelines.)

University of Georgia Press oversees its own distribution.

Query letters and SASEs should be directed to:

Nancy Grayson, Associate Director and Editor-in-Chief

Derek Krissoff, Acquisition Editor

Christa Frangiamore, Acquisitions Editor

Andrew Berzanskis, Assistant Editor

Mark Steudel, Acquisitions Assistant

UNIVERSITY OF HAWAII PRESS

2840 Kolowalu Street, Honolulu, HI 96822-1888

1-800-956-8255   fax: 808-988-6052

www.uhpress.hawaii.edu   e-mail: uhpbooks@hawaii.edu

Areas of University of Hawaii Press publishing interest include cultural history, economics, social history, travel, arts and crafts, costume, marine biology, natural history, botany, ecology, religion, law, political science, anthropology, and general reference; particular UHP emphasis is on regional topics relating to Hawaii, and scholarly and academic books on East Asia, South and Southeast Asia, and Hawaii and the Pacific.

University of Hawaii Press (started in 1947) publishes books for the general trade, as well as titles keyed to the academic market. UHP also issues a series of special-interest journals. The house maintains an established backlist.

On the University of Hawaii list: *The Oahu Snorkelers and Shore Divers Guide* by Francisco B. de Carvalho; *The Ethnography of Vietnam's Central Highlanders: A Historical Contextualization, 1850–1990* by Oscar Salemink; *Women Through the Lens: Gender and Nation in a Century of Chinese Cinema* by Shuqin Cui; *The Scriptures of Won Buddhism: A Translation of Wonbulgyo Kyojon* by Bongkil Chung; *Samoan Art and Artists* by Sean Mallon; *Angelwings: Contemporary Queer Fiction from Taiwan* translated by Fran Martin; *Century of the Tiger: One Hundred Years of Korean Culture in America* edited by Jenny Ryun Foster, Heinz Insu Fenkl and Frank Stewart; *Tongans Overseas: Between Two Shores* by Helen Morton Lee; *Empire of Emptiness: Buddhist Art and Political Authority in Qing China* by Patricia Berger; *Unfolding the Moon: Enacting Women's Kastom in Vanuatu* by Lissant Bolton; *Don Francisco de Paula Marin* by Ross H. Gast and Agnes C. Conrad; *Integrated Korean: Advanced Intermediate Level 1* by KLEAR, edited by Ho-min Sohn and Eun-Joo Lee; *Hawaiian Legends of the Guardian Spirits* by Caren Loebel-Fried; *The Rise of Modern Japan* by Linda K. Menton, Noren W. Lush, Eileen H. Tamura, Chance I. Gusukuma; *Half a Century of Japanese Theater, 1980s: Part 2* edited by the Japan Playwrights Association; *The Blessings of Bhutan* by Russ and Blyth Carpenter; *My Brother Hideo Kobayashi* by Junko Takamizawa.

A notable UHP series is *Talanoa: Contemporary Pacific Literature*, which makes the writing of Pacific Islanders available to a wider audience. Sample titles: *Deep River Talk: Collected Poems* by Hone Tuwhere; *Once Were Warriors* by Alan Duff; *Leaves of the Banyan Tree* by Albert Wendt.

The University of Hawaii Press handles its own distribution via a network that includes in-house fulfillment services, as well as independent sales representatives.

Query letters and SASEs should be directed to:

Keith Leber, Acquisitions Editor—Natural history and science of Hawaii and the Pacific. E-mail: kleber@ hawaii.edu

Pamela Kelley, Acquisitions Editor—Pacific studies, Southeast Asian studies, and Asian literature. E-mail: pkelley@hawaii.edu

Patricia Crosby, Executive Editor—East Asia history, philosophy, religion, art history, and social sciences. E-mail: pcrosby@hawaii.edu

Masako Ikeda, Acquisitions Editor—Hawaiiana, Pacific literature, and Asian American studies. E-mail: masakoi@hawaii.edu

William Hamilton, Director

Cheri Dunn, Managing Editor

Ann Ludeman, Managing Editor

UNIVERSITY OF ILLINOIS PRESS

1325 South Oak Street, Champaign, IL 61820

217-333-0950   fax: 217-244-8082

www.press.uillinois.edu   e-mail: uipress@uillinois.edu

University of Illinois Press (founded in 1918) publishes books of general and scholarly nonfiction, with strong emphasis on American studies (especially history, literature, and music), communications, film studies, folklore, gender studies, African American studies, regional studies, law and political science, religion and philosophy, labor studies, and athletics. University of Illinois Press also publishes poetry (submissions accepted in February only).

Representative of the University of Illinois program: *Abbas Kiarostami* by Mehmaz Saeed-Vafa & Jonathon Rosenbaum; *All Abraham's Children* by Armand Mauss; *Art and Freedom* by E. E. Sleinis; *Arts of a Cold Sun*, poems by G. E. Murray; *Bluegrass Breakdown* by Robert Cantwell; *The Brass Check* by Upton Sinclair; *The Consumer Trap* by Michael Dawson; *Contesting Identities* by Aaron Baker; *Dynamic Structure of Reality* by Xavier Zubiri; *Engaging Humor* by Elliott Oring; *Gambling Life* by Thomas Malaby; *Lost Legacy* by Irene Bates and E. Gary Smith; *Making Truth* by Theodore L. Brown; *The Nazi Olympics* edited by Arnd Kruger and William Murray; *Passing for Spain* by Barbara Fuchs; *Reading Nietzsche* translated by Greg Whitlock; *Tales and Trails of Illinois* by Stu Fliege; *The Unlevel Playing Field* by David K. Wiggins and Patrick B. Miller; *African American Mayors*; *American Opera*; *Ancient Records of Egypt*; *Bluegrass Odyssey*; *Chicago and the Old Northwest*; *Damnedest Radical*; *Desirable Body*; *Early Encounter with Tomorrow*; *Elliot Coues*; *Enemies Within*; *Gold and the American Country Club*; *The Graying of America*; *Haunting Violations*.

The University of Illinois Press has been chosen as one of the publishers for the National Poetry Series. New poetry titles: *Grazing* by Ira Sadoff; *Walt Whitman Bathing* (poems) by David Wagoner; *To the Bone* (new and selected poems) by Sydney Lea; *The Tracks We Leave: Poems on Endangered Wildlife of North America* by Barbara Helfgott Hyett (illustrated by Robert W. Treanor); *The Broken World* (poems) by Marcus Cafagna; *Dance Script with Electric Ballerina* (poems) by Alice Fulton; *Bruised Paradise* (poems) by Kevin Stein.

Of literary note: *"I Cease Not to Yowl": Ezra Pound's Letters to Olivia Rossetti Agresti* edited by Demetres P. Tryphonopoulos and Leon Surette; *Unbought Spirit: A John Jay Chapman Reader* edited by Richard Stone; *The Urban Sublime in American Literary Naturalism* by Christophe Den Tandt; *Taking It Home: Stories from the Neighborhood* by Tony Ardizzone; *Flights in the Heavenlies* by Ernest J. Finney; *The New World* by Russell Banks; *Walter Burley in America* (photographs and essay by Mati Maldre; essay, catalog, and selected bibliography by Paul Kruty).

University of Illinois Press distributes its own list, as well as books from other university publishers, including Vanderbilt University Press.

Query letters and SASEs should be directed to:

Joan Catapano, Associate Director and Editor-in-Chief—Women's studies, history, African American studies, film

Ann Lowry, Journals Manager and Senior Editor—Literature

Elizabeth G. Dulany, Editor—Western Americana, religious studies, archaeology, anthropology

Judith M. McCulloh, Executive Editor—Music, folklore, pop culture

Richard J. Martin, Executive Editor—Political science, sociology, law, philosophy, architecture, economics

Richard L. Wentworth, Editor—American history, black history, communications, sports history, and regional books

Willis G. Regier, Director—Literature, Near Eastern studies, foodways

UNIVERSITY OF IOWA PRESS

100 Kuhl House, Iowa City, IA 52242-1000

319-335-2000   fax: 319-335-2055

www.uiowapress.org   e-mail: uipress@uiowa.edu

University of Iowa Press (established in 1938) produces a solid list in selected categories that includes scholarly works, general-interest nonfiction, and regional titles in the areas of archaeology, anthropology, and history. The house also produces short stories, literary criticism, creative nonfiction, and poetry.

Iowa series include American Land and Life; Sightline Books: The Iowa series in literary nonfiction; Kuhl House Poets; and publications from Studies in Theatre History and Culture, the annual Iowa Poetry Prize competition.

Iowa nonfiction: *King James and Letters of Homoerotic Desire* by David M. Bergeron; *Of Cabbages and Kings County: Agriculture and the Formation of Modern Brooklyn* by Marc Linder and Lawrence S. Zacharias; *Soldier Boy: The Civil War Letters of Charles O. Musser, 29th Iowa* edited by Barry Popchock; *Sickness, Recovery, and Death: A History and Forecast of Ill Health* by James C. Riley; *After the West Was Won: Homesteaders and Town-Builders in Western South Dakota* by Paula M. Nelson; *China Dreams: Growing Up in Jewish Tientsin* by Isabelle Maynard (foreword by Albert E. Stone); *Okoboji Wetlands: A Lesson in Natural History* by Michael J. Lannoo; *Fourteen Landing Zones: Approaches to Vietnam War Literature* edited by Philip K Jason; *Beyond Homelessness: Frames of Reference* by Benedict and Jeffrey Giamo.

Iowa fiction and literature: *Shiny Objects* by Dianne Benedict; *Friendly Fire* by

Kathryn Chetkovich; *Old Wives' Tales* by Susan M. Dodd; *Igloo Among Palms* by Rod Val Moore; *Traps* by Sondra Spatt Olsen; *The Black Velvet Girl* by C. E. Poverman; *Between the Heartbeats* (poems and prose by nurses; edited by Cortney Davis and Judy Schaefer); *Uncertainty and Plenitude: Five Contemporary Poets* by Peter Stitt.

Literary criticism and the arts are areas in which Iowa has traditionally produced a strong list. Titles: *Jazz Country: Ralph Ellison in America* by Horace A. Porter; *Fly in the Buttermilk: The Life Story of Cecil Reed* by Cecil A. Reed, with Priscilla Donovan; *Tight Spaces* by Kesho Scott, Cherry Huhanji, and Egyirba High; *My Iowa Journey: The Life Story of the University of Iowa's First African American Professor* by Philip G. Hubbard; *The Making of a Black Scholar: From Georgia to the Ivy League* by Horace A. Porter; *The Penultimate Suitor* by Mary Leader; *Stand Up Poetry: An Expanded Edition* by Charles Harper Webb; *Love in a Global Village* by Jessie Carroll; *Liberal Education and the Public Interest* by James O. Freedman; *Coloring Locals: Racial Formation in Kate Chopin's Youth's Companion Stories* by Bonnie James Shaker; *Gothic Passages: Racial Ambiguity and the American Gothic* by Justin D. Edwards; *Modern Hamlets and Their Soliloquies: An Expanded Edition* by Mary Z. Maher; *Montane Foragers: Asana and the South-Central Andean Archaic* by Mark S. Aldenderfer; *Metafiction: A Community of Writers* by Paul Engle and the Iowa Writer's Workshop; *Interpreting the Theatrical Past: Essays in the Historiography of Performance* by Thomas Postlewait and Bruce McConachie.

Winners of the Iowa Poetry Prize include *Wake* by Bin Ramke; *The Oval Hour* by Kathleen Peirce and *Try* by Cole Swensen.

University of Iowa Press books are distributed by the University of Chicago Distribution Center.

Query letters and SASEs should be directed to:

Holly Carver, Director and Editor

Prasenjit Gupta, Humanities Editor

Charlotte Webb, Managing Editor

UNIVERSITY OF MICHIGAN PRESS

839 Greene Street, Ann Arbor, MI 48104-3209

734-764-4388   fax: 734-615-1540

www.press.umich.edu

University of Michigan Press publishes trade nonfiction and works of scholarly and academic interest. Topic areas and categories include: African American studies, anthropology, archaeology, Asian studies, classical studies, literary criticism and theory, economics, education, German studies, history, linguistics, law, literary biography, literature, Michigan and the Great Lakes region, music, physical sciences, philosophy and religion, poetry, political science, psychology, sociology, theater and drama, women's studies, disability studies, and gay and lesbian studies.

University of Michigan Press (founded in 1930) executes a major program to publish an abundant list of textbooks, monographs, academic literature, undergraduate texts, and a wide variety of books for general readers. Subject areas here encompass disciplines within the behavioral sciences, as well as the humanities. University of Michigan Press publishes in hardcover and paperback editions. Ann Arbor Paperbacks is an imprint geared toward the general trade market.

From the Michigan list: *The Case for the Prosecution in the Ciceronian Era* by Michael Alexander; *The Culture of San Sepolcro During the Youth of Piero Della Francesca* by James R. Banker; *The Morality of Laughter* by F. H. Buckley; *Robert Mugabe: A Life of Power and Violence* by Stephen Chan; *Volatile States: Institutions, Policy, and the Performance of American State Economies* by W. Mark Crain; *Soul Barnacles: Ten More Years with Ray* by Tess Gallagher and Greg Simon; *The Well-Being of the Elderly on Asia: A Four-Country Comparative Study* edited by Albert Hermalin; *Greek Syntax: Volume 3, Early Greek Poetic and Herodotean Syntax* by K. W. Kruger; *Is Rational Choice Theory All of Social Science?* by Mark I. Lichbach; *A Fly in the Soup: Memoirs* by Charles Simic; *Reinventing the State: Economic Strategy and Institutional Change in Peru* by Carol Wise; *On the Banks of the Ganga: When Wastewater Meets a Sacred River* by Kelly D. Alley; *China: Adapting the Past, Confronting the Future* edited by Thomas Buoye, Kirk Denton, Bruce Dickson, Barry Naughton, and Martin K. Whyte; *Adoption in America: Historical Perspectives* edited by E. Wayne Carp; *Tony Kushner in Conversation* edited by Robert Vorlicky; *Approaching the Millennium: Essays on Angels in America* edited by Deborah R. Geis and Steven F. Kruger; *Health Benefits at Work: An Economic and Political Analysis of Employment-Based Health Insurance* by Mark V. Pauly; *Coltrane: His Life and Music* by Lewis Porter.

University of Michigan Press handles distribution through a worldwide network of independent sales representatives.

Query letters and SASEs should be directed to:

Ellen McCarthy, Senior Editor—Economics, anthropology, social issues

Kelly Sippell, English as a Second Language Manager—ESL, applied linguistics, regional studies, and sports titles

Christopher J. Collins, Acquiring Editor—Classical studies, archaeology, medieval history, Renaissance studies, and German studies

LeAnn Fields, Executive Editor—Literature, performance studies, gender studies, disability studies

James F. Reische, Acquiring Editor—Political science, law, American studies, and American history

Mary Erwin, Assistant Director— Regional studies

Chris Hebert, Acquisitions Editor—Music and distributed titles

UNIVERSITY OF MINNESOTA PRESS

111 Third Avenue South, Suite 290, Minneapolis, MN 55401-2520

612-627-1970   fax: 612-627-1980

www.upress.umn.edu   e-mail: ump@umn.edu

The University of Minnesota Press (founded in 1927) is a not-for-profit publisher of academic books for scholars and selected general interest titles. They do not publish original fiction or poetry. Areas of emphasis include American studies, anthropology, art and aesthetics, cultural theory, film and media studies, gay and lesbian studies, geography, literary theory, political and social theory, race and ethnic studies, sociology, and urban studies. The Press also maintains a long-standing commitment to publishing books that focus on Minnesota and the Upper Midwest, including regional nonfiction, history, and natural science.

Recent notable titles: *Plague of Frogs* by William Souder; *Masking and Power* by Gerald Aching; *Border Women* by Debra A. Castillo and Maria Socorro Tabuenca Cordoba; *Shakespeare's Hand* by Jonathan Goldberg; *Against the Romance of Community* by Miranda Joseph; *World Bank Literature* edited by Amitava Kumar; *Entry Denied* by Eithne Luibheid; *A Political Science* edited by Warren Magnusson and Karena Shaw; *Touch* by Laura U. Marks; *Deathwork* by Michael Mello; *Noir Anxiety* by Kelly Oliver and Benigno Trigo; *Lusosex* edited Susan Canty Quinlan and Fernando Arenas; *City Requiem* by Ananya Roy; *Ghosts of Slavery* by Jenny Sharpe; *Error, Misuse, Failure* by Julian Yates; *The Dubious Spectacle*; *A Queer Mother for the Nation*; *Being Political*; *Reading Autobiography*; *The Unfinished System of Nonknowledge*; *Bodies in Technology*; *Christopher and His Kind*; *My Guru and His Disciple*; *Cyberculture*; *American Studies in a Moment of Danger*.

University of Minnesota Press order fulfillment is handled by the Chicago Distribution Center and in the U.K. and Europe through Plymbridge Distributors, Ltd.

Query letters and SASEs should be directed to:

Richard Morrison, Humanities—American studies, cultural theory, gay and lesbian studies, humanities

Carrie Mullen, Executive Editor—Political science, geography, urban studies, environmental studies, sociology, anthropology

Douglas Armato, Acquisitions—Digital culture, philosophy, reprints

Beverly Kaemmer, Acquisitions—MMPI, psychology

Todd Orjala, Regional Upper Midwestern studies, Native American studies

Pieter Martin, Architecture, public art and culture

Andrea Kleinhuber, Cinema and media studies, art and visual culture

UNIVERSITY OF MISSOURI PRESS

2910 LeMone Boulevard, Columbia, MO 65201

573-882-7641   fax: 573-884-4498

www.umsystem.edu/upress   e-mail: upress@umsystem.edu

The University of Missouri Press (founded in 1958) accents scholarly books, general-interest trade titles, fiction, and regional works. Specific areas within the UMP publishing range include African American studies, cultural studies, folklore, gender studies, intellectual history, journalism, and photography. University of Missouri Press publishes in hardback and trade paperback editions.

Highlights of the Missouri line: *A Place Between Stations* by Stephanie Allen; *From Fugitive Slave to Free Man: The Autobiographies of William Wells Brown* edited by William L. Andrews; *Searching for Their Places: Women in the South Across Four Centuries* edited by Thomas H. Appleton Jr., and Angela Boswell; *Romanticism and Transcendence: Wordsworth, Coleridge, and the Religious Imagination* by J. Robert Barth, S.J.; *Mark Twain and the American West* by Joseph L. Coulombe; *Knut Hamsun Remembers America: Essays and Stories, 1885–1949*, edited and translated by Richard Nelson Current; *Muriel Rukeyser's "The Book of the Dead"* by Tim Dayton; *Southern Womanhood and Slavery: A Biography of Louisa S. McCord, 1810–1879* edited and translated by Richard Nelson Current; *Mary McLeod Bethune and Black Women's Political Activism* by Joyce A. Hanson; *Heartland Heroes: Remembering World War II* by Ken Hatfield; *Prophesying Daughters: Black Women Preachers and the Word, 1823–1913* by Chanta M. Haywood; *African American Life in the Rural South, 1900–1950* edited by R. Douglas Sanders; *What I Cannot Say to You: Stories* by Vanessa Furse Jackson; *Mark Twain: Social Philosopher* by Louis J. Budd; *The Soledades, Gongora's Masque of the Imagination* by Marsha A. Collins; *A Consuming Faith: The Social Gospel and Modern American Culture* by Susan Curtis.

University of Missouri Press handles its own distributional services.

Query letters and SASEs should be directed to:

Beverly Jarrett, Director and Editor-in-Chief

Clair Willcox, Acquisitions Editor

Jane Lago, Managing Editor

John Brenner, Editor

Sara Davis, Editor

Gary Kass, Editor

Julie Schroeder, Editor

UNIVERSITY OF NEBRASKA PRESS

233 North 8th Street, Lincoln, NE 68588- 0255

402-472-3584   fax: 402-472-3584

http://www.nebraskapress.unl.edu   e-mail: pressmail@unl.edu

The program at University of Nebraska Press encompasses anthropology, environmental studies, history, literature and criticism, Native American studies, philosophy, wildlife and environment, and general reference works. The house further accents the literature and history of the Trans-Missouri West, the American Indian, contemporary and modern literary trends, sports, and the environment (especially emphasizing Western United States and American Indian tie-in topics).

University of Nebraska Press (founded in 1941) publishes general trade titles in hardcover and paperback, as well as selected scholarly nonfiction. Many UNP titles and subject areas overlap categories and thus are provided wider marketing exposure. University of Nebraska Press has successfully established niches in each of its targeted market sectors; a solid showcase of Nebraska titles has garnered book-club sales in both mainstream and specialty venues.

The University of Nebraska literary horizon features leading-edge criticism and theory, works keyed to the American West and the American Indian, and historical as well as current writers worldwide, including European women and French literature in translation. The house offers a strong selection of scholarly writings on the life and works of Willa Cather.

University of Nebraska Press produces the Women in the West series and works on Western history and literature; American Indian topics; and the great outdoors. Bison Books is Nebraska's imprint for popularly oriented trade titles.

Nebraska's American Indian studies include biography and memoirs, literature and legend, society and culture, and history, as well as a line of titles for young readers. Series listed in this area are American Indian Lives, Sources of American Indian Oral Literature, Studies in the Anthropology of North American Indians, Indians of the Southeast, and The Iroquoians and Their World. The press also offers the North American Indian Prose Award, in conjunction with the Native American Studies Program at the University of California, Berkeley. (Detailed information is available from the publisher upon request.) A recent winner of this award is *Boarding School Seasons* by Brenda Child.

Representative of the Nebraska publishing program: *Local Wonders* by Ted Kooser; *Monte Walsh* by Jack Schaefer; *Come on Seabiscuit!* by Ralph Moody; *Collision of Home Plate* by James Reston Jr; *Arabs at War* by Kenneth M. Pollack; *Pieces from Life's Crazy Quilt* by Marvin Arnett; *In the Shadow of Memory* by Floyd Skloot; *Phantom Limb* by Janet Sternburg; *Turning Bones* by Lee Martin; *Secret Frequencies* by John Skoyles; *They*

Cleared the Lane by Ron Thomas; *Out West: A Journey Through Lewis and Clark's America* by Dayton Duncan; *Standing Up to the Rock* by T. Louise Freeman-Toole; *Thoughts from a Queen-Sized Bed* by Mimi Schwartz; *How Nancy Jackson Married Kate Wilson and Other Tales of Rebellious Girls and Daring Young Women* by Mark Twain (edited by John Cooley).

The Bison Frontiers of Imagination Series features reprints of classic speculative fiction, ranging from Edgar Rice Burroughs's *Land That Time Forgot* to Wylie and Balmer's *When Worlds Collide*. Other titles include: *Gulliver of Mars* by Edwin Arnold; *Under the Moons of Mars* by Edgar Rice Burroughs; *The Nightmare & Other Tales of Dark Fantasy* by Francis Stevens; *Tales of Wonders* by Mark Twain; *Before Adam* by Jack London.

Query letters and SASEs should be directed to:

Elizabeth Demers, Acquisitions Editor—History

Ladette Randolf, Senior Editor—Humanities

Rob Taylor, Acquisitions Editor—Sports

Gary Dunham, Editor-in-Chief—Native studies

UNIVERSITY OF NEW MEXICO PRESS

1720 Lomas Boulevard, NE, Albuquerque, NM 87131

1-800-249-7737   fax: 505-277-9270

www.unmpress.com   e-mail: unmpress@unm.edu

University of New Mexico Press (begun in 1929) is a publisher of general, scholarly, and regional trade books in hardcover and paperback editions. Among areas of strong New Mexico interest are archaeology, folkways, literature, art and architecture, photography, crafts, biography, women's studies, travel, and the outdoors. UNM Press offers a robust list of books in subject areas pertinent to the American Southwest, including native Anasazi, Navajo, Hopi, Zuni, and Apache cultures; Nuevomexicano (New Mexican) culture; the pre-Columbian Americas; and Latin American affairs. UNMP also publishes works of regional fiction and belles lettres, both contemporary and classical. The press commands a staunch backlist.

Representative of the University of New Mexico Press list: *Voices of the Buffalo Soldier: Records, Reports, and Reconciliation of Military Life and Services in the West* by Frank N. Schubert; *Trophy Husband: A Survival Guide to Working at Home* by Steve Brewer; *Gone: Photographs of Abandonment on the High Plains* by Steve Fitch; *Cuba: Picturing Change* by E. Wright Leadbetter; *Moony's Road to Hell* by Manuel Ramos; *La Mordida* by Jim Sanderson; *At Ease with the Dead* by Walter Satterthwait; *The Deadly Canyon* by Jack Page; *Raptor* by Judith Van Gireson; *Hot Biscuits* edited by Max Evans and Candy

Moulton; *West of Babylon* by Eduardo Garrigues; *The Algarrobos Quartet* by Gerardo Mario Golobaff; *Millie Cooper's Ride* by Marc Simmons; *Peter Becomes a Trail Man* by William C. Carson; *The Great Game of the Birds and Animals* by Deborah Duvall; *Swept Under the Rug* by Kathy M'Claskey; *World War II and the American Indian* by Kenneth Townsend; *Dine* by Peter Iverson; *For Our Navajo People* edited by Peter Iverson; *The Indian Frontier, 1763-1846* by R. Douglas Hurt; *Racial Frontiers* by Arnoldo De Lean; *Nuclear Reactions* by Chuck McCutchean; *Justice Betrayed* by Ralph Melnick; *Remote Beyond Control* edited by John L. Kessell; *"Sin Nombre" Hispana and Hispano Artists of the New Deal Era* by Tey Marianna Nun; *Navajo Trading: The End of an Era* by Willow Roberts Powers; *Salt Dreams: Land and Water in Low-Down California* by William deBuys and Joan Myers; *Coal Camp Days: A Boy's Remembrance* by Ricardo L. Garcia; *Crossing Guadalupe Street: Growing Up Hispanic and Protestant* by David Maldonadao Jr.; *Finding the West: Explorations with Lewis and Clark* by James P. Ronda; *The Great Maya Droughts: Water, Life and Death* by Richardson B. Gill.

New Mexico fiction/poetry titles: *Poetry Lover* by Gary Soto; *Losers and Keepers in Argentina: A Work of Fiction* by Nina Barragan; *Miracles of Sainted Earth* (poems) by Victoria Edwards Tester; *Cavern* by Jake Page.

The press is home to the literary journal *Blue Mesa Review*. The Pasó por Aquí series makes available texts from the Nuevomexicano literary heritage (many editions in bilingual format). Diálogos is a series in Latin American studies, specializing in books with crossover potential in both academic and general markets.

University of New Mexico Press handles distribution for its own list and also works through regional sales representatives.

Query letters and SASEs should be directed to:

David Holtby, Associate Director

UNIVERSITY OF NORTH CAROLINA PRESS

116 South Broadway Street, Chapel Hill, NC 27514-3808

919-966-3561   fax: 919-966-3829

www.uncpress.unc.edu   e-mail: uncpress@unc.edu

University of North Carolina Press (founded in 1922) publishes works of general nonfiction, scholarly titles, and regional books, as well as a selection of general-interest trade titles. The house has a broad array of books on a firm backlist.

University of North Carolina Press publishing interest encompasses African American studies, American studies, British history, business history, Civil War, folklore, Latin American studies, literary studies, anthropology, nature, political science, social issues, legal history, sports and sports history, and gender studies.

North Carolina highlights: *The Free State of Jones* by Victoria E. Bynum; *Drawing on*

America's Past by Virginia Tuttle Clayton, Elizabeth Stillinger, Erika Doss, and Deborah Chotner; *The Imagined Civil War* by Alice Fahs; *Conflicting Missions* by Piero Gleijeses; *Martin R. Delany* edited by Robert S. Levine; *Omaha Beach* by Adrian R. Lewis; *Window on Freedom* edited by Brenda Gayle Plummer; *Pickett's Charge in History and Memory* by Carol Readon; *A History of Small Business in America* by Mansel G. Blackford; *Jefferson and Monroe* by Noble E. Cunningham; *The Cult of Nothingness* by Roger-Pol Droit; *Behind the Backlash* by Kenneth D. Durr; *Bittersweet* by Chris Feudtner; *The Maya of Morganton* by Leon Fink; *Confronting the War Machine* by Michael S. Foley; *Germany's Cold War* by William Glenn Gray; *Colored Pictures* by Michael D. Harris; *Conversations with the High Priest of Coosa* by Charles M. Hudson; *Staff Officers in Gray* by Robert E. L. Krick; *At America's Gates* by Erika Lee; *Working the Garden* by William Conlogue; *A World of Its Own* by Matt Garcia; *The Mormon Question* by Sarah Barringer Gordon; *Scientists, Business and the State, 1890–1960* by Patrick J. McGrath; *A Blessed Company* by John K. Nelson; *Black Identity and Black Protest in the Antebellum North* by Patrick Rael; *Forged Genealogies* by Carol Rigolot.

University of North Carolina Press handles its own distribution with the assistance of regional sales representatives.

Query letters and SASEs should be directed to:

David Perry, Assistant Director and Editor-in-Chief—History, regional trade, Civil War

Kate Douglas Torrey, Director—Gender studies

Mark Simpson-Vos, Associate Editor and Assistant to the Editor-in-Chief

Charles Grench, Assistant Director and Senior Editor—History, classics, economics and business history, law and legal studies, political science

Amanda McMillan, Assistant Editor and Assistant to the Senior Editor

Elaine Maisner, Editor

Sian Hunter, Editor

UNIVERSITY OF OKLAHOMA PRESS

1005 Asp Avenue, Norman, OK 73019-6051

405-325- 2000

www.oupress.com

University of Oklahoma Press highlights the fields of Americana, regional topics (especially the American West), anthropology, archaeology, history, military history, political science, literature, classical studies, and women's studies. University of Oklahoma Press series include the Western Frontier Library, the American Indian Literature and Critical Studies series, and the Bruce Alonzo Goff Series in Architecture.

University of Oklahoma Press (founded in 1928) publishes a wide range of scholarly nonfiction, with crossover trade titles primarily in popular history and the arts; the house's prowess is particularly renowned in the arena of the native cultures of North, Central, and South America—the extensive backlist as well as new and current offerings in these fields embrace a wellspring of over 250 titles.

On Oklahoma's list: *A Pipe for February* by Charles H. Red Corn; *American Gypsy* by Diane Glancy; *Ancient Egyptian Medicine* by John F. Nunn; *Before Lewis and Clark* by A. P. Nasatir; *Black Masculinity and the Frontier Myth in American Literature* by Michael K. Johnson; *Blackfeet Tales from Apikuni's World* by James Willard Schultz; *Blood of the Prophets* by Will Bagley; *Bravo of the Brazos* by Robert K. DeArment; *Cheyennes and Horse Soldiers* by William Y. Chalfant; *Chief Daniel Bread and the Oneida Nation of Indians of Wisconsin* by Laurence M. Hauptman and L. Gordon McLester III; *Coquelle Thompson, Athabaskan Witness* by Lionel Youst and William R. Seaburg; *Fort Union and the Upper Missouri Trade* by Barton H. Barbour; *Four Creations* by Gary H. Gossen; *Haunted by Home* by Phyllis Cole Braunlich; *Indian Fights* by J. W. Vaughn; *The Indian Reorganization* by Vine Deloria.

Query letters with SASEs should be directed to:

Charles Rankin, Associate Director, Editor-in-Chief

Karen Wieder—Literature, Natural history

John Drayton, Director—Classical studies

UNIVERSITY OF SOUTH CAROLINA PRESS

718 Devine Street, Columbia, SC 29208

1-800-768-2500   fax: 1-800-868-0740

www.sc.edu/uscpress/

University of South Carolina Press covers Southern studies, military history, contemporary and modern American literature, maritime history, religious studies, and speech and communication. University of South Carolina Press (founded in 1944) publishes a strong academic and scholarly list, with some crossover general trade titles. The press publishes in hardcover, as well as trade paperback, and maintains an extensive backlist.

Indicative of the South Carolina program: *Against the Stream* by Anna Elisabeth Rosmus; *Aging in the New Millenium* by Terry Tirrito; *Baruch ben Neriah* by J. Edward Wright; *Clergymen and Chiefs* by Alexander Quattlebaum McQueen; *Colors of the Robe* by Anada Abeysekara; *Cultural Values in the Southern Sporting Narrative* by Jacob Rivers; *Dark Hours* by Randolph Kirkland Jr.; *A Day of Gladness* by Herold Weiss; *The Great Cooper River Bridge* by Jason Annan and Pamela Gabriel; *In the Great Maelstrom* by Charles Holden; *Islamic Ethics of Life* edited by Jonathan Brockopp; *James Louis Petigru* by William H. Pease and Jane H. Pease; *Lean Down Your Ear Upon the Earth and Listen* by Robert Taylor Ensign; *Memory and Identity* edited by Bertland and Randy J. Sparks; *Narrating Knowledge in Flannery O'Connor's Fiction* by Donald E. Hardy; *The Papers of John C. Calhoun* by Clyde N. Wilson and Shirley B. Cook; *Pitchfork Ben Tillman* by Francis Butler Simkins; *Sir John Fisher's Naval Revolution* by John Gordon; *South Carolina Negroes* by George B. Tindall; *Understanding Robert Coover* by Brian K. Evenson; *Before Gatsby: The First Twenty-Six Stories by F. Scott Fitzgerald* edited by Matthew J. Bruccoli, with the assistance of Judith S. Baughman; *Between North and South: The Letters of Emily Wharton Sinkler, 1842–1865* edited by Anne Sinkler Whaley LeClercq; *Charleston in My Time: The Paintings of West Fraser* by West Fraser; *The Duchess of Malfi's Apricots, and Other Literary Fruits* by Robert Palter.

University of South Carolina Press oversees its own distribution.

Query letters and SASEs should be directed to:

Barry Blose, Acquisitions Editor—Literary studies, rhetoric, religious studies, studies in social work

Alexander Moore, Acquisitions Editor—Southern history, regional studies, Civil War studies, maritime history

---

UNIVERSITY OF TENNESSEE PRESS

110 Conference Center Building, Knoxville, TN 37996-4108

865-974-3321   fax: 865-974-3724

www.utpress.org

The University of Tennessee Press publishes scholarly and general interest books in American studies, in the following subdisciplines: African American studies, Appalachian studies, literature, religion (history, sociology, anthropology, biography), folklore, history, architecture, material culture, and historical archaeology. Submissions in other fields, and submissions of poetry, textbooks, and translations, are not invited.

The University of Tennessee Press (founded in 1940) has earned a national reputation for excellence, with titles representing both traditional and cutting-edge scholarship. The press's editorial point of view reflects an awareness of social and quality-of-life issues and results in books that inform thought and policy, as well as contribute to scholarship.

Recent books published by UT Press include: *You Gotta Laugh to Keep from Cryin'* by Sam Venable; *The Tennessee Encyclopedia of History and Culture* by Van West; *Waiting for Elijah* by Gari-Anne Patzwald; *Dark Symbols, Obscure Signs* by Riggins R. Earl; *Elevating the Race* by Albert G. Miller; *Graceful Women* by Constance Waeber Elsberg; *Rights for a Season* by Lewis A. Randolph and Gayle T. Tate; *The Politics of Injustice* by David Niven; *Bruce Grit* by William Seraile; *How Boston Played* by Stephen Hardy; *Charles Faulkner Bryan* by Carolyn Livingston; *Twisted from the Ordinary* edited by Mary E. Papke; *The Appalachian Frontier* by John Anthony Caruso; *The World Moves, We Follow* by William J. Dewey; *Divided Loyalties* by Digby Gordon Seymour; *Valley So Wild* by Alberta and Carson Brewer; *A Separate Circle: Jewish Life in Knoxville, Tennessee* by Wendy Lowe Besmann; *Thinking Confederates: Academia and the Idea of Progress in the New South* by Dan R. Frost; *Rac(e)ing to the Right: Selected Essays of George S. Schuyler* edited by Jeffrey B. Leak; *Spiritual Merchants: Religion, Magic and Commerce* by Carolyn Long; *Bound to Be a Soldier: The Letters of Private James T. Miller, 111th Pennsylvania Infantry, 1861–1864* edited by Jedediah Mannis and Galen R. Wilson; *The African American Aeneas: Classical Origins of the American Self* by John C. Shields.

Books from the University of Tennessee Press are distributed by the Chicago Distribution Center.

Query letters and SASEs should be directed to:

Joyce Harrison, Acquisitions Editor

UNIVERSITY OF TEXAS PRESS

PO Box 7819, Austin, TX 78713-7819

512-471-7233   fax: 512-232-7178

www.utexas.edu/utpress   e-mail: utpress@uts.cc.utexas.edu

Areas of University of Texas Press publishing scope include international and regional studies, gender studies, Latin America, American Southwest, Native America, Texana, Mesoamerica, applied language and Latino literature (including Latin American and Middle Eastern works in translation), the environment and nature, art and architecture, classics, film studies, social sciences, and humanities.

University of Texas Press (founded in 1950) is among the largest of American university presses. UTP publishes in a wide range of general nonfiction fields, offering titles of popular interest and for scholarly and academic readers produced in hardcover and trade paperback.

On the UTP list: *Las Tejanas* by Teresa Palomo Acosta and Ruthe Wingarten; *Postethnic Narrative Criticism* by Frederick Luis Aldama; *Demosthenes, Speeches 50-59* translated by Victor Bers; *The Dawn at My Back* by Carroll Parrott Blue; *Handbook of Latin American Studies No. 59* edited by Lawrence Boudon and Katherine D. McCann; *We're the Light Crust Doughboys from Burrus Mill* by Jean A. Boyd; *New Art of Cuba* by

Luis Camnitzer; *Felix Longoria's Wake* by Patrick Carroll; *Maya Palaces and Elite Residences* edited by Jessica Joyce Christie; *Understanding the Language of Science* by Steven Darian; *Defiance and Deference in Mexico's Colonial North* by Susan Deeds; *Big Bend Pictures* by James Evans; *Shadowed Ground* by Kenneth E. Foote; *Baetica Felix* by Evan W. Haley; *The French in Texas* edited by Francois Lagarde; *Kiowa, Apache, and Comanche* by William C. Meadows; *The Rise of Cable Programming in the United States* by Megan Mullen; *Collecting Latin American Art for the 21st Century* edited by Mari Carmen Ramirez, with Theresa Papanikolas and Gabriela Rangel; *Concept and Controversy* by W. W. Rostow; *Planning the Family in Egypt*; *Staying Sober in Mexico City*; *The Collected Poems and Selected Prose* by Stanley Burnshaw; *Imagining Texas*.

University of Texas Press handles its own distribution.

Query letters and SASEs should be directed to:

Jim Burr, Sponsoring Editor—Classics and ancient world, film and media studies, Middle East studies, Old World archaeology, architecture

William Bishel, Sponsoring Editor—Texana, ornithology, botany, marine science, natural history, geography, environmental studies

Theresa May, Editor-in-Chief—Latin American studies, Chicano/a studies, Native American studies, anthropology, New World archaeology, applied language, art

Allison Faust, Associate Editor: Assistant to Theresa May

Wendy Moore, Assistant Editor: Assistant to William Bishel and Jim Burr

Tim Staley, Sponsoring Editor

UNIVERSITY OF WASHINGTON PRESS

1326 Fifth Avenue, suite 555, Seattle, WA 98145-5096

206-543-4050   fax: 206-543-3932

www.washington.edu/uwpress/   e-mail: uwpord@u.washington.edu

The program at University of Washington Press is particularly strong in the fields of the publisher's major academic concentrations, which encompass fine arts (including a special interest in the arts of Asia), regional America (with an emphasis on Seattle and the Pacific Northwest), and Native American studies. University of Washington Press maintains a solid backlist.

University of Washington Press (established in 1920) is a midsize house with a primarily scholarly list that features select titles geared toward the general-interest trade market. The house produces books in hardcover and paperback (including reprint editions) and distributes adjunct visual resources (including videotapes, films, and filmstrips). University of Washington also handles a line of scholarly imports (primarily fine arts titles). UWP enters into joint-publication projects with a variety of museums and cultural foundations and produces a large number of fine arts books and exhibition catalogues.

On the Washington list: *Distant Corner: Seattle Architects and the Legacy of H. H. Richardson* by Jeffrey Karl Ochsner and Dennis Alan Andersen; *Hobnobbing with a Countess and Other Okanagan Adventures: The Diaries of Alice Barrett Parke, 1891–1900* edited by Jo Fraser Jones; *Knowledge Across Cultures: A Contribution to Dialogue Among Civilizations* edited by Ruth Hayhoe and Julia Pan; *Natural Grace: The Charm, Wonder, and Lessons of Pacific Northwest Animals and Plants* by William Dietrich; *Never Late for Heaven: The Art of Gwen Knight* by Sheryl Conkelton and Barbara Thomas; *The Prince and the Salmon People: A Tale* by Claire Rudolph Murphy; *New Version of the Gandhari Dharmapada and a Collection of Previous-Birth Stories: British Library Kharosthi Fragments* by Timothy Lenz with Andrew Glass and Bhikshu Dharmamitra; *Where Land and Water Meet: A Western Landscape Transformed* by Nancy Langston; *Art and Home: Dutch Interiors in the Age of Rembrandt* by Mariet Westermann; *Family Mediation: Theory and Practice with Chinese Families* by Howard H. Irving; *Matsuri! Japanese Festival Arts* by Gloria Granz Gonick; *One Room Out West: The Story of the Jore School and Its Student* by Rita Seedorf.; *Afghanistan's Endless War: State Failure and Regional Politics* by Larry P. Goodson; *Saving the Reservation: Joe Garry and the Battle to Be Indian* by John Fahey; *Ways of Being Ethnic in Southwest China* by Stevan Harrell; *Women in Pacific Northwest History, Revised Edition* edited by Karen J. Blair; *The Woven Coverlets of Norway* by Katherine Larson.

Weyerhaeuser Environmental Books series (under the general editorship of William Cronon) titles: *Landscapes of Promise: The Oregon Story, 1800–1940* by William Robbins; *World Fire: The Culture of Fire on Earth* and *Fire in America: A Cultural History of Wildland and Rural Fire*, both by Stephen J. Pyne.

University of Washington Press handles its own distribution via its home office and a number of regional sales representatives, and also distributes for a number of other specialist publishers and arts institutions, including the Tate Gallery, Asian Art Museum of San Francisco, Reaktion Books, Columbus Museum of Art, National Portrait Gallery of the Smithsonian Institution, Exhibitions International, and Idaho State Historical Society.

Query letters and SASEs should be directed to:

Michael Duckworth, Acquisitions Editor—Asian studies, Middle East studies, Russian and East European studies

Naomi Pascal, Associate Director and Editor-in-Chief—Western studies, Asian American studies, Western history, regional history

Lorri Hagman, Acquisitions Editor

Jacqueline Ettinger, Acquisitions Editor

UNIVERSITY OF WISCONSIN PRESS

1930 Monroe Street, 3rd Floor, Madison, WI 53711-2059

773-702-7000   fax: 773-702-7212

www.wisc.edu/wisconsinpress/   e-mail: uwiscpress@uwpress.wisc.edu

University of Wisconsin Press catalogues such fields as African studies, autobiography, art, American studies, anthropology and folklore, biography, contemporary issues, classical studies, environmental studies, European studies, gay studies, geography, history, criminology, Latin American studies, law, literature and criticism, medicine, music, poetry, sociology, Wisconsin regional studies, and women's studies. The press hosts a steadfast backlist.

Titles from UWP: *Apostles of Culture* by Lora Dee Garrison; *The Army of Truth* by Henrik Wergeland; *Bejing* by Philip Gambone; *Brooklyn Boy* by Alan Lelchuk; *Building Fiction* by Jesse Lee Kercheval; *The Centaur in the Garden* by Moacyr Scliar; *A Childhood Under Hitler and Stalin* by Michael Wieck; *The Classical Epic Tradition* by John Kevin Newman; *The Dane County Farmer's Market* by Mary Carpenter with Quentin Carpenter; *The End of Prussia* by Gordon A. Craig; *The England of Elizabeth* by A. L. Rowse; *Everyday and Prophetic* by Nick Halpern; *Family and Farm in Pre-Famine Ireland* by Kevin O'Neill; *A Fiddler's Tale* by Louis Kaufman with Annette Kaufman; *The Good Life* by Yi-Fu Tuan; *Gut Feelings* by Merrill Joan Gerber; *The Heretic* by Lewis Weinstein; *How It Was Done in Paris* by Leonid Livak; *The Imperial Sublime* by Harsha Ram; *Iran* by Michel M. J. Fischer; *Irish Peasants* edited by Samuel Clark and James S. Donnelly; *Isaac Bashevis Singer* by Janet Hadda; *Latin Moon in Manhattan* by Jaime Manrique; *The Low End of Higher Things* by David Clewell; *Mercy Mercy Me* by Elena Georgiou; *The Museum of Happiness* by Jesses Lee Kercheval; *Old World Wisconsin* by Fred L. Holmes; *Pluralism at Yale* by Richard M. Merelman; *An Aran Keening* by Andrew McNeillie; *The Autobiographical Documentary in America* by Jim Lane; *The Craft of Old-Master Drawings* by James Watrous; *A Deeper Freedom* by Charles W. Anderson.

University of Wisconsin Press (founded in 1937) is a midsize house that specializes in nonfiction and scholarly books and journals, with a growing and vigorous list of crossover titles geared to mainstream trade interest.

Distribution for University of Wisconsin Press publications is through the Chicago Distribution Center; trade sales are garnered nationwide by the press's formidable lineup of regional field representatives.

Query letters and SASEs should be directed to:

Raphael Kadushin, Acquisitions Editor—Gay and lesbian studies, autobiography, film studies, classics, environmental studies, history, Holocaust studies, dance, and performance art

Sheila McMahon Moermond, Acquisitions Assistant

Tricia Brock, Editor—Pop culture

VANDERBILT UNIVERSITY PRESS

112 21st Avenue South, Nashville, TN 37203

615-322-3585   fax: 615-343-8823

www.vanderbilt.edu/vupress   e-mail: vupress@vanderbilt.edu

Founded in 1940, Vanderbilt University Press is the publishing arm of one of the nation's leading research universities. The Press publishes intellectually provocative and socially significant books in the humanities, health care, social sciences, education, and regional studies for both academic and general audiences.

Notable titles include: *An Improbable Life* by Robert Craft; *Heartaches by the Number* by Bill Friskics-Warren and David Cantwell; *Exile and Cultural Hegemony* by Sebastian Faber; *Beyond Realism and Antirealism* by David L. Hildebrand; *Fateful Shapes of Human Freedom* by Vincent Colapietro; *Making Morality* by Todd Lekan; *Peabody College* by Paul K. Conkin; *Singing in the Saddle: A History of the Singing Cowboy* by Douglas B. Green; *Invisible Work* by Efrain Kristal; *Cervantes in Algiers: A Captive's Tale* by Maria Antonia Garces; *Reading Novels* by George Hughes; *The Holocaust and Other Genocides* edited by Helmut Walser Smith; *The Clinton Wars: The Constitution, Congress and War Powers* by Ryan C. Hendrickson; *To Give Their Gifts: Health, Community, and Democracy* by Richard A. Couto with Stephanie C. Eken; *Fatherhood Arrested: Parenting from Within the Juvenile Justice System* by Anne M. Nurse; *Families at Work: Expanding the Bounds* edited by Naomi Gerstel, Dan Clawson, and Robert Zussman.

Warehousing and worldwide order fulfillment are provided by the University of Oklahoma Press in Norman, Oklahoma.

Query letters and SASEs should be directed to:

Michael Ames, Director

YALE UNIVERSITY PRESS

302 Temple Street, New Haven, CT 06511

PO Box 209040, New Haven, CT 06520-9040

203-432-0960   fax: 203-432-0948

www.yale.edu/yup/   e-mail: yupmkt@yalevm.cis.yale.edu

The Yale publishing program offers both trade and academically oriented titles in the fields of the arts, the humanities, and the social sciences. Particular general-interest areas include contemporary issues, culture, and events; architecture, art criticism, and art history; history of America (with additional focus on the American West); literature and literary criticism; and political science, economics, and military studies. Yale produces hardcover and trade paper editions.

Yale University Press sponsors the annual Yale Younger Poets Competition and publishes the winning manuscript. Yale series include Composers of the Twentieth Century and Early Chinese Civilization.

Yale University Press (established in 1908) is at the forefront of university publishing. The house is one of the major academic houses, and Yale's commercial presence is evident in the catalogs of book clubs, as well as on national, regional, and specialty bestseller lists.

Notable titles from Yale: *The Art of Structural Design* by David P. Billington; *Renoir and Algeria* by Roger Benjamin; *Art in France* by Christopher Green; *Turner* by James Hamilton; *Tina Modotti* by Letizia Argenteri; *J. M. Barrie & The Lost Boys* by Andrew Birkin; *Sir John Hawkins* by Harry Kelsey; *Jonathan Edwards* by George Marsden; *Science as Autobiography* by Thomas Soderqvist; *Trying Neaira* by Debra Hamel; *Every Farm a Factory* by Deborah Fitzgerald; *Doing School* by Denise C. Pope; *The Corset* by Valerie Steele; *Visions of a New Land* by Emma Widdis; *Downtown* by Robert M. Fogelson; *The Two Reformations* by Heiko A. Oberman, edited by Donald Weinstein; *Ghetto Diary* by Janusz Korczak; *Reading Between the Lines* edited by Peter C. Patrikis; *The American Jury System* by Randolph N. Jonakait; *Kenneth Tynan* by Dominic Shellard; *The Oboe* by Geoffrey Burgess and Bruce Haynes; *The Moral Foundations of Politics* by Ian Shapiro; *The Christians As the Romans Saw Them* by Robert L. Wilken; *Bull's-Eye* by Jonathan A. Edlow, M. D.; *How Class Works* by Stanley Aronowitz; *Dr. Beach's Survival Guide* by Stephen P. Leatherman; *The Archaeology of Athens*; *You Look Beautiful Like That*; *The Art of Mu Xin*; *The Tumultuous Fifties*; *The Battle for Realism*; *Candace Wheeler*; *Great British Paintings from American Collections*; *Queen Anne (A Biography)*; *Selected Letters of Robert Louis Stevenson (A Biography)*; *Household and City Organization at Olynthus*; *The Five "Confucian" Classics*; *Loss of Happiness in Market Economies*; *Corporate Irresponsibility*.

Yale University Press handles its own distribution.

Query letters and SASEs should be directed to:

Jean E. Thomson Black, Acquisitions Editor—Science and medicine

Jonathan Brent, Editorial Director—Literature, literary studies, theater, Slavic studies.

Robert T. Flynn, Acquisitions Editor—Religion, law, and philosophy

Keith Condon, Assistant Editor—History

Patricia Fidler, Publisher—Art and architecture

Michelle Komie, Assistant Editor—Art and architecture

Michael O'Malley, Editor—Business, economics, and law

Mary Jane Peluso, Publisher—Languages and ESL (contactfor special instructions on how to submit a proposal for languages and ESL)

Lara Heimert, Senior Editor—History, intellectual history, women's studies

John Kulka, Senior Editor—Literature, philosophy, and political science

RELIGIOUS, SPIRITUAL & INSPIRATIONAL PRESSES

THE WRITER'S JOURNEY

THEMES OF THE SPIRIT & INSPIRATION

DEBORAH LEVINE HERMAN

If you have decided to pursue writing as a career instead of as a longing or a dream, you might find yourself falling into a pattern of focusing on the goal instead of the process. When you have a great book idea, you may envision yourself on a book-signing tour or as a guest on Oprah before you've written a single word.

It's human nature to look into your own future, but too much projection can get in the way of what the writing experience is all about. The process of writing is like a wondrous journey that can help you cross a bridge to the treasures hidden within your own subconscious. Some people believe that it's a way for you to link with the collective or universal consciousness, the storehouse of all wisdom and truth, as it has existed since the beginning of time.

Many methods of writing bring their own rewards. Some people can produce exceptional prose by using their intellect and their mastery of the writing craft. They use research and analytical skills to help them produce works of great importance and merit.

Then there are those who have learned to tap into the wellspring from which all genius flows. They are the inspired ones who write with the intensity of an impassioned lover. They are the spiritual writers who write because they have to. They may not want to, they may not know how to, but something inside them is begging to be let out. It gnaws away at them until they find a way to set it free.

Although they may not realize it, spiritual writers are engaged in a larger spiritual journey toward ultimate self-mastery and unification with God.

Spiritual writers often feel as if they're taking dictation. It is as though their thoughts have a life of their own, and the mind is merely a receiver. Some people refer to this as "channeling" and believe disembodied spirits take over and write through them. Although I sincerely doubt that Gandhi or other notables have authored as many channeled books as people have claimed, truly spiritual writing does have an otherworldly feeling and can often teach writers things they would otherwise not have known.

Writing opens you up to new perspectives, much like self-induced psychotherapy. Although journals are the most direct route for self-evaluation, fiction and nonfiction also serve as vehicles for a writer's growth. Writing helps the mind expand to the limits of the imagination.

Anyone can become a spiritual writer. There are many benefits to doing so, not the least of which is the development of your soul. On a more practical level, it is much less difficult to write with flow and fervor than it is to be bound by the limitations of logic and analysis. If you tap into the universal source, there is no end to your potential creativity.

The greatest barrier to becoming a spiritual writer is the human ego. We treat our words as if they were our children—only we tend to be neurotic parents. Children are not owned by parents, but rather must be loved, guided, and nurtured until they can carry on, on their own.

The same is true for our words. If we try to own and control them like property, they will be limited by our vision for them. We will overprotect them and will not be able to see when we may be taking them in the wrong direction for their ultimate well-being.

Another ego problem that creates a barrier to creativity is our need for constant approval and our tendency toward perfectionism. We may feel the tug toward free expression, but will erect blockades to ensure appropriate style and structure. We write with a "schoolmarm" hanging over our shoulders, waiting to tell us what we are doing wrong.

Style and structure are important to ultimate presentation, but that is what editing is for. Ideas and concepts need to flow like water in a running stream.

The best way to become a spiritual writer is to relax and have fun. If you are relaxed and are in a basically good mood, you'll be open to intuition. Writers tend to take themselves too seriously, which causes anxiety, which exacerbates fear, which causes insecurity, which diminishes our self-confidence and leads ultimately to mounds of crumpled papers and lost inspiration.

If you have faith in a Supreme Being, the best way to begin a spiritual writing session is with the following writer's prayer:

Almighty God (Jesus, Allah, Great Spirit, etc.), Creator of the Universe, help me to become a vehicle for your wisdom so that what I write is of the highest purpose and will serve the greatest good. I humbly place my (pen/keyboard/Dictaphone) in your hands so that you may guide me.

Prayer helps to connect you to the universal source. It empties the mind of trash, noise, and potential writer's blocks. If you are not comfortable with formal prayer, a few minutes of meditation will serve the same purpose.

Spiritual writing as a process does not necessarily lead to a sale. The fact is that some people have more commercial potential than others, no matter how seemingly unimportant their message might be. Knowledge of the business of writing will help you make a career of it. If you combine this with the spiritual process, it can also bring you gratification and inner peace.

If you trust the process of writing and allow the journey to take you where it will, it may bring you benefits far beyond your expectations.

ABINGDON PRESS

DIMENSIONS FOR LIVING

KINGSWOOD BOOKS

201 Eighth Avenue South, PO Box 801, Nashville, TN 37202-0801

615-749-6290

www.Abingdonpress.com

Abingdon Press is the book-publishing division of the United Methodist Publishing House (founded in 1789). Abingdon produces hardcover, trade paperback, and mass-market paperback editions, covering a wide range of religious specialty, religious trade, and popular markets. Areas of concentration include professional reference and resources for the clergy; academic and scholarly works in the fields of religious and Biblical history and theory; inspirational and devotional books; and titles with contemporary spiritual and ethical themes intended for a wider readership. Abingdon's publishing presence includes software and works on CD-ROM.

Abingdon also issues several series of books for children and resources for Sunday school and general Christian education, as well as church supplies (posters, calendars, certificates, maps, buttons, music, and dramatic scripts). Dimensions for Living is an Abingdon imprint dedicated to titles with a popular orientation (see separate subentry further on). Abingdon reprints a number of its bestselling titles in mass-market paperback editions and tends a formidable backlist.

On the Abingdon list: *The Organization of the United Methodist Church* by Jack Tuell; *The Passion Driven Congregation* by Kent Millard and Carver McGriff; *The Works of John Wesley (Volume 24), Journal and Diaries* by Richard Heitzenrater; *Tween Spirituality; A Year's Worth of Children's Church* by Lisa Flinn; *African American History Month* by Tyrone Gordon; *And Then Mark Died* by Susan Vogel; *Badger's Easter Surprise (Oaktree Wood series)* by Alan Parry and Linda Parry; *At the End of the Day* by James Moore; *Jesus' Claims—Our Promises* by Maxine Dunnam; *Essential Bible Passages for Youth Leaders* by Nan Duerling; *An Introduction to Christian Theology* by Zaida Meldondo Perez; *And You Welcomed Me* by Amy Oden; *Counseling Families Across the Stages of Life* by George Harold Koenig, Linda Revilla, and Andrew Weaver; *Her Own Story* by Paul Chilcote;

John Wesley on Christian Beliefs by Kenneth Cain Kinghorn; *Pastor* by William H. Willimon; *Public Reading of Scripture* by Clay Schmit; *New Tools for a New Century* by John Jewell; *Nurturing Faith in Families* by Jolene Rochlkepartain; *A Day of Rest* by Martha W. Hickman.

The Grand Sweep series by Ellsworth Kalas is a Bible study program that moves in canonical sequence, based on Ellsworth Kalas's book *365 Days from Genesis Through Revelation*. Titles: *The Grand Sweep: Bible Study for Individuals and Groups*; *The Grand Sweep: Daily Response Book*; *The Grand Sweep: Sermon Ideas for 52 Weeks*.

New Fortress press titles: *In Justice: Women and Global Economics* by Ann-Cathrin Jarl; *Terror and Triumph: The Nature of Black Religion* by Anthony B. Pinn; *It Ain't Over Till It's Over: A User's Guide for the Second Half of Life* by William Diehl and Judith Ruhe Diehl.

Body & Soul: A Disciplined Approach to a Healthy Lifestyle is a series of programs for Christians seeking a healthful lifestyle. Body & Soul focuses on the spiritual, physical, mental, emotional, and social aspects of persons for a powerful approach to behavior change. Titles: *Health Yourself*; *Second Helpings*; *Wonderfully Healthy*; *Caring & Sharing*; *Stepping Forward*.

In addition to distributing its own books, Abingdon Press handles the lists of several other smaller religious publishers. Query letters and SASEs should be directed to:

Dr. Rex D. Matthews, Editor, Academic Books—Books for Sunday and parochial schools and seminaries

Jack Keller, Editor, Professional Books and Reference Books—Methodist doctrine and church practices for clergy and laity. Dictionaries and general reference guides relevant to Methodist history and policy

Mary Catherine Dean, Editor, Trade Books—Nonfiction books that help families and individuals live Christian lives; contemporary social themes of Christian relevance

DIMENSIONS FOR LIVING

Dimensions for Living is an Abingdon imprint devoted to general-interest religious trade books on practical Christian living. Dimensions for Living publishes in the popular categories of inspiration, devotion, self-help, home, and family, as well as gift volumes. The concept behind the Dimensions for Living imprint—"quality books that celebrate life"—was developed in response to market research. The editorial approach is to combine contemporary themes with mainstream Christian theology.

Titles from Dimensions for Living: *A Day of Rest* by Martha Hickman; *African Prayers* by Robert Van De Weyer; *Blessings for Today* by Susan Skinner; *From Eve to Esther* by Nell Mohney; *From Mary to Lydia* by Nell Mohney; *God Sightings* by Bass M. Mitchell; *God Was Here and I Went Out to Lunch* by James W. Moore; *Lord of the Evening* by Frank Topping; *Personal Prayers for Seniors* by Alan W. Schreiber; *Personal Prayers for Women* by Grace Simpson.

Query letters and SASEs should be directed to:

Sally Sharpe, Editor, Dimensions for Living—Quality books that celebrate life and affirm the Christian faith

KINGSWOOD BOOKS

Kingswood books is an Abingdon imprint that publishes scholarly works in all areas of Methodist and Wesleyan studies. The imprint honors John Wesley's lifelong commitment to the Christian lifestyle. This commitment, which found expression in his extensive writing and publishing, took form in his establishment of the Kingswood School, near Bristol, England.

New titles from Kingswood include: *Politics in the Order of Salvation* by Theodore Weber; *Trinity, Community and Power* by Douglas Meeks; *The Episcopacy of American Methodism* by James E. Kirby; *Methodism and the Shaping of American Culture* by John H. Wigger and Nathan O. Hatch.

AMERICAN FEDERATION OF ASTROLOGERS, INC.

6535 South Rural Road, Tempe, AZ 85283-3746

480-838-1751   fax: 480-838-8293

www.astrologers.com   e-mail: AFA@msn.com

The American Federation of Astrologers (founded in 1938) is a specialist publisher of books on astrology for everyone from the beginner to the professional. The house also offers astrological software, charts, and other astrological aids, but does not publish these.

As an organization, the American Federation of Astrologers (AFA) aims to further astrological education and research. The AFA is an astrological membership organization, as well as a major publisher and distributor of astrological books and related supplies. AFA books are written by a variety of talented astrologers from all over the globe.

The AFA encourages and promotes the science and art of astrology and advocates freedom of thought and speech in the astrological arena. The house offers a monthly membership bulletin, *Today's Astrologer*, and hosts periodic conventions. The organization's publishing program has generally produced a short list of new titles each year and supports an extensive publications backlist.

From the American Federation of Astrologers: *Child Astrology* by M. J. Abadie; *Discrimination of Birth* by John Addey; *The Zodiac* by Omraam Aivanhov; *Daily Use of the Ephemeris* by Elizabeth Aldrich; *Planets in Signs* by Skye Alexander; *The 90 Degree Disc: Handbook* by Karl Ambjornson; *Astrology, Psychology and the 4 Elem* by Stephen Arroyo; *You in a Modern World* by Doris Chase Doane; *First Survive, Then Thrive: The Journey from Crisis to Transformation* by John F. Eddington and Beth Rosato; *Phases of the Moon* by Marilyn Busteed and Dorothy Wergin; *Freudian Astrology, Lilith, and Libido* by Elizabeth Greenwood; *Zodiac Explorer's Handbook* by Helene Hess; *The Living Stars* by Dr. Eric Morse; *Sun Sign Success* by Joseph Polansky; *Cosmopsychology: Engine of Destiny* by Marc Robertson; *The Book of Lovers* by Carolyn Reynolds.

Authors please note: the American Federation of Astrologers wishes to consider only completed manuscripts for publication—and does not wish to consider queries, outlines, samples, or proposals. Manuscripts may be submitted along with copies on diskette (other than Macintosh), in text format.

American Federation of Astrologers distributes its own list, as well as publications of other houses.

Send completed manuscripts to:

Kris Brandt Riske, Production Manager

JASON ARONSON INC., PUBLISHERS

This revered publisher, of important and serious books relevant to psychology, sociology and Judaica, has ceased to acquire and publish new works.

AUGSBURG FORTRESS PUBLISHING

FORTRESS PRESS

100 South Fifth Street, Suite 700, Minneapolis, MN 55402

612-330-3300/1-800-426-0115   fax: 612-330-3455

www.augsburgfortress.org

Mailing address:

PO Box 1209, Minneapolis, MN 55440-1209

Augsburg Fortress publishes titles in popular and professional religious categories. The Augsburg Fortress list accents works of interest to general readers, in addition to books that appeal primarily to a mainstream religious readership and a solid selection of works geared to professional clergy and practitioners of pastoral counseling.

Categories include theology and pastoral care, Biblical and historical academic studies, the life and tradition of Martin Luther, self-improvement and recovery, and books for younger readers from nursery and preschoolers through young adult.

The Fortress Press imprint accents issues of contemporary cultural, theological, and political impact. In addition, Augsburg Fortress produces computer software, recordings, artwork, and gift items. Augsburg Fortress also vends a line of liturgical vestments and supplies. The house is widely known for its full range of Bibles, produced in a variety of editions and styles.

Augsburg Fortress's ecumenical emphasis enables the house to address a broad range of issues and views within a diversified booklist. Augsburg Fortress Publishing (founded in 1890) is a subsidiary of the Publishing House of the Evangelical Lutheran Church in America.

Representative of the Augsburg list: *Jesus' Lonely Road* by Robert C. Bankhead; *At the Cross with Jesus* by Carl B. Rife; *The First Step Bible* by Mack Thomas; *The Rhyme Bible Storybook* by L. J. Sattgast; *Welcome Aboard* by Tim Wright; *Acts of Faith 2: Dramas for God's People* by Brad Kindell; *Everyone Who Is Thirsty, Come!* by Jay Beech; *The Gifts of Lent* by Donald H. Neidigk; *Conversations with the Savior* by Donald H. Neidigk; *Gathering at Golgotha* by Katherine Bailey Babb; *Thespian Theology* by John A. TenBrook.

Children's selections include the line of Good News Explorers Sunday school curriculum series, the Rejoice series, and the Witness series, as well as individual titles. Samples include: *Swamped!* by Nathan Aaseng; *So I Can Read* by Dandi Mackall (illustrated by Deborah A. Kirkeeide); *Ms. Pollywog's Problem-Solving Service* by Ellen Javernick (illustrated by Meredith Johnson).

Authors should note: Augsburg Fortress prefers to receive a proposal rather than a completed manuscript; the house receives over 3,000 submissions per year—a finely honed book proposal may therefore be considered essential.

Augsburg Fortress has a potent distribution network with sales representatives operating via offices nationwide.

FORTRESS PRESS

Fortress Press focuses on the ever-changing religious worldview of the contemporary world. The Fortress list is keyed to issues of topical interest, tackled with vision and precision; these works address political and cultural issues and are often on the cusp of current religious debate. The Fortress market orientation tilts toward both the general trade and the religious trade.

Titles from Fortress Press: *God Beyond Gender: Feminist Christian God Language* by Gail Ramshaw; *The Crucifixion of Jesus: History, Myth, Faith* by Gerard S. Sloyan; *The Paradoxical Vision: A Public Theology for the Twenty-First Century* by Robert Benne; *The Spirituality of African Peoples: The Search for a Common Moral Discourse* by Peter J. Paris; *Theology for a Scientific Age: Being and Becoming—Natural, Divine, and Human* by Arthur Peacocke; *Womanism and Afrocentrism in Theology* by Cheryl J. Sanders; *X-odus: An African-American Male Journey* by Garth Kasimu Baker-Fletcher.

Query letters and SASEs should be directed to:

Marshall Johnson, Editorial Director

Robert Klausmeier, Senior Acquisitions Editor

BAKER BOOK HOUSE

CHOSEN BOOKS

FLEMING H. REVELL

SPIRE BOOKS

Twin Brooks Industrial Park, 6030 East Fulton Road, Ada, MI 49301

616-676-9185   fax: 616-676-9573

www.bakerbooks.com

Mailing address:

PO Box 6287, Grand Rapids, MI 49516-6287

Baker Book House (founded in 1939) produces works across the spectrum of general religious subject areas (from Protestant and ecumenical perspectives). Baker Book House is a preeminent distributor in the religious publishing field. Baker Book House distributes its own list (including its diverse imprints).

Query letters and SASEs should be directed to:

Rebecca Cooper, Assistant Editor

BAKER BOOK HOUSE

The publishing division of Baker Book House issues titles of general trade interest, as well as a wide selection of books for ministers, students, schools, libraries, and church workers.

Highlighting the Baker program: *Long Road to LaRosa* by Paul Bagdon; *Stallions at Burnt Rock* by Paul Bagdon; *Stuffed Animals on the Ceiling Fan* by Silvana Clark; *How Can I Help?* by Linda Elliot; *Fresh Elastic for Stretched Out Moms* by Barbara Johnson; *Quiet in His Presence* by Jan Harris; *When to Speak Up (and When Not To)* by Dr. Michael Sedler; *The Fisherman* by Larry Huntsperger; *Getting the Gospel Right* by R. C. Sproul; *Each New Day, 25th ann. Ed.* by Corrie ten Boom; *And Then I had Kids* by Susan Alexander Yates; *Building a Home Full of Grace* by John and Susan Yates; *Ruth Bell Graham's Collected Poems* by Ruth Bell Graham; *Messenger of Hope: Becoming Agents of Revival for the Twenty-First Century* by David Bryant; *Willing to Believe: The Controversy Over Free Will* by R. C. Sproul; *Yearning Minds and Burning Hearts: Rediscovering the Spirituality of Jesus* by Glendion Carney and William Long; *A Time to Heal: John Perkins, Community Development, and Racial Reconciliation* by Stephen E. Berk; *Masterpieces of the Bible: Insights into Classical Art of Faith* by Keith White; *Teaching in Tough Times* by Judy Nichols; *Treasured Friends: Finding and Keeping True Friendships* by Ann Hibbard.

CHOSEN BOOKS/FLEMING H. REVELL/SPIRE BOOKS

This Baker wing specializes in spiritually oriented works for the popular religious audience, including a wide range of fiction. Offerings from the Revell program include the Treasury of Helen Steiner Rice line of inspirational titles. The Chosen Books imprint produces evangelical Christian books for personal growth and enrichment. Spire accents an inspirational list of personal stories told through autobiography and memoir.

Chosen titles include: *Twilight Labyrinth: Why Does Spiritual Darkness Linger Where It Does?* by George K. Otis, Jr.; *The Love Every Woman Needs: Intimacy with Jesus* by Jan McCray; *I Give You Authority* by Charles H. Kraft; *Blessing or Curse* by Derek Prince.

From Revell: *The New Birth Order Book* by Dr. Kevin Leman; *The Menopause Manager: Balancing Medical Knowledge and Botanical Wisdom for Optimal Health* by Mary Ann and Joseph L. Mayo; *Happily Ever After: And 21 Other Myths About Family Life* by Karen Scalf Linamen; *Love Busters: Overcoming the Habits That Destroy Romantic Love* by Willard F. Harley, Jr.; *What Kids Need Most Is Mom* by Patricia H. Rushford; *When Your Best Is Never Good Enough: The Secret of Measuring Up* by Kevin Leman.

On the Spire roster: *Jonathan, You Left Too Soon* by David B. Biebel; *Getting the Best of Your Anger* by Les Carter; *Making Peace with Your Past* by H. Norman Wright; *Those Turbulent Teen Years* by Jeenie Gordon.

Baker Book House does not accept unsolicited manuscripts. We recommend that you submit your work to First Edition, an online service of the Evangelical Christian Publishers' Association, and The Writer's Edge. We subscribe to both these services and regularly review the proposals posted there. You may contact these organizations at these addresses:

First Edition: www.ecpa.org/FE/ or e-mail: FirstEdition@ECPA.org

The Writer's Edge: www.writersedgeservice.com or e-mail: info@WritersEdge-Service.com; PO Box 1266, Wheaton, IL 60189

BETHANY HOUSE PUBLISHERS

11400 Hampshire Avenue South, Bloomington, MN 55438

952-829-2500   fax: 952-829-2572

www.bethanyhouse.com

In early 2003, Bethany House Publishers became an imprint of Baker Book House. Editorial offices will continue operation in Minnesota, but the warehouse and fulfillment operations will be moved to Baker Book's Grand Rapids facility.

Bethany House Publishers (founded in 1956) issues hardcover and trade paperback titles in evangelical Christian fiction (with an accent on historicals) and nonfiction, as well as a powerful youth lineup. Areas of Bethany House nonfiction interest include devotional works, relationships and family, and biblical reference.

Bethany's fiction authors include such bestselling names as Janette Oke, Judith Pella, and Gilbert Morris. The program accents titles with American prairie and Western themes, historical romances, and works with contemporary settings; the house also offers boxed series sets. Among Bethany fiction features are the series by the father/daughter writing team Lynn Morris and Gilbert Morris.

The house's trade credo is: "God's light shining through good books." Bethany's traditional devotion to bookmaking is evident in its enduring backlist.

Titles from Bethany: *Across the Years* by Tracie Peterson; *Angels Watching Over Me* by Michael Phillips; *Sutter's Cross* by W. Dale Cramer; *God's Pathway to Healing Joints and Arthritis* by Reginald B. Cherry, M.D.; *The Christian Wedding Planner*; *The New Bride Guide* by Ellie Kay; *Frugal Families* by Jonni McCoy; *Thrive!: A Woman's Guide to a Healthy Lifestyle* by Dr. Carrie Carter; *Daughter of the Loom* by Tracie Peterson and Judith Miller; *A Rush of Wings* by Kristen Heitzmann; *A Greater Glory* by James Scott Bell; *At the Name of Jesus* by Tricia McCary Rhodes.

Children's and young adult fiction: *The Birthday Present Mystery* (Young Cousins Mysteries) by Elspeth Campbell Murphy; *About Face Space Race* (AstroKids series) by Robert Elmer; *Cross My Heart* (The Hidden Diary series) by Sandra Byrd; *Promise Breaker* (Promise of Zion series) by Robert Elmer.

Bethany House distributes to the trade through Ingram, Baker & Taylor, and other wholesalers.

Bethany House Publishers will no longer accept unsolicited manuscripts and book proposals. We will continue to accept queries, proposals, and manuscripts through established literary agents, recognized manuscript services, and writers' conferences attended by BHP editorial staff. We will also accept one-page only facsimile proposals directed to Adult Nonfiction, Adult Fiction, or YA/children editors. Check our Web site for current numbers.

Query letters and SASEs should be directed to:

Donna Birky, Administrative Editorial Assistant

Sharon Madison, Acquisitions Editor

BEYOND WORDS

20827 N. W. Cornell Rd., Suite 500

Hillsboro, Oregon 97124-9808

503-531-8700   fax: 503-531-8773

www.beyondword.com   e-mail: info@beyondword.com

Beyond Words is a publishing company for authors, artists, and readers who share a love of words and images that inspire, delight, and educate. Founded in 1984 by owners

Richard and Cindy Rags, Beyond Words has sold over half a million titles and has over 100 books currently in print. Beyond Words has also published books in over thirty different languages.

Beyond Words accepts manuscripts year round, specifically in the areas of Photography, Personal Growth, Women's Issues, Spirituality, and Children's. They also have periodic writing contests.

Recent titles include: *The Gordon House: Lore of the Dolphin* by Natalia Burn; *The Book of Intentions* by Dianne Martin; *The Letter Box* by Mark Button; *Path of the Pearl* by Mary Olsen-Kelly; *The Widening Stream* by David Ulrich; *Noble Red Man* by Harvey Arden; *Wisdom's Choice* by Kathryn Adams Shapiro; *Your Authentic Self* by Ric Giardina; *Midlife Clarity*; *The Art of Thank You* by Connie Leas.

Children's Books: *Elizabeth's Song*; *Meet Niche*; *It's Your Rite*; *Generation Fix*; *Authors by Request*; *Going Places*.

Send query and SASEs to:

Cindy Black, Acquisitions Editor

COOK COMMUNICATIONS

FAITH KIDZ BOOKS, TOYS & MEDIA

HONOR BOOKS

CHURCH ALIVE

FAITH PARENTING

LIFE JOURNEY

RIVER OAK

VICTOR BOOKS

4050 Lee Vance View, Colorado Springs, CO 80918

719-536-3271   fax: 719-536-3296

Cook Communications produces mainstream Christian religious titles in books and other media. Divisions include: Victor Books, Faith Marriage, Faith Parenting, Faithful Woman, Lion, Faith Kidz Bookz, and Faith Kidz Toys & Media.

Cook Communications and its imprints reflect the merger (in July of 1996) of Chariot Family Publishing and Scripture Press Publications/Victor Books, along with the operation's relocation from Illinois to Colorado.

The house mission is to assist in the spiritual development of people by producing and distributing consumer-driven, centrist Christian products that foster discipleship, increase understanding of the Bible, and promote the application of Christian values in everyday life.

Cook Communications products are prayerfully crafted to fit its prime audience. They are inspirational, fun, and creative and provide sound Christian education. They are easy and simple for parents, teachers, and others to use effectively. The nature of the house product and its marketing will encourage linking church and home.

Cook Communications markets lines that target broad sectors of the market: youth (primarily from the Faith Kidz Brand), adult (Victor Books, Faith Marriage, Faith Parenting, and Faithful Woman), and general religious trade (Lion Publishing).

Cook Communications distribution utilizes a network of field representatives and services that includes its own in-house catalog and marketing operations.

FAITH KIDZ BOOKS, TOYS & MEDIA

Faith Kidz produces a strong list of titles with a religious orientation in the publishing areas of juvenile fiction, inspirational and devotional reference (most of them works for young readers), as well as works for a general religious readership. Chariot markets a line of illustrated Bibles and illustrated inspirational and devotional readings.

As the editors of Faith Kidz Books note: "We have been called by Christ to foster the spiritual development of children. That is why, through Faith Kidz Books & Toys, we focus on training children in and through the family. We exist to help parents evangelize and discipline their children as a part of everyday life as commanded in Deuteronomy 6:5–9. We will facilitate family discipleship by providing an organized Christian growth program of market-sensitive, exemplary products."

Faith Kidz Books offers a wide range of reading materials for ages birth to teen. Faith Kidz Toys offers gift and educational items that are inspirational and fun—toys, games, and gift products for ages birth to teen. Each book/product contains a Faith Building or Faith Parenting Guide that is designed to help children understand God's word through sight, sound, and touch/action. Some titles include: *Missing Manger Mystery* by Jerry Thomas; *Room In the Stable* by Crystal Bowman; *A Knight in the Forest* by Dan Foote; *What Do You See When You See Me?* by Jeannie St. John Taylor; *I Have a Friend* by Heather Gemmen; *Mystery At Crestwater Camp* by Jeanne Gowen Dennis and Shelia Seifert.

HONOR BOOKS

Honor publishes books that inspire readers and help them feel closer to God. Readers should be impressed by the wide array of gift and motivational books offered. Honor titles: *Quiet Moments With God For Teens*; *Quiet Moments With God for African Americans*; *Quiet Moments with God for Teachers*; *Minute Motivations for Leaders*; *Minute Motivations for Teachers*; *Minute Motivations for Teens*; *Minute Motivations for Dieters*.

CHURCH ALIVE

Church Alive books are designed to aid church ministries by producing VBS and children's church programs and books on learning styles and methods of teaching. Readers will find everything needed to enhance the learning experience inside a church. Titles include: *Joy of Eating Right* by Dee Brestin; *Every Season Kid Pleasin' Children's Sermons* by Susan Martins Miller; *Teaching With All Your Heart* by David Fessenden; *Flowers From God* by Marlene LeFever; *Life and Lessons of Jesus, Vol. 1: Jesus' Early Years; Gifts of Gold* by Betty Huizenga.

FAITH PARENTING

Faith Parenting is designed to help parents with the Biblical mandate of passing on their Christian faith to their children. Central to this effort are books that encourage family devotions, such as the *Family Night Tool Chest* line.

LIFE JOURNEY

Life Journey offers books for every facet of a busy Christian life including the subjects of life, marriage, parenting, leadership, inspiration, and even some fiction titles. Titles include: *Two Great Christmas Stories* by Gary E. Parker; *Holidays Family Nights Tool Chest* by Kurt Bruner and Jim Weidmann; *When Your World Falls Apart* by Mike Macintosh; *Slices of Life: Unexpected Blessings from Everyday Life* by Ellie Lofaro; *In a Heartbeat* by Dawn Siegrist Waltman; *Courage to Connect: A Journey Toward Intimacy in Relationships* by Rich Hurst.

RIVER OAK

River Oak publishes titles to captivate the heart, mind and imagination of the reader. Their books try to challenge and entertain the reader through fictional titles that are great stories, written by great writers. River Oak books are designed to be well packaged page-turners. Titles include: *Avenged* by Ken Boa; *Malchus* by William G. Griffiths; *A Place Called Wiregrass* by Michael Morris; *Mutiny's Curse* by Dan Thrapp; *Tuesdays With Matthew* by Mike Nappa; *At Home In Mitford* by Jan Karon.

VICTOR BOOKS

Victor Books (founded in 1934) offers a wide range of books keyed to spiritual, religious, philosophical, and social topics for the adult, as well as educational materials and supplies.

Categories of publishing interest include family spiritual growth, women's spiritual growth, books of the Bible, Bible characters, group builder resources, and general topics. The Victor Books imprint marks the trade-directed portion of the program. Victor is the imprint that marks games and gifts for adults.

The Victor product line meets various personal needs of the market. Victor reaches evangelicals with the purpose of aiding the intended audience in its spiritual formation. Victor adult fame and media adult products facilitate fun learning of Bible truths through adult group and family interaction with such items as games, puzzles, and activities.

More than just entertaining, Cook Publishing hopes to inspire you to fulfill the great commandment: to love God with all your heart, soul, mind, and strength and your neighbor as yourself. Toward that end, many of our books contain a personal note from the author. Titles include: *Mary: The Mother of Jesus* by Wendy Virgo; *Desert of Hardship, Water of Hope* by Jill Briscoe and Judy Briscoe Golz; *Be Series: Be Distinct* by Warren Wiersbe; *Choices of the Heart—Repackage* by Kathy Collard Miller.

Query letters and SASEs should be directed to:

Karen Athen, Secretary Department Head

COUNCIL OAK BOOKS

1615 S. Baltimore, Suite 3, Tulsa, OK 74119

918-587-6454/1-800-247-8850   fax: 918-583-4995

www.counciloakbooks.com   e-mail: jclark@counciloakbooks.com

Council Oak Books, founded in 1984, is a publisher of distinguished nonfiction books based in personal, intimate history (letters, diaries, memoirs); Native American history and spiritual teachings; African American history and contemporary experience; small illustrated inspirational gift books; and unique vintage photo books and Americana. We're looking for those unique, eloquent voices whose history, teachings, and experiences illuminate our lives. No fiction, poetry, or children's books. Check our website at: www.counciloakbooks.com.

Titles from Council Oak: *The Blessing* by Gregory Orr; *Being & Vibration* by Joseph Rael and Mary Elizabeth Marlow; *The Journey Home* by Clifton L. Taulbert; *Secrets From an Inventor's Notebook* by Maurice Kanbar; *Native New Yorkers* by Evan T. Pritchard; *Fools Crow* by Thomas E. Mails; *The Route 66 Cookbook* by Marion Clark; *Strongman* (edited by Robert Mainardi); *Of Unknown Origin* by Debra Levi Holtz; *Vow* by Kay Leigh Hagan; *No Word for Time: The Way of the Algonquin People* by Evan T. Pritchard; *Beyond Fear: The Toltec Guide to Freedom and Joy, the Teachings of Don Miguel Ruiz*, as recorded by Mary Carroll Nelson; *When the Night Bird Sings* by Joyce Sequichie Hifler; *A Cherokee Feast of Days* by Joyce Sequichie Hifler; *The Hoop and the Tree* by Chris Hoffman.

Send a brief query letter describing your book with SASE, or a full proposal including table of contents or chapter outline, sample chapter, and author bio, with either sufficient postage for return or a notation that the material may be recycled if declined. Unsolicited manuscripts cannot be returned. Query or proposal should be directed to:

Kevin Bentley, Editor in Chief

THE CROSSING PRESS

PO Box 7123, Berkeley, CA 94707

510-524-1052   fax: 510-524-1052

www.crossingpress.com   e-mail: order@tenspeed.com

The Crossing Press is now a part of Ten Speed Press (see listing in Independent U.S. Presses.)

The Crossing Press publishes a wide range of hardcover and trade paperback editions and is dedicated to publishing books, videos, and audios on natural healing, spirituality, alternative healing practices, pet care, general nonfiction, and cookbooks. Our subjects include astrology, aromatherapy, body image, meditation, shamanism, and women's issues, to name a few. It is our hope that the power of information is a catalyst for change and development, not only for the self but for the global community as well.

The Crossing Press was established in upstate New York in 1972 as a modest, veritable cottage press, run from the farmhouse of the founders, Elaine Goldman Gill and John Gill, who were teaching at Cornell University at the time. Relocated to the central California coastal region in the 1980s, the Crossing Press retains its personalized editorial touch and small press savvy.

Titles from the Crossing Press include: *Living Feng Shui* by Carol J. Hyder; *Essential Wicca* by Paul Tuitean and Estelle Daniels; *Overcoming Headaches* by Pat Thomas; *The Wisdom of Negative Thinking* by Tony Humphreys; *Reliance on the Light* by Diane Stein; *Men's Health* by Joe Armstrong; *Pocket Herbal Reference Guide* by Debra St. Claire; *Natural Healing for Dogs & Cats* by Diane Stein; *Aromatherapy: A Complete Guide* by Kathi Keville & Mindy Green; *The Healing Energy of Your Hands* by Michael Bradford; *Essential Reiki* by Diane Stein; *A Magical Guide to Love & Sex: How to Use Rituals, Spells, and Nature's Energies to Bring Love into Your Life* by Cassandra Eason; *Explorations in Consciousness* by Atala Dorothy Toy; *Understanding and Overcoming Depression* by Tony Bates; *Inner Radiance, Outer Beauty* by Ambika Wauters; *Stein's Guide to Goddess Craft* by Diane Stein; *Healing Spirits* by J. Joslow Rodewald and P. West Barker.

The Crossing Press distributes through Publisher's Group West. The Crossing Press accepts unsolicited manuscripts. Query letters, proposals, and manuscripts (SASEs included) should be directed to:

Caryle Hirshberg, Managing Editor

Elaine Gill, Acquisitions Editor

CROSSROAD PUBLISHING COMPANY

CROSSROAD HERDER

481 Eighth Avenue, Suite 1550, New York, NY 10001

212-868-1801   fax: 212-868-2171

www.crossroadpublishing.com

Crossroad Publishing Company (founded in 1980) publishes scholarly and general-interest titles in religion, philosophy, spirituality, and personal improvement. Crossroad offers books in spirituality, religion, and counseling for general and popular religious markets. The Crossroad Herder imprint publishes books in theology, religious studies, and religious education for professionals and active members of Catholic and mainline Protestant churches.

Crossroad and sibling imprint Crossroad Herder (formerly Herder & Herder) is a United States-based wing of the international firm Verlag Herder (founded in 1798). The programs of Crossroad and Crossroad Herder offer books by some of the most distinguished authors in the United States and abroad in the fields of theology, Biblical studies, spirituality, religious education, women's studies, world religions, psychology, and counseling. Crossroad supports a strong backlist.

Crossroad and Continuum, now two completely separate entities sharing the same address, were corporate affiliates within the Crossroad/Continuum Publishing Group from 1980 through the early 1990s. Even through the dual-house years, each publisher retained its distinct identity. (For Continuum, please see the entry in the U.S. Publishers section.)

Crossroad is an entrepreneurial house of modest size, with a tightly focused program that takes advantage of diverse marketing channels; as such, this publisher provides an excellent environment for authors looking for personalized and long-term publishing relationships.

Titles from Crossroad: *God at the Ritz* by Lorenzo Albacete; *Violence Unveiled* by Gil Bailie; *And Now I See...* by Robert Barron; *Beauty for Ashes* by John Farina; *Rhythms and Cycles* by Nancy Bruning; *The Rule of St. Benedict* by Joan Chittister; *A New Set of Eyes* by Paula D'Arcy; *Mary: Art, Culture, and Religion through the Ages* by Caroline Ebertshauser; *Tender Fires: The Spiritual Promise of Sexuality* by Fran Ferder and John Heagle; *Daring Promise* by Richard Gaillardetz; *Beyond the Mirror: Reflections of Life and Death* by Henri J. Nouwen; *Finding My Way Home: Pathways to Life and the Spirit* by Henri J. Nouwen; *Beyond the Empire* by Desmond O'Grady; *The Christian Family Toolbox* by David Robinson; *Intimacy with God* by Thomas Keating; *Eyes on the Cross: A Guide for Contemplation* by Michael Kennedy; *On the Body: A Contemporary Theology of Sexuality* by Maria Carlo Martini; *The Doctors of the Church* by Bernard McGinn; *All Saints: Daily Reflections on Saints, Prophets and Witnesses for Our Time* by Robert Ellsberg;

Post Traumatic Stress Disorder: The Victim's Guide to Healing and Recovery by Raymond B. Flannery, Jr.; *Spiritual Passages: The Psychology of Spiritual Development "For Those Who Seek"* by Benedict Groeschel, Jr.; *Educating for Life: A Spiritual Vision for Every Teacher and Parent* by Thomas Groome; *Consider Jesus: Waves of Renewal in Contemporary Christology* by Elizabeth Johnson.

An ongoing Crossroad line is the Adult Christian Education Program, which issues series titles in scripture study, theology and church history, Christian living, and world religious traditions.

Crossroad has sponsored the Crossword Women's Studies Award and the Cross-road Counseling Book Award, both of which bestow publication under the house imprimatur. (Details are available upon request from the publisher.) Crossroad distributes via Spring Arbor Distributing.

Query letters and SASEs should be directed to:

Alison Donohue, Editor

Paul McMahon, Editor

CROSSROAD HERDER

Books published under the Crossroad Herder imprint mark the cutting edge of theology. Each volume presents fresh perspectives on a topic of interest, expands discussion on an issue of concern, and is accessible to the theologian and interested readers alike.

Titles from Crossroad Herder: *The Mystical Thought of Meister Eckhart* by Bernard McGinn; *Christian Hope and Christian Life* by Rowan A. Greer; *Paul in Chains* by Richard J. Cassidy; *She Who Is, Tenth Anniversary Edition* by Elizabeth A. Johnson; *The Dictionary of Popes and the Papacy* by Steimer and Parker, eds.; *The Ethical Thought of Hans Urs von Balthasar* by Christopher W. Steck; *Catholics and American Culture* by Mark Massa, S.J.

Query letters and SASEs should be directed to:

Michael Parker, Editor

CROSSWAY BOOKS

1300 Crescent Street, Wheaton, IL 60187-5883

630-682-4300   fax: 630-682-4785

e-mail: info@gnpcb.org

Crossway produces a small list of books with an evangelical Christian perspective aimed at both the religious and general audience, including issue-oriented nonfiction, evangelical works, inspiration, and fiction. Crossway Books (founded in 1938) is a division of Good News Publishers.

From the Crossway list: *Best of All* by Max Lucado; *God Knows My Name* by Debby Anderson; *God's Greater Glory: The Exalted God of the Historic Biblical Faith* by Bruce Ware; *The Vanishing Word: The Veneration of Visual Imagery in the Postmodern World* by Arthur Hunt; *The Second Coming: Signs of Christ's Return and the End of the Age* by John MacArthur; *Holiness by Grace: Delighting in the Joy That Is Our Strength* by Bryan Chapell; *Beyond the Bounds: Open Theism and the Undermining of Biblical Christianity* edited by John Piper, Justin Taylor, and Paul Kjoss Helseth; *Think Biblically: Recovering a Christian Worldview* edited by John MacArthur; *Evidence and Truth: Foundations for Christian Truth* by Robert Morgan; *Pastoral Leadership for Manhood and Womanhood* edited by Wayne Grudem and Dennis Rainey; *The Word of God in English: Criteria for Excellence in Bible Translation* by Leland Ryken; *Jesus Driven Ministry* by Ajith Fernando; *The Case for Classical Christian Education* by Douglas Wilson.

Sample children's books: Lewis and Clark Squad series by Stephen Bly; *You Are Mine* by Max Lucado.

Crossway Books is interested in nonfiction areas of books on the deeper Christian life, issue-oriented books, and a select number of academic and professional volumes. It feels called to publish fiction works that fall into these categories: historical, youth/juvenile, adventure, action, intrigue, thriller, and contemporary and Christian realism.

Crossway handles its own distribution. Crossway Books invites query letters regarding works written from an evangelical Christian perspective. Please send a synopsis (one to two pages, double-spaced) and no more than two chapters. No entire manuscripts; such submissions will be returned. Query letters and SASEs should be directed to:

Marvin Padgett, Vice President, Editorial

DISCIPLESHIP RESOURCES

Delivery address:

1908 Grand Avenue, Nashville TN 37212

Mailing address:

PO Box 840, Nashville, TN 37202-0840

1-800-814-7833

www.discipleshipresources.org   e-mail: discipleshipresources@gbod.org

Discipleship Resources (founded in 1951) is the publishing component of the General Board of Discipleship, one of the major program boards of the United Methodist

Church. Areas of publishing interest encompass United Methodist history, doctrine, and theology, as well as Bible study, Christian education, ethnic church concerns, evangelism, ministry of the laity, stewardship, United Methodist men, and worship.

Discipleship Resources issues a varied inventory, including books, booklets, manuals, audiovisuals, packets, and supplies directed to local church members and leaders, lay and clergy, men and women, children, youth, and adults—as well as to district and conference leaders and others serving the congregation. Some resources guide the leader of an area of work or particular program, while others are aimed toward individual study and enrichment.

Titles from Discipleship Resources: *Lay Speakers Preach* by John P. Gilbert; *Go Preach!* by John P. Gilbert; *Lay Speakers Lead Bible Study* by Evelyn Laycock; *Lay Speakers Lead Prayers* by Jim Roy; *Lay Speaking: Basic Ministries: Basic Course 2001-2004* by John P. Gilbert and Nan C. Zoller; *Lay Speaking Ministries: Guide for Conference & District Committees 2001-2004* by James W. Lane; *Cultivating Christian Community* by Thomas R. Hawkins; *Lay Speakers Lead in Worship* by Hoyt L. Hickman; *The Heart's Journey* by Barb Nardi Kurtz; *Spouts* by Edie Genung Harris & Shirley L. Ramsey; *Accountable Discipleship* by Steve W. Manskar; *Guide for Covenant Discipleship Groups* by Gayle Turner Watson; *Start Here* by Barbara Bruce; *Keeping In Touch* by Carol F. Krau; *Designing an Older Adult Ministry* by Richard H. Gentzler, Jr.; *Baby Boomer Spirituality* by Craig Kennet Miller; *Couples Who Care* by Jane P. Ives; *Starting Again* by Sandra Scott.

Discipleship handles its own distribution. Writers who wish to submit materials to Discipleship Resources for publishing consideration may acquire editorial guidelines upon request from the publisher. The guide includes versatile tips that are broadly applicable to manuscript preparation in general. Query letters and SASEs should be directed to:

Mary Gregory, Business and Operations Director

WILLIAM B. EERDMANS PUBLISHING COMPANY

EERDMANS BOOKS FOR YOUNG READERS

255 Jefferson Avenue SE, Grand Rapids, MI 49503

616-459-4591/1-800-253-7521

www.eerdmans.com   e-mail: info@eerdmans.com

Eerdmans publishes books of general interest; religious, academic, and theological works; books for young readers; regional histories, and American religious history. Eerdmans Publishing offers a Christian handle on such areas as anthropology, Biblical studies, and religious approaches to biography, African American studies, church administration, music, philosophy, psychology, science, social issues, current and historical theology, and women's interests.

The Eerdmans catalog also highlights general reference works, such as Bible commentaries and theological dictionaries, as well as titles in Old and New Testament studies.

William B. Eerdmans Publishing Company (founded in 1911) is one of the largest independent nondenominational Christian religious publishers in the United States.

On the Eerdmans list: *Captain American and the Crusade against Evil* by Robert Jewett and John Shelton Lawrence; *Paul, the Letter Writer* by M. Luther Stirewalt; *Song of Songs* by Judith Ernst; *Scarred by Struggle* by Joan D. Chittister; *Gather into One: Praying and Singing Globally* by Michael Hawn; *Abraham Lincoln: Redeemer President* by Allen Guelzo; *The Archaeology of Qumran and the Dead Sea Scrolls* by Jodi Magness; *The Dead Sea Scrolls Today* by James Vanderkam; *The Confessions of St. Augustine* (edited by Carolinne White); *Women in Scripture* (edited by Carol Meyers); *Building a Healthy Culture* (edited by Don Eberly); *Religions of the Hellenistic-Roman Age* by Antonia Tripolitis; *Eerdmans Dictionary of the Bible* (edited by David Noel Freedman); *The Book of Marriage* (edited by Dana Mack and David Blankenhorn).

A special Eerdmans project is the beautifully produced *The Leningrad Codex: A Facsimile Edition* (Astrid B. Beck, Managing Editor; David Noel Freedman, General Editor; James A. Sanders, Publication Editor).

Query letters and SASEs should be directed to:

Charles van Hof, Managing Editor

Jon Pott, Editor in Chief

EERDMANS BOOKS FOR YOUNG READERS

Eerdmans Books for Young Readers, an imprint of William B. Eerdmans Publishing Company founded in 1995, seeks to publish beautifully written and illustrated books that nurture children's faith in God and help young people to explore and understand the wonder, joy, and challenges of life. The house considers manuscripts that address spiritual themes in authentic and imaginative ways without being didactic.

Some recent titles include picture books *The Song of the Whooping Crane* by Eileen Spinelli, illustrated by Elsa Warnick; *What Does the Sky Say* by Nancy White Carlstrom, illustrated by Tim Ladwig; and *Jesus*, written and illustrated by Brian Wildsmith. Two recently published young adult novels include *Secrets in the House of Delgado* by Gloria Miklowitz and *Maggie in the Morning* by Elizabeth Van Steenwyk.

Eerdmans Books for Young Readers publishes between 12 and 16 books a year, with about 5 to 10 percent from first-time authors. The subcategories of books include picture books, novels, biographies, and Bible stories. Sample titles: *The Octave of Angels* by Margaret McAllister; *When Daddy Prays* by Nikki Grimes; *Especially Heroes* by Virginia Kroll and Tim Ladwig.

Query letters and SASEs should be directed to:

Judy Zylstra, Editor-in-Chief

FELDHEIM PUBLISHERS

200 Airport Executive Park, Nanuet, NY 10954

845-356-2282   fax: 845-425-1908

www.feldheim.com   email: questions@feldheim.com

Feldheim Publishers (founded in 1954) is among the leading houses in areas of publishing activity that include works of contemporary authors in the field of Orthodox Jewish thought, translations from Hebrew of Jewish classical works, dictionaries and general reference works, textbooks, and guides for Sabbaths and festivals, as well as literature for readers ages three and up (Young Readers Division). The Feldheim publishing program is expanding, and the house releases an increasing number of new titles each season. Feldheim retains a comprehensive backlist.

From Feldheim: *Stay on Target* by Rabbi Moshe Goldberger; *The Travels and Tales of Dr. Emanuel J. Mitzvah* by Yaffa Ganz; *The Midrash Rabbah on Megillas Esther* by the Midrash Rabbah Ha'mevoar Institute; *Guidelines: Purim* by Rabbi Elozor and Rabbi Yitzchok Jaeger; *The Commentators' Al Hanissim—Purim* by Rabbi Yitzchak Sender; *The Malbim Esther* by Jonathan Taub; *Turnabout: The Malbim on Megillas Esther* by Rabbi Mendel Weinbach; *127 Insights into Magillas Esther* by Rabbi Mendel Weinbach; *Megillath Shushan* by Itshak Yallouz and N. Ashlag; *A Purim Story* by Linda Davis; *Malka's Kosher Cookbook* by Malka Padwa-Engel; *In the Beginning* by Rosie Einhorn and Sherry Zimmerman; *Of Times Past* by Arlene Chavel and Sara Farkas.

Feldheim Publishers handles its own distribution and offers books of additional publishers such as American Yisroel Chai Press and Targum Press. Query letters and SASEs should be directed to:

Yitzchak Feldheim, President

FRIENDSHIP PRESS

475 Riverside Drive, Room 860, New York, NY 10115-0050

212-870-2496   fax: 212-870-2550

www.ncccusa.org/friend/fphome

The Friendship list encompasses religious books, as well as mainstream trade titles in the public-interest realm that address contemporary topics including: cultural pluralism, the media, global awareness, health and wholeness, technology and the environment, human rights, and world peace. Friendship also produces ecumenical religious, spiritual, inspirational, and educational program materials intended for the use of adults, youths, and children. The house offers several lines of videos, maps, notecards, and informational posters.

Friendship Press was established in 1902 as a missionary education movement in the United States and Canada. Now part of the National Council of the Churches of Christ USA, Friendship Press is a leading ecumenical publisher of educational materials for schools and parishes.

Noted Friendship authors include Margaret Mead, Pearl Buck, Joseph Diescho, Wole Soyinka, Rogoberta Menchu, John R. Mott, Phillip Potter, Leslie Newbigin, Masao Takenaka, and Emilio Castro. Friendship Press books have been reviewed by the *New York Times* and *Publishers Weekly* and are recommended for use in colleges, universities, and seminars.

Friendship Press distributes its own list. Friendship Press publishes a limited number of new titles per season—most of which are commissioned additions to the house's ongoing curriculum series.

General titles include: *Swallow's Nest* by Marchiene Vroon Rienstra; *By Faith* by John Lindner, Alva Cox and Linda-Marie Delloff; *All Quite Beautiful* by N. Lynne Westfield; *Families Valued* by Jack Nelson-Pallmeyer; *Study Guide to Families Valued* by Joe Leonard and Jack Nelson-Pallmeyer.

Please note: Friendship Press is no longer accepting new manuscripts for publication. We are marketing our current stock only.

Mary Byrne Hoffman, Editor

GLENEIDA PUBLISHING GROUP

See Baker Book House and Liguori Publications.

GOSPEL LIGHT PUBLICATIONS

REGAL BOOKS

RENEW BOOKS

2300 Knoll Drive, Ventura, CA 93003

805-644-9721/1-800-446-7735

Founded in 1933 by Dr. Henrietta Mears, Gospel Light is committed to providing effective resources for evangelism, discipleship, and Christian education through Sunday school and Vacation Bible school curricula, videos, children's music, and Regal and Renew Books. Divisions of Gospel Light include: Regal Books (founded in 1965) specializes in needs-oriented books and building efforts; Renew Books (founded in 1997) serves the fastest-growing segment of the Church worldwide—those experiencing awakening and renewal with an expectancy for revival.

The mission of Gospel Light is to know Christ and make Him known; to provide His Church with effective Bible teaching and learning resources for use in making disciples, empowering them for godly living, equipping them for ministry and the evangelism of the world. Gospel Light is headquartered in Ventura, California with distribution facilities in Cincinnati, Ohio.

Gospel Light highlights include: *Secrets of the Koran* by Don Richardson; *The Biblical Guide to Alternative Medicine* by Dr. Neil Anderson and Dr. Michael Jacobson; *Prayer: Dare to Ask* by Ralph Moore; *The Dream Releasers* by Wayne Cordeiro; *The Worship Warrior* by Chuck Pierce; *Blessing Your Children* by Jack W. Hayford; *What Every Pastor Should Know About Sunday School* by Elmer L. Towns and Stan Toler; *Grow Your Church from the Outside In* by George Barna; *Simple Prayers for a Powerful Life* by Ted Haggard; *River of Delight* by Dick Eastman; *Praying the Bible* by Wesley and Stacey Campbell; *Moments Together for Parents* by Dennis and Barbara Rainey; *Moments Together for Intimacy* by Dennis and Barbara Rainey; *The Heart of Worship Files* by Matt Redman; *On Daddy's Shoulders* by Tommy Tenney and Amie Dockery; *Single Focus* by George Barna; *Spiritual House Cleaning* by Eddie Smith; *The Secret Place of Joy* by Lindell Cooley; *Praying the Bible: The Pathway to Spirituality* by Wesley Campbell; *Pastors at Greater Risk* by H.B. London and Neil Wiseman; *I'll Hold You in Heaven* by H.B. London and Neil Wiseman; *I'll Hold You in Heaven Remembrance Journal* by Debbie Heydrick; *Before You Live Together* by Dr. Dave Gudel; *Communication: Key to Your Marriage* by H. Norman Wright; *Always Daddy's Girl* by H. Norman Wright; *Churchquake!* by Peter Wagner; *Prayer Shield* by Peter Wagner; *Intercessory Prayer* by Dutch Sheets; *God's Dream Team* by Tommy Tenney; *God's Secret to Greatness* by Tommy Tenney and David Cape.

On the Regal list: *Moments Together for Couples* by Dennis and Barbara Rainey; *So What's the Difference?* by Fritz Ridenour; *What the Bible Is All About* by Henrietta Mears; *The Unquenchable Worshipper* by Matt Redman; *Today Is the First Day* edited by Carole Lewis; *Victory Over the Darkness* by Neil T. Anderson; *Intercessory Power* by Dutch Sheets; *The Marriage Checkup* by Norman H. Wright; *The Bible-Based Weight Loss Plan* by Carole Lewis; *Stomping Out the Darkness* by Neil Anderson and Dave Park; *Stomping Out Depression* by Neil Anderson and Dave Park; *Surviving Adolescence* by Jim Burns; *What Hollywood Won't Tell You About Love, Sex and Dating* by Susie Shellenburger and Greg Johnson.

Gospel Light overseas its own distribution. Unsolicited manuscripts are not accepted. Query letters and SASEs should be directed to:

Kyle Duncan, Acquisitions

HARPERSANFRANCISCO

353 Sacramento Street, Suite 500, San Francisco, CA 94111-3653

415-477-4400   fax: 415-477-4444

www.harpercollins.com

HarperSanFrancisco (HSF) strives to be the preeminent publisher of the most important books across the full spectrum of religious and spiritual literature, adding to the wealth of the world's wisdom by respecting all traditions and favoring none. It publishes books in the areas of spirituality, religion, and inspiration from the full family of religious and spiritual traditions.

HSF focuses on books that inspire and nurture the mind, body, and spirit; explore the essential religious, spiritual, and philosophical questions; present a rich and diverse array of cultures and their wisdom traditions; and support readers in their ongoing personal discovery and enrichment.

It is the policy of HarperSanFrancisco to publish books that represent important religious groupings, express well-articulated thought, combine intellectual competence and felicitous style, add to the wealth of religious literature irrespective of creedal origin, and aid the cause of religion without proselytizing for any particular sect.

HSF has featured works by Martin Luther King, Jr., Huston Smith, Billy Graham, Mother Teresa, Marcus Borg, John Shelby Spong, the Dalai Lama, C. S. Lewis, Richard Foster, Philip Gulley, John Dominic Crossan, Diana Eck, and Melodie Beattie. The house is corporately affiliated with the editorially independent Zondervan, a subsidiary of HarperCollins (see separate Zondervan listing), which focuses on books for the evangelical Christian market.

HarperSanFrancisco is a division of the international HarperCollins corporate family of publishers (which includes imprints emanating from the HarperCollins New York offices; see HarperCollins in U.S. Publishers section). HarperSanFrancisco benefits directly from core HarperCollins marketing, sales, and power and retains its editorial and marketing independence and identity.

Frontlist trade books from HarperSanFrancisco: *A Thousand Pieces of Gold* by Adeline Yen Mah; *Chasing Rumi* by Roger Housden; *The Future of Peace* by Scott Hunt; *The Invitation* and *The Dance* by Oriah Mountain Dreamer; *Celebration of Discipline* by Richard Foster; *The Measure of a Man* by Sidney Poitier; *The Legacy of Luna* by Julia Butterfly Hill; *A New Christianity for a New World* and *Why Christianity Must Change or Die* by John Shelby Spong; *The Alchemist* by Paulo Coelho; *The Historical Jesus* and other Jesus books by John Dominic Crossan; *Why Religion Matters* and *The World's Religions* by Huston Smith; *The Soul of Rumi* and *The Essential Rumi*, translated by Coleman Barks; *Mere Christianity* and other classics by C. S. Lewis; *Catholicism* by Richard McBrien; *Everyday Zen* by Jako Beck; *The Tibetan Book of Living and Dying* by Sogyal Rinpoche; *The Jew in the Lotus* by Roger Kamenetz; *The Gospel of Thomas*, translated by Marvin Meyer; *The Divine Conspiracy* by Dallas Willard.

HarperSanFrancisco titles are distributed by HarperCollins Publishers in Scranton, Pennsylvania. HSF does not accept unsolicited manuscripts. Query letters and SASEs should be directed to:

Gideon Weil, Editor—Literary spiritual fiction and nonfiction, self-help, inspiration

John V. Loudon, Executive Editor—Religious studies, biblical studies, psychology/personal growth, inspiration, Eastern religions, Buddhist and Christian spirituality

Renee Sedliar, Associate Editor—Literary inspirational fiction and nonfiction, popular inspiration

Eric Brandt, Senior Editor

Julia Roller, Assistant Editor

HARVEST HOUSE PUBLISHERS

HARVEST HOUSE BOOKS FOR CHILDREN AND YOUNG ADULTS

990 Owen Loop North, Eugene, OR 97402

541-343-0123   fax: 541-302-0731

www.harvesthousepubl.com

Harvest House produces religion-oriented nonfiction and fiction, resources for Bible study and theological thought, and educational and devotional resources. Harvest House frontlist titles address topics of current interest, often with widespread implications on the social-religious front. Subjects include media, technology, and politics; parenting, youth, relationships, and the family; Christian living and contemporary values; cults and the occult; personal awareness, inspiration, and spiritual growth; Christian history and heritage; and humor.

The publisher's nondenominational list features many works that offer an evangelical Christian perspective and includes a number of notably individualist author voices. Harvest House publishes books in hardcover, trade paperback, and mass-market paperback editions.

The house issues a number of strong lines directed toward the children's-and-youth market (please see separate subentry further on). Harvest House also produces books in the Spanish language, as well as audiobooks, calendars, and daily planners.

Harvest House Publishers (founded in 1974) holds the following credo for books and other product lines: "Helping people grow spiritually strong."

Sample titles: Top-selling titles by Stormie Oamrtian: *The Power of a Praying Woman*; *The Power of a Praying Wife*; *The Power of a Praying Parent*; *The Power of a Praying Husband*. Other top selling titles: *The Daily Bible* by LaGard Smith; *The Rescue* by

Lori Wick; *Life Management for Busy Women* by Elizabeth George; *Men Are like Waffles—Women Are like Spaghetti* by Bill Farrel and Pam Farrel; *Before You Say "I Do"* by Wes Roberts and H. Norman Wright; *The Resurrection File* by Craig Parshall; *Secrets of an Irresistible Woman* by Michelle McKinney Hammond; *The Bondage Breaker* by Neil T. Anderson; *How to Study Your Bible* by Kay Arthur; *A Sanctuary for Your Soul* by Kay Arthur; *Heaven Sent* by Kathryn Andrews Fincher; *A Garden Full of Love* by Sandra Kuck; *Friends of the Heart* by Emilie Barnes and Donna Otto; *Whispers of Prayer* by Emilie Barnes; *How Big Is God's Love* by David and Helen Haidle; *Moms Who Have Changed the World* by Lindsey O'Connor; *Just Enough Light for the Step I'm On* by Stormie Omartian; *Unquenchable Love* by David and Heather Kopp; *Hidden Agendas for the New Millennium* by Dave Hunt; *Foreshadows of Wrath and Redemption* by William T. James; *Bruce and Stan's Guide to the End of the World* by Bruce Bickel and Stan Jantz.

Special Harvest House project: *Simpler Times* by Thomas Kinkade, an artist renowned for light-infused paintings of nostalgic, heartwarming scenes, who combines his visual talents with thoughtful narrative in this exquisitely designed gift book. More than 20 full-color paintings are accompanied by Thomas Kinkade's thoughts on living in a complex age, keeping perspective, and creating balance. Additional titles in the Lighted Path Collection include: *Home Is Where the Heart Is*; *Glory of Creation*; *I'll Be Home for Christmas, Romantic Hideaways*; *Beyond the Garden Gate.*

Fiction from Harvest House includes mainstream novels with a religious accent; historical adventure tales; Bible-based stories; books geared toward a women's readership (including romances); occult thrillers; mystery and suspense fiction; and futuristic works.

Biblical and historical fiction from Harvest House: *The Princess* by Lori Wick; *Island Bride* by Linda Chaikin; *Magnolia Dreams* by Virginia Gaffney; *Promise Me Tomorrow* by Lori Wick; *The Moment I Saw You* by Lisa Samson; *Captive Heart* by Linda Chaikin.

Harvest House manages its own distributional network.

HARVEST HOUSE BOOKS FOR CHILDREN AND YOUNG ADULTS

Harvest House produces a selection of books directed toward a youthful readership, as well as titles of interest to teachers and parents. The solid list encompasses boardbooks, picture books, storybooks, interactive books, joke books, general nonfiction, and novels (including a number of successful series).

On the Harvest House children's-and-youth list: *Let's Make Something Fun* by Emilie Barnes; *Nighty Night, Sleep Tight* (boardbook) by Michael Sparks; *The Bondage Breaker Youth Edition* by Neil T. Anderson and Dave Park; *Extremely Good Clean Jokes for Kids* by Bob Phillips.

Harvest House no longer accepts unsolicited query letters.

HAZELDEN PUBLISHING AND EDUCATIONAL SERVICES

HAZELDEN FOUNDATION

PO Box 11 C03, Center City, MN 55012-0011

651-213-4000

www.hazelden.org   email: info@hazelden.org

Hazelden publishes books for a consumer and professional readership in such areas as recovery, personal and spiritual growth, self-help, spirituality, substance abuse, and compulsive behaviors. The house's backlist represents all areas of the Hazelden publishing program.

The Hazelden publications and marketing vision encompass books, pamphlets, audiocassettes and videocassettes, computer software, calendars, and books for young readers, along with a gift line.

Hazelden's motto is "A Mission in Motion". When Hazelden opened its doors 50 years ago, the mission seemed simple: to rehabilitate clients and restore self-worth and dignity to their lives. Hazelden still commits to this mission as a multidimensional organization involved in public policy, research, education, evaluation, and many other areas of chemical dependency. Hazelden has become a respected leader in the chemical-dependency field and the premier publisher of bibliotherapy. As a pioneer in addiction research and education, Hazelden's clinical expertise is reflected in educational materials that cover a wide range of topics in the treatment of chemical dependency and other addictions. Core to the success of the treatment process, Hazelden materials interact with clients. The matrix of materials reinforces important information to clients. Most of all, these materials are a concrete way for clients to retain the concepts they learn in treatment.

Hazelden was established as a publishing operation (in 1954, as Hazelden Educational Materials) with the hardcover release of *Twenty-Four Hours a Day* by Rich W (still in print in hardcover and paperback editions). Hazelden is a division of the Hazelden Foundation, which also operates a network of recovery centers. The publisher has a major concentration in materials related to the 12-Step approach.

In early 1994, Hazelden purchased CompCare and Parkside, two former niche publishers with strong backlists in areas consistent with Hazelden's publishing range—particularly in treatment and recovery titles, as well as titles in the broader general-interest trade arena. Hazelden also bought Johnson Institute, a publisher that specialized in prevention issues related to chemical dependency. These titles address parenting topics, K–12 educational needs, and recovery issues.

In addition to the aforementioned *Twenty-Four Hours a Day*, Hazelden's bestselling trade entrants include *Codependent No More* and *The Language of Letting Go* (both by Melody Beattie), and *Each Day a New Beginning*.

From Hazelden: *Alcohol: Cradle to Grave* by Eric Newhouse; *A Bar On Every Corner* by Jack Erdmann; *A Moment to Reflect Series* by Veronica Ray; *Accepting Ourselves and Others* by Sheppard Kominars and Kathryn Kominars; *Fat is a Family Affair* by Judi Hollis; *A Relapse Prevention Workbook for Women* by Karen Mattson; *Contrary to Love* by Patrick Carnes Ph.D.; *A Guide for Parents and Families* by Stephen Biddulph; *A Woman's Journal* by Stephanie Covington; *A Parent's Guide to Sex, Drugs, and Flunking Out* by Joel Epstein; *Aging and Addiction* by Carol Colleran and Debra Jay; *Chronic Illness and the Twelve Steps* by Martha Cleveland; *Facts about Hepatitis C* by David Paulson; *Fighting Invisible Tigers* by Earl Hipp; *Highs!* by Alex Packer; *Losing Your Shirt* by Mary Heineman; *Miles To Go Before I Sleep* by Jackie Nink Pflug; *A Journey Through Grief* by Alla Renee Bozarth; *Field Notes* by Sharon White; *Grieving* by Peter McDonald.

Hazelden furnishes its titles to the bookstore trade directly and has made inroads into the gift-distribution world. Additional marketing avenues for Hazelden trade titles include the house's direct-to-the-consumer mail-order business. Hazelden books are popular items worldwide, with a foreign distribution network that includes Russia and Canada.

Other areas to which Hazelden markets include: structured care (Hazelden develops and markets print, audio, and visual materials for treatment centers, hospitals, and professional markets); prevention, education, and professional training (the publisher accesses the markets of primary and secondary schools, counselor-training programs, and community prevention and treatment programs); and corrections (the publisher addresses the needs of county, state, and federal corrections facilities).

Hazelden Foundation books are distributed by the Florida based trade publisher, Health Communications, Inc.

Query letters and SASEs should be directed to:

Rebecca Post, Editorial Director

Kristin Buzick, Manuscript Coordinator

HEBREW PUBLISHING COMPANY

PO Box 222, Spencertown, NY 12165

518-392-3322   fax: 518-392-4280

Hebrew Publishing Company (established in 1901) offers a wide range of titles in such categories as reference materials and dictionaries; religion, law, and thought; Rabbinic literature; literature; history and biography; children's books; Hebrew-language textbooks and Hebrew culture; Yiddish; the Bible in Hebrew/English and English only; prayers and liturgy, including: daily (Hebrew only, and Hebrew/English); Sabbath, high holidays, and festivals; memorial; Purim; and general prayers and liturgy; Hanukkah items; Haggadahs; educational materials; sermons and aids of the rabbi;

and calendars. The house publishes a limited number of new titles and maintains an established backlist.

On the HPC list: *Yom Kippur* by Philip Birnbaum; *Judaism as a Civilization* by Mordecai Kaplan; *Acharon Hamohikanim (The Last of the Mohicans)* by James Fenimore Cooper; *Business Ethics in Jewish Law* (Jung/Levine); *Encyclopedia of Jewish Concepts* by Philip Birnbaum; *Rahel Varnhagen: The Life of a Jewess* by Hannah Arendt; *Torah and Tradition* by Orenstein and Frankel; *Jewish Tales and Legends* by Menachem Glen.

Hebrew Publishing Company oversees its own distribution, utilizing the services of independent fulfillment and distribution firms. Query letters and SASEs should be directed to:

Charles Lieber, Editor in Chief

HEBREW UNION COLLEGE

3101 Clifton Avenue, Cincinnati, OH 45220-2488

513-221-1875

e-mail: hucpress@huc.edu   e-mail: www.huc.edu/press

Hebrew Union publishes scholarly Judaica, along with some frontlist titles of broader appeal. Within the Hebrew Union College scope are books representing a variety of divisions, institutions, and programs: Klau Library, Skirball Museum, Kuntresim (Hebrew texts copublished with Ben-Zion Dinur Center of the Hebrew University), the journals Hebrew Union College Annual and American Jewish Archives, and special-interest projects (such as books and videotapes) from HUC-UC Ethics Center.

Hebrew Union College Press (founded in 1921) publishes a select list of new titles covering a full range of its list, while tending a full backlist. HUC engages in copublishing projects with other institutions, including Harvard University Press, KTAV Publishing House, University of Alabama Press, and Yale University Press.

From Hebrew Union College Press: *Modern Jewish Mythologies* edited by Glenda Abramson; *Profane Scriptures* by Menashe Kadishman; *Beyond Survival and Philanthropy* edited by Allon Gal and Alfred Gottschalk; *The Jew in the Medieval World* by Marc Saperstein; *German Jews Beyond Judaism* by George Mosse; *Theology and Poetry* by Jakob Petuchowski; *To Reveal Our Hearts: Jewish Women Writers in Tsarist Russia* by Carole Balin; *A Letter That Has Not Been Read: Dreams in the Hebrew Bible* by Shaul Bar; *In the Service of the King: Officialdom in Ancient Israel and Judah* by Nili S. Fox.

Hebrew Union College Press is distributed by Wayne State University Press. HUC welcomes the submission of scholarly manuscripts in all areas of Judaica. For further information, contact Professor Michael Meyer, Chair, Publications Committee, at the publisher's address. Query letters and SASEs should be directed to:

Barbara Selya, Managing Editor

HORIZON PUBLISHERS/CORNERSTONE

50 South 500 West, Bountiful, UT 84011-0490

801-295-9451   fax: 801-295-0196

www.horizonpublishers.com   e-mail: horizonp@burgoyne.com

Horizon Publishers (founded in 1971) was purchased in August 2000 by Cornerstone Publishing & Distribution, Inc. Cornerstone will continue to distribute Horizon's list and use the Horizon Publishers imprint on selected works. The combined companies form a smaller house that produces hardcover and paperback works with emphasis in the areas of religion, inspiration, youth and adult fiction, cooking and food storage, emergency preparedness, outdoor living, music and art, marriage and family, children's books, and crafts (especially cross-stitch).

Cornerstone is a privately owned corporation with no ecclesiastical ties. The main readership of the house's theological works is the Latter-Day Saint (Mormon) community, so most of its religious works are compatible with that doctrinal perspective, but many are aimed at a wider Christian audience. Cornerstone/Horizon's publishing interest encompasses books on doctrine and church history, children's religious teaching, inspirational and doctrinal talk tapes, religious music, and art. Its list includes religious humor, faith-promoting experiences, historical works, biographies of well-known leaders, doctrinal studies, and fiction for middle-grade, young adult, and adult readers.

Representative of the Cornerstone/Horizon list: *The Axe Wielder's Handbook* by Michael Beaudry; *Born to Save Mankind—New Insights on Events Surrounding the Birth of Christ* by Duane Crowther; *Every Person in the New Testament* by Lynn Price; *Evidences of the True Church* by Dennis Brown; *For Times and For Seasons—Great Ideas for Family Devotionals* by John-Charles Duffy; *Forever* by Jack Weyland; *Great Are the Words of Isaiah* by Monte Nyman; *The Longing* by Shari Gibson; *One in a Billion* by Sharlee Mullins Glenn; *Preparing the Elders of Israel to Save the Constitution* by Steve Thomas; *Testifying of the Prophet Joseph* by Mark Forester.

Fiction titles: *Thy Kingdom Come, Volume 1: Prodigal Journey* by Linda Paulson Adams; *Singled Out* by Eric Samuelsen; *The Wise Man in the Checkered Shirt* by Michael Drake; *Crescendo* by Terry J. Moyer.

Family-oriented books: *How to Raise Kids Without Climbing the Walls* by Larry G. Brady, Ph.D.; *Making Marriage Magnificent* by Reed and Lorena Markham; *Family Home Evenings for Dads* by Dianne Friden, Carolyn Seimers, and Barbara Thackeray.

Cornerstone/Horizon handles its own distribution. The house's guidelines for authors are filled with apt advice for all writers. Query letters and SASEs should be directed to:

The Editorial Board

INNER OCEAN

PO Box 1239, Makawao, Maui Hawaii, 96768-1239

808-573-8000   fax: 808-573-0700

www.innerocean.com   e-mail: info@innerocean.com

Inner Ocean was founded in 1999 by two successful businessmen who wanted to publish the kinds of books that have brought about such positive change in their own lives. Founders John Elder and Chip McClelland seek to publish books that expand consciousness, present alternative philosophies, and explore our vast human potential.

They also hope to publish books that help: create common goals for humanity, particularly as the goals relate to brining better communication and peaceful co-existence; readers evolve as more conscious and purposeful beings; explore new and socially conscious business models for the twenty-first century; inspire readers to experience their lives with passion as well as intellect; people integrate more courage and risk-taking in their lives. They do not publish adult fiction, short stories, poetry or children's titles.

Recent titles include: *High Country* by David Alderman; *In the High-Energy Zone* by Paul Deslaurier; *Perfect Madness* by Donna Lee Gorrell; *Sacred Selfishness* by Bud Harris; *Mystical Dogs* by Jean Houston; *Anyway: The Paradoxical Commandments* by Kent Keith; *Choosing to Be Well* by Haven Logan; *Swimming Where Madmen Drown* by Robert Master; *Miracle in Maui* by Paul Pearsall; *The Initiation* by Donald Schnell; *Web Thinking* by Linda Seger; *The Gift of a Child* by Mary Ann Thompson; *The Soul in the Computer* by Barbara Waugh.

See website for submission guidelines.

INNER TRADITIONS INTERNATIONAL, BEAR AND COMPANY

HEALING ARTS PRESS BOOKS

One Park Street, Rochester, VT 05767

802-767-3174   fax: 802-767-3726

www.InnerTraditions.com   e-mail: info@gotoit.com

Inner Traditions publishes across such subject areas as acupuncture, anthroposophy, aromatherapy, the arts, astrology, bodywork, cookbooks, crafts, cultural studies, earth studies, Egyptian studies, gemstones, health and healing, homeopathy, indigenous cultures, African American traditions, inner traditions of the West and the East, myth and legend, massage, natural medicine, self-transformation, sacred sexuality, spirituality, and travel.

Inner Traditions International (founded in 1975) produces hardcover trade books and trade paperbacks, illustrated gift books, and mass-market paperback editions, as well as a line of audioworks and selected videotapes. The house also packages specialty items such as boxed sets and tarot decks.

Special imprints include Destiny Books, Destiny Recordings, Healing Arts Press, and Park Street Press. Inner Traditions en Español is a line published in the Spanish language. Inner Traditions India issues works aimed at the Indian market. The house has announced a forthcoming slate of multimedia titles. Inner Traditions International publishes a medium-sized list each year and maintains a strong backlist.

The Inner Traditions imprint accents works that represent the spiritual, cultural, and mythic traditions of the world, focusing on inner wisdom and the perennial philosophies.

Inner Traditions titles: *A Brief History of India* by Alain Danielou; *The Cherokee Herbal* by J. T. Garrett; *Teen Feng Shui* by Susan Levitt; *The Lost Tomb of Viracocha* by Maurice Cotterell; *From Magical Child to Magical Teen* by Joseph Chilton Pearce; *Rituals and Practices with the Motherpeace Tarot* by Vicki Noble; *Shamanic Experience* by Kenneth Meadows; *El Corazon del Yoga* by T. K. V. Desikachar; *The Kabbalah of the Soul* by Leonora Leet, Ph.D.; *The Templar Treasure at Gisors* by Jean Markale; *Sir Gawain* by John Matthews; *Rumi: Gazing at the Beloved* by Will Johnson; *Abs on the Ball* by Colleen Craig; *Coyote Healing* by Lewis Mehl-Madrona, M.D., Ph.D.; *Painting the Dream* by David Chethlahe Paladin; *Sexual Reflexology* by Mantak Chia and William Wei; *The Tarot Court Cards* by Kate Warwick-Smith; *Indian Mythology* by Devdutt Pattanaik; *Guardians of the Celtic Way* by Jill Kelly, Ph.D; *The Celtic Wisdom of Tarot* by Caitlin Matthews; *The Lost Treasure of the Knights Templar: Solving the Oak Island Mystery* by Steven Sora; *Sacred Woman, Sacred Dance: Awakening Spirituality Through Movement and Ritual* by Iris J. Stewart; *A Yoga of Indian Classical Dance: The Yogini's Mirror* by Roxanne Kamayani Gupta; *The Heart of Yoga: Developing a Personal Practice* by T. K. V. Desikachar; *Transfigurations* by Alex Greg; *Pilates on the Ball* by Colleen Craig; *Advanced Bach Flower Therapy: A Scientific Approach to Diagnosis and Treatment* by Gotz Blome, M.D.

Destiny Books are contemporary metaphysical titles for a popular audience, with special emphasis on self-transformation, the occult, and psychological well-being. Destiny Recordings are cassettes and compact discs of spiritual and indigenous music traditions. Destiny Audio Editions include Inner Traditions books on tape, as well as original spoken-word cassettes.

HEALING ARTS PRESS BOOKS

Healing Arts Press publishes works on alternative medicine and holistic health that combine contemporary thought and innovative research with the accumulated knowledge of the world's great healing traditions.

Park Street Press produces books on travel, psychology, consumer and environmental issues, archaeology, women's and men's studies, and fine art.

Inner Traditions en Español is the house's Spanish-language publishing program, in cooperation with Lasser Press of Mexico City. This line includes popular titles from a variety of Inner Tradition imprints.

Bear and Company titles: *The Lost Book of Enki* by Zecharia Sitchin; *Catastrophobie* by Barbara Hand Clow; *Time and the Technoscope* by Jose Arguelles; *Gods of Eden* by Andrew Collins.

Selections from the Inner Traditions en Español list: *Secretos Sexuales (Sexual Secrets)* by Nik Douglas and Penny Slinger; *El Cáñamo para la Salud (Hemp for Health)* by Chris Conrad.

Kits and gift packages from Inner Traditions: *The Lakota Sioux Sweat Lodge Cards* by Chief Archie Fire Lame Deer and Helene Sarks; *Leela: The Game of Self-Knowledge* by Harish Johari.

Inner Traditions supervises its own distribution. Query letters and SASEs should be directed to:

Jon Graham, Acquisitions Editor

INNISFREE PRESS

136 Roumfort Road, Philadelphia, PA 19119-1632

215-247-4085/1-800-367-5872   fax: 215-247-2343

www.innisfreepress.com   e-mail: InnisfreeP@aol.com

Innisfree is a creative publishing forum for books that feature the area of personal growth with spiritual and feminine dimensions. The editorial sphere encompasses self-discovery, relationships, nutrition, writing and journaling, healing and inspiration, transition and renewal, Bible study, and meditation. Innisfree acquired LuraMedia in late 1996.

From the Innisfree list: *Give to Your Heart's Content* by Linda Harper, Ph.D.; *Practicing Your Path* by Holly Whitcomb; *One Anothering* by Richard Meyer; *Stumbling Toward God* by Margaret McGee; *The Haunt of Grace* by Ted Loder; *Mending the World* by Rev. Bruce Epperly and Rabbi Lewis Solomon; *Braided Streams*; *Bridge to Wholeness*; *Call to the Soul*; *Circle of Stones*; *The Circle Continues*; *Dream Theatres of the Soul*; *Family Puzzles*; *The God Between Us*; *God's Forgotten Daughter*; *Guerrillas of Grace*; *I Asked for Intimacy*; *I Sit Listening to the Wind*; *The Job Hunter's Spiritual Companion*; *Just a Sister Away*; *Leading Ladies*; *Mother Love*; *My Heart in My Mouth*; *Nobody Owns Me*; *Prayers to Sophia*; *Raising Up Queens*; *Red Fire*; *Return to the Sea*; *Sabbath Sense*; *Seasons of Friendship*; *Silence*; *Slow Miracles*; *Spiritual Lemons*; *The Star in My Heart*; *The Tao of Eating*; *This Is My Body*; *Tracks in the Straw*; *Whole Earth Meditation*; *The Wisdom of Daughters*; *Woman's Book of Money and Spiritual Vision*; *The Woman Who Found Her Voice*; *The Woman Who Lost Her Heart*; *Wrestling the Light*; *Writing and Being*.

LuraMedia, Inc. (founded in 1982), was known as a small house that undertook to select, design, produce, and distribute its list with care and flair; the publisher's stated goal was to provide materials that foster healing and hope, balance and justice. Effective November 15, 1996, LuraMedia was sold to Innisfree Press in Philadelphia, Pennsylvania, and the San Diego office of LuraMedia closed. LuraMedia books are available through the new company.

Innisfree distributes to the trade via Consortium. Query letters and SASEs should be directed to:

Marcia Broucek, Publisher

INTERVARSITY PRESS

InterVarsity Christian Fellowship of the USA

PO Box 1400, Downers Grove, IL 60515

630-734-4000   fax: 630-734-4200

www.ivpress.com   e-mail: mail@ivpress.com

InterVarsity Press publications embrace the main fields of Bible study guides, reference books, academic and theological books, and issue-oriented books of general interest to educated Christians.

Nonfiction categories in areas of contemporary religious interest include titles in self-improvement, spirituality, and interpersonal relations. The house also produces humor.

InterVarsity Press (founded in 1947) is the publishing arm of InterVarsity Christian Fellowship of the USA. The press operates within IVCF's framework and publishes interdenominational books (in hardback and paperback) under the banner "Heart. Soul. Mind. Strength."

Indicative of the InterVarsity Press nonfiction frontlist: *LifeGuide Bible Studies* by Cindy Bunch; *Dancing in the Desert* by Marsha Crockett; *Down-to-Earth Spirituality* by R. Paul Stevens; *Getting Honest With God* by Mark Littleton; *Hope* by J. I. Packer and Carolyn Nystrom; *Job* by Paul Stevens; *Kingdom Ethics* by Glen Stassen and David Gushee; *Meeting the Spirit* by Douglas Connelly; *The Message of Heaven and Hell* by Bruce Milne; *Praying the Psalms* by Juanita Ryan; *The Smell of Sin* by Don Everts; *Transformation* by Rebecca Manley Pippert; *Wisdom* by Bill Hybels; *Women of the New Testament* by Phyllis Le Peau; *Making Life Work* by Bill Hybels; *The Wedge of Truth* by Phillip E. Johnson; *Soul Craft* by Douglas Webster; *Habits of the Mind* by James W. Sire; *The Holy Spirit* by Donald Bloesch; *The Challenge of Jesus* by N. T. Wright; *Church Next* by Eddie Gibbs; *Love, Honor & Forgive* by Bill and Pam Fanel; *Never Beyond Hope* by J. I. Packer.

LifeGuide Bible Studies introduces new titles that focus on particular scriptural areas and specific books of the Bible. Other Bible studies are published each year.

A full set of guidelines for manuscript submission to InterVarsity Press is available upon request from the publisher. Query letters and SASEs should be directed to:

Andrew T. Le Peau, Editorial Director

JEWISH LIGHTS PUBLISHING

PO Box 237, Sunset Farm Offices, Route 4, Woodstock, VT 05091

802-457-4000   fax: 802-457-4004

www.jewishlights.com   e-mail: editorial@jewishlights.com

Jewish Lights Publishing shows a vigorous approach to titles "for people of all faiths, all backgrounds." Its books cover Jewish spirituality, life cycles, self-help/healing, theology, history, and contemporary culture, all within the trade motto "Words for the soul— made in Vermont." Jewish Lights offers books in hardcover, quality paperback, and gift editions.

Jewish Lights features authors at the forefront of spiritual thought. Each voice is unique, and each speaks in a way readers can hear. Jewish Lights books are judged as successful not only by whether they are beautiful and commercially successful, but by the difference they make in their readers' lives.

Jewish Lights Publishing (founded in 1990), a division of LongHill Partners, Inc., describes itself as publishing books that reflect the Jewish wisdom tradition for people of all faiths and all backgrounds. Its books really focus on the quest for the self, seeking meaning in life. These are books that help you to understand who you are and who you might become as a Jewish person, or as a person who is part of a tradition that has its roots in the Judeo-Christian world. The books deal with issues of personal growth and issues of religious inspiration.

Jewish Lights' principal goal is to stimulate thought and help all people learn about who the Jewish People are, where they come from, and what the future can be made to hold. Although people of diverse Jewish heritage are the primary audience, Jewish Lights books speak to people in the Christian world as well and will broaden their understanding of Judaism and the roots of their own faith.

Jewish Lights seeks out materials about the unity and community of the Jewish People and the relevance of Judaism to everyday life. To help in these efforts, respectful of the rich diversity of Jewish heritage, the publisher has established an Advisory Board representing a broad range of Jewish perspectives. The Advisory Board helps seek out new material and provides insights into the publishing needs of the Jewish community.

The press publishes the award-winning Kushner Series: Classics of Modern Jewish Spirituality by Lawrence Kushner. A related special-edition project is *The Book of Letters: A Mystical Hebrew Alphabet* (designed by Lawrence Kushner).

From Jewish Lights: *Women of the Wall* edited by Phyllis Chesler and Rivka Haut;

Ehyeh by Arthur Green; *An Orphan in History* by Paul Cowan; *My People's Prayer Book, Vol. 6* edited by Rabbi Lawrence Hoffman; *Making a Successful Jewish Interfaith Marriage* by Rabbi Kerry Olitzky with Joan Peterson Littman; *The Jewish Family Fun Book* by Danielle Dardashti and Roni Sarig; *The Rituals and Practices of a Jewish Life* edited by Rabbi Kerry Olitzky and Rabbi Daniel Judson; *The Book of Words: Talking Spiritual Life, Living Spiritual Talk* and *Eyes Remade for Wonder* by Lawrence Kushner; *Finding Joy: A Practical Spiritual Guide to Happiness* by Daniel L. Schwartz with Mark Hass; *How to Claim the Spiritual Meaning of Your Bar or Bat Mitzvah; Moses—The Prince, the Prophet: His Life, Legend & Message for Our Lives* by Rabbi Levi Meier, Ph.D.

The Art of Jewish Living series, from the Federation of Jewish Men's Clubs, provides the following titles: *A Time to Mourn, a Time to Comfort: A Guide to Jewish Bereavement and Comfort; The Shabbat Seder;* and *Hanukkah* by Dr. Ron Wolfson.

The Jewish Thought Series, from Israel's MOD Books, is distributed exclusively by Jewish Lights. A part of Israel's Broadcast University Series, the books are written by leading experts and authors in their respective fields. Titles are published jointly by Tel Aviv University, the Chief Education office of the IDF, and IDF Radio. Selected series offerings: *Jerusalem in the 19th Century* by Yehoshua Ben-Arieh; *Jewish Reactions to the Holocaust* by Yehuda Bauer; *Lectures on the Philosophy of Spinoza* by Professor Yosef Ben-Shlomo; *The Spiritual History of the Dead Sea Sect* by David Flusser; *The World of the Aggadah* by Avigdor Shinan; *Human Rights in the Bible and Talmud* by Haim H. Cohn.

Children's titles and books for the family from Jewish Lights: *A Prayer for the Earth: The Story of Naamah, Noah's Wife* by Sandy Eisenberg Sasso (illustrated by Bethanne Andersen); *When a Grandparent Dies: A Child's Own Workbook for Dealing with Shiva and the Year Beyond* by Nechama Liss-Levenson; *The New Jewish Baby Book: A Guide to Choices for Today's Families* by Anita Diamant.

Jewish Lights Publishing handles its own distribution. Query letters and SASEs should be directed to:

Stuart M. Matlins, Editor-in-Chief

THE JEWISH PUBLICATION SOCIETY

2100 Arch Street, 2nd floor, Philadelphia, PA 19103

215-832-0608/1-800-234-3151   fax: 215-568-2017

www.jewishpub.org   e-mail: jewishbook@jewishpub.org

The Jewish Publication Society specializes in hardcover and trade paperback books of Jewish interest, especially traditional religious works (including the Torah), as well as relevant commentaries and resources for Jewish life.

The Jewish Publication Society (founded in 1888) upholds a commitment to the English-speaking Jewish community by publishing works of exceptional scholarship, contemporary significance, and enduring value. The publisher traditionally assumes a demanding balancing act among the various denominations of Jewish institutional life, between academic and popular interests, and between past and present visions of Judaism.

Recently published: *The JPS Guide to Jewish Women* by Emily Taitz, Sondra Henry, Cheryl Tallan; *The Rebbe's Daughter* by Malkah Shapiro; *Folktales of Joha, Jewish Trickster* collected by Matilda Koen-Sarano; *Legends of the Jews* by Louis Ginzberg; *Not to Worry* by Michele Klein; *Raising a Mensch* by Shelley Kapnek Rosenberg; *Discovering Jewish Music* by Marsha Bryan Edelman; *Jerusalem* by Lee I. Levine; *Studies in the Meaning of Judaism* by Eugene B. Borowitz; *Pesikta De-Rab Kahana* translated by William G. Braude and Israel J. Kapstein; *The Day the Rabbi Disappeared: Jewish Holiday Tales of Magic* retold by Howard Schwartz; *Tanakh; The Holy Scriptures; Trees, Books, and Torah* edited by Ari Elon, Naomi Hyman, and Arthur Waskow; *A Survivors Haggadah* edited by Saul Touster; *Preparing Your Heart for Passover* by Kerry M. Olitzky; *Preparing Your Heart for the High Holy Days* by Kerry M. Olitzky and Rachel T. Sabath; *Swimming in the Sea of Talmud* by Michael Katz and Gershon Schwartz; *The "Shabbes Goy"* by Jacob Katz; *Epistles of Maimonides* translations and notes by Abraham Halkin; *Daughters of the King* edited by Susan Grossman.

Indicative of JPS nonfiction: *In the Year 1096: The First Crusade and the Jews* by Robert Chazen; *Reclaiming the Dead Sea Scrolls* by Lawrence Schiffman; *On the Possibility of Jewish Mysticism in Our Time* by Gershom Scholem; *On Family and Feminism* by Blu Greenberg; *Blessings* (a prayer book) by Melanie Greenberg.

The Jewish Publication Society is a not-for-profit educational institution that distributes its own list and, through its book club, offers to its membership Judaica from other publishers as well.

Query letters and SASEs should be directed to:

Jewishbook@jewishpub.org, Attn: Acquisitions

KAR-BEN COPIES

6800 Tildenwood Lane, Rockville, MD 20852

301-984-8733/1-800-4-KARBEN   fax: 301-881-9195

www.karben.com   e-mail: editorial@karben.com

Kar-Ben Copies offers an expansive Jewish library for young children and families, as well as teachers. The Kar-Ben list encompasses presentations keyed to high holidays,

RELIGIOUS, SPIRITUAL & INSPIRATIONAL

the Sabbath, culture and tradition, and general-interest concepts.

Sample titles: *The Mouse in the Matzah Factory* by Francine Medoff; *The Shapes of My Jewish Year* by Marji Gold-Vokson; *The Sounds of My Jewish Year* by Marji Gold-Vokson; *Sammy Spider's First Tu B'Shevat* by Sylvia Rouss; *A Seder for Tu B'Shevat* by Harlene Appleman and Jane Shapiro; *Sammy Spider's First Purim* by Sylvia Rouss; *Make Your Own Megillah* by Judyth Groner and Madeline Wikler; *A Costume for Noah* by Susan Remick Topek; *Purim Fun* by Judy Groner and Madeline Wikler.

Kar-Ben's children's books are handsomely produced volumes that often incorporate fine illustrative work. The Kar-Ben catalog highlights books especially for toddlers, as well as a reference line for youngsters (the "All About" Jewish Holiday series). The house also offers audiocassettes and calendars.

Kar Ben's list of over 95 books on Jewish themes include such recent titles as *The Hardest Word* by Jacqueline Jules, *The Shabbat Box* by Lesley Simpson, *Hanukkah Cat* by Chaya Burnstein; and *Clap and Count—Jewish Action Rhymes* by Jacqueline Jules. Bestsellers include the six popular Sammy Spider books for Hanukkah, Passover, Purim, Tubshevar, Rosh Hashanah, and Sabbat.

A special Kar-Ben line consists of book-and-cassette packages, with accompanying leader's guides for family services keyed to the high holidays (Selichot, Rosh Hashanah, and Yom Kippur). These works are written by Judith Z. Abrams, designed and illustrated by Katherine Janus Kahn, with original music by Frances T. Goldman.

Kar-Ben (founded in 1976) welcomes comments, kudos, and manuscripts. Query letters and SASEs should be directed to:

Madeline Wikler, Editor-in-Chief

KTAV PUBLISHING HOUSE

930 Newark Avenue, Jersey City, N.J. 07306

201-963-9524   fax: 201-963-0102

www.ktav.com   e-mail: questions@ktav.com

KTAV Publishing House (founded in 1924) features books of Jewish interest, including scholarly Judaica, sermonica, textbooks, and books for a younger readership. KTAV also markets religious educational materials (including books), as well as gifts and decorative items. Many KTAV titles in the scholarly vein relate the history of Jewish thought and culture within the context of broader issues—some of global scope—and are of appeal to the interested general reader.

KTAV's catalog embraces the categories of Judaica, Biblica, Torah study, Jewish law, contemporary Halachic thought, sermonica, Jewish history, Jewish thought, contemporary Jewry, and Torah and science.

Titles from KTAV: *Leaves of Faith: Vol 1 The World of Jewish Learning* by Aharon

Lichtenstein; *The Jews of Kaifeng China* by Xu Xin; *Thinking God: The Mysticism of Rabbi Zadok Hakohen Oflublin* by Alan Brill; *Worship of the Heart: Essays on Jewish Prayer* by Soloveitchik edited by Shalom Carmy; *The New Jewish Experiential Book* by Bernard Reisman; *Exploring Sephardic Customs and Traditions* by Marc Angel; *Out of the Whirlwind: Essays on Suffering, Mourning and the Human Condition* edited by David Shatz, Joel Wolowelsky and Reuven Ziegler; *The Second How to Handbook for Jewish Living* by Kerry Olitzky and Ronald Isaacs; *Children of Abraham: An Introduction to Judaism for Muslims* by Ruvn Firestone; *Children of Abraham: An Introduction to Islam for Jews* by Khalid Duran; *The Third How to Handbook for Jewish Living* by Kerry Okitzky; *Blessings of Freedom: Chapters in American Jewish History* by Michael Feldberg; *The World of Jewish Learning* by Rabbi Aharon Lichtenstein; *Charlie Reminisces: The Stories of Charles H. Bendheim* by Charles Bendheim; *The Jewish Experiential Book* by Bernard Reisman; *Understanding the Talmud: A Dialogic Approach* by Jacob Neusner.

KTAV distributes its own list; in addition, the house distributes the books of Yeshiva University Press. Query letters and SASEs should be directed to:

Bernard Scharfstein, Publisher

LIGUORI PUBLICATIONS

LIGUORI TRIUMPH BOOKS

One Liguori Drive, Liguori, MO 63057-9999

636-464-2500/1-800-325-9526   fax: 636-464-8449

www.liguori.org

Liguori Publications and its trade imprint Liguori Triumph represent a twofold approach to religious publishing. Liguori (run by Redemptionist priests) produces books and pamphlets focused on the needs of Catholic parishes and specialized religious-bookstore markets and publishes *Liguorian* magazine. Liguori Triumph Books publishes for the mainstream religious-trade-book market. Under the rubric of Liguori Faithware, the publisher supplies computer resources for Catholics.

Liguori initiated its book program in 1968 and met with immediate success with *Good Old Plastic Jesus* by Earnest Larsen and *Keeping Your Balance in the Modern Church* by Hugh O'Connell.

Though Liguori, America's largest producer of Catholic publications, is assuredly a business, it is primarily a ministry. Through publications—in print and through electronic media—Liguori is able to reach people in ways that are not available in ordinary day-to-day ministry.

Liguori titles: *The Rosary of Pope John Paul II* by Haris Christoffersen; *Raising Kids Who Care About Themselves, About Their World, About Each Other Revised and Updated* by Kathleen O'Connell Chesto; *Grow Old Along with Me* by William Rabior and Susan

Rabior; *Do This in Rememberance of Me* by Rev. Seamus Doyle; *Handbook for Today's Catholic Children* by Francine O'Connor; *Blessed Are the Peacemakers* by Mary Latela; *Our Lady of Holy Saturday* by Cardinal Carlo Martini; *The Way of the Cross* by Caryll Houselander; *Journey to Glory: Lent 2003* by Francine O'Connor; *Angels All Around Us: The Catholic Belief and Experience; Daily Strength: One Year of Experiencing the Psalms* by Victor M. Parachin; *For Men Only: Strategies for Living Catholic* by Mitch Finley; *In the Womb of God: Creative Nurturing for the Soul* by Celeste Snowber Schroeder; *A Call to Peace: 52 Meditations on the Family Pledge of Nonviolence* by James McGinnis; *Out of the Ordinary: Awareness of God in the Everyday* by Peter Verity.

Highlights from Liguori include *Mother Teresa: In My Own Words* by Mother Teresa; *Family Planning: A Guide for Exploring the Issues* by Charles and Elizabeth Balsam; *Sex and the Christian Teen* by Jim Auer.

Liguori Publications promotes and markets through such vehicles as catalog mailings and listings in Liguorian magazine, circulates bookstore and parish newsletters, and utilizes flyers and self-mailers. Authors interested in Liguori or Triumph may request from the publisher a brochure covering submission guidelines. Query letters and SASEs should be directed to:

Rev. Harry Grile, Publisher, Editor in Chief, Book and Pamphlet Department

LIGUORI TRIUMPH BOOKS

Liguori Triumph Books emphasizes an ecumenical perspective in the religious trade market. Liguori Triumph reaches a wide readership through books in a variety of areas, including psychology, spirituality, inspiration, awareness, theology, and Christian living.

Liguori Triumph Books asserts the impact of social and cultural developments on readers' values and religious faith and reflects this stance in its selection of new titles. The publishing program accents topics of contemporary controversy and debate. Liguori Triumph was formerly part of Gleneida Publishing Group.

From Liguori Triumph: *Testimony of the Cross* by His Holiness Pope John Paul II; *Making Your Way After Your Parents' Divorce* by Lynn Cassella; *Blessings of the Daily* by Brother Victor-Antoine d'Avila Latourrette; *Do I Have to Go to Church* by Jim Auer; *Handbook's for Today's Catholic Children* by Francine O'Connor; *The Search for Happiness Four Levels of Emotional and Spiritual Growth* by Oscar Lukefahr; *Jesus: An Unconventional Biography* by Jacques Duquesne; *Shaking a Fist at God: Struggling with the Mystery of Undeserved Suffering* by Katharine Dell; *Happy Are They . . . Living the Beatitudes in America* by Jim Langford; *On Living Simply: The Golden Voice of John Chrysostom* (compiled by Robert Van de Weyer); *Lift Up Your Heart: A Guide to Spiritual Peace* by Fulton J. Sheen. Query letters and SASEs should be directed to:

Fr. Bill Parker, Editorial Director

Cecelia Portlock, Production Editor

John Cleary, Associate Editor (Book Submissions)

Judy Bauer, Administrative Editor

LLEWELLYN PUBLICATIONS

PO Box 64383, St. Paul, MN 55164-0383

651-291-1790/1-800-The-Moon   fax: 651-291-1908

www.llewellyn.com   e-mail: lwlpc@llewellyn.com

Traditional areas of Llewellyn publishing concentration include astrology, magic, the occult, self-improvement, self-development, spiritual science, alternative technologies, nature religions and lifestyles, spiritist and mystery religions, divination, phenomena, and tantra. These works are brought out under the lustrous Llewellyn logo: a crescent moon. Llewellyn's trade motto—"new worlds of mind and spirit"—indicates the publisher's openness to explore new territory.

Llewellyn Publications (established in 1901) is a venerable house with a historical emphasis on the practical aspects of what today may be termed New Age science—how it works, and how to do it.

Llewellyn catalogs a full stock of new seasonal releases, along with a prolific backlist in hardcover, trade paper, and mass-market editions. Llewellyn also issues tarot decks and divination kits. The house's expanded program includes Spanish-language trade paperbacks.

New titles from Llewellyn: *Witchcraft: An Alternative Path* by Ann Moura; *Designing Your Own Tarot Spreads* by Teresa Michelsen; *Playing with Fire* by Dotti Enderle; *Astral Projection Plain & Simple: Out-of-Body Experience* by Osborne Phillips; *Buddhist Astrology from a Buddhist Perspective* by Jan Angel; *Cunningham's Encyclopedia of Wicca in the Kitchen* by Scott Cunningham; *Cooking by Moonlight: A Witch's Guide to Culinary Magic* by Karri Ann Alrich; *The Quest Tarot* by Joseph Martin; *Tarot & Magic* by Donald Kraig; *Meditation* by Jose Lorenzo-Fuentes; *The Art of Predictive Astrology* by Carol Rushman; *Nostradamus, World War III, 2002* by David Montaigne; *Ostara* by Edain McCoy; *Charting Your Spiritual Path with Astrology* by Stephanie Clement.

Backlist favorites from Llewellyn include: *Astrology for the Millions* by Grant Lewi; *Auras: See Them in Only 60 Seconds!* by Mark Smith; *The Intimate Enemy: Winning the War Within Yourself* by Guy Finley and Ellen Dickstein, Ph.D.; *In the Presence of Aliens: A Personal Experience of Dual Consciousness* by Janet Bergmark; *Magical Gardens: Myths, Mulch and Marigolds* by Patricia Monaghan; *Feng Shui for Beginners: Successful Living by Design* by Richard Webster; *Peaceful Transition: The Art of Conscious Dying & the Liberation of the Soul* by Dr. Bruce Goldberg; *How to Develop and Use Psychic Touch* by Ted Andrews; *Strange but True: From the Files of FATE Magazine* (edited by Corine Kenner and Craig Miller); *100 Days to Better Health, Good Sex & Long Life: A Guide to Taoist Yoga* by Eric Steven Yudelove; *Experiencing the Kabbalah: A Simple Guide to Spiritual Wholeness* by Chic Cicero and Sandra Tabatha Cicero.

Llewellyn has produced a limited number of fiction titles. Among them: *Murder at Witches' Bluff* by Silver Ravenwolf; *Beneath a Mountain Moon* by Silver Ravenwolf; *Playing with Fire* by Dotti Enderle; *The Lost Scrolls of King Solomon* by Richard Behrens;

RELIGIOUS, SPIRITUAL & INSPIRATIONAL

Visions of Murder by Florence Wagner McClain; *Lilith* by D. A. Heeley; *Cardinal's Sin: Psychic Defenders Uncover Evil in the Vatican* by Raymond Buckland.

Llewellyn is a specialty house and looks for projects (books and audiotapes, as well as videos and computer software) that will have extended sales viability; Llewellyn is not geared toward academic or scholarly publishing, and its products are aimed at general audiences without specialist knowledge or training. Authors may request the house's writers' guidelines, which contain valuable tips generally applicable to structuring and proposing publishing projects.

To request a copy of the Llewellyn Writers' Guidelines for book publication, send an SASE to Nancy Mostad, Acquisitions Manager. Only writers who request and adhere to the writers' guidelines will be considered for publication.

An aggressive marketer and promoter, Llewellyn publications and authors are given full house support, including the areas of arranging author interviews and appropriate advertising and subsidiary rights. Often incorporated into the schedule is placement in Llewellyn's magazines (*New Times*) and primarily promotional venues (*New Worlds*). Llewellyn's marketing network encompasses distributional arrangements worldwide.

Query letters and SASEs should be directed to:

Nancy J. Mostad, Acquisitions Manager

Barbara Wright, Acquisitions Editor—Tarot and kits

LOTUS PRESS

PO Box 325, Twin Lakes, WI 53181

262-889-8561   fax: 262-889-8591

Lotus Press produces works in the fields of health, yoga, and Native American and New Age metaphysics.

Lotus Press (founded in 1981) is a division of Lotus Brands, Inc.

On the Lotus Press list: *The Healing Power of Grapefruit Seed* by Shalila Sharamon and Bodo J. Baginski; *The Healing Power of Essential Oils* by Rololphe Balz; *Abundance Through Reiki* by Paula Horan; *Ayurveda Secrets of Healing* by Maya Tiwari; *Reiki: Way of the Heart* by Walter Lubeck; *New Eden: For People, Animals, Nature* by Michael W. Fox (illustrated by Susan Seddon Boulet); *Rainforest Remedies: One Hundred Healing Herbs of Belize* by Rosita Arvigo and Michael Balick; *Stargazer: A Native American Inquiry into Extraterrestrial Phenomena* by Gerald Hausman.

Lotus Press distributes primarily through special product outlets such as health-food stores and spiritual-interest booksellers. Query letters and SASEs should be directed to:

Cathy Hoselton, Assistant to the President

MESORAH PUBLICATIONS

4401 Second Avenue, Brooklyn, NY 11232

718-921-9000   fax: 718-680-1875

www.artscroll.com   e-mail: info@artscroll.com

Mesorah Publications produces books of contemporary Jewish interest written by authors with sophisticated firsthand knowledge of Orthodox religious practices, history, and culture. It is also noted for its works in traditional Judaica, Bible study, Talmud, liturgical materials, Jewish history, and juvenile literature. Founded in 1976, Mesorah Publications, Ltd., remains true to tradition in all of its publications, as expressed in its motto: "Mesorah Publications . . . helping to preserve the heritage, one book at a time."

From Mesorah: *Noble Lives Noble Deeds* by Rabbi Dovid Silber; *Understanding People* by Rabbi Yisroel Reisman; *Women in the Talmud* by Rabbi Dr. Aaron Glatt; *Light at the End of the Tunnel* by Rabbi Abraham J. Twerski; *Searching for Comfort* by Rabbi Meir Munk; *Harmony With Others* by Rabbi Zelig Pliskin; *Parsha Perceptions* by Rabbi Yissocher Frand; *Is It Kosher* by Rabbi Yissocher Frand; *Rabbi Miller Speaks* by Rabbi Simcha Bunim Cohen; *The Torah Treasury* by Rabbi Moshe Lieber; *A Promise Fulfilled* by Menachem Kagan; *Creative Communications* by Rabbi Paysach Krohn; *Sensitivities* by Rabbi Paysach Krohn; *Living Jewish* by Rabbi Berel Wein; *Reflections of the Maggid* by Rabbi Paysach Krohn; *Chinuch in Turbulent Times* by Rabbi Dov Brezak; *The Rubin Edition of the Prophets: Samuel I and II* by Rabbi Nosson Scherman; *Journey to Virtue* by Rabbi Avrhohom Ehrman; *The Jewish Theory of Everything* by Max Anteby; *The Gentle Voice of Hashem* by Rabbi Yisroel Reisman.

Mesorah catalogs books from such other houses as Shaar Press, Tamar Books, and OU/NCSY Publications. Query letters and SASEs should be directed to:

Charlotte Friedland, Acquisitions Editor

MOODY PRESS

820 North LaSalle Boulevard, Chicago, IL 60610-3284

312-329-2101   800-678-8812

www.moodypress.org   e-mail: pressinfo@moody.edu

In addition to general-interest religious titles (Bible-based interdenominational), Moody produces a list that includes Bibles, books for children and youths, novels, biographies, educational resources, and works for religious professionals. Moody's books are issued in clothbound editions, trade paperback, and mass-market paperback. Moody also catalogs computer software, audiotapes, and videocassettes. Moody Press (founded in 1894) serves as the publishing ministry of Moody Bible Institute.

Moody produces a number of targeted and successful lines that encompass the spectrum of the house's publishing interests. This portion of the Moody program offers such series as Men of Integrity, Moody Acorns, Golden Oldies, Healing for the Heart, Quiet Time Books for Women, and Salt & Light Pocket Guides.

Representative Moody titles: *The 10 Commandments of Marriage* by Ed Young; *Becoming a Woman Who Pleases God* by Pat Ennis and Lisa Tatlock; *Beyond Expectations* by Nancy Sebastian Meyer; *The Brother's Keeper* by Tracy Groot; *City on a Hill* by Philip Graham Ryken; *Different by Design* by H. Dale Burke; *Foundational Faith* by John Koessler; *Gospel Trailblazer* by Edward Gilbreath; *Helper By Design* by Elyse Fitzpatrick; *If You Only Knew...* by O. Sonny Acho; *A Journey to Victorious Praying* by Bill Thrasher; *Leading Talents, Leading Teams* by Lee Ellis; *The Love Languages of God* by Gary Chapman; *Ricky and Friends Go To Africa* by Tony and Tracey Van Dyke; *Seven Secrets to Sexual Purity* by Dannah Gresh; *Unlocking Your Legacy* by Paul J. Meyer; *Winning the Race to Unity* by Clarence Shuler; *Almost Home* by Wendy Lawton; *Amazing Faith* by Thomas A. Shaw and Dwight A. Clough; *Angels Watchin'* by A. Shelton Rollins; *The Art of Storytelling* by John Walsh; *Confessions of an Ex-Crossmaker* by E. K. Bailey; *Empowering Choices* by Kendra Smiley; *Equally Yoked* by Perry Moore; *From Dust to Ashes* by Tricia Goyer; *Holy Transformation* by Chip Ingram; *Last Chance* by Greg Stier; *Nothing to Fear* by Larry Burkett; *Trouble with Jesus* by Joseph M. Stowell; *Seven Words to Change Your Family... While There's Still Time* by James MacDonald; *Sought by Grace* by R. Kent Hughes; *Totally Saved: Understanding, Experiencing and Enjoying the Greatness of Your Salvation* by Tony Evans; *Unlocking Your Legacy: 25 Keys for Success* by Paul J. Meyer.

Northfield Publishing, an imprint of Moody Press, is a line of books for non-Christians in your life, those who are exploring the Christian faith or acquaintances who identify themselves as Christians but may not be active in a local church. While the books remain true to biblical principles, certain Christian wording and Scripture book references are eliminated to avoid reader confusion. Covering such areas as finances, relationships, and business, Northfield authors are professionals in their field who write with relevance and offer wide-ranging perspectives.

Some Northfield titles: *The Five Love Languages: How to Express Heartfelt Commitment to Your Mate* by Gary Chapman; *Reinventing Your Career: Surviving a Layoff and Creating New Opportunities* by Stephen P. Adams; *The Relaxed Parent: Helping Your Kids Do More As You Do Less* by Tim Smith.

Fiction from Moody includes historicals, high-tech espionage, and contemporary mysteries. Larry Burkett Products is a line of books and tapes accenting the social/financial sphere.

Query letters and SASEs should be directed to:

Mark Tobey, Director of Acquisitions: acquisitions@moody.edu

MULTNOMAH PUBLISHERS

204 West Adams Avenue, PO Box 1720, Sisters, OR 97759

541-549-1144/1-800-929-0910   fax: 541-549-2044

www.multnomahpublishers.com   e-mail: information@multnomahbooks.com

Multnomah covers the major categories of Christian trade publishing in general non-fiction and fiction.

Multnomah produces books and audiocassettes with a contemporary verve in Christian living and family enrichment, as well as lines of devotional titles and gift books.

Sample titles: *30 Days to Discovering Personal Victory Through Holiness* by Bruce Wilkinson; *A Life God Rewards* by Bruce Wilkinson; *Be Intolerant* by Ryan Dobson; *Desiring God* by John Piper; *Did You Get What You Prayed For?* by Nancy Jo Sullivan and Jane A. G. Kise; *Generation Esther* by Lisa Ryan; *How To Get Your Teen To Talk To You* by Kent Julian and Connie Grigsby; *I Kissed Dating Goodbye Study Guide* by Joshua Harris; *Is the Antichrist Alive Today?* by Mark Hitchcock; *Lists to Live By: The Fourth Collection* by Alice Gray, Steve Stephens, and John Van Diest; *My Name is Chloe* by Melody Carlson; *Overcoming Overload* by Mary Farrar and Steve Farrar; *Point Man* by Steve Farrar; *Right with God: Loving Instruction from the Father's Heart* by Ron Mehl; *Secrets of the Vine for Teens* by Bruce Wilkinson; *Set Apart: Discovering Personal Victory Through Holiness* by Bruce Wilkinson; *So You're Thinking About Homeschooling: Fifteen Families Show How You Can Do It* by Lisa Whelchel.

Multnomah also offers a strong list of fiction, including contemporary and historical novels.

Sample fiction titles: *Along Came Jones* by Linda Windsor; *Antonia's Choice* by Nancy Rue; *Autumn Dreams* by Gayle Roper; *Danger in the Shadows* by Dee Henderson; *High Stakes: The Baxter Series #4* by Kathy Herman; *Out of the Ruins* by Sally S. Wright; *Steal Away: Terri Blake-Addison Mystery Series, book one* by Linda Hall; *The Lights of Tenth Street* by Shaunti Feldhahn; *The Little Sparrows* by Al Lacy and JoAnna Lacy; *The Rescuer* by Dee Henderson.

Multnomah is currently not accepting unsolicited manuscripts, proposals, or queries. Queries will be accepted through agents and at writer's conferences at which a Multnomah representative is present. Query letters and SASEs should be directed to the Editorial Department or to:

David Webb, Editorial Director

THOMAS NELSON PUBLISHERS

501 Nelson Place, PO Box 141000, Nashville, TN 37214-1000

615-889-9000

www.thomasnelson.com

Thomas Nelson Publishers is an editorially independent product group of Thomas Nelson, Inc. (founded in Scotland in 1798 and purchased by Sam Moore in 1969). Thomas Nelson Publishers produces Christian trade books in hardcover and trade paperback in the areas of health, inspiration, self-help, psychology, family concerns, parenting, charismatic interest, leadership and motivation, contemporary issues and interests, and healing and recovery. Oliver-Nelson is a trade-oriented imprint.

Already among the major players in the religious-publishing arena, Nelson enjoys its current phase of corporate exuberance. The house bought Here's Life Publishers from Campus Crusade for Christ and expanded its evangelism and discipleship markets.

Titles from Thomas Nelson: *Experiencing the Heart of Jesus* by Max Lucado; *Hermie, the Common Caterpillar Board Book* by Max Lucado; *Signature Series King Bible*; *Blink* by Ted Dekker; *Wild at Heart Field Manual* by John Eldredge; *High Trust Selling* by Todd Duncan; *Grace for the Moment Journal* by Max Lucado; *Something Worth Leaving Behind* by Brett Beavers and Tom Douglas; *Louisiana Gardener's Guide—Revised Edition* by Dan Gill and Joe White; *Cuando la tragedia ocurre* by Charles Stanley; *A Thousand Goodbyes* by Jim Huber; *Edge of the Wilderness: A Novel* by Stephanie Grace Whitson; *Forever Ruined for the Ordinary* by Joy Dawson; *The One: A Realistic Guide to Choosing Your Soul Mate* by Ben Young; *What If Jesus Had Never Been Born?* by D. James Kennedy; *Attack on America: New York, Jerusalem, and the Role of Terrorism in the Last Days* by John Hagee; *The Blood of the Moon: Understanding the Historic Struggle Between Islam and Western Civilization* by George Grant; *Trust and Tragedy: Encountering God in Times of Crisis* by Tommy Tenney; *When Tragedy Strikes* by Dr. Charles Stanley; *The Red Sea Rules* by Robert J. Morgan; *Let Love Change Your Life: Growing in Intimacy, Growing in Love* by Becky Tirabassi; *Islam Revealed: A Christian Arab's View of Islam* by Anis Shorrosh; *Financially Secure: An Easy-to-Follow Money Program for Women* by Deborah McNaughton.

Bestsellers from Thomas Nelson: *The 17 Indisputable Laws of Teamwork* and *The 17 Essential Qualities of a Team Player* by John C. Maxwell; *Beside Still Waters: A Devotional* by Thomas Kinkade; *Falling Forward: How to Make the Most Out of Your Mistakes* by John C. Maxwell; *How to Live Through a Bad Day: Seven Powerful Insights from Christ's Words on the Cross* by Jack Hayford; *Into His Presence: An In Touch Devotional* by Dr. Charles Stanley; *Kingdom Come: A Novel* by Larry Burkett; *Lord, I Want to Be Whole: The Power of Prayer and Scripture in Emotional Healing* by Stormie Omartian; *On the Brink: Breaking*

Through Every Obstacle into the Glory of God by Rod Parsley; *The God Catchers: Experiencing the Manifest Presence of God* by Tommy Tenney; *Under Cover: The Key to Living in God's Provision and Protection* by John Bevere.

Thomas Nelson Publishers does not accept unsolicited query letters, proposals, or manuscripts.

Thomas Nelson handles its own distribution. Query letters and SASEs should be directed to:

Laura Minchew, Editor

NEW HARBINGER PUBLICATIONS

5674 Shattuck Avenue, Oakland, CA 94609

www.newharbinger.com

New Harbinger owners Matt McKay and Patrick Fanning started their company in 1978, publishing *The Relaxation and Stress Reduction Workbook* with no capital and a $9.95 box of stationery. Since that time the company has grown to employ over twenty-five people and has 180 titles currently in print.

Despite experiencing tremendous growth, New Harbinger still models its current titles after the original release. With each title they publish they seek a broad important problem, proven techniques, simplicity, a step-by-step format with lots of examples and exercises, and a book that teaches people skills, rather than merely inspires or entertains.

More than just another "self-help" focused publisher, New Harbinger has an excellent reputation with the mental health and medical communities. They are the only psychology publishing house associated with a large mental health clinic. Matt McKay, along with being the co-founder of New Harbinger, is the co-founder and clinical director of a non-profit, low-fee clinic called Haight Ashbury Psychological Services.

Recent titles include: *You, Your Relationship & Your ADD* by Michael T. Bell, Ed.S.; *The BDD Workbook* by James Claiborn, Ph.D, and Cherry Pedrick, RN; *Stop Feeling Tired!* by George D. Zgourides, Psy.D. and Christie S. Zgourides, MA; *Don't Let Your Emotions Run Your Life* by Scott E. Spradlin, MA; *Your Depression Map* by Randy J. Paterson, PhD.; *Drugs & Your Kid* by Peter D. Rogers, Ph.D. and Lea Goldstein, Ph.D.

Send query and SASEs to:

Catherine Sutker, Acquisitions Manager

Jueli Gastwirth, Acquisitions Editor

Tesilya Hanauer, Acquisitions Editor

Spencer Smith, Acquisitions Editor

NEW LEAF AND MASTER BOOKS

PO Box 726, Green Forest, AR 72638

870-438-5288   fax: 870-438-5120

www.masterbooks.net   e-mail: nlp@newleafpress.net.

Areas of New Leaf publishing include Christian living, prophecy and eschatology, theology, applied Christianity, Bible study, family/home/marriage, friendship and love, education, evangelism, devotional works (including daily readings), and humor. Master Books is the house's imprint for its children's and creation science, titles. The house has a solid backlist.

New Leaf Press (founded in 1975) publishes primarily for the Christian religious market, with some trade-religious crossover titles. New Leaf produces in hardcover and paperback (trade paper and mass-market); many New Leaf books are priced economically.

On the New Leaf list: *Come Home to Comfort* by Sharon Hoffman; *The Joyous Gift of Puppy Love*; *The Life Story of Lester Sumrall*; *First Comes Love, Then Comes Money* by Roger Gibson; *First Thing Monday Morning* by Dianna Booher; *Reasons for Believing: A Seeker's Guide to Christianity* by Frank Harper; *Recapturing Your Dreams* by David Shibley; *Bible Comes Alive, volume 2*, by Drs. Clifford and Barbara Wilson; *The Fragrance of Christmas* and *A Cup of Devotion with God*, by Dan and David Davidson; *Success Without Guilt* by Robert Strand; *When Hollywood Says Yes, How Can America Say No?* by Gene Wolfenbarger.

Master titles: *Exploring the World Around You* by Dr. Gary Parker; *God and the Nations* by Dr. Henry Morris; *Grand Canyon: A Different View* by Tom Vail; *Is the Big Bang Biblical* by Dr. John D. Morris; *Refuting Evolution 2* by Jonathan Sarfati; *The Story of "In God We Trust"* by John Hudson Tiner; *The Story of Noah's Ark* by Tom Dooley and Bill Looney; *Whale of a Story* by Buddy Davis. *Buried Alive* by Dr. Jack Cuozzo; *The Great Alaskan Dinosaur Adventure* by Buddy Davis, Mike Liston, and John Whitmore.

New Leaf Press distributes its own list; New Leaf also provides distribution services for other publishers with related market outlooks. Query letters and SASEs should be directed to:

Roger Howerton, Acquisitions

Jim Fletcher, Editor-in-Chief

NEW WORLD LIBRARY

H J KRAMER

STARSEED PRESS

NATARAJ PUBLISHING

14 Pamaron Way, Novato, CA 94949

1-800-972-6657 ext.52   fax: 415-884-2199

www.newworldlibrary.com

Founded in 1977 as Whatever Publishing, Inc., New World Library is a solid midsize publisher focusing on titles that awaken individual and global potential through inspirational and practical nonfiction books and audio cassettes. The most common subjects include: personal growth, spirituality, health and wellness, business and prosperity, religion, parenting, multicultural studies, and women's studies. They also have a growing Spanish language publishing program.

Even though it currently employees only fifteen people, New World Library has an impressive track record of sales and well received spiritual titles. Among them are *Creative Visualization* by Shakti Gawain, which has sold over 3 million copies in over thirty foreign editions; *The Seven Spiritual Laws of Success* by Deepak Chopra (co-published with Amber-Allen Publishing), which has sold over 2 million copies; and *The Power of Now* by Eckhart Tolle, a recent release that has already sold 200,000 copies since November 1999.

New World Library sometimes publishes books in association with other companies. Beside co-publishing titles with Amber-Allen, New World also co-publishes with, and releases the entire catalog for, another inspirational publisher called Nataraj Publishing. In 2000 New World began a joint venture program with the publisher H. J. Kramer. Under the terms of the agreement, New World handles Kramer's sales, marketing, subsidiary rights, fulfillment, production and accounting needs. Though H. J. Kramer has ceased accepting manuscripts indefinitely, they still produce an impressive line of titles. New World Library has taken over H. J. Kramer's backlist, and it distributes Kramer's new titles as well as those of its imprint, Starseed Press. Starseed Press focuses on children's subjects.

H. J. Kramer titles include: *100 Ways to Build Self-Esteem and Teach Values* by Diana Loomans with Julia Loomans; *Movement for Self-Healing* by Meir Schneider; *No Regrets* by Barry Neil Kaufman; *Answers From the Angels* by Terry Lynn Taylor; *Guardians of Hope* by Terry Lynn Taylor; *Moments of Union* by Hal Kramer; *You the Healer* by Jose Silva and Robert B. Stone, Ph.D; *Talking With Nature* by Michael J. Roads; *The Blue Dolphin* by Robert Barnes.

H. J. Kramer/Starseed Press titles: *Bless Your Heart* by Holly Bea; *The Chief's Blanket* by Michael Chanin; *Dragon Soup* by Arlene Williams; *Good Night God* by Holly Bea;

The Land of the Blue Flower by Frances Hodgson Burnett; *The Lovables in the Kingdom of Self-Esteem* by Diane Loomans; *My Spiritual Alphabet Book* by Holly Bea; *Positively Mother Goose* by Diane Loomans, Karen Kolberg, and Julia Loomans.

General titles from New World Library: *Sake & Satori* by Joseph Campbell; *The Architecture of All Abundance* by Lenedra J. Carroll; *Ready for Romance* by Leslie Caplan and Jimmy Caplan; *Money Magic* by Deborah L. Price; *The Love Compatibility Book* by Edward Hoffman, Ph.D., and Marcella Bakur Weiner, Ph.D.; *Essential Aromatherapy* by Susan Worwood and Valerie Ann Worwood; *The Gift* by Echo Bodine; *The Red-Haired Girl from the Bog* by Patricia Monaghan.

Send submissions and SASE's to:

Alex Slagg, Submissions Editor

Georgia Hughes, Editor

Jason Gardner, Senior Editor

PAULIST PRESS, INC.

997 Macarthur Boulevard, Mahwah, NJ 07430

201-825-7300/1-800-218-1903   fax: 201-825-6921

www.paulistpress.com   e-mail: info@paulistpress.com

Paulist Press publishes Roman Catholic as well as ecumenical titles in Bible study, biography, women's studies, spirituality, current issues, self-help and personal growth, Catholicism, liturgy, theology, philosophy, ethics, Jewish–Christian relations, world religions, youth ministry, and education. The Paulist list ranges from popularly oriented traditionalist works to provocative frontiers of religious thought. In addition to books, Paulist offers a multimedia line.

Titles from Paulist Press include: *Touching God* by Ellyn Sanna; *Guia sobre la Misa para ninos* by Sue Stanton; *My Catholic Pray and Play Activity Book* by Jennifer Galvin; *A Sorrowful Joy* by Kimberly C. Patton; *Genetic Engineering, Christian Values and Catholic Teaching* by Paul Flaman; *Living the Days of Advent and the Christmas Season 2002* by Stephanie Collins; *Martin de Porres: A Saint for Our Time* by Joan Monahan; *Everyday Virtues* by John W. Crossin; *Reading the Pentateuch: An Historical Introduction* by John J. McDermott; *Soundbyte Spirituality: Sayings to Awaken Faith* by Brett C. Hoover and Frank Sabatte; *Angelic Spirituality: Medival Perspectives on the Ways of Angels* by Steven Chase; *Don't Tell Me What to Do!* by Father Dave Heney; *Making Peace with Motherhood…And Creating a Better You* by Heidi Brattone.

Query letters and SASEs should be directed to:

Rev. Lawrence Boadt, C.S.P., Editorial Director

Susan Heyboer O'Keefe, C.S.P., Children's Book Editor

THE PILGRIM PRESS

700 Prospect Avenue, East Cleveland, OH 44115-1100

216-736-3764   fax: 216-736- 2207

www.pilgrimpress.com   e-mail: pilgrim@ucc.org

The Pilgrim Press is a Christian-related imprint that focuses on three areas: theological ethics (including science, technology, and medicine); human identity, relationships, and sexuality (including feminist and gay/lesbian issues); and activist spirituality (having a social dimension).

Pilgrim Press (begun in 1645 and established in the United States in 1895) is the book-publishing banner of the publishing wing of the United Church of Christ. United Church Press is a Pilgrim imprint geared primarily toward readers of inspirational materials.

Pilgrim's trade motto: Books at the Nexus of Religion and Culture.

The house has a tradition of publishing books and other resources that challenge, encourage, and inspire, and are crafted in accordance with fine standards of content, design, and production.

Indicative of the Pilgrim list: *Amistad: The Slave Uprising Aboard the Spanish Schooner* by Helen Kromer; *Celebrating Her: Feminist Ritualizing Comes of Age* by Wendy Hunter Roberts; *Crossing the Soul's River: A Rite of Passage for Men* by William O. Roberts, Jr.; *Now That You're Out of the Closet, What About the Rest of the House?* by Linda Handel; *Forgiving Our Grownup Children* by Dwight Lee Wolter; *Prayers for the Common Good* by A. Jean Lesher; *Just Peacemaking: Ten Practices for Abolishing War* by Glen Stassen; *Meditations on the Way of the Cross* by Mother Teresa of Calcutta and Brother Roger of Taize; *The Wealth or Health of Nations: Transforming Capitalism from Within* by Carol Johnston; *Sacred Texts and Authority* by Jacob Neusner; *The Great Commandment: A Theology of Resistance and Transformation* by Eleanor H. Haney.

The Pilgrim Library of World Religions is a series designed for both classroom and general use, written by authorities in each tradition. The series addresses how five great world religions—Judaism, Hinduism, Buddhism, Islam, and Christianity—approach a certain critical issue. Titles include: *God* (edited by Jacob Neusner). Projected titles include: *Evil and Suffering; Women and Families; Death and the Afterlife; Sacred Texts and Authority.* A representative title from Pilgrim Library of Ethics: *Abortion: A Reader* (edited by Jacob Neusner).

The Pilgrim Press oversees its own distribution. Query letters and SASEs should be directed to:

Timothy Staveteig, Publisher

PRESBYTERIAN PUBLISHING CORPORATION

WESTMINSTER/JOHN KNOX

100 Witherspoon Street, Louisville, KY 40202

502-569-5060   fax: 502-569-5113

www.wjkbooks.com

The Presbyterian Publishing Corporation (PPC), the denominational publisher of the Presbyterian Church (USA), publishes under the imprints Westminster/John Knox Press and Geneva Press. PPC's three primary objectives are: (1) To develop and publish high-quality, useful resources for congregations, both within the Presbyterian Church (USA) and ecumenically; (2) To expand the scope of the Westminster/John Knox Press academic publishing program in order to better facilitate the training of clergy and scholars; and (3) To publish books for lay and general readers that "contribute to the broader conversation about religion, society, and moral values."

Sample titles: *To God Alone Be Glory* by Harold M. Daniels; *Witness Without Parallel* by Earl S. Johnson; *Is It I Lord?* by James O. Chatham; *Let Us Pray* edited by Martha S. Gilliss.

Bestsellers: *The Gospel According to The Simpsons* by Mark I. Pinsky; *P.S. God, Can You Fly?* by R. Wayne Willis; *Come Worship With Me* by Ruth L. Boiling; *Proclaim Jubilee!* by Maria Harris; *Soul Feast* by Marjorie Thompson; *The Weekend that Changed the World* by Peter Walker; *Clergy Killers* by G. Lloyd Rediger; *Revolution and Renewal* by Tony Campolo; *Cadences of Hope* by Walter Brueggemann; *Soul Survivors* by Carlyle Stewart; *The Book of Reformed Prayers* by Howard L. Rice and Lamar Williamson; *Soul Among Lions* by Will D. Campbell; *Looking for Jesus* by Virginia Owens.

With a publishing heritage that dates back over 160 years, PPC publishes more than 100 new works each year, while maintaining a backlist of more than 1,000 titles sold around the world. PPC, located in Louisville, Kentucky, with offices in the United Kingdom and the Netherlands, characterizes its publishing program with the theme "Challenging the Mind, Nourishing the Soul."

Query letters and SASEs should be directed to:

Angela Jackson, Editor

WESTMINSTER/JOHN KNOX

Westminster/John Knox publishes general-interest religious trade books, as well as academic and professional works in Biblical studies, theology, philosophy, ethics, history, archaeology, personal growth, and pastoral counseling. Among its series are Literary Currents in Biblical Interpretation, Family Living in Pastoral Perspective, Gender and the Biblical Tradition, and the Presbyterian Presence: The Twentieth-Century Experience.

Westminster/John Knox Press represents the publications unit of the Presbyterian Church (USA). The house unites the former independents Westminster Press and John Knox Press, which were originally founded as one entity in 1838, then separated into distinct enterprises, and again merged as WJK following the reunion of the Northern and Southern Presbyterian Churches in 1983.

Selected titles from Westminster/John Knox: *Dark the Night, Wild the Sea* by Robert McAfee Brown; *Speaking the Truth in Love: Prophetic Preaching to a Broken World* by J. Philip Wogaman; *Our Testament Wisdom: An Introduction* (revised and enlarged) by James L. Crenshaw; *Theology of the Prophetic Books: The Death and Resurrection of Israel* by Donald E. Gowan; *Honor and Shame in the Gospel of Matthew* by Jerome H. Neyrey; *Jesus as a Figure in History: How Modern Historians View the Man from Galilee* by Mark Allan Powell; *Athena's Disguises: Mentors in Everyday Life* by Susan Ford Wiltshire; *Both Feet Planted in Midair: My Spiritual Journey* by John McNeill; *Equipping the Saints: Teacher Training in the Church* by Sara Covin Juengst; *Survival or Revival: Ten Keys to Church Vitality* by Carnegie Samuel Calian; *We Have Seen the Lord!: The Passion and Resurrection of Jesus Christ* by William Barclay.

WJK's Studies in the Family, Religion, & Culture series offers informed and responsible analyses of the state of the American family from a religious perspective and provides practical assistance for the family's revitalization. Titles: *For the Love of Children: Genetic Technology and the Future of the Family* by Ted Peters; *Religion, Feminism, and the Family* (edited by Anne Carr and Mary Steward Van Leeuwen); *Faith Traditions and the Family* (edited by Phyllis D. Airhart and Margaret Lamberts Bendroth).

Westminster/John Knox distributes its list through Spring Arbor. The house also represents titles from other publishers, including Orbis Books, Pilgrim Press, Saint Andrew Press of Scotland, and Presbyterian Publishing Corporation.

Query letters and SASEs should be directed to:

Angela Jackson, Assistant Editor

RED WHEEL/WEISER BOOKS

368 Congress Street, 4th Floor, Boston, MA 02210

617-542-1324   fax: 617-482-9676

www.redwheelweiser.com

Areas of Weiser publishing interest include self-transformation, alternative healing methods, meditation, metaphysics, consciousness, magic, astrology, tarot, astral projection, Kabbalah, earth religions, Eastern philosophy and religions, Buddhism, t'ai chi, healing, and Tibetan studies.

The publisher has observed the many paths that lead to personal transformation and strives to publish books to help many different people find the path that is right for them. Weiser Books specializes in books relating to all facets of the secret and hidden teachings worldwide.

Sample titles: *Stillness, Daily Gifts of Solitude* by Richard Mahler; *Be Generous* by Marell; *The Celestial Guide to Every Year of Your Life* by Z Budapest & Diana L. Paxson; *Gay Witchcraft* by Christopher Penczak; *The Office Sutras* by Maria Menter; *Will Work for Food or $* by Bruce Moody; *One God, Shared Hope* by Maggie Oman Shannon; *The Woman's Book of Courage* by Sue Patton Thoele; *Wonderful Ways to Love a Child* by Judy Ford (foreword by Amanda Ford); *The Naptime Book* by Cynthia MacGregor; *How to Get a Good Reading from a Psychic Medium* by Carole Lynne; *A Witch's Book of Answers* by Eileen Holland & Cerelia; *Heart Sense* by Paula M. Reeves, Ph.D.; *The Celtic Book of Seasonal Meditations* by Claire Hamilton; *Sacred Beat* by Patricia Telesco and Don Two Eagles Waterhawk; *Tarot D' Amour* by Kooch Daniels and Victor Daniels; *The Power to Write* by Caroline Joy Adams; *Once and Future Myths* by Phil Cousineau; *Soul Mission, Life Vision* by Alan Seale; *Single Female Pilgrim Seeks Spiritual Sustenance* by Suzanne Clores; *Safe Passage* by Molly Fumia; *A Way Forward* by Anna Voigt and Nevill Drury; *Spiritual Cleansing* by Draja Mickaharic; *Reality Works* by Chandra Alexander; *Intuition @ Work & at Home and Play* by James Wanless.

Frontlist Weiser titles characteristically revamp age-old themes into new and vibrant works of contemporary sensibility. In addition to new titles, Weiser publishes classic references and tracts in reprint; Weiser also offers a particularly distinguished selection of titles pertinent to the life and works of Aleister Crowley, as well as a strong line of Gurdjieff studies. The house publishes in hardcover and paperback editions and maintains a thriving backlist. Weiser Books was founded in 1955.

Weiser Books handles its own distribution and distributes selected titles from other houses; the Weiser distribution catalog lists titles from over 200 publishers. Weiser Books is the exclusive distributor of Nicolas-Hays, Inc., titles, as well as Binkey Kok. Weiser utilizes the services of several national trade distributors.

Query letters and SASEs should be directed to:

Eliot Stearnes, Editor

Ms. Robyn Heisey, Editor

ST. ANTHONY MESSENGER PRESS AND FRANCISCAN COMMUNICATIONS

28 West Liberty Street, Cincinnati, OH 45210

513-241-5615   fax: 513-241-0399

www.AmericanCatholic.org   e-mail: lisab@americancatholic.org

Areas of St. Anthony Messenger publishing interest include Franciscan topics, Catholic identity, family life, morality and ethics, parish ministry, pastoral ministry, prayer helps, sacraments, saints and Christian heroes, Scripture, seasonal favorites, small-group resources, spirituality for every day, children's books, and youth ministry. The house produces books (hardcover and paperback, many in economically priced editions), magazines, audiotapes and videocassettes, as well as educational programs and an award-winning Web site.

St. Anthony Messenger Press (founded in 1970) and Franciscan Communications publishes Catholic religious works and resources for parishes, schools, and individuals. The house also owns the video/print imprints Ikonographics and Fischer Productions.

Titles: *A Retreat with John the Evangelist: That You May Have Life* by Raymond E. Brown, S.S.; *A Retreat with Mark: Embracing Discipleship* by Stephen C. Doyle, O.F.M.; *Living God's Word—Reflections on the Weekly Gospels: Cycle A* by David Knight; *Thresholds to Prayer* by Kathy Coffey; *Jesus of the Gospels: Teacher, Storyteller, Friend, Messiah* by Arthur E. Zannoni; *Jesus' Plan for a New World: The Sermon on the Mount* by Richard Rohr, O.F.M., with John Bookser Feister; *Following Francis of Assisi: A Spirituality for Daily Living* by Patti Normile; *Journeys into Matthew: 18 Lessons of Exploration and Discovery* by Raymond Apicella; *Marriage and the Spirituality of Intimacy* by Leif Kehrwald; *God Is Close to the Brokenhearted: Good News for Those Who Are Depressed* by Rachael Callahan, C.S.C., and Rea McDonnell, S.S.N.D.; *Harvest Us Home: Good News As We Age* by Rachel Callahan, C.S.C., and Rea McDonnell, S.S.N.D.; *The Blessing Candles: 58 Simple Mealtime Prayer-Celebrations* by Gaynell Bordes Cronin and Jack Rathschmidt; *Thomas Merton's Paradise Journey: Writings on Contemplation* by William H. Shannon; *The Lay Contemplative: Testimonies, Perspectives, Resources* edited by Virginia Manss and Mary Frolich; *Twelve Tough Issues: What the Church Teaches—And Why* by Archbishop Daniel E. Pilarczyk.

St. Anthony Messenger Press also offers music CDs, computer software, videos, and audiocassettes.

St. Anthony Messenger Press distributes books through Ingram, Spring Arbor, Riverside Distributors, Appalachian Inc., Baker & Taylor, and ABS/Guardian. Query letters and SASEs should be directed to:

Lisa Biedenbach, Editorial Director, Books

SHAMBHALA PUBLICATIONS

300 Massachussetts Avenue, Boston, MA 02115

617-424-0030   fax: 617-236-1563

www.shambhala.com   e-mail: editors@shambhala.com

Shambhala publishes hardcover and paperback titles on creativity, philosophy, psychology, medical arts and healing, mythology, folklore, religion, art, literature, cooking, martial arts, and cultural studies. Shambhala generally issues a modest list of new titles each year and tends a flourishing backlist; the house periodically updates some of its perennial sellers in revised editions.

The house packages a number of distinct lines, including gift editions and special-interest imprints. Shambhala Dragon Editions accents the sacred teachings of Asian masters. Shambhala Centaur Editions offers classics of world literature in small-sized gift editions. The New Science Library concentrates on titles relating to science, technology, and the environment. Shambhala copublishes C. G. Jung Foundation Books with the C. G. Jung Foundation for Analytical Psychology. Shambhala Redstone Editions are fine boxed sets composed of books, postcards, games, art objects, and foldouts. Shambhala Lion Editions are spoken-word audiotape cassette presentations.

Shambhala Publications is a foremost representative of the wave of publishers specializing in the arena of contemporary globalized spiritual and cultural interest. Since Shambhala's inception (the house was founded in 1969), the field has blossomed into a still-burgeoning readership, as underscored by the many smaller independent presses and large corporate houses that tend this market.

Titles from Shambhala: *Buddha of Infinite Light* by D. T. Suzuki; *Imagery in Healing: Shamanism and Modern Medicine* by Jeanne Acherberg; *Lady of the Lotus-Born: The Life and Enlightenment of Yeshe Tsogyal* by Gyalwa Changchub, Namkhai Nyingpo (translated by Padmakara Translation Group); *Lightning at the Gate: A Visionary Journey of Healing* by Jeanne Achterberg; *The Myth of Freedom and the Way of Meditation* by Chogyam Trungpa; *Toward a Psychology of Awakening: Buddhism, Psychotherapy, and the Path of Personal and Spiritual Transformation* by John Welwood; *Twilight Goddess: Spiritual Feminism and Feminine Spirituality* by Thomas Cleary and Sartaz Aziz; *Being Zen: Bringing Meditation to Life* by Ezra Bayda; *The Five Wisdom Energies: A Buddhist Way of Understanding Personality, Emotions, and Relationships* by Irini Rockwell; *Infinite Circle: Teachings in Zen* by Bernie Glassman; *Spacecruiser Inquiry: True Guidance for the Inner Journey* by A. H. Almaas.

Shambhala distributes to the trade via Random House. Shambhala services individual and special orders through its own house fulfillment department. Query letters and SASEs should be directed to:

David O'Neal, Managing Editor

SIGNATURE BOOKS

564 West 400 North Street, Salt Lake City, UT 84116-3411

801-531-1483   fax: 801-531-1488

www.signaturebooks.com   e-mail: people@signaturebooks.com

The Signature list emphasizes contemporary literature, as well as scholarly works relevant to the Intermountain West. Signature Books (established in 1981) publishes subjects that range from outlaw biographies and Mormonism to speculative theology, from demographics to humor. In addition to a wide range of nonfiction, Signature publishes novels and collections of poetry. The common objective of the selections on Signature's roster is to provide alternatives to the institutional agendas that underlie many of the publications in the region.

Indicative of Signature nonfiction: *Red Stocking* and *Out-of-Towners* edited by Stanford J. Layton; *The Angel Acronym* by Paul M. Edwards; *The Articles of Faith* by James E. Talmage; *Baha'I* by Margit Warburg; *Vernal Promises* by Jack Harrell; *Early Mormon Documents* by Dan Vogel; *History's Apprentice* edited by John Sillito; *A Winter with the Mormons* edited by David L. Bigler; *Elder Statesman* by D. Michael Quinn; *American Apocrypha* edited by Dan Vogel and Brent Metcalfe; *Mormon Mavericks* by John Sillito and Susan Staker; *Conflict in the Quorum* by Gary James Bergera; *Being Different* edited by Stanford J. Layton; *The Mysteries of Godliness* by David John Buerger; *An Insider's View of Mormon Origins* by Grant H. Palmer; *Heresies of Nature* by Margaret Blair Young; *The House of James & Other Stories* by Lewis B. Horne; *The Marketing of 'Sister B'* by Linda Hoffman Kimball; *Salamander: The Story of the Mormon Forgery Murders* by Linda Sillitoe and Allen Roberts (George J. Throckmorton, forensic analysis); *Remembering Brad: On the Loss of a Son to AIDS* by H. Wayne Schow; *The Sanctity of Dissent* by Paul James Toscano; *Waiting for the World's End: The Diaries of Wilford Woodruff* (edited by Susan Staker); *A Sculptor's Testimony in Bronze and Stone: Sacred Sculpture of Avard T. Fairbanks*; *"Wild Bill" Hickman and the Mormon Frontier* by Hope A. Hilton; *Aspen Marooney* and *The Backslider* by Levi S. Peterson; *Beyond the River: A Novel* by Michael Fillerup.

Signature Publications oversees distribution of its titles via in-house ordering services and a national network of wholesalers. Signature Books does not accept unsolicited manuscripts. Query letters and SASEs should be directed to:

Ron Priddcs, Director

TYNDALE HOUSE PUBLISHERS

351 Executive Drive, Carol Stream, IL 60188

630-668-8300   fax: 630-668-3245

www.tyndale.com

Tyndale offers a comprehensive program in Christian living: devotional, inspirational, and general nonfiction, from a nondenominational evangelical perspective. Tyndale's publishing interest also encompasses religious fiction. The house publishes the best-selling *Left Behind* series. Tyndale house offers a strong line of Bibles. Tyndale House Publishers (founded in 1962) produces hardcover, trade paperback, and mass-market paperback originals, as well as reprints. Tyndale also catalogs audio and video products.

New titles from Tyndale: *130 Questions Children Ask About War and Terrorists* by Stephen Arterburn and David Stoop; *How to Study the Bible and Enjoy It* by Skip Heitzig; *Loving Your Body* by Deborah Newman; *Mama Says . . . Cookies Cure a Lot of Things* by Rita Maggart; *The Never Alone Church* by David Ferguson; *No Fear Guide for First Time Parents* by Focus; *The No-Brainer's Guide to How Christians Live* and *The No-Brainer's Guide to What Christians Believe* by Stan Campbell and James S. Bell, Jr.; *Protecting Your Child in an X-rated World* by Frank York and Jan LaRue; *Rag Baby* by Karyn Henley; *Sacred Journeys* by Wendy Murray Zoba; *Why Believe?* by Greg Laurie; *Why You Can't Stay Silent* by Tom Minnery; *First Century Diaries: The Gaius Diary* by Gene Edwards; *Heart to Heart Series: Heart to Heart Stories for Sisters* by Joe Wheeler.

In a publishing partnership with the American Association of Christian Counselors, Tyndale offers books written by leading Christian counselors that integrate counseling principles and Biblical theology as they offer authoritative analysis and research for the Professional Counseling Library. Titles include: *Counseling Children Through the World of Play* by Daniel Sweeney, Ph.D.; *Psychology, Theology, and Spirituality in Christian Counseling* by Mark R. McMinn; *Counseling Through the Maze of Divorce* by George Ohlschlager; *Treating Sex Offenders* by Daniel Henderson; *Brief Counseling* by Gary J. Oliver; *Treating Victims of Sexual Abuse* by Diane Langberg.

Tyndale fiction includes mainstream novels, as well as a number of inspirational romance series, including works set in Revolutionary War and Civil War milieus. The house is interested in evangelical Christian-theme romance in other historical periods (including Regency), as well as those with a humorous twist.

Tyndale fiction list: *Looking for Cassandra Jane* by Melody Carison; *They Shall See God* by Athol Dickson; *Heartquest: English Ivy* by Catherine Palmer.

The Tyndale program of books for children and young adults is in a transitional phase; currently, the house is not interested in fiction geared for this younger age group.

Tyndale House oversees its own distribution. Tyndale also distributes books from Focus on the Family. Tyndale does not accept unsolicited manuscripts. For manuscript submissions, send SASE to the Manuscript Review Committee, requesting a copy of the committee's writers' guidelines—and query first. Query letters and SASEs should be directed to:

Jan Axford—Children's and gift

Janelle Howard—Adult nonfiction and fiction

Jan Stob—Adult fiction

Anne Goldsmith—Women's fiction and romance

UNION OF AMERICAN HEBREW CONGREGATIONS/UAHC PRESS

Union of American Hebrew Congregations

633 Third Avenue, New York, NY 10017-6778

212-650-4000   fax: 212-650-4119

http://uahcpress.com   e-mail: press@uahc.org

Union of American Hebrew Congregations/UAHC Press publishes in the areas of religion (Jewish), Reform Judaism, textbooks, audiovisual materials, social action, biography, and life cycles and holidays. In its trade categories, UAHC Press accents juvenile fiction and adult nonfiction books, as well as titles in basic Judaism and inspirational works. The house catalogs books, audiocassettes, videotapes, and multimedia products.

The UAHC Press provides the highest quality in religious educational materials and has done so for well over 100 years. The publications of the press are suitable for all ages, from preschool through adult, for use in both the classroom and at home. The publishers are committed to providing their readers with the foremost in materials and service, to be a continuing resource for books, publications, audiocassettes, videotapes, and multimedia.

Founded in 1873, UAHC Press is a division of Union of American Hebrew Congregations. The UAHC Press publishing program includes the Reform Judaism magazine.

Indicative of UAHC Press interests: *Out of the Whirlwind* by Albert H. Friedlander; *Hello, Hello, Are You There, God?* by Rosalind Charney; *Chocolate Chip Challah* by Lisa Rauchwerger; *Until the Messiah Comes* by Kenneth Roseman; *Duties of the Soul* edited by Niles E. Goldstein and Peter S. Knobel; *A Shabbat Reader* edited by Dov Peretz Elkins; *When There Is No Other Alternative* by Sanford Seltzer; *Shemonah Perakim* by Kerry M. Olitzky and Leonard S. Kravitz; *The Torah: A Modern Commentary* (edited by W. Gunther Plaut); *Meeting at the Well: A Jewish Spiritual Guide to Engagement* by Daniel Judson and Nancy Wiener; *Mishlei: A Modern Commentary on Proverbs* (edited and translated by Leonard S. Kravitz and Kenny M. Olizky).

Children's titles from UAHC: *Good Night, Lilah Tov* by Michelle Shapiro Abraham; *The High Holy Days* by Camille Kress; *Good Morning Boker Tov* by Michelle Shapiro Abraham; *Night Lights: A Sukkot Story* by Barbara Kiamond Goldin; *Holy Days, Holy Ways* by Sharon D. Halper.

UAHC Press handles its own distribution. Query letters and SASEs should be directed to:

Kenneth Gesser, Publisher

Rabbi Hara Person, Editor

RELIGIOUS, SPIRITUAL & INSPIRATIONAL

VEDANTA PRESS

Vedanta Society of Southern California

1946 Vedanta Place, Hollywood, CA 90068

1-800-816-2242

www.vedanta.com   e-mail: info@vedanta.com

Vedanta's publishing interests include meditation, religions and philosophies, and women's studies. In addition to its list of titles imported from the East (primarily from Indian publishers), Vedanta's program embraces works of Western origin. The publisher catalogs titles from other publishers and also sells audiotapes and videotapes.

The house publishes books on the philosophy of Vedanta, with an aim to engage a wide variety of temperaments, using a broad spectrum of methods, in order to attain the realization of each individual personality's divinity within. Vedanta Press (founded in 1947) is a subsidiary of the Vedanta Society of Southern California.

Backlist from the press: *The Compassionate Mother* translated by Swami Tanamayananda; *The Essential Rumi* by Rumi; *Mahabharata for Children* by Swami Raghaveshananda; *Myths and Legends of the Hindus and Buddhists* by Sister Nivedita and Ananda and K. Coomaraswamy; *Principles of Tantra* by Sir John Woodroffe; *Ramakrishna and Christ: The Supermystics* by Paul Hourihan; *Ramakrishna and His Gospel* by Swami Bhuteshananda; *The World Sri Ramakrishna Knew* by Dr. Jaladhi Kumar Sarkar; *Yoga for Beginners* by Swami Gnaneswarananda; *How to Know God: The Yoga Aphorisms of Patanjali* (translated by Swami Prabhavananda and Christopher Isherwood); *The Upanishads: Breath of the Eternal* (translated by Swami Prabhavananda and Frederick Manchester); *Women Saints: East and West* (edited by Swami Ghanananda and Sir John Stewart-Wallace); *The Sermon on the Mount According to Vedanta* by Swami Prabhavananda; *Seeing God Everywhere: A Practical Guide to Spiritual Living* by Swami Shraddhananda; *Six Lighted Windows: Memories of Swamis in the West* by Swami Yogeshananda. Vedanta publishes many classic Vedic works in a variety of editions and translations. Among them: *Bhagavad Gita: The Song of God* (translated by Swami Prabhavananda and Christopher Isherwood; introduction by Aldous Huxley).

Vedanta Press handles its own distribution.

Vedanta's books originate in-house, though the publisher is open to considering additional projects that may fall within its program. Vedanta does not wish to receive unsolicited manuscripts. Before you submit a query letter, be sure your book is within our niche. We don't do personal spiritual biographies and subjects outside the Vedanta tradition. Please do your research before writing to us or, for that matter, any publisher. Query letters and SASEs should be directed to:

Bob Adjemian, Manager

WISDOM PUBLICATIONS

199 Elm Street, Somerville, MA 02144

617-776-7416   fax: 617-776-7841

www.wisdompubs.org   e-mail: info@wisdompubs.org

Wisdom Publications, a not-for-profit publisher, is dedicated to making available authentic Buddhist works for the benefit of all. The house publishes translations of the sutras and tantras, commentaries and teachings of past and contemporary Buddhist masters, and original works by the world's leading Buddhist scholars. In 1996, Wisdom Publications was named one of the top 10 fastest-growing small publishers in the country (the company has been in the United States since 1989) by *Publishers Weekly*.

Wisdom titles are published in appreciation of Buddhism as a living philosophy and with the commitment to preserve and transmit important works from all the major Buddhist traditions. Wisdom products are distributed worldwide and have been translated into a dozen foreign languages.

Wisdom publishes the celebrated Tibetan Art Calendar, containing 13 full-color reproductions of the world's finest Indo-Tibetan thangka paintings, accompanied by detailed iconographical descriptions.

Wisdom highlights: *Faces of Compassion* by Taigen Dan Leighton; *Longing for Certainty* by Bhikkhu Nyanasobhano; *Essence of Jung's Psychology & Tibetan Buddhism* by Radmila Moacanin; *The Fine Arts of Relaxation, Concentration and Meditation* by Joel Levey and Michelle Levey; *Awesome Nightfall* by William Lafleur; *Nyingma School of Tibetan Buddhism* by Dudjom Rinpoche and Gyurme Dorje; *The Svantantrika-Prasangika Distinction* edited by Sara McClintock and George Dreyfus.

Wisdom Publications is distributed to the trade in the United States and Canada by National Book Network (NBN). Query letters and SASEs should be directed to:

Acquisitions Editor

ZONDERVAN PUBLISHING HOUSE

5300 Patterson Avenue SE, Grand Rapids, MI 49530

616-698-6900   fax: 616-698-3454

www.zondervan.com

Zondervan Publishing House (founded in 1931) became a division of HarperCollins in 1988. Zondervan publishes both fiction and nonfiction books that have a strong emphasis on Christianity. Zondervan is the number one publisher of the Bible world-wide and has held at least 5 (and as many as 10) out of the top 10 positions on the Christian Booksellers bestseller lists since 1995.

Although Zondervan specializes in publishing Bibles and books, the house also produces a wide variety of resources, including audio books, eBooks, videos, CD-ROMs, and inspirational gifts. Zondervan has six primary product-group departments. These include: Bibles; Books; New Media, which publishes electronic format books, Bibles, and software products; Zonderkidz; Inspirio; and Vida Publishers, Zondervan's multilingual publishing and distribution unit.

In 2000, Zondervan released the industry's first two e-Books, including the first Christian book published exclusively in electronic format, Leonard Sweet's *The Dawn Mistaken for Dusk*. Also in 2000 Zondervan launched its gift program, Inspirio, specializing in inspirational gift products.

Zonderkidz was formed in 1998 to represent the children's and juvenile division at Zondervan. Zonderkidz is now the leading publisher of children's Bibles, children's Christian books, and other related products.

As the world's largest Bible publisher, Zondervan holds exclusive publishing rights to the New International Version of the Bible—the most popular translation of the Bible—and has distributed more than 150 million copies worldwide. Zondervan publishes approximately 50 Bible products, 150 books, 80 gifts, and 50 new media products each year.

Sample titles: *The Purpose Driven Life* by Rick Warren; *The Case for Christ* by Lee Strobel; *Season of Blessing* by Beverly LaHaye and Terri Blackstock; *Mere Christianity* by C. S. Lewis; *Cape Refuge* by Terri Blackstock; *Women of the Bible* by Ann Spangler and Jean E. Syswerda; *The Women of Faith Daily Devotional* by Patsy Clairmont, Barbara Johnson, Marilyn Meberg, Luci Swindoll, Sheila Walsh, and Thelma Wells; *The Screwtape Letters* by C. S. Lewis; *Boundaries* by Dr. Henry Cloud and Dr. John Townsend; *Stories Behind the Best-Loved Songs of Christmas* by Ace Collins; *The Case for Faith* by Lee Strobel; *Streams in the Desert* by Mrs. Charles E. Cowman and James Reimann.

Bestsellers from Zondervan include: *The Case for Christ* and *The Case for Faith* by Lee Strobel; *Emerald Windows* by Terri Blackstock; *He's Been Faithful* by Carol Cymbala; *How People Grow* by Dr. Henry Cloud and Dr. John Townsend; *If You Want to Walk on Water, You've Got to Get Out of the Boat* by John Ortberg; *The Life God Blesses* by Jim Cymbala, Stephen Sorenson, and Amanda Sorenson; *Mere Christianity* by C. S. Lewis; *Streams in the Desert* by James Reimann; *The Strongest Strong's Exhaustive Concordance* by James Strong, John R. Kohlenberger, and James A. Swanson; *Women of the Bible* by Jean Syswenda.

Zondervan distributes its own titles to the general market, the book trade, and the CBA. Zondervan asks that interested authors write to request submissions guidelines before submitting manuscripts or other material.

Manuscripts and SASEs to:

First Edition, The ECPA Manuscript Service (www.ECPA.org).

CANADIAN BOOK PUBLISHERS

CANADIAN BOOK PUBLISHING
AND THE CANADIAN MARKET

GREG IOANNOU

Canadian and U.S. writers who consider submitting inquiries to Canadian publishers should keep a few important points in mind. In most cases, Canadian book publishers are looking for material of Canadian interest. However, this does not mean they are not interested in queries from writers who reside in or are native to other countries.

Indeed, a rich current in the Canadian publishing stream features the Canadian experience from outlander or expatriate perspectives. Canadian reader interests are also keyed into a number of broader market sectors, such as North American pop culture and British Commonwealth concerns.

Appropriate queries (see the listings for these publishers) will be considered. Keep in mind the markets, as well as the mandates, of each house.

Publishing in Canada is markedly different from the industry in the United States. A large percentage of Canadian-owned publishing houses are small- to medium-sized, with net sales that may seem low to those accustomed to the standards of the U.S. marketplace. (Remember, the English-language Canadian market is only one-tenth the size of the U.S. market.)

Canada is a separate market, and some writers are able to sell the Canadian rights to their books separately from the U.S. rights. Before you sign a contract for "North American rights," consider whether your book would likely sell enough copies in Canada that it would be of interest to a Canadian publisher.

Don't just blithely sell the Canadian rights to a hockey book or a biography of a Canadian celebrity (such as Faye Wray, Neil Young, or Peter Jennings) to a U.S. publisher for the blanket "foreign rights" or "world English-language rights" rate—the Canadian rights alone may be worth more than the U.S. or the rest of the worldwide rights are!

The Canadian government directly subsidizes the book industry to help ensure that Canadian writers get their works published domestically and to keep the national market from being overwhelmed by the publishing giants to the south. The government grant system makes possible a greater independence on the part of Canadian-owned houses, which comprise the creative heart of publishing in Canada.

Never send an unsolicited manuscript to a Canadian publisher. Many Canadian publishers will send them back unopened because of a court ruling that forced Doubleday Canada to pay a writer thousands of dollars in compensation for losing the only copy of an unsolicited manuscript. Send query letters only!

It is a nice touch for American writers to remember that Canada is not part of the United States, so Canadian publishers cannot use U.S. stamps to return anything you send them. Use International Reply Coupons (available at any post office) instead.

ANVIL PRESS

6 West 17th Ave. (REAR), Vancouver, BC V5Y 1Z4, Canada

604-876-8710   fax: 604-879-2667

www.anvilpress.com   e-mail: info@anvilpress.com

Anvil Press began in 1988 as the publisher for *sub-TERRAIN* Magazine. In 1991, it expanded into the book-publishing field with the mandate to discover and nurture new talent in Canada. It now publishes 8–12 titles a year and sponsors the International Novel Contest every Labour Day long weekend (more information about the contest is available on its website: www.anvilpress.com). Although it does occasionally publish nonfiction, Anvil specializes in contemporary literary fiction, poetry, and drama; it does not publish genre fiction.

Recent Anvil titles: *Tight Like That* by Jim Christy; *The Fed Anthology: Brand New Fiction & Poetry from the Federation of BC Writers* edited by Susan Musgrave; *Sideways* by Heather Haley; *Knucklehead* by W. Mark Giles; *The Dreamlife of Bridges* by Robert Strandquist; *In the Trenches* edited by Brian Kaufman; *The Beautiful Dead End* by Clint Hutzulak; *Socket* by David Zimmerman; *Snatch* by Judy Macinnes Jr.; *Skin* by Bonnie Bauman; and Lyle Neff's book of poetry, *Full MagPie Dodge*.

For fiction/nonfiction submissions, Anvil requests a brief, one-page synopsis of the entire manuscript and 20–30 pages of the manuscript itself. For poetry, 8–12 poems should be submitted. Anvil requests the entire manuscript for works of drama, unless excessively long. Anvil publishes only Canadian authors. Only manuscripts accompanied by an SASE will be considered. Query letters and SASEs should be directed to:

Brian Kaufman, Publisher

ARSENAL PULP PRESS

103 – 1014 Homer Street, Vancouver, BC V6B 2W9, Canada

604-687-4233/1-888-600-PULP   fax: 604-687-4283

www.arsenalpulp.com

Arsenal Pulp Press is a publisher in Vancouver, Canada with over 160 titles in print in categories including fiction, poetry, cultural, gender, multicultural studies, and cookbooks. Founded in the early seventies by university students seeking a publishing voice independent of the Canadian academic establishment, it continues today as one of the most well-respected publishers of progressive titles and subjects. In 1993 Arsenal published the first gay male prose text ever in Canada. Additionally in recent years Arsenal has found success publishing cookbooks, specifically How It All Vegan, published in 1998, now in its 6th printing.

In regard to submissions, Arsenal seeks titles in these subjects: Literary Fiction (no genre fiction, such as sci-fi, thrillers, or romance), cultural studies, pop culture, political/sociological studies, regional studies and guides, in particular for British Columbia; cookbooks, gay and lesbian literature, visual art, multicultural literature.

Current titles include: *I, Shithead* by Joey Keithley; *Spree* by Pamela Klaffke; *The Garden of Vegan* by Tanya Barnard and Sarah Kramer; *Vancouver: The Unknown City* by John Mackie and Sarah Reeder; *Tongue Twisters* by Gord Martin; *The Toronto City* by Howard Akler and Sarah Hood; *Quickies 3* by James Johnstone; *Hot & Bothered 4* edited by Karen Tulchinsky; *Chef in Your Backpack* by Nicole Bassett.

BEACH HOLME PUBLISHING

Suite 1010, 409 Granville Street, Vancouver, BC V6C 1T2, Canada

604-733-4868   fax: 604-733-4860

www.beachholme.bc.ca   e-mail: bhp@beachholme.bc.ca

Beach Holme Publishing, so named in honor of the owner's house, is a small Vancouver publisher with a mandate "to promote indigenous creative writing to the wider Canadian public." Its literary roots began with its former incarnation, Press Porcepic, which published such renowned authors as Dorothy Livesay and James Reaney. Porcepic Books continues as an imprint of Beach Holme and has built its own niche in the Canadian literary heritage with newer talents like Evelyn Lau and Jane Urquhart. Novels, plays, poetry, and short fiction are all featured under the Porcepic Books imprint. Beach Holme also publishes young adult fiction (Sandcastle Books). Under its new imprint, Prospect Books, Beach Holme publishes creative nonfiction.

Titles typical of the list: Fiction: *The View From Tamischeira* by Richard Cumyn; *The Moor Is Dark Beneath the Moon* by David Watmough; *Hail Mary Corner* by Brian Payton; *Cold Clear Morning* by Lesley Choyce. Poetry: *The Alchemy of Happiness* by Marilyn Bowering; *Words for Trees* by Barbara Folkart; *Helsinki Drift* by Douglas Burnet Smith; *Iron Mountain* by Mark Frutkin; *Purity of Absence* by Dave Margoshes. Nonfiction: *101 Top Historical Sites of Cuba* by Alan Twigg; *One Russia, Two Chinas* by George Fetherling; *Lost Province: Adventures in a Moldovan Family* by Stephen Henighan; *Little White Squaw: A White Woman's Story of Abuse, Addiction, and Reconciliation* by Eve Mills Nash and Kenneth J. Harvey; *House Inside the Waves* by Richard Taylor. Young Adult: *Death by Exposure* by Eric Walters and Kevin Spreekmeester; *Chasing the Arrow* by Charles Reid; *Tiger Town* by Eric Walters; *Ben Franklin's War* by Stephen Eaton Hume; *What the Small Day Cannot Hold* by Susan Musgrave; *Tiger in Trouble* by Eric Walters; *Viking Quest* by Tom Henighan; *The Self-Completing Tree* by Dorothy Livesay.

Beach Holme Publishing produces only work by Canadian authors resident in Canada; foreign manuscripts will not be considered and should be directed elsewhere. Additionally, Beach Holme does not accept manuscripts via fax or email. Query letters and SASEs should be directed to:

Michael Carroll, Publisher

Jen Hamilton, Production Manager

Sarah Warren, Publicity and Marketing Coordinator

CORMORANT BOOKS

215 Spadina Ave., Studio 230, Toronto, ON M5T 2C7, Canada

416-929-4957   fax: 416-929-3596

www.cormorantbooks.com

Cormorant Books publishes a small, select list of literary fiction and trade nonfiction. This small press also produces several works of fiction in translation.

Notables from the Cormorant catalogue: *Lives of the Saints* by Nino Ricci; *Kitchen Music* by Charles Foran; *Gaff Topsails* by Patrick Kavanagh; *The Good Body* by Bill Gaston; *Purple Forsky* by Carol Bruneau; *Drowning in Darkness* by Peter Oliva.

Recent nonfiction titles: *Living in the World as If It Were Home* by Tim Lilburn; *A Very Large Soul: Selected Letters from Margaret Laurence to Canadian Writers*, edited by J. A. Wainwright; *Invisible Among the Ruins: Field Notes of a Canadian in Ireland* by John Moss.

Query letters and SASEs should be directed to:

Marc Cote, Publisher

COTEAU BOOKS

401 2206 Dewdney Avenue, Regina, SK S4R 1H3, Canada

306-777-0170   fax: 306-522-5152

www.coteaubooks.com   e-mail: coteau@coteaubooks.com

Coteau Books publishes a range of Canadian works, with a particular focus on the literary genres—novels, short fiction, poetry, drama, and juvenile fiction. Coteau presents an annual list that reflects literary quality across the country, including First Nations authors, with a focus on prairie voices of all kinds. Nonfiction work, especially memoir, is a growing interest as well.

Coteau has recently launched a new poetry series called Open Eye, with the intent to feature new, young poetic voices and attract a broad readership to the genre.

The Coteau list features such titles as the international short fiction anthology *Two Lands Two Visions* (edited by Janice Kulyk Keefer and Solomea Pavlychko); Open Eye poetry title *My Flesh the Sound of Rain* by Heather MacLeod; and *The Intrepid Polly McDoodle*, the second in a juvenile novel series by Edmonton author Mary Woodbury.

Recent titles include Governor General's Award-winner Anne Szumigalski's greatest hits, *On Glassy Wings*, which received the Canadian Authors Association Poetry Prize; Barbara Nickels's first poetry book, *The Gladys Elegies*, which was awarded the Pat Lowther Memorial Prize as the best book of poetry by a woman; and the short fiction collection *In the Misleading Absence of Light* by Regina author Joanne Gerber (which has received five national and provincial awards to date).

Sample titles include: Winner of the 2002 Governor General's Award for Fiction: *A Song for Nettie Johnson* by Gloria Sawai; *Teaching Mr. Cutler* by Robert Currie; *They Shouldn't Make You Promise That* by Lois Simmie; *Children of Paper* by Martha Blum; *Great Gift of Tears* edited by Heather Hodgson; *Street Wheat* by Mansel Robinson; *A Secret Envy of the Unsaved* by Rebecca Frederickson; *Variations of Eve* by Treena Kortje. Young Readers: *Return of the Grudstone Ghosts: A Moose Jaw Mystery* by Arthur Slade; *Andrei and the Snow Walker* by Larry Warwaruk; *Jason and the Wonder Horn* by Linda Hutsell-Manning.

Coteau also publishes the annual daybook *Herstory: The Canadian Women's Calendar*, compiled annually by the Saskatoon Women's Calendar Collective.

Coteau only publishes books by Canadian authors.

Queries and SASEs should be directed to:

Nik Burton, Managing Editor, Regina

DOUGLAS & MCINTYRE PUBLISHING GROUP

GROUNDWOOD BOOKS

GREYSTONE BOOKS

Suite 201, 2323 Quebec Street, Vancouver, BC V5T 2S7, Canada

604-254-7191

Toronto office:

Suite 500 720, Bathurst Street, Toronto, ON M5S 2R4, Canada

416-537-2501

www.douglas-mcintyre.com   e-mail: dm@douglas-mcintyre.com

Douglas & McIntyre is the original part of the entire publishing group. They have been publishing books in Canada and abroad since 1971. Publishing roughly 25 books a year, the house's strongest subjects are First Nations art and culture, Canadian art and architecture, Canadian biography, history and social issues, literary fiction, popular memoir, food and wine, and British Columbiana, though they also pride themselves on a wide cross section of books.

Nonfiction titles: D & M recent award winners: *The Trade* by Fred Stenson; *A Story as Sharp as a Knife* by Robert Bringhurst; *Krieghoff: Images of Canada* by Dennis Reid; *The Clouded Leopard* by Wade Davis; *Why I Hate Canadians* by Will Ferguson; *Across the Top of the World* by James Delgado.

Sample titles: *How to Be a Canadian* by Will Ferguson and Ian Ferguson; *David Blackwood* by William Gough; *Waiting for Gertrude* by Bill Richardson; *Light at the Edge of the World* by Wade Davis; *Lost Worships* by James P. Delgado; *Inuksuit* by Norman Hallendy.

GREYSTONE BOOKS

Greystone Books publishes in Canada but sells around the world. Almost half of the books are sent overseas and published in more than 15 countries. Since 1993 Greystone has built a strong list of books publishing in the subjects of natural history, natural science and environmental issues, popular culture, health, and sports with titles aimed at both children and adults.

From Greystone: Major successes: *Wolves* by Candace Savage; *Sacred Balance* by David Suzuki; *Gordie: A Hockey Legend* by Roy MacSkimming; *Hockey the NHL Way* by Sean Rossiter; *Fishing with Old Guy* by Paul Quarrington; *The Bear's Embrace* by Patricia Van Tighem.

Sample titles: *In the Arms of Morpheus* by Barbara Hodson; *Mario Lemieux* by Sean Rossiter; *Nature of Lions* by Eric S. Grace; *Sacred Hunt* by David F. Pelly; *Fishing for Brookies, Browns and Bows* by Gord Deval; *Zamboni Rodeo* by Jason Cohen.

GROUNDWOOD BOOKS

Since 1978 Groundwood Books has been publishing children's books for all ages, including fiction, nonfiction, and picture books. Other Groundwood books seek to tell the stories of people who have been overlooked by society and whose contributions have been discounted or forgotten. They also publish books by the First Peoples of this hemisphere. Groundwood books has been publishing books by Latin Americans living in the Americas since 1998. Libros Tigrillo, a Spanish imprint, is part of this initiative.

Award winning books include: *The Maestro* (Governor General's Award Winner) by Tim Wynne-Jones; *Stella, Star of the Sea*; *Stella, Queen of the Snow* by Marie-Louise Gay. Other titles: *The Pot of Wisdom* by Adwoa Badoe; *Snow Bear* by Liliana Stafford; *Ghost Cat* by Mark Abley; *The Race of Toad and Deer* by Pat Mora.

Douglas & McIntyre handles its own distribution, as well as purveying books from additional houses and institutions, including the Canadian Museum of Civilization, the Mountaineers, the New Press, Sierra Club Books, and Thames and Hudson.

Query letters and SASEs should be directed to the Editorial Panel.

FITZHENRY & WHITESIDE LTD.

195 Allstate Parkway, Markham, ON L3R 4T8, Canada

905-477-9700/800-1387-9776   fax: 905-477-9179 800-260-9777

www.fitzhenry.ca   www.trifoliumbooks.com

Fitzhenry & Whiteside Ltd. (founded in 1966) specializes in trade nonfiction and children's books. The firm also offers a textbook list and a small list of literary/fiction.

Fitzhenry & Whiteside nonfiction titles range throughout Canadian history, biography, native studies, nature, and antiques and collectibles. The children's book list includes early readers, picture books, and middle-grade and young adult novels. Markets include trade, school, library, professional and reference, college, mail order, and specialty.

F & H distributes several imprints within its publishing group. Trifolium Books specializes in publishing teacher and student resources in science, mathematics, information technology, design & technology, and language arts. They also publish a limited number of books in science, health, and psychology for college age adults.

Trifolium titles: *Active Learning in the Digital Age Classroom* by Ann Heide and Dale Henderson; *Stardust: Teacher's Resource* by Julie E. Czerneda and Annette Griessman; *Tales From the Wonder Zone: Explorer* by Julie E. Czerneda; *The Internet Handbook for Writers, Researchers, & Journalists, 2002-2003 Edition* by Mary McGuire, Linda Stillborne, Melinda McAdams, and Laurel Hyatt.

From Fitzhenry & Whiteside: *Just Another Indian* by Warren Goulding; *The World Is Our Witness* by Tom Molloy; *Five Pennies* by Irene Morck; *Aunt Mary in the Granary* by

Eileen Comstock; *On the Road with David Thompson* by Joyce and Peter McCart; *The Calgary Gardener* by The Calgary Horticultural Society; *Skippers of the Sky* edited by William Wheeler; *A Hikers Guide to the Rocky Mountain Art of Lawren Harris* by Lisa Christensen; *Saskatchewan In Sight* by John L. Perret; *Keepers of the Earth* by Michael J. Caduto and Joseph Bruchac; *The Native Stories From Keepers of Life* by Michael J. Caduto and Joseph Bruchac; *Park Prisoners* by Bill Waiser; *Eternal Prairie* by Randy Adams; *Prairie Skies* by Courtney Milne; *Looking West* by Brock V. Silversides; *Wild Birds Across the Prairies* by Wayne Lynch; *But It's a Dry Cold!* by Elaine Wheaton; *Shooting Cowboys* by Brock V. Silversides.

Stoddart Kids and Brady Brady are Fitzhenry & Whiteside's lines of children's books. Brady Brady is a cartoon hockey player. Brady Brady author, Mary Shaw, is the wife of former hockey star, Brad Shaw. Brady Brady Titles: *Brady Brady and the Great Link*; *Brady Brady and the Runaway Goalie*; *Brady Brady and the Twirlin' Torpedo*; *Brady Brady and the Singing Tree*.

On the children's list: *Rebound* by Eric Walters; *Maybe Tomorrow* by Joan Weir; *Too Young to Fight* compiled by Priscilla Galloway; *Storm at Batoche* by Maxine Trottier; *The Twelve Months* by Rafe Martin and Vladyana Langer Krykorka; *The World of Gubbio* by Michael Bedard and Murray Kimber; *There Have Always Been Foxes* by Maxine Trottier; *We'll All Go Sailing* by Maggee Spicer and Richard Thompson (illustrated by Kim La Fave); *Number 21* by Nancy Hundal (illustrated by Brian Deines); *The Adventures of Baby Bear* by Aubrey Lang (photographs by Wayne Lynch).

Fitzhenry & Whiteside distributes its own list and provides distribution services in Canada for a number of U.S. publishers.

Query letters and SASEs should be directed to:

Sharon Fitzhenry, President and Publisher

Gail Winskill, Children's Book Publisher

GOOSE LANE EDITIONS

469 King Street, Fredericton, NB E3B 1E5, Canada

506-450-4251   fax: 506-459-4991

e-mail: gooselane@gooselane.com

Goose Lane Editions is a small Canadian publishing house that specializes in literary fiction, poetry, and a select list of nonfiction titles. It does not publish commercial fiction, genre fiction, or confessional works of any kind. Occasionally, one of its books will appeal to young adults, but it does not publish books specifically for that market, nor does it publish books for children.

Recent Goose Lane titles: *Elle* by Douglas Glover; *Wanting the Day* by Brian Bartlett; *A Sharp Tooth in the Fur* by Darryl Whetter; *Trails of Greater Moncton* by Kate

Merlin; *Amazing Medical Stories* by George Burden and Dorothy Grant; *Strong Hollow* by Linda Little; *Tent of Blue* by Rachael Preston; *Hallowed Timbers* by Susan Hyde and Michael Bird; *A Good Enough Life* by Susan Gabori; *50 Things to Make with a Broken Hockey Stick* by Peter Manchester; *Tracking Doctor Lonecloud* by Ruth Holmes Whitehead; *Coastline* edited by Anne Compton, Laurence Hutchman, Ross Leckie and Robin McGrath; *The Coasts of Canada* by Lesley Choyce; *16 Categories of Desire* by Douglas Glover.

As a member of the Literary Press group, Goose Lane Editions has a Canada-wide sales force serving the book trade, and the company employs several regional sales representatives to nontraditional outlets such as gift stores. Academic sales are handled by Irwin Publishing. General Distribution Services takes care of order fulfillment.

Goose Lane considers submissions from outside Canada only rarely, and only when both the author and the material have significant Canadian connections and the material is of extraordinarily high interest and literary merit. Writers should submit a synopsis, outline, and sample (30–50 pages) with an SASE if in Canada; international authors should include an SASE and international reply coupons with submission. Please query by mail or phone before submitting; direct queries to:

Laurel Boone, Editorial Director

HARLEQUIN ENTERPRISES LIMITED

HARLEQUIN BOOKS (CANADA)

MILLS & BOON/HARLEQUIN ENTERPRISES LTD.

WORLDWIDE LIBRARY

225 Duncan Mill Road, Don Mills, ON M3B 3K9, Canada

416-445-5860

The Harlequin Enterprises home base in Ontario, Canada, issues the greater portion of Harlequin Books series, while the New York office issues several Harlequin series, as well as the Silhouette list (please see listing for Harlequin Books in the directory of United States publishers and editors). Harlequin Enterprises Limited also publishes the Worldwide Library, which accents titles in the mystery/suspense and thriller mode.

Each of the various lines within the Harlequin series of romance novels published in Canada, like their American counterparts, stakes out particular market-niche segments of reader interest within the overall categories of romance fiction and women's fiction.

The editorial acquisitions departments for Harlequin Romance and Harlequin Presents are located at the operation's United Kingdom offices (the address for which is listed farther on). Following are overviews of some of the editorial guidelines supplied to authors:

HARLEQUIN BOOKS (CANADA)

MIRA Books is dedicated to mainstream single-title women's fiction in hardcover and mass-market paperback editions. MIRA titles assume no particular genre designation, though the works are considered to be of interest to a primarily women's readership. MIRA Books hosts a wide variety of authors and approaches.

Harlequin Temptation introduces strong, independent heroines and successful, sexy heroes who overcome conflict inherent to their heated relationships and in the end decide to marry. The books in this series are known for their wit, as well as for emotional strength. They are sensuous romances about choices ... dilemmas ... resolutions ... and, above all, the fulfillment of love. This is the most highly charged and most sensual Harlequin series.

Harlequin Superromance is a line of longer, contemporary romance novels. These are realistic stories with emotional depth and intensity ... more involving plots ... more complex characters. Superromance women are confident and independent, yet eager to share their lives. This series is generally mainstream in tone, with romance, of course, being the propelling theme. Love scenes may be explicit, so long as they exhibit good taste.

Detailed information is available upon request from the publisher. Harlequin will send prospective authors full editorial guidelines with suggested heroine and hero profiles, as well as information pertaining to manuscript length, setting, and sexual approach and content.

Make sure your query is clear as to which line it is intended for: Harlequin Romance, Harlequin Presents, Harlequin Temptation, Harlequin Superromance, or Harlequin Duets.

Query letters and SASEs should be directed to:

Amy Moore-Benson, Editor—MIRA Books

Birgit Davis Todd, Senior Editor—Harlequin Temptation

Brenda Chin, Editor—Harlequin Temptation, Duets

Dianne Moggy, Editorial Director— MIRA Books

Laura Shin, Editor—Harlequin Superromance

Bev Sotelov, Editor—Harlequin Superromance

Paula Eykelhof, Senior Editor—Harlequin Superromance

Susan Sheppard, Editor—Harlequin Temptation, Duets

Zilla Soriano, Editor—Harlequin Superromance

Martha Keenan, Associate Editor—MIRA Books

Valerie Gray, Editor—MIRA Books

MILLS & BOON/HARLEQUIN ENTERPRISES LTD.

HARLEQUIN PRESENTS

HARLEQUIN ROMANCE

Eton House, 18-24 Paradise Road, Richmond, Surrey TW9 1SR, United Kingdom

Acquisitions for Harlequin Romance and Harlequin Presents are through the United Kingdom offices. Query the offices to request a set of editorial guidelines supplied to prospective authors.

Harlequin Romance is the original line of romance fiction, the series that started it all—more than 35 years ago. These are warm, contemporary novels, filled with compassion and sensitivity, written by world-famous authors.

Harlequin Presents is overall the bestselling Harlequin line, published in 16 different languages and sold in almost every country of the world. This line features heartwarming romance novels about bright, capable women who are taking charge of their own lives, set in exotic locales.

To query the U.K. divisions, write (and enclose SASE) in care of the Editorial Department (especially to request guidelines), or direct inquiries to the following individual editors:

Lesley Stonehouse, Senior Editor—Silhouette

Karin Stoecker, Editorial Director—All Mills & Boon series

Linda Fildew, Senior Editor—Historical Romance and MIRA

Samantha Bell, Senior Editor—Mills and Boons Enchanted and Harlequin Romance

Sheila Hodgson, Senior Editor—Medical

Tessa Shapcott, Senior Editor—Harlequin Presents (contemporary romances)

WORLDWIDE LIBRARY

WORLDWIDE MYSTERY

GOLD EAGLE BOOKS

The Worldwide Library division of Harlequin Enterprises hosts two major imprints, Worldwide Mystery and Gold Eagle Books. Worldwide Library emphasizes genre fiction in the categories of mystery and suspense, action-adventure, futuristic fiction, war drama, and post-holocaust thrillers. The house gives its titles (primarily mass-market paperbacks) solid marketing and promotional support.

The Worldwide Mystery imprint specializes in mainstream commercial mystery and detective fiction in reprint. This imprint has not been issuing previously unpublished, original fiction; however, Worldwide is not to be overlooked as a resource regarding potential reprint-rights sales in this field. The house generally keeps lines of popular writers' ongoing series in print for a number of seasons, sometimes indefinitely.

Titles in reprint at Worldwide: *Zero at the Bone* by Mary Willis Walker; *Time of Hope* by Susan B. Kelly; *The Hour of the Knife* by Sharon Zukowski; *Murder Takes Two* by Bernie Lee; *Hard Luck* by Barbara D'Amato; *A Fine Italian Hand* by Eric Wright.

Gold Eagle Books is known for a fast-and-furious slate of men's action and adventure series with paramilitary and future-world themes. Series include Deathlands, the Destroyer, the Executioner, and Stony Man. Gold Eagle also publishes Super Books keyed to the various series—longer novels with more fully developed plots. Prospective authors should be familiar with the guidelines and regular characters associated with each series.

Query letters and SASEs should be directed to:

Feroze Mohammed, Senior Editor and Editorial Coordinator—Gold Eagle Books

Heather Locker, Associate Editor

HOUSE OF ANANSI PRESS

110 Spadina Ave., 801, Toronto, ON M5V 2K4, Canada

416-363-4343   fax: 416-363-1017

www.anansi.ca

House of Anansi Press is a literary press, founded in 1967 by Dennis Lee and David Godfrey, with a mandate to publish innovative literary works in fiction, nonfiction, and poetry by Canadian writers. Anansi acquired a reputation early on for its editors' ability to spot talented writers who push the boundaries and challenge the expectations of the literary community. This continues to be a part of the press's mandate, while it also maintains its rich backlist and keeps important works by Canadian writers in print.

Anansi has published works by such Canadian authors as Northrop Frye, Margaret Atwood, Michael Ondaatje, and Dennis Lee. The house emphasizes literary fiction, trade nonfiction, poetry, politics, philosophy, social thought, literary criticism, theory, autobiography, biography, and women's studies. Anansi also publishes *Alphabet City*, an annual journal of cultural theory, literature, philosophy, and architecture.

Representative of the list: *Open* by Lisa Moore; *Hypothesis* by John Barton; *Finding Peace* by Jean Vanier; *Science and Society* by Martin Moskovits; *Ireland's Ire* by Mark Anthony Jarman; *Ground Works* by Christian Bok; *Appropriate Place* by Lise Bissonnette; *Fine Passage* by France Daigle; *Beyond Fate* by Margaret Visser; *UN* by Dennis Lee; *No Pain Like This Body* by Harold Sonny Ladoo; *Five Legs* by Graeme Gibson; *Crowd of Sounds* by Adam Sol; *The Real World of Technology* by Ursula M. Franklin; *Becoming Human* by Jean Vanier; *Mean* by Ken Babstock; *The Plight of Happy People in an Ordinary World* by Natalee Caple; *Ruin and Beauty* by Patricia Young.

Do not send electronic submissions. Direct query letters and SASEs to:

Martha Sharpe, Publisher

Andrew Heintzman

Gordon Johnston

Janice Kulyk Keefer

Esta Spalding

INSOMNIAC PRESS

192 Spadina Avenue, Suite 403, Toronto, ON M5T 2C2, Canada

416-504-6270   fax: 416-504-9313

www.insomniacpress.com

Insomniac Press publishes a small, eclectic list of books, most of which have an experimental bent. Though focused primarily on literary fiction, Insomniac also produces select nonfiction and popular trade titles. The Press celebrated its 10th anniversary in 2002.

Poetry and graphic novels round out the catalog of this unique press. Nonfiction areas of interest include: architecture, social commentary, political science, business, personal finance, travel and food, black studies, and pop culture. Insomniac also publishes literature of gay and lesbian interest and is celebrated for its high-caliber spoken word anthologies.

Works representative of the nonfiction list: *If I Knew, Don't You Think I'd Tell You?* by Jann Arden; *The Patron Saint of Business Management* by Anna Farago; *Harmattan* by Marcello Di Cintio; *Method of Madness* by Brad Kelln; *Black Coffee Night* by Emily Schult; *Tell Him You're Married* by Stan Rogal; *Reforming the Prophet* by W. R. Clement; *Breaking Out* by Kevin Alderson; *Scouts Are Cancelled* by John Stiles; *Side/Lines: A New Canadian Poetics* by Rob McLennan.

Insomniac does not accept unsolicited manuscripts; send queries and SASEs to:

Mike O'Connor, Publisher

Richard Amonte, Marketing Coordinator, Editor

Adrienne Weiss, Marketing Coordinator, Editor

KEY PORTER BOOKS LTD.

70 The Esplanade, Toronto, ON M5E 1R2, Canada

416-862-7777   fax: 416-862-2304

www.keyporter.com

Key Porter Books Ltd. (founded in 1981) is a midsize house that publishes a primarily nonfiction list with a Canadian twist. Key Porter produces titles in current affairs, science and health, travel, the environment, ecology, politics, sports, and a solid line of money books and entrepreneurial guides. In addition, the house offers coffee-table and gift editions, as well as occasional fiction and literary works.

Frontlist Key Porter titles are provided full promotional support that spotlights targeted review venues, national media exposure, magazine advertising (including co-op arrangements), and foreign-rights sales. The house maintains a strong backlist.

Among Key Porter highlights: *The 3 AM Handbook* by William Feldman, MD, FRCPC; *The Ability to Forget* by Norman Levine; *Anne Lindsay's Lighthearted Cookbook* by Anne Lindsay; *The Atlas of Dinosaurs* by "Dino" Don Lessem; *The Autobiography of Willie O'Ree* by Willie O'Ree; *Body Harmony* by Terry Willard; *Clueless in the Garden* by Yvonne Cunnington; *The Complete Guide to Home Water & Moisture Problems* by Gary Branson; *The Complete Guide to Natural Healthcare for Children* by Karen Sullivan; *Duet for Three* by Joan Barfoot; *The Encyclopedia of Owls* by James R. Duncan, Ph.D; *Walking on Land* by Farley Mowat; *Can Asians Think?* by Kishore Mahbubani; *The Hiding Place* by Trezza Azzopardip; *The Dog Rules* by William Thomas; *When Eve Was Naked* by Josef Skvorecky; *The Truth About Love* by Patrick Roscoe; *The Jasmine Man* by Lola Lemire Tostevin; *Always Give a Penny to a Blind Man* by Eric Wright; *Odjig: The Art of Daphne Odjig 1966–2000* by Daphne Odjig with Carol Podedworny; *Civilians* by Felipe Fernandez-Armstrong.

Key Porter handles its own distribution. Send queries and SASEs to:

Clare McKeon, Vice-President, Editor-in-Chief

LOBSTER PRESS LTD.

1620 Sherbrooke St. West, Suites C & D, Montreal, QC H3H 1C9, Canada

514-904-1100   fax: 514-904-1101

www.lobsterpress.com

Lobster Press Ltd. is a publisher of high-quality books for children based in Montreal. Their books are distributed by the University of Toronto Press in Canada and PGW in the U.S. Publishing both fiction and nonfiction books for children and their parents, Lobster Press also publishes a best-selling series of family guidebooks available in bookstores across Canada. Some of the travel guides include: *The Lobster Kids' Guide to Exploring Halifax*; *The Lobster Kids' Guide to Exploring New Orleans*; *The Lobster Kids' Guide to Exploring San Diego*.

The fiction list at Lobster includes picture books and other light-hearted series for children. Their most visible of these series of titles is the Abbey & Tess Pet Sitters Club. Other fiction titles include: The Max-a-Million series; The Step Chain series; The Generation Norah series. Picture books include: *Rainy Day with Bear*; *My Great-great-great-great-great-grandfather Was a Warrior!*

The nonfiction list challenges readers to appreciate the history of Canada and also challenges kids to think for themselves. Titles include: *Our Song: The Story of O Canada, The Canadian National Anthem*; *Think for Yourself*; *Make Things Happen*; *7 Secrets of Highly Successful Kids*.

MCGILL-QUEEN'S UNIVERSITY PRESS

Montreal office:

McGill University, 3430 McTavish Street, Montreal, QC H3A 1X9, Canada

514-398-3750   fax: 514-398-4333

e-mail: mqup@mqup.ca

Kingston office:

Queen's University, Kingston, ON K7L 3N6, Canada

fax: 613-533-6822

www.mqup.mcgill.ca   e-mail: mqup@post.queensu.ca

Publications from McGill-Queen's University Press include works on architecture, biography, British studies, business history, Canadian history, Canadian politics, economics, environment, French history, housing policy, international history, Irish history, Judaica, literature and literary criticism, Loyalist history, native studies, philosophy, political economy, psychology, Quebec history, sociology, urban geography, women's studies, poetry, and general-interest works, primarily in areas of current interest in international and cultural affairs. McGill-Queen's publishes no hard sciences.

McGill-Queen's University Press (founded in 1969) produces trade books with scholarly market crossover, as well as titles geared specifically for the academic market. The press is a conjoint publishing endeavor of Queen's University (Kingston) and McGill University (Montreal). Many of McGill-Queen's books have a Canadian subject slant; in addition, the house is strong in a variety of fields in the international arena,

CANADIAN PUBLISHERS

as well as in the social sciences and humanities. McGill-Queen's publishes in the English language and occasionally in French.

On the McGill-Queen's list: *Blood Ground* by Elizabeth Elbourne; *Village Politics and the Mafia in Sicily* by Filippo Sabetti; *The Irish War of Independence* by Michael Hopkinson; *Determining Boundaries in a Conflicted World* by Suzanne N. Lalonde; *Steps on the Road to Medicare* by C. Stuart Houston; *Lieutenant Owen William Steele of the Newfoundland Regiment* edited by David R. Facey-Crowther; *The University* edited by F. King Alexander and Kern Alexander; *Silent Surrender* by Kari Levitt; *Enemy Aliens, Prisoners of War* by Bohdan S. Kordan; *Arctic Justice* by Shelagh D. Grant; *Apocalypse Soon?* by Stephen F. Haller; *Marguerite Bourgeoys and Montreal 1640–1665* by Patricia Simpson; *Canada Enters the Nuclear Age: A Technical History of Atomic Energy of Canada Limited as Seen from Its Research Laboratories* by E. Critoph, et al.; *Degrees of Freedom: Canada and the United States in a Changing World* (edited by Keith Banting, George Hoberg, and Richard Simeon); *The Secession of Quebec and the Future of Canada* by Robert A. Young; *A Long Way from Home: The Tuberculosis Epidemic Among the Inuit* by Pat Sandiford Grygier; *The Virtual Marshall McLuhan* by Donald F. Theall; *Stranger Gods: Salman Rushdie's Other Worlds* by Roger Y. Clark; *The Distant Relation: Time and Identity in Spanish American Fiction* by Eoin S. Thomson.

The McGill-Queen's literary purview embraces criticism, memoir, biography, and letters. *Lying About the Wolf: Essays in Culture and Education* by David Solway; *Aesthetics* by Colin Lyas; *African Exploits: The Diaries of William Stairs 1887–1892* (edited by Roy MacLaren); *The Cassock and the Crown: Canada's Most Controversial Murder Trial* by Jean Monet; *Cold Comfort: My Love Affair with the Arctic* by Graham W. Rowley; *Mapping Our Selves: Canadian Women's Autobiography* by Helen M. Buss; *The Birth of Modernism: Ezra Pound, T. S. Eliot, W. B. Yeats, and the Occult* by Leon Surette.

Distribution for McGill-Queen's University Press is handled by General Distribution Services in Canada and by Cornell University Press Services (CUPS) in the United States.

Query letters and SASEs should be directed to:

Donald H. Akenson, Senior Editor (Kingston)

Joan Harcourt, Editor (Kingston)

Roger Martin, Editor (Kingston)

Kyle Madden, Editor (Kingston)

Philip J. Cercone, Executive Director of Press and Senior Editor (Montreal)

Aurele Parisien, Editor (Montreal)

John Zucchi, Editor (Montreal)

Joan McGilvray, Coordinating Editor (Montreal)

Joanne Pisano, Editorial Assistant (Montreal)

Brenda Prince, Editorial Assistant (Montreal)

MCGRAW-HILL RYERSON LIMITED

300 Water Street, Whitby, ON L1N 9B6, Canada

905-430-5116

www.mcgrawhill.ca

McGraw-Hill Ryerson Limited prides itself on being one of the "liveliest Canadian publishers." Though founded on its educational division, McGraw-Hill Ryerson also has a thriving trade arm. This division publishes general interest books by, about, and for Canadians.

Notable from the McGraw-Hill list: *More Than a Pink Cadillac* by Jim Underwood; *How to Make Money In Stocks: A Winning System in Good Times or Bad* by William O'Neil; *Windows XP for Professionals: A Beginner's Guide* by Martin Matthews; *Hacking Exposed: Network Security Secrets and Solutions, Fourth Edition* by Stuart McClure; *HVAC Instant Answers* by Peter Curtiss; *Project Management* by William Pinkerton; *DVD Confidential: Hundreds of Hidden Easter Eggs Revealed* by Mark Saltzman; *The Complete Fat Flush Program* by Ann Gittleman; *Current Diagnosis & Treatment in Gastroenterology* by Scott Friedman; *Harrison's Manual of Medicine, 15/e for PDA* by Eugene Braunwald; *Canadian Consumer Alert: 101 Ways to Protect Yourself and Your Money* by Pat Foran; *On Course with Mike Weir* by Mike Weir; *Make Sure It's Deductible* by Evelyn Jacks.

McGraw-Hill Ryerson concentrates on personal finance, management, and small business books.

Query letters and SASEs should be directed to:

Lynda Walthert, Assistant to the Publisher

NC PRESS LIMITED

345 Adelaide Street West, Toronto, ON M5V 1R5, Canada

416-593-6284

NC Press publishes a broad range of topics covering the spectrum of general trade interest in areas such as cooking, health, Canadian history, politics, poetry, art and performance, literature and literary criticism, folkways and lifeways, the natural world, self-help, and popular psychology.

NC Press Limited (incorporated in 1970) is a trade publisher of Canadian books dedicated to the social, political, economic, and spiritual health of the human community. This is a small press—currently publishing a frontlist of 6 to 10 new books each year—with an expansive vision: "To make a difference." NC Press thus strives to present complex ideas in ways accessible to a wide readership. Among NC Press books are numerous literary-award winners. The press has served as an agent for non-Canadian publishers and catalogs a substantial backlist.

In 1988 Gary Perly, president of Perly's Maps, purchased a majority interest in NC Press Limited; the house now produces the Perly's map and atlas series, which offers a strong line of urban atlases and street guides to such environs as Toronto, Montreal, and Quebec City.

NC Press nonfiction: *Ninety-Nine Days: The Ford Strike in Windsor in 1945* by Herb Colling; *Living and Learning with a Child Who Stutters: From a Parent's Point of View* by Lise G. Cloutier-Steele; *Eating Bitterness: A Vision Beyond Prison Walls* by Arthur Solomon; *A Woman in My Position: The Politics of Breast Implant Safety* by Linda Wilson, with Dianne Brown.

Literary works and works of cultural note: *Voices from the Odeyak* by Michael Posluns; *Folktales of French Canada* by Edith Fowke; *One Animal Among Many: Gaia Goats and Garlic* by David Walter-Toews; *Images: Thirty Stories by Favorite Writers* (compiled and with paintings by Len Gibbs).

NC Press books are distributed via the publisher's network, which involves independent sales representatives worldwide and the fulfillment services of University of Toronto Press.

Query letters and SASEs should be directed to:

Caroline Walker, President and Publisher

ORCA BOOK PUBLISHERS

PO Box 5626, Station B, Victoria, BC V8R 6S4, Canada

250-380-1229   fax: 250-380-1892

www.orcabook.com   e-mail: orca@orcabook.com

Orca publishes an eclectic mix of children's picture books, chapter books, and juvenile and young adult fiction. At the present, Orca only considers manuscripts by Canadian authors.

Pick of the Orca list: *Jo's Triumph* by Nikki Tate; *Birdie for Now* by Jean Little; *TJ and the Cats* by Hazel Hutchinn; *Before Wings* by Beth Goobie; *Ballerinas Don't Wear Glasses* by Ainslie Manson; *In the Clear* by Anne Carter; *Red Moon Follows Truck* by Stephen Eaton Hume; *Daughter of Light* by Martha Attema.

Orca is accepting picture book manuscripts in the following areas: stories derived from the author's own childhood experiences, carefully researched historical tales, and modern stories situated within Canada, but with universal appeal. Manuscripts should be limited to 1,500 words in length.

In the juvenile and young adult fiction genres, Orca seeks manuscripts that meet the following criteria: regional stories, challenging language and themes, stories based on historical subjects, or contemporary stories that are issue-oriented. These manuscripts should be between 20,000 and 45,000 words in length. Chapter books should be between 8,000 and 15,000 words in length.

For picture books, submit a manuscript without artwork unless you are a trained artist; do not send any originals. For juvenile or young adult projects, send a query first, along with a synopsis and the first few chapters. All submissions should include an SASE. Do not query by e-mail or fax.

These and other guidelines can be found on the Orca Web site.

Query letters and SASEs should be directed to:

Maggie de Vries, Children's Book Editor—Picture books, chapter books, juvenile fiction

Bob Tyrrell, Publisher—Teen fiction

PENGUIN BOOKS CANADA LIMITED

10 Alcorn Avenue, Suite 300, Toronto, ON M4V 3B2, Canada

416-925-2249

www.penguin.ca

Penguin Books Canada Limited operates independently of its American affiliate Penguin/Putnam USA. Founded in 1974, Penguin Canada's mandate is to publish Canadian authors; the house does so with fine style, covering a mother lode of original trade nonfiction, as well as a golden seam of mainstream and category fiction and literary works.

Penguin Canada purveys, via its catalog and distribution network, featured titles from the parent company's various international divisions, including Penguin USA, Viking Australia, and Viking UK. The house also distributes for W. W. Norton and Faber and Faber UK. Viking Canada and Puffin Canada are the house's juvenile imprints.

From the Penguin Canada list: *The Art of Living Well* by Rose Reisman; *Pattern Recognition* by William Gibson; *Journals* by Kurt Cobain; *Hateship, Friendship, Courtship, Loveship, Marriage* by Alice Munro; *Birds* by Robert Bateman; *Gynecological Health* by Dr. M. Sara Rosenthal; *Saint Maybe* by Anne Tyler; *The Young Wan* by Brendan O'Carroll; *Danny Boy* by Malachy McCourt; *Almost There* by Nuala O'Faolain; *Kit's Law* by Donna Morrissey; *The Girl in the Picture* by Denise Chong; *Titans* by Peter C. Newman; *Paper Shadows* by Wayson Choy; *Parenting with Wit & Wisdom* by Barbara Coloroso; *Notes from the Hyena's Belly* by Nega Mezlekia; *Dagmar's Daughter* by Kim Echlin; *Cold Is the Grave* by Peter Robinson; *The Saratine Mosaic* by Guy Gavriel Kay; *Home from the Vinyl Café* by Stuart McLean.

Penguin Books Canada's titles are distributed by Canbook Distribution. Query letters and SASEs should be directed to:

Barbara Berson, Children's Books and Fiction Editor

Cynthia Good, Publisher/President

Diane Turbide, Editorial Director

Michael Schellenberg, Editor—Genre fiction, general nonfiction

---

PLAYWRIGHTS CANADA PRESS

215 Spadina Avenue, suite 230, Toronto, ON M5T 2C7, Canada

416-703-0013   fax: 416-408-3402

www.playwrightscanada.com   e-mail: angela@puc.ca

Playwrights Canada Press is an award-winning drama publisher. The press publishes 12 to 15 titles annually, specializing in Canadian plays and selected drama theory and history.

Playwrights Canada Press accepts submissions to its editorial committee all year round. Plays submitted must have had at least one professional production in the past 10 years. Include first production information, including cast and crew, with the manuscript.

Recent titles include: *Alien Creature* by Linda Griffiths; *Angelique* by Lorena Gale; *Belle* by Florence Gibson; *Cake-Walk* by Colleen Curran; *Colours in the Storm* by Jim Betts; *The Drawer Boy* by Michael Healey; *Easy Lenny Lazmon and the Great Ascension* by Anton Piatigorsky; *Illegal Entry* by Clem Martini; *Inuk* by Henry Beissel; *It's All True* by Jason Sherman; *Perfect Pie* by Judith Thompson; *Questionable Activities: The Best* edited by Judith Rudakoff; *Strangers Among Us* by Aaron Bushkowsky; *Whylah Falls* by George Elliott Clarke; *The Drawer Boy* by Michael Healey; *The Duchess* by Wallace Simpson.

U.S. Distributor: Theatre Communications Group.

Query letters and SASEs should be directed to:

Angela Reberio, Publisher

Betony Main, Editor

POLESTAR BOOKS

Polestar Books has been purchased by Raincoast Books.

THE PORCUPINE'S QUILL

68 Main Street, Erin, ON N0B 1T0, Canada

519-833-9158   fax: 519-833-9845

www.sentex.net/~pql/

The Porcupine's Quill is a leading Canadian small press producing a handpicked list of literary works (short story collections, novels, juvenile fiction, and poetry) by both emerging and veteran writers. The press is proud to have produced several books that have been shortlisted for awards, including the prestigious Governor General's Award. The Porcupine's Quill also produces a selection of trade and critical works, as well as a handful of books on the visual arts.

The Porcupine's Quill roster includes: *The Deep* by Mary Swan; *The Stand-In* by David Helwig; *Planet Earth* by P.K. Page; *The Understanding* by Jane Barker Wright; *A Tourist's Guide to Glengarry* by Ian McGillis; *The Syllabus* by Mike Barnes; *Uncomfortably Numb* by Sharon English; *Girls and Handsome Dogs* by Norm Sibum; *13* by Mary-Lou Zeitoun; *The Fragments* by Stavros Tsimicalis; *When Words Deny the World* by Stephen Henighan; *Back Flip* by Anne Denoon; *Seasoning Fever* by Susan Kerslake; *A Kind of Fiction* by P. K. Page; *An Artist's Garden* by G. Brender à Brandis; *Done Legend* by Richard Outram; *Southern Stories* by Clark Blaise.

Now a popular destination for submissions, the Porcupine's Quill is swamped with manuscripts; as such, it does not accept unsolicited work. Instead, the Porcupine's Quill often seeks out writers whose work has appeared in literary magazines such as *The New Quarterly*. All submissions should include an SASE, short biography, and bibliography. They should be directed to:

John Metcalf, Senior Editor

Tim Inkster, Publisher

RAINCOAST BOOKS

9050 Shaughnessy Street, Vancouver, BC V6P 6E5, Canada

604-323-7100   fax: 604-323-2600

www.raincoast.com   e-mail: info@raincoast.com

Raincoast Books publishes intelligent, topical, and beautifully designed books of a regional, national, and international nature in the areas of food, travel, creative nonfiction, picture books, arts and photography, pop culture, biography, and the outdoors.

Raincoast also has launched a new national fiction imprint publishing Canadian novels, short fiction, and young adult books.

Raincoast has recently acquired Polestar Books, which will remain an imprint and continue to publish literary fiction, poetry, feminist works, and sports titles.

Sample titles: *Mount Appetite* by Bill Gaston; *Stay* by Aislinn Hunter; *Baudolino* by Umberto Eco; *Tiger Dreams* by Almeda Glenn Miller; *The Cameraman* by Bill Gaston; *Please* by Peter Darbyshire; *The Moon in the Pines* translated by Jonathan Clements; *Shaken by Physics* by John MacKenzie; *Drawn & Quarterly* by Drawn & Quarterly; *Hamilton Sketchbook* by David Collier; *Commuter Waiting Games* by Hal Bowman; *Shunju* by Takashi Sugimoto and Marcia Iwatate; *Tilting, Newfoundland* by Robert Mellin; *A Good House Is Never Done* by John Wheatman; *Studies in Design* by Christopher Dresser; *Hawaii* by Conner Gorry and Julie Jones; *(Un)London* edited by Clare Cumberlidge; *Escape From Fire Island* by Jim English; *Night of a Thousand Boyfriends* by Miranda Clarke; *The Physics of Hockey* by Alain Hache; *Maple Leaf Legends* by Mike Leonetti; *Crossing Over* by John Edward.

Other titles: *Harry Potter I–III* by J. K. Rowling; *Fire into Ice* by Verne Frolick; *The Mermaid's Muse* by Dave Bouchard; *Shocking Beauty* by Thomas Hobbs; *Zest for Life* by Diane Clement; *The Sensualist* by Barbara Hodgson.

Queries and SASEs should be directed to:

Lynn Henry, Executive Editor

Joy Gugeler, Editorial Director—Fiction

Michelle Benjamin, Associate Publisher

RANDOM HOUSE CANADA

One Toronto Street, Suite 300, Toronto, ON M5C 2V6, Canada

416-364-4449   fax: 416-364-6863

www.randomhouse.ca

A division of Random House of Canada Limited, Random House Canada produces a select list of trade fiction and nonfiction. Publications include Canadian and international titles, with a major concentration on books that appeal to the Canadian market.

Nonfiction areas include popular topical interest and current events, cooking, lifestyle and the arts, history and politics, biography and memoir, travel narrative, popular science, and business and economics. Nonfiction titles include *The Water in Between* by Kevin Patterson; *Bones* by Elaine Dewar; *The Lion, the Fox, and the Eagle* by Carol Off; *Hot Sour Salty Sweet* by Jeffrey Alford and Naomi Duguid; *The Nature of Economies* by Jane Jacobs; *Anti Diva* by Carole Pope.

Other titles include: *Life of Pi* by Yann Martel; *Our Father Who Art in a Tree* by Judy Pascoe; *The Skating Pond* by Deborah Joy Corey; *Madame Proust and the Kosher Kitchen* by Kate Taylor; *Mercy* by Alissa York; *Rush Home Road* by Lori Lansens; *Death's Jest-Book* by Reginald Hill; *The Perpetual Ending* by Kristen den Hartog; *The Treatment* by Mo Hayder; *The Blue Roan Child* by Jamieson Findlay; *Adam and Eve Pinch Me* by Ruth Rendell; *Saints of Big Harbour* by Lynn Coady; *White Lily* by Xing-Ting Ye; *A Rhinestone Button* by Gail Anderson-Dargatz; *Smart Couples Finish Rich* by David Bach; *The Joy of Writing* by Pierre Berton; *A Time to Die* by Robert Moore; *On the Natural History of Destruction* by W. G. Sebald; *AWOL* edited by Jennifer Barclay and Amy Logan; *Rory & Ita* by Roddy Doyle; *The Procrastinating Child* by Rita Emmett; *Forever Summer* by Nigella Lawson; *Home of Dinner* by Lucy Waverman; *Maud's House of Dreams* by Janet Lunn; *The Snow Geese* by William Fiennes.

The Random House Canada fiction program is known for its mix of established literary titans and exciting new talent. The list includes Canadian authors such as Douglas Coupland, Katherine Govier, Paul Quarrington, John MacLachlan Gray, Elyse Friedman, Billie Livingston, and Pulitzer Prize winner Carol Shields. Internationally, Random House Canada publishes authors who include Julian Barnes, Peter Carey, Eleanor Bailey, Barry Lopez, and Booker Prize winners Graham Swift and Arundhati Roy.

Query letters and SASEs should be directed to:

Anne Collins, Vice President and Publisher

SOMERVILLE HOUSE BOOKS LIMITED

24 Dinnick Crescent, Toronto, ON M4N 1L5, Canada

416-489-7769

e-mail: sombooks@goodmedia.com and somer@sympatico.ca

Somerville House specializes in interactive books and kits for young readers. In 1997, Somerville House announced a joint-venture partnership with Penguin Putnam Inc. In 1999, Somerville House became the official youth publisher of the NHL. These new efforts continue to produce the same kind of fun and educational children's titles typical of the Somerville list.

Titles: *The Holographic Night Sky Book & Kit* by Kenneth Hewitt-White; *The Titanic Book and Submersible Model* by Susan Hughes and Steve Santini; *A Century of Hockey Heroes* by James Duplacey and Eric Zweig; *Chess for Kids* by Kevin F. R. Smith and Daniel C. Macdonald; *The Bones Book & Skeleton* by Stephen Cumbaa.

Children's nonfiction submissions are welcome. Please include an SASE. Due to the volume of submissions, Somerville House discards materials after three months if insufficient postage is enclosed. Direct all queries to:

Harry Endrulat, Manager, Editorial and Product Development

UNIVERSITY OF BRITISH COLUMBIA PRESS

2029 West Mall, Vancouver, BC V6T 1Z2, Canada

604-822-5959   fax: 604-822-6083

www.ubcpress.ubc.ca   e-mail: info@ubcpress.ubc.ca

Categories of UBC Press interest include Canadian culture and history, political science, Asian studies, Native studies with emphasis on the Northwest Coast, gender studies, Pacific Rim studies, global geography, fisheries and forestry, environmental studies, Northern studies, and Canadian sociology.

UBC Press (founded in 1971) publishes academic books, as well as general-interest works, with an emphasis on Canadian subjects.

On the UBC Press list: *Birds of the Yukon Territory* edited by Pamela H. Sinclair, Wendy A. Nixon, Cameron D. Eckert and Nancy L. Hughes; *Stepping Stones to Nowhere* by Galen Roger Perras; *At Home with Bella Coola Indians* edited by John Barker and Douglas Cole; *Not the Slightest Chance* by Tony Banhaml; *Growth and Governance of Canadian Universities* by Howard C. Clark; *Japan at the Millennium* by David Edgington; *Pilgrims, Patrons, and Place* edited by Phyllis Granoff and Koichi Shinohara; *A War of Patrols* by William Johnston; *The Integrity Gap* edited Eugene Lee and Anthony Perl; *In the Long Run We're All Dead* by Timothy Lewis; *Taking Stands* by Maureen G. Reed; *New Perspectives on the Public-Private Divide* by Law Commission of Canada; *The Vancouver Achievement* by John Punter.

UBC Press distribution is handled by Raincoast Books (e-mail: custserv@raincoast.com).

Query letters and SASEs should be directed to:

Jean Wilson, Associate Director, Editorial

Emily Andrew, Acquisitions Editor

Randy Schmidt, Acquisitions

UNIVERSITY OF TORONTO PRESS

10 Saint Mary Street, Suite 700, Toronto, ON M4Y 2W8, Canada

416-978-2239   fax: 416-978-4738

University of Toronto Press publishes in a range of fields, including history and politics; women's studies; health, family, and society; law and crime; economics; workplace communication; theory/culture; language, literature, semiotics, and drama; medieval studies; Renaissance studies; Erasmus; Italian-language studies; East European studies; classics; and nature. The list includes topical titles in Canadian studies, native studies, sociology, anthropology, urban studies, modern languages, and music, as well as travel and touring guides.

University of Toronto Press produces titles for the general trade, as well as academic works. UTP issues a series of specialist journals of note, including *Scholarly Publishing*. The house produces no original contemporary fiction or poetry.

Representing the University of Toronto list: *Fields of Fire* by Terry Copp; *Caring for Lesbian and Gay People* by Allan D. Perkins and Cathy Risdon; *Hunting the 1918 Flu* by Kirsty E. Duncan; *Sceneography in Canada* by Natalie Rewa; *Judging Bertha Wilson* by Ellen Anderson; *Renegade Lawyer* by Laurel Sefton; *Guardian of the Gulf* by Brian Tennyson; *The Politics of Population* by Bruce Curtis; *Before Malory* by Richard J. Moll; *Pride and Prodigies* by Andy Orchard; *John Selden* by Reid Barbour; *The Butterflies of Canada* by Ross A. Layberry, Peter W. Hall, and J. Donald Lafontaine (with specimen plates by John T. Fowler); *Working for Wildlife: The Beginning of Preservation in Canada* by Janet Foster; *The Illuminated Page: Ten Centuries of Manuscript Painting in the British Library* by Janet Backhouse; *Conduct Unbecoming: The Story of the Murder of Canadian Prisoners of War in Normandy* by Howard Margolian; *The Socially Concerned Today* by John Kenneth Galbraith; *Kaiser and Führer: A Comparative Study of Personality and Politics* by Robert G. L. Waite; *Werewolf! The History of the National Socialist Guerrilla Movement 1944–1946* by Perry Biddiscombe; *The Science of War: Canadian Scientists and Allied Military Technology During the Second World War* by Donald H. Avery.

University of Toronto Press oversees a distributional network encompassing offices and sales agents worldwide; it handles titles from other book publishers, as well as for institutions such as Royal Ontario Museum and Canadian Museum of Nature.

Query letters and SASEs should be directed to:

Gerald Hallowell, Editor—Canadian history and Canadian literature

Joan Bulger, Editor—Art and classics, architecture

Kieran Simpson, Editor—Department of Directories

Ron Schoeffel, Senior House Editor—Romance languages, native languages, religion and theology, education, philosophy

Suzanne Rancourt, Editor—Medieval studies, medieval and Old English literature

Virgil Duff, Executive Editor—Social sciences, scholarly medical books, law and criminology, women's studies

Jill McConkey, Editor

Siobhan McMenemy, Editor—Cultural Studies

Len Husband, Editor—Canadian History

Lauren Freeman, Assistant Editor—Social Sciences

WHITECAP BOOKS

351 Lynn Avenue, North Vancouver, BC V7J 2C4, Canada

604-980-9852 fax: 604-980-8197

www.whitecap.ca

Whitecap Books, established in 1977, was created with one thing in mind: "survival." As such, Whitecap Books is a commercial press, with a strong marketing program to showcase its publications.

Whitecap produces trade nonfiction, with a strong focus on cookbooks by chefs, gardening, large-format photography, and books on local interest subjects. Whitecap also maintains a children's list of nonfiction and fiction.

Representative titles include: *The Lazy Gourmet* by Susan Mendelson; *The Blooming Great Gardening Book* by Steve Whysall; *Secret Coastline* by Andrew Scott; *Hiking Ontario's Heartland* by Shirley Teasdale.

Books from the children's list: *Whose House Is This?* by Wayne Lynch; *Gilbert de la Frogponde* by Jennifer Rae (illustrated by Rose Cowles).

Query letters and SASEs should be directed to:

Leanne McDonald, Foreign Rights and Acquisitions Associate

Marial Shea, Editorial Director

SECTION SIX

LITERARY AGENTS

WHAT MAKES THIS AGENT DIRECTORY SPECIAL?

AGENTS AND THEIR INTERESTS, EXPERIENCE, & PERSONALITIES

JEFF HERMAN

No other listing of literary agents comes anywhere close to this one. We don't just tell you who the agents are and where to find them; we get the agents to actually talk to you and reveal a slice of their personalities as well. These surveys also reveal what agents want to (and don't want to) represent, when and where they were born and educated, their career history, and their agenting track record. Memorize some of these tidbits and you can be something of a gossip.

About 200 exceptionally well-qualified agents are included in this listing. Each year I invite the 200-plus members of the Association of Author Representatives, as well as many excellent nonmember agents, to be in the book.

As you might expect, many of the most successful agents are not overly hungry for unsolicited new submissions, and some of them therefore do not wish to participate. We listed no agents against their wishes, and we allowed all agent contributors to be as terse or expansive as they pleased.

I made the best effort to include only legitimate agencies. Please let me know about any negative experiences you encounter, though I hope there won't be any.

AEI ATCHITY ENTERTAINMENT INTERNATIONAL, INC.

no

9601 Wilshire Boulevard, Box 1202, Beverly Hills, CA 90210

323-932-0407   fax: 323-932-0321

www.AEIonline.com   e-mail: submissions@aeionline.com

Agents: Ken Atchity, AEI Partner/CEO; Chi-Li Wong, AEI Partner/COO; Brenna Lui, VP Development: Jennifer Pope; Margaret O' Connor (Books), Michael Kuciak (Scripts).

Born: Atchity: Eunice, Louisiana.

Education: Atchity: B.A., Georgetown; Ph.D. in Comparative Literature, Yale.

Career history: Atchity: Professor of comparative literature (classics, medieval, Renaissance creative writing), Occidental College (1970–1987); Instructor, UCLA Writer's Program (1970–1987). Author of 13 books, including *How to Escape Lifetime Security to Pursue Your Impossible Dream: A Guide to Transforming Your Career* (Forthcoming, Allworth); *How to Publish Your Novel* (SquareOne Books, 2004); *A Writer's Time: A Guide to the Creative Process, from Vision Through Revision* (Norton); *The Mercury Transition: Career Change through Entrepreneurship* (Longmeadow); and *Writing Treatments That Sell* (with Chi-Li Wong; Owl Books). Producer of 21 films, including *Life or Something Like It* (Angelina Jolie, Ed Burns), *Joe Somebody* (Tim Allen, Jim Belushi, Julie Bowen), *Champagne for Two* (Cinemax-HBO), *Amityville: The Evil Escapes* (NBC) *Shadow of Obsession* (NBC), and *Falling Over Backwards*. Sold Ripley's Believe-It-Or-Not! franchise to Paramount Pictures, AEI to coproduce with Alphaville (producers of *The Mummy*).

Hobbies/personal interests: Atchity: Collecting autographed editions, pitchers; tennis; travel.

Areas most interested in agenting: We are especially interested in (a) celebrity or "branded" books and films that can be series; (b) successfully self-published books that can be taken to the national market; (c) nonfiction with national impact and national platform and business nonfiction with corporate tie-in potential; (d) novels with a fresh contemporary voice and/or film potential; (e) pop culture, music books, and music-related films; and (f) celebrity biographies. Aside from that, we're dying to discover (a) the next Michael Chabon and/or (b) the next Hispanic American, Asian American, or African American novelist. Nonfiction: Entrepreneurial business books by distinguished business leaders; personal achievements by nationally-known names; visionary, heroic, and true stories of every kind, including true crime; general interest and/or narrative nonfiction, especially true stories with TV or film potential; non-religious inspirational; branded self-help; branded reference books. The key is combining a major platform with a major message for the general public. Fiction: Mainstream commercial novels (action, thrillers, suspense, mainstream romance, espionage, outstanding science fiction) that can also be made into TV or feature films; dramatic fiction with fresh, original voice. Screenplays: All motion picture, as well as specific television movie, categories. Especially adaptations of classics to modern times; teen action, comedy, horror; heroic true stories (past or present), especially involving families in crisis; action, thrillers, serious drama for big stars, romantic comedy, science fiction with strong characters, female-driven heroic stories.

Areas not interested in agenting: Drug-related, fundamental religious, category romance, category mystery or Western, poetry, children's, "interior" confessional fiction, novelty books.

If not agenting, what would you be doing? Atchity: If I weren't a literary manager, writer, and producer, I'd be doing the same thing and calling it something else. A story merchant: finding, perfecting, selling and producing stories by serious storytellers determined to become globally known for their art and craft.

Best way to initiate contact: Query letter, including synopsis (with SASE), or brief e-mail stating subject matters to submissions@aeionline.com. Nothing, including scripts, will be returned without an SASE. See info under "Submit" on www.aeionline.com. Please note: All submissions to Jennifer Pope.

Representation by category: Nonfiction, 40%; Fiction, 40%; Screenplays, 20%.

Commission: Books: 15% of all domestic sales, 25-30% foreign. Scripts: 10-15%. If we exercise our manager's option to produce your project for film or television, commission on dramatic rights sale is refunded to you upon our receipt of producer's fees.

Number of titles sold last year: 22.

Rejection rate: 95%.

Most common mistakes authors make with your agency: Asking us to hold their hands instead of focusing on our work to develop and sell their books or scripts. Our aim is to become partners with our clients, raising them to the level of brand-recognition in either film or publishing, or both. For that reason, we remain intensely focused on the selling process until a client is launched.

The most costly and time-consuming mistake is remaining ignorant of where your work fits into the market and of who your reader might be. Sending the kind of work (romances, light mysteries, episodic scripts) we're specifically not looking for.

What can writers do to enhance their chances of getting you as manager? Persist, heighten their self-expectation and ambition, perfect their writing, learn more about the business, commit to marketing your work and, most of all, read commercial novels and see commercial films.

Description of the client from Hell: He or she is so self-impressed it's impossible to provide constructive criticism; makes his package impossible to open, provides return envelope too small to be used, and tells us how to run our business.

Description of a dream client: He or she comes in with an outstanding thriller or high-concept nonfiction book, plus an outline for two more, is delighted to take commercial direction on the writing and the career, markets his or her book relentlessly. The higher the concept the better.

Why did you become a manager? Nearly two decades of teaching comparative literature and creative writing at Occidental College and the UCLA Writers Program, reviewing for the *Los Angeles Times Book Review*, and working with the dreams of creative people through DreamWorks (which I co-founded with Marsha Kinder) provided a natural foundation for this career. I made the transition from academic life through producing, but continued my publishing-consulting business by connecting my authors with agents. As I spent more and more time developing individuals' writing careers, as well as working directly with publishers in my search for film properties, it became obvious that literary management was the next step. True or fiction, what has always turned me on is a good story.

How would you describe what you actually do for a living? We're story merchants. We find stories, help perfect them, and introduce them to the marketplace in New York, Los Angeles, and throughout the world. When the stories are dramatic, we produce them for our storytellers with an eye toward building them eventually as filmmakers themselves so that they can produce and direct their own stories.

What do you think about other agents and managers? I think some of them are wonderful and some of them are awful, and many of them are in between. We work with other managers and agents every day, and often have clients referred to us by them—on both coasts.

What do you think about editors? Same as above, except to note that they're busier today then ever before, and more than ever before focused on marketing and distribution issues—with, as a result, radically less time to work with writers on an editorial or development basis. Work submitted to them must be virtually ready for publication.

What do you think about publishers? They've become strictly business for the most part (when it comes to the majors in New York), focused on bottom lines and, as result, brands. They need us to bring something of "added value" to the table, and we work with our nonfiction and fiction clients to discover what that might be.

What were your favorite films last year? *Mystic River, Intolerable Cruelty, Lost in Translation, The Italian Job, Secretary, The Guru, Chicago, Whalerider, Seabiscuit, Love Actually…*

Do you watch *The Sopranos*? Nope, not anymore.

Comments: My most exciting experience is discovering that I'm reading what could be a bestselling proposal or manuscript. Everything else pales into insignificance compared with this moment of discovery. The only "bad feeling" that equals this high feeling is finding out that the writer has just signed with someone else. When you send a query, don't make a decision without letting us know whether you're submitting exclusively to us (which we prefer and give priority handing to).

Representative titles: Fiction: *Meg* (Walt Disney Pictures, Bantam-Doubleday; Literary Guild Main Selection), *The Trench* (Kensington-Zebra), *Domain, Goliath,* and *Primal Waters* (Tor) by Steve Alten , *The Loch; Sign of the Watcher* by Brett Bartlett (Propaganda Films); *Patent to Kill* and *Buffalo Medicine* by April Christofferson (Forge); *Mama's Baby, Daddy's Maybe* and *Pushing Up Daisies* by Jamise Dames (Atria); *Midnight Carol* by Patricia Davis (St. Martin's Press); *The Tenth Muse* by Nancy Freedman (St.

Martin's Press); *Strange Gifts and River of Summer* by Lois Gilbert (NAL Dutton); *The Cruelest Lie* by Milt Lyles (AEI/Calcasieu Press); *180 Seconds at Willow Park* by Rick Lynch (New Line Pictures; Dove Books); Michael Murray's *InsurrectionRed, BlackLight, ForceGold* (Putnam-Signet); Shirley Palmer's *Danger Zone* and *The Trade* (Mira); James Michael Pratt's *The Last Valentine, The Lighthouse Keeper, Ticket Home, Paradise Bay* (St. Martin's Press); *NANO* by John Robert Marlow (Tom Doherty Associates); *Spirits of the High Mesa* by Floyd Martinez (Arte Publico); *The Hong Kong Sanction* by Mitch Rossi (Kensington/Pinnacle); Cheryl Saban's *Sins of the Mother, Moral Obligations*, and *Telephone Tag* (Dove Books); John Scott Shepherd's *Henry's List of Wrongs* and *Dead Father's Guide to Sex and Marriage* (New Line Cinema; Warner Bros; Pocket); Tracy Price-Thompson, *Knockin' Boots* and *G-Spot* (Random House).

Nonfiction: Barbara Berg's *How to Escape the No-Win Trap* (McGraw-Hill); Peter S. Bielagu's *Getting Loaded: Get Ready. Get Set. Get Rich.* (NAL); Howard Bonham's *Dictionary for Investors* (Adams Media); Gary Buffone's *The Myth of Tomorrow* (McGraw-Hill); Abbott George Burke's *Simply Heavenly, The Monastery Vegetarian Cookbook* (Macmillan); Clint Greenleaf's *Gentleman's Guide* series (Adams Media); Paul Grangaard's *The Grangaard Strategy* and *Plan Right for Retirement* (Perigee); Tim Hoerr's *Thank God It's Monday Morning* (Celebrity Press); Dr. Mark Huston, Nadine Fox, Barry Taylor's *What Your Doctor Won't Tell You About Hypertension* (Warner Books); *The Learning Annex* series (Wiley); *The Pleasure of Wine, Uncluttering Your Space, Feng Shui, Upgrade Your Brain, Stop Being Nice*; Gary & Joy Lundberg's *I Don't Have to Make Everything All Better* and *Marriage for Better Not Worse* (Viking-Penguin; Book of the Month Club Selection); Elizabeth Mason's *The Rag Street Journal: A Guide to Thrift Shops in North America* (Owl) and *Valuable Vintage* (Random House/Clarkson-Potter); Alison McMillen's *When I Loved Myself Enough* (St. Martin's Press); Audrey Nelson and Susan K. Golant's *You Don't Say* (Prentice-Hall); Lucy Papillon's *When Hope Can Kill* (Celebrity Press); Ripley Entertainment's *The Amazing World of Robert Ripley* and *Ripley's Encyclopedia of the Bizarre* (Black Dog & Leventhal). Jim Sagner's *Success through Cashflow Reengineering* (American Management Association); Carole Smith's *The Magic Castle: My Son Was a Multiple* (St. Martin's Press; Rosemont Productions); *Mary Taylor's Bedroom Games* (Three Rivers/Random House); Nadine Taylor's *Hormonal Therapy* (NAL); Suzi Parker's *Sex in the South*; Governor Jesse Ventura's *I Ain't Got Time to Bleed: Reworking the Body Politic from the Bottom Up* (Villard) and *Do I Stand Alone?* (Pocket).

Scripts and Dramatic Rights being produced by AEI: *Ripley's Believe-It-Or-Not!* (Alphaville/Paramount); Marc Gardner's *Death on the Hospital Lawn* (Zide-Perry; HBO); Steve Alten's *MEG* (Larry Gordon Productions), *The Loch* (David Foster Productions); Patricia Davis's *Midnight Carol* (HBO); John Scott Shepherd's *Henry's List of Wrongs* (Zide-Perry Films; New Line Pictures), *The Kill Martin Club* (Red Hour/Warner Bros.), *Favorite Son* (Donald De Line Pictures/Sony); *Life, or Something Like It* (Davis Entertainment/New Regency); Michael S. Simpson and William Diehl's *Zombie Squad* and *Bullet Proof* (HBO/ABC); Krishna Shah's *Taj Mahal* (Ramoji Film City/Double Helix).

ALTAIR LITERARY AGENCY, LLC

PO Box 11656, Washington D.C., 20008

202-237-8282

www.altairliteraryagency.com

Agents: Nicholas Smith, Andrea Pedolsky

Born: Smith: St. Louis, Missouri. Pedolsky: 1951, New York, New York.

Education: Smith: Languages, Vassar, 1973–1974; Arts Management, SUNY/Purchase, 1985. Pedolsky: B.A. in American Studies, CUNY/Queens College; M.S. in Library Science, Columbia University.

Career history: Smith: Bookseller, Editor, Publisher, Marketing and Sales Manager (publishing), Director, New Product Development (packager/agency); Independent Agent; Agent/Co-Founder Altair Literary Agency. Pedolsky: Editor, reference and professional books, Neal Schuman Publishers, 1978–1988; Acquisitions Editor, Director of Editorial Development and Production, Amacom Books; Executive Editor (created and launched) Peterson's/Pacesetter Books, 1994–1996; Agent/Co-Founder Altair Literary Agency. Also, Editor/Co-Editor/Co-Author of *Continuing Education for Businesspeople*, *The Small Business Sourcebook*, and *Creating a Financial Plan*.

Hobbies/personal interests: Smith: Music, reading, museums (art, science, and natural history exhibitions), travel, history. Pedolsky: Art, reading, walking, travel, old cities.

Areas most interested in agenting: Smith: American history (only pre-20th century); exploration, history (a wide variety of eras, subjects, and places); illustrated books (topic-centered); science and invention (especially history of); style and design books. Fiction: Literary historical fiction and historical mysteries (only pre-20th century settings for both categories). Activity books (especially interested in formats such as clue books, pop-ups, die-cuts, reveals, etc.). Pedolsky: Art (biography, history of), biography (prominent and historical figures); contemporary issues, illustrated books, multicultural topics, religion and spirituality (history of, new ideas about), sports (women's and men's), women's issues. IMPORTANT: All prospective nonfiction authors MUST have professional and/or academic expertise in their topic.

Areas not interested in agenting: No memoir, true crime, sci-fi/fantasy, thrillers, children's or YA fiction.

Best way to initiate contact: Visit our website to send an electronic query (no attachments), and for guidelines. Nonfiction: A well-thought out and composed query letter, citing your related credentials and why you are the best person to write your book, and/or a complete proposal. Fiction: A query letter, including a brief, compelling synopsis of the story, and a bio/c.v. with writing credits. Please note: we will only respond and/or return materials when you include an SASE.

Client representation by category: Smith: Nonfiction, 85%; Fiction (historical only), 10%; Children's (activity only), 5%. Pedolsky: Nonfiction, 95%; Fiction, 5%.

Commission: 15% domestic, 20% foreign.

Rejection rate (all submissions): 90%.

Most common mistakes authors make: Not demonstrating, either through your proposal or synopsis, that you have the background, knowledge, savvy, and ability to write your proposed book. Also, failing to understand and demonstrate how you can help your potential publisher to take advantage of the marketplace for your book. Another common mistake is querying by telephone or fax.

Description of the client from Hell: There have not been many. Those who come to mind have little or no understanding of the book marketplace and require too much handholding.

Description of a dream client: First and foremost, be a great writer and storyteller. Be someone who has the knowledge, skill, creativity, and expertise to write and support your book; who understands the collaborative aspects of working with an agent and editor; who takes responsibility for meeting deadlines; and who has a sense of humor.

Why did you become an agent? Smith: I love ideas and books, enjoy encountering interesting authors with both, and particularly like to bring authors and editors together over a great book—then mediate the process to everyone's benefit. Pedolsky: When I was an editor, I had to confine and align my acquiring efforts to a particular house's list and interests. It became clear to me that if I wanted to work with a variety of authors with unique voices, styles, and concerns, being an agent was the way to go.

Representative titles: *Wormwood: A Natural History of Chernobyl* by Mary Mycio (Joseph Henry Press); *Unlocking Your Family's Medical & Genetic History* by Thomas Shawker with the National Genealogical Society (Rutledge Hill Press); *A Fierce Storm Rising: Women, Sex, and Power—and the Catholic Church* by Angela Bonavoglia (Regan-Books); *How Herbs Work* by Holly Phaneuf (Marlowe & Company); *The Bright Promise of Introverted Children* by Marti Laney (Workman Publishing); *How to Say It When You Don't Know What to Say* by Robbie Miller Kaplan (Penguin USA); *Marni Nixon* by Marni Nixon (Billboard Books); *The Cutting-Edge Runner* by Matt Fitzgerald (Rodale); *One Thing at a Time* by Cindy Glovinsky (St. Martin's Press); *Successful Joint Venturing* by Robert Wallace (Dearborn); *Daunting Legacies: Artists' Estates and Art Market* by Magda Salvesen (Rutgers University Press).

MIRIAM ALTSHULER LITERARY AGENCY

53 Old Post Road North, Red Hook, NY 12571

845-758-9408

Agent: Miriam Altshuler
Born: New York, New York.
Education: B.A., Middlebury College.

Career history: Agent for 11 years at Russell & Volkening. Started my own agency in 1994.

Hobbies/personal interests: Skiing, horses, the outdoors, my children, reading.

Areas most interested in agenting: Literary and commercial fiction, narrative nonfiction, popular culture.

Areas not interested in agenting: No sci-fi, Westerns, romance, horror, genre mysteries.

Best way to initiate contact: Query letter with SASE. No fax or e-mail queries, no unsolicited manuscripts.

Most common mistakes authors make with your agency: Send unsolicited manuscripts; don't include SASEs with query letters; do not research the type of books we represent; calling in place of a query; sending fax or e-mail query; multiple calls checking up on a query letter.

Reading-fee policy: No reading fee.

Client representation by category: Nonfiction, 50%; Fiction, 50%.

Commission: 15% books and movies; 20% foreign; 17.5% England.

BETSY AMSTER LITERARY ENTERPRISES

PO Box 27788, Los Angeles, CA 90027-0788

323-662-1987

Agent: Betsy Amster

Education: B.A., University of Michigan.

Career history: Before opening my agency in 1992, I spent ten years as an Editor at Vintage Books and Pantheon and two years as Editorial Director of the Globe Pequot Press.

Hobbies/personal interests: Reading, movies, art, swimming, hiking, poking into odd corners of Los Angeles

Areas most interested in agenting: Literary fiction; high quality commercial women's fiction (i.e., the next Elinor Lipman); narrative nonfiction, especially by journalists; psychology and self-help; popular culture; women's issues; health; parenting; literary gardening; clever gift books by illustrators or photographers who can also write.

Areas not interested in agenting: Children's or YA titles, category romance, science fiction, fantasy, Westerns, horror, computers, poetry, screenplays.

If not agenting, what would you be doing? I'd be a lawyer.

Best way to initiate contact: No phone calls or faxes. For fiction, please send the first three pages of your manuscript; for nonfiction, please send a query letter or your proposal. No response without SASE.

Reading-fee policy: No reading fee.

Commission: 15% domestic; 20% foreign.

Number of titles sold last year: 25.

Most common mistakes authors make: Nonfiction: Failing to research the competition. Fiction: Submitting a first draft.

Description of a dream client: Writes well, takes direction gracefully, moves easily from book to book. Meets deadlines. Rises to the challenge of helping the publisher promote the book. Knows the difference between a big problem and a little one. Calls and faxes only during business hours. Likes to laugh. A mensch!

Why did you become an agent? I can't keep my nose out of books.

What can writers do to enhance their chances of getting you as an agent? If you're writing nonfiction, read the books on how to write a book proposal. If you're writing fiction, join (or start) a writers' group to get feedback on your work. Study story structure. Be prepared to go through drafts and drafts. Ripeness is all.

How would you describe what you actually do for a living? I'm constantly on the lookout for writers whose work moves or enlightens me, which means I read everything in sight. Once I take writers on, I work with them to make sure that their proposal or manuscript is polished and persuasive. I keep track of which editors are doing what types of books and make sure that I understand their taste. I jump up and down on the phone with editors (or in their offices or over lunch) to share my enthusiasm for my clients' work. I nudge publishers as required, to see that they live up to their promises.

Representative titles: *Rejuvenile: How a New Species of Reluctant Adults is Redefining Maturity* by Christopher Noxon (Crown); *The Great Black Way: Central Avenue and the Legacy of African-American Los Angeles*, by RJ Smith (PublicAffairs); *The Reluctant Tuscan* by Phil Doran (Gotham); *My Therapist's Dog* by Diana Wells (Algonquin); *Lexi James & The Council of Girlfriends* by Melissa Jacobs (Avon); *Pen on Fire* by Barbara DeMarco-Barrett (Harcourt); *Garrett In Wedlock* by Paul Mandelbaum (Berkley); *Carry Ons: Traveling Chihuahuas* by Sharon Montrose (Stewart, Tabori & Chang); *Secrets of The Renaissance Soul: How to Make "Too Many Interests" Work for You* by Margaret Lobenstine (Gotham); *The Highly Sensitive Child* by Elaine N. Aron, Ph.D. (Broadway); *The Blessing of a Skinned Knee* by Wendy Mogel (Scribner/Penguin).

MARCIA AMSTERDAM AGENCY

maybe

41 West 82nd Street, New York, NY 10024

212-873-4945

Agent: Marcia Amsterdam
Education: B.A. in English and Journalism, Brooklyn College.
Career history: Editor; agent (1960–present).

Hobbies/personal interests: Reading, theater, movies, art, travel, discovering wonderful new writers.

Areas most interested in agenting: An eclectic list of mainstream and category fiction and popular nonfiction. I enjoy medical and legal thrillers, character-driven science fiction, mysteries, horror, historical romance, contemporary women's fiction, and quality young-adult fiction.

Areas not interested in agenting: Children's books, poetry, short stories, technical books, thrillers about drug cartels.

If not agenting, what would you be doing? Reading published books more, traveling more.

Best way to initiate contact: A query letter (with SASE).

Reading-fee policy: No reading fee.

Client representation by category: Nonfiction, 20%; Fiction, 70%; Children's, 10%.

Commission: 15% domestic; 20% on foreign sales and movie and television sales (split with subagents); 10% on screenplays.

Number of titles sold last year: A fair number.

Rejection rate (all submissions): Alas, most.

Most common mistakes authors make: Spelling and grammar still count, as does a comfortable, legible typeface.

Description of the client from Hell: I wouldn't know. I've never had one.

Description of a dream client: One who trusts the reader, is professional, adaptable, has a sense of humor, and has confidence in my judgment.

Why did you become an agent? When I was an editor, other editors often came to me for suggestions about books they were working on. I found that I enjoyed giving editorial and career advice. One editor said, "You keep selling my books. Why don't you become an agent?" So I did.

Representative titles: *China Dome* (Kensington); *Flash Factor* (Kensington); *Moses Sees a Play* (Farrar, Straus & Giroux); *Rosey in the Present Tense* (Walker & Co.); *The Haunting* by Ruby Jean Jensen (Kensington).

THE ANDERSON LITERARY AGENCY INC.

395 Riverside Drive, Suite 12AH, New York, NY 10025

fax: 646-414-7639

e-mail: gilesa@rcn.com

Agent: Giles Anderson
Born: March 23, 1973, Princeton, New Jersey.

Education: B.A. in Philosophy and the History of Math and Science, St. John's College, Annapolis, Maryland.

Career history: Giles Anderson began his publishing career at Boston's Zephyr Press, a small publisher of Russian and Ukrainian literature in translation. In 1997 he joined Scott Waxman to found the Scott Waxman Agency Inc., and in September 2000, he left to form The Anderson Literary Agency Inc.

Areas most interested in agenting: Narrative nonfiction, biography, science, memoir, spirituality, books in translation, and religion.

Areas not interested in agenting: Romance, science fiction, Westerns, genre mystery, and most children's material.

Best way to initiate contact? Brief e-mail query only.

Reading-fee policy: No reading fee.

Commission: 15% domestic, 25% foreign.

Number of titles sold last year: 20.

Rejection rate: 99%.

Do you watch *The Sopranos?* No.

Representative titles: *Kepler's Witch* and *The Harmonies of the Universe: Spiritual Science in the First Days of the Modern World* (Harper San Francisco); *Death's Acre: Inside the Legendary Forensics Lab The Body Farm: Where the Dead Do Tell Tales* (Putnam), *The Guiding Night: A Modern Vision of the Dark Night of the Soul* by Gerald May (Harper San-Francisco); *The Chess Artist: Genius, Obsession, and the World's Oldest Game* (St. Martin's Press); *The White House, Inc. – Employee Handbook: A Staffer's Guide To Success, Profit & Salvation Inside George W. Bush's Executive Branch* (Plume); *The Great Beyond: A History of Higher Dimensions from Einstein's Universe to Brane Worlds* (Wiley); *Victories of Reason: How Christianity, Freedom, and Capitalism Led to Western Success* (Random House, 2005); *The Mindset Mystery: How Our Thinking Creates Success or Failure* (Random House, 2005).

ARCADIA

31 Lake Place North, Danbury CT 06810

203-797-0993 fax: 203-730-2594

e-mail: arcadialit@att.net

Agent: Victoria Gould Pryor
Place of Birth: Manhattan.
Educational History: B.A. Pembroke College/Brown University (Modern Literature/History); M.A. (Modern Literature), NYU.

Career History: John Cushman Agency, Sterling Lord Agency, Harold Matson Agency, Literistic, Ltd., Arcadia.

Hobbies/personal interests: Science, medicine, nature, gardening, classical music and singing, current/foreign affairs, reading, law, art.

Areas most interested in agenting: Literary and commercial fiction. Nonfiction: science/medicine, current affairs/popular culture, history, psychology, true crime, investigative journalism, women's issues, biography, music, or any book that is intriguing, challenging or life-altering.

Areas not interested in agenting: Children's/YA, science fiction/fantasy, horror.

If not agenting, what would you be doing? I'd be an unhappy and reasonably solvent doctor or lawyer, a happy and struggling woodworker or landscape architect, or if I had a much better voice, an ecstatic and prosperous Wagnerian opera singer.

Best way to initiate contact: Detailed query letter with sample material and SASE. No faxed queries, please, though e-mail queries without attachments are fine.

Reading-fee policy: No reading fee.

Client representation by category: Nonfiction 75%, fiction 25%.

Commission structure: 15% commission.

Rejection rate: 99.9% rejection rate.

Most common mistakes authors make with your agency: Long, rambling pitch letters; not studying the market and knowing one's niche; showing work half-cocked; forgetting the SASE. Fiction writers who believe that because their novel concerns something timely, that automatically makes it readable and saleable.

Description of the client from Hell: The client from Hell delivers late or not at all, is not respectful of an agent's or editor's time, telephones to deliver complex information that should be put in writing. He/she is unable to hear or apply whatever information or advice is offered, and assumes that business ground rules will be set aside for his/her work. Fortunately I don't represent anyone who resembles this.

Description of the dream client: The dream author, like most of my current clients, is a hardworking mensch, behaves professionally and delivers writing that is thoughtful, intelligent, enticing, and grabs you in the heart and gut.

How did you become an agent? The luck of the draw; I stumbled into the perfect field for me, which combines a love of reading, people, and business with a smattering of law and social work thrown in on the side.

What can writers do to enhance their chances of getting you as an agent? Other than being exceptionally talented, dedicated and ambitious, it helps if you're realistic and are looking for a long-term relationship based on professional success and mutual respect. Non-fiction authors: credentials in your field are crucial; research the competition thoroughly, and understand the importance of self-promotion.

How would you describe what you actually do for a living? Combination of talent scout, business manager/career planner, developmental editor, cheerleader, and handholder.

What do you think about other agents? Most agents I'm acquainted with are hardworking, talented, devoted professionals.

What do you think about editors? Ditto for the editors. Their role is especially difficult, and they're often caught in a squeeze between trying to do right by an author and obligations to their employer's bottom line.

Comments: It's a rough, tough business. Prepare yourself for anything and everything. Have stamina, a sturdy ego, a high threshold for frustration, and a well-developed sense of adventure and humor. You'll need it all.

Representative titles: Nonfiction: Jonathan Weiner: *The Beak of the Finch* and *Time, Love, Memory* (Knopf); Dr. Frank T. Vertosick, Jr.: *When the Air Hits YourBrain: Tales of Neurosurgery* (Norton) and *Why We Hurt: The Natural History of Pain* and *The Genius Within: Discovering the Intelligence of Every Living Thing* (Harcourt); Dr. Bernie Siegel: *Love, Medicine and Miracles; Peace, Love and Healing; How to Live Between Office Visits; Prescriptions for Living* (HarperCollins), *Help Me to Heal* (Hay House); Jane Anne Staw: *Unstuck: A Supportive and Practical Guide to Working Through Writer's Block*; Dr. Mary Sue Miller: *No Visible Wounds: Identifying Nonphysical Abuse of Women by Their Men* (Contemporary); Perdita Kirkness Norwood with Teri Wingender: *The Enlightened Stepmother* (Avon). Fiction: Anjana Appachana: *Listening Now* (Random House); Suzanne Hamilton Free: *The Blue Nature* (St. Martin's); Jeanne Mackin: *Dreams of Empire* (Kensington); *The Sweet By and By* (St. Martin's).

AUTHENTIC CREATIONS LITERARY AGENCY, INC.

X—No

Maybe

875 Lawrenceville-Suwanee Road, Suite 310-306, Lawrenceville, GA 30043

770-339-3774   fax: 770-339-7126

e-mail: Ron@authenticcreations.com

Agents: Mary Lee Laitsch, Ronald E. Laitsch

Born: Mary Lee: Baraboo, Wisconsin. Ronald: Milwaukee, Wisconsin.

Education: Mary Lee: B.S. in Education, University of Wisconsin. Ronald: J.D., University of Wisconsin Law School; B.S., University of Wisconsin School of Business.

Career history: Mary Lee: Taught library science. Established my literary agency in 1995. Ronald: Attorney. Established literary agency in 1995. Active member of AAR and Authors Guild.

Hobbies/personal interests: Mary Lee: Family, reading, crafts, sewing. Ronald: Golf, reading, gardening.

Areas most interested in agenting: Mary Lee: Fiction: Adventure, historical, murder mysteries, romance, suspense, and, of course, literary fiction. Nonfiction: Business, crafts, how-to, humor, political, sports, true crime, and women's issues. Ronald: Fiction: Adventure, murder mysteries, suspense, mainstream, and literary fiction. Nonfiction: Business, how-to, political, sports, true crime, and ethnic works.

Areas not interested in agenting: Mary Lee: Poorly crafted works. Ronald: Projects that are not well written.

If not agenting, what would you be doing? Mary Lee: I totally enjoy what I am doing and cannot imagine getting into any other line of work. Ronald: Writing and painting, things I have very little time for at the moment.

Best way to initiate contact: Query letter with SASE.

Reading-fee policy: No reading fee.

Client representation by category: Mary Lee: Nonfiction, 30%; Fiction, 65%; Children's, 5%. Ronald: Nonfiction, 50%; Fiction, 50%.

Commission: 15% domestic, 20% foreign.

Number of titles sold last year: Mary Lee: The exact number of manuscripts sold varies from year to year. The only constant is that each year has seen a steady increase over the number of manuscripts sold during the previous year. Ronald: 21.

Rejection rate: 99%.

Description of the client from Hell: Mary Lee: We have clients from all over the world, but none of them, to our knowledge, comes from Hell. We attempt to treat all of our clients as the unique and talented artists they are and in return expect them to respect our professional opinion on how to get their books published. So far this system has worked out well for us. Ronald: One whose writing is wonderful but is impossible to work with to the point we have to part company.

Description of a dream client: Mary Lee: A talented writer who has carefully proofread the manuscript before submitting it to us. Ronald: A person who loves to write and lets the agent do the selling.

Most common mistakes authors make with your agency: Ronald: Not providing sufficient information about their project or their qualifications to write the manuscript.

Why did you become an agent? Mary Lee: I enjoy working with new writers to develop their initial works into publishable manuscripts.

What can authors do to enhance their chances of getting you as an agent? Mary Lee: I like working with enthusiastic writers. Let that show through in your query letter.

How would you describe what you actually do for a living? Ronald: I view the role of the agent as working with the author to perfect a marketable manuscript and then matching that manuscript with a publisher capable of maximizing the sales of the ensuing book.

How did you become an agent? Ronald: From a frustrated writer to a person in a position to remove that frustration for other writers. I know from experience how hard it is to write a good manuscript. I enjoy being in a position to help a writer get that effort into a published book.

What do you think about other agents? Like any other profession, some are better than others. However, it is more important that the author and agent trust and like one another to form a strong marketing team.

What do you think about publishers? They are the ones we all need to please in order to get the manuscript into print. For this reason it is imperative to understand the publishers may need changes in the work to put it into publishable form.

What do you think about editors? Ronald: Good editors make all the difference between a successful book and a large number of remainders in a discount bookstore. They are the key to a successful writing career.

Do you watch *The Sopranos*? Ronald: Who watches television when there are so many great books to read?

Comments: Mary Lee: It takes an enormous amount of dedication and effort to write a marketable manuscript. It takes the same effort by the literary agent to find just the right publisher. We prefer to establish a long-term relationship with those authors who appreciate and respect the contributions made by each half of what will become a successful partnership. Ronald: An agent and a writer are a partnership with the same ultimate goal, namely to get the manuscript published. Each has to trust the other to get the job done or the project is doomed for failure. Placing and selling a manuscript takes time and perseverance. The author must have the patience while the agent carries out his end of the partnership with a minimum amount of contact with the author. If the agent spends all his time on the phone with the author, then he can't be on the phone with the editor, the person in position to offer the author a publishing contract.

Representative titles: *Secret Agent* by Robyn Spizman and Mark Johnston (Simon & Schuster); *Cooking Outside the Pizza Box* by Danae Campbell and Jean Patterson (Barron's).

BA LITERARY AGENCY

1062 Manila Drive, Barefoot Bay, Florida 32976

e-mail: phildotd@aol.com

Maybe

Agent: Phil Raia, President.

Born: Brooklyn NY.

Education: BA, Columbia University.

Career history: Eighteen years as a freelance editor in NY. Major portion of my work was for the traditional publishers in the New York area.

Areas most interested in agenting: Espionage thrillers, mysteries, romance, women's issues.

Areas not interested in agenting: Poetry, short stories, children's books.

Best way to initiate contact: E-mail preferred, but I do accept postal queries with an SASE. Queries are to contain no more than a four-page synopsis and a short bio of the author.

Reading-fee policy: No reading or editing fees, but the cost of copying and postage for submissions is absorbed by the author.

Client representation: Nonfiction, 25%; fiction, 50%, other areas, 25%.

Commission: 15% domestic, 20% foreign.

Number of titles sold last year: Three, all previously unpublished authors.

Rejection rate: 85%.

Most common mistakes authors make: Send unsolicited manuscripts; expect agency to download entire manuscript or queries that are comprised of more than 4 pages; trying to impress the agent with his/her prowess as a writer. I prefer to let your writing impress me.

Description of a dream client: The finest writers have yet to be discovered, a point that most agencies overlook. The next Dan Brown, John Grisham, and Tom Clancy are out there and I want to be the agent that discovers them.

Description of a client from Hell: Constant e-mails and phone calls as to what's happening. The need for ego stroking and hand holding. Expectations that are simply not realistic. At best this business is like the lotto, but you cannot win if you don't play.

Comments: The challenge facing unpublished authors reads like a catch-22. Publishers rarely accept submissions from authors and most agents arbitrarily reject new authors. So it becomes a neverending circle of frustration. My list of clients includes 75% unpublished authors. Without them and the challenge to get them published, I would be bored stiff.

MEREDITH BERNSTEIN LITERARY AGENCY, INC.

2112 Broadway, Suite 503A, New York, NY 10023

212-799-1007   fax: 212-799-1145

Agents: Meredith Bernstein, Elizabeth Cavanaugh

Born: Bernstein: July 9, 1946, Hartford, Connecticut; Cavanaugh: October 16, 1962.

Education: Bernstein: B.A., University of Rochester, 1968; Cavanaugh: B.A. in Literature and Creative Writing, Ohio University (Athens).

Career history: Bernstein: Many jobs before becoming an agent: freelance reader, story editor; worked for another agency for five years before starting my own in 1981. Cavanaugh: Before working in publishing, I held a number of positions that were "book"-related, including working for a period as a librarian. I began in publishing with the Bernstein Agency in the mid-1980s and was instrumental in the development of our foreign rights activity.

Hobbies/personal interests: Bernstein: I am a collector of vintage and contemporary costume jewelry and clothing, along with ceramics and fiber art as well as photography, and many other works from the contemporary craft movement in the U.S.; almost any cultural event (I'm an avid theatergoer); spending time with friends; travel, adventure, and personal-growth work. Cavanaugh: I am interested in all forms of art and love museums, movies, dance, music (I studied the violin for 10 years), and, of course, reading. I am also an avid cook, love gardening, and am currently renovating a

70-year-old house. I am a strong environmentalist and love animals and nature, and enjoy camping, hiking, and canoeing.

Areas most interested in agenting: Bernstein: Nonfiction: Psychology, self-help, health/fitness, memoir, current events, business, biography, celebrity. Cavanaugh: Narrative nonfiction, parenting, pop-science, general nonfiction, mysteries, literary fiction, mainstream fiction.

Areas not interested in agenting: Bernstein: Children's books, Westerns (men's), sci-fi. Cavanaugh: Science fiction, children's, poetry, screenplays.

If not agenting, what would you be doing? Bernstein: (1) Curating the American Craft Museum; (2) Replacing Oprah; (3) Running a top fashion house in Paris. Cavanaugh: It would most likely involve some aspect of books or publishing (maybe editing or even writing), or perhaps be as far afield as environmental science or catering.

Best way to initiate contact: A query letter with SASE.

Reading-fee policy: No reading fee.

Client representation by category: Nonfiction, 50%; Fiction, 50%.

Commission: 15% domestic; 20% on foreign sales (split with subagents).

Number of titles sold last year: A lot!

Rejection rate (all submissions): Unsure, but probably fairly high because we must truly believe in the projects we represent and, therefore, are selective about what we request to see.

Most common mistakes authors make: Bernstein: Poor presentation, no SASE. Cavanaugh: Poorly researched projects (which includes not knowing the market in terms of what is already on the shelves for the type of book they are writing), sloppy presentation.

Description of the client from Hell: Bernstein: Pushy, demanding, inflexible, calls too much, sloppy presentation of material, egomaniacal. Cavanaugh: Those who do not take a professional approach to their career and who do not appreciate the role of an agent.

Description of a dream client: Bernstein: Professional, courteous; dream clients see our relationship as teamwork, respect how hard I work for them. Cavanaugh: Great writers whose talent and passion for their work bring the project to life and who want us to work together to reach their potential.

How did you become an agent? Bernstein: Sold my first book overnight(!) almost 25 years ago.

Why did you become an agent? Bernstein: I was born to do this! Cavanaugh: As an agent, the diversity of projects I represent allows me to work within the creative process in many different genres and with many different publishers.

How would you describe what you actually do for a living? Bernstein: I actualize the experience of the authors' dreams.

What do you think about editors? Bernstein: I wish they would stop becoming agents!

What do you think about publishers? Bernstein: We need them and they need us.

Comments: Bernstein: The saddest thing for me about publishing today is that "the bottom line is king." I see so many beautiful pieces of work that I am told are "too small." In the old days, there was "a wing and a prayer"—the loss of that belief system is a failure to envision.

Representative titles: *Romantic Suspense* by Sharon Sala a.k.a. Dinah McCall; *And Other Romances* by Sandra Hill, Janis Reems Hudson, and Julia London; *The Nature of Animal Healing* by Dr. Martin Goldstein (Knopf); *The Whole Truth* by Nancy Pickard (Pocket); *Hormone Deception* by Lindsay Berkson (Contemporary); *The Swampwalker's Journal* by David Carroll (Houghton-Mifflin); *The No-Cry Sleep Solution* by Elizabeth Pantley (Contemporary). Additionally, numerous mystery writers like Nancy Pickard, Troy Soos, Joel Goldman, and Michael Jahn. Many new nonfiction titles in health, spirituality, "how-to," business ,and relationships.

DANIEL BIAL AGENCY

41 West 83rd Street, Suite 5-C, New York, NY 10024

212-721-1786

e-mail: dbialagency@juno.com

Agent: Daniel Bial

Education: B.A. in English, Trinity College.

Career history: Editor for 15 years, including 10 years at HarperCollins. Founded agency in 1992.

Hobbies/personal interests: Travel, cooking, music, parenting.

Areas most interested in agenting: Nonfiction: Popular reference, business, popular culture, science, history, humor, Judaica, sports, psychology, cooking. Fiction: Quality fiction, mysteries.

Areas not interested in agenting: Nonfiction: Academic treatises, crafts, gift books. Fiction: Romances, horror, medical thrillers, children's books, poetry, novels by authors with no publishing credits.

Best way to initiate contact: Query letter with SASE. I accept e-mail queries, without attached files.

Reading-fee policy: No reading fee.

Client representation by category: Nonfiction, 95%; Fiction, 5%.

Commission: 15% domestic; 25% foreign.

Most common mistakes authors make with your agency: A surprising number of writers devote time in their query letter to telling me about their previous failures. They essentially reject themselves.

What gets you excited? I get excited by authors who are excited about their projects. I love authors who know they're on to something special, and who can share their enthusiasm.

Description of the client from Hell: Clients from Hell are almost always wrapped up in private grievances and needs. They talk when they should listen, try force when they should use tact, and get involved in personal gamesmanship when much of publishing calls for team play. They suspect the worst and often cause crises simply through their own closed-mindedness.

Description of a dream client: Dream clients produce trim, tight, ready-to-sell material. They know the business and how to get ahead. They recognize the importance of marketing and know that good intentions don't sell books—hard work does. They take pride in their work and their relationships.

Why did you become an agent? I became an agent for the same reason I first became an editor: because I loved the discovery of new authors and books, loved helping create a sellable project, and loved negotiating big advances. I switched desks because I wanted to be my own boss.

Comments: While I am always looking for authors who write beautifully without any outside help, I am also an experienced book doctor. As a former editor, I can be demanding of some authors, insisting that they rework and rewrite their proposal until it represents the best book they can write. I will also work with less experienced writers to help them prepare their work for others to agent.

LITERARY AGENTS

BLEECKER STREET ASSOCIATES, INC.

532 LaGuardia Place, #617, New York, NY 10012

212-677-4492   fax: 212-388-0001

Agent: Agnes Birnbaum
Place of birth: Budapest, Hungary, but have lived most of my life in the United States.
Education: Educated in Europe and America.
Career history: Spent 16 years as an Editor before starting my own agency in 1984. Senior Editor at Pocket Books and NAL; Editor-in-Chief of Award Books, later a part of Berkley.
Hobbies/personal interests: Reading, classical music, movies, theater, travel.
Areas most interested in agenting: Nonfiction: History, biography, science, investigative reporting, health, women's issues, popular psychology, nature and outdoor writing, true adventure, New Age/spirituality. Fiction: Mystery and suspense thrillers, women's novels.
Areas not interested in agenting: Poetry, science fiction, Westerns, children's books, film/TV scripts, plays, professional, and academic books.

If not agenting, what would you be doing? I'd still be an editor.

Best way to initiate contact: With a short letter about the book and the author. An SASE is a must. No faxes or e-mails, please.

Reading-fee policy: We have no reading fee.

Client representation by category: Fiction, 15%; nonfiction, 80%; children's 5%.

Rejection rate: 90%

Commission: 15% on domestic sales; 25% on foreign and film/TV if a co-agent is used (who gets 10% commission)—it's 15% on foreign and film/TV if Bleecker is the sole agent.

Most common mistakes authors make: They call, fax, or e-mail; send handwritten, ungrammatical letters; they tell you the book is great because their husband/mother/children all loved it.

Description of the client from Hell: Writers with unreasonable and unrealistic expectations; people who don't know the market they're writing for; someone who is unprofessional—late in delivery of work, refuses to make editorial changes, falls apart from rejection or critiques. The person who asks for a personal meeting prior to sending in material for professional evaluation.

Description of a dream client: The writer with talent and creative new ideas. Writers who are passionate about their work, are willing to self-promote, and understand the pros and cons of the business behind the books.

Why did you become an agent? I love books. I enjoyed being an editor and I wanted to go into business for myself. This was the logical next profession that still involved reading and writers.

What can writers do to enhance their chances of getting you as agent? They can send a great short letter (an art form in itself)—a writer who knows how to convince me the idea is saleable by listing facts instead of adjectives. Authors who have proven expertise on the topics of their books and are familiar with the market for them, know the competition, and can point out how their books are wonderfully different.

What do you think about other agents? I belong to AAR, the agents group, and find my colleagues helpful, friendly, thoughtful.

How would you describe what you actually do for a living? Wonderful fun—I really enjoy what I do. And I think I'm good at it. I'm good at the negotiating process, good at helping writers shape their work. Bleecker has an excellent track record with first-time authors, for example.

What do you think about editors? I like them. I used to be one so I can relate to their problems and points of view. It's helpful when an agent who was once on the other side of the desk can anticipate the objections in the deal-making process and have the answers handy in advance.

What do you think about publishers? They can be too tough on writers. However, ultimately I think that publishers and authors share a common goal: a terrific book that is also successful.

Comments: I wish that beginning writers read more on the topic of the genre they themselves are working in. Bestselling authors are especially worthwhile to dissect and study—there are inevitably good reasons why someone attracts a large following.

Representative titles: *Boys into Men: Raising African-American Male Teenagers* by Nancy Boyd-Franklin, Ph.D., and A. J. Franklin, Ph.D. (Dutton/Plume); *The Women's Pharmacy* by Julie Catalano (Dell); *Strange Skies* by Patricia Barnes-Svarney and Thomas Svarney (Fireside/Touchstone); *Bright Minds—Poor Grades* by Michael Whitley, Ph.D. (Perigee/Putnam); *The Encyclopedia of the Occult* by Brad Steiger (Gale); *How Hitler Could Have Won WWII* by Bevin Alexander (Crown); *Ophelia Speaks* by Sara Shandler (Harper); *The Irish Manor House Murder* by Dicey Deere (St. Martins); *Angel's Crime* by Preston Pairo (NAL); *Smart Guide to Time Management* by Lisa Rogak (Wiley); *Her Father's Daughter* by Mollie Poupeney (Random House); *The Dim Sum of All Things* by Kim Wong Keltner (Harper); *Storm on The Horizon* by David Morris (Free Press/S&S); *Sojourner: Mission to Mars* by Andrew Mishkin (Berkley); *Alpine Circus* by Michael Finkel (Lyons Press); *The Forgotten War* by David Methurst (Random House).

THE BLUMER LITERARY AGENCY, INC.

350 Seventh Avenue, Suite 2003, NY, NY 10001-5013

212-947-3040   fax: 212-947-0460

Yes ?

4/2/05

Agent: Olivia Blumer
Place of birth: Long Island, NY
Education: BA, Goucher College
Career history: Doubleday, Scribner Book Companies.
Hobbies/personal interests: Food, travel, tennis, cats.
Areas most interested in agenting: Quality fiction, practical nonfiction, memoir, narrative nonfiction.
Areas not interested in agenting: Science fiction, fantasy, children's.
Best way to initiate contact: Query letter (hard copy, not e-mail).
Reading-fee policy: No fee.
Client representation by category: 65% nonfiction; 35% fiction
Commission: 15% domestic, 20% foreign.
Number of titles sold last year: 15.
Rejection Rate: 95%
Most common mistakes authors make: Sending partial manuscripts, unrequested.
Description of the client from Hell: Requires constant feedback, not self-sufficient/professional.
Description of a dream client: Positive attitude, self-promoter who respects boundaries. Original thinker. Professional in dealing with others.
How did you become an agent? When *Simple Abundance*, a book I aquired, became a bestseller, I quit to invest in myself.

Why did you become an agent? To sell what I believe in.

What would you be doing if you weren't an agent? A little of this, and a little of that.

What can writers do to enhance their chances of getting you as agent? Write well, establish a "platform," think outside the box.

How would you describe what you actually do for a living? Help talented people achieve their potential.

What do you think about other agents? Some good, some bad, all complicated.

What do you think about editors? Some good, some bad, all complicated.

What do you think about publishers? Some good, some bad, all complicated.

Representative titles: *A Year by the Sea* by Joan Anderson (Broadway); *Hot Sour Salty Sweet* by Alford Dreguid (Artisan/Workman); *The Miracles of Santo Fico* by Dennis L. Smith (Warner); *What Happened to Henry* by Sharon L. Pywell (Putnam).

BOOKENDS, LLC

136 Long Hill Road, Gillette, NJ 07933

www.bookends-inc.com   e-mail: editor@bookends-inc.com

Agents: Jessica Faust, Jacky Sach, Kim Lionetti

Born: Faust: March 24, 1971, Minnesota. Sach: June 9, 1964, United Kingdom. Lionetti: September 1, 1973, York, Pennsylvania.

Education: Faust: B.A. in Journalism, Marquette University. Sach: B.A. in English, Oneonta, New York. Lionetti: BA in English, minor in business, Penn State University.

Career history: Faust: Berkley Publishing: 1994–1998 (Associate Editor); Macmillan Publishing 1998–1999 (Senior Editor). Sach: Berkley Publishing/Penguin Putnam: 1986–2000. Lionetti: Assistant, Leisure Books, 1995; Senior Editor, Berkley Publishing Group, 1995-2004.

Hobbies/personal interests: Faust: Yoga, walking the dog, decorating my home, cooking, reading, and travel. Sach: Yoga, Zen meditation, walking the dog, hiking, traveling, reading, writing, cooking, and crafts. Lionetti: Piano, calligraphy, crafts, reading.

Areas most interested in agenting: Faust: Romance (romantic suspense, contemporary romance, paranormal, historical, romantic comedy), chick-lit, women's fiction, cozy mysteries with a strong hook, self-help and how-to nonfiction, women's interest, parenting, business, finance, health, sex and relationships, pets, and psychology. Sach: Mysteries (intense thriller, romantic suspense, cozies with a strong hook, police procedurals, anything with a great, original hook), women's fiction, chick lit, family dramas. Self-help and how-to nonfiction, including intelligent spirituality, women's nonfiction, health, pets. Edgy nonfiction; platform-driven, original nonfiction. Lionetti: True crime, pop science, thrillers, romance, mystery, general fiction.

Areas not interested in agenting: Faust: Children's, science fiction, fantasy. Sach:

Children's, science fiction and fantasy, textbooks and religion, techno-thrillers, military fiction. Lionetti: Science fiction/fantasy.

If not agenting, what might you be doing? Faust: I would be an editor. I spent seven years in publishing as an acquisitions editor and I loved every minute of it. There is no doubt in my mind that if I were to leave agenting, it would only be because I've made a decision to rejoin a publishing house. Sach: Writing, editing, service work of some capacity, or traveling. Lionetti: Own my own bookstore.

Best way to initiate contact: Query letters are accepted via snail mail and e-mail. However, if you know the material you are submitting fits a category our agency represents, feel free to send along a partial. Always include a brief query letter, outlining your book and giving your credentials as a writer, a synopsis of the book, and an SASE. The agency does not accept e-mail attachments and will only look at short letters.

Client representation by category: Nonfiction, 60%; Fiction, 40%.

Commission: 15% English language; 20% British and foreign translation; 15% television, movie, and so on.

Number of titles sold last year: Approximately 75 agency total.

Rejection rate (all submissions): 90%.

Most common mistakes authors make: Faust: Not including a cover letter. I don't know how many times I'll request a manuscript after getting an e-mail or snail mail query, only to receive the material and nothing else. I get hundreds of submissions and queries a month and can't always remember which I've requested and which were just sent to me. It is important to remind me in a short letter not only that I've requested your material, but who you are, what your background is, and a brief two-sentence synopsis of your book. Sach: Clients forget that we look at hundreds of submissions and cannot always keep track of random communications and submissions. I appreciate a potential client who is clear with every piece of communication with me, detailing who the client is, what the client is sending me, conversations we may have had, dates submissions were sent, and titles of submissions.

Description of the client from Hell: Faust: Clients from Hell already know everything there is to know and don't need an editor. They usually think the book is perfect just as they wrote it and will refuse to accept any editorial suggestions their agent or editor might make. In addition, their primary goal is to be a star and they expect their editor and agent to make them one, without doing any work themselves. Sach: Clients from Hell think they have written the perfect book that needs no help whatsoever and are resistant to changes and input from editors and agents. These clients also think that everything should be dropped immediately for them and have no understanding of time and patience. The client from Hell is egotistical, self-centered, and impatient. Lionetti: Eager to sell without a willingness to learn.

Description of a dream client: Faust: My dream clients understand the need for an editor or an agent. They know that their book is not perfect and relish the look of a second pair of eyes, someone who isn't so close to the characters that she can't see their flaws. They take the time to know the industry and ask questions of things they don't understand. Dream clients write because they love to write, not just because they want to be published. And whether they are published or not, they are always writing. Sach:

My dream clients understand the symbiotic relationship between writers and agents/editors. The clients are open to suggestion and change and want their books to be the best they can be. The clients rely on the hard-earned experience and knowledge of their editors and agents, while communicating their own ideas, dreams, and suggestions. Dream clients are patient and eager to learn and grow. Dream clients want thriving/positive relationships with their agents and strive first and foremost to make the best books possible. Dream clients also are willing to learn about the publishing industry. I believe that knowledgeable clients are good clients. Dream clients are writers at heart. They are most interested in writing; getting published is a wonderful benefit but not the reason they write. Most of all, these clients write, write, write! Lionetti: One who is prepared to work and to learn in order to get published, and understands that the effort must last far beyond that first sale.

How did you become an agent? Faust: In 1999, Jacky Sach and I were sitting in her Brooklyn apartment discussing our jobs and careers when, out of the blue, I wondered if she would ever consider starting a business. Boom! Five months later we were the proud owners of BookEnds, LLC, a book packaging company. After just a short year in business, we were proud to say we had sold 10 books, but for some reason neither of us felt we were getting what we wanted from the business. That's when it hit us. What we really missed was working with the authors. We missed the romance and intrigue (literally) of working on fiction and nonfiction and helping authors craft the work they created. That's when we decided it was time to present ourselves as agents. We'd already had a number of requests for representation, so in 2001 we made it official. Sach: I'll rely on my partner's (Jessica Faust's) words for this one. Well said! Lionetti: Invited to join two of my former Berkley colleagues, Jessica Faust and Jacky Sach, at their company, BookEnds.

Why did you become an agent? Faust: I really love working with authors. I love helping them shape the book, and I love brainstorming during its inception. While I was able to achieve these things as an editor, I felt hemmed in by the confines of the publishing house. As an agent, I can take on almost any project that interests me because I have a huge variety of publishing houses to offer it to. Sach: I love reading and I love representing writers. I love the idea of helping someone fulfill a dream and build a career in writing. I also enjoy the creative input I have as an agent. Lionetti: I enjoy working with authors and helping them to develop their ideas.

What can writers do to enhance their chances of getting you as their agent? Faust: Build your platform as a writer and an expert in your field. Authors with contest wins certainly move to the top of my reading pile, as do those with expertise and a strong platform in their field (primarily for nonfiction), those who present workshops, appear in the media, and write articles. And of course, the most important thing, write a really strong, interesting and original book or book proposal. Sach: First of all, write the best book you can. Then know your market: I love an educated, proactive, market-savvy writer. Know what distinguishes your book from the crowd of books. Familiarize yourself with bookstores. Build your platform: you should be an expert in your field with utmost market exposure. Enter contests, submit for awards and magazine publication. I appreciate originality. Lionetti: Present a case as to why their book is marketable, not just good.

How would you describe what you do for a living? Faust: I am an advocate for authors. It is my job to coach authors (as needed) through writing the book and then negotiate the contract and deal with the publishing house on their behalf. Sach: Author advocate. Lionetti: Give aspiring writers the opportunity to share their work with the bookbuying public.

What do you think about editors? Faust: Since I was an editor for many years, I think they are wonderful. I have a good relationship with many editors, and 90 percent of them do their job out of love. They love books and they love helping authors shape their manuscript. Unfortunately, editors are often restrained by the confines of the company they work for. Not all publishing houses handle cozy mysteries or historical romances, and for that reason editors are not always able to take on a project they love. It is a frustrating job at times, and editors are often given a bad rap for these reasons. Sach: I think today's editors are extremely overworked. A large percentage of them are wonderful, dedicated, hardworking individuals who have an honest desire to find a great writer and develop that writer's career—not just for the bestseller status but also for the joy of producing something notable. I believe that many talented editors are out there. Lionetti: Having been one, I think they're hardworking and smart, but too often overburdened.

What do you think about publishers? Faust: They are businesspeople and, while what they deal with is often considered art, the publishers themselves only look at it from a business perspective. This is an important thing for all writers to remember. Sach: There are fewer publishers left, as consolidation becomes more frequent—I wish there were more publishers! I wish the bottom line didn't weigh as heavily as it does. I wish writing as an art were more appreciated. But all in all, I do think publishers are doing a good job of getting writers out there. Although I do wish there were more opportunities for new writers and the publishers were more willing to take big chances. I also think many publishers feel this way themselves. Lionetti: Publishing is a business, and like every business it's all about the bottom line. They're looking for books that they know will sell, not just books that are well written.

What were your favorite films last year? Faust: Unfortunately, I'm not much of a movie buff. *My Big Fat Greek Wedding*. Sach: *Signs* and *My Big Fat Greek Wedding*.

Do you watch *The Sopranos*? Faust: No. Sach: No.

Comments: Faust: There are so many amazing writers out there with wonderful stories to tell, but those who really hit home with me are the writers who are doing it from the heart. They are writing about something they know and writing because of their love for writing. I love being an agent and I'm looking forward to, more than anything, working with and meeting so many new and terrific writers and helping them make their dreams come true. Sach: What rocks my world is when I know I am reading the truth; when the truth just rings out from the plate, whether it's a novel or a nonfiction work, honesty speaks to me. That moment when you read something and you know it is absolutely right, completely perfect . . . nothing is more beautiful than that.

Representative titles: *The Bestseller: Success Stories from Top Authors, Editors, Agents, and the Booksellers Behind Them* by Dee Power and Brian Hill (Dearborn); *8 Weeks to*

Fabulous Foreplay by Dr. Patti Britton (Rodale); *The Night She Died* by Jennifer Patrick (Soho); *Atthea's Chance* by Barbara Gale (Harlequin); *Hoe Lot of Trouble* by Heather Webber (Avon); *HR Confidential* by Cynthia Shapiro (St. Martin's Press); *Resilience at Work* by Salvatore R. Maddi and Deborah M. Khashaba (Amacom); *Restylane* by Dr. Alan Engler and Sonia Weiss (Berkley).

CURTIS BROWN LTD.

Ten Astor Place, New York, NY 10003

212-473-5400

Agents: Ellen Geiger, Elizabeth Harding, Ginger Knowlton, Laura Blake Peterson, Douglas Stewart, Mitchell Waters

The following information pertains to Ellen Geiger:

Born: New York, New York.

Education: Graduate Degree in Anthropology.

Career history: Former PBS Executive before becoming a literary agent.

Hobbies/personal interests: Tennis, reading, growing perfect tomatoes, travel, film, theater, arts.

Areas most interested in agenting: Nonfiction of all kinds, especially narrative, and high-quality commercial and literary fiction, cutting-edge issues, journalists, Asia and Asian-American subjects, religion, science, history.

Areas not interested in agenting: Romance, New Age, children's, poetry, cookie-cutter thrillers, right-wing propaganda.

Best method to initiate contact: Query letter with SASE, sample chapters (if novel) or proposal (if nonfiction).

If not agenting, what would you be doing? I'll always be an agent.

Client representation by category: Nonfiction, 75%; Fiction, 25%.

What is your commission structure? 15% domestic; 20% Canadian/overseas.

Rejection rate (all submissions): 95%.

Most common mistakes authors make: Sending a whole manuscript with a query letter without being requested, sloppy mistakes and typos in proposals, calling repeatedly for status reports, telling me what a great film their book will make.

Description of the client from Hell: Someone who can't be pleased, no matter what happens. An overanxious author who calls or e-mails all the time; suspicious authors who can't trust their agents.

Description of the dream client: A writer who is talented, patient, hard working, self-confident. A writer with a track record of some sort. A genius who is also a nice person.

How did you become an agent? I was mentored into the business by a top agent.

Why did you become an agent? It's immensely satisfying to bring good work to the public.

What can writers do to enhance their chances of getting you as an agent? Write a dynamite query letter, have some expertise on the subject (if nonfiction) or a publishing track record (if fiction).

How would you describe what you actually do for a living? Among other clichés: mine for gold, storm the barricades, pour oil on the waters, throw caution to the winds, tilt at windmills.

What do you think about editors? They are under tremendous pressure to justify their acquisitions before their Editorial Boards, so submissions need to be truly excellent. They are also seriously understaffed and cannot do the kind of in-depth editing and hand-holding they'd like to do.

What do you think about publishers? They should all tithe at the shrine of St. Oprah for popularizing literature and creating new readers.

Comments: I love it when unusual books become hits, like *Tuesdays with Morrie* or *Longitude*. This happens often enough in publishing to give me hope.

Representative titles: *Body RX* by Dr. Scott Connelly (Putnam); *Lillian Gish* by Charles Affron (Scribner); *God at the Edge* by Niles Goldstein (Bell Tower); *Murder with Puffins, Flamingos, etc.* by Donna Andrews (St. Martin's Press).

The following information pertains to Elizabeth Harding:

Education: B.A. in English, University of Michigan (Ann Arbor)

Areas most interested in agenting: Children's literature.

Best method to initiate contact: Query letter or sample chapters.

Client representation by category: Children's, 100%.

Commission: 15% domestic; 20% foreign; 15% dramatic

The following information pertains to Ginger Knowlton:

Born: Before the 1960s in Princeton, New Jersey.

Education: Questionable, Navy brat quality.

Career history: I worked in a factory assembling display cases in Mystic, Connecticut, for a time. Gained numerous pounds one summer working in a bakery in Mendocino, California. I've taught preschool and I directed an infant and toddler child-care center. That means I organized a lot of fundraisers. I started working at Curtis Brown in 1986.

Areas most interested in agenting: Middle-grade and teenage novels.

Areas not interested in agenting: I prefer to remain open to all ideas.

Best method to initiate contact: A simple, straightforward letter with a return envelope works well.

If not agenting, what might you be doing? I love my job, but if I had the luxury of not having to work, I would play tennis even more than I already do; I would tend my gardens more fastidiously; and I would spend more time playing with others.

Client representation by category: Nonfiction, 5%; Fiction, 5%; Children's, 90%.

Commission: 15% domestic; 20% foreign.

Rejection rate (all submissions): 98%.

Most common mistakes authors make: Expecting an answer within a week, but mostly poor quality writing.

Description of the client from Hell: Happy to report that I still don't have first-hand experience with a "client from Hell," so once again I will refrain from describing one (for fear of a self-fulfilling prophecy).

Description of a dream client: Professional authors who respect my job as I respect theirs, who will maintain an open dialogue so we may learn from each other and continue to grow, who are optimistic and enthusiastic, and who continue to write books worthy of publication.

How did you become an agent? I asked Dad for money for graduate school. He offered me a job at Curtis Brown instead.

What do you think about editors? I have a lot of respect for editors and I think they have an incredibly difficult job. As in all professions, some are more gifted than others.

The following information pertains to Laura Blake Peterson:

Education: B.A., Vassar College.

Career history: 1986–present, Curtis Brown, Ltd.

Hobbies/personal interests: Gardening, pets, regional equestrian competitions.

Areas most interested in agenting: Exceptional fiction, narrative nonfiction, young adult fiction, anything outstanding.

Areas not interested in agenting? Fantasy, science fiction, poetry.

Best way to initiate contact: The best way is through a referral from either a client of mine or an editor with whom I work.

Client representation by category: Nonfiction, 40%; Fiction, 40%; Children's, 20%.

Commission: 15% domestic; 20% foreign.

Rejection rate (all submissions): 98%.

Common mistakes authors make: Calling, rather than sending a query letter.

Description of the client from Hell: Authors who call incessantly, preventing me from accomplishing anything on their behalf.

Description of the dream client: A talented writer who knows the idiosyncrasies of the publishing business yet nonetheless remains determined to be a part of it; a writer with the skills and patience to participate in an often frustrating and quirky industry.

Why did you become an agent? I love language. I can't imagine a better job than helping to bring a skilled writer to the attention of the book-buying public.

If not agenting, what might you be doing? Teaching, gardening, who knows?

What can writers do to enhance their chances of getting you as an agent? Do their homework. Find out what I (or whoever they're contacting) like to read and represent, what books I've sold in the past, etc. Read this survey!

The following information pertains to Douglas Stewart:

Born: 1971, Wisconsin.

Education: B.A., Vassar College.

Areas most interested in agenting: Literary fiction, serious nonfiction.

Areas not interested in agenting: Romance, how-to, health, children's, spirituality.

Best way to initiate contact: Query letter and one sample chapter (fiction), or just a query letter (nonfiction).

Client representation by category: Nonfiction, 50%; Fiction, 50%.

Rejection rate (all submissions): 98%.

Representative titles: *Shadow Baby* by Alison McGhee (Harmony Books); *Lit Life* by Kurt Wenzel (Random House); *Mountain City* by Gregory Martin (FSG/North Point); *Ghostwritten* by David Mitchell (Random House); *Humanity* by Jonathan Glover (Yale University Press); *The Colors of Nature* by Alison Deming and Laucet Savog (Milkweed).

The following information pertains to Mitchell Waters:

Born: June 19, 1957, Brooklyn, New York.

Education: M.A. in English Literature, Fordham University.

Hobbies/personal interests: Tennis, theater, opera.

Areas most interested in agenting: Literary fiction, narrative nonfiction, mystery, suspense, health, social sciences, gay and lesbian fiction, nonfiction.

Areas not interested in agenting: Science fiction, romance.

Best way to initiate contact: Query letter.

Client representation by category: Nonfiction, 60%; Fiction, 35%; Children's, 5%.

Commission: 15% domestic sales.

Number of titles sold last year: 25.

Rejection rate (all submissions): 95%.

Most common mistakes authors make: Frequent follow-up phone calls.

Why did you become an agent? To be an advocate for talented writers.

If not agenting, what might you be doing? Teaching literature.

What can writers do to enhance their chances of getting you as an agent? Be patient, but remind me they are there.

Unlikely

SHEREE BYKOFSKY ASSOCIATES, INC.

16 W. 36th St, 13th Floor, New York, NY 10018

212-244-4144

Agent: Sheree Bykofsky

Born: September 1956, Queens, New York.

Education: B.A., State University of New York, Binghamton; M.A. in English and Comparative Literature, Columbia University.

Career history: Executive Editor/Book Producer, the Stonesong Press (1984–1996); Freelance Editor/Writer (1984); General Manager/Managing Editor, Chiron Press, 1979–1984. Author and co-author of a dozen books, most notably *The Complete Idiot's Guide to Getting Published* (Alpha/Macmillan).

Hobbies/personal interests: Tournament Scrabble, poker, racquetball, movies, bridge.

Areas most interested in agenting: Popular reference, adult nonfiction (hardcovers and trade paperbacks), quality fiction (highly selective).

Areas not interested in agenting: Genre romances, science fiction and fantasy, Westerns, occult and supernatural, children's books, screenplays, plays.

If not agenting, what would you be doing? Writing and editing.

Best way to initiate contact: Send a well-written, detailed query letter with an SASE. Please, no phone calls.

Reading-fee policy: No reading fee.

Client representation by category: Nonfiction, 80%; Fiction, 20%.

Commission: 15%.

Number of titles sold last year: 100.

Rejection rate (all submissions): 90%.

Most common mistakes authors make: Excessive hubris; not explaining what the book is about; paranoia (we're not going to steal your idea); sloppy grammar, punctuation, and spelling.

Description of the client from Hell: I only take on an author if I feel we can work well together.

Description of a dream client: One who is not only a talented writer but also who is a professional in every sense—from writing the proposal to promoting the book. Also, writers who appreciate my hard work on their behalf. I love when authors read my book *The Complete Idiot's Guide to Getting Published.*

How did you become an agent? I managed a small textbook publishing company. Then I was a book producer and author, then an agent.

Why did you become an agent? It suits me, and I feel I have the talent and experience to do it well.

Comments: In addition to being an agent, I have been a book packager and an author. This gives my clients and me a perspective that most agents do not have. Often, I match my clients with publishers' ideas.

Representative titles: *Niche and Grow Rich* by Jennifer Basye Sander and Peter Sander; *365 Ways to Become a Millionaire Without Being Born One* by Brian Koslow (Dutton); *Love Types: Discover Your Romantic Style and Find Your Soul Mate* by Alexander Avila (Avon); *Multicultural Manners* by Norine Dresser (Wiley); *Race Manners* by Bruce Jacobs (Arcade); *The Bearded Lady* by Sharlee Dieguez (Hill Street); *The Complete Idiot's Guide to Getting Published* by Sheree Bykofsky (Alpha/Macmillan); *Dealers, Healers, Brutes & Saviors* by Gerald and Susan Meyers (Wiley); *In All the Wrong Places* by Donna Anders (Pocket); *22 Ways to Creating a Meaningful Work Place* by Tom Terez (Adams); *Breast Cancer Survival Manual* by John Link, M.D. (Holt); *Create Your Own Luck* by Azriela Jaffe (Adams); *The Bhaghavad Gita for Westerners* by Jack Hawley (New World Library); *The Toltec Way* by Susan Gregg (Renaissance); *Christmas Windows in New York: A Pictorial Look at 100 Years of Christmas Windows* by Sheryll Bellman (Rizzoli).

MARIA CARVAINIS AGENCY, INC.

X - NO
Maybe

1350 Avenue of the Americas, Suite 2905, New York, NY 10019

212-245-6365   fax: 212-245-7196

e-mail: mca@mariacarvainisagency.com

Agents: Maria Carvainis, President; Moira Sullivan, Literary Associate; David Harvey, Literary Assistant

Born: Carvainis: March 24, 1946, Brisbane, Australia.

Education: Carvainis: B.A., in History, City College of New York, 1967.

Career history: Maria Carvainis established Maria Carvainis Agency, Inc., in 1977 and the agency has expanded and been profitable ever since. Prior to 1977, she worked for 10 years in the publishing industry as an Editor and then Senior Editor at Macmillan Publishing, Basic Books, Avon Books, and Crown Publishing. She has been active in the Association of Authors' Representatives, serving as a Board Member, Treasurer, and Chair of the AAR Contracts Committee, and currently is a member of the AAR Royalty Committee.

Hobbies/personal interests: Carvainis: Reading literary fiction, biographies, and mysteries; gardening, gourmet cooking, wine appreciation, and international travel. Maria is a Conservator of the New York Public Library, Member of Literary Partners, President and Board Member of Bidwell House Museum, and devotee of vintage English cars, especially Bentleys.

Areas most interested in agenting: The agency represents both fiction and nonfiction, with special interest in general fiction/mainstream, literary fiction, mystery and suspense, thrillers, historicals, young adult, contemporary women's fiction, biography and memoirs, business, psychology, and popular science.

Areas not interested in agenting: Carvainis: Science fiction.

If not agenting, what would you be doing? Carvainis: I have never considered an alternative profession.

Best way to initiate contact: Carvainis: An articulate and succinct query letter with SASE. Include a one- or two-paragraph description of the project, mention writing credits, if any, and describe where your project fits in the marketplace. In addition, identify what material is available: complete manuscript, sample chapters, or synopsis.

Reading-fee policy: No reading fee.

Client representation by category: Carvainis: Nonfiction, 40%; Fiction, 60%.

Commission: 15% domestic, 20% foreign.

Number of titles sold last year: Confidential.

Rejection rate (all submissions): Carvainis: 99%, but new original writers should never be discouraged by the statistics.

Most common mistakes authors make: Carvainis: Some writers view their queries as form letters.

Description of a dream client: Carvainis: A writer who is intelligent, has original ideas, and is informed about the marketplace, in addition to having the ability to write and willingness to rewrite.

How did you become an agent? Carvainis: I wanted to be an entrepreneur and used my 10 years of editorial experience to do so.

Why did you become an agent? Carvainis: After 10 years on the corporate side of the desk, I found myself more identified with the authors and their interests than with the corporate mission. Furthermore, I wanted to be an independent businessperson, responsible only to my clients and myself. I was willing to take a risk for greater personal and financial rewards and have had the satisfaction of helping many writers fulfill their aspirations and establish careers.

What can writers do to enhance their chances of getting you as an agent? Writers should be able to crystallize the originality of their work. Clarity is a sign of competence and confidence.

How would you describe what you actually do for a living? Carvainis: I believe that I am a long-term business partner with the writer to build a successful career. Each writer has unique strengths. My job is to complement the author. Authors vary in how much creative direction they need. Authors who are still building a readership can often benefit from editorial direction as they shape the next project. The role of agents always involves vigorously trying to sell projects they represent because they believe in the author. After the sale, it is all about negotiating the best contract and protecting the author's rights.

What do you think about editors? Carvainis: Editors today vary tremendously in their abilities. Because the corporate structure uses agents as readers or screeners of material, the editor is primarily in an acquisition role, often spending more time in meetings than in working with authors and manuscripts.

What do you think about publishers? Carvainis: There is tremendous confusion in the industry among publishers. The great uncertainty is whether the traditional role of a publisher has value or whether a publisher is simply a content provider. And the emergence of electronic commerce and the electronic book, combined with globalized consolidation, seems at times to totally preoccupy them.

What were your favorite films last year? Carvainis: *Master and Commander.*

Do you watch *The Sopranos?* Carvainis: Yes—on video.

Representative titles: *Simply Dangerous* by Mary Balogh (Delacorte); *The Mourning Sexton* by Michael Baron (Doubleday); *White Hot* by Sandra Brown (Simon & Schuster); *In the Shadow of Fame* by Sue Erikson Bloland (Viking); *Winterset* by Candace Camp (Mira); *To the Limit* by Cindy Gerard (St. Martin's); *A Perfect Bride and A Perfect Groom* by Samantha James (Avon); *To Collar a Killer* by Lee Charles Kelley (Avon); *The Killing Rain* by P. J. Parrish (Kensington); *Some Danger Involved* by Will Thomas (Simon & Schuster/Touchstone).

MARTHA CASSELMAN, LITERARY AGENT

PO Box 342, Calistoga, CA 94515

707-942-4341

Agent: Martha Casselman
In response to my query, Ms. Casselman sent the following:
Dear Friends:
Here's the news from Calistoga: I am going to close the office to new projects, although I will continue to review statements, make disbursements, and follow up on contractual, in-process, and on-publication logistics. Proposals under consideration will, of course, get my full attention.

This is an exciting decision for me, and one I have thought about for a long time. I have no plans to do anything different with my life; that's the best time to close the door on this chapter—twenty-five years as an agent. I've made wonderful friends, and, while there have been some disappointing experiences, there have been many, many extremely satisfying ones. My writers have always inspired me. I owe them a lot, for their smarts, integrity, and faith in me.

My office door will be open for occasional editing projects (my first love) and some editorial consulting.

I feel a keen sense of separation from an amazing publishing community and a sense of accomplishment all mixed together.

CASTIGLIA LITERARY AGENCY

yes

1155 Camino Del Mar, Suite 510, Del Mar, CA 92014

858-755-8761   fax: 858-755-7063

Agents: Julie Castiglia, Winifred Golden. Sally Van Haitsma, Associate Agent
Education: Castiglia: Educated in England.
Career history: Castiglia: Published writer (three book titles—hundreds of magazine articles, essays, poetry in literary anthologies), Freelance Editor (past 14 years).
Hobbies/personal interests: Castiglia: Traveling, hiking, skiing, gardening, animals, decorative arts, books.
Areas most interested in agenting: Castiglia: Mainstream, literary, and ethnic fiction. Nonfiction: Psychology, science and health, biography, women's issues, niche books, contemporary issues, narrative nonfiction, how-to. Golden: Mainstream fiction and nonfiction, literary and ethnic fiction, narrative nonfiction, pop culture, true crime, suspense, science fiction.

Areas not interested in agenting: Castiglia: Horror and science fiction; formula romance. Golden: Poetry, romance, fantasy.

Best way to initiate contact: Query letter with SASE.

Reading-fee policy: No reading fee.

Client representation by category: Nonfiction, 50%; Fiction, 50%.

Commission: 15% domestic.

Number of titles sold last year: 25.

Rejection rate (all submissions): 95%.

Why did you become an agent? Castiglia: I've always loved books and knew the publishing business well, having sold my own three books and edited other writers' work. It was a natural step.

What can writers do to enhance their chances of getting you as an agent? We prefer potential clients to be referred by editors, professional writers, or clients. Otherwise, the query letter has to knock our socks off.

Representative titles: *The Orphanage* by Robert Buettner (Warner Books); *Maya Running* by Anjali Banerjee (Bantam); *The Companion* by Susan Squires (St. Martin's); *Courtyards* by Douglas Keister (Gibbs Smith); *Destined for the Throne* by Julia Gelardi (St. Martin's); *The New Vegan* by Janet Hudson; (Thorsons/HarperCollins); *Whitman A-Z* by Charles Oliver (Facts on File); *Orwell A-Z* by Bader/Rasmussen (Facts on File); *Scalamandre* by Brian Coleman & Doug Mayers (Gibbs Smith).

WM CLARK ASSOCIATES

355 West 22nd Street, New York, NY 10011

212-675-2784   fax: 646-349-1658

www.wmclark.com   e-mail: wcquery@wmclark.com

Agent: William Clark

Born: Roanoke, Virginia.

Education: College of William and Mary.

Career history: Virginia Barber Agency (1992–1993); William Morris Agency (1993–1997).

Areas most interested in agenting: Mainstream literary fiction and quality nonfiction, especially memoirs, popular culture, and current events.

Areas not interested in agenting: Horror, science fiction, fantasy, children's or young adult, how-to.

If not agenting, what would you be doing? I would be a Buddhist monk.

Best way to initiate contact: E-mail queries (to wcquery@wmclark.com). E-mail queries should include a general description of the work, a synopsis/outline, biographical information, and publishing history, if any. I will respond whether or not I am interested in your work or idea, or if I feel it is not right for me.

Reading-fee policy: No fee.

Client representation: Nonfiction, 40%; Fiction, 60%.

Number of titles sold last year: 35.

Rejection rate: 90%

Commission: 15% domestic, 20% foreign.

Description of the client from Hell: I have no clients from Hell.

Description of the dream client: Clients who understand the market for their book, and their role in the publication of the book, beyond actually writing the book.

Representative titles: *River Town* by Peter Hessler (HarperCollins); *Nine Hills to Nambonkaha* by Sara Erdman (Henry Holt), *Apples of Gold in Settings of Silver: Dinner as a Work of Art* by Carolin Young (Simon & Schuster); *Stardust Melodies* by Will Friedwald (Pantheon); *Fallingwater Rising: E. J. Kaufmann and Frank Lloyd Wright Build the Most Exciting House on Earth* by Franklin Toker (Alfred A. Knopf); *Behind Deep Blue* by Feng-hsiung Hsu (Princeton); *The Answer is Never* by Jacko Weyland (Grove Press); *Fashion Victim* by Michelle Lee (Broadway Books); *Tha Doggfather* by Snoop Dogg (William Morrow); *Dante's Path* by Richard and Bonney Schaub (Gotham Books); *Bjork* by Bjork (Bloomsbury Books).

CLAUSEN, MAYS & TAHAN LITERARY AGENCY

PO Box 1015, New York, NY 10276

212-239-4343   fax: 212-239-5248

Agents: Stedman Mays, Mary M. Tahan.

Education: Mays: M.A. in English, University of Virginia. Tahan: M.A. in Near East Studies, New York University.

Areas most interested in agenting: Mostly nonfiction: women's issues, relationships, men's issues, parenting, spirituality, religion, history, memoirs, biography, autobiography, true stories, medical, health/nutrition, psychology, how-to, business/financial, fashion/beauty, style, humor, novels (both genre and literary); rights for books optioned for TV movies and feature films.

Areas not interested in agenting: Although the majority of our list is nonfiction, we are actively looking for novels.

Best way to initiate contact: For nonfiction, a query letter (containing proposed book concept and author bio) or proposal (containing the following sections: Concept; Market Analysis; Competition; Author's Publicity Platform; Author's Credentials, and Chapter-by-Chapter Outline), including self-addressed stamped envelope for return of materials. For fiction, a brief synopsis plus first 10 pages of novel. Do not fax queries, proposals, or excerpts of manuscripts.

Reading-fee policy: No reading fees.

Client representation by category: Nonfiction, 95%; Fiction, 5%.

Commission: 15%.

Rejection rate (all submissions): 95%.

Description of a dream client: An author with a vision who listens to constructive suggestions. (It is also important for an author to be willing to promote the book aggressively, resourcefully, and creatively. Publishers look for authors skilled at generating publicity.)

Why did you become an agent? Love publishing—learn with every book.

Representative titles: *Eating the Okinawa Way* by Bradley Willcox, M.D., Craig Willcox, Ph.D., and Makoto Suzuki, M.D. (Clarkson Potter); *The Anti-Inflammation Diet* by Richard Fleming, M.D. with Tom Monte (Putnam); *And if I Perish: Frontline US Army Nurses in WWII* by Evelyn Monahan, Ph.D. and Rosemary Neidle-Greenlee, MSN (Knopf); *Case Files Civil Servant* (Penguin) and *Resident Alien: The New York Diaries* (Alyson), both titles by Quentin Crisp; *Help Your Baby Talk, Grow Your Baby's Mind* by Robert Owens, Ph.D. with Leah Feldon; (Perigee); *The Emotionally Abusive Relationship* by Beverly Engel (Wiley & Sons); *Does This Make Me Look Fat?* by Leah Feldon (Villard/Random House); *The Rules and The Rules II* (Warner Books) and *The Rules for On-Line Dating* (Pocket Books), all titles by Ellen Fein and Sherrie Schneider; *How to Write a Movie in 21 Days* by Viki King (HarperCollins); *Cosmic Banditos: A Novel* by Ann Warren & Joan Lilly (Doubleday); *Your Hands Can Heal You* by Master Stephen Co and Eric Robins, M.D. with John Merryman (Free Press).

RUTH COHEN, INC.

PO Box 2244, La Jolla, CA 92038

858-456-5805

Agent: Ruth Cohen

Areas most interested in agenting: Very selective women's fiction (contemporary themes of modern women), mysteries (different settings with fascinating characters), juvenile literature (quality picture books, middle-grade fiction/nonfiction, young-adult novels, thrillers (no drugs or Mafia).

Areas not interested in agenting: Films, scripts, poetry, books in rhyme or verse, science fiction, Westerns, how-to books.

Best way to initiate contact: Send a query letter (must send SASE), which also includes the opening 10 to 15 pages of the manuscript. Please, no unsolicited full manuscripts.

Reading-fee policy: No reading fee. Charge for foreign mailings and copying manuscripts.

Client representation by category: Nonfiction, 5%; Fiction, 60%; Children's, 35%.

Commission: 15% domestic; 20% foreign.

Number of titles sold last year: 56.

Description of the client from Hell: There aren't really any clients from Hell. There are clients who grow disappointed and who despair of the publishing world as it merges and alters and leaves fewer opportunities for new writers to succeed in work they love—writing.

Description of a dream client: Clients who understand that our combined efforts generally will advance both our careers, and that patience and stamina are the preferred attributes for getting published well—now and always.

Comments: Keep trying—and keep trying to detach yourself from your own writing so that you can view it objectively. Then reassess, revise, rework, and resubmit.

FRANCES COLLIN, LITERARY AGENT

PO Box 33, Wayne, PA 19087-8033

610-254-0555

fran@francescollin.com

Agent: Fran Collin

Areas not interested in agenting: Cookbooks, gardening books, illustrated books (coffee-table books, that is).

If not agenting, what would you be doing? Haven't a clue.

Best way to initiate contact: Query letter by mail with SASE, unless recommended by editors, writers (clients), or other professionals, in which case, telephone. Please no faxes, phone or e-mail unsolicited queries.

Client representation by category: Nonfiction, 49%; Fiction, 49%; Textbooks, 1%; Poetry, 1%.

Commission: 15% on U.S. deals; 20% on foreign, translation, film, and permissions.

Rejection rate (all submissions): 99.44/100%.

How did you become an agent? Went for an interview to a large agency as a secretary and never looked back.

Why did you become an agent? I discovered that I could be paid for introducing my writer friends to editors—that is, I found that there was a profession devoted to my avocation.

Comments: Member of the AAR.

DON CONGDON ASSOCIATES, INC.

156 Fifth Avenue, Suite 625, New York, NY 10010-7002

fax: 212-727-2688

e-mail: DCA@doncongdon.com

> **Agents:** Don Congdon, Michael Congdon, Susan Ramer, Cristina Concepcion.
> **Areas not interested in agenting:** Romance, how-to, textbooks.
> **Best way to initiate contact:** Send a query letter with SASE.
> **Client representation:** Nonfiction, 55%; Fiction, 45%.
> **Commission:** 15% domestic; 19% foreign.
> **Most common mistakes authors make:** Not sending an SASE, sending material as an attachment to e-mail instead of copying and pasting it to the e-mail (which we require for security reasons), not providing enough description of the work(s), not revealing the query is being sent simultaneously to other agents.
> **Representative titles:** *Let's All Kill Constance* by Ray Bradbury (HarperCollins); *Cold Case Squad* by Edna Buchanan (Simon & Schuster); *Eisenhower* by Carlo D'Este (Henry Holt); *Bachelor Girl* by Betsy Israel (William Morrow); *Fashionistas* by Lynn Messina (Red Dress Ink); *Lincoln's War* by Geoffrey Perret (Random House); *The Path to Victory* by Douglas Porch (Farrar, Straus & Giroux); *Dress Your Family in Corduroy and Denim* by David Sedaris.

CREATIVE MEDIA AGENCY INC.

240 West 35th Street, Suite 500, New York, NY 10001

212-560-0909

> **Agent:** Paige Wheeler
> **Education:** Boston University Magna cum Laude.
> **Career history:** Euromoney Publications, London; Harlequin/Silhouette Books; Artists Agency Inc.; Creative Media Agency Inc.
> **Areas most interested in agenting:** Fiction: commercial fiction, women's fiction, romance, mysteries, thrillers. Nonfiction: popular reference, self-help, how-to, pop culture, women's issues.
> **Areas not interested in agenting:** Horror, sci-fi, fantasy, Westerns, children's, biographies.
> **Best way to initiate contact:** Send a query letter with an SASE.
> **Reading-fee policy:** No reading fee.

Client representation by category: Nonfiction, 20%; Fiction, 80%.

Commission: 15% domestic, 20% foreign.

Rejection rate (all submissions): 90%.

Description of the client from Hell: Uncooperative, impatient—doesn't understand the nature of publishing.

Description of a dream client: Cooperative, patient, brilliant, willing to work as a partner to build a solid career.

Why did you become an agent? It is a great combination of many talents. You are an editor, salesperson, and businessperson simultaneously. Also, I can't stop reading, so I may as well get paid for it.

Representative titles: *32AA* by Michelle Cunnah (Avon Books); *Fear Itself* by Barret Schumacher (Tor/Forge); *An Affair Most Wicked* by Julienne Mocheen (Avon Books); *Putt to Death* by Roberta Isleib (Berkley Prime Crime); *Once Upon a Time in Great Britain* by Melanie Wentz (St. Martin's Press); *Kick Off Your Career* by Kate Wendleton (Career Press); *The Brush Off* by Laura Bradley (Pocket Books); *Psychic Cup* by Kim Allen (Andrews McMeel); *On the Edge of the Woods* by Diane Tyrrel.

CROSSMAN LITERARY AGENCY

65 East Scott, Suite 12E, Chicago, IL 60610

312-664-6470   fax: 312-664-7137

e-mail: crossmanla@aol.com

Agent: Nancy Crossman

Career history: V.P.; Editorial Director; Associate Publisher, Contemporary Books, Inc.

Hobbies/personal interests: Travel, golf, reading.

Areas most interested in agenting: General nonfiction, self-help, women's issues, gift books.

Areas not interested in agenting: Children's or young adult titles; fiction; poetry.

Best way to initiate contact: Query with synopsis and SASE.

Reading-fee policy: No reading fee.

Commission: 15% domestic, 25% foreign.

Number of titles sold last year: 20.

Client representation: Nonfiction 95%; other 5%.

Most common mistakes authors make: Not doing their marketing/promotion and competition homework.

Description of a dream client: Dream clients are professional, work as team players, are talented writers, and are passionate about their work.

Why did you become an agent? After 16 years as the director of a publishing house, I left so that I could work on a variety of projects that personally interested me and spend more time with my two young children.

What can writers do to enhance their chances of getting you as an agent? Be patient and have a good sense of humor.

Representative titles: *The Cake Mix Doctor* cookbook series by Anne Byrn (Workman); *Breast Fitness: An Optimal Exercise and Health Plan for Reducing Your Risk of Breast Cancer* by Drs. Anne McTiernan and Julie Gralow (St. Martin's Press); *The Pocket Parent* by Gail Reichlin & Caroline Winkler (Workman); *What Women Don't Learn in Business School* by Susan Abrams (Prima); *A Golfer's Education* by Darren Kilfara (Algonquin); *What Your Doctor May Not Tell You…Fibroids* by Drs. Michael Broder and Scott Goodwin (Warner); *The Baby Bistro Cookbook* by J. Muromcew, (Rodale).

RICHARD CURTIS ASSOCIATES, INC.

171 East 74th Street, New York, NY 10021

212-772-7363

Agent: Richard Curtis

Born: June 23, 1937.

Education: B.A. in American studies, Syracuse University; M.A. in American studies, University of Wyoming.

Career history: A leading author advocate and author of *How To Be Your Own Literary Agent* and other books about publishing. First president of Independent Literary Agents Association (1977-1978), President of Association of Authors' Representatives (1995-1997).

Hobbies/personal interests: Watercolor painting, composing and listening to classical music, watching and playing sports, attending ballet, reading biography and science.

Areas most interested in agenting: Fantasy and science fiction, romance and "chick-lit," mysteries and thrillers, health and medicine, business, history, biography, pop culture, some young adult fiction.

Areas not interested in agenting: Children's literature, cookbooks, poetry, memoirs by authors who are not famous.

If not agenting, what would you be doing? Traveling, reading, painting.

Best way to initiate contact: One-page query letter submitted by US post, plus no more than a one-page synopsis and accompanied by an SASE. No faxed or e-mailed queries. No consideration of manuscripts or sample chapters unless specifically requested. If requested, submission must be accompanied by SASE or we will recycle your material.

Number of titles sold last year: Approximately 150.

Reading-fee policy: No reading fee.

Client representation by category: Nonfiction, 75%; Fiction, 25%.

Commission: 15% on basic sale to US publisher; 15% on dramatic rights (movies, television, audio, multimedia), 25% on British and foreign publication rights.

Rejection rate (all submissions): 99.9%.

Most common mistakes authors make: Phone queries instead of a letter. Want to see us before we've read material. Don't proofread their work.

Description of the client from Hell: High PITA factor. (PITA stands for Pain In The Ass.) Divide commissions earned into time dealing with complaints.

Description of a dream client: Low PITA factor.

Why did you become an agent? Love authors, love publishers, love books, love being in the middle.

How would you describe what you actually do for a living? When asked if she knew what her daddy did for a living, my (then) little daughter said, "He's a book sender." I'm not sure I've heard a better description. But I do think of myself more as an artists' manager than an agent in the old 10-percenter sense.

How did you become an agent? An employment agent sent me to an agency when I graduated and, having fallen in, I never wanted to get out.

What do you think about editors? Like authors, many editors have become disenfranchised from the publishing process.

What do you think about publishers? They have become increasingly conservative and afraid to take risks or invest time developing talent.

Comments: Due to economic pressures, the publishing industry has become increasingly resistant to new books and authors, and as a result literary agents including ours have been forced to become ever more selective. Nevertheless, Richard Curtis Associates remains committed to helping new authors to break into the system and has introduced some original talents into the marketplace. At the same time, electronic delivery of text has created the potential for an exciting alternative publishing industry. To meet that challenge, Richard Curtis has launched e-reads, an online publisher dedicated to reissuing previously published books. Contact info@ereads.com.

Representative titles: *Ilium* by Dan Simmons (HarperCollins), *Suspicion of Madness* by Barbara Parker (Dutton/NAL), *Dead Lines* by Greg Bear (Random House/Del Rey), *Rhapsody* by Elizabeth Haydon, *Why Men Never Remember and Women Never Forget* by Marianne Legato, M.D., *Movies on TV* by Leonard Maltin (Penguin), *Safely Rest* by David Colley (Berkley), *Calder Promise* by Janet Dailey (Kensington).

THE CYPHER AGENCY

816 Wolcott Avenue, Beacon, NY 12508-4261

845-831-5677   fax: 845-831-5677

http://pages.prodigy.net/jimcypher   e-mail: jimcypher@prodigy.net

Agent: Jim Cypher

Born: April 5, 1935; Osceola, Florida.

Educational History: BA and MA in English, San Jose State University; doctoral program in Media Studies at New York University.

Career History: Founded The Cypher Agency in 1994 after having spent nearly three decades (1961-1989) with the IBM Corporation, serving in corporate communications and public relations professional and management assignments.

Hobbies/Personal Interests: Photography, travel, reading, food, classical music.

Areas most interested in agenting: Popular culture, contemporary issues, sports (NASCAR, golf, football, baseball), biography/autobiography, history, health/medicine, government/politics/law, and true crime/investigative.

Areas not interested in agenting: Fiction, poetry, gardening, "kiddy lit," business/management, computers, religious/spiritual, screenplays, crafts/hobbies, cooking, food, nutrition, money/finance/economics.

Best way to initiate contact: Query letter with SASE; e-mail is welcome too, but don't include an attatchment (for virus protection reasons).

Reading-fee guidelines: No reading fee, per AAR guidelines.

Client representation by category: Nonfiction, 100%.

Commision: 15% domestic; 20% foreign.

Rejection rate: 99%; furthermore, as I begin to enjoy my new senior-citizen status more and more, I find I am taking on very few new projects now, only those that really ring my chimes.

Most common mistakes authors make: Overlooking the vital importance of creating a solid nonfiction book proposal. Expecting publishers to produce their books in only a few months. Hyping their submissions as "sure bestsellers." Doing insufficient research about competitive titles already available.

How did you become an agent? After taking advantage of an IBM early retirement incentive and deciding to make a mid-life career change, I took several courses at New York University's Center for Book Publishing to learn all about the book biz and establish my "agenting" career credentials.

What would you be doing if you weren't an agent? Hanging out in neighborhood bars, becoming a "couch potato."

What can writers do to enhance their chances of getting you as an agent? Come up with a truly "commercially viable" project, one that acquisitions editors are likely to salivate over because it's one of a kind and will fill a niche in the marketplace.

How would you describe what you actually do for a living? I help writers reach print by working closely with them to give acquisitions editors what they want.

What do you think about other agents? In the main, they're a likeable bunch of formidable competitors. Unfortunately, there are a few "sharks" out there who take advantage of budding writers and should be exposed for what they are.

What do you think about editors? They're vastly overworked and underpaid for the long hours they devote to their trade.

What do you think about publishers? Couldn't exist without 'em. I won't bother to complain about ever-increasing conglomerization, because it won't help a whit to stem the tide.

Representative titles: *Inside Sudan: Political Islam, Conflict and Catastrophe and Revolution in Zanzibar, An American's Cold War Tale* by US Ambassador Donald Patterson (Westview Press/Perseus); *Gay Perspectives: Things Our Homosexuality Tells Us About the Nature of God* and *Gay Spirituality: The Role of Gay Identity in the Transformation of Human Consciousness* by Toby Johnson (Alyson); *Open Lands: Travels Through Russia's Once Forbidden Places* by Mark Taplin (Streerforth Press); *Taco Titan: The Glen Bell Story* by Debra Lee Baldwin (Legacy Books); *Plan Now or Pay Later: Judge Jane's No-Nonsense Guide to Estate Planning* by Jane B. Lucal (Bloomberg Press); *Living with Chronic Fatigue Syndrome: A Personal Story for Recovery* by Timothy Kenny (Thunder's Mouth Press); *The Heart Disease Sourcebook, The Brain Disease Sourcebook* and *The Cancer Pain Sourcebook* by Roger S. Cicala, MD (McGraw-Hill/Contemporary); *The Masters: A Hole-by-Hole History of America's Golf Classic* by David Sowell (Brassey's); *The Super Bowl's Most Wanted: The Top 10 Book of Big Game Heroes, Football Zeroes and Championship Oddities* by Walter Harvey (Brassey's); *Postcards from Pit Road: Inside NASCAR's 2002 Season, Rebel with a Cause: A Season with NASCAR Star Tony Stewart* and *At Speed: Up Close and Personal with the People, Places, and Fans of NASCAR* by Monte Dutton (Brassey's); *Deadly Cuts: The Crimes of True Believers* and *Murder 101: Homicide and Its Investigation* by Robert L. Snow (Praeger/Greenwood); *Killer with a Badge* by Charles Hustmyre (Berkley); *Witch* by Glenn Puit (Berkley); *Perfect Poison* and *Lethal Guardian* by William Phelps (Kensington); *September Sacrifice* by Mark A Horner (Kensington).

LIZA DAWSON ASSOCIATES

Yes
4/30

240 West 35th Street, Suite 500

New York, New York 10001

212-465-9071 (LD)/212-868-1365 (CB)

e-mail: Ldawson@LizaDawsonAssociates.com and Caitlinblasdell@yahoo.com

Agents: Liza Dawson, Caitlin Blasdell

Education: Dawson: B.A. in History, Duke University; graduate of Radcliffe's Publishing Procedures Course. Blasdell: BA in English from Williams College, 1989.

Career history: Dawson: Founded Liza Dawson Associates in 1998 after 20 years as Executive and Senior Editors at William Morrow and Putnam. Blasdell: Editor and Senior Editor at HarperCollins and William Morrow/Avon from 1994 to 2000, specializing in commercial fiction; joined agency in 2001.

Hobbies/personal interests: Dawson: Local and national politics, ancient history, gardening.

Areas most interested in agenting: Dawson: Nonfiction: academics, specifically historians, psychologists, anthropologists; doctors who have a fresh angle on popular subjects, journalists who have found their niche, media personalities, true crime written with flair, business books, travel, parenting, politics and memoirs. Fiction: literary as well as commercial fiction with a distinctive voice. This would include domestic dramas, fiction written by African Americans, historicals, sophisticated thrillers as well as stories set in Asia, India and the Middle East. Blasdell: Quality commercial and literary fiction, including science fiction and fantasy, high-concept thrillers, mysteries, women's fiction, young adult, and historical. Quality narrative nonfiction.

Areas not interested in agenting: Dawson: Poetry, Westerns, science fiction, children's. Blasdell: Category romance, Westerns, children's picture books, textbooks, poetry, New Age.

Best way to initiate contact: Both: Query letter with SASE.

Client representation by category: Dawson: 40% fiction; 60% nonfiction. Blasdell: 80% fiction; 20% nonfiction.

Commission structure: 15% domestic; 20% foreign.

Rejection rate: Both: 99%.

Representative titles: Dawson: *Mayada: Daughter of Iraq* by Jean Sasson (Dutton); *Warrior-King* by John Bonifaz (The Nation Books); *....And a Time to Die: How Patients Experience Death in American Hospitals* by Dr. Sharon Kaufman (Scribners); *It's So Much Work to be Your Friend: How to Improve Your Child's Social Skills at Home, School and in the Community* by Richard Lavoie (Fireside); *Ida B.* by Karen Miller (Simon and Schuster); *The Nanny Murders* by Merry Jones (Thomas Dunne Books/St. Martin's). Blasdell: *Black Tiger* by Robert Brace (Putnam); *Singularity Sky* by Charles Stross (Putnam).

THE JENNIFER DECHIARA LITERARY AGENCY

254 Park Avenue South suite 2L, New York, NY 10010

212-777-2702

www.jdlit.com   e-mail: jenndec@aol.com

Agent: Jennifer DeChiara
Born: New York City

Career History: Freelance book editor for Simon & Schuster and Random House; writing consultant for several major New York City corporations; literary agent with Perkins, Rubie Literary Agency; founded The Jennifer DeChiara Literary Agency in 2001.

Hobbies/personal interests: Reading, movies, music, ballet, photography, sports, travel.

Areas most interested in agenting: Children's books (picture books, middle-grade, young adult); literary fiction; commercial fiction; mysteries/thrillers; self-help; parenting; celebrity biographies; humor; pop-culture; in general, almost any well-written book, either fiction or non-fiction.

Areas not interested in agenting: Romance; erotica/porn; horror; science fiction; fantasy; poetry.

Best way to initiate contact: Query letter with SASE.

Client representation: Nonfiction, 20%; Fiction, 20%; Children's 60%.

Commission: 15% domestic; 20% on foreign sales (split with subagents).

Number of titles sold last year: 20.

Rejection rate (all submissions): 95%.

Description of the Client from Hell: Someone who calls or e-mails constantly for news; expects a phone call when there's nothing to discuss, expects me to perform according to their timetable, has no knowledge of the publishing business and doesn't think it's their job to learn, doesn't want to work on next book until the first one is sold, can't accept rejection or criticism, needs a lot of hand-holding, has a negative attitude; fails to work as part of a team. Every once in while a Client from Hell slips into the agency, but once they show us their horns, we send them back to the inferno.

Description of a dream client: Someone who is passionate about writing; thoroughly professional; appreciative and understanding of my efforts; and who works as part of a team.

Most common mistakes authors make: Phoning, e-mailing, or faxing queries; calling to check that we received query letter or manuscript; expecting to meet me or showing up uninvited before I've agreed to represent them; interviewing me instead of the other way around; someone who raves about their material when the work has to speak for itself; someone who is more concerned about possible movie deals and marketing angles and the prestige of being an author rather than the actual writing; queries and manuscripts that are poorly written or that have typos; not sending an SASE.

How would you describe what you actually do for a living? I help make dreams come true.

JOELLE DELBOURGO ASSOCIATES, INC.

450 Seventh Avenue, Suite 3004, New York, NY 10123

fax: 212-279-8863

www.Delbourgo.com   e-mail: info@Delbourgo.com

Yes 4/30 (handwritten)

Agent: Joelle Delbourgo

Education: B.A. Magna Cum Laude, Phi Beta Kappa, Williams College (double major in History and English Literature); M.A. with Honors in English Literature from Columbia University.

Career history: Fall 1999 to present: President and Founder of Joelle Delbourgo Associates, Inc. 1996–1999: HarperCollins 1996–1997: Vice President, Editorial Director; 1997–1999: Senior Vice President, Editor in Chief and Associate Publisher; 1980–1996: Held various positions from Senior Editor to Vice President, Editor-in-Chief of Hardcover and Trade Paperback; 1976–1980: Various editorial positions at Bantam Books.

Hobbies/personal interests: Cooking, Latin and ballroom dancing, travel.

Areas most interested in agenting: Serious nonfiction, including history, psychology, women's issues, medicine and health, business, thesis-based books and interdisciplinary approaches to nonfiction subjects, literary fiction, some commercial fiction, some historical fiction. I handle some high-end lifestyle and fine art titles. I'm interested in serious thinkers and original ideas.

Areas not interested in agenting: No category fiction (including romance, Westerns, science fiction, and fantasy), very few thrillers, no children's books or technical books.

Best way to initiate contact: By writing an intelligent query letter, preferably one page in a readable type, that shows that you've done your homework.

Reading-fee policy: We do not charge to read submissions, but by the same token, we are not obligated to analyze your work for you unless you become a client.

Client representation by category: Nonfiction, 80%; Fiction, 20%.

Commission: 15% domestic; 20% on foreign and film.

Number of titles sold last year: 15.

Rejection rate: 95%.

Description of the Client from Hell: The client who approaches me by phone, sends materials in minuscule type without an SASE or by disc, calls to find out if the package has arrived, won't take no for an answer. Clients with a smattering of publishing knowledge that makes them second-guess the agent every step.

Description of a dream client: The client who has been thinking about the idea or book for a long time; who is passionate, committed, serious, respectful, and works hard over the long term to do right by the book. The client who understands that this is a partnership, between agent and client at first, and then with the editor and publisher.

My role is to guide, advise, cheer, facilitate, boost egos, and be there when the going gets rough.

Most common mistakes authors make: Pretending they know me when they don't, not sending an SASE, writing letters telling me how many other agents have rejected them already or how little they know about the process. Good-bye!

What can writers do to enhance their chances of getting you as their agent? Read books and articles about publishing to gain an understanding of the process. Be professional. Listen to advice, and understand that it comes from years of experience. Be kind. I am impressed by serious credentials or life experience, and, of course, it helps if the author has already established a platform, has contacts, media experience, been published previously, or won awards and/or grants. Write me a fabulous and respectful query and follow the guidelines on my website.

Why did you become an agent? I had put in 25 years on the corporate side, climbing the ladder from Editorial Assistant to many years as a top executive. I loved the publishing process, but it also grinds you down. I wanted to get back to what got me into publishing in the first place: working with writers and editors again. I also wanted to work for a company in which I could set the tone, one that is professional and generous and respectful, and the best way to do it seemed to be to create it myself!

If not agenting, what might you be doing? I would be a college professor or dean, perhaps, or a writer myself. Anything that involves life as learning. Publishing has been a continuous graduate school for me and has allowed me to hone my skills and knowledge, while pushing the envelope in those areas I'm curious about. My authors are often pioneers in their fields, and I get a firsthand education working with them. It really works both ways.

How would you describe what you do for a living? That's always tough to do. I see myself as helping to shape the culture, by choosing to support and develop ideas I find exciting, bodies of information that need to be shared, and literary experiences that will touch readers' hearts and minds. I like being a catalyst in people's lives, occasionally helping them to live their dreams. I am a muse, mother, therapist, advocate, CEO, and friend. Sometimes I wish I had someone like that in my life!

How did you become an agent? I left a high-level job I loved and the next day sat down and worked for eight hours, trying to figure out how to translate my deep experience into a company that specialized in literary management and some consulting. I am really an editor and publisher in drag; agenting allows me to continue having the conversations I've always loved to have, but from a different vantage point, which I think is immeasurably valuable to authors.

Why did you become an agent? I perceived that agents had taken on more and more of the creative editorial and marketing role for authors as their advocates within publishing houses have less and less time to edit books and develop their authors' careers. So it made sense to shift my experience and knowledge to helping authors earlier in the process.

What do you think about other agents? Many are wonderful; some are frauds. It's important for an author to do the homework required to determine who is reputable and who is not.

What do you think about editors? I'm nuts about them. Occasionally, you meet those who aren't smart or good at their job, but most are exceptional. They love what they do and live every day in the hope that they'll discover something wonderful, something worthy, something that can sell. I love the older, wiser, experienced ones, who have perfected their craft, but I'm also very impressed with the taste and talents of the many young editors in the business who have the ear of their management and take their responsibilities very seriously.

What do you think about publishers? They face a very tough challenge. I have a great deal of compassion for them (especially since I've been one!). There's enormous pressure to make margins that simply don't exist for the most part in publishing. It's an antiquated formula. And not many other businesses have to define every single "product" as distinct from every other every day. There is some franchise publishing, of course, but most publishers have to strike some balance between reducing books to formulas and highlighting what makes each one special, and that message has to be translated down the line, every step of the way, to booksellers and to the consumer.

What were your favorite films last year? *The House of Sand and Fog, Something's Gotta Give, Cold Mountain.*

Do you watch *The Sopranos?* No, I just didn't get into it. But I do confess to loving *Sex and the City.*

Comments: I get really irritated by all the gloom and doom about publishing. It's true that the traditional world of book publishing is shrinking, but it's equally true that there are marvelous new opportunities if you keep your eyes open. I'm fascinated with the opportunity that university presses have, for example, to develop what the "big" firms call "mid-list," or by the new trade lists being developed by McGraw-Hill, which was formerly thought of primarily as a business publisher, and Rodale Books, which is rapidly expanding beyond direct mail. While I'm a realist, my philosophy is to think positively and go where the opportunity is. I hate it when people don't agree with me, but, hopefully, I'm right about books more often then I'm wrong; no one "owes" you anything. You want to sell books because they are good and because someone at the publishing house has a vision for how to bring them to market. When it works correctly, it's a beautiful thing.

Representative titles: *Deflation* by Chris Farrell (HarperBusiness); *Dr. Yoga* by Nirmala Heriza (Tarcher/Penguin); *Now What: 90 Days to Change Your Life Direction* by Laura Berman Fortgang (Tarcher/Penguin); *The New Anti-Semitism* by Phyllis Chesler (Jossey-Bass/Wiley); *Seven Masters—One Path* by John Selby (HarperSan Francisco); *Feeling Unreal: Depersonalization Disorder and the Loss of the Self* by Dr. Daphne Simeon and Jeffrey Abugel (Oxford University Press); *Hurricane Season* by Pamela Duncan (Bantam Delacorte/Random House); *Mavericks, Miracle and Medicine* by Julie Fenster (Carroll & Graf/Avalon); *What Color is the Medicine? For My Sick Kid,* by Geeta Anand (Regan Books/HarperCollins).

DH LITERARY, INC.

PO Box 990, Nyack, NY 10960

212-753-7942

e-mail: dhendin@aol.com

Agent: David Hendin

Born: December 16, 1945.

Education: B.S. in Biology, Education, University of Missouri, 1967; M.A. in Journalism, University of Missouri, 1967.

Career history: United Feature Syndicate/United Media; Senior Vice President and Chief Operating Officer of United Feature Syndicate; President and Chief Operating Officer of World Almanac, Pharos Books (1970–1993). Author of 11 nonfiction books, including *Death as a Fact of Life* (Norton, Warner), *The Life Givers* (Morrow), and co-author of *The Genetic Connection* (Morrow, Signet).

Hobbies/personal interests: Archaeology.

Areas most interested in agenting: We are not accepting new clients at this time, though the agency remains active.

Areas not interested in agenting: Fiction submissions by referral only.

If not agenting, what would you be doing? Excavating ruins in the Middle East or teaching journalism at a university (both of which I've done).

Best way to initiate contact: E-mail: dhendin@aol.com

Reading-fee policy: No reading fee. We're members of the AAR.

Client representation by category: Nonfiction, 85%; Fiction, 10%; Textbooks, 5%.

Commission: 15%.

Number of titles sold last year: 15.

Rejection rate: 99.9%.

Most common mistakes authors make: Send too much material before being asked; don't write a good query letter; don't enclose SASE; start the query by telling me they have 14 unpublished projects...

Description of the client from Hell: I have no clients from Hell.

Description of a dream client: Great ideas, prompt delivery, at least a passing interest in the business side of publishing.

Why did you become an agent? I have been a newspaper columnist, book author, and president of a publishing company. Becoming an agent was the next logical extension of my professional life—not to mention that some of my best friends are writers!

Comments: Writers—send me your fabulous ideas. I have a relatively small number of clients and love to work on projects I like.

Representative titles: Two mystery series by Elaine Viets (Signet/Penguin); *Miss Manners Guide to Excruciatingly Correct Behavior* by Judith Martin (W. W. Norton & Co.); *Time Machines* by David Toomey (W.W. Norton & Co.).

DHS LITERARY, INC.

10711 Preston Road, Suite 100, Dallas, TX 75230

214-363-4422   fax: 214-363-4423

e-mail: submissions@dhsliterary.com

Agents: David Hale Smith
Born: July 9, 1968.
Education: B.A. in English, Kenyon College, 1990.
Career history: Copyeditor, one year, *Southwest NewsWire, Inc.*, Dallas; Assistant Agent/Agent, three years, Dupree/Miller & Associates, Dallas; founded DHS Literary Agency, March 1994.

Hobbies/personal interests: Reading, writing, camping, hiking, travel.

Areas most interested in agenting: Mainstream fiction: thrillers, suspense, mystery, historical fiction. Literary fiction. Business nonfiction. Multicultural interests. Pop culture, music, film and television, technology. General nonfiction and gift books.

Areas not interested in agenting: Short stories, poetry, and children's.

If not agenting, what would you be doing? I would also like to travel around the world with my family one day.

Best way to initiate contact: We no longer accept unsolicited queries. We only consider manuscripts recommended by published authors and other industry contacts.

Reading-fee policy: No reading fee.

Client Representation: Nonfiction, 65%; Fiction, 35%.

Commission: 15% domestic sales; 20% on foreign (via subagents).

Number of titles sold last year: 28.

Rejection rate: 99%.

Most common mistakes authors make: The biggest mistake we see people making is coming on too strong without backing up their claims of "sure-fire" success. We think that people must be aggressive to get noticed in this business—but if you're all style and no substance, it is a waste of everybody's time. Another common blunder we see is just a general lack of preparedness. Spend some time learning about the business before contacting agents and publishers.

Description of the client from Hell: Unprofessional people who think that once they have an agent, their role in placing and selling their work is finished. We had a client who made the mistake of thinking this agency was his personal secretarial and counseling firm, without ever realizing that all the time we spent talking to him and doing his busywork was time we couldn't spend selling his stuff. He is no longer a client.

Description of a dream client: A professional in every phase of the business, who believes that the agent–author relationship is a team endeavor. A successful publishing experience is the result of a collaborative effort. We work extremely hard for our clients—and we work even harder for those who make it easier for us to do our job by working with us, not against us.

Why did you become an agent? I have always loved books, reading good ones, and talking about them with other people—that's the best part of the job. When I learned that agents get to see the good stuff even before the publishers do, that's where I wanted to be.

What can writers do to enhance their chances of getting you as an agent? See our description of the "dream client." We actually have an "Ideal Client Profile": talented, passionate, professional, progressive thinker, articulate communicator, and financially independent. If you fit that profile, we want to hear from you.

How would you describe what it is you do for a living? We manage the careers of professional writers.

Representative titles: *A Fistful of Rain* by Greg Rucka (Bantam); *As Luck Would Have It* by Josh Piven (Villard).; *The Neiman Marcus Cookbook* by Kevin Garvin with John Harrisson (Clarkson Potter); *City on Fire* by Bill Minutaglio (Harper).

JIM DONOVAN LITERARY

4515 Prentice, Suite 109, Dallas, TX 75206

214-696-9411

Agent: Jim Donovan
Education: B.S., University of Texas.
Career history: In books since 1981 as a bookstore manager; chain-store buyer; published writer (*Dallas: Shining Star of Texas*, 1994, Voyageur Press; *The Dallas Cowboys Encyclopedia*, 1996, Carol Publishing; *Elvis Immortal*, 1997, Legends Press; *Custer and the Little Bighorn*, 2001, Voyager Press); Freelance Editor; Senior Editor, Taylor Publishing, five years. Literary Agent since 1993.

Areas most interested in agenting: Fiction: Thriller, mystery (not cozy), contemporary. Nonfiction: Sports, history, popular culture, biography, business, military, popular reference, and narrative nonfiction.

Areas not interested in agenting: Children's, poetry, short stories, romance, religious/spiritual, technical books, computer books, screenplays, science fiction and fantasy.

If not agenting, what would you be doing? A publisher.

Best way to initiate contact: Nonfiction: Query with synopsis and SASE. Fiction: Query with 2–5 page synopsis, first 30–40 pages, and SASE.

Reading-fee policy: No reading fee.

Client representation by category: Nonfiction, 70%; Fiction, 30%.

Commission: 15%.

Number of titles sold last year: About 24.

Rejection rate (all submissions): 98%.

Most common mistakes authors make: The top 10 query letter turnoffs: (1) Don't use a form letter that begins with "To whom it may concern" or "Dear editor." (2) Don't say your writing is better than bestselling writers'. (3) Don't mention your self-published books unless they've sold several thousand copies. (4) Don't refer to your "fiction novel." (5) Don't brag about how great or how funny your book is. (6) Don't quote rave reviews from your relatives, friends, or editors whom you've paid. (7) Don't tell the agent how you're positive your book will make both of you rich. (8) Don't say it's one of five novels you've finished. (9) Don't tell the editor that he'll be interested because it will make a great movie. (10) Don't ask for advice or suggestions (if you don't think it's ready, why should they?).

What do you think about editors? Editors are the miners of the publishing world—they spend days and nights digging through endless layers of worthless material for the occasional golden nugget. Anything the agent or the writer can do to make their job easier is greatly appreciated, so I stress that to potential writers.

Comments: Most aspiring authors don't want to put in the time and effort necessary to become published—they think that if they attend enough writers' conferences and read enough books on how to become published that somehow, through some form of osmosis or alchemy, they will become published. I'm not interested in working with someone who doesn't understand that the key to publication is revision . . . and more revision . . . and more revision. The #1 problem with the unsolicited material I receive is that it's almost always not well-written enough—buy a copy of *The Elements of Style* and master those 85 pages before you go any further.

Representative titles: *The Art of Client Service* by Robert Solomon (Dearborn); *Dead Man Rise Up Never* by Ron Faust (Bantam); *Streetcar* by Sam Staggs (St. Martin's); *The Killing Ground* by Bill Sloan (Simon & Schuster); *Hinterland* by Carlton Stowers (De Capo); *The Tuna Went Down to Texas* by Mike Shropshire.

DUNHAM LITERARY, INC.

156 Fifth Avenue, Suite 625, New York, NY 10010-7002

212-929-0994   fax: 212-929-0904

www.dunhamlit.com

Agents: Jennie Dunham
The Rhoda Weyr Agency is now a division of Dunham Literary, Inc.
Dunham Literary, Inc. has an alliance with the Denise Marcil Literary Agency and Don Congdon Associates.
Born: April 1969.
Education: Magna Cum Laude, Anthropology major, Princeton University.

Career history: One year at John Brockman Associates, one year at Mildred Marmur Associates, six years at Russell & Volkening, started Dunham Literary in August 2000.

Hobbies/personal interests: Book arts and paper making, movies, photography, Old English, language and linguistics, feminist/women's studies, travel, science, history, health, religion and spirituality. I'm an animal lover, but I'm partial to dogs (I have a Newfoundland). I also collect first printings of first editions of books.

Areas most interested in agenting: Quality fiction and non-fiction for adults, and children's books for all ages.

Areas not interested in agenting: Romance, science fiction, poetry, horror, Westerns, and individual short stories. Also, we don't represent plays or screenplays (but we do represent books into movies and plays).

Best way to initiate contact: Write a letter describing the project and the author's qualifications for the project and enclose the customary self-addressed, stamped envelope for a response. If the project seems as if we might be interested, we will request it. Please do not send sample material unless requested. We do not accept phone calls for query pitches, and we do not accept e-mail or faxed queries. Please visit our website, www.dunhamlit.com, for lots of details and FAQ about submitting to this agency.

Client representation : Adult fiction and nonfiction 50%; children's 50%.

Commission: 15% domestic, motion picture, and other dramatic contracts; 20% foreign contracts.

Number of titles sold last year: 25.

Rejection rate (all submissions): We reject the vast majority of query letters sent to us, but we read each one and respond usually within a week. So many people write to us with books about topics that we don't handle. Just doing this little bit of research will substantially increase a writer's chance of finding the right match with an agent.

Description of the client from Hell: A client who says one thing and does another, who doesn't listen or trust an agent's advice, who doesn't know or pay attention to the market, and who tries to tell an agent how to handle his or her business.

Description of the dream client: A client who is productive, dedicated, talented, successful, interesting, and pleasant is a good client. It's also good if the client wins awards and is a self-promoter. A sense of humor that accompanies realistic expectations given the market is also appreciated.

Most common mistakes authors make: In this day of computers, it's a mistake to send a form query letter without a specific person's name in the salutation. Also, sometimes writers address agents familiarly, as if they knew them, which really should be reserved for people who do know them personally. The grammar, spelling, and punctuation should all be correct. It's really best to send the query letter in writing rather than to call first and ask to send it. That does not constitute a solicited manuscript. It's also a mistake to call and interview agents before submitting a query letter.

What can writers do to enhance their chances of getting you as an agent? Professionalism, good writing, good ideas, and the willingness to work with an agent to manage the writer's career make us enthusiastic about a client. More people try to write bestsellers than good books, and if they concentrated on writing a good book, they'd be closer to having a bestseller. We look closely at a writer's previous experience, especially in magazines and books.

How did you become an agent? By accident. Isn't that how most things happen? I graduated from college at a time when few jobs were available. I knew I wanted to have a job where I worked with books, so I found an internship at a publishing company. They recommended me to a headhunter. I was sent on one interview, and when offered the job I took it.

Why did you become an agent? Did you read the answer to that last question? I wanted a paycheck, and I'd be offered one. It was during that first job at an agency that I knew that this is what I wanted for a career. As an agent I like helping authors to bring their books to the world. In this sense I like to think of myself as a midwife of creativity or someone who can make a writer's dream come true. I like the variety of book projects I handle as an agent. I receive great satisfaction in protecting authors by negotiating contracts for them. I also collect books.

If not agenting, what would you be doing? Maybe I would be an anthropologist or a professor of English, folklore, or communications.

How would you describe what you do for a living? I connect writers and publishers.

What do you think about editors? Editors help guide an author to create his or her best work. They're an invaluable part of the publishing process, and they're not appreciated enough.

What do you think about publishers? Publishers provide visibility, credibility, and distribution channels for author's books. They're an important part of getting good books into readers' hands.

What were your favorite films last year? *O Brother, Where Art Thou?*; *Chocolat*; *Shrek*; *Harry Potter and the Sorcerer's Stone*.

Do you watch *The Sopranos?* No, as a matter of fact I do not watch *The Sopranos*. I tend to watch the Discovery Channel, the Learning Channel, and the History Channel.

Comments: It takes talent and hard work to capture human truths in words, and to me that is what makes good writing, fiction and non-fiction, vital to our lives.

Because the business is one of having a few, lucrative clients rather than a lot of clients, most agents need to be extremely selective with the clients they take on. One agent may turn down the same writer who is snapped up by a different agent.

Representative titles: *Living Dead Girl* by Tod Goldberg (Soho Press); *In My Mother's House* by Margaret McMullan (Thomas Dunne Books); *Road Work* by Mark Bowden (Grove/Atlantic); *Baby Massage* by Michelle Kluck (Running Press); *Covenants* by Lorna Freeman (ROC); *Alice in Wonderland* (pop-up) by Robert Sabuda (Little Simon); *Dahlia* retold and illustrated by Barbara McClintock (Farrar, Straus & Giroux); *Clever Beatrice and the Best Little Pony* by Margaret Willey and illustrated by Heather Solomon (Atheneum); *Who Will Tell My Brother?* by Marlene Carvell (Hyperion).

ELLENBERG LITERARY AGENCY

548 Broadway, #5E, New York, NY 10012

fax: 212-941-4652

www.ethanellenberg.com   e-mail: agent@ethanellenberg.com

Agents: Ethan Ellenberg, Michael Psaltis
Place of birth: Psaltis: New York.
Educational History: University of Maryland.
Career History: Prior to joining the Ellenberg Literary Agency, worked at a book marketing firm, for a book publicist, for Newmarket Press and for the Book Industry Study Group.
Areas most interested in agenting: Psaltis: Serious nonfiction, cooking and food-related books, health, science and many other areas of narrative nonfiction; literary fiction and all types of commercial fiction.
Areas not interested in agenting: Psaltis: Poetry, short stories, children's books.
Best way to initiate contact: E-mail or via postal mail.
Reading-fee policy: No reading or other fees of any kind.
Client representation: 40% fiction; 60% nonfiction.
Commission structure: 15%, except when co-agent is involved on foreign and other subsidiary rights deals the commission is 10% (and 10% for the co-agent).
Number of titles sold last year: Agency sold over 100 titles last year.
Rejection rate: At least 95% rejected.
Most common mistakes authors make with your agency: Send material that we do not handle.
What can writers do to enhance their chances of getting you as an agent? Be professional in all aspects.
Representative titles: Steven Shaw's *Restaurants Revealed*; Elizabeth Crane and Sharon Chandler's *Aim High* (Perigee/Penguin); Elaine Gavalas' *Yogi in the Kitchen* (Avery/Penguin); David Smith's *Why We Lie* (St. Martin's Press); Bev Vincent's *The Road to the Dark Tower* (NAL/Dutton).

FARRIS LITERARY AGENCY, INC.

PO Box 570069, Dallas, TX 75357-0069

972-203-8804

www.farrisliterary.com   e-mail: farris1@airmail.net; agent@farrisliterary.com

Agents: Michael D. Farris, Susan Morgan Farris

Born: Michael: June 30, 1955, Baton Rouge, Louisiana. Susan: September 23, 1958, Dallas, Texas.

Education: Michael: B.A. in Political Science, University of Texas at Arlington; J.D. (Cum Laude), Texas Tech University School of Law. Susan: B.A. (Cum Laude) in English, Stephen F. Austin State University; J.D., Texas Tech University School of Law.

Career history: Michael: Attorney since 1983, freelance editor. Susan: Attorney since 1983, freelance editor, college instructor.

Hobbies/personal interests: Michael: Reading, travel, movies, sports. Susan: Gardening, traveling, reading.

Areas most interested in agenting: Fiction: Thrillers, suspense, mysteries, romance, mainstream, horror, action/adventure, literary, Christian, Westerns. Nonfiction: How-to, law, true crime, self-help, current affairs, popular culture, women's issues, biography, history, political, travel, sports, theater/film, spiritual, inspirational.

Areas not interested in agenting: Poetry, children's, fantasy, New Age, occult, gay/lesbian, erotica, science fiction, technical, computer.

Best way to initiate contact: Send a one-page query letter with SASE or an e-mail query letter.

Client representation by category: 60% fiction; 40% non-fiction

Rejection rate: 99%.

Commission: 15% domestic; 20% foreign.

Description of the client from Hell: Those who fail to follow through on what they need to do, but who make outrageous demands on others.

Description of the dream client: Clients who write well, tell a good story, are articulate and personable, and allow agents to do their job.

Common mistakes authors make: Failing to proofread and/or not knowing how to properly use the English language.

What can writers do to enhance their chances of getting you as their agent? Have more than one book in them, and be able to sell themselves as well as their writing.

Why did you become an agent? Michael: I have loved reading my entire life. I decided to do something that combines my legal training and skills with that love. Susan: With my English degree and love of literature, it was a natural progression to add "literary agent" to "attorney at law."

If not agenting what might you be doing? Lounging on a beach in Hawaii.

How would you describe what you do for a living? Helping people tell their stories to the world.

How did you become an agent? It was a natural transition from our backgrounds as attorneys, including some entertainment law practice.

What do you think about editors? Editors are all looking for that next great writer. We hope to be able to help them find several.

What do you think about publishers? Publishing has become a bottom-line-oriented business. We'd like to help with their bottom lines by bringing them talented new writers.

What were your favorite films last year? *Mystic River, Seabiscuit, Master and Commander, The Missing.*

Do you watch *The Sopranos?* No.

Comments: The only ones who accomplish their dreams are those who dare to dream. So dream.

Representative titles: *The Proud Bastards* by E. Michael Helms (Pocket Books); *The I Don't Know How to Cook Book* by Mary-Lane Kamberg (Adams Media); *Balaam Gimble's Gumption* by Mike Nichols (John M. Hardy Publishing Company).

THE FOGELMAN LITERARY AGENCY

7515 Greenville Avenue, Suite 712, Dallas, TX 75231

214-361-9956   fax: 214-361-9553

www.Fogelman.com   e-mail: foglit@aol.com

Agents: Evan M. Fogelman, Linda M. Kruger, Helen C. Brown

Born: Fogelman: May 1, 1960. Kruger: May 16, 1967.

Education: Fogelman: B.A. with Honors, Tulane University, 1982; J.D., Tulane University, 1985; Stanford Publishing Course. Kruger: B.A. in Media Theory and Criticism, University of Texas at Austin, 1989. Brown: B.A. Brown University.

Career history: Fogelman: Entertainment attorney, book reviewer, author publicist. Kruger: Has been with the agency since its inception. Brown: Marketing, TV, VH-1, MTV.

Hobbies/personal interests: Fogelman: Enjoying the company of my wife and children, laughter, French bulldogs, distance running, history, issues of constitutional law, investing. Kruger: Walking, dogs, reading, home projects, movies.

Areas most interested in agenting: Fogelman: Romantic suspense, mysteries, romance with humor/idiosyncrasy, thrillers, all matter of nonfiction, business subjects. Brown: Nonfiction, literary fiction.

Areas not interested in agenting: Fogelman: Anything not listed previously. Kruger: Poetry, short stories, true Westerns, science fiction, historical fiction, action adventure, New Age, mysteries. Brown: historical romance, science fiction, children's, humor.

If not agenting, what would you be doing? Fogelman: I'd be in the oil business. Book deals are often a lot like wildcat oil wells, actually. Kruger: Taking way too many pictures of my two Labs.

Best way to initiate contact: Fogelman: E-mail or snail mail. Kruger: A query letter with SASE will be responded to within five business days. Published authors are invited to call. No unsolicited material, please. Please check out our website at www.Fogelman.com. Brown: E-mail or snail mail.

Reading-fee policy: No reading fee.

Client representation by category: Fogelman: Nonfiction, 50%; Fiction, 50%. Kruger: Nonfiction, 10%; Fiction, 90%.

Commission: 15% domestic, including all agency-negotiated subsidiary-rights deals; 10% foreign.

Number of titles sold last year: Fogelman: 75-plus; Kruger: 50-plus.

Rejection rate (all submissions): 99.5%.

Most common mistakes authors make: Fogelman: Seeking representation too early in the process. If you're a new novelist, finish the book first. If you're a nonfiction writer, do a formal proposal first. Kruger: When writers cannot tell me what type of a book they have written. One writer described his book as (and this is an actual quote), "A non-genre erotic contemporary mainstream men's fantasy action/adventure romantic sexual comedy novel, or, if you really need a category, call it Romance Novel, Male Division." In helping writers categorize their books, I always ask one question: If you had one copy of your manuscript and you had to put it on one bookshelf at the bookstore, where would it go? Also, I hate unsolicited material.

What can writers do to enhance their chances of getting you as an agent? Kruger: Research the agency and know what I am looking for and what types of work I represent. Our website really helps!

Description of the client from Hell: Fogelman: Authors who would rather complain to me about how unfair publishing is instead of finishing their book; authors who scream for all the rest of us to make our deadlines, yet demand an extension on every contracted manuscript delivery date. Kruger: A writer who does not realize that this is a creative, yet professional, business.

Description of a dream client: Fogelman: Authors who love to write more than they like to tell others, "I'm a writer." Kruger: Someone who keeps the lines of communication open. This is a two-way relationship. As for the creative process, my dream client creates characters and then releases those characters to tell the story.

How did you become an agent? Kruger: I met Evan Fogelman when he opened the doors to the agency. His enthusiasm and love of the business were contagious and my schooling and background made agenting second nature for me. Fogelman: As an entertainment lawyer, I started negotiating book deals and became enthralled. Brown: The business of books fascinates me.

Why did you become an agent? Fogelman: I completely enjoy the crossroads of art and commerce. Kruger: There are many reasons I became an agent, but what keeps me in this business is the chance to work with such creative individuals. This is an exciting business, one unlike any other profession. The atmosphere of our agency is always entertaining and challenging. I wouldn't change a thing.

How would you describe what you actually do for a living? Kruger: I wear many hats. I'm an editor, a listener, a cheerleader, a reader, a salesman, a negotiator. At times, I am a pit bull and at other times, I let silence work for me. Fogelman: Negotiating commerce for art!

What do you think about editors? Kruger: As long as they are acquiring my clients' books, I love them. Fogelman: What—are you a comedian? I love editors.

Without them, I wouldn't have a job. Brown: It's co-dependency!

What were your favorite films last year? Fogelman/Kruger/Brown: Any film that was adapted from a book!

Do you watch *The Sopranos?* Fogelman: No. But I watch my wife watching *The Sopranos*—now that's interesting! Kruger: No.

Comments: Fogelman: Spending four hours each day in a chat room will do very little to help turn your book into a screenplay. Remember, writing is better than a regular-type job—that's one of the reasons you got into it, right? Share what you do with your children—they will look at reading in a whole new way. Kruger: I've heard it said that there are those who are compelled to write and those who love to write. My clients are compelled to write—and I love what they write.

Representative titles: The Agency's clients include Terri Brisbin, Lisa Cach, Alice Duncan, Anne Eames, Elizabeth Eliot, Jane Graves, Leann Harris, Candice Hern, Victoria Chancellor, Caroline Rose Hunt, Joni Johnston, Karon Karter, April Kihlstrom, Sylvie Kurtz, Karen Leabo, Delia Parr, Pam McCutcheon, Laurel O'Donnell, Gwen Pemberton, Susan Plunkett, Louise B. Raggio, Laura Renken, Larry Shriner, Teresa Southwick, Crystal Stovall, Katherine Sutcliffe, RaeAnne Thayne, Ronda Thompson, and Cathy Yardley.

FORTHWRITE LITERARY AGENCY/KELLER MEDIA, INC.

100 Wilshire Boulevard, Suite 625 Santa Monica, CA 90401

1-866-62-WRITE   fax: 310-456-6589

www.kellermedia.com   e-mail: query@kellermedia.com

Agents: Senior Agent: Wendy Keller; Associate Agent: Deborah Charles; Editorial Director: Alex Schnitzler

Born: Keller: Chicago, Illinois.

Education: Arizona State University, Journalism.

Career history: Agent since 1988, founded ForthWrite 1989, incorporated Keller Media, Inc. 2003.

Hobbies/personal interests: Reading, learning Italian, shopping with my pre-teen.

Areas most interested in agenting: Self-help (from how to have a happier life to overcoming eating disorders to living pain-free, etc), parenting, pop psych, health/alternative health/healing, Metaphysical/Universal wisdom, Buddhism, inspirational, how-to (do anything from train a puppy to grow better tomatoes), Business (sales, management, marketing, entrepreneurship, career, finance). We also resell self-published books to major US publishers, and sell many foreign rights into and out of the USA. Multilingual: Fluent French, limited Italian, Spanish, and Polish.

Areas not interested in agenting: We *never* do *any* fiction *nor* first person stories like, "I got over this or that medical or mental problem." We don't handle anything channeled by Jesus, Princess Di, Mother Teresa, your dead granny, or the Great Pumpkin. We don't handle screenplays (despite our location) and we don't handle coffee table books or books meant for children.

Best way to initiate contact: E-mail query first.

Reading-fee policy: No reading fee.

Client representation by category: Nonfiction, 100%.

Commission: 15% life of property; 20% foreign we place.

Number of titles sold last year: 17

Rejection rate (all submissions): 92%.

Most common mistakes authors make: (1) Telling me their book is better than anything ever published in the history of mankind. (2) Not knowing there have to be more than three other people in the United States interested in their topic for me to sell it. (3) Forgetting that publishing is a business, not a hobby, for those of us on this side of the desk.

Description of the client from Hell: I don't take on "clients" from Hell! But there are apparently thousands of unpublished writers from Hell! They're the ones who didn't research their topic before writing; who have no credentials for their topic; who don't understand that there are competitive books; or who start their query letter with "I'm a bestseller to be!"

Description of a dream client: My list of authors. (*Awwww!*)

Why did you become an agent? Lightning bolt struck me…twice…in front of a bookstore.

If not agenting, what might you be doing? Rereading *The Alchemist* on the patio of my palazzo in Firenze.

How did you become an agent? Mother Teresa came to me in a vision, wearing galoshes and a pink boa. Each step she made left an impression similar to newsprint on the white marble floor. She channeled the idea that the publishing industry contained my ultimate destiny. I looked at the floor and read the words, and together they said, "You Help Should Published Get Authors." Then I realized it was a word scramble. The rest is history!

What can writers do to enhance their chances of getting you as an agent? Research your competition and be prepared to adapt your concept if necessary to make it worth more money. Be a public speaker or have the intent to become one. Be a long-term thinker when it comes to your book and its surrounding success. You'll probably make more money from the things you do around the book, than from the book itself: e.g, speaking, consulting, special sales, grow your business or practice, etc.

How would you describe what you actually do for a living? My team and I help would-be authors position themselves as marketable people in the eyes of publishers. We turn them into speaker/author/consultants with a direct, proven method. We are "forced" to do all of this while watching 9 miles of azure Pacific Coastline from our office windows, luxuriating in an exquisite environment and working with really cool, motivated people, on your side of publishing and on ours.

What do you think about other agents? I think there are many good agents. I have many friends who also sell books with integrity and respect for authors. However, I have also met many "housewife agents"–people who do this part time trying to make a few bucks. I started out that way, with a baby at my feet and #2 on the way. But the reality is, my clients are much better served now by me being a real, professional agent instead of a homespun "nice person who likes the book."

What do you think about editors? I think the world would come to a screeching halt without their dedication to content. Seriously, they work very, very hard for their money, often putting in hours that would make most people faint. They usually have a keen eye for content and work to keep their finger on the pulse of national interest so the books they publish not only succeed but help their intended audience.

What do you think about publishers? I love every single one who sends accurate checks by their due date.

Do you watch *The Sopranos?* Never. But I can sing it.

Comments: If you're a writer who wants to get published and you've spent the time to read this book, write your idea, and know how your book contributes to this crowded market, good for you. But if you haven't done your research—that is, you don't know who will buy your book and why—buy Jeff Herman's guide. Before you discourage yourself and waste our time and yours, find out what your book contributes: Is it new? Different? Better? More? How does it compare with all the other similar books? Why will anyone buy it? Why? Find an agent when you can answer that question because you won't before.

Representative titles: *Powerful Presentations for the Sales Professional* by Gary Hankins, (Dearborn); *The Acorn Principle* by Jim Cathcart (Russian and Swedish rights); *The Seven Principles of Conscious Parenting* by Shirley Yuen (Tuttle Publishing); *Raising a Secure Child: Creating an Emotional Connection between You and Your Child* by Dr. Zeynep Biringen (Viking/Penguin/Putnam/Perigee).

FOSTER LITERARY AGENCY

PO Box 939, West Jordan, UT 84084-0939

801-280-3890

e-mail: tinajazz@aol.com

Agent: Tina Foster
Born: 4/21/45, Salt Lake City, Utah.
Education: University of Utah/Journalism; Salt Lake Community College/Police Academy.
Career History: South Jordan Police Department for 5 years/writer for 20 years/ taught fiction writing classes for 7 years/editor for 6 years.

Hobbies/ personal interests: Reading, theater, music, travel, movies

Areas most interested in agenting? Romance, mystery, thrillers, suspense, historicals, western, mainstream, women's fiction.

Areas not interested in agenting? Horror, short stories, poetry.

Best way to initiate contact: Query with a self-addressed, stamped envelope. May send first three chapters and synopsis with SASE.

Client representation by category: Nonfiction, 20%; Fiction, 80%

Commission: 15% U.S. sales

Number of titles sold last year: Started in February of 2003.

Rejection rate (all submissions): About 90%- maybe higher.

Description of the client from Hell: People who call and try to pitch their novel over the phone. Or expect me to call them back in answer to a query because they didn't include an SASE. One who needs a lot of hand holding, expects editors at a publishing house to critique their work and tell them why they didn't like their writing. Thinks they are supposed to get results within a couple of weeks.

Description of a dream client: One who sends a well-written query, an intriguing synopsis, and a polished and professional manuscript that is properly formatted. One who knows that the wheels of publishing turn slowly and that everything takes time.

Most common mistakes authors make: Not including an SASE for a reply. An improperly formatted manuscript, i.e. single spacing, no page numbers, header, lots of spelling errors and typos.

What can writers do to enhance their chances of getting you as an agent? Make sure manuscripts are properly formatted, double check spelling and typos. Be patient. It takes a while to read through all the manuscripts. Have a polished and professional manuscript, an intriguing story that is told well.

Why did you become an agent? After teaching a fiction writing class for the last several years, I saw a lot of talent slip through.

What might you be doing if you weren't an agent? Still teaching fiction writing and writing my own stuff.

How would you describe what it is that you actually do for a living? Basically I read books for a living. If I read a really good one, then I want to share it with publishers.

How did you become an agent? I couldn't find any agents listed in Utah, so I decided to open up this untapped market.

What do you think about editors? They are your first audience.

What do you think about publishers? Without them, there wouldn't be all the diverse selection of books out there.

What were your favorite films last year? *Gangs of New York* and *The Pianist*.

Do you watch *The Sopranos?* Sorry, I don't have HBO.

Representative titles: Being new, it takes awhile to get started, but I have at least 12 novels under consideration. Hopefully by the next edition I'll have more details to report.

JEANNE FREDERICKS LITERARY AGENCY, INC.

221 Benedict Hill Road, New Canaan, CT 06840

voice/fax: 203-972-3011

e-mail: jfredrks@optonline.net

Agent: Jeanne Fredericks

Born: April 19, 1950.

Education: B.A., Mount Holyoke College, 1972; Radcliffe Publishing Procedures Course; M.B.A., New York University Graduate School of Business Administration, 1979.

Career history: Assistant to Editorial Director and Foreign/Subsidiary Rights Director, Basic Books (1972–1974); Managing Editor and Acquisitions Editor, Macmillan (1974–1980); Editorial Director, Ziff-Davis Books (1980–1981); Literary Agent, Susan P. Urstadt Agency (1990–1996); Acting Director, Susan P. Urstadt Agency (1996–1997); established own agency, February 1997. Member of AAR.

Hobbies/personal interests: Crew, family activities, tennis, swimming, yoga, reading, cooking, traveling, gardening, casual entertaining.

Areas most interested in agenting: Practical, popular reference by authorities, especially in health, sports, science, business, cooking, parenting, travel, antiques and decorative arts, gardening, women's issues.

Areas not interested in agenting: Horror, occult fiction, true crime, juvenile, textbooks, poetry, essays, plays, short stories, science fiction, pop culture, computers and software guides, politics, pornography, overly depressing or violent topics, memoirs that are more suitable for one's family or that are not compelling enough for the trade market, romance, manuals for teachers.

If not agenting, what would you be doing? A trade book publisher or a writer.

Best way to initiate contact: Please query (with SASE) by mail, with outline, description of project, author biography, sample writing. No phone calls. No fax. E-mail queries should be short and without attachments.

Reading-fee policy: No reading fee.

Client representation by category: Adult Nonfiction, 98%; Fiction, 2%

Commission: 15% domestic (20% movie, TV, video); 20% foreign (if direct); 25% foreign (if with co-agent).

Number of titles sold last year: 15.

Rejection rate (all submissions): 95%.

Most common mistakes authors make: Calling me to describe their proposed books and giving far too much detail. I'd much rather see that potential clients can write well before I spend valuable phone time with them. Also, claiming to have the only book on a subject when a quick check on the Internet reveals that there are competitive titles.

Description of the client from Hell: Arrogant, pushy, self-centered, unreliable writers who don't understand publishing or respect my time, and who vent their anger in an unprofessional way.

Description of a dream client: Creative, cooperative, professional writers who are experts in their fields and who can offer information and guidance that are new and needed by a sizable audience.

Why did you become an agent? I enjoy working with creative writers who need my talents to find the right publishers for their worthy manuscripts and to negotiate fair contracts on their behalf. I'm still thrilled when I open a box of newly published books by one of my authors, knowing that I had a small role in making it happen. I'm also ever hopeful that the books I represent will make a difference in the lives of many people.

How did you become an agent? While I was a full-time mom with young children, an agent who used to send me proposals when I was an editorial director asked me to work part-time with her as an independent agent. The position allowed me to return to publishing in a gradual way as my children spent increasing amounts of time in school.

What can writers do to enhance their chances of getting you as an agent? Show me that they have thoroughly researched the competition and can convincingly explain why their proposed books are different, better, and needed by large, defined audiences. Be polite, patient, and willing to work hard to make their proposals ready for submission.

What would you be doing if you weren't an agent? Reading and traveling more for pleasure, or perhaps writing or running a publishing company.

How would you describe what you actually do for a living? Putting together the right authors with the right publishers, negotiating contracts on behalf of authors, checking royalty statements and monitoring the flow of money from publishers to authors, acting as the diplomat if problems arise during the publishing process.

What do you think about editors? Having been on the editorial side of publishing for about 10 years, I have great respect for the demands on the time of a busy editor. I therefore try to be targeted and to the point when I telephone them and provide them with a one-page pitch letter that gives them the essence of what they need to make a proposal to management. I also make sure that the proposals I represent are focused, complete, and professional to make it easy for an editor to grasp the concept quickly and have a good sense of what the book will be like and why it will sell well. With few exceptions, editors value the creativity and hard work of authors and are intelligent and well-meaning. Since they are often overwhelmed with manuscripts, paperwork, and meetings, though, they sometimes neglect some of their authors and need an agent's nudging and reminders.

Representative titles: *Lilias! Yoga Gets Better with Age* by Lilias Folan (Rodale), *Creating Optimism: A Proven Seven-Step Program for Overcoming Depression* by Bob Murray, Ph.D. and Alicia Fortinberry, M. S. (Contemporary Books); *What's That You're Eating?: What the Food Industry Does to Your Food and How to Eat Well Anyway* by Carol Hart, Ph.D. (Avery); *Melanoma* by Catherine Poole with Dupont Guerry, M.D. (Yale); *Outdoors: The Perfect Fit* by Anne Halpin (Rodale); *From Storebought to Homemade* by Emyl

Jenkins (QVC); *The Complete Greenhouse Book* by Roger Marshall (Storey); *How to Invest in Real Estate* by Carolyn Janik (Kiplinger); *The Art and Craft of Pounding Flowers* by Laura Martin (Rodale); *Getting Ready for Baby* by Helene Tragos Stelian (Chronicle); *The Internet Legal Guide* by Dennis Powers (John Wiley & Sons); *Cowboys and Dragons: Shattering Cultural Myths to Achieve Better Chinese-American Business Relations* by Charles Lee, Ph.D. (Dearborn); *Yoga for Men* by Thomas Claire (Career Press); *Handbook to Life in the Medieval World* by Madeleine Cosman.

SARAH JANE FREYMANN LITERARY AGENCY

59 West 71st Street, Suite 9B, New York, NY 10023

fax: 212-501-8240

e-mail: sjfs@aol.com

Agent: Sarah Jane Freymann

Born: London, England.

Education: Although educated mostly in New York, I went to a French school, the Lycée Français, which is why I am fluent in many languages; and I traveled a great deal from a very early age.

Career history: My first job was with the United Nations; I also worked as a model and as an editor.

Hobbies/personal interests: Inner and outer journeys; adventures of all kinds that generate insight, growth, a greater appreciation for our world, passion, an inquisitive mind, and a fiercely gentle heart; wonderful food and laughter shared with good friends; listening to my daughter's beautiful voice and savoring her delicious cooking.

Areas most interested in agenting: Nonfiction: Spirituality, psychology, body/mind/spirit, self-help; women's/men's issues; health (conventional and alternative); cookbooks; narrative nonfiction; natural science, nature; memoirs, biography; cutting-edge current events; multicultural issues; popular culture. Fiction: Quality mainstream and literary fiction.

Areas not interested in agenting: Science fiction, fantasy, horror, genre romance, young adult, genre mysteries, screenplays, anything channeled.

If not agenting, what would you be doing? This year, whether agenting or not, one of my first priorities is to participate in some form of political activism. After that, doing my writing/meditation/therapy work; working with children and adolescents; to start ballroom dancing; and, wishfully thinking, to cultivate a quiet haven somewhere by the sea.

Best way to initiate contact: Via e-mail (no attachments). Or via query with SASE.

Reading-fee policy: No reading fee.

Client representation by category: Nonfiction, 85%; Fiction, 15%.

Commission: 15% domestic; 20% foreign.

Rejection rate (all submissions): 85%.

Most common mistakes authors make: Calling us and attempting to describe your work over the telephone. Submitting to more than one agent at a time and not letting us know you have.

Description of the client from Hell: I wouldn't know—we've never had one.

Description of a dream client: Someone who is not only a natural storyteller and writes beautifully, with passion and intelligence, but who is also a human being—a "mensch." Someone with a sense of humor, who also has the patience and willingness to rewrite and rework their material if necessary. And last, but not least, clients who have enough confidence in themselves and in us not to call us too often, and who realize that if we spend all our time talking to them on the phone, we won't have that time to spend selling their work.

Why did you become an agent? Probably in the genes. I'm a natural matchmaker and a physician's daughter. I like to think that thanks to my intervention, this author and that publisher met, formed a relationship, and that I am the midwife to this wonderful book.

How did you become an agent? Thinking back, all I can say is that it was a case of, leap before you look, or of angels rushing in where fools would have feared to tread.

What can writers do to enhance their chances of getting you as an agent? Submit a strong, clear, well-written query letter that sells both the book and its author, with the promise of substance rather than hype.

How would you describe what you actually do for a living? I'm a treasure hunter constantly in search of hidden gems and undiscovered talent; I'm an editor who helps clients shape their manuscripts and proposals; I'm a matchmaker, a deal-maker, and a negotiator; and finally, I'm a believer with the conviction that stories (in all forms) are still our most powerful magic.

What would you be doing if you weren't an agent? I love being an agent, but I probably would have made a good doctor in which case I'd be working for Doctors Without Borders.

What do you think about editors? I have enormous respect for editors. They are intelligent, often surprisingly idealistic, well informed, incredibly hardworking, devoted to their books and to their authors, and among my dearest friends.

What do you think about publishers? The challenge is to balance "business as usual" with an appropriate response to these extraordinary times; to create books that reach across borders and transcend differences, while also safeguarding our freedom of speech and of thought. I believe that by this common bond, we are all—author, agent, publisher, and reader—united.

What were your favorite films last year? *Lord of the Rings; Whale Rider; Cold Mountain.*

Do you watch *The Sopranos?* Of course. And *West Wing*. But the most breathtakingly wonderful event on television this past year was *Angels In America.*

Comments: Agents have to keep their fingers on the pulse of and respond to the current realities of the publishing world. We are the bridge between the creative and the commercial; between the world of the writer and the world of the publisher. This makes an agent's job pretty tricky, because we have to be aware of how the industry works: know which editors are looking for what kinds of books. . .What the competition is. . .What the sales possibilities are. . .And how to pitch the publisher in an arresting and compelling way. But at the same time, we still have to be willing to be seduced: by a writer's passion, by an extraordinary story, by memorable characters, by powerful ideas. We have to be willing to take a chance on a project or a writer we believe in. This requirement to be both a clear-headed businessperson and a dreamer is a balancing act, but in order to represent clients in the best way possible, it's necessary.

Representative titles: *Cooking One on One: Kitchen Secrets from a Master Teacher* by John Ash with Amy Mintzer (Clarkson Potter); *Private Rio: The Great Houses and Gardens* by Tomas de Elia and Juan Pablo Queiroz (Rizzoli); *Around the Bloc: My Life in Moscow, Beijing, and Havana* by Stephanie Elizondo Griest (Villard/Random House); *Mexicocina: Kitchens and Recipes of Mexico* by Melba Levick and Elizabeth McNair (Chronicle); *Kitchen Gatherings: Perfect Recipes for Sharing Meals with Friends* by Pam Anderson (Houghton Mifflin).

MAX GARTENBERG LITERARY AGENCY

12 Westminster Drive, Livingston, NJ 07039

973-994-4457

e-mail: gartenbook@att.net

Agent: Max Gartenberg
Associate Agents: Anne Devlin, Will Devlin
912 N. Pennsylvania Avenue, Yardley, PA 19067

Agency history: For many years a one-agent operation, this agency has recently expanded, adding two new associates, who are attuned to a wider range of contemporary interests and more receptive to new writers. Anne Devlin has had a distinguished career in newspaper journalism, Will Devlin in law.

Areas most interested in agenting: This agency's hallmark has been, and will continue to be, solid non-fiction in all areas. However, with the expansion, it intends to be a more visible presence in fiction than heretofore.

Areas not interested in agenting: Category fiction, novelty books, and personal memoirs of illness, victimhood, and alien abduction.

Best way to initiate contact: With a one- or two-page, first-class letter accompanied by an SASE if the writer wishes any sort of reply. Agents usually don't read sample pages or chapters, if included, and are absolutely turned off by cold calls and faxed queries.

Client representation by category: 90% non-fiction, 10% fiction.

Reading-fee policy: No reading fee.

Commission: 15% on initial sale; thereafter, 10% on sales in the United States, 15–20% elsewhere.

Rejection rate (all submissions): 95%.

Most common mistakes authors make: What most turns an agent off is a solicitation that tells almost nothing about the writer or his or her material but requests detailed information about the agency and its services, information which is readily available in such books as the *Writer's Guide*.

What gets you excited? A sense that the writer knows his subject because he or she has thoroughly researched it, and has written a book that is genuinely fresh and new.

Description of the client from Hell: Client who demands unceasing attention, who is never satisfied with the deal the agent brings him (he always has friends whose agents got twice as much), who delivers his manuscript late and blames the agent for the mess. This is not an imaginary character.

Description of a dream client: A writing professional who can be counted on to produce a well-made, literate, enlightening, and enjoyable book with a minimum of Sturm und Drang. Fortunately, this is not an imaginary character, either.

Why did you become an agent? We love good books. They are the pillars of our civilization. We feel it a privilege to work with those who create them.

Representative titles: *Unorthodox Warfare* by Ralph D. Sawyer (Westview Press); *Passing Gas and Other Towns Along the the American Highway* by Gary Gladstone (Tenspeed Press); *Ogallala Blue* by William Ashworth (W.W. Norton and Company).

GELFMAN SCHNEIDER LITERARY AGENTS, INC.

250 West 57th St.

fax: 212-245-8678

e-mail: Deborah@gelfmanschneider.com

Agent: Deborah Schneider

Born: Chicago.

Career history: John Farauharson, Ltd.; Gelfman Schneider Literary Agents.

Areas most interested in agenting: General adult hardcover fiction and nonfiction.

Areas not interested in agenting: Children's, romance, science fiction, screenplays

If not agenting, what would you be doing? Rescuing greyhounds.

Best way to initiate contact: Query letter, with SASE.

Reading-fee policy: No.

Client representation by category: Nonfiction, 40%; Fiction, 60%.

Commission: 15% domestic and film, 20% foreign.

Number of titles sold last year: 55

Most common mistakes authors make: E-mail queries, wrong name, sending the entire manuscript unsolicited.

How did you become an agent: Scouting for movie studios.

Why did you become an agent? I wanted to work directly with writers and be able to work for myself, not a corporation.

What would you be doing if you weren't an agent? I love my work and wouldn't do anything else.

What do you think about other agents? I have many good friends and colleagues in the agent community.

What do you think about publishers? I have spent over twenty years in this business and value enormously the relationships I have built over this time with editors and publishers.

THE SEBASTIAN GIBSON AGENCY

PO Box 13350, Palm Desert, CA 92255-3350

760-322-2446   fax: 760-322-3857

Agent: Sebastian Gibson

Born: December 8, 1950.

Education: B.A. (Cum Laude), UCLA; L.L.B. (Magna Cum Laude), University College Cardiff, Great Britain; J.D., University of San Diego School of Law.

Career history: Author of two novels, six screenplays, the lyrics and music to a stage musical, and hundreds of copyrighted songs. Author of published legal articles in both the United States and England. Performed as a stage musician on tour in the United States and Europe, and in a national television special. Obtained law degrees in both the United States and Great Britain. Practiced law in San Diego for four years, subsequently in England and the Middle East, and in 1984 began the Law Offices of Sebastian Gibson in Palm Springs, California. Presently practices law and represents literary and entertainment clients from law offices in Palm Springs, California.

Hobbies/personal interests: Reading well-written books, traveling to book fairs, discovering new talent.

Areas most interested in agenting: All categories of fiction, particularly suspense and contemporary action novels with interesting characters and well-woven plots. Especially interested in psychological thrillers, historical novels, mystery/suspense and action/adventure or espionage with romance subplots and interesting twists, crime/police with humorous/gritty elements, medical dramas, women's fiction, sagas, and any well-written novel with unusual characters. Nonfiction with unusual approaches or written by celebrities, cookbooks or photography with a novel twist, humorous diet books, controversial issues, biographies, current affairs, "kiss and tell" books, and women's issues. What really gets us excited is when we read something fresh and new, with a genre all its own, or a story told in a way that has never been told before. If it grabs our imagination, it will grab the imagination of a publisher and the buying public as well.

Areas not interested in agenting: Poetry, textbooks, essays, short stories, how-to books, books in verse, computer, gardening, pornography, autobiographies by non-celebrities, drug recovery.

If not agenting, what would you be doing? Sipping piña coladas on a beach in Greece, far away from telephones, car phones, beepers, pagers, and computers.

Best way to initiate contact: Fiction: Send query letter or book proposal with two-page synopsis of full story including the ending and the first three chapters, up to one pound, with SASE. Proposals and sample chapters without postage will be trashed. No disks, please. Sample chapters should already be edited and without typographical errors or incorrect grammar. Due to postal rules, no foreign submissions over one pound and without sufficient IRCs will be accepted under any circumstances.

Reading-fee policy: No reading fee as such. We do, however, request a bush-league, small potato, hardly worth mentioning but ever so popular contribution to our efforts of $15 per submission, which in the past has been used to pay for guard dogs to keep other agents away from our authors, to send those delightfully tacky pens and coasters that publishers like so much, and to pay for all those cocktails at the pools in Palm Springs and Las Vegas where we do our reading (eat your hearts out, you agents who winter in New York). Seriously, each year we receive more and more submissions, and to give each one the time it deserves increases our overhead dramatically.

Client representation by category: Nonfiction, 10%; Fiction, 90%.

Commission: 20% domestic; 30% foreign (split with foreign agents).

Rejection rate (all submissions): 99.9%

Most common mistakes authors make: Sending first drafts, no SASE, faxing queries, incessant calls, sending autobiographies and travel memoirs of trips to Orlando or Tijuana. Sending entire manuscripts or more than one submission at a time.

Description of the client from Hell: We don't have any over-demanding clients with unrealistic expectations. Five years ago we buried them all alive in killer anthills in the desert. Recently, one was dug up and found to still be typing away.

Description of a dream client: Bestselling authors who leave their present uncaring agent for the personal care our agency can provide.

Why did you become an agent? With my background in music and literature, as well as interests in Europe and the law, it was a natural progression to add a literary agency to our law firm.

Comments: A good book must grab the reader (and the publisher and certainly an agent) from the very first time. The first paragraph must be your best paragraph, the first page your best page, and the first chapter best chapter. If it isn't, you're kidding yourself if you think an agent will overlook a poorly written first paragraph, first page or first chapter in hopes that by the end of the submission, your writing skills, style or format will improve. You need to have invested some time reading the style books at your local bookstore and not expect that an agent has the time to teach you these skills or to respond to a call or letter asking why we passed on your submission.

GRAYBILL & ENGLISH, LLC

1875 Connecticut Avenue, NW Suite 712 Washington, DC 20009-5726

202-588-9798   fax: 202-457-0662

www.GraybillandEnglish.com

Graybill & English is a literary agency and law firm. As a literary agency, we represent literary properties, both fiction and nonfiction, before publishers nationwide. We are constantly adding new and talented writers to our list of literary clients and matching collaborators with projects in need of authors or editors. We do not charge reading fees, and are members of the Association of Authors' Representatives. Our foreign rights (U.K., Europe, Asia, South America, etc.) are handled by international rights agents in most foreign countries around the world. Dramatic rights are handled through sub-agents in New York and Los Angeles.

Agents: Nina Graybill, Elaine English, Jeff Kleinman, Lynn Whittaker, Kristen Auclair

Born: English: Asheville, NC; Kleinman: Cleveland, OH; Whittaker: October 24; Auclair: Boston, MA.

Education: Graybill: J.D., George Washington Law School, 1987. English: Undergraduate in Latin (Magna Cum Laude) at Randolph Macon Woman's College, J.D., National Law Center at George Washington University. Kleinman: B.A. with High Distinction, University of Virginia (English/Modern Studies) M.A., University of Chicago (Italian Language/Literature), J.D., Case Western Reserve University; Whittaker: Undergraduate in English and Political Science at University of Georgia; M.A. in English, University of Georgia. Auclair: B.A., Magna Cum Laude, James Madison University (English/Human Communication).

Career History: Graybill: For the past 15 years, I have been an attorney specializing in publishing and entertainment law and a literary agent. Graybill & English began in 1997. Prior to becoming a lawyer, I was a freelance editor and writer, working on presidential and congressional investigations and commissions; the final one being the House-Senate Iran-Contra Committee in 1987. I am also the co-author of six cookbooks. English: After pursuing careers in teaching, social services, and personnel management, I completed law school and began working as an attorney for a public interest organization, Reporters Committee for Freedom of the Press, on open government and media issues. I then joined a small firm with a publishing law/agenting practice.

Throughout my practice, I have concentrated on media and publishing issues. I recently expanded my practice to include agenting of commercial fiction. Kleinman: After graduating from the University of Virginia, I lived in Italy for about three years, studying the Italian Renaissance. Previously an associate at the art and literary law firm of Kaufman & Silverberg in Washington, DC., I'm now an agent (and attorney) with this firm, where I've been since 1998. Whittaker: Many years as an Editor and Publications Director in academic and educational publishing, several years as a Publisher and Editor-in-Chief of a small press, co-author of two women's history books. Auclair: I began working in publishing more than ten years ago, first with the science publisher W.H. Freeman, then as an editor for HarperCollins, then as the publicist for The Lyons Press. I became a literary agent in 1999.

Hobbies/personal interests: Graybill: Reading, cooking, antiques, design and architecture, art. English: Reading, hiking, nature photography. Kleinman: Art, history, horses (train dressage and event horses). Auclair: Running, snowboarding, cooking.

Areas most interested in agenting: Graybill: Narrative nonfiction, very readable serious nonfiction (e.g., health, psychology, science, culture and race, history, politics), some light nonfiction, literary fiction, and very limited mystery and suspense. English: Women's fiction, including romances (single title, both contemporary and historical), mysteries, and thrillers. Kleinman: Prescriptive nonfiction: health, parenting, aging, nature, pets, how-to, etc. Narrative nonfiction; especially books with an historical bent, but also travel, art, nature, ecology, politics, military, espionage, cooking, equestrian, pets, memoir, biography. Fiction: very well-written, character-driven novels, some SF&F, suspense, thrillers. Otherwise mainstream commercial and literary fiction. Whittaker: Creative and narrative nonfiction of all kinds; serious nonfiction, especially history and biography; nature and science writing; literary fiction; mysteries; how-to/self-help; celebrity. Subjects of particular interest include women's stories and issues, U.S. history, multicultural and African American subjects, race relations, dogs, sports, health/nutrition, psychology, business/career, pop culture, writing. Also academics who can write for the trade market. Auclair: Practical nonfiction including health, parenting, and women's issues. Also pop culture, well-written narrative nonfiction, accessible serious nonfiction, books about animals. Literary fiction.

Areas not interested in agenting: Graybill: How-tos, children's, genre fiction (except some mysteries and suspense), poetry, New Age, spirituality, screenplays, stage plays. English: Non-fiction and childrens' projects, also no science fiction or time travel romances, and no inspirational fiction. No Westerns, time travel, or paranormal romances and no nonfiction. Kleinman: No mysteries, romance, Westerns, children's or young adult, poetry, plays, screenplays. Whittaker: Children's/young adult, romance, Westerns, science fiction, screenplays, and scripts. Auclair: children's or young adult, thrillers, science fiction, fantasy, screenplays.

If not agenting, what would you be doing? Graybill: I am also an attorney, a sometime cookbook writer, and a part-time interior design consultant. English: simply practicing law. Kleinman: practicing intellectual property law.

Best ways to initiate contact: Graybill: Query letter, with a one-page synopsis and sample chapters for fiction, and a proposal or detailed explanation of the book and a bio for nonfiction, and an SASE. English: Query letter with one-page synopsis (can be sent by regular mail or e-mail, no attachments please). Kleinman: Snail-mail or e-mail (no attachments please). Nonfiction: Cover letter, proposal, including author credentials and sample chapter and/or outline. Fiction: Cover letter and the first few pages of the novel. Whittaker: A query letter that outlines book and author credentials, sent by regular mail or e-mail (no attachments please). Okay to send sample of up to 30 pages with mailed query letter. I also love to meet writers at writing conferences and to hear from writers who have heard me speak on panels. And I love getting referrals. Auclair: Written or e-mail but no attachments. Nonfiction: Query letter, proposal, and sample chapter and/or outline. Fiction: Query letter and the first few chapters of the novel.

Reading-fee policy: AAR members; no reading fees.

Client representation: Nonfiction, 80%, Fiction, 20%. No children's, other.

Commission: 15% domestic; 25% first serial; 20% foreign.

Rejection rate: (all submissions): 95%.

Most common mistakes authors make: Graybill: Overhyped letters about how wonderful they and their certain-to-be bestselling book are; query letters and first pages (even paragraphs) of a manuscript that are full of typos, grammatical errors, misspellings (which to me indicates a lack of professionalism). Kleinman: Groveling—just pretend this is a job application, and act like a professional; providing too much information—telling too much about the project, rather than being able to succinctly summarize it; sending a poorly formatted, difficult to read manuscript. Whittaker: Handing me a list of 10 books they're writing and asking me to choose which one I'd like to see. Querying me about types of books I don't represent. English: Rushing their manuscript to an agent or editor before they have completed editing, critiquing, and proofreading. Auclair: Sending me proposals in categories I don't represent or have any interest in, or sending me a proposal without taking time to carefully edit it first.

Description of the client from Hell: Graybill: I try to spot these coming and step aside: Writers with an overblown sense of their talent and value, writers who don't want to put in the time and hard work a proposal or a manuscript requires. I don't mind big egos or artistic temperament, I just ask that there be some valid underpinnings for them. Kleinman: Someone who doesn't listen, doesn't incorporate suggestions, and believes that the world "owes" him (or her) a bestseller.

Description of the dream client: Graybill: Dream clients are enthusiastic; eager to make their work even better; considerate; prompt, and very, very talented. Kleinman: Someone who writes beautifully, who has marketing savvy and ability, who is friendly, accessible, easy to work with, fun to talk to, can follow directions and guidance without taking offense.

How did you become an agent? Kleinman: My law firm shared offices with an agency, and I did several book contracts. Gradually, I started reading manuscripts, talking to writers, and before long, there I was—a literary agent. English: Deliberate decision made after intensive study of market.

Why did you become an agent? Graybill: I became a lawyer/agent because I wanted to combine my interest and background in books and writing with my new law degree. English: Because I love books, enjoy working with authors, and wanted to contribute, in even a small way, to the creative process by which the reading public is entertained. Kleinman: Agentry is a great marriage of law and writing—both of which I love. Agenting's a lot of fun—it allows me to work on (and learn about) a wide variety of subjects, meet an incredible range of people, and generally participate in the business of books—which is very rewarding for me. Whittaker: I've loved reading all my life and believe in the power of books to affect people's lives. I like the combination of solitary work (reading, thinking, evaluating, editing) and social interaction (with writers, editors, booksellers, and others in the book world). I love my clients and enjoy learning from them, making them happy by selling their work, and giving them whatever advice and support they need to develop their careers. I also really enjoy the eclectic variety of books I share with my clients. Auclair: To see an idea grow into a manuscript and ultimately turn into a book is such a rewarding experience; every project is a little adventure.

What can writers do to enhance their chances of getting you as an agent? Graybill: If writers are referred by someone I know, I will look at their project a little more closely than I might a stranger's. But mostly, I am interested in a query letter offering a fresh treatment of an intriguing topic by someone with the appropriate credentials to write such a book. In the case of fiction, I look for writers who, their natural talent aside, have read many, many good books in their area of interest, such as literary fiction or mysteries, and who have studied fiction writing enough—through reading, courses, workshops, writing groups—to understand the demands of their chosen type of fiction. English: Know their target market and have a well-written, solid manuscript, with an inventive plot, good pacing, strong dialogue, and realistic, strong characters. Kleinman: ENHANCE YOUR CREDENTIALS. Get published, or have some kind of platform or fresh perspective that really stands out above the crowd. Show me (so I can show a publisher) that you're a good risk for publication. Whittaker: Most of all, be good writers. Also, have books on topics I love. Teach me about something new. Auclair: Do the research, know what goes into a good book proposal, understand that it takes a lot of work and that going the extra mile can make all the difference.

How would you describe what you actually do for a living? Kleinman: Soothe egos, expedite situations, hold hands and make sure things remain on track. And read —read—read.

What do you think about editors? Graybill: I really admire strong, hands-on editors who understand what a book and its author are about and only seek to make it better and those who stay actively involved throughout the entire process, from acquisition through launch. Kleinman: I think that too often they're overworked and underpaid, and often don't have the time to really "connect the dots" in a manuscript or a proposal—so it's crucial that we (the writer and I) connect the dots for them. Auclair: I used to be one myself, so I know the pressures they are under and the workload they're facing. The best ones are some of the most intelligent and creative people I know.

What do you think of publishers? Graybill: I've never heard any writers say that their publishers did enough to promote their books. I am distressed about the takeover of so many publishers by a few conglomerates because the competition among publishes is far less intense and the emphasis is on trendy books that sell in huge numbers at the expense of smaller but worthwhile books. Kleinman: Probably by the time this book comes out, there will only one publisher left, and it will only publish 2 or 3 mega-authors.

Comments: Kleinman: From personal experience, I know how frustrating it can be to work with literary agents: your manuscript disappears for months at a time, only to return to you with a polite little "sorry, not for us" scrawled on your original cover letter. Or an agent agrees to take you on, and a year goes by with no word—only to have your manuscript returned to you with "sorry, I'm just not enthusiastic enough about this one." Was it submitted to publishers? If not, just what was your agent doing for the past year? Who knows? Don't expect that from me. My turnaround time, at the moment, is about two months for fiction (solicited manuscripts) and about three weeks for non-fiction proposals. If I have your manuscript on an exclusive basis, and if I return the manuscript to you, I do my best to write you one to two pages of comments about the problems I found—I rarely resort to the "sorry, not for me" theme unless the only reason I decide not to take on a project is because it's simply not right for me or if I'm just utterly buried in manuscripts. However, because I work with four other agents, it's also possible that your manuscript might be "right" for one of them, and I will pass it along to them. Because I do not require exclusivity, I'll rarely pencil in comments directly on your solicited manuscript— unless you do provide it to me on an exclusive basis (say, for six to eight weeks). If I have your manuscript exclusively, and if I am enthusiastic enough to consider representing it, I'll often line-edit the first hundred pages or so, just to give you an idea of what your manuscript may need to work out some of the kinks. Everyone will tell you that one of the most important criteria for a good agent is that s/he is enthusiastic about your work. Believe it. You must find some-one who loves the project, and will fight to get it published. In my case, this means that I'll only read a manuscript twice: if I read it any more than that, I lose that edge of enthusiasm. So only send your material to me when you think it's as good as you can get it.

Representative Titles: *The Memory of Running* by Ron McLarty (Viking); *Secret Soldiers* by Philip Gerard (Dutton); *Gentleman's Blood* by Barbara Holland (Blooms-bury USA)' *The Man Who Changed How Boys & Toys Were Made* by Bruce Watson (Viking/Penguin); *Learning to Speak Alzheimer's* by Joanne Koenig-Coste (Houghton-Mifflin); *Trim Kids in Twelve Weeks* by Melinda Sothern, Kris von Almen, & Heidi Schumacher (HarperCollins); *Bombproofing Your Horse* by Rick Pelicano (Trafalgar Square; *A Telling of Stars* by Caitlin Sweet (Penguin Putnam); *I May be Wrong But I Doubt It* by Charles Barkley, edited & with introduction by Michael Wilbon (Random House); *The White House Nannies* by Barbara Kline (Tarcher;, *A Sister's Breastfeeding Handbook* by Katherine Barber (Sourcebooks); *Body Check* and *Fair Play* by Deirdre Martin (Berkley); *Straight from the Heart* by Bettye Griffin (BET Books); *Never Say Never* by Phyllis George (McGraw-Hill); *The Persia Café* by Melany Neilson; *One Hell of a Candidate* by William F. Gavin (St. Martin's Press).

THE CHARLOTTE GUSAY LITERARY AGENCY

10532 Blythe Avenue, Los Angeles, CA 90064

phone: 310-559-0831   fax: 310-559-2639

www.mediastudio.com/gusay   e-mail for brief queries only: gusay1@aol.com

(*Note: We hardly ever look at this e-mail address as it has hundreds of queries on it at any given time. Best to contact us by snail mail with SASE.*)

Agent: Charlotte Gusay

Education: B.A. in English Literature/Theater; M.A. in Education.

Career history: Taught in secondary schools for several years. Interest in filmmaking developed. Founded (with partners) a documentary film company in the early 1970s. Soon became interested in the fledgling audio-publishing business. Became the Managing Editor for the Center for Cassette Studies/Scanfax, producing audio programs, interviews, and documentaries. In 1976 founded George Sand, Books, in West Hollywood, one of the most prestigious and popular bookshops in Los Angeles. It specialized in fiction and poetry, sponsored readings and events. Patronized by the Hollywood community's glitterati and literati, George Sand, Books, was the place to go when looking for the "best" literature and quality books. It was here that the marketing of books was preeminent. It closed in 1987. Two years later the Charlotte Gusay Literary Agency was opened.

Hobbies/personal interests: Gardens and gardening, magazines (a magazine junkie), good fiction, reading, anything French, anything Greek.

Areas most interested in agenting: I enjoy both fiction and nonfiction. Prefer commercial, mainstream—but quality—material. Especially like books that can be marketed as film material. Also, material that is innovative, unusual, eclectic, nonsexist. Will consider literary fiction with crossover potential. The agency is a signatory to the Writers' Guild and so represents screenplays and screenwriters selectively. I enjoy unusual children's books and illustrators, but have begun to limit children's projects to young adult novels especially if they have film possibilities.

Areas not interested in agenting: Does not consider science fiction or horror, poetry or short stories (with few exceptions), or the romance genres per se.

If not agenting, what would you be doing? I would write a book called *Zen and the Art of Gardening with a Black Thumb* (I'm kidding!). I would travel to Istanbul and become a foreign agent. I would finish all of Proust. I would re-read Jane Austen. Work on my French. Study Greek. Play the piano. Tap dance.

Best way to initiate contact: Send one-page query letter with SASE. Then if we request your material (book, proposal, whatever it is), note the following guidelines: For fiction: Send approximately the first 50 pages and a synopsis, along with your credentials (i.e., list of previous publications, and/or list of magazine articles, and/or any pertinent information, education, and background). For nonfiction: Send a proposal consisting of an overview, chapter outline, author biography, sample chapters, marketing and audience research, and survey of the competition. Important note: Material will not be returned without an SASE. Second important note: Seduce me with humor and intelligence.

Reading fee policy: No reading fee. No editorial fees. When a client is signed, the client and I share 50/50% out-of-pocket expenses. In certain cases, I charge a nominal processing fee—especially when considering unsolicited submissions—decided upon as and when queries arrive in my office.

Client representation by category: Nonfiction, 40%; Fiction, 15%; Children's, 10%; Books to Film/Screenplays, 35%.

Commission: 15% books; 10% screenplays.

Most common mistakes authors make: Clients must understand the role of agents and that agents represent only the material they feel they can best handle. Potential clients must understand that any given agent may or may not be an editor, a sounding board, a proposal writer, or a guidance counselor. Because of the enormous amount of submissions, queries, and proposals, the agent most often has only the time to say yes or no to your project. Above all, when clients don't understand why in the world I can't respond to a multiple submission with regard to their "900-page novel" within a few days, all I can do is shake my head and wonder if that potential client realizes I am human.

Description of the client from Hell: The one who does not understand the hard work we do for our clients. Or the one who refuses to build a career in a cumulative manner, but rather goes from one agent to the next and so on. Or clients who circulate their manuscripts without cooperating with their agents. Or those who think it all happens by magic. Or those who do not understand the nuts and bolts of the business.

Description of the dream client: The one who cooperates. The one who appreciates how hard we work for our clients. The one who submits everything on time, in clean, edited, proofed, professional copies of manuscripts and professionally prepared proposals. Clients who understand the crucial necessity of promoting their own books until the last one in the publisher's warehouse is gone. Those who work hard on their book selling in tandem with the agent. The author-agent relationship, like a marriage, is a cooperative affair, and it's cumulative. The dream client will happily do absolutely whatever is necessary to reach the goal.

How did you become an agent? With a great entrepreneurial spirit, cold calls, seat-of the pants daring, 12 years in the retail book business (as founder and owner of a prestigious book shop in LA), and 20 years of business experience, including producing films and editing spoken-word audio programs; agenting is the most challenging and rewarding experience I've ever had.

Why did you become an agent? I became an agent because I know how to sell books and movies. Above all, I am knowledgeable and experienced, and I love agenting.

How would you describe what you actually do for a living? My job is essentially that of a bookseller. I sell books. To publishers, producers, and ultimately to the retail book trade. Sometimes, I develop a book idea. Sometimes, I develop someone's story, help the writer get a proposal written. I've even written proposals myself because I believed strongly in the book, or the person's story, or the saleability of an idea. For fiction writers with potential, I sometimes make cursory suggestions, but most often I help them to find a professional editor to work on their novel before it is submitted to a publishing house.

What do you think about other agents: I have many agent friends. We laugh together and cry on each other's shoulders and help each other out. We talk a great deal about how difficult the publishing business is and how "writers" don't understand that.

What do you think about editors? Editors are overworked and underpaid. Therefore, if you wish to have the best chance of having your work accepted, you must do their work for them and don't complain. That is the reality of the editor's milieu. Editors are usually very smart. Most always, if they're any good, they are temperamental, and they know their particular publisher's market. If interested, they know how to make your work fit into their list. Do what your editor (and agent) tells you. No argument.

What do you think about publishers? Publishers are having a very difficult time these days. The "conglomeratizing" of the publishing business is extremely worrisome and publishers are feeling the pressure. However, publishers are always looking for the next great writer, the next great book, and a way to make both successful. (That means making money.)

What were your favorite films last year? Recent films and not-so-recent films I liked: *Pieces of April, Something About Mary, Shakespeare in Love*. A few of my all-time favorite films are *Runaway Train, The English Patient, Rebel Without a Cause, Woman in the Dunes*.

Do you watch *The Sopranos?* I subscribed to HBO so I could watch *The Sopranos*. I watched it a few times. It's very clever. I prefer to listen to Mozart or Saul Williams or watch a movie or HGTV or MasterpieceTheatre.

Comments: Be professional. Be courteous. Be patient. Understand that we are human. Pay careful attention to the kinds of projects we represent. Query us only if you feel your project fits with our agency profile. Know what we are overworked, always swamped with hundreds of queries. Know that we love and understand writers. Take us to lunch. Send flowers (just kidding).

Representative titles: *Imperial Mongolian Cooking: Recipes from the Kingdoms of Genghis Khan* by Marc Cramer (Hippocrene Publishers); *Somebody's Child: Stories from the Private Files of an Adoption Attorney* by Randi Barrow (Perigee/Penguin Putnam, Inc.); *Retro Chic: A Guide to Fabulous Vintage and Designer Resale Shopping in North America & Online* by Diana Eden & Gloria Lintermans (Really Great Books); *Other Sorrows, Other Joys: The Marriage of Catherine Sophia Boucher and William Blake* by Janet Warner (St. Martin's Press); *, said the shotgun to the head* by Saul Williams (Atria/MTV Books); *The Spoken Word Revolution: An essay, poem and an audio contribution* by Saul Williams (SourceBooks). Films: *Somebody's Child: Stories from the Private Files of an Adoption Attorney* by Randi Barrow (Perigee/Penguin Putnam, Inc). Optioned by Green/Epstein/Bacino/Productions for a television series; *A Place Called Waco: A Survivor's Story* by David Thibodeau and Leon Whiteson (Public Affairs/ Perseus Book Group).

In turn-around to Showtime for a Television Movie; *Love Groucho: Letters from Groucho Marx to His Daughter Miriam*, edited by Miriam Marx Allen (Faber & Faber, Straus & Giroux U.S., and Faber & Faber U.K.). Sold to CBS: *A Place Called Waco: A Survivor's Story*; *Rio L.A.:Tales from the Los Angeles River* by Patt Morrision, with photographs by Mark Lamonica (Angel City Press). We have ten books in development at this writing.

JEANNE K. HANSON LITERARY AGENCY

6708 Cornelia Drive, Edina, MN 55435

voice/fax: 952-920-8819

e-mail: jkhlit@aol.com

Agent: Jeanne K. Hanson
Born: August 12, 1944.
Education: B.A. in Philosophy and English, Wellesley College; M.A.T. in English and Education, Harvard; M.A. in Journalism, University of Minnesota; Radcliffe Publishing Course.
Career history: Teacher for 2 years; Journalist for 15 years; Literary Agent for 19 years.
Hobbies/personal interests: Running, reading, going to arts events.
Areas most interested in agenting: Nonfiction books written by journalists, science books for the general public written by professors and journalists, authors of published books for ages 8-12.
Areas not interested in agenting: Celebrity books; New Age; memoirs; self-help, humor, religion/spirituality,and manifestos.
If not agenting, what would you be doing? Probably being a writer.
Best way to initiate contact: Query letter with a table of contents and 1–3 pages of sample writing from the book.
Client representation by category: Nonfiction, 95%; Fiction, 5%.
Commission: 15% with no extra fees.
Number of titles sold last year: 20.
Rejection rate (all submissions): 99%.
Most common mistakes authors make: Large multiple submissions (agents can just tell); self-absorbed authors who may be a little nuts, even.
Description of the client from Hell: Someone who is really late delivering the book to the publisher; someone who sends me a proposal sealed so tightly with layers and layers of paper and tape that it takes forever to open it!
Description of a dream client: A great journalist or professor who understands how to write for an audience and how to analyze trends; a professor who really, really knows something really interesting and can write about it in a wonderful way.

How did you become an agent? I wrote a book and liked my agent, long ago.

Why did you become an agent? Because I love books and love doing deals for them that make everybody happy!

What can writers do to enhance their chances of getting you as an agent? Have a great idea.

How would you describe what you actually do for a living? Getting to yes.

What do you think about editors? Nice.

What do you think about publishers? O.K.

Representative titles: *Cancer Club* by Christine Clifford (Putnam); *Politicking* by Bill Rauch (FSG); *Extreme Geology* (Facts on File series).

THE JOY HARRIS LITERARY AGENCY

156 Fifth Avenue, Suite 617, New York, NY 10010

fax: 212-924-6609

Agents: Joy Harris; Leslie Daniels

Educational History: Daniels: BA Linguistics; MA Psychology; MFA Fiction Writing.

Career History: Daniels: Over a decade with Joy Harris.

Areas most interested in agenting: Literary fiction and narrative nonfiction. Daniels: Good narrative, good writing, fiction and nonfiction.

Areas not interested in agenting: Romance, science fiction. Daniels: Genre, textbook, Christian, and mythical.

If not agenting, what would you be doing? Editing, writing.

Best way to initiate contact: Send a query letter via mail with a sample chapter. Daniels: Write me a letter with a SASE.

Reading-fee policy: None.

Client representation by category: Nonfiction, 50%; Fiction, 50%. Daniels: 60% fiction; 40% nonfiction.

Commision structure: 15%.

Rejection rate (all submissions): 95%. Daniels: Shockingly high.

Description of a dream client: Imaginative, creative, psychologically sound, with a sense for marketing.

How did you you become an agent? Mentored by Joy Harris.

Why did you become an agent? I love to read, I respect writers.

What can writers do to enhance their chances of getting you as an agent? Write a great first page.

How would you describe what you do for a living? Invent books and/or midwife them.

What do you think about other agents? Lots of variety is a good thing.

What do you think about editors? Much respect and some great friendships.

Do you watch *The Sopranos?* Yes.

Representative titles: *Ahab's Wife* by Sena Jeter Naslund (HarperCollins); *Juno & Juliet* by Julian Gough; *I Don't Know How She Does It* by Allison Pearson (Knopf); *Sons of Camelot* by Larry Leamer (Harper); *The Dirty Girls Social Club* by Alisa Valves-Rodriguez (St. Martins); *Natalie Wood: A Life* by Gavin Lambert (Knopf); *Schopenhauer's Porcupine* by Dr. Deborah Lepuitz (Basic Books); *If Nights Could Talk* by Marsha Recknagel (Thomas Dunne Books); *The Bad and the Beautiful* by Katherine MacNair (W. W. Norton).

JOHN HAWKINS & ASSOCIATES

71 West 23rd Street, Suite 1600, New York, NY 10010

fax: 212-807-9555

www.jhaliterary.com

Agents: Warren Frazier, Anne Hawkins, William Reiss, Elly Sidel

Born: Reiss: September 14, 1942.

Education: Frazier: B.A., Princeton. Reiss: B.A., Kenyon College. Hawkins: A.B., Bryn Mawr College.

Career history: Reiss: Freelance Researcher; Editorial Assistant to Lombard Jones (a graphic designer and editor); Encyclopedia Editor, Funk & Wagnall's Standard Reference Library; Literary Agent.

Hobbies/personal interests: Sidel: Reading; going to the ballet, movies, theater; hanging out; playing with friends and family; walking; swimming; politics; travel. Hawkins: Music, collecting tribal art, hiking, gardening—almost any excuse to be outdoors.

Areas most interested in agenting: Frazier: Fiction: literary and commercial. Nonfiction: biography, travel, natural history, science. Reiss: Biographies, nonfiction historical narratives, archaeology, science fiction and fantasy, mysteries and suspense, true-crime narrative, natural history, children's fiction, adult fiction. Hawkins: Literary and commercial fiction, including mystery suspense, and thrillers. Non-fiction; history, science, current affairs, medicine, women's and family issues.

Areas not interested in agenting: Frazier: Romance. Reiss: Romance novels, poetry, plays. Hawkins:. Fiction: children's books, romance, horror, Westerns. Nonfiction: cookbooks, "how-to", and self-help. Other: poetry, plays, screenplays.

If not agenting, what might you be doing? Hawkins: Hard to say, since I really love being a literary agent. Other dream jobs might be working as a curator in a major museum or running an experimental nursery for exotic trees, shrubs, and perennials.

Best way to initiate contact: Frazier: frazier@jhaliterary.com; short description of project, brief bio. Reiss: Telephone or send a letter describing project, with a few sample pages to provide a sense of writing style. Hawkins: Query letter and sample pages.

Reading-fee policy: No reading fee.

Client representation by category: Frazier: Nonfiction, 50%; Fiction, 50%. Hawkins: Nonfiction, 40%; Fiction, 60%.

Commission: 15% domestic; 20% foreign.

Rejection rate (all submissions): 95%.

Most common mistakes authors make: Hawkins: Two extremes here—the under-promoter and the over-promoter. The under-promoter throws together a sloppy query package with a rambling, unconvincing letter and/or sample chapters riddled with errors. The over-promoter makes extravagant claims about the project—"a sure pick for Oprah's Book Club" or "guaranteed to be a #1 national bestseller." It's hard to take either seriously.

Description of a dream client: Sidel: A talented, flexible, creative professional writer who understands that this is a process. Someone with a sense of humor and a Pulitzer Prize. Hawkins: Dream clients take the trouble to educate themselves about the realities of the publishing business and enter the process armed with good sense, good manners, and good humor.

What can writers do to enhance their chances of getting you as an agent? Hawkins: As a practical matter, projects directly referred by people I know always rise to the top of the pile, since they are more likely to be a good fit with my taste and areas of expertise. But there's also the occasional cold-call query letter that shows so much personality, intelligence, and professionalism that I'm predisposed to like the sample materials. An agent and an author work together for a long time, and I want to feel that I will enjoy representing writers as much as their work.

Representative titles: Frazier: *House of Leaves* by Mark Z. Danielewski; Reiss: *The Madman's Tale* by John Katzenbach; *The Good Neighbor* by William Kowalski; *The Ghost Heart* by Cecilia Samartin.

THE JEFF HERMAN AGENCY, LLC

P.O. Box 1522, 9 South Street, Stockbridge, MA 01262

413-298-0077   fax: 413-298-8188

www.jeffherman.com   e-mail: jeff@jeffherman.com

Agents: Jeff Herman, Deborah Levine Herman

Born: J. Herman: December 17, 1958, Long Island, New York. D. L. Herman: October 4, 1958, Long Island, New York.

Education: J. Herman: Liberal Arts, B.S., Syracuse University, 1981. D. L. Herman: Too much. B.A., Ohio State University; Master's of Journalism, Ohio State University Graduate School in a dual degree with the College of Law. Got Juris Doctorate, passed the bar, and have been in recovery ever since.

Career history: J. Herman: Publicity Department—Schocken Books, Account Executive for a public relations agency, founded my own PR agency, founder of literary agency in 1988. D. L. Herman: An Assistant Attorney General for Ohio, private litigator—civil matters, writer neophyte, rejection-letter expert (recipient), ghostwriter, author, book proposal/book doctor/literary agent/rejection-letter expert (purveyor).

Hobbies/personal interests: J. Herman: Eating, sleeping, walking, staring at nothing. D. L. Herman: My three children, low-brow entertainment, yard sales, antiques, flea markets, oil painting, karaoke, gossip magazines, celebrities, spiritual development, horses, my pets.

Areas most interested in agenting: J. Herman: I could answer this, but by tomorrow, I'll change my mind. D. L. Herman: Popular culture, unique nonfiction. I like books that usher in the trends rather than trail behind.

Areas not interested in agenting: J. Herman: As above. D. L. Herman: Anything pompous, judgmental, or boring. Autobiographies are difficult to place, but they can be used as the backdrop for exceptional projects. No matter how wonderful or tragic your life might be, it will take a lot for it to compete as straight autobiography.

If not agenting, what would you be doing? J. Herman: I'd get a job with Fed Ex.

Best way to initiate contact: J. Herman: Letters, e-mails, faxes.

Reading-fee policy: J. Herman: As per AAR rules, we don't charge any.

Client representation by category: J. Herman: Nonfiction, 90%; Children's Textbooks, 10%. D. L. Herman: Nonfiction, 95%.

Commission: 15% on domestic sales; still 10% for foreign.

Number of titles sold last year: 25.

Rejection rate (all submissions): In the high 90s.

Most common mistakes authors make: J. Herman: Muddying their pitch. Putting their expectations beyond their value. D. L. Herman: Asking me to sell myself to them. I'm too busy. Being rude or demanding on the phone. We all answer phones to cover each other. Those of you who try to get past our screening process by behaving like royalty might just find yourself talking to me and pitching yourself right into embarrassment. Another mistake is to try to pitch by phone unless we know you or are related to you. This is a hard-copy business; follow protocol.

Description of the client from Hell: J. Herman: There are several archetypes that come to mind, such as: manic egomaniacs who really don't have much to sell other than their own wind, people who nag me so that I either have to fire them or make them a close relative. People who interminably obsess about what others were "supposed" to do for them or did to them. D. L. Herman: Those who view their manuscript as a destination and not a process. We can each be messengers of the greater light. The trick is to know when to get out of the way. There are no real clients from Hell because, if they are too arrogant to accept direction, I send them back to the Universe for further polishing and education.

Description of a dream client: J. Herman: They know how to punch a hole through unfortunate circumstances and walk through to the other side. And they know how to see and embrace a good thing. D. L. Herman: Those who listen to and find their own inner voice. This is where the best writing is found. A person like this understands that time and space are not always what we want them to be. Sometimes the Universe has its own agenda.

How did you become an agent? J. Herman: I started by pitching manuscripts written by my public relations clients. I would just cold-call publishers and get editors on the phone. I didn't know that made me a literary agent until much later.

Why did you become an agent? J. Herman: I have a weak back and strong eyes. D. L. Herman: To learn to become a writer. Then I married Jeff Herman to ensure representation. He still makes me put it in writing!

What can writers do to enhance their chances of getting you as an agent? J. Herman: Don't give up. D. L. Herman: Focus on writing from a business perspective. If no one would ever buy your book, how can we possibly sell it for you? If your project is well-thought-out and commercially meaningful, you have as much chance as anyone else does.

How would you describe what you actually do for a living? J. Herman: I help get books published.

What do you think about editors? J. Herman: That's a tough job, because there are so many people they have to answer to, so many people they have to cover for, so many they have to appease, and so many details to attend to. They are underappreciated.

What do you think about publishers? J. Herman: Ask me again next year.

Comments: J. Herman: Seriously, none of this is rocket science. Please enjoy what you do, and educate yourself about what it takes to succeed.

Representative titles: *The Aladdin Factor* by Mark Victor Hansen and Jack Canfield (Berkley); *Blackroots: An African American Guide to Tracing the Family Tree* by Tony Burroughs (Simon & Schuster); *Driving Your Woman Wild in Bed* by Staci Keith (Warner Books); *Pocket Guide to Saints* by Annette Sandoval (Dutton); *The Angry Child* by Timothy Murphy (Random House); *The Complete Idiot's Guide to Investing Like a Pro* by Ed Koch and Debra DeSalvo (Macmillan); *The Unauthorized Story of the Beatles' Get Back Sessions* by Doug Sulpy (St. Martin's Press); *The 10 Habits of Naturally Slim People* by Jill Podjasek (Contemporary); *Southern Invincibility: Why the South Lost the Civil War* by Wiley Sword (St. Martin's Press); *Words of Wisdom: Selected Quotes From His Holiness the Dalai Lama* (book and calendar) by Margaret Gee (Andrews McMeel); *Exploring Meditation* by Susan Shumsky (Career Press); *Born to Be Wild: Freeing the Spirit of the Hyper-Active Child* by Kristi Boylan (Penguin/Putnam); *Tom Hopkin's Complete Guide to Sales Success* by Tom Hopkins (Warner Books); *The Toastmaster's Guide to Public Speaking* by Michael Aun and Jeff Slutsky (Dearborn); *The Weekend Millionaires Guide to Real Estate* by Mike Summey (McGraw-Hill).

JULIE HILL MEDIA AND LITERARY AGENCY

1155 Camino del Mar, suite #530, Del Mar, CA 92014

fax: 858-259-2777

e-mail: Hillagent@aol.com

Agent: Julie Hill

Education: B.A., University of Arizona; graduate work, UCLA; Publishing Program, University of California–Berkeley.

Career History: I come to agenting from writing. I have written for magazines and Internet sites such as Citysearch/Microsoft, and I wrote a nonfiction book some years ago. I also learned book publicity during my career as an author, and the tutelage of Arielle Ford of the Ford Group prepared me well for understanding what authors must do to market their work. I also used to be an Interior Designer, thus my interest in all books that have a visual component.

Hobbies/personal interests: Art, fine cuisine, horticulture, long-distance travel.

Areas most interested in agenting: Nonfiction of any kind, especially how-to, self-help. I have had a fair number of successes with art and architecture books and would like to represent more experts in those fields. Travel and health books are always welcome. Astrology, family and gender issues, and snappy commercial reference books are what I am searching for!

Areas not interested in agenting: Fiction, poetry, screenplays, large coffee-table books, cookbooks, textbooks.

Best way to initiate contact: Send a book proposal with a market analysis and an SASE. E-mail submissions? No thank you. "Snail mail" only, 1st class or priority please. Please do not send anything that requires a signature.

Client representation by category: Nonfiction, 90%; fiction 10%

Commission: 15% domestic; 20% foreign.

Number of titles sold: 21.

Rejection rate: 90%.

Description of the client from Hell: They call to chat. Call to complain. Want their lawyer to read everything (this last comment is really about lawyers, not the client).

Description of the dream client: They have a perfectly finished and researched book proposal and know they must market their work after publication, with or without a hired publicist. Their synopsis and market survey are above reproach. They realize that the book is not just the fruit of their creativity and hard work, but it is a business unto itself and they treat it as such.

Why did you become an agent? After I published my book, I understood how tough and how much fun being a published author is. I like making authors happy and successful.

How did you become an agent? Writer friends suggested I'd be good at it.

What would you be doing if you weren't an agent? Traveling, cooking, entertaining, writing.

What can writers do to enhance their chances of getting you as an agent? Make sure their work doesn't need further tweaking, that it is fully ready to market.

How would you describe what you actually do for a living? Some days I feel like I am back in graduate school, reading reading reading. Some days I feel like it's one big party on the phone with editors and clients I love.

What do you think about other agents? Depends on the agent. The ones I know well work hard and are sometimes underappreciated by their clients.

What do you think about editors? Overworked, underpaid, and I appreciate them enormously.

What do you think about publishers? Many of them seem to need a time-out at Business School. I don't mean the editors, I mean the high-up financial decision-makers who write the gospel on how money is allotted.

Comments: I like this business with all its faults. Good authors make my day. Good editors make my day. Good publishers keep my bank balance happy. Thanks!

Representative titles: *Art and Healing* by Barbara Ganim (Three Rivers/Random House); *Visual Journaling* by Barbara Ganim and Susan Fox (The Theosophical Press/Quest Books); *American Gargoyles, Spirits in Stone* by Darlene Crist and Robert Llewellyn (Clarkson Potter/Random House); *Café Life: Rome, Café Life: Florence* and *Café Life: Venice* by Joe Wolff and Roger Paperno (Interlink Books), *Drawing from the Heart, When it Hurts Too Much to Talk* (Theosophical Press) by Barbara Ganim, *Florida for Families* by Laura Lee Miller, (UPress Florida). Many others in the works!

HORNFISCHER LITERARY MANAGEMENT, INC.

PO Box 50544, Austin, TX 78763

e-mail: jim@hornfischerlit.com

Agent: Jim Hornfischer
Born: 1965, Massachusetts.
Education: J.D./M.B.A., University of Texas at Austin; B.A., Colgate University.
Career history: President, Hornfischer Literary Management, Inc., founded 2001; Agent, Literary Group International, 1993–2001; Editorial positions, McGraw-Hill General Books Division & HarperCollins Adult Trade Division, 1987–1992.

Hobbies/personal interests: Books. What else is there? (Okay, there's sports, too, and maybe music, and the occasional movie.)

Areas most interested in agenting: All types of high-quality narrative nonfiction, biography and autobiography, current events, U.S. history, military history, world history, political and cultural subjects, science, medicine/health, business/management, finance, academic writing and research that has a general-interest audience.

Areas not interested in agenting: Poetry, fiction.

Best way to initiate contact: A smartly tailored personal letter that suggests professionalism and/or accomplishment, together with 30-50 pages of good material that supports your optimism. Please include a thorough overview of the book and its market, author bio/c.v., chapter summaries, and two sample chapters. With fiction, please send a one-page synopsis and the first 30-35 pages of the manuscript.

Reading fee policy: No.

Client representation by category: Nonfiction, 95%; Fiction, 5%.

Commission: 15% domestic; 20% foreign.

Number of titles sold last year: 16

Rejection rate (all submissions): The same parade-drenching number as the rest of them.

Description of the dream client: Thinks big, drinks from glasses that are half full, writes even grocery lists with narrative momentum, keeps an open ear for useful advice, and runs with it in brilliant and surprising ways.

Common mistakes authors make: Succumbing to "Hollywood fever" by insisting on making their pitch in person or via telephone. Demanding an editorial critique of their work. (Agents can't spend time providing gratis critiques; reading time is simply too scarce.) Requiring us to audition for the role of their agent before we're even remotely interested. Not enclosing return postage, then becoming indignant over lack of response.

What can writers do to enhance their chances of getting you as their agent? Grasp the rudiments of the business (even if as an artist you'd prefer not to bother), temper your ambition with patience and a long view, and refine and improve your craft continuously.

Why did you become an agent? Getting a good book published, especially one that might not otherwise have been, can be rewarding in a life-affirming sort of way.

If not agenting, what might you be doing? Practicing law and suing the tar out of those who take advantage of innocent, hard-working writers.

How would you describe what you actually do for a living? My wife always tells me that I shatter dreams for a living, because I send back so many rejections. I prefer to think that for those writers for whom I do useful work, I make them.

What do you think about editors? The best ones are the heart and soul of their companies, and management should listen to them more closely.

What do you think of publishers? They are patrons to their authors who believe in them and make the market for their work. But most publishers are under financial pressures that have little to do with publishing, and hence sometimes can lose the all-important long-term view of an author's career development.

Representative titles: *Flags of Our Fathers* by James Bradley with Ron Powers (Bantam); *Lone Star Nation* by H. W. Brands (Doubleday); *The Most Exclusive Club: A History of the U.S. Senate* by Lewis L. Gould (Basic); *Raising Cole* by Marc Pittman with Mark Wangrin (HCI); *All American: The Rise and Fall of Jim Thorpe* by Bill Crawford (Wiley); *A Good Forest for Dying* by Patrick Beach (Doubleday); *The Pleasure Instinct* by Gene Wallenstein (Wiley); *Global War, Secret War* by George Friedman (Doubleday); *Why Things Break* by Mark Eberhart (Scribner); *My Life Had Stood a Loaded Gun* by Theo Padnos (Miramax).

IMPRINT AGENCY, INC.

5 West 101 Street, Suite 8-B, New York, NY 10025

212-666-1688

e-mail: imprintagency@@earthlink.net

Agent: Stephany Evans; Gary Heidt
Born: October 11, 1957, West Chester, Pennsylvania. Heidt: Born: October 12, 1970, Houston, TX.
Education: Evans: Communications/theater arts, Elizabethtown College, Elizabethtown, PA. Assorted art (drawing, painting), writing, and filmmaking classes at various NYC schools and institutions. Heidt: Graduated from Columbia University with a BA in psychology.
Career history: Evans: Co-founder/producer/actress Zemmel theater company, NYC. Assorted acting gigs in theater and film. Assistant to Editorial Direct, S&S Audio; Editor of alternative health/personal growth magazine *Free Spirit*, have done freelance editing in a wide range of categories, and ghostwritten books in the spiritual category. Began agenting with Sandra Martin/Paraview; founded own agency in 1993. Heidt: He is/has been a free jazz musician and a theatre administrator.
Hobbies/personal interests: Painting, mosaics, flea-marketing, restoring several old adobe houses in West Texas, traveling, going to the movies.
Areas most interested in agenting: Evans: I have eclectic tastes, but have especially enjoyed working with spirituality, New Age, alternative health/healing, parenting, psychology/transpersonal psychology, multicultural, women's issues, lifestyle and popular reference; and would love to find some really good fiction—either literary or commercial, especially women's. Heidt: Interested in representing fiction—both literary and commercial, including genre; spirituality (especially interested in Gnosticism); music; history; humor and Fortean/hermetic/paranormal and other arcane subject matter.
Areas not interested in agenting: Poetry, children's picture books, sci-fi, thrillers.
Best way to initiate contact: Query letter via e-mail or letter (with SASE). Please do not send full proposals or manuscripts via e-mail.

Reading-fee policy: Imprint does not charge reading fees.

Client representation by category: Nonfiction, 90%; Fiction, 10%. 98% of what we represent is for the adult market.

Commission: 15% domestic; 20% foreign (when using a subagent).

Number of titles sold last year: 18.

Rejection rate (all submissions): At least 95%.

Description of the client from Hell: Writers with unrealistic notions about the potential of their projects and also about what a publisher can/will do for them. Loose cannons who do end runs around the agent, firing off calls, e-mails, or letters to their editors when feeling insecure. Those who send their material in bits and pieces or who fail to update on important teaching/promotional work they are doing.

Description of the dream client: One who supplies all necessary info in a timely way without incessant micro-updates; one who is a lovely person, as well as being a terrific writer with a fresh, interesting point of view.

How did you become an agent? At a party, I met another agent who needed help. The work, as she described it, sounded right up my alley so I offered to help in order to learn.

Most common mistakes authors make: Expecting the agent to be a mind-reader and not supplying crucial information about their background or marketing platform; or, not caring about their presentation—spelling, grammar, typos, single-spaced type. Or, not disclosing that they have sent their work to several agents at once, or, worse, have already sent their material to several publishers on their own. Or, they have no idea of what the competition is for their book.

What can writers do to enhance their chances of getting you as an agent? They should do all of their homework—have a timely concept in a beautifully organized package. Know their competition, and have a great platform in place. And be nice.

Why did you become an agent? I have been an avid reader all my life and after dabbling in several areas of the arts, while growing sicker and sicker of waitressing and bartending, found that this is the first job that never bores me. I love being among the first to hear an author's new idea, and I also love the people who make up the publishing industry.

If not agenting, what might you be doing? Making art, establishing a gallery to show and sell other artists' work, traveling . . . reading, maybe publishing?

What do you think about other agents? They are (mostly) saints.

What do you think about editors? They also are (mostly) saints.

What do you think about publishers? They are (mostly) brave for business-folk, but some can be frustratingly limited in vision.

Representative titles: *Something Borrowed* by Emily Giffin (St. Martins); *Wide Awake: A Buddhist Guide for Teens* by Diana Winston (Perigee); *Encyclopedia of the Harlem Renaissance* by Aberjhani and Sandra L. West (Facts on File); *Ina May's Guide to Childbirth* by Ina May Gaskin (BantamDell); *365 Yoga* by Julie Rappaport (Tarcher); *1001 Questions to Ask BEFORE You Get Married*, Monica Mendez Leahy (McGraw-Hill); *Everything and the Kitchen Sink: Remodel Your Kitchen without Losing Your Mind* by Janice Costa and Daina Manning (Andrews & McMeel); *365 Kabbalah* by Rabbi Gershon Winkler (Andrews & McMeel); *Dancing on Quicksand: A Transforming Friendship in the Age of Alzheimer's* by Marilyn Mitchell (Johnson Books); *Dunwich's Guide to Gemstone Sorcery* by Gerina Dunwich (New Page Books); *Designing A Home With Wood* by Heather Adams (Stewart, Tabori, & Chang); *Horses Don't Lie: What Horses Teach Us About Our Natural Capacity for Awareness, Confidence, Courage, and Trust* by Chris Irwin, with Bob Weber (Marlowe & Company); *Unconditional Bliss: Finding Happiness in Times of Hardship* by Raphael Cushnir (Quest Books); *Healing Mantras and Shakti Mantras* by Thomas Ashley-Farrand (Ballantine).

INTELLECTUAL PROPERTY MANAGEMENT GROUP (IPMG)

PO Box 503, Kensington, MD 20895-0503

fax: 815-550-0842

www.ipmg.net   e-mail: query_ipmg@yahoo.com

Managing Agent: Christina Arneson
Associates: Jon Russell, Elizabeth Russell
Assistants: Karen Harvey, Carol Stigger, Mike Walden
Born: Arneson: 1965, Spokane, Washington. J. Russell: 1958, Tipton, Indiana. E. Russell: 1961, Tipton, Indiana.
Education: Arneson: Florida State University and New York University. J. Russell: University of Minnesota. E. Russell: Earlham College, University of California Los Angeles, and San Francisco Law School.
Career history: Christina Arneson has 17 years of book publishing experience in subsidiary rights, marketing, and as an author, editor, agent and book packager. Most recently, she founded the Intellectual Property Management Group, a publishing and media cooperative agency where she has helped self-and subsidy-published authors make it onto the bestseller list and even the Oprah Winfrey Show. Christina established the Christina Arneson Agency in 1995, finding immediate success when her first, previously unpublished client was nominated for the National Book Award. Christina held positions as Director of Subsidiary Rights at Simon & Schuster and was a founding member of Hyperion, and spent 6 years developing that start-up. At Putnam, Christina worked in Production and Marketing. Christina is the author of two books of humor (the second still in print 6 years post-publication) with over a quarter of a million copies in print, and is the former Managing Director of *South Of The Highway Magazine*, circulation 70,000 throughout the Hamptons and NYC. Christina is a regular speaker at writers' conferences and workshops, and is a member of the Faith Popcorn BrainReserve and Mensa.
Hobbies/personal interests: Book packaging, marketing, e-commerce, reading,

cooking, biking, tennis, and sailing.

Areas most interested in agenting: Commercial/mass market nonfiction; Latina/Latino fiction and nonfiction, business, science, technology.

Areas not interested in agenting: Genre fiction, poetry, and children's literature.

Best way to initiate contact: Via e-mail only! If you don't or can't submit via e-mail, we will be of little use to you. We are working from the four corners of the United States and need to have all initial contacts transmittable via the Internet.

Reading-fee policy: We do not charge reading fees of any sort.

Client representation by category: Nonfiction, 65%; Fiction, 20%; Film/television 10%; textbooks 5%.

Commission: 15%.

Number of titles sold last year: 16.

Rejection rate: 99%.

Description of the client from Hell: Well, we hate to include anyone in this category because we know that they are just trying to protect their own interests or don't know any better, but there are some annoyances we can mention: people who think we're going to steal their idea so they behave coyly, prospective clients who find our home numbers and call us, people who use all caps in e-mails, those who believe editors at large publishing houses should be able to make snap decisions not realizing that the editor has to sell a manuscript internally to dozens of people, ranging from marketing, to legal, to subsidiary rights, as well as to other senior editorial staff members. And my new favorite is perspective clients who claim that they have been recommended to us— we check!

Description of the dream client: Someone who writes well and sells even better.

Most common mistakes authors make: We don't want to know if you have kids or a spouse unless it's relevant to your work. We also need the truth without elaboration. When you tell us about your potential market in a book proposal, give realistic numbers. Read our website to learn more. There is quite a bit of incorrect information out there that can ruin your chances of being published. If anyone can find the source that says you should start a query letter by delving into the story or asking questions, please let me know, I would like to straighten them out. That calls for an immediate rejection.

What can writers do to enhance their chances of getting you as an agent? Know your market. Pay close attention to your competition and marketing sections of your proposal. Know what you're getting into. Expect to spend your own money on marketing. Regardless of who publishes your book, you will need to work if you want to realize your full potential.

Why did you become an agent? Helping people get their work published, recognized, and purchased is a very rewarding experience.

If not agenting, what might you be doing? We would write more books ourselves.

How would you describe what you do for a living? Network, read, research, hand-hold, predict the future, find solutions, network some more, make phone calls!

How did you become an agent? Christina started her agency as a hobby, a way to stay connected to the publishing world while she took time off to care for her two new babies. When her first author (a previously unpublished 24-year-old) was nominated for the National Book Award, she thought, "Oh, this is easy." She was wrong, of course.

What do you think about other agents? I admire them. I would like to hang out with them more. We need a support group.

What do you think about editors? We love them! Editors are in a tough position right now. The job has changed so much. Their job now requires them to read the minds of the marketing and sales people. It's not about the "really good book," it's about the "really good sell."

What do you think about publishers? We love them! And we love to see that as the larger houses merge, so many new smaller publishers are appearing as real competition. We also love to see so many people self-publishing now. It's not easy, but it's a wonderful way to learn about the biz and set yourself up for a larger publishing house.

What were your favorite films last year? Who has time for movies?

Do you watch *The Sopranos?* We're honoring Omerta on this one.

Comments: Whether you are submitting to us or not, visit our website, and explore all our valuable information.

Representative titles: *Leaps of Faith* by Rachel Kranz (Farrar, Straus & Giroux); *RepoGirls* by Laverne Harvey (Film rights Lary Simpson Productions, Television rights Fox Network, Book rights sale pending); *Statistics Unplugged* by Sally Caldwell (Wadsworth Press); *From This High Place* by Ken Standley (Putnam); *How To Aggravate a Man* by Christina Arneson (Adams Media); *The Vintner's Luck* by Elizabeth Knox (Farrar, Straus & Giroux).

INTERNATIONAL LITERARY ARTS

RR 5, Box 5391 A, Moscow, PA 18444

570-689-2692

www.internationalliteraryarts.com   query@internationalliteraryarts.com

Agents: Founding Agent Pamela K. Brodowsky, Evelyn Fazio

Born: Brodowsky: October 1967, Midland Park, New Jersey.

Education: Brodowsky: Business. Fazio: M.A. in History, University of Connecticut; B.A. in History, University of Bridgeport.

Career history: Brodowsky: Sales and Marketing, Business Consultant, Literary Agent and Author. Fazio: Vice President & Publisher, Editorial Director, Executive Editor, Managing Editor.

Hobbies/personal interests: Literature, film, art, and classical music.

Areas most interested in agenting: Agency covers across the spectrum. Fiction: Literary, commercial fiction with screen potential, mystery, suspense, thrillers, romance. Any exceptionally well crafted project. Nonfiction: Agency covers across the spectrum in all areas of nonfiction.

Areas not interested in agenting: Anything poorly written, dull or average; be unique, rise above.

Best way to initiate contact: Send a query letter with SASE; enclose the first 15 pages of the manuscript. Please do not send full, unsolicited manuscripts. You may use e-mail for query only, no attachments.

Reading-fee policy: Agency does not charge reading fees.

Client representation: Nonfiction, 50%; Fiction, 50%.

Commission: 15%.

Number of titles sold last year: 10.

Rejection rate: 98%.

Description of the client from Hell: A person who listens to you when you're talking, but doesn't hear what you're saying.

Description of the dream client: A writer who has the determination and ability to succeed. A true professional. One who knows it's not as easy as 1-2-3.

Most common mistakes authors make: Queries that don't provide me with enough information; bad grammar; they don't enclose an SASE with the query letter.

What can writers do to enhance their chances of getting you as their agent? A well-written query letter is a good place to start.

Why did you become an agent? There is only one answer to this question and that is I have a great love for the written word.

How did you become an agent? After seventeen years in sales, in 2000 I opened my own agency.

If not agenting, what might you be doing? I would likely be a sales executive.

How would you describe what you do for a living? Challenging—and I love a challenge.

What do you think about other agents? I feel agents have one of the most difficult yet rewarding careers, discovering new talent and making dreams a reality.

What do you think about editors? I think most are underpaid.

What do you think about publishers? I think they are the cores of our apple.

Comments: Know the market, know the process, nothing worthwhile in life comes without hard work.

NATASHA KERN LITERARY AGENCY, INC.

PO Box 2908, Portland, OR 97208-2908

503-297-6190

www.natashakern.com

Agent: Natasha Kern

Education: University of North Carolina, Chapel Hill; Columbia University, New York; graduate work, New York University.

Career history: Editor for New York publishers and agents prior to founding her own agency in 1986.

Hobbies/personal interests: Gardening, animals and birds, yoga, performing arts, history, geology, and, of course, and reading.

Areas most interested in agenting: Fiction: Commercial and mainstream women's, romances, historicals, paranormal thrillers, suspense, chick-lit, lady-lit, romantic comedy, paranormal romance and inspirational fiction. Nonfiction: Body, mind, spirit subjects, popular science, inspirational subjects, multi-cultural, investigative journalism, health, science, women's issues, parenting, spirituality, psychology, business, self-help, gardening, current issues, animals/nature, controversial subjects, and narrative nonfiction.

Areas not interested in agenting: Fiction: Horror, sci-fi and fantasy, true crime, short stories, children's or young adult. Nonfiction: Sports, cookbooks, poetry, illustrated or coffee-table books, computers; technical, scholarly or reference; stage plays, scripts, screenplays, or software.

If not agenting, what would you be doing? I did everything else I ever wanted to do before becoming an agent. Agenting is truly a calling for me, and I would not be as happy doing anything else. It is a case of "Do what you love (and are good at) and the money follows." I also have a deep commitment to bringing new knowledge, new ideas, and new writing into the world. I believe storytelling is powerful and a great book truly can change the world.

Best way to initiate contact: Go to our website at www.natashakern.com for updates on our interests and how to submit. Go to fiction or nonfiction.

Reading-fee policy: No reading fee charged.

Client representation by category: Nonfiction, 40%; Fiction, 60%.

Commission: 15% domestic and film; 20% foreign.

Number of titles sold last year: 54.

Rejection rate (all submissions): 99% unsolicited mail; 85% solicited or submitted via website. Write a good query! We are selective, but we do want to find successful writers of the future. Go to the website and follow the instructions. This greatly increases your chance of success.

Most common mistakes authors make: Not describing their material or project adequately. Querying by fax, or phone. Sending unrequested material. Exaggerated claims or credentials. Comparing themselves favorably to current bestselling authors. Querying about books in areas we do not represent. Lack of professionalism. Omitting the end from a synopsis. Failing to follow instructions.

Description of the client from Hell: I do not have any clients like this. All of my clients are people I respect and admire as individuals, as well as writers. They are committed to their own success, and I am committed to helping them to achieve it. They understand the complex tasks involved in agenting, including sales, negotiations, editorial, arbitration, foreign and film rights, and so forth, and we work as a team to ensure the best outcome for their work.

Description of a dream client: One who participates in a mutually respectful business relationship, is clear about needs and goals, and communicates about career planning. If we know what you need and want, we can help you to achieve it. A dream client has a gift for language and storytelling, a commitment to a writing career, a desire to learn and grow, and a passion for excellence. This client understands that many people have to work together for a book to succeed and that everything in publishing takes far longer than one imagines. Trust and communication are truly essential. How wonderful that so many of my clients are dream clients.

Why did you become an agent? When I left New York, I knew that I wanted to stay in publishing. However, editorial work was not sufficiently satisfying by itself. I knew I could acquire and develop saleable properties and that my background gave me expertise in sales and running a company. I wanted to work with people long-term and not just on a single project or phase of one. Plus, I had an entrepreneurial temperament and experience negotiating big-money deals from raising venture capital for high-tech firms. When I developed literary projects for other agents that did not sell, I knew I could sell them myself—so I did. I've never regretted that decision. Agenting combined my love of books, my affinity for deal making, and my preference for trusting my own intuition. I sold 28 books the first year the agency was in business, and have sold 600 books since.

What can writers do to enhance their chances of getting you as an agent? Read all the advice we provide gratis on the website. We are doing our best to help you succeed! In nonfiction, the author's passionate belief in the subject, as well as expertise and a defined audience, are appealing. Be a client who is willing to listen, learn, and work hard to succeed. If there are writing problems, I will get this author help, in order to produce a saleable proposal. In fiction, I look for a wonderful, fresh, authorial voice, a page-turning plot that really does keep me up at night after a long day, well-structured chapters, and imaginative prose. A writer who can pull me into another point of view and another world I don't want to leave. In fiction, the writing is everything. We are glad to encourage promising writers who still need to master some aspects of craft, if they are willing to work with an editor.

How would you describe what you actually do for a living? Unpublished writers often think an agent's job is only sales and negotiations. I am often involved in a book's development from the initial concept through preparation of a proposal; provide editorial advice; select appropriate editors; handle submissions and negotiations; troubleshoot publication problems, including reviewing publicity planning, distribution concerns, creating a website, and working with private publicists; long-term career planning and strategies; handle an author's financial affairs, audit royalty statements, collect unpaid monies, deal with tax documents and legal issues of many kinds; subsidiary sales, including foreign rights, film rights, audio, video, and other rights; handle career crises or conflicts with publishers; assist authors in earning a livelihood with their writing; provide expertise at writers' conferences; educate clients about the publishing industry and its vicissitudes; keep in touch with editors and their acquisitions interests or concerns about clients; attend industry events like Book Expo; meet personally with clients, editors, and others in the industry; answer hundreds of e-mails each week; talk on the phone a great deal; reading the work of clients and prospective clients and keep up with trends; work with office staff to upgrade corporate procedures and technical support; supervise the bookkeeper and accountants; arrange articles and interviews for trade publications, and so on. It's a long day.

What do you think about editors? Editors are indispensable, and every writer should be blessed with a good one. It is one of my primary goals to match each client with the perfect editor. I often succeed and the result is magical, like all great collaborations: Fred Astaire and Ginger Rogers, or Maxwell Perkins and Thomas Wolfe. Writers are more successful in great partnerships. No one can be objective about his or her own work or realistically expect to recognize all of his or her own flaws. Most successful endeavors require a coach—a voice coach, a dance teacher, an Olympic coach. Writing is no exception. There are gifted editors, both private editors and those at publishing houses, who can turn a strong manuscript into a great one, a gifted author into a bestselling one. I want all my clients to have that opportunity.

What do you think about publishers? They are going to have some interesting times ahead in the volatile new world of publishing, with challenges at every turn. Developing new talent and valuing the writers who are creating their long-term success would seem to be prerequisites for meeting these challenges. We keep up with changes in the industry and also work with new emerging presses, as well as major publishers. We can help authors to understand the publisher's point of view (and vice versa) in all situations so that a win-win deal will result.

Comments: Believe in yourself and your own gifts. Keep in mind that the challenge for every writer is twofold—to have something to say and to have the mastery of the craft to say it well. Study and practice plotting, pacing, point of view, and so forth—so you can express exactly what you want to say. Nothing is more important than being true to your own artistic vision and understanding the requirements of the medium you have chosen to express it, whether you are writing a symphony, a haiku, or a novel. Keep in mind that in imitating other writers, you can only be second-rate at being them. Expressing your own inner thoughts, feelings, and stories in your own way is the only path to real success. Your world, your history, your experiences, your insights cannot be duplicated by anyone else. Bring us in to share your vision, your imagination. No one can do it better than you can, because the truth of your uniqueness is what you are here to offer everyone else. It is what moves us and takes us outside of our own lives when we read what you have written.

Representative titles: *American Nightmare: The History of Jim Crow* by Jerrold Packard (St. Martin's Press); *Hope Is the Thing with Feathers* by Christopher Cokinos (Tarcher/Warner); *Identity Is Destiny* by Laurence Ackerman (Berrett-Koehler); *The Ecological Garden* by Toby Hemenway (Chelsea Green); *The Quiet Game* by Greg Iles (Dutton); *DaVinci Legacy* by Lewis Perdue (Forge/TOR); *The Power of Losing Control* by Joe Caruso (Gotham/Putnam); *Embrace The Dawn* by Kathleen Morgan (Tyndale); *With Serious Intent* by Maureen McKade (Putnam); *The Waiting Child* by Cindy Champnella (St. Martin's); *The Sacred Bedroom* by Jon Robertson (New World

Library); *Beautiful Ghosts* by Eliot Pattison (St. Martin's); *Beyond the Shadows* by Robin Hatcher (Tyndale); *The Hunger for Ecstasy* by Jalaja Bonheim (Rodale); *Biocosm* by Jim Gardner (Inner Ocean); *The Diamond Conspiracy* by Nick Kublicki (Sourcebooks); *Spirit Babies* by Walter Makichen (Bantam); *Kiss Me Once, Kiss Me Twice* by Kimberly Raye (Warner); *Sweet Release* by Pamela Clare (Leisure); *Blood Rein* by Mike Jones (St. Martin's).

LINDA KONNER LITERARY AGENCY

10 West 15th Street, Suite 1918, New York, NY 10011

212-691-3419

Agent: Linda Konner

Born: Brooklyn, New York.

Education: B.A. in Modern Languages, Brooklyn College; M.A.T. in Sociology and Urban Education, Fordham University.

Career history: 1976–1981, Editor at *Seventeen* magazine; 1981–1983, Managing Editor, and 1983–1985, Editor-in-Chief at *Weight Watchers Magazine*; 1985–1986, Entertainment Editor at *Redbook*; 1986–1993, Entertainment Editor at *Woman's World magazine*; 1996–present, Literary Agent. Author of eight books.

Hobbies/personal interests: Movies, theater, travel, exploring New York City, poker.

Areas most interested in agenting: Nonfiction only: Especially health, self-help, fitness and nutrition, relationships, parenting, pop psychology, celebrities, how-to, career, personal finance, African American

Areas not interested in agenting: Fiction, children's, illustrated books

If not agenting, what would you be doing? Writing books; in particular, a book I can't sell for the life of me, called *Apartners: Living Apart and Loving It* (my honey of 26 years and I are not married and don't live together).

Best way to initiate contact: Send a brief query letter along with SASE.

Reading-fee policy: No reading fee.

Client representation by category: Nonfiction, 100%.

Commission: 15% domestic, 25% foreign (my foreign rights subagents collect 15%).

Number of titles sold last year: About 20.

Rejection rate: 90%.

What gets you excited? See description of a dream client.

Description of the client from Hell: Clients from Hell don't follow through. Say they will turn in a proposal promptly/do a rewrite promptly/come up with ideas for the next book but then never do. Schmooze endlessly with me on the phone, either out of loneliness or to get my help coming up with a new idea. Think that "fun" multicolored proposals with lots of (needless) visuals are great (they do not save an otherwise poor idea or poor writing).

Description of a dream client: Those who write well and have a steady stream of good, commercial nonfiction ideas. Are experts in their field (or have access to one) and have media experience. Not afraid to think big. They have a sense of the marketplace—what's happening in the publishing world and what is likely to sell. They follow directions. Turn things around promptly. Keep phone conversations brief and to the point. Appreciate the efforts I'm making on their behalf.

Why did you become an agent? I wanted a change from book writing. I had successfully sold and negotiated contracts for several books of my own and my friends (often getting better deals for myself than my agents had gotten), and I enjoyed the process. Also, I had always had many more good book ideas than I ever had the time to write myself, and now I can see some of my ideas (such as *The Wedding Dress Diet*) blossom into books written by other talented people, who may be good writers but don't have a concrete book idea at the moment.

Representative titles: *Date Like a Man. . .to Get the Man You Want* (HarperCollins) by Myreah Moore and Jodie Gould; *Six Questions That Can Change Your Life* by Joseph Nowinski, Ph.D. (Rodale); *Change Your Mind, Change Your Body* by Ann Kearney-Cooke, Ph.D., and Florence Isaacs (Atria); *The Ultimate Body* by Liz Neporent (Ballantine); *More Money Than God: Living a Rich Life Without Losing Your Soul* by Steven Z. Leder; *Getting Elected* by Congresswomen Loretta and Linda Sanchez; *No More Type-2 Diabetic Kids* by Sheri Colberg-Ochs, PhD and Mary Friesz; *Like a Lampshade in a Whorehouse: My Story* by Phyllis Diller with Richard Buskin.

BARBARA S. KOUTS, LITERARY AGENT

PO Box 560, Bellport, NY 11713

631-286-1278

Agent: Barbara S. Kouts
Born: October 24, 1936.
Education: B.A. in English, New York University; M.A. in English, SUNY at Stony Brook.
Career history: Freelance editoral work at book publishers and magazines; began working in literary agency 1980; founded own agency in 1991.
Hobbies/personal interests: Walking, swimming, reading, bicycle riding, gardening, spending time with my family and friends.

Areas most interested in agenting: Children's, fiction and nonfiction.

Areas not interested in agenting: Science fiction and romance novels, adult fiction and nonfiction.

If not agenting, what would you be doing? Traveling, sailing around the world, working with children, reading, and writing.

Best way to initiate contact: Query letter and description of project (with SASE).

Reading-fee policy: No reading fee (only photocopying expenses).

Client representation by category: 100% children's fiction and non-fiction.

Commission: 15%.

Number of titles sold last year: Lost count!

Rejection rate: 90% of new submissions and queries.

Most common mistakes authors make: Calling on the phone over and over again to find out about everything! Constantly! Sending sloppy and unprofessional work!

What gets you excited? A wonderful manuscript.

Description of the client from Hell: Expecting much too much—instant reads, instant dollars, instant attention! A feeling of nontrust, quibbling over everything.

Description of a dream client: Hardworking, reliable, consistent in writing, willing to rewrite and revise, kind and considerate. Upbeat and cheerful.

How did you become an agent? Studied English literature, studied editorial procedures. Worked for a book publisher and a magazine publisher.

Why did you become an agent? Great love of books! And good reads! I love to see a manuscript turn into a published book. And children need good books now.

How would you describe what you actually do for a living? I work for writers to better their careers. I work to serve writers.

What do you think about other agents? I know about many who are very good!

What do you think about editors? I admire a good editor, and there are many in the field now.

What do you think about publishers? A good publisher publishes good books, books of fine quality!

Comments: Keep on writing—never give up! "To one's own self be true." Write from the heart and soul!

Representative titles: *Dancing on the Edge* by Han Nolan; *Sacajawea* by Joseph Bruchac; *Cinderella Skeleton* by Robert San Souci; *Froggy's First Christmas* by Jonathan London; *Hidden Roots* by Joseph Bruchac (Scholastic); *Hector Springs Loose* by Elizabeth Shreeve (Aladdin, S&S); *Froggy's Baby Sister* by Jonathan London (Viking); *When We Were Saints* by Han Nolan (Harcourt).

IRENE KRAAS AGENCY

Irene Kraas: 256 Rancho Alegre, Santa Fe, NM 87508

fax: 505-438-7783

Ashley Kraas: 507 NW 22nd Ave., Suite 104 Portland, OR 97210

503-319-0900

Agent: Irene W. Kraas, Principal; Ashley Kraas, Associate
Born: August 16, is this necessary?
Education: B.A. in Psychology; M.Ed. in Educational Psychology.
Career history: Career Counselor; Management Consultant and Trainer to business, universities, and government; Literary Agent (1990–present).
Hobbies/personal interests: Reading, hiking, and enjoying life.
Areas most interested in agenting: At the moment, Irene is looking for psychological thrillers, medical thrillers, mysteries and literary fiction. Ashley is interested in romance, women's fiction, historical fiction, and nonfiction (including but not limited to memoirs, biographies, self-help and spiritual). Material by unpublished authors will be accepted in those areas only. Published authors seeking representation may contact us regarding material in any area except children's picture books and chapter books. Please send appropriate submissions to the correct address.
Areas not interested in agenting: Please see above.
If not agenting, what would you be doing? I've done what I've wanted all along and this is the ultimate. However, if I had to choose, I would be a rich publisher and publish all those great books that I've had rejected! Ashley: I love this work. I'd do exactly the same thing, but from Paris. Oh wait, I think that falls under what will you be doing in the future, not instead of.
Best way to initiate contact: Send either of us a short cover letter, the first 50 pages of a completed manuscript and return postage. Remember to send the right submission to the right address. And, please, no query letters!
Reading-fee policy: No reading fee.
Client representation by category: Irene: Fiction 80%, Nonfiction 5%, Young Adult 15%. Ashley: Romance 70%, Women's Fiction 20%, Nonfiction 10%.
Commission: 15%.
Number of titles sold last year: Varies from year to year.
Rejection rate (all submissions): 99%.
Most common mistakes authors make: No return postage or no cover letter. Also, an envelope too small for returns. Of course, I can ignore everything if it's a great manuscript.
Description of the client from Hell: I'll take the fifth, thanks.
Description of a dream client: Great writers who trust me to do the very best for them.

Why did you become an agent? I went from 20 years in business consulting to becoming the great American writer to agenting. I love using my business acumen in helping first-time authors get a break.

How would you describe what you actually do for a living? I read, read, read. Then sell, sell, sell.

What do you think about editors? Mostly, they are top-notch people interested in good writing.

What do you think about publishers? Well, let's just say they don't always see the picture clearly and don't always have the writer's best interests in mind. But that's why we have agents!

Do you watch *The Sopranos*? Without a doubt!

Representative titles: *Ty Merrick* by Denise Vitola (Berkley/Ace); *The Edge on the Sword*, a trilogy by Rebecca Tingle (YA-Putnam); *St. Germain Series*, 5 books by Chelsea Quinn Yarbro (Warner Books); *No Place Like the Chevy* by Janet Lee Carey (Atheneum); *Tales of Goblyn Woods* by Hilari Bell (Harper/Avon); *The Farsala Trilogy* by Hilari Bell (Simon & Schuster); *Any Kind of Luck* by Bill Sibley (Kensington); *Night Terror* by Chandler McGrew (Bantam); *The Snake Dancer* by Kimberley Griffiths Little (Knopf); *Alexandra Gladstone Series* by Paula Paul (Berkley); *The Fixer* by Jon Merz (Kensington); *Patriots in Petticoats* by Shirley Raye Redmond (Simon & Schuster); *The Dog Who Dug for Dinosaurs* by Shirley Raye Redmond (Simon & Schuster); *Song of the Land* by Noel-Anne Brennan (Berkley/Ace).

LAURA LANGLIE, LITERARY AGENT

275 President Street, Apartment 3, Brooklyn, NY 11231

718-858-0659   fax: 718-858-6161

e-mail: ljlangliel@aol.com

Agent: Laura Langlie

Born: January 21, 1964, Minneapolis, Minnesota.

Education: University of Iowa.

Career history: Associate Production Manager at Kensington; Editorial, Subrights, Production, Publicity, etc., Carroll & Graf; Kidde, Hoyt & Picard Literary Agency, Agent.

Hobbies/personal interests: Going to the movies and the theater. Cooking and ice-skating.

Areas most interested in agenting: I'm most enthusiastic about representing a book that appeals to me as a reader. Any good story well told, whether it be a romance, mystery, or literary novel, truly excites me. The same can be said for nonfiction. I look for books about a fascinating time, event, or person—something unique or an established subject revisited in a new fashion.

Areas not interested in agenting: Male adventure, military novels, most science fiction, poetry, and erotica.

Best way to initiate contact: Send me a brief query letter, accompanied by an SASE. Make sure you tell me about your book—what's the hook?—why is it worthwhile?—and about yourself.

Client representation: Nonfiction, 50%; Fiction, 25%; Children's, 25%.

Commission: 15%.

Number of titles sold last year: 25.

Rejection rate (all submissions): 90%.

Description of the client from Hell: My clients from Hell are unrealistic, not open to suggestions on how to improve their work, those who don't realize that once a book is accepted, their work is only just beginning.

Description of the dream client: My dream clients are optimistic, eager, and willing to work hard with me to reach their goals.

Common mistakes authors make: They don't tell me enough about themselves in their query letter. Remember to address why you're the right author for this book.

What can writers do to enhance their chances of getting you as their agent? Kindly write to me; don't telephone. Be a pleasant, patient, straightforward person. No one wants to work hard for someone who's unpleasant and difficult.

Why did you become an agent? I enjoy helping people. There's nothing more satisfying than making a deal on an author's behalf and seeing it work out in the end for all three parties.

If not agenting, what might you be doing? I'd be involved in publishing in some capacity. I've been reading *Publishers Weekly* since I was in high school.

How would you describe what you do for a living? I'm a matchmaker. Sometimes it works; sometimes the matches result in a divorce. On the whole, however, I've got a pretty good track record.

How did you become an agent? I was asked if I wanted to become an agent. At that time, I was working as a freelance editor and thought to take advantage of the opportunity. I always enjoyed my relationships with authors. It appears that it was what I was meant to do.

What do you think about editors? Editors are really partners with agents. A good editor is a true find. An editor's enthusiasm and dedication can make all the difference to a book's success.

What do you think about publishers? I think it's a tough market for publishers today. Books have never been a big moneymaking industry, but since many publishers are now owned by large corporations, there's considerable pressure on the publishing divisions to deliver a profit. I like working with a variety of publishers. Often, smaller publishers can surprise you with their creativity and passion for what they do.

What were your favorite films last year? *Lord of the Rings: Return of the King* and *Lost in Translation.*

Do you watch *The Sopranos*? Not much this year.

Comments: What "rocks my world" is to help clients realize their dreams.

Representative titles: *Someplace Like This* by Renee Ashley (Permanent Press); *The Angel Whispered Danger* by Mignon F. Ballard (St. Martin's Press/Berkley); *The Accidental Duchess* by Jessica Benson (Pocket Books); Loman Princess Diaries novels, *Princess in the Spotlight*, *Princess in Love*, and *Boy Meets Girl* by Meg Cabot (HarperCollins); *In the Wake of Madness* (Algonquin) and *A Watery Grave* (St. Martin's Press) by Joan Druett; *The Lobotomist* by Jack El-Hai (John Wiley and Sons); *Chasing the Devil's Tail* by David Fulmer (Poisoned Pen Press/ Harvest); *Satan's Pony* and *Scarecrow* by Robin Hathaway (Thomas Dunne Books/St. Martin's Press); *The Serious Kiss* by Mary Hogan (HarperCollins); *Tigers of the Snow* and *Himalaya* by Jonathan Neale (Thomas Dunne Books/St. Martin's Press); *Lost at Sea* by Jonathan Neale (Houghton Mifflin); *Fire and Ice* by Eric Pinder (Algonquin); *Unveiled: The Hidden Loves of Nuns* by Cheryl L. Reed (Berkley); *The Pact* by Jennifer Sturman (Red Dress).

MICHAEL LARSEN—ELIZABETH POMADA LITERARY AGENTS

1029 Jones Street, San Francisco, CA 94109-5023

415-673-0939

www.larsen-pomada.com   e-mail: larsenpoma@aol.com

Agents: Michael Larsen, Elizabeth Pomada

Born: Larsen: January 8, 1941, New York, New York. Pomada: June 12, 1940, New York, New York.

Education: Larsen: City College of New York, 1965. Pomada: Cornell University, 1962.

Career history: Larsen: Worked at Bantam, William Morrow, and Pyramid (now part of Berkley). Pomada: Worked at Holt, David McKay, and the Dial Press. Members: AAR. Sold books to more than 100 publishers. Started Northern California's oldest literary agency in 1972. Written or co-authored 15 books. Larsen wrote *How to Write a Book Proposal*; *Literary Agents: What They Do, How They Do It, and How to Find and Work with the Right One for You*; and, with Jay Conrad Levinson and Rick Frishman, co-authored *Guerrilla Marketing for Writers: 100 Weapons for Selling Your Work.* I speak at the Learning Annex and writers' conferences, including Maui and Santa Barbara. We present seminars on "Get Paid to Write Your Book! 3 Steps to Writing an Irresistible Book Proposal," "Guerrilla Marketing for Writers," "3 Ways to Make Yourself Irresistible to Any Agent or Publisher," "Taking the Guesswork Out of Publishing: 15 Ways to Test-Market Your Books to Guarantee Their Success.," "Publishing, A to Z."

Hobbies/personal interests: Larsen: Reading books between covers without the phone ringing, jazz and classical music, France, movies and other media, technology and the future. (After all, it is where I'm going to spend the rest of my life.) Pomada:

France, traveling and writing about it; and reading for pleasure.

Areas most interested in agenting: General fiction and nonfiction. Larsen: Beautiful writing, new ideas with social or esthetic value, anything that large and medium-sized houses will buy, how-tos, self-help, business, technology, trends, visions of the future, health, spirituality, pop culture, history, architecture, illustrated books. Pomada: Nonfiction: books for women, travel, food, the arts, and narrative nonfiction, including memoirs and biographies. Fiction: General, women's, historical and contemporary, commercial, literary, thrillers, suspense, and genre: romance, mystery, fantasy.

Areas not interested in agenting: Articles, short stories, poetry, screenplays, children's and young adult, textbooks, stories of abuse, books that will only interest small houses. Agents and editors want to look forward to working with the books and authors they take on. This makes them less receptive to books that are only depressing. Like the readers they are surrogates for, agents and editors like happy endings or a positive slant on a depressing subject. If possible, don't sell a problem; sell a solution.

Best way to initiate contact: Fiction: Elizabeth is eager to see the first 10 pages of a completed novel, followed by a 2-page synopsis after you have gotten feedback from people who know writing. Please include an SASE, and your daytime phone number. Nonfiction: Michael's book on proposals describes what we need to see. If your book will be aimed at a wide national audience and will depend on your promotional efforts to keep selling, please mail your title and promotion with an SASE or e-mail them as a letter, not as an attachment. If it's a serious or narrative book, please send the first three chapters followed by a 2-page synopsis, an SASE, and your daytime phone number.

Client representation by category: Nonfiction, 70%; Fiction, 30%.

Commission: 15% domestic, which includes film and most expenses; foreign 20%, except Asia 30%.

Number of titles sold last year? 15–20.

Rejection rate (all submissions): More than 90%.

Description of the client from Hell: We have an eccentric California approach to agenting. We like to handle books we like by writers we like and sell them to editors we like. So we don't even have a client from Heck.

Description of the dream client: Dream clients are alchemists who have a clear vision of their literary and financial goals, which they pursue with relentlessness tempered by passion, professionalism, optimism, and grace. They make nothing in their lives more important than achieving their goals; have a steady stream of brilliant ideas they can transform into gold; write exquisite prose that gives us, the editors and the book buyers who read it, chills; understand that agents and writers don't sell books—books sell themselves; understand that publishing a book is an imperfect process that will create problems so they make the best of any situation by taking the long view as well as the short view; they are lifelong learners about writing, publishing and their field; are motivated more by love than money, by art than commerce; inspire passion and excellence in everyone who comes into contact with them and their work; believe that the right book will change the world and use their literary gifts to make a difference as well as a living; balance their personal and professional lives without sacrificing one to the other; call us when they have a problem; understand that as writers, we endure the same problems they do, so we try to balance truth and charity; understand that since they are free to leave us at any time, we always have an incentive to keep them satisfied.

Most common mistakes authors make: Not following the advice in this book.

What can writers do to enhance their chances of getting you as an agent? Come as close as they can to the ideal of the dream client. Check our website or send a #10 SASE for our free brochure "3 Ways to Make Yourself Irresistible to Any Agent or Publisher" to find out about us. There are 1,200 agents out there. Tell us why you want us.

Why did you become an agent? We love books, and we love helping writers make their work 100 percent and then reap the rewards and recognition they deserve.

If not agenting, what would you be doing? Larsen: Writing. Pomada: Traveling the world and writing about it.

How would you describe what you do for a living? We are mediators between you and the marketplace, scouts who know what publishers want, midwives who help you give birth to your ideas and make sure your work is ready before submitting it, matchmakers who arrange working marriages between you and the best possible editor and publisher for your books, negotiators who hammer out the best contract for you, advocates between you and your publisher throughout the publication process, and mentors who advise you about publishing, promotion, your writing, and your career— an oasis of encouragement when you need it.

How did you become an agent? Larsen: The Symbionese Liberation Army made me an agent. When the SLA kidnapped Patricia Hearst, I sold a book about it in four phone calls and thought, "Gee, this looks easy. I should do it for a living!" Pomada: When we moved to San Francisco, I registered with an employment agency that specialized in writers. The owner couldn't find me a job, but she had all these manuscripts and didn't know what to do with them. We did.

What do you think about editors? People become editors for the same reason they become agents: because they like books and people. We wouldn't be agents if we didn't know a lot of wonderful editors who are dedicated to acquiring good books, editing them well, and being the in-house agent for the books they buy by stirring up as much enthusiasm for their books as they can inside and outside of the house. Editors are the ultimate middle-people, trying to please publishers, authors, agents, and themselves. The overworked and underpaid editors who do this, while balancing art and commerce so they can keep their jobs, deserve to be regarded as the heroes of the business.

What do you think about publishers? Consolidation, conglomerization, technology, and the globalization of culture and commerce are transforming the industry, but no one knows into what. Competition, stockholders, and rising costs force the six conglomerates that dominate the industry to be more concerned about the bottom line than about supporting new writers while they build the audience for their books. This creates opportunities for small and niche publishers, university presses, and self-publishers.

Do you watch *The Sopranos?* No. There's too much violence in the real world. We don't want more violence in our lives. And certainly don't want those people in our home.

Comments: You have at least 17 options for getting your books published (they're listed on our website). Large and medium-sized houses are only one of them, but they are the only way that agents can make a living. More than 90 percent of agents must find new writers to make a living. But even though they can't make a living saying no, they reject more than 90 percent of the material they receive. Despite this paradoxical situation, we think it's easier than ever to get an agent. What's getting harder is writing something strong enough to convince large and medium-sized houses to take a chance on it. If you can, it will be easier than ever for you to find an agent and a publisher, because the more challenging publishing becomes, the easier it is to sell books that meet that challenge. If you want to be published by a large- or medium-sized house, follow these steps: Learn how agents and publishers work. Read what you love to read and write what you love to read. Read competitive books so you can use the one you love as models. You can only write as well as you read. Accept the bad news that you won't get your proposal or manuscript right by yourself and be glad about the good news: You don't have to. Understand that publishing is based on relationships. Build on- and off-line networks of publishing people and professionals in your field who can help you with feedback on your idea, your work, finding an agent, promotion, sources of information, and connections to other potential members of your networks. Come up with a new idea or an exciting new twist on an old one. Write the manuscript for a novel or a proposal for a nonfiction book. Whether you're writing fiction or nonfiction, prepare a promotion plan. Revise your work as often as needed. Share it with many readers: friends and family, potential buyers, literate readers, authors of books like yours, experts on the subject, and a devil's advocate who can spot whatever needs to be improved or removed. Approach agents or publishers the way their listings in directories recommend. Do everything you can for your books. Look at your career, not as being based on 1 book but based on 10 or 20, each better than the last. You are the most important person in the publishing process because you make it go. If you are writing to meet the needs of the marketplace and you can promote your books, now is the best time ever to be a writer. There are more subjects for you to write about, more ways to build your networks and learn about writing and publishing, more books and authors to serve as models for you to emulate, more options for getting your books published, and more ways to promote your books and profit from them than ever. Proceed as if success is inevitable. Persistence rewards talent.

Representative titles: *Freedom: Passages in Independence and the Power of Choice* by Leonard Roy Frank (Random House, July 4th, 2003); *The Silver Wyrm*, the 13th volume of the Deverry Series, by Katherine Kerr (Daw); *Fox on the Front*, a thriller by Michael Dobson and Doug Niles (Tor); *Join the Money Club: Fiscal Fitness for Women* by Candace Bahr and Ginita Wall, CP, CFP, (John Wiley); *Permission to Play: Taking Time* *to Create Fun in Your Life* by Jill Murphy Long (Sourcebooks); *The Only Negotiating Book You'll Ever Need: 101 Tactics for Win-Winning at Home and At Work* by Peter Stark and Jane Flaherty (Broadway Books); *Stuff Happens (And Then You Fix It): 9 Reality Rules to Steer Your Life Back in the Right Direction* by John Alston CPAE and Lloyd Thaxton (Wiley); *Say It Again, Sam: A Compiled Compendium of Repetitive Redundancies* by Richard Kallan, Ph.D. (Pantheon/Anchor); *Snoopy's Guide to the Writing Life* edited by Barnaby Conrad and Monte Schulz with words of wisdom from 30 top storytellers including Sue Grafton, Ray Bradbury and Elmore Leonard.

LEVINE GREENBERG LITERARY AGENCY, INC

(formerly James Levine Communications, Inc.)

307 Seventh Avenue, Suite 1906, New York, NY 10001

212-337-0934

www.levinegreenberg.com

West Coast Office:

112 Auburn Street, San Rafael, CA 94901

415-785-1582

Agents: James A. Levine, Arielle Eckstut (West Coast Office), Daniel Greenberg, Stephanie Kip Rostan.

Born: Levine: April 20, 1946. Eckstut: August 25, 1970. Greenberg: October 13, 1970. Rostan: March 7, 1973.

Education: Levine: B.A., Amherst College; M.A. C. Phil. (English Literature), University of California, Berkeley; Ed.D., Harvard University. Eckstut: B.A., University of Chicago. Greenberg: B.A. (History), University of Wisconsin at Madison. Rostan: Phillips Academy; B.A. (English/Creative Writing), Princeton.

Career History: Levine: Spent much of my career doing what I do now: putting together ideas, people, and money; identifying, nurturing, and marketing talent; creating projects that make a difference. As an entrepreneur in the not-for-profit and academic sectors, including a decade as Vice President at the Bank Street College of Education in New York City, I channeled people's expertise into a variety of media: print, software, video, multimedia, and audio. Eckstut: Pastry chef prior to becoming literary agent. Greenberg: Penguin Books and then in Italy with the Roberto Santachiara Literary Agency. Rostan: Editor, Bantam Books and then Book Producer, iVillage.com.

Hobbies/personal interests: Levine: Jazz, sports (playing them), photography, travel, hiking, voracious reading in a wide range of areas. More than twenty years as founder/director of The Fatherhood Project, a nonprofit research and educational initiative now located at the Families and Work Institute in New York City. Have written seven books, most recently *Working Fathers: New Strategies for Balancing Work and Family*, two software manuals, and more than one hundred articles for leading magazines. Also produced the PBS documentary *Fatherhood U.S.A.* Eckstut: Working with writers as an agent at James Levine Communications has fostered my own writing, and I have co-authored two books: *Pride and Promiscuity: The Lost Sex Scenes of Jane Austen* and *Satchel Sez: The Wit and Wisdom of Leroy "Satchel" Paige*, with an introduction by Bob Costas. I also love to cook, bake, and make art (I have a design background). I'm also an avid moviegoer and former member of an improvisational theatre group. Greenberg: When I'm not standing in the middle of the room on one leg balancing 1,500 page manuscripts on my head (my all time favorite hobby!), I'm watching movies, cooking meals, riding my bicycle, or doing yoga. Rostan: Red Sox baseball fan, green belt in karate, travel, writing, animals.

Areas most interested in agenting: Levine: I love the challenge of working with smart people who have great ideas. Eckstut: First, great writing. Second, great recipes. Greenberg: For fiction, any piece of solid writing interests me, no matter what the genre. I also look at credentials and publishing history. I keep my eyes open for a sharp sense of humor. Rostan: Commercial and literary fiction, including mystery/suspense and women's fiction, smart self-help, psychology.

Areas not interested in agenting: Levine: Anything that's poorly written. Eckstut: Romance, children's, true crime, academic, and professional books. Greenberg: Romances. Rostan: Business, cookbooks, science fiction, children's, academic.

If not agenting, what would you be doing? Levine: Writing and working in some other organizational setting to develop people's talent. Eckstut: Industrial designer? Director? Chef? Who knows! Greenberg: Impossible to conceive of such a scenario. Rostan: Writing (can't say whether it would be published!) and traveling everywhere.

Best way to initiate contact: Fill out the easy-to-use submission form on our website, www.jameslevine.com. It's listed under How We Work/Submission.

Client representation by category: Nonfiction 80%, Fiction 20%.

Commission: 15%.

Rejection rate: 99%.

Most common mistakes authors make: Send a whole manuscript, unsolicited, with no SASE, then keep calling—wanting to know why they have not gotten their manuscript back. Forget to explain who they are, why they're qualified to write, and, most important, who the audience is for their work.

Describe the client from Hell: Calls all the time for unnecessary reasons and never once says thanks.

Description of a dream client: Organized, thoughtful, easy to get along with, conscientious, reliable, cordial, and fun!

Why did you become an agent? We feel passionately about feeling passionately about the projects we take on. Levine: I was an agent before I ever knew I was an agent. Eckstut: Pure luck. Greenberg: I enjoy working with talented and interesting people. There is also nothing quite as exciting as the huge deal! Rostan: To be involved in the creative process of bringing books to market and the business aspects of making deals.

What can writers do to enhance their chances of getting you as an agent? Send us chocolate. (Just kidding.) Be organized and easy to work with—this will go a long way with your editor, too.

Representative titles: *Our Dumb Century* by The Onion (Crown); *Crossing the Chasm* by Geoffrey Moore (HarperBusiness); *Queen Bees & Wannabes* by Ross Wiseman (Crown); *Non-Campus Mentis* by Anders Henriksson (Workman); *Chicken* by David Henry Sterry (Regan); *Resurrecting Mingus* by Jenoyne Adams (Simon &Schuster); *Act Natural* by Ken Howard (Random House); *Piloting Palm* by Andrea Butter and David Pogue (Wiley); *Fruitflesh* by Gayle Brandeis (HarperSanFrancisco); *CNBC 24/7 Trading* (Wiley); *The Root Worker* by Rainelle Burton (Overlook); *Customers.com* by Patricia Seybold (Crown); *The Common Thread* by Martha Manning (Morrow); *Why God Won't Go Away* by Andrew Newberg, M.D., Eugene D'Aquili, M.D. Ph.D., and Vince Rause (Ballantine); *Raising Fences: A Black Man's Love Story* by Michael Datcher (Riverhead); *Reinventing Medicine* by Larry Dossey, M.D. (HarperSanFrancisco); *How to Quit Golf: A 12-Step Program* by Craig Brass (Dutton); *Room Redux* by Joanne Eckstut and Sheran James (Chronicle); *How to Raise a Family on Less Than Two Incomes* by Denise Topelnicki (Broadway); *The Complete Cancer Survival Guide* by Peter Teeley and Philip Bashe (Doubleday); *Run Catch Kiss* by Amy Sohn (Simon & Schuster); *Undoing Depression* by Richard O'Connor (Little, Brown); *Satchel Sez: The Wit, Wisdom and World of Leroy "Satchel" Paige* by David Sterry and Arielle Eckstut (Crown); *The Quest for Immortality: Science at the Frontiers of Aging* by S. Jay Olshansky and Bruce Carnes (W.W. Norton).

PAUL S. LEVINE LITERARY AGENCY

1054 Superba Avenue, Venice, CA 90291-3940

310-450-6711   fax: 310-450-0181

e-mail: pslevine@ix.netcom.com

Agent: Paul S. Levine
Born: March 16, 1954, New York.
Education: B.Comm., Concordia University, Montreal (1977); M.B.A., York University, Toronto (1978); J.D., University of Southern California, Los Angeles (1981).
Career history: Attorney for more than 22 years.
Areas most interested in agenting: Commercial fiction and nonfiction for adults, children, and young adults.
Areas not interested in agenting: Science fiction, fantasy, and horror.
If not agenting, what would you be doing? Practicing entertainment law.
Best way to initiate contact: Query by snail mail (with SASE), e-mail, fax.
Reading-fee policy: No reading fee.

Client representation: Nonfiction, 50%; Fiction, 35%; Children's, 10%; Other, 5%.
Commission: 15%.
Number of titles sold last year: 50.
Rejection rate: 97%.
Most common mistakes authors make: Writing bad query letters.
What gets you excited? See description of a dream client.
Description of the client from Hell: One who calls, faxes, e-mails, or otherwise tries to contact me every day. One who constantly needs reassurance that each rejection letter does not mean the client's project lacks merit and that the client is an awful person.
Description of a dream client: The opposite of above.
Why did you become an agent? I have loved the book business ever since I started practicing law in 1980. My first client was a major book publisher.
What can writers do to enhance their chances of getting you as an agent? Contact me in a professional manner. Be referred by an existing client, colleague, or friend.
How would you describe what you actually do for a living? I represent writers—book authors, screenwriters, television writers, and writer-producers.
What do you think about other agents? They're great people, as long as they don't practice entertainment/publishing law without a license.
What do you think about editors? I love them.
What do you think about publishers? I love them, too.
Comments: I always tell my clients that the only thing that I know how to write is a contract. I envy writers who can actually write.

LINDSEY'S LITERARY SERVICES

7502 Greenville Avenue, Suite 500, Dallas, Texas 75231

fax: 214-890-9295

bonedges001@aol.com

Agents: Emily Armenta; Bonnie James
Education: Armenta: MBA, University of Texas; James: M.A., University of California-Berkeley.
Career History: Armenta: Independent Film Editing. James: Magazine and film editing.
Hobbies/personal interests: Armenta: Travel, working out, yoga. James: Travel, cooking, hiking.
Areas most interested in agenting: Armenta: Nonfiction: New Age/metaphysics, self-help, psychology, women's issues, memoir, true crime. Fiction: Mystery/suspense, thriller, horror, literary, mainstream, romance. James: Nonfiction: New age/meta-

physics, self-help, psychology, women's issues, memoir, true crime. Fiction: mystery/suspense, thriller, horror, literary, mainstream, romance.

Areas not interested in agenting: Text books; children's books; poetry; juvenile.

Best way to initiate contact: Query or e-mail. Please no telephone calls. For nonfiction include proposal, writing sample, and brief biography, listing credentials and platform details. For fiction include synopsis, first three chapters, and brief biography.

Client representation by category: Nonfiction 75%; Fiction 25%.

Commission: 15% domestic, 20% foreign.

Number of titles sold last year: Seven.

Rejection rate (all submissions): 98%

Description of the client from Hell: Writers with unrealistic expectations, writers who won't listen and refuse to take advice.

Description of the dream client: Writers dedicated to the craft of writing. Writers who know their market and are constantly trying to improve.

Most common mistakes authors make: Poorly written material, unprofessional submission packages.

What can writers do to enhance their chances of getting you as an agent? Be professional with presentations, be willing to learn and take advice.

Why did you become an agent? Armenta: I love books. James: Wanted to go in business for myself, and I love well-written books.

What might you be doing if you weren't an agent? Editing magazines or films. James: Open an independent bookstore.

How would you describe what you actually do for a living? Hard work, but fun.

How did you become an agent? Natural progression from what we were doing.

What do you think about other agents? Hardworking people who love books.

What do you think about editors? Most are capable professionals.

What do you think about publishers? Most believe in terrific books; a few put more emphasis on a writer's name than quality writing.

What were your favorite films last year? Armenta: *Pirates of the Caribbean*. James: *Thirteen* (but it was terribly depressing).

Do you watch *The Sopranos?* No.

Miscellaneous Comments: Be sure your query and presentation of material is the best it can be. All too often writers tend to be sloppy querying agents. It's a real turn off.

Representative titles: *Hands of Vengeance*, Richard Sand (Durban House); *Crisis Pending*, Steve Cornell (Durban House).

THE LITERARY GROUP INTERNATIONAL

270 Lafayette Street, Suite 1505, New York, NY 10012

212-274-1616   fax: 212-274-9876

www.theliterarygroup.com   e-mail: litgrpfw@aol.com

Agents: Frank Weimann, Ian Kleinert

Hobbies/personal interests: Weimann: Ice hockey.

Areas most interested in agenting: Weimann: Categories include sports, science, how-to, mystery, romance, suspense, African-American subjects, politics, memoirs, history. All types of high-quality narrative nonfiction, current events, military history, U.S. history, world history, political subjects, science, medicine/health, business/management/finance, and all genres of mainstream fiction.

Areas not interested in agenting: Poetry.

If not agenting, what would you be doing? Weimann: This is all I ever wanted to do.

Best way to initiate contact: The ideal way to initiate contact is by sending us a clear, concise, compelling query letter.

Reading-fee policy: No reading fee.

Client representation by category: Weimann: Nonfiction, 55%; Fiction, 45%.

Commission: 15% domestic; 20% foreign.

Number of titles sold last year: Agency: 75.

Rejection rate (all submissions): Weimann: 99%.

Most common mistakes authors make: The most common mistake is to insist on meeting with an agent. It is what's on the page that counts, not a wonderful personality.

Description of the client from Hell: The worst thing a client can do, in my mind, is to constantly bombard the agency and/or publisher with needless phone calls.

Description of a dream client: Most of our authors fit into this category. Dream clients are willing to listen to our suggestions, make a decision, and trust that we will do what is in their best interest.

How did you become an agent? My first client, Thomas "Hollywood" Henderson, asked me to represent him after publishers loved his story and hated the proposal I wrote for him.

Why did you become an agent? Very simple—I don't have the ability to write books, but have the ability to help those who can.

How would you describe what you do for a living? I have the greatest job in the world.

What can writers do to enhance their chances of getting you as their agent? It is important to us that an author has confidence in our ability to help shape their writing career.

What do you think about editors? I believe editors are the most overworked and underpaid people in the creative arts.

What do you think about publishers? Where would we be without them?

Representative titles: *The Darwin Awards I* and *II* by Wendy Northcutt (E. P. Dutton); *Flags of Our Fathers* by James Bradley (Bantam Doubleday Dell); *October Sky* by Homer Hickam (Dell); *Keep it Simple* by Terry Bradshaw (Pocket); *Hunting the Jackal* by Billy Waugh (William Morrow); *Body by God* by Ben Lerner (Thomas Nelson); *The Good Guys* by Bill Bonanno & Joe Pistone (Warner); *The Manor* by Scott Nicholson (Pinnacle); *God Still Don't Like Ugly* by Mary Monroe (Dafina); *What a Girl Wants* by Kristin Billerbeck (W Publishing); *A Quarter for a Kiss* by Mindy Starns-Clark (Harvest House); *Inside Delta Force* by Eric Haney (Bantam).

TONI LOPOPOLO LITERARY MANAGEMENT

8837 School House Lane, Coopersburg, PA 18036

215-679-0560   fax: 215-679-0561

e-mail: LopopoloBooks@aol.com

Agent: Toni Lopopolo

Born: July 18, Los Angeles.

Education: M.A.

Career history: 1972–1973, Publicity Associate, Bantam Books; 1973–1975, Paperback Marketing Manager, Houghton-Mifflin; 1975–1981, Executive Editor, Macmillan; 1981–1990, Executive Editor, St. Martin's Press; 1990–present, Literary Agency.

Hobbies/personal interests: Reading, anything about Rudolph Valentino and Nelson Eddy, my dogs, restoring houses, interior design.

Areas most interested in agenting: Narrative nonfiction; biography, psychology, health, parenting, women's interest, Self-health, dog health and training, and any of today's most important subjects. Fiction: mysteries with unique, ethnic protagonists, historical, family sagas. The truly quirky novel with unusual characters.

Areas not interested in agenting: Try me.

Best way to initiate contact: Terrific query letter and excellent credentials.

Client representation by category: Nonfiction, 80%; Fiction, 20%.

Commission structure: 15% domestic; 20% foreign.

Number of titles sold last year: 8.

Rejection rate (all submissions): 95%.

Common mistakes authors make: Fiction writers who have not mastered the skills that make up the craft of book-length fiction; phoning to tell me their "idea" for a book; wannabe writers who have not done their homework such as learning how to write a query letter and enclose an SASE, who do not have the credentials or the platform for the nonfiction subject they propose; those who balk at writing a proposal; fiction writers who send a 10-page synopsis, and much more.

Description of the client from Hell: The terminally insecure.

Description of the dream client: The true professional writers who trust and believe in their agent and themselves.

How did you become an agent? It was a natural segue after 20 years in book publishing.

Why did you become an agent? Becoming an agent was a natural follow-up to a long publishing career. The love of good books.

How would you describe what you do for a living? I search for talented writers and manage their careers. This includes a lot of editing.

What can writers do to enhance their chances of getting you as their agent? For nonfiction, submitting an excellently crafted proposal. For fiction, writers who have mastered the skills that make up the craft of book-length fiction and the craft of meticulous self-editing. Writers who have done their homework in how to correctly submit to an agent and who show strong self-confidence are welcome.

If not agenting, what would you be doing? I'd like to go back to teaching. I'd be refurbishing fixer-upper houses. I love the process. Plus, I'd have more than three dogs. And reading already published books by the hundreds.

What do you think about editors? Because I worked as an editor for many years, I am very empathetic to their workload and plight in the machinery of a publishing house. Many are great talents.

What do you think about publishers? It is daunting to walk into a bookstore and see the thousands of books sitting on the shelves. These books live or die with little help from the publishers who put them there. Conglomerate publishing has not helped the old sink-or-swim philosophy and that's discouraging, but we press on, don't we? And, as long as publishers publish and readers keep reading, agents will sell books.

What were your favorite films last year? I collect old films from the 1930s; I especially like early James Cagney, I own every available film with Rudolph Valentino, I now own every George Raft (Valentino wannabe) film but one that I haven't located yet called *It Had To Happen*, (I'm also searching for 1937's *Fifty Roads To Town*) and I'm crazy for Nelson Eddy. I own many movies about dogs including *The Biscuit Eater*. I enjoyed a recent film, *Seabiscuit*.

Do you watch *The Sopranos*? Every episode. Never miss it. How about that Janice? And the fight between Tony and Ralphie. Whew! And I do hope the ducks come back. Can't wait for the new season!

Representative titles: *Organizing From The Right Side of the Brain* by Lee Silber; *Self-Promotion for Creative People* by Lee Silber (Crown); *Real-Life Home Schooling* by Rhonda Barfield (Pocket Books); *Five Steps to Emotional Healing* by Gloria Arenson (Simon & Schuster); The Starletta Duval mystery series (*Green Money* and *Reckless Eyeballin'*; Ballantine).

NANCY LOVE LITERARY AGENCY

250 E. 65th Street Suite #4A, New York, NY 10021

212-980-3499

Agent: Nancy Love; Miriam Tager

Education: Tager: MS in Education; MA in Writing.

Career history: Book/Magazine writer before she opened her agency 20 years ago.

Hobbies/personal interests: Cooking/Gardening/Hiking. Tager: Writing young adult books.

Areas most interested in agenting: Health, parenting, women's issues, current affairs, bio, history, relationships, self-help. Tager: Mysteries/thrillers.

Areas not interested in agenting: All fiction except mysteries/thrillers, children's, poetry. Tager: Science fiction, fantasy, supernatural, occult, horror.

If not agenting, what might you be doing? Travel writing. Tager: Writing on the beach.

Best way to initiate contact: Send query. No e-mail/fax queries, please. Tager: Send query and first 3 chapters (around 40 pages) and a synopsis.

Reading-fee policy: None.

Client representation by category: 85% nonfiction; 15% mysteries, thrillers.

Commission structure: 15%.

Number of titles sold last year: 8.

Rejection rate (all submissions): 95% unsolicited. Tager: 95%.

Common mistakes authors make: Sending a query about a genre that we do not handle. Tager: Sending a chapter from the end of their book, vague query letters and a very long synopsis.

Description of the client from hell: Tager: A client that thinks and acts like they are above revisions.

Description of the dream client: They take direction well, have great ideas and meet deadlines. Tager: A client who is open, receptive and willing to make changes.

How did you become an agent? It was a natural transition from being a writer/editor. Tager: I made a career change, from burnt-out elementary school teacher to agent.

Why did you become an agent? It utilizes all of my abilities. I also like being responsible for the development of a book. Tager: I wanted to get back to my writing life.

What would you be doing if you weren't an agent? Tager: Be a full-time writer.

How would you describe what you do for a living? I get to help struggling authors fulfill their dreams of getting published. What could be more satisfying?

What can writers do to enhance their chances of getting you as their agent? They need to have a platform and a good idea. Tager: Be clear and concise in query letters. Do not talk about being the next Michael Connelly! Make sure something dramatic happens in the first three chapters and make your main characters likeable.

How would you describe what you actually do for a living? I like to make it possible for writers to come up with a marketable product.

Comments: Never give up! If you don't have a pile of rejection letters then you are not a writer!

Representative titles: *All The Shah's Men* by Stephen Kinzer (John Wiley); *7 Tools to Beat Addiction* by Stanton Peele, PhD (Crown); *Say Goodbye to Back Pain* by Emile Hiesiger, MD & Marian Betancourt (Pocket); *Bone Dry* by Ben Rehder (St. Martin's Press); *The Cemetery Yew* by Cynthia Riggs (St. Martin's Press); *Raising Courageous Kids* by Charles Smith (Sorin Books).

DONALD MAASS LITERARY AGENCY

160 West 95th Street, Suite 1B, New York, NY 10025

fax: 212-866-8181

e-mail: info@maassagency.com

Agents: Donald Maass, Jennifer Jackson, Rachel Vater, Cameron McClure

Born: Maass: 1953, Columbus, Georgia. Jackson: 1971, Cambridge, New York. Vater: 1975, Covington, Kentucky. McClure: 1979, Huntington Beach, California.

Education: Maass: B.A., St. Lawrence University, 1975; Jackson: B.A., St. Lawrence University, 1993. Vater: B.A., Northern Kentucky University, 1998. McClure: B.A., University of California at Santa Barbara, 2001.

Career history: Maass: 1977–1978, Editor, Dell Publishing; 1979, Agent, Scott Meredith Literary Agency, Inc.; 1980, founded Donald Maass Literary Agency. Jackson: 1993–present, Donald Maass Literary Agency. Vater: 1999–2003, Editor, Writer's Digest Books; 2003–present, Donald Maass Literary Agency. McClure: 2002–2004, Assistant Agent, Curtis Brown Ltd.; 2004–present, Donald Maass Literary Agency.

Hobbies/personal interests: Maass: Reading, theater, sailing, squash, antiques, stock market. Jackson: Cooking, criminology, website design, RPGs, ectophilic music. Vater: Reading, writing, playing the piano and flute, singing, theater, art, women's studies, religious studies. McClure: Reading, soccer, running, biking, music, history channel, movies.

Areas most interested in agenting: Maass: Fiction specialist. Concentration in science fiction, fantasy, mystery, suspense, horror, frontier, mainstream, and literary. Jackson: Fiction specialist in all genres, especially mystery, suspense, thrillers, science fiction, and fantasy, romance, women's fiction. Vater: Fiction: literary, mainstream, especially chick lit, romance, suspense and fantasy. McClure: Fiction: literary and historical, mystery and suspense, fantasy, women's fiction. Narrative nonfiction.

Areas not interested in agenting: Maass: Pop psychology, how-to, true crime, humor/novelty, juvenile. Jackson: Nonfiction, poetry, and children's books. Vater: non-fiction, horror, children's books. McClure: Poetry, how-to, children's books.

If not agenting, what would you be doing? Maass: Oh, Lord, it's too late to think about that now. Jackson: There's something besides agenting? Vater: I've wanted to be an agent more than anything, so this isn't a job I accidentally fell into. If I weren't an agent, I would be an editor or a writer. McClure: Brain surgery.

Best way to initiate contact: One-page query letter (with SASE), that includes a description of the book and any prior book or short story credits, along with first five pages.

Reading-fee policy: No reading fee.

Client representation by category: Fiction, 100%. Jackson: Nonfiction, 1%; Fiction, 99%.

Commission: 15% domestic; 20% foreign.

Number of titles sold last year: Maass: 75. Jackson: 55.

Rejection rate (all submissions): 99%.

Most common mistakes authors make: Long summaries. You need only three things to hook me on your story: setting, protagonist, problem. Brevity is also good in your bio and career plans.

Description of a dream client: Patient, passionate, dedicated to craft, writes for the joy of it, works well with others, enjoys the publishing game.

Why did you become an agent? Maass: I love books, and I believe that fiction matters. Jackson: It grew very naturally out of my love for reading and storytelling. I've never looked back. Vater: As a former editor, I wanted to continue working with authors beyond one book, to have a chance to guide their careers and help them take their writing to the next level and be a part of their success. McClure: I love to read, and it is enormously satisfying to help ensure that stories I like will be read.

Comments: Maass: I currently serve on the Board of Directors of the AAR. Interested writers may want to read my book *The Career Novelist*, published in 1996 by Heinemann or *Writing the Breakout Novel* published by Writer's Digest Books. Vater: I also edit the annual *Agents Directory* published by Emmis Books.

Representative titles: *Down and Out in the Magic Kingdom* by Cory Doctorow; *The Longest Night* by Greg Keizer (G.P. Putnam's Sons); *The Salt Roads* by Nalo Hopkinson (Warner Books); *Shoulder the Sky* by Anne Perry (Ballantine); *Furies of Calderon* by Jim Butcher (Penguin/Ace); *Hammered* by Elizabeth Bear (Bantam Spectra); *Depth Perception* by Linda Castillo (Penguin/Berkley); *The Famous Flower of Serving Men* by Deborah Grabien (St. Martin's Press); *Staying Dead* by Laura Anne Gilman (Harlequin Luna).

MANUS & ASSOCIATES LITERARY AGENCY, INC.

425 Sherman Ave. suite 200, Palo Alto, CA 94306

650-470-5151   fax: 650-470-5159

www.ManusLit.com   e-mail: ManusLit@ManusLit.com

Agents: Janet Manus, Jillian Manus, Jandy Nelson, Stephanie Lee, Donna Levin

Born: Janet Manus: Hartford, Connecticut. Jillian Manus: April 26 —That's all you get, in New York City. Nelson: November 25, 1965, New York. Lee: August 6, Palo Alto, California. Levin: September 4, Oakland, CA.

Education: Janet Manus: B.A. and M.A. Jillian Manus: NYU Film School and life. Nelson: B.A., Cornell University; M.F.A., Brown University. Lee: B.A. in Literature, Stanford University. Donna Levin: B.A., University of California at Berkeley, J.D., Hastings College of Law.

Career history: Janet Manus: Foreign Rights Agent for British and foreign publishers; East Coast Rep. for the Guinness Book of World Records. Jillian Manus: TV agent at ICM, Director of Development at Warner Bros. & Universal Studios, VP of Production for Dino Delaurentis, VP of Media Acquisitions at Trender AG in Zurich, Associate Publisher of two national magazines dealing in entertainment and technology sectors. Nelson: I worked in academic teaching, creative writing, and drama and also worked in theater and film, doing everything from stage management to dramatizing. Lee: I worked in this office during college and never left. Levin: Author of four published books; has ghostwritten several books; long-time writing instructor at University of California–Berkeley Extension; Former reviewer for CA Bay Area radio and TV stations.

Hobbies/personal interests: Janet Manus: Travel, arts, football, interrelating with three adult daughters, two grandsons, and husband. Jillian Manus: Yoga, old movies, classic literature, boxing, ballet, gymnastics, critiquing, movies, water skiing; all sports, political efforts, child rearing, and children's health and welfare. Nelson: Books, film, theater, hiking, traveling, festivity, poetry. Lee: Movies, books, music, pop culture, sculpture, kitsch, camping.

Areas most interested in agenting: Janet Manus: True crime with TV/film potential; parenting; unique mysteries. Jillian Manus: Women's commercial literary fiction, fiction that I can successfully sell into the movie/TV marketplace, health and nutrition, sports, prescriptive self-help and self-esteem, biographies/memoirs, dramatic narrative fiction, politics, parenting, high-concept suspense/thrillers, child rearing. Nelson: Literary fiction, multicultural fiction, memoirs, thrillers, commercial fiction, women's fiction; narrative nonfiction; women's issues; intelligent, prescriptive self-help; health; pop culture. Lee: Commercial literary fiction, dark/quirky fiction, prescriptive self-help memoirs, narrative nonfiction, Gen X/Gen Y issues, young voices. Levin: mysteries, thrillers, literary and commercial fiction, self-help, how to, memoirs, chick lit, multi-cultural.

Areas not interested in agenting: Entire Agency: Romance, science fiction, poetry, espionage, textbooks, computer books, Westerns, magazine articles, horror, fantasy, children's, cookbooks, screenplays, young adult.

If not agenting, what would you be doing? Janet Manus: Secret Service agent, educator. Jillian Manus: I would love to be a teacher, an honest politician, a child psychologist, or an Olympic gymnast. Nelson: Teaching, climbing Mt. Everest, being a rock star! Lee: Writing, editing, filmmaking, or launching a new magazine.

Best way to initiate contact: Fiction: query by e-mail or letter, or send a compelling pitch letter with the first 30 pages and SASE. Nonfiction: Send a proposal and SASE. Refer to our website (www.manuslit.com) for additional information. *Do not* query call. Please note: if you include an SASE, we will respond to you. Please do not call to check the status.

Reading-fee policy: No reading fee.

Client representation by category: Janet Manus: Nonfiction, 70%; Fiction, 30%. Lee: Nonfiction, 40%; Fiction, 60%; Jillian Manus: Nonfiction, 75%; Fiction, 25%. Nelson: Nonfiction, 70%; Fiction, 30%. Levin: Nonfiction, 40%; Fiction, 60%.

Commission: 15% for domestic publication and worldwide motion pictures and TV; 25% for foreign publication, only if co-agented.

Number of titles sold last year: A lot!

Rejection rate (all submissions): 98.5%.

Most common mistakes authors make: Calling instead of introducing themselves and their projects through queries. Following the latest trends instead of listening to their inner voice. Sending their work before it is ready. Serial killer's point of view.

Description of a dream client: A talented and well-rounded writer who plays well with others.

How did you become an agent? Janet Manus: My husband (a publishing lawyer) talked me into it. Jillian Manus: My mother talked me into it! Nelson: I badgered Jillian Manus. Lee: I badgered Jandy Nelson.

Why did you become an agent? Janet Manus: I love books and think it is a wonderful calling. Jillian Manus: I love working with writers, as I truly respect their dedication and craft. Nelson: To work with writers and to help bring writing into the world that will move, enrich, inspire, and delight the reading public. Lee: Because books are magical and working with writers is equally so.

What can writers do to enhance their chances of getting you as an agent? Fiction: We rely on the quality of the writing. Nonfiction: It is helpful for a nonfiction writer to have a platform and additional avenues of marketing and distribution, such as lecture circuits, seminars, and so forth.

How would you describe what you actually do for a living? Janet Manus: I keep my eyes open, nurture, and enjoy. Jillian Manus: I search, nurture, sell, and celebrate. Nelson: Rejoicing in writers and their words. Lee: Treasure hunting. Bradford: I search for diamonds in the rough.

What do you think about editors? Janet Manus: A talented and caring editor means everything. Jillian Manus: I think savvy editors are worth their weight in gold. Nelson: They are the wizards behind the curtains.

What do you think about publishers? Janet Manus: I respect them for having a tough time in the present climate of publishing. Jillian Manus: I respect and pity them at the same time.

Representative titles: *One Minute Millionaire* by Robert Allen and Mark Victor Hansen (Harmony); *The Territory of Men* by Joelle Frasier (Villard); *Dream of the Walled City* by Lisa Huang Fleischman (Pocket); *Catfish and Mandala* by Andrew Pham (FSG); *Cane River* by Lalita Tadmey (Warner); *Gettysburg* by Newt Gingrich and Bill Fortschen (St. Martin's/ Thomas Dunne); *Grant Comes East* by Newt Gingrich and Bill Fortschen (St. Martin's/ Thomas Dunne) *Air Force One: A History of the Presidents and Their Planes* by Kenneth T. Walsh (Hyperion); *All The Presidents' Children* by Doug Wead (Atria Books); *Raising A President* by Doug Wead (Atria Books); *Geisha, A Life* by Mineko Iwasaki with Rande Brown (Atria Books); *Missed Fortune* by Doug Andrew (Warner Books); *Space Between the Stars* by Deborah Santana (Villard); *Lily Dale: The Town That Talks to the Dead* by Christine Wicker (HarperSanFrancisco); *Avoiding Prison and Other Noble Vacation Goals: Adventure in Love and Danger* by Wendy Dale (Three Rivers Press); *The Love Clinic* by Dr. Sheron Patterson (Perigee); *Within These Walls: Memoirs of a Death House Chaplain* by Rev. Carroll Pickett with Carlton Stowers (St. Martin's).

MARCH TENTH, INC.

4 Myrtle Street, Haworth, NJ 07641

201-387-6551

Agent: Sandra Choron
Born: March 10, 1950, New York City.
Education: B.A., Lehman College, New York.
Career history: As an Editor, Publisher, Author, and Book Producer, I have had experience in all aspects of book publishing at both large (Dell) and small (Hawthorn) firms.
Hobbies/personal interests: Popular culture, music, folk art, painting.
Areas most interested in agenting: Popular culture, history, general nonfiction, music, commercial fiction, fine fiction, self-help (those without credentials need not apply), biography, new trends, novelties.
Areas not interested in agenting: Genre fiction, techno-thrillers, politics, personal memoirs of people who never did anything interesting, special interest, picture books, short fiction, poetry.

If not agenting, what would you be doing? Writing.

Best way to initiate contact: Submit a query letter (with SASE).

Reading-fee policy: No reading fee.

Client representation by category: Nonfiction, 70%; Fiction, 30%.

Commission: 15% domestic; 20% foreign or dramatic rights.

Number of titles sold last year: 20.

Rejection rate (all submissions): 90%.

Most common mistakes authors make: They fail to describe the project in a concise way. They fail to state their credentials. I don't like being hyped. Facts and sales ammunition are great, but if there are three exclamation points in your first paragraph, my BS-detector goes crazy!

Description of the client from Hell: Someone who is convinced that "everyone" will buy his book.

Description of a dream client: Tall, dark. . .

How did you become an agent? It's a long story. . .

Why did you become an agent? As an editor, my interests always exceeded the capabilities of any one publisher. Agenting allows me great range and flexibility.

What can writers do to enhance their chances of getting you as an agent? Know your audience.

How would you describe what you actually do for a living? I make books happen.

What do you think about editors? They come in too many shapes and sizes to generalize.

What do you think about publishers? See above.

What were your favorite films last year? Home movies of my vacation in Mexico; *Being John Malkovich.*

Do you watch *The Sopranos?* Fuggetaboudit.

Comments: Publishing a book is an incredibly gratifying experience. It can also be unbelievably grueling. Enter at your own risk.

Representative titles: *Songs* by Bruce Springsteen (HarperCollins); *The Appalachians* (PBS tie-in) edited by Mari-Lynn Evans, et al (Random House); *And My Shoes Keep Walking Back to You* by Kathi Kamen Goldmark (Chronicle); *The Future of Zionism* by Rabbi Arthur Hertzberg (Harper San Francisco); *100 Simple Secrets of Happy Families* by David Niven (Harper San Francisco); *The Uncollected Henry James* edited by Floyd Horowitz (Avalon).

MARGRET MCBRIDE LITERARY AGENCY

7744 Fay Avenue, Suite 201, La Jolla, CA 92037

858-454-1550   fax: 858-454-2156

www.mcbrideliterary.com   www.oneminuteapology.com

e-mail: staff@mcbridelit.com

Agent: Margret McBride; Associate Agent: Donna DeGutis

Career history: Random House, Ballantine Books, Warner Books. Opened Agency in 1980.

Hobbies/personal interests: Reading, writing, lecturing, flower gardens, flower arranging, photography, home remodeling and selling, skiing, biking.

Areas most interested in agenting: Commercial and literary fiction and nonfiction, business books.

Areas not interested in agenting: Childrens' books

If not agenting what would you be doing? Reading other agents' clients' books and writing and lecturing on my next works.

Best way to initiate contact: Write a letter describing your work, emphasizing what you will do to promote your work. We do not edit works—we sell them. Let us know that you know it's ready to be published and why. Please follow submission guidelines on our website.

Reading-fee policy: No reading fees. If we turn your project down, it's because we only work on a very select number of books a year. We look for exceptional writing, and in the case of nonfiction, exceptional writers with outstanding credentials, a strong speaking platform and something new and fresh to say. We get five thousand submissions a year, so there is no time to explain why we don't feel we can best represent your work.

Commission Structure: The standard 15% for domestic sales. Foreign: 25% (co-agents).

Number of titles sold last year: Twelve.

Most common mistakes authors make with my agency: Being rude to people in my agency, or assuming they don't communicate with me. Asking to meet before we review the project. Submitting unedited work.

Description of the Client from Hell: We've seen a few clients from purgatory— but the ones from Hell we avoid.

Description of a dream client: An author who remembers that he or she is writing a book for readers to love, enjoy. . .a book to inform and possibly transform. An author who takes up media training prior to publicity and has professional assistance to improve their manuscript if needed. Someone who is willing to invest in his or her career, create a website, take speech classes, speak in front of groups about his or her book. Most successful books are author-driven.

How did you become an agent? A lot of people I knew in publishing told me that I was a natural salesperson and that I should become an agent. So I tried it, and sold *The One Minute Manager*. Then, I began to believe them.

Why did you become an agent? I've always loved reading and love new ideas. I have an enormous amount of enthusiasm when I read something fresh and new. I become unstoppable.

What can authors do to enhance their chances of getting you as an agent? Show they care about producing the best work they are capable of. Never send me something that's not their best.

How would you describe what you actually do for a living? I make the world a better place to live in.

What do you think about other agents? I think that everyone has something unique to contribute to the literary world.

What do you think about editors? Hardworking, brilliant, and should get more credit for their work. Every publisher's catalog should list the editor who championed the book through the process.

What do you think about publishers? Need to adapt a new way of learning what the public wants so they won't be so surprised when books sell millions of copies because of a "fluke." Market research is the one missing ingredient. Publishers as a whole are really special people who do their work because they really want to make the world think from time to time. They want to make a difference. They should all be named for saints when they move on.

Comments: Publishers should give incentives to the PR department so they will feel motivated not to take no for an answer. This is the one weak link at most publishers. More time needs to be spent on making authors more promotable. A publisher will spend half a million dollars on an author and never suggest media training.

Representative titles: *Fish! for Life* by Stephen C, Lundin, John Christensen, and Harry Paul (Hyperion); *The One Minute Apology* by Ken Blanchard and Margret McBride (William Morrow); *The One Minute Manager* by Ken Blanchard and Spencer Johnson, MD (William Morrow); *Step Wars: Overcoming the Perils and Making Peace in Adult Stepfamilies* by Jean Lipman Blumen, Ph.D. and Grace Gabe M.D. (St. Martins); *Fierce Conversations* by Susan Scott (Penguin Putnam Viking); *The Present* by Spencer Johnson, MD. (Doubleday); *Leverage Your Best, Ditch The Rest: A Master Coach's Guide to Your Phenomenal Success* by Scott Blanchard and Madeleine Homan (William Morrow); *Burro Genius* by Victor Villasenor (Harper Collins Rayo); *The Confession* by Sheldon Siegel (Putnam); *Love on a Rotten Day* by Hazel Dixon Cooper; *Kingdomality* by Sheldon Bowles, Richard Silvano, and Susan Silvano (Hyperion), *Breakthrough* by Bill Davidson.

MARTIN LITERARY AGENCY

17328 Ventura Blvd., Suite 138, Encino, CA 91316

e-mail: Sharlene@MartinLiteraryManagement.com

www.MartinLiteraryManagement.com

818-595-1130

Agent: Sharlene Martin

Born: New Haven, CT, sometime in the '50s.

Educational History: Graduate of the University of Bridgeport.

Career History: It all started in high school when I was made Editor of my Literary Magazine, the *West Whims*. After college, I followed my wanderlust and was a 'Stewardess' for American Airlines based out of NY. Moved into management, and ultimately became one of 12 Recruiters nationwide and handling hiring for AA out of my NY office in the Chrysler Building. I have the distinction of hiring the very first Male Flight Attendant in the mid-'70s.

After AA, I followed my entrepreneurial heart and became the founder and President of Helping Hands, Inc.—the country's first American Nanny Agency. That earned me the title of HomeBased Entrepreneur of the Year from *Entrepreneur* magazine, and Small Businessperson of the Year from the CT Chamber of Commerce. I sold the business in 1989 and moved to California and began work in the Entertainment industry in Hollywood. A brief stint as a talent agent and manager, and then a Casting Director led me to my work with writers for film and television as an Independent Producer. After several successful options and sales, I ran the Acquisitions and Management Dept. of a well-known reality company and worked daily with writers in developing treatments and scripts for the television market. When I realized I loved working with writers but didn't enjoy the phony world of entertainment, I decided to re-invent myself and my love of books, and start a literary management company. And, I've never been happier.

Hobbies: Reading (yes, reading. . .a perfect weekend is sitting by my pool with a stack of manuscripts or proposals or a great non-fiction book that I can learn from). Also enjoy skiing, movies, and fine food with a great Cabernet.

Most interested in agenting: Nonfiction (memoirs, celebrity-based books, self-help, inspirational, pop-culture, chick lit, women's issues, entrepreneurial/business books).

Not interested in agenting: Screenplays, poetry, children's books, art, history, sports, and most novels.

If not agenting, what might you be doing? I can't imagine after all my careers that I'd want to do anything else.

Best way to initiate contact: I love e-mail! Save the trees, save postage, and send me a great query letter e-mail. No attachments please, just cut and paste to the body of the e-mail. See my website for more info: www.MartinLiteraryManagement.com.

Reading fee policy: No fees.

Representation by category: 5% fiction, 95% non-fiction.

Commission structure: 15% domestic/25% foreign.

Number of titles sold last year: Haven't been doing this for a year yet, so I'll wait until next year to report that.

Rejection Rate: 95% rejection rate but don't despair, what's someone's poison is another's pleasure!

Most common mistakes: Calling and pitching me on the phone. No, no, no. Put it in writing. I don't care how well you speak, it's your writing I want to learn about first.

Describe the Client from Hell: I don't have any. I handpick them carefully so each is a special gem.

Describe your dream client: Meets deadlines, takes advice, builds their platform, hires professional editors when warranted, gives me some breathing room to do the best job I can for them.

What can writers do to enhance their chances of getting you as an agent? Be a dream client.

Describe what you do for a living: I'm a matchmaker—I match talented writers with great books to the right publishers and editors.

What do you think about other agents? Bless them, it's not an easy business.

What do you think about editors? I love Editors. Most are kind and responsive and know that I'll only contact them when it's a good fit. You can't cry wolf too often or you'll never get their attention when you *really* want it.

What do you think about publishers? They're what makes my job possible. Bless them.

Representative titles: *But you knew that already* by Dougall Fraser (Rodale); *The Mommy Chronicles* by Sara Behnke and Stephanie Triplett (Hay House).

E. J. MCCARTHY AGENCY

21 Columbus Ave. Ste. 210

San Francisco, CA 94111

415-296-7706

ejmagency@mac.com

Agent: Mr. E. J. McCarthy

Education: Bachelor of Arts degree in English, Fordham University, New York, NY.

Career History: I began my career in book publishing in 1988 as an editorial assistant for Doubleday Book Clubs. After that I worked for several years as an editor at Dell Publishing, where I acquired works of fiction and nonfiction. For eight years (1995-2003), I worked as executive editor of Presidio Press, a commercial military history book publisher, which is an imprint of Random House. I was in charge of Presidio's editorial program, and acquired and edited more than 150 books.

Hobbies/personal interests: Current events, politics, baseball, movies, literature, history, music, running, television, travel, newspapers, magazines.

Areas most interested in agenting: Narrative nonfiction, history, biography, military history, political science, literary fiction, humor, thrillers, crime.

Areas not interested in agenting: Children's books, poetry, science fiction, horror, fantasy.

Best way to initiate contact: Query via letter or e-mail. E-mail query is preferred.

Commission structure: 15% on all domestic sales, including film and subsidiary sales. Commissions on foreign sales vary, usually 20%.

Reading-fee policy: No reading fee.

Client representation by category: Nonfiction: 90%, Fiction: 10%.

Commission structure: 15% domestic, 20% foreign.

Number of titles sold last year: 4.

Rejection rate: 99.9%.

Most common mistakes authors make with your agency: Sending works outside of my purview; not telling me that their work has been submitted to other agents, and worse, to publishers.

Description of the client from Hell: Someone who does not respect the expertise and judgment of a publishing professional. Someone with a bad temper; one who spends a lot of time writing angry e-mails and leaving long phone messages; one who is ready to blame others for his or her own mistakes; one who has an unrealistic expectation of what a publisher will do in the way of marketing. Someone who fails to be consistently polite; one who is not willing to go the extra mile.

Description of the dream client: A patient, intelligent, good-humored, understanding writer who will consider suggestions and will respond to requests in a timely and professional manner. A writer who possesses authentic passion for his work. Someone who trusts his agent to do a good job.

Most common mistakes authors make: Sending single-spaced manuscripts, using small type, stapling chapters together, not numbering a manuscript successively. Not describing succinctly what the manuscript is about, assuming a publisher will make their book an instant bestseller. Saying things like "that should be the publisher's job"— no, it's your book, it's part of your life, it's your job.

What can writers do to enhance their chances of getting you as their agent? Make sure that your proposal is neatly typed, clearly written, and succinct. Tell me who you are: your background, past writing credits. Make sure the rest of your material is finished and ready to send to me. Read books about the publishing process by such authors as Jeff Herman, Michael Larsen, Noah Lukeman, and Susan Rabiner and Al Fortunato.

Why did you become an agent? I've wanted to be in the book business since I was sixteen, when I read the biography of Max Perkins by Scott Berg. It's exciting to be the first one to read and champion a manuscript that will ultimately get published, read, reviewed, and talked about. I like working with publishing people, and because I have been an editor for nearly fifteen years, I have credibility with editors and authors. I know what editors look for. I can help writers think of ways to make their work irresistible to a publisher.

What might you be doing if you weren't an agent? I would start my own publishing company.

How would you describe what it is you actually do for a living? I find a publisher for a writer's book, and try to make sure that the books are published well.

How did you become an agent? I wanted to be an agent for several years; the time came. I called everyone in publishing I knew, and told them I was starting my own agency. I have no doubt that it is the right thing for me to do.

What do you think about other agents? I have many friends who are agents. As a newcomer to agenting, I have benefited from their good advice and expertise.

What do you think about editors? I respect and like editors. It is a good and important profession. Editors tend to be overworked and underpaid. I think it's best for the agent and writer to do everything they can to make things a little easier for them.

What do you think about publishers? Good publishers tend to sift through all the various business matters and try to do what's best for their company, its editors, authors, readers, and sales and distribution channels. It's not an easy job; I have great respect for publishers.

Miscellaneous Comments: Never give up hope, but if a consensus of publishing professionals wants a revised manuscript, leave your ego behind and start working.

Truly good books will get published. It can take a long time, and a lot of work, but someone, somewhere will recognize good writing. Perseverance is crucial. Once a book is published, word of mouth is everything.

Representative titles: *Broken Eagle* by Thomas Hammes (Motorbooks); *Hammer From Above* by Jay Stout (Random House).

SALLY HILL MCMILLAN & ASSOCIATES

429 East Kingston Avenue, Charlotte, NC 28203

704-334-0897   fax: 704-334-1897

e-mail: mcmagency@aol.com

Agent: Sally McMillan
Education: M.A. in English, University of North Carolina-Charlotte.
Career history: After teaching English a few years, I started my publishing career in the marketing department of UNC Press, Chapel Hill, in 1974. Then I started up a

small publishing company, East Woods Press, and ran it from 1977–1987, sold it to Globe Pequot Press, stayed on as editor from 1987–1990, and began my literary agency in 1990.

Hobbies/personal interests: Travel, French language, cruising, reading.

Areas most interested in agenting: Southern fiction, women's mainstream fiction, mystery/suspense, health, psychology, history, Americana.

Areas not interested in agenting: Romance, science fiction, fantasy, children's books, cookbooks.

Best way to initiate contact: Fiction: Query with SASE. Nonfiction: Proposal with SASE.

Client representation by category: Nonfiction, 60%; Fiction, 40%, children's 0%.

Commission: 15%; 20% on co-agented subrights sales.

Rejection rate: 95%

Description of the client from Hell: Although I don't have any clients from Hell, I imagine one to be someone who thinks only of herself and is not appreciative of the time and effort I and others expend on her behalf. I find that my more successful clients are those who understand the business from multiple points of view, including mine, and realize that they need to care for and feed their agent in order to be cared for and fed in return.

Description of the dream client: My dream clients are those who are considerate of my time, listen to and follow my advice, provide all information requested and offer more if needed, work hard to promote their books, work even harder to write the best books possible, and are ambitious and realistic about their careers.

Most common mistakes authors make: Calling and asking to take me to lunch before sending me their work, sending the wrong kind of projects to me.

What can writers do to enhance their chances of getting you as their agent? Follow my advice about the dream client.

Why did you become an agent? I love working directly with writers and found that running a growing press meant that I had to give that up more and more. As an agent, I get to be as proactive as I want to be in shaping a book. I also love the flexibility of the job and the variety of work experience that goes along with it.

If not agenting, what might you be doing? I would be writing or teaching if I weren't so consumed by other people's writings and teachings.

How would you describe what you do for a living? I play matchmaker all day long and help make people's dreams come true. It's a wonderfully satisfying job.

How did you become an agent? Some of my former authors asked me to place their books. I did it for love and got hooked.

What do you think about other agents? Most agents I know are wonderful people who have their clients' best interests at heart.

What do you think about editors? Most editors I know care very much about writers and are often frustrated because they cannot make things happen for them.

What do you think about publishers? Most publishers I know have the finest intentions. I know from experience that they have a very difficult job and an enormous responsibility.

Comments: I don't claim to have created it, but my favorite advice to writers is "Perseverance rewards talent."

Representative titles: *Friendship Cake, The Things I Know Best, Hope Springs, Forever Friends, The Last Odd Day* by Lynne Hinton (HarperSanFrancisco); *Fire in the Rock* by Joe Martin (Ballantine); *Home Across the Road* by Nancy Peacock (Bantam); *Sins of the Brother, Dog Island,* and *A Clean Kill* by Mike Stewart (Putnam); *Life a la Mode* by Linda Lenhoff (Kensington); *Don't Let Your Mind Stunt Your Growth* by Bryan Robinson (New Harbinger); *Wedding Etiquette for Divorced Families* by Martha Woodham (Contemporary/McGraw Hill); *20,000 Secrets of Tea* by Victoria Zak (Dell).

CLAUDIA MENZA LITERARY AGENCY

1170 Broadway Suite 807, New York, NY 10001

212-889-6850

Agent: Claudia Menza

Career history: 1969–1973, Assistant Editor, Evergreen Review; 1973–1983, various titles, Managing Editor before leaving, Grove Press; 1983–present, President, Claudia Menza Literary Agency; published writer; member, Academy of American Poets; member, Italian-American Writers Association; member, P.E.N; member, AAR.

Areas most interested in agenting: African-American fiction and nonfiction, general nonfiction that concerns social and political issues, literary fiction.

Areas not interested in agenting: Science fiction, poetry, plays, mysteries, thrillers, memoir, romance, textbooks, children's books.

If not agenting, what would you be doing? Being a publisher.

Best way to initiate contact: Query letter, outline, and 20-page sample if nonfiction. Query letter and 25-page sample if fiction. SASE must be included with both. No phone calls.

Reading-fee policy: No reading fee.

Client representation by category: Nonfiction, 50%; Fiction, 50%.

Commission: 15% on all rights represented, except in case of a co-agent being used (film, dramatic, or foreign rights) and then it's 20%.

Rejection rate (all submissions): 80%.

Most common mistakes authors make: Calling to solicit interest in their manuscripts. Calling us to see if we've either received or read their manuscripts. Not including an SASE with submissions. Asking if they can deliver the manuscript in person.

What can writers do to enhance their chances of getting you as an agent? Be understanding about our time; we receive between 10 and 20 manuscripts per day.

Description of the client from Hell: A client who calls several times a week for updates on a book's submission status or calls with questions several times a week instead of saving all questions for one call. A client who makes unreasonable requests of a publisher: a 15-city author tour when sales don't warrant it; a full-page ad in the *New York Times* when a book has sold 5,000 copies; a car to take the author to a meeting with a publisher (yes, someone actually has requested that); a six-figure advance for a second book when the first book sold 5,000 copies.

Description of a dream client: Writers who keep in mind the realities of the publishing business (it is a business); who make their phone calls short, unless a long call is warranted; who trust what the agent is telling them and don't try to convince the agent to do something that is not in the their best interests. After all, why hire a professional if you don't want to follow that person's advice? Having said that, dream clients also come up with imaginative ideas as to how best to promote their work and themselves.

Why did you become an agent? I love books. I love writers.

How would you describe what you do for a living? Represent the work of writers and manage their careers. Help them to develop into the kinds of writers they want to be.

DORIS S. MICHAELS LITERARY AGENCY, INC.

1841 Broadway, Suite 903, New York, NY 10023

212-265-9474   fax: 212-265-9480

www.dsmagency.com

Agents: Doris S. Michaels

Born: May 1955, Lodi, California.

Education: B.A. in English and German Literature, University of California at Santa Cruz; M.A.T. in German and English, University of California at Berkeley; Certificate in Computer Technology, Columbia University; Certificate in Book and Magazine Publishing, Summer Publishing Institute, New York University.

Career history: Acquisitions Editor for Prentice Hall, 1982–1984; Technology Consultant and Trainer for PHINET and Prudential-Bache, 1984–1987; International Information Center Manager for Union Bank of Switzerland, based in Zurich, 1987–1992; independent literary agent based in NYC, 1994–present.

Hobbies/personal interests: Reading, music, especially listening to classical music and playing the violin. Sports, especially mountain biking, skiing, and swimming. Computers.

Areas most interested in agenting: Fiction: commercial fiction, literary fiction, women's fiction, novels with strong screen potential. Adult nonfiction (hardcovers and trade paperbacks): Biographies, business, classical music, sports, women's issues. Multimedia electronic works for computers.

Areas not interested in agenting: Science fiction, fantasy, mysteries, thrillers, romances, Westerns, occult and supernatural, horror stories, poetry, textbooks, religion, film scripts, cookbooks, diet books, short stories, articles, humor, professional manuals.

If not agenting, what would you be doing? Touring as a concert violinist.

Best way to initiate contact: E-mail: query@dsmagency.com. Please, no calls.

Reading-fee policy: No reading fee.

Client representation by category: Nonfiction, 50%; Fiction, 50%.

Commission: 15%.

Number of titles sold last year: 30.

Rejection rate (all submissions): 98%.

Most common mistakes authors make: They send an unprofessional query e-mail.

Description of the client from Hell: I only work with clients with whom I can develop a good working relationship.

Description of a dream client: Someone who has talent, understands the publishing process, appreciates the hard work I do, and listens carefully.

How did you become an agent? After attending New York University's Summer Publishing Institute, I began my own agency in 1994.

Why did you become an agent? I enjoy reading good fiction and the process of helping talented writers get published.

How would you describe what you actually do for a living? I seek out talented writers and help them get published. I work closely with them to help them grow and build their careers. My time is spent maintaining the connections that I have with some of the industry's top editors, reading the projects of my clients and projects from potential clients, and giving my best efforts to ensure the production of high-quality work and the most professional image possible for my agency.

What do you think about editors? The best editors are those who respond in a timely manner to submissions. They are willing to negotiate contracts to ensure the best deal possible for all parties concerned. They are passionate about their projects, and they are willing to work closely with both the author and me as a team to help build the author's career.

Representative titles: *Cycles: How We'll Live, Work and Buy* by Maddy Dychtwald (Free Press); *How to Become a CEO* series by Jeffrey Fox (Hyperion); *The Neatest Little Guide to Do-It-Yourself Investing* by Jason Kelly (Plume).

RANDI MURRAY LITERARY AGENCY, INC

804 Vista Road, Hillsborough, CA 94010

650-347-8121

www.murrayagency.com   e-mail: murrayr@aol.com

Agent: Randi Glass Murray

Born: Fort Belvoir, Virginia; raised in Baltimore, Maryland.

Education: B.S. and M.B.A., Wharton School, University of Pennsylvania.

Career history: After graduate school I worked for Goldman Sachs in New York, in both investment banking and equity research, where I followed stocks in the media industry. My husband and I moved to San Francisco in 1987, and I worked for Cornerstone Research, a litigation consulting firm specializing in securities fraud cases, eventually becoming chief administrative officer of that firm. I have always been a passionate reader, and formed a still-going-strong book club 17 years ago! I recently formed my own agency, and feel so fortunate to have discovered a field which combines my love for books with my business, client service, and legal experience.

Areas most interested in agenting: Literary and commercial fiction, narrative and prescriptive nonfiction, popular culture. I have a special fondness for biography and historical fiction.

Areas not interested in agenting: Children's, science fiction, romance, Westerns, poetry, horror, thrillers.

Best way to initiate contact: Please visit my website—www.murrayagency.com. Electronic submission guidelines are available there.

Reading-fee policy: No reading fee.

Commission: 15% domestic; 20% foreign.

Why did you become an agent? It is incredibly gratifying to me to get a writer published—it still gives me goosebumps! And there's nothing that beats the feeling when I'm reading a terrific submission—my heart starts pounding and I can't turn the pages fast enough.

JEAN V. NAGGAR LITERARY AGENCY, INC.

216 East 75th Street, 1E, New York, NY 10021

212-794-1082

Agents: Jean V. Naggar, Jennifer Weltz, Anne Engel, and Alice Tasman

Born: Tasman: May 26, 1967, Philadelphia, Pennsylvania. Weltz: NYC.

Education: Naggar: B.A., with Honors, London University. Engel: Bachelor of

Laws, London University. Tasman: B.A., Brown University, 1989; M.F.A., Sarah Lawrence College, 1994. Weltz: Cornell University.

Career history: Naggar: Writer, Editor, Translator, Book Reviewer. Engel: 20 years as an Editor in British publishing houses. Tasman: Jean V. Naggar Literary Agency in subrights and agenting my own list from 1995–present. Mediator until 1993; at JUNCA since.

Hobbies/personal interests: Naggar: Parenting, reading, music, business, travel, cooking. Wide-ranging other interests that do not include sports and politics. Engel: Looking at cities, cooking, and entertaining.

Areas most interested in agenting: Naggar: Fiction: strong, well-written mainstream fiction, literary fiction, contemporary, suspense, historical fiction, mysteries. Nonfiction: biography, literary autobiography or memoirs, science for the layperson, psychology, and sophisticated self-help. Engel: Science, biography, exclusively nonfiction. Tasman: Literary/commercial nongenre fiction, literary thrillers, multicultural nonfiction, celebrity biographies. Weltz: Children, middle grade and young adult.

Areas not interested in agenting: Naggar: Sports, politics, category fiction, most science fiction, KGB/South American drug-cartel espionage. Engel: Fiction, children's books, coffee-table books, children's books. Tasman: Science fiction, fantasy fiction, romance, self-help. Weltz: Adult.

Best way to initiate contact: Naggar: Query letter. Engel: An enthusiastic, balanced letter. Tasman: Query letter. Weltz: Letter snail mail.

Reading-fee policy: No reading fee.

Client representation by category: Naggar: Nonfiction, 45%; Fiction, 45%; Children's, 10%. Engel: Nonfiction, 100%. Tasman: Nonfiction, 10%; Fiction, 90%; Weltz: 100% children's.

Commission: 15% domestic; 20% international.

Number of titles sold last year: Naggar: 47.

Rejection rate (all submissions): 96%.

Most common mistakes authors make: Naggar: Not doing any background research on agents before contacting; asking, Do you want to see my work? without describing it; calling every five minutes to check up on things—a sure precursor of the client from Hell! Tasman: Too many calls before we've agreed to take them on. Weltz: E-mail queries to multiple agents.

Description of the client from Hell: Naggar: An author who has chosen me as an agent but never quite trusts me. Tasman: Clients who ask to read and/or write their submission letters. Unpublished authors who ask if they can quit their jobs. An unemployed client. An unpublished author who is banking on a six-figure advance. Weltz: Not trusting my actions.

Description of a dream client: Naggar: Talented, appreciative, intelligent, knowledgeable. Tasman: A client who lets you do your job; a relationship based on trust and faith. Weltz: Working with me as a team to make a successful career.

How did you become an agent? Tasman: I was getting my M.F.A. at Sarah Lawrence College. I worked as an intern for the Wendy Weil Agency. I was extremely interested in books and film. Wendy strongly suggested I look for a job in subrights, which is where I started at this agency. Weltz: I started in the agency as the subsidiary rights manager and financial person.

Why did you become an agent? Naggar: I love reading and respect writers. I enjoy being an advocate for writers I respect. Tasman: I love books and people. I thought I wanted to be a writer, but realized that I am much more effective and happy being part of someone else's creative process. Weltz: I have always loved children's books and enjoy helping them get published.

What can writers do to enhance their chances of getting you as an agent? Tasman: Give me time to thoroughly assess their work. Naggar: Present themselves well, have patience to wait out my heavy reading schedule, and make no early outrageous claims for their work. Weltz: Give me your best work.

How would you describe what you actually do for a living? Tasman: I represent writers; I am the liaison between a writer and a publisher. I read manuscripts, edit manuscripts, pitch manuscripts to editors, and place them with the appropriate publishing house. Naggar: Indulge my reading enthusiasms and then enlist the world to take pleasure with me! Read and negotiate strong contracts. Supervise and set in motion every possible venue to enhance a client's career.

What do you think about editors? Tasman: I am grateful for editors. They're vital.

What do you think about publishers? Tasman: Ditto.

Comments: Tasman: How difficult it is to find a home for literary fiction and good quality fiction in general!

Representative titles: *Lucky in the Corner* by Carol Anshaw (Houghton Mifflin); *The Shelters of Stone* by Jean M. Auel (Crown); *China Run* by David Ball (Simon & Schuster); *In the Yikes Zone: A Conversation with Fear* by Mermer Blakeslee (Plume); *Drastic* by Maud Casey (Morrow); *Self-Coaching: How to Heal Anxiety and Depression* by Joe Luciani (Wiley); *The Associate* by Phillip Margolin (HarperCollins); *Wild Justice* by Phillip Margolin (HarperCollins); *Fiona Range* by Mary McGarry Morris (Viking); *Greenwichtown* by Joyce Palmer (St. Martin's Press); *Rashomon Gate* by Ingrid Parker (St. Martin's Press); *Nectar* by Lily Prior (Ecco Press/HarperCollins); *Eyes of the Albatross* by Carl Safina (Holt); *Saving Your Brain* by Jeff Victoroff (Bantam Dell); *Half Broken Things* by Morag Joss (Bantam).

THE NEVILLE AGENCY

15 West 12th Street, Suite 5G, New York, NY 10011

Agent: Barret Neville

Career History: Nearly ten years as an editor at Penguin Group, St. Martin's Press, and McGraw-Hill, acquiring and developing a range of bestselling nonfiction as well as mysteries; launched the agency in 2004.

Areas most interested in agenting: Commercial and literary nonfiction; mysteries and thrillers (particularly historicals).

Areas not interested in agenting: Literary fiction.

If not agenting, what would you be doing? Working as an editor and pursuing my own writing projects.

Best way to initiate contact: E-mail.

Reading-fee policy: None.

Client representation by category: 70% nonfiction, 25% fiction, 5% YA/children's.

Commission structure: 15% of domestic royalties, 20% of international royalties.

Number of titles sold last year: N/A.

Rejection rate: 75%.

Most common mistakes authors make with your agency: Sometimes authors lose sight of the fact that a book is a product that must be marketed, as well as a labor of love to be cherished. Though it may have nothing to do with the art of writing, it's important for authors to be receptive to the marketing side of the publishing business.

What can writers do to enhance their chances of getting you as an agent? It all comes down to the writing. That said, sometimes a great project can be obscured by a rambling cover letter, so make sure you explain what's special about your book by the end of the first paragraph.

Your description of the client from Hell: One who rejects any feedback that doesn't agree with their idea of how things should be.

Your description of a dream client: One who enters into the author-agent relationship in a spirit of authentic collaboration.

How did you become an agent? My most successful books as an editor were the ones I developed and acquired on my own, without going through agents. Eventually, after watching a few of these books take off, I decided that since what I was doing was very much like agenting, I should make it official.

Why did you become an agent? I wanted the experience of working with an author over the course of a career, as opposed to just one or two books.

How would you describe what you actually do for a living? I partner with authors to help them develop their projects and then find the right home for their books. I focus on my clients' needs and helping them achieve their particular goals. When you get right down to it, I'm a cross between a nurturing editor and a blood-thirsty marketer.

What do you think about other agents? It's like any industry: There are a lot of competent people out there, and your challenge as an author is to find one you click with.

What do you think about editors? Having been one myself, I know that they're often staggering under an enormous amount of administrative baggage, but for the most part they never lose sight of their passion or their authors—even at the expense of their own nights and weekends.

What do you think about publishers? They're our business partners in all this. Their goal is to make a profit, as is ours. And as with any business partner, sometimes there are disagreements. However, as long as these are resolved through pragmatic negotiation, we can both achieve our goals.

Representative titles: *QBQ! The Question Behind the Question* and second untitled book by John Miller (Putnam/Penguin Group); *How to Be a Superhero* by Doctor Metropolis (Plume/Penguin Group).

NEW ENGLAND PUBLISHING ASSOCIATES, INC.

PO Box 5, Chester, CT 06412

860-345-7323   fax: 860-345-3660

www.nepa.com   e-mail: nepa@nepa.com

Agents: Elizabeth Frost-Knappman, Edward W. Knappman, Ron Formica
Born: EFK: October 1, 1943. EWK: November 17, 1943. RF: July 3, 1971.
Education: EFK: B.A. in Anthropology, George Washington University, 1965; graduate work at University of Wisconsin and New York University. EWK: B.A. in History, George Washington University, 1965; M.S. in Journalism, Columbia University, 1966. RF: B.A. in Journalism, University of Connecticut, 1994; graduate work in history at Central Connecticut State University.
Career history: EFK: Senior Editor, William Morrow; Senior Editor, Doubleday; Editor, William Collins & Sons (London); Associate Editor, Natural History Press. Author of *Courtroom Drama* Vols. 1–3: *Women's Suffrage in America, Women's Rights on Trial: 101 Historic Trials from Anne Hutchinson to The Virginia Military Institute Cadets; World Almanac of Presidential Quotations, ABC-CLIO History of Women's Progress in America,* and *The Quotable Lawyer.* EWK: Publisher of Facts on File; Executive Vice President of Facts on File. Editor of *Great World Trials, Great American Trials, American Jobs Abroad* (with V. Harlow), and *Sex, Sin, and Mayhem.* RF: Managing Editor of New England Publishing 1996-2003. Editor of *Famous First Facts About the Environment,* co-editor of *American Presidents: Year by Year,* contributor to the *Wilson Calendar of World History, Facts About China,* and *The Chronology of American Literature.*
Hobbies/personal interests: EFK: Swimming, knitting, gardening, and tennis. EWK: Reading in the areas of history and politics. RF: Biking, golf, reading, music, films, history.
Areas most interested in agenting: EFK: Women's subjects, science, biographies, current events, literature. EWK: Reference, history, business, information, self-help, biographies, narrative nonfiction. RF: Current events, world and U.S. history, sports, entertainment, and health and exercise.
Areas not interested in agenting: Personal memoirs, fiction, children's books, screenplays.
If not agenting, what would you be doing? EFK: Traveling. EWK: Traveling.
Best way to initiate contact: Send a well-thought-out proposal with a sample

chapter and resume. Check our submission guidelines page at www.nepa.com and follow them.

Reading-fee policy: No reading fee.

Client representation by category: Adult nonfiction, 95%.

Commission: 15%, unless co-agents must be employed for dramatic or foreign rights.

Number of titles sold last year: 70.

Rejection rate (all submissions): 95%.

Most common mistakes authors make: It's important to put in the time and effort to perfect a proposal. The key is to carefully research your competition, not just in the bookstores, but in the libraries, union catalog, and Books in Print. Make substitutions in materials after submission process has started; call too soon for a decision; treat the competition too cavalierly; phone and e-mail us or their editors excessively.

Description of the client from Hell: There are no clients from Hell, just nervous ones, although those who think they know how to sell a book better than we do should spend some time in purgatory.

Description of a dream client: Professional, flexible about revisions, patient, friendly.

How did you become an agent? In 1982 EFK found it easier to be a parent while working from home, starting a new business.

Why did you become an agent? After many years as an editor (EFK) and publisher (EWK), we wanted to start our own business and move midway between Boston and New York City. Our combined literary agency, book-producing business, and consulting operations allow us to do this. What started as a small business in 1983 has grown to a good-sized one, with five employees to serve clients.

What can writers do to enhance their chances of getting you as an agent? Follow our guidelines for preparing proposals; request a sample proposal if you need a model; make certain your qualifications match the book you wish to write; make your sample chapters the best literary quality you can.

How would you describe what you actually do for a living? Read, edit, query editors, submit your work to publishers, negotiate the best possible sale and contracts, make subsidiary rights sales (foreign, dramatic), do all bookkeeping for the life of your book, problem solve day in, day out.

What do you think about editors? Editors are well-read, hardworking, underpaid people who are under constant pressure to turn a profit for the conglomerates that employ them.

What do you think about publishers? Working with most publishers today is like dealing with the Department of Agriculture. No one has sufficient power, efficiency is not at a premium, and decisions are made by committee. So authors would be wise not to try to go it alone.

Comments: The world of publishing has changed so radically in the last 30 years that the business is difficult for authors, agents, and editors alike. Presses want the same genre or brand-name books. Advances are less competitive than ever before. Fortunately, each year start-ups and new imprints emerge to breathe new life into our industry, taking more chances on a first book or a writer without a "platform." Still, our advice to authors is, Don't give up your day job and build up your credits in magazines, newspapers, and journals before embarking on books.

Representative titles: *The Night Attila Died* (Berkley); *Dissecting Death: Secrets of a Medical Examiner* (Broadway); *The Letters of Noël Coward* (Pantheon); *A Hanging Offense: The Strange Affair of the Warship Somers* (The Free Press); *The Princeton Murders* (Berkley); *Breast Cancer for Dummies* (John Wiley); *Carnegie* (John Wiley); *Natural Stomach Care* (Avery Putnam); *Eating for Life: The Total Health Impact Diet* (Berkley); *Crusaders on the Nile* (Harvard University Press); *60 Million Frenchman Can't Be Wrong* (Sourcebooks); *How to Succeed as a Lifestyle Entrepreneur* (Dearborn); *Why CRM Doesn't Work* (Bloomberg); *Winning Habits* (FT/Prentice Hall); *51 Easy Ways to Prevent Global Warming* (Andrews McMeel); *The Secret Life of Sharks: A Leading Marine Biologist Reveals the Mysteries of Shark Behavior* (Simon & Schuster).

JAMES PETER ASSOCIATES, INC.

PO Box 358, New Canaan, CT 06840

203-972-1070

Agent: Gene Brissie
Born: New York City.
Education: Princeton University.
Career history: Farrar, Straus and Giroux; Simon & Schuster; G. P. Putnam's Sons; Contemporary Books; Prentice Hall; James Peter Associates.
Hobbies: Reading, music, history, pop culture, science, sports.
Areas most interested in agenting: All nonfiction areas.
Areas not interested in agenting: Fiction/children's books, YA, poetry.
Best way to initiate contact: Query letter with SASE.
Client representation by category: Nonfiction, 100%.
Commission: 15% domestic; 20% foreign.
Number of titles sold last year: 35–40.
Rejection rate: 90%.
Description of the client from Hell: An author who views the writer/publisher relationship as an adversarial one.
Description of the dream client: An author who writes a solid proposal and delivers a good manuscript, on time.
What can writers do to enhance their chances of getting you as an agent? The most saleable authors have a strong understanding of the marketplace and they know what has a good chance of selling.
Why did you become an agent? I worked on the other side of the desk as an editor, editor-in-chief, and publisher for close to 25 years, and I wanted to try this side.

I know how to sell to editors and publishers.

If not agenting, what would you be doing? I'd be a publisher.

How would you describe what you do for a living? I help mold proposals, submit and sell them to editors and publishers, negotiate the contracts, and collect and dispense the proceeds for a group of very talented authors.

How did you become an agent? I was fortunate to buy JPA from its founder, Bert Holtje, one of the best.

What do you think about editors? I love them.

What do you think about publishers? I love them.

Do you watch *The Sopranos?* Not regularly; I've seen it a few times.

Representative titles: *Nothing to Fear: Lessons in Leadership from Franklin Delano Roosevelt* by Alan Axelrod (Prentice Hall); *The Encyclopedia of Submarines* by Wilbur Cross (Facts on File); *The Penguin Dictionary of American Folklore* by Harry Oster and Alan Axelrod (Penguin); *Unsolved Mysteries of Science* by John Malone (John Wiley & Sons); *Encyclopedia of the American West* (3 volumes), Zenda Inc. (Macmillan); *Walkin' the Line: A Journey from the Past to the Present Along the Mason Dixon Line* by William Ecenbarger (M. Evans & Co.); *Hepatitis C: The Silent Killer* by Carol Turkington (Contemporary Books); *The Complete Idiot's Guide to Latino History and Culture* by Danilo Figueredo (Alpha Books); *American History ASAP* by Alan Axelrod (Penguin); *The Flying Circus* by Speaker of the House James C. Wright; *The Lazy Person's Guide to Investing* by Paul Farrell (Warner); *The Official Handbook of the Vast Right Wing Conspiracy* by Mark W. Smith (Regenery); *How to Get Started in Commerical Real Estate* by Jack Cummings (John Wiley); *The Subject is Left Handed* by Danney Rosset (Algonquin); *Wheel, Deal, and Steal* by D. Quinn Mills (Financial Times/Prentice Hall).

PMA LITERARY AND FILM MANAGEMENT, INC.

45 West 21st Street, 6th floor, New York, NY 10010

212-929-1222

www.pmalitfilm.com

e-mail: queries@pmalitfilm.com and Scott@pmalitfilm.com

Agents: Peter Miller, Scott Hoffman, Lisa Silverman

Born: Miller: Atlantic City, New Jersey. Hoffman: Livingston, NJ. Silverman: Springfield, Massachusetts.

Education: Miller: B.A., Monmouth College. Hoffman: B.A. College of William and Mary, M.B.A., New York University's Leonard N. Stern School of Business. Silverman: B.A., Wesleyan University.

Career history: Miller: Founded Writers House, a literary agency, 1972; founded the Peter Miller Agency, 1974; incorporated agency in 1981; founded PMA Literary and Film Management, Inc., 1992. Founded 21st Millennium Lion, Inc. (a production company) in 1996. Have now been in business for almost 30 years. Hoffman: Founding Partner of Janus-Merritt Strategies, LLC, a Washington, DC Strategic Consulting and Lobbying firm. Joined PMA in 2003. Silverman: Literary agent at The Tantleff Office and Bockworks Inc. from 1996-2001. Developmental Editor at McGraw-Hill from 2001-2003. Recently joined PMA.

Hobbies/personal interests: Miller: Traveling, gourmet food and wine, reading, fishing, playing with my daughters (Liseanne and Margo). Hoffman: Politics, wine, chess, bridge, opera. Silverman: Literature, film history, piano, reading, yoga, baseball.

Areas most interested in agenting: Miller: Action/suspense fiction, thrillers and legal thrillers, history, serious journalism, current events, pop culture. Hoffman: Nonfiction (particularly political nonfiction), literary fiction, commercial fiction. Silverman: Commercial and literary fiction, nonfiction dealing with pop culture, social/cultural subjects, health/fitness, women's issues.

Areas not interested in agenting: Poetry, pornography, children's books.

What might you be doing if you weren't an agent? Miller: A publisher or film producer, executive at a film studio. Hoffman: Running a private equity fund. Silverman: Editor or high school English teacher.

Best way to initiate contact: Miller: Send a query or an e-mail to my attention, detailing the essence of the book and why it is commercial, along with a biography of the author. Hoffman: E-mail queries only to Scott@Pmalitfilm.com. Silverman: Query by mail or e-mail, to lisa@pmalitfilm.com.

Reading-fee policy: No.

Client representation by category: Miller: Nonfiction, 20%; Fiction, 60%; Screenplays, 30%. Hoffman Nonfiction: 40%, Fiction, 60%: Silverman: Nonfiction 40%, Fiction 60%

Commission: Domestic 15%; film rights 10–15%; foreign rights 20–25%.

Number of titles sold last year: Miller: 20. Hoffman: 6.

Rejection rate (all submissions): 95%

Most common mistakes authors make: Miller: Many authors express a negative attitude toward agents and the publishing industry in general. What a way to win your potential agent's confidence! Sending me too much material or following up too soon or too often while being aggressive. It makes me wary of working with them. Hoffman: Sending revisions before I've had a chance to take a look at the original manuscript. Please don't send an agent or a manager a manuscript that isn't close enough to perfect to stand on its own. Silverman: A lack of professionalism and care; whether through spelling/grammar errors, submitting a manuscript with no synopsis or no contact information, or trying to get our attention with gimmicks and packaging rather than good writing.

Description of the client from Hell: Miller: The client who sends you a handwritten manuscript and calls you every day to see if you have read it. Hoffman: No such thing. People from Hell don't get to be clients. We love our writers. Silverman: The client from Heaven who leaves you for another agency.

Description of a dream client: Miller: Clients who trust your judgment and let you work for them. After all, I've been selling books for almost 30 years and I've sold over 800, so I must be doing something right. The writer who delivers a professional product on time and who understands my limitations.

Why did you become an agent? Miller: I had always wanted to be involved with films and I figured out early on that a great way to find properties was in the book world. I'm glad it happened this way because I think I'm good at it. I love my work. Hoffman: My two favorite things in life have always been books and deals—now I get to do book deals for a living. What could be better? Silverman: I've always had a knack for working with writers, and I'd rather be making deals on behalf of writers than on behalf of publishers.

How did you become an agent: Silverman: It wasn't something I planned. My first job out of college was as an assistant at an agency, and it stuck.

What can writers do to enhance their chances of getting you as an agent? Miller: Submit a professional, well-thought-out query letter with a polished synopsis and/or manuscript presentation. Hoffman: Figure a way around the usual blind query process; get a recommendation. Silverman: Write a good book. That's the bottom line. Take writing classes, join a writing group, do anything you can to make your writing more polished and effective.

How would you describe what you actually do for a living? Miller: Dealmaker. Hoffman: Venture Capitalist; I identify promising books and find a way to bring them to the world. Silverman: Facilitator— matching a talented writer to the right publisher, then dealing with the business side so they can get down to the business of creating.

What do you think about other agents? We don't have much contact with other agents, since we mainly deal with publishers. Obviously, they are the competition, but we have to like and respect our competition because they are in this business for the same reasons we are.

What do you think of editors? Miller: They're brilliant, God-like, and I highly respect them. Hoffman: After dealing with politicians in my previous career, editors are a breath of fresh air. Silverman: I love them because they love books. Unfortunately, they don't have the same decision-making power or ability to nurture unknown authors that they once did.

What do you think about publishers? Miller: Publishers are in the business to make money! The times are changing so we have to too. Hoffman: I'm encouraged to see publishers beginning to publish books that appeal to traditionally underserved markets—the trend is most easily identifiable with books that appeal to African-American and Latino audiences, and to conservative and Christian audiences. Silverman: The big ones are consolidating, but many small ones are flourishing, and new imprints are being created all the time—it seems there's a place for any good book if you look hard enough.

What were your favorite films last year? Silverman: *Lost in Translation; The Triplets of Belleville.*

Do you watch *The Sopranos?* Miller: If I'm near a TV, yes. Hoffman: I'm Italian and from Jersey— fuhgeddaboutit; of course I watch *The Sopranos*. Silverman: I'm the only member of this staff who's not an Italian from New Jersey, but I watch it anyway.

Comments: Writers, write on!

Representative titles: *1906* by James Dalessandro (Chronicle); *How to be Invisible* by J.J. Luna (Thomas Dunne); *The Virgin's Knot* by Holly Payne (Dutton); *As We Lay* by Darlene Johnson (Striver's Row); *Mister S: The Last Word on Frank Sinatra* by George Jacobs and William Stadiem (Harper Entertainment); *A Travel Guide to Heaven* by Anthony DeStefano (Doubleday); *Slow Hands* by Lynne Kaufman (MIRA); *I'm Telling* by Karen W. Quinones Miller (Simon & Schuster); *Police Heroes* by Chuck Whitlock (Tom Dunne/SMP); *Miss Julia* series by Ann Ross (Viking); *A Man Finds His Way* by Freddie Lee Johnson, III (One World/Ballantine); *The New York Cabbie Cookbook* by Mary Ellen Winston and Holly Garrison (Running Press); *Le Colonial* by Kien Nguyen (Little Brown); *Chocolate for a Woman's Soul II* by Kay Allenbaugh (Fireside, Simon & Schuster); *Walking to Canterbury* by Jerry Ellis (Ballantine); *Final Verdict: The Simple Truth in the Killing of JFK* by Vincent Bugliosi (W. W. Norton); *The Secret Universe of Names* by Roy Feinson (Overlook Press); *Between Black and White* by Nicole Bailey-Williams (Doubleday). *Hoffman: The Preservationist* by David Maine (St. Martin's); *Hyping Hope: How the Self-Help Movement Made America Helpless* by Steve Salerno (Crown Forum); *Xombies* by Walter Greatshell (Berkley).

SUSAN ANN PROTTER, LITERARY AGENT

110 West 40th Street, Suite 1408, New York, NY 10018

212-840-0480

Agent: Susan Ann Protter

Career history: Associate Director, Subsidiary Rights Dept., Harper & Row Publishers, Inc.; founded Susan Ann Protter Agency in 1971.

Hobbies/personal interests: Sailing, film, opera, travel, languages.

Areas most interested in agenting: Suspense fiction, including mysteries and thrillers; women's fiction; science fiction; exotic fiction. Nonfiction: (by recognized experts only); general and women's health; parenting; how-to; popular science and medicine; alternative medicine; history and biography, narrative nonfiction.

Areas not interested in agenting: Science fiction, romance, Westerns, children's books, high fantasy, dark fantasy, horror and textbooks.

Best way to initiate contact: One-page query letter with SASE (no e-mail), which gives overview, brief synopsis, author's background. If interested, will request first 30 pages and outline with an SASE. No reply without SASE.

Reading-fee policy: No reading fee.

Client representation by category: Nonfiction, 45%; Fiction, 55%.

Commission: 15%.

Number of titles sold last year: 20.

Rejection rate (all submissions): 97%. The agency can accommodate very few new authors; prior publication is an asset.

Most common mistakes authors make: They do not do their homework.

Comments: As an agent, I am looking for writers with whom I believe I will be able to connect for the long haul. The author and agent need to share a sense of joined vision and goals. Without that, they are unlikely to succeed as a team.

Representative titles: *House of Storms* by Ian R. Maclead (Ace); *Growing and Changing: Revised Edition* by Kathy McCoy, Ph.D. and Charles Wibbelsman, MD (Perigee/Putnam); *Write to the Point* by Salvatore J. Iacone (Career Press); *Perfect Planet, Clever Species* by William C. Burger (Prometheus); *Ghost Eater* by Frederick Highland (Thomas Dunne/St. Martin's); *Beyond the Mirage: Americans in Saudi Arabia* by Thomas W. Lippman (Westview/Perseus); *Getting Organized (New Ed)* by Stephanie Winston (Warner Books); *Operation Solomon: The Evacuation of the Ethiopian Jews to Israel* (Oxford); *Night Falls on Damascus* by Frederick Highland (Thomas Dunne/St. Martin's).

RAINES & RAINES

103 Kenyon Road Medusa, NY 12120

518-239-8311   518-239-6029

Agents: Theron Raines, Joan Raines, Keith Korman

Educational History: T. Raines: Columbia, Oxford.

Best way to intiate contact: One page letter.

Commission Structure: 15% domestic; 20% foreign.

Miscellaneous Comments: TR and JR are both authors of 3 books.

Representative Titles: *Die Hard* by Roderick Thorp; *Deliverance* by James Dickey; *Forrest Gump* by Winston Graham; *The Destruction of the European Jews* by Fial Jenkins; *Ordinary Men* by Christopher Brenning; *TAPS* by Willie Norris; *The Man Who Walked Between the Towers* by Mordicai Gerstein ('04 Caldecott winner); *Legacy* by Rich Lowry; *Active Faith* by Ralf Reed.

HELEN REES LITERARY AGENCY

376 North Street, Boston, MA 02113-2103

617-227-9014   fax: 617-227-8762

e-mail: reesliterary@aol.com

Agents: Helen Rees; Joan Mazmanian; Ann Collette; Lorin Rees
Born: October 2, 1936.
Education: B.A. in History, George Washington University.
Career history: Director of Office of Cultural Affairs, City of Boston (1978–1982); Literary Agent (1983–present).
Hobbies/personal interests: Horseback riding, opera, theater, hiking.
Areas most interested in agenting: Collette: Literary fiction, women's studies, health, biography, history. Rees: Business, money/finance, economics; government/politics, law; contemporary issues; literary fiction. Considers these nonfiction areas: Biography/autobiography; business/economics; current affairs; government/politics/law/; health/medicine; history; money/finance; women's issues/studies. Considers these fiction areas: Contemporary issues; historical; literary; mainstream contemporary; mystery/suspense; thriller.
Areas not interested in agenting: Children's books, young adult, science fiction, poetry, cookbooks, gardening books, photography.
Best way to initiate contact: Query with SASE, outline, and 2 sample chapters. No e-mail or fax queries. Responds in 2-3 weeks. Obtains most new clients through recommendations from others, solicitations, conferences.
Reading-fee policy: No reading fee.
Client representation by category: Nonfiction, 65%; Fiction, 15%; Other, 20%.
Commission: 15% domestic; 20% foreign.
Number of titles sold last year: 30.
Rejection rate (all submissions): 85%.
Most common mistakes authors make: In a query letter, they unrealistically hype their material.
Description of the client from Hell: Someone who sends a manuscript over and calls an hour later to see if I've read it.
Description of a dream client: Someone who listens and is talented.
Comments: Established 1983. Member of AAR and PEN America. Represents approximately 80 clients. 50% are new/unpublished writers. Currently handles: 60% nonfiction books; 40% novels.
Representative titles: Untitled new book by Senator John Kerry (Viking); *The Case for Israel* by Alan Dershowitz (Wiley); *Why Businesses Fail* by Sydney Finklestein (Viking); *Remember Who You Are: Harvard Business Professors on Life and Leadership* by Daisy Wademan (HBSP); *Claire Fontaine: Crime Fighter* by Tracy Enright (Thomas Dunne Books).

JODY REIN BOOKS, INC.

7741 South Ash Court, Centennial, CO 80122

303-694-4430

www.jodyreinbooks.com

Agent: Jody Rein

Career history: Spent 13 years in publishing at Contemporary Books (Senior Editor), Bantam Doubleday Dell (Executive Editor), and Morrow/Avon Books (Executive Editor). Incorporated Jody Rein Books in 1994.

Areas most interested in agenting: Very commercial nonfiction written by people who have both media contacts/experience and true expertise in their chosen subject matter. Serious and compelling narrative nonfiction. An amazing work of literary fiction by an award-winning short-story writer.

Areas not interested in agenting: Category fiction (mystery, romance, science fiction, horror, etc.), poetry, children's books.

Best way to initiate contact: A recommendation from someone I trust. A one-page query letter.

Reading-fee policy: No reading fee.

Client representation by category: Nonfiction, 85%; Fiction, 15%.

Commission: 15%.

Number of titles sold last year: 7.

Rejection rate (all submissions): 90–95%.

Most common mistakes authors make: Fax me; e-mail me; send me something I know nothing about; call me; say, "I can write about anything!"; say, "Well, I don't really know if this has been done before . . ."

Description of the client from Hell: Anyone who believes an agent is a necessary evil. An author who expects a perfect publishing experience but doesn't expect to do any work on his own.

Description of a dream client: Someone with a fabulous idea and the requisite writing experience, life experience, education, and passion to pull it off. Plus, media experience and contacts. Plus, a real willingness to do whatever he can to work with the agent and publisher to make his book a bestseller. Plus, respect for himself, for the book, for the publisher, and for me.

Why did you become an agent? I had been in the publishing business at an executive level for 13 years when I moved to Denver. I love this business. Being an agent was the only way to stay in the business, working with the top professionals in New York—and still live in the Rocky Mountains.

Comments: You can find good agents anywhere in the country, but make sure you protect yourself by doing adequate research. Ask the agent who wants to represent you if she has New York experience, how you would work together, and so on. But don't ask these questions until she has offered to represent you. If she doesn't want to sell your work, it doesn't matter what her experience is.

Representative titles: *Skeletons on the Zahara* by Dean King (Little Brown, optioned by Baltimore/Spring Creek); *The Big Year* by Mark Obmascik (The Free Press, optioned by DreamWorks); *The Seashell on the Mountaintop* by Alan Cutler (Penguin Putnam); *8 Simple Rules for Dating my Teenage Daughter* by W. Bruce Cameron (Workman, sold to ABC/Disney).

THE AMY RENNERT AGENCY, INC.

Address: 98 Main Street, #302, Tiburon, CA 94920

415-789-8955   fax: 415-789-8944

Agent: Amy Rennert
Place of birth: Brooklyn, New York.
Career History: Award-winning writer and editor. Editor-in-Chief of *San Francisco Focus* magazine and *Women's Sports* magazine, author of three books.
Areas most interested in agenting: Narrative nonfiction, especially memoirs, business, pop culture, health, adventure, sports, psychology. Literary fiction, mysteries, thrillers.
Areas not interested in agenting: Religious fundamentalism, gag gifts, romance novels, science fiction, self-help, children's, Westerns, fantasy.
Best way to initiate contact: For nonfiction, send a cover letter and a proposal, including at least one sample chapter. For fiction, a cover letter and the first 50-75 pages. We do not need to see a query letter first. We do not accept e-mail or disks, and we do not respond unless writers send self-addressed stamped envelopes.
Reading fee policy: No reading fee.
Client representation by category: Nonfiction 65%; Fiction 35%.
Commission structure: 15% domestic; 20% foreign.
Number of titles sold last year: 25+.
Rejection rate (all submissions): 95%.
Most common mistakes authors make with your agency: Not including appropriate SASE for materials wanted back; using envelopes that are impossible to open; using those padded envelopes that spray gray stuff all over the office; not taking care to write a compelling, professional letter; faxing over revised pages soon after submission.
Your description of a dream client: Dream clients write like a dream and are professional in all dealings. They learn a little or a lot about the publishing business before approaching the agency. Dream clients don't need money desperately right now, but are interested in a writing career and let their hard work lead them in the right direction. The dream client has talent, patience and perseverance.
Why did you become an agent? For the opportunity to bring books that matter into the world, so that I could use both my editorial and my business skills, so that I

didn't have to work for anybody else, and so that I could help writers achieve their dreams while realizing my own.

What do you think about editors? I think that most of them care about books. They are smart and market-savvy and are too pressured by the bottom line these days. I wish, and they wish too, that they had more time to edit books.

Representative titles: *The Prizewinner of Defiance, Ohio: How My Mother Raised Ten Kids on 25 Words or Less* by Terry Ryan (Simon & Schuster); *A Slant of Sun* and *Still Love in Strange Places* by Beth Kephart (Norton); *Why I'm Like This* by Cynthia Kaplan (William Morrow); *Offer of Proof* by Robert Heilbrun (William Morrow); *The Travel Detective* by NBC Today Show correspondent Peter Greenberg (Villard); *The Rabbi & the Hitman* by Arthur Magida (HarperCollins); *Maisie Dobbs* by Jacqueline Winspear (Soho); *The Sex Lives of Teenagers* by Dr. Lynn Ponton (Dutton); *Blood Washes Blood* by Frank Viviano (Pocket Books); *Class Dismissed* (St. Martin's) and *Dirty* (HarperSan Francisco) both by Meredith Maran; *God's Breath: Sacred Scriptures of the World* edited by John Miller & Aaron Kenedi (Marlowe); *Arousal* by Dr. Michael Bader (St. Martin's); *The Orange Curtain* and *City of Strangers* by John Shannon (Otto Penzler/Carroll & Graf); *A Mouthful of Air* by Amy Koppelman (MacAdam/Cage); *Tumbling After* by Susan Parker (Crown).

JODIE RHODES LITERARY AGENCY

8840 Villa La Jolla Drive, Suite 315, La Jolla, CA 92037

858-625-0544

e-mail: jrhodes1@san.rr.com

Agent: Jodie Rhodes, President; Clark McCutcheon, fiction editor at large; Bob McCarter, nonfiction editor at large; Vicki Satlow, foreign rights, Milan, Italy. Contact for all queries: Jodie Rhodes.

Born: Montreal, Canada.

Education: B.A. Ohio Wesleyan University. Pursued M.A. at Ohio State concurrently with my husband pursuing his Ph.D. at Ohio State, but ended up doing his research and papers instead of my own.

Career History: Advertising—started as a copywriter at a small agency in Columbus, Ohio. Went to W.B. Doner in Detroit as a media buyer, then to Hoeffer, Dietrich and Brown in San Francisco and ended up as Vice President, media director of N.W. Ayer's West Coast operation.

Hobbies/Personal Interests: A hobby that grew into a vice was option trading. I was an active trader in the market for many years, concurrent with my positions in advertising. The day I realized I was in trouble was when I had so much money rolling in from option trades that I began regarding my salary as chump change. I now only hold stocks that pay strong dividends. Love bridge and am a Life Master. Am a passionate but rather inept tennis player. Have always loved horses and riding. Bike regularly.

Areas most interested in agenting: Multicultural literature, both fiction and non-fiction, makes my eyes light up. Books that have something important to say and characters with substance. Voice is everything to me in a novel. I'm fascinated by science and have sold many books by a variety of scientists and academics. Mainstream fiction, memoirs, biography, history, literary novels, world literature, politics, military, international affairs, women's issues, parenting, health, medicine.

I am rightly known as an agent who welcomes new writers and the vast majority of books I've sold have been authored by new writers, in the sense that it was their first published book.

However, good books come from intelligent, hardworking, interesting people who've done things with their lives. I expect every writer who contacts me to have thoroughly researched the subject matter of their book, novel or nonfiction, to write with palpable knowledge and authority, to have practiced and honed the craft of writing which is demonstrated by their winning awards, having short stories published in well-known literary magazines, articles in magazines and newspapers. I also expect a cogent and intriguing query letter.

Areas not interested in agenting: No romances, religious or spiritual books, no self help or inspirational books, no children's books (although I'm interested in YA/teen literary novels), no erotic works, no science fiction, fantasy, or horror unless it's a brilliantly creative work.

If not agenting, what might you be doing? Writing. I always wanted to be a writer and in the eighties had two books published: *American Beauties* by Bantam and *Winners and Losers* by Putnam. The latter made the LA bestsellers list its first week in print.

Best way to initiate contact: Despite my use of e-mail to pitch books, I don't accept queries by e-mail or fax and do wish writers would not call to tell me about their book and ask if I'd like to see it. Submission guidelines are clear and available in many sources. Send a query letter, a brief synopsis with the emphasis on brief (I can't begin to tell you how many 20- and 30-page synopses I receive). In addition, since the bottom line is all about the writing, I invite writers to include the opening 50 or so pages of their book. I reply only if an SASE is enclosed. I reply to queries in less than a week in the majority of cases—and that includes queries that include 50 pages of MS.

Client representation by category: 30% fiction, 65% nonfiction, 5% YA/teen. I might add this is not my choice. I would prefer 60% fiction and 40% the rest. The magic of fiction is that the author creates life. I love my brilliant scientists, doctors, and academics, but a truly great novel is my passion.

Commission structure: 15% in all cases except 20% for foreign sales if it's placed through a subagent.

Number of titles sold last year: 32.

Rejection rate: 99%.

Most common mistakes authors make: They don't think before they write. They just let it pour out. The result is illogical plots, inconsistent characters, clichéd, superficial writing and a bored agent. A writer should spend at least two hours of research for every hour of writing. They should know their characters as well as they know their secret thoughts. They should know everything about the situations they put their characters in, including what the streets they walk on look like.

Description of the client from Hell: A client who e-mails or calls you every week after the first round of submissions has been mailed out—who falls apart emotionally when the first reflections come in, who acts as though they're the only client you have, who repeatedly asks what you're going to do after every rejection, who tries to make you feel you and only you are responsible for selling the book—the actual book they wrote has nothing to with it.

Description of a dream client: Intelligent, appreciative, patient, a genuine grown-up who realizes a good agent works as hard as a writer and has enormous demands on their time from many areas—who even tries to help by getting name people to endorse his or her book and does research to find possible small publishers the agent can contact if the major and midsize houses have all rejected it.

How did you become an agent? Through more work than I ever thought I was capable of. Most everything in my life has come easy to me. When I started my agency in late 1998, I was (and still am) living in La Jolla, California, 3,000 miles from the heart of the publishing business. I didn't have a single writer or know a single editor. I'd never worked as an editor in a New York trade house (although I had worked as an editor years and years ago in a subsidiary of McGraw-Hill in Columbus, Ohio). I knew nobody and nobody knew me. In addition, they didn't care. For the first six months I received nothing but the most ghastly imaginable mss, all of which I rejected, and began to think seriously of quitting this insane idea. But I've always been a bulldog. So the first thing I did was convince some regional and national writers' magazines to publish my columns. Then I wrote the head of every major New York house and said I'd like to interview their editors. I will be grateful all my life to Sally Richardson at St. Martins and Emily at Atria/Pocket/Simon & Schuster who, out of the kindness of their hearts, personally called me on the phone and offered me each some 5 or 6 editors. After that, everybody was willing to talk to me.

The other thing I did was make what I hoped would be a short-term sacrifice for a long-term benefit. There are about 3,000 people who call themselves agents in this country and I started out as 3,001. Major talented polished writers were not querying me. So I took the best of the raw talent and edited their mss into saleable books.

Above all, I owe New York editors, and I'm talking major editors, for their unbelievable kindness. I had several writers who told me their previous agents never received a single response from editors when they sent submissions. That was the fate I feared. So I introduced myself. I wrote them about myself. They were so gracious! I'll never forget Jane Von Mehren, now VP Editor-in-Chief of Viking Penguin, calling me one day simply to ask—had I sold a book yet. Carolyn Marino is a saint. She has cheered me on for years, never letting the fact she has yet to take one of my books deter her from encouraging me to keep sending. The brilliant editor of Ecco Press, Dan Halpren, has taked the time to write notes like, "I'm sorry this one won't work for Ecco but I remain hopeful." Michael Pietsch, Brian Tart and Wendy Lamb wrote wonderful recommendation letters to LMP so I could get listed—and I'd never come close to selling them a book. I probably shouldn't start naming editors because there are so many others who reached out a helping hand.

Why did you become an agent? I had been doing writer workshops and seminars at the Learning Annex for several years. It hurt me to see how totally ignored they were by agents simply because they were new. I mean, no one would give them a chance. I figured maybe an underdog like myself might just be able to help underdogs like themselves. My mission from the inception of my agency was to get new writers published. In the past two and a half years I've sold 65 books (including series) and all but one were by previously unpublished writers, the majority of whom had been rejected by everyone else for years. Now of course I'm selling published writers but they're writers I got published and we're now placing their second books.

What can writers do to enhance their chances of getting you as their agent? Be honest, be professional, do your homework before you contact me, research your book, hone your writing craft, don't write for the market (meaning if you're written a book motivated simply by the desire to sell a book, go to some other agent). Write because you had to—because your story, fiction or nonfiction, was that important to you. If you've written a novel and not once during the time you wrote it did you feel excitement, fear, desire, hope, desperation, curiosity, determination—if you never laughed or cried, then you never got inside your book. If you felt nothing, the reader will feel nothing.

How would you describe what you actually do for a living? Making people's dreams come true.

What do you think about other agents? They run the gamut from ghastly to superb, unfortunately. I get horror stories constantly from writers who've been badly hurt by agents. Anyone can call him or herself an agent. We're not even licensed. I've been told there are 3,000 literary agents in this country. Ninety percent of the books are sold by 10% of us. That leaves a lot of agents scratching to survive and too many make their money by charging writers outrageous fees for reading mss, editing, marketing fees, etc. My advice is to never consider an agent who asks you for money except for specifically itemized submission costs after they've offered you representation and you've seen their contract.

What do you think about editors? With rare exceptions, I love them. They are so bright. Have gained so much knowledge (from their writers, actually), most really deeply care about books and they're all under such pressure all the time—they work enormously long hours and have demands on them writers can't even begin to imagine—yet they will always give new writers a chance.

What do you think about publishers? It makes me sad that making money is so important to them. I guess to stay in the business, they have to. But it didn't used to be that way before all the mergers and acquisitions.

I wish they'd reward writers who make money for them by considerably more generous royalties—they know what their break-even point is—after that why not let the author share more fairly in the profits?

What were your favorite films last year? I work 17 hours a day, 7 days a week and before I became an agent, I read a minimum of 10 books a week and saw a movie at least once a week. Now I never see movies and never get to read real books. It's horrible, because I need to know what's out there. Thank God for *Publishers Weekly* and editors who send me their writers' books so I can at least scan them.

Do you watch *The Sopranos*? Actually I did a few times when it first appeared but no time now. When they're on, I'm reading manuscripts.

Comments: I think I've already made more than you ever wanted to read; however, I'd like to tell writers that in fiction authors write bad books and characters write good books—in memoir never remember, reflect, recall or reminisce—relive what you write! That's the only way it will have power. The key to good novels is a simple, clear focused plot and engaging complex characters. Most writers write convoluted plots with simple-minded characters. Put intelligence, wit and charm into your characters. Stop with the banal dialogue. Don't copy life or imitate life in your books—99% of life is meaningless chaos. Give life order and meaning and distill its essence. That's what readers want.

Representative titles: *Village Bride in Beverly Hills* by Kavita Daswani (Penguin, U.S., HarperCollins, UK); *The Myrtles* by Frances Kermeen (Warner); *Inside the Crips* by Ann Pearlman (St. Martin's Press); *Home is East* by Many Ly (Delacorte); *Last of the Roundup Boys* by Debra Seely (Holiday House); *Science of Circumstance* by Suzanne Bell (Rutgers University Press); *The Dwarf in Louis XIV's Court* by Paul Weidner (University of Wisconsin, US; Kinneret-Zamora, Israel); *Biology for a New Century* by Stan Rice (John Wiley & Sons); *Changing Course* by Jeanne Lutz (New Horizon Press); *Raising Healthy Eaters* by Henry Joseph Legeres (DaCapo Press); *Down and Dirty Justice* by Gary Lowenthal (New Horizon Press); *Epiphanies* by Terry Bennett (Toby Press); *Forensic Chemistry* by Suzanne Bell (Prentice Hall); *The Darkest Clearing* by Brian Railsback (High Sierra Press).

JONNE RICCI LITERARY AGENCY

PO Box 13410, Palm Desert, CA 92255

www.jonnericciliteraryagency.net

Individual Agents: Sole Proprietorship
Date/Place of birth: Denver, Colorado
Educational History: Cherry Creek High School and Hollywood Institute of Arts.

Career History: Housewife, business owner.

Hobbies/Personal interests: Golf, bridge, computer.

Areas most interested in agenting: Fiction, children's and Christian books.

Areas not interested in agenting: Nonfiction secular writers.

If not agenting, what would you be doing? Hobbies and other church activities.

Best way to initiate contact: My website tells how to contact me.

Reading-fee policy: I do not charge a reading fee.

Client representation by category: 70% fiction, 20% children's, and 10% Christian.

Commission structure: 15%.

Number of titles sold last year: 1.

Rejection rate: 97%.

Most common mistakes authors make with your agency: Sending submissions that have way too many errors in their writing.

What can writers do to enhance their chances of getting you as an agent? Send a clean package, neatly organized, with good writing skills.

Your description of the client from Hell: One that doesn't take no for an answer and keeps trying to stay in contact with me.

Your description of a dream client: Good writing skills, clean submission with a marketable product, and easy to work with.

How did you become an agent? I spent 7 years learning the trade.

Why did you become an agent? My husband is a published author. I enjoy being in the field of writing and want to help other authors get published.

How would you describe what you actually do for a living? Editing submissions from potential authors and being able to offer representation to an author whom I feel has written a good and marketable product.

What do you think about other agents? I really have no opinion on other agents. I am just concerned with my agency and being an ethical person in my field.

What do you think about editors? I know they have many submissions and I only hope they will be able to see the potential I see in my clients.

What do you think about publishers? They are the company that can put the novels in the book stores and I fully understand why most of them only accept submissions from agents.

Miscellaneous Comments: I only accept material that I feel is a saleable product. I won't waste the publishers' time by sending poorly written novels.

Representative titles: This year, I have 6 clients and I'm in the process of submitting their work to publishers.

THE ANGELA RINALDI LITERARY AGENCY

PO Box 7877, Beverly Hills, CA 90212-7877

310-842-7665   fax: 310-837-8143

e-mail: amr@rinaldiliterary.com

Agent: Angela Rinaldi

Career history: Editor at New American Library/Signet, Pocket Books, Bantam. Manager Book Publishing, the *Los Angeles Times*.

Areas most interested in agenting: Literary and mainstream fiction and upmarket commercial women's fiction. Narrative non-fiction, women's issues/studies, current issues, biography, popular reference, prescriptive and pro-active self-help, business, career, personal finance, medical/health and books written by journalists, academics, doctors and therapists, based on their research.

Areas not interested in agenting: Category romances, gift books, science fiction, fantasy, westerns, techno or Cold War thrillers, horror, cookbooks, poetry, children's books, young adult, and film scripts.

Best way to initiate contact: Fiction: Send first three chapters with brief synopsis. Non-fiction: Query with detailed letter or proposal. E-mail inquiries but please, no attachments. Allow 4-6 weeks response time. No phone calls or faxes. Include SASE with the correct postage. Please don't use metered mail, don't send anything certified mail or ask for anything to be returned that weighs more than one pound.

Reading fee: None.

Client representation by category: 50% fiction.

Commission: 15% domestic; 20% foreign.

Representative titles: *Who Moved My Cheese?* by Dr. Spencer Johnson (Putnam); *Zen Golf: Mastering the Mental Game* by Dr. Joseph Parent (Doubleday); *Calling In the One: 7 Weeks to Attract the Love of Your Life* by Katherine Woodward Thomas (Three Rivers); *The Thyroid Solution* by Dr. Ridha Arem (Ballantine); *The Starlite Drive-in* by Marjorie Reynolds (Morrow); *Blind Spot* by Stephanie Kane (Bantam); *The Seventh Sin* by Eben Paul Perison (NAL); *Blood Orange* by Drusilla Campbell (Kensington); *Reflections from the Heart: What Our Animal Companions Tell Us* by Deborah DeMoss Smith (Wiley); *My First Crush* by Linda Kaplan (The Lyons Press).

ANN RITTENBERG LITERARY AGENCY, INC.

1201 Broadway, Suite 708, New York, NY 10001

212-684-6936   fax: 212-684-6929

www.rittlit.com

Agent: Ann Rittenberg, Ted Gideonse

Born: Rittenberg: 1957, New York, New York. Gideonse: 1974, Cincinnati, Ohio.

Education: Rittenberg: B.A., Eckerd College; Gideonse: B.A., Harvard University; MFA, The New School University.

Career history: Rittenberg: 1979–1980, *St. Petersburg Times*; 1980–1986, Editor, Atheneum Publishers; 1986–1992, Agent, Julian Bach Agency; 1992–present, President, Ann Rittenberg Literary Agency, Inc. Gideonse: 1997-1999, *Newsweek*; 1999-2002, freelance writer and editor; 2002-present, Ann Rittenberg Literary Agency, Inc.

Hobbies/personal interests: Rittenberg: Gardening, travel, ballet/theater, entertainment, cabaret, New York. Gideonse: film, theater, design.

Areas most interested in agenting: Rittenberg: Literary fiction, serious narrative nonfiction, biography/autography/memoir, cultural history, social history, upmarket contemporary women's fiction. Gideonse: Serious nonfiction/journalism, literary fiction, gay and lesbian culture and history, upmarket novelty books.

Areas not interested in agenting: Rittenberg: Sci-fi, genre fiction, romance, how-to, gift books. Gideonse: Romance, how-to, anything derivative and dull.

If not agenting, what would you be doing? Rittenburg: Traveling the world, playing tennis and golf, studying art and languages, writing literary criticism—in other words, pursuing leisure activities! There's no other job I'd want to have. Gideonse: Reading the classics, going to movies, hanging out in dive bars—that's what I do when I'm not at work and what I'd do if I didn't have a job. But I love my job, I love my clients, and I love making books happen.

Best way to initiate contact: Write me a letter.

Client representation by category: Nonfiction, 50%; Fiction, 50%.

Commission: 15% domestic, 15% film (split with subagent), 20% foreign (spilt with sub-agent).

Number of titles sold last year: 25

Rejection rate (all submissions): 98%.

Most common mistakes authors make: When writers say, "I've just finished a novel. . ." I wonder why they haven't put it through another draft before approaching agents. I also don't like letters that focus more on marketing than they do on the work.

Description of the client from Hell: Rittenberg: Those who don't want to revise their work until after it's sold to a publishing house. Those who never call, then complain about lack of attention. Gideonse: Arrogant, unbending, un-editable folks who don't like to chat on the phone with their agent.

Description of a dream client: All of our clients are dream clients. They are hard-working, enthusiastic, dedicated to writing, convinced that the work comes first, conscious that the author-agent relationship flourishes when it is a partnership based on mutual respect and trust.

Why did you become an agent? Rittenberg: When I worked in a publishing house, I saw that it wasn't politic to put the author's needs before the needs of the publicity department, the sales department, the rights department, even the book-ordering department. That didn't seem right to me, and I became an agent so that I could advocate for writers. Gideonse: I love finding and developing original, exciting writers and then getting them published. It's fun, and it makes me feel as if I'm enriching culture.

What can writers do to enhance their chances of getting you as an agent? Keep their letters short.

How would you describe what you actually do for a living? Advocating for authors, with all that entails: Coping with an avalanche of paperwork and a cacophony of telephone calls, faxes, and e-mails; meeting editors, film producers, and foreign publishers and staying current with their interests and the demands of the marketplace. We also spend a lot of time talking to clients so we can get to know them and their hopes and needs, as well as their work, and we strategize about when to submit work, how to get the best work out of a writer, how to raise a writer's profile, and how to get the publishers to focus on how to best publish each book we represent.

What do you think about editors? They are smart, wonderful, creative, caring people who are swamped by work and the demands of the corporations so many of them work for.

What do you think about publishers? They're too big and are inefficient as a result of streamlining and merging in a quest for economic efficiency. Some of them are too small, and while they can give personal attention at every stage in a way that the big publishers can't, their distribution arrangements can be a source of frustration.

Representative titles: *Improbable* by Adam Fawer (William Morrow & Co); *A Certain Slant of Light* by Laura Whitcomb (Houghton Mifflin); *The New York Night: Mystique and its History* by Mark Caldwell (Scribner); *Mystic River* by Dennis Lehane (William Morrow & Co); *Seven Blessings* by Ruchama King (St. Martin's Press).

JUDITH RIVEN, LITERARY AGENT/EDITORIAL CONSULTANT

250 West 16th St., #4F, New York, NY 10011

212-255-1009

e-mail: Rivenlit@att.net

   Agent: Judith Riven

Education: B.A.; M.A. in English Literature.

Career history: Majority of experience as an Acquiring Editor for several major trade publishers. Independent Agent since mid-1993.

Areas most interested in agenting: Practical self-help, particularly medical/health, both conventional and alternative; history, natural history (am particularly interested in the Southwestern U.S.) cooking and food writing, social issues; narrative nonfiction. Fiction—both serious and commercial.

Areas not interested in agenting: Gratuitous violence, genre fiction other than mysteries.

Best way to initiate contact: E-mail brief query—no attachments. Snail-mail brief query letter with SASE. No faxes.

Reading-fee policy: None.

Client representation by category: Nonfiction, 95%; Fiction, 5%. I don't represent children's books.

Commission: 15% of all monies; 10% of foreign (foreign agent commissions at 15% for a total of 25%).

Number of titles sold last year: 15.

Rejection rate (all submissions): 95%.

Most common mistakes authors make: Not having a clear focus on what they want to say; not understanding the importance of developing their concepts into well-articulated proposals.

Description of the client from Hell: Writers who are unwilling to listen—and to hear feedback on their work. Anyone who believes that working hurriedly is more important than working thoroughly.

Description of a dream client: Most of my clients are dream clients. I try to represent people whose work I admire and who share a vision of working collaboratively, who have high aspirations and realistic goals and are willing to commit themselves to achieving them.

Why did you become an agent? It was a natural evolution from being an acquisitions editor. As publishing became more corporate, I found I wanted the ability to work more independently. I have always loved publishing and agenting. I was offered the perfect situation to continue working with the author helping to shape ideas and negotiate book deals.

What can writers do to enhance their chances of getting you as an agent? Very thoughtfully and carefully develop their proposal before getting in touch with me.

How would you describe what you do for a living? I get to work with many wonderful and special people who are excited about and committed to what they're doing, whether they're cancer researchers, psychologists, chefs, entomologists, or novelists, and I represent their ideas to another group of exceptional people: editors.

What do you think of editors? Most are seriously smart, very committed, and enormously overworked. They have a broad and deep perspective on what's happening in the marketplace.

What do you think about publishers? They're in a more and more difficult situation. The large ones tend to get bogged down in corporate bureaucracy. The smaller ones are hard-pressed to compete both in acquiring and getting their books into the marketplace.

What were your favorite films last year? Among the films I enjoyed and admired last year were: *Capturing the Friedmans*; *Spellbound*; *City of God*; *The Cooler*; *In America*; *Something's Gotta Give*; *The Station Master*; *Bend it Like Beckham*. But no single film emerged as a favorite.

Do you watch *The Sopranos*? Yes—but not as enthusiastically as in years past.

Representative titles: *Delivering Dr. Amelia* by Dan Shapiro (Harmony/Vintage); *Nightmusic* by Harrison Slater (Harcourt); *The Roosevelts and the Royals* by Will Swift (Wiley); *Bloodbath: A Human and Social History of WWI* by Gerald L. Meyers (Bantam); *Wine for Women* by Leslie Sbrocco (William Morrow); *Tom Douglas' Big Dinners* by Tom Douglas (William Morrow); *Delicate* by Mary Sojourner (Scribner); *Is Something Wrong With My Child?* By Laurie LeComer (Perigee); *Happy Mealtimes* by Linda Pilette (Three River Press).

B. J. ROBBINS LITERARY AGENCY

5130 Bellaire Avenue, North Hollywood, CA 91607

fax: 818-760-6616

e-mail: Robbinsliterary@aol.com

Agent: B. J. Robbins
Born: New York City.
Education: B.A. (Magna Cum Laude with Highest Distinction) in English, Phi Beta Kappa, University of Rochester.

Career history: Worked in book publishing for 15 years before moving to LA and opening my agency in 1992. Started in publicity at Simon & Schuster and M. Evans before going to Harcourt, where I spent 7 years, in New York and San Diego, in jobs ranging from Publicity Manager to Marketing Director and Senior Editor.

Hobbies/personal interests: Basketball (I play in a mom's league), baseball (which I don't play); does shopping with my teenage daughter count as a hobby?

Areas most interested in representing: I look for projects that are fresh and original and have literary merit, whether they're novels or narrative nonfiction. I also look for experts who can impart important information in a unique way.

Areas not interested in agenting: I don't do most genre fiction: romance, science fiction, fantasy, horror, westerns, techno-thrillers, anything apocalyptic. No screenplays, poetry, children's books. No books about dating.

Best way to initiate contact: Don't call or fax. E-mail queries are ok, but do not include attachments. For mailed submissions, send a short cover letter accompanied by a small sample of your writing (first three chapters or so for fiction, a proposal for nonfiction) with an SASE .

Client representation by category: Nonfiction, 50%; Fiction, 50%.

Commission: 15% domestic; 20% foreign.

Rejection rate (all submissions): 95%.

Description of the client from Hell: Clients who don't understand how the business works, who have unrealistic expectations, who call constantly or at inappropriate times. Fortunately, I have eliminated all Clients from Hell and have developed excellent CFH radar.

Description of the dream client: All of mine fit this category. They behave professionally; they know how publishing works, even if they're first-timers, because they've taken the time to do their homework.

Most common mistakes authors make: The list is long, but here are a few pet peeves: including random chapters instead of the first three; telling me we're going to make a million dollars; any kind of gimmick; calling your work a fiction novel or, for that matter, a nonfiction novel; not including return postage; having spelling and grammatical errors in the cover letter; including a synopsis/outline longer than three pages.

What can writers do to enhance their chances of getting you as an agent? Write a simple, straightforward cover letter that includes a brief description of your work, the reasons why you are soliciting my agency, and a short bio. I also like to see a sample of your writing, so include 50 pages or so and an SASE.

Why did you become an agent? I had just moved to LA and was looking for a way to use my varied publishing experience in order to continue to work with writers while working for myself.

If not agenting, what might you be doing? Reading books for fun.

What do you think about editors? All the editors I work with are exceptionally smart, work hard, and really care about authors.

What do you think about publishers? Same as above.

Do you watch *The Sopranos?* Yes.

Representative titles: *The Sex Lives of Cannibals: Adrift in the Equatorial Pacific* by J. Maarten Troost (Broadway); *Snow Mountain Passage* by James D. Houston (Knopf); *The Last Summer* by John Hough Jr. (Simon & Schuster); *Coffee and Kung Fu* and *Separation Anxiety* by Karen Brichoux (NAL).

LINDA ROGHAAR LITERARY AGENCY, INC.

133 High Point Drive, Amherst, MA 01002

413-256-1921   fax: 413-256-2636

www.lindaroghaar.com   e-mail: contact@lindaroghaar.com

Agent: Linda L. Roghaar

Born: September 11, 1947, Winchester, Massachusetts.

Education: B.A. in Religion, Miami University (Ohio), 1969; M.A. in Liberal Studies, Vanderbilt University, 1997.

Career history: I've worked in publishing since 1974, first as a bookseller and bookstore manager, then as a publisher's sales rep. Established the agency in 1997.

Areas most interested in agenting: I am a generalist.

Areas not interested in agenting: Children's, horror, science fiction.

If not agenting, what would you be doing? Selling books in another division of the publishing industry.

Best way to initiate contact: Query letter with SASE or an e-query.

Reading-fee policy: No reading fee.

Client representation by category: Nonfiction, 90%; Fiction, 10%.

Commission: 15% domestic, 20% foreign.

Rejection rate (all submissions): 99%.

Most common mistakes authors make: Calling me to tell me about the book. Sending an incomplete, confusing package, not enough postage, or a metered envelope.

Description of a dream client: Writers who are friendly, patient, organized. A sense of humor always helps, along with a realistic perspective of their place in publishing. Those who have thought through the idea (for nonfiction) or polished the manuscript (for fiction) before contacting me.

How did you become an agent? I've been an entrepreneur for so long! My 30 years of experience in the publishing business have been invaluable in my everyday dealings with writers and publishers.

Why did you become an agent? I love making the connection between writer and publisher and seeing worthy projects find their way into print. Years ago, I made that connection between the bookstore customer and a book, and then for many years as a publisher's rep between publisher and bookseller. Now, it's between writer and publisher, and that is a natural progression for me. I really love my work.

What can writers do to enhance their chances of getting you as an agent? Present the material in a clear, complete package.

What do you think about editors? Overall, a delightful and interesting group of people who deal remarkably well with the frustrations of their jobs.

What do you think about publishers? I divide publishers into two groups: The Big Guys (maybe by the time you read this, it will be One Big Guy) and the Independents. The Big Guys: They can really get things done and continue to produce quality lists. My biggest frustration with them is this—they want something new and different, but with a track record. They are less likely to take chances and therefore miss some very good opportunities. The Independents: They publish some of the most interesting and important books today and now, finally, get better review attention. The quality of their production is excellent, and each book gets a lot of in-house attention. My frustrations are less precise, less timely publishing schedules; long lead times to decide on a manuscript; smaller advances. Generally, though, at all publishing houses people are overworked, a bit frantic, and totally committed to their work.

Representative titles: *Tea At the Blue Lantern Inn* by Jan Whitaker (St. Martin's

Press); *What Would Buffy Do? The Vampire Slayer as Spiritual Guide* by Jana Riess (Jossey-Bass); *Mindful Knitting* by Tara Jon Manning (Tuttle); *The Green Mountain Spinnery Knitting Book* by Margaret Klein Wilson and the Green Mountain Spinnery (Countryman/WW Norton); *Cat vs. Cat: Keeping the Peace When You Have More than One Cat* by Pam Johnson Bennett (Penguin).

THE ROSENBERG GROUP

23 Lincoln Avenue, Marblehead, MA 01945

781-990-1341

www.rosenberggroup.com

Agent: Barbara Collins Rosenberg
Born: The Bronx, New York.
Education: B.A. in Theater and English, Montclair State University.
Career history: Senior Acquisitions Editor for eight years at Harcourt; agent since June 1998.

Areas most interested in agenting: Romance, women's fiction, "chick lit," literary fiction. Any commercial nonfiction and college textbooks for first- and second-year courses.

Areas not interested in agenting: Anything that's not listed above.

If you weren't agenting, what might you be doing? Something in publishing, most likely acquiring.

Best way to initiate contact: Well-written query letter.

Client representation: Nonfiction, 40%; Fiction, 40%. Textbooks, 20%.

Commission: 15% domestic.

Number of titles sold last year: 28.

Rejection rate (all categories): 95%.

Most common mistakes authors make: Not paying attention to the areas of fiction I represent.

Description of the client from Hell: I haven't had one—I can sense early on who will be trouble.

Description of the dream client: A client who meets deadlines, knows his or her market, works well within the editorial process and doesn't complain too much about covers.

How did you become an agent? I have always thought of publishing as an accidental career.

Why did you become an agent? I became an agent because I saw a need for textbook authors to have someone looking out for them.

What can writers do to enhance their chances of getting you as their agent? Know their market and write a great book.

Representative titles: *Chasing Steinbrenner* by Rob Bradford (Brassey's); *The Conception Chronicles* by Patty Debano, Courtney Menzel and Shelly Sutphen (HCI); *How to Do Everything with HTML, 2e* by James Pence (McGraw-Hill); *Music of the Peoples of the World* by Bill Alves (Wadsworth); 3 romantic suspense novels (titles to come) by Dee Davis (HQN); 3 military romances, Catherine Mann (HQN).

RITA ROSENKRANZ LITERARY AGENCY

440 West End Avenue, Suite 15D, New York, NY 10024-5358

212-873-6333

Agent: Rita Rosenkranz

Career history: Editor at various New York publishing houses before becoming an agent in 1990.

Areas most interested in agenting: All areas of nonfiction, with emphasis on biography, business, parenting, cooking, current affairs, cultural issues, health, history, how-to, self-help, theater/film, popular culture, religious/inspirational, science, women's issues.

Areas not interested in agenting: Fiction and children's books.

Best way to initiate contact: Send an outline/proposal with an SASE. I do not accept queries by e-mail or fax. I consider simultaneous queries and submissions.

Client representation by category: Nonfiction, 98%; Fiction, 1%; Children's, 1%.

Commission: 15% on domestic sales; 20% on foreign sales.

Number of titles sold last year: 40.

Rejection rate (all submissions): 95%.

Representative titles: *Flowers, White House Style* by Dottie Temple and Stan Finegold (Simon & Schuster); *Saving Beauty from Beast: How to Protect Your Daughter from an Unhealthy Relationship* by Vicki Crompton and Ellen Kessner (Little Brown); *Wolf Pack: The American Submarine Strategy That Helped Defeat Japan* by Steven Trent Smith (John Wiley & Sons); *An Exaltation of Soups, as told in More Than 100 Recipes* by Pat Solley (Three Rivers Press).

CAROL SUSAN ROTH LITERARY

1824 Oak Creek Drive, Suite 416, Palo Alto, CA 94304

(or)

PO Box 620337 Woodside, CA 94062

650-323-3795

e-mail: carol@authorsbest.com

Agent: Carol Susan Roth

Born: October 22, New Brunswick, New Jersey.

Education: B.A., New York University; M.A., East West Counseling and Psychotherapy; California Institute of Integral Studies, San Francisco; Stanford University Professional Publishing Program, Mark Victor Hansen, "Building Your Speaking and Publishing Empire."

Career history: Trained as a psychotherapist specializing in motivational training seminars. More than a decade producing and promoting public events (100+) with the "who's who" in personal growth, spirituality, health, and business (bestselling authors, including John Gray, Scott Peck, Bernie Siegal, Thomas Moore). In 1987, produced the first Spirituality and Business Conference—"The Heart of Business"—with more than a dozen multimillionaire entrepreneurs who had followed their hearts to great success.

Hobbies/personal interests: Warm-water sailing, Siddha yoga, the Dalai Lama.

Areas most interested in agenting: 100% Nonfiction only; my specialty is spirituality, health, personal growth, business. I represent many first-time authors, as well as clients who have been published before and several who have been published with 20 to 30 books each.

Areas not interested in agenting: Sorry, no fiction/no channeling, or any book written by an author without credentials, groundbreaking new content, charisma, and dedication to making it a bestseller.

If not agenting, what would you be doing? Book development, marketing strategy, and promotion for authors (which I also do now).

Best way to initiate contact: Please send your query and proposal with several sample chapters and a marketing plan with SASE. Also, your media kit, seminar brochures, videos. Please don't send e-mail files. Please use Jeff Herman's *Write the Perfect Book Proposal*.

Reading-fee policy: No reading fee. Consulting available for proposal development, marketing strategy, and promotion. I also refer out to book doctors/ghostwriters.

Client representation by category: Nonfiction, 100%.

Commission: 15%. I arrange for the publisher to set up separate accounts so that the author is paid directly.

Number of titles sold last year: 17.

Rejection rate (all submissions): 95%.

Most common mistakes authors make: They don't realize that publishing is a fiercely competitive business, that their book is seen as a product by editors. Publishers now are more interested in the ability of authors to promote themselves and their work than even in the book concept itself!

Description of the client from Hell: An author without credentials, exciting new content, or charisma who thinks that becoming a bestselling author is a hobby.

Description of a dream client: My clients! They have hearts. They inspire and educate me. Hardworking—willing to do whatever it takes—brilliant and fun.

Why did you become an agent? I promoted many authors on their way to the bestseller lists. It was thrilling. I find it even more exciting to work directly with authors, collaborating with them to develop their work and their careers.

What can writers do to enhance their chances of getting you as an agent? Be original! Be willing to work hard to develop your celebrity and your audience. Love yourself, your work, your world.

How would you describe what you actually do for a living? I'm a visionary, confidante, developer, coach, cheerleader, matchmaker, and marketer.

What do you think about editors? I deeply respect great editors. They are the vital link in bringing my clients' work to the public.

What do you think about publishers? Publishers all have their own personality or flavor. It's great fun identifying and matching what they want with my authors' expertise.

Comments: I want to make you a star if you have a great message that serves humanity on this beautiful blue pearl Earth.

Representative titles: *Two Questions* by Michael Ray (Scribner); *Healing Zen* by Ellen Birx (Viking); *Yoga RX* by Larry Payne (Broadway); *Kindling the Celtic Spirit* by Mar Freeman (HarperSanFrancisco); *Changewave Investing 2.0* by Tobin Smith (Doubleday/Currency); *Investing in Biotech* by Jim McCamant (Perseus); *Extreme Success* by Frank McKinney (John Wiley & Sons); *Power Yoga for Dummies* by Doug Swenson (Wiley); *Networking for Dummies* by Donna Fisher (Hungry Minds); *Advertising for Dummies* by Gary Dahl (Wiley); *Career Change for Dummies* by Carol McMelland (Wiley); *Drums for Dummies* by Jeff Strong (Wiley); *The Infertility Cure* by Randine Lewis (Little Brown); *Pilates Fusion* by Shirley Ancher (Chronicle Books); *Tough Issues, Great Results!* by Don Maruscka (Amacom).

THE PETER RUBIE LITERARY AGENCY

240 West 35th Street, Suite 500, New York, NY 10001

212-279-1776/212-279-1282   fax: 212-279-0927

www.prlit.com

Agents: Peter Rubie; June Clark (pralit@aol.com); Hanna Rubin; Jodi Weiss; Caren Johnson (sendmanuscript@aol.com).

Born: Rubie: May 3, 1950; Clark: March 1, 1957, New York City. Johnson: 9/3/81, Bronx, New York.

Education: Rubie: Journalism degree, NCTJ, England. Clark: B.A. in Creative Writing/Mass Communications, Queens College, NY. M.A. in Writing & Publishing, Emerson College, Boston, M.A. Johnson: B.A., English Lit, City College of NY.

Career history: Rubie: Fleet Street newspapers (England); BBC radio news (England); Fiction Editor, Walker & Co. (New York City); book doctor (New York City); literary agent; published novelist, and nonfiction writer. Adjunct Professor at New York University. Clark: Marketing and production in Cable TV (Showtime, Time Warner Cable); professional copywriter; published author, playwright. Rubin: Magazine editor prior to joining agency.

Hobbies/personal interests: Rubie: Movies, chess, politics/world affairs, music, science. Clark: Writing, reading, traveling, food and wine, socializing, and relaxing.

Areas most interested in agenting: Pop culture, business, history, pop science, strong narrative nonfiction, New Age, literate thrillers, literate crime novels, literate science fiction and fantasy, literary fiction, biography, women's issues, cooking and lifestyles, health and fitness, and parenting. Clark: Nonfiction: Commerical/perspective New Age; film, TV, music; health and beauty; reference, how-to; women's issues; sexuality and relationships; food and wine; topical issues for teens; biography; pets; and travel. Fiction: I rarely, if ever, represent fiction, as I'm incredibly picky and have little time to read manuscripts. Will occasionally be swayed by a page-turning mystery/thriller, "chick-lit" for women over 30, or something offbeat for a niche market. Rubin: History, travel, memoir. Johnson: Latino-based genre fiction (spec. romance, chick-lit, and mystery), Latino-based nonfiction, literary fiction, mystery, romance, narrative.

Areas not interested in agenting: Clark: Sci-fi, horror, fantasy; "boy" books; science; military history; Westerns; poetry; children's books; "I survived [whatever]" memoirs; short stories/novellas; anthologies of previously published "columns". Rubin: Romance, children's. Johnson: Poetry, science fiction, fantasy, screenplays, short stories.

If not agenting, what would you be doing? Rubie: Writing full-time. Clark: Writing full-time or working as a stand-up comedian. Rubin: Editing. Johnson: I'd be a book editor, own a bookstore, or be a professional shopper at Bergdorf.

Best way to initiate contact: Prefer query letter; e-mail occasionally. Rubin: E-mail or snail mail. Johnson: E-mail query or send letter by mail, query/proposal, and chapters 1–3.

Reading-fee policy: No reading fee.

Client representation: Nonfiction, 60%: Fiction, 40%. Rubin: Non-fiction, 50%; Fiction, 50%. Johnson: 80% fiction; 20% nonfiction.

Commission: 15% domestic; 20% foreign.

Number of titles sold last year: Rubie: 50; Clark: 35.

Rejection rate (all submissions): 95%. Rubin: I reject about 95%. Johnson: 90%.

Most common mistakes authors make: Overly cute approach, putting form over substance, unrealistic view of publishing, and being unprofessional. Clark: We get at least a dozen calls a day from authors wanting to verify our address. They can find this on our website or through information or this book! Also, when authors send us queries, they rarely tell us about their credentials as writers or their expertise in the area they are writing about. Who they are and what they know is as important as the book they are writing. Johnson: They don't treat their writing as a career. They don't submit queries/proposals with enough info for agent to make an informed decision.

Description of the client from Hell: Unprofessional, unrealistic expectations, no knowledge of the publishing industry, calls every day for news, does not listen to advice, and a control freak. Clark: Authors I'm considering taking on who want to brainstorm and/or get my input/advice on their project and then spring the news that they're going to work with another agent (after extracting all my ideas); aspiring authors whose egos are larger than their talents or who want the kudos without doing the work; having a client take a contract I spend a long and hard time negotiationg and having it reviewed by his/her attorney who usually knows nothing about publishing contracts; authors who don't tell me they are having problems (at home, at work, with family, with health, etc.) and can't deliver their manuscript on time until the day before their manuscript is contractually due to be delivered; check Amazon.com every five minutes to see their ranking and panic over it; being called or e-mailed relentlessly as to the "status" of their proposal/manuscript with publishers—if I had an offer, don't you think I'd call and tell you?! Rubin: Not writing clear query letters. One who persistently argues with advice. Johnson: One who treats an agent like a servant—constantly calling with lists of demands and for updates.

Description of a dream client: Dream clients know the market and how to present their material; take editorial input well; have patience. They call every six weeks or so, work with the agent as part of an effective team; are responsive, responsible, and thoroughly professional. Clark: Thankfully, I represent many "dream clients". They are the ones who are respectful of my time and input, enjoy the process of brainstorming, are game for working on any idea I present to them, are easy-going, enthusiastic, meet deadlines, write killer proposals quickly and fluidly, and most importantly, earn the respect and admiration of their editors who, in turn, keep coming back to them for more and more books. Rubin: One who is willing to carefully hone/revise/strengthen a proposal. Johnson: One who understands the publishing process & does everything in his or her power to assist both agent and publisher with making their book a success.

How did you become an agent? Was helping my agent/friend, Peter Rubie, read through the "slush pile" and found several book projects I liked. Was encouraged to pursue them and sold my first book in a few weeks—hence a new career was born. Rubin: I wanted to move into books and Peter spoke at a course I took. Johnson: I met Peter through a pub program at CCNY and started as an intern, progressed to agenting my own books.

Why did you become an agent? Rubie: To help discover new talent and help further the careers of established writers. As a writer, I try to be the sort of agent I would like to have. Clark: Initially, for the fun of it—it's a very sociable job and I love to meet new people with interesting ideas, talk on the phone and brainstorm, and "do lunch". I still find the work and the people stimulating—I learn something new every day from everyone I work with. I understand what makes a good book proposal as well as a good book (after studying writing and being a published writer in my own right) and feel I can be helpful to others. It's exciting to see a work progress from a seed of an idea to a finished product. Rubin: Because I love working closely with writers. Johnson: I enjoy working with authors both creatively and professionally to nurture and promote their work.

What can writers do to enhance their chances of getting you as an agent? Be mindful of the types of books I already represent so as not to waste my time or be disappointed by my rejection. Put together an intelligent cover letter that tells me, in a compelling way, about the merits of your book, your credentials and experience that directly relate to your book, and why I am the right agent to represent it. Rubin: Be polite, write, and report well, be willing to really craft work and learn the competition, not ignore it. Johnson: Writers should be professional, eager, and have a damn good idea to sell.

How would you describe what you actually do for a living? I like to say that I read for a living. It sounds quite scholarly and respectable.

What do you think about other agents? They are the mirror opposites of editors, and probably enjoy their job a lot more.

What do you think about editors? They are some of the most energetic, overworked, and interesting people I've worked with.

Comments: Rubie: I wish more writers considered themselves professionals and looked at their careers accordingly. To understand my philosophy of writing, read my books *The Elements of Storytelling* (John Wiley, 1996) or *Telling the Story* (HarperCollins).

Representative titles: *The Equity Culture* by B. Mark Smith (Farrar, Straus & Giroux); *On Night's Shore* by Randall Silvis (St. Martin's Press); *Jew Boy* by Alan Kaufman (Fromm); *The Emperor and the Wolf* by Stuart Galbrayth (Farber); *Soupy Sez* by Soupy Sales and Charles Sazberg (M. Evans & Co.); *Hope's End* by Stephen Chambers (TOR); *Einstein's Refrigerator* by Steve Silverman (Andrews McMeel); *Jaco* by Bill

Milkaoski (Backbeat); *An Askew View: The Films of Kevin Smith* by John Muir (Applause); *The Hope Valley Hubcap King* by Sean Murphy (Dell); *Walking Money* by James Born (Putnam); *Finishing Business* by Harlon Ullman (Naval Institute Press). Clark: *The Saucy Sisters Guide to Wine* by Barbara Nowak and Beverly Wicham (NAL); *BodyScopes* by Gabrielle Lichterman (AndrewsMcMeel); *Parenting Your Pooch* by Lynn Lott, Jane Nelson, and Therry Jay (Rodale); *Best in Show: The Films of Christopher Guest and Company* by John Kenneth Muir (Applause); *The Goddess Orgasm* by Jon P. Bloch (St. Martin's Press); *Mean Chick's Cliques and Dirty Tricks: A Girls Guide* by "Dr. Erika" Shearin Karres (Adams); and *A Hundred Years, A Million Laughs: The Friars Club 100th Anniversary* by Barry Doughtery (Emmis).

RUSSELL & VOLKENING, INC.

50 West 29th Street, Suite 7, New York, NY 10001

212-684-6050   fax: 212-889-3026

Agent: Joseph Regal

Education: English (Magna Cum Laude), Columbia College.

Career history: Professional musician after college; have been at Russell & Volkening for 11 years.

Hobbies/personal interests: Music (classical, rock, funk, blues, jazz, etc.), sports (basketball, tennis), art, anthropology, photography, science, philology, spirituality, travel, and design.

Areas most interested in agenting: I am interested in good stories, whether fiction (commonly called "literary") or nonfiction. I am especially interested in cultures with which I am unfamiliar—be they Pakistani, Greek, Irish, Thai, inner-city Cleveland, or the American South. In nonfiction, those stories tend to be narratives from science, history, and memoir—even photobooks and cookbooks. I look for voice more than subject.

Areas not interested in agenting: I don't handle romance, science fiction, or horror. Nor do I handle self-help, diet books, or prescriptive nonfiction.

If not agenting, what might you be doing? I'd be a musician, physicist, or priest.

Best way to initiate contact: Send a query letter with SASE, and if it's fiction, include a synopsis and the first five pages.

Client representation by category: Nonfiction, 50%; Fiction, 50%.

Commission: 15% commission, except on foreign contracts, which are 20%.

Number of titles sold last year: 22.

Rejection rate (all submissions): 99%.

Most common mistakes authors make: Because of the tremendous drain on our time and resources, the little things mean a lot when we look at query letters. It is truly astounding how many people send poorly written letters, rife with typos and grammatical errors. Why would we show your work more respect than you do? If you can't write a good letter, we're not going to be too enthusiastic about the prospects for the book.

Description of the client from Hell: There is no client from Hell. The relationship between author and agent is like any other: it flourishes when there are clear ground rules each party respects. If boundaries are transgressed, it is up to one party to communicate that to the other. While no one's perfect (including me), this almost always works.

Description of a dream client: Dream clients show me the same respect, patience, enthusiasm, and care I show them and their work.

How did you become an agent? Pretty much by accident; I was singing in a band in New York City and needed a day job. Since I loved books, I wanted to get into publishing and was lucky enough to land at a very fine agency. I had planned to remain an assistant, but within my first year I fell in love with three novels the other agents were rejecting and was allowed to offer my assistance to the writers. I sold all three (eventually) and found myself hooked.

Why did you become an agent? I love books and the next best thing to being a mother is being a midwife. I enjoy being involved in every stage of the publishing process and find it very satisfying to think that I have made a contribution through my advocacy of writers I admire.

What can writers do to enhance their chances of getting you as their agent? Good writing is what it always comes down to. Sometimes there might be something special that makes a difference if we're on the fence—a fascinating career, the support of a famous writer, incredible life experiences, being a 25-year-old ex-cover girl—but in the end, we'll take on anyone if the writing moves us.

How would you describe what you actually do for a living? I juggle: at any given moment I'm a talent scout, editor, psychologist, art consultant, lawyer, or salesman.

What do you think about editors? I don't have any thoughts about editors as a group. As with any group, there are good, bad, and indifferent. I do know it's not an easy job balancing the needs of your publishing house, your authors, and your passions.

What do you think about publishers? I think the publishing industry is slightly out of touch with the real world. When all you do is read books for a living, you can lose sight of how the average reader comes to books and how little time most people have for reading. This is manifested in different ways, but most obviously in marketing and publicity. In what other industry would the newest, least-experienced employees be in charge of promoting a product? Of course, that's if the product is actually promoted, which quite often it isn't—especially if it's literary fiction, which needs the most promotion, but often gets the least. Publishers need to re-imagine the whole promotional structure; a sea change is possible, but only if people believe it is possible.

Comments: It's a very exciting time for books; I feel that the threat of electronic publishing has helped awaken publishers from their collective slumber. Because of e-books and the Internet, everyone has begun to think about publishing in a slightly different way. I don't think most publishers or agents (including me) have grasped fully what the information revolution will mean—certainly not the end of books, as some fear—but there is a lot of energy now, and positive things are happening. One of the most cheering aspects is that publishers have begun to realize how important it is that they establish themselves as a brand, an arbiter of quality, in a world where any authors can put their work online and invite people to read it and buy it. If the means of delivery and distribution begins to slip away, it ironically places a greater emphasis on some of the old-fashioned aspects of publishing, editorial work in particular. One nice benefit has been a slight renaissance in the publishing of literary fiction, but there are bound to be other unexpected results. Where does that leave you? Do good work. Strive for excellence. Take pleasure in the work itself. The world will still recognize quality; it's only a question of how long it takes.

Representative titles: *Back When We Were Grownups* by Anne Tyler (Knopf); *The Pickup* by Nadine Gordimer (FSG); *Warriors of God* by James Reston Jr. (Doubleday); *No Certain Rest* by Jim Lehrer (Random House); *Daddy Says* by Ntozake Shange (Simon & Schuster); *Conscious Style Home* by Danny Seo (St. Martin's Press); *Veiled Courage* by Cheryl Benard (Broadway); *Hollow Ground* by Stephen Marion (Algonquin); *The Watermelon King* by Daniel Wallace (Houghton Mifflin); *Dirt Music* by Tim Winton (Scribner); *The First Americans* by Dr. James Adovasio and Jake Page (Random House); *Interrogation* by Thomas H. Cook (Bantam).

THE SAGALYN LITERARY AGENCY

7201 Wisconsin Ave, Suite 675, Bethesda, MD 20814

301-718-6440

Agent: Raphael Sagalyn
Areas most interested in agenting: Adult fiction and nonfiction.
Areas not interested in agenting: Cookbooks, children's, screenplays, poetry.
Best way to initiate contact: Send a query letter outlining your professional experience and a brief synopsis by e-mail to agency@sagalyn.com.
Representative titles: *When Pride Still Mattered* and *First In His Class* by David Maraniss (Simon & Schuster); *The Long Gray Line* and *An Army at Dawn* by Rick Atkinson (Henry Holt); *Agents of Innocence, a novel* by David Ignatius; *Spin Cycle* by Howard Kurtz (Free Press); *Innumeracy* by John Allen Paulos (FSG); *The Moral Animal* and *Nonzero* by Robert Wright (Pantheon); *Rising Tide* by John Barry (Simon & Schuster); *The Corner* by David Simon (Broadway); *Strange Justice* by Jill Abramson and Jane Mayer (HMCo); *Generations* by Bill Strauss and Neil Howe (Morrow) ; *See No Evil* by Bob Baer (Crown); *The Work of Nations* and *Locked In the Cabinet* by Robert Reich (Knopf); *Bowling Alone* by Robert Putnam (Simon & Schuster).

VICTORIA SANDERS & ASSOCIATES

241 Avenue of the Americas, New York, NY 10014

212-633-8811

e-mail: queriesvsa@hotmail.com

Agent: Victoria Sanders
Born: Hollywood, California.
Education: B.F.A., New York University, 1983; J.D., Benjamin N. Cardozo School of Law, 1988.
Areas most interested in agenting: Fiction: literary and commercial. Nonfiction: history, biography, politics, sociology, psychology. Special interests: African-American, Latin, women's, gay and lesbian work.
Areas not interested in agenting: Hard science, children's, textbooks, and poetry.
If not agenting, what would you be doing? A producer or furniture designer.
Best way to initiate contact: Only accepting e-mail queries. Send query to queriesvsa@hotmail.com.
Reading-fee policy: No reading fee.
Client representation by category: Nonfiction, 50%; Fiction, 50%.
Commission: 15% straight; 20% if co-agented foreign; 20% film; and 15% TV commission.
Number of titles sold last year: 22.
Rejection rate (all submissions): 90%.
Most common mistakes authors make: Rambling queries, typos, no SASE, multiple books printed in a letter.
Description of the client from Hell: Negative personality.
Description of the dream client: Hardworking, dedicated writers with their heads screwed on tight.
What can writers do to enhance their chances of getting you as an agent? Well-written, attention-grabbing letter. Knowledge of other authors we represent and reasons why they believe they would fit in well.
How would you describe what you actually do for a living? I am an advocate for writers.
How did you become an agent? After law school I worked in the contracts/legal department of Simon & Schuster for almost three years. I was very unhappy in the corporate world but loved publishing. I went into agenting because I felt that writers have historically been treated poorly.
Why did you become an agent? It's the best of both worlds. I get to read manuscripts and negotiate deals. I came from L.A. and film and, after getting a law degree, realized that the best part of the entertainment business was in bridging the gap between the writer or artist and the producer or publisher. I love being the representative and friend of my clients.

What do you think about editors? They are an incredibly smart, dedicated, and mostly underpaid group.

What do you think about publishers? A few great ones still exist.

What were your favorite films last year? *Monsters Ball; Far From Heaven; Songcatcher.*

Do you watch *The Sopranos?* Oh, yeah.

Representative titles: *Can't Stop, Won't Stop: Portraits of Hip Hop Generation* by Jeff Chang (St. Martin's Press); *Indelible* by Karin Slaughter; *Partners to History* by Donzaleigh Abernathy; *My Jim* by Nancy Rawles.

SCHIAVONE LITERARY AGENCY, INC.

236 Trails End, West Palm Beach, FL 33413-2135

voice/fax: 561-966-9294

e-mail: profschia@aol.com

Agent: James Schiavone, Ed.D.

Born: New York City.

Education: B.S., M.A., New York University; Ed.D., Nova University; Professional Diploma, Columbia University.

Career history: Professor Emeritus of Developmental Skills at the City University of New York; Literary Agent.

Areas most interested in agenting: Celebrity biography; autobiography; memoirs; nonfiction. Fiction: mainstream, commercial, and literary; thrillers and mysteries; romances, historical. Children's: all genres of fiction and nonfiction.

Areas not interested in agenting: Poetry; short stories.

If not agenting, what would you be doing? Teaching graduate courses in the psychology of reading; writing nonfiction.

Best way to initiate contact: Queries only via post. Include brief bio-sketch, synopsis, previous books published. No response without SASE. No phone calls, faxes. One-page e-mail queries are acceptable, absolutely NO attachments.

Reading-fee policy: No reading fee.

Client representation by category: Nonfiction, 51%; Fiction, 41%; Children's, 5%; Textbooks, 3%.

Commission: 15% domestic; 20% foreign.

Number of titles sold last year: 17.

Rejection rate (all submissions): 90%.

Most common mistakes authors make: Failure to query first, no SASE, send unsolicited manuscript, expect agency to download entire manuscript via e-mail, make initial contact via phone/fax.

Description of a dream client: One who is a published, successful author.

How did you become an agent? It was a natural segue from academia.

Why did you become an agent? I have enjoyed a lifetime love of books and reading. I served as a reading specialist in schools and colleges and authored five trade books and three textbooks. I enjoy representing creative people and helping them to sell their work.

How would you describe what you actually do for a living? Sell creative work of authors/clients to major publishing houses; negotiate contracts; handle business details—enabling authors to concentrate on the craft of writing.

What do you think about editors? I have been fortunate in working with the best editors in the industry. Generally, they are conscientious, indefatigable, and sincere in bringing an author's work to press. Agenting would be impossible without them.

What do you think about publishers? They are the backbone of the industry. I am grateful for the serious consideration they give to my highly selective submissions.

Comments: While I prefer working with authors published by major houses, I do encourage submissions from highly creative, talented first-time authors.

Representative Titles: *The Lightning Shrikes* (novel) by Devon Mihesuah (Lyons Press); *A Short History of Taiwan: The Case for Independence* by Gary Marvin Davison, Ph.D. (Praeger, Greenwood Publishing Group); *From Ace to Zummo: A Dictionary of Numerologically Based Names for Your Pet* by Ellin Dodge, America's foremost numerologist (Fireside/Simon & Schuster); *Friendly Persuasion* by David Yount (Sterling House).

WENDY SCHMALZ AGENCY

Box 831, Hudson NY, 12534

515-672-7697   fax: 518-672-7662

e-mail: wschmalz@earthlink.net

Agent: Wendy Schmalz

Education: Barnard, B.A.

Career history: I was an agent at Harold Ober Associates for several years. I opened my own agency in June 2002.

Areas most interested in agenting: Adult and children's fiction and nonfiction.

Areas not interested in agenting: Sci-fi, fantasy, picture books for children, romance.

Reading-fee policy: No fee.

Client representation by category: 50% children's; 25% adult fiction; 25% adult non-fiction.

Commission: 15% domestic; 20% foreign.

Number of titles sold last year: 25.
Rejection rate (all submissions): 95%.

SUSAN SCHULMAN—A LITERARY AGENCY

454 West 44th Street, New York, NY 10036

212-713-1633   fax: 212-581-8830

Second Office: 2 Bryan Plaza, Washington Depot, CT 06794

860-868-3700   fax: 860-868-3704

www. SchulmanAgency.com   e-mail: Schulman@aol.com

Agents: Owner, Susan Schulman; Rights Director, Eleanora Tevis; Submissions Editor, Linda Migalti; Acqusitions Editor, Emily Rhea; Business Affairs, Sandra Gannon

Educational History: B.A. Summa Cum Laude; M.A. Summa Cum Laude, Phi Beta Kappa.

Career History: Former college teacher specializing in History of the English Language, Linguistics, and and Old English.

Areas most interested in agenting: Books for, by, and about women; psychology, popular culture, contemporary history, business and management, and health-related topics, children's books. Our agency also represents playwrights and composers and lyricists for the stage. We also act as foreign rights agents for Millbrook Press, Mid-List Press, Inner Ocean Publications, and Fairview Press, among other small publishers.

Areas not interested in agenting: Religion, fantasy, technical books.

Best way to initiate contact: The best contact is through personal recommendation or a letter of inquiry, including a synopsis of the work and an SASE.

Reading-fee policy: No reading fee. We are a member of the AAR.

Commission: 15% new clients; 20% for foreign sales.

Client representation: 20% fiction, 50% nonfiction, 20% children's, 10% plays and screenplays.

Rejection rate (all submissions): 95%. I regret that most submissions are returned for work or forwarded to another agent. About 3% of the unsolicited submissions become active.

Most common mistakes authors make: The most common mistakes are calling to inquire about their letter of inquiry or to pitch their project over the phone, and failure to include SASE. The larger mistakes include unfinished work, unpolished writing, and ill-prepared proposals.

Why did you become an agent? I love business and I love to read. Literary representation is like Christmas to me. Each new package offers the potential to enjoy the read and to sell it so others may as well.

What can writers do to enhance their chances of getting you as an agent? We appreciate writers who have done their homework—writers who have taken the time to educate themselves on the publishing industry and a bit about the process of literary representation. We seek enthusiastic self-starters.

Representative titles: *Rise of the Creative Class* by Richard Florida (Basic Books); *The Half Empty Heart* by Alan Downs (St. Martin's Press); *The Candymen* by Nile Southern (Arcade Books); *The History of Xerography* by David Owen (Simon and Schuster); *Ungodly: Madlyn Murray O'Hare* by Theodore Dracos; *Along the Coast* by Jim Arnosky (HarperCollins Childrens Books); *Holes: The Play* by Louis Sachar, *Lilly's Purple Plastic Purse* adapted for the stage by Kevin Kling.

SEBASTIAN LITERARY AGENCY

172 E. Sixth Street, #2005, St. Paul, MN 55101-1978

651-224-6670

www.sebastianagency.com

Agents: Laurie Harper, Founder and Agent; Dawn Frederick, Associate Agent; Hillary Smith, Assistant Agent

Born: Harper: September 1954; Frederick: March 1975; Smith: October, 1980.

Education: Harper: Business and finance, with pre-law studies. Frederick: Bachelor's in Early Childhood Education and a Master's in Information Sciences. Smith: Bachelor's in English Literature and Art History.

Career history: Harper: The literary agency was founded in 1985. It evolved simultaneously with the closing of my small Bay Area regional publishing company (Sebastian Publishing), which published gift books, selling to B. Dalton, Waldenbooks, and independents throughout the West Coast. After I placed books with other publishers for authors I could not publish, I discovered my strengths as an agent. Frederick: I joined the agency in early 2003. Previously I was a bookseller, worked for a YA nonfiction publisher, and interned at a University Press (during my college studies). Smith: I joined the agency in late 2003 after completing the Denver publishing program. I also interned in the Editorial department for *Twin Cities Business Monthly Magazine* and was a staff writer for a local newspaper.

Hobbies/personal interests: Harper: Sailing, rollerblading, shooting hoops, movies, but mostly riding my motorcycle. Frederick: Reading, movies, darts, *Buffy the Vampire Slayer*, travel—so many ways to have fun, so little time. Smith: Running, reading, traveling, good conversation, cooking, independent films. Special personal interest in political history, art history, biographies, art culture in the 1920s.

Areas most interested in agenting: Harper: Narrative nonfiction across a broad spectrum (though not family memoirs); consumer reference; health, nutrition, medical issues; psychology/sociology, current affairs/journalism, business (management, careers, business stories), and various books/topics that target mainstream educated readers. Frederick: Biography (Historical, media-related, professional, political), Fiction (Women's Literature, Genre, Mainstream Fiction), Young Adult (Fiction and Nonfiction), Popular Culture (especially Americana), Sports, Social Issues/Current Affairs, and History. Smith: At this early stage, my focus is on literary fiction, as well as serious and creative nonfiction appealing to those in their 20s and 30s (including popular culture), though I am taking on few authors this first year.

Areas not interested in agenting: No poetry, children's, original screenplay material, gift books, religious, academic, or scholarly. We would also note that most memoirs will not work for us, unless the author is established.

If not agenting, what would you be doing? Harper: I would most likely be in contract law, perhaps working for the Authors Guild. Frederick: I would start my own business, of some kind! Smith: I would more than likely be living in a foreign country, teaching English or helping out where my capabilities would be put to good use.

Best way to initiate contact: Send a query letter explaining the project, who you are, and why you are doing this book. Feel free to include the proposal, outline, and a sample chapter. And, of course, the SASE. We do not want phone calls unless the author has been referred to us by a client or colleague. E-mail queries are fine without attachments (see website for further information).

Reading-fee policy: No reading fee or editorial fee.

Client representation by category: Nonfiction, 99%; Fiction, 1%.

Commission: 15% domestic; 20% foreign.

Number of titles sold last year: It usually averages 20-25.

Rejection rate (all submissions): 98%. The majority of new clients come from referrals from our clients or industry professionals and colleagues. However, every submission is read and considered on its own merit.

Most common mistakes authors make: It is a costly mistake to use anything other than the current year's resource material when exploring potential agents, due to the constant changes in the industry. It is also counterproductive to query without providing the agent with sufficient orientation and information. We are reading the proposal cold. The author has to make it make sense; give it a proper framework. Demonstrate that you know the market for your book; what's been published, how your book fits into the scheme of things. You must answer the obvious questions: Who cares? Why? Are these book-buying people? How many are there? Can anyone find them? What do you specifically have to offer a publisher who would invest in this project? Publishing is, after all, first and foremost a business. . .not an endowment for the arts or for hobbyists.

Description of the client from Hell: The first thing has to be unrealistic expectations: financial and promotional expectations that are simply not realistic for as-yet-unproven authors. For previously unpublished authors, it's understandable that they don't know the industry, but it is incumbent upon prospective authors to inform themselves on the basics. Attend some conferences; do some reading; talk to other published authors. I'm happy to coach an author about strategy or problem solving, to help plan out a realistic publishing career path, but the agent can't be in charge of teaching Publishing 101. Another difficulty comes if the author expects the agent to perform miracles: We can't sell what isn't saleable. It is the author's responsibility to consider and reflect upon the feedback given by agents and publishers and to use that to improve the manuscript's potential for publication. We expect our clients to be mature professional adults, capable of approaching this process positively and constructively.

Your description of a dream client: Professional, focused, market-driven writers who are flexible enough to work with the whole "team" that a publisher brings to the book publishing process. And patient—patience and persistence are big pluses in publishing, as is a sense of humor.

Comments: The challenge facing every author and publisher (and therefore agent) is how to reach a readership, how to get people to buy this particular book. It isn't a matter of "Put it out there and they will come." Accordingly, our decisions about which authors to partner with are based on many elements. Aside from the book itself, we consider the talents of the writer and what the writer brings to the marketing and promotion of that book. We also have to balance our overall client list. And, certainly, we evaluate the timing of your book for the specific category and market. The best advice we can give a writer is to only write the books you have to write, that book for which you have passion, skill, and ability to promote and market over many years. As agents, we are focused on books and authors that can compete at a national level for readers' precious attention.

Representative titles: An as-yet-untitled Betty Crocker biography by Susan Marks (Simon & Schuster); *The Other Side of Eden* by John Steinbeck IV and Nancy Steinbeck (Prometheus); *Forget Perfect!* by Lisa McLeod (Perigee-Putnam); *Two in The Field* by Darryl Brock (Plume); *Short Cycle Selling* by Jim Kasper (McGraw-Hill); *Bounce Your Body Beautiful* by Liz Applegate (Prima/Random); *It Ends With You* by Tina Tessina (New Page Books); *The Warren Buffett Way, Second Edition* by Robert Hagstrom (Wiley); *The Third Age: 6 Principles for Growth and Renewal After Forty* by William Sadler (Perseus Books); *Too Nice For Your Own Good* by Duke Robinson (Warner); *The Art of the Advantage* by Kaihan Krippendorf (Texere).

THE SEYMOUR AGENCY

475 Miner Street, Canton, NY 13617

315-386-1831   fax: 315-386-1037

www.theseymouragency.com   e-mail: marysue@slic.com

Agent: Mary Sue Seymour
Born: September 21.
Education: B.S., State University of Potsdam, New York; postgraduate work with

Potsdam State, Ithaca College.

Career history: Taught 11 years in the public school system; former professional artist; former freelance writer published in national magazines.

Hobbies/personal interests: Piano, reading, alpine skiing, swimming, hiking, camping in the Adirondacks.

Areas most interested in agenting: Christian romance, Christian self-help, romance, Westerns, and general nonfiction, business books, prescriptive books, literary novels, young adult fiction.

Areas not interested in agenting: Short stories, screenplays, poetry.

If not agenting, what would you be doing? Writing and painting.

Best way to initiate contact: Short query letter and first 50 pages of novel or nonfiction proposal w/sample chapter.

Reading-fee policy: No.

Client representation by category: Nonfiction, 40%; Fiction, 50%; Children's, 5%; Textbooks, a few.

Commission: 12.5% published authors; 15% unpublished.

Number of titles sold last year: Several.

Rejection rate (all submissions): 95%.

Description of the client from Hell: Never had one.

Description of the dream client: Dream clients are those who write a lot, use suggestions, are enthusiastic about their writing, appreciate what we try to do for them, and send us books we can sell.

How did you become an agent? I listed myself in a writer's guide and sold a four-book contract with our first submission. I guess it was just meant to be.

Why did you become an agent? I love books—reading and learning—and I enjoy each of the diverse challenges of publishing. Books are fundamental to our society, and I take pride in being part of their contribution. There is enormous satisfaction from creating a successful team—making the right match between author and publisher, negotiating a fair contract that promotes a successful venture, and assisting in every way to build long-lasting relationships.

What can writers do to enhance their chances of getting you as an agent? Being professionally polite, and a sense of humor doesn't hurt either.

Common mistakes authors make: Send a fax. Include no SASE and expect me to call them. Try to write a snappy cover letter without actually describing their project. For example, is it fiction or nonfiction? If it's fiction, what genre is it?

How would you describe what you actually do for a living? Attend conferences such as Romancing the Rockies in 2003, The London Book Fair in 2003, Christian Booksellers Association in Orlando 2003, Romance Writers of America National in NYC 2003, Put Your Heart in a Book in NJ 2003, the Chesapeake Bay Romance Writers Conference 2003, Star Bright/Star Write in Houston 2003, BEA in Los Angeles 2003. Work seven days a week, try to keep our clients feeling good about themselves, work with contracts and royalties, and keep accurate records of all of the above.

What do you think about editors? Editors are professionals who know their stuff. They work long hours and bring too much work home (any is too much).

What were your favorite films last year? The only movie I saw last year was *Pirates of the Caribbean*. Loved the beautiful scenery and escapist plot! *My Fair Lady*, *Phantom of the Opera*, and *Stomp* were musicals I saw in London last spring. Would love to see *My Fair Lady* and *Stomp* again. I also saw *42nd Street* and *The Producers* in NYC last summer. Loved Tom Wopat in *42nd Street* and *The Producers* was really funny.

Comments: If a writer wants to get published, he/she needs to study the market and target a book to a publisher that is buying that type of book. The publishing industry isn't (unfortunately) what it was ten years ago. It's a tough business. If an agent or editor rejects your project, keep in mind the house may have really liked it but couldn't take it on in present economic conditions. Mary Sue is a member of RWA, The Author's Guild and AAR.

While in school we learned rules of writing that don't apply in today's commercial market. Keep your writing crisp and to the point. A rejection isn't a judgement of your character; writing is a business. You must approach industry professionals with projects that will make money for their company. Remember agents work on commission. They won't take a new project on that has only a minimal chance of selling.

Representative titles: Award-winning author Gail Sattler's four-book inspirational romance deal; Christie Craig's *250 Questions Every Home Buyer Should Ask*; Sandra Detrixhe's *The Zen and Art of Sewing*; Barbara Cameron's *The Everything Robert's Rules Book*; Betty Alt and Sandra Wells's *Cops in Skirts*; Sandra Detrixhe's *The Everything Sewing Book*; Brent Manley's *The Bridge Book* and *The Tao and Art of Bridge*; Shelley Sabga's *Finding Love in Payton*; Carolyn Jewel's historical romance titled *The Spare*; Meg and Sean Clemens's *The Math Puzzle Book*; Betty Alt's *Fleecing Grandma and Grandpa*.

THE ROBERT E. SHEPARD AGENCY

1608 Dwight Way, Berkeley, CA 94703

510-849-3999

www.shepardagency.com   e-mail: query@shepardagency.com

Agent: Robert Shepard

Education: B.A., M.A. in English, University of Pennsylvania.

Career history: Last year, I celebrated the Agency's 10th anniversary and my 20th year in the publishing industry. Much has changed since I started out in the trade division of Addison-Wesley, a respected publisher that has since passed into history. But my background on the editorial, sales, and marketing sides of publishing gave me a good understanding of the "business" side, including managing millions of dollars in sales, and excellent working relationships with scores of acquisitions editors. I bring all of that, a passion for nonfiction, and a healthy skepticism about the state of the publishing industry to bear in working with my clients. I enjoy helping them craft their proposals, sharing ideas with them as they write their books, helping them decide on the topics for their future works, and working with them to build their writing careers. I enjoy the process of actually selling their books, and celebrating with my clients when the contract is signed and the advance check issued. The role of agents in the work of authors has become ever more critical. I'm proud of the close rapport I've established with authors and remain committed to the idea that books are the foundation of our culture; everything else springs from them. Since I love nonfiction, it's especially gratifying to see literary nonfiction works enjoying renewed success. This is an excellent time to be a nonfiction author, and I believe the works on my list have played a role in that.

Hobbies/personal interests: Hiking, biking, trains, raptors, and diagramming sentences.

Areas most interested in agenting: I represent only nonfiction, and under that heading I've cultivated two separate categories of books. The first consists of works driven by an exceptionally strong, unified, literary narrative—books intended to make complex ideas accessible to a wider public; to shed new light on aspects of history, society, or popular culture; or to provide fresh insights into people, places, or concepts we may think of as commonplace. On this side of the practice, my subject headings include history, contemporary affairs and politics, science for laypeople, and topics in culture, sexuality, urbanism, and even sports. The other general category of books I represent tends to be driven less by narrative and more by hard information; on this side, I have a core interest in personal finance and investing, business, and series-oriented works in such areas as music and general reference. It's safe to say that I'm interested in neither the most commercial nor the most abstruse kinds of books; but I'm happy to represent works that change readers' minds, that may require a somewhat more intellectually curious audience, or about which someone might say, "I never thought this would be an interesting subject, but this book was a super read!"

Areas not interested in agenting: I never handle fiction, poetry, screenplays, or textbooks, and in general I'm not interested in autobiographical works—even when they relate in some way to my regular categories. (In other words, I most likely wouldn't represent a book on your sailing trip through the South Pacific, during which you played the clarinet; but I might represent a history of that region—or a biography of Benny Goodman). Robert E. Shepard Agency titles are usually aimed at a broad audience, so that highly specialized works (such as ones that examine religious writings in detail, or whose intended readers are mainly in a single profession) are not appropriate. As a general rule, I'm also not interested in works on New Age spirituality, self-help, or recovery.

If not agenting, what would you be doing? It could go one of three ways: Either I would go back and get that Ph.D. and write papers on 19th-century authors who were extremely prominent in their day but who paradoxically have become totally obscure (probably due to bad marketing), or I would be conducting a symphony orchestra, or I would be riding trains somewhere in an attempt to escape my job as publisher of a distinguished literary nonfiction house. I'm not picky.

Best way to initiate contact: Never call or fax; neither will speed consideration of your proposal. I encourage authors to mail a query letter or proposal or to e-mail a relatively brief query describing the proposed work, its intended audience, and the author's own credentials and reason for writing on this subject. Don't just refer me to a website; I want to see how you present your ideas in the succinct form demanded by a query letter, whether by mail or e-mail. Please do not attach any computer files to e-mail messages; for security purposes, they'll be deleted. If you use regular mail, always enclose a postage-paid return envelope capable of holding everything you sent me, without which you will not receive a reply.

Reading-fee policy: No reading fee.

Client representation by category: Nonfiction, 100%.

Commission: 15% domestic, 20% for "subagented" foreign rights.

Number of titles sold last year: 10. I have deliberately kept the practice small in order to devote time to my clients. I am happy to see proposals from new authors or from authors whose previous works may have been in genres other than general nonfiction. However, your credentials and expertise should be suited to the kind of book you're proposing.

Rejection rate (all submissions): 99%.

Most common mistakes authors make: A big one is failing to share the proposal with a friend, another writer, or a trusted adviser before sending it out. Authors who work in a vacuum risk losing perspective. In the many months you've been working on your book proposal—and very often they really do take that long to write—has your focus shifted inadvertently? Have you failed to discuss some aspect of your topic that an agent or editor might find fascinating—simply because you're too immersed in writing to realize you'd missed it? Have you cited a date or name incorrectly, making yourself look careless even though you really do know your facts? A trusted adviser, particularly one with experience in writing books, can help you improve your proposal or even catch mistakes before you send it to agents. Not to sound like the English teacher I sometimes think I should have been, but bad spelling and grammar often guarantee rejection slips, too. Proofread your work, and if you don't trust your proofreading skills, find someone you do trust to help you. I also counsel authors to avoid proposal clichés. A big one is "there's no competition for my book." You should always try to find works that others might consider competitive, and then describe what's new, different, and better about yours. Finally, there are two important housekeeping issues: Always enclose a return envelope large enough to hold your material, with the proper postage (without which you won't get a response); and always provide your return address.

Description of the client from Hell: One who's good at selling an agent or editor on a book but doesn't want to actually write it. Writing is tough and an agent tries to help, but in the end the responsibility is the author's.

Description of a dream client: Those who are passionate about writing, passionate about their subjects, and appreciative when things go right.

Why did you become an agent? I love books and believe they can and should still be central to our cultural life, even in an era when they're being joined by new sources of entertainment and information all the time. But the consolidations of leading publishers during the 1990s resulted in the loss of many editors, the very people who traditionally worked the closest with authors, helped them craft better books, and made sure that the marketing got done. The vast majority of today's editors are as talented and dedicated as ever but find themselves with more books to edit and less time to spend with authors. So although authors create the intellectual property that fuels our culture, they can feel lost in the publishing shuffle, confused by business aspects of their writing careers, and even disillusioned by the paradoxical demand of publishers to write "fresh" books that nonetheless don't deviate much from the constraints of established categories. I see my role as an agent as that of a mentor and advocate for my clients and their work, as a diplomat who can moderate the author-publisher relationship, as a business adviser who watches over royalty statements, and, in the end, as someone who helps authors feel good about the writing experience, so they can write more books in the future. The bad news, unfortunately, is that a good part of an agent's day is still spent saying "no." The good news is that great books by new and established authors are written and published every day. When everything works as it should, the wealth of media outlets available to us in the Internet age means that books can be more, rather than less, influential.

What can writers do to enhance their chances of getting you as an agent? Go to a good independent bookstore. It's essential for authors to have some perspective on their work, and that means knowing all about books that are similar, or that an agent might mistake as being similar, and (in another vein) being able to talk about authors you respect whose work is in some ways akin to yours. There's nothing more helpful to me than a short overview that answers questions like these: Why did you write this book? What need does it fill? What audience do you envision? What are some books like yours, even if they are terrible (and say why)? Why are you the right person to write this book? What would you like your work to achieve that hasn't been achieved before? Browsing in bookstores, and buying and reading a few recent works, can be very helpful as you answer those questions. I recommend libraries, too, but it's essential to stay current.

Representative titles: *Word Freak: Heartbreak, Triumph, Genius, and Obsession in the World of Competitive Scrabble Players* by Stefan Fatsis (Houghton Mifflin HC, Penguin PB—a bestseller, soon to be a feature film); *Coal: A Human History* by Barbara Freese (Penguin—also a bestseller); *Leave the Office Earlier* by Laura Stack (Broadway Books); *The Root of Wild Madder: Journeys Into the Passion, Lore and Soul of the Persian Carpet* by Brian Murphy (Simon & Schuster); *In the Court of Public Opinion* by James F Haggerty (John Wiley & Sons); *Wine & War: The French, the Nazis, and the Battle for France's Greatest Treasure* (Broadway Books—an international bestseller); *The Biotech Investor* by Tom Abate (Times Books/ Henry Holt).

WENDY SHERMAN ASSOCIATES, INC.

450 Seventh Avenue, Suite 3004, New York, NY 10123

212-279-9027   fax: 212-279-8863

www.wsherman.com   e-mail: wendy@wsherman.com

Agent: Wendy Sherman
Born: New York City.
Education: Bachelor's Degree in Special Education.
Career history: Opened this agency in 1999. Was previously with the Aaron Priest Agency. Vice President Executive Director at Henry Holt, Vice President Associate Publisher at Owl Books, Vice President Sales and Subsidiary Rights (1988–1999). Also worked at Simon & Schuster and Macmillan.

Hobbies/personal interests: Reading, skiing, walking, traveling.
Areas most interested in agenting: Quality fiction, thrillers, suspense, narrative nonfiction.
Areas not interested in agenting: Genre fiction such as science fiction, fantasy, horror, mysteries, romance, and children's books.
If not agenting, what would you be doing? I could be back in corporate publishing, but choose not to pursue that career path.
Best way to initiate contact: Query letter via regular mail to agency.
Reading-fee policy: No.
Client representation by category: Nonfiction, 50%; Fiction, 50%.
Commission: 15% domestic; 20% foreign.
Number of titles sold last year: 18.
Rejection rate (all submissions): 99%.
Most common mistakes authors make: The most common mistake is not properly targeting the right agent. Writers should do their research as to who seems to be a good fit for their material. I would also have to say that prospective clients should have some patience. We receive 100+ submissions per week and read them all. In addition, it's important to remember that what counts is finding the right agent—one who really sees the potential for the book—not just finding any agent. We no longer accept e-mail queries, and do not open attachments. I like to be informed if other agencies are being queried at the same time. Once we ask to read the manuscript, we prefer exclusivity for a reasonable time period.
Description of the client from Hell: The client from Hell is unreasonably demanding and doesn't trust my judgment and experience.
Description of a dream client: The perfect collaboration between agent and author is one of mutual goals and respect.

How did you become an agent? After leaving Henry Holt, I had the opportunity to work for the Aaron Priest Agency. I had thought about agenting for some time, and it seemed like the perfect way to make the change from working for a publisher to becoming an agent.

Why did you become an agent? 20+ years as a publisher led me to this career. I sold subsidiary rights for most of my career and love selling and negotiating, I opened this agency because I wanted to be able to offer my clients the benefit of my publishing experience, while enjoying the opportunities and challenges associated with owning one's own business.

How would you describe what you actually do for a living? We bring writers to the attention of the best possible/most enthusiastic editor and publisher. We then do our best to ensure the book is published with the utmost enthusiasm.

What do you think about editors? More than ever, editors have a very tough job. They not only have to find manuscripts they want to publish, but then convince in-house colleagues in editorial, marketing, and sales to support the acquisitions.

What do you think about publishers? It's tougher than ever for publishers to make money these days. We need to work together and have mutually respectful and collaborative relationships.

Comments: For me, being an agent is the best of all worlds. I get to work with writers I care about and help make their dreams come true. In my role as an agent I have been able to expand upon my relationships with editors and publishers. I am always looking for the next amazing novel or nonfiction project. While most of our new clients come from referrals, we consider every query we receive and in spite of the enormous amount of material we have to decline, I never lose my optimism that I'll find something wonderful. The challenge as an agent is to take on what you feel strongly about and what you are confident you can sell. Not just take on clients to say you have them. That said, we are very selective.

Representative titles: Fiction: *Massachusetts, California, Timbuktu* by Stephanie Rosenfeld (Ballantine); *Crawling at Night* and *The Good Remains* by Nani Power (Grove/Atlantic); *Flashover* by Suzanne Chazin (Putnam); *Star Witness* and *Breach of Trust* by DW Buffa (Putnam); *Fatal Flaw* and *Past Due* by William Lashner (Morrow) *The Ice Chorus* by Sarah Stonich (Little, Brown); *Househusband* and *Southern Living* by Ad Hudler (Ballantine); *The Cloud Atlas* by Liam Callanan (Delacorte); *Schopenhauer's Telescope* by Gerard Donovan (Counterpoint); *The Real Minerva* by Mary Sharratt (Houghton Mifflin). Nonfiction: *Alvin Ailey Dance Moves!* by Lise Friedman (Stewart Tabori and Chang) ; *Ten on Sunday* by Alan Eisenstock (Atria Books); *Why Does He Do That?* and *When Dad Hurts Mom* by Lundy Bancroft; *Real Love* by Dr. Greg Baer (Gotham Books); *Still With Me* by Andrea King Collier (Simon & Schuster); *The Holy Thief* by Rabbi Mark Borovitz and Alan Eisenstock (Morrow).

JACQUELINE SIMENAUER LITERARY AGENCY, INC.

PO Box A.G., Mantoloking, NJ 08738

732-262-0783   fax: 732-262-0825

Agents: Fran Pardi, Jacqueline Simenauer

Born: Simenauer: February 23, 1949, New York. Pardi: 1949, Pittsburgh, Pennsylvania.

Education: Simenauer: Fordham University. Pardi: B.A. in English.

Career history: Simenauer: Editor, World Wide Features, Inc.; President, Psychiatric Syndication Service, Inc.; freelance writer and co-author: *Beyond the Male Myth* (Times Books); *Husbands and Wives* (Times Books); *Singles: The New Americans* (Simon & Schuster); *Not Tonight Dear* (Doubleday); *Singles Guide to Cruise Vacations* (Prima Publishing). Pardi: Strong journalism background; freelance writer, and editor.

Hobbies/personal interests: Simenauer: Cruising the world. Pardi: Music, reading, dance, theater.

Areas most interested in agenting: Simenauer: I like a wide range of strong commercial nonfiction books that includes medical, health, nutrition, popular psychology, how-to, self-help, parenting, women's issues, spirituality, men's issues, relationships, social sciences, fashion, beauty, business, computers, reference. Pardi: Cookbooks, medical books, and fiction.

Areas not interested in agenting: Poetry, crafts, children's books.

If not agenting, what would you be doing? Simenauer: Become an entrepreneur. Pardi: Probably sitting on a beach or in front of a fireplace reading published books, as opposed to unpublished books.

Best way to initiate contact: Simenauer: I prefer a query letter with SASE. Pardi: Query letter with SASE.

Reading-fee policy: No reading fee.

Client representation by category: Nonfiction, 95%; Fiction, 5%.

Commission: 15%.

Rejection rate (all submissions): Simenauer: 95%. Pardi: 98%.

Most common mistakes authors make: Simenauer: Call and tell you that other agents are interested and want to know what you will do for them if they decide to go with you (and this is before you have even had a chance to see their material). Pardi: Cute gimmicks or self-platitudes. What's on the paper is the only thing that matters.

Description of the client from Hell: Simenauer: One who keeps calling for all sorts of reasons. Doesn't send SASE, yet demands material back. Calls collect. Calls with long-winded query and expects you to make a decision over the phone. Sends in handwritten, illegible query. Pardi: The one who thinks I can read 250 pages a minute and keeps calling back to check on status. This is one case where the squeaky wheel does not get oiled. It just gets annoying.

Description of a dream client: Simenauer: Sends in a terrific outline—well-written, great idea, easy to work with. Follows through. Has patience and loyalty. Pardi: The one who trusts that I will do everything in my power to represent the book without being badgered.

Why did you become an agent? Simenauer: I have been an articles editor, journalist, freelance writer, and co-author. Agenting seemed the next step. Pardi: I sort of fell into it, but quickly realized that it does satisfy my "readaholic" compulsion. The only time I am not reading is when I am driving (although I do manage to absorb a few paragraphs at traffic lights).

Comments: Simenauer: I think my background as a freelance writer and co-author makes me even more sympathetic to struggling writers. I understand what it feels like to see your name on a book jacket and appear on a major TV show, and if I can help you achieve your dream, then it becomes mine as well. But understand that it takes a great deal of perseverance to go from an idea to a proposal strong enough to get the attention of the publishing world. I hear good ideas all day long, yet few ever go anywhere. Pardi: I love to be surprised when I read a manuscript, and I love to become emotionally involved. Also, I am a little partial to Pittsburgh Steelers fans.

MICHAEL SNELL LITERARY AGENCY

PO Box 1206, Truro, MA 02666-1206

508-349-3718

Agents: Michael Snell, President; Patricia Snell, Executive Vice President

Born: Michael: August 16, 1945, Denver, Colorado. Patricia: March 6, 1951, Boston, Massachusetts.

Education: Michael: B.A., DePauw University, Phi Beta Kappa. Patricia: Fine Arts, Pratt Institute.

Career history: Michael: Editor, Wadsworth Publishing Company (1967–1978); Executive Editor, Addison-Wesley (1978–1979); Owner, Michael Snell Literary Agency (1979–present). Patricia: Financial Officer; Editor; Executive V.P., H. Michael Snell, Inc. (1986–present).

Hobbies/personal interests: Michael: Tennis, golf, shell-fishing, fishing, gardening. Patricia: Tennis, organic vegetable and flower gardening.

Areas most interested in agenting: Nonfiction books that offer readers genuine, tangible benefits, especially practical, applied self-help and how-to titles in all areas: health and fitness, parenting, relationships, sex, travel, gardening, sports, psychology, communication, writing and publishing, and pets. Michael specializes in business, management, leadership, finance, computers, technology, entrepreneurship, motivation, careers at all levels, from professional/reference to low-level how-to. Both Michael and Patricia emphasize books by women, for women on all subjects, from workplace issues and entrepreneurship and management to dating, marriage, relationships, communication, sex, and parenting.

Areas not interested in agenting: Personal memoirs, science fiction, children's books, noncommercial fiction.

If not agenting, what would you be doing? Almost any creative career (painting, sculpture, fiction-writing, teaching) where something solid and valuable arises from applying skill and endures long after you die. Then again, it's nice to get paid for your accomplishments.

Best way to initiate contact: New authors can obtain a brochure, "How to Write a Book Proposal," by sending an SASE. We also urge prospective clients to read our 1997 book *From Book Idea to Bestseller* (Prima Publishing). Keep query letters concise and focused: your topic, your credentials, and your intended audience. Always include an SASE for response. We only consider new clients on an exclusive basis.

Reading-fee policy: No, we work strictly on a commission basis.

Client representation by category: Nonfiction, 90%; Fiction, 10%.

Commission: 15% of all income from primary and subsidiary rights, with higher percentages arranged for developmental editing, rewriting, line editing, collaborating, and ghostwriting.

Number of titles sold last year: 30.

Rejection rate (all submissions): 93%.

Most common mistakes authors make: Authors who do not respect the etiquette that multiple queries are okay, but multiple submissions are not. Too many ambitious would-be authors engage in their quest for an agent as if they were looking for a plumber rather than for a mentor and friend. They forget that we invest valuable time, expertise, and resources every minute we spend reacting to, critiquing, developing, editing, and shaping a project. Manipulation, playing one agent off against another while gaining value from both, usually backfires. It certainly derails the crucial building of a trusting relationship.

Description of the client from Hell: Subject experts who assume expertise in writing and publishing and do not appreciate that they can learn from our 40 years of book development experience. Eager authors who do not take the time to develop the full potential of their books and grow impatient with the inherently slow, deliberate nature of book publishing. Writers so intent on making money that they forget that bestsellers benefit readers' lives first and foremost and make money only when they solve problems and change readers' lives. Hastiness, inattention to detail, manipulativeness, greediness, dishonesty and lack of integrity, and humorlessness drive us crazy, just as they drive any businessperson crazy.

Description of a dream client: Any writers, regardless of their background and areas of expertise, who take time to listen and learn about project development and publishing; who take time to develop and write a valuable book proposal and manuscript; who enter into a relationship with us in a spirit of partnership; who work hard but patiently; who, above all, maintain a sense of perspective and humor. Dream clients display all the traits we expect from friends and family: trust, honesty, integrity, respect, and a genuine caring. Without those qualities, no relationship can flourish. With them,

Agent: Philip Spitzer

Born: August 6, 1939, New York City.

Education: M.A., New York University Graduate Institute of Book Publishing; M.A. in French, University of Paris, France.

Career history: New York University Press, 1961–1962; McGraw Hill Book Company, trade sales, Sales Promotion Manager, art book department, 1963–1966; John Cushman Associates/Curtis Brown Ltd. Literary Agency, 1966–1969; Philip G. Spitzer Literary Agency, 1969–present.

Hobbies/personal interests: Sports and travel.

Areas most interested in agenting: Fiction: literary and suspense. Quality nonfiction, including sports, biography, current events.

Areas not interested in agenting: Most category fiction, most how-to.

If not agenting, what might you be doing? Book sales representative.

Best way to initiate contact: Query letter with SASE.

Reading fee policy: No reading fee.

Client representation by category: Nonfiction, 40%; Fiction, 60%.

Commission: 15% domestic; 20% foreign.

Number of titles sold last year: 25.

Rejection rate (all submissions): 95%.

Most common mistakes authors make: Telephoning is a mistake.

Description of the client from Hell: Daily phone calls; impossible to satisfy; if book doesn't sell—either to publisher or subsequently in bookstores—agent is to blame.

Description of the dream client: Informed, respectful, and loyal.

Why did you become an agent? An opportunity to work closely with both authors and publishers.

How did you become an agent? I was recommended for a job in an agency.

Why did you become an agent? I wanted the above-mentioned job.

What can writers do to enhance their chances of getting you as an agent? Write a great book.

How would you describe what you actually do for a living? Consuming; there is little time for anything else.

What do you think about other agents? I don't think about other agents.

What do you think about editors? I can't imagine describing editors as a group, any more than I would agents.

What do you think about publishers? See above.

Do you watch *The Sopranos*? No.

Representative titles: *The Narrows* by Michael Connelly (Little, Brown); *In the Moon of Red Ponies* by James Lee Burke (Simon & Schuster); *Nine* by Jan Burke (Simon & Schuster); *Allah's Torch: A Report from Behind the Scenes in Asia's War on Terror* by Tracy Dahlby (William Morrow); *Hank Aaron and the Home Run that Changed America* by Tom Stanton (William Morrow); *Eleanora Duse, a Biography* by Helen Sheehy; *Shadow Men* by Jonathon King (Dutton); *Missing Justice* by Alafair Burke (Henry Holt & Co.).

STEELE-PERKINS LITERARY AGENCY

26 Island Lane, Canandaigua, NY 14424

fax: 585-396-3579

e-mail: pattiesp@aol.com

Agent: Pattie Steele-Perkins

Education: B.A. in English, Nazareth College; M.S. in Communications, Syracuse University, New House School.

Career history: 15 years as a literary agent.

What subjects/categories are you most enthusiastic about agenting? Romance and women's fiction.

What subjects are you not interested in agenting? Science fiction, paranormal, children's books.

What is the best way to contact you? Through the mail. Send a synopsis and first three chapters with an SASE.

Client representation by category: Fiction, 100%.

Commission: 15%.

Rejection Rate: 95% of what we receive is not what we handle and is rejected before getting to my desk.

What are some common mistakes writers make? They send their work before it's ready.

Description of the client from Hell: The unpublished author who calls every day and e-mails twice a day.

Description of the dream client: The published author who is so busy writing books she doesn't know I'm alive except at contract time.

What can writers do to enhance their chances of getting you as an agent? Writers should study the marketplace and submit work to those agents who specialize in the author's genre.

What do you think of editors? Editors love books and are in constant search of "The Book."

STIMOLA LITERARY STUDIO

308 Chase Court, Edgewater, NJ 07020

voice/fax: 201-945-9353

e-mail: LtryStudio@aol.com

Agent: Rosemary B. Stimola

Born: November 6, 1952, Queens, New York.

Education: B.A. in Elementary Education/Theoretical Linguistics; M.A. in Applied Linguistics; Ph.D. in Linguistics and Educational Psych; all from NYU.

Career history: Teacher, children's bookseller, freelance editor, education consultant, agent.

Hobbies/personal interests: Beach combing, Latin dance.

Areas most interested in agenting: Preschool through young adult fiction/nonfiction.

Areas not interested in agenting: Adult fiction.

Best way to initiate contact: E-mail query.

Client representation: Children's, 75% fiction/15% nonfiction; Other, 10%.

Commission: 15%.

Number of titles sold last year: 21.

Rejection rate (all submissions): 90% or more.

Description of the client from Hell: Desperate for money, has unrealistic expectations and a major ego.

Description of the dream client: Talented, flexible, and realistic, keeps deadlines.

Most common mistakes authors make: "I've published for adults so I can certainly write for children."

What can writers do to enhance their chances of getting you as an agent? Referrals through editors, other clients, or agents.

Why did you become an agent? I like it, it likes me. The potential for achieving something great is ever-present.

If not agenting, what might you be doing? Working in publishing as an editor or marketing director.

How would you describe what you actually do for a living? I make the best possible deal for a book and then work collaboratively with a writer, editors, and others to produce the best possible book.

How did you become an agent? Editors kept referring clients to me even before I had formalized the studio!

What do you think about other agents? In general, mixed as any other group. I am fortunate enough to belong to a small agents consortium that meets once a month to discuss deals, business and more. Wonderful, talented and experienced in different areas, they are a solid touchtone and a great source of advice and support.

What do you think about editors? A mixed bag . . . from the sublime to the absurd.

What do you think about publishers? Too bottom line-oriented right now; often view P&Ls as a firm predictor of future sales.

What were your favorite films last year? *Return of the King, Mystic River, Cold Mountain.*

Do you watch *The Sopranos?* Every single week.

Comments: No need to make things more difficult than necessary. I love dealing with straight shooters who answer calls and don't waste their time or mine.

Representative titles: *The Beacon Hill Boys* by Ken Mochizuki (Scholastic Press); *The Many Adventures of Johnny Mutton* by James Proimos (Scholastic Press); *Undersea Encounters* by Mary Jo Rhodes and David Hall (Franklin Watts); *Sweet Talkin' Board Book Series* by Jackie Reinach (Random House); *The Secret To Freedom* by Marcia Vaughan (Lee & Low Books); *Gregor the Overlander* by Suzanne Collins (Scholastic Press).

STRATEGIC SOLUTIONS, INC. LITERARY AGENTS

17820 Pheasant Lane, Little Rock, AR 72206

501-888-4702   fax: 501-888-8589

e-mail: strategicsolns@aol.com

http://4dw.net/strategics/lit.html

Agents: Marissa J. Carter, Bonnie S. Hibschman
Born: Carter: March 2, 1952, London, England. Hibschman: August 14, 1951, Michigan City, Indiana.
Education: Carter: B.A. in Biochemistry, Oxford University, 1974; Ph.D. in Chemistry, Brandeis University, 1985. Hibschman: B.S. in Education (English), Eastern Illinois University, 1974; Persuasive, Expository and Technical Writing, University of Arkansas at Little Rock, 1999.
Career history: Carter: Scientist for more than 25 years (research & development), manufacturing, sales, marketing, technical writing); Writer and Editor since 1999. Hibschman: Teacher for three years, sales and marketing for years when not cooking, cleaning, coaching, chauffeuring, sewing, or working on fundraising projects for two terrific daughters throughout their school years. I've written all my life, but finally turned it into a writing/editing business degree in 1999.
Hobbies/personal interests: Carter: Technology, travel, aviation, and playing foosball with Bonnie in the lunch hour. Hibschman: Writing, movies, reading, talking with interesting people.
Areas most interested in agenting: Carter: Thrillers (especially espionage and technothrillers), military adventure, spiritual novels, science fiction, science and technology, general business, exposés (especially David and Goliath stories), investigative crime, and biographic material (especially scientists). Hibschman: Exposés, autobiographies, contemporary events, literary and mainstream fiction, human interest, and spiritual understanding.
Areas not interested in agenting: Carter: Children's books, erotica, sports, cooking, art books, Westerns, and please no more stories about drugs, trafficking, and gangs. Hibschman: Historical nonfiction, cooking, erotica, children's books, arts, and pets.

Best way to initiate contact: Send a query letter, including a bio. For fiction: send first three chapters, plus synopsis; nonfiction: outline, plus first three chapters.

Client representation by category: Carter: Nonfiction, 50%; Fiction, 50%. Hibschman: Nonfiction, 75%; Fiction, 25%.

Commission: 15% domestic; 20% foreign rights.

Rejection rate (all submissions): Carter: We reject a very high percentage of manuscripts on the first go-around, although several have subsequently been accepted after considerable rework. Hibschman: Nearly all first-time submissions need some work to be ready for representation. If an author is serious and wants to pursue publication, critiques are valuable tools that can help an author with the "weak" spots. Even though I might like a manuscript, the first submission is usually rejected with comments on improvement.

Description of the client from Hell: Carter: Those who don't do their homework, demand to be constantly updated, and don't follow up on our suggestions in a timely manner. We try to screen out these types ahead of time, but if you see any lifeless bodies on the front page of the *Arkansas Democratic Gazette*, you'll know our screening process broke down. Hibschman: Funny you should ask. A client who sends a genre that we do not represent, who tells me how to do my job, who demands answers that cannot be given, who tries to throw monkey wrenches into the timeline, who doesn't have the foggiest idea about the processes involved, or who throws a temper tantrum on the phone.

Description of the dream client: Carter: Someone who takes our suggestions to heart and goes the extra mile; a good writer who wants to put in the time to become a great writer; someone who is patient and understands that the publishing process can be a long and arduous course. Hibschman: Imaginative, witty, creative; a person who takes great pains and pleasure in the craft and has a unique, developed style; a person who can incorporate constructive criticism, knowing that improvement and enhancement of the writing is the goal; a person who understands that less is sometimes more.

What are common mistakes authors make? Carter: Sending manuscripts in single-spaced format, not properly paginated, and with weird scene/chapter formats. Sending a "circular"-type query letter, indicating this is the hottest bestseller since *Gone with the Wind*, and little else. Hibschman: Sending an e-mail saying, "I have a bestseller," but saying nothing about the book or the author. Sending a manuscript in less that 12-pt. type. . .my eyes get mighty sore by by the end of the day, and I'm liable to throw it aside if the type is too small to read. Authors should always follow the submission protocol.

What can writers do to enhance their chances of getting you as an agent? Both: Following proper protocol; learn how to write an attention-getting query letter, and include supplementary material in the proper format. What really impresses us is when authors have researched their market and indicate how their works fit in, AND have had their work well edited. See website: http://4dw.net/strategics/lit.html for submissions protocol, fiction writing tips, tips on presentations to literary agents.

Why did you become an agent? Carter: A combination of things: I was tired of the corporate scene and constant travel and frustrated with other agents dismissing my books with a curt "not for us." I wanted a completely different career. I wanted to be an agent who was approachable and who could nurture writing talent. . .a writing coach, I guess. Hibschman: I'm happiest when working with words, someone else's or my own. It was a natural progression, like learning to swim after wading in the pond.

If not agenting, what might you be doing? Carter: Probably inventing new and exotic pyrotechnic mixtures and plastics in my garage laboratory. Hibschman: Finishing the gazebo in my backyard that was started about six years ago.

How would you describe what you do for a living? Carter: I write, read, and edit all kinds of written material, talk on the phone, deal with morons, run down to Office Depot and the Post Office, and learn the idiosyncrasies of computer programs. Once in a while I yell "Yahoo!" when I discover fresh talent. Hibschman: Grading papers on a grander scale—but the writers actually like to write. Writing, proofreading, printing, and packaging.

How did you become an agent? Carter: My business partner and I founded an editing, writing, and translation company in 2000. We began acquiring clients in the course of our editing and writing activities, and several urged us to become literary gatekeepers and represent them. We decided to start literary agent activities in the fall of 2001, with the premise of helping promising writers any way we could. We haven't looked back. Hibschman: We were editing one of the best manuscripts we'd ever seen, and when we sent it back to the author, he asked, "Well. . .why don't you represent it for me? I don't see any reason to find someone else when I already like to work with you." We looked at each other, lightbulbs flashing in our brains as if to say, "Hello? Are you listening? Pay attention." And we said in unison, "Why not?" Jumping right in, it took us a while to get started, so it's just been the last six months or so that we feel we've actually made progress.

What do you think about editors? Carter: They should hire competent assistants. Hibschman: If they'd rather be doing something else, then they better go do it. It's an occupation that's either in the bones or isn't. We have found that the majority are quite friendly and helpful; they are quick to respond and tell us what they do or do not like.

What do you think about publishers? Carter: Becoming more and more focused on the bottom line. . .which is okay, but I would like to see publishers take more risks with first-time authors who have something to say in a fresh and imaginative way. Seeing the same authors again and again on the bestseller lists bothers me a lot. While some bestselling material is good, a lot of it isn't. Publishers are hyping money-making big-time authors and lowering the standards of publishing at the same time. Perversely, the bar is set even higher for new authors. Most authors will reach a certain number of books and become stale because they are on the deadline treadmill. I find it sad that sales and marketing have triumphed over good editorial judgment. Hibschman: They are human beings, covering the spectrum of human behavior. No one's perfect. Everyone makes a few mistakes along the way. But, many terrific first-time authors are overlooked, and the audiences are left with just a few best-selling authors to choose from. If given a choice, the audiences would probably like to have more variety.

What were your favorite films last year? Carter: *Insomnia, K-PAX, Behind Enemy Lines.* Hibschman: Robert Redford (*Spy Game*), could still come to my house for dinner (or breakfast, or lunch, or brunch) at his convenience, even though it was last year's film. Definitely, *K-PAX.* I'm a schmuck for tear-jerkers, so *Pearl Harbor* is still at the top of my list.

Do you watch *The Sopranos?* Carter: Nope. Hibschman: Uh-uh!

Comments: Carter: Rissy's diatribes: "Service" has become an oxymoron; lack of ethics and corruption in the corporate world and in government; the almighty dollar, and those dedicated to chasing it; jingoism usurping human rights, diversity, and tolerance of others. Whatever happened to "Love thy neighbor as thyself"? Hibschman: A few disturbances in the business are: Seeing the same authors in the top 20, year after year, even if their writing has gone downhill (and some whose writing started on a downhill slide and never recovered). Publishers who wouldn't give an excellent new author a break, even if their lists have been drenched in soggy soup for years. Editors of publishing houses who won't respond to submissions; who guard their offices, identities, and phone numbers like Fort Knox. Sometimes, it takes a new agent to discover a new author of bestseller magnitude. Fresh eyes are valuable assets. Oh, and publishers who send back pithy letters that an editor is no longer on their staff, even when the editor left the day before.

PAM STRICKLER AUTHOR MGMT.

P.O. Box 429, Accord, New York 12404

845-687-0186

www.pamstrickler.com

Agent: Pamela Dean Strickler

Place of Birth: Berkeley, California, 1950.

Career History: Senior editor for sixteen years at Ballantine Books, five years at Avon before that. Also 1995-99 an independent manuscript editor. First work as an agent began in 1997, later associated with the Scovil Chichak Galen Agency. Started own agency in 2001.

Education History: B.A. University of California.

Hobbies: Reading, gardening, dancing, long walks. Serving as an education volunteer for a nature preserve.

Areas most interested in agenting: Mystery, Women's fiction, Romance, mainstream fiction.

Areas not interested in agenting: Children's, poetry, how-to.

Best way to initiate contact: E-mail query. Please check webpage for up-to-date information, www.pamstrickler.com

LITERARY AGENTS

PAM STRICKLER AUTHOR MGMT. 681

Reading fee policy: No reading fee.

How do you describe what you actually do for a living? Very much what I did as an editor, a job I always loved: think about each book carefully, think about the author's career long term, worry about all aspects of publishing each book, work in partnership with the author. Writers are smart, fun people, so I've always enjoyed this. Plus, of course, I have a major passion for books.

Representative titles: Nicola Cornick's *Englishmen Make the Worst Lovers in the World* (Harlequin/HQN); Seressia Glass's *Three Wishes* (Genesis Press); Elena Greene's *Saving Lord Verwood* (New American Library); Ginger Hanson's *Tennessee Waltz* (Kensington); Patricia Harwin's first novel *Arson and Old Lace* (Pocket); Wendy Wax's *Leave it to Cleavage* (Bantam); Karen White-Owens's *Circles of Love* (BET/Arabesque); Sally Wright's *Out of the Ruins* (Multnomah and Ballantine).

First published projects as an agent included an Edgar Award finalist, *Pursuit and Persuasion* by Sally Wright, and a *New York Times* bestseller by a first-time novelist, *Sullivan's Island* by Dorothea Benton Frank.

THE JOHN TALBOT AGENCY, INC.

540 West Boston Post Road, PMB 266, Mamaroneck, NY 10543 -3437

914-777-4000

www.johntalbotagency.com   e-mail: talbotagency@mac.com

Agent: John Talbot
Education: B.A., DePauw University.
Career history: I am a Literary Agent and former book Editor with 19 years of experience in corporate book publishing. Prior to becoming an Agent, I spent seven years as a Senior Editor with the Putnam Berkley Group, where I edited such *New York Times* bestselling authors as Tom Clancy, W. E. B. Griffin, and Jack Higgins, as well as rising literary stars like Tom Perrotta, author of *Election* (Putnam), the novel upon which the film of the same title was based, and Fred Haefele, author of *Rebuilding the Indian: A Memoir* (Riverhead). I published national bestsellers in hardcover, trade paperback, and mass market paperback, along with five *New York Times* Notable Books. I began my career at Simon & Schuster and worked at Pocket Books and Putnam Berkley before moving on to the Anita Diamant Literary Agency, and then forming my own agency in 1998. I represent clients who write in most commercial and literary genres, with narrative nonfiction, suspense, women's fiction, and literary fiction being my areas of emphasis. I am a member of the Authors Guild and as such adhere to the Canon of Ethics as recommended to the Guild by the AAR.

Hobbies/personal interests: Sailing, boating, and related water sports. I am a published poet and have had a novel optioned for film. Church is a growing influence in my life.

Areas most interested in agenting: I am most enthusiastic about representing narrative nonfiction, novels of suspense, and literary and women's fiction. Narrative nonfiction can cover almost any subject, but adventure and personal journey are particular interests of mine. *Rebuilding the Indian* (see above) is a good example of both. Newspaper and magazine experience can be helpful in this area; many books are generated from concepts first tried out in articles. In fiction, I am looking for the fresh and occasionally edgy voice, no matter the subject or genre. Writers with minority backgrounds and unusual experiences and perspectives interest me, as do, perhaps conversely, writers of what Sue Miller calls domestic realism. Previous publication in literary journals and magazines is a plus.

Areas not interested in agenting: I do not represent children's books, science fiction, fantasy, genre romance, Westerns, poetry, or screenplays.

Best way to initiate contact: Query via e-mail only. See website for instructions.

Reading-fee policy: I do not charge reading fees.

Client representation by category: Nonfiction, 50%; Fiction, 50%.

Commission: 15% on all domestic sales, including film and subsidiary sales. Commissions on foreign rights sales vary; they are usually 20%, but can go to 25%, depending on co-agent.

Number of titles sold last year: I sold approximately 25 titles last year.

Rejection rate (all submissions): My acceptance rate for cold queries has been 1 in 500.

Most common mistakes authors make: Not carefully following the submission guidelines as posted on my website. Pitching multiple projects in one query letter. Rambling queries. Trying to pressure me or have me justify my agency before an offer of representation is made. Knocking published authors or comparing yourself favorably to bestsellers. Not trusting me or the business in general, thinking someone's going to steal your idea. Relaying incomplete representation, submission, or publishing histories. Not being truthful or straightforward.

Description of the client from Hell: Clients from Hell don't respect my time. They fail to recognize the publisher's justly proprietary attitude toward marketing, book design, and other facets of publication. They won't take suggestions for change, no matter how small or well-reasoned; complain about writing; and treat being published as a right instead of the privilege that it is.

Description of a dream client: Dream clients respect my personal and professional lives. They trust me. They are open to input from their editor. They love to read and they love to write. They are enthusiastic about their ideas and about what they do.

Why did you become an agent? Becoming an agent was a natural progression from being an editor. It's the same type of work, but I'm able to spend less time in meetings and more time working with authors. I can also handle a more eclectic range of material, and I get to work with editors throughout the industry who share my passions and enthusiasms.

What can writers do to enhance their chances of getting you as an agent? Try to respect my time. Make sure your proposal is clear, succinct, and well organized. Make sure the rest of your material is finished and ready to go if I'm interested.

How would you describe what you actually do for a living? I help authors manage their careers for the long term. I find and put projects that I'm passionate about into the hands of equally enthusiastic editors.

What do you think about editors? Editors without a doubt are the hardest working and most idealistic people in book publishing.

What do you think about publishers? Publishers represent the best opportunity for gifted writers to get wide distribution, readership, and money in what is an often difficult business.

Comments: A large part of success comes with a proper attitude. The most successful authors I know enjoy the process of learning and got into the business for the pleasure and challenge of writing. Impatience, mistrustfulness, and competitiveness with other writers can be very damaging to a career. Focus on your own content, find your own best voice, and enjoy the ride. This can be a wonderful business.

Representative titles: Fiction: *Straits of Power* by Joe Buff (Morrow/Avon); *Department Thirty* by David Kent (Pocket Books); *One Flesh* by Clarence Major (Dafina Books); *Crossing the Line* by Clinton McKinzie (Delacorte/Dell); *The Opposite Shore* by Maryanne Stahl (NAL Accent); *Becoming Finola* by Suzanne Strempek Shea (Pocket Books); *Leave Myself Behind* by Bart Yates (Kensington). Non-Fiction: *Keep Going Till You Get There, Then Keep Going* by General Ezell Ware, Jr. with Joel Engel (Dutton/NAL); *No Backup: My Life as a Female FBI Special Agent,* by Rosemary Dew and Pat Pape (Carroll & Graf); *Negotiating Without a Net: Unbeatable Real-World Strategies from the NYPD's Top Hostage Negotiator* by Dominick Misino, NYPD (Ret.) and Jim DeFelice (McGraw-Hill); *Shelf Life: Romance, Mystery, Drama, and Other Page-Turning Adventures From a Year in a Bookstore* by Suzanne Strempek Shea (Beacon); *This Pats Year: A Season-Long Trek Through Patriots Nation* by Sean Glennon (Taylor).

SCOTT TREIMEL NY

434 Lafayette Street, New York, NY 10003

fax: 212-505-0664

e-mail: ST.NY@Verizon.net

Agent: Scott Treimel, assistant agent Ari Hopkins

Career history: Curtis Brown, Scholastic, United Features Syndicate, Warner Bros., HarperCollins Children's Books.

Best way to initiate contact: Scott Treimel NY submission policy: We average 3,000 unsolicited submissions yearly and must hold strictly to these policies. Send submissions via post. Text must be in standard manuscript form: double-spaced type in a standard-size font. No multiple submissions or queries are considered. We require 90 days exclusivity from our receipt of materials. Submissions received without S.A.S.E. are recycled upon receipt. Complete picture book texts may be submitted, no more than two. Picture book dummies and/or thumbnail storyboards may be submitted only if the author is also the illustrator. A standard-formatted manuscript must also be included. Complete chapter books of 60 or fewer pages may be submitted. Queries are required for manuscripts of 60 or more pages; include a story synopsis, with attention to character development, and two sample chapters.

Illustrators may submit no more than six pictures—never original art—showing people, animals, and environments. Note: if all pictures are still lifes, we cannot evaluate narrative potential. No film scripts are considered. No toy projects are considered.

Number of titles sold last year: 19.

Client Representation: 100% children's.

Most common mistakes authors make with your agency: Writing from a sentimentalized recollection of childhood; writing didatic stories; inadequate technique and skills.

What would you be doing if you weren't an agent? Editor.

What can writers do to enhance their chances of getting you as an agent? Be exceptional writers.

Commission: 15–20% domestic; 20–25% foreign.

Rejection rate (all submissions): 99%; most new clients have already published at least one book.

What do you think about other agents? I am hearing tales of shocking maleficence. An author wanting representation might benefit from checking a prospective agent's background credentials.

Comments: Scott Treimel NY sells and administers intellectual property rights—print, electronic, foreign, dramatic, film, composition, broadcast, merchandise, promotion—for children's book creators. Agency Founded in 1995. Member: Association of Authors Representatives; The Authors Guild; Society of Children's Book Writers and Illustrators.

Representative titles: Novels: *Open Ice* by Pat Hughes (Random House/Wendy Lamb); *The Stupendous Dodgeball Fiasco* by Janice Repka (Dutton); *Theories of Relativity* by Barbara Haworth-Attard (Harper Canada); *From Charlie's Point of View* by Richard Scrimger (Tundra, Canada/Dutton, US); *Dear Canada* by Barbara Haworth-Attard (Scholastic Canada). Picture Books: *Papa, Do You Love Me* by Barbara Joosse (Chronicle Books); *What To Do? What To Do?* By Toni Teeven (Clarion); *Please Is a Good Word to Say* by Barbara Joosse (Philomel); *My Life as Chicken* by Ellen Kelley (Harcourt); *Blueberry Mouse* by Alice Low (Mondo). Non-Fiction: *Killer Ants* by Nicholas Nirgiotis (Holiday House); *Maple Syrup Spring* by Ann Purmell (Holiday House); *A Pieplate In the Sky* by Alice Low (Holiday House).

UNITED TRIBES MEDIA INC

240 West 35th Street, #500, New York, NY 10001

212-244-4166   212-534-7646

e-mail: janguerth@aol.com

Agent: Jan-Erik Guerth
Born: 1965, in a Volkswagen Beetle.
Education: M.Ph. in Cultural Studies, New York University.
Career history: Comedian (one of five funny Germans!), journalist, radio producer, film distributor, before discovering my true passion—publishing.
Areas most interested in agenting: Only nonfiction—including ethical, social, gender, and cultural issues; comparative religion; spirituality; self-help and wellness; science and arts; history and politics; nature and travel; and any fascinating future trends and other serious nonfiction.
Areas not interested in agenting: Depends on each project, but most certainly not agriculture, animals, military, war, sports, and needlework.
Best way to initiate contact: Outline with one sample chapter, resume, and SASE. E-mailed preferred.
Reading-fee policy: No reading fee.
Client representation by category: Nonfiction, 100%.
Commission: 15%; 20% on foreign rights sales.
Description of the client from Hell: Has two little horns on forehead, hides bushy tail and horse's hoof, and smells of sulfur and roses.
Description of a dream client: Look in your mirror.

THE RICHARD R. VALCOURT AGENCY, INC.

177 East 77th Street PPHC, New York, NY 10021

Agent: Richard R. Valcourt
Born: November 29, 1941, Fall River, Massachusetts.
Education: B.A., Roger Williams College; M.A., New York University; ABD, City University Graduate School; L.L.B., LaSalle Extension University.
Career history: Radio-television Journalist (1961–1980); Program Administration, City University of New York (1980–1995); Instructor, Department of Political Science, Hunter College (1981–1995); founded Richard Valcourt Agency (1995), Consulting Faculty, American Military University (1996–present). Editor-in-Chief, International Journal of Intelligence (1998–present), Executive Editor (1986–1998).

Areas most interested in agenting: Now represent exclusively professional and scholarly works in international relations, national security, and related aspects of United States government and politics.

Areas not interested in agenting: All works not included in the above category.

Best way to initiate contact: Letter of inquiry (with SASE), brief biography, summary of material.

Reading-fee policy: No reading fee. May charge for photocopying, mailing, and phone calls if excessive.

Client representation by category: Nonfiction, 100%.

Commission: 15% domestic, 20% foreign.

Rejection rate (all submissions): 99.5%.

What can writers do to enhance their chances of getting you as an agent? Be experienced practitioners, academics, or journalists in the fields I represent.

THE VINES AGENCY, INC.

648 Broadway, Suite 901, New York, NY 10012

212-777-5522   fax: 212-777-5978

e-mail: JV@vinesagency.com

Agent: James C. Vines

Born: May 1, 1966, Huntsville, Alabama.

Education: Auburn University.

Career history: Raines & Raines, Literary Agent, 1989–1992; Virginia Barber Literary Agency, Literary Agent, 1993–1995; The Vines Agency, Inc., Literary Agent, 1995–present.

Hobbies/personal interests: Sailing, music.

Areas most interested in agenting: Quality commercial fiction, thrillers, women's fiction, quality commercial nonfiction, adventure, relationship books.

Areas not interested in agenting: If it's well written, I want to see it.

If not agenting, what would you be doing? I am an agent because I can't be anything else.

Best way to initiate contact: Query with one-page letter describing the story, along with SASE.

Reading-fee policy: No reading fees whatsoever.

Client representation by category: Nonfiction, 50%; Fiction, 50%.

Commission: 15% domestic, 25% foreign commission.

Number of titles sold last year: 30.

Rejection rate (all submissions): I reject 80% of the "over the transom" submissions I receive.

Most common mistakes authors make: Writing 12-page cover letters (single-spaced); sending chapters from the middle of the novel, claiming "those are the best"; and calling to see if I've had a chance to read the material yet.

Description of the client from Hell: I do not represent hellish clients.

Description of a dream client: See my list of authors under "representative titles."

How did you become an agent? I had met some brilliant authors who needed a good business manager, and I couldn't find anything else in this world nearly as exciting as helping them to develop their careers.

Why did you become an agent? I love great authors and want to help them reach their goals.

What can writers do to enhance their chances of getting you as an agent? Write on subjects about which you are passionate. Research the marketplace to make sure the same book hasn't already been written by somebody else. Don't pack your manuscript in plastic "peanuts" that will require us to vacuum the office after opening the box containing your manuscript.

How would you describe what you actually do for a living? I identify the largest and best audience for a book and then arrange deals on the author's behalf with the publishers and film producers best positioned to deliver that book to its audience.

What do you think about editors? I love editors, if they're good.

What do you think about publishers? The right publisher for the right author is a dream come true.

Comments: Please don't write for the money because if you do write for the money, you'll be intolerable once you finally get it.

Representative titles: *The Ring* by Koji Suzuki (Vertical); *Before I Let Go* by Darren Coleman (HarperCollins); *Camilla's Roses* by Bernice L. McFadden (Dutton/Plume); *Things Will Get As Good As You Can Stand* by Laura Doyle (Simon & Schuster); *Ecstasy* by Beth Saulnier (Warner Books); *Sunset and Sawdust* by Joe R. Lansdale (Knopf); *The Power of the Dog* by Don Winslow (Knopf); *The Iron Coffin* by John Mannock (New American Library); *A Fountain Filled With Blood* by Julia Spencer-Fleming (St. Martin's); *The Book Lover's Cookbook* by Shaunda Kennedy Wenger (Ballantine); *The Book of Flying* by Keith Miller (Riverhead).

STEPHANIE VON HIRSCHBERG LITERARY AGENCY, LLC

1385 Baptist Church Road (A), Yorktown Heights, NY 10598

914-243-9250   fax: 914-962-7285

Agent: Stephanie von Hirschberg
Born: December 18, 1950, Pretoria, South Africa.
Education: B.A. in English, Comparative Literature (Magna Cum Laude), Finch College; M.A. in English Literature, St. John's University.

Career history: I began my career as an Editor at Doubleday, working on fiction and general nonfiction. In 1984, I joined *New Woman* magazine because I wanted to do more hands-on editorial work. For the next 14 years, I worked on all kinds of stories—psychology, celebrities, finance, health, careers. I wrote articles, surveys, a book review column, and an alternative health column. I also freelanced as a book editor. In 1994, I received the Editor of the Year award from the American Society of Journalists and Authors, in recognition of my support of writers. I am co-author of the off-Broadway play *We Are Your Sisters*, an adaptation of a biography of African-American women in the nineteenth century. In 1998, I moved to *Reader's Digest* to work on narrative and dramatic nonfiction stories. I launched my literary agency in 1999.

Hobbies/personal interests: Reading, animals, ecology, music.

Areas most interested in agenting: Biography, psychology, medicine, popular science, food, religion (ecumenical), mythology, nature, environmental issues, animals, true-life adventure, literary fiction, mainstream women's fiction.

Areas not interested in agenting: Children's books, horror, sci-fi, fantasy.

If not agenting, what would you be doing? I'd probably be a farmer (organic foods only) and run a small publishing company out of my barn.

Best way to initiate contact: Send a query letter with an SASE. No email queries, please.

Reading-fee policy: No reading fee.

Client representation by category: Nonfiction, 75%; Fiction, 25%.

Commission: 15%; 25% if a co-agent is involved (e.g., for film or foreign rights).

Number of titles sold last year: 6.

Rejection rate (all submissions): 98%.

Most common mistakes authors make: Not doing enough homework about the competition and similar books. Poorly written queries and proposals.

Description of a dream client: Someone who is talented, highly motivated, appreciates editorial suggestions, and has a sense of humor and a positive, realistic outlook.

Why did you become an agent? I love books and the whole, crazy business of publishing. Also, I enjoy being a catalyst—developing talent, bringing great stories and ideas into the world, making dreams come true.

What can writers do to enhance their chances of getting you as an agent? For nonfiction projects, I look for writers who have something truly original and relevant to say and who have strong credentials in their field. Similarly, for fiction, originality and a distinctive voice will get my attention, especially if you have published short stories in literary journals.

Representative titles: *Shakespeare by Another Name: The Literary Biography of Edward de Vere, 17th Earl of Oxford* by Mark K. Anderson (Gotham/Penguin Putnam, 2005); *Effortless Pain Relief* by Ingrid Bacci, Ph.D. (Free Press, 2005); *Ordinary Genius* (F), by Thomas Fox Averill (University of Nebraska Press, 2005); *The Hopes of Snakes* by Lisa Couturier (Beacon Press); *Healthy Helpings: 800 Fast and Fabulous Recipes for the Kosher (or not) Cook* by Norene Gilletz (Woodland, 2004); *Healing from Family Rifts* by Mark Sischel CSW (McGraw Hill, 2004); *The Women Who Danced by the Sea* by Marsha Mirkin PhD (Monkfish, 2004); *The Slow Air of Ewan MacPherson* (F) by Thomas Fox

Averill (Penguin, 2003); *Toddler* by Jennifer Margulis, ed. (Seal Press 2003); *Healing Hurt, Restoring the Hope* by Suzy Yehl Marta (Rodale, 2004); *The Secret Spiritual Life of Children* by Tobin Hart, Ph.D. (Inner Ocean, 2004).

VRATTOS LITERARY AGENCY

708 Gravenstein Highway North, Suite 185, Sebastopol, CA 95472

phone/fax: 707-570-2720

e-mail: VrattosLitAgency@aol.com

Agent: Francesca Vrattos
Date/Place of birth: 04/15/52, Boston, MA.
Educational History: Central Florida Junior College.
Career History: Co-founder of Writers' Showplace Inc., an online literary referral agency connecting writers with agents from 1998-2003, assistant to the Vice President of Penguin Putnam Inc., Western Division 2000-2002, founder of The Writer's Guide.Com, a literary referral agency, 2003.

Hobbies/Personal interests: Cooking, reading, sewing, painting.
Areas most interested in agenting: Adult fiction and nonfiction.
Areas not interested in agenting: Erotica, children's, young adult.
If not agenting, what would you be doing: Writing, reading, cooking.
Best way to initiate contact: E-mail or phone.
Reading-fee policy: No reading fees.
Client representation by category: 40% Fiction, 60% Nonfiction.
Commission structure: 15%; 20% foreign.
Number of titles sold last year: Our agency is only 4 months old and no sales yet.
Rejection rate: 98%.
Most common mistakes authors make with your agency: Expecting results overnight. I always encourage my clients to work on the next project and be patient.
What can writers do to enhance their chances of getting you as an agent? Being an excellent writer, knowing the business and acting professional.
Your description of the client from Hell: The client that e-mails or calls regarding the status of their manuscript, despite the fact that we have only had it one week!
Your description of a dream client: A client who treats me and the industry with respect.
How did you become an agent? Got tired of finding agents for authors and thought I'd make a good agent myself.
Why did you become an agent? After years of writing and submitting I decided to jump the fence and try it from this side. Much more fun!
How would you describe what you actually do for a living? I feel like I'm on a

treasure hunt when I open a query letter or begin reading a manuscript. There's no telling when I'm going to find that big prize.

What do you think about other agents? I admire them.

What do you think about editors? Without them we'd be out of business.

What do you think about publishers? Without them we'd ALL be out of business.

WALES LITERARY AGENCY, INC.

PO Box 9428, Seattle, WA 98109-0428

206-284-7114

www.waleslit.com   e-mail: waleslit@waleslit.com

Agent: Elizabeth Wales

Born: March 30, 1952.

Education: B.A., Smith College; graduate work in English and American Literature, Columbia University.

Career history: Worked in the trade sales departments at Oxford University Press and Viking Penguin; worked in city government and served a term on the Seattle school board; also worked as a Bookseller and Publisher's Representative.

Areas most interested in agenting: A wide range of narrative nonfiction and literary fiction titles. Especially interested in nonfiction projects that could have a progressive cultural or political impact. In fiction, looking for talented mainstream storytellers, both new and established. Especially interested in writers from the Northwest, Alaska, the West Coast, and what have become known as the Pacific Rim countries.

Areas not interested in agenting: Children's books, almost all genre projects (romance, sci-fi, mystery historicals, true crime, horror, action/adventure), how-to, self-help.

Best way to initiate contact: Send a query letter, briefly describing your book project and your publishing history, and a writing sample from the project, with SASE.

Reading-fee policy: No reading fee.

Client representation by category: Nonfiction, 60%; Fiction, 40%.

Commission: 15% domestic.

Number of titles sold last year: 14.

Rejection rate (all submissions): Most of our projects and authors come from referrals, but several times a year we "discover" a beauty of a book from the submissions pile.

Why did you become an agent? For the adventure and the challenge; also, I am a generalist—interested in variety.

Comments: I am interested in writers who are dedicated to writing and/or who have a particularly compelling story to tell.

Representative titles: *Michelangelo's Mountain* by Eric Scigliano (Simon & Schuster); *In Praise of Small Things* by Lyanda Lynn Haupt (Little, Brown & Co); *Against Gravity* by Farnoosh Moshiri (Penguin).

JOHN A. WARE LITERARY AGENCY

392 Central Park West, New York, NY 10025

Agent: John A. Ware

Born: May 21, 1942.

Education: B.A. in Philosophy, Cornell University; graduate work in English Literature, Northwestern University.

Career history: Editor, eight years, Doubleday & Company; Literary agent, one year, James Brown Associates/Curtis Brown Ltd.; founded John A. Ware Literary Agency in 1978.

Hobbies/personal interests: Music, Italy, and running.

Areas most interested in agenting: Biography and history; investigative journalism, social commentary, and contemporary affairs; bird's eye views of phenomena; literary and suspense fiction; Americana and folklore; nature and science.

Areas not interested in agenting: Technothrillers and women's romances; men's action-adventure; how-tos, save the area of medicine and health; guidebooks and cookbooks; science fiction; personal memoirs; reference; and young adult.

If not agenting, what would you be doing? Teaching philosophy or working as a sportswriter, or in some position in race relations.

Best way to initiate contact: Query letter only with SASE.

Reading-fee policy: No reading fee. Only for Xeroxing, authors' copies of galleys and books, and unusual mailing expenses—for example, messengers.

Client representation by category: Nonfiction, 80%-90%; Fiction, 10%-20%.

Commission: 15% on all sales, save foreign, which are 20%.

Rejection rate (all submissions): 99%.

Description of the client from Hell: Untrusting and accordingly nudging.

Description of a dream client: Dream clients are professional in all aspects of their chosen writing area; trusting; in possession of a sense of humor.

Why did you become an agent? I like working with writers, editorially and otherwise, outside the corporate realms of meetings and red tape, inside of which I worked as an editor.

What do you think about other agents? I surely respect my peers; "innocent," anyway until proven...

Do you watch *The Sopranos?* Yes.

Comments: In what remains of our genteel world of books, I would encourage a shoring up of the realm of common courtesy, returning phone calls, saying please and thank you, and so forth and so on.

Representative titles: *Under The Banner of Heaven* by Jon Krakauer [Fundamentalist Mormons] (Doubleday/Anchor); *The Butterfly Hunter* by Chris Ballard (Broadway); *Sarah's Quilt: A Novel* by Nancy E. Turner (Thomas Dunne Books/St. Martin's); *Better Off: Pulling the Plug on Technology* by Eric Brende (HarperCollins); *Hunger: A Novel* by Elise Blackwell (Little, Brown/Back Bay); *The Traveller: A Biography of John Ledyard* by William Gifford (Harcourt).

WATERSIDE PRODUCTIONS, INC.

The Waterside Building, 2187 Newcastle Avenue, #204, Cardiff-by-the-Sea, CA 92007

760-632-9190   fax: 760-632-9295

www.waterside.com

Agents: Matt Wagner, David Fugate, Margot Maley Hutchison, Christian Crumlish, Kimberly Valentini, Jawahara K. Saidullah, William E. Brown and Craig Wiley.

Education: Fugate: B.A. in Literature, University of California, San Diego. Maley: Literature, University of California, San Diego. Wagner: B.A. in Literature/Creative Writing, University of California, Santa Cruz.

Career history: Fugate: Agent with Waterside Productions since 1994. Maley: Literary Agent with Waterside since 1992. Wagner: I've been a Library Clerk, a Bookbinder, a Bookstore Clerk, and a Buyer. I've been a Literary Agent for eight years.

Hobbies/personal interests: Fugate: Biking, cooking, reading, running. Wagner: Yoga, tennis, golf, lots of reading.

Areas most interested in agenting: Fugate: Computer books and compelling nonfiction in many areas, including business, technology, sports, and pop culture. Wagner: Computer books, Internet-specific programming titles, sports, culture and technology, general how-to, business, and management. Maley: Computer books, business, technology, parenting, health and fitness, and online courses. Crumlish: Music, computer, business, and reference books. Saidullah: Computer books, certification, business, technology, medical and biotechical. Valentini: All areas of non-fiction including pop culture, health and fitness, self-help, and business. Also interested in compelling fiction. Brown: Technology, programming, security, biotech, networking, and web technologies, nanotechnology, miscellaneous technology topics. Non-fiction: Judeo-Christian inspirational, parenting/family studies, leadership, systems thinking, biographies, historical accounts, social commentaries. Fiction: I am only interested in well crafted, well written proposals or manuscripts. Prefer young adult, adult Christian fiction, science fiction, mysteries, romance, and historical drama. Wiley: politics/current affairs, Christian/religious, business, technical/computer, legal.

Areas not interested in agenting: Wagner: Fiction, poetry, self-help. Fugate: Fiction, New Age, children's, religious, romance, poetry, short stories. Maley Hutchison: Fiction, New Age, religious. Crumlish: First novels, short stories, poetry (there are not enough hours in the day). Saidullah: Fiction, religion, poetry. Valentini: Short stories and poetry. Brown: New Age or Occult spirituality.

If not agenting, what would you be doing? Fugate: I would be the sixth man for some mediocre professional basketball team in Greece, or a nomadic ski bum, or a project-development person at Miramax, or on the editorial side of the publishing industry. Maley: I would be leading safaris in East Africa. Wagner: Editor, publisher, or packager. I would love to run a bookstore someday.

Best way to initiate contact: Query letter or proposal either by e-mail or regular mail. Wagner: mwagner@waterside.com. Fugate: david@waterside.com. Maley Hutchison: mmaley@waterside.com. Crumlish: xian@waterside.com. Valentini: Kimberly@waterside.com. Wiley: cwiley@waterside.com.

Reading-fee policy: No reading fee.

Client representation by category: Fugate: Nonfiction, 100%. Maley: Nonfiction, 100%. Wagner: Nonfiction, 95%; Textbooks, 5%.

Commission: 15% domestic, 20% film, 25% foreign.

Number of titles sold last year: Fugate: 110. Maley: 110. Wagner: 100.

Rejection rate (all submissions): 95%.

Most common mistakes authors make: Fugate: Not researching their market thoroughly. Maley: A poorly written proposal or query letter or too many phone calls to check on the status of their proposal. Wagner: Telling me the book is sure to sell several million copies because the market is everyone. Insufficient market research.

Description of the client from Hell: Fugate: The client from Hell is unprofessional, confrontational, and fails to meet deadlines. Maley: A rude, arrogant, pushy, and impatient person who has completely unrealistic expectations. Wagner: What they said!

Description of a dream client: Fugate: Talented writers who are professional, maintain positive relationships with their editors, and look to resolve problems in a positive way. Maley: A great writer with good ideas who meets deadlines and is friendly and pleasant to deal with. Wagner: Professional, open-minded, creative, honest, and disciplined.

Why did you become an agent? Fugate: I like books, words, and ideas. Maley: Growing up, I always seemed to have either a book or a phone in my hand. Wagner: Probably because I can talk really fast. Also, I love books and like dealing with writers and publishers. It helps to be on the cutting edge.

Comments: Waterside is the world's premiere literary agency for computer and technology authors. We are passionate about representing authors' interests and we've agented more bestselling authors and more bestselling books than all other agencies combined. Since our founding in 1982, Waterside agents have successfully represented more than 5,000 books to over 50 publishers, generating more than $150 million dollars for authors. Waterside is also a long time supporter of the authoring community as the host of the computer book industry's annual gathering, the Waterside Publishing Conference. For more than 10 years the top authors and publishers have met to discuss the computer book industry's most pressing issues.

Waterside agents also represent a wide range of nonfiction titles including business, parenting, humor, health and fitness, pop culture, sports, body, mind, spirit, cookbooks and much more.

Representative titles: Maley: *Dreamweaver Magic* by Al Sparber (New Riders Press); *A+ Certification for Dummies* by Ron Gilster (Hungry Minds, Inc.); *The Digital Photography Bible* by Ken Milburn (Hungry Minds, Inc.); *Inside Business Incubators and Corporate Ventures* by Sally Richards (Wiley); *John Chambers and the Cisco Way* by John K. Waters (Wiley); *Fed Up! Dr. Oliver's Ten Step No Diet Fitness Plan* by Dr. Wendy Oliver (Contemporary Books). Wagner: *KISS Guide to Windows* by Rich Levin (Dorling Kindersly); *Poor Richard's Building Online Communities* by Margy Levine Young (Top Floor Publishing); *PCs for Dummies* by Dan Gookin (Hungry Minds). Fugate: *The JavaScript Bible* by Danny Goodman (Hungry Minds); *The Flash 6 Bible* by Rob Reinhardt (Hungry Minds); *Inside XML* by Steven Holzner (New Riders); *Hack Attacks Revealed* by John Chirillo (Wiley Technical Publishing).

TED WEINSTEIN LITERARY MANAGEMENT

287 Duncan Street, San Francisco, CA 94131

www.twliterary.com

Agent: Ted Weinstein

Education: Bachelor's degree in Philosophy from Yale College, Master's degree in Public and Private Management from Yale School of Management.

Career: Ted Weinstein has broad experience on both the business and editorial sides of publishing. Before founding his agency he held senior publishing positions in licensing, marketing, publicity and business development, including VP Marketing & Business Development at Nolo Press and the head of electronic publishing and licensing for Miller Freeman. Also a widely published author, Ted has been the music critic for NPR's *All Things Considered* and a commentator for the *San Francisco Chronicle* and many other publications.

Areas most interested in agenting: Wide range of intelligent nonfiction, especially narrative nonfiction, current affairs, politics, biography, history, business, science, technology, environment, pop culture, lifestyle, travel, self-help, health and medicine.

Areas not interested in agenting: Fiction, stage plays, screenplays, poetry, or books for children or young adults.

Best way to initiate contact: E-mail query or full proposal—see website for detailed submission guidelines.

Client representation by category: 90% nonfiction; 10% fiction.

Commission: 15% commission on domestic sales; 20% on overseas and translation.

Rejection rate (all submissions): 98%, but I carefully review every submission I receive because of the 2% that is destined for great success.

Description of the Client from Hell: A client who doesn't act like a professional—missing deadlines, personalizing business issues. Publishing is a business, and success is always more likely to come to those who are disciplined and who treat the people they work with respectfully.

Description of a dream client: Talented, communicative, disciplined, professional, hard working and who treats his or her writing like a career (even if it isn't their only career).

Most common mistakes authors make: Submitting a proposal for a type of work I do not represent. Sending a proposal that isn't polished, professional, and proofread. Making a first query contact by phone.

What can writers do to enhance their chances of getting you as their agent? Treat their writing as a long term career, not just a one book opportunity. Constantly improve their writing by getting feedback from writing groups, editors, and other thoughtful coaches. Increase their public profile by publishing their words and ideas via newspapers, magazines, and radio.

Why did you become an agent? Before becoming an agent I spent many years in different areas of publishing—editorial, marketing, business development, licensing—and agenting is an endlessly fascinating and rewarding combination of all these areas.

What might you be doing if you weren't an agent? I have so much fun as an agent that I can't imagine doing anything else.

How would you describe what you do for a living? I am a consultant to my clients—on their ideas, their writing, their careers, and more.

What do you think about other agents? Every agent is an individual, with different strengths. Authors should be self-aware about the kind of assistance they most need and rigorous in searching for the right agent for them.

What do you think about editors? They are some of the smartest readers around. My clients and I carefully review every comment we receive from editors, especially when it is a rejection. No two editors will have the same reaction to any proposal, but the insights from each one are enormously valuable in helping my clients impove their work.

What do you think about publishers? They are smart businesspeople, without whom talented authors are not likely to reach the audience they deserve.

Representative titles: *American Nightingale: The True Story of Frances Slanger, the Forgotten Heroine of Normandy* by Bob Welch (Atria/Simon & Schuster); *Paris in Mind* by Jennifer Lee (Vintage Books/ Random House); *The Skeptic's Dictionary* by Robert Carroll, Ph.D. (John Wiley & Sons); *The Weight Loss Diaries* by Courtney Rubin (Contemporary/McGraw-Hill); *Hear Where We Are: Reawakening to the Sensuality of Sound* by Michael Stocker (University of California Press).

WIESER & ELWELL, INC.

80 Fifth Avenue, #1101, New York, NY 10011

212-260-0860

Agents: Olga B. Wieser, Jake Elwell

Born: Elwell: July 23, 1964, Milton, Massachusetts.

Education: Elwell: B.A., Lake Forest College.

Career history: O. Wieser: NYU Press; Agent since 1975. Elwell: House painter; high school English teacher; Wieser & Wieser: Assistant, 1989–1994; Agent, 1994–present.

Hobbies/personal interests: Elwell: Antiques, book collecting, hockey, fishing, travel.

Areas most interested in agenting: O. Wieser: Well-written, challenging books of all kinds. Strong commercial and literary fiction; holistic, medical, and psychological issues are of particular interest. Elwell: Commercial fiction, including mysteries, historicals, military, suspense, romance. Nonfiction backed by a strong author profile: history, true crime, biography, Americana, books about New England.

Areas not interested in agenting: O. Wieser: Category romance; historicals. Elwell: Science fiction, self-published books that did poorly.

If not agenting, what would you be doing? O. Wieser: Writing. Elwell: Teaching, traveling, trying to be a writer, painting houses.

Best way to initiate contact: Through a referral from someone we know well or by mail with a well-presented outline and opening 50 pages with SASE. Please, no phone or faxed queries.

Reading-fee policy: No reading fee.

Client representation by category: Nonfiction, 45%; Fiction, 50%; Children's, 5%.

Commission: 15% domestic; 20% foreign.

Number of titles sold last year: 50.

Rejection rate (all submissions): 97%.

Most common mistakes authors make: Showing material that is incomplete in planning or presentation. Pitches that try to shock or impress with coolness. We avoid faxed proposals, spiral (or otherwise) bound manuscripts, and solicitations that include past rejection letters from agents and editors (yes, it happens!) like the plague.

Description of the client from Hell: Pitches numerous, disparate ideas and expects reaction or action on all of them. Never is satisfied.

Description of a dream client: Knowledgeable of the realities of publishing (good and bad). Appreciative, receptive to our input, resourceful, and trustworthy.

Why did you become an agent? O. Wieser: There's no job more rewarding, enriching, and exciting. Elwell: I like working in an entrepreneurial setting, and I love books. And there's nothing like playing a role in bringing a book to life.

Representative titles: *Cyclops One* by Jim DeFelice (Pocket); *Terminal Run* by

Michael DiMercurio (NAL); *A Hero's Homecoming* by Kate Huntington (Zebra); *Havoc's Sword* by Dewey Lambdin (St. Martin's Press); *Disaster by the Bay* by H. Paul Jeffers (Lyons Press); *The Battle of Kursk* by Edwin P. Hoyt (Tor/Forge); *Hell Wouldn't Stop: An Oral History of the Battle of Wake Island* by Chet Cunningham (Carroll & Graf); *Agent 146* by Erich Gimpel (St. Martin's Press); *Negotiate and Win* by Dominick Misino (McGraw-Hill); *Frogmen of World War II* by Chet Cunningham (Pocket).

WRITERS HOUSE LLC

21 West 26th Street, New York, NY 10010

212-685-2400   fax: 212-685-1781

Agents: Steven Malk, Susan Ginsburg, Michele Rubin, Albert J. Zuckerman, Merrilee Heifetz, Amy Berkower, Jennifer Lyons (jlyons@writershouse.com), Susan Cohen, Simon Lipskar, Jodi Reamer

Born: Ginsburg: New York. Lebowitz: Baltimore, Maryland. Lyons: August 30, 1961, New York City. Cohen: June 27, 1958.

Education: Ginsburg: Yale University. Zuckerman: D.F.A. in Dramatic Literature, Yale. Heifetz: B.A., Sarah Lawrence College. Lyons: B.A., Sarah Lawrence College; M.A., Middlebury College. Cohen: B.A., Princeton University.

Career history: Ginsburg: Editor-in-Chief, Atheneum; Executive Editor, St. Martin's; Executive Editor, Simon & Schuster/Pocket Books. Zuckerman: Naval officer; Foreign Service officer, U.S. State Department; Assistant Professor of Playwriting, Yale Drama School; winner of Stanley Drama Prize for best new American play of 1964; author of two published novels and of *Writing the Blockbuster Novel*; writer for *The Edge of Night* on TV; Broadway producer. Heifetz: Taught writing to children; Literary Agent. Lyons: Began as an Assistant to Joan Daves. Became Director in 1995. I also work as a senior Writer's House Agent. Cohen: 20 years at Writer's House.

Hobbies/personal interests: Zuckerman: Helping writers; tennis, antique textiles and furniture. Heifetz: Cooking, art, sports. Lyons: Dance, rare books, travel.

Areas most interested in agenting: Ginsburg: Fiction: commercial fiction of any type and literary fiction that is accessible. Nonfiction: broad range of topics chosen purely by interest and marketability. Narrative nonfiction, women's issues, science, biography/autobiography, cookbooks. Zuckerman: Fiction: wonderful novels of all kinds, especially those accessible and attractive to a large readership. Nonfiction: history, biography, narrative nonfiction.. Lyons: Literary fiction and nonfiction. Cohen: Children's books; both authors and illustrators; adults, selected number of nonfiction projects.

Areas not interested in agenting: Ginsburg: Children's books, science fiction. Zuckerman: Scholarly, professional. Heifetz: Men's adventure. Lyons: Romance. Cohen: Science fiction, fantasy, educational, inspirational, academic, financial, business.

If not agenting, what would you be doing? Heifetz: Living in Italy. Lyons: I like what I'm doing. I would also teach.

Best way to initiate contact: Ginsburg: Through written correspondence—query letter (with SASE). Zuckerman: An interesting, intelligent letter (with SASE). Heifetz: Letter (with SASE). Lyons: Send a query letter and three sample chapters. Cohen: Query letter.

Reading-fee policy: No reading fee.

Client representation by category: Agency as a whole has about 500 clients. Ginsburg: 40–50 clients; Nonfiction, 60%; Fiction, 40%. Zuckerman: About 70 clients; Nonfiction, 50%; Fiction, 50%. Heifetz: Nonfiction, 10%; Fiction, 80%; Children's, 10%. Lyons: Nonfiction, 50%; Fiction, 45%, Children's, 5%. Cohen: Nonfiction, 15%; Fiction, 5%; Children's, 80%.

Commission: 15% domestic and film; 20% foreign.

Number of titles sold last year: Agency: More than 400. Lyons: 65. Cohen: 100.

Rejection rate (all submissions): 50%. Cohen: 90%. Lyons: 90%.

Most common mistakes authors make: Lyons: Pink paper. Cohen: Telling me they were referred by someone I've never heard of, sending photos of themselves, sending unprofessional illustrations with their stories.

Description of the client from Hell: Heifetz: I don't have any. Lyons: Calls all the time.

Description of a dream client: Heifetz: Talented, professional, pleasant to deal with, prolific. Lyons: Polite.

What can writers do to enhance their chances of getting you as an agent? Lyons: Build platforms.

How did you become an agent? Lyons: Met an agent who thought I'd make a good one. Cohen: I started at an entry-level position, became an agent's assistant, and after learning how to represent authors, started doing so.

Why did you become an agent? Heifetz: I like reading and I like writers. Lyons: Love the fusion of literary and business.

How would you describe what you actually do for a living? Cohen: I help authors navigate the world of trade publishing.

Comments: Well-known clients are: Octavia E. Butler, Nora Roberts, F. Paul Wilson, Tim Willocks, Ridley Pearson, Ann Martin, Francine Pascal, James Howe, Bruce Sterling, Joan D. Vinge, Cynthia Voigt, Colin Wilson, Robin McKinley, Ed Humes, Robert Anton Wilson, Lora Brody, Jane Feather, Ken Follett, Michael Lewis, Stephen Hawking, V. C. Andrews, Linda Howard, Paula Danziger, Banana Yoshimoto, Barbara Delinsky, Eileen Goudge, Sydney Omarr, David Berlinski, Jessica Harris, Leigh and Leslie Keno, Neil Gairman, Laurell Hamilton, Rosanne Cash.

Representative titles: *The Universe in a Nutshell* by Stephen Hawking (Bantam); *Coast Road* by Barbara Delinsky (Simon & Schuster, first in a three-book mystery series); *Inner Harbor* by Nora Roberts (Berkley); *Inside Intel* by Tim Jackson (Dutton); *Monitor* by James DeKay (Walker); *American Gods* by Neil Gaiman (Avon); *Style and the Man* by Alan Flusser (Harper); *Sunflower* by Martha Powers (Simon & Schuster); *The First Wives' Club* by Olivia Goldsmith (Simon & Schuster); *The Hammer of Eden* by

Ken Follett (Crown); *The Swan Maiden* by Susan King (Penguin Putnam); *Tired of Nagging (30 Days to Positive Parenting)* by Virginia Stowe with Andrea Thompson; *Next* by Michael Lewis (Knopf). Cohen: *MacLean Trilogy* by Janice Johnson (Harlequin); *The World* by Roni Schotter (Atheneum); *The Pickle Museum* by Debbie Tilley (Harcourt).

THE ZACK COMPANY, INC.

243 West 70th Street, Suite 8D, New York, NY 10023-4366

www.zackcompany.com

Agent: Andrew Zack
Born: 1966, Massachusetts.
Education: B.A. in English and Political Science, University of Rochester, 1988.
Career history: I began my publishing career on the retail side as the Evening Manager of an independent bookstore in Massachusetts. While attending the University of Rochester in Rochester, New York, I continued working on the retail side at the university's Barnes & Noble bookstore. Later, I served as an Editor on several student publications, including two years as the Managing Editor of the university yearbook, *Interpres.* I graduated in 1988 with a B.A. and the summer following attended the Radcliffe Publishing Course at Harvard University, an intensive publishing "boot camp" led by numerous publishing veterans. In September of 1988, I began work at Simon & Schuster Trade Division as a Foreign Rights Assistant, where I worked with S&S's foreign subagents in the licensing of foreign editions. Not long thereafter, I moved to Warner Books as an Editorial Assistant. While there, I edited a number of titles and began acquiring on my own. I next worked at Donald I. Fine, Inc., as an Assistant Editor and Rights Associate. Within six months, I was promoted to Associate Editor and Rights Manager. I acquired numerous titles and sold subsidiary rights to the entire Fine list, including serial, book club, reprint, large print, film, and television. I also served as liaison with Fine's British and foreign subagents. The Berkley Publishing Group was my next home, my having been recruited as an Editor. I was eventually responsible for more than 40 titles and brought a number of first-time authors to the list. I left Berkley during a corporate downsizing and entered the world of freelance. As a freelance Editor, I worked with a number of different clients, including several literary agencies and major publishers such as the Berkley Publishing Group, Donald I. Fine, Inc., Avon Books, Dell Publishing, and Tom Doherty Associates. I also reviewed for Kirkus and the Book-of-the-Month Club. I became a Literary Agent in September of 1993, joining the then recently formed Scovil Chichak Galen Literary Agency as a full Agent. I launched the Andrew Zack Literary Agency in March of 1996, which I then incorporated as The Zack Company, Inc., in May 1997.

Hobbies/personal interests: Indoor rowing, biking, film, investing, computers, jazz, reading, racquetball.

Areas most interested in agenting: Serious narrative nonfiction; history and oral history, particularly military history and intelligence services history; politics and current affairs works by established journalists and political insiders or pundits; science and technology and how they affect society, by established journalists, science writers, or experts in their fields; biography, autobiography, or memoir by or about newsworthy individuals, individuals whose lives have made a contribution to the historical record; personal finance and investing; parenting by established experts in their field; health and medicine by doctors or established medical writers; business by nationally recognized business leaders or established business writers, for example, from *The Wall Street Journal*; relationship books by credentialed experts, that is, psychiatrists, psychologists, and therapists with prior publishing credits. Commercial fiction (but not "women's fiction"); thrillers in every shape and form—international, serial killer, medical, scientific, computer, psychological, military, legal; mysteries and not-so-hard-boiled crime novels; action novels, but not action/adventure; science fiction and fantasy, preferably hard science fiction or military science fiction (I was a huge Robert Heinlein fan when I was younger) and big, elaborate fantasies (not coming-of-age fantasies) that take you to a new and established world; horror novels that take you on a roller-coaster ride; historical fiction (but not Westerns).

Areas not interested in agenting: Women's fiction, romance novels, and anything that is intended primarily for a woman reader; genre horror novels, Westerns, religious words, Christian fiction or nonfiction, gay or lesbian fiction; humor (unless by an established humorist, columnist, or comedian); any work of nonfiction in a specialized field that is not by a qualified expert in the field; anything that is supposed to be a novel but is less than 65,000 words; previously self-published books that have sold less than 20,000 copies; any novel featuring drug dealers or drug conspiracies or using AIDS as a weapon; medical thrillers about the evils of HMOs.

If not agenting, what would you be doing? I would likely still be an editor, or I might have gone to law school and pursued a career in entertainment law.

Best way to initiate contact: Best way to initiate contact: Visit our website at www.zackcompany.com and click on How to Query Us.

Reading-fee policy: No reading fee.

Client representation by category: Nonfiction, 35%; Fiction, 65%. (I want more nonfiction by leading authorities in their areas of expertise.)

Commission: 15% or 20% domestic, 20% or 25% foreign, depending on publishing history.

Rejection rate (all submissions): 99.95%.

Most common mistakes authors make: Calling instead of writing; writing a query letter for a work of fiction that doesn't describe the book! My website contains an article on how to write a good query letter.

Description of the client from Hell: Clients from Hell have probably published two or three, or maybe three or four, books. These are likely fiction but might be nonfiction. They have "fired" their previous agent because their career is going nowhere and that is, of course, the agent's fault. They are looking for an agent who can "make things happen"; and just to make sure those things happen, they call a minimum of three or four times a week for updates. They regularly pitch ideas to their old editors, to the point where those editors call me and ask me to stop my clients from doing this constantly. These clients are convinced that their ideas are future bestsellers and can't understand why no one agrees with them. They want instant feedback from me or their editors and never once consider that I may have other clients or that the editors may have books on production schedules ahead of theirs. These clients send proposals via e-mail and don't understand why there isn't an instant response (the one downside to e-mail is that it creates a presumption that because it's almost instantaneous in delivery, the reply to it should be instantaneous). Bottom line: Clients from Hell believe that their needs outweigh everyone else's—their agent's, their editor's, their publicist's, and the needs of all the other authors with whom those people may be working.

Description of a dream client: Dream clients act like professionals. They prepare their material according to publishing standards. They keep me updated on the progress of the work and on their career. They send me an updated biography when something significant happens, as well as copies of reviews of published books if the reviews reach them before getting to my office. They call with news, or fax or e-mail me with news, but generally are aware that time spent "chatting" is time that could be spent selling their works. And, of course, they are *New York Times* bestselling authors.

Why did you become an agent? I had been in the publishing business as an editor and subsidiary rights salesperson for a number of years. I had the opportunity to move into representation with a start-up firm that held a lot of promise. It seemed to be the next, natural step in my career.

How would you describe what you actually do for a living? I represent authors in the sale of their works to publishers, film studios, audio companies, and so on. That means reviewing materials to see if I believe there is a market for them, locating the best markets for them, concluding the sale, negotiating the contract on behalf of my client, and continuing to follow up with the buyer to ensure that the process goes well and that the buyer is using the best efforts to make the work a success.

What do you think of other agents? I think most agents are trying to do the best for their clients, but often they are inclined not to push contractual issues as strongly as they might, out of fear of alienating a publisher and inhibiting their ability to sell future works to that publisher. Often during contract negotiations, I hear that "no other agent but you has ever asked us for that" and my reaction is, "Well, those agents aren't doing the best they can for the client." Publishers' boilerplate contracts are not written to favor authors; they are written to favor publishers. Thus it's important that an agent make best efforts to revise the agreement to make it more equitable. When seeking an agent, ask what, in his or her opinion, the most important contractual issues are? How long does it take to negotiate a contract? If they say a week or so, then they aren't going to the mat to get you the best terms, in my opinion.

What do you think about editors? In today's publishing world, editors have become more like product managers. Because of the demands on them to meet with marketing, publicity, and art departments, there is little time to brainstorm with their authors to help develop the work. In addition, technology has made it mechanically easier to write books, which has resulted in an explosion in the number of books that are submitted. The sheer amount of reading required has made it that much more difficult for editors to look for "diamonds in the rough." Instead, they are looking for more "perfect" books that need little editorial work.

What do you think about publishers? Publishers today are looking for the biggest bang for their buck. They seem more willing to spend $100,000–$1 million on a book and put a big push behind it than to spend $10,000–$25,000 on several books and advertise and promote these books. I would guess that even with a $100,000 advance, publishers are going to do a lot less to push a book than an author might want. Publishers are loath to spend money to make money and will only invest heavily in promotion if a large advance is involved. This forces agents and authors to seek larger and larger advances that frequently do not earn out, which in some cases means the publisher loses money. When the publisher loses money, that means it is less likely to take risks and, strangely enough, it is the smaller books that are seen as risks, not the big-money books. This makes it more and more difficult for first-time authors to be sold, unless publishers perceive the author as the "next big thing." In the end, if authors are not the "next big thing," and the publisher loses money on their books, it is very likely those authors will have a very difficult time selling their second book. A vicious cycle is at work, but it is generally one that was started by publishers and can only be ended by publishers.

Do you watch *The Sopranos*? Yes, as well as *The West Wing, JAG, ER, Stargate: SG-1, Sex and the City, Six Feet Under, Frasier, CSI,* and *Farscape.*

Comments: The agent–author relationship is a business partnership. Agents have their role and authors have their role. Neither is an employee of the other. Interestingly enough, I never hear about agents or authors hiring each other, but I hear about them firing one another all the time. Agents, obviously, are businesspeople. Authors need to be businesspeople, too. Authors should do their best to be as informed as possible about the nature of the publishing business. They should subscribe to *Publishers Weekly,* or at least read it in the library every week. They should talk to their local independent bookseller (and if they really want to learn a few things, they should get a part-time job working in a bookstore). My best client is an educated client. I find that the hardest thing about the agent-author relationship is communication. E-mail has become an important mode of communication for me. It's quick and easy and almost instantaneous as a form of communication. Authors should be able to ask their agents all the questions they want, and if an author's agent disagrees with that, it's time to find another agent. But authors also need to recognize that every minute spent on the phone with them is a minute that could be spent selling their projects. As long as authors understand the job they have and the job agents have in the author-agent relationship, the business partnership will flourish and be profitable.

Representative titles: Please visit my website at: www.zackcompany.com.

SUSAN ZECKENDORF ASSOCIATES, INC.

171 West 57th Street, New York, NY 10019

212-245-2928

Agent: Susan Zeckendorf
Born: New York City.
Education: B.A., Wellesley College; M.Ed., Columbia Teachers College.
Career History: Former Counseling Psychologist.
Hobbies/Personal Interests: Music, reading, cooking.
Areas most interested in agenting: Mysteries, literary fiction, biography, social history, mainstream fiction, science, music.
Areas not interested in agenting: Sci-fi, romance, economics.
If not agencting: Counseling patients.
Best way to initiate contact: Query letter with SASE.
Client representation by category: Nonfiction, 25%; Fiction, 75%.
Commission: 15% U.S.; 20% foreign.
Rejection rate (all submissions): 95%.
Number of titles sold last year: 3.
Description of the client from Hell: Pushy and aggressive.
Description of the dream client: Professional attitude.
How did you become an agent? Through a friend who was an agent.
Why did you become an agent? I love books.
How would you describe what you actually do for a living? I'm the middle man between the client and publisher.
What do you think about other agents? I like them.
What do you think about editors? Fine
What do you think about publishers? Fine
Representative titles: *Back in Shape* by Jaffe and Cooper (Fireside); *The First Four Hundred* by Mrs. Astor's Nework (Rizzoli); *Mabelleen: Literary Fiction* by Kathleen Wallace King (Holt).

ADVICE FOR AUTHORS

THE BATTLE OF THE "UNS"
(UNAGENTED/UNSOLICITED SUBMISSIONS)

JEFF HERMAN

Most major publishing houses claim to have policies that prevent them from even considering unagented/unsolicited submissions. "Unagented" means that a literary agent did not make the submission. "Unsolicited" means that no one at the publisher asked for the submission.

It's possible that you, or people you know, have already run into this frustrating roadblock. You may also be familiar with the rumor that it's more difficult to get an agent than it is to get a publisher—or that no agent will even consider your work until you have a publisher. On the surface, these negatives make it seem that you would have a better shot at becoming a starting pitcher for the Yankees or living out whatever your favorite improbable fantasy might be.

But, as you will soon learn, these so-called policies and practices are often more false than true, especially if you develop creative ways to circumvent them.

I have dubbed the previous obstacle course the Battle of the "UNs."

If you're presently unagented/unsolicited, you're one of the UNs.

Welcome! You're in good company.

Nobody is born published. There is no published author who wasn't at one time an UN. Thousands of new books are published each year, and thousands of people are needed to write them. You can be one of them.

In this chapter I'll show you how to win the Battle of the UNs. But first let me clarify an important distinction. When I use the word "win" here, I don't mean to say that you'll necessarily get your work published. What I mean is: You'll gain reasonable access to the powers-that-be for your work, and you'll learn how to increase the odds—dramatically—that your work will in fact be acquired.

Please be realistic. For every published writer, there are, at minimum, several thousand waiting in line to get published. "Many are called, but few are chosen."

It's completely within your power to maximize your chances of getting published. It's also within your power to minimize those chances. There are reasons why some highly talented people habitually underachieve, and those reasons can often be found within them. If you fail, fail, and fail, you should look within yourself for possible answers. What can you do to turn it around? If you find some answers, then you haven't failed at all, and the lessons you allow yourself to learn will lay the groundwork for success in this and in other endeavors.

Having an agent greatly increases the likelihood that you will be published. For one thing, on the procedural level, established agents can usually obtain relatively rapid (and serious) consideration for their clients. One basic reason for this is that editors view agents as a valuable screening mechanism—that is, when a project crosses the editor's desk under an agent's letterhead, the editor knows it's undergone vetting from someone in the industry who is familiar with the applicable standards of quality and market considerations.

I usually recommend that unpublished writers first make every attempt to get an agent before they start going directly to the publishers.

It's significantly easier to get an agent than it is to get a publisher—not the other way around. Most agents I know are always on the lookout for fresh talent. Finding and nurturing tomorrow's stars are two of our functions.

However, one of my reasons for writing and researching this book is to reveal to you that as a potential author, not having an agent does not necessarily disqualify you from the game automatically. Before I show you ways to win the Battle of the UNs, I'd like you to have a fuller understanding of the system.

YOU ARE THE EDITOR

Imagine that you're an acquisitions editor at one of America's largest publishing firms in New York City. You have a master's degree from an Ivy League college and you, at least, think you're smarter than most other people. Yet you're earning a lot less money than most of the people who graduated with you. Your classmates have become lawyers, accountants, bankers, and so forth, and they all seem to own large, well-appointed apartments or homes—whereas you, if you fall out of bed, might land in the bathtub of your minuscule New York flat.

On the other hand, you love your job. For you, working in publishing is a dream come true. As in other industries and professions, much of your satisfaction comes from advancement—getting ahead.

To move up the career ladder, you'll have to acquire at least a few successful titles each year. To find these few good titles, you'll be competing with many editors from other publishers and perhaps even with fellow editors within your own firm. As in any other business, the people who make the most money for the company will get the choice promotions and the highest salaries. Those who perform less impressively will tend to be passed over. (Of course, being a good editor and playing politics well are also important.)

There are two tried-and-true sources for the titles that publishers acquire: literary agents and direct solicitations.

LITERARY AGENTS

As an editor on the move, you'll cultivate relationships with many established literary agents. You'll want them to know what you like and what you don't like. And, by showing these agents you're disposed to acquiring new titles to build your position in the company, you'll encourage them to send you projects they think are right for you.

When you receive material from agents, you usually give it relatively fast consideration—especially if it's been submitted simultaneously to editors at other houses, which is usually the case.

When something comes in from an agent, you know it's been screened and maybe even perfected. Established agents rarely waste your time with shoddy or inappropriate material. They couldn't make a living that way because they'd quickly lose credibility with editors.

DIRECT SOLICITATIONS

If you're an ambitious editor, you won't just sit back passively and wait to see what the agents might bless you with. When you're resourceful, the opportunities are endless. Perhaps you'll contact your old American history professor and ask her to do a book showcasing her unique perspectives on the Civil War.

Or maybe you'll contact that young, fresh fiction writer whose short story you just read in a leading literary journal. You might even try reaching that veteran United States senator who just got censured for sleeping with his young aides.

One place you'll tend not to use is the "slush pile." This is the room (more like a warehouse) where all the unagented/unsolicited submissions end up.

Looking through the slush pile isn't a smart use of your limited time and energy. The chances that anything decent will be found there are much less than 1 percent. You have less-than-fond memories of your first year in the publishing business, when, as an editorial assistant (which was basically an underpaid secretarial job), one of your tasks was to shovel through the slush. Once in a great while, something promising could be found; but most of the stuff wasn't even close. At first, you were surprised by how unprofessional many of the submissions were. Many weren't addressed to anyone in particular; some looked as if they had been run over by Mack trucks; others were so poorly printed they were too painful for tired eyes to decipher—the list of failings is long.

No, the slush pile is the last place—or perhaps no place—to find titles for your list.

Now you can stop being an editor and go back to being whoever you really are. I wanted to show you why the system has evolved the way it has. Yes, though it's rational, it's cold and unfair, but these qualities aren't unique to publishing.

You're probably still wondering when I'm going to get to that promised modus operandi for winning the Battle of the UNs. Okay, we're there.

OUT OF THE SLUSH

The following steps are intended to keep you out of the infamous slush pile. Falling into the slush is like ending up in jail for contempt of court; it's like being an untouchable in India; it's like being Frank Burns on *M*A*S*H*. My point is that nobody likes the Slushables. They're everyone's scapegoat and nobody's ally.

Once your work is assigned to the slush pile, it's highly unlikely that it will receive effective access. Without access, there can be no acquisition. Without acquisition, there's no book.

Let's pretend that getting published is a board game. However, in this game you can control the dice. Here are several ways to play.

GET THE NAMES!

If you submit to nobody, it will go to nobody. Sending it to "The Editors," "Gentlemen," or the CEO of a $100-million publishing house equals sending it to no one.

Use the directory in this book to get the names of the suitable contacts.

In addition to using this directory, there are two other proven ways to discover who the right editors may be:

1. Visit bookstores and seek out recent books that are in your category. Check the acknowledgments section of each one. Many authors like to thank their editors here (and their agents). If the editor is acknowledged, you now have the name of someone who edits books like yours. (Remember to call to confirm that the editor still works at that publishing house.)

2. Simply call the publisher and ask for the editorial department. More often than not, a young junior editor will answer the phone with something like, "Editorial." Like people who answer phones everywhere, these people may sound as if they are asleep, or they may sound harried, or even as if they're making the most important declaration of their lives.

    Luckily for you, publishers plant few real secretaries or receptionists in their editorial departments, since it's constantly reconfirmed that rookie editors will do all that stuff for everyone else—and for a lot less money! Hence, real editors (although low in rank) can immediately be accessed.

Returning to the true point of this—once someone answers the phone, simply ask, "Who edits your business books?" (Or whatever your category is.)

You can also ask who edited a specific and recent book that's similar to yours. Such easy but vital questions will bring forth quick and valuable answers. Ask enough times and you can build a list of contacts that competes with this book.

DON'T SEND MANUSCRIPTS UNLESS INVITED TO DO SO!

Now that you're armed with these editors' names, don't abuse protocol (editors yell at me when you do—especially when they know where you've gotten their names). Initiate contact by sending a letter describing your work and encouraging the editor to request it.

This letter, commonly referred to as a query letter, is in reality a sales pitch or door-opener. (Please see the following chapter in this book about query letters for a full overview of this important procedure.) In brief, the letter should be short (less than $1\frac{1}{2}$ pages), easy to read and to the point, personalized, and well printed on good professional stationery. Say what you have, why it's hot, why you're a good prospect, and what's available for review upon request.

In addition to the letter, it's okay to include a resume/bio that highlights any writing credits or relevant professional credentials; a brief summary (2-3 pages) if the book is nonfiction, or a brief synopsis if it's fiction; a photo, if you have a flattering one; and promotional materials. Be careful: At this stage your aim is merely to whet the editor's appetite; you don't want to cause information overload. Less is more.

Also include a self-addressed stamped envelope (SASE). This is an important courtesy; without it, you increase your chances of getting no response. Editors receive dozens of these letters every week. Having to address envelopes for all of them would be very time-consuming. And at 37 cents a pop, it's not worth doing.

The SASE is generally intended to facilitate a response in the event of a negative decision. If the editor is intrigued by your letter, he may overlook the missing SASE and request to see your work—but don't count on it.

You may be wondering: If I have the editor's name, why not just send her my entire manuscript? Because you're flirting with the slush pile if you do. Even though you have the editor's previously secret name, you're still an UN, and UNs aren't treated kindly. An editor is inundated with reams of submissions, and her problem is finding good stuff to publish. If you send an unsolicited manuscript, you'll just be perceived as part of that problem. She'll assume you're just another slushy UN who needs to be sorted out of the way so she can go on looking for good stuff.

A bad day for an editor is receiving a few trees' worth of UN manuscripts; it deepens her occupational neurosis.

On the other hand, a professional letter is quite manageable. It is, at least, likely to be read. It may be screened initially by the editor's assistant, but will probably be passed upstairs if it shows promise.

If the editor is at all intrigued by your letter, she will request to see more material, and you will have earned the rank of being solicited.

Even if your work is not ultimately acquired by this editor, you will have at least challenged and defeated the UNs' obstacle course by achieving quality consideration. Remember: Many people get published each year without the benefits of being agented or initially solicited.

It's okay, even smart, to query several editors simultaneously. This makes sense because some editors may take a very long time to respond or, indeed, may never respond. Querying editors one at a time might take years.

If more than one editor subsequently requests and begins considering your work, let each one know that it's not an exclusive. If an editor requests an exclusive, that's fine—but give him a time limit (4 weeks is fair).

Don't sell your work to a publisher before consulting everyone who's considering it and seeing if they're interested. If you do sell it, be sure to give immediate written and oral notification to everyone who's considering it that it's no longer available.

The query-letter stage isn't considered a submission. You only need to have follow-up communications with editors who have gone beyond the query stage, meaning those who have requested and received your work for acquisition consideration. If you don't hear back from an editor within 6 weeks of sending her your letter, it's safe to assume she's not interested in your work.

If you send multiple queries, don't send them to more than one editor at the same house at the same time. If you don't hear back from a particular editor within 6 weeks of your submission, it's probably safe to query another editor at that house. One editor's reject is another's paradise; that's how both good and bad books get published.

We've just covered a lot of important procedural ground, so don't be embarrassed if you think you've forgotten all of it. This book won't self-destruct (and now, presumably, you won't either).

COLD CALLS BREED COLD HEARTS

One more thing: It's best not to cold-call these editors. Don't call them to try to sell them your work. Don't call them to follow up on query letters or submissions. Don't call them to try to change their minds.

Why? Do you like it when someone calls you in the middle of your favorite video to sell you land in the Nevada desert, near a popular nuclear test site?

Few people like uninvited and unscheduled sales calls. In some businesses, such as public relations, calling contacts is a necessary part of the process—but not in publishing. Furthermore, this business is based on hard copy. You may be the greatest oral storyteller since Uncle Remus, but if you can't write it effectively and engagingly, nobody will care. You'll end up soliciting their hostility. Of course, once they are interested in you on the basis of your hard copy, your oral and physical attributes may be of great importance to them.

On the other hand, some people are so skilled on the telephone that it's a lost opportunity for them not to make maximum use of it as a selling method. If you're one of these extremely rare and talented people, you should absolutely make use of whatever tools have proved to work best for you.

Everything I've said is my opinion. This is a subjective industry, so it's likely—no, it's for certain—that others will tell you differently. It's to your advantage to educate yourself to the fullest extent possible (read books, attend workshops, and so forth)—and in the end, to use your own best instincts about how to proceed.

I'm confident that my suggestions are safe and sound, but I don't consider them to be the beginning and the end. The more you know, the simpler things become; the less you know, the more complex and confusing they are.

BREAKING THE RULES

Taken as a whole, this book provides a structure that can be considered a set of guidelines, if not hard-and-fast rules. Some people owe their success to breaking the rules and swimming upstream—and I can certainly respect that. Often such people don't even know they're breaking the rules; they're just naturally following their own unique orbits (and you'll find a few illustrations of this very phenomenon elsewhere in these essays). Trying to regulate such people can often be their downfall.

On one hand, most of us tend to run afoul when we stray from established norms of doing business; on the other hand, a few of us can't succeed any other way (Einstein could have written an essay about that).

If you're one of those few, hats off to you! Perhaps we'll all learn something from your example.

Keep reading!

WRITE THE PERFECT QUERY LETTER

DEBORAH LEVINE HERMAN
JEFF HERMAN

The query is a short letter of introduction to publishers or agents, encouraging them to request to see your fiction manuscript or nonfiction book proposal. It is a vital tool, often neglected by writers.

If done correctly, it can help you to avoid endless frustration and wasted effort. The query is the first hurdle of your individual marketing strategy. If you can leap over it successfully, you're well on your way to a sale.

The query letter is your calling card. For every book that makes it to the shelves, thousands of worthy manuscripts, proposals, and ideas are knocked out of the running by poor presentation or inadequate marketing strategies. Don't forget that the book you want to sell is a product that must be packaged correctly to stand above the competition.

A query letter asks the prospective publisher or agent if she would like to see more about the proposed idea. If your book is fiction, you should indicate that a manuscript or sample chapters are available on request. If nonfiction, you should offer to send a proposal and, if you have them, sample chapters.

The query is your first contact with the prospective buyer of your book. To ensure that it's not your last, avoid common mistakes. The letter should be concise and well written. You shouldn't try to impress the reader with your mastery of all words over three syllables. Instead, concentrate on a clear and to-the-point presentation with no fluff.

Think of the letter as an advertisement. You want to make a sale of a product, and you have very limited space and time in which to reach this goal.

The letter should be only one page long if possible. It will form the basis of a query package that will include supporting materials. Don't waste words in the letter describing material that can be included separately. Your goal is to pique the interest of an editor who has very little time and probably very little patience. You want to entice her to keep reading and ask you for more.

The query package can include a short resume, media clippings, or other favorable documents. Do not get carried away, or your package will quickly come to resemble junk mail. Include a self-addressed stamped envelope (SASE) with enough postage to return your entire package. This will be particularly appreciated by smaller publishing houses and independent agents.

For fiction writers, a short (1- to 5-page), double-spaced synopsis of the manuscript will be helpful and appropriate.

Do not waste money and defeat the purpose of the query by sending an unsolicited manuscript. Agents and editors may be turned off by receiving manuscripts of 1,000+ pages that were uninvited and that are not even remotely relevant to what they do.

The query follows a simple format (which can be reworked according to your individual preferences):

1. lead;

2. supporting material/persuasion;

3. biography; and

4. conclusion/pitch.

YOUR LEAD IS YOUR HOOK

The lead can either catch the editor's attention or turn him off completely. Some writers think getting someone's attention in a short space means having to do something dramatic. Editors appreciate cleverness, but too much contrived writing can work against you. Opt instead for clear conveyance of thoroughly developed ideas and get right to the point.

Of course, you don't want to be boring and stuffy in the interest of factual presentation. You'll need to determine what is most important about the book you're trying to sell, and write your letter accordingly.

You can begin with a lead similar to what you'd use to grab the reader in an article or a book chapter. You can use an anecdote, a statement of facts, a question, a comparison, or whatever you believe will be most powerful.

You may want to rely on the journalistic technique of the inverted pyramid. This means that you begin with the strongest material and save the details for later in the letter. Don't start slowly and expect to pick up momentum as you proceed. It will be too late.

Do not begin a query letter like this: "I have sent this idea to 20 agents/publishers, none of whom think it will work. I just know you'll be different, enlightened, and insightful, and will give it full consideration." There is no room for negatives in a sales pitch. Focus only on positives—unless you can turn negatives to your advantage.

Some writers make the mistake of writing about the book's potential in the first paragraph without ever stating its actual idea or theme. Remember, your letter may never be read beyond the lead, so make that first paragraph your hook.

Avoid bad jokes, clichés, unsubstantiated claims, and dictionary definitions. Don't be condescending; editors have egos, too, and have power over your destiny as a writer.

SUPPORTING MATERIAL: BE PERSUASIVE

If you are selling a nonfiction book, you may want to include a brief summary of hard evidence, gleaned from research, that will support the merit of your idea. This is where you convince the editor that your book should exist. This is more important for non-fiction than it is for fiction, where the style and storytelling ability are paramount. Non-fiction writers must focus on selling their topic and their credentials.

You should include a few lines showing the editor what the publishing house will gain from the project. Publishers are not charitable institutions; they want to know how they can get the greatest return on their investment. If you have brilliant market-ing ideas or know of a well-defined market for your book where sales will be guaran-teed, include this rather than other descriptive material.

In rereading your letter, make sure you have shown that you understand your own idea thoroughly. If it appears half-baked, the editors won't want to invest time fleshing out your thoughts. Exude confidence so that the editor will have faith in your ability to carry out the job.

In nonfiction queries, you can include a separate table of contents and brief chapter abstracts. Otherwise, it can wait for the book proposal.

YOUR BIOGRAPHY: NO PLACE FOR MODESTY

In the biographical portion of your letter, toot your own horn, but in a carefully calcu-lated, persuasive fashion. Your story of winning the third-grade writing competition (it was then that you knew you wanted to be a world-famous writer!) should be saved for the documentary done on your life after you reach your goal.

In the query, all you want to include are the most important and relevant creden-tials that will support the sale of your book. You can include, as a separate part of the package, a resume or biography that will elaborate further.

The separate resume should list all relevant and recent experiences that support your ability to write the book. Unless you're fairly young, your listing of academic accomplishments should start after high school. Don't overlook hobbies or non-job-related activities if they correspond to your book story or topic. Those experiences are often more valuable than academic achievements.

Other information to include: any impressive print clippings about you; a list of your broadcast interviews and speaking appearances; and copies of articles and reviews about any books you may have written. This information can never hurt your chances and could make the difference in your favor.

There is no room for humility or modesty in the query letter and resume. When corporations sell toothpaste, they list the product's best attributes and create excitement about the product. If you can't find some way to make yourself exciting as an author, you'd better rethink your career.

HERE'S THE PITCH

At the close of your letter, ask for the sale. This requires a positive and confident conclusion with such phrases as "I look forward to your speedy response." Such phrases as "I hope" and "I think you will like my book" sound too insecure. This is the part of the letter where you go for the kill.

Be sure to thank the reader for his or her attention in your final sentence.

FINISHING TOUCHES

When you're finished, reread and edit your query letter. Cut out any extraneous information that dilutes the strength of your arguments. Make the letter as polished as possible so that the editor will be impressed with you, as well as with your idea. Don't ruin your chances by appearing careless; make certain your letter is not peppered with typos and misspellings. If you don't show pride in your work, you'll create a self-fulfilling prophecy; the editor will take you no more seriously than you take yourself.

Aesthetics are important. If you were pitching a business deal to a corporation, you would want to present yourself in conservative dress, with an air of professionalism. In the writing business, you may never have face-to-face contact with the people who will determine your future. Therefore, your query package is your representative.

If editors receive a query letter on yellowed paper that looks as if it's been lying around for 20 years, they will wonder if the person sending the letter is a has-been or a never-was.

You should invest in a state-of-the-art letterhead—with a logo!—to create an impression of pride, confidence, and professionalism. White, cream, and ivory paper are all acceptable, but you should use only black ink for printing the letter. Anything else looks amateurish.

Don't sabotage yourself by letting your need for instant approval get the best of you. Don't call editors. You have invited them to respond, so be patient. Then prepare yourself for possible rejection. It often takes many nos to get a yes.

One more note: This is a tough business for anyone—and it's especially so for greenhorns. Hang in there.

QUERY TIPS

If you have spent any time at all in this business, the term *query letter* is probably as familiar to you as the back of your hand. Yet no matter how many courses you've attended and books you've read about this important part of the process, you may still feel inadequate when you try to write one that sizzles. If it's any consolation, you're far from being alone in your uncertainties. The purpose of the query letter is to formally introduce your work and yourself to potential agents and editors. The immediate goal is to motivate them to promptly request a look at your work, or at least a portion of it.

In effect, the letter serves as the writer's first hurdle. It's a relatively painless way for agents and editors to screen out unwanted submissions without the added burden of having to manhandle a deluge of unwanted manuscripts. They are more relaxed if their in-boxes are filled with 50 unanswered queries, as opposed to 50 uninvited 1,000-page manuscripts. The query is a very effective way to control the quality and quantity of the manuscripts that get into the office. And that's why you have to write good ones.

The term *query letter* is part of the lexicon and jargon of the publishing business. This term isn't used in any other industry. I assume it has ancient origins. I can conjure up the image of an English gentleman with a fluffy quill pen composing a most civilized letter to a prospective publisher for the purpose of asking for his work to be read and, perchance, published. Our environments may change, but the nature of our ambitions remains the same.

Let's get contemporary. Whenever you hear the term *query letter*, you should say to yourself "pitch" or "sales" letter. Because that's what it is. You need the letter to sell.

QUERY LETTER TIPS

- *Don't be long-winded.* Agents/editors receive lots of these things, and they want to mow through them as swiftly as possible. Ideally, the letter should be a single page with short paragraphs. (I must admit I've seen good ones that are longer than a page.) If you lose your reader, you've lost your opportunity.

- *Get to the point; don't pontificate.* Too many letters go off on irrelevant detours, which makes it difficult for the agent/editor to determine what's actually for sale—other than the writer's soapbox.

- *Make your letter attractive.* When making a first impression, the subliminal impact of aesthetics cannot be overestimated. Use high-quality stationery and typeface. The essence of your words is paramount, but cheap paper and poor print quality will only diminish your impact.

- *Don't say anything negative about yourself or your attempts to get published.* Everyone appreciates victims when it's time to make charitable donations, but not when it's time to make a profit. It's better if you can make editors/agents think that you have to fight them off.

WHY NOT SIMPLY SUBMIT MY MANUSCRIPT?

Q: Why can't I bypass the query hurdle by simply submitting my manuscript?
A: You may—and no one can litigate against you. But if you submit an unsolicited manuscript to a publisher, it's more likely to end up in the so-called slush pile and may never get a fair reading. If it's sent to an agent, nothing negative may come of it. However, most agents prefer to receive a query first.

Sending unsolicited nonfiction book proposals is in the gray zone. Proposals are much more manageable than entire manuscripts, so editors/agents may not particularly mind.

But you may want to avoid the expense of sending unwanted proposals. After all, the query is also an opportunity for you to screen out those who clearly have no interest in your subject.

Also, you shouldn't be overly loose with your ideas and concepts.

These pointers, in combination with the other good information in this book and all the other available resources, should at least give you a solid background for creating a query letter that sizzles.

THE KNOCKOUT NONFICTION BOOK PROPOSAL

JEFF HERMAN

The nonfiction book proposal is very similar to a sales brochure; viewed as such, and given its due and primary importance in the process of editorial acquisition and book publishing in general, mastery of proposal writing will give you more than a mere leg up: It will invariably make the difference between success and failure.

Before agents and publishers will accept a work of fiction (especially from a newer writer), they require a complete manuscript.

However, nonfiction projects are different: A proposal alone can do the trick. This is what makes nonfiction writing a much less speculative and often more lucrative endeavor (relatively speaking) than fiction writing.

You may devote five years of long evenings to writing a 1,000-page fiction manuscript, only to receive a thick pile of computer-generated rejections. Clearly, writing nonfiction doesn't entail the same risks.

On the other hand, writing fiction is often an emotionally driven endeavor in which rewards are gained though the act of writing and are not necessarily based on rational, practical considerations. Interestingly, many successful nonfiction writers fantasize about being fiction writers.

Fiction writing, whether it be pulp or literary, is one of the most creative things a person can do. And there is a market for fiction: Millions of Americans read fiction voraciously. As is covered elsewhere in this book, the fiction market has a category structure through which agents and publishers can be approached.

Nevertheless, as an author, you should understand that writing nonfiction is the easier road to getting published.

As you'll learn, the proposal's structure, contents, and size can vary substantially, and it's up to you to decide the best format for your purposes. Still, the guidelines given here serve as excellent general parameters.

A topnotch excellent model proposal is featured later in this chapter.

APPEARANCE COUNTS

- Your proposal should be printed in black ink on clean, letter-sized (8½" x 11"), white paper.

- Avoid slick-surfaced computer paper. Be sure to type or print out your manuscript on bond paper—and to separate and trim the pages if they are generated from a fanfold tractor-fed printer.

- Letter-quality printing is by far the best. Make sure the ribbon or toner or ink cartridge is fresh and that all photocopies are dark and clear enough to be read easily. Be wary of old manual typewriters—have the proposal retyped on up-to-date equipment if necessary. Publishing is an image-driven business, and you will be judged, perhaps unconsciously, on the physical and aesthetic merits of your submission.

- Always double-space, or you can virtually guarantee reader antagonism—eyestrain makes people cranky.

- Make sure your proposal appears fresh and new and hasn't been dog-eared, marked-up, and abused by previous readers. No editor will be favorably disposed if she thinks that everyone else on the block has already sent you packing. You want editors to suppose that you have lots of other places you can go, not nowhere else to go.

- Contrary to common practice in other industries, editors prefer not to receive bound proposals. If an editor likes your proposal, she will want to photocopy it for her colleagues, and your binding will only be in the way. If you want to keep the material together and neat, use a paper clip; if it's a lengthy proposal, clip each section together separately.

THE TITLE PAGE

The title page should be the easiest part, but it can also be the most important, since, like your face when you meet someone, it's what is seen first.

Try to think of a title that's attractive and effectively communicates your book's concept. A descriptive subtitle, following a catchy title, can help to achieve both goals.

It's very important that your title and subtitle relate to the book's subject, or an editor might make an inaccurate judgment about your book's focus and automatically dismiss it.

For instance, if you're proposing a book about gardening, don't title it *The Greening of America*.

Examples of titles that have worked very well are:

How to Win Friends and Influence People by Dale Carnegie
Think and Grow Rich by Napoleon Hill
Baby and Child Care by Dr. Benjamin Spock
How to Swim with the Sharks Without Being Eaten Alive by Harvey Mackay

And, yes, there are notable exceptions: An improbable title that went on to become a perennial success is *What Color Is Your Parachute?* by Richard Bolles. Sure, you may gain freedom and confidence from such exceptional instances. By all means let your imagination graze during the brainstorming stage.

However, don't bet on the success of an arbitrarily conceived title that has nothing at all to do with the book's essential concept or reader appeal.

A title should be stimulating and, when appropriate, upbeat and optimistic. If your subject is an important historic or current event, the title should be dramatic. If a biography, the title should capture something personal (or even controversial) about the subject. Many good books have been handicapped by poorly conceived titles, and many poor books have been catapulted to success by good titles. A good title is good advertising. Procter & Gamble, for instance, spends thousands of worker-hours creating seductive names for its endless array of soap-based products.

The title you choose is referred to as the "working title."

Most likely, the book will have a different title when published. There are two reasons for this:

1. A more appropriate or arresting title (or both) may evolve with time; and

2. The publisher has final contractual discretion over the title (as well as over a lot of other things).

The title page should contain only the title; your name, address, and telephone number—and the name, address, and phone number of your agent, if you have one. The title page should be neatly and attractively spaced. Eye-catching and tasteful computer graphics and display-type fonts can contribute to the overall aesthetic appeal.

OVERVIEW

The overview portion of the proposal is a terse statement (one to three pages) of your overall concept and mission. It sets the stage for what's to follow. Short, concise paragraphs are usually best.

BIOGRAPHICAL SECTION

This is where you sell yourself. This section tells who you are and why you're the ideal person to write this book. You should highlight all your relevant experience, including media and public-speaking appearances, and list previous books, articles, or both, published by or about you. Self-flattery is appropriate—so long as you're telling the truth. Many writers prefer to slip into the third person here, to avoid the appearance of egomania.

MARKETING SECTION

This is where you justify the book's existence from a commercial perspective. Who will buy it? For instance, if you're proposing a book on sales, state the number of people who earn their livings through sales; point out that thousands of large and small companies are sales-dependent and spend large sums on sales training, and that all sales professionals are perpetually hungry for fresh, innovative sales books.

Don't just say something like "My book is for adult women and there are more than 50 million adult women in America." You have to be much more demographically sophisticated than that.

COMPETITION SECTION

To the uninitiated, this section may appear to be a set-up to self-destruction. However, if handled strategically, and assuming you have a fresh concept, this section wins you points rather than undermines your case.

The competition section is where you describe major published titles with concepts comparable to yours. If you're familiar with your subject, you'll probably know those titles by heart; you may have even read most or all of them. If you're not certain, check *Books in Print*—available in virtually every library—which catalogues all titles in print in every category under the sun.

Don't list everything published on your subject—that could require a book in itself.

ADVICE FOR AUTHORS

Just describe the leading half-dozen titles or so (backlist classics, as well as recent books) and *explain why yours will be different.*

Getting back to the sales-book example, there is no shortage of good sales books. There's a reason for that—a big market exists for sales books. You can turn that to your advantage by emphasizing the public's substantial, insatiable demand for sales books. Your book will feed that demand with its unique and innovative sales-success program. Salespeople and companies dependent on sales are always looking for new ways to enhance sales skills (it's okay to reiterate key points).

PROMOTION SECTION

Here you suggest possible ways to promote and market the book. Sometimes this section is unnecessary. It depends on your subject and on what, if any, realistic promotional prospects exist.

If you're proposing a specialized academic book such as *The Mating Habits of Octopi*, the market is a relatively limited one, and elaborate promotions would be wasteful.

But if you're proposing a popularly oriented relationship book along the lines of *The Endless Orgasm in One Easy Lesson*, the promotional possibilities are also endless. They would include most major electronic broadcast and print media outlets, advertising, maybe even some weird contests.

You want to guide the publisher toward seeing realistic ways to publicize the book.

CHAPTER OUTLINE

This is the meat of the proposal. Here's where you finally tell what's going to be in the book. Each chapter should be tentatively titled and clearly abstracted.

Some successful proposals have fewer than 100 words per abstracted chapter; others have several hundred words per chapter. Sometimes the length varies from chapter to chapter. There are no hard-and-fast rules here; it's the dealer's choice.

Sometimes less is more; at other times a too-brief outline inadequately represents the project.

At their best, the chapter abstracts read like mini-chapters—as opposed to stating "I will do . . . and I will show . . ." Visualize the trailer for a forthcoming movie; that's the tantalizing effect you want to create.

Also, it's a good idea to preface the outline with a table of contents. This way, the editor can see your entire road map at the outset.

SAMPLE CHAPTERS

Sample chapters are optional. A strong, well-developed proposal will often be enough. However, especially if you're a first-time writer, one or more sample chapters will give you an opportunity to show your stuff and will help dissolve an editor's concerns about your ability to actually write the book, thereby increasing the odds that you'll receive an offer—and you'll probably increase the size of the advance, too.

Nonfiction writers are often wary of investing time to write sample chapters since they view the proposal as a way of avoiding speculative writing. This can be a short-sighted position, however, for a single sample chapter can make the difference between selling and not selling a marginal proposal. Occasionally, a publisher will request that one or two sample chapters be written before he makes a decision about a particular project. If the publisher seems to have a real interest, writing the sample material is definitely worth the author's time, and the full package can then be shown to additional prospects, too.

Many editors say that they look for reasons to reject books and that being on the fence is a valid reason for rejecting a project. To be sure, there are cases where sample chapters have tilted a proposal on the verge of rejection right back onto the playing field!

Keep in mind that the publisher is speculating that you can and will write the book upon contract. A sample chapter will go far to reduce the publisher's concerns about your ability to deliver a quality work beyond the proposal stage.

WHAT ELSE?

There are a variety of materials you may wish to attach to the proposal to further bolster your cause. These include:

- Laudatory letters and comments about you.

- Laudatory publicity about you.

- A headshot (but not if you look like the Fly, unless you're proposing a humor book or a nature book).

- Copies of published articles you've written.

- Videos of TV or speaking appearances.

- Any and all information that builds you up in a relevant way, but be organized about it—don't create a disheveled, unruly package.

LENGTH

The average proposal is probably between 15 and 30 double-spaced pages, and the typical sample chapter an additional 10 to 20 double-spaced pages. But sometimes proposals reach 100 pages, and sometimes they're 5 pages total. Extensive proposals are not a handicap.

Whatever it takes!

MODEL SUCCESSFUL NONFICTION BOOK PROPOSAL

What follows is a genuine proposal that won a healthy book contract. It's excerpted from *Write the Perfect Book Proposal* by Jeff Herman and Deborah Adams (John Wiley & Sons) and includes an extensive critique of its strongest and weakest points. All in all, it's an excellent proposal and serves as a strong model.

The book is titled *Heart and Soul: A Psychological and Spiritual Guide to Preventing and Healing Heart Disease* and is written by Bruno Cortis, M.D. This project was sold to the Villard Books division of Random House.

Every editor who saw this proposal offered sincere praise. Ironically, several of these editors regretted not being able to seek the book's acquisition. From the outset I was aware this might happen. The past few years have given us numerous unconventional health and healing books—many of which are excellent. Most publishers I approached felt that their health/spirituality quota was already full and that they would wind up competing with themselves if they acquired any more such titles.

Experienced agents and writers are familiar with the market-glut problem. In many popular categories it's almost endemic. If you're prepared for this reality from the outset, there are ways to pave your own road and bypass the competition. Dedicated agents, editors, and writers want to see important books published, regardless of what the publishers' lists dictate.

Furthermore, it is not necessary for every publisher to want your book (though that is the proven way to maximize the advance).

In the end, you need only the right publisher and a reasonable deal.

Let's look first at the title page from the book proposal.

HEART AND SOUL

(This is a good title. It conjures up dramatic images similar to a soulful blues melody. And it has everything to do with what this proposal is about. The subtitle is scientific and provides a clear direction for the patients.)

Psychological and Spiritual Guide to Preventing and Healing Heart Disease
by
Bruno Cortis, M.D.
Book Proposal

The Jeff Herman Agency
PO Box 1522, 9 South Street
Stockbridge, MA
telephone: 413-298-8188

(The title page is sufficient overall. But it would have been better if the software had been available to create a more striking cover sheet. To a large degree, everything does initially get judged by its cover.)

OVERVIEW

(One minor improvement here would have been to shift the word "Overview" to the center of the page—or otherwise styling the typeface for such headings and subheadings throughout the proposal to make them stand out from the body text.)

Heart disease is the number-one killer of Americans over the age of 40. The very words can sound like a death sentence. Our heart, the most intimate part of our body, is under siege. Until now, most experts have advised victims of the disease, as well as those who would avoid it, to change avoidable risk factors, like smoking, and begin a Spartan regimen of diet and exercise. But new research shows that risk factors and lifestyle are only part of the answer. In fact, it is becoming clear that for many patients, emotional, psychological, and even spiritual factors are at least as important, both in preventing disease and in healing an already damaged heart.

(This is a powerful lead paragraph. The author knows a lot of books are out there about heart disease. The first paragraph of the overview immediately distinguishes this book proposal and draws attention to "new research." Anything that is potentially cutting edge is going to catch the eye of a prospective publisher.)

ADVICE FOR AUTHORS

THE KNOCKOUT NONFICTION BOOK PROPOSAL   727

Like *Love, Medicine, and Miracles* by Bernie Siegel, which showed cancer patients how to take charge of their own disease and life, *Heart and Soul* will show potential and actual heart patients how to use inner resources to form a healthy relationship with their heart, actually healing circulatory disorders and preventing further damage.

(The preceding paragraph contains the central thesis for the project, and it is profoundly important. In retrospect, this could have worked exceedingly well as the first paragraph of the proposal, thereby immediately setting the stage. This is a clever comparison to a highly successful book. It indicates an untapped market that has already proved itself in a similar arena. Instead of merely making unsubstantiated claims based on the success of Dr. Siegel's work, the author shows what this book will do to merit the same type of attention.)

The author, Bruno Cortis, M.D., is a renowned cardiologist whose experience with hundreds of "exceptional heart patients" has taught him that there is much more to medicine than operations and pills.

(It is good to bring the author's credentials into the overview at this juncture. A comparison has been made with a highly successful and marketable doctor/author—which will immediately raise questions as to whether this author has similar potential. The author anticipates this line of editorial reasoning and here makes some strong statements.)

Dr. Cortis identifies three types of heart patients:

♦   Passive Patients, who are unwilling or unable to take responsibility for their condition. Instead, these patients blame outside forces, withdraw from social contacts, and bewail their fate. They may become deeply depressed and tend to die very soon.

♦   Obedient Consumers, who are the "A" students of modern medicine. Following doctors' orders to the letter, these patients behave exactly as they are supposed to, placing their fates in the hands of the experts. These patients tend to die exactly when medicine predicts they will.

♦   Exceptional Heart Patients, who regard a diagnosis of heart disease as a challenge. Although they may have realistic fears for the future, these patients take full responsibility for their situation and actively contribute to their own recovery. While they may or may not follow doctors' orders, these patients tend to choose the therapy or combination of therapies that is best for them. They often live far beyond medical predictions.

(This is an exceptional overview—especially where it defines the three patient types.)

It is Dr. Cortis's aim in this book to show readers how to become exceptional heart patients, empowering them to take responsibility for their own health and well-being.

(The remaining paragraphs of this overview section show a highly focused and well-thought-out plan for the book. The writing collaborator on this project had to condense and assimilate boxes and boxes of material to produce this concise and to-the-point overview that leaves no questions unanswered. Although it took a great deal of effort for the writer to write such a good proposal, there is no struggle for the editor to understand exactly what is being proposed and what the book is going to be about.)

Although Dr. Cortis acknowledges the importance of exercise, stress management, and proper nutrition—the standard staples of cardiac treatment—he stresses that there is an even deeper level of human experience that is necessary in order to produce wellness. Unlike other books on heart disease, *Heart and Soul* does not prescribe the same strict diet and exercise program for everyone. Instead it takes a flexible approach, urging readers to create their own unique health plan by employing psychological and spiritual practices in combination with a variety of more traditional diet and exercise regimens.

While seemingly revolutionary, Dr. Cortis's message is simple: You can do much more for the health of your heart than you think you can. This is true whether you have no symptoms or risk factors whatsoever, if you have some symptoms or risk factors, or if you actually already have heart disease.

MARKET ANALYSIS

Heart and Soul could not be more timely. Of the $1^1/_2$ million heart attacks suffered by Americans each year, nearly half occur between the ages of 40 and 65. Three-fifths of these heart attacks are fatal. While these precise statistics may not be familiar to the millions of baby boomers now entering middle age, the national obsession with oat bran, low-fat foods, and exercising for health shows that the members of the boomer generation are becoming increasingly aware of their own mortality.

(The writer would be well advised to ease off the use of the term baby boomer. It is so often used in book proposals that many editors are undoubtedly sick of it. It might have been better merely to describe the exceptional number of people in this pertinent age bracket—without attempting to sound trendy. Good use of facts, trends, and the public's receptivity to what some would characterize as an unorthodox treatment approach.)

This awareness of growing older, coupled with a widespread loss of faith in - doctors and fear of overtechnologized medicine, combine to produce a market that is ready for a book emphasizing the spiritual component in healing, especially in reference to heart disease.

Most existing books on the market approach the subject from the physician's point of view, urging readers to follow doctor's orders to attain a healthy heart. There is very little emphasis in these books on the patient's own responsibility for wellness or the inner changes that must be made for the prescribed regimens to work. Among the best known recent books are:

(Not a big deal in this instance—but ordinarily it would be better to have identified this portion of the proposal as the competition section, set it off under a separate heading.)

Healing Your Heart, by Herman Hellerstein, M.D., and Paul Perry (Simon & Schuster, 1990). Although this book, like most of the others, advocates proper nutrition, exercise, cessation of smoking, and stress reduction as the road to a healthy heart, it fails to provide the motivation necessary to attain such changes in the reader's lifestyle. Without changes in thinking and behavior, readers of this and similar books will find it difficult, if not impossible, to follow the strict diet and exercise program recommended.

In Heart Talk: Preventing and Coping with Silent and Painful Heart Disease (Harcourt Brace Jovanovich, 1987), Dr. Peter F. Cohn and Dr. Joan K. Cohn address the dangers of "silent" (symptomless) heart disease. While informative, the book emphasizes only one manifestation of heart disease and does not empower readers with the motivational tools needed to combat that disease.

(This section is termed the market analysis, which in this proposal actually departs from the approach of the typical marketing section of most proposals. Instead of telling the publisher how to sell the book, the writing collaborator [see the About the Authors section further on] shows special insight into the target audience. The key is that this analysis is not merely a statement of the obvious. This type of in-depth analysis of the potential reader can be very persuasive.)

The Trusting Heart, by Redford Williams, M.D. (Times Books, 1989), demonstrates how hostility and anger can lead to heart disease, while trust and forgiveness can contribute to wellness. While these are important points, the holistic treatment of heart disease must encompass other approaches as well. The author also fails to provide sufficient motivation for behavioral changes in the readers.

(The author does a good job of demonstrating the invaluable uniqueness of this particular project—especially important when compared with the strong list of competitors.)

The best book on preventing and curing heart disease is Dr. Dean Ornish's *Program for Reversing Heart Disease* (Random House, 1990). This highly successful book prescribes a very strict diet and exercise program for actually reversing certain types of coronary artery disease. This still-controversial approach is by far the best on the market; unfortunately, the material is presented in a dense, academic style not easily accessible to the lay reader. It also focuses on Dr. Ornish's program as the "only way to manage heart disease," excluding other, more synergistic methods.

(The writer collaborator directly analyzed the competition, highlighting the most relevant books on the market without listing each one directly. Although you do not want to present the editor with any unnecessary surprises, if there are too many similar books out in your particular subject area, you might want to use this approach. The writer confronts the heaviest competition directly by finding specific distinguishing factors that support the strength of his proposed project.)

APPROACH

Heart and Soul will be a 60,000- to 70,000-word book targeted to health-conscious members of the baby boom generation. Unlike other books on heart disease, it will focus on the "facts of the connection between the mind and the body as it relates to heart disease, showing readers how to use that connection to heal the heart." The book will be written in an informal but authoritative style, in Dr. Cortis's voice. It will begin with a discussion of heart disease and show how traditional medicine fails to prevent or cure it. Subsequent chapters will deal with the mind-body connection, and the role in healing of social support systems, self-esteem, and faith. In order to help readers reduce stress in their lives, Dr. Cortis shows how they can create their own "daily practice" that combines exercise, relaxation, meditation, and use of positive imagery. Throughout the book, he will present anecdotes that demonstrate how other Exceptional Heart Patients have overcome their disease and gone on to lead healthy and productive lives.

In addition to a thorough discussion of the causes and outcomes of coronary artery disease, the book will include tests and checklists that readers may use to gauge their progress, and exercises, ranging from the cerebral to the physical, that strengthen and help heal the heart. At the end of each chapter readers will be introduced to an essential "Heartskill" that will enable them to put the advice of the chapter into immediate practice.

Through example and encouragement *Heart and Soul* will offer readers a variety of strategies for coping with heart disease, to be taken at once or used in combination. Above all an accessible, practical book, *Heart and Soul* will present readers with a workable program for controlling their own heart disease and forming a healthy relationship with their hearts.

(This is a good summary statement of the book.)

ABOUT THE AUTHORS

Bruno Cortis, M.D., is an internationally trained cardiologist with more than 30 years' experience in research and practice. A pioneer of cardiovascular applications of lasers and angioscopy, a Diplomate of the American Board of Cardiology, contributor of more than 70 published professional papers, Dr. Cortis has long advocated the need for new dimensions of awareness in health and the healing arts. As a practicing physician and researcher, his open acknowledgment of individual spirituality as the core of health puts him on the cutting edge of those in traditional medicine who are beginning to create the medical arts practices of the future.

(This is a very good description of the author. The writing collaborator establishes Dr. Cortis as both an expert in his field and a compelling personality. All of this material is relevant to the ultimate success of the book.)

Dr. Cortis has been a speaker at conferences in South America, Japan, and Australia, as well as in Europe and the United States. His firm, Mind Your Health, is dedicated to the prevention of heart attack through the development of human potential. Dr. Cortis is the cofounder of the Exceptional Heart Patients program. The successful changes he has made in his own medical practice prove he is a man not only of vision and deeds, but an author whose beliefs spring from the truths of daily living.

(A formal vita follows in this proposal. It is best to lead off with a journalistic-style biography and follow up with a complete and formal resume—assuming, as in this case, the author's professional credentials are inseparable from the book.)

Kathryn Lance is the author of more than 30 books of nonfiction and fiction (see attached publications list for details). Her first book, *Running for Health and Beauty* (1976), the first mass-market book on running for women, sold half a million copies. *The Setpoint Diet* (1985), ghosted for Dr. Gilbert A. Leveille, reached the *New York Times* bestseller list for several weeks. Ms. Lance has written widely on fitness, health, diet, and medicine.

(Though she wasn't mentioned on the title page, Lance is the collaborator. This brief bio and the following resume reveal a writer with virtually impeccable experience. Her participation served to ensure the editors that they could count on the delivery of a high-quality manuscript. Her bio sketch is also strong in its simplicity. Her writing credits are voluminous, but she does not use up space here with a comprehensive listing. Instead she showcases only credits that are relevant to the success of this particular project. Comprehensive author resumes were also attached as addenda to the proposal package.)

HEART AND SOUL
by
Bruno Cortis, M.D.
Chapter Outline

(Creating a separate page [or pages] for the entire table of contents is a useful and easy technique to enable the editor to gain a holistic vision for the book before delving into the chapter abstracts. In retrospect, we should have had one here.)

(The following is an exceptional outline because it goes well beyond the lazy and stingy telegraph approach that many writers use, often to their own detriment. [Telegrams once were a popular means of communication that required the sender to pay by the word.] Here each abstract reads like a miniature sample chapter unto itself. It proves that the writers have a genuine command of their subject, a well-organized agenda, and superior skills for writing about it. Together they are a darn good team. Whatever legitimate reasons a publisher may have had for rejecting this proposal, it had nothing to do with its manifest editorial and conceptual merits. Some writers are reluctant to go this editorial distance on spec. However, if you believe in your project's viability and you want to maximize acquisition interest and the ultimate advance, you'll give the proposal everything you've got.)

Contents

Introduction: Beating the Odds: Exceptional Heart Patients
(See sample chapter.)

Chapter One
YOU AND YOUR HEART
Traditional medicine doesn't and can't "cure" heart disease. The recurrence rate of arterial blockage after angioplasty is 25-35 percent, while a bypass operation only bypasses the problem, but does not cure it. The author proposes a new way of looking at heart disease, one in which patients become responsible for the care and well-being of their hearts, in partnership with their physicians. Following a brief, understandable discussion of the physiology of heart disease and heart attack, further topics covered in this chapter include:

(This is a good technique for a chapter abstract. The writer organizes the structure as a listing of chapter topics and elaborates with a sample of the substance and writing approach that will be incorporated into the book. The editor cannot, of course, be expected to be an expert on the subject, but after reading this abstract will come away with a good sense of the quality of the chapter and the depth of its coverage.)

Heart disease as a message from your body. Many of us go through life neglecting our bodies' signals, ignoring symptoms until a crisis occurs. But the body talks to us and it is up to us to listen and try to understand the message. The heart bears the load of all our physical activity as well as our mental activity. Stress can affect the heart as well as any other body system. This section explores the warning signs of heart disease as "messages" we may receive from our hearts, what these messages may mean, and what we can do in response to these messages.

Why medical tests and treatments are not enough. You, the patient, are ultimately responsible for your own health. Placing all faith in a doctor is a way of abdicating that responsibility. The physician is not a healer; rather, he or she sets the stage for the patient's body to heal itself. Disease is actually a manifestation of an imbalance within the body. Medical procedures can help temporarily, but the real solution lies in the patient's becoming aware of his own responsibility for health. This may involve changing diet, stopping smoking, learning to control the inner life.

(Although the abstracts are directed to the editor who reviews the proposal, the writer incorporates the voice to be used in the book by speaking directly to the reader. This is an effective way to incorporate her writing style into the chapter-by-chapter outline.)

Getting the best (while avoiding the worst) of modern medicine. In the author's view, the most important aspect of medicine is not the medication but the patient/physician relationship. Unfortunately, this relationship is often cold, superficial, professional. The patient goes into the medical pipeline, endures a number of tests, then comes out the other end with a diagnosis, which is like a flag he has to carry for life. This view of disease ignores the patient as the main component of the healing process. Readers are advised to work with their doctors to learn their own blood pressure, blood sugar, cholesterol level, and what these numbers mean. They are further advised how to enlist a team of support people to increase their own knowledge of the disease and learn to discover the self-healing mechanisms within.

How to assess your doctor. Ten questions a patient needs to ask in order to assure the best patient-doctor relationship.

Taking charge of your own medical care. Rather than being passive patients, readers are urged to directly confront their illness and the reasons for it, asking themselves: How can I find a cause at the deepest level? What have I learned from this disease? What is good about it? What have I learned about myself? Exceptional heart patients don't allow themselves to be overwhelmed by the disease; rather, they realize that it is most likely a temporary problem, most of the time self-limited, and that they have a power within to overcome it.

Seven keys to a healthy heart. Whether presently healthy or already ill of heart disease, there is a great deal readers can do to improve and maintain the health of their hearts. The most important component of such a plan is to have a commitment to a healthy heart. The author offers the following seven keys to a healthy heart: respect your body; take time to relax every day; accept, respect, and appreciate yourself; share your deepest feelings; establish life goals; nourish your spiritual self; love yourself and others unconditionally. Each of these aspects of heart care will be examined in detail in later chapters.

Heartskill #1: *Learning to take your own pulse.* The pulse is a wave of blood sent through the arteries each time the heart contracts; pulse rate therefore provides important information about cardiac function. The easiest place to measure the pulse is the wrist: place your index and middle finger over the underside of the opposite wrist. Press gently and firmly until you locate your pulse. Don't use your thumb to feel the pulse, because the thumb has a pulse of its own. Count the number of pulse beats in fifteen seconds, then multiply that by four for your heart rate.

This exercise will include charts so that readers can track and learn their own normal pulse range for resting and exercising, and be alerted to irregularities and changes that may require medical attention.

(The inclusion of this technique shows how specific and practical information will be included in the book—important for a nonfiction book proposal. Editors look for what are called the program aspects of a book, because they can be used in promotional settings—and may also be the basis for serial-rights sales to magazines.)

Chapter Two
YOUR MIND AND YOUR HEART

This chapter begins to explore the connection between mind and body as it relates to heart disease. Early in the chapter readers will meet three Exceptional Heart Patients who overcame crushing diagnoses. These include Van, who overcame a heart attack (at age 48), two open-heart surgeries, and "terminal" lung cancer. Through visualization techniques given him by the author, Van has fully recovered and is living a healthy and satisfying life. Goran, who had a family history of cardiomyopathy, drew on the support and love of his family to survive a heart transplant and has since gone on to win several championships in an Olympics contest for transplant patients. Elaine, who overcame both childhood cancer and severe heart disease, is, at the age of 24, happily married and a mother. The techniques used by these Exceptional Heart Patients will be discussed in the context of the mind-body connection.

(The authors do not save the good stuff for the book. If you have interesting case studies or anecdotes, include them here: The more stimulating material you can include, the more you can intrigue your editor. In general, this chapter-by-chapter synopsis is exceptionally detailed in a simplified fashion, which is important for this type of book.)

How your doctor views heart disease: Risk factors v. symptoms. Traditional medicine views the risk factors for heart disease (smoking, high blood cholesterol, high blood pressure, diabetes, obesity, sedentary lifestyle, family history of heart disease, use of oral contraceptives) as indicators of the likelihood of developing illness. In contrast, the author presents these risk factors as *symptoms* of an underlying disease, and discusses ways to change them. Smoking, for example, is not the root of the problem, which is, rather, fear, tension, and stress. Smoking is just an outlet that the patient uses to get rid of these basic elements, which he or she believes are uncontrollable. Likewise high cholesterol, which is viewed by the medical establishment as largely caused by poor diet, is also affected by stress. (In a study of rabbits on a high-cholesterol diet, narrowing of arteries was less in rabbits that were petted, even if the diet remained unhealthful.) Other elements besides the traditional "risk factors," such as hostility, have been shown to lead to high rates of heart disease.

A mind/body model of heart disease. It is not uncommon to hear stories like this: They were a very happy couple, married 52 years. Then, suddenly, the wife developed breast cancer and died. The husband, who had no previous symptoms of heart disease, had a heart attack and died two months later. All too often there is a very close relationship between a traumatic event and serious illness. Likewise, patients may often become depressed and literally will themselves to die. The other side of the coin is the innumerable patients who use a variety of techniques to enlist the mind-body connection in helping to overcome and even cure serious illnesses, including heart disease.

Rethinking your negative beliefs about heart disease. The first step in using the mind to help to heal the body is to rethink negative beliefs about heart disease. Modern studies have shown that stress plays a most important role in the creation of heart disease, influencing all of the "risk factors." Heart disease is actually a disease of self, caused by self, and is made worse by the belief that we are its "victims." Another negative and incorrect belief is that the possibilities for recovery are limited. The author asserts that these beliefs are untrue, and that for patients willing to learn from the experience, heart disease can be a path to recovery, self-improvement, and growth.

The healing personality: tapping into your body's healing powers. Although the notion of a "healing personality" may sound contradictory, the power of healing is awareness, which can be achieved by anyone. The author describes his own discovery of spirituality in medicine and the realization that ultimately the origin of disease is in the mind. This is why treating disease with medicine and surgery alone does not heal: because these methods ignore the natural healing powers of the body/mind. How does one develop a "healing personality"? The starting point is awareness of the spiritual power within. As the author states, in order to become healthy, one must become spiritual.

Writing your own script for a healthy heart. Before writing any script, one must set the stage, and in this case readers are urged to see a cardiologist or physician and have a thorough checkup. This checkup will evaluate the presence or absence of the "risk factors" and assess the health of other body organs as well. Once the scene is set, it is time to add in the other elements of a healthy heart, all of which will be explored in detail in the coming chapters.

Making a contract with your heart. We see obstacles only when we lose sight of our goals. How to make (either mentally or on paper) a contract with one's heart that promises to take care of the heart. Each individual reader's contract will be somewhat different; for example, someone who is overweight might include in the contract the desire that in six months she would weigh so much. The point is to set realistic, achievable goals. Guidelines are provided for breaking larger goals down into small, easily achievable, steps. Creating goals for the future makes them a part of the present in the sense that it is today that we start pursuing them.

What to say when you talk to yourself. In the view of the author, the greatest source of stress in life is negative conversations we have with ourselves. These "conversations," which go on all the time without our even being aware of them, often include such negative suggestions as "When are you going to learn?" "Oh, no, you stupid idiot, you did it again!" When we put ourselves down, we reinforce feelings of unworthiness and inadequacy, which leads to stress and illness. Guidelines are given for replacing such negative self-conversation with more positive self-talk, including messages of love and healing.

Heartskill #2: Sending healing energy to your heart. In this exercise, readers learn a simple meditation technique that will help them get in touch with their natural healing powers and begin to heal their hearts.

Chapter Three
THE FRIENDSHIP FACTOR:
PLUGGING INTO YOUR SOCIAL SUPPORT SYSTEM

Heart disease is not an isolated event, and the heart patient is not an isolated human being. Among the less medically obvious "risk factors" involved in coronary disease are social isolation. In this chapter the author discusses the importance of maintaining and strengthening all the social support aspects of the patient's life, including family, friendship, community, and sex. He shows how intimacy and connection can be used not just for comfort but also as actual healing tools.

Sexual intimacy: the healing touch. Following a heart attack, many patients may lose confidence due to a fear of loss of attractiveness or fear of death. Citing recent studies, the author points out that there is a difference between making sex and making love. The desire for sex is a human need and is not limited to healthy people. Anybody who has had a heart problem still has sexual needs and ignoring them may be an additional cause of stress. Guidelines for when and how to resume sexual activity are offered. Other topics covered in this chapter include:

Keeping your loved ones healthy, and letting them keep you healthy
How you may be unwittingly pushing others out of your life
The art of nondefensive, nonreactive communication
Accepting your loved ones' feelings and your own
How to enlist the support of family and friends
Joining or starting your own support group

Heartskill #3: *Mapping your social support system*

Chapter 4
OPENING YOUR HEART:
LEARNING TO MAKE FRIENDS WITH YOURSELF

In addition to enlisting the support of others, for complete healing it is necessary for the patient to literally become a friend to himself or herself. This may entail changing old ways of thinking and responding, as well as developing new, healthier ways of relating to time and other external stresses. In this chapter the author explores ways of changing Type A behavior, as well as proven techniques for dealing with life's daily hassles and upsets. An important section of the chapter shows readers how to love and cherish the "inner child," that part of the personality that needs to be loved, to be acknowledged, and to have fun. Equally important is the guilt that each of us carries within, and that can lead not only to unhealthy behaviors but also to actual stress. The author gives exercises for learning to discover and absolve the hidden guilts that keep each of us from realizing our true healthy potential. Topics covered in this chapter include:

A positive approach to negative emotions
Checking yourself out on Type A behavior: a self-test
Being assertive without being angry
Keeping your balance in the face of daily hassles and major setbacks
Making a friend of time
Identifying and healing your old childhood hurts
Letting go of hurts, regrets, resentments, and guilt
Forgiving yourself and making a new start
The trusting heart

Heartskill #4: *Forgiveness exercise*

Chapter 5
IDENTIFYING AND ELIMINATING STRESS IN YOUR LIFE

The science of psychoneuroimmunology is beginning to prove that the mind and body are not only connected, but also inseparable. It has been demonstrated that changes in life often precede disease. Lab studies have shown that the amount of stress experienced by experimental animals can induce rapid growth of a tumor that would ordinarily be rejected. For heart patients, the fact of disease itself can become another inner stress factor that may worsen the disease and the quality of life. One out of five healthy persons is a "heart reactor," who has strong responses under stress that induce such unhealthful physiological changes as narrowing of the coronary arteries, hypertrophy of the heart muscle, and high blood pressure. In this chapter the author shows readers how to change stress-producing negative beliefs into constructive, rational beliefs that reduce stress. Included are guidelines to the five keys for controlling stress: diet, rest, exercise, attitude, and self-discipline.

Why you feel so stressed-out
Where does emotional stress come from and how does it affect your heart?
Your stress signal checklist
Staying in control
Calculating your heart-stress level at home and on the job
Stress management

Heartskill #5: *Mapping your stress hotspots*

Chapter 6
YOUR FAITH AND YOUR HEART

As the author points out, there are few studies in the field of spirituality and medicine, because physicians, like most scientists, shy away from what is called "soft data." Soft data are anything outside the realm of physics, mathematics, etc.: the "exact sciences." As a physician, the author has grown ever more convinced of the body's natural healing power, which is evoked through mind and spirit. No matter how "spirit" is defined, whether in traditional religious terms or as a component of mind or personality, the truth is that in order to become healthy, it is necessary to become spiritual.

In a 10-month study of 393 coronary patients at San Francisco General Hospital, it was proven that the group who received outside prayer in addition to standard medical treatment did far better than those who received medical treatment alone. Those in the experimental group suffered fewer problems with congestive heart failure, pneumonia, cardiac arrests, and had a significantly lower mortality rate. This chapter explores the possible reasons for this startling result and illuminates the connection between spirit and health.

The difference between spirituality and religion. A discussion of the differences between traditional views of spirituality and the new holistic approach that sees mind, body, and spirit as intimately connected and interdependent.

Faith and heart disease. The healing personality is that of a person who takes care of his own body. He may also use such other "paramedical" means to get well as physical exercise, a proper diet, prayer, meditation, positive affirmations, and visualization techniques. The author surveys these techniques that have been used for centuries to contribute to the healing of a wide variety of diseases. Other topics exploring the connection between faith and a healthy heart include:

> *Tapping into your personal mythology*
> *Forgiving yourself for heart disease*
> *Keeping a psychological-spiritual journal*

Heartskill #6: *Consulting your inner adviser*

Chapter 7
PUTTING IT ALL TOGETHER: HOW TO DEVELOP YOUR OWN DAILY PRACTICE FOR A HEALTHY HEART

Daily Practice as defined by the author is a personalized program in which readers will choose from among the techniques offered in the book to create their own unique combination of mental and physical healing exercises. Each component of the daily practice is fully explained. The techniques range from the familiar—healthful diet and exercise—to the more spiritual, including prayer, meditation, and visualization. Included are examples of use of each of these techniques as practiced by Exceptional Heart Patients.

> *The benefits of daily practice*
> *Meditation: how to do it your way*
> *Stretching, yoga, and sensory awareness*
> *Hearing with the mind's ear, seeing with the mind's eye*
> *The psychological benefits of exercise*
> *Healthy eating as a meditative practice*
> *The healing powers of silent prayer*
> *Creating your own visualization exercises*
> *Creating your own guided-imagery tapes*
> *Using other types of positive imagery*

Heartskill #7: *Picking a practice that makes sense to you*

Chapter 8
LEARNING TO SMELL THE FLOWERS

In our society, pleasure is often regarded as a selfish pursuit. We tend to feel that it is not as important as work. And yet the key element in health is not blood pressure, or cholesterol, or blood sugar; instead it is peace of mind and the ability to enjoy life. Indeed, this ability has been proven to prevent illness. In this chapter the author focuses on the ability to live in the moment, savoring all that life has to offer, from the simple physical pleasures of massage to the more profound pleasures of the spirit. Topics covered in this chapter include a discussion of Type B behavior, which can be learned. The secrets of this type of behavior include self-assurance, self-motivation, and the ability to relax in the face of pressures. The author shows how even the most confirmed Type A heart patient can, through self-knowledge, change outer-directed goals for inner ones, thus achieving the emotional and physical benefits of a Type B lifestyle. Other topics discussed in this chapter include:

Getting the most out of the present moment
Taking an inventory of life's pleasures
Counting down to relaxation
Hot baths, hot showers, hot tubs, and saunas
Touching; feeding the skin's hunger for human touch
Pets, plants, and gardens as healing helpers

Heartskill #8: *Building islands of peace into your life*

Chapter 9
CREATING YOUR FUTURE

The heart may be viewed in many different ways: as a mechanical pump, as the center of circulation, as the source of life. The author suggests viewing the heart above all as a spiritual organ, the center of love, and learning to figuratively fill it with love and peace. A positive result of heart disease is the sudden knowledge that one is not immortal, and the opportunity to plan for a more worthwhile, fulfilling life in the future. In this final chapter, Dr. Cortis offers guidelines for setting and achieving goals for health—of mind, body, and spirit. For each reader the goals, and the means to achieve them, will be different. But as the author points out, this is a journey that everyone must take, patients as well as doctors, readers as well as the author. No matter how different the paths we choose, we must realize that truly "our hearts are the same."

The Art of Happiness
Choosing your own path to contentment
Goals chosen by other exceptional heart patients

(Appendixes are always a valuable bonus.)

(It is great to be able to include an actual endorsement in your proposal package. Quite often, writers state those from whom they intend to request endorsements—but do not actually have them lined up. Perhaps unnecessary to say, but valuable to reiterate, is that editors and agents are not overly impressed by such assertions. They do, however, nod with respect to those authors who demonstrate that they can deliver on their claims. The inclusion of at least one such blurb creates tremendous credibility.)

GERALD G. JAMPOLSKY, M.D.
Practice Limited to Psychiatry
Adults and Children

April 1, 1998

Mr. Jeff Herman
The Jeff Herman Agency, Inc.
140 Charles Street, Suite 15A
New York, NY 10014

Dear Jeff:
You may use the following quote for Bruno's book:

> *"Dr. Bruno Cortis writes from the heart—for the heart. This is a much-needed and very important book."*

Gerald Jampolsky, M.D.
Coauthor of *Love Is the Answer*

With love and peace,
Jerry
Gerald Jampolsky, M.D.

(The author, Dr. Cortis, is very well connected in his field. He solicited promises from several prominent persons to provide cover endorsements like this one. Having these promises to provide such blurbs at the time I marketed the proposal further enhanced the agency's sales position.)

REJECTED . . . AGAIN

THE PROCESS AND THE ART OF PERSEVERANCE

JEFF HERMAN

Trying to sell your writing is in many ways similar to perpetually applying for employment; it's likely you will run into many walls. And that can hurt. But even the Great Wall of China has a beginning and an end—for it's simply an external barrier erected for strategic purposes. In my experience, the most insurmountable walls are the ones in our own heads. Anything that is artificially crafted can and will be overcome by people who are resourceful and determined enough to do it.

Naturally, the reality of rejection cannot be completely circumvented. It is, however, constructive to envision each wall as a friendly challenge to your resourcefulness, determination, and strength. There are many people who got through the old Berlin Wall because for them it was a challenge and a symbol—a place to begin, not stop.

The world of publishing is a potentially hostile environment, especially for the writer. Our deepest aspirations can be put to rest without our having achieved peace or satisfaction. But it is within each of us to learn about this special soil and blossom to our fullest. No rejection is fatal until the writer walks away from the battle, leaving the written work behind, undefended and unwanted.

WHY MOST REJECTION LETTERS ARE SO EMPTY

What may be most frustrating are the generic word-processed letters that say something like: "not right for us." Did the sender read any of your work? Did that person have any personal opinions about it? Could she not have spared a few moments to share her thoughts?

As an agent, it's part of my job to reject the vast majority of the submissions I receive. And with each rejection, I know I'm not making someone happy. On the other hand, I don't see spreading happiness as my exclusionary purpose. Like other agents and editors, I make liberal use of the generic rejection letter.

Here's why: Too much to do, too little time. There just isn't sufficient time to write customized, personal rejection letters. To be blunt about it, the rejection process isn't a profit center; it does consume valuable time that otherwise could be used to make profits. The exceptions to this rule are the excessive-fee-charging operations that make a handsome profit with each rejection.

In most instances, the rejection process is "giveaway" time for agents and editors since it takes us away from our essential responsibilities. Even if no personal comments are provided with the rejections, it can require many hours a week to process an ongoing stream of rejections. An understaffed literary agency or publishing house may feel that it's sufficiently generous simply to assign a paid employee the job of returning material as opposed to throwing it away. (And some publishers and literary agencies do in practice simply toss the greater portion of their unsolicited correspondence.) Agents and editors aren't Dear Abby, though many of us wish we had the time to be.

Therefore, your generic rejection means no more and no less than that particular agent/editor doesn't want to represent/publish you and (due to the volume of office correspondence and other pressing duties) is relaying this information to you in an automated, impersonal way. The contents of the letter alone will virtually never reveal any deeper meanings or secrets. To expect or demand more than this might be perceived as unfair by the agent/editor.

KNOW WHEN TO HOLD, KNOW WHEN TO FOLD

It's your job to persevere. It's your mission to proceed undaunted. Regardless of how many books about publishing you've read, or how many writers' conferences you've attended, it's up to no one but you to figure out how and when to change your strategy if you want to win at the book-publishing game.

If your initial query results are blanket rejects, then it may be time to back off, reflect, and revamp your query presentation or overall approach. If there are still no takers, you may be advised to reconceive your project in light of its less-than-glorious track record. Indeed, there might even come a time for you to use your experience and newfound knowledge of what does and doesn't grab attention from editors and agents—and move on to that bolder, more innovative idea you've been nurturing in the back of your brain.

AN AUTHENTIC SUCCESS STORY

Several years ago, two very successful, though unpublished, gentlemen came to see me with a nonfiction book project. My hunch was that it would make a lot of money. The writers were professional speakers and highly skilled salespeople, so I arranged for them to meet personally with several publishers, but to no avail.

All told, we got more than 20 rejections—the dominant reason being that editors thought the concept and material weak. Not ones to give up, and with a strong belief in their work and confidence in their ability to promote, the authors were ultimately able to sell the book for a nominal advance to a small Florida publishing house—and it was out there at last, published and in the marketplace.

As of this writing, *Chicken Soup for the Soul*, by Jack Canfield and Mark Victor Hansen, has sold millions of copies and has been a *New York Times* bestseller for several years straight. Furthermore, this initial success has generated many bestselling sequels.

We all make mistakes, and the book rascals in New York are definitely no exception. Most important, Canfield and Hansen didn't take no for an answer. They instinctively understood that all those rejections were simply an uncomfortable part of a process that would eventually get them where they wanted to be. And that's the way it happened.

A RELENTLESS APPROACH TO SELLING YOUR BOOK

I once heard a very telling story about Jack Kerouac, one from which we can all learn something. Kerouac was a notorious literary figure who reached his professional peak in the 1950s. He's one of the icons of the Beat Generation and is perhaps best remembered for his irreverent and manic travel-memoir-as-novel *On the Road*.

SALES TALES FROM THE BEAT GENERATION

The story begins when Kerouac was a young and struggling writer, ambitiously seeking to win his day in the sun. He was a charismatic man and had acquired many influential friends. One day Kerouac approached a friend who had access to a powerful publishing executive. Kerouac asked the friend to hand-deliver his new manuscript to the executive, with the advice that it be given prompt and careful consideration.

When the friend handed the manuscript to the executive, the executive took one glance and began to laugh. The executive explained that two other people had hand-delivered the very same manuscript to him within the last few weeks.

What this reveals is that Kerouac was a master operator. Not only did he manage to get his work into the right face, but also he reinforced his odds by doing it redundantly. Some might say he was a manipulator, but his works were successfully published, and he did attain a measure of fame in his own day, which even now retains its luster.

. . . AND FROM THE BEATEN

I will now share a very different and more recent story. It starts in the 1940s, when a bestselling and Pulitzer Prize-winning young-adult book was published. Titled *The*

Yearling, this work was made into an excellent movie starring Gregory Peck. The book continues to be a good backlist seller.

In the 1990s, a writer in Florida, where *The Yearling*'s story takes place, performed an experiment. He converted the book into a raw double-spaced manuscript and changed the title and author's name—but the book's contents were not touched. He then submitted the entire manuscript about 20 publishers on an unagented/unsolicited basis. I don't believe the submissions were addressed to any specific editors by name.

Eventually, this writer received many form rejections, including one from the book's actual publisher. Several publishers never even responded. A small house in Florida did offer to publish the book.

What is glaringly revealed by this story? That even a Pulitzer Prize-winning novel will never see the light of day if the writer doesn't use his brain when it's time to sell the work.

HOW TO BEAT YOURSELF—AND HOW NOT TO

People who are overly aggressive do get a bad rap. As an agent and as a person, I don't like being hounded by salespeople—whether they're hustling manuscripts or insurance policies. But there are effective ways to be heard and seen without being resented. Virtually anyone can scream loud enough to hurt people's ears. Only an artist understands the true magic of how to sell without abusing those who might buy. And we all have the gift to become artists in our own ways.

Here's an example of what not to do:

It's late in the day and snowing. I'm at my desk, feeling a lot of work-related tension. I answer the phone. It's a first-time fiction writer. He's unflinchingly determined to speak endlessly about his work, which I have not yet read.

I interrupt his meaningless flow to explain courteously that while I will read his work, it's not a good time for me to talk to him. But he will not let me go; he's relentless. Which forces me to be rude and cold as I say "Bye" and hang up.

I then resent the thoughtless intrusion upon my space and time. And I may feel bad about being inhospitable to a stranger, whatever the provocation.

Clearly, the previous scenario does not demonstrate a good way to initiate a deal. I'm already prejudiced against this writer before reading his work.

Here's a more effective scenario:

Same conditions as before. I answer the telephone. The caller acknowledges that I must be busy and asks for only 30 seconds of my time. I grant them. He then begins to compliment me; he's heard I'm one of the best, and so forth. I'm starting to like this conversation; I stop counting the seconds.

Now he explains that he has an excellent manuscript that he is willing to give me the opportunity to read and would be happy to send it right over. He then thanks me for my time and says good-bye.

I hang up, feeling fine about the man; I'll give his manuscript some extra consideration.

In conclusion, relentless assertiveness is better than relentless passivity. But you want your style to be like Julie Andrews's singing voice in *The Sound of Music*, as opposed to a 100-decibel boom box on a stone floor.

THE LITERARY AGENCY FROM A TO Z
HOW LITERARY AGENTS WORK

JEFF HERMAN

L iterary agents are like stockbrokers, marketing or sales directors, or real-estate agents: They bring buyers and sellers together, help formulate successful deals, and receive a piece of the action (against the seller's end) for facilitating the partnership.

Specifically, literary agents snoop the field for talented writers, unearth marketable nonfiction book concepts, and discover superior fiction manuscripts to represent. Simultaneously, agents cultivate their relationships with publishers.

When an agent detects material she thinks she can sell to a publisher, she signs the writer as a client, works on the material with the writer to maximize its chances of selling, and then submits it to one or more appropriate editorial contacts.

The agent has the contacts. Many writers don't know the most likely publishers; even if the writers do have a good overview of the industry and some inside contacts, the typical agent knows many more players and also knows which editors like to see what material.

And the agent may even be aware of finesse elements such as recent shifts in a publisher's acquisition strategy.

HOW AGENTS WORK FOR THEIR CLIENTS

A dynamic agent achieves the maximum exposure possible for the writer's material, which greatly enhances the odds that the material will be published—and on more favorable terms than a writer is likely to yield.

Having an agent gives the writer's material the type of access to the powers-that-be that it might otherwise never obtain. Publishers assume that material submitted by an agent has been screened and is much more likely to fit their needs than is the random material swimming in the slush pile.

If and when a publisher makes an offer to publish the material, the agent acts on the author's behalf and negotiates the advance (the money paid up front), table of royalties, control of subsidiary rights, and many other important and marginal contract clauses that may prove to be important down the line. The agent acts as the writer's advocate with the publisher for as long as the book remains in print or licensing opportunities exist.

The agent knows the most effective methods for negotiating the best advance and other contract terms and is likely to have more leverage with the publisher than the writer does.

There's more to a book contract than the advance-and-royalty schedule. There are several key clauses that you, the writer, may know little or nothing about, but would accept with a cursory perusal in order to expedite the deal. Striving to close any kind of agreement can be intimidating if you don't know much about the territory; ignorance is a great disadvantage during a negotiation. An agent, however, understands every detail of the contract and knows where and how it should be modified or expanded in your favor.

Where appropriate, an agent acts to sell subsidiary rights after the book is sold to a publisher. These rights can include: serial rights, foreign rights, dramatic and movie rights, audio and video rights, and a range of syndication and licensing possibilities. Often, a dynamic agent will be more successful at selling the subsidiary rights than the publisher would be.

THE AGENT'S PERSPECTIVE

No agent sells every project she represents. Even though authors are signed on the basis of their work's marketability, agents know from experience that some projects with excellent potential are not necessarily quick-and-easy big-money sales. And, yes, each and every agent has at least on occasion been as bewildered as the author when a particularly promising package receives no takers. Some projects, especially fiction, may be marketed for a long time before a publisher is found (if ever).

THE AUTHOR'S EXPECTATIONS

What's most important is that you, the author, feel sure the agent continues to believe in the project and is actively trying to sell it.

For his work, the agent receives a commission (usually 15 percent) against the writer's advance and all subsequent income relevant to the sold project.

Although this is an appreciable chunk of your work's income, the agent's involvement should end up netting you much more than you would have earned otherwise. The agent's power to round up several interested publishers to consider your work opens up the possibility that more than one house will make an offer for it, which means you'll be more likely to get a higher advance and also have more leverage regarding the various other contractual clauses.

The writer-agent relationship can become a rewarding business partnership. An agent can advise you objectively on the direction your writing career should take. Also, through her contacts, an agent may be able to get you book-writing assignments you would never have been offered on your own.

SCOUT FOR THE BEST AGENT FOR YOU

There are many ways to get an agent; your personal determination and acumen as a writer will be two of your most important assets. The best way to gain access to potential agents is by networking with fellow writers. Find out which agents they use and what's being said about whom. Maybe some of your colleagues can introduce you to their agents or at least allow you to drop their names when contacting their agents. Most agents will be receptive to a writer who has been referred by a current and valued client.

This book features a directory of literary agencies, including their addresses, the names of specific agents, and agents' specialty areas, along with some personal remarks and examples of recent titles sold to publishers.

QUERY FIRST

The universally accepted way to establish initial contact with an agent is to send a query letter. Agents tend to be less interested in—if not completely put off by—oral presentations. Be sure the letter is personalized: Nobody likes generic, photocopied letters that look like they're being sent to everyone.

Think of the query as a sales pitch. Describe the nature of your project and offer to send additional material—and enclose a self-addressed stamped envelope (SASE). Include all relevant information about yourself—along with a resume if it's applicable. When querying about a nonfiction project, many agents won't mind receiving a complete proposal. But you might prefer to wait and see how the agent responds to the concept before sending the full proposal.

For queries about fiction projects, most agents prefer to receive story-concept sheets, plot synopses, or both; if they like what they see, they'll request sample chapters or ask you to send the complete manuscript. Most agents won't consider manuscripts for incomplete works of fiction, essentially because few publishers are willing to do so.

If you enclose an SASE, most agents will respond to you, one way or another, within a reasonable period of time. If the agent asks to see your material, submit it promptly with a polite note stating that you'd like a response within 4 weeks on a non-fiction proposal, or 8 weeks on fiction material. If you haven't heard from the agent by that time, write or call to find out the status of your submission.

CIRCULATE WITH THE FLOW

You're entitled to circulate your material to more than one agent at a time, but you're obligated to let each agent know that such is the case. If and when you do sign with an agent, immediately notify other agents still considering your work that it's no longer available.

At least 200 literary agents are active in America, and their individual perceptions of what is and isn't marketable will vary widely—which is why a few or even several rejections should never deter writers who believe in themselves.

BUYER AND SELLER REVERSAL

When an agent eventually seeks to represent your work, it's time for her to begin selling herself to you. When you're seeking employment, you don't necessarily have to accept the first job offer you receive; likewise, you do not have to sign immediately with the first agent who wants you.

Do some checking before agreeing to work with a particular agent. If possible, meet the agent in person. A lot can be learned from in-person meetings that can't be gathered from telephone conversations. See what positive or negative information you can find out about the agent through your writers' network. Ask the agent for a client list and permission to call certain clients. Find out the agent's specialties.

Ask for a copy of the agent's standard contract. Most agents today will want to codify your relationship with a written agreement; this should protect both parties equally. Make sure you're comfortable with everything in the agreement before signing it. Again, talking with fellow writers and reading books on the subject are excellent ways to deepen your understanding of industry practices.

When choosing an agent, follow your best instincts. Don't settle for anyone you don't perceive to be on the level, or who doesn't seem to be genuinely enthusiastic about you and your work.

SELF-REPRESENTATION: A FOOL FOR A CLIENT?

Agents aren't for everyone. In some instances, you may be better off on your own. Perhaps you actually do have sufficient editorial contacts and industry savvy to cut good deals by yourself. If so, what incentive do you have to share your income with an agent?

Of course, having an agent might provide you the intangible benefits of added prestige, save you the hassles of making submissions and negotiating deals, or act as a buffer through whom you can negotiate indirectly for tactical reasons.

You might also consider representing yourself if your books are so specialized that only a few publishers are potential candidates for them. Your contacts at such houses might be much stronger than any agent's could be.

ATTORNEYS: LITERARY AND OTHERWISE

Some entertainment/publishing attorneys can do everything an agent does, though there's no reason to believe they can necessarily do more. A major difference between the two is that the lawyer may charge you a set hourly fee or retainer, or any negotiated combination thereof, instead of an agency-type commission. In rare instances, writer-publisher disputes might need to be settled in a court of law, and a lawyer familiar with the industry then becomes a necessity.

BOTTOM-LINE CALCULATIONS

The pluses and minuses of having an agent should be calculated like any other business service you might retain—it should benefit you more than it costs you. Generally speaking, the only real cost of using an agent is the commission. Of course, using the wrong agent may end up causing you more deficits than benefits, but even then you may at least learn a valuable lesson for next time.

Your challenge is to seek and retain an agent who's right for you. You're 100 percent responsible for getting yourself represented and at least 50 percent responsible for making the relationship work for both of you.

MORE QUESTIONS AND ANSWERS

ABOUT AGENTS, EDITORS, AND
THE PUBLISHING INDUSTRY

JEFF HERMAN

In the course of my ongoing participation in publishing workshops, seminar presentations, and panels at writers' conferences, certain questions arise time and again. Many of these requests for information go straight to the heart of the world of book publishing.

The following questions are asked from the gut and replied to in kind. In order to be of value to the author who wishes to benefit from an insider view, I answer these serious queries in unvarnished terms, dispensing with the usual sugarcoating in order to emphasize the message of openness and candor.

Q: I have been at this for a long time, and can't get published. How come?
Well, your stuff may not be good. That's the easy answer, which probably applies to most of what gets written and, frankly, to some of what actually gets published. After all, books get published for many reasons, including the possibility that they are of high quality. But lack of quality is not, never has been, and never will be the only factor as to why books do or don't get published. That said, it's good to make your product the best it can be.

It's safe to say that everyone who works in publishing will agree that countless works of excellence don't make it to publication. That's unfortunate. But is it unfair? Who's to say?

Many works get published because the writer managed to get them to the right people at the right time. How and why did that happen?

Other fine works fail to "connect", in spite of the diligent efforts made by the writer to sell it. Why? I don't know. Why are some people very pretty, while others are very ugly? I don't know. Some consequences can be logically traced backwards to a cause or causes, or a lack of necessary acts.

But sometimes there is no apparent pathology behind what does and doesn't happen. And that's when we must simply surrender. There's an ancient Jewish saying, "Man plans, God laughs." Some things are left to our discretion and control, whereas other things obviously are not. It's possible that that may be why you did not sell your manuscript. But I don't know.

Q: Why are memoirs and autobiographies hard to sell?
Because the vast majority of us lead lives of quiet desperation that would bore even a 300-year-old turtle. None of us ever truly listen to each other. That's why a lot of us pay strangers $90 or more an hour to listen to us. Or at least we think they're listening.

So why should someone actually pay you to read about your life? If you can effectively answer that question, you may be qualified to write a book about YOU.

Now, there are ways to maneuver around this conundrum. For instance, you can place your life within the context of fascinating events. People do connect to events and situations that mirror their own lives and feelings right back at them.

You can think ahead by doing something notable or outrageous for the sole purpose of having a platform for writing about yourself. A lot of us do ridiculous things anyway, so why not do them in a planned conscious way? It's said that we all write our own script in life. So, if you are the designer of your own life, who do you have to blame for leading a boring life? Think about your life as a feature film, and start living it within that context. Pre-empt the cutting room floor whenever possible. Become someone that other people will pay to watch, read about, and listen to.

Even if you don't get anything sold, you may still end up with more friends.

Q: Why do editors, agents and some writers seem so snobby?
Because maybe they are. Why should you care? Because you want validation and snobs counter that. A long time ago, when I was young and a bit more stupid, I told a snobby editor to come clean my bathroom for me. He didn't. Neither did I; I hired a housekeeper. To this day I enjoy foiling people who think they are better then the rest. Sometimes, I think I'm better than the rest. But my better angels take care of that by hiding my car in a parking lot, or causing me to wash my mouth with shampoo. My list of due personal humiliations is infinite, and appreciated.

Snobbery is a burden, and a punishment unto itself. Let the snobs have their burden, and keep writing.

Q: Is it more difficult to get an agent than it is to get a publisher?
I believe it's substantially easier to get an agent than it is to get a publisher.

The primary reason for this is that no agent expects to sell 100 percent of the projects she chooses to represent. Not because any of these projects lack merit (though some of them may), but because only so many titles are published per year—and many excellent ones just won't make the cut. This is especially true for fiction by unknown or unpublished writers, or for nonfiction in saturated categories. As a result, many titles will be agented but never published.

Naturally, a successful agent prefers to represent projects that she feels are hot and that publishers will trample each other to acquire. But few, if any, agents have the luxury of representing such sure-bet projects exclusively. In fact, the majority of their projects may be less than "acquisition-guaranteed," even though they are of acquisition quality.

The agent assumes that many of these projects will eventually be sold profitably, but probably doesn't expect all of them to be. Every experienced agent knows that some of the best cash cows were not easily sold.

Make no mistake—it's not easy to get a reputable agent. Most agents reject 98 percent of the opportunities that cross their desks. They accept for representation only material they believe can be sold to a publisher. That is, after all, the only way for them to earn income and maintain credibility with publishers. If an agent consistently represents what a publisher considers garbage, that will become her professional signature—and her undoing as an agent.

But don't despair. This is a subjective business, composed of autonomous human beings. One agent's reject can be another's gold mine. That's why even a large accumulation of rejections should never deter you as a writer.

Some people get married young, and some get married later!

Q: Is there anything I can do to increase my odds of getting an agent?
Yes.

First consider the odds quoted in the previous answer. The typical agent is rejecting 98 percent of everything he sees. That means he's hungry for the hard-to-find 2 percent that keeps him in business.

If you're not part of that 2 percent, he'll probably have no use for you or your project. Your challenge is to convince him that you're part of that select 2 percent.

Q: What do agents and editors want? What do they look for in a writer? What can I do to become that kind of writer?
Let's back up a step or two and figure out why agents want to represent certain projects and why editors want to buy them. This industry preference has little to do with quality of writing as such.

Many highly talented writers never get published. Many mediocre writers do get published—and a number of them make a lot of money at it. There are reasons for this. The mediocre writers are doing things that more than compensate for their less-than-splendid writing. And the exceptional writers who underachieve in the publishing arena are (regardless of their talents) most likely doing things that undermine them.

In other words, being a good writer is just part of a complex equation. Despite all the criticism the educational system in the United States has received, America is exceedingly literate and has a mother lode of college graduates and postgraduates. Good, knowledgeable writers are a dime a dozen in this country.

Profitable writers, however, are a rare species. And agents and editors obviously value them the most. Once more: Being an excellent writer and a financially successful writer don't necessarily coincide. Ideally, of course, you want to be both.

To maximize your success as a writer, you must do more than hone your ability to write; you must also learn the qualifiers and the disqualifiers for success. Obviously, you wish to employ the former and avoid the latter. Publishing is a business, and agents tend to be the most acutely business-oriented of all the players. That's why they took the risk of going into business for themselves (most agents are self-employed).

If you wish, wear your artist's hat while you write. But you'd better acquire a business hat and wear it when it's time to sell. This subtle ability to change hats separates the minority of writers who get rich from the majority who do not.

In my opinion, rich writers didn't get rich from their writing (no matter how good it is); they got rich by being good at business.

Many good but not-so-wealthy writers blame various internal or external factors for their self-perceived stagnation. My answer to them is: Don't blame anyone, especially yourself. To lay blame is an abdication of power. In effect, when you blame, you become a car with an empty gas tank, left to the elements. The remedy is to fill the tank yourself.

Learn to view mistakes, whether they be yours or those of the people you relied upon, as inconvenient potholes—learning to move around them will make you an even better driver. Remember the old credo: Only a poor workman blames his tools.

Observe all you can about those who are successful—not just in writing, but in all fields—and make their skills your skills. This is not to insist that making money is or should be your first priority. Your priorities, whatever they are, belong to you. But money is a widely acknowledged and sought-after emblem of success.

If an emphasis on personal gain turns you off, you may, of course, pursue other goals. Many successful people in business find the motivation to achieve their goals by focusing on altruistic concepts—such as creating maximum value for as many people as possible. Like magic, money often follows value even if it wasn't specifically sought. If you're unfortunate enough to make money you don't want, there's no need to despair: There are many worthy parties (including charities) that will gladly relieve you of this burden.

Here are specific ways to maximize your ability to get the agent you want:

- *Don't start off by asking what the agent can do for you.* You're a noncitizen until the agent has reason to believe that you may belong to that exclusive 2 percent club the agent wants to represent. It's a mistake to expect the agent to do anything to sell herself to you during that initial contact. You must first persuade her that you're someone who's going to make good money for her business. Once you've accomplished that, and the agent offers you representation, you're entitled to have the agent sell herself to you.

- *Act like a business.* As you're urged elsewhere in this book, get yourself a professional letterhead and state-of-the-art office equipment. While rarely fatal, cheap paper and poor-looking type will do nothing to help you—and in this business you need all the help you can give yourself.
  Virtually anyone—especially the intellectually arrogant—is apt to be strongly affected on a subliminal level by a product's packaging. People pay for the sizzle, not the steak. There is a reason why American companies spend billions packaging, naming, and advertising such seemingly simple products as soap. We would all save money if every bar of soap were put into a plain paper box and

just labeled "Soap." In fact, the no-frills section does sell soap that way—for a lot less. But few people choose to buy it that way. Understand this human principle, without judging it and use it when packaging yourself.

- *Learn industry protocol.* I never insist that people follow all the rules. As Thomas Jefferson wisely suggested, a revolution every so often can be a good thing. But you should at least know the rules before you break them—or before you do anything.

  For instance: Most agents say they don't like cold calls. I can't say I blame them. If my rejection rate is 98 percent, I'm not going to be enthusiastic about having my ear talked off by someone who is more than likely part of that 98 percent. Just like you, agents want to use their time as productively as possible. Too often, cold calls are verbal junk mail. This is especially true if you are a writer selling fiction; your hard copy is the foot you want to get through the door.

  Speaking for myself, most cold calls have a neutral effect on me (a few turn me off, and a few rouse my enthusiasm). I try to be courteous, because that's how I would want to be treated. I will allow the caller to say whatever he wants for about one minute before I take over to find out what, if anything, the person has in the way of hard copy. If he has some, I invite him to send it with an SASE. If he doesn't have any, I advise him to write some and then send it. Usually, I don't remember much about what he said on the phone; I may not even remember that he called. But that doesn't matter; it's the hard copy that concerns me at first. This is the way it works with most agents. We produce books, not talk.

  An agent's time is an agent's money (and therefore his clients' money). So don't expect any quality access until the agent has reason to believe you're a potential 2 percenter. If you're the CEO of General Motors, for instance, and you want to write a book, then all you need to do is call the agent(s) of your choice and identify yourself; red carpets will quickly appear. But the vast majority of writers have to learn and follow the more formalized procedures.

- *As explained elsewhere in this book, view the query letter as a sales brochure.* The best ones are rarely more than $1\frac{1}{2}$-2 pages long and state their case as briefly and efficiently as possible.

Here are the most common query mistakes:

1. Long, unfocused paragraphs.

2. Pontificating about irrelevancies (at least, matters that are irrelevant from the agent's perspective).

3. Complaining about your tribulations as a writer. We all know it's a tough business, but nobody likes losers—least of all, shrewd agents. Always be a winner when you're selling yourself, and you'll be more likely to win.

Most agents are hungry for that golden 2 percent, and they dedicate a great deal of time shoveling through mounds of material looking for it. You must be the first to believe that you are a 2 percenter, and then you must portray yourself that way to others. Reality begins in your own head and is manifested primarily through your own actions—or lack thereof.

Every agent and editor has the power to reject your writing. But only you have the power to be—or not to be—a writer.

Q: Should I query only one agent at a time?
Some of my colleagues disagree with me here, but I recommend querying 5 to 10 agents simultaneously, unless you already have your foot in the door with one. I suggest this because some agents will respond within 10 days, while others may take much longer or never respond at all. Going agent by agent can eat up several months of valuable time before a relationship is consummated. And then your work still has to be sold to a publisher.

To speed up this process, it's smart to solicit several agents at a time, though you should be completely upfront about it. If you go the multiple-submissions route, be sure to mention in your query letters to each agent that you are indeed making multiple submissions (though you needn't supply your agent list).

When an agent responds affirmatively to your query by requesting your proposal or manuscript, it's fine then to give the agent an exclusive reading. However, you should impose a reasonable time frame—for instance, 2 weeks for a nonfiction proposal and 4 weeks for a large manuscript. If it's a nonexclusive reading, make sure each agent knows that's what you want. And don't sign with an agent before talking to all the agents who are reading your work. (You have no obligation to communicate further with agents who do not respond affirmatively to your initial query.)

Most agents make multiple submissions to publishers, so they should be sensitive and respectful when writers have reason to use the same strategy agents have used with success.

Q: How do I know if my agent is working effectively for me? When might it be time to change agents?
As I remarked earlier, agents don't necessarily sell everything they represent, no matter how persistent and assertive they may be. In other words, the fact that your work is unsold doesn't automatically mean that your agent isn't doing his job. To the contrary, he may be doing the best job possible, and it may be incumbent upon you to be grateful for these speculative and uncompensated efforts.

Let's say 90 days pass and your work remains unsold. What you need to assess next is whether your agent is making active and proper attempts to sell your work.

Are you receiving copies of publisher rejection letters regarding your work? Generally, when an editor rejects projects submitted by an agent, the work will be returned within a few weeks, along with some brief comments explaining why the project was declined. (In case you're wondering, the agent doesn't have to include an SASE; the editors want agent submissions.) Copies of these rejection letters should be sent to you on a regular basis as the agent receives them. While no one expects you to enjoy these letters, they at least document that your agent is circulating your work.

If you have received many such rejection letters within these 90 days, it's hard to claim that your agent isn't trying. If you've received few or none, you might well call the agent for a status report. You should inquire as to where and when your work has been submitted, and what, if anything, the results of those submissions have been. In the end, you will have to use your own best judgment as to whether your agent is performing capably or giving you the run-around.

If it ever becomes obvious that your agent is no longer seriously trying to sell your work (or perhaps never was), you should initiate a frank discussion with the agent about what comes next. If the agent did go to bat for you, you should consider the strong possibility that your work is presently unmarketable and act to preserve the agent relationship for your next project. Remember, if your work remains unsold, your agent has lost valuable time and has made no money.

If the evidence clearly shows that your agent has been nonperforming from day one, then your work has not been tested. You should consider withdrawing it and seek new representation.

Agent-hopping by authors is not rampant, but it's not uncommon either. Often the agent is just as eager as you—or more so—for the break-up to happen. One veteran colleague once told me that when he notices he hates to receive a certain client's phone calls, then it's time to find a graceful way to end the relationship.

The wisdom of agent-jumping must be assessed on a case-by-case basis. The evidence shows that many writers have prospered after switching, while others have entered limbo or even fallen far off their previous pace.

Before you decide to switch agents, you should focus on why you are unhappy with your current situation. It may be that if you appeal to your agent to discuss your specific frustrations—preferably in person, or at least by phone—many or all of them can be resolved, and your relationship will be given a fresh and prosperous start.

Agents are not mind readers. You only have one agent, but your agent has many clients. It is therefore mostly your responsibility as a writer client to communicate your concerns and expectations effectively to your agent. Your relationship may require only occasional adjustments, as opposed to a complete break-up.

Q: Who do agents really work for?
Themselves! Always have and always will.

True, agents serve their clients, but their own needs and interests always come first. Of course, this is the way it is in any business relationship (and in too many personal ones). You should never expect your lawyer, accountant, or stockbroker (and so on) to throw themselves into traffic to shield you from getting hit.

As long as the interests of the agent and the writer are in harmony, everything should work out well. However, on occasion the writer may have expectations that could be detrimental to the agent's own agenda (not to mention state of mind). Writers must never lose sight of the truth that publishers are the agent's most important customers. Only a foolish agent would intentionally do serious damage to her relationships with individual editors and publishing houses. It should be further noted that there is, therefore, a fine line that an agent will not cross when advocating for her clients.

Q: What do agents find unattractive about some clients?
Agents are individuals, so each will have his own intense dislikes. But, generally speaking, a certain range of qualities can hamper any and all aspects of an agent's professional association with a client—qualities that often have similarly negative effects in realms other than publishing. Here's a litany of displeasing client types and their characteristics.

+ The Pest. Nobody likes a nag, whether at home or at the office. A squeaky wheel may sometimes get the grease—not that anyone likes the effect—but more often this person gets the shaft.

+ The Complainer. Some people can never be satisfied, only dissatisfied. It seems to be their mission in life to pass along their displeasure to others. These folks are never any fun—unless you're an ironic observer.

+ The BS Artist. These clients believe everything even remotely connected with themselves is the greatest—for example, their fleeting ideas for books should win them millions of dollars up front. Of course, if they actually produce the goods, then the BS part of the term doesn't apply to them.

+ The Screw-Up. These clients miss trains, planes, and deadlines. Their blunders can create major hassles for those who count on them.

+ The Sun God. Some people believe they are more equal than others and will behave accordingly. It's a real pleasure to see Sun Gods humbled.

+ The Liar. Need I say more?

Sometimes these wicked traits combine, overlap, and reinforce themselves in one individual to create what an agent may rate as a veritable client from hell. Enough said on this subject for now, except that I would be remiss if I did not insist that no trade or professional class is immune to this nefarious syndrome—not even literary agents.

Q: How does someone become an agent?
For better or worse, anyone in America can declare himself an agent—at any time. But what people say and what they do are different things. Legitimate literary agents earn most or all of their income from commissions. The less-than-legitimate agencies most often depend on reading and management fees for their cash, with few, if any, actual book sales to their credit.

Most agents earn their stripes by working as editors for publishers. But that is by no means the only route, nor is it necessarily the most effective training ground. Good agents have emerged from a variety of environments and offer a broad range of exceptional credentials. What's most important is the mix of skills they bring to their agenting careers, such as:

1. Strong relationship skills—the ability to connect with people and earn their confidence.

2. Sales and marketing skills—the ability to get people to buy from them.

3. Persuasion and negotiating skills—the ability to get good results in their dealings.

4. An understanding of the book market and of what publishers are buying.

5. An ability to manage many clients and projects at the same time.

Q: Who owns book publishing?
Many decades ago, book-publishing entities were customarily founded by individuals who had a passion for books. Though they obviously had to have business skills to make their houses survive and thrive, money was not necessarily their primary drive (at least, not in the beginning), or they would have chosen more lucrative endeavors.

The vestiges of these pioneers can be found in the family names still extant in the corporate designations of most of today's publishing giants. But apart from the human-sounding names, these are very different companies today. Much of the industry is owned by multinational, multibillion-dollar conglomerates that have priorities other than the mere publication of books. The revenues from book operations are barely noticeable when compared with such mass-market endeavors as movies, TV/cable, music, magazines, sports teams, and character licensing. Stock prices must rise, and shareholders must be optimally satisfied for these firms to feel in any way stable.

Q: How does this type of ownership affect editors and the editorial-acquisition process?
This rampant corporate ownership translates into an environment in which book editors are pressured to make profitable choices if their careers are to prosper. At first look, that doesn't sound radical or wrongheaded, but a downside has indeed developed—editors are discouraged from taking risks for literary or artistic rationales that are ahead of the market curve or even with an eye toward longer-term development and growth of a particular writer's readership.

The bottom line must be immediately appeased by every acquisition, or the non-performing editor's career will crumble. The editor who acquires blockbusters that the culturally elite disdain is an editor who is a success. The editor whose books lose money but are universally praised by critics is an editor who has failed.

Of course, the previous comparison is extreme. Most editors are not single-minded money-grubbers and do their best to acquire meaningful books that also make commercial sense. Where the cut becomes most noticeable is for the thousands of talented fiction writers who will never write big money-makers. While slots still exist for them, large publishers are increasingly reluctant to subsidize and nurture these marginally profitable writers' careers. Commercially speaking, there are better ways to invest the firm's resources.

Q: What, if any, are a writer's alternatives?
Yes, the big kids are dominant on their own turf and intend to extend their claim to as much of book country as they can. But this isn't the end of the story. The heroes are the thousands of privately owned "Mom and Pop" presses from Maine to Alaska who only need to answer to themselves. Every year, small presses, new and old, make an important contribution to literate culture with books that large publishers won't touch. It's not uncommon for some of these books to become bestsellers. University presses also pump out important (and salesworthy) books that would not have been published in a rigidly commercial environment.

Q: Is there anything positive to say about the current situation?
I don't mean to imply that the corporate ownership of the bulk of the book industry is absolutely bad. Indeed, it has brought many benefits. Publishers are learning to take better advantage of state-of-the-art marketing techniques and technologies and have more capital with which to do it. The parent entertainment and communications firms enable the mainstream commercial publishers to cash in on popular frenzies, as with dinosaur mania, the latest and most salacious scandals, fresh interest in the environment or fitness, or celebrity and other pop-culture tie-ins, such as Gump and Madonna books.

The emergence of superstores enables more books to be sold. The stores create very appealing environments that draw much more traffic than conventional old-style bookstores. Many people who hang out at the superstores were never before motivated to go book shopping. But once they're in one of these well-stocked stores—whether at the bookshelves, ensconced in a reading-seat, or perched by a steaming mug at an in-store cafe—they're likely to start spending.

The unfortunate part is that many small independent bookshops cannot compete with these new venues. However, many others are finding clever ways to hang on, by accenting special reader-interest areas or offering their own individual style of hospitality.

Q: How profitable is publishing?
One way to measure an industry's profitability is to look at the fortunes of those who work in it. By such a measure, the book business isn't very profitable, especially when compared to its twentieth-century sisters in entertainment and information industries: movies, television, music, advertising, and computers. Most book editors require a two-income family if they wish to raise children comfortably in New York or buy a nice home. The vast majority of published authors rely upon their day jobs or

spouse's earnings. A handful of authors make annual incomes in the six and seven figures, but it's often the movie tie-ins that get them there and in turn push even more book sales.

A fraction of book editors will climb the ranks to the point at which they can command six-figure incomes, but most never attain this plateau. Almost all of those writers just starting in the business earn barely above the poverty level for their initial publishing endeavors—if that.

A well-established literary agent can make a lot of money. The trick is to build a number of backlist books that cumulatively pay off healthy commissions twice a year, while constantly panning for the elusive big-advance books that promise short-term (and perhaps long-term) windfalls.

In many ways, the agents are the players best positioned to make the most money. As sole proprietors, they're not constrained by committees and can move like lightning. When everything aligns just right, the agent holds all the cards by controlling access to the author (product) and the publisher (producer).

The publishing companies themselves appear at least adequately profitable, averaging about 5 to 10 percent return on revenues (according to their public balance sheets). The larger companies show revenues of between $1 billion and $2 billion, sometimes nudging higher.

These are not sums to sneeze at. But most of those sales derive from high-priced nonbookstore products like textbooks and professional books. Large and midsize publishers alike are dependent upon their cash-cow backlist books for much of their retail sales. These books entail virtually no risk or investment, since their customer base is essentially locked in for an indefinite period, and the publisher has long ago recouped the initial investment. Many backlist books are legacies from editors and business dynamics that current employees may know nothing about.

The real risk for the current regime is their frontlist, which is the current season's crop. Large houses invest tens of millions of dollars to acquire, manufacture, market, and distribute anywhere from 50 to a few hundred "new" books. A small number of big-ticket individual titles will by themselves represent millions of dollars at risk. Most titles will represent less than $50,000 in risk on a pro-rata basis.

In practice, most of these frontlist titles will fail. The publisher will not recoup its investment and the title will not graduate to the exalted backlist status. But like the fate of those innumerable turtle eggs laid in the sand, it's expected that enough spawn will survive to generate an overall profit and significant backlist annuities well into the future.

In the fairness of a broader picture, it is known that most motion pictures and television shows fail, as do most new consumer products (such as soap or soft drinks) that have engendered enormous research-and-development costs. It's the ones that hit—and hit big—that make the odds worth enduring for any industry.

SCAMS AND BOOK DOCTORS

IN THAT ORDER

JEFF HERMAN

Publishing scams have become an epidemic. I read somewhere that writers are getting ripped off for more than $50 million a year, and some scam artists have even gone to jail.

Let's start by looking at ethics. I don't like ethics. They're like organized religion—prone to promoting arrogance, subjective judgment, and hypocrisy. I do like honesty. Honesty's best defense is the fast and consistent enforcement of consequences against those people who harm others.

The best defense is not to be a victim in the first place. Without becoming a paranoid lunatic, you must accept that bad deeds are hovering around waiting to happen. Sometimes, you may be tempted into being a perpetrator. That's why houses have glass windows and why the universe can't stay angry, or else we'd all have to go to Hell. It's more likely, however, that you'll be a victim, not a "do-er," on any given day; though it's hoped you'll be neither. Both extremes may be mostly, or completely, within your power to be or not to be. For instance, I'll never understand why women jog by themselves in Central Park when it's dark out. And I'll never understand why writers send fat checks to virtual strangers.

To what extent should society protect its citizens from making stupid choices? I've seen smart men and women date and marry morons, with predictably disastrous results. I've done enough stupid things in my life to qualify for the Infra-Mensa society many times over. How about you? Should someone have stopped us? And if we were stopped, might we not have been even more stupid the next time?

Basically, I'm praising stupidity as a natural right and gift. It's unnatural to overly protect people from themselves. We all see what happens to individuals who are excessively parented or to entire communities that are enabled to subsist in perpetual poverty and social decay.

So what about writers who get scammed? Well, they should stop doing it.

- They should stop sending money to get people to "read" their work, since there are several hundred real agents who will do that for free.

- They should stop smoking and stop eating other fat mammals.

- They should stop giving money to unproven strangers who promise to get them published, since there are several hundred real agents who will do that on a contingency.

- They should wear seatbelts, especially when in New York taxis.

- They should stop giving money to unproven strangers who promise to "fix" the work, especially since there are at least dozens of real former book editors who can genuinely fix your work.

- They should stop maintaining balances on their credit cards.

- They should always ask for evidence of ability whenever asked for money.

If we, as writers, walk the previous line, then parasitic acts could not exist and thrive. We would not need more laws, more people working for government, or any ethics. Such things only exist in the absence of honesty and in the dissonance that follows.

As a service, I have attached information about specific "Book Doctor" organizations and individuals that I'm familiar with and trust. These are people who either have deep experience working as real editors at real publishers, have "doctored" many manuscripts to the point of publication, or both. Retaining their skills will often make the difference between getting a deal or being a "close call."

I endorse none of these people or the expectations they might create. I simply want you to have a safe place to turn if you need help and are ready to receive.

The following is an actual pitch letter from a fee-charging agency, with only the names and other identifying information changed. Such correspondence is typical of the alluring invitations writers often receive in response to their agent submissions.

If a writer chooses to explore this route, I strongly advise following these preliminary steps:

1. Ask for references. You're being asked to shell out hundreds of dollars to a virtual stranger. Get to know those who would eat your money.

2. Ask for a list of titles sold. Find out whether the so-called agency actually has an agenting track record. Or is this particular operation just a high-priced reading service with an agency façade?

3. Better yet, call or write to non-fee charging agents and ask them to recommend book doctors, collaborative writers, or editorial freelancers whom they use to shape and develop their own clients' works, or see the "Book Doctor" section in this book. This may be a better place to spend your money.

BEWARE OF SHARKS!

The following correspondence is genuine, though all names and titles have been altered. My purpose for exposing these ever-so-slightly personalized form letters isn't to condemn or ridicule anyone. I simply wish to show how some subsidy publishers hook their clients.

SHARK HOUSE PUBLISHERS

Mr. Bourne Bate
Brooklyn Bridge
East River, NY 00000

Dear Mr. Bate:

Your manuscript *A Fish's Life* is written from an unusual perspective and an urgent one. In these trying economic times that have created despair and anguish, one must give thought to opportunities, and this upbeat and enthusiastic book makes us realize that those opportunities are out there! My capsule critique: Meticulous aim! With a surgeon's precision we're taught how to work through everything from raising money to targeting areas. There is a sharp eye here for all of the nuances, studded with pointers and reasoning, making it a crucial blueprint.

What can I say about a book like this? It stopped me in my tracks. I guess all I can do is thank you for letting me have the opportunity to read it.

The editors who read this had a spontaneous tendency to feel that it was imbued with some very, very good electricity and would be something very special for our list and saw such potential with it that it was given top priority and pushed ahead of every other book in house. The further problem is that publishing being an extremely rugged business, editorial decisions have to be based on hard facts, which sometimes hurt publishers as much as authors. Unfortunately, we just bought several new nonfiction pieces . . . yet I hate to let this one get away. Publishing economics shouldn't have anything to do with a decision, but unfortunately, it does and I was overruled at the editorial meeting.

Still I want you to know that this is a particularly viable book and one that I really would love to have for our list. Furthermore, this might be picked up for magazine serialization or by book clubs because it is so different. Our book *Enraptured* was serialized six times in *International Inquirer* and sold to Andorra. *The Devil Decided* sold well over 150,000 copies, and we have a movie option on it. *Far Away*, serialized in *Places* magazine and *Cure Yourself* was taken by a major book club.

I really want this book for our list because it will fit into all the areas that we're active in. Therefore, I'm going to make a proposition for you to involve yourself with us. What would you think of the idea of doing this on a cooperative basis? Like many New York publishers these days, we find that sometimes investors are interested in the acquisition of literary properties through a technique that might be advantageous under our tax laws. There is no reason that the partial investor cannot be the writer, if that person so chooses. Tax advantages may accrue.

I'd be a liar if I promised you a bestseller, but I can guarantee that nobody works as hard promoting a book as we do: We nag paperback, book clubs, magazines, and foreign publishers with our zeal and enthusiasm. We do our PR work and take it seriously because this is where we're going to make the money in the long run. One of our authors hired a top publicist on his own for $50,000. He came limping back to us, saying they didn't do the job that we did, and which we don't charge for. This made our office feel very proud of all our efforts.

I feel that your book deserves our efforts because it is something very special. Think about what I've written to you, and I will hold the manuscript until I hear from you. I truly hope that we can get together because I really love this book and believe it is something we can generate some good action for vis-à-vis book clubs, foreign rights, etc., because it is outstanding and has tremendous potential.

Sincerely,

Eda U. Live

Eda U. Live
Executive Editor

The writer of *A Fish's Life* wrote back to Shark House (all names have been changed) and informed the vanity press that he did not want to pay any money to the publisher to have his book published.

The vanity house responded with the following letter.

(This publisher has probably learned from experience that some exhausted writers will return to them with open wallets after fruitless pursuit of a conventional commercial publishing arrangement.)

SHARK HOUSE PUBLISHERS

Mr. Bourne Bate
Brooklyn Bridge
East River, NY 00000

Dear Mr. Bate:

I have your letter in front of me and I want you to know that I think very highly of the book. Before I go any further, I want to tell you that it is a topnotch book and it hits the reader.

In order for us to do a proper job with a book, there is a great deal of PR work involved and this is very costly. To hire an outside agent to do a crackerjack job would cost you upward of $50,000. Yet here we do not charge for it because it is part of our promotion to propel a book into the marketplace, and it is imperative that this be done. The author has to be booked on radio and TV, stores have to be notified, rights here and abroad have to be worked on, reviewers contacted, autograph parties arranged, and myriad details taken care of.

In view of this, why did I ask you to help with the project? I think the above is self-explanatory, especially when we are in the midst of a revolution between books and television. Publishers are gamblers vying for the same audience. Just because a publisher loves a book is no guarantee that the public is going to love it. In times when bookstores are more selective in the number of books they order, the best of us tremble at the thought of the money that we must put out in order to make a good book a reality.

Be that as it may, I have just come from another editorial meeting where I tried to re-open the case for us, but unfortunately, the earlier decision stands.

As a result, I have no choice but to return the manuscript with this letter. I would also like to tell you that you must do what the successful writers do. Keep sending it out. Someone will like it and someone will buy it.

I wish you every success. Live long and prosper.

Sincerely,

Eda U. Live

Eda U. Live
Executive Editor

NINE SIGNS OF A SCAM BOOK DOCTOR

JERRY GROSS

Working with an expert, ethical book doctor can often make the difference between being published or remaining unpublished. Conversely, working with an unqualified, unethical book doctor can often be hazardous—even fatal—to your career.

You've worked hard to save the money to hire a book doctor. Make sure that the book doctor you hire will turn out to be a good investment. Here are 9 signs that someone who claims to be a professional book doctor may be trying to scam you.

1. **A scam book doctor states that you can't get published unless you hire a book doctor.** You may hear that editors and publishers demand that a manuscript be professionally edited before they will consider it for publication, or that agents won't take on a client unless the writer first works with a book doctor to polish the manuscript.

    Not true. Agents and editors still take on manuscripts that need a lot of work, but, to be candid, they don't do it too often because they are usually overworked and overwhelmed by the volume of material submitted to them. That's why working with a good book doctor can at least improve your odds of being accepted by an agent and an editor.

2. **A scam book doctor guarantees, or at least implies, that his editing will get you accepted by an agent.**

    Not true! No reputable book doctor can make this statement because no book doctor can persuade an agent to represent a project that the agent does not like, believe in, or see as commercially viable. Beauty is in the eye of the beholder, and editors and agents often see a manuscript's potential through very different eyes.

3. **A scam book doctor guarantees, or strongly implies, that once she's edited your manuscript, an agent will definitely be able to sell it.**

    Not true. The vagaries, shifts of taste, and trends in the publishing marketplace are such that agents themselves cannot be sure which manuscripts will be salable.

4. **A scam book doctor admits (or you discover) that he has a "financial arrangement" with the person or company who referred you to him.** In plain English, this means that he kicks back part of his fee for the referral.

    This is inarguably unethical. There should be no financial relationship between the book doctor and the referring party. If one exists, it can adversely affect the honesty and integrity of his evaluation of your manuscript, or both.

5. **A scam book doctor does not guarantee that she will edit your manuscript personally.**

    Since you are hiring the editor for her specific expertise, insist that she guarantee in writing that she will edit the manuscript herself. If she won't do this, look elsewhere for an editor.

6. **A scam book doctor tells you that he can't take on your project, but will subcontract it.**

    However, he won't tell you who will edit it, and he won't provide you with that editor's background, samples of that editor's work, or any references. And he does not give you the right to accept or refuse the editor he suggests.

    If you do decide to work with another editor because the one you wanted is overbooked or otherwise unavailable, then you have every right to know as much about the person recommended by him as you know about the editor making the recommendation. You also have every right to decide whether you want to work with the editor whom he recommends.

7. **A scam book doctor won't provide references from authors or agents she's worked with.**

    Obviously, the editor won't provide you with names of dissatisfied clients, but you can learn a lot by gauging the enthusiasm (or lack of it) with which the client discusses working with the book doctor. Ask questions: "Was she easy and friendly to work with?"; "Was she receptive to ideas?"; "Was she available to discuss her approach to line-editing, critique of the manuscript, or both?"; "Did you feel that you got good value for your money?"

8. **A scam book doctor won't provide samples of his editing or critiques.**

    Engaging in a book doctor without seeing how he line-edits or problem-solves a manuscript is akin to buying oceanfront property in Arizona from a real estate salesman on the phone or on the Web. Talk is cheap, but good editing is expensive. Make sure you are buying the expertise you need; demand to see samples of the editor's work. If he balks, hang up the phone!

9. **A scam book doctor sends you an incomplete Letter of Agreement** that does not specify all the costs you will incur, what she will do for each of her fees, a schedule of payment, and a due date for delivery of the edited or critiqued manuscript.

Every one of your contractual obligations to each other should be spelled out clearly in the Letter of Agreement before you sign it. If changes are agreed upon during the course of the author-editor relationship, these changes should either be incorporated into a new Letter of Agreement that both parties sign or be expressed in rider clauses added to the Agreement that are initialed by both editor and author. There should be no hidden or "surprise" costs at the time of the final payment to the book doctor.

A final caution: Be convinced that you are hiring the right book doctor before signing the Letter of Agreement. Not only your money, but also your career is at stake!

Jerry Gross has been a fiction and nonfiction editor for many years, the last seventeen as a freelance editor/book doctor. He is Editor of the standard work on trade-book editing *Editors on Editing: What Writers Need to Know About What Editors Do*. He also creates and presents workshops and panels on editing and writing at writers' conferences. He can be reached at 63 Grand Street, Croton-on-Hudson, NY 10520-2518.

BOOK DOCTORS

THE REAL DEAL

SUSAN SCHWARTZ

Most writers are aware that publishers have become much more business-oriented and competitive in this age of consolidation. What these writers may not know is that the movers and shakers in the publishing industry increasingly rely on independent editors—sometimes called "book doctors"—to transform promising material into publishable books and magazine articles and provide writers with their professional expertise.

Words into Print is one of three currently thriving alliances of top New York publishing professionals who provide independent editorial services to publishers, literary agents, book packagers, content providers, and—most important—directly to writers. In addition to our affiliation with such organizations as ASJA, the Author's Guild, the Women's National Book Association, PEN, and the NWU, Words into Print also offers a Web site (www.wordsintoprint.org) that lists our members and their e-mail addresses, credentials, and recently completed projects. It also provides direct links to related sites. A writer accessing our Web site can approach any editor directly or send a general query to determine which editor or editors are best suited to and available for a particular project.

The editors affiliated with Words into Print have diverse publishing backgrounds. Some of us specialize in fiction, some in nonfiction; some are terrific proposal writers; some are conscientious line editors; some of us function as project developers, matching subjects with appropriate writers and, from there, finding agents and in some cases publishers to handle projects. We offer ghostwriting and other collaborative services, as well as general consultation to writers.

Independent editors who make up groups such as Words into Print can save writers time and heartache by steering them in the right direction at the outset. We work hard for the writers who hire us, as we shape their material, give advice, and meet regularly with the on-staff professionals who make today's publishing decisions. By tapping our expertise, writers acquire the tools they need to navigate the submission and publishing process. While we can't guarantee that every writer's project will find an agent or result in a sale to a publisher, our track record speaks for itself in the number of projects that come our way, are rewritten or reshaped, and then are sold.

If you are engaging a freelance editor or "book doctor," here are some questions to consider:

- Does the editor have on-staff experience? The best book doctors spent decades on staff at major New York publishers and have inside knowledge of what publishers are looking for, how they view manuscripts and proposals, and what it takes to make them notice yours.

- Does the editor's experience mesh with the kind of project you are attempting to publish? Does that person's initial comments about your project make sense? The best editors don't necessarily tell writers what they want to hear; they evaluate material with a clear idea of the competition and marketing climate facing the project and can often suggest ways to reshape and restructure to enhance marketability.

- Is the editor a member of an independent editors' group, such as Words into Print, or affiliated with one of the established professional writers' groups (ASJA, the Author's Guild, the Women's National Book Association, PEN, and the NWU)? Belonging to at least one of these groups is a mark of professionalism.

- How many projects did the editor complete in the past year, and what kind of assignments were they? The best independent editors receive assignments from a wide variety of sources: literary agents, publishers, other editors, and directly from writers who contact them via personal recommendation or over the Internet.

- What specifically does the editor's fee include? Many independent editors charge a reading or consultation fee up front to determine your project's needs. After making that determination, the editor negotiates fees, depending on the time and level of editing the project requires. Some editors charge by the hour; others offer a "package deal."

- What other services can the editor provide? Not only do independent editors have the expertise to help you shape a project, but also, once an agent is on board, that editor can be helpful in guiding the project through the submission process to successful publication and beyond. One of my clients calls me her "secret weapon" in dealing with her agent and her publisher. I'm often called upon to interpret everything from a rushed agent phone call to baffling letters she receives from her on-staff editor (a former colleague of mine). While it was her agent who brought us together several projects ago, neither the agent nor the editor has any idea that I'm still involved behind the scenes, nor do they need to. In this case, I work for the author, helping her get the most out of the professionals involved in her book's success.

In an increasingly competitive marketplace, the difference between capturing a publisher's attention and being relegated to the "slush pile" often rests on the kind of professional polish and presentation that only industry professionals can provide. Independent editors' groups, such as Words into Print, provide the services that writers need before they approach agents or publishers with their projects. We have the credentials and the track record vital to getting writers' work noticed and gaining entry into the sometimes baffling, always formidable publishing world.

WORDS INTO PRINT (www.wordsintoprint.org)

WiP is an alliance of top New York publishing professionals who have pooled our talents and resources to provide a broad range of editorial services. Whatever your needs, we can help you realize your writing and publishing goals. Working with authors, publishers, literary agents, book packagers, and content providers worldwide, our members are available to:

+ Develop book proposals and other editorial projects

+ Evaluate, critique, troubleshoot, and "doctor" manuscripts

+ Line-edit and rewrite text for all media

+ Coauthor and ghostwrite for commercial, professional, and academic markets

+ Write original text for books, magazines, websites, and corporate publications

+ Manage illustrated projects, from conception to delivery of art and text on disk

+ Advise writers on the publishing process

+ Offer referrals to literary agents, book packagers, and publishers

+ Offer referrals for other publishing services, including graphic design, research (text and photo), translation, copyediting, proofreading, and indexing

WiP's members specialize in the following subject areas:

Nonfiction: alternative health, anthologies, anthropology, architecture, art, autobiography, biography, business, cookbooks, crafts, criticism, cultural issues, current affairs, divorce, education, film/television, geography, health/fitness, history, humor, illustrated books, journalism, Judaica, law, lifestyle, memoir, music, nature, parenting, performing arts, philosophy, photography, politics, popular culture, psychology, reference, religion, science, self-help, social issues, spirituality, theater, travel/adventure, true crime, women's studies.

Fiction: action, adventure, literary novels, mysteries, poetry, popular novels, short stories, suspense, thrillers, young adult.

Brief profiles of our members, along with contact information, follow. We welcome all queries and contacts to individual members or to our group e-mail or mailing address, but please do not send unsolicited manuscripts. With our diverse backgrounds and experience, we can match you with the right editor for you. Our client lists, resumes, references, portfolios, and fees are available upon request. For the best in the business, look no further. The editors at WiP look forward to working with you!

Janet Bryne: Biography, memoir, politics, culture, art, fiction, library reference.

Bonny V. Fetterman Popular and scholarly nonfiction: biography/memoir, history, Judaica. General social sciences with special expertise in Jewish history, literature, and culture; biblical studies; anthologies; and translations.

Penelope Franklin General nonfiction, including autobiography/memoir, diaries and letters, women's issues, travel, art, history, psychology, humor, health, natural history, food, paranormal phenomena, anthologies.

Ruth Greenstein Literary fiction, illustrated nonfiction, biography, memoir, social and cultural issues, travel and adventure, nature, religion and spirituality, health, psychology, visual and performing arts, architecture, media tie-ins, anthologies, reference, poetry.

Rob Kaplan: General nonfiction, including business, self-help, popular psychology, parenting, history, and other subjects.

Diane O'Connell Autobiography/memoir, self-help, psychology, health/fitness, parenting, divorce, education, film, theater, journalism, crafts, cooking, narrative nonfiction, and young adult and mainstream fiction.

Susan A. Schwartz Ghostwriting: fitness, memoirs. Editing: popular nonfiction (health, parenting, business, relationships, memoirs); popular reference books (all subjects); book proposals and assessments; corporate and marketing publications (histories, biographies, conference materials); website content; fiction (women's fiction; medical, legal, and political thrillers; general categories).

Katharine Turok Literary and popular fiction, biography/memoir, general nonfiction, film and theater, translations, photography, poetry, psychology, travel, women's issues, art and architecture, reference, anthologies.

Daniel Zitin Fiction: most popular genres, including literary novels, mysteries, thrillers, and novels of action and suspense.

Susan A. Schwartz, former Editor at Doubleday, Facts On File, and Contemporary Books, is currently a member of the independent editors' group Words into Print (www.wordsinto-print.org). She has served as a book doctor and ghostwriter for the past four years.

INDEPENDENT EDITORS GROUP (www.bookdocs.com)

The Independent Editors Group is a professional affiliation of highly select, diverse, experienced freelance editors/book doctors who work with writers, editors, and agents in trade book publishing. They are: Sally Arteseros, Maureen Baron, Carolyn Blakemore, Deborah Chiel, Paul De Angelis, Joyce Engelson, Jerry Gross, Susan Leon, Richard Marek, Joan S. Pollack, James O'Shea Wade, and Genevieve Young.

Years of distinguished tenure at major publishing houses made them eminently qualified to provide the following editorial services on fiction and nonfiction manuscripts.

+ In-depth evaluations and detailed critiques

+ Problem-solving

+ Plot restructure

+ Developmental and line editing

+ Reorganization, revision, and rewriting

+ Book proposals and development

+ Ghostwriting and collaboration

If any editor is unavailable, referrals will be made to other appropriate IEG members. Inquiries are welcomed; please do not send manuscripts. Fees, references, and resumes are available from editors on request.

Whenever you have a project calling for freelance editorial expertise, get in touch with the best editors in trade book publishing today to solve your manuscript problems.

Sally Arteseros
2 Fifth Avenue, Suite 10-T
New York, NY 10011
Fax: 212-982-2053
Edits all kinds of fiction; literary, commercial, women's, historical, contemporary, inspirational. A specialist in short stories. And in nonfiction: biography, autobiography, memoir, psychology, anthropology, business, regional books, and academic books. Editor at Doubleday for more than 25 years.

Maureen Baron
150 West 87th Street, #6C
New York, NY 10024
212-787-6260

Former Vice President/Editor in Chief of NAL/Signet Books continues to work with established and developing writers in all areas of mainstream fiction and nonfiction. Specialties: medical novels and thrillers; women's issues; health matters; African American fiction; biography; memoirs. Knows the market and has good contacts. Book club consultant.

Carolyn Blakemore
242 East 19th Street
New York, NY 10003
Fax: 212-228-6835
A hardcover book Editor for more than 30 years, specializing in commercial fiction, history, and biography, research, and outlines. Has worked with S. M. Alsop, Barbara T. Bradford, James Dickey, Kitty Carlisle, Kitty Kelley, Joseph Lash, John D. MacDonald, Alexandra Ripley, John Toland, Thomas Fleming, Lawrence Grobel, and William Morris.

Deborah Chiel
180 West End Avenue, #23
New York, NY 10023
Fax: 212-362-1104
Freelance writer, book doctor, and Editor whose ghostwriting credits include a major work of alternative medicine for a leading New York oncologist and a legal thriller inspired by a real-life corporate courtroom battle. Also coauthored a glitzy romantic novel and has written more than a dozen novelizations based on feature film and television scripts.

Paul De Angelis Book Development
PO Box 97
Cornwall Bridge, CT 06754
Fax: 860-672-6861
Manuscript evaluations, rewriting or ghostwriting, and editing. Thirty years' experience in key positions at St. Martin's Press, E. P. Dutton, and Kodansha America. Special expertise in history, current affairs, music, biography, literature, translations, popular science. Authors worked with: Delany sisters, Mike Royko, Peter Guralnick, Barbara Pym, Alexander Dubcek.

Joyce Engelson
1160 Fifth Avenue, #402
New York, NY 10029
Fax: 212-860-9095
Sympathetic, hands-on editing; goal: commercial publication. Forty years' experience. Concentrations: thrillers, mysteries, literary and first novels; health, psychology, mind/body, women's issues, American history, pop culture, sports, comedy ("best sense

of humor in the biz"—try me!). Authors include Richard Condon, Norman Cousins, Gael Greene. And me.

Jerry Gross
63 Grand Street
Croton-on-Hudson, NY 10520-2518
Fax: 914-271-1239
More than 40 years of specific, problem-solving critiquing, line editing, restructuring, and rewriting of mainstream and literary fiction and nonfiction manuscripts and proposals. Specialties: male-oriented escape fiction, popular psychology, and pop culture. My goal is to make the manuscript as effective and salable as possible.

Susan Leon
21 Howell Avenue
Larchmont, NY 10538
Fax: 914-833-1429
Editor specializing in preparation of book proposals and collaborations, including two *New York Times* bestsellers. Fiction: All areas—commercial, literary, historical, and women's topics. Nonfiction: history, biography, memoir, autobiography, women's issues, family, lifestyle, design, travel, food. Also, law, education, information, and reference guides.

Richard Mark
29 East 9th Street
New York, NY 10003
Fax: 212-420-1819
Former President and Publisher of E. P. Dutton specializes in editing and ghostwriting. Edited Robert Ludlum's first nine books, James Baldwin's last five, and Thomas Harris's *The Silence of the Lambs*. As ghostwriter, collaborated on six books, among them a novel that sold 225,000 copies in hardcover and more than 2 million in paperback.

Joan S. Pollack
890 West End Avenue, #14B
New York, NY 10025
Fax: 212-666-4219
Specializing in autobiography, biography, memoirs, and fiction; any manuscripts with a narrative line. Collaborative ghosting of celebrity biographies—for example, Douglas Fairbanks, Jr., *The Salad Days* (Doubleday) and *A Hell of a War* (St. Martin's Press); Jack Benny and Joan Benny, *Sunday Nights at Seven* (Warner Books).

James O'Shea Wade
1565 Baptist Church Road
Yorktown Heights, NY 10598
Voice/fax: 914-962-4619

With 30 years' experience as Editor-in-Chief and Executive Editor for major publishers, including Crown/Random House, Macmillan, Dell, and Rawson-Wade, I edit and ghostwrite in all nonfiction areas and specialize in business, science, history, biography, and military. Also edit all types of fiction, prepare book proposals, and evaluate manuscripts.

Genevieve Young
30 Park Avenue
New York, NY 10016
Fax: 212-683-9780
Detailed analysis of manuscripts, including structure, development, and line editing. Areas of special interest include biography, autobiography, medicine, animals, modern Chinese history, and all works with a story line, whether fiction or nonfiction.

ASSOCIATION OF AUTHOR REPRESENTATIVES (AAR)

Attached here is the Canon of Ethics from the Association of Author Representatives (AAR). Even though I make fun of ethics as a ruling concept and don't know which high horse imposed the use of the word *Canon* in this instance, these are excellent guidelines that all agents should follow and that clients should expect and demand that agents follow.

Membership within the AAR implies complete compliance with these guidelines. The AAR is not an agency of enforcement or endorsement. It can simply grant or deny membership in the organization. It's not a so-called trade group. It could be seen as a collective "study" group composed of people who share common pursuits and mutual interests—in this case, book agenting.

Many good agents have chosen to be nonaffiliated with the AAR, including yours truly, for various reasons. In my case, I do a number of "packaged" deals, and my wife does a number of collaboration or "work-for-hire" arrangements, which puts us outside the narrow membership parameters. Excellent agencies that do other "things" beyond simple agenting will not be members for the same reason.

Therefore, membership in the AAR is a pretty good indication of legitimacy. But nonmembership, in and of itself, may indicate nothing.

ABOUT THE AAR

The AAR was formed in 1991 through the merger of the Society of Authors' Representatives (founded in 1928) and the Literary Agents Association (founded in 1977).

The AAR's objectives include keeping agents informed about conditions in publishing, the theater, the motion picture and television industries, and related fields; encouraging cooperation among literary organizations; and assisting agents in representing their author-clients' interests.

To qualify for membership in the AAR, an agent must meet professional standards specified in the organization's bylaws and agree to its Canon of Ethics.

The AAR cannot regulate the commissions, fees, services, or other competitive business practices of its members.

MEMBERSHIP QUALIFICATIONS

Membership in the AAR is restricted to agents whose primary professional activity for the two years preceding application for membership in the AAR has been as an authors' representative or a playwrights' representative.

To qualify for membership, the applicant for membership in the literary branch of the AAR must have been the agent principally responsible for executed agreements concerning the grant of publication, translation, or performance rights in 10-different literary properties during the 18-month period preceding application.

Alternatively, if the applicant is a dramatic agent, the agent must have been principally responsible for executing agreements for the grant of rights for at least five stage productions before live audiences (in First Class theaters, off-Broadway theaters, LORT theaters, or major institutional theaters in New York City) during the preceding two-year period. At least one such grant must have used either the Approved Production Contract of the Dramatists Guild, Inc., or have been a grant for the production of the play off-Broadway in New York City.

Member agents must conduct their business in such a manner as to be in compliance with legal and fiduciary duties to their clients, and each member agent must agree, in writing, to adhere to the AAR's Canon of Ethics.

Associate members are full-time employees of a sponsoring agent member. They do not themselves qualify for full membership, but are actively engaged in the selling of rights to literary or dramatic properties.

The previous qualifications are merely a digest of some of the requirements for membership. The full requirements are set forth in the Bylaws of the Association of Authors' Representatives, Inc.

CANON OF ETHICS

1. The members of the Association of Authors' Representatives, Inc., are committed to the highest standard of conduct in the performance of their professional activities. While affirming the necessity and desirability of maintaining their full individuality and freedom of action, the members pledge themselves to loyal service to their clients' business and artistic needs and will allow no conflicts of interest that would interfere with such service. They pledge their support to the Association itself and their principles of honorable coexistence, directness, and honesty in their relationships with their co-members. They undertake never to mislead, deceive, dupe, defraud, or victimize their clients, other members of the Association, the general public, or any person with whom they do business as a member of the Association.

2. Members shall take responsible measures to protect the security and integrity of clients' funds. Members must maintain separate bank accounts for money due their clients so that there is no commingling of clients' and members' funds. Members shall deposit funds received on behalf of clients promptly upon receipt and shall make payments of domestic earnings due clients promptly, but in no event later than 10 business days after clearance. Sums under $50 shall be paid within a reasonable time of clearance. However, on stock and similar rights, statements of royalties and payments shall be made not later than the month following the member's receipt, each statement and payment to cover all royalties received to the 25th day of the previous calendar month. Payments for amateur rights shall be made not less frequently than every six months. A member's books of account must be open to the client at all times with respect to transactions concerning the client.

3. In addition to the compensation for agency services that is agreed upon between a member and a client, a member may, subject to the approval of the client, pass along charges incurred by the member on the client's behalf, such as copyright fees, manuscript retyping, photocopies, copies of books for use in the sale of other rights, long distance calls, special messenger fees, etc. Such charges shall be made only if the client has agreed to reimburse such expenses.

4. A member shall keep each client apprised of matters entrusted to the member and shall promptly furnish such information as the client may reasonably request.

5. Members shall not represent both buyer and seller in the same transaction. Except as provided in the next sentence, a member who represents a client in the grant of rights in any property owned or controlled by the client may not accept any compensation or other payment from the acquirer of such rights, including but not limited to so-called packaging fees, it being understood that the member's compensation, if any, shall be derived solely from the client. Notwithstanding the foregoing, a member may accept (or participate in) a so-called packaging fee paid by an acquirer of television rights to a property owned or controlled by a client if the member: (a) fully discloses to the client at the earliest practical time the possibility that the member may be offered such a "packaging fee," which the member may choose to accept; (b) delivers to the client at such time a copy of the Association's statement regarding packaging and packaging fees; and (c) offers the client at such time the opportunity to arrange for other representation in the transaction. In no event shall the member accept (or participate in) both a packaging fee and compensation from the client with respect to the transaction. For transactions subject to the Writers Guild of America (WGA) jurisdiction, the regulations of the WGA shall take precedence over the requirements of this paragraph.

6. Members may not receive a secret profit in connection with any transaction involving a client. If such profit is received, the member must promptly pay over the entire amount to the client. Members may not solicit or accept any payment or other things of value in connection with their referral of any author to any third party for any purpose, provided that the foregoing does not apply to arrangements made with a third party in connection with the disposition of rights in the work of a client of the member.

7. Members shall treat their clients' financial affairs as private and confidential, except for information customarily disclosed to interested parties as part of the process of placing rights, as required by law, or, if agreed with the client, for other purposes.

   The AAR believes that the practice of literary agents charging clients or potential clients for reading and evaluating literary works (including outlines, proposals, and partial or complete manuscripts) is subject to serious abuse that reflects adversely on our profession. For that reason, members may not charge clients or potential clients for reading and evaluating literary works and may not benefit, directly or indirectly, from the charging for such services by any other person or entity. The term *charge* in the previous sentence includes any request for payment other than to cover the actual cost of returning materials.

SELF PUBLISHING

JEFF HERMAN

Many books in print have sold hundreds of thousands of copies but will never appear on any lists, nor will they ever be seen in a bookstore, nor will the authors ever care. Why? Because these authors are self-publishers and make as much as a 90 percent profit margin on each copy they sell.

Their initial one-time start-up cost to get each of their titles produced may have been $15,000, but after that, each 5,000-copy print run of a hardcover edition costs about $1.25 per unit. The authors sell them for $25 each. When they do a high-volume corporate sale, they're happy to discount the books 20 percent or more off the $25 list price.

Now, we said that no bookstores are in the picture. Then how and where are the authors selling their books? The answer to this question is also the answer to whether it makes sense for you to self-publish. Here's what these authors do:

1. A well-linked Web site designed to sell and upsell.

2. A well-oiled corporate network, which translates into frequent high-volume orders by companies that distribute the book in-house as an educational tool or distribute them at large as a sales vehicle (customized printings are no problem).

3. Frequent public speaking events where backroom sales happen.

4. Frequent and self-generated publicity that's designed to promote the books and leads people to the Web site, a toll free number, or both.

Obviously, most of us don't have this kind of in-house infrastructure, which brings us back to the most important question: How will you sell copies of your self-published book? If you don't have a realistic answer in place, then self-publishing may not be a viable option after all, or at least your initial expectations have to be reoriented.

Why can self-publishers make so much money? Because they get to keep it. Here's how a conventional book publisher's deal gets divided up:

+ Start with a trade paperback listed at $20.

- $10 goes to the retailer.

- $1.50 goes to the author.

- The first $15,000 goes to set the book up.

- $1.00 goes to printing each copy.

- $? Corporate overhead. (If the publisher overpaid on the advance, then this number goes higher.)

- $?? Publisher's profit. (This is a real wild card. If a publisher is an inefficient operation, than any profit may be out of reach. If too few books sell, there are only losses, no matter how lean and mean the publisher may be.)

A secondary source of no-overhead revenues for both publishers and self-publishers is ancillary rights, which includes exports, translations, and audio editions.

What's clear is that the published author makes a tiny fraction of the per-unit sale versus what the self-publisher makes. But the publisher also absorbs all the risks. And then there's the distribution factor . . .

WHAT'S DISTRIBUTION?

AND WHY DO SELF-PUBLISHERS HAVE A TOUGH TIME WITH IT?

Because everyone else does, too. Distribution is the process that gets books onto shelves, theoretically. Strong distribution does not ensure that bookstores will elect to stock the title. Too many books are published, compared to the quantity and quality of shelf space to accommodate them. You can have a big-name publisher and an invisible book. Distribution only generates the potential for the book to be available in stores, and nonexistent distribution deletes that potential.

All established book publishers have proven distribution channels in place, consisting of warehouses, fulfillment and billing operations, and traveling or regional salespeople who pitch the stores.

Smaller-sized presses may not be able to afford all of that, so they'll pay a 15 percent commission to a large house to handle it for them, or they will retain an independent distributor that does nothing but distribute for small presses.

Brick and mortar bookstores are not eager to open accounts with self-publishers. It's too much of a hassle. Same goes for independent distributors.

Several brilliant self-publishing consultants have devised ways to bypass these distribution obstacles. Look for their books in the "Suggested Resources" section of this book.

Vanity publishing is for morons. I don't mean to be insulting. It's just that you end up spending so much more than necessary, all for the illusion that you've been published in the conventional sense. In truth, the only thing you'll get out of the deal are boxes of expensive books that were probably not edited or well produced.

Hiring qualified editors, consultants, and so on, to help you make the best self-published book possible does not fall under the vanity label.

WHEN THE DEAL IS DONE

HOW TO THRIVE AFTER SIGNING
A PUBLISHING CONTRACT

JEFF HERMAN

ongratulations! You've sold your book to an established publishing house. You've gained entry to the elite club of published authors. You'll discover that your personal credibility is enhanced whenever this achievement is made known to others. It may also prove a powerful marketing vehicle for your business or professional practice.

Smell the roses while you can. Then wake up and smell the coffee. If your experience is like that of numerous other writers, once your book is actually published, there's a better-than-even chance you'll feel a bit of chagrin. Some of these doubts are apt to be outward expressions of your own inner uncertainties. Others are not self-inflicted misgivings—they are most assuredly ticked off by outside circumstances.

Among the most common author complaints are: (1) Neither you nor anyone you know can find the book anywhere. (2) The publisher doesn't appear to be doing anything to market the book. (3) You detest the title and the jacket. (4) No one at the publishing house is listening to you. In fact, you may feel that you don't even exist for them.

As a literary agent, I live through these frustrations with my clients every day, and I try to explain to them at the outset what the realities of the business are. But I never advocate abdication or pessimism. There are ways for every author to substantially remedy these endemic problems. In many cases this means first taking a deep breath, relaxing, and reaching down deep inside yourself to sort out the true source of your emotions. When this has been accomplished, it's time to breathe out, move out, and take charge.

What follows are practical means by which each of these four most common failures can be preempted. I'm not suggesting that you can compensate entirely for what may be a publisher's defaults; it's a tall order to remake a clinker after the fact. However, with lots of smarts and a little luck you can accomplish a great deal.

A PHILOSOPHY TO WRITE BY

Let me introduce a bit of philosophy that applies to the writer's life, as well as it does to the lives of those who are not published. Many of you may be familiar with the themes popularized by psychotherapists, self-awareness gurus, and business motivators that assert the following: To be a victim is to be powerless—which means you don't have the ability to improve your situation. With that in mind, avoid becoming merely an author who only complains and who remains forever bitter.

No matter how seriously you believe your publisher is screwing up, don't fall into the victim trap. Instead, find positive ways to affect what is or is not happening for you.

Your publisher is like an indispensable employee whom you are not at liberty to fire. You don't have to work with this publisher the next time, but this time it's the only one you've got.

There are a handful of perennially bestselling writers, such as John Grisham, Anne Rice, Mary Higgins Clark, and Michael Crichton, whose book sales cover a large part of their publisher's expense sheet. These writers have perhaps earned the luxury of being very difficult, if they so choose (most of them are reportedly quite the opposite).

But the other 99.98 percent of writers are not so fortunately invested with the power to arbitrate. No matter how justified your stance and methods may be, if you become an author with whom everyone at the publishing house dreads to speak, you've lost the game.

The editors, publicists, and marketing personnel still have their jobs, and they see no reason to have you in their face. In other words: Always seek what's legitimately yours, but always try to do it in a way that might work for you, as opposed to making yourself persona non grata till the end of time.

ATTACKING PROBLEM NO. 1: NEITHER YOU NOR ANYONE YOU KNOW CAN FIND THE BOOK ANYWHERE

This can be the most painful failure. After all, what was the point of writing the book and going through the whole megillah of getting it published if it's virtually invisible?

Trade book distribution is a mysterious process, even for people in the business. Most bookstore sales are dominated by the large national and regional chains, such as Waldenbooks, B. Dalton, Barnes & Noble, and Borders. No shopping mall is complete without at least one of these stores. Publishers always have the chain stores in mind when they determine what to publish. Thankfully, there are also a few thousand independently owned shops throughout the country.

Thousands of new titles are published each year, and these books are added to the seemingly infinite number that are already in print. Considering the limitations of the existing retail channels, it should be no surprise that only a small fraction of all these books achieves a significant and enduring bookstore presence.

Each bookstore will dedicate most of its visual space to displaying healthy quantities of the titles it feels are safe sells: books by celebrities and well-established authors, or books that are being given extra-large printings and marketing budgets by their publishers, thereby promising to create demand.

The rest of the store will generally provide a liberal mix of titles, organized by subject or category. This is where the backlist titles reside and the lower-profile newer releases try to stake their claims. For instance, the business section will probably offer two dozen or so sales books. Most of the displayed titles will be by the biggest names in the genre, and their month-to-month sales probably remain strong, even if the book was first published several years ago.

In other words, probably hundreds of other sales books were written in recent years that, as far as retail distribution is concerned, barely made it out of the womb. You see, the stores aren't out there to do you any favors. They are going to stock whatever titles they feel they can sell the most of. There are too many titles chasing too little space.

It's the job of the publisher's sales representative to lobby the chain and store buyers individually about the merits of her publisher's respective list. But here, too, the numbers can be numbing. The large houses publish many books each season, and it's not possible for the rep to do justice to each of them. Priority will be given to the relatively few titles that get the exceptional advances.

Because most advances are modest, and since the average book costs about $20,000 to produce, some publishers can afford to simply sow a large field of books and observe passively as some of them sprout. The many that don't bloom are soon forgotten, as a new harvest dominates the bureaucracy's energy. Every season, many very fine books are terminated by the publishing reaper. The wisdom and magic these books may have offered are thus sealed away, disclosed only to the few.

I have just covered a complicated process in a brief fashion. Nonetheless, the overall consequences for your book are in essence the same. Here, now, are a few things you may attempt in order to override such a stacked situation. However, these methods will not appeal to the shy or passive:

- Make direct contact with the publisher's sales representatives. Do to them what they do to the store buyers—sell 'em! Get them to like you and your book. Take the reps near you to lunch and ballgames. If you travel, do the same for local reps wherever you go.

- Make direct contact with the buyers at the national chains. If you're good enough to actually get this kind of access, you don't need to be told what to do next.

- Organize a national marketing program aimed at local bookstores throughout the country.

There's no law that says only your publisher has the right to market your book to the stores. (Of course, except in special cases, all orders must go through your publisher.) For the usual reasons, your publisher's first reaction may be "What the hell are you doing?" But that's okay; make the publisher happy by showing her that your efforts work. It would be wise, however, to let the publisher in on your scheme up front.

If your publisher objects—which she may—you might choose to interpret those remarks simply as the admonitions they are, and then proceed to make money for all. This last observation leads to ways you can address the next question.

ATTACKING PROBLEM NO. 2: THE PUBLISHER DOESN'T APPEAR TO BE DOING ANYTHING TO MARKET THE BOOK

If it looks as if your publisher is doing nothing to promote your book, then it's probably true. Your mistake is being surprised and unprepared.

The vast majority of published titles receive little or no marketing attention from the publisher beyond catalog listings. The titles that get big advances are likely to get some support, since the publisher would like to justify the advance by creating a good seller.

Compared to those in other Fortune 500 industries, publishers' in-house marketing departments tend to be woefully understaffed, undertrained, and underpaid. Companies like Procter & Gamble will tap the finest business schools, pay competitive salaries, and strive to nurture marketing superstars. Book publishers don't do this.

As a result, adult trade book publishing has never been especially profitable, and countless sales probably go unmade. The sales volumes and profits for large, diversified publishers are mostly due to the lucrative—and captive—textbook trade. Adult trade sales aren't the reason that companies like Random House can generate more than $1 billion in annual revenues.

Here's What You Can Do

Hire your own public relations firm to promote you and your book. Your publisher is likely to be grateful and cooperative. But you must communicate carefully with your publishing house.

Once your manuscript is completed, you should request a group meeting with your editor and people from the marketing, sales, and publicity departments. You should focus on what their marketing agenda will be. If you've decided to retain your own PR firm, this is the time to impress the people at your publishing house with your commitment and pressure them to help pay for it. At the very least, the publisher should provide plenty of free books.

Beware of this common problem: Even if you do a national TV show, your book may not be abundantly available in bookstores that day—at least, not everywhere. An obvious answer is setting up 800 numbers to fill orders, and it baffles me that publishers don't make wider use of them. There are many people watching Oprah who won't ever make it to the bookstore, but who would be willing to order then and there with a credit card. Infomercials have proved this.

Not all talk or interview shows will cooperate, but whenever possible you should try to have your publisher's 800 number (or yours) displayed as a purchasing method, in addition to the neighborhood bookstore. If you use your own number, make sure you can handle a potential flood.

If retaining a PR firm isn't realistic for you, then do your own media promotions.

There are many good books in print about how to do your own PR. (A selection of relevant titles may be found in this volume's "Suggested Resources" section.)

ATTACKING PROBLEM NO. 3: YOU DETEST THE TITLE AND JACKET

Almost always, your publisher will have final contractual discretion over title, jacket design, and jacket copy. But that doesn't mean you can't be actively involved. In my opinion, you had better be. Once your final manuscript is submitted, make it clear to your editor that you expect to see all prospective covers and titles. But simply trying to veto what the publisher comes up with won't be enough. You should try to counter the negatives with positive alternatives. You might even want to go as far as having your own prospective covers professionally created. If the publisher were to actually choose your version, the house might reimburse you.

At any rate, don't wait until it's after the fact to decide you don't like your cover, title, and so forth. It's like voting: Participate or shut up.

ATTACKING PROBLEM NO. 4: NO ONE AT THE PUBLISHING HOUSE SEEMS TO BE LISTENING TO YOU

This happens a lot—though I bet it happens to certain people in everything they do. The primary reasons for this situation are either (1) that the people you're trying to access are incompetent; (2) that you're not a priority for them; or (3) that they simply hate talking to you.

Here are a few things you might try to do about it:

- If the contact person is incompetent, what can that person really accomplish for you anyway? It's probably best to find a way to work around this person, even if he begins to return your calls before you place them.

- The people you want access to may be just too busy to give you time. Screaming may be a temporary remedy, but eventually, they'll go deaf again. Obviously, their time is being spent somewhere. Thinking logically, how can you make it worthwhile for these people to spend more time on you? If being a pain in the neck is your best card, then perhaps you should play it. But there's no leverage like being valuable. In fact, it's likely that the somewhere else they're spending their time is with a very valuable author.

- Maybe someone just hates talking to you. That may be this person's problem. But, as many wise men and women have taught, allies are better than adversaries. And to convert an adversary is invaluable. Do it.

CONCLUSION

This essay may come across as cynical. But I want you to be realistic and be prepared. Many publishing success stories are out there, and many of them happened because the authors made them happen.

For every manuscript that is published, probably a few thousand were rejected. To be published is a great accomplishment—and a great asset. If well tended, it can pay tremendous dividends.

Regardless of your publisher's commitment at the outset, if you can somehow generate sales momentum, the publisher will most likely join your march to success and allocate a substantial investment to ensure it. In turn, the publisher may even assume all the credit. But so what? It's to your benefit.

THE SECRETS OF GHOSTWRITING AND COLLABORATION SUCCESS

TONIANNE ROBINO

Thousands of people in the world have valuable information to share or incredible stories to tell. But only a few of them have the ability or the time to write their own books. That's where you—the professional writer—come into the picture. If you're a strong, clear writer, have the ability to organize thoughts and ideas into a logical order, and can put your ego in the back seat, you may have what it takes to be a successful ghostwriter or collaborator.

The life of a professional writer has its share of pains, but it also has an ample amount of perks. To begin with, it provides a means of escape from the Monday through Friday, 9 to 5 grind. The pay is good, and as you improve your skills and broaden your network, it gets better. In addition to being paid to learn and write about interesting people, philosophies, and methods, being a professional writer puts you in touch with a wide array of fascinating people.

I've had the chance to interview some of the planet's most brilliant people and to explore the work of trendsetters and pioneers in the fields of business, psychology, health, fitness, relationship building, astrology, and metaphysics. I have been flown to Paris to meet with leaders in the field of innovation, wined and dined at some of New York's most exclusive restaurants, and collected agates on the Oregon coast, all in the name of "work." If this sounds appealing, keep reading.

WHAT'S THE DIFFERENCE BETWEEN GHOSTWRITING AND COLLABORATING?

One of the most common questions I'm asked is "What's the difference between a ghostwriter and a collaborator?" The answer can vary from project to project. But, typically, a ghostwriter gathers the author's original materials and research and turns them into a book, based on the author's specifications (if the book will be self-published) or the publisher's specifications (if the book has been sold through the proposal process.)

Theoretically, although ghostwriters do conduct interviews and undertake additional research, they do not contribute their own thoughts or ideas to the content of the book.

In reality, the boundaries of the ghostwriter are not always so clear. As a ghostwriter, I have created 80 percent of the exercises in a number of self-help books, provided many original ideas for content, and "given away" plenty of great title ideas. I don't regret these choices because they felt right and, in the cases mentioned, I was being fairly paid for my ideas, as well as for my services. My being generous with my contributions also made my clients happy and helped to build the foundation of my business. But don't take this too far. For one thing, it's not always a wise choice—particularly if you're giving away original ideas that are perfect for your own book. For another thing, the author you're working with may not appreciate this type of input from you. Do not overstep your boundaries as a ghostwriter by adding your own thoughts to a book, unless the author specifically asks you to do this.

In my more naïve days, and following two glasses of Chardonnay, I made the mistake of sharing my unsolicited input with the author of a health book that I was ghostwriting. In the midst of my enthusiasm, I started brainstorming ideas that she might use to illustrate some of the book's major points. Suddenly, she sprung out of her chair, pointed at me, and declared, "Let's get something straight. This is MY book!" Ouch! I was offering ideas without being asked, but on the other hand, I was only suggesting. Even so, take the word of an initiate and tread softly on your client's turf.

Nowadays, if an author wants me to contribute my own ideas and create original material to support the book, I work with that person as a collaborator and generally receive a coauthor credit, either on the cover or on the title page. Getting credit isn't the most important thing when you're starting out, but if you want to publish your own books in the future, stringing together a list of credits can give you a considerable advantage.

If a book cover says "by John Doe and Jane Smith," they were probably equal collaborators. That can mean:

- they're both experts and one or both of them wrote the book,

- they're both experts and they hired a ghostwriter to write the book, or

- the first author is the expert and the second is a professional writer.

If a book cover says "by John Doe with Jane Smith," Jane probably wrote the book. It could also mean that Jane was a contributor to the book.

Whether you will be serving as a ghostwriter or a collaborator should be clarified up front. Which way to go depends on the project and the people involved. Some of my clients want me to be a "ghost" because they want exclusive cover credit, or they want people to think they wrote their own book. (If this bothers you, now would be a good time to bail out.) Other clients say, "I'm not a writer. This is my material, but I don't want to pretend I wrote this book," or "You deserve credit for what you're doing." On the flip side of the coin, you may be willing to write some books that you don't want your name on. Let's hope this is not because you haven't done a good job! Perhaps you're trying to establish yourself in a particular field of writing and may not want to be linked with projects outside of your target area. That's a judgment call, and you're the best one to make it.

BEING "INVISIBLE" HAS ITS ADVANTAGES

Years ago, after signing my first contract to ghostwrite a book about personal development, I called a friend to share the great news. But instead of being happy for me, she said, "That's not fair. Why should you write a book and not get any credit for it? You teach that stuff in your seminars. Why don't you write the book yourself?" She was also upset that I wouldn't divulge the name of the "mystery author."

She had no way of knowing how challenging it can be to publish your first book flying solo. The author whom I was writing for was well-known and regularly spoke to huge crowds of people all around the world. He had created the perfect platform for this book and was in the prime position to make it a success. He had been previously published and his depth of knowledge in this topic was far greater than my own.

For me, it was a chance to learn more about one of my favorite topics from one of the best sources available. It was also a chance to slip into the publishing world through the back door. I dashed in and never looked back. Once I completed that book, the author referred me to a friend who hired me to write a book about her spiritual journey. She, in turn, introduced me to a professional speaker who wanted to self-publish a book on personal coaching, but could never find the time to write it. And so it goes. If you do a good job, one book can easily lead to the next.

Besides that, being invisible has its advantages. I can zip into the grocery store in purple sweatpants, hair in a ponytail on top of my head, and not a stitch of make-up, and nobody notices or cares! I can kiss my husband in public without camera flashes going off around us, and nobody shows up at my door uninvited, except my mother-in-law.

WHEN CREDIT IS DUE

After you've ghostwritten your first book or two, you'll have more confidence in yourself and your abilities. You will probably start fantasizing (if you haven't already) about seeing your name on the cover, instead of tucked into the acknowledgments section—if that! My name didn't even appear in the first few books that I wrote. Beginning with the fourth book, I asked for a credit in the acknowledgments. Since then, I've been thanked for being a wordsmith, editorial adviser, writing coach, editor, and a "great friend." At least, that was a step in the right direction. However, as much as I relish my anonymity, I also look forward to the day when I'm writing more of my own books than other people's! For that reason, most of the professional writing that I do now is as a collaborator/coauthor.

TEN STEPS TO SUCCEEDING AS A PROFESSIONAL WRITER

There are a number of things to consider before quitting your job and striking out as a professional writer. Writing is a constant process and no matter how good a writer may be, that individual can always get better. Another point to consider is that being a great writer doesn't ensure your success. Writing is a business, and the more you learn about running a business, the better off you'll be. If you're stagnating in a job you abhor, reframe your situation so that you see it as an opportunity to continue earning an income while you make the transition to your writing career. Meanwhile, focus on polishing your writing and interpersonal skills and learn as much about operating a business as you can. The more you learn now, the fewer mistakes you'll make later.

1. ASSESS YOUR WRITING SKILLS

Now is the time to be as objective about your writing as possible. Regardless of where you believe you could or should be along your writing path, what counts at the moment is where you are right now. What writing experience do you have? Have you taken any writing courses? Does your writing flow from one thought logically to the next, or does it need to be better organized? Is your writing smooth and conversational, or does it sound stiff or overly academic? What sorts of positive and negative comments have you received about your writing? Have you had anything published? If not, get going!

If you're too close to your writing to be objective, hire an editor, book doctor, or writing coach to give you some forthright feedback. This assessment will help you to learn where you excel and where you should focus your efforts for improvements. The good news is that there's a market for writers at all points on the professional spectrum. You may not be ready to take on your first book, but you could be qualified to ghost-write an article, collaborate on a chapter, or polish someone else's work. Begin at your current skill level and commit to a path of improvement. By doing this, you will increase your abilities and your income.

2. MAKE YOUR FIRST LIST

Everyone knows at least a few experts. Whether the experts in your life are doctors, professors, psychologists, interior decorators, photographers, archaeologists, or magicians, chances are that some of them have a goal to write a book. Unless these people are good writers and have a lot of free time, which very few experts have, their book will remain on their "wish list" until someone like you shows up to help them. So begin to make a "potential author" list by answering the following questions. For each question, list as many names as you can think of.

Do you know people who are pioneers or experts in their field?
Do you know people who are famous, either in general or in their area of expertise?
Who are the experts, celebrities, or trendsetters whom your friends or associates know?

Once you've made your list, number the names, starting with number one for the person you would most like to work with. Resist the urge to contact these people until you have professionally prepared for your meeting, by learning more about them and taking Steps 3 and 4.

3. PREPARE A PROFESSIONAL PACKAGE

Put together a promotional package for yourself, or hire a professional to help you do it. This package should include your resume or bio, the services you offer, and a variety of writing samples, showing different styles and topics. You might also insert a page of testimonials from people you have helped with your writing skills or from teachers and coaches who can attest to your abilities. If you've been published, include clean copies of a few of your best clips. If you haven't, enclose a few essays that demonstrate your ability to write clearly and deliver a message effectively.

When you send out your promotional package, enclose a personal pitch letter.. Basically, you are telling people what you believe they have to offer the world through their experience or expertise. You're also telling them why you are the perfect person to write the article, manuscript, or book proposal.

4. SET YOUR RATES

Some writers enclose a rate sheet in their promotional package, but I don't recommend it. I do recommend that you make a rate sheet for your own reference. This will be your guide when you are deciding what to charge your clients. Since every project is a little different, don't commit to a price until you estimate how much time and money it will take for you to do the job well.

Calculate how fast you can write final copy, by keeping track of the actual hours spent writing, editing, and proofreading an article or sample chapter. When the piece is completed to your satisfaction, follow this formula:

Total number of words in final copy
Divided by
Total number of hours to complete final copy
Equals:
Your average speed per hour

The idea isn't to race. This exercise is designed to give you a reality check. If you don't know your average speed for producing final copy, you won't be able to create realistic deadline schedules and you'll have no idea how much you're earning for a day of work.

While you may be able to speed through a first draft, the chapter isn't finished until you've edited, polished, and proofread it.

In addition to estimating your actual writing time, build in time for research, interviews, and meetings with the author. You should also estimate the amount of postage, phone charges, faxes, audio tapes, transcription services, and anything else that will be money out of your pocket. Once you've done your homework, you can present the client with a Letter of Agreement (see Step 7) that includes what you will charge and what they will get for your fee.

Writers' rates vary wildly. I was paid $10,000 for the first few books that I ghost-wrote, and this is still a great starter rate for a nonfiction book ranging from 70,000 to about 85,000 words. You may not be able to charge this much the first time or two, but with each publication that you add to your list, you can inch up your price. When you reach the point where you are earning $15,000 or more on a book, you will be in the company of some of the most successful ghostwriters. The average fee to write a book proposal can range from $1,000 up to $8,000 or more. When you turn writing into a full-time adventure and write several proposals and books each year, while perhaps editing others, you'll be well on your way to ongoing financial and publishing success!

Many times, if you are working as a "writer for hire," you are paid a flat fee and do not receive royalties from book sales. If you are ghostwriting the book, you may be able to negotiate for royalties. (Royalties for ghostwriting can range from 10 percent of the author's royalties to 50 percent.) If you're a collaborator, in most cases you're entitled to a percentage of the book sales. However, many contracts state that the writer does not begin to receive royalties until the publisher has recouped the initial advance for the book. In some cases, the writer's royalties do not begin until the author has recouped the amount invested in the writer. The bottom line is that most ghostwriters don't receive a dime in royalties until thousands of books have been sold. I suggest that you charge what you're worth up front and think of royalties as icing on the cake.

5. POLISH YOUR INTERPERSONAL SKILLS

Unfortunately, some of the best writers are not comfortable talking to people or selling themselves to potential clients. If you see this as a possible pitfall in building your business, make it a priority to develop your interpersonal skills. Plenty of books, tapes, and seminars address personal development, communication skills, networking, and conflict resolution. Devote yourself to learning how to be more comfortable and effective in your interactions with others.

Practice listening closely to what your client is saying, without interrupting. Growing up in an Italian family with everyone talking at once, I had no problem paying attention to what my clients were saying. (If you can listen to three people at once, you can easily hear one at a time!) However, mastering the discipline to keep my mouth shut until it was my turn to talk was another matter entirely. While interjecting and simultaneous talking is considered par for the course in some settings, many people are offended by interruptions and consider them rude. If you have an exciting idea or pertinent question on the tip of your tongue, jot it down, and wait until your clients complete their thoughts, before chiming in.

Learn how to communicate with your clients in a way that is open and caring. For example, rather than telling an author that the file of notes she sent you was so disorganized that dealing with it was like "stumbling blindfolded through a maze," tell her you appreciate her ability to think of so many things at once. Then tell her what you want her to do. "Please put all of your notes under specific category headings, so I can keep all of your great ideas organized." The rule is to think before you speak. There are usually better ways to communicate a thought than the first words that pop into your head or out of your mouth!

Another skill that is essential for a ghostwriter and important for a collaborator is learning how to keep your ego in check. It's not uncommon for a writer to start feeling attached to a project and have a desire for greater freedom or control of the content or writing style. Remind yourself that this book is not yours. Your day will come, and working as a professional writer is paving the way for that to happen.

One of the surest ways to nip your ghostwriting career in the bud is to break the code of confidentiality that you have with the author of the book. Degrees of "invisibility" differ by project, but if the author doesn't want anyone to know you are writing the book, zip your lips. Other than perhaps your spouse, there is no one, and I mean no one, that you should tell. You can say you're writing a book, and you can divulge the general topic, but that has to be the end of the conversation. To this day, my best friends have no idea who I've ghostwritten books for—except in the cases where the authors have publicly acknowledged me for my participation.

Finally, one of the most beneficial interpersonal skills that a writer or anyone else can possess is a sense of humor. Things are bound to go wrong somewhere along the way, and being able to laugh together with your client will ease tension and stress and make the project a whole lot more fun. It's also valuable to learn to laugh at yourself. My father always said, "If you can look at yourself in the mirror at the end of the day and laugh, you'll make it in life." Oftentimes, when I write a book I create a blooper file, just for my own entertainment. This file contains all of the funny, startling, and obscene typos that I find when I proofread my work.

Keep in mind that there are scores of great writers in the world. Why would an author choose to work with someone who's cranky, arrogant, or self-absorbed if it's possible to work with someone equally talented who is also pleasant, down to earth, and fun?

6. KNOW WHEN TO RUN!

Some day, in the not too distant future, you will have a chance to write a book that you know in your gut is not a good match. This might be because it's a topic that bores your pants off, the point of view is in direct opposition to your own beliefs, or the material is leagues away from your scope of knowledge, experience, or ability for comprehension. In spite of all this, you may be tempted to leap into this "opportunity." Maybe your rent is due, the phone company is threatening to disconnect you, or maybe you just can't wait any longer to write your first book. Before you rationalize this decision or override your instincts, take a step back and think about it for at least two days before you commit. For instance, I should have failed algebra class, but my professor gifted me with the lowest passing grade. Even so, when I was offered a chance to ghostwrite *Understanding the Intrigue of Calculus*, I was tempted to do it. Fortunately, two bounced check notices (caused by my math errors) snapped me back to reality, and I graciously declined the offer.

Aside from making a good match with a topic, it is imperative that you feel good about the book's author. It usually takes about nine months to write a book and doing it with someone else can be compared to having a baby together—minus the sex. If you like each other, it can be a wonderful journey filled with creative energy. If you don't like each other, it can be a recurring nightmare that doesn't go away when you wake up.

Years ago, I took on the daunting task of "saving a book." The complete manuscript was due in three months and the author's writing team had mysteriously jumped ship. When I spoke with author for the first time, she was both friendly and enthusiastic, but she also seemed a little desperate. I ignored my instincts, and two days later I was sitting in her apartment discussing the book. Several things happened that day, and each one of them should have set off warning flares in my mind. To begin with, the author's materials were in complete disarray. (No problem, I told myself. I'm a great organizer.) Second, in between telling me how important it is to speak to our mates with respect, she was berating her husband for his lack of photocopying abilities and sundry other things that he couldn't do right to save his life. (She's just stressed out, I justified.) And third, as I leafed through the disheveled stacks of unnumbered pages, I came across a few very cryptic and angry-sounding notes from the writing team that had bailed out. (I reassured myself that even if others had failed, I would not.)

These rationalizations would soon come back to bite me. And not just once. As it turned out, nine writers had attempted to complete this manuscript before I was contacted. Four writers quit, one writer had a nervous breakdown, three of them disappeared into thin air, and another had his phone disconnected. Ironically, the week the book was released, I had the pleasure of meeting one of the writers who had wisely run for her life. We traded our "Crazy-Author Horror Stories" over steaming plates of fried rice and laughed until tears streamed down our cheeks. At that point it was funny, but not a moment before! If you connect with an author who enters the scene waving red flags, run for your life!

7. CLOSE THE DEAL

Verbal agreements are not enough. If you're working with a publishing house, the author or the author's agent will usually have a contract for you to sign. Make sure you understand this agreement before you sign it. Don't be afraid to ask questions. These contracts are written in "legalese" and can be daunting the first time you encounter one. If you're working with an author who plans to self-publish, create a "letter of agreement" that specifies exactly what services you are providing, the fees involved, the date of delivery, and any other considerations that should be put into writing. This document should be signed by both you and the author; it will help to prevent assumptions or other misunderstandings concerning your business agreement.

8. CAPTURE THE AUTHOR'S VOICE

Whether you're working as a ghostwriter or a collaborator, one of your jobs is to capture the voice of the author. Simply put, you want to write in a way that makes it sound like the author is talking. It shouldn't sound like another author whose style you admire, and it most certainly should not sound like you!

Practice reading a few paragraphs from a favorite book, and then write a few of your own, mimicking the author's voice. Do this with a wide variety of authors, and over time, you will develop an "ear" for others' voices.

One of the best ways to write in the author's voice is to conduct taped interviews with the author and have them transcribed onto computer disk. You can cut and paste the pertinent information into each chapter, in the author's own words, and then smooth it out and expand it as needed.

9. CREATE AND KEEP DEADLINES

There are nearly as many methods of meeting deadlines as there are writers. I tend to take a very methodical approach, dividing up the work into equal parts, circling my "days off," and carefully penciling each chapter deadline on my desk calendar. (I can't help it, I was born this way.) Other writers would go mad with this approach. One of the best writers I know creates 10 percent of the book the week she signs the contract and the other 90 percent the month before the manuscript is due. I couldn't even conceive of this approach and would never have believed it could be done if I hadn't witnessed it personally. The secret is to find out what works best for you. But don't kid yourself. Very few writers can write a great book in less than six months. At least until you settle into your own rhythm, pace yourself. Set reasonable deadlines and find a way to stay accountable to those dates.

Staying accountable to my own deadline schedule was initially much harder than I thought it would be. (There are so many tempting diversions in life!) Frequently, when I was supposed to be writing, I was toying with an art project, combing the forest floor in search of gourmet mushrooms, or just staring out the window. My sense of urgency wasn't ignited until my cash flow began to dwindle. That was when I discovered my motivation. Food, shelter, electricity. It may sound like common sense, but for me it was an "aha" moment. I do have some built-in motivation, but it's keeping my cash flow going that moves me from the sunroom to my office each day.

Linking your productivity with your payments works very well. Ask for one-third of your fee up front. This assures you that the author is serious and provides income so you can focus on the book. Schedule your second payment of one-third to coincide with turning in 50 percent of the manuscript. The final one-third is slated for the date you deliver the final manuscript to the author. If you feel you need more deadlines, divide your fee into four or more payments, each contingent on completing a certain amount of work.

10. ASK FOR REFERRALS

I don't have a business card that says "writer." I don't advertise my writing or editing services, and networking requires an hour's drive from the sanctuary of my forest home into the nearest city—which translates into: I rarely do it. By all sensible accounts, I shouldn't be making it as a ghostwriter. And yet I am, and have been for more than a decade. The secret to my success is word of mouth marketing. My clients are happy with my work and me, so they hire me again. They also tell their friends and associates about me, and the wheel continues to spin, seemingly of its own volition.

I know there are many more approaches to marketing, but I've learned that personal referrals usually provide clients whom I want to work with. It's possible for a satisfied client to refer you to an author whom you'd rather eat glass than work with, but most of the time, personal referrals increase your chances of connecting with authors and projects that are interesting and appealing.

When you've completed your work and satisfied your client, ask for referrals. If you've delivered the goods, they'll be happy to brag about you to their friends and associates who "just can't seem to find the right writer."

MAINTAIN YOUR BRIDGES

After the manuscript is complete, the author will be busy with promotional plans and getting back to regular business. You will be focusing on your next project. It's easy to get caught up in the day-to-day happenings and neglect to maintain the bridges that you've already built.

Make it a point to connect with satisfied clients from time to time. Hearing from you will help them think of you for future projects and will increase the likelihood that they'll remember to refer you to someone else. Every couple of months, send a card, a funny e-mail, or an upbeat fax. I phone previous clients only on occasion, and when I do, I call them at their office and keep it short. You want to be the person they look forward to hearing from, not the one who won't go away!

FICTION DICTIONARY

JAMIE M. FORBES

In book publishing, people describe works of fiction as they relate to categories, genres, and other market concepts, which, coming from the mouths of renowned industry figures, can make it sound as if there's a real system to what is actually a set of arbitrary terminology. Categories are customarily viewed as reflecting broad sectors of readership interest. Genres are either subcategories (classifications within categories) or types of stories that can pop up within more than one category—though genre and category are sometimes used interchangeably.

For instance, suspense fiction (as a broad category) includes the jeopardy story genre (typified by a particular premise that can just as easily turn up in a supernatural horror story). Or, again within the suspense fiction category, there's the police procedural (a subcategory of detective fiction, which is itself a subcategory of suspense that is often spoken of as a separate category). The police procedural can be discussed as a distinct genre with its own special attributes; and there are particular procedural genre types, such as those set in the small towns of the American plains or in a gritty urban environment. As a genre-story type, tales of small-town American life also surface in the context of categories as disparate as literary fiction, horror stories, Westerns, and contemporary and historical romance.

As we can see, all of this yakety-yak is an attempt to impose a sense of order onto what is certainly a muddy creative playing field.

The following listing of commonly used fiction descriptives gives an indication of the varieties of writing found within each category. This is not meant to be a strict taxonomy. Nor is it exhaustive. The definitions associated with each category or genre are fluid and personalized in usage and can seem to vary with each author interview or critical treatise, with each spate of advertising copy or press release, or they can shift during the course of a single editorial conference. One writer's "mystery" may be a particular editor's "suspense," which is then marketed to the public as a "thriller."

Then, too, individual authors do come up with grand, original ideas that demand publication and thereby create new categories or decline to submit to any such designation. But that's another story—maybe yours.

ACTION-ADVENTURE

The action-oriented adventure novel is best typified in terms of premise and scenario trajectory. These stories often involve the orchestration of a journey that is essentially exploratory, revelatory, and (para)military. There is a quest element—a search for a treasure in whatever guise—in addition to a sense of pursuit that crosses over into thrillerdom. From one perspective, the action-adventure tale, in story concept if not explicit content, traces its descent from epic-heroic tradition.

In modern action-adventure we are in the territory of freebooters, commandos, and mercenaries—as well as suburbanites whose yen for experience of the good life, and whose very unawareness in the outback, takes them down dangerous trails. Some stories are stocked with an array of international terrorists, arms-smugglers, drug-dealers, and techno-pirates. Favorite settings include jungles, deserts, swamps, and mountains—any sort of badlands (don't rule out an urban environment) that can echo the perils that resound through the story's human dimension.

There can be two or more cadres with competing aims going for the supreme prize—and be sure to watch out for lots of betrayal and conflict among friends, as well as the hitherto unsuspected schemer among the amiably bonded crew.

Action-adventures were once thought of as exclusively men's stories. No more. Writers invented new ways to do it, and the field is now open.

COMMERCIAL FICTION

Commercial fiction is defined by sales figures—either projected (prior to publication, even before acquisition) or backhandedly through actual performance. Commercial properties are frontlist titles, featured prominently in a publisher's catalog and given good doses of publicity and promotion.

An agent or editor says a manuscript is commercial, and the question in response is apt to be: How so? Many books in different genres achieve bestseller potential after an author has established a broad-based readership and is provided marketing support from all resources the publisher commands.

Commercial fiction is not strictly defined by content or style; it is perhaps comparative, rather than absolute. Commercial fiction is often glitzier, more stylishly of the mode in premise and setting; its characters strike the readers as more assuredly glamorous (regardless of how highbrow or lowlife).

A commercial work offers the publisher a special marketing angle, which changes from book to book or season to season—this year's kinky kick is next year's ho-hum. For a new writer in particular, to think commercially is to think ahead of the pack and not jump on the tail-end of a bandwagon that's already passed. If your premise has already played as a television miniseries, you're way too late.

Commercial works sometimes show elements of different categories, such as detective fiction or thrillers, and may cut across or combine genres to reach out toward a vast readership. Cross-genre books may thus have enticing hooks for the reading public at large; at the same time, when they defy category conventions they may not satisfy genre aficionados. If commercial fiction is appointed by vote of sales, most popular mysteries are commercial works, as are sophisticated bestselling sex-and-shopping oh-so-shocking wish-it-were-me escapades.

CRIME FICTION

Related to detective fiction and suspense novels, in subject matter and ambiance, are stories centered on criminal enterprise. Crime fiction includes lighthearted capers that are vehicles in story form for the portrayal of amusingly devious aspirations at the core of the human norm. Crime stories can also be dark, black, noir, showing the primeval essence of tooth-and-nail that brews in more than a few souls.

Some of the players in crime stories may well be cops of one sort or another (and they are often as corrupt as the other characters), but detection per se is not necessarily the story's strong suit. It is just as likely that in the hands of one of the genre's masters, the reader's lot will be cast (emotionally, at least) in support of the outlaw characters' designs.

DETECTIVE FICTION

Varieties of detective fiction include police procedurals (with the focus on formal investigatory teamwork); hard-boiled, poached, or soft-boiled (not quite so tough as hard-boiled); and the cozy (a.k.a. tea-cozy mysteries, manners mysteries, manor house mysteries).

Detectives are typically private or public pros; related professionals whose public image, at least, involves digging under the surface (reporters, journalists, computer hackers, art experts, psychotherapists, and university academics, including archaeologists); or they may be rank amateurs who are interested or threatened via an initial plot turn that provides them with an opportunity (or the necessity) to assume an investigatory role.

The key here is that the detective story involves an ongoing process of discovery that forms the plot. Active pursuit of interlocking clues and other leads is essential—though sometimes an initial happenstance disclosure will do in order to kick off an otherwise tightly woven story.

The manifold denominations of modern detective fiction (also called mysteries, or stories or novels of detection) are widely considered to stem from the detective tales composed by the nineteenth-century American writer Edgar Allan Poe. Though mysterious tracks of atmosphere and imagery can be traced in the writings of French symbolists (Charles Baudelaire was a big fan of Poe), the first flowering of the form was in Britain, including such luminaries as Arthur Conan Doyle, Agatha Christie, and Dorothy L. Sayers. Indeed, in one common usage, a traditional mystery (or cozy) is a story in the mode initially established by British authors.

The other major tradition is the American-grown hard-boiled detective story, with roots in the tabloid culture of America's industrial growth and the associated institutions of yellow journalism, inspirational profiles of the gangster-tycoon lifestyle, and social-action exposés.

The field continues to expand with infusions of such elements as existentialist character conceits, the lucidity and lushness of magic-realists, and the ever-shifting sociopolitical insights that accrue from the growing global cultural exchange.

Occasionally, detective fiction involves circumstances in which, strictly speaking, no crime has been committed. The plot revolves around parsing out events or situations that may be construed as strange, immoral, or unethical (and are certainly mysterious), but which are by no means considered illegal in all jurisdictions.

FANTASY FICTION

The category of fantasy fiction covers many of the story elements encountered in fables, folktales, and legends; the best of these works obtain the sweep of the epic and are touched by the power of myth. Some successful fantasy series are set within recognizable museum-quality frames, such as those of ancient Egypt or the Celtic world. Another strain of fantasy fiction takes place in almost-but-not-quite archaeologically verifiable regions of the past or future, with barbarians, nomads, and jewel-like cities scattered across stretches of continent-sized domains of the author's imagination.

Fair game in this realm are romance, magic, and talking animals. Stories are for the most part adventurous, filled with passion, honor, vengeance—and action. A self-explanatory subgenre of fantasy fiction is termed sword-and-sorcery.

HORROR

Horror has been described as the simultaneous sense of fascination and terror, a basic attribute that can cover significant literary scope. Some successful horror writers are admired more for their portrayal of atmosphere than for attention to plot or character development. Other writers do well with the carefully paced zinger—that is, the threat-and-delivery of gore; in the hands of skilled practitioners, sometimes not much more is needed to produce truly terrifying effects.

The horror genre has undergone changes—there is, overall, less reliance on the religiously oriented supernatural, more utilization of medical and psychological concepts, more sociopolitical and cultural overtones, and a general recognition on the part of publishers that many horror aficionados seek more than slash-and-gore. Not that the readers aren't bloodthirsty—it is just that in order to satisfy the cravings of a discerning audience, a writer must create an augmented reading experience.

The horror itself can be supernatural in nature, psychological, paranormal, or techno (sometimes given a medical-biological slant that verges on sci-fi), or can embody personified occult/cultic entities. In addition to tales of vampires, were-creatures, demons, and ghosts, horror has featured such characters as the elemental slasher/stalker (conceived with or without mythic content), a variety of psychologically tormented souls, and just plain folks given over to splatterhouse pastimes. Whatever the source of the horror, the tale is inherently more gripping and more profound when the horrific beast, force, or human foe has a mission, is a character with its own meaningful designs and insights—when something besides single-minded bloodlust is at play.

At times, the horror premise is analogous to a story of detection (especially in the initial setup); often the horror plot assumes the outlines of the thriller (particularly where there is a complex chase near the end); and sometimes the horror-story scenario ascribes to action-adventure elements. However, rather than delineating a detailed process of discovery (as in a typical mystery) or a protracted hunt throughout (as in the thriller), the horror plot typically sets up a final fight to the finish (until the sequel) that, for all its pyrotechnics and chills, turns on something other than brute force.

LITERARY FICTION

The term literary describes works that feature the writer's art expressed at its most refined levels; literary fiction describes works of literature in such forms as the novel, novella, novelette, short story, and short-shorts (also known as flash fiction). In addition to these fictional formats, literary works include poetry, essays, letters, dramatic works, and superior writing in all nonfiction varieties, covering such areas as travel, food, history, current affairs, and all sorts of narrative nonfiction, as well as reference works.

Literary fiction can adhere to the confines of any and all genres and categories, or suit no such designation. A work of fiction that is depicted as literary can (and should) offer the reader a multidimensional experience. *Literary* can designate word selection and imagery that is careful or inspired or that affects an articulated slovenliness. A literary character may be one who is examined in depth or is sparsely sketched to trenchant effect. Literature can postulate philosophical or cultural insights and portray fresh ideas in action. Literary works can feature exquisitely detailed texture or complete lack of sensory ambiance.

Structurally, literary fiction favors story and plot elements that are individualistic or astonishingly new, rather than tried-and-true. In some cases the plot as such does not appear important, but beware of quick judgment in this regard: Plotting may be subtle, as in picking at underlying psychology or revelation of character. And the plot movement may take place in the reader's head, as the progressive emotional or intellectual response to the story, rather than demonstrated in external events portrayed on paper.

To say that a work is literary can imply seriousness. Nonetheless, many serious works are not particularly sober, and literary reading should be a dynamic experience—pleasurably challenging, insightful, riveting, fun. A work that is stodgy and boring may not be literary at all, for it has not achieved the all-important aim of being fine reading.

Obviously, a book that is lacking with respect to engaging characters, consciousness of pace, and story development, but that features fancy wordplay and three-page sentences, is hardly exemplary of literary mastery. Though such a work may serve as a guidepost of advanced writing techniques for a specialized professional audience, it is perhaps a more limited artifice than is a slice-and-dice strip-and-whip piece that successfully depicts human passion and offers a well-honed story.

Commercial literature, like commercial fiction in general, is essentially a back-definition; commercial literature indicates works of outstanding quality written by authors who sell well, as opposed to just plain literature, which includes writers and works whose readership appeal has not yet expanded beyond a small core. Noncommercial literary works are staples of the academic press and specialized houses, as well as of selected imprints of major trade publishers.

When a literary author attracts a large readership or manages to switch from the list of a tiny publisher to a mammoth house, the publisher might decide a particular project is ripe for a shot at the big-time and slate the writer for substantial attention, accompanied by a grand advance. If you look closely, you'll note that literary authors who enter the commercial ranks are usually not just good writers: Commercial literary works tap into the cultural pulse, which surges through the editorial avenues into marketing, promotion, and sales support.

In day-to-day commercial publishing discourse, to call a piece of work literary simply means it is well written. As a category designation, literary fiction implies that a particular book does not truly abide by provisos of other market sectors—though if the work under discussion does flash some category hooks, it might be referred to in such catch-terms as a literary thriller or literary suspense.

MAINSTREAM FICTION

A mainstream work is one that can be expected to be at least reasonably popular to a fairly wide readership. In a whim of industry parlance, to various people in publishing the label *mainstream* signifies a work that is not particularly noteworthy on any count—it's a work of fiction that's not literary, according to circumscribed tastes, and not something easily categorized with a targeted, predictable base of readership. Maybe not particularly profitable, either, especially if the publishing house is bent on creating bestsellers. A mainstream work may therefore be seen as a risky proposition, rather than a relatively safe bet.

Let this be a cautionary note: In some publishing minds, a plain-and-simple mainstream book signifies midlist, which equals no sale. In a lot of publishing houses, midlist fiction, even if it's published, gets lost; many commercial trade houses won't publish titles they see as midlist (see Midlist Fiction).

A mainstream work may be a good read—but if that's all you can say about it, that's a mark against its prospects in the competitive arena. When a story is just a good story, the publisher doesn't have much of a sales slant to work with; in publishing terms that makes for a dismal enough prognosis for an editor or agent to pass.

If a manuscript has to sell on storytelling merits or general interest alone, it most likely won't sell to a major publisher at all. If mainstream fiction is what you've got, you, the writer, are advised to return to the workshop and turn the opus into a polished piece with a stunning attitude that can be regarded as commercial, or redesign the story line into a category format such as mystery, suspense, or thriller. A mainstream mystery or mainstream thriller may contain characters who aren't too wacko and milieus that aren't overly esoteric. Such works are eminently marketable, but you might suppress the mainstream designation in your query and just call your work by its category or genre moniker.

If you've got the gifts and perseverance to complete a solid story, and you find yourself about to say it's a mainstream book and no more, you'll be farther along faster if you work to avoid the midlist designation. Think commercially and write intrepidly.

Please note: Many editors and agents use the term *mainstream fiction* more or less synonymously with commercial fiction (see Commercial Fiction).

MIDLIST FICTION

Midlist books are essentially those that do not turn a more-than-marginal profit. That they show a profit at all might testify to how low the author's advance was (usually set so the publisher can show a profit based on projected sales). Midlist books may be category titles, literary works, or mainstream books that someone, somewhere believed had commercial potential (yet to be achieved).

The midlist is where no one wants to be: You get little if any promotion, few reviews, and no respect. Why publish this kind of book at all? Few publishers do. A midlist book was most likely not intended as such; the status is unacceptable unless the writer is being prepped for something bigger and is expected to break through soon. When a writer or series stays midlist too long, they're gone—the publishers move on to a more profitable use of their resources.

If the publishers don't want you, and the readers can't find you, you're better off going somewhere else, too. (See Commercial Fiction or any of the other category designations.)

MYSTERY

Many people use the term *mystery* to refer to the detective story (see Detective Fiction). When folks speak of traditional mysteries, they often mean a story in the British cozy mold, which can be characterized—but not strictly defined—by an amateur sleuth (often female) as protagonist, a solve-the-puzzle story line, minimal body count (with all violence performed offstage), and a restrained approach to language and tone. Sometimes, however, a reference to traditional mysteries implies not only cozies, but also includes stories of the American hard-boiled school, which are typified by a private eye (or a rogue cop), up-front violence as well as sex, and vernacular diction.

On the other hand, mysteries are seen by some to include all suspense fiction categories, thereby encompassing police procedurals, crime capers, thrillers, and even going so far afield as horror and some fantasy fiction.

In the interests of clarity, if not precision, here we'll say simply that a mystery is a story in which something of utmost importance to the tale is unknown or covert at the outset and must be uncovered, solved, or revealed along the way. (See Crime Fiction, Detective Fiction, Fantasy Fiction, Horror, Suspense Fiction, and Thriller.)

ROMANCE FICTION

The power of love has always been a central theme in literature, as it has in all arts, in all life. For all its importance to the love story genre, the term *romance* does not pertain strictly to the love element. The field can trace its roots through European medieval romances that depicted knights-errant and women in distress, which were as much tales of spiritual quest, politics, and action as love stories. The Romantic movement of the nineteenth century was at its heart emblematic of the heightened energy lent to all elements of a story, from human passion, to setting, to material objects, to psychological ramifications of simple acts.

Thanks to the writers and readers of modern romances, they've come a long way from the days of unadulterated heart-stopping bodice-rippers with pampered, egocentric heroines who long for salvation through a man. Today's romance most often depicts an independent, full-blooded female figure in full partnership with her intended mate.

Modern romance fiction is most assuredly in essence a love story, fueled by the dynamics of human relationships. From this core, writers explore motifs of career and family, topical social concerns, detective work, psychological suspense, espionage, and horror, as well as historical period pieces (including European medieval, Regency, and romances set in the American West) and futuristic tales. Romance scenarios with same-sex lovers are highlighted throughout the ranks of vanguard and literary houses, though this theme is not a priority market at most trade publishers or romance-specialist presses.

Among commercial lead titles tapped for bestseller potential are those books that accentuate the appeal of romance within the larger tapestry of a fully orchestrated work. (See also Women's Fiction.)

SCIENCE FICTION

Take humankind's age-old longings for knowledge and enlightenment and add a huge helping of emergent technology, with the twist that science represents a metaphysical quest—there you have the setup for science fiction. Though the basic science fiction plot may resemble that of action-adventure tales, thrillers, or horror stories, the attraction for the reader is likely to be the intellectual or philosophical questions posed, in tandem with the space-age glitter within which it's set. In terms of character interaction, the story line should be strong enough to stand alone when stripped of its technological trimmings.

In the future fiction genre, the elements of science fiction are all in place, but the science tends to be soft-pedaled, and the story as a whole is character-based. In a further variation, the post-apocalyptic vision presents the aftermath of a cataclysm (either engendered by technology or natural in origin) that sets the survivors loose on a new course that demonstrates the often-disturbing vicissitudes of social and scientific evolution. Such scenarios are generally set in the not-too-distant future, are usually earth-based, or are barely interstellar, with recognizable (but perhaps advanced) technology as the norm.

Purity of genre is at times fruitless to maintain or define. Is Mary Shelley's *Frankenstein* a science fiction tale or a horror story, or is it primarily a literary work? Is Jules Verne's *20,000 Leagues Under the Sea* science fiction or a technothriller—or a futuristic action-adventure?

Stories of extraterrestrial exploration, intergalactic warfare, and other exobiological encounters are almost certain to be placed within the science fiction category, until the day when such endeavors are considered elements of realism.

SUSPENSE FICTION

Suspense fiction embraces many literary idioms, with a wide range of genres and sub-divisions categorized under the general rubric of suspense. Indeed, in broad terms, all novels contain suspense—that is, if the writer means for the reader to keep reading and reading, and reading on . . . way into the evening and beyond.

Suspense fiction has no precise formula that specifies certain character types tied to a particular plot template. It is perhaps most applicable for a writer to think of suspense as a story concept that stems from a basic premise of situational uncertainty. That is: Something horrible is going to happen! Let's read! Within suspense there is considerable latitude regarding conventions of style, voice, and structure. From new suspense writers, editors look for originality and invention and new literary terrain, rather than a copycat version of last season's breakout work.

However, that said, writers should note that editors and readers are looking for works in which virtually every word, every scene, every blip of dialog serves to heighten suspense. This means that all imagery—from the weather to social setting, to the food ingested by the characters—is chosen by the writer to induce a sense of unease. Each scene (save maybe the last one) is constructed to raise questions or leave something unresolved. Every sentence or paragraph contains a possible pitfall. A given conversational exchange demonstrates edgy elementals of interpersonal tension. Everything looks rosy in one scene? Gotcha! It's a setup to reveal later what hell lurks underneath. Tell me some good news? Characters often do just that, as a prelude to showing just how wrong things can get.

The jeopardy story (or, as is often the case, a woman-in-jeopardy story) reflects a premise, rather than being a genre per se. A tale of jeopardy—a character under continuous, increasing threat and (often) eventual entrapment—can incorporate what is otherwise a psychological suspense novel, a medical thriller, an investigatory trajectory, or a slasher-stalker spree.

Additional subdivisions here include romantic suspense (in which a love relationship plays an essential or dominant role (see Romance Fiction), erotic suspense (which is not necessarily identical to neurotic suspense), and psychological suspense (see immediately following).

SUSPENSE/PSYCHOLOGICAL

When drifts of character, family history, or other psychodynamics are central to a suspense story's progress and resolution, the tale may aptly be typified as psychological. Sometimes superficial shticks or gimmicks suffice (such as when a person of a certain gender turns out to be cross-dressed—surprise!), but such spins work best when the suspense is tied to crucial issues the writer evokes in the characters' and readers' heads and then orchestrates skillfully throughout the story line.

There are, obviously, crossover elements at play here, and whether a particular work is presented as suspense, psychological suspense, or erotic suspense can be more of an advertising-copywriting decision than a determination on the part of editor or author.

THRILLER

The thriller category is exemplified more by plot structure than by attributes of character, content, or story milieu. A thriller embodies what is essentially an extended game of pursuit—a hunt, a chase, a flight worked fugue-like through endless variations.

At one point in the history of narrative art, thrillers were almost invariably spy stories, with international casts and locales, often set in a theater of war (hot or cold). With shifts in political agendas and technical achievement in the real world, the thriller formula has likewise evolved. Today's thriller may well involve espionage, which can be industrial or political, domestic or international. There are also thrillers that favor settings in the realms of medicine, the law, the natural environs, the human soul, and the laboratory; this trend has given rise to the respective genres of legal thriller, medical thriller, environmental thriller, thrillers with spiritual and mystical themes, and the technothriller—assuredly there are more to come.

The thriller story line can encompass elements of detection or romance and certainly should be full of suspense, but these genre-specific sequences are customarily expositional devices or may be one of many ambient factors employed to accentuate tension within the central thriller plot. When you see a dust jacket blurb that depicts a book as a mystery thriller, it likely connotes a work with a thriller plot trajectory that uses an investigatory or detective-work premise to prepare for the chase.

WESTERN FICTION

The tradition of Western fiction is characterized as much by its vision of the individualist ethic as it is by its conventional settings in the frontier milieu of the American West during the period from the 1860s to the 1890s, sometimes extending into the early 1900s. Though the image of the lone, free-spirited cowpoke with an internalized code of justice has been passed down along the pulp-paper trail, it has long been appreciated by historians that the life of the average itinerant ranch-hand of the day was anything but glamorous, anything but independent.

Whatever the historical record, editors by and large believe readers don't want to hear about the lackluster aspects of saddle tramps and dust-busting ruffians. Nevertheless, there have been inroads by books that display the historically accurate notions that a good chunk of the Western scene was inhabited by women and men of African American heritage, by those with Latino cultural affinities, by Asian expatriates, and by

European immigrants for whom English was a second language, as well as by a diversity of native peoples.

Apart from the traditional genre Western, authors are equipped for a resurgence in a variety of novels with Western settings, most notably in the fields of mystery, crime, action-adventure, suspense, and future fiction. Among the newer Western novels are those replete with offbeat, unheroic, and downright antiheroic protagonists; and the standardized big-sky landscape has been superseded by backdrops that go against the grain.

Family sagas have long included at least a generation or two who drift, fight, and homestead through the Western Frontier. In addition, a popular genre of historical romance is set in the American West (see Romance Fiction).

Many contemporary commercial novels are set in the Western United States, often featuring plush resorts, urban and suburban terrain, as well as the remaining wide country. The wide variety of project ideas generated by writers, as well as the reader response to several successful ongoing mystery series with Western elements, indicates a lively interest out there.

WOMEN'S FICTION

When book publishers speak of women's fiction, they're not referring to a particular genre or story concept (even if they think they are). This category—if it is one—is basically a nod to the prevalence of fiction readers who are women. Women's fiction is a marketing concept. As an informal designation, women's fiction as a matter of course can be expected to feature strong female characters and, frequently, stories offered from a woman's perspective.

As for the writers of books in this category—many (if not most) are women, but certainly not all of them are; the same observation applies to readers. Men can and do read these works, too—and many professional male writers calculate potential readership demographics (including gender) as they work out details of story and plot.

In essence, what we've got is storytelling that can appeal to a broad range of readers, but may be promoted principally to the women's market. It makes it easier to focus the promotion and to pass along tips to the publisher's sales representatives.

Many women writers consider their work in abstract compositional terms, regardless of whom it is marketed to. Other women writers may be publicized as cultural pundits, perhaps as feminists, though they don't necessarily see their message as solely women-oriented. Are they women writers or simply writers? So long as sales go well, they may not even care.

Some women writers adopt the genderless pose of the literary renegade as they claw their way through dangerous domains of unseemly characterization, engage in breakthrough storytelling techniques, and explore emergent modes of love. (After all, how can a force of nature be characterized by sex?) Any and all of these female word-smiths may find themselves publicized as women authors.

Romantic fiction constitutes one large sector of the women's market, for many of the conventions of romance tap into culturally significant areas of the love relationship of proven interest to women bookbuyers.

Descriptive genre phrases pop in and out of usage; some of them trip glibly from the tongue and are gone forevermore, while others represent established literary norms that endure: kitchen fiction, mom novels, family sagas, domestic dramas, historical romances, chick lit, lipstick fiction, erotic thrillers. When these popular titles are written, promoted, or both, in ways intended to pique the interest of women readers, whatever else they may be, they're automatically women's fiction.

THE AUTHOR-AGENT AGREEMENT

JEFF HERMAN

The author-agent relationship is a business relationship. Substantial sums and complex deals may be involved. It's to everyone's advantage to explicitly codify the rules and parameters of the relationship in a brief, plain-English agreement. It's true that the author-agent relationship can become unusually cozy. Still, there's no reason why even the best of friends can't have written business agreements without diminishing their mutual trust and affection. From at least one perspective, explicitly written agreements can be seen to go hand in hand with—and serve to underscore or amplify—existing bonds of confidence, faith, and friendship.

Some agents prefer oral understandings and handshakes, but most use a standard written agreement. It's unlikely that any two agencies will use the same agreement, but most agreements overlap each other closely in their intent and spirit.

Several aspects of the author-agent arrangement are covered by the typical agreement. Here are some of the major points of consideration, along with some key questions you might reflect on as you peruse the materials your prospective agent has submitted to you:

1. REPRESENTATION

What precisely will the agency be representing? Will it be a per-project representation? Or will it include all future works as well? Will it automatically cover all nonbook sales, such as magazine or newspaper articles? The extent of the representation should be spelled out so that there are no memory lapses or misunderstandings down the line.

2. AGENCY COMMISSION

The agency will receive a commission for all sales it makes against the work's advance and on any subsequent income derived from royalties and the licensing of various rights. According to a recent study by the Authors' Guild, most agencies charge new clients 15 percent for domestic sales. Many agencies charge 20-30 percent for foreign sales, since the commission often has to be split with local subagents (the agent in the foreign country who actually expedites the sale).

3. DURATION AND POTENTIAL TERMINATION OF THE AGREEMENT

When does the agreement end? How can the author or agency act to terminate the agreement? What happens after it's terminated?

Are agency agreements negotiable? Probably. It's a case-by-case situation. Don't be afraid to question, or attempt to reword, some aspects of the agreement. It will be better if such discussions are held in a friendly manner, directly between you and the agent. As a cautionary note: It is a common observation that the involvement of third parties—especially lawyers—can backfire and ignite issues that are irrelevant to the traditional ground rules of the author-agent understanding. It's fine to consult a lawyer, but you should be the point person.

The following is the standard agreement that I use with my clients. It's provided for your reference. It's not the only way an agreement can be or should be.

SAMPLE LETTER OF AGREEMENT

This Letter of Agreement between The Jeff Herman Agency, LLC, ("Agency") and _____ ("Author"), entered into on (date), puts into effect the following terms and conditions:

REPRESENTATION

* The Agency is hereby exclusively authorized to seek a publisher for the Author's work, hereby referred to as the "Project," on a per-project basis. The terms and conditions of this Agreement will pertain to all Projects the Author explicitly authorizes the Agency to represent, through oral and written expression, and that the Agency agrees to represent. Separate Agreements will not be necessary for each single project, unless the terms and conditions differ from this Agreement.

COMMISSION

* If the Agency sells the Project to a publisher, the Agency will be the Agent-of-Record for the Project's income-producing duration and will irrevocably keep 15 percent of all the Author's income relevant to sold Project. The due Agency commission will also pertain to all of the Project's subsidiary rights sales, whether sold by the Agent, Author, or Publisher. In the event the agency uses a subagent to sell foreign or film rights, and the subagent is due a commission, the Agency commission for such will be 10 percent, and the subagent's commission will not be more than 10 percent. All Project income will be paid by the publisher to the Agency. The Agency will pay the Author all due monies within a reasonable time, upon receipt and bank clearance, with full accounting

provided. The Agency will not be required to return any legitimately received commissions should the Author-Publisher contract be terminated or if the Author's work is unacceptable to the Publisher. There will be an Agency Clause in the Author-Publisher contract stating the Agency's status, the wording of which shall be subject to Author approval. These terms will be binding on the Author's estate in the event of his/her demise.

EXPENSES

+ The Agency will be entitled to receive reimbursement from the Author for the following specific expenses relevant to its representation of the Project: Manuscript/proposal copying costs; long-distance telephone calls and faxes between Author and Agency; necessary overnight deliveries and local messenger costs; postage and handling for manuscripts, foreign shipping and communications costs. An itemized accounting and records of all such items will be maintained by the Agency and will be shown to the Author. No significant expenses (in excess of $25.00) will be incurred without the Author's prior knowledge and consent. The Agency will have the option to either bill the Author for these expenses, regardless of whether or not the Project in question is sold to a publisher, or to charge such expenses against the Author's account.

PROJECT STATUS

+ The Agency agrees to forward to the Author copies of all correspondence received from publishers in reference to the Author's Project(s).

REVISIONS

+ This Agreement can be amended or expanded by attaching Rider(s) to it, if all parties to this Agreement concur with the terms and conditions of the Rider(s) and sign them.

TERMINATION

+ This Agreement can be terminated in writing by any party to it by writing to the other parties, at any time following its execution. However, the Agency shall remain entitled to due commissions that may result from Agency efforts implemented prior to the termination of this Agreement and will remain entitled to all other due monies as stated in this Agreement. Termination of the Agency representation of one or more Author Projects will not imply termination of this Agreement, unless such is specifically requested in writing.

Signatures below by the parties named in this Agreement will indicate that all parties concur with the terms and conditions of this Agreement.

_____   _____
The Jeff Herman Agency, Inc.   Author
                                            Social Security No.:
                                            Date of birth:
Specific project(s) being represented at this time:

Q & A

Q: If you, Mr. Herman, were the writer, what are some of the key points that would most concern you about an agent's agreement?
If I were a writer, I would prefer to see the following incorporated into my agreement with the literary agency:

1. I would want the representation to be on a per-project basis. I would not want to be automatically obligated to be represented by the agent on my next project.

2. I would want a liberal termination procedure. If at any point after signing the agreement I change my mind, I want the ability to immediately end the relationship.

Of course, I realize that the agent will be entitled to his commission relevant to any deals I accept that result from his efforts on the project's behalf—even if the deal is consummated after my termination of the agent.

THE COLLABORATION AGREEMENT

JEFF HERMAN

A ny book that is written by two or more writers is a collaborative effort. Such collaborative endeavors are predominately nonfiction works, though collaborative fiction is by no means unheard of (typically, a novel featuring a celebrity author that is for the most part written by someone else, or two bestselling novelists looking to synergize their reader base). There are several reasons why a writer might choose to collaborate with another, as opposed to writing the book alone.

The most common reasons are:

- A person may have the essential expertise, professional status, and promotability to author a book, but may lack time, ability, interest, or any combination of these, to do the actual writing. Therefore, retaining someone to do the writing is a sensible—even preferable—alternative.

- Some nonfiction projects, especially academic or professionally oriented ones, cover a broad range of material, and few individuals may have the requisite depth to write the book unilaterally. Therefore, two or more writers with complementary specializations may team up. For exceptionally technical books, such as medical texts, there can be several collaborators.

Many writers earn handsome incomes writing other people's books. When they are collaborative writers, their names are flashed along with the primary author of the project (and given second billing, usually preceded by "and," "with," or "as told to"). If they are true ghostwriters, they may well have the same level of input and involvement as collaborators, but will generally receive no public recognition for their work (other than perhaps a subtle pat on the back in the acknowledgments section).

WHAT ARE COLLABORATION AGREEMENTS?

As with any business relationship, it's wise for the collaborators to enter into a concise agreement (written in plain English) that spells out all the terms and conditions of the relationship—especially each party's respective responsibilities and financial benefits.

A collaboration agreement can run from 1 to more than 20 pages, depending on how much money is at issue and the complexity of the other variables. Most of the time we in the industry can keep these agreements down to an easy-to-read 2 pages. It's probably not necessary to go to the expense of retaining a lawyer for this task. If you have an agent, he can probably draw up an agreement for you or at least show you several samples.

The following is a sample collaboration agreement that is similar to ones used by many of my clients.

(Disclaimer: This sample collaboration agreement is intended only as a reference guide.)

SAMPLE COLLABORATION AGREEMENT

This collaboration agreement (Agreement), entered into on [date], by and between John Doe (John) and Jane Deer (Jane), will put into effect the following terms and conditions, upon signing by both parties.

(1) Jane will collaborate with John in the writing of a book about [subject or brief description goes here].

(2) In consultation with John, Jane will prepare a nonfiction book proposal and sample chapter for the purpose of selling the book to a publisher.

(3) Jane and John will be jointly represented by [name of literary agent/agency].

(4) John will be the book's spokesperson. John's name will appear first on the cover and in all publicity, and his name will be more prominently displayed than Jane's.

(5) Following the sale of the project proposal to a publisher, if, for any reason, Jane does not wish to continue as a collaborator, she shall be entitled to [monetary amount goes here] against the book's first proceeds in consideration of her having written the successful proposal, and she will forfeit any future claims against the book and any connection thereto.

(6) Jane's and John's respective estates will be subject to the terms and conditions of this Agreement, in the event of either's demise.

(7) John agrees to indemnify and hold Jane harmless from any liability, claim, or legal action taken against her as a result of her participation in the book proposal or book. Such exoneration includes but is not limited to costs of defending claims, including reasonable counsel fees. John agrees that any funds derived from sale of the proposal or book may be utilized to pay such claims.

(8) This Agreement can be amended or expanded by attaching riders to it, if such riders are signed by Jane and John.

(9) No other claims or representations are made by either party; both agree that this Agreement fully integrates their understanding. No other representations, promises, or agreements are made except as may be in writing and signed by the party to be held responsible.

(10) Jane shall receive the first [monetary amount goes here] of the book's proceeds when sold to a publisher. John shall receive the next [monetary amount goes here]. All

income thereafter shall be evenly received (50/50). All subsidiary rights income shall be split 50/50.

(11) John will own the book's copyright.

(12) John will be responsible for paying expenses relevant to the preparation of the proposal (photocopying; telephone; deliveries; travel, etc.). Upon the book's sale to a publisher and the receipt of the first part of the advance, John will be reimbursed for 50 percent of these expenses by Jane. John and Jane will equally split (50/50) costs relevant to writing the book following its sale to a publisher.

_____   _____

Jane Deer   John Doe

Q & A

Q: What about agent representation if it's a collaborative effort?
There are two possibilities:

1. The same agent will represent both parties. However, this requires the agent to be equal in her dealings with both parties. For instance, the agent should avoid tilting toward John while he's negotiating the collaboration agreement with Jane. What I do is provide both parties with accurate advice and then step aside as they—hopefully—work things out between themselves and then come back to me with all issues resolved.

   More important: the agent should not "double-dip." In other words, my commission will only pertain to the work's income. I will not touch any money that one collaborator may pay to the other, even if such payments exceed the work's advance.

2. Some collaborations can be coagented. Each collaborator may already have a different agent. Or it may be felt that there will be a conflict of interest for the same agent to represent both parties.

   When this happens, both agents will negotiate the collaboration agreement with each other in behalf of their respective clients. All parties will then work out a strategy to determine which agent is to be out front selling and negotiating the deal. Each agent will receive a commission only against her client's respective share.

As with any other business relationship, collaboration agreements generally have the best chance to produce a productive and successful outcome when they reasonably and realistically reflect the rights, responsibilities, special talents, and good interests of all involved parties.

MAKING IT HAPPEN

DEBORAH LEVINE HERMAN

Nothing is better than having your first book published. You may want to believe that spouses, friends, children, and world peace are more important, but when you see your name and your words in print it is nothing short of ego ecstasy.

Your publisher gives you a release date and you wait expectantly for the fanfare, but unless you're well known already (and remember, this is your first book), chances are your publisher will devote only modest publicity to your book.

It will be exciting if you are asked to do radio or television interviews, but do not expect Oprah fresh out of the gate. There are exceptions, of course, but it's important for you to know that most books don't receive extensive publisher support. It may not seem logical that a publisher would take you all the way to the mountain and not help you climb your way to the top, but it is the reality of the business. The reality is that the destiny of your book remains largely in your hands. With the right combination of drive, know-how, and chutzpah, you can make it happen for yourself.

IDEAS FOR MAKING IT HAPPEN

Here are some ideas for making it happen.

You can always hire a publicist. If you have the means, there are many publicists who can help you promote your book and who will do a lot of the work for you. You will have many great bragging opportunities when you work it into conversations that your publicist is setting your book tour.

Publicists are expensive and don't always deliver. You may want to check out our book *Make It Big Writing Books* to become publicist-savvy. This book contains interviews with top publicists, as well as some great promotion ideas. You can also read about how some bestselling authors made it to the top.

If you don't take the publicist route, you can do many things for yourself. Work with your publisher's publicity department. Its staff members may not invest their time and resources, but they should support your efforts.

As soon as you know the approximate date your book will be released to the bookstores, start your campaign. Ask your publicity department for review copies of your book and create a target list of possible magazines, newsletters, Web sites, and newspapers that might want to review your book. Don't sit on this. Magazines work months in advance. If your book is coming out in April, you should be contacting magazines as early as you possibly can; six months in advance isn't too soon. March is way too late. If you can't get review copies, you should still find ways to query the magazines. You may be able to get copies of your book covers and provide sample chapters.

It will be helpful for you to create an attractive publicity packet. You will need a biography of yourself, a good photograph, a copy of the book cover or the material your publisher uses to sell your book to the bookstores, a news release about your book, and any other relevant information. Do not forget to put in contact information. Book endorsements are also great, if you have them.

This packet can be used for magazines and any other print media, as well as for television and radio. If you want to spare some expense, create a one-page information sheet that you can fax to prospects whom you also contact by phone. Lists of radio stations are available in the reference department of your public library. Radio interviews can be done by phone. The key is to create a hook that will entice radio producers to use you on their shows. Think in terms of a short explanatory sentence that captures the essence of your book in as few words as possible.

For book signings, contact the promotions person at the bookstores you target. If you plan to visit various cities on a self-designed book tour, contact bookstores and local media well in advance so they can publicize the event. Maximize your visit to each city with a coordinated plan that will help promote your signing.

If your book is fiction, you can arrange for events in which you read portions of your book for an audience. Venues are available beyond the bookstores, but you will need to be creative in determining what they are.

If your book is nonfiction, create a topic stemming from your book that can be the subject of a workshop or lecture. Many venues are available that could help you publicize the event. Don't worry if you don't make money through lectures. If you are part of a seminar company, the exposure it will give your book in the promotional materials alone will be valuable.

Be creative. Don't let your ego trick you into believing you are above the hard work it takes to make a book successful. Roll up your sleeves. If you are passionate about your book, you are the one who can best "make it happen."

TIME MANAGEMENT

DEBORAH LEVINE HERMAN

It is probably more difficult for writers who do not have a separate day job to manage time and to meet deadlines. If you are a full-time writer, you are not confined to a structured day and have to be self-disciplined and self-motivated.

If you are by nature a methodical writer who keeps an orderly home and an efficient calendar, is always prompt, and never misses appointments, I truly envy you. If you are like me, all of the above require great effort and are probably much more challenging than writing itself.

I love any kind of creative endeavor and am passionate about writing. I am also easily distracted. If I am not under deadline, I work at home and am just as likely to wallpaper my house as I am to write a book proposal, query letter, or fiction piece. As you know, there are many things writers can be doing between assignments to further their careers. You can write, research, plan, or promote existing projects. You can also promote yourself to gain a forum for your ideas and future projects. Unfortunately, I sometimes like to procrastinate to the point that I am not even aware of how much time I may be wasting.

I do not recommend the unofficial Deborah Herman method of kamikaze writing. As my career has developed, I have been learning to improve my time-management techniques. I am a work-in-progress, but I can share what works for me.

TIME MANAGEMENT TECHNIQUES

If writing is what you do, you need to treat it as a job. It is fine if you want to think about it all the time and define yourself by it. But it is important for you to delineate between the work of writing and your life. Otherwise, you will wind up looking at the basic activities of life management as something akin to playing hooky from what you really "should" be doing. There are even times when I view housework as a treat because I am stealing time from my work. For anyone who knows me, that is truly a pitiful concept.

You need to set up a schedule that allows you to leave your work behind. If you commit to a deadline, you must evaluate approximately how many work hours you will need to do the job. Some people write quickly and prolifically, and some write as if they are constipated. You have to be honest in determining how much time you will need for actual writing and how much time you will need to pace, twist your hair, or play solitaire on your PC until you are able to focus. You don't need to feel guilty if you have some writing rituals, but be sure to consider them part of your overall schedule.

It is best if you schedule your writing and writing-related activities at the same time every day. Writing is a very concentration-intensive activity so you may not be able to devote eight straight hours to it. If you can be productive for two hours, that may be enough time per day. If you need to do more, I suggest you work in two-hour blocks with a substantial break in between them.

You need to listen to your own writing rhythms. Sometimes I can work for 2 to 3 hours that seem like 1 hour, and other times 1 hour can seem like 10. As long as you set aside the same time each day, you will be consistently productive and will use your time well.

When you finish your writing or writing-related activities for the day or business week, forget about them. Have a life. Have fun. Get some exercise. Stretch. Take care of your home and laundry. Do the things everyone else does to create balance. Writing takes a lot out of you emotionally, physically, and mentally.

You do not want to use up your energy all at once, or you will become miserable and will no longer love to write. If you do not love to write, get out of the business. Writing is not glamorous. Sometimes it can be tedious and grueling. But if you can't imagine doing anything else with your life, make sure to be good to yourself so that you can be effective.

Do not wait for inspiration to strike before you write. If you have chosen writing as a profession, you need to be professional. You can't just wait for the right mood to strike before you get down to business. If you wake up feeling a little down, don't give into it. Kick yourself in the rear and get to your desk or computer.

Do not listen to your inner voice if it tells you your work stinks. Nothing will mess up your writing schedule more than your little inner demons. Go to work anyway, or you will never make any progress.

The unfortunate thing about writing is that we do not get the kind of instant feedback we would get at a standard job. If we do a good job, no one is there to tell us so, and we do not believe our friends and family anyway. If we do a bad job, we may not know it and will still not believe anyone who tells us so. We work in a vacuum. So plod along. You will get the feedback you need when you obtain contracts for your work or when you hand in the completed manuscripts to your publisher.

The irony about writing as a profession is that we need such strong egos and are probably among the least-secure members of the human population. So view yourself as a business producing a product. As long as it meets acceptable standards for the marketplace, do not worry if it is not perfect. Once you relax about the work, you will see how much more productive you can be.

You may even find you enjoy the process and produce higher-quality work. If you relax within the schedule you have created, you give yourself the chance to develop your craft and hone your skills and voice. Whether you are a ghostwriter, a novelist, or a specialist in nonfiction, you will develop a signature style. You can't do this if you are so uptight that you can't breathe.

So managing your time is really a state of mind. There are many books that will teach you specific techniques for organization, calendar usage, and time management to the minute. But for writers, the most important factor is how you feel about your writing, your career, and your life. If you seek balance and want to be productive, you will create a system that works for you. If you want to drive yourself crazy and wind up drinking yourself to an early grave so that you can be immortalized as an "arteest," let your time manage you.

I vote for balance. I love to be free-spirited and eccentric. It is my most comfortable persona. But when I am under deadline, I do not think the anxiety is worth it. I also do not think it is worth it if my house is ready to be condemned, my children are running away to Grandma's, and my husband is ready to commit justifiable homicide.

So take control of your time and see what a difference it will make.

THE STATE OF BOOK PUBLISHING

TODAY AND TOMORROW

JEFF HERMAN

For several years the big question for everyone in publishing has been: "How will the Internet affect the book business?"

I'm going to go out on a limb here and say that new technologies don't and won't matter, because it's all about delivery and production systems. It has nothing to do with the evolution of the creative process or the measure of America's appetite for reading books. Whether you're composing your verse with a chisel on a limestone tablet or orally dictating to a computer that will immediately generate your hard copy (or cyber copy), it's still all about creating.

Cassettes and LPs quickly disappeared when CDs appeared. But the producers, distributors, and artists remained the same. Napster did threaten to overthrow the status quo by enabling consumers to acquire products without having to pay, but that was obviously illegal and unsustainable.

One day consumers may routinely buy and read books without touching a piece of paper (*Star Trek*'s Captain Picard was deemed eccentric for his tendency to read books the "old fashioned" way). Yet what hasn't been clearly explained is why this, in and of itself, is revolutionary.

A revolution is when the existing power structure is abruptly overthrown and replaced by something much different. Do we see that happening? It's true that anyone with a computer can virtually self-publish his or her book in cyberspace. But then how do you get people to know about it and motivate them to buy it? Online self-publishing saves you the trouble and expense of printing and storing thousands of copies in your garage, all on spec, but one hundred thousand words written by WHO? is likely to be forever lost in cyberspace.

The only really important issue is working out a reasonable compensation structure for writers, as publishers shift their front- and backlists to electronic "books."

We need to pay closer attention to the fallout from the "globalization" of America's publishing infrastructure, which began more than 10 years ago and has managed to consolidate the largest piece of the publishing pie into a few hands, most of which are as American as a Volkswagen. Independently owned "boutique" houses will always emerge and thrive, but they can act only from the margins. The sky hasn't fallen, but the atmosphere is different.

In the past, most books were acquired not so much for their immediate success, but because it was hoped they would nourish the "backlist," which was the surest way for a publisher to bolster its existence into the future. But that isn't today's publishing model. The large houses and the bookstore chains want megaselling, supernova brands, not a smorgasbord of delicacies. You can almost see these words written across the proverbial transoms of editors' offices: "Only bestselling writers need apply."

This is not to suggest that the midlist book is dead; far from it. Publishers can't afford to kill the midlist. But they are disrespecting it by refusing to adequately support it. The race is on to consolidate resources and place bets on the Derek Jeters of publishing. That's what gets noticed and rewarded by the corporate overlords.

But here's a silly little secret: If large houses stopped betting the farm on flaky blockbusters and mostly concentrated on feeding their healthy backlists with smart midlist acquisitions, they would be much more profitable today and tomorrow, and many more writers could make decent money from writing. And there would be a lot more good books to sell, buy, and read.

Yet an even more systemic issue pre-exists today's regime: We are a nation of readers. Tens of millions of us avidly read *People* and many other mass-market publications each week. But only a tiny fraction of this dedicated readership routinely buys books. What a shame, especially for writers, since an expanding market would mean more book contracts.

Why? There are many reasons, but I believe the most important one is historical. Two hundred years ago only a few people could actually read, and the vast majority of the population was functionally illiterate. Furthermore, only a few people could actually afford to buy books. It follows that book publishing, at its very genesis, could and would only serve the nation's most affluent and educated layer, which formed a narrow slice of the whole.

Things are much different today, and most of us are decent and active readers. But publishing as an institution has never caught up with the fact that the "rest of us" now read and have a few bucks. In fact, the most profitable book sectors, like mass-market romance, are treated as proletarian baggage, even though they subsidize many of the million-dollar acquisition mistakes made by the "smart" people.

The day that book publishers can see the *National Enquirer* as a role model instead of a joke, editors will all be earning healthy six-figure incomes, bookstores will be as common as drugstores, and many more writers will actually be writing during the day.

THE PATH TO PUBLICATION IN THE NEW MILLENNIUM

MORRIS ROSENTHAL

Imagine sending a query letter offering an unfinished manuscript to eight publishers and receiving four positive responses within the week. Or, out of the blue, the managing editor of a major imprint contacting you to ask whether you need a publisher for your work? These scenarios may sound like an advertisement in a writer's magazine intended to separate you from your money, but they actually happened to me, thanks to the Internet.

WHY PUBLISH ON THE INTERNET?

The vast majority of writers today have exchanged their typewriters for personal computers, but their sole focus remains sending that double-spaced manuscript off to New York City with an SASE. That's a shame, because by simply skipping down an extra item in the File menu of your word processor, you can save that document as HTML, a form ready for instant publication on the Internet. "Why should I give my work away for free?" you argue. "What if someone steals it?"

Your primary challenge, as an unpublished writer, is getting people to read your work and respond to it. After all, you need to convince editors and agents that you really know your market, but how can you do that if your market has never heard of you? Whether you write plumbing books or poetry, an audience for your work exists on the Internet, and if you can fix people's leaky pipes or hearts, they will show their appreciation. The main pay-offs of Web publishing for the unknown writer are reader feedback and traffic (visitors to your site).

Testimonial e-mails from visitors to your site can carry real weight with an acquisitions editor. In fact, McGraw-Hill used excerpts from nine such letters as a marketing tool on the back cover of my first published book, *The Hand-Me-Down PC*. Feedback from Web surfers is valuable for another reason; this audience isn't tied to you by friendship or blood. Even criticism is useful because these people are your market, and compliments from Mom are rarely as uplifting as those from a complete stranger. Traffic on your site can be used to prove that you do have an audience and, even more important for smaller publishers, that you know how to promote yourself. By the way, a copyright is a copyright, so if someone does plagiarize your work, take it as a compliment and threaten to sue.

WHAT TO PUT ON YOUR SITE

Building a Web site is something that anyone can do. Before you rush out and buy the latest book on the subject, try setting up a free Web site using one of the online providers, like Geocities, which will lead you through the process step by step. This doesn't have to be your permanent site. In fact, there are many good reasons to host your site on a commercial server for anywhere from $10 to $50 per month, but the main point is to get started. Unlike paper publishing, Web publishing is flexible by its very nature. If you make a spelling mistake, want to change something you said, add a picture, or even close down the site, you can do it instantly any time of the day or night!

The critical components (2 Cs) for any Web site are content and contact—content is the work you want people to see and contact is the means through which they can react to it, normally e-mail. As I said, it only takes one click of the mouse to save your manuscript in Web format, but you might want to produce material specifically targeted for the Web. Many people who surf the Web are looking for answers, so if you write nonfiction, you could offer to answer readers' e-mailed questions about your subject of expertise. This can take some time, but you will definitely learn what your audience is interested in rather than what you think they are interested in. This "hands-on" experience really carries weight with editors.

For example, back in 1995 I signed up for a $14.95/month Internet account with a national service that was later acquired by AOL. Learning that it came with space for a Web site, I posted a short guide titled "Troubleshooting and Repairing Clone PCs," which I had previously written for some co-op students I had trained. My primary motivation in posting the computer material was to attract people to read the short fiction and poetry I had also posted on the site. People who didn't find an answer to their problems but who thought I might be able to help them began sending me questions. Recognizing that this was "content," I began adding a new question and answer to the Web site each night. This section of the site, titled "The Midnight Question," became the most popular draw during the years that I maintained it and had a large number of repeat visitors. That original short guide and the material from the "Midnight Question" became the core of my first published book.

Many journalists now depend on the Internet for material to fill out their articles, and the questions and answers I posted on my site brought me two generous helpings of free publicity. The first was a front-page story in *The Investor's Business Daily*, which described me as a "Digital Age Dear Abby" and the second was an interview and a link on the *Dateline MSNBC* site, which sent 10,000 visitors to my site in a single day. These cases may be extreme, but I continue to receive regular exposure in both online and traditional publications due to material I have posted online.

When it comes to fiction and poetry, you have little choice other than to publish whole works on the Web. In some documented cases, individuals began by Web publishing a novel, responded to reader demand by self-publishing their own books, and eventually landed real publishing contracts, but this kind of success is rare. Publishing fiction and poetry on the Internet is less likely to bring an unknown author the kind of instant exposure that can result from a well-planned information site, but the feedback, when it comes, is all the more welcome for that reason. The modest successes I've experienced with fiction on the Web, like having a short story picked up for a printed zine or adopted onto a genre site, have worked wonders for my bruised fiction ego.

Once I got an e-mail from a guy with a corporate return address, asking if I could send him my online novel, which was then posted in twenty-six individual HTML documents, as a Word file. I wrote back asking why he wanted the novel in Word format when he could already get it in any Web browser. He replied, "Nothing sinister, I'm reading it at the office and if it's in Word, I can act like I'm working."

GETTING PEOPLE TO COME TO YOUR SITE

"Even if you build it, they won't come unless you tell them it's there!"

Morris Rosenthal—March 21, 2000

From Fortune 500 ghost sites to Aunt Millie's home page with pictures of the cat, the Web is crowded with sites that nobody visits. As you have read in many sections of this book, publishing is a business, and in business you can't escape from marketing. The good news is that on the Web, the only type of marketing you need is free, as long as you provide the labor. This marketing of your site can be broken into three basic areas: search engines and directories, link trading (including Web rings), and discussion groups.

Search engines and directories, once very different beasts, have been integrated to the point where I'll treat them as one subject. Examples of these are: Yahoo, Altavista, Infoseek, Excite, Lycos, Webcrawler, Snap, Google, and so on. The pure search engine concept is one in which you type certain key words into a box and the search engine returns some or all of the sites containing those key words in one combination or another, depending on the search conditions you apply. A pure directory is a hierarchical catalog in which you choose a general subject, like "Arts and Humanities," and continually narrow down your search in layer after layer of categories until you reach "Bronze casting techniques in Ancient Greece." The key is for you to get listed in the major search engines and directories, and not to get taken in by an ad for a service that will list you in 1,000 search engines for $19.95. Most search traffic is directed by a handful of search engines and directories, primarily those listed herein. Make sure that you submit to any search engines and directories that you use, and just hope that your potential readers think the same way.

If you want to be published, you must undertake one exercise in market research: try to put yourself in the shoes of your target audience and search the Web for the sort of work you hope to publish. You'll quickly get a feel for the type of key words you should include on your pages, not to mention valuable insight into the "competition," which makes up an important part of any sales pitch to a traditional publisher. You may be astounded by the number of sites that already offer almost exactly what you planned to be first with, but don't be discouraged. In publishing, the bigger the existing market, the more likely a publisher will want to produce another title for it. Competing with other Web sites will help you hone your skills for the big battle, which is competing with other books.

Getting listed in search engines is easy. Simply go to the search engine site, look for a link that says "Submit your URL" or "Add your site," and click on it. This will bring you to a submissions page where you type in the address of your new Web page. Take note of any search engine you visit so that you can return in two weeks to see if it listed you, and resubmit if it didn't. Repeat as needed. Directories take a little more thought and persistence. You need to carefully choose which category you want to be listed in, and again, the best way to do this is to pretend you are a potential reader looking for whatever it is you write about. Directory entries are handled by human beings rather than by automated software, so only a small number of submissions are ever actually looked at. Sound familiar? Some directories even offer a guaranteed consideration of your site for a flat fee, around $100, but Yahoo is the only one I would even consider paying, and then only for a commercial site.

A link is essentially an address holder that shows up in most browsers as an underlined word or phrase. Link exchanges work on the old principle of "You scratch my back, I'll scratch yours." You find another site with content related to your own site, and you and the other webmaster negotiate an exchange of links via e-mail. When visitors to your site click on a link you have made to another site, they're gone. I'm not a big fan of link exchanges because they can easily get out of hand to the point where your site is no more than a revolving door.

If you provide good content and make sure you are listed in the big search engines, people who maintain "all links" sites, essentially small targeted directories, will eventually find and link you. WebRings, on the other hand, are a nice way to join an online community of people who share your writing interests. For an index of WebRings and how to join, visit www.webring.com.

Discussion groups and news groups are a highly targeted way to announce the existence of your site. There are tens of thousands of public news or user groups, not to mention those discussion groups hosted on individual sites. Odds are, somebody out there is interested in what you are doing. It was by way of a technology discussion group that I received an unsolicited offer from a major imprint to publish a book based on my online material, although I eventually turned them down in favor of McGraw-Hill. The editor was apparently in the habit of checking the group for new trends or potential material, and a message I had posted to the group about new online material brought her to my site.

THIS IS THE FUTURE

Maybe you secretly hate your computer, though you avoid thinking about it while you're working for fear it will read your mind and trash your documents. There will always be room for a small number of eccentrics whose quirks are part and parcel of their attraction, but it's a tough role to break in with.

The Internet is the future, and a Web strategy will be an integral part of any query letter in the coming years. The best way to learn about the Web and its potential is to get online and experiment with it. Even if you never post material to the Internet, you will need to understand how the publishing industry uses this tool.

Lest you think, "This is all great and fine for writing about technology, but what about my special field?" let me relate a final anecdote. For the past couple of years I've worked on translations of my great-grandmother's Hebrew books and wanted to get a short piece published about how she came to learn Hebrew in 1860s Latvia. This is definitely not "high tech" stuff. A Web search conducted with Altavista turned up a list of possible publications, and I sent queries to those that listed e-mail addresses for the editor.

Of the three or four responses, I submitted the article, via e-mail, to the most enthusiastic, where it was accepted for publication in the next issue. The edited copy was sent for my approval, via e-mail, and the only time paper or postage entered the process was when the publisher sent me five complimentary copies of the magazine.

Once you have a Web site of your own, you'll wonder how you lived without one. For example, you can access your own material from any Internet-connected computer in the world! No more missed opportunities because the dog ate the manuscript and the editor you met on vacation wants to see it yesterday.

I have written and submitted material for publication from a friend's computer on the other side of the Atlantic, and with e-mail, you'll never worry about missing a phone call. A popular Web site can actually pay! You can sell self-published books to people for less than the cost of the inkjet cartridge they would use up printing it or you can sell yourself as a consultant, speaker, writer, and so on.

Last but not least, you can sign up as an Amazon associate, referring your visitors to Amazon.com for books you suggest, have reviewed, or have written. Currently, Amazon is putting over $100 per month into my pocket, which more than pays the freight for a commercial Web site.

WEBSITES FOR AUTHORS

WEBSITES FOR AUTHORS

One of the most valuable aspects of the World Wide Web for writers is that it provides the opportunity to explore the world of publishing. The following annotated list of websites offers descriptions of some of the most useful sites for writers. For your convenience, sites are grouped according to the following categories:

RESOURCE CATEGORIES

- Anthologies
- Children's Literature
- E-Publishing
- Funding Sources
- Horror
- Mystery
- Poetry
- Romance
- Science Fiction
- Screenwriting
- Western

ANTHOLOGY RESOURCES

ANTHOLOGIES ONLINE

http://www.AnthologiesOnline.com

Writers will find more than great articles and frequent postings of calls for manuscripts. From *Chicken Soup* to horror, anthology publishers post their calls for writers. Subscribers have advance notice of calls for manuscripts and may apply for a free promotional page. The site has a comprehensive, up-to-date list of paying markets for writers of science fiction, fantasy, horror, and slipstream. One page lists all markets; other pages break out markets by pro, semi-pro, anthologies, and contests, as well as by print and electronic formats. Listings include summaries of guidelines and indications of markets' "aliveness," plus website URLs.

CHILDREN'S LITERATURE RESOURCES

CHILDREN'S BOOK COUNCIL, THE

http://www.cbcbooks.org/

"CBC Online is the website of the Children's Book Council—encouraging reading since 1945." It provides a listing of articles geared toward publishers, teachers, librarians, booksellers, parents, authors, and illustrators—all those who are interested in the children's book field.

CHILDREN'S WRITING RESOURCE CENTER

http://www.write4kids.com/

"Whether you're published, a beginner, or just someone who's always dreamt of writing for kids," here you'll find a free library of how-to information, opportunities to chat with other children's writers and illustrators, links to research databases, articles, tips for beginners, secrets for success as a children's writer, message boards, a children's writing survey, the chance to ask questions of known authors, and the opportunity to register in the website's guestbook to receive free e-mail updates filled with news. The site features a listing of favorite books, Newberry Medal winners, Caldecott Award winners, current bestsellers, and a link to its own children's bookshop.

THE SOCIETY OF CHILDREN'S BOOK WRITERS AND ILLUSTRATORS

http://www.scbwi.org/

This website "has a dual purpose: It exists as a service to our members, as well as offering information about the children's publishing industry and our organization to non-members." It features a listing of events, awards and grants, publications, information for members, information on how to become a member, and a site map.

VERLA KAY'S WEBSITE FOR CHILDREN'S WRITERS

http://www.verlakay.com

This site is packed with information to assist writers of children's stories. Whether you are a beginner or a multi-published writer, there is something here for you. A chat room with nightly chats with other children's writers, online workshops and transcripts of past workshops, a Getting Started page, and a Published Writers page are just some of the features of this award-winning website.

E-PUBLISHING RESOURCES

BOOKBOOTERS.COM

http://www.bookbooters.com

Bookbooters Press is a full-service digital publisher specializing in the electronic and print-on-demand publication of high-quality works of fiction and nonfiction. Through our website, www.bookbooters.com, customers may securely purchase titles by some of today's bestselling authors in e-book, CD-ROM, and paperback formats. The Authors Area includes a community area to meet other authors and to submit manuscripts for consideration by our team of professional acquisition editors.

EKIDNA EBOOKS

http://www.eKIDna.com.au

eKIDna eBooks is a small but growing publisher of e-books for children at home and at school. Based in Australia, eKIDna has strong ties with North American e-book publishers and is concentrating on its educational list for early English reading. Paying high royalties, it is a writer-friendly site limited mostly by its difficulty in finding illustrators who are willing to work for royalty-only; if you are an illustrator, too—or can take an illustrator with you—your chances of publication are immensely advanced.

XC PUBLISHING

http://www.xcpublishing.com

XC Publishing is a royalty-paying electronic publisher of high-quality original science fiction, fantasy, romance, and mystery electronic books. Authors can count on solid editorial support and a long shelf life for their titles. The site also offers book-related extras, as well as several book review e-mail newsletters. The site includes author's guidelines and a sample contract.

ZANDER EBOOKS

http://www.ZanderEbooks.com

Zander eBooks is a royalty-paying electronic publisher and e-book seller offering a high-quality selection of fiction, nonfiction, and children's e-books in the widest variety of formats available. Customers can choose from HTML, Adobe PDF, Microsoft Reader, Palm/Pocket PC, Franklin Reader, RocketBook, and paperback editions of our titles. A portion of the proceeds from each e-book sale is donated to reforestation programs, in an effort to educate the public about the ecological benefits of e-books.

FUNDING RESOURCES

ART DEADLINE, THE

http://custwww.xensei.com/adl/

The Art Deadline is a "monthly newsletter providing information about juried exhibitions and competitions, call for entries/proposals/papers, poetry and other writing contests, jobs, internships, scholarships, residencies, fellowships, casting calls, auditions, tryouts, grants, festivals, funding, financial aid, and other opportunities for artists, art educators, and art students of all ages. Some events take place on the Internet."

AT-A-GLANCE GUIDE TO GRANTS, THE

http://www.adjunctadvocate.com/nafggrant.html

The At-a-Glance Guide to Grants offers information about grants, including a glossary of terms in grant forms, sample contracts, links to grant-related sites, a database of funding opportunities, and related agencies, foundations, and organizations. The site also includes a tutorial section with information on how to write a proposal and how to win a grant.

BOOKZONE

http://www.bookzone.com

This site offers information on writing, marketing, business, and legal issues for publishing professionals. It features forums, publishing news, and online subscriptions to journals "at the guaranteed lowest prices on the Web. For design, development, e-commerce solutions, promotion, and exposure, BookZone is the busiest and best Web host for publishers, authors, and other publishing professionals."

FOUNDATION CENTER, THE

http://fdncenter.org/

The Foundation Center website is dedicated to assisting writers in finding grants. It offers "over 200 cooperating sites available in cities throughout the United States. Of particular note is its large online library, with a wonderful interactive orientation to grant seeking. You'll even find application forms for several funding sources here."

FUNDSFORWRITERS

http://www.fundsforwriters.com and

http://www.chopeclark.com/fundsforwriters.htm

FundsforWriters specializes in leading writers to grants, awards, contests, fellowships, markets, and jobs. The two websites and three newsletters provide a weekly abundance of sources for writers to reference and put checks in the bank. The other sites teach you how to write. FundsforWriters tells you where to make a living doing it.

NATIONAL WRITERS UNION

http://www.nwu.org/

The union for freelance writers working in U.S. markets offers grievance resolution, industry campaigns, contract advice, health and dental plans, member education, job banks, networking, social events, and much more.

WESTERN STATES ARTS FEDERATION

http://www.westaf.org/

The WSAF is a "nonprofit arts service organization dedicated to the creative advancement and preservation of the arts. Focused on serving the state arts agencies, arts organizations, and artists of the West, WSAF fulfills its mission by engaging in innovative approaches to the provision of programs and services and focuses its efforts on strengthening the financial, organizational, and policy infrastructure of the arts in the West."

HORROR RESOURCES

DARK ECHO HORROR

http://www.darkecho.com/darkecho/index.html

Dark Echo Horror features interviews, reviews, a writers' workshop, dark links, and a newsletter. Articles relate to topics such as the perception and psychology of the horror writer, the "best" horror, and reviews of dark erotica. The site also offers information and links to fantasy writing.

HORROR WRITERS ASSOCIATION

http://www.horror.org/

The Horror Writers Association (HWA) was formed to "bring writers and others with a professional interest in horror together, and to foster a greater appreciation of dark fiction in general." Bestower of the Bram Stoker Awards, HWA offers a newsletter, late-breaking market news, informational e-mail bulletins, writers' groups, agents, FAQ, and links.

MASTERS OF TERROR

http://www.mastersofterror.cjb.net/

Masters of Terror offers information about horror fiction, book reviews, new authors, horror movies, author message boards, HorrorNet chat room, and a reference guide and critique of horror fiction that features some 500 authors and 2,500 novels. The site also includes exclusive author interviews, book and chapbook reviews, and horror news.

MYSTERY RESOURCES

CLOCKTOWER FICTION

http://www.clocktowerfiction.com/

Clocktower Fiction aims to "provide free quality original fiction for avid readers." Clocktower Fiction publishes *Outside: Speculative and Dark Fiction*, which is a freelance, paying, online publication that is published three times a year. The site provides links to grammar, writing, and other writers' resources and covers a variety of genres, including mystery, science fiction, macabre, suspense thrillers, and noir fiction.

CLUELASS HOME PAGE

http://www.cluelass.com

The ClueLass Home Page offers awards for mystery fiction and nonfiction, information about conferences and conventions, and mystery groups for writers and fans. It includes information about markets, other contests, reference material, and online support, as well as listings of mystery magazines and newsletters, an international directory of mystery booksellers and publishers, and factual links about crime, forensics, and investigation.

MYSTERY ON-LINE

http://www.webinspect.com/mystery.htm

Mystery On-Line is a site that is a work-in-progress of a mystery novel on the Web. Amateur and published writers may submit chapters for the Mystery On-Line continuing story. Each month a new chapter is selected and published on the site from the submissions. The site also includes mystery writing links and book reviews.

MYSTERY WRITERS OF AMERICA

http://www.mysterywriters.org

Mystery Writers of America "helps to negotiate contracts, watches development in legislation and tax law, sponsors symposia and mystery conferences, and publishes books." The site includes mystery links, awards, a calendar of events, writers' discussions, and a new online mystery every day. It was established to promote and protect "the interests and welfare of mystery writers and to increase the esteem and the literary recognition given to the genre."

SHORT MYSTERY FICTION SOCIETY

http://www.thewindjammer.com/smfs/

The Short Mystery Fiction Society "seeks to actively recognize writers and readers who promote and support the creative art form of short mysteries in the press, in other mystery organizations, and through awards." The site offers a newsletter and other resources.

SISTERS IN CRIME

http://www.sinc-ic.org

Sisters in Crime is a website that vows to "combat discrimination against women in the mystery field, educate publishers and the general public as to inequities in the treatment of female authors, raise awareness of their contribution to the field, and promote the professional advancement of women who write mysteries." The site includes information about local chapters of Sisters in Crime and offers mystery links and online bookstores.

THE MYSTERIOUS HOME PAGE

http://www.webfic.com/mysthome/mysthome.htm

The Mysterious Home Page is "a guide to mysteries and crime fiction on the Internet." The site offers newsgroups, mailing lists, information on conferences and conventions, publishers, book dealers, interactive fiction, reviews, and electronic mysteries.

THE MYSTERY WRITERS' FORUM

http://www.zott.com/mysforum

The Mystery Writers' Forum consists of "mystery writers and aspiring mystery authors who are sharing our trials, tribulations, and research problems and triumphs on a supportive, threaded bulletin board system." The site includes a bookstore, Internet links, and cyber crime references.

POETRY RESOURCES

ACADEMY OF AMERICAN POETS

http://www.poets.org/index.cfm

The Academy of American Poets website offers news regarding contest opportunities and winners, an online poetry classroom, the first-ever poetry book club, events calendars, and a search feature to find a specific poet or poem. Users can also listen to an author read a poem in RealAudio. The "My Notebook" feature allows visitors to keep a file of favorite poems or readings from the site. There are also discussion groups and literary links sections.

ALIENFLOWER

http://www.xdrom.com/alienflower/

AlienFlower is a site that offers poetry essays and virtual art, a discussion forum, literary links, video poetry readings, and more.

ATLANTIC UNBOUND POETRY PAGES

http://www.theatlantic.com/atlantic/atlweb/poetry/poetpage.htm

The Atlantic Unbound Poetry Pages are brought to you from the *Atlantic Monthly*, a literary magazine. The website offers reviews of new poetry, a discussion forum, and the Audible Anthology, which is a collection of poetry sound files, poetry articles, links, and poetry from the *Atlantic Monthly* online zine. It is a searchable site and offers poetry and literature links.

ELECTRONIC POETRY CENTER

http://wings.buffalo.edu/epc/

There are perhaps more poetry websites online than any other literary genre, so picking one representative site is really quite pointless. But we do recommend the Electronic Poetry Center at the University of New York at Buffalo, which is the heart of the contemporary poetry community online, having been around since the early days of gopher space—practically the Dark Ages in computer time. Of particular note are the active and well-respected poetics mailing list, the large collection of audio files, and an extensive listing of small press poetry publishers.

NATIONAL POETRY ASSOCIATION

http://www.nationalpoetry.org/

The National Poetry Association website, supported in part by Grants for the Arts and Maya Angelou, offers an online poetry journal called Poetry USA and aims to "promote poets and poetry to wider audiences by all possible means, serving both the literary community and the general public." The site is dedicated to the memory of William Burroughs, Allen Ginsberg, Denise Levertov, and Jack Micheline. It includes information about the National Poetry Association's current projects and offers contests for poets.

PERIHELION ROUND TABLE DISCUSSIONS

http://www.webdelsol.com/Perihelion/p-discussion3.htm

The Perihelion Round Table Discussions is a site that brings to the public the thoughts of established poets and editors on issues of the Internet and its effect on poetry and the writing of poetry. There is also a discussion area where readers and visitors may add their insight to the discussions.

POETRY SOCIETY OF AMERICA

http://www.poetrysociety.org/

The Poetry Society of America website includes information about the newest developments in the Poetry in Motion project, which posts poetry to seven million subway and bus riders in New York City, Chicago, Baltimore, Portland, and Boston. It also includes news about poetry awards, seminars, the tributes in libraries program, the poetry in public program, and poetry festivals.

POETS & WRITERS

http://www.pw.org/

Poets & Writers is an online resource for creative writers that includes publishing advice, message forums, contests, a directory of writers, literary links, information on grants and awards, news from the writing world, trivia, and workshops.

THE INTERNATIONAL LIBRARY OF POETRY

http://www.poetry.com

The International Library of Poetry website offers information about its writing competitions, which focus on "awarding large prizes to poets who have never before won any type of writing competition." The site also includes Internet links, a list of past winners, anthologies of winning poems, and chat rooms.

THE WRITER'S LIFE

http://www.thewriterslife.net

The Writer's Life is an online interactive writing and resource site where published, as well as nonpublished, authors submit their articles/short stories/poetry for publication. It is the site's goal to help writers achieve their dreams and goals of becoming published. The site provides publishing links, author interviews, Literary Link-of-the-Week awards, great writing sites, e-publishing links, freelancing opportunities, conference and workshops information, author quotes, chat, newsletter, in-house writing group, and more.

ROMANCE RESOURCES

ROMANCE WRITERS OF AMERICA

http://www.rwanational.org

Romance Writers of America (RWA) is a national nonprofit genre writers' association—the largest of its kind in the world. It provides networking and support to individuals seriously pursuing a career in romance fiction.

USEFUL LINKS FOR ROMANCE WRITERS AND READERS

http://www.jaclynreding.com/links/

If you're interested in writing fiction, particularly in the romance genre, consider this website the launching pad for getting you where you need to go on the Internet. Hundreds of websites have been arranged in easy-to-navigate categories, covering all aspects of the craft of writing—from research to publishers to booksellers to bestseller lists—this place has it all. New sites are constantly being added and you can even submit your own favorite sites! Voted one of the 101 Best Websites for Writers by *Writer's Digest*.

SCIENCE FICTION RESOURCES

SCIENCE FICTION AND FANTASY WRITERS OF AMERICA

http://www.sfwa.org

The official website of the Science Fiction and Fantasy Writers of America offers information about the organization, its members and affiliated publications, an art gallery, and various awards.

SFNOVELIST

http://www.sfnovelist.com/index.htm

SFNovelist is "an online writing group dedicated to novelists who write 'hard science' SF." It is a highly structured and organized system for the exchange of science fiction manuscripts for consideration by other writers. Its goals are to: become in the marketplace a premier source of novelists who write "believable/hard science" SF; garner the attention of SF publishers, SFWA, and other writers' organizations for SF novelists; and develop a cadre of strong novelists, most of whom become published. Behind every great SF writer is usually a group of fellow writers who are equally serious about their writing, establish a presence at major SF writer conferences and conventions, and provide services and information to members that will help them in their search for self-improvement and in getting published. This includes contacts with other known writers and publishers and sources of distribution and marketing.

SCREENWRITING RESOURCES

HOLLYWOOD CREATIVE DIRECTORY, THE

www.hcdonline.com

The Hollywood Creative Directory's mission is to be the preferred and preeminent source of professional and educational information to, for, and about the entertainment industry, not only to the current entertainment industry professional community, but to aspiring professionals as well. HCD publishes the Producers Directory, "the phone book to Hollywood," a must-have directory for screenwriters. HCD offers screenwriter and film directories in an online subscription database. The website maintains one of the best entertainment job boards for the industry. HCD also publishes many how-to screenwriting books under the imprint of Lone Eagle Publishing, including the bestselling *Elements of Style for Screenwriters* and *How Not to Write a Screenplay.*

HOLLYWOOD SCRIPTWRITER

http://www.hollywoodscriptwriter.com

Hollywood Scriptwriters is an international newsletter that offers articles on craft and business "to give screenwriters the information they need to work at their careers." The site includes low-budget and indie markets available for finished screenplays, as well as a listing of agencies that are currently accepting submissions from readers of Hollywood Scriptwriter. According to Hollywood Scriptwriter, "people like Harold Ramis, Francis Ford Coppola, and Larry Gelbart have generously given of their time, knowledge, and experiences to share with HS's readers."

SCREENWRITER'S HOME PAGE, THE

http://home.earthlink.net/~scribbler/

The Screenwriter's Home Page offers "articles and interviews by people who work, day in and day out, in the movie business." Its aim is to help "not only with writing, but with the reality of the entertainment world." It includes agent listings, best ways to have your script rejected, professionals' thoughts on screenwriting, and industry news.

SCREENWRITER'S RESOURCE CENTER

http://www.screenwriting.com

The Screenwriters Resource Center aims to "provide links to products and services for screenwriters, compiled by the staff at the National Creative Registry." It includes links to many screenwriting sites and offers advice and copyright words of warning for writers posting original work on the Internet.

SCREENWRITER'S UTOPIA

http://www.screenwritersutopia.com/

Screenwriter's Utopia includes "helpful hints for getting screenplays produced, script development services, and contest information." The site includes a screenwriters' work station, tool kit, agent listings, and creative screenwriting magazines. Interviews with the screenwriters of *Sleepless in Seattle*, *Blade*, and *The Crow: City of Angels* are featured, and other interviews are archived. The site also includes chat rooms, message boards, a writer's directory, and a free newsletter.

SCREENWRITER'S WEB, THE

http://breakingin.net

The site offers screenwriters and filmmakers tips, tools, and resources to help them get their scripts read and recommended to the movies. Special features: interviews with film pros, screenplay tutorials, script marketing tips, and insider information from an experienced LA screenwriter.

SCREENWRITERS & PLAYWRIGHTS HOME PAGE

http://www.teleport.com/~cdeemer/scrwriter.html

The Screenwriters & Playwrights Home Page "is designed to meet the special needs of screenwriters and playwrights." Features of the site include screenwriting basics, marketing tips, screenplay formats, agent listings, pitches and query letters, producer listings, writing for actors, and tips from pros. It also offers a free newsletter and Internet resources.

WESTERN RESOURCES

WESTERN WRITERS OF AMERICA, INC.

http://www.westernwriters.org

"WWA was founded in 1953 to promote the literature of the American West and bestow Spur Awards for distinguished writing in the Western field." The site offers information about Old West topics, a listing of past Spur Award winners, and opportunities to learn about WWA and the Spur Award, to apply for membership in WWA, to subscribe to *Roundup* Magazine, or to contact Western authors whose work interests you.

GENERAL RESOURCES

1001 WAYS TO MARKET YOUR BOOKS

http://www.bookmarket.com/1001bio.html

1001 Ways to Market Your Books is a site that offers a book marketing newsletter, consulting services, and book marketing updates. Other topics include success letters, author bios, sample chapters, and tables of contents.

ABSOLUTE WRITE

http://www.absolutewrite.com/

Absolute Write is the "one-stop Web home for professional writers." It offers specific resources for freelance writing, screenwriting, playwriting, writing novels, nonfiction, comic book writing, greeting cards, poetry, songwriting, and more. The site also features interviews, articles, announcements, and a newsletter.

AMERICAN BOOKSELLERS ASSOCIATION

http://www.bookweb.org

The American Booksellers Association is a trade association representing independent bookstores nationwide. The site links members to recent articles about the industry and features Idea Exchange discussion forums.

AMERICAN DIALECT SOCIETY

http://www.americandialect.org/

The American Dialect Society website offers discussion lists, a newsletter, and a contacts list. Writers will find the "Dialect in Literature Bibliography" useful, as well as CD-ROM dictionaries and style and grammar guides.

AMERICAN SOCIETY OF JOURNALISTS AND AUTHORS

http://www.asja.org/

The American Society of Journalists and Authors is "the nation's leading organization of independent nonfiction writers." It offers its members professional development aids, such as confidential market information, an exclusive referral service, seminars and workshops, and networking opportunities. The site offers all visitors a newsletter, legal updates from the publishing world, and professional links.

AMERICAN JOURNALISM REVIEW

http://www.ajr.org/

This redeveloped site includes more editorial content, updated links to news industry sites, an improved job search function called "The Employment Section," and other interactive features.

ASSOCIATED WRITING PROGRAMS, THE

http://www.awpwriter.org/

The Associated Writing Programs website offers information about the AWP annual conference, a list of writers' conferences, a list of AWP member schools, articles and information on writing and writing programs, and a sample of articles and news from the AWP magazine *The Writer's Chronicle*. Members of AWP enjoy career advice, a subscription to *The Writer's Chronicle*, and notice of contests and awards.

ASSOCIATION OF AMERICAN PUBLISHERS, INC.

http://www.publishers.org/index.htm

The Association of American Publishers "is the principal trade association of the book publishing industry." The site includes information and registration for annual meetings and conferences, industry news, info about book publishing, industry stats and issues, and copyright data.

AUTHOR NETWORK

http://www.author-network.com

Author Network is a flourishing international community for writers. The site includes articles, monthly columns, a newsletter, message board, discussion group, critique service, and thousands of links to other writing sites. The writer in residence, Paul Saevig, provides a regular supply of instructional essays that may help new writers or even established authors. Other material and articles are provided by regular contributors, who are generally published authors themselves. Author Network promotes individual writers and other sites of interest to writers, as well as competitions, conferences, and courses.

AUTHOR'S GUILD, THE

http://www.authorsguild.org/

For more than 80 years the Guild has been the authoritative voice of American writers....its strength is the foundation of the U.S. literary community. This site features contract advice, a legal search, information on electronic rights and how to join the organization, a bulletin index, publishers' row, a listing of board members, and current articles regarding the publishing field. There is also a link for Back-in-print.com, an online bookstore featuring out-of-print editions made available by their authors.

AUTHORLINK

http://www.authorlink.com/

This information service for editors, literary agents, and writers boasts more than 165,000 loyal readers per year. Features include a "Manuscript Showcase" that contains 500+ ready to publish, evaluated manuscripts.

AYLAD'S CREATIVE WRITING GROUP

http://www.publication.com/aylad

This site provides a forum for "people to get their work read and critiqued by fellow writers in a friendly atmosphere." The service is free and all writing forms are welcome. The site includes links to other resources for writers.

BLACK WRITERS ALLIANCE

http://www.blackwriters.org/

The Black Writers Alliance is the "first literary arts organization to utilize the power of the online medium to educate, inform, support and empower aspiring and published Black writers. The Black Writers Alliance (BWA) is dedicated to providing information, news, resources, and support to Black writers, while promoting the Internet as a tool for research and fellowship among the cultural writing community." The site offers users access to its media kit, a forum, a directory of speakers, a photo album, mailing lists, and chat rooms. The Black Writers Alliance is the first online community that has hosted an annual conference for its members.

BOOKLIST

http://www.ala.org/booklist/index.html

Booklist is a "digital counterpart of the American Library Association's *Booklist* magazine." In the site is a current selection of reviews, feature articles, and a searchable cumulative index. Review topics include books for youth, adult books, media, and reference materials. The site also includes press releases, the best books list, and subscription information.

BOOKNOTE

http://www.booknote.com/

Booknote specializes in custom-designed websites for authors, book titles, literary agents, and publishers. Its award-winning sites are individually designed to capture the creativity of the unique individuals they feature. Booknote also extensively target-markets each site to all relevant special-interest or news groups on the Web, to increase both the person's recognition and World Wide Web sales.

BOOKREPORTER

http://www.bookreporter.com/brc/index.asp

Bookreporter is a site that offers book reviews and a perspectives section that deals with such topics as when a book becomes a movie. It features a daily quote by a famous author.

BOOKTALK

http://www.booktalk.com/

Want to find out how to click with the people who talk books? Booktalk is a site where writers and readers learn more about the publishing industry. Besides an extensive literary agent list, there are articles about how to get published, writing tips from authors, and a bulletin board. The host for many author homepages, Booktalk allows readers to interact with bestselling authors, learn about new releases, read book excerpts, and see what's upcoming. A slushpile section lists conferences and publishing links.

BOOKWIRE

http://www.bookwire.com/

Partners with *Publishers Weekly*, *Literary Market Place*, and the *Library Journal*, among others, BookWire is a site that offers book industry news, reviews, original fiction, author interviews, and guides to literary events. The site features publicity and marketing opportunities for publishers, authors, booksellers, and publicists, and it includes a list of the latest BookWire press releases.

BOOKZONE

http://www.bookzone.com/

BookZone was created "to increase book sales and profits for publishers." The site features a Super Catalog of books, thousands of book-related links, industry insights and resources, publishing news, and site hosting, development, and online marketing.

BURRY MAN WRITERS CENTER, THE

http://www.burryman.com/

With members and visitors in 104 countries, the Burry Man truly is "a worldwide community of writers." Working professionals and beginning writers find exclusive articles on the craft and business of writing, an extensive list of freelance job resources, a vast section focusing on Scotland, and links to more than 3,000 primary sources of information, giving writers the chance to speak to one another and use the Internet to hone their skills.

COFFEEHOUSE FOR WRITERS

http://www.coffeehouse4writers.com/

The Coffeehouse for Writers is an "online writer's colony; a place where writers—from novice to professional—gather to critique, advise, and encourage each other." The site provides links to other resources for writers and a list of suggested books.

E-BOOKS CAFÉ

http://www.topzone.com/ebookscafe/

E-books Café is dedicated to helping fellow writers reach out and touch the world through words. It provides an assortment of books to the public in the e-book and POD format in all genres of fiction, as well as nonfiction. It also offers authors worldwide the opportunity to promote and sell their e-books and POD books for free at its site.

ECLECTIC WRITER, THE

http://www.eclectics.com/writing/writing.html

This site is an information source for those interested in crime, romance, horror, children's, technical, screen, science fiction, fantasy, mystery, and poetry writing. It features articles, a fiction writer's character chart, resources by genre, reference materials, research, general writing resources, online magazines and journals, writing scams, awards, and a writing-related fun page.

EDITOR'S PEN, THE

http://users.myepath.com/dwlacey/default.htm

The Editor's Pen site exists to connect "sites for and about Writers, Editors, and Indexers." It includes links to lists of freelancers and online dictionaries. Other interesting links include an "Edit challenge" and "Quotable words of editorial wisdom."

EDITORIAL EYE, THE

http://www.eei-alex.com

The Editorial Eye website consists of a sampler of articles originally printed in the newsletter by the same name. The articles discuss techniques for writing, editing, design, and typography, as well as information on industry trends and employment. The Eye has been providing information to publication professionals for 18 years.

ENCYCLOPAEDIA BRITANNICA

http://www.eb.com/

This service is subscription-based and allows the user to search the *Encyclopaedia Britannica*. New users can try a "sample search."

FORWRITERS.COM

http://www.forwriters.com/

This "mega-site" provides numerous links to writing resources of all kinds. It lists conferences, markets, agents, commercial services, and more. The "What's New" feature allows the user to peruse what links have recently been added under the various categories.

GRANTA

http://www.granta.com/

The *Granta* website offers information about the most current issue of this highly regarded literary journal. The introduction is an explanation and background info about the topic around which the issue is based. The contents of the issue are listed, and visitors to the site may read a sample from the issue, as well as obtain subscription and ordering information. It also offers similar information about back issues and a readers' survey.

HOLLYLISLE.COM

http://hollylisle.com/

HollyLisle.com offers a community of supportive writers helping each other reach their writing goals. Led by full-time novelist Holly Lisle, the community includes crit circles, discussion and research boards, workshops, free real-time writing classes with professional writers and people who can offer their expertise in areas of interest to writers, writing articles, free writing e-books and the award-winning free e-zine *Vision: A Resource for Writers*, plus chapters, cover art, works-in-progress, and surprises for readers.

INSCRIPTIONS

http://www.inscriptionsmagazine.com

Inscriptions is the weekly e-zine for professional writers. For the past four years, each jam-packed issue has featured writing and publishing-related articles, interviews with experts, job opportunities, writing contests, paying markets, book reviews, and links. Sign up for the e-mail version and receive more than 70 pages of useful information each week, perfect for the freelancing writer or telecommuting editor. Learn how to earn money for your stories. Find your next job opportunity. Or enter the monthly writing contest and win cash prizes.

LITERARY MARKET PLACE

http://www.literarymarketplace.com/

The *Literary Market Place* website offers information about publishers, which are categorized as U.S. book publishers, Canadian book publishers, and small presses, as well as literary agents, including illustration and lecture agents. The site also offers trade services and resources.

LOCAL WRITERS WORKSHOP

http://members.tripod.com/~lww_2/introduction.htm

The Local Writers Workshop is an Internet forum for works in progress, especially those "in the early stages of revision." The creators of this membership-based site pride themselves on its community ethic.

MIDWEST BOOK REVIEW

http://www.execpc.com/~mbr/bookwatch/

Responsible for Bookwatch, a weekly television program that reviews books, videos, music, CD-ROMs, and computer software, as well as five monthly newsletters for community and academic library systems and much more, the Midwest Book Review was founded in 1980. This site features its reviews.

MISC.WRITING

http://www.scalar.com/mw/

"Misc.writing is a Use Net newsgroup that provides a forum for discussion of writing in all its forms—scholarly, technical, journalistic, and mere day-to-day communication." Website resources include a writer's bookstore and market information.

NATIONAL ASSOCIATION OF WOMEN WRITERS—NAWW

http://www.naww.org/

The National Association of Women Writers—NAWW was founded to support, encourage, entertain, motivate, and inspire women writers. NAWW offers a free weekly inspirational/how-to e-magazine, an online Member Portfolio, a Member Publications page, a quarterly member publication (*The NAWW Writer's Guide*), a Discussion List, a Member Only Online Critique Group, Daily Inspiration, a Writer's Resource Library, and much more.

NATIONAL WRITERS UNION, THE

http://www.nwu.org/

The National Writers Union is the trade union for freelance writers of all genres. The website provides links to various services of the union, including grievance resolution, insurance, job information, and databases.

NEWSLINK

http://newslink.org/

NewsLink offers exceptionally well-organized links to newspapers, broadcasters, and magazines. Users can search by name, or browse by state or national papers, major metros, dailies, nondailies, major networks, subject, or country. NewsLink also has a JobLink feature, where users can post a job or search for a job. The site makes hundreds of updates each week, so you can be sure you are getting up-to-the-minute information.

NOVELIST, THE

http://novelnow.cjb.net/

The Novelist is dedicated to helping novel writers get published, tackling issues such as querying agents and the nature of the business, independent publishers versus the Big Six, and marketing. In the section for writer's conference notes, you can read "what went on" at the venues. Includes thousands of links to writer resources, including agents and publishers and an open message board where writers can blow off steam or post news.

PAINTED ROCK

http://www.paintedrock.com/memvis/memvis1.htm

"Painted Rock provides services to nonpublished writers, published writers, and readers." Free features on the site include information on a free 12-week Artist's Way program, message boards, goal writing groups, writing topics, a book discussion group, a research listserv, and *The Rock* online magazine. In addition to their free services, the site offers paid online writing classes, a subscription-based newsletter, and two bookstores, as well as advertising, promotion for authors, and website hosting and design.

PARA PUBLISHING

http://www.parapublishing.com/

The Para Publishing Book Publishing Resources page offers "the industry's largest resources/publications guide," a customized book writing/publishing/promoting information kit, as well as current and back issues of its newsletter. The site also includes research links, a listing of suppliers, and mailing lists.

PEN AMERICAN CENTER

http://www.pen.org/

PEN is an international "membership organization of prominent literary writers and editors. As a major voice of the literary community, the organization seeks to defend the freedom of expression wherever it may be threatened, and to promote and encourage the recognition and reading of contemporary literature." The site links to information about several PEN-sponsored initiatives, including literary awards.

PUBLISHERS WEEKLY ONLINE

http://publishersweekly.reviewsnews.com/

Publishers Weekly Online offers news about the writing industry, as well as special features about reading and writing in general and genre writing. The site also includes news on children's books, book-selling, interviews, international book industry news, and industry updates.

PUT IT IN INK

http://www.putitinink.com

Put It In Ink brings you articles, tips, books, software, and information about the craft of writing and getting published. Find information about newsletters (both print and online), e-zines, self-publishing and traditional publishing, freelancing, freelance jobs/markets, marketing tips, article writing, ideas to write about, and more.

R. R. BOWKER

http://www.bowker.com/

R. R. Bowker is a site that offers a listing of books in print on the Web, books out of print, an online directory of the book publishing industry, a data collection center for R. R. Bowker publications, and a directory of vendors to the publishing community.

REFERENCE SHELF

http://Alabanza.com/kabacoff/Inter-Links/reference.html

The Reference Shelf site provides quick access to words, facts, and figures that are useful when writing and fact-checking. A special "Words" section features dictionaries, acronym finders, and links to computer-jargon.

SENSIBLE SOLUTIONS FOR GETTING HAPPILY PUBLISHED

http://www.happilypublished.com/

This site is "designed to help writers, publishers, self-publishers, and everyone else who cares about reaching readers, including editors, agents, booksellers, reviewers, industry observers and talk show hosts. . .and aims to help books get into the hands of the people they were written for." It includes information about finding a publisher, how to boost a book's sales, and sensible solutions for reaching readers.

SHARPWRITER.COM

http://www.sharpwriter.com/

SharpWriter.Com is a practical resources page for writers of all types—a "writer's handy virtual desktop." Reference materials include style sheets, dictionaries, quotations, and job information. The Office Peacemaker offers to resolve grammar disputes in the workplace.

SHAW GUIDES, INC., WRITER'S CONFERENCES

http://www.writing.shawguides.com/

Shaw Guides: Writer's Conferences is a subscription-based listing of sponsors and the following month's writer's conferences calendar. The Shaw Site for Writer's Conferences allows the user to search for information about 400 conferences and workshops worldwide. An e-mail service can be used to get updates about conferences that meet user criteria for dates, topics, and locations. Other resources include Quick Tips, links to organizations, and information about residencies and retreats.

SMALL PUBLISHERS OF NORTH AMERICA

http://www.spannet.org/home.htm
Small Publishers of North America is a site for "independent presses, self-publishers, and savvy authors who realizethat if their books are to be successful, they must make them so." The site offers pages for "fun, facts, and financial gain." It also offers a newsletter.

STORY BASE

www.storybase.net

Storybase net explores over 2,000 narrative situations that suggest multiple story possibilities depending on what you project onto them. It is a computer program that can be purchased at the storybase.net website.

UNITED STATES COPYRIGHT OFFICE

www.copyright.gov

The United States Copyright Office site allows the user to find valuable information about copyright procedures and other basics. In addition, the user can download publications and forms, then link to information about international copyright laws.

WELL, THE

http://www.well.com/

The WELL (Whole Earth 'Lectronic Link) is an online gathering place that its creators call a "literate watering hole for thinkers from all walks of life."

WOMEN WHO WRITE

http://members.aol.com/jfavetti/womenww/www.html

Women Who Write is a "collage of women based all over the United States with a passion for writing." The site provides useful links and a large dose of encouragement to women writers of all experience levels.

WOODEN HORSE PUBLISHING

http://www.woodenhorsepub.com/

Wooden Horse Publishing is a complete news and resource site for article writers. Visitors get news about markets, including planned, new, and folding magazines; editor assignments; and editorial changes. The site features a searchable market database of over 3,000 U.S. and Canadian consumer and trade magazines. Entries include full contact information, writer's guidelines, and—only at Wooden Horse—reader demographics and editorial calendars. Newsletter describes new markets and industry trends.

WRITE FROM HOME

http://www.writefromhome.com/

Whether you're a freelance writer, author, or writing from home but employed by a publication, this site strives to offer work-at-home writer's tips, information, and resources to help you balance your writing career and children under one roof. You'll also find lots of writing and marketing resources to help you achieve the success you desire. It features a chat room, e-mail discussion list, and a monthly e-zine.

WRITELINKS

http://www.writelinks.com/

The site provides an array of services that include workshops, personalized tutoring, and critique groups. "WriteLinks is designed to be of value to all writers, regardless of their experience, genre, or focus."

WRITER'S EXCHANGE, THE

http://www.writers-exchange.com/

The Writers Exchange is a community designed to share and enrich the lives of writers. The site features articles, writing links, a listing of writing books, jobs/markets, book and software reviews, ask the experts, author interviews, authors' homepages, author services, announcements, and awards. The site offers a monthly e-zine, which includes book reviews, writing tips, marketing ideas, and website reviews.

WRITER'S MANUAL

http://www.writersmanual.com/

Writer's Manual is an online writer-related information warehouse. It receives information from writers, publishers, and agents worldwide, which includes links, announcements, articles, book reviews, press releases, and more. The site features free writer-related articles, links and resources, recommended books, and a vast job board that lists jobs for traditional and online publishing markets, syndication markets, publishers, grants/fellowships, and contests. The site hosts contests on a monthly basis, including the Writer Critique Contest, in which a published author edits and critiques the writing of one winner.

WRITER'S CENTER, THE

http://www.writer.org/

The Writer's Center is a Maryland-based nonprofit that "encourages the creation and distribution of contemporary literature." The website provides information on the organization's 200+ yearly workshops and links to its publication Poet Lore and Writer's Carousel.

WRITERS GUILD OF AMERICA

http://www.wga.org/

The WGA West site provides information about the Guild and its services, such as script registration. Other links to writing resources are provided as well.

WRITERS NET

http://www.writers.net/

Writers Net is a site that "helps build relationships between writers, publishers, editors, and literary agents." It consists of two main sections, "The Internet Directory of

Published Writers," which includes a list of published works and a biographical statement, and "The Internet Directory of Literary Agents," which lists areas of specialization and a description of the agency. Both are searchable and include contact information. It is a free service that hopes to "become an important, comprehensive matchmaking resource for writers, editors, publishers, and literary agents on the Internet."

WRITERS ON THE NET

http://www.writers.com/

"Writers on the Net is a group of published writers and experienced writing teachers building an online community and resource for writers and aspiring writers." A subscription to the mailing list provides a description and schedule of classes offered by the site and a monthly newsletter.

WRITERS WRITE

http://www.writerswrite.com/

This "mega-site" provides myriad resources, including a searchable database of online and print publications in need of submissions. The Writers Write chat room is open 24 hours a day for live discussion.

WRITERS' BBS, THE

http://www.writers-bbs.com/home.shtml

The Writers' BBS is intended for "authors, poets, journalists, and readers" and highlights writers' chat rooms, discussion forums, and an e-zine for beginning writers called *Fish Eggs for the Soul*. It also includes games, personal ads, copyright information, mailing lists, Internet links, an adults-only section, and the online *King James Bible*.

WRITERS-EDITORS NETWORK

http://www.writers-editors.com/

The Writers-Editors Network has been "linking professional writers with those who need content and editorial services since 1982." The site features agent listings, articles on marketing tools, and a database of over 10,000 e-mail addresses of editors and book publishers. The site also links to fabulous how-to e-books of dream jobs for writers.

WRITERSPACE

http://www.writerspace.com/

"Writerspace specializes in the design and hosting of websites for authors. We also provide Web services for those who may already have websites but wish to include more interactivity in the way of bulletin boards, chat rooms, contests, and e-mail newsletters." The site features an author spotlight, contests, workshops, mailing lists, bulletin boards, chat rooms, romance links, a guestbook, information on adding your link, Web design, Web hosting, its clients, and rates.

WRITERSWEEKLY.COM

http://www.writersweekly.com/

This is the home of the most current paying markets to be found online. WritersWeekly publishes a free weekly e-zine featuring new paying markets and freelance job listings. Serving more readers than any other freelance writing e-zine it is dedicated to teaching writers how to make more money writing.

WRITING CORNER

http://www.writingcorner.com/

Writing Corner is dedicated to the reader and writer alike, providing a one-stop place for author sites, chats, and giveaways, along with articles on all aspects of writing. The weekly "JumpStart" newsletter is designed to motivate writers at every level, while the "Author's Corner" newsletter keeps readers apprised of author events. The site features market information, resource listings, book reviews, and vast archives of writing information for fiction, nonfiction, and corporate writers.

WRITING-WORLD.COM

http://www.writing-world.com/

This site offers more than 250 articles on the craft and business of writing, in such categories as freelancing, fiction, genres, skill-building, children's writing, self-publishing, and more. It features a regularly updated list of writers' contests, a "writers wanted" section, and a free biweekly e-mail newsletter with articles, publishing news, and market information.

YOUCANWRITE

http://www.youcanwrite.com/

YouCanWrite is one of *Writer's Digest's* 101 Best Sites for Writers and is the brainchild of two long-time publishing professionals who know the business from the inside out. Aspiring nonfiction writers can get the real story on what agents and editors look for in a salable manuscript. The site offers a wealth of free information, and its Insider Guides are practical, fun to read e-books that cover all the bases—from agents to books proposals to contracts.

ZUZU'S PETALS LITERARY RESOURCE, THE

http://www.zuzu.com/

The Zuzu's Petals Literary Resource is a site that focuses on a comprehensive list of writers' resource links and information. It includes a bookstore; discussion forums; its literary magazine, *Zuzu's Petals Quarterly Online*; art news, which reports on news in the literary world; and contests.

BOOKS FOR AUTHORS

BOOKS FOR AUTHORS

SELF-PUBLISHING RESOURCES

All-By-Yourself Self-Publishing
by David H. Li (Premier Pub Company)
PO Box 341267, Bethesda, MD 20827
e-mail: davidli@erols.com

The Art of Self-Publishing
by Bonnie Stahlman Speer (Reliance Press)
60-64 Hardinge Street, Deniliquin, NSW, 2710; Australia
e-mail: reliance@reliancepress.com.au

Book Production: Composition, Layout, Editing & Design.
Getting It Ready for Printing
by Dan Poynter (Para Publishing)
PO Box 8206-240, Santa Barbara, CA 93118-8206
805-968-7277; fax: 805-968-1379; cell: 805-680-2298
e-mail: DanPoynter@aol.com; 75031.3534@compuserve.com

Business and Legal Forms for Authors and Self-Publishers
by Tad Crawford (Allworth Press)
10 East 23rd Street, Suite 210, New York, NY 10010
212-777-8395

The Complete Guide to Self-Publishing: Everything You Need to Know
to Write, Publish, Promote and Sell Your Own Book
by Tom Ross, Marilyn J. Ross (Writer's Digest Books)
1507 Dana Avenue, Cincinnati, OH 45207
513-531-2222; fax: 513-531-4744

The Complete Guide to Successful Publishing
by Avery Cardoza (Cardoza Pub)
132 Hastings Street, Brooklyn, NY 11235
800-577-WINS, 718-743-5229; fax: 718-743-8284; e-mail: cardozapub@aol.com

The Complete Self-Publishing Handbook
by David M. Brownstone, Irene M. Franck (Plume)
375 Hudson Street, New York, NY 10014
212-366-2000

The Economical Guide to Self-Publishing: How to Produce and
Market Your Book on a Budget
by Linda Foster Radke, Mary E. Hawkins, Editor (Five Star Publications)
PO Box 6698, Chandler, AZ 85246-6698
480-940-8182

Exports/Foreign Rights, Selling U.S. Books Abroad
by Dan Poynter (Para Publishing)
PO Box 8206-240, Santa Barbara, CA 93118-8206
805-968-7277; fax: 805-968-1379; cell: 805-680-2298
e-mail: DanPoynter@aol.com; 75031.3534@compuserve.com

A Guide to Successful Self-Publishing
by Stephen Wagner (Prentice Hall Direct)
240 Frisch Court, Paramus, NJ 07652
201-909-6200

How to Make Money Publishing from Home, Revised 2nd Edition: Everything
You Need to Know to Successfully Publish Books, Newsletters, Web Sites,
Greeting Cards, and Software
by Lisa Shaw (Prima Publishing)
3000 Lava Ridge Court, Roseville, CA 95661

How to Publish Your Own Book and Earn $50,000 Profit
by Gordon Burgett (Communication Unlimited)
PO Box 6405, Santa Maria, CA 93456
800-563-1454; fax: 805-937-3035; e-mail: gordon@sops.com

How to Publish, Promote, and Sell Your Own Book
by Robert Lawrence Holt (St. Martin's Press)
175 Fifth Avenue, New York, NY 10010
212-674-5151

How to Self-Publish & Market Your Own Book: A Simple Guide for Aspiring Writers
by Mark E. Smith, Sara Freeman Smith (U R Gems Group)
PO Box 440341, Houston, TX 77244-0341
281-596-8330

How to Self-Publish Your Book with Little or No Money! A Complete Guide to Self-Publishing at a Profit!
by Bettie E. Tucker, Wayne Brumagin (Rainbow's End Company)
354 Golden Grove Road, Baden, PA 15005 US
724-266-2346; fax: 724-266-2346

How You Can Become a Successful Self-Publisher in America and Elsewhere
by Paul Chika Emekwulu (Novelty Books)
PO Box 2482, Norman, OK 73070
voice/fax: 405-447-9019; e-mail: novelty@telepath.com

Make Money Self-Publishing: Learn How from Fourteen Successful Small Publishers
by Suzanne P. Thomas (Gemstone House Publishing)
PO Box 19948, Boulder, CO 80308
800-324-6415

The Prepublishing Handbook : What You Should Know Before You Publish Your First Book
by Patricia J. Bell (Cats Paw Press)
9561 Woodridge Circle, Eden Prairie, MN 55347
952-941-5053; fax: 952-941-4759; e-mail: catspawpress@aol.com

The Publish It Yourself Handbook (25th Anniversary Edition)
by Bill Henderson (Introduction); (W. W. Norton & Company)
500 Fifth Avenue, New York, NY 10110
212-354-5500

Publish Your Own Novel
by Connie Shelton, Lee Ellison, Editor (Intrigue Press)
PO Box 27553, Philadelphia, PA 19118
800-996-9783

The Self-Publisher's Writing Journal
by Lia Relova (Pumpkin Enterprises)
12 Packet Road, Palos Verdes, CA 90275
e-mail: princesslia@hotmail.com

The Self-Publishing Manual: How to Write, Print & Sell Your Own Book
by Dan Poynter (Para Publishing)
PO Box 8206-240, Santa Barbara, CA 93118-8206
805-968-7277; fax: 805-968-1379; cell: 805-680-2298
e-mail: DanPoynter@aol.com, 75031.3534@compuserve.com

A Simple Guide to Self-Publishing: A Step-by-Step Handbook to Prepare, Print, Distribute & Promote Your Own Book—3rd Edition
by Mark Ortman (Wise Owl Books)
PO Box 29205, Bellingham, WA 98228
360-671-5858; e-mail: publish@wiseowlbooks.com

Smart Self-Publishing: An Author's Guide to Producing a Marketable Book
by Linda G. Salisbury (Tabby House)
4429 Shady Lane, Charlotte Harbor, FL 33980-3024
941-629-7646; fax: 941-629-4270

The Woman's Guide to Self-Publishing
by Donna M. Murphy (Irie Publishing)
301 Boardwalk Drive, PO Box 273123, Fort Collins, CO 80527-3123
970-482-4402; fax: 970 482-4402; e-mail: iriepub@verinet.com

INDUSTRY RESOURCES

30 Steps to Becoming a Writer and Getting Published: The Complete Starter Kit for Aspiring Writers
by Scott Edelstein (Writer's Digest Books)
1507 Dana Avenue, Cincinnati, OH 45207
513-531-2222; fax: 513-531-4744

500 Ways to Beat the Hollywood Script Reader: Writing the Screenplay the Reader Will Recommend
by Jennifer M. Lerch (Fireside)
1230 Avenue of the Americas, New York, NY 10020
212-698-7000

1001 Ways to Market Your Books: For Authors and Publishers: Includes Over 100 Proven Marketing Tips Just for Authors
by John Kremer (Open Horizons)
PO Box 205, Fairfield, IA 52556

1,818 Ways to Write Better & Get Published
by Scott Edelstein (Writer's Digest Books)
1507 Dana Avenue, Cincinnati, OH 45207
513-531-2222; fax: 513-531-4744

2005 Children's Writer's & Illustrator's Market (annual)
by Alice Pope, Editor (Writer's Digest Books)
1507 Dana Avenue, Cincinnati, OH 45207
513-531-2222; fax: 513-531-4744

2005 Novel & Short Story Writer's Market (annual)
by Anne Bowling, Editor (Writer's Digest Books)
1507 Dana Avenue, Cincinnati, OH 45207
513-531-2222; fax: 513-531-4744

2005 Poet's Market (annual)
by Nancy Breen, Editor (Writer's Digest Books)
1507 Dana Avenue, Cincinnati, OH 45207
513-531-2222; fax: 513-531-4744

2005 Writer's Market (annual)
by Kathryn Brogan, Editor (Writer's Digest Books)
1507 Dana Avenue, Cincinnati, OH 45207
513-531-2222; fax: 513-531-4744

Advice to Writers: A Compendium of Quotes, Anecdotes, and Writerly Wisdom
from a Dazzling Array of Literary Lights
by John Winoker, Compiler (Vintage Books)
299 Park Avenue, New York, NY 10171
212-751-2600

The American Directory of Writer's Guidelines:
What Editors Want, What Editors Buy (3rd ed.)
by John C. Mutchler (Quill Driver Books)
1831 Industrial Way, #101, Sanger, CA 93657
fax: 559-876-2170; e-mail: sbm12@csufresno.edu

The Art and Science of Book Publishing
by Herbert S. Bailey Jr. (Ohio University Press)
Scott Quadrangle, Athens, OH 45701

The Author's Guide to Marketing Your Book:
From Start to Success, for Writers and Publishers
by Don Best, Peter Goodman (Stone Bridge Press)
PO Box 8208 , Berkeley, CA 94707
800-947-7271; fax: 510-524-8711; e-mail: sbporter@stonebridge.com

An Author's Guide to Publishing
by Michael Legat (Robert Hale Ltd.)
Clerkenwell House 45-47, Clerkenwell Green, London, England EC1R 0HT
0171-251-2661

The Big Deal: Hollywood's Million-Dollar Spec Script Market
by Tom Taylor (William Morrow & Company)
1350 Avenue of the Americas, New York, NY 10019
212-261-6500

Book Blitz: Getting Your Book in the News: 60 Steps to a Best Seller
by Barbara Gaughen, Ernest Weckbaugh (Best Seller Books)
7456 Evergreen Drive, Santa Barbara, CA 93117
800-444-2524

Book Business: Publishing: Past, Present, and Future
by Jason Epstein (W. W. Norton & Company)
500 Fifth Avenue, New York, NY 10110
212-354-5500; fax: 212-869-0856

Book Editors Talk to Writers
by Judy Mandell (John Wiley & Sons)
605 Third Avenue, New York, NY 10158-0012
212-850-6000; fax: 212-850-6088
e-mail: info@wiley.com

Book Promotion for the Shameless: 101 Marketing Tips that Really Work (3.5 diskette)
by Lorna Tedder (Spilled Candy Publications)
PO Box 5202, Niceville, FL 32578-5202
850-897-4644
e-mail: orders@spilledcandy.com

Book Promotion for Virgins:
Answers to a New Author's Questions About Marketing and Publicity
by Lorna Tedder (Spilled Candy Publications)
PO Box 5202, Niceville, FL 32578-5202
850-897-4644
e-mail: orders@spilledcandy.com

The Book Publishing Industry
by Albert N. Greco (Allyn & Bacon)
75 Arlington Street, Suite 300, Boston, MA 02116
617-848-6000

Book Publishing: The Basic Introduction
by John P. Dessauer (Continuum Publishing Group)
370 Lexington Avenue, New York, NY 10017
212-953-5858

Breaking into Print: How to Write and Publish Your First Book
by Jane L. Evanson, Luanne Dowling (Kendall/Hunt Publishing Company)
4050 Westmark Drive, PO Box 1840, Dubuque, IA 52004-1840
800-228-0810, 319-589-1000

Business and Legal Forms for Authors and Self-Publishers
by Tad Crawford (Allworth Press)
10 East 23rd Street, New York, NY 10010
fax: 212-777-8261; e-mail: groberts@allworth.com

The Career Novelist: A Literary Agent Offers Strategies for Success
by Donald Maass (Heinemann)
22 Salmon Street, Port Melbourne, Victoria 3207, Australia
e-mail: customer@hi.com.au

The Case of Peter Rabbit: Changing Conditions of Literature for Children
by Margaret MacKey (Garland Publishing)
29 W. 35th Street, New York, NY 10001-2299
212-216-7800; fax: 212-564-7854; e-mail: info@taylorandfrancis.com

Complete Guide to Book Marketing
by David Cole (Allworth Press)
10 East 23rd Street, New York, NY 10010
fax: 212-777-8261; e-mail: groberts@allworth.com

The Complete Guide to Book Publicity
by Jodee Blanco (Allworth Press)
10 East 23rd Street, Suite 210, New York, NY 10010
212-777-8395

The Complete Guide to Writer's Groups, Conferences, and Workshops
by Eileen Malone (John Wiley & Sons)
605 Third Avenue, New York, NY 10158-0012
212-850-6000; fax: 212-850-6088; e-mail: info@wiley.com

The Complete Guide to Writing Fiction and Nonfiction—And Getting It Published
by Patricia Kubis, Robert Howland (Prentice Hall Direct)
240 Frisch Court, Paramus, NJ 07652
201-909-6200

A Complete Guide to Writing for Publication
by Susan Titus Osborn, Editor (ACW Press)
5501 N. 7th Ave., # 502, Phoenix, AZ 85013
877-868-9673; e-mail: editor@acwpress.com

The Complete Idiot's Guide to Getting Published
by Sheree Bykofsky, Jennifer Basye Sander (Alpha Books)
201 West 103rd Street, Indianapolis, IN 46290
317-581-3500

The Complete Idiot's Guide to Getting Your Romance Published
by Julie Beard (Alpha Books)
4500 E. Speedway, Suite 31, Tucson, AZ 85712
fax: 800-770-4329

Complete Idiot's Guide to Publishing Children's Books
by Harold D. Underdown, et al. (Alpha Books)
4500 E. Speedway, Suite 31, Tucson, AZ 85712
fax: 800-770-4329

The Copyright Permission and Libel Handbook:
A Step-by-Step Guide for Writers, Editors, and Publishers
by Lloyd J. Jassin, Steve C. Schecter (John Wiley & Sons)
605 Third Avenue, New York, NY 10158-0012
212-850-6000; fax: 212-850-6088; e-mail: info@wiley.com

Desktop Publishing & Design for Dummies
by Roger C. Parker (IDG Books Worldwide, Inc.)
919 E. Hillsdale Boulevard, Suite 400, Foster City, CA 94404-2112
800-762-2974

The Directory of Poetry Publishers: 2001–2002 (Directory of Poetry Publishers, 17th Ed.)
by Len Fulton, Editor (Dustbooks)
PO Box 100, Paradise, CA 95967
530-877-6110, 800-477-6110; fax: 530-877-0222

Directory of Small Press/Magazine Editors & Publishers, 31st Ed
by Len Fulton, Editor (Dustbooks)
PO Box 100, Paradise, CA 95967
530-877-6110, 800-477-6110 ; fax: 530-877-0222

Editors on Editing: What Writers Need to Know About What Editors Do
by Gerald Gross, Editor (Grove Press)
841 Broadway, New York, NY 10003
212-614-7850

The First Five Pages: A Writer's Guide to Staying Out of the Rejection Pile
by Noah T. Lukeman (Fireside)
1230 Avenue of the Americas, New York, NY 10020
212-698-7000

Formatting & Submitting Your Manuscript (Writer's Market Library Series)
by Jack Neff (Writer's Digest Books)
1507 Dana Avenue, Cincinnati, OH 45207
513-531-2222; fax: 513-531-4744

From Book Idea to Bestseller: What You Absolutely, Positively Must Know to Make Your Book a Success
by Michael Snell, et al. (Prima Publishing)
3000 Lava Ridge Court, Roseville, CA 95661

From Pen to Print: The Secrets of Getting Published Successfully
by Ellen M. Kozak (Henry Holt)
115 West 18th Street, New York, NY 10011
212-886-9200; fax: 212-633-0748; e-mail: publicity@hholt.com

Get Published: Top Magazine Editors Tell You How
by Diane Gage (Henry Holt)
115 West 18th Street, New York, NY 10011
212-886-9200; fax: 212-633-0748; e-mail: publicity@hholt.com

Get Your First Book Published: And Make It a Success
by Jason Shinder, Jeff Herman, Amy Holman (Career Press)
3 Tice Road, PO Box 687, Franklin Lakes, NJ 07417
201-848-0310

Getting Your Book Published for Dummies
by Sarah Parsons Zackheim (IDG Books Worldwide, Inc.)
919 E. Hillsdale Boulevard, Suite 400
Foster City, CA 94404-2112
800-762-2974

*Getting Your Manuscript Sold: Surefire Writing and Selling Strategies
That Will Get Your Book Published*
by Cynthia Sterling, M. G. Davidson (Empire Publishing Service)
PO Box 717, Madison, NC 27025-0717
fax: 336-427-7372

How to Be Your Own Literary Agent: The Business of Getting a Book Published
by Richard Curtis (Houghton Mifflin Company)
222 Berkeley Street, Boston, MA 02116-3764
617-351-5000

How to Get Happily Published (5th ed.)
by Judith Appelbaum (HarperCollins)
10 East 53rd Street, New York, NY 10022-5299
212-207-7000

How to Publish, Promote, and Sell Your Own Book
by Robert Lawrence Holt (St. Martin's Press)
175 Fifth Avenue, New York, NY 10010
212-674-5151

How to Write a Book Proposal
by Michael Larsen (Writers Digest Books)
1507 Dana Avenue, Cincinnati, OH 45207
513-531-2222; fax: 513-531-4744

How to Write a Damn Good Novel
by James N. Frey (St. Martin's Press)
175 Fifth Avenue, New York, NY 10010
212-674-5151

How to Write and Sell Your First Nonfiction Book
by Oscar Collier, Frances Spatz Leighton (St. Martin's Press)
175 Fifth Avenue, New York, NY 10010
212-674-5151

How to Write Irresistible Query Letters
by Lisa Collier Cool (Writer's Digest Books)
1507 Dana Avenue, Cincinnati, OH 45207
513-531-2222; fax: 513-531-4744

How to Write & Sell Your First Novel
by Oscar Collier (Writer's Digest Books)
1507 Dana Avenue, Cincinnati, OH 45207
513-531-2222; fax: 513-531-4744

How to Write What You Want and Sell What You Write
by Skip Press (Career Press)
3 Tice Road, PO Box 687, Franklin Lakes, NJ 07417
201-848-0310

In the Company of Writers: A Life in Publishing
by Charles Scribner (Scribner)
1230 Avenue of the Americas, New York, NY 10020
212-698-7000

The Insider's Guide to Getting an Agent
by Lori Perkins (Writer's Digest Books)
1507 Dana Avenue, Cincinnati, OH 45207
513-531-2222; fax: 513-531-4744

The Joy of Publishing
by Nat G. Bodian (Open Horizons)
PO Box 205, Fairfield, IA 52556

Jump Start Your Book Sales: A Money-Making Guide for Authors,
Independent Publishers and Small Presses
by Marilyn Ross, Tom Ross (Writers Digest Books)
1507 Dana Avenue, Cincinnati, OH 45207
513-531-2222; fax: 513-531-4744

Kirsch's Guide to the Book Contract: For Authors, Publishers, Editors and Agents
by Jonathan Kirsch (Acrobat Books)
PO Box 870, Venice, CA 90294
fax: 310-823-8447

Kirsch's Handbook of Publishing Law: For Authors, Publishers, Editors and Agents
by Jonathan Kirsch (Acrobat Books)
PO Box 870, Venice, CA 90294
fax: 310-823-8447

Literary Agents: A Writer's Introduction
by John F. Baker (IDG Books Worldwide, Inc.)
919 E. Hillsdale Boulevard, Suite 400, Foster City, CA 94404-2112
800-762-2974

*Literary Agents: What They Do, How They Do It, and How to Find and
Work with the Right One for You, Revised and Expanded*
by Michael Larsen (John Wiley & Sons)
605 Third Avenue, New York, NY 10158-0012
212-850-6000; fax: 212-850-6088; e-mail: info@wiley.com

*Literary Marketplace (annual): The Directory of the American Book
Publishing Industry with Industry Yellow Pages*
by R. R. Bowker Staff (R. R. Bowker)
630 Central Avenue, New Providence, NJ 07974
888-269-5372; e-mail: info@bowker.com

Making It in Book Publishing
by Leonard Mogel (IDG Books Worldwide, Inc.)
919 E. Hillsdale Boulevard, Suite 400, Foster City, CA 94404-2112
800-762-2974

Marketing Strategies for Writers
by Michael H. Sedge (Allworth Press)
10 East 23rd Street, Suite 210, New York, NY 10010
212-777-8395

Merriam-Webster's Manual for Writers and Editors
Merriam Webster
47 Federal Street, PO Box 281, Springfield, MA 01102
413-734-3134; fax: 413-731-5979; e-mail: mwsales@m-w.com

Negotiating a Book Contract: A Guide for Authors, Agents and Lawyers
by Mark L. Levine (Moyer Bell Ltd.)
Kymbolde Way, Wakefield, RI 02879
401-789-0074, 888-789-1945; fax: 401-789-3793; e-mail: sales@moyerbell.com

*Nonfiction Book Proposals Anybody Can Write:
How to Get a Contract and Advance Before Writing Your Book*
by Elizabeth Lyon (Blue Heron Pub)
1234 SW Stark Street, Suite 1, Portland, OR 97205
fax: 503-223-9474; e-mail: bhp@teleport.com

Poet Power! The Practical Poet's Complete Guide to Getting Published (and Self-Published)
by Thomas A. Williams (Venture Press)
PO Box 1582, Davis, CA 95617-1582
530-756-2309; fax: 530-756-4790; e-mail: wmaster@ggweb.com

The Portable Writers' Conference: Your Guide to Getting and Staying Published
by Stephen Blake Mettee, Editor (Word Dancer Press)
1831 Industrial Way, #101, Sanger, CA 93657
voice/fax: 559-876-2170; e-mail: sbm12@csufresno.edu

Publish to Win: Smart Strategies to Sell More Books
by Jerrold R. Jenkins, Anne M. Stanton (Rhodes & Easton)
35 Clark Hill Road, Prospect, CT 06712-1011
203-758-3661; fax: 603-853-5420; e-mail: biopub@aol.com

The Screenwriter's Bible: A Complete Guide to Writing, Formatting, and Selling Your Script
by David Trottier (Silman-James Press)
3624 Shannon Road, Los Angeles, CA 90027
323-661-9922; fax: 323-661-9933

Secrets of a Freelance Writer: How to Make $85,000 a Year
by Robert W. Bly (Henry Holt)
115 West 18th Street, New York, NY 10011
212-886-9200; fax: 212-633-0748; e-mail: publicity@hholt.com

Self-Editing for Fiction Writers
by Renni Browne, Dave King (HarperCollins)
10 East 53rd Street, New York, NY 10022-5299
212-207-7000

A Simple Guide to Marketing Your Book:
What an Author and Publisher Can Do to Sell More Books
by Mark Ortman (Wise Owl Books)
24425 Fieldmont Place, West Hills, CA 91307
818-716-9076; e-mail: apweis@pacbell.net

The Shortest Distance Between You and a Published Book
by Susan Page (Broadway Books)
841 Broadway, New York, NY 10003
212-614-7850

Telling Lies for Fun & Profit
by Lawrence Block, introduction by Sue Grafton (William Morrow & Company)
1350 Avenue of the Americas, New York, NY 10019
212-261-6500

This Business of Books: A Complete Overview of the Industry from Concept Through Sales
by Claudia Suzanne, Carol Amato & Thelma Sansoucie, Editors (Wambtac)
17300 17th Street, #J276, Tustin, CA 92780
800-641-3936; fax: 714-954-0793; e-mail: bookdoc@wambtac

This Business of Publishing: An Insider's View of Current Trends and Tactics
by Richard Curtis (Allworth Press)
10 East 23rd Street, Suite 210, New York, NY 10010
212-777-8395

What Book Publishers Won't Tell You:
A Literary Agent's Guide to the Secrets of Getting Published
by Bill Adler (Citadel Press)
3300 Business Drive, Sacramento, CA 95820
fax: 916-732-2070

The Whole Picture: Strategies for Screenwriting Success in the New Hollywood
by Richard Walter (Plume)
375 Hudson Street, New York, NY 10014
212-366-2000

Writer Tells All: Insider Secrets to Getting Your Book Published
by Robert Masello (Owl Books)
115 West 18th Street, New York, NY 10010
212-886-9200

Write the Perfect Book Proposal: 10 Proposals That Sold and Why
by Jeff Herman, Deborah M. Adams (John Wiley & Sons)
605 Third Avenue, New York, NY 10158-0012
212-850-6000; fax: 212-850-6088
e-mail: info@wiley.com

A Writer's Guide to Overcoming Rejection:
A Practical Sales Course for the As Yet Unpublished
by Edward Baker (Summerdale Publishing Ltd.)

The Writer's Handbook (annual)
by Elfrieda Abbe, editor (The Writer Books)
21027 Crossroads Circle, PO Box 1612, Waukesha, WI 53187
800-533-6644

Writer's International Guide to Book Editors, Publishers, and Literary Agents: Make the Whole English-Speaking Publishing World Yours with This One-of-a-Kind Guide
by Jeff Herman (Prima Publishing)
3000 Lava Ridge Court. Roseville, CA 95661

The Everything Get Published Book
By Peter Rubie (Adams Media)

The Writer's Legal Companion: The Complete Handbook for the Working Writer
by Brad Bunnin, Peter Beren (Perseus Press)
11 Cambridge Center, Cambridge, MA 02142
e-mail: info@perseuspublishing.com

The Writer's Legal Guide (2nd ed.)
by Tad Crawford, Tony Lyons (Allworth Press)
10 East 23rd Street, Suite 210, New York, NY 10010
212-777-8395

The Writer's Little Instruction Book: 385 Secrets for Writing Well and Getting Published
by Paul Raymond Martin, Polly Keener (Writer's World Press)
35 N. Chillecothe Road, Suite D, Aurora, OH 44202
330-562-6667; fax: 330-562-1216; e-mail: Writersworld@juno.com

The Writer's Market Companion
by Joe Feiertag, Mary Carmen Cupito (Writer's Digest Books)
1507 Dana Avenue, Cincinnati, OH 45207
513-531-2222; fax: 531-531-4744

Writer's & Illustrator's Guide to Children's Book Publishers and Agents
by Ellen R. Shapiro (Prima Publishing)
3000 Lava Ridge Court, Roseville, CA 95661

Writing Down the Bones: Freeing the Writer Within
by Natalie Goldberg (Shambhala Publications)
PO Box 308, Boston, MA 02117
617-424-0030; fax: 617-236-1563

Writing Successful Self-Help and How-To Books
by Jean Marie Stine (John Wiley & Sons)
605 Third Avenue, New York, NY 10158-0012
212-850-6000; fax: 212-850-6088; e-mail: info@wiley.com

Writing the Breakout Novel
By Donald Maass (Writer's Digest Books)

Writing the Nonfiction Book
by Eva Shaw, Ph.D. (Rodgers & Nelsen Publishing Company)
PO Box 700, Loveland, CO 80537
970-593-9557

You Can Make It Big Writing Books:
A Top Agent Shows How to Develop a Million-Dollar Bestseller
by Jeff Herman, Deborah Levine Herman, Julia DeVillers (Prima Publishing)
3000 Lava Ridge Court, Roseville, CA 95661

Your Novel Proposal: From Creation to Contract: The Complete Guide to
Writing Query Letters, Synopses and Proposals for Agents and Editors
by Blythe Camenson (Writer's Digest Books)
1507 Dana Avenue, Cincinnati, OH 45207
513-531-2222; fax: 513-531-4744

E-PUBLISHING RESOURCES

A Cheap and Easy Guide to Self-Publishing E-Books
by Wayne F. Perkins (1st Books Library)
2595 Vernal Pike, Bloomington, IN 47404
800-839-8640; fax: 812-339-6554
outside USA and Canada: 812-339-6000

The Columbia Guide to Digital Publishing
by William E. Kasdorf (Columbia University Press)

Electronic Books and Epublishing: A Practical Guide for Authors
by Harold Henke (Springer Verlag)

Electronic Publishing: Avoiding the Output Blues
by Taz Tally (Prentice Hall)

Electronic Publishing: The Definitive Guide
by Karen S. Wiesner (Avid Press)
5470 Red Fox Drive, Brighton, MI 48114
810-801-1177; e-mail: cgs@avidpress.com

ePublishing for Dummies
by Victoria Rosenborg (Hungry Minds, Inc.)
909 Third Avenue, New York, NY 10022

*The Freelance Writer's E-Publishing Guidebook: 25+ E-Publishing Home-Based
Online Writing Businesses to Start for Freelancers*
by Anne Hart (iUniverse.com)
800-376-1736; e-mail: publisher@iuniverse.com

How to Get Your E-Book Published
by Richard Curtis, W. T. Quick (Writer's Digest Books)
1507 Dana Avenue, Cincinnati, OH 45207
513-531-2222; fax: 513-531-4744

How to Publish and Promote Online
by M. J. Rose, Angela Adair-Hoy (Griffin Trade Paperback)
175 Fifth Avenue, New York, NY 10010
212-647-5151

Official Adobe Electronic Publishing Guide
by Adobe Creative Team (Adobe Press)
345 Park Avenue, San Jose, CA 95110-2704
408-536-6000

Real ePublishing, Really Publishing!: How to Create Digital Books by and for All Ages
by Mark W.F. Condon and Michael McGuffee (Heinemann)

*U-Publish.Com: How Individual Writers Can Now Effectively Compete
with the Giants of Publishing*
by Dan Snow, Danny O. Poynter (Unlimited Publishing)
PO Box 3007, Bloomington, IN 47402
e-mail: publish@unlimitedpublishing.com

*What Every Writer *Must* Know About E-Publishing*
by Emily A. Vander Veer (Emily A. Vander Veer)
e-mail: emily@emilyv.com

Writing.Com: Creative Internet Strategies to Advance Your Writing Career
by Moira Anderson Allen (Allworth Press)
10 East 23rd Street, Suite 210, New York, NY 10010
212-777-8395

Your Guide to E-book Publishing Success: How to Create and Profitably Sell Your Writing on the Internet
by James Dillehay (Warm Snow Publishers)
50 Sufi Road, PO Box 75, Torreon, NM 87061
e-mail: service@craftmarketer.com

GLOSSARY

GLOSSARY

abstract A brief sequential profile of chapters in a nonfiction book proposal (also called a synopsis); a point-by-point summary of an article or essay. In academic and technical journals, abstracts often appear with (and may serve to preface) the articles themselves.

adaptation A rewrite or reworking of a piece for another medium, such as the adaptation of a novel for the screen. (*See also* **screenplay**.)

advance Money paid (usually in installments) to an author by a publisher prior to publication. The advance is paid against royalties: If an author is given a $5,000 advance, for instance, the author will collect royalties only after the royalty moneys due exceed $5,000. A good contract protects the advance if it should exceed the royalties ultimately due from sales.

advance orders Orders received before a book's official publication date, and sometimes before actual completion of the book's production and manufacture.

agent The person who acts on behalf of the author to handle the sale of the author's literary properties. Good literary agents are as valuable to publishers as they are to writers; they select and present manuscripts appropriate for particular houses or of interest to particular acquisitions editors. Agents are paid on a percentage basis from the moneys due their author clients.

American Booksellers Association (ABA) The major trade organization for retail book-sellers, chain and independent. The annual ABA convention and trade show offers a chance for publishers and distributors to display their wares to the industry at large and provides an incomparable networking forum for booksellers, editors, agents, publicists, and authors.

American Society of Journalists and Authors (ASJA) A membership organization for professional writers. ASJA provides a forum for information exchange among writers and others in the publishing community, as well as networking opportunities. (*See also* **Dial-a-Writer**.)

anthology A collection of stories, poems, essays and/or selections from larger works (and so forth), usually carrying a unifying theme or concept; these selections may be written by different authors or by a single author. Anthologies are compiled as opposed to written; their editors (as opposed to authors) are responsible for securing the needed reprint rights for the material used, as well as supplying (or providing authors for) pertinent introductory or supplementary material and/or commentary.

attitude A contemporary colloquialism used to describe a characteristic temperament common among individuals who consider themselves superior. Attitude is rarely an esteemed attribute, whether in publishing or elsewhere.

auction Manuscripts a literary agent believes to be hot properties (such as possible best-sellers with strong subsidiary rights potential) will be offered for confidential bidding from multiple publishing houses. Likewise, the reprint, film, and other rights to a successful book may be auctioned off by the original publisher's subsidiary rights department or by the author's agent.

audio books Works produced for distribution on audio media, typically audiotape cassette or audio compact disc (CD). Audio books are usually spoken-word adaptations of works originally created and produced in print; these works sometimes feature the author's own voice; many are given dramatic readings by one or more actors, at times embellished with sound effects.

authorized biography A history of a person's life written with the authorization, cooperation, and, at times, participation of the subject or the subject's heirs.

author's copies/author's discount Author's copies are the free copies of their books the authors receive from the publisher; the exact number is stipulated in the contract, but it is usually at least 10 hardcovers. The author will be able to purchase additional copies of the book (usually at 40% discount from the retail price) and resell them at readings, lectures, and other public engagements. In cases where large quantities of books are bought, author discounts can go as high as 70%.

author tour A series of travel and promotional appearances by an author on behalf of the author's book.

autobiography A history of a person's life written by that same person, or, as is typical, composed conjointly with a collaborative writer ("as told to" or "with"; *see also* **coauthor**; **collaboration**) or ghostwriter. Autobiographies by definition entail the authorization, cooperation, participation, and ultimate approval of the subject.

B

backlist The backlist comprises books published prior to the current season and still in print. Traditionally, at some publishing houses, such backlist titles represent the publisher's cash flow mainstays. Some backlist books continue to sell briskly; some remain bestsellers over several successive seasons; others sell slowly but surely through the years. Although many backlist titles may be difficult to find in bookstores that stock primarily current lists, they can be ordered either through a local bookseller or directly from the publisher.

backmatter Elements of a book that follow the text proper. Backmatter may include the appendix, notes, glossary, bibliography and other references, lists of resources, index, author biography, offerings of the author's and/or publisher's additional books and other related merchandise, and colophon.

bestseller Based on sales or orders by bookstores, wholesalers, and distributors, best-sellers are those titles that move the largest quantities. List of bestselling books can be local (as in metropolitan newspapers), regional (typically in geographically keyed trade or consumer periodicals), or national (as in *USA Today*, *Publishers Weekly*, or the *New York Times*), as well as international. Fiction and nonfiction are usually listed separately, as are hardcover and paperback classifications. Depending on the list's purview, additional industry-sector designations are used (such as how-to/self-improvement, religion and spirituality, business and finance); in addition, bestseller lists can be keyed to particular genre or specialty fields (such as bestseller lists for mysteries, science fiction, or romance novels, and for historical works, biography, or popular science titles)—and virtually any other marketing category at the discretion of whoever issues the bestseller list (for instance African-American interests, lesbian and gay topics, youth market).

bibliography A list of books, articles, and other sources, that have been used in the writing of the text in which the bibliography appears. Complex works may break the bibliography down into discrete subject areas or source categories, such as General History, Military History, War in the Twentieth Century, or Unionism and Pacifism.

binding The materials that hold a book together (including the cover). Bindings are generally denoted as hardcover (featuring heavy cardboard covered with durable cloth and/or paper, and occasionally other materials) or paperback (using a pliable, resilient grade of paper, sometimes infused or laminated with other substances such as plastic). In the days when cloth was used lavishly, hardcover volumes were conventionally known as clothbound; and in the very old days, hardcover bindings sometimes featured tooled leather, silk, precious stones, and gold and silver leaf ornamentation.

biography A history of a person's life. (*See also* **authorized biography**; **autobiography**; **unauthorized biography**.)

blues (or bluelines) Photographic proofs of the printing plates for a book. Blues are reviewed as a means to inspect the set type, layout, and design of the books pages before it goes to press.

blurb A piece of written copy or extracted quotation used for publicity and promotional purposes, as on a flyer, in a catalog, or in an advertisement (*See also* **cover blurbs**).

book club A book club is a book-marketing operation that ships selected titles to subscribing members on a regular basis, sometimes at greatly reduced prices. Sales of a work to book clubs are negotiated through the publisher's subsidiary rights department (in the case of a bestseller or other work that has gained acclaim, these rights can be auctioned off). Terms vary, but the split of royalties between author and publisher is often 50%/50%. Book club sales are seen as blessed events by author, agent, and publisher alike.

book contract A legally binding document between author and publisher that sets the terms for the advance, royalties, subsidiary rights, advertising, promotion, publicity—plus a host of other contingencies and responsibilities. Writers should therefore be thoroughly familiar with the concepts and terminology of the standard book-publishing contract.

book distribution The method of getting books from the publisher's warehouse into the reader's hands. Distribution is traditionally through bookstores but can include such means as telemarketing and mail-order sales, as well as sales through a variety of special-interest outlets such as health-food or New Age venues, sports and fitness emporiums, or sex shops. Publishers use their own sales forces as well as independent salespeople, wholesalers, and distributors. Many large and some small publishers distribute for other publishers, which can be a good source of income. A publisher's distribution network is extremely important, because it not only makes possible the vast sales of a bestseller but also affects the visibility of the publisher's entire list of books.

book jacket (*See* **dust jacket.**)

book producer or **book packager** An individual or company that can assume many of the roles in the publishing process. A book packager or producer may conceive the idea for a book (most often nonfiction) or series, bring together the professionals (including the writer) needed to produce the book(s), sell the individual manuscript or series project to a publisher, take the project through to manufactured product—or perform any selection of those functions, as commissioned by the publisher or other client (such as a corporation producing a corporate history as a premium or giveaway for employees and customers). The book producer may negotiate separate contracts with the publisher and with the writers, editors, and illustrators who contribute to the book.

book review A critical appraisal of a book (often reflecting a reviewer's personal opinion or recommendation) that evaluates such aspects as organization and writing style, possible market appeal, and cultural, political, or literary significance. Before the public reads book reviews in the local and national print media, important reviews have been published in such respected book-trade journals as *Publishers Weekly*, *Kirkus Reviews*, *Library Journal*, and *Booklist*. A gushing review from one of these journals will encourage booksellers to order the book; copies of these raves will be used for promotion and publicity purposes by the publisher and will encourage other book reviewers nationwide to review the book.

Books in Print Listings, published by R. R. Bowker, of books currently in print; these yearly volumes (along with periodic supplements such as Forthcoming Books in Print) provide ordering information, including titles, authors, ISBN numbers, prices, whether the book is available in hardcover or paperback, and publisher names. Intended for use by the book trade, Books in Print is also of great value to writers who are researching and market-researching their projects. Listings are provided alphabetically by author, title, and subject area.

bound galleys Copies of uncorrected typesetter's page proofs or printouts of electronically produced mechanicals that are bound together as advance copies of the book (compare **galleys**). Bound galleys are sent to trade journals (*see* **book review**) as well as to a limited number of reviewers who work under long lead times.

bulk sales The sale at a set discount of many copies of a single title (the greater the number of books, the larger the discount).

byline The name of the author of a given piece, indicating credit for having written a book or article. Ghostwriters, by definition, do not receive bylines.

C

casing Alternate term for binding (*see* **binding**).

category fiction Also known as genre fiction. Category fiction falls into an established (or newly originated) marketing category (which can then be subdivided for more precise target marketing). Fiction categories include action-adventure (with such further designations as military, paramilitary, law enforcement, romantic, and martial arts); crime novels (with points of view that range from deadpan cool to visionary, including humorous capers as well as gritty urban sagas); mysteries or detective fiction (hard-boiled, soft-boiled, procedurals, cozies); romances (including historicals as well as contemporaries); horror (supernatural, psychological, or technological); thrillers (tales of espionage, crisis, and the chase), Westerns, science fiction, and fantasy. (*See also* **fantasy**, **horror**, **romance fiction**, **science fiction**, **suspense fiction**, and **thriller**.)

CD or **computer CD** High-capacity compact discs for use by readers via computer technology. CD-ROM is a particular variety; the term is somewhere between an acronym and an abbreviation (CD-ROMs are compact computer discs with read-only memory, meaning the reader is not able to modify or duplicate the contents). Many CDs are issued with a variety of audiovisual as well as textual components. When produced by publishers, these are sometimes characterized as books in electronic format. (*See also* **multimedia**.)

children's books Books for children. As defined by the book-publishing industry, children are generally readers aged 17 and younger; many houses adhere to a fine but firm editorial distinction between titles intended for younger readers (under 12) and young adults (generally aged 12 to 17). Children's books (also called juveniles) are produced according to a number of categories (often typified by age ranges), each with particular requisites regarding such elements as readability ratings, length, and inclusion of graphic elements. Picture books are often for very young readers, with such designations as toddlers (who do not themselves read) and preschoolers (who may have some reading ability). Other classifications include easy storybooks (for younger school children), middle-grade books (for elementary to junior high school students), and young adult (abbreviated YA, for readers through age 17).

coauthor One who shares authorship of a work. Coauthors all have bylines. Coauthors share royalties based on their contributions to the book. (Compare **ghostwriter**.)

collaboration Writers can collaborate with professionals in any number of fields. Often a writer can collaborate in order to produce books outside the writer's own areas of formally credentialed expertise (for example, a writer with an interest in exercise and nutrition may collaborate with a sports doctor on a health book). Though the writer may be billed as a coauthor (*see* **coauthor**), the writer does not necessarily receive a byline (in which case the writer is a **ghostwriter**). Royalties are shared, based on respective contributions to the book (including expertise or promotional abilities as well as the actual writing).

colophon Strictly speaking, a colophon is a publisher's logo; in bookmaking, the term may also refer to a listing of the materials used, as well as credits for the design, composition, and production of the book. Such colophons are sometimes included in the backmatter or as part of the copyright page.

commercial fiction Fiction written to appeal to as broad-based a readership as possible.

concept A general statement of the idea behind a book.

cool A modern colloquial expression that indicates satisfaction or approval, or may signify the maintenance of calm within a whirlwind. A fat contract for a new author is definitely cool.

cooperative advertising (co-op) An agreement between a publisher and a bookstore. The publisher's book is featured in an ad for the bookstore (sometimes in conjunction with an author appearance or other special book promotion); the publisher contributes to the cost of the ad, which is billed at a lower (retail advertising) rate.

copublishing Joint publishing of a book, usually by a publisher and another corporate entity such as a foundation, a museum, or a smaller publisher. An author can copublish with the publisher by sharing the costs and decision making and, ultimately, the profits.

copyeditor An editor, responsible for the final polishing of a manuscript, who reads primarily in terms of appropriate word usage and grammatical expression, with an eye toward clarity and coherence of the material as presented, factual errors and inconsistencies, spelling, and punctuation. (*See also* **editor**.)

copyright The legal proprietary right to reproduce, have reproduced, publish, and sell copies of literary, musical, and other artistic works. The rights to literary properties reside in the author from the time the work is produced—regardless of whether a formal copyright registration is obtained. However, for legal recourse in the event of plagiarism or other infringement, the work must be registered with the U.S. Copyright Office, and all copies of the work must bear the copyright notice. (*See also* **work-for-hire**.)

cover blurbs Favorable quotes from other writers, celebrities, or experts in a book's subject area, which appear on the dust jacket and are used to enhance the book's point-of-purchase appeal to the potential book-buying public.

crash Coarse gauze fabric used in bookbinding to strengthen the spine and joints of a book.

curriculum vitae (abbreviated **c.v.**) Latin expression meaning "course of life"—in other words, the résumé.

D

deadline In book publishing, this not-so-subtle synonym is used for the author's due date for delivery of the completed manuscript to the publisher. The deadline can be as much as a full year before official publication date, unless the book is being produced quickly to coincide with or follow up a particular event.

delivery Submission of the completed manuscript to the editor or publisher.

Dial-a-Writer Members of the American Society of Journalists and Authors may be listed with the organization's project-referral service, Dial-a-Writer, which can provide accomplished writers in most specialty fields and subjects.

direct marketing Advertising that involves a "direct response" (which is an equivalent term) from a consumer—for instance, an order form or coupon in a book-review section or in the back of a book or mailings (direct-mail advertising) to a group presumed to hold a special interest in a particular book.

display titles Books that are produced to be eye-catching to the casual shopper in a bookstore setting. Often rich with flamboyant cover art, these publications are intended to pique bookbuyer excitement about the store's stock in general. Many display titles are stacked on their own freestanding racks; sometimes broad tables are laden with these items. A book shelved with its front cover showing on racks along with diverse other titles is technically a display title. Promotional or **premium** titles are likely to be display items, as are massmarket paperbacks and hardbacks with enormous bestseller potential. (Check your local bookstore and find a copy of this edition of this *Guide*—if not already racked in "display" manner, please adjust the bookshelf so that the front cover is displayed poster-like to catch the browser's eye—that's what we do routinely.)

distributor An agent or business that buys books from a publisher to resell, at a higher cost, to wholesalers, retailers, or individuals. Distribution houses are often excellent marketing enterprises, with their own roster of sales representatives, publicity and promotion personnel, and house catalogs. Skillful use of distribution networks can give a small publisher considerable national visibility.

dramatic rights Legal permission to adapt a work for the stage. These rights initially belong to the author but can be sold or assigned to another party by the author.

dust jacket (also **dustcover** or **book jacket**) The wrapper that covers the binding of hardcover books, designed especially for the book by either the publisher's art department or a freelance artist. Dust jackets were originally conceived to protect the book during shipping, but now their function is primarily promotional—to entice the browser to actually reach out and pick up the volume (and maybe even open it up for a taste before buying) by means of attractive graphics and sizzling promotional copy.

dust-jacket copy Descriptions of books printed on the dust-jacket flaps. Dust-jacket copy may be written by the book's editor but is often either recast or written by in-house copywriters or freelance specialists. Editors send advance copies (*see also* **bound galleys**) to other writers, experts, and celebrities to solicit quotable praise that will also appear on the jacket. (*See also* **cover blurb**.)

E

editor Editorial responsibilities and titles vary from house to house (often being less strictly defined in smaller houses). In general, the duties of the editor-in-chief or executive editor are primarily administrative: managing personnel, scheduling, budgeting, and defining the editorial personality of the firm or imprint. Senior editors and acquisitions editors acquire manuscripts (and authors), conceive project ideas and find writers to carry them out, and may oversee the writing and rewriting of manuscripts. Managing editors have editorial and production responsibilities, coordinating and scheduling the book through the various phases of production. Associate and assistant editors edit; they are involved in much of the rewriting and reshaping of the manuscript and may also have acquisitions duties. Copyeditors read the manuscript and style its punctuation, grammar, spelling, headings and subheadings, and so forth. Editorial assistants, laden with extensive clerical duties and general office work, perform some editorial duties as well—often as springboards to senior editorial positions.

Editorial Freelancers Association (EFA)   This organization of independent professionals offers a referral service, through both its annotated membership directory and its job phone line, as a means for authors and publishers to connect with writers, collaborators, researchers, and a wide range of editorial experts covering virtually all general and specialist fields.

el-hi   Books for elementary and/or high schools.

endnotes   Explanatory notes and/or source citations that appear either at the end of individual chapters or at the end of a book's text; used primarily in scholarly or academically oriented works.

epilogue   The final segment of a book, which comes "after the end." In both fiction and nonfiction, an epilogue offers commentary or further information but does not bear directly on the book's central design.

F

fantasy   Fantasy is fiction that features elements of magic, wizardry, supernatural feats, and entities that suspend conventions of realism in the literary arts. Fantasy can resemble prose versions of epics and rhymes or it may be informed by mythic cycles or folkloric material derived from cultures worldwide. Fantasy fiction may be guided primarily by the author's own distinctive imagery and personalized archetypes. Fantasies that involve heroic-erotic roundelays of the death-dance are often referred to as the sword-and-sorcery subgenre.

film rights   Like **dramatic rights**, these belong to the author, who may sell or option them to someone in the film industry—a producer or director, for example (or sometimes a specialist broker of such properties)—who will then try to gather the other professionals and secure the financial backing needed to convert the book into a film. (*See also* **screenplay**.)

footbands   (*See* **headbands**.)

footnotes   Explanatory notes and/or source citations that appear at the bottom of a page. Footnotes are rare in general-interest books, the preferred style being either to work such information into the text or to list informational sources in the bibliography.

foreign agents   Persons who work with their United States counterparts to acquire rights for books from the U.S. for publication abroad. They can also represent U.S. publishers directly.

foreign market   Any foreign entity—a publisher, broadcast medium, etc.—in a position to buy rights. Authors share royalties with whoever negotiates the deal or keep 100% if they do their own negotiating.

foreign rights   Translation or reprint rights that can be sold abroad. Foreign rights belong to the author but can be sold either country-by-country or en masse as world rights. Often the U.S. publisher will own world rights, and the author will be entitled to anywhere from 50% to 85% of these revenues.

foreword An introductory piece written by the author or by an expert in the given field (*see* **introduction**). A foreword by a celebrity or well-respected authority is a strong selling point for a prospective author or, after publication, for the book itself.

Frankfurt Book Fair The largest international publishing exhibition—with five hundred years of tradition behind it. The fair takes place every October in Frankfurt, Germany. Thousands of publishers, agents, and writers from all over the world negotiate, network, and buy and sell rights.

Freedom of Information Act Ensures the protection of the public's right to access public records—except in cases violating the right to privacy, national security, or certain other instances. A related law, the Government in the Sunshine Act, stipulates that certain government agencies announce and open their meetings to the public.

freight passthrough The bookseller's freight cost (the cost of getting the book from the publisher to the bookseller). It is added to the basic invoice price charged the bookseller by the publisher.

frontlist New titles published in a given season by a publisher. Frontlist titles customarily receive priority exposure in the front of the sales catalog—as opposed to backlist titles (usually found at the back of the catalog), which are previously published titles still in print.

frontmatter The frontmatter of a book includes the elements that precede the text of the work, such as the title page, copyright page, dedication, epigraph, table of contents, foreword, preface, acknowledgments, and introduction.

fulfillment house A firm commissioned to fulfill orders for a publisher—services may include warehousing, shipping, receiving returns, and mail-order and direct-marketing functions. Although more common for magazine publishers, fulfillment houses also serve book publishers.

G

galleys Printer's proofs (or copies of proofs) on sheets of paper, or printouts of the electronically produced setup of the book's interior—the author's last chance to check for typos and make (usually minimal) revisions or additions to the copy (*see* **bound galleys**).

genre fiction (*See* **category fiction**.)

ghostwriter A writer without a byline, often without the remuneration and recognition that credited authors receive. Ghostwriters often get flat fees for their work, but even without royalties, experienced ghosts can receive quite respectable sums.

glossary An alphabetical listing of special terms as they are used in a particular subject area, often with more in-depth explanations than would customarily be provided by dictionary definitions.

H

hardcover Books bound in a format that uses thick, sturdy, relatively stiff binding boards and a cover composed (usually) of a cloth spine and finished binding paper. Hardcover books are conventionally wrapped in a dust jacket. (*See also* **binding; dust jacket.**)

headbands Thin strips of cloth (often colored or patterned) that adorn the top of a book's spine where the signatures are held together. The headbands conceal the glue or other binding materials and are said to offer some protection against accumulation of dust (when properly attached). Such bands, placed at the bottom of the spine, are known as footbands.

hook A term denoting the distinctive concept or theme of a work that sets it apart as being fresh, new, or different from others in its field. A hook can be an author's special point of view, often encapsulated in a catchy or provocative phrase intended to attract or pique the interest of a reader, editor, or agent. One specialized function of a hook is to articulate what might otherwise be seen as dry albeit significant subject matter (academic or scientific topics; number-crunching drudgery such as home bookkeeping) into an exciting, commercially attractive package.

horror The horror classification denotes works that traffic in the bizarre, awful, and scary in order to entertain as well as explicate the darkness at the heart of the reader's soul. Horror subgenres may be typified according to the appearance of were-creatures, vampires, human-induced monsters, or naturally occuring life forms and spirit entities—or absence thereof. Horror fiction traditionally makes imaginative literary use of paranormal phenomena, occult elements, and psychological motifs. (*See* **category fiction; suspense fiction.**)

how-to books An immensely popular category of books ranging from purely instructional (arts and crafts, for example) to motivational (popular psychology, self-awareness, self-improvement, inspirational) to get-rich-quick (such as in real estate or personal investment).

hypertext Works in hypertext are meant to be more than words and other images. These productions (ingrained magnetically on computer diskette or CD) are conceived to take advantage of readers' and writers' propensities to seek out twists in narrative trajectories and to bushwhack from the main path of multifaceted reference topics. Hypertext books incorporate documents, graphics, sounds, and even blank slates upon which readers may compose their own variations on the authored components. The computer's capacities to afford such diversions can bring reader and hypertext literature so close as to gain entry to each other's mind-sets—which is what good books have always done.

I

imprint A separate line of product within a publishing house. Imprints run the gamut of complexity, from those composed of one or two series to those offering full-fledged and diversified lists. Imprints also enjoy different gradations of autonomy from the parent company. An imprint may have its own editorial department (perhaps consisting of as few as one editor), or house acquisitions editors may assign particular titles for release on appropriate specialized imprints. An imprint may publish a certain kind of book (juvenile or paperback or travel books) or have its own personality (such as a literary or contemporary tone). An individual imprint's categories often overlap with other imprints or with the publisher's core list, but some imprints maintain a small-house feel within an otherwise enormous conglomerate. The imprint can offer the distinct advantages of a personalized editorial approach, while availing itself of the larger company's production, publicity, marketing, sales, and advertising resources.

index   An alphabetical directory at the end of a book that references names and subjects discussed in the book and the pages where such mentions can be found.

instant book   A book produced quickly to appear in bookstores as soon as possible after (for instance) a newsworthy event to which it is relevant.

international copyright   Rights secured for countries that are members of the International Copyright Convention (*see* **International Copyright Convention**) and that respect the authority of the international copyright symbol, ©.

International Copyright Convention   Countries that are signatories to the various international copyright treaties. Some treaties are contingent upon certain conditions being met at the time of publication, so an author should, before publication, inquire into a particular country's laws.

introduction   Preliminary remarks pertaining to a piece. Like a foreword, an introduction can be written by the author or an appropriate authority on the subject. If a book has both a foreword and an introduction, the foreword will be written by someone other than the author; the introduction will be more closely tied to the text and will be written by the book's author. (*See also* **foreword**.)

ISBN (International Standard Book Number)   A 10-digit number that is linked to and identifies the title and publisher of a book. It is used for ordering and cataloging books and appears on all dust jackets, on the back cover of the book, and on the copyright page.

ISSN (International Standard Serial Number)   An 8-digit cataloging and ordering number that identifies all U.S. and foreign periodicals.

J

juveniles   (*See* **children's books**.)

K

kill fee   A fee paid by a magazine when it cancels a commissioned article. The fee is only a certain percentage of the agreed-on payment for the assignment (no more than 50%). Not all publishers pay kill fees; a writer should make sure to formalize such an arrangement in advance. Kill fees are sometimes involved in work-for-hire projects in book publishing.

L

lead The crucial first few sentences, phrases, or words of anything—be it a query letter, book proposal, novel, news release, advertisement, or sales tip sheet. A successful lead immediately hooks the reader, consumer, editor, or agent.

lead title A frontlist book featured by the publisher during a given season—one the publisher believes should do extremely well commercially. Lead titles are usually those given the publisher's maximum promotional push.

letterhead Business stationery and envelopes imprinted with the company's (or, in such a case, the writer's) name, address, and logo—a convenience as well as an impressive asset for a freelance writer.

letterpress A form of printing in which set type is inked, then impressed directly onto the printing surface. Now used primarily for limited-run books-as-fine-art projects. (*See also* **offset**.)

libel Defamation of an individual or individuals in a published work, with malice aforethought. In litigation, the falsity of the libelous statements or representations, as well as the intention of malice, has to be proved for there to be libel; in addition, financial damages to the parties so libeled must be incurred as a result of the material in question for there to be an assessment of the amount of damages to be awarded to a claimant. This is contrasted to slander, which is defamation through the spoken word.

Library of Congress (LOC) The largest library in the world is in Washington, D.C. As part of its many services, the LOC will supply a writer with up-to-date sources and bibliographies in all fields, from arts and humanities to science and technology. For details, write to the Library of Congress, Central Services Division, Washington, DC 20540.

Library of Congress Catalog Card Number An identifying number issued by the Library of Congress to books it has accepted for its collection. The publication of those books, which are submitted by the publisher, are announced by the Library of Congress to libraries, which use Library of Congress numbers for their own ordering and cataloging purposes.

Literary Market Place (LMP) An annual directory of the publishing industry that contains a comprehensive list of publishers, alphabetically and by category, with their addresses, phone numbers, some personnel, and the types of books they publish. Also included are various publishing-allied listings, such as literary agencies, writer's conferences and competitions, and editorial and distribution services. *LMP* is published by R. R. Bowker and is available in most public libraries.

literature Written works of fiction and nonfiction in which compositional excellence and advancement in the art of writing are higher priorities than are considerations of profit or commercial appeal.

logo A company or product identifier—for example, a representation of a company's initials or a drawing that is the exclusive property of that company. In publishing usage, a virtual equivalent to the trademark.

M

mainstream fiction   Nongenre fiction, excluding literary or avant-garde fiction, that appeals to a general readership.

marketing plan   The entire strategy for selling a book: its publicity, promotion, sales, and advertising.

mass-market paperback   Less-expensive smaller-format paperbacks that are sold from racks (in such venues as supermarkets, variety stores, drugstores, and specialty shops) as well as in bookstores. Also referred to as rack (or rack-sized) editions.

mechanicals   Typeset copy and art mounted on boards to be photocopied and printed. Also referred to as pasteups.

midlist books   Generally mainstream fiction and nonfiction books that traditionally formed the bulk of a publisher's list (nowadays often by default rather than intent). Midlist books are expected to be commercially viable but not explosive bestsellers—nor are they viewed as distinguished, critically respected books that can be scheduled for small print runs and aimed at select readerships. Agents may view such projects as a poor return for the effort, since they generally garner a low-end advance; editors and publishers (especially the sales force) may decry midlist works as being hard to market; prospective readers often find midlist books hard to buy in bookstores (they have short shelf lives). Hint for writers: Don't present your work as a midlist item.

multimedia   Presentations of sound and light, words in magnetically graven image—and any known combination thereof as well as nuances yet to come. Though computer CD is the dominant wrapper for these works, technological innovation is the hallmark of the electronic-publishing arena, and new formats will expand the creative and market potential. Multimedia books are publishing events; their advent suggests alternative avenues for authors as well as adaptational tie-ins with the world of print. Meanwhile, please stay tuned for virtual reality, artificial intelligence, and electronic end-user distribution of product.

multiple contract   A book contract that includes a provisional agreement for a future book or books. (*See also* **option clause/right of first refusal**.)

mystery stories or **mysteries**   (*See* **suspense fiction**.)

N

net receipts   The amount of money a publisher actually receives for sales of a book: the retail price minus the bookseller's discount and/or other discount. The number of returned copies is factored in, bringing down even further the net amount received per book. Royalties are sometimes figured on these lower amounts rather than on the retail price of the book.

New Age An eclectic category that encompasses health, medicine, philosophy, religion, and the occult—presented from an alternative or multicultural perspective. Although the term has achieved currency relatively recently, some publishers have been producing serious books in these categories for decades.

novella A work of fiction falling in length between a short story and a novel.

O

offset (offset lithography) A printing process that involves the transfer of wet ink from a (usually photosensitized) printing plate onto an intermediate surface (such as a rubber-coated cylinder) and then onto the paper. For commercial purposes, this method has replaced letterpress, whereby books were printed via direct impression of inked type on paper.

option clause/right of first refusal In a book contract, a clause that stipulates that the publisher will have the exclusive right to consider and make an offer for the author's next book. However, the publisher is under no obligation to publish the book, and in most variations of the clause the author may, under certain circumstances, opt for publication elsewhere. (*See also* **multiple contract.**)

outline Used for both a book proposal and the actual writing and structuring of a book, an outline is a hierarchical listing of topics that provides the writer (and the proposal reader) with an overview of the ideas in a book in the order in which they are to be presented.

out-of-print books Books no longer available from the publisher; rights usually revert to the author.

P

package The package is the actual book; the physical product.

packager (*See* **book producer.**)

page proof The final typeset copy of the book, in page-layout form, before printing.

paperback Books bound with a flexible, stress-resistant, paper covering material. (*See also* **binding.**)

paperback originals Books published, generally, in paperback editions only; sometimes the term refers to those books published simultaneously in hardcover and paperback. These books are often mass-market genre fiction (romances, Westerns, Gothics, mysteries, horror, and so forth) as well as contemporary literary fiction, cookbooks, humor, career books, self-improvement, and how-to books—the categories continue to expand.

pasteups (*See* **mechanicals.**)

permissions The right to quote or reprint published material, obtained by the author from the copyright holder.

picture book A copiously illustrated book, often with very simple, limited text, intended for preschoolers and very young children.

plagiarism The false presentation of someone else's writing as one's own. In the case of copyrighted work, plagiarism is illegal.

preface An element of a book's frontmatter. In the preface, the author may discuss the purpose behind the format of the book, the type of research upon which it is based, its genesis, or underlying philosophy.

premium Books sold at a reduced price as part of a special promotion. Premiums can thus be sold to a bookseller, who in turn sells them to the bookbuyer (as with a line of modestly priced art books). Alternately, such books may be produced as part of a broader marketing package. For instance, an organization may acquire a number of books (such as its own corporate history or biography of its founder) for use in personnel training and as giveaways to clients; or a nutrition/recipe book may be displayed along with a company's diet foods in non-bookstore outlets. (*See also* **special sales**.)

press agent (*See* **publicist**.)

press kit A promotional package that includes a press release, tip sheet, author biography and photograph, reviews, and other pertinent information. The press kit can be put together by the publisher's publicity department or an independent publicist and sent with a review copy of the book to potential reviewers and to media professionals responsible for booking author appearances.

price There are several prices pertaining to a single book: The invoice price is the amount the publisher charges the bookseller; the retail, cover, or list price is what the consumer pays.

printer's error (**PE**) A typographical error made by the printer or typesetting facility, not by the publisher's staff. PEs are corrected at the printer's expense.

printing plate A surface that bears a reproduction of the set type and artwork of a book, from which the pages are printed.

producer (*See* **book producer**.)

proposal A detailed presentation of the book's concept, used to gain the interest and services of an agent and to sell the project to a publisher.

public domain Material that is uncopyrighted, whose copyright has expired, or that is uncopyrightable. The last includes government publications, jokes, titles—and, it should be remembered, ideas.

publication date (or **pub date**) A book's official date of publication, customarily set by the publisher to fall 6 weeks after completed bound books are delivered to the warehouse. The publication date is used to focus the promotional activities on behalf of the title—so that books will have had time to be ordered, shipped, and be available in the stores to coincide with the appearance of advertising and publicity.

publicist (**press agent**) The publicity professional who handles the press releases for new books and arranges the author's publicity tours and other promotional venues (such as interviews, speaking engagements, and book signings).

publisher's catalog   A seasonal sales catalog that lists and describes a publisher's new books; it is sent to all potential buyers, including individuals who request one. Catalogs range from the basic to the glitzy and often include information on the author, on print quantity, and on the amount of money slated to be spent on publicity and promotion.

publisher's discount   The percentage by which a publisher discounts the retail price of a book to a bookseller, often based in part on the number of copies purchased.

Publishers' Trade List Annual   A collection of current and backlist catalogs arranged alphabetically by publisher, available in many libraries.

Publishers Weekly (PW)   The publishing industry's chief trade journal. *PW* carries announcements of upcoming books, respected book reviews, interviews with authors and publishing-industry professionals, special reports on various book categories, and trade news (such as mergers, rights sales, and personnel changes).

Q

quality   In publishing parlance, the word "quality" in reference to a book category (such as quality fiction) or format (quality paperback) is a term of art—individual works or lines so described are presented as outstanding products.

query letter   A brief written presentation to an agent or editor designed to pitch both the writer and the book idea.

R

remainders   Unsold book stock. Remainders can include titles that have not sold as well as anticipated, in addition to unsold copies of later printings of bestsellers. These volumes are often remaindered—that is, remaining stock is purchased from the publisher at a huge discount and resold to the public.

reprint   A subsequent edition of material that is already in print, especially publication in a different format—the paperback reprint of a hardcover, for example.

résumé   A summary of an individual's career experience and education. When a résumé is sent to prospective agents or publishers, it should contain the author's vital publishing credits, specialty credentials, and pertinent personal experience. Also referred to as the curriculum vitae or, more simply, vita.

returns   Unsold books returned to a publisher by a bookstore, for which the store may receive full or partial credit (depending on the publisher's policy, the age of the book, and so on).

reversion-of-rights clause   In the book contract, a clause that states that if the book goes out of print or the publisher fails to reprint the book within a stipulated length of time, all rights revert to the author.

review copy   A free copy of a (usually) new book sent to electronic and print media that review books for their audiences.

romance fiction or **romance novels**   Modern or period love stories, always with happy endings, which range from the tepid to the torrid. Except for certain erotic specialty lines, romances do not feature graphic sex. Often mistakenly pigeonholed by those who do not read them, romances and romance writers have been influential in the movement away from passive and coddled female fictional characters to the strong, active modern woman in a tale that reflects areas of topical social concern.

royalty   The percentage of the retail cost of a book that is paid to the author for each copy sold after the author's advance has been recouped. Some publishers structure royalties as a percentage payment against net receipts.

S

sales conference   A meeting of a publisher's editorial and sales departments and senior promotion and publicity staff members. A sales conference covers the upcoming season's new books, and marketing strategies are discussed. Sometimes sales conferences are the basis upon which proposed titles are bought or not.

sales representative (sales rep)   A member of the publisher's sales force or an independent contractor who, armed with a book catalog and order forms, visits bookstores in a certain territory to sell books to retailers.

SASE (self-addressed stamped envelope)   It is customary for an author to enclose SASEs with query letters, with proposals, and with manuscript submissions. Many editors and agents do not reply if a writer has neglected to enclose an SASE with correspondence or submitted materials.

satisfactory clause   In book contracts, a publisher will reserve the right to refuse publication of a manuscript that is not deemed satisfactory. Because the author may be forced to pay back the publisher's advance if the complete work is found to be unsatisfactory, the specific criteria for publisher satisfaction should be set forth in the contract to protect the author.

science fiction   Science fiction includes the hardcore, imaginatively embellished technological/scientific novel as well as fiction that is even slightly futuristic (often with an after-the-holocaust milieu—nuclear, environmental, extraterrestrial, genocidal). An element much valued by editors who acquire for the literary expression of this cross-media genre is the ability of the author to introduce elements that transcend and extend conventional insight.

science fiction/fantasy   A category fiction designation that actually collapses two genres into one (for bookseller-marketing reference, of course—though it drives some devotees of these separate fields of writing nuts). In addition, many editors and publishers specialize in both these genres and thus categorize their interests with catchphrases such as sci-fi/fantasy.

screenplay   A film script—either original or one based on material published previously in another form, such as a television docudrama based on a nonfiction book or a movie thriller based on a suspense novel. (Compare with **teleplay**.)

self-publishing   A publishing project wherein an author pays for the costs of manufacturing and selling his or her own book and retains all money from the book's sale. This is a risky venture but one that can be immensely profitable (especially when combined with an author's speaking engagements or imaginative marketing techniques); in addition, if successful, self-publication can lead to distribution or publication by a commercial publisher. (Compare with **subsidy publishing**.)

self-syndication   Management by writers or journalists of functions that are otherwise performed by syndicates specializing in such services. In self-syndication, it is the writer who manages copyrights, negotiates fees, and handles sales, billing, and other tasks involved in circulating journalistic pieces through newspapers, magazines, or other periodicals that pick up the author's column or run a series of articles.

serial rights   Reprint rights sold to periodicals. First serial rights include the right to publish the material before anyone else (generally before the book is released, or coinciding with the book's official publication)—either for the U.S., a specific country, or for a wider territory. Second serial rights cover material already published, either in a book or another periodical.

serialization   The reprinting of a book or part of a book in a newspaper or magazine. Serialization before (or perhaps simultaneously with) the publication of the book is called first serial. The first reprint after publication (either as a book or by another periodical) is called second serial.

series   Books published as a group either because of their related subject matter (such as a biographical series on modern artists or on World War II aircraft) and/or single authorship (a set of works by Djuna Barnes, a group of books about science and society, or a series of titles geared to a particular diet-and-fitness program). Special series lines can offer a ready-made niche for an industrious author or compiler/editor who is up to date on a publisher's program and has a brace of pertinent qualifications and/or contacts. In contemporary fiction, some genre works are published in series form (such as family sagas, detective series, fantasy cycles).

shelf life   The amount of time an unsold book remains on the bookstore shelf before the store manager pulls it to make room for newer incoming stock with greater (or at least untested) sales potential.

short story   A brief piece of fiction that is more pointed and more economically detailed as to character, situation, and plot than a novel. Published collections of short stories— whether by one or several authors—often revolve around a single theme, express related outlooks, or comprise variations within a genre.

signature   A group of book pages that have been printed together on one large sheet of paper that is then folded and cut in preparation for being bound, along with the book's other signatures, into the final volume.

simultaneous publication   The issuing at the same time of more than one edition of a work, such as in hardcover and trade paperback. Simultaneous releases can be expanded to include (though rarely) deluxe gift editions of a book as well as mass-market paper versions. Audio versions of books are most often timed to coincide with the release of the first print edition.

simultaneous (or multiple) submissions   The submission of the same material to more than one publisher at the same time. Although simultaneous submission is a common practice, publishers should always be made aware that it is being done. Multiple submissions by an author to several agents is, on the other hand, a practice that is sometimes not regarded with great favor by the agent.

slush pile   The morass of unsolicited manuscripts at a publishing house or literary agency, which may fester indefinitely awaiting (perhaps perfunctory) review. Some publishers or agencies do not maintain slush piles per se—unsolicited manuscripts are slated for instant or eventual return without review (if an SASE is included) or may otherwise be literally or figuratively pitched to the wind. Querying a targeted publisher or agent before submitting a manuscript is an excellent way of avoiding, or at least minimizing the possibility of, such an ignoble fate.

software   Programs that run on a computer. Word-processing software includes programs that enable writers to compose, edit, store, and print material. Professional-quality software packages incorporate such amenities as databases that can feed the results of research electronically into the final manuscript, alphabetization and indexing functions, and capabilities for constructing tables and charts and adding graphics to the body of the manuscript. Software should be appropriate to both the demands of the work at hand and the requirements of the publisher (which may contract for a manuscript suitable for on-disk editing and electronic design, composition, and typesetting).

special sales   Sales of a book to appropriate retailers other than bookstores (for example, wine guides to liquor stores). This classification also includes books sold as premiums (for example, to a convention group or a corporation) or for other promotional purposes. Depending on volume, per-unit costs can be very low, and the book can be custom-designed. (*See also* **premium**.)

spine   That portion of the book's casing (or binding) that backs the bound page signatures and is visible when the volume is aligned on a bookshelf among other volumes.

stamping   In book publishing, the stamp is the impression of ornamental type and images (such as a logo or monogram) on the book's binding. The stamping process involves using a die with a raised or intaglioed surface to apply ink stamping or metallic-leaf stamping.

subsidiary rights   The reprint, serial, movie and television, and audiotape and videotape rights deriving from a book. The division of profits between publisher and author from the sales of these rights is determined through negotiation. In more elaborately commercial projects, further details such as syndication of related articles and licensing of characters may ultimately be involved.

subsidy publishing   A mode of publication wherein the author pays a publishing company to produce his or her work, which may thus appear superficially to have been published conventionally. Subsidy publishing (alias vanity publishing) is generally more expensive than self-publishing, because a successful subsidy house makes a profit on all its contracted functions, charging fees well beyond the publisher's basic costs for production and services.

suspense fiction Fiction within a number of genre categories that emphasize suspense as well as the usual (and sometimes unusual) literary techniques to keep the reader engaged. Suspense fiction encompasses novels of crime and detection (regularly referred to as mysteries. These include English-style cozies, American-style hard-boiled detective stories, dispassionate law-enforcement procedurals, crime stories, action-adventure, espionage novels, technothrillers, tales of psychological suspense, and horror. A celebrated aspect of suspense fiction's popular appeal—one that surely accounts for much of this broad category's sustained market vigor—is the interactive element: The reader may choose to challenge the tale itself by attempting to outwit the author and solve a crime before detectives do, figure out how best to defeat an all-powerful foe before the hero does, or parse out the elements of a conspiracy before the writer reveals the whole story.

syndicated column Material published simultaneously in a number of newspapers or magazines. The author shares the income from syndication with the syndicate that negotiates the sale. (*See also* **self-syndication**.)

syndication rights (*See also* **self-syndication; subsidiary rights**.)

synopsis A summary in paragraph form, rather than in outline format. The synopsis is an important part of a book proposal. For fiction, the synopsis portrays the high points of story line and plot, succinctly and dramatically. In a nonfiction book proposal, the synopsis describes the thrust and content of the successive chapters (and/or parts) of the manuscript.

T

table of contents A listing of a book's chapters and other sections (such as the front matter, appendix, index, and bibliography) or of a magazine's articles and columns, in the order in which they appear; in published versions, the table of contents indicates the respective beginning page numbers.

tabloid A smaller-than-standard-size newspaper (daily, weekly, or monthly). Traditionally, certain tabloids are distinguished by sensationalism of approach and content rather than by straightforward reportage of newsworthy events. In common parlance, "tabloid" is used to describe works in various media (including books) that cater to immoderate tastes (for example, tabloid exposé, tabloid television; the tabloidization of popular culture).

teleplay A **screenplay** geared toward television production. Similar in overall concept to screenplays for the cinema, teleplays are nonetheless inherently concerned with such TV-loaded provisions as the physical dimensions of the smaller screen, and formal elements of pacing and structure keyed to stipulated program length and the placement of commercial advertising. Attention to these myriad television-specific demands are fundamental to the viability of a project.

terms The financial conditions agreed to in a book contract.

theme A general term for the underlying concept of a book. (*See also* **hook**.)

thriller   A thriller is a novel of suspense with a plot structure that reinforces the elements of gamesmanship and the chase, with a sense of the hunt being paramount. Thrillers can be spy novels, tales of geopolitical crisis, legal thrillers, medical thrillers, technothrillers, domestic thrillers. The common thread is a growing sense of threat and the excitement of pursuit.

tip sheet   An information sheet on a single book that presents general publication information (publication date, editor, ISBN, etc.), a brief synopsis of the book, information on relevant other books (sometimes competing titles), and other pertinent marketing data such as author profile and advance blurbs. The tip sheet is given to the sales and publicity departments; a version of the tip sheet is also included in press kits.

title page   The page at the front of a book that lists the title, subtitle, author (and other contributors, such as translator or illustrator), as well as the publishing house and sometimes its logo.

trade books   Books distributed through the book trade—meaning bookstores and major book clubs—as opposed to, for example, mass-market paperbacks, which are often sold at magazine racks, newsstands, and supermarkets as well.

trade discount   The discount from the cover or list price that a publisher gives the bookseller. It is usually proportional to the number of books ordered (the larger the order, the greater the discount), and typically varies between 40% and 50%.

trade list   A catalog of all of a publisher's books in print, with ISBNs and order information. The trade list sometimes includes descriptions of the current season's new books.

trade (quality) paperbacks   Reprints or original titles published in paperback format, larger in dimension than mass-market paperbacks, and distributed through regular retail book channels. Trade paperbacks tend to be in the neighborhood of twice the price of an equivalent mass-market paperback version and about half to two-thirds the price of hardcover editions.

trade publishers   Publishers of books for a general readership—that is, nonprofessional, nonacademic books that are distributed primarily through bookstores.

translation rights   Rights sold either to a foreign agent or directly to a foreign publisher, either by the author's agent or by the original publisher.

treatment   In screenwriting, a full narrative description of the story, including sample dialogue.

U

unauthorized biography   A history of a person's life written without the consent or collaboration of the subject or the subject's survivors.

university press   A publishing house affiliated with a sponsoring university. The university press is generally nonprofit and subsidized by the respective university. Generally, university presses publish noncommercial scholarly nonfiction books written by academics, and their lists may include literary fiction, criticism, and poetry. Some university presses also specialize in titles of regional interest, and many acquire projects intended for commercial book-trade distribution.

unsolicited manuscript   A manuscript sent to an editor or agent without being requested by the editor/agent.

V

vanity press   A publisher that publishes books only at an author's expense—and will generally agree to publish virtually anything that is submitted and paid for. (*See also* **subsidy publishing**.)

vita   Latin word for "life." A shortened equivalent term for *curriculum vitae* (*see also* **résumé**).

W

word count   The number of words in a given document. When noted on a manuscript, the word count is usually rounded off to the nearest 100 words.

work-for-hire   Writing done for an employer, or writing commissioned by a publisher or book packager who retains ownership of, and all rights pertaining to, the written material.

Y

young-adult (YA) books   Books for readers generally between the ages of 12 and 17. Young-adult fiction often deals with issues of concern to contemporary teens.

young readers or **younger readers**   Publishing terminology for the range of publications that address the earliest readers. Sometimes a particular house's young-readers' program typifies books for those who do not yet read; which means these books have to hook the caretakers and parents who actually buy them. In certain quirky turns of everyday publishing parlance, *young readers* can mean anyone from embryos through young adults (and "young" means *you* when you want it to). This part may be confusing (as is often the case with publishing usage): Sometimes *younger adult* means only that the readership is allegedly hip, including those who would eschew kid's books as being inherently lame and those who are excruciatingly tapped into the current cultural pulse, regardless of cerebral or life-span quotient.

Z

zombie (or **zombi**)   In idiomatic usage, a zombie is a person whose conduct approximates that of an automaton. Harking back to the term's origins as a figure of speech for the resurrected dead or a reanimated cadaver, such folks are not customarily expected to exhibit an especially snazzy personality or be aware of too many things going on around them; hence some people in book-publishing circles may be characterized as zombies.

INDEX

INDEX

Philomel Books, 53, 56–57

Philosophy, 32, 33, 67, 76, 80, 99, 157, 165, 170, 272, 274, 281, 289, 320, 341, 344, 352, 354, 357, 358, 363, 369, 373, 375, 379, 408, 412, 442, 444, 447, 452, 471

Photography, 76, 96, 155, 229, 258, 268, 287, 314, 319, 323, 354, 365, 378, 380, 403, 477, 482

Phyllis Fogelman Books, 53

Picador USA, 29, 31

Picturebacks, 82

Pilgrim Press, The, 443–445

Pinnacle Books, 221–222

Playwrights Canada Press, 476

Plume, 40, 48–49

PMA Literary and Film Management, Inc., 623–625

Pocket books, 84–86

Poetry, 18, 19, 20, 52, 79, 106, 124, 133, 140, 144, 157, 159, 160, 166, 177, 185, 186, 189, 192, 207, 213, 224, 244, 247, 250, 259, 262, 271, 274, 295, 301, 330, 349, 354, 357, 362, 367, 371, 373, 374, 376, 388, 449, 458, 459, 461, 464, 468, 469, 471, 473, 477, 478

Polestar Books, 476, 478

Politics/political science, 9, 14, 19, 20, 21, 23, 30, 31, 32, 33, 68, 74, 75, 76, 80, 85, 86, 87, 88, 89, 99, 100, 129, 131, 157, 170, 173, 177, 189, 253, 258, 264, 272, 277, 281, 286, 298, 351, 352, 353, 354, 356, 358, 360, 363, 367, 369, 372, 373, 376, 381, 383, 390, 417, 470, 471, 473, 478, 480

Pomegranate Communications, Inc., 279– 280

Popular culture, 27, 5, 9, 14, 22, 25, 26, 27, 38, 43, 48, 65, 71, 73, 74, 75, 87, 89, 98, 99, 107, 120, 129, 155, 173, 189, 204, 212, 234, 281, 290, 295, 323, 328, 342, 352, 360, 367, 368, 369, 462, 469, 477

Portfolio, 40, 49

Presbyterian Publishing Corporation, 444–445

Presidio Press, 65–67, 280

Price Stern Sloan, 40, 49, 53, 57

Prima Games, 62

Prime Crime, 40, 50

Princeton Review, 61

Princeton University Press, 336, 360–361

Professional Publications, Inc., 281

Professional writers. See also Collaborators

    advantages of, 795

    assessing skills, 796

    closing the deal, 800–801

    collaboration agreement, 820–822

    credit for, 795–796

    deadlines, meeting, 801–802

    in the new millennium, 830–834

    interpersonal skills and, 798–799

    professional package, preparing, 797

    rates, setting, 797–798

    referrals, asking for, 802

    refusing books, 799–800

    royalties for, 798

    success and, 823–824

    time management, 825–827

    voice of author, capturing, 801

Programming, 237, 243, 310

Prometheus Books, 28–284

Susan Ann Protter, Literary Agent, 626

Psychiatry, 116, 237

Psychology, 10, 21, 26, 27, 46, 47, 49, 52, 65, 67, 68, 74, 80, 85, 89, 98, 101, 111, 117, 120, 125, 129, 131, 165, 200, 210, 212, 218, 237, 255, 258, 272, 296,

John Wiley & Sons, 218, 324–326
Wiley Children's Books, 324–326
William Morrow, 5, 14–15
Williamson Publishing Company, 326–327
Willow Creek Press, 327
Wine, 7, 44
Wisdom Publications, 453
Women's fiction, 15, 27, 33, 43, 50, 52, 65, 68, 69, 75, 99, 192, 221, 418, 465
    definition of, 814–815
Women's issues, 26, 27, 43, 46, 48, 52, 65, 74, 76, 88, 89, 98, 99, 120, 200, 305, 312, 403, 407, 412
Women's studies, 79, 87, 134, 165, 234, 295, 298, 345, 365, 376, 380, 383, 388, 408, 424, 441, 442, 452, 471, 480
Woodworking, 182, 308, 311
Workman Publishing Company, 113–114, 328–329
Worldwide Library, 465, 467–468
Worldwide Mystery, 467
Wright Group/McGraw-Hill, 236, 330–331
The Writer Books, 220
Writer's Digest Books, 182, 331
Writers House LLC, 698–700
Writing, books on, 89, 220, 331. *See also* Resources for Writers

Y

Yale University Press, 336, 389–390, 421
Yoga, 434
Young adult books, 15, 43, 58, 59, 91, 92, 242, 293, 324, 345, 398, 402, 422, 459, 463, 474, 478

Z

Zack Company, The, 700–703
Zebra Books, 221–222
Susan Zeckendorf Associates, Inc., 704

Zonderkidz, 454
Zondervan Publishing House, 4, 453–454